HOLT McDOUGAL
a division of Houghton Mifflin Harcourt

Eastern Hemisphere

Christopher L. Salter

HOLT McDOUGAL
a division of Houghton Mifflin Harcourt

Author

Dr. Christopher L. Salter

Dr. Christopher L. "Kit" Salter is Professor Emeritus of geography and former Chair of the Department of Geography at the University of Missouri. He did his undergraduate work at Oberlin College and received both his M.A. and Ph.D. degrees in geography from the University of California at Berkeley.

Dr. Salter is one of the country's leading figures in geography education. In the 1980s he helped found the national Geographic Alliance network to promote geography education in all 50 states. In the 1990s Dr. Salter was Co-Chair of the National Geography Standards Project, a group of distinguished geographers who created *Geography for Life* in 1994, the document outlining national standards in geography. In 1990 Dr. Salter received the National Geographic Society's first-ever Distinguished Geography Educator Award. In 1992 he received the George Miller Award for distinguished service in geography education from the National Council for Geographic Education. In 2006 Dr. Salter was awarded *Lifetime Achievement Honors* by the Association of American Geographers for his transformation of geography education.

Over the years, Dr. Salter has written or edited more than 150 articles and books on cultural geography, China, field work, and geography education. His primary interests lie in the study of the human and physical forces that create the cultural landscape, both nationally and globally.

ISBN-13: 978-0-55-402392-2
ISBN: 0-55-402392-X

1 2 3 4 5 6 7 8 9 032 13 12 11 10 09 08

Reviewers

Academic Reviewers

Elizabeth Chako, Ph.D.
Department of Geography
The George Washington University

Altha J. Cravey, Ph.D.
Department of Geography
University of North Carolina

Eugene Cruz-Uribe, Ph.D.
Department of History
Northern Arizona University

Toyin Falola, Ph.D.
Department of History
University of Texas

Sandy Freitag, Ph.D.
Director, Monterey Bay History and
    Cultures Project
Division of Social Sciences
University of California,
    Santa Cruz

Oliver Froehling, Ph.D.
Department of Geography
University of Kentucky

Reuel Hanks, Ph.D.
Department of Geography
Oklahoma State University

Phil Klein, Ph.D.
Department of Geography
University of Northern Colorado

B. Ikubolajeh Logan, Ph.D.
Department of Geography
Pennsylvania State University

Marc Van De Mieroop, Ph.D.
Department of History
Columbia University
New York, New York

Christopher Merrett, Ph.D.
Department of History
Western Illinois University

Thomas R. Paradise, Ph.D.
Department of Geosciences
University of Arkansas

Jesse P. H. Poon, Ph.D.
Department of Geography
University at Buffalo–SUNY

Robert Schoch, Ph.D.
CGS Division of Natural Science
Boston University

Derek Shanahan, Ph.D.
Department of Geography
Millersville University
Millersville, Pennsylvania

David Shoenbrun, Ph.D.
Department of History
Northwestern University
Evanston, Illinois

Sean Terry, Ph.D.
Department of Interdisciplinary
    Studies, Geography and
    Environmental Studies
Drury University
Springfield, Missouri

Educational Reviewers

Dennis Neel Durbin
Dyersburg High School
Dyersburg, Tennessee

Carla Freel
Hoover Middle School
Merced, California

Tina Nelson
Deer Park Middle School
Randallstown, Maryland

Don Polston
Lebanon Middle School
Lebanon, Indiana

Robert Valdez
Pioneer Middle School
Tustin, California

Teacher Review Panel

Heather Green
LaVergne Middle School
LaVergne, Tennessee

John Griffin
Wilbur Middle School
Wichita, Kansas

Rosemary Hall
Derby Middle School
Birmingham, Michigan

Rose King
Yeatman-Liddell School
St. Louis, Missouri

Mary Liebl
Wichita Public Schools USD 259
Wichita, Kansas

Jennifer Smith
Lake Wood Middle School
Overland Park, Kansas

Melinda Stephani
Wake County Schools
Raleigh, North Carolina

Teacher's Edition

Contents

Contents

Part A

UNIT 1 Introduction to the Eastern Hemisphere 1

Geography's Impact Video Series
Impact of a System of Laws

Part B

Geography's Impact Video Series
Impact of Desertification

 **Europe** 547

CHAPTER 17 **Physical Geography of Europe** 560

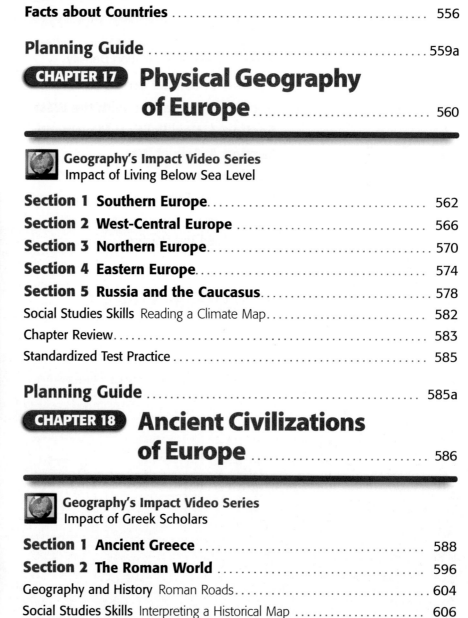

Geography's Impact Video Series
Impact of Living Below Sea Level

CHAPTER 18 **Ancient Civilizations of Europe** 586

Geography's Impact Video Series
Impact of Greek Scholars

CASE STUDY **The Celts** 610

Reference

Features

Satellite View

See the Eastern Hemisphere through satellite images and explore what these images reveal.

Social Studies Skills

Learn, practice, and apply the skills you need to study and analyze geography.

CONNECTING TO . . .

Explore the connections between geography and other subjects.

Literature

Learn about the Eastern Hemisphere through literature.

Writing Workshop

Learn to write about geography and history.

FOCUS ON READING

Learn and practice skills that will help you read your social studies lessons.

FOCUS ON WRITING AND SPEAKING

Use writing and speaking skills to reflect on the Eastern Hemisphere and its people.

Primary Sources

Learn about the Eastern Hemisphere through important documents and personal accounts.

BIOGRAPHIES

Meet the people who have influenced the Eastern Hemisphere and learn about their lives.

Charts and Graphs

The **World Almanac and Book of Facts** is America's largest-selling reference book of all time, with more than 81 million copies sold since 1868.

FACTS ABOUT COUNTRIES

Study the latest facts and figures about countries.

FACTS ABOUT THE WORLD

Study the latest facts and figures about the world.

Quick Facts and Infographics

Quick Facts and Infographics *(continued)*

Charts and Graphs

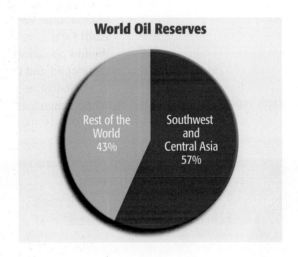

World Oil Reserves

Rest of the World 43%

Southwest and Central Asia 57%

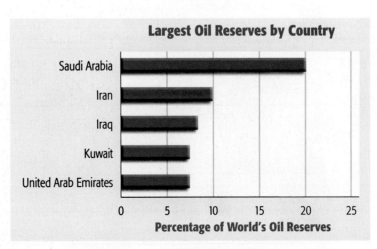

Largest Oil Reserves by Country

Saudi Arabia

Iran

Iraq

Kuwait

United Arab Emirates

0   5   10   15   20   25

Percentage of World's Oil Reserves

Charts and Graphs *(continued)*

February 1945
Allied leaders plan the final defeat of the Axis Powers.

April 1945
Allied troops begin liberation of Nazi concentration camps.

1944   1945   1946

June 6, 1944
Allied forces launch D-Day invasion in Normandy, France.

May 7, 1945
Germany surrenders to Allied Powers.

Geography Skills
With map zone geography skills, you can go online to find interactive versions of the key maps in this book. Explore these interactive maps to learn and practice important map skills and bring geography to life.

To use map zone interactive maps online:

1. Go to go.hrw.com.
2. Enter the KEYWORD shown on the interactive map.
3. Press return!

Interactive Maps

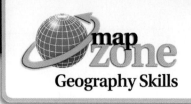

Maps

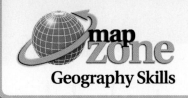
Maps *(continued)*

Atlas

Italy, 500 BC

Romans
Etruscans
Greeks
Carthaginians

0   30   60 Miles
0   30   60 Kilometers

Ligurian Sea
Adriatic Sea
Rome
Tyrrhenian Sea
Ionian Sea
Mediterranean Sea
Carthage

Holt McDougal integrates **standards-based content, reading instruction,** and **active learning** so students understand and experience geography

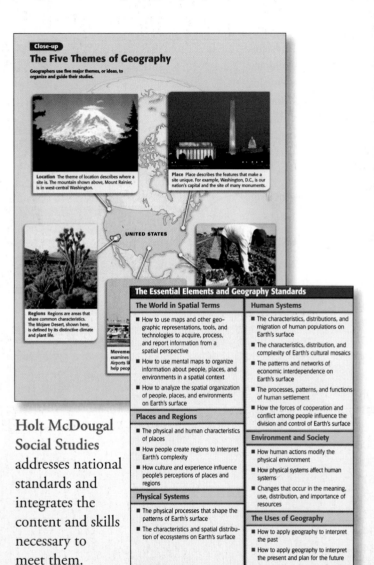

Close-up
The Five Themes of Geography

Geographers use five major themes, or ideas, to organize and guide their studies.

Location The theme of location describes where a site is. The mountain shown above, Mount Rainier, is in west-central Washington.

Place Place describes the features that make a site unique. For example, Washington, D.C., is our nation's capital and the site of many monuments.

UNITED STATES

Regions Regions are areas that share common characteristics. The Mojave Desert, shown here, is defined by its distinctive climate and plant life.

Movement examines Airports li help peop

The Essential Elements and Geography Standards

The World in Spatial Terms	Human Systems
■ How to use maps and other geographic representations, tools, and technologies to acquire, process, and report information from a spatial perspective	■ The characteristics, distributions, and migration of human populations on Earth's surface
■ How to use mental maps to organize information about people, places, and environments in a spatial context	■ The characteristics, distribution, and complexity of Earth's cultural mosaics
■ How to analyze the spatial organization of people, places, and environments on Earth's surface	■ The patterns and networks of economic interdependence on Earth's surface
	■ The processes, patterns, and functions of human settlement
Places and Regions	■ How the forces of cooperation and conflict among people influence the division and control of Earth's surface
■ The physical and human characteristics of places	**Environment and Society**
■ How people create regions to interpret Earth's complexity	■ How human actions modify the physical environment
■ How culture and experience influence people's perceptions of places and regions	■ How physical systems affect human systems
Physical Systems	■ Changes that occur in the meaning, use, distribution, and importance of resources
■ The physical processes that shape the patterns of Earth's surface	**The Uses of Geography**
■ The characteristics and spatial distribution of ecosystems on Earth's surface	■ How to apply geography to interpret the past
	■ How to apply geography to interpret the present and plan for the future

Holt McDougal Social Studies addresses national standards and integrates the content and skills necessary to meet them.

Chapter 1 A Geographer's World
Using Prior Knowledge

FOCUS ON READING

When you put together a puzzle, you search for pieces that are missing to complete the picture. As you read, you do the same thing when you use prior knowledge. You take what you already know about a subject and then add the information you are reading to create a full picture. The example below shows how using prior knowledge about computer mapping helped one reader fill in the pieces about how geographers use computer mapping.

In the past, maps were always drawn by hand. Many were not very accurate. Today, though, most maps are made using computers and satellite images. Through advances in mapmaking, we can make accurate maps on almost any scale, from the whole world to a single neighborhood, and keep them up to date.

From Section 3, The Branches of Geography

Computer Mapping	
What I know before reading	What else I learned
• My dad uses the computer to get a map for trips.	• Maps have not always been very accurate.
• I can find maps on the Internet of states and countries.	• Computers help make new kinds of maps that are more than just cities and roads.
	• These computer maps are an important part of geography.

READING SOCIAL STUDIES

Reading Social Studies lessons focus on the reading skills students need to access information that they will learn. A consistent reading and vocabulary development strategy is integrated into every section, and makes content accessible to **all** students

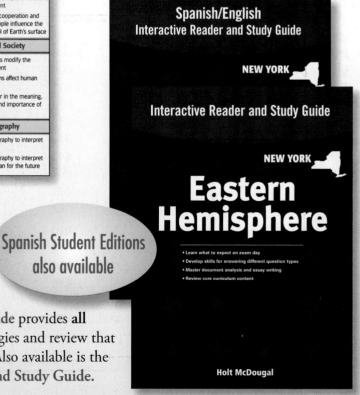

Spanish/English
Interactive Reader and Study Guide

NEW YORK

Interactive Reader and Study Guide

NEW YORK

Eastern Hemisphere

• Learn what to expect on exam day
• Develop skills for answering different question types
• Master document analysis and essay writing
• Review core curriculum content

Holt McDougal

Spanish Student Editions also available

The **New York Interactive Reader and Study Guide** provides **all** students with additional support including strategies and review that ensure they master both content and standards. Also available is the New York Spanish/English Interactive Reader and Study Guide.

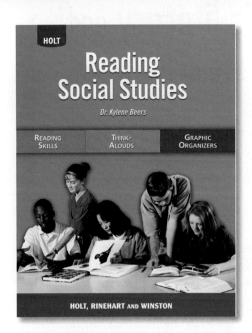

Written by Dr. Kylene Beers, **Reading Social Studies** helps students in every social studies course develop content-area reading skills. It includes reading skills practice, think-aloud strategies, and graphic organizers.

Graphic Organizer Transparencies with Support for Reading and Writing and **Online Interactive Graphic Organizers** provide lesson plans and transparencies that help students organize notes, prepare to write, and improve reading comprehension.

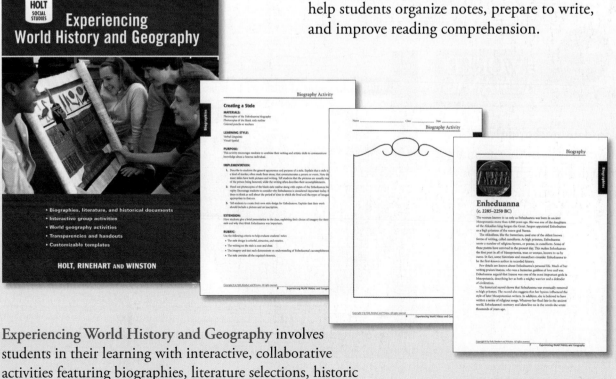

Experiencing World History and Geography involves students in their learning with interactive, collaborative activities featuring biographies, literature selections, historic documents, and map transparencies.

Holt McDougal fosters **geographic literacy** and helps students discover the world they live in today

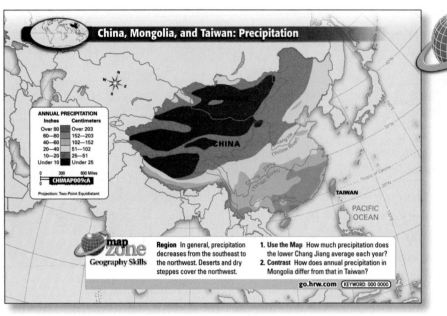

China, Mongolia, and Taiwan: Precipitation

ANNUAL PRECIPITATION

Inches	Centimeters
Over 80	Over 203
60—80	152—203
40—60	102—152
20—40	51—102
10—20	25—51
Under 10	Under 25

0 300 600 Miles

CHIMAP009cA

Projection: Two-Point Equidistant

CHINA

TAIWAN

PACIFIC OCEAN

map zone
Geography Skills

Region In general, precipitation decreases from the southeast to the northwest. Deserts and dry steppes cover the northwest.

1. **Use the Map** How much precipitation does the lower Chang Jiang average each year?
2. **Contrast** How does annual precipitation in Mongolia differ from that in Taiwan?

go.hrw.com   KEYWORD: 000 0000

Geography Skills

The Map Zone System introduces basic map skills, includes a variety of highly visual maps, promotes geographic literacy, and extends learning with interactive online maps.

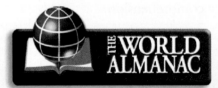

THE WORLD ALMANAC

Up-to-date, authoritative, real-world data in this program is provided through our partnership with the World Almanac Education Group.

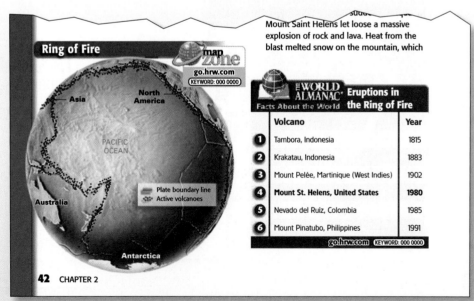

Ring of Fire

map zone
go.hrw.com
KEYWORD: 000 0000

Asia

North America

PACIFIC OCEAN

Australia

Antarctica

Plate boundary line
Active volcanoes

Mount Saint Helens let loose a massive explosion of rock and lava. Heat from the blast melted snow on the mountain, which

THE WORLD ALMANAC
Facts About the World
Eruptions in the Ring of Fire

	Volcano	Year
1	Tambora, Indonesia	1815
2	Krakatau, Indonesia	1883
3	Mount Pelée, Martinique (West Indies)	1902
4	**Mount St. Helens, United States**	**1980**
5	Nevado del Ruiz, Colombia	1985
6	Mount Pinatubo, Philippines	1991

go.hrw.com   KEYWORD: 000 0000

42 CHAPTER 2

Instructional Visuals bring people, places, and concepts to life.

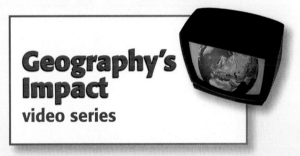

If YOU lived there...

Your parents own a small farm in the Chinese countryside in the mid-1950s. China's new leaders are making changes, however. They are taking people's farms and combining them to create large government-run farms. Your family and neighbors will now work a large farm together. China's leaders will tell you what to grow and pay you based on how much the farm produces.

How do you feel about these changes?

If You Lived There scenarios introduce each section and challenge students with a provocative question designed to make the study of geography, culture, and history relevant to students.

Geography's Impact Video Program captures students' imaginations and helps students see the impact of physical and human geography, as well as historical events, on the world they live in today. Available on VHS, DVD, and on the *New York Interactive Online Edition.*

Holt McDougal ensures you can
differentiate instruction for all students

New York Teacher One Stop™ on DVD-ROM provides easy-to-use print and technology resources that allow teachers to maximize their effectiveness and save time in planning, teaching, and assessing students' understanding of each lesson. It also includes the powerful ExamView® Version 6 Assessment Suite.

English-Language Learner Strategies and Activities, written by Dr. Julie Chan, supports every social studies course with teaching methods and application activities that improve comprehension and understanding of key concepts.

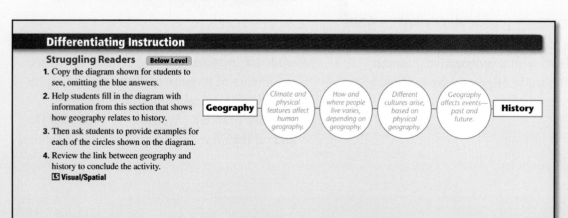

Differentiating Instruction

Struggling Readers   Below Level

1. Copy the diagram shown for students to see, omitting the blue answers.

2. Help students fill in the diagram with information from this section that shows how geography relates to history.

3. Then ask students to provide examples for each of the circles shown on the diagram.

4. Review the link between geography and history to conclude the activity.
   Visual/Spatial

Geography → Climate and physical features affect human geography. → How and where people live varies, depending on geography. → Different cultures arise, based on physical geography. → Geography affects events—past and future. → **History**

In the *New York Teacher's Edition,* **Differentiating Instruction Activities** provide teaching strategies for English-language learners, advanced learners, and special education students.

New York Differentiated Instruction Teacher Management System offers a wide variety of planning and instructional strategies in one convenient location.

The system includes:
- Instructional Benchmarking Guides
- Section Lesson Plans
- Lesson Plans for Differentiated Instruction
- Interactive Reader and Study Guide Teacher's Guide and Answer Key

New York Differentiated Instruction Modified Worksheets and Tests CD-ROM provides modified key resources to meet the specifications for students' **Individualized Education Plans (IEPs.)**

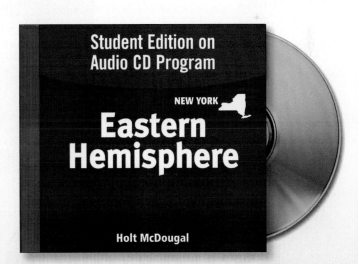

Student Edition on Audio CD Program is a direct read of the *New York Student Edition* that offers extra support for auditory learners, English-language learners, and reluctant readers. **Spanish Chapter Summaries Audio CD Program** is also available.

Holt McDougal includes a range of **assessment options** to effectively monitor students' progress

New York Progress Assessment Support System includes assessment for every chapter and helps you monitor students' progress.

The system includes
- Test-Taking Tips
- Diagnostic Test
- Section Quizzes
- Chapter Tests
- Unit Tests
- End-of-Year Test
- Answer Keys

ExamView® Version 6 Assessment Suite, on the New York Teacher One Stop™, makes it easy for you to reteach and offer support to those students who need it.

MindPoint® Quiz Show, located on the **New York Teacher One Stop**™ on DVD-ROM, is an interactive game that assesses student understanding, tracks student performance, and makes learning fun. Also available on the **Quiz Game CD-ROM.**

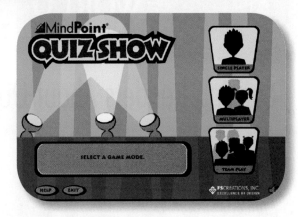

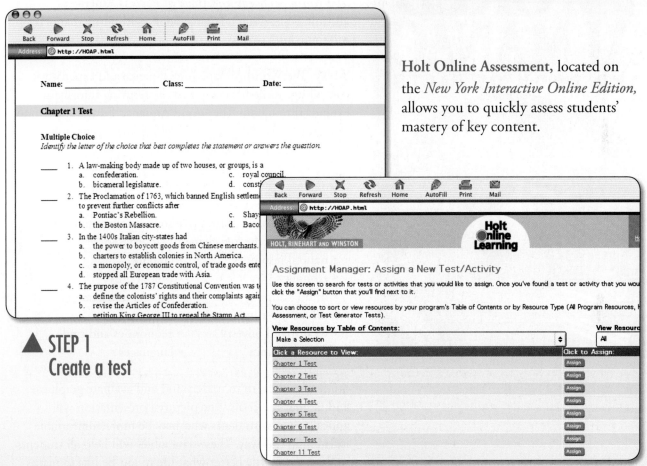

Holt Online Assessment, located on the *New York Interactive Online Edition*, allows you to quickly assess students' mastery of key content.

▲ **STEP 1**
Create a test

▲ **STEP 2**
Assign a test

◀ **STEP 3**
View and print progress reports

THE WORLD ALMANAC EDUCATION GROUP

Teaching Readers About Our World Since 1868

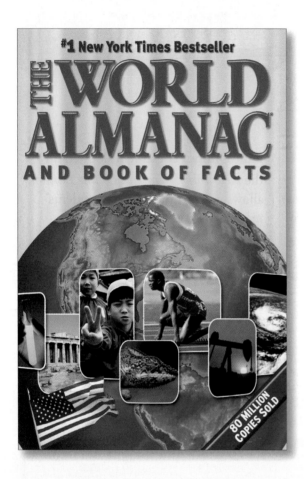
The World Almanac and Book of Facts has been delivering information about our world since the presidency of Johnson—Andrew Johnson! First published in 1868, *The World Almanac and Book of Facts* is America's all-time best-selling reference book, with more than 81 million copies sold.

Today, The World Almanac's experience and expertise at compiling, authenticating, and distributing information extends throughout The World Almanac Education Group. The group specializes in helping illuminate geography and the other social studies for students.

Throughout the *Student Edition,* you'll find dozens of tables compiled by the editors of *The World Almanac.* Drawing on only the most authoritative sources, these tables teach students about the key elements of geography:

- natural resources
- ethnicity
- immigration
- urban and rural areas
- wealth and poverty
- demographics
- climate
- topography
- natural disasters
- religion
- economics and trade
- languages

Students will learn to understand and evaluate graphical and tabular materials. The pictorial presentation will appeal to many students who may be more comfortable learning in this way. These data tables will help all students understand a little better what life might be like in places few of us will ever have the opportunity to visit.

These tables are also available at **go.hrw.com,** where they will be updated annually. If you have any suggestions or questions about the tables, please e-mail us at wa-ms-geo@waegroup.com.

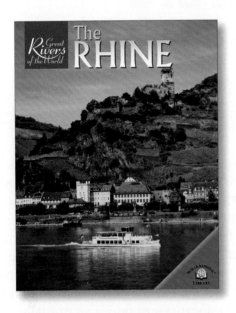

Social Studies Books, Kits, and Databases for Your Classroom and Library

The World Almanac Education Group comprises *World Almanac Books, Facts On File News Services, World Almanac Education Library Services,* and *Gareth Stevens Inc.* These companies all offer valuable resources for geography and the other social studies. From engaging worksheet activities to supplemental classroom books that delve deeper into key curriculum areas to on-line database subscriptions, these materials can help you inspire your students to inquire about the world around them.

Social Studies Books

Gareth Stevens publishes acclaimed middle-school books series (with Teacher's Guides) in U.S. and World Geography, American and World History, and American Government. Popular series include: *Great Cities of the World, Places in History, Great Rivers of the World, World Almanac Library of American Government,* and the *World Almanac Library of the States.*

Teaching Kits

World Almanac Education Library Services offers middle school skills kits that combine class sets of authoritative reference works with worksheets, videos, and posters to teach students valuable map and research skills. With a set of almanacs or atlases at hand, students quickly learn how to find and use information, while discovering the world around the corner and around the globe. The *World Almania* game is a fun way to teach world facts.

On-line Databases

Facts On File News Services delivers award-winning online subscription databases at **FACTS.com** and **FactsforLearning.com**. These easy-to-use, accessible-from-anywhere databases teach kids about current events, topical issues, and science news. For a free trial visit: **www.facts. com/geography**. Teachers also love the *Issues & Controversies Yearbooks,* which give students a quick understanding of more than 60 of the year's most talked-about topics.

The World Almanac & World Almanac for Kids

Of course the World Almanac Education Group is founded on the reputation of *The World Almanac and Book of Facts,* the perennial number-one bestseller. Many middle schoolers also enjoy the colorful, fun *World Almanac for Kids.*

The Importance of a Geographic Perspective

By Dr. Christopher L. Salter

Dr. Christopher L. Salter is one of the country's leading figures in Geography Education. In the 1980s, he helped found the National Geographic Alliance network to promote Geography Education. In the 1990s, Dr. Salter was Co-Chair of the National Geography Standards Project, a group of distinguished geographers who created Geography for Life in 1994, the document outlining national standards in geography. In 2006 Dr. Salter was awarded Lifetime Achievement Honors by the Association of American Geographers for his transformation of geography education.

Geography is often simply defined as "location, location, location." Geography—and a geographic perspective of the world—deals with far more, however. A geographic perspective is a way of looking at the world that blends an understanding of location, resources use, landscape change, and human use of the world into a way of thinking—a way of seeing how Earth is, how it has been shaped, and why it matters to people. A geographic perspective also provides ideas about how future landscapes should be modified and maintained.

Having a geographic perspective is important for many reasons. For example, a geographic perspective helps us understand the spatial character-istics of the world around us. At the personal and local level, something as basic as finding a good parking spot requires a solid spatial knowledge of a neighborhood. If you know a neighborhood's street network, traffic patterns, and parking laws, you will have a major advantage in finding a great parking space. At the global level, understanding spatial characteristics such as the patterns of human migration and the locations of resources can help leaders and societies make better decisions for the future. As geographers know, societies must not only think in terms of the immediate consequences of our human transformation of the world and its landscapes. They must also look well down the road and think about what might be around each turn.

A geographic perspective can help us better understand how human settlement and patterns of human migration shape the world around us. The engine of such migrations is a blend of human perceptions of place and the human fascination with moving to new places, seeking new futures. For thousands of years, people have been curious about what might exist just over the next mountain or across the seas or beyond a nearby border. Human migration patterns are not driven just by people's objective knowledge. The images people have of various places are shaped by many factors—stories they hear, information from TV, or impressions from exposure to all sorts of media. These varied and often random bits of information help make up people's 'mental maps' of places they may never have seen. People rely on their stored database of knowledge when undertaking the difficult process of migration. Such movement leads to geographic change both at the origin and destination of such geographic shifts. Understanding the origin and significance of our powerful mental maps is also part of a geographic perspective.

Likewise, a geographic perspective can help us think about resources and the location and nature of environmental features that are likely to be modified by human actions. The resources we depend on—that is, the various elements essential for life—are all geography. From the most basic resources of water and farmland to the more complex goods that we associate with city centers, malls, or technology (computers, new medicines, mountain bicycles), all are part of the power of geography. Consider where we get the vital raw materials for energy and the manufacturing of important goods. In the process from the discovery of resources to the final production and selling of goods, the geography of location, transportation, human settlements, population, and popular culture are all at steady interplay.

For example, look at the country-of-origin label (e.g, "Made in China") on your clothes, computer, or cell phone. The distance from your home to the place where those things were manufactured had to be overcome by transport, by international agreements, by some sort of advertising that caused you—or someone—to decide which specific item to buy. Geographic influences were at work throughout every aspect of the creation, shipping, and marketing of those goods. At the same time, geographic images of other places likely stimulated people living in the countryside in places such as China, India, or Mexico to move from rural areas to cities to seek jobs in the very factories that made those goods. Furthermore, American companies often increase their profits by using global trade networks

to have goods such as cell phones or T-shirts manufactured by foreign companies. The geographic impact of such decisions might be felt negatively in the United States if factories close and felt positively in places where global trade is booming.

In this textbook, the Five Fundamental Themes and the Six Essential Elements of Geography all work together to influence, shape, and teach us how to understand, maintain—and one hopes, improve—the human, cultural, and geographic landscape. We are all responsible for the intelligent management of the environment and the broader cultural landscapes around us. If you utilize a geographic perspective that focuses on the ways in which humans transform and manage Earth, you will be making a productive use of geography.

A Geographic Perspective

- is a way of looking at the world that blends an understanding of location, resource use, landscape change, and human use of the world.

- is a way of seeing how Earth is, how it has been shaped, and why it matters to people.

- provides ideas about how future landscapes should be modified and maintained.

Making Social Studies Accessible to English Learners

by Dr. Julie M.T. Chan

Dr. Julie M.T. Chan, Ed.D., is Director of Literacy Instruction in the Newport-Mesa Unified School District, located in Costa Mesa, California. She is a member of the California Reading and Literature Project (CRLP), UCI/Orange County region, and serves on the state-level CRLP Secondary Academic Literacy Tools development team. In addition, Dr. Chan teaches graduate courses on "The Socio-cultural Contexts of Literacy and Learning" in the Masters of Reading program at California State University, Fullerton, and "Linguistics in Action in the Multicultural Classroom" at Concordia University in Irvine, California.

As increasing numbers of English-Language Learners (ELLs) enter the nation's secondary schools each year, it is incumbent upon all of us to help each student fully access the Social Studies curriculum.

Social Studies instruction relies heavily on language—oral language (listening/speaking) and written language (reading/writing). Because of their limited—but developing—proficiency in the English language, ELLs have a difficult time grasping the information presented orally by the teacher. In addition, they struggle when reading the printed text in Social Studies textbooks.

Chamot and O'Malley (1994) identified six areas where teachers can support ELLs: (1) Conceptual understanding, (2) Vocabulary, (3) Language functions and discourse, (4) Structures, (5) Academic language skills, and (6) Study skills and learning strategies. Here are some ways that teachers can make Social Studies accessible to English-Language Learners.

Conceptual Understanding While all students need to develop the concepts of time, chronology, distance, and differing ways of life, some ELLs may have never studied geography. Teachers could approach unfamiliar concepts and content by reading aloud trade books to build background knowledge or to provide a mental model at the beginning of a unit of study.

Vocabulary Students need to learn the content-specific, specialized terminology of Social Studies in order to discuss and report on the ideas studied. As students move up through the grades, the academic vocabulary of Social Studies becomes increasingly difficult because of the complexity of the concepts it represents. Thus, knowing which words to introduce and how and when to introduce them is critical.

Language Functions and Discourse In most school districts, students are expected to analyze, compare, contrast, and make judgments about social studies information. In contrast to the narrative discourse of texts designed for English language development, Social Studies materials feature expository patterns across various text structures. By using graphic organizers or mind maps that match the different text structures, teachers can make abstract ideas, concepts, and content visible and concrete for ELLs.

Differentiating Instruction

At Level

English-Language Learners

1. Copy the table shown for students to see, omitting the blue answers.

2. Help students fill in the table with information from this and other sections that helps describe each area.

3. Review the link between physical geography and population to conclude the activity.

LS Visual/Spatial, Verbal/Linguistic

Alternative Assessment Handbook, Rubric 6: Charts

Areas with Low Population			
	Climate	Water	Soil and Land
Far North America	Very cold	Little water	Frozen soil
Australia	Very hot	Little water	Desert
Northern Asia	Very cold	Little water	Frozen soil
North Africa	Very hot	Little water	Desert

Lessons designed to support instructions for English-Language Learners can be found throughout the Teacher's Editions.

Structures Oral and written language structures present special challenges to ELLs. When teachers use research-based effective strategies to support oral and written language as well as published text structures, they can nudge their ELLs toward thinking, talking, reading, and writing like geographers.

Academic Language Skills Students typically learn Social Studies through the receptive modes of listening and reading. In contrast, they "show what they know" through the productive modes of class discussion, oral presentations and written products such as projects, reports, and expository/analytical essays. When the academic vocabulary of the content/concept to be studied is explicitly taught, ELLs can be more productive and therefore more successful at showing what they know.

Study Skills and Learning Strategies Chamot and O'Malley (1994) note that study skills, thinking skills, and social skills are also important components of the Social Studies curriculum. ELLs may not have, as yet, developed the learning strategies essential to these three skill areas. Thus, teachers should help ELLs develop these skills so they can be better prepared to cope with the growing demands of new and abstract information found in grade-level Social Studies classrooms, textbooks, print materials, and primary source documents.

Teachers who are aware of the difficulties that ELLs encounter in their Social Studies classes will use this as an opportunity to explicitly teach those skills and strategies needed to be successful learners. Whether a teacher instructs regular Social Studies classes or a sheltered section, the result will be ELLs who have greater access to the Social Studies curriculum and who experience greater success as students moving toward the mainstream.

Billmeyer, Rachel (1996). *Teaching Reading in the Content Areas: If Not Me, Then Who?* Aurora, CO: McREL.

Buehl, Doug (2001). *Classroom Strategies for Interactive Learning.* Newark, DE: International Reading Association.

Chamot, Anna Uhl and J. Michael O'Malley (1994). *The CALLA Handbook: Implementing the Cognitive Academic Language Learning Approach.* Reading, MA: Addison-Wesley Publishing Company.

Roe, Betty, et al (1991). *Secondary School Reading Instruction: The Content Areas.* Boston, MA: Houghton Mifflin.

Tompkins, Gail E. (1997). *Literacy for the Twenty-First Century: A Balanced Approach.* Upper Saddle River, N.J.: Merrill.

ELL Instructional Support Services

- Use graphic organizers to teach abstract ideas.

- Teach specialized Social Studies vocabulary and usage.

- Promote development of study skills, thinking skills, and social skills.

- Read aloud content-related materials to help students build background knowledge.

Teaching Vocabulary and Comprehension

by Dr. Kylene Beers

Dr. Kylene Beers is Senior Reading Advisor to Secondary Schools for Teachers College Reading and Writing Project, Columbia University. A former middle school teacher, Dr. Beers has turned her commitment to helping struggling readers into the major focus of her research, writing, speaking, and teaching. She is the author of *When Kids Can't Read/What Teachers Can Do* (Heinemann, 2002) and co-editor of *Adolescent Literacy: Turning Promise into Practice* (Heinemann, 2007). The former editor of the National Council of Teachers of English (NCTE) literacy journal *Voices from the Middle*, Dr. Beers is the senior program author of Holt, Rinehart and Winston's *Elements of Literature*, grades 6–12, and *Holt Literature and Language Arts,* grades 6–11 and is co-editor of *Into Focus: Understanding and Creating Middle School Readers* (Christopher-Gordon, 1998). She is a recognized authority on struggling readers, has written articles for numerous journals, and speaks nationally and internationally. Dr. Beers is the 2001 recipient of the Richard W. Halley Award given by NCTE for outstanding contributions to middle school literacy.

Effective Vocabulary Instruction

"Preteaching vocabulary . . . requires that the words to be taught must be key words, . . . be taught in semantically and topically related sets, . . . and that only a few words be taught per lesson."

—Tierney and Cunningham

The Right Words and the Right Number

The more vocabulary words we give students to learn weekly, the less chance students have of learning a word to the level needed to move it from short-term to long-term memory. Keeping the number between 5 and 10 means students have a better chance of retaining that word beyond the end of the week.

Consequently, choose wisely the words to be taught. Avid readers benefit by studying rare words—those highly unusual ones—because these students already have a solid vocabulary of the more common words. Struggling readers, however, benefit by focusing on high-utility words—those more common words that they are likely to see in other contexts. So, in the sentence, "The boys banked the canoe to the lee side of the rock," the inclination might be to teach the word *lee,* a rare word. However, if students don't know what *banked* means in this context or don't know the word *canoe,* it matters little what *lee* means. For struggling readers, a focus on high-utility words is more beneficial than a focus on rare words.

The Right Instructional Approach

Tierney and Cunningham (1984) explain that offering students a list of vocabulary words with their definitions is not as effective as placing each word within a semantic context. Students learn how to use words as they read or hear them used correctly. The Reading Social Studies features in this textbook list the key terms and academic vocabulary for each chapter. Defining these terms and using them in a sentence provide students with the semantic placement that most helps them learn words. Choosing the right number of the right words and presenting words in a semantic context help students build their vocabulary and, as a consequence, improve their comprehension.

Improving Comprehension

"Comprehension is both a product and a process, something that requires purposeful, strategic effort on the reader's part as he or she predicts, visualizes, clarifies, questions, connects, summarizes, and infers."

—Kylene Beers

When the Text is Tough

"Comprehension is only tough when you can't do it," explained the eleventh-grader. I almost dismissed his words until I realized what truth they offered. We aren't aware of all the thinking we do to comprehend a text until faced with a difficult text. Then all too clearly, we're aware of what words we don't understand, what syntax seems convoluted, and what ideas are beyond our immediate grasp. As skilled readers, we know what to do—we slow our pace, reread, ask questions, connect whatever we do understand to what we don't understand, summarize what we've read thus far, and make inferences about what the author is saying. In short, we make that invisible act of comprehension visible as we consciously push our way through the difficult text. At those times, we realize that, indeed, comprehension is tough.

Reading Strategies for Struggling Readers

Comprehension is even tougher if you lack strategies that would help you through the difficult text. Many struggling readers believe they aren't successful readers because that's just the way things are. They believe successful readers know some secret that they haven't been told. While we don't mean to keep comprehension a secret, at times that is what we do. For example, though we tell students to "reread," we haven't shown them how to alter their reading. We tell them to "make inferences," or "make predictions," but we haven't taught them how to do such things. In other words, we tell them what to do, but don't show them how to do it, in spite of several decades of research showing the benefit of direct instruction in reading strategies to struggling readers.

Direct Instruction

Direct instruction means telling students what you are going to teach them, modeling it for them, providing assistance as they practice it, then letting them practice it on their own. It's not saying, "visualize while you read," but, instead, explaining, "today, I'm going to read this part aloud to you. I'm going to focus on seeing some of the action in my mind as I read. I'm going to stop occasionally and tell you what I'm seeing and what in the text helped me see that." When we directly teach comprehension strategies to students by means of modeling and repeated practice, we show students that good readers don't just get it. They work hard to get it. Direct instruction takes the secret out of comprehension as it provides teachers the support they need to reach struggling readers.

Baumann, J. 1984.
"Effectiveness of a Direct Instruction Paradigm for Teaching Main Idea Comprehension." *Reading Research Quarterly,* 20: 93–108.

Beers, K. 2002.
When Kids Can't Read—What Teachers Can Do. Portsmouth: Heinemann.

Dole, J., Brown, K., and Trathen, W. 1996.
"The Effects of Strategy Instruction on the Comprehension Performance of At-Risk Students." *Reading Research Quarterly,* 31: 62–89.

Duffy, G. 2002.
"The Case for Direct Explanation of Strategies." *Comprehension Instruction: Research-Based Best Practices.* Eds. C. Block and M. Pressley. New York: Guilford Press. 28–41.

Pearson, P. D. 1984.
"Direct Explicit Teaching of Reading Comprehension." *Comprehension Instruction: Perspectives and Suggestions.* Eds. G. Duffy, L. Roehler, and J. Mason. New York: Longman. 222–233.

Tierney, R. J., and Cunningham, J. W. 1984.
"Research on Teaching Reading Comprehension." *Handbook of Reading Research.* Eds. P. D. Pearson, R. Barr, M. Kamil, P. Mosenthal. New York: Longman. 609–656.

Standard English Learners
Language Acquisition as a Scaffold to the Geography Curriculum
by Dr. Noma LeMoine

Dr. Noma LeMoine, Ph.D., is a nationally recognized expert on issues of language variation and learning in African American and other students for whom Standard English is not native. She is Director of Academic English Mastery and Closing the Achievement Gap Branch for the Los Angeles Unified School District. She is a member of the National Citizen's Commission on African American Education, an arm of the Congressional Black Caucus Education Brain Trust. Dr. LeMoine is also the author of *English for Your Success: A Language Development Program for African American Students.*

Who are Standard English Learners?

Standard English Learners (SELs) are students for whom Standard English is not native or whose home language—the language acquired between infancy and five years of age—structurally does not match the language of school. Standard English Learners include African American, Hawaiian American, Mexican American, and Native American students that have in common a linguistic history grounded in languages other than English. Prior to coming in contact with English their ancestors spoke African languages, Hawaiian languages, Latin American Spanish, or Native American languages. In each case these "involuntary minorities" combined English vocabulary with their native language and fashioned new ways of communicating in their new environments. These language forms, African American Language (often referred to as Black English); Hawaiian American Language (referred to as Hawaiian Pidgin English); Mexican American Language (referred to as Chicano English); and Native American Language (sometimes referred to as Red English) incorporate English vocabulary, but differ in structure and form from standard American English.

Standard English Learners arrive at school in kindergarten as competent users of the language of their home but demonstrating limited proficiency in the language of school, that is, Standard American English. They are generally classified as English Only on school language surveys even though many of the rules that govern their home language are based in languages other than English. Because of their designation as English Only, these students' need for structured programs that support their acquisition of standard and academic English is often overlooked.

Language Variation and Learning in SELs

In order for culturally and linguistically diverse Standard English Learners to succeed academically they must acquire the language, culture, and literacies of school. They must become literate in the forms of English that appear in newspapers, magazines, textbooks, voting materials, and consumer contracts. How best to facilitate this learning in Standard English Learners has proven elusive for most American public educational institutions and

Struggling Readers

1. Review with students the three cultures described in this section. Have them take out three sheets of paper and write the name of one culture at the top of each sheet.

2. On each sheet of paper, have students write at least two important words that help to describe the culture. Have them write a definition for each word, looking words up in the dictionary if necessary.

3. Have students then draw a picture illustrating at least one of the defined words. The picture should be labeled with a caption describing the illustration. The caption can be a few words or two or three short sentences.

LS Verbal/Linguistic, Visual/Spatial

Alternative Assessment Handbook, Rubrics 3: Artwork; and 40: Writing to Describe

Lessons designed to support instructions for Standard English Learners can be found throughout the Teacher's Editions.

minimal emphasis has been placed on identifying instructional methodologies that scaffold SELs' access to core curricula. Learning is viewed as a social phenomenon and knowledge is recognized as a social construction that is influenced by the cultural and linguistic experiences, perspectives, and frames of reference both students and teachers bring to the learning environment. For Standard English Learners this suggests that an instructional model that validates and builds on prior knowledge, experiences, language and culture while supporting the acquisition of school language through content learning is an appropriate pedagogy.

A good Geography curriculum provides students with opportunities to investigate and study Earth's natural features, climate, products and inhabitants. It should therefore apprentice students through authentic learning activities that provide opportunities for them to think, write, speak and act as geographers. For Standard English Learners, whose language and learning styles often do not match mainstream expectations, engaging in authentic learning activities that emphasize critical thinking, problem solving, writing and speaking relative to content leaning, is essential to success in mastering core curricula. As teachers assist Standard English Learners and other students with developing skills as geographers, they can at the same time provide corresponding opportunities to develop skills as speakers, readers, and writers.

SELs must be provided opportunities to add school language and literacy to their repertoire of skills using instructional approaches that build on the culture and language they bring to the classroom. In order for SELs to experience greater success in accessing core curricula, teachers will need to construct learning environments that are authentic and culturally responsive, and that support language acquisition and build upon the experiences, learning styles, and strengths these students bring to the classroom.

SEL Instructional Support Strategies

- Incorporate applicable strategies into instruction in English including utilization of visuals, manipulatives, graphic organizers, media and other tools to explain concepts.

- Provide continuous and varied opportunities for students to use language to interact with each other and the content through instructional conversations.

- Provide 30 to 45 minutes per day of Mainstream English Language Development (MELD) instruction that promotes the development of listening, speaking, reading, and writing skills in standard and academic English.

- Establish classroom libraries that include culturally relevant books and provide opportunities for SELs to be read to and to engage in free voluntary reading (FVR) on a daily basis.

- Encourage student/classroom development of a personal thesaurus of conceptually coded words to support the acquisition of academic vocabulary.

- Convey knowledge of the impact of diverse cultures on the modern world with an emphasis on historical and contemporary achievers.

- Make connections to students' prior knowledge, experiences, and cultural funds of knowledge to support learning and retention of learned concepts.

New York

New York Social Studies Middle School Standards

What are the New York Social Studies Middle School Standards?

Learning standards are simply the things you are expected to know, understand, and be able to do as a result of your education. Learning standards are usually organized by subject and grade. So standards for your United States history course, for example, focus on the knowledge and skills you will need to gain in your social studies class this school year.

How can New York Social Studies Middle School Standards help me?

These learning standards are helpful because they give you a clear picture of what you will be expected to learn. This can help you to focus on key material as you work through the school year. You can think of the standards as a kind of checklist—and you can even check off important subjects and skills as you master them. Another advantage of becoming familiar with the standards is that teachers often base lesson plans and tests on these standards. That means that the standards can give you a preview of what to expect in this course.

How are the New York Social Studies Middle School Standards organized?

New York educators have organized the teaching of social studies by creating different kinds of standards at several levels. At the top level are New York State Learning Standards for Social Studies. These are very broad standards—each one covers a large amount of learning. Because they are so broad, there are only five of them, and only one refers to the study of United States and New York history. You can read it below. On the next page, you will read more detailed parts of the standard.

Each Standard is divided into Key Ideas. These Key Ideas give you a description of the main categories of information you will be learning, as well as the kinds of skills you will be practicing.

Standard 1—History of the United States and New York

Students will use a variety of intellectual skills to demonstrate their understanding of major ideas, eras, themes, developments, and turning points in the history of the United States and New York.

1. The study of New York State and United States history requires an analysis of the development of American culture, its diversity and multicultural context, and the ways people are unified by many values, practices, and traditions.

Student Performance Indicators:

1.1a: explore the meaning of American culture by identifying the key ideas, beliefs, and patterns of behaviors, and traditions that help define it and unite all Americans

1.1b: interpret the ideas, values, and beliefs contained in the Declaration of Independence and the New York State Constitution and United States Constitution, Bill of Rights, and other important historical documents

Central Park, New York City

2. Important ideas, social and cultural values, beliefs, and traditions from New York State and United States history illustrate the connections and interactions of people and events across time and from a variety of perspectives.

Student Performance Indicators:

1.2a: describe the reasons for periodizing history in different ways

1.2b: investigate key turning points in New York State and United States history and explain why these events or developments are significant

1.2c: understand the relationship between the relative importance of United State domestic and foreign policies over time

1.2d: analyze the role played by the United States in international politics, past and present

3. Study about the major social, political, economic, cultural, and religious developments in New York State and United States history involves learning about the important roles and contributions of individuals and groups.

Student Performance Indicators:

1.3a: complete well-documented and historically accurate case studies about individuals and groups who represent different ethnic, national, and religious groups, including Native American Indians, in New York State and the United States at different times and in different locations

1.3b: gather and organize information about the important achievements and contributions of individuals and groups living in New York State and the United States

1.3c: describe how ordinary people and famous historic figures in the local community, state, and the United States have advanced the fundamental democratic values, beliefs and traditions expressed in the Declaration of Independence, the New York State and United States Constitutions, the Bill of Rights, and other important historic documents

4. The skills of historical analysis include the ability to: explain the significance of historical evidence; weigh the importance, reliability, and validity of evidence; understand the concept of multiple causation; understand the importance of changing and competing interpretations of different historical developments.

Standard 2—World History

Students will use a variety of intellectual skills to demonstrate their understanding of major ideas, eras, themes, developments, and turning points in world history and examine the broad sweep of history from a variety of perspectives.

1. The study of world history requires an understanding of world cultures and civilizations, including an analysis of important ideas, social and cultural values, beliefs, and traditions. This study also examines the human condition and the connections and interactions of people across time and space and the ways different people view the same event or issue from a variety of perspectives.

Student Performance Indicators:

2.1a: know the social and economic characteristics, such as customs, traditions, child-rearing practices, ways of making a living, education and socialization practices, gender roles, foods, and religious and spiritual beliefs that distinguish different cultures and civilizations

2.1b: interpret and analyze documents and artifacts related to significant developments and events in world history

2. Establishing timeframes, exploring different periodizations, examining themes across time and within cultures, and focusing on important turning points in world history help organize the study of world cultures and civilizations.

Student Performance Indicators:

2.2a: develop timelines by placing important events and developments in world history in their correct chronological order

2.2b: measure time periods by years, decades, centuries, and millennia

2.2c: study about major turning points in world history by investigating the causes and other factors that brought about change and the results of these changes

3. Study of the major social, political, cultural, and religious developments in world history involves learning about the important roles and contributions of individuals and groups.

Student Performance Indicators:

2.3a: investigate the roles and contributions of individuals and groups in relation to key social, political, cultural, and religious practices throughout world history

Brooklyn Bridge

Social Studies Curriculum Standards

2.3b: interpret and analyze documents and artifacts related to significant developments and events in world history

2.3c: classify historic information according to the type of activity or practices: social/cultural, political, economic, geographic, scientific, technological, and historic

4. The skills of historical analysis include the ability to investigate differing and competing interpretations of the theories of history, hypothesize about why interpretations change over time, explain the importance of historical evidence, and understand the concepts of change and continuity over time.

Student Performance Indicators:

2.4a: explain the literal meaning of a historical passage or primary source document, identifying who was involved, what happened, where it happened, what events led up to these developments, and what consequences or outcomes followed

2.4b: analyze different interpretations of important events and themes in world history and explain the various frames of reference expressed by different historians

2.4c: view history through the eyes of those who witnessed key events and developments in world history by analyzing their literature, diary accounts, letters, artifacts, art, music, architectural drawings, and other documents

2.4d: investigate important events and developments in world history by posing analytical questions, selecting relevant data, distinguishing fact from opinion, hypothesizing cause-and-effect relationships, testing these hypotheses, and forming conclusions

Standard 3—Geography

Students will use a variety of intellectual skills to demonstrate their understanding of the geography of the interdependent world in which we live—local, national, and global—including the distribution of people, places, and environments over the Earth's surface.

1. Geography can be divided into six essential elements which can be used to analyze important historic, geographic, economic, and environmental questions and issues. These six elements include: the world in spatial terms, places and regions, physical settings (including natural resources), human systems, environment and society, and the use of geography. (Adapted from The National Geography Standards, 1994: Geography for Life)

Student Performance Indicators:

3.1a: map information about people, places, and environments

3.1b: understand the characteristics, functions, and applications of maps, globes, aerial and other photographs, satellite-produced images, and models

3.1c: investigate why people and places are located where they are located and what patterns can be perceived in these locations

3.1d: describe the relationships between people and environments and the connections between people and places

2. Geography requires the development and application of the skills of asking and answering geographic questions; analyzing theories of geography; and acquiring, organizing, and analyzing geographic information. (Adapted from The National Geography Standards, 1994: Geography for Life)

Standard 4—Economics

Students will use a variety of intellectual skills to demonstrate their understanding of how the United States and other societies develop economic systems and associated institutions to allocate scarce resources, how major decision-making units function in the U.S. and other national economies, and how an economy solves the scarcity problem through market and nonmarket mechanisms.

1. The study of economics requires an understanding of major economic concepts and systems, the principles of economic decision making, and the interdependence of economies and economic systems throughout the world.

Student Performance Indicators:

4.1a: explain how societies and nations attempt to satisfy their basic needs and wants by utilizing scarce capital, natural, and human resources

4.1b: define basic economic concepts such as scarcity, supply and demand, markets, opportunity cost, resources, productivity, economic growth, and systems

4.1c: understand how scarcity requires people and nations to make choices which involve costs and future considerations

Grand Central Station New York

4.1d: understand how people in the United States and throughout the world are both producers and consumers of goods and services

4.1e: investigate how people in the United States and throughout the world answer the three fundamental economic questions and solve basic economic problems

4.1f: describe how traditional, command, market, and mixed economies answer the three fundamental economic questions

4.1g: explain how nations throughout the world have joined with one another to promote economic development and growth

2. Economics requires the development and application of the skills needed to make informed and well-reasoned economic decisions in daily and national life.

Student Performance Indicators:

4.2a: identify and collect economic information from standard reference works, newspapers, periodicals, computer databases, textbooks, and other primary and secondary sources

4.2b: organize and classify economic information by distinguishing relevant from irrelevant information, placing ideas in chronological order, and selecting appropriate labels for data

4.2c: evaluate economic data by differentiating fact from opinion and identifying frames of reference

4.2d: develop conclusions about economic issues and problems by creating broad statements which summarize findings and solutions

4.2e: present economic information by using media and other appropriate visuals such as tables, charts, and graphs to communicate ideas and conclusions

Standard 5—Civics, Citizenship, and Government

Students will use a variety of intellectual skills to demonstrate their understanding of the necessity for establishing governments; the governmental system of the U.S. and other nations; the U.S. Constitution; the basic civic values of American constitutional democracy; and the roles, rights, and responsibilities of citizenship, including avenues of participation.

1. The study of civics, citizenship, and government involves learning about political systems; the purposes of government and civic life; and the differing assumptions held by people across time and place regarding power, authority, governance, and law. (Adapted from The National Standards for Civics and Government, 1994)

Student Performance Indicators:

5.1a: analyze how the values of a nation affect the guarantee of human rights and make provisions for human needs

5.1b: consider the nature and evolution of constitutional democracies

5.1c: explore the rights of citizens in their parts of the hemisphere and determine how they are similar to and different from the rights of American citizens

5.1d: analyze the sources of a nation's values as embodied in its constitution, statutes, and important court cases

2. The state and federal governments established by the Constitutions of the United States and the State of New York embody basic civic values (such as justice, honesty, self-discipline, due process, equality, majority rule with respect for minority rights, and respect for self, others, and property), principles, and practices and establish a system of shared and limited government. (Adapted from The National Standards for Civics and Government, 1994)

Student Performance Indicators:

5.2a: understand how civic values reflected in United States and New York State Constitutions have been implemented through laws and practices

5.2b: understand that the New York State Constitution, along with a number of other documents, served as a model for the development of the United States Constitution

5.2c: compare and contrast the development and evolution of the constitutions of the United States and New York State

5.2d: define federalism and describe the powers granted the national and state governments by the United States Constitution

5.2e: value the principles, ideals, and core values of the American democratic system based upon the promises of human dignity, liberty, justice, and equality

5.2f: understand how the United States and New York State Constitutions support majority rule but also protect the rights of the minority

3. Central to civics and citizenship is an understanding of the roles of the citizen within American constitutional democracy and the scope of a citizen's rights and responsibilities.

Student Performance Indicators:

5.3a: explain what citizenship means in a democratic society, how citizenship is defined in the Constitution and other laws of the land, and how the definition of citizenship changed in the United States and New York State over time

5.3b: understand that the American legal and political systems guarantee and protect the rights of citizens and assume that citizens will hold and exercise certain civic values and fulfill certain civic responsibilities

5.3c: discuss the role of an informed citizen in today's changing world

5.3d: explain how Americans are citizens of their state and of the United States

4. The study of civics and citizenship requires the ability to probe ideas and assumptions, ask and answer analytical questions, take a skeptical attitude toward questionable arguments, evaluate evidence, formulate rational conclusions, and develop and refine participatory skills.

Student Performance Indicators:

5.4a: respect the rights of others in discussions and classroom debates regardless of whether or not one agrees with their viewpoint

5.4b: explain the role that civility plays in promoting effective citizenship in preserving democracy

5.4c: participate in negotiation and compromise to resolve classroom, school, and community disagreements and problems

Making This Book Work for You

Studying geography will be easy for you with this textbook. Take a few minutes now to become familiar with the easy-to-use structure and special features of your book. See how it will make the Eastern Hemisphere come alive for you!

Unit

Each unit begins with a satellite image. In Units 2 through 5, this image is followed by atlas and a table with facts about each country. Use these pages to get an overview of the region you will study.

Regional Atlas

The maps in the regional atlas show some of the key physical and human features of the region.

Facts about Countries See which countries are included in each region and learn some important facts about them with these helpful tables.

Chapter

Each regional chapter begins with a preview of what you will learn and a map of the region. Special instruction is also given in reading and skills.

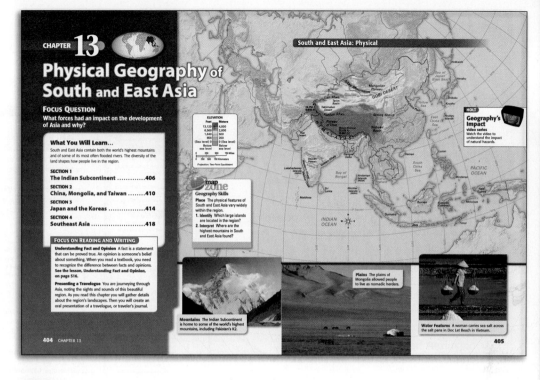

Reading Social Studies

Chapter reading lessons give you skills and practice to help you read the textbook. More help with each lesson can be found in the back of the book. Margin notes and questions in the chapter make sure you understand the reading skill.

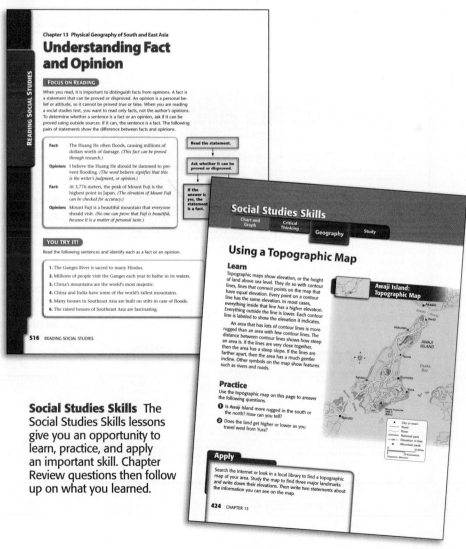

Social Studies Skills The Social Studies Skills lessons give you an opportunity to learn, practice, and apply an important skill. Chapter Review questions then follow up on what you learned.

Section

The section opener pages include Main Ideas, an overarching Big Idea, and Key Terms and Places. In addition, each section includes these special features:

If YOU Lived There . . . Each section begins with a situation for you to respond to, placing you in a place that relates to the content you will be studying in the section.

Building Background Building Background connects what will be covered in each section with what you already know.

Short Sections of Content The information in each section is organized into small chunks of text that you can easily understand.

Taking Notes Suggested graphic organizers help you read and take notes on the important ideas in the section.

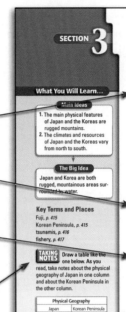

SECTION 3

Japan and the Koreas

What You Will Learn...

Main Ideas

1. The main physical features of Japan and the Koreas are rugged mountains.
2. The climates and resources of Japan and the Koreas vary from north to south.

The Big Idea

Japan and Korea are both rugged, mountainous areas surrounded by water.

Key Terms and Places

Fuji, p. 415
Korean Peninsula, p. 415
tsunamis, p. 416
fishery, p. 417

TAKING NOTES Draw a table like the one below. As you read, take notes about the physical geography of Japan in one column and about the Korean Peninsula in the other column.

Physical Geography	
Japan	Korean Peninsula

If YOU lived there...

You are a passenger on a very fast train zipping its way across the countryside. If you look out the window to your right, you can see the distant sparkle of sunlight on the ocean. If you look to the left, you see rocky, rugged mountains. Suddenly the train leaves the mountains, and you see hundreds of trees covered in delicate pink flowers. Rising above the trees is a single snowcapped volcano.

How does this scenery make you feel?

BUILDING BACKGROUND The train described above is one of the many that cross the islands of Japan every day. Japan's mountains, trees, and water features give the islands a unique character. Not far away, the Korean Peninsula also has a distinctive landscape.

Physical Features

Japan, North Korea, and South Korea are on the eastern edge of the Asian continent, just east of China. Separated from each other only by a narrow strait, Japan and the Koreas share many common landscape features.

Physical Features of Japan

Japan is an island country. It is made up of four large islands and more than 3,000 smaller islands. These islands are arranged in a long chain more than 1,500 miles (2,400 km) long. This is about the same length as the eastern coast of the United States, from southern Florida to northern Maine. All together, however, Japan's land area is slightly smaller than the state of California.

About 95 percent of Japan's land area is made up of four large islands. From north to south, these major islands are Hokkaido (hoh-KY-doh), Honshu (HAWN-shoo), Shikoku (shee-KOH-koo), and Kyushu (KYOO-shoo). Together they are called the home islands. Most of Japan's people live there.

Resources

Resources are not evenly distributed among Japan and the Koreas. Neither Japan nor South Korea, for example, is very rich in mineral resources. North Korea, on the other hand, has large deposits of coal, iron, and other minerals.

Although most of the region does not have many mineral resources, it does have other resources. For example, the people of the Koreas have used their land's features to generate electricity. The peninsula's rocky terrain and rapidly flowing rivers make it an excellent location for creating hydroelectric power.

In addition, Japan has one of the world's strongest fishing economies. The islands lie near one of the world's most productive fisheries. A **fishery** is a place where lots of fish and other seafood can be caught. Swift ocean currents near Japan carry countless fish to the islands. Fishers then use huge nets to catch the fish and bring them to Japan's many bustling fish markets. These fish markets are among the busiest in the world.

This fish market in Tokyo, Japan, is the busiest in the world. People gather here every morning to buy freshly caught fish.

SUMMARY AND PREVIEW The islands of Japan and the Korean Peninsula share many common features. In the next section, you will see similar features in the region of Southeast Asia and learn how those features affect life in that region.

READING CHECK Analyzing What are some resources found in Japan and the Koreas?

Reading Check Questions end each section of content so you can check to make sure you understand what you just studied.

Summary and Preview The Summary and Preview connects what you studied in the section to what you will study in the next section.

Section Assessment Finally, the section assessment boxes make sure that you understand the main ideas of the section. We also provide assessment practice online!

Section 3 Assessment

go.hrw.com
Online Quiz
KEYWORD: SK9 HP8

Reviewing Ideas, Terms, and Places

1. a. **Identify** What types of landforms cover Japan and the **Korean Peninsula**?
   b. **Compare and Contrast** How are the physical features of Japan and Korea similar? How are they different?
   c. **Predict** How do you think natural disasters affect life in Japan and Korea?
2. a. **Describe** What kind of climate is found in the northern parts of the region? What kind of climate is found in the southern parts?
   b. **Draw Conclusions** Why are **fisheries** important to Japan's economy?

Critical Thinking

3. **Categorizing** Draw a chart like this one. In each row, describe the region's landforms, climate, and resources.

	Japan	Korean Peninsula
Landforms		
Climate		
Resources		

FOCUS ON SPEAKING

4. **Thinking about Nature** Nature is central to the art and culture of both Japan and Korea. How will you describe the natural environments of this region in your travelogue? Jot down some ideas.

Features

Your book includes many features that will help you learn about the Eastern Hemisphere such as Close-up and Satellite View.

Satellite View See and explore the world through satellite images.

Close-up

Communist China

China celebrates the beginnings of Chinese Communism on National Day, October 1. It was on October 1, 1949 that Mao Zedong created the People's Republic of China. The celebration includes a huge parade in Beijing's Tiananmen Square.

Beijing
CHINA
PACIFIC OCEAN

The Gate of Heavenly Peace displays Mao Zedong's portrait above the entrance.

The parades include couples married on National Day, a popular time to wed.

A military parade of soldiers, tanks, and other equipment shows China's power.

Satellite View

Namib Desert

One of the world's most unusual deserts, the Namib lies on the Atlantic coast in Namibia. As this satellite image shows, the land there is extremely dry. Some of the world's highest sand dunes stretch for miles along the coast.

In spite of its harsh conditions, some insects have adapted to life in the desert. They can survive there because at night a fog rolls in from the ocean. The insects use the fog as a source of water.

Drawing Conclusions How have some insects adapted to living in the Namib Desert?

Close-up These features help you see how people live and what places look like around the world.

Chapter Review

At the end of each chapter, the Chapter Review will help you review key concepts, analyze information critically, complete activities, and show what you have learned.

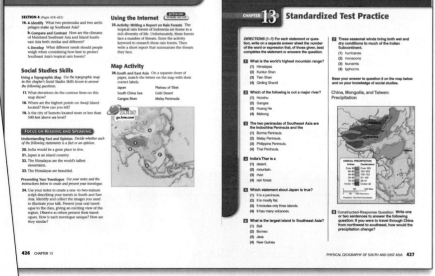

Standardized Test Practice Practice for standardized tests with the last page of each chapter before moving on to another region of the world!

Scavenger Hunt

Are you ready to explore the world of geography? **Holt McDougal Eastern Hemisphere New York, Part A** is your ticket to this exciting world. Before you begin your journey, complete this scavenger hunt to get to know your book and discover what's inside.

On a separate sheet of paper, fill in the blanks to complete each sentence below. In each answer, one letter will be in a yellow box. When you have answered every question, copy these letters in order to reveal the answer to the question at the bottom of the page.

1 According to the Table of Contents, the title of Chapter 7 is Religions of the Ancient Middle East— J u d a i s m , Christianity, and Islam. What else does the Table of Contents show?
the title of each section, page numbers

2 The two main ideas listed on page 138 explain what you will learn in that section. The first word of the second of these main ideas is r e l i g i o n .

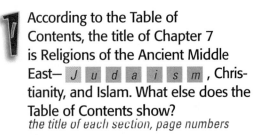

3 The Geography and History feature on pages 152–153 is called Crossing the S a h a r a . What other features can you find in this book?
Case Study, Focus on Culture, Close-up, Satellite View

4 The Eye on Earth feature on pages 44–45 is called The Ring of F i r e . What is this feature about?
volcanoes and earthquakes

5 Look at the English and Spanish Glossary. The first term listed there is absolute l o c a t i o n . How will use this glossary?
to look up the definitions of unfamiliar words

6 Look up Gao in the Gazetteer. According to the entry, it was the capital of the S o n g h a i Empire.

7 Page R1 is the beginning of the E c o n o m i c s Handbook. What will you find in this section of the book?
glossary of economic terms, questions and activities for review

Fact!

The oldest known permanent settlement in the world is in Southwest Asia. What is it called?

J e r i c h o

Geography and Map Skills Handbook

Contents

Throughout this textbook, you will be studying the world's people, places, and landscapes. One of the main tools you will use is the map—the primary tool of geographers. To help you begin your studies, this Geography and Map Skills Handbook explains some of the basic features of maps. For example, it explains how maps are made, how to read them, and how they can show the round surface of Earth on a flat piece of paper. This handbook will also introduce you to some of the types of maps you will study later in this book. In addition, you will learn about the different kinds of features on Earth and about how geographers use themes and elements to study the world.

✳Interactive Maps

Geography Skills With map zone geography skills, you can go online to find interactive versions of the key maps in this book. Explore these interactive maps to learn and practice important map skills and bring geography to life.

To use map zone interactive maps online:

1. Go to go.hrw.com.

2. Enter the KEYWORD shown on the interactive map.

3. Press return!

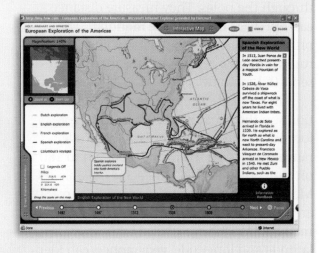

Mapping the Earth
Using Latitude and Longitude

A **globe** is a scale model of the Earth. It is useful for showing the entire Earth or studying large areas of Earth's surface.

To study the world, geographers use a pattern of imaginary lines that circles the globe in east-west and north-south directions. It is called a **grid**. The intersection of these imaginary lines helps us find places on Earth.

The east-west lines in the grid are lines of **latitude**, which you can see on the diagram. Lines of latitude are called **parallels** because they are always parallel to each other. These imaginary lines measure distance north and south of the **equator**. The equator is an imaginary line that circles the globe halfway between the North and South Poles. Parallels measure distance from the equator in **degrees**. The symbol for degrees is °. Degrees are further divided into **minutes**. The symbol for minutes is ´. There are 60 minutes in a degree. Parallels north of the equator are labeled with an N. Those south of the equator are labeled with an S.

The north-south imaginary lines are lines of **longitude**. Lines of longitude are called **meridians**. These imaginary lines pass through the poles. They measure distance east and west of the **prime meridian**. The prime meridian is an imaginary line that runs through Greenwich, England. It represents 0° longitude.

Lines of latitude range from 0°, for locations on the equator, to 90°N or 90°S, for locations at the poles. Lines of longitude range from 0° on the prime meridian to 180° on a meridian in the mid-Pacific Ocean. Meridians west of the prime meridian to 180° are labeled with a W. Those east of the prime meridian to 180° are labeled with an E. Using latitude and longitude, geographers can identify the exact location of any place on Earth.

Lines of Latitude

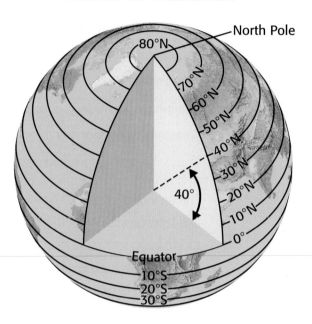

Lines of Longitude

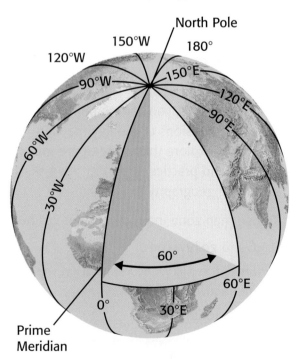

The equator divides the globe into two halves, called **hemispheres**. The half north of the equator is the Northern Hemisphere. The southern half is the Southern Hemisphere. The prime meridian and the 180° meridian divide the world into the Eastern Hemisphere and the Western Hemisphere. Look at the diagrams on this page. They show each of these four hemispheres.

Earth's land surface is divided into seven large landmasses, called **continents**. These continents are also shown on the diagrams on this page. Landmasses smaller than continents and completely surrounded by water are called **islands**.

Geographers organize Earth's water surface into major regions too. The largest is the world ocean. Geographers divide the world ocean into the Pacific Ocean, the Atlantic Ocean, the Indian Ocean, and the Arctic Ocean. Lakes and seas are smaller bodies of water.

Northern Hemisphere

Southern Hemisphere

Western Hemisphere

Eastern Hemisphere

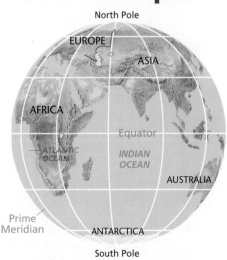

Mapmaking
Understanding Map Projections

A **map** is a flat diagram of all or part of Earth's surface. Mapmakers have created different ways of showing our round planet on flat maps. These different ways are called **map projections**. Because Earth is round, there is no way to show it accurately on a flat map. All flat maps are distorted in some way. Mapmakers must choose the type of map projection that is best for their purposes. Many map projections are one of three kinds: cylindrical, conic, or flat-plane.

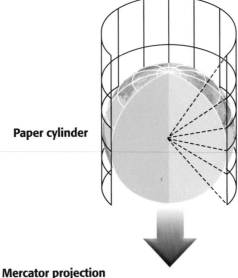

Paper cylinder

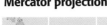

Cylindrical Projections

Cylindrical projections are based on a cylinder wrapped around the globe. The cylinder touches the globe only at the equator. The meridians are pulled apart and are parallel to each other instead of meeting at the poles. This causes landmasses near the poles to appear larger than they really are. The map below is a Mercator projection, one type of cylindrical projection. The Mercator projection is useful for navigators because it shows true direction and shape. However, it distorts the size of land areas near the poles.

Mercator projection

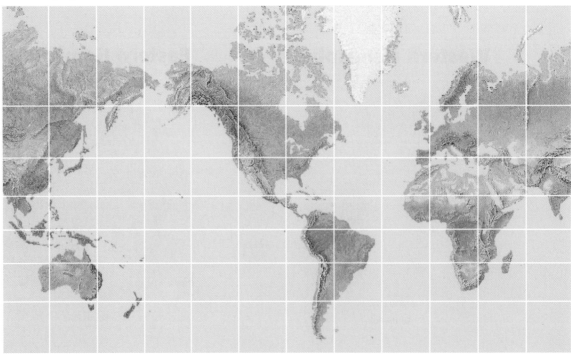

Conic Projections

Conic projections are based on a cone placed over the globe. A conic projection is most accurate along the lines of latitude where it touches the globe. It retains almost true shape and size. Conic projections are most useful for showing areas that have long east-west dimensions, such as the United States.

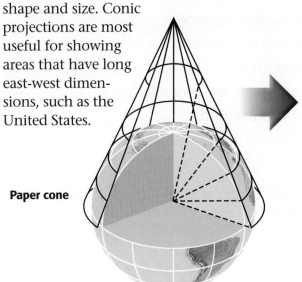

Paper cone

Conic projection

Flat-plane Projections

Flat-plane projections are based on a plane touching the globe at one point, such as at the North Pole or South Pole. A flat-plane projection is useful for showing true direction for airplane pilots and ship navigators. It also shows true area. However, it distorts the true shapes of landmasses.

Flat-plane projection

Flat plane

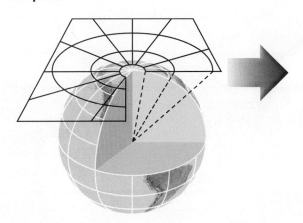

Map Essentials
How to Read a Map

Maps are like messages sent out in code. To help us translate the code, mapmakers provide certain features. These features help us understand the message they are presenting about a particular part of the world. Of these features, almost all maps have a title, a compass rose, a scale, and a legend. The map below has these four features, plus a fifth—a locator map.

❶ Title

A map's **title** shows what the subject of the map is. The map title is usually the first thing you should look at when studying a map, because it tells you what the map is trying to show.

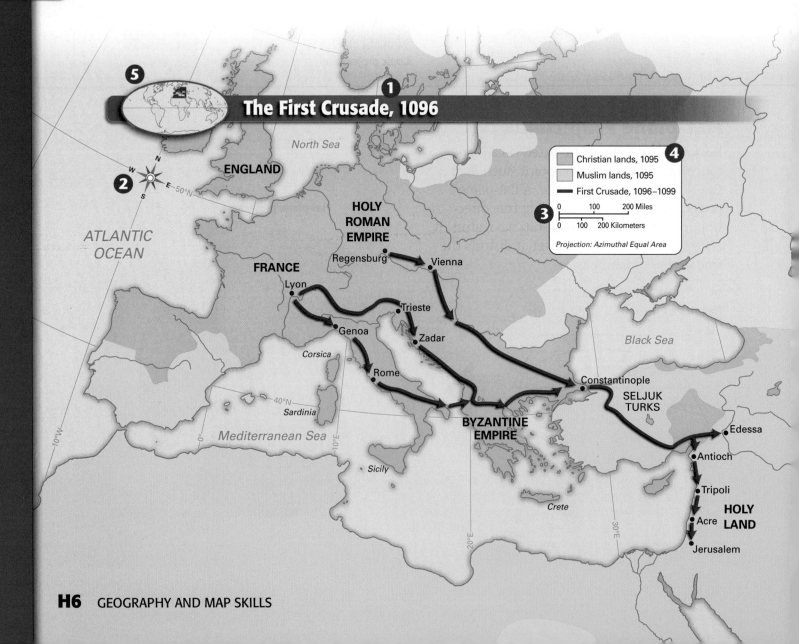

The First Crusade, 1096

Christian lands, 1095
Muslim lands, 1095
First Crusade, 1096–1099

0   100   200 Miles
0   100   200 Kilometers

Projection: Azimuthal Equal Area

North Sea

ENGLAND

ATLANTIC OCEAN

50°N

HOLY ROMAN EMPIRE

FRANCE

Regensburg

Vienna

Lyon

Trieste

Genoa

Zadar

Corsica

Rome

Black Sea

Constantinople

SELJUK TURKS

40°N

Sardinia

BYZANTINE EMPIRE

Edessa

Mediterranean Sea

Antioch

Sicily

Tripoli

Crete

HOLY LAND

Acre

Jerusalem

10°W

0°

10°E

20°E

30°E

❷ Compass Rose

A directional indicator shows which way north, south, east, and west lie on the map. Some mapmakers use a "north arrow," which points toward the North Pole. Remember, "north" is not always at the top of a map. The way a map is drawn and the location of directions on that map depend on the perspective of the mapmaker. Most maps in this textbook indicate direction by using a compass rose. A **compass rose** has arrows that point to all four principal directions.

❸ Scale

Mapmakers use scales to represent the distances between points on a map. Scales may appear on maps in several different forms. The maps in this textbook provide a **bar scale**. Scales give distances in miles and kilometers.

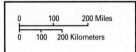

To find the distance between two points on the map, place a piece of paper so that the edge connects the two points. Mark the location of each point on the paper with a line or dot. Then, compare the distance between the two dots with the map's bar scale. The number on the top of the scale gives the distance in miles. The number on the bottom gives the distance in kilometers. Because the distances are given in large intervals, you may have to approximate the actual distance on the scale.

❹ Legend

The **legend**, or key, explains what the symbols on the map represent. Point symbols are used to specify the location of things, such as cities, that do not take up much space on the map. Some legends show colors that represent certain features like empires or other regions. Other maps might have legends with symbols or colors that represent features such as roads. Legends can also show economic resources, land use, population density, and climate.

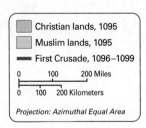

❺ Locator Map

A **locator map** shows where in the world the area on the map is located. The area shown on the main map is shown in red on the locator map. The locator map also shows surrounding areas so the map reader can see how the information on the map relates to neighboring lands.

Working with Maps
Using Different Kinds of Maps

As you study the world's regions and countries, you will use a variety of maps. Political maps and physical maps are two of the most common types of maps you will study. In addition, you will use special-purpose maps. These maps might show climate, population, resources, ancient empires, or other topics.

Political Maps

Political maps show the major political features of a region. These features include country borders, capital cities, and other places. Political maps use different colors to represent countries, and capital cities are often shown with a special star symbol.

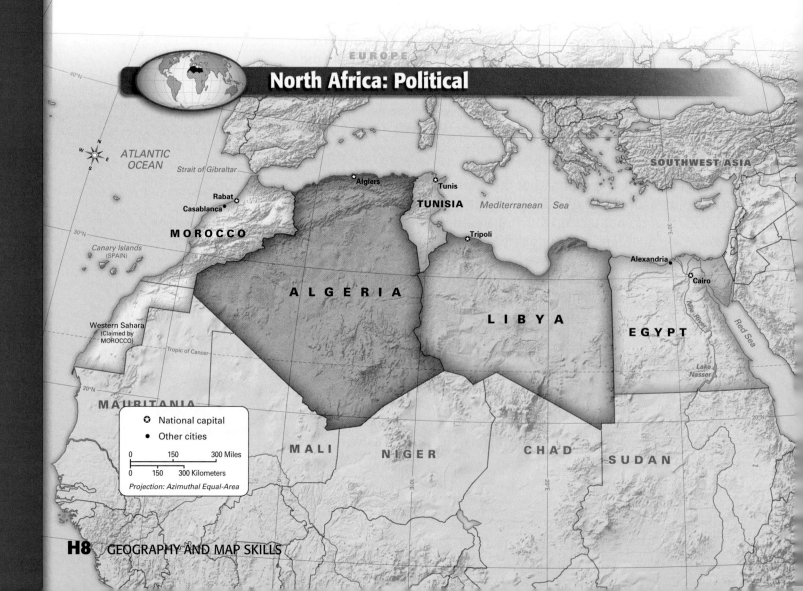

North Africa: Political

National capital
Other cities

0   150   300 Miles
0 150 300 Kilometers
Projection: Azimuthal Equal-Area

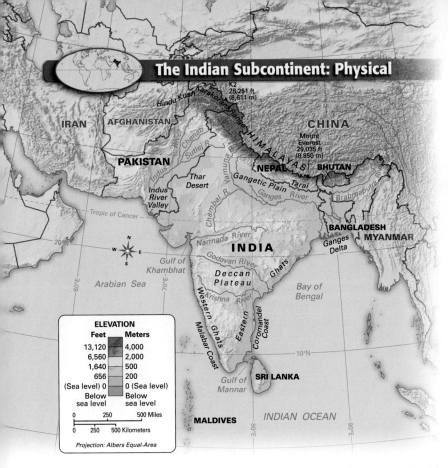

The Indian Subcontinent: Physical

K2
28,251 ft
(8,611 m)

Hindu Kush

Karakoram Range

IRAN

AFGHANISTAN

CHINA

Mount Everest
29,035 ft
(8,850 m)

HIMALAYAS

PAKISTAN

NEPAL

BHUTAN

Chenab R.

Sutlej R.

Indus R.

Thar Desert

Gangetic Plain

Tarai

Ganges

Yamuna R.

BANGLADESH

Indus River Valley

MYANMAR

Tropic of Cancer

Chambal R.

Narmada River

INDIA

Ganges Delta

Brahmaputra

Godavari River

Ghats

20°N

Gulf of Khambhat

Deccan Plateau

Bay of Bengal

Arabian Sea

Krishna River

Western Ghats

Eastern Ghats

Coromandel Coast

10°N

ELEVATION

Feet	Meters
13,120	4,000
6,560	2,000
1,640	500
656	200
(Sea level) 0	0 (Sea level)
Below sea level	Below sea level

Malabar Coast

Gulf of Mannar

SRI LANKA

0   250   500 Miles

0   250   500 Kilometers

Projection: Albers Equal-Area

MALDIVES

INDIAN OCEAN

Physical Maps

Physical maps show the major physical features of a region. These features may include mountain ranges, rivers, oceans, islands, deserts, and plains. Often, these maps use different colors to represent different elevations of land. As a result, the map reader can easily see which areas are high elevations, like mountains, and which areas are lower.

Special-Purpose Maps

Special-purpose maps focus on one special topic, such as climate, resources, or population. These maps present information on the topic that is particularly important in the region. Depending on the type of special-purpose map, the information may be shown with different colors, arrows, dots, or other symbols.

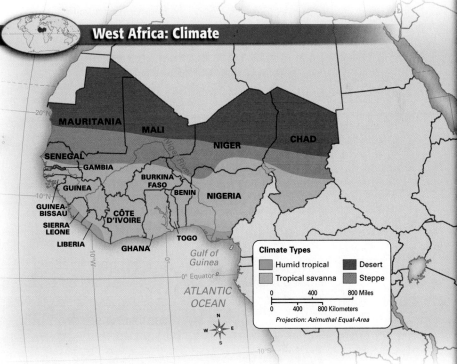

West Africa: Climate

20°N

MAURITANIA

MALI

Niger River

NIGER

CHAD

SENEGAL

GAMBIA

GUINEA

BURKINA FASO

BENIN

NIGERIA

GUINEA-BISSAU

CÔTE D'IVOIRE

10°N

SIERRA LEONE

LIBERIA

GHANA

TOGO

Gulf of Guinea

0° Equator

ATLANTIC OCEAN

10°S

Climate Types

Humid tropical		Desert
Tropical savanna		Steppe

0   400   800 Miles

0   400   800 Kilometers

Projection: Azimuthal Equal-Area

Using Maps in Geography The different kinds of maps in this textbook will help you study and understand geography. By working with these maps, you will see what the physical geography of places is like, where people live, and how the world has changed over time.

Geographic Dictionary

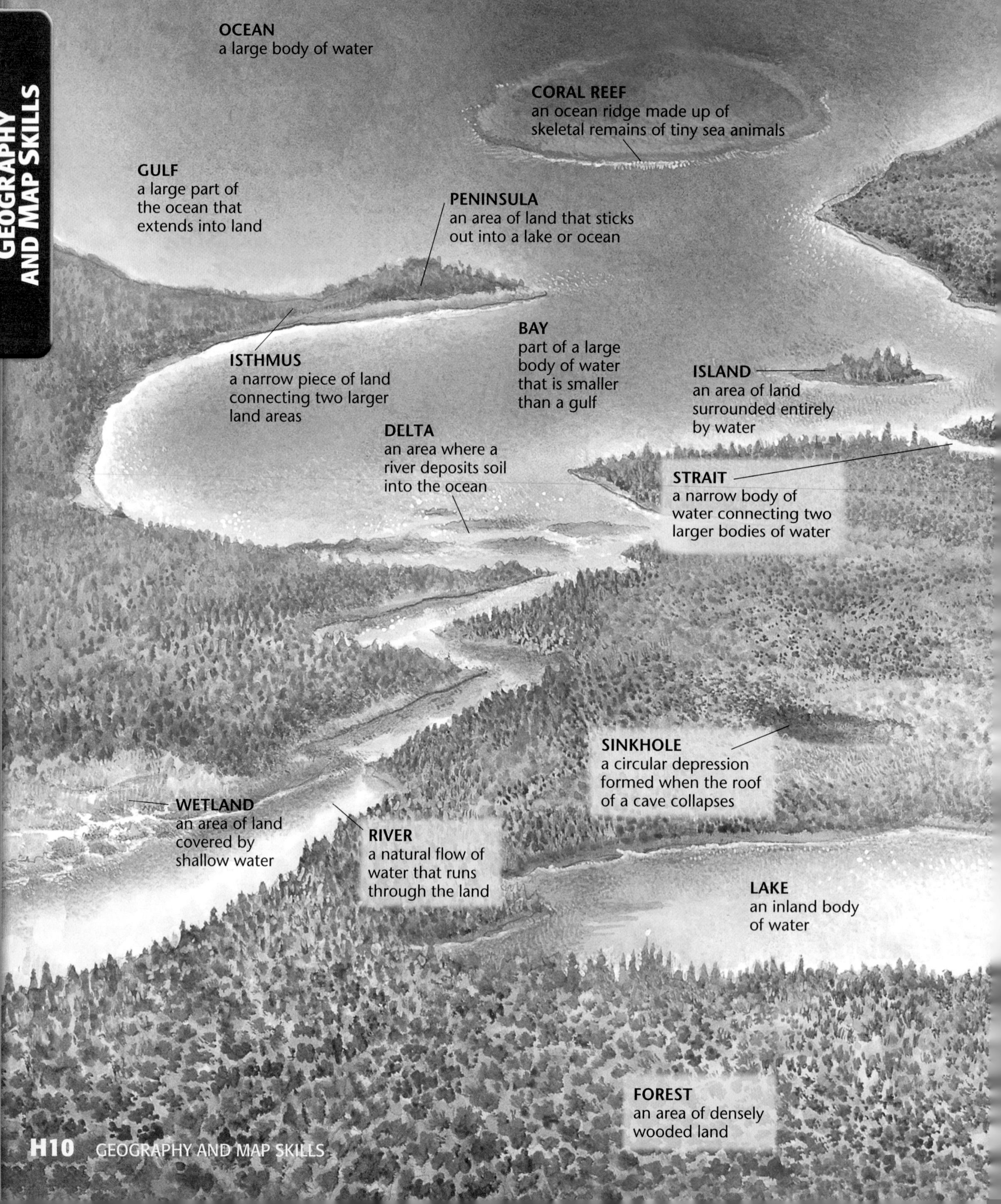

OCEAN
a large body of water

CORAL REEF
an ocean ridge made up of
skeletal remains of tiny sea animals

GULF
a large part of
the ocean that
extends into land

PENINSULA
an area of land that sticks
out into a lake or ocean

ISTHMUS
a narrow piece of land
connecting two larger
land areas

BAY
part of a large
body of water
that is smaller
than a gulf

ISLAND
an area of land
surrounded entirely
by water

DELTA
an area where a
river deposits soil
into the ocean

STRAIT
a narrow body of
water connecting two
larger bodies of water

SINKHOLE
a circular depression
formed when the roof
of a cave collapses

WETLAND
an area of land
covered by
shallow water

RIVER
a natural flow of
water that runs
through the land

LAKE
an inland body
of water

FOREST
an area of densely
wooded land

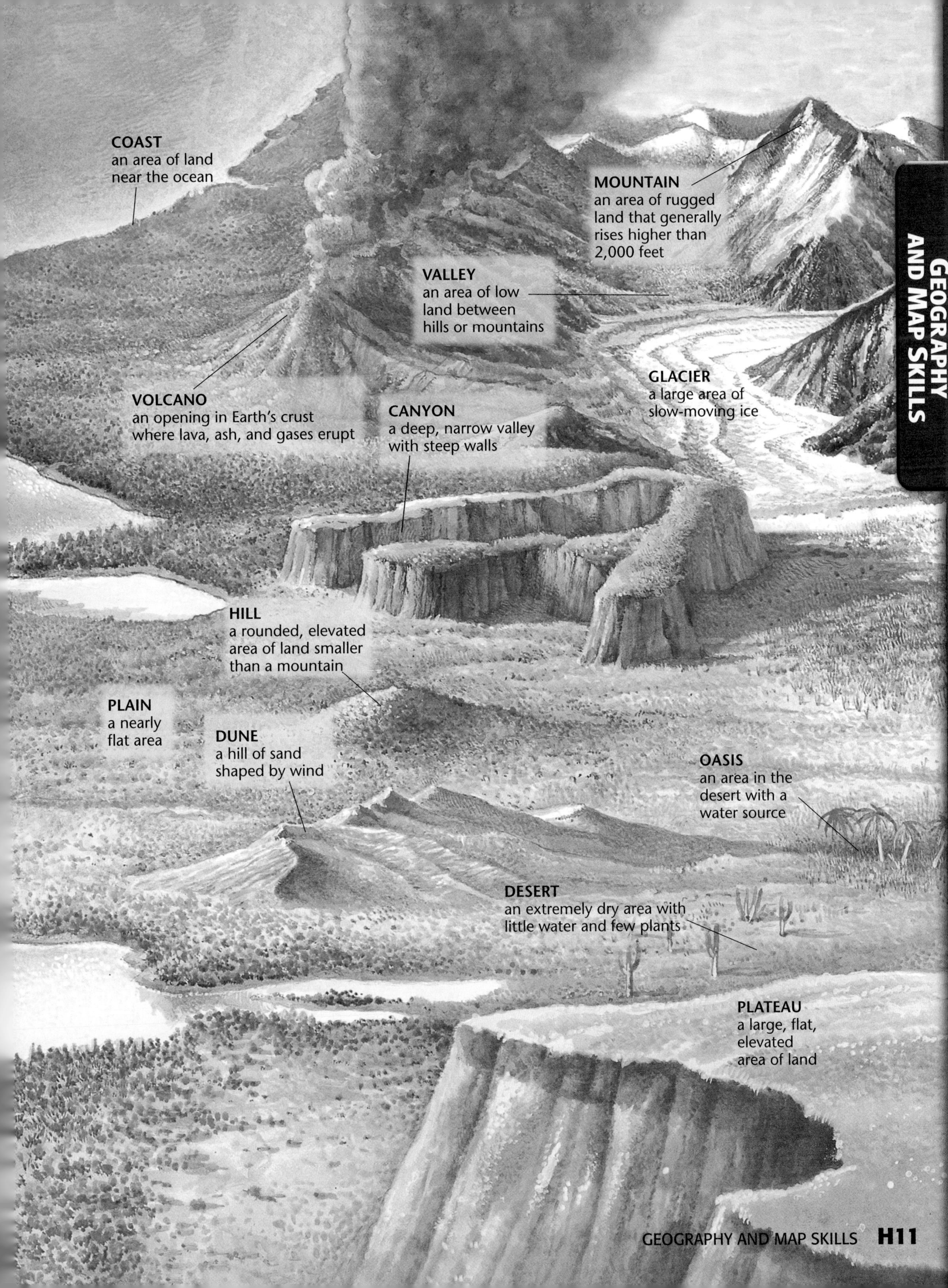

COAST
an area of land
near the ocean

MOUNTAIN
an area of rugged
land that generally
rises higher than
2,000 feet

VALLEY
an area of low
land between
hills or mountains

GLACIER
a large area of
slow-moving ice

VOLCANO
an opening in Earth's crust
where lava, ash, and gases erupt

CANYON
a deep, narrow valley
with steep walls

HILL
a rounded, elevated
area of land smaller
than a mountain

PLAIN
a nearly
flat area

DUNE
a hill of sand
shaped by wind

OASIS
an area in the
desert with a
water source

DESERT
an extremely dry area with
little water and few plants

PLATEAU
a large, flat,
elevated
area of land

Themes and Essential Elements of Geography

by Dr. Christopher L. Salter

To study the world, geographers have identified 5 key themes, 6 essential elements, and 18 geography standards.

"How should we teach and learn about geography?" Professional geographers have worked hard over the years to answer this important question.

In 1984 a group of geographers identified the 5 Themes of Geography. These themes did a wonderful job of laying the groundwork for good classroom geography. Teachers used the 5 Themes in class, and geographers taught workshops on how to apply them in the world.

By the early 1990s, however, some geographers felt the 5 Themes were too broad. They created the 18 Geography Standards and the 6 Essential Elements. The 18 Geography Standards include more detailed information about what geography is, and the 6 Essential Elements are like a bridge between the 5 Themes and 18 Standards.

Look at the chart to the right. It shows how each of the 5 Themes connects to the Essential Elements and Standards. For example, the theme of Location is related to The World in Spatial Terms and the first three Standards. Study the chart carefully to see how the other themes, elements, and Standards are related.

The last Essential Element and the last two Standards cover The Uses of Geography. These key parts of geography were not covered by the 5 Themes. They will help you see how geography has influenced the past, present, and future.

5 Themes of Geography

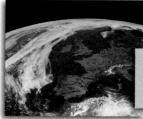

Location The theme of location describes where something is.

Place Place describes the features that make a site unique.

Regions Regions are areas that share common characteristics.

Movement This theme looks at how and why people and things move.

Human-Environment Interaction People interact with their environment in many ways.

6 Essential Elements

18 Geography Standards

1. How to use maps and other tools
2. How to use mental maps to organize information
3. How to analyze the spatial organization of people, places, and environments

I. The World in Spatial Terms

4. The physical and human characteristics of places
5. How people create regions to interpret Earth
6. How culture and experience influence people's perceptions of places and regions

II. Places and Regions

7. The physical processes that shape Earth's surface
8. The distribution of ecosystems on Earth

9. The characteristics, distribution, and migration of human populations
10. The complexity of Earth's cultural mosaics
11. The patterns and networks of economic interdependence on Earth
12. The patterns of human settlement
13. The forces of cooperation and conflict

III. Physical Systems

IV. Human Systems

14. How human actions modify the physical environment
15. How physical systems affect human systems
16. The distribution and meaning of resources

V. Environment and Society

17. How to apply geography to interpret the past
18. How to apply geography to interpret the present and plan for the future

VI. The Uses of Geography

Become an Active Reader

by Dr. Kylene Beers

Did you ever think you would begin reading your social studies book by reading about *reading*? Actually, it makes better sense than you might think. You would probably make sure you knew some soccer skills and strategies before playing in a game. Similarly, you need to know something about reading skills and strategies before reading your social studies book. In other words, you need to make sure you know what- ever you need to know in order to read this book successfully.

Tip #1

Read Everything on the Page!

You can't follow the directions on the cake-mix box if you don't know where the directions are! Cake-mix boxes always have direc- tions on them telling you how many eggs to add or how long to bake the cake. But, if you can't find that information, it doesn't mat- ter that it is there.

Likewise, this book is filled with information that will help you understand what you are reading. If you don't study that informa- tion, however, it might as well not be there. Let's take a look at some of the places where you'll find important information in this book.

The Chapter Opener
The chapter opener gives you a brief over- view of what you will learn in the chapter. You can use this information to prepare to read the chapter.

The Section Openers
Before you begin to read each section, pre- view the information under What You Will Learn. There you'll find the main ideas of the section and key terms that are important in it. Knowing what you are looking for before you start reading can improve your under- standing.

Boldfaced Words
Those words are important and are defined somewhere on the page where they appear— either right there in the sentence or over in the side margin.

Maps, Charts, and Artwork
These things are not there just to take up space or look good! Study them and read the information beside them. It will help you understand the information in the chapter.

Questions at the End of Sections
At the end of each section, you will find questions that will help you decide whether you need to go back and re-read any parts before moving on. If you can't answer a question, that is your cue to go back and re- read.

Questions at the End of the Chapter
Answer the questions at the end of each chapter, even if your teacher doesn't ask you to. These questions are there to help you figure out what you need to review.

Tip #2

Use the Reading Skills and Strategies in Your Textbook

Good readers use a number of skills and strategies to make sure they understand what they are reading. In this textbook you will find help with important reading skills and strategies such as "Using Prior Knowledge," and "Understanding Main Ideas."

We teach the reading skills and strategies in several ways. Use these activities and lessons and you will become a better reader.

- First, on the opening page of every chapter we identify and explain the reading skill or strategy you will focus on as you work through the chapter. In fact, these activities are called "Focus on Reading."

- Second, as you can see in the example at right, we tell you where to go for more help. The back of the book has a reading handbook with a full-page practice lesson to match the reading skill or strategy in every chapter.

- Third, we give you short practice activities and examples as you read the chapter. These activities and examples show up in the margin of your book. Again, look for the words, "Focus on Reading."

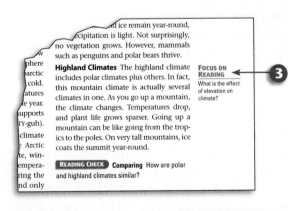

- Finally, we provide another practice activity in the Chapter Review at the end of every chapter. That activity gives you one more chance to make sure you know how to use the reading skill or strategy.

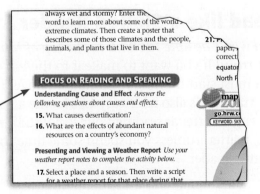

Tip #3

Pay Attention to Vocabulary

It is no fun to read something when you don't know what the words mean, but you can't learn new words if you only use or read the words you already know. In this book, we know we have probably used some words you don't know. But, we have followed a pattern as we have used more difficult words.

- First, at the beginning of each section you will find a list of key terms that you will need to know. Be on the lookout for those words as you read through the section. You will find that we have defined those words right there in the paragraph where they are used. Look for a word that is in boldface with its definition highlighted in yellow.

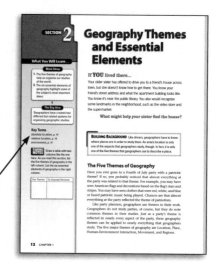

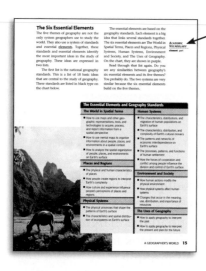

- Second, when we use a word that is important in all classes, not just social studies, we define it in the margin under the heading Academic Vocabulary. You will run into these academic words in other textbooks, so you should learn what they mean while reading this book.

Tip #4

Read like a Skilled Reader

You won't be able to climb to the top of Mount Everest if you do not train! If you want to make it to the top of Mount Everest then you must start training to climb that huge mountain.

Training is also necessary to become a good reader. You will never get better at reading your social studies book—or any book for that matter—unless you spend some time thinking about how to be a better reader.

Skilled readers do the following:

1. They preview what they are supposed to read before they actually begin reading. When previewing, they look for vocabulary words, titles of sections, information in the margin, or maps or charts they should study.

2. They get ready to take some notes while reading by dividing their notebook paper into two parts. They title one side "Notes from the Chapter" and the other side "Questions or Comments I Have."

3. As they read, they complete their notes.

4. They read like **active readers**. The Active Reading list below shows you what that means.

5. Finally, they use clues in the text to help them figure out where the text is going. The best clues are called signal words. These are words that help you identify chronological order, causes and effects, or comparisons and contrasts.

Chronological Order Signal Words: *first, second, third, before, after, later, next, following that, earlier, subsequently, finally*

Cause and Effect Signal Words: *because of, due to, as a result of, the reason for, therefore, consequently, so, basis for*

Comparison/Contrast Signal Words: *likewise, also, as well as, similarly, on the other hand*

Active Reading

There are three ways to read a book: You can be a turn-the-pages-no-matter-what type of reader. These readers just keep on turning pages whether or not they understand what they are reading. Or, you can be a stop-watch-and-listen kind of reader. These readers know that if they wait long enough, someone will tell them what they need to know. Or, you can be an active reader. These readers know that it is up to them to figure out what the text means. Active readers do the following as they read:

Predict what will happen next based on what has already happened. When your predictions don't match what happens in the text, re-read the confusing parts.

Question what is happening as you read. Constantly ask yourself why things have happened, what things mean, and what caused certain events. Jot down notes about the questions you can't answer.

Summarize what you are reading frequently. Do not try to summarize the entire chapter! Read a bit and then summarize it. Then read on.

Connect what is happening in the section you're reading to what you have already read.

Clarify your understanding. Be sure that you understand what you are reading by stopping occasionally to ask yourself whether you are confused by anything. Sometimes you might need to re-read to clarify. Other times you might need to read further and collect more information before you can understand. Still other times you might need to ask the teacher to help you with what is confusing you.

Visualize what is happening in the text. In other words, try to see the events or places in your mind. It might help you to draw maps, make charts, or jot down notes about what you are reading as you try to visualize the action in the text.

Social Studies Words

As you read this textbook, you will be more successful if you learn the meanings of the words on this page. You will come across these words many times in your social studies classes, like geography and history. Read through these words now to become familiar with them before you begin your studies.

Social Studies Words

WORDS ABOUT TIME

AD	refers to dates after the birth of Jesus
BC	refers to dates before Jesus's birth
BCE	refers to dates before Jesus's birth, stands for "before the common era"
CE	refers to dates after Jesus's birth, stands for "common era"
century	a period of 100 years
decade	a period of 10 years
era	a period of time
millennium	a period of 1,000 years

WORDS ABOUT THE WORLD

climate	the weather conditions in a certain area over a long period of time
geography	the study of the world's people, places, and landscapes
physical features	features on Earth's surface, such as mountains and rivers
region	an area with one or more features that make it different from surrounding areas
resources	materials found on Earth that people need and value

WORDS ABOUT PEOPLE

anthropology	the study of people and cultures
archaeology	the study of the past based on what people left behind
citizen	a person who lives under the control of a government
civilization	the way of life of people in a particular place or time
culture	the knowledge, beliefs, customs, and values of a group of people
custom	a repeated practice or tradition
economics	the study of the production and use of goods and services
economy	any system in which people make and exchange goods and services
government	the body of officials and groups that run an area
history	the study of the past
politics	the process of running a government
religion	a system of beliefs in one or more gods or spirits
society	a group of people who share common traditions
trade	the exchange of goods or services

Academic Words

What are academic words? They are important words used in all of your classes, not just social studies. You will see these words in other textbooks, so you should learn what they mean while reading this book. Review this list now. You will use these words again in the chapters of this book.

Academic Words

acquire	to get	**implement**	to put in place
advocate	to plead in favor of	**implications**	consequences
authority	power or influence	**implicit**	understood though not clearly put into words
circumstances	conditions that influence an event or activity	**incentive**	something that leads people to follow a certain course of action
classical	referring to the cultures of ancient Greece or Rome	**innovation**	a new idea or way of doing something
complex	difficult, not simple	**interpret**	to explain the meaning of something
consequences	the effects of a particular event or events	**method**	a way of doing something
contracts	binding legal agreements	**policy**	rule, course of action
development	creation; the process of growing or improving	**primary**	main, most important
distinct	clearly different and separate	**principle**	basic belief, rule, or law
distribute	to divide among a group of people	**procedure**	a series of steps taken to accomplish a task
efficient	productive and not wasteful	**process**	a series of steps by which a task is accomplished
element	part	**purpose**	the reason something is done
establish	to set up or create	**rebel**	to fight against authority
ethical	related to rules of conduct or proper behavior	**role**	a part or function
explicit	fully revealed without vagueness	**strategy**	a plan for fighting a battle or war
facilitate	to make easier	**structure**	the way something is set up or organized
factor	cause	**traditional**	customary, time-honored
features	characteristics	**values**	ideas that people hold dear and try to live by
function	work or perform	**vary**	to be different
ideals	ideas or goals that people try to live up to		
impact	effect, result		

Multiple Choice

A multiple-choice test item is a question or an incomplete statement with several answer choices. To answer a multiple-choice test item, select the choice that best answers the question or that best completes the statement.

Learn

Use these strategies to answer multiple-choice test items:

❶ Carefully read the question or incomplete statement.

❷ Look for words that affect the meaning, such as *all, always, best, every, most, never, not,* or *only.* For example, in Item 1 to the right, the word *all* tells you to look for the answer in which all three choices are correct.

❸ Read *all* the choices before selecting an answer—even if the first choice seems right.

❹ In your mind, cross off any of the answer choices that you know for certain are wrong.

❺ Consider the choices that are left and select the *best* answer. If you are not sure, select the choice that makes the most sense.

For each statement or question, write the number of the word or expression that, of those given, best completes the statement or answers the question.

❶ ❷

1 **Which of the following are *all* physical features of geography?**
(1) landforms, climates, people
(2) landforms, climates, soils
(3) landscapes, climates, plants
(4) landscapes, communities, soils ❸

2 **A region is an area that has**
(1) one or more common features. ❺
(2) no people living in it. ❹
(3) few physical features.
(4) set physical boundaries.

Practice

For each statement or question, write the number of the word or expression that, of those given, best completes the statement or answers the question.

1 **Which of the following is part of the study of human geography?**
(1) bodies of water
(2) communities
(3) landforms
(4) plants

2 **The economy of North Korea is *best* described as a**
(1) command economy.
(2) developed economy.
(3) market economy.
(4) traditional economy.

Primary Sources

Primary sources are materials, often called documents, created by people who lived during the times you are reading about. Examples of primary sources include text documents, such as letters and diaries, and visual documents, such as photographs.

Learn

Use these strategies to answer test questions about primary sources:

1 Note the document's title and source line. This information can tell you the document's author, date, and purpose.

2 Skim the document. Get an idea of its main focus.

3 Read the question about the document. Note what information you are being asked to find.

4 Read or examine the document carefully. As you do, identify the main idea and key details.

5 Compare the question and answer choices to the document. Look for similar words. Then read between the lines. Use your critical-thinking skills to draw conclusions.

6 Review the question and select the best answer.

Base your answer to the following question on the text excerpt and on your knowledge of social studies.

1

Geography for Life

"Geography is a field of study that enables us to find answers to questions about the world around us—about where things are and how and why they got there…With a strong grasp of geography, people are better equipped to solve issues at not only the local level but also the global level."

— from *Geography for Life*, by the Geography Education Standards Project

4

2

1

1 Which statement below *best* summarizes the main idea of the above passage?

3

(1) Geography helps people to read and make maps.

(2) Geography helps people to get where they are going.

6

(3) Geography helps people to understand the world better and to solve problems.

5

(4) Geography helps people explore Earth.

Practice

Base your answers to the following questions on the text excerpt above and on your knowledge of social studies.

1 What is one question geography can answer for us?

(1) when events happened

((2)) where things are

(3) why people act how they do

(4) why the sky is blue

2 What are two levels at which geography helps people solve issues?

(1) global and strong

(2) equipped and global

(3) strong and equipped

((4)) local and global

H21

Charts and Graphs

Charts and graphs are tables or drawings that present and organize information or data. Some standardized tests include questions about charts and graphs. These questions require you to interpret the information or data in the chart or graph to answer the question.

Learn

Use these strategies to answer test questions about charts and graphs:

❶ Read the title of the chart or graph. Identify the subject and purpose of the information shown.

❷ Read all the other labels. Note the types of information the chart or graph is showing and how the information is organized.

❸ Analyze the information or data. Look for patterns, changes over time, and similarities or differences. For example, in the graph at right, world population growth rises dramatically after 1900.

❹ Read the question carefully. Note key words in the question.

❺ Review the chart or graph to find the correct answer.

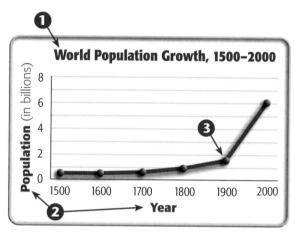

World Population Growth, 1500–2000

Source: *Atlas of World Population History*

❶ **Based on the graph above, during which period did the world population <u>increase</u> the <u>most</u>?** **❹**

(1) 1600 to 1700

(2) 1700 to 1800

(3) 1800 to 1900

❺ (4) 1900 to 2000

Practice

Base your answer to the following question on the chart and on your knowledge of social studies.

❶ **Which country in the Ring of Fire had two major volcanic eruptions?**

(1) Colombia

(2) Indonesia

(3) Philippines

(4) United States

Major Eruptions in the Ring of Fire

THE WORLD ALMANAC
Facts about the World

Volcano	Year
Tambora, Indonesia	1815
Krakatau, Indonesia	1883
Mount Saint Helens, United States	1980
Nevado del Ruiz, Colombia	1985
Mount Pinatubo, Philippines	1991

Maps

Standardized tests may include questions that refer to information in maps. These maps might show political features such as cities and states, physical features such as mountains and plains, or information such as climate, land use, or settlement patterns.

Learn

Use these strategies to answer questions about maps.

❶ Read the map title to identify the map's subject and purpose. The map below shows levels of government freedom around the world.

❷ Study the legend. It explains information in the map, such as what different colors or symbols mean.

❸ Note the map's direction and scale. The scale shows the distance between points in the map.

❹ Examine the map closely. Read all the labels and study the other information, such as colors, borders, or symbols.

❺ Read the question about the map.

❻ Review the map to find the answer.

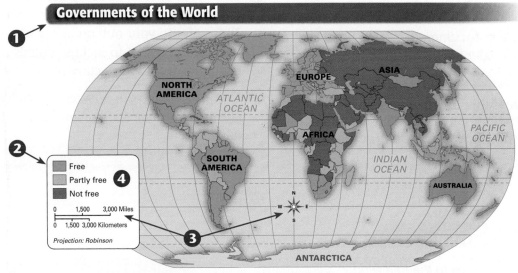

Governments of the World

Free
Partly free
Not free

0   1,500   3,000 Miles
0 1,500 3,000 Kilometers

Projection: Robinson

Source: *Freedom House*

Practice

Base your answers to the following questions on the map and on your knowledge of social studies.

1 Which two continents have the least government freedom?

(1) Africa and Asia
(2) Africa and Europe
(3) Australia and Europe
(4) Europe and Asia

2 The continents with the most freedom are Australia and

(1) Africa.
(2) Europe.
(3) North America.
(4) South America.

Constructed Response

Constructed response questions usually require you to examine a document, such as a letter, chart, or map. You then use the information in the document to write an extended answer, often a paragraph or more in length.

Learn

Use these strategies to answer extended response questions:

1 Read the directions and question carefully to determine the purpose of your answer. For example, are you to explain, identify causes, summarize, or compare? To help determine the purpose, look for key words such as *compare, contrast, describe, discuss, explain, interpret, predict,* or *summarize.*

2 Read the title of the document. Identify its subject and purpose.

3 Study the document carefully. Read all the text. Identify the main idea or focus.

4 If allowed, make notes on another sheet of paper to organize your thoughts. Jot down information from the document that you want to include in your answer.

5 Use the question to create a topic sentence. For example, for the practice question below, a topic sentence might be, "Earth's tilt and revolution cause the seasons to change at about the same time each year in the Northern Hemisphere."

6 Create an outline or graphic organizer to help organize your main points. Review the document to find details or examples to support each point.

7 Write your answer in complete sentences. Start with your topic sentence. Then refer to your outline or organizer as you write. Be sure to include details or examples from the document.

8 Last, proofread your answer. Check for correct grammar, spelling, punctuation, and sentence structure.

Practice

Base your answers to the following question on the diagram and on your knowledge of social studies.

1 **Constructed-Response Question** Write a paragraph explaining how the movement of plates on Earth's crust leads to the formation of volcanoes.

The separation of plates can allow magma to rise up and create volcanoes.

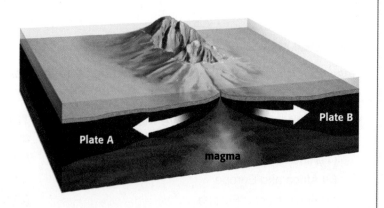

Plate A

Plate B

magma

Introduction to the Eastern Hemisphere

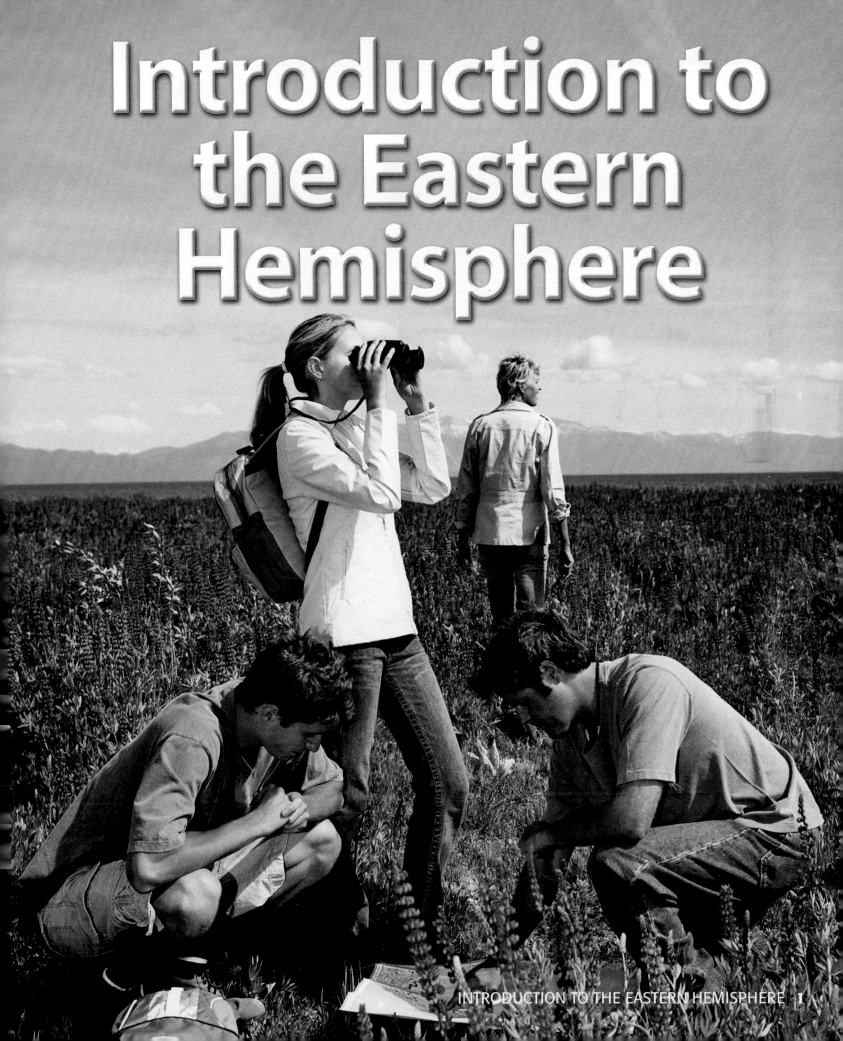

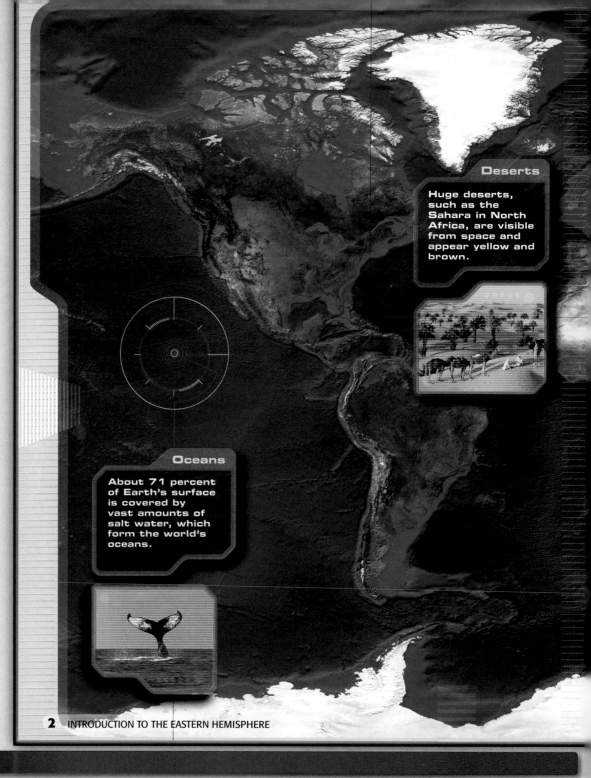

Unit Preview

Introduce the Unit

Share the information in the chapter overviews with students.

Chapter 1 Geography is the study of the world's people and places. Geographers use many tools to study the main branches of geography—human and physical. They organize their studies by using the five themes and the six essential elements of geography.

Chapter 2 The Eastern Hemisphere lies east of the prime meridian and is home to a variety of countries and cultures. Water is a dominant feature in the Eastern Hemisphere and is essential for life. Processes below and on Earth's surface shape the Eastern Hemisphere's physical features.

Chapter 3 The weather and climate of the Eastern Hemisphere are affected by various forces, including sun, location, wind, water, and mountains. The Eastern Hemisphere has five major climate zones. The Eastern Hemisphere's natural resources have many uses.

Chapter 4 Prehistoric people of the Eastern Hemisphere learned to adapt to their environment, to make simple tools, to use fire, and to use language. As people migrated around the world they learned to adapt to new environments. The development of agriculture in the Eastern Hemisphere brought great changes to human society.

Deserts

Huge deserts, such as the Sahara in North Africa, are visible from space and appear yellow and brown.

Oceans

About 71 percent of Earth's surface is covered by vast amounts of salt water, which form the world's oceans.

2 INTRODUCTION TO THE EASTERN HEMISPHERE

Unit Resources

Planning

- Differentiated Instruction Teacher Management System: Pacing Guide
- OSP Teacher's One-Stop Planner: Calendar Planner
- Power Presentations with Video CD-ROM
- Virtual File Cabinet

Differentiating Instruction

- Differentiated Instruction Teacher Management System: Lesson Plans for Differentiated Instruction
- Differentiated Instruction Modified Worksheets and Tests CD-ROM

Enrichment

- RF: Interdisciplinary Projects, Diagram an Ecosystem
- RF: Geography and History, Migration of Early Humans
- Geography, Science, and Culture Activities with Answer Key

Assessment

- PASS: Benchmark Test
- OSP ExamView Test Generator: Benchmark Test
- Holt Online Assessment Program, in the Holt Interactive Online Student Edition
- Alternative Assessment Handbook

UNIT 1
Introduction to the Eastern Hemisphere

Explore the Satellite Image
Human-made machines that orbit Earth, called satellites, send back images of our planet like this one. What can you learn about Earth from studying this satellite image?

Frozen Lands
Earth's icy poles are frozen year-round and appear a brilliant white from space. These frozen lands contain much of Earth's freshwater.

Explore the Pictures

Point out that the photographs and satellite image on these pages show some of Earth's major contrasts—ice and water, desert and forest. Ask students where they think most people on Earth live, and why. *possible answer—in the temperate regions, where the weather is mild and where there is water and vegetation*

🗺 Map Zone Transparency: Introduction to the Eastern Hemisphere

Connect to the Unit

Activity **Hold a Job Fair** Have students imagine that they are planning a career in geography. Assign small groups various career options for geographers and have students research the qualifications and possible projects that geographers in each field might have. Students might find information on the Internet or by interviewing a geographer about his or her work.

Then hold a class job fair. Have students in each group present information about each field of geography. Ask students to narrow down their choices. What aspect of geography interests them the most? Are they more interested in studying human or physical geography? Would they prefer to work in a laboratory, office, or in the field? Would they like to teach geography?

During their study of the unit, have students reconsider their choices, asking themselves whether their preferences or interests have shifted, and if so, to what. **LS** **Interpersonal**

📓 Alternative Assessment Handbook, Rubric 11: Discussions

Critical Thinking: Interpreting Maps   At Level

Analyze Satellite Technology

1. Point out the relative size of Antarctica compared to the rest of Earth as pictured in this satellite image. Then ask students to find Antarctica on a globe and on a world map. How is Antarctica represented in these sources? Which gives the most accurate representation of the continent?

2. Have students research satellite images of the poles over the last 30 years or so. One source for these images is the Web site of the U.S. Geological Survey. Ask students to write

a report based on their findings, including conclusions drawn by scientists about the causes of the shrinking polar ice caps.

3. Have students speculate about what other long-term changes might be tracked by satellites (e.g., urban growth, deforestation, and desertification). Discuss the potential impact of satellite imagery on public policy debates. **LS** **Visual/Spatial, Verbal/Linguistic**

📓 Alternative Assessment Handbook, Rubrics 21: Map Reading; and 42: Writing to Inform

Answers

Explore the Satellite Image *possible answers—types of landforms, such as deserts, mountains, and plains; distribution of vegetation; proportion of water to land; depth of oceans; extent of ice packs; the fact that there is less vegetation at the equator and none at the poles; the lands between those regions generally have more temperate climates*

3

Chapter 1 Planning Guide

A Geographer's World

Chapter Overview	Reproducible Resources	Technology Resources
CHAPTER 1 pp. 4–25 **Overview:** In this chapter, students will learn about the study of geography, the geography themes and essential elements, and the branches of geography.	**OSP Differentiated Instruction Teacher Management System:*** • Instructional Pacing Guides • Lesson Plans for Differentiated Instruction **Interactive Reader and Study Guide:** Chapter Summary Graphic Organizer **Resource File*** • Chapter Review • Focus on Reading: Using Prior Knowledge • Focus on Writing: Writing a Job Description • Social Studies Skills: Analyzing Satellite Images **Experiencing World History and Geography**	**OSP Teacher's One-Stop Planner:** Calendar Planner **Power Presentations with Video CD-ROM** **Differentiated Instruction Modified Worksheets and Tests CD-ROM** **Interactive Skills Tutor CD-ROM** **Student Edition on Audio CD Program** **Music of the World Audio CD Program** **Geography's Impact Video Series (VHS/DVD):** Impact of Studying Geography* **World Outline Maps: Transparencies and Activities**
Section 1: **Studying Geography** **The Big Idea:** The study of geography and the use of geographic tools helps us view the world in new ways.	**OSP Differentiated Instruction Teacher Management System:** Section 1 Lesson Plan* **Interactive Reader and Study Guide:** Section 1 Summary **Resource File*** • Vocabulary Builder: Section 1 • Biography: Claudius Ptolemy	**Daily Bellringer Transparency:** Section 1* **Map Zone Transparency:** High School Soccer Participation*
Section 2: **Geography Themes and Essential Elements** **The Big Idea:** Geographers have created two different but related systems for organizing geographic studies.	**OSP Differentiated Instruction Teacher Management System:** Section 2 Lesson Plan* **Interactive Reader and Study Guide:** Section 2 Summary **Resource File*** • Vocabulary Builder: Section 2 • Geography and History: Migration of Early Humans	**Daily Bellringer Transparency:** Section 2* **Map Zone Transparency:** Italy*
Section 3: **The Branches of Geography** **The Big Idea:** Geography is divided into two main branches—physical and human geography.	**OSP Differentiated Instruction Teacher Management System:** Section 3 Lesson Plan* **Interactive Reader and Study Guide:** Section 3 Summary **Resource File*** • Vocabulary Builder: Section 3 • Literature: *The Wind Makes Dust* by Carl Sagan • Biography: Ellen Churchill Semple • Primary Source: *The Travels of Marco Polo* by Marco Polo	**Daily Bellringer Transparency:** Section 3*

Review, Assessment, Intervention

- **Quick Facts Transparency:** Visual Summary: A Geographer's World*
- **Spanish Chapter Summaries Audio CD Program**
- **Progress Assessment Support System (PASS):** Chapter Test*
- **Differentiated Instruction Modified Worksheets and Tests CD-ROM:** Modified Chapter Test
- **OSP Teacher's One-Stop Planner:** ExamView Test Generator (English/Spanish)
- **Alternative Assessment Handbook**
- **HOAP Holt Online Assessment Program (HOAP),** in the Holt Interactive Online Student Edition

- **PASS:** Section 1 Quiz*
- **Online Quiz:** Section 1
- **Alternative Assessment Handbook**

- **PASS:** Section 2 Quiz*
- **Online Quiz:** Section 2
- **Alternative Assessment Handbook**

- **PASS:** Section 3 Quiz*
- **Online Quiz:** Section 3
- **Alternative Assessment Handbook**

Power Presentations with Video CD-ROM

Power Presentations with Video are visual presentations of each chapter's main ideas. Presentations can be customized by including Quick Facts charts, images from the text, and video clips.

Holt Online Learning

go.hrw.com Teacher Resources KEYWORD: SK9 TEACHER

go.hrw.com Student Resources KEYWORD: SK9 CH1

- Interactive Multimedia Activities
- Current Events
- Chapter-based Internet Activities
- and more!

Holt Interactive
Online Student Edition
Complete online support for interactivity, assessment, and reporting
- Interactive Maps and Notebook
- Standardized Test Prep
- Homework Practice and Research Activities Online

CHAPTER 1 PLANNING GUIDE

Differentiating Instruction

How do I address the needs of varied learners?
The Target Resource acts as your primary strategy for differentiated instruction.

ENGLISH-LANGUAGE LEARNERS & STRUGGLING READERS

Graphic Organizer Transparencies with Support for Reading and Writing

Spanish Resources

Spanish Chapter Summaries Audio CD Program

Teacher's One-Stop Planner:
- ExamView Test Generator, Spanish
- PuzzlePro, Spanish

Additional Resources

Differentiated Instruction Teacher Management System: Lesson Plans for Differentiated Instruction

Resource File:
- Vocabulary Builder Activities
- Social Studies Skills: Analyzing Satellite Images

Quick Facts Transparency:
- Visual Summary: A Geographer's World

Student Edition on Audio CD Program

Interactive Skills Tutor CD-ROM

English-Language Learner Strategies and Activities

SPECIAL NEEDS LEARNERS

Differentiated Instruction Modified Worksheets and Tests CD-ROM

- Vocabulary Flash Cards
- Modified Vocabulary Builder Activities
- Modified Chapter Review
- Modified Chapter Test

Additional Resources

Differentiated Instruction Teacher Management System: Lesson Plans for Differentiated Instruction

Interactive Reader and Study Guide

Resource File: Social Studies Skills: Analyzing Satellite Images

Student Edition on Audio CD Program

Interactive Skills Tutor CD-ROM

Graphic Organizer Transparencies with Support for Reading and Writing

ADVANCED/GIFTED AND TALENTED STUDENTS

Resource File

The Resource File activities allow students to extend their knowledge of chapter-related places and people and to practice geography skills.
- Focus on Reading: Using Prior Knowledge
- Focus on Writing: Writing a Job Description
- Literature: *The Wind Makes Dust* by Carl Sagan

Additional Resources

Differentiated Instruction Teacher Management System: Lesson Plans for Differentiated Instruction

World History and Geography Document-Based Questions Activities

Geography, Science, and Cultures Activities

Experiencing World History and Geography

Quiz Game CD-ROM

Differentiated Activities in the Teacher's Edition

- Geography Graphic Organizer
- Describing Pictures
- Analyzing Malawi Image
- Using Food to Understand Culture
- Identifying Main Idea

Differentiated Activities in the Teacher's Edition

- Describing Fruit
- Creating a Geography Puzzle

Differentiated Activities in the Teacher's Edition

- Researching the Channel Tunnel
- Comparing Monuments
- Examine Eratosthenes's Process

HOLT Teacher's One-Stop Planner®

How can I manage the lesson plans and support materials for differentiated instruction?

With the Teacher's One-Stop Planner, you can easily organize and print lesson plans, planning guides, and instructional materials for all learners.

The Teacher's One-Stop Planner includes the following materials to help you differentiate instruction:

- **· Interactive Teacher's Edition**
- **· Calendar Planner and pacing guides**
- **· Editable lesson plans**
- **· All reproducible ancillaries in Adobe Acrobat (PDF) format**
- **· ExamView Test Generator (English & Spanish)**
- **· Transparency and video previews**

Professional Development

What teacher training resources are available to help me grow professionally?

- **· In-service and staff development** as part of your Holt Social Studies product purchase
- **· Quick Teacher Tutorial Lesson Presentation CD-ROM**
- **·** Intensive tuition-based **Teacher Development Institute**
- **· Convenient Holt Speaker Bureau –** face-to-face workshop options
- **· 24/7 Ask A Professional Development Expert** at http://www.hrw.com/prodev/

4   CHAPTER 1

● Chapter Preview ●

Chapter Big Ideas

Section 1 The study of geography and the use of geographic tools helps us view the world in new ways.

Section 2 Geographers have created two different but related systems for organizing geographic studies.

Section 3 Geography is divided into two main branches—physical and human geography.

Focus on Reading and Writing

Reading The Resource File provides a worksheet to help students practice using prior knowledge.

📝 **RF:** Focus on Reading, Using Prior Knowledge

Writing The Resource File provides a worksheet to help students organize and write their job description.

📝 **RF:** Focus on Writing, Writing a Job Description

Key to Differentiating Instruction

Below Level

Basic-level activities designed for all students encountering new material

At Level

Intermediate-level activities designed for average students

Above Level

Challenging activities designed for honors and gifted and talented students

Standard English Mastery

Activities designed to improve standard English usage

CHAPTER 1

A Geographer's World

FOCUS QUESTION

How did geography influence the development of the Eastern Hemisphere?

What You Will Learn...

In this chapter you will learn about the field of geography, the study of the world's people and places. You will also learn why people study geography and how they organize their studies.

FOCUS ON READING AND WRITING

Using Prior Knowledge Prior knowledge is what you already know about a subject. Before you read a chapter, review the chapter and section titles. Then make a list of what you already know. Later, you can compare your prior knowledge with what you learned from the chapter. **See the lesson, Using Prior Knowledge, on page S2.**

Writing a Job Description Geographers are people who study geography, but what is it exactly that they do? As you read this chapter you will learn about the work that geographers do. Then you will write a job description that could be included in a career-planning guide.

Studying the World Exploring the world takes people to exciting and interesting places.

4   CHAPTER 1

Introduce the Chapter

At Level

Through a Geographer's Eyes

1. Ask students to imagine that they are geographers studying the area in which they live. Have them write down several things they think a geographer would want to learn about and the methods and tools they might use.

2. Ask volunteers to state a topic or method they wrote down, and why they think it is important to their area. Write the answers on the board or a flip chart.

3. After the answers are written down, ask students if they see any patterns in the kinds of things geographers might be interested in studying.

4. Explain that geography looks at physical and human features, in regions large and small, using specific methods and tools. Encourage students to think about how they might adapt or expand the list as they learn.

LS Verbal/Linguistic, Visual/Spatial

📝 Alternative Assessment Handbook, Rubric 11: Discussions

This village is in the country of Nepal. It rests high in the Himalayas, the highest mountains in the world.

What is the land around the village like? How can you tell that people live in this area?

HOLT
Geography's Impact
video series
Watch the video to understand the impact of studying geography.

Human Geography Geography is also the study of people. It asks where people live, what they eat, what they wear, and even what kinds of animals they keep.

Physical Geography Geography is the study of the world's land features, such as this windswept rock formation.

5

• Chapter Preview •

Explore the Pictures

Nepal Some of the world's highest mountains, part of the Himalayas, lie within or border Nepal. Strong rivers run from these mountains to create lush valleys. But clearing mountain lands for new fields or wood for fuel has led to serious problems with erosion.

Analyzing Visuals

What do the girl's clothes tell you about the climate in her country? *The climate is cool—at least for part of the year.*

go.hrw.com
Online Resources
Chapter Resources:
KEYWORD: SK9 CH1
Teacher Resources:
KEYWORD: SK9 TEACHER

HOLT

Geography's Impact
▶ video series
See the Video Teacher's Guide for strategies for using the chapter video to teach about the impact of studying geography.

Critical Thinking: Comparing and Contrasting   At Level

Understanding Location

1. Bring a globe to the front of the class. Ask for a volunteer to locate Nepal, Norway, and Indonesia. Discuss where each country is in relation to the equator and what the climate might be like there.

2. Ask students to discuss how people's lives might be similar or different in each place due to location. Discuss how features such as mountains and bodies of water might affect people's lives.

3. Organize students into small, mixed-ability groups. Have groups discuss the similarities and differences between the climate and features of your home state and those of Nepal, Norway, and Indonesia.

4. As a class, go over the groups' findings.
   LS **Verbal/Linguistic, Visual/Spatial**
   Alternative Assessment Handbook, Rubrics 9: Comparing and Contrasting; and 11: Discussions

Answers

Analyzing Visuals *Answers will vary but may note the snow-capped mountains and terraced landscape; the houses, walkways, and gardens are signs that people live in this area.*

Studying Geography

Bellringer

If YOU lived there... Use the **Daily Bellringer Transparency** to help students answer the question.

 Daily Bellringer Transparency, Section 1

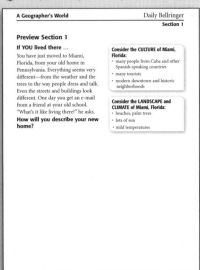

A Geographer's World   Daily Bellringer
Section 1

Preview Section 1

If YOU lived there ...
You have just moved to Miami, Florida, from your old home in Pennsylvania. Everything seems very different—from the weather and the trees to the way people dress and talk. Even the streets and buildings look different. One day you get an e-mail from a friend at your old school. "What's it like living there?" he asks. **How will you describe your new home?**

Consider the CULTURE of Miami, Florida:
• many people from Cuba and other Spanish-speaking countries
• many tourists
• modern downtown and historic neighborhoods

Consider the LANDSCAPE and CLIMATE of Miami, Florida:
• beaches, palm trees
• lots of sun
• mild temperatures

Key Terms and Places

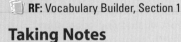 **RF:** Vocabulary Builder, Section 1

Taking Notes

Have students copy the graphic organizer onto their own paper and then use it to take notes on the section. This activity will prepare students for the Section Assessment, in which they will complete a graphic organizer that builds on the information using the Critical Thinking Skill: Summarizing.

What You Will Learn...

Main Ideas

1. Geography is the study of the world, its people, and the landscapes they create.
2. Geographers look at the world in many different ways.
3. Maps and other tools help geographers study the planet.

The Big Idea

The study of geography and the use of geographic tools helps us view the world in new ways.

Key Terms

geography, *p. 6*
landscape, *p. 6*
social science, *p. 7*
region, *p. 8*
map, *p. 10*
globe, *p. 10*

TAKING NOTES Draw a large circle like the one below in your notebook. As you read this section, write a definition of geography at the top of the circle. Below that, list details about what geographers do.

Geography is ___

If YOU lived there...

You have just moved to Miami, Florida, from your old home in Pennsylvania. Everything seems very different—from the weather and the trees to the way people dress and talk. Even the streets and buildings look different. One day you get an e-mail from a friend at your old school. "What's it like living there?" he asks.

How will you describe your new home?

> **BUILDING BACKGROUND** Often, when you are telling someone about a place they have never been, what you are describing is the place's geography. What the place looks like, what kind of weather it has, and how people live there are all parts of its geography.

What Is Geography?

Think about the place where you live. What does the land look like? Are there tall mountains nearby, or is the land so flat that you can see for miles? Is the ground covered with bright green grass and trees, or is the area part of a sandy desert?

Now think about the weather in your area. What is it like? Does it get really hot in the summer? Do you see snow every winter? How much does it rain? Do tornadoes ever strike?

Finally, think about the people who live in your town or city. Do they live mostly in apartments or houses? Do most people own cars, or do they get around town on buses or trains? What kinds of jobs do adults in your town have? Were most of the people you know born in your town, or did they move there?

The things that you have been thinking about are part of your area's geography. **Geography** is the study of the world, its people, and the landscapes they create. To a geographer, a place's **landscape** is all the human and physical features that make it unique. When they study the world's landscapes, geographers ask questions much like the ones you just asked yourself.

Teach the Big Idea   At Level

Studying Geography

1. **Teach** Ask students the questions in the Main Idea boxes under Direct Teach.

2. **Apply** Have students work in small groups to create a poster describing their community for a geographer who will be studying it. The group should agree on labels for physical and human characteristics. For each label, students should provide visual or written information, indicate known regional or global connections (such as the names of rivers or immigrant groups), and suggest a method of study (make observations).

3. **Review** Have each group present its poster to the class.

4. **Practice/Homework** Have students draw a map of their neighborhood. Tell students to include a compass rose and a legend.
   LS Verbal/Linguistic, Visual/Spatial

   Alternative Assessment Handbook, Rubrics 20: Map Creation; and 28: Posters

Geography as a Science

Many of the questions that geographers ask deal with how the world works. They want to know what causes mountains to form and what creates tornadoes. To answer questions like these, geographers have to think and act like scientists.

As scientists, geographers look at data, or information, that they gather about places. Gathering data can sometimes lead geographers to fascinating places. They might have to crawl deep into caves or climb tall mountains to make observations and take measurements. At other times, geographers study sets of images collected by satellites orbiting high above Earth.

However geographers gather their data, they have to study it carefully. Like other scientists, geographers must examine their findings in great detail before they can learn what all the information means.

Geography as a Social Science

Not everything that geographers study can be measured in numbers, however. Some geographers study people and their lives. For example, they may ask why countries change their governments or why people in a place speak a certain language. This kind of information cannot be measured.

Because it deals with people and how they live, geography is sometimes called a social science. A **social science** is a field that studies people and the relationships among them.

The geographers who study people do not dig in caves or climb mountains. Instead, they visit places and talk to the people who live there. They want to learn about people's lives and communities.

READING CHECK **Analyzing** In what ways is geography both a science and a social science?

What Is Geography?

Geography is the study of the world, its people, and the landscapes they create. To study a place's geography, we look at its physical and human features.

The physical features of Algeria include huge deserts full of tall sand dunes.

Many Algerians live in small villages like this one. The village is one of Algeria's human features.

Together, Algeria's physical and human features create the country's landscape.

ANALYSIS SKILL **ANALYZING VISUALS**
What is the landscape of this part of Algeria like?

Differentiating Instruction

At Level

Struggling Readers

1. To help students understand that geography is both a science and a social science, draw the graphic organizer for students to see. Omit the blue, italicized answers.

2. Have each student copy and complete the graphic organizer. When students are finished, review the answers with the group.
   LS **Verbal/Linguistic, Visual/Spatial**
   Alternative Assessment Handbook, Rubric 13: Graphic Organizers

```
                    Geography
                   /          \
              Science      Social Science
             /   |   \        /        \
        Observe Measure View    Visit places  Talk to
                      satellite  people live   people
                      images
```

Direct Teach

Main Idea

❶ **What Is Geography?**

Geography is the study of the world, its people, and the landscapes they create.

Identify What are three ways that geographers can gather scientific data about places? *make observations, take measurements, study satellite images*

Explain Why is geography sometimes called a social science? *It deals with people and how they live.*

Summarize What are some types of work a geographer might do? *study places close-up, such as caves and mountains; study the earth using images taken from a distance; study the lives of people in a certain place*

Predict In what ways could studying geography be useful? *help communities plan change; learn how people protect themselves from weather; see how world regions affect each other*

Connect to English/Language Arts

Geography The word *geography* comes from the Greek *geographein*, meaning "to describe the earth's surface"; "geo" means "earth" and "graphein" means "to write." Can you think of another type of study of the earth that begins with "geo"? *geology*

Answers

Reading Check *Like scientists, geographers gather and study data. Geographers also study people and how they live, like social scientists.*

Analyzing Visuals *small village, huge desert, tall sand dunes*

7

❷ Looking at the World

Geographers look at the world in many different ways.

Recall What two types of characteristics can define a region? *physical, human*

Contrast What might a geographer study at the local, regional, and global levels? *local—how people in a community or town live; regional—how the landscape affects people's lives, how people in the region interact; global—how people interact all over the world, how people's actions in one place affect other parts of the world*

Identify Cause and Effect What do you think will happen as communication and transportation systems improve? *global relationships will become more common*

📑 **RF:** Biography, Claudius Ptolemy

Looking at the World

Whether they study volcanoes and storms or people and cities, geographers have to look carefully at the world around them. To fully understand how the world works, geographers often look at places at three different levels.

Local Level

Some geographers study issues at a local level. They ask the same types of questions we asked at the beginning of this chapter: How do people in a town or community live? What is the local government like? How do the people who live there get around? What do they eat?

By asking these questions, geographers can figure out why people live and work the way they do. They can also help people improve their lives. For example, they can help town leaders figure out the best place to build new schools, shopping centers, or sports complexes. They can also help the people who live in the city or town plan for future changes.

Regional Level

Sometimes, though, geographers want to study a bigger chunk of the world. To do this, they divide the world into regions. A **region** is a part of the world that has one or more common features that distinguish it from surrounding areas.

Some regions are defined by physical characteristics such as mountain ranges, climates, or plants native to the area. As a result, these types of regions are often easy to identify. The Rocky Mountains of the western United States, for example, make up a physical region. Another example of this kind of region is the Sahara, a huge desert in northern Africa.

Other regions may not be so easy to define, however. These regions are based on the human characteristics of a place, such as language, religion, or history. A place in which most people share these kinds of characteristics can also be seen as a region. For example, most people in Scandinavia, a region in northern Europe, speak similar languages and practice the same religion.

Looking at the World

Geographers look at the world at many levels. At each level, they ask different questions and discover different types of information. By putting information gathered at different levels together, geographers can better understand a place and its role in the world.

ANALYZING VISUALS Based on these photos, what are some questions a geographer might ask about London?

Local Level This busy neighborhood in London, England, is a local area. A geographer here might study local foods, housing, or clothing.

Critical Thinking: Identifying Frame of Reference
At Level

Using a Globe

1. Bring a globe to the front of the class. Ask students what *global* means. Be sure they understand it refers to the whole planet.

2. Ask what *local* means. Ask for a volunteer to point on the globe to their town or city. Ask the class if everyone agrees this location is correct.

3. Ask what *regional* means. Ask a volunteer to show the region the school community is part of (for example, surrounding cities or states). Have the student explain why this is a region (for example, shared land features). You

may want to have other volunteers cite other shared features.

4. Ask volunteers to show on the globe the local and regional locations for cities in other countries.

5. Lastly, name some physical and human characteristics. Then ask for volunteers to identify a region on the globe that shares those characteristics. **LS Verbal/Linguistic, Visual/Spatial**

📝 Alternative Assessment Handbook, Rubric 9: Comparing and Contrasting

Answers

Analyzing Visuals *Students' questions should focus on images that refer to the local, regional, and global levels of London.*

Regions come in all shapes and sizes. Some are small, like the neighborhood called Chinatown in San Francisco. Other regions are huge, like the Americas. This huge region includes two continents, North America and South America. The size of the area does not matter, as long as the area shares some characteristics. These shared characteristics define the region.

Geographers divide the world into regions for many reasons. The world is a huge place and home to billions of people. Studying so large an area can be extremely difficult. Dividing the world into regions makes it easier to study. A small area is much easier to examine than a large area.

Other geographers study regions to see how people interact with one another. For example, they may study a city such as London, England, to learn how the city's people govern themselves. Then they can compare what they learn about one region to what they learn about another region. In this way, they can learn more about life and landscapes in both places.

Global Level

Sometimes geographers do not want to study the world just at a regional level. Instead they want to learn how people interact globally, or around the world. To do so, geographers ask how events and ideas from one region of the world affect people in other regions. In other words, they study the world on a global level.

Geographers who study the world on a global level try to find relationships among people who live far apart. They may, for example, examine the products that a country exports to see how those products are used in other countries.

In recent decades, worldwide trade and communication have increased. As a result, we need to understand how our actions affect people around the world. Through their studies, geographers provide us with information that helps us figure out how to live in a rapidly changing world.

READING CHECK **Finding Main Ideas** At what levels do geographers study the world?

Regional Level As a major city, London is also a region. At this level, a geographer might study the city's population or transportation systems.

.London

Global Level London is one of the world's main financial centers. Here a geographer might study how London's economy affects the world.

A GEOGRAPHER'S WORLD **9**

The Geographer's Tools

Geographers use many tools to study the world. Each tool provides part of the information a geographer needs to learn what a place is like.

ANALYZING VISUALS What information could you learn from each of these tools?

A geographer can use a globe to see where a place, such as the United States, is located.

High School Soccer Participation

Participation in High School Soccer
- More than 9%
- 5–9%
- 3–5%
- Fewer than 3%
- Data not available

Maps usually give geographers more information about a place than globes do. This map, for example, shows rates of soccer participation in the United States.

The Geographer's Tools

FOCUS ON READING
What do you already know about maps and globes?

Have you ever seen a carpenter building or repairing a house? If so, you know that builders need many tools to do their jobs correctly. In the same way, geographers need many tools to study the world.

Maps and Globes

The tools that geographers use most often in their work are maps and globes. A **map** is a flat drawing that shows all or part of Earth's surface. A **globe** is a spherical, or ball-shaped, model of the entire planet.

Both maps and globes show what the world looks like. They can show where mountains, deserts, and oceans are. They can also identify and describe the world's countries and major cities.

There are, however, major differences between maps and globes. Because a globe is spherical like Earth, it can show the world as it really is.

A map, though, is flat. It is not possible to show a spherical area perfectly on a flat surface. To understand what this means, think about an orange. If you took the peel off of an orange, could you make it lie completely flat? No, you could not, unless you stretched or tore the peel first.

The same principle is true with maps. To draw Earth on a flat surface, people have to distort, or alter, some details. For example, places on a map might look to be farther apart than they really are, or their shapes or sizes might be changed slightly.

Still, maps have many advantages over globes. Flat maps are easier to work with than globes. Also, it is easier to show small areas like cities on maps than on globes.

In addition, maps usually show more information than globes. Because globes are more expensive to make, they do not usually show anything more than where places are and what features they have.

10 CHAPTER 1

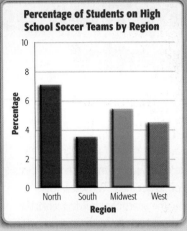

Percentage of Students on High School Soccer Teams by Region

Charts and graphs are also tools geographers can use to study information. They are often used when geographers want to compare numbers, such as the number of students who play soccer in each region of the country.

Other Tools

Geographers also use many other tools. For example, they use computer programs to create, update, and compare maps. They also use measuring devices to record data. In some cases, the best tools a geographer can use are a notebook and tape recorder to take notes while talking to people. Armed with the proper tools, geographers learn about the world's people and places.

READING CHECK **Summarizing** What are some of the geographer's basic tools?

SUMMARY AND PREVIEW Geography is the study of the world, its people, and its landscapes. In the next section, you will learn about two systems geographers use to organize their studies.

Maps, on the other hand, can show all sorts of information. Besides showing land use and cities, maps can include a great deal of information about a place. A map might show what languages people speak or where their ancestors came from. Maps like the one on the opposite page can even show how many students in an area play soccer.

Satellite Images

Maps and globes are not the only tools that geographers use in their work. As you have already read, many geographers study information gathered by satellites.

Much of the information gathered by these satellites is in the form of images. Geographers can study these images to see what an area looks like from above Earth. Satellites also collect information that we cannot see from the planet's surface. The information gathered by satellites helps geographers make accurate maps.

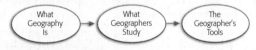

Section 1 Assessment

go.hrw.com
Online Quiz
KEYWORD: SK9 HP1

Reviewing Ideas, Terms, and Places

1. **a. Define** What is **geography**?
   b. Explain Why is geography considered a science?
2. **a. Identify** What is a **region**? Give two examples.
   b. Elaborate What global issues do geographers study?
3. **a. Describe** How do geographers use satellite images?
   b. Compare and Contrast How are maps and globes similar? How are they different?

Critical Thinking

4. **Summarizing** Draw three ovals like the ones shown here. Use your notes to fill the ovals with information about geography, geographers, and their tools.

What Geography Is → What Geographers Study → The Geographer's Tools

FOCUS ON WRITING

5. **Describing the Subject** Based on what you have learned, what might attract people to work in geography? In your notebook, list some details about geography that might make people interested in working in the subject.

A GEOGRAPHER'S WORLD **11**

Bellringer

If YOU lived there. . . Use the **Daily Bellringer Transparency** to help students answer the question.

🎲 Daily Bellringer Transparency, Section 2

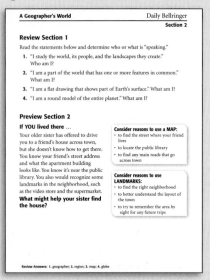

A Geographer's World   Daily Bellringer
                                                              Section 2

Review Section 1

Read the statements below and determine who or what is "speaking."

1. "I study the world, its people, and the landscapes they create." Who am I?
2. "I am a part of the world that has one or more features in common." What am I?
3. "I am a flat drawing that shows part of Earth's surface." What am I?
4. "I am a round model of the entire planet." What am I?

Preview Section 2

If YOU lived there ...

Your older sister has offered to drive you to a friend's house across town, but she doesn't know how to get there. You know your friend's street address and what the apartment building looks like. You know it's near the public library. You also would recognize some landmarks in the neighborhood, such as the video store and the supermarket. **What might help your sister find the house?**

Consider reasons to use a MAP:
• to find the street where your friend lives
• to locate the public library
• to find any main roads that go across town

Consider reasons to use LANDMARKS:
• to find the right neighborhood
• to better understand the layout of the town
• to try to remember the area by sight for any future trips

Review Answers: 1. geographer; **2.** region; **3.** map; **4.** globe

Academic Vocabulary

Review with students the high-use academic term in this section.

element part (p. 15)

📝 **RF:** Vocabulary Builder, Section 2

Taking Notes

Have students copy the table onto their own paper and then use it to take notes on the section. This activity will prepare students for the Section Assessment, in which they will complete a table that builds on the information using the Critical Thinking Skill: Categorizing.

Geography Themes and Essential Elements

What You Will Learn...

Main Ideas

1. The five themes of geography help us organize our studies of the world.
2. The six essential elements of geography highlight some of the subject's most important ideas.

The Big Idea

Geographers have created two different but related systems for organizing geographic studies.

Key Terms

absolute location, *p. 14*
relative location, *p. 14*
environment, *p. 14*

TAKING NOTES Draw a table with two columns like the one here. As you read this section, list the five themes of geography in the left column. List the six essential elements of geography in the right column.

Five Themes	Six Essential Elements

If YOU lived there...

Your older sister has offered to drive you to a friend's house across town, but she doesn't know how to get there. You know your friend's street address and what the apartment building looks like. You know it's near the public library. You also would recognize some landmarks in the neighborhood, such as the video store and the supermarket.

What might help your sister find the house?

BUILDING BACKGROUND Like drivers, geographers have to know where places are in order to study them. An area's location is only one of the aspects that geographers study, though. In fact, it is only one of the five themes that geographers use to describe a place.

The Five Themes of Geography

Have you ever gone to a Fourth of July party with a patriotic theme? If so, you probably noticed that almost everything at the party was related to that theme. For example, you may have seen American flags and decorations based on the flag's stars and stripes. You may have seen clothes that were red, white, and blue or heard patriotic music being played. Chances are that almost everything at the party reflected the theme of patriotism.

Like party planners, geographers use themes in their work. Geographers do not study parties, of course, but they do note common themes in their studies. Just as a party's theme is reflected in nearly every aspect of the party, these geography themes can be applied to nearly everything that geographers study. The five major themes of geography are Location, Place, Human-Environment Interaction, Movement, and Regions.

Teach the Big Idea

At Level

Geography Themes and Essential Elements

1. **Teach** Ask students the questions in the Main Idea boxes under Direct Teach.

2. **Apply** Organize students into groups. Each group will create a brochure introducing the school's buildings and grounds to a new student. Have groups organize their brochures by geography theme and write or draw information about the school related to that theme. Then have students review the essential elements. If an element relates to a theme, students should add that information to their brochures.

3. **Review** Discuss how this project illustrates the "Uses of Geography" element. Display the brochures in the classroom.

4. **Practice/Homework** Have students repeat this project using as a subject their home, yard, or another place of their choosing. 🅛🅢 **Verbal/Linguistic, Visual/Spatial**

   📝 Alternative Assessment Handbook, Rubrics 14: Group Activity; and 37: Writing Assignments

The Five Themes of Geography

Geographers use five major themes, or ideas, to organize and guide their studies.

go.hrw.com KEYWORD: SK9 CH1

Location The theme of location describes where something is. The mountain shown above, Mount Rainier, is in west-central Washington.

Place Place describes the features that make a site unique. For example, Washington, D.C., is our nation's capital and has many great monuments.

UNITED STATES

Regions Regions are areas that share common characteristics. The Mojave Desert, shown here, is defined by its distinctive climate and plant life.

Movement This theme looks at how and why people and things move. Airports like this one in Dallas, Texas, help people move around the world.

Human-Environment Interaction People interact with their environments in many ways. Some, like this man in Florida, use the land to grow crops.

ANALYSIS SKILL **ANALYZING VISUALS**

Which of the five themes deals with the relationships between people and their surroundings?

A GEOGRAPHER'S WORLD **13**

Main Idea

❶ The Five Themes of Geography

The five themes of geography help us organize our studies of the world.

Explain How are the five themes of geography helpful to geographers? *can be applied to nearly everything geographers study; helps geographers organize their work*

Identify What are some common interactions between people and their environments? *agriculture, fishing, building a place to live*

Analyze Which one of the following does not belong: location, place, human-environment interaction, language, movement, regions? *language—the others are the five themes of geography*

Elaborate Why do you think it is helpful to use themes for studying geography? *possible answer—helps you remember to consider all important aspects; helps to compare and contrast studies of different places by looking at the same topics*

Did you know. . .

The story of the Lincoln Memorial (shown at left in the picture of Washington, D.C.) gives us a window into other places and times. The memorial was built to resemble an ancient Greek temple. It has 36 columns, one for each state at the time of Lincoln's death.

Differentiating Instruction

English-Language Learners
At Level

1. To help students apply their understanding of the themes, have students read a picture caption aloud and describe it.

2. Then ask each student to write two paragraphs, the first starting with, "In this picture you see . . ." and the second starting with "The geography theme this picture shows is . . ." Students should give a reason that links the theme and the picture. **LS Verbal/Linguistic, Visual/Spatial**

Alternative Assessment Handbook, Rubric 40: Writing to Describe

Advanced/Gifted and Talented
Above Level
Research Required

1. Have students research a building or monument in Washington, D.C., and one in ancient Greece, Egypt, or Rome. How are they alike? Different?

2. Have students use their research to create a presentation, including artwork, on their findings.

3. Ask students to make a presentation to the class. Have their classmates offer constructive feedback. **LS Verbal/Linguistic, Visual/Spatial**

Alternative Assessment Handbook, Rubric 29: Presentations

Answers

Analyzing Visuals *Human-environment interaction deals most directly with this theme.*

13

Main Idea

1 The Five Themes of Geography, *continued*

The five themes of geography help us organize our studies of the world.

Identify Give an example of absolute location. *a street address*

Define What is relative location? *expressing location in general terms, such as the U.S. being south of Canada*

Identify Cause and Effect What are two examples of people's actions that are an effect of their environment? *wearing heavy clothing in cold areas, finding ways to protect homes from river or ocean flooding*

📖 **RF:** Geography and History, Migration of Early Humans

Info to Know

Lots of Land? According to "The World Factbook" at the CIA Web site, the total land area of the world is 148.94 million square kilometers (km). Of that land, only 10.73% is arable (fit for or used for growing crops).

Connect to Math

How Much Land? One kilometer is equal to about 0.62 miles. How many square miles is the total land area of the world? How many square miles of arable land are there? *about 57.5 million square miles of total land; about 6.17 million square miles of arable land*

Answers

Focus on Reading *Students' responses should reflect their understanding of Earth's land, water, climate, plants, and animals.*

Reading Check *location, place, human-environment interaction, movement, regions*

Analyzing Visuals *Students' responses will vary but may include all elements except for The World in Spatial Terms.*

Location

Every point on Earth has a location, a description of where it is. This location can be expressed in many ways. Sometimes a site's location is expressed in specific, or absolute, terms, such as an address. For example, the White House is located at 1600 Pennsylvania Avenue in the city of Washington, D.C. A specific description like this one is called an **absolute location**. Other times, the site's location is expressed in general terms. For example, Canada is north of the United States. This general description of where a place lies is called its **relative location**.

Place

Another theme, Place, is closely related to Location. However, Place does not refer simply to where an area is. It refers to the area's landscape, the features that define the area and make it different from other places. Such features could include land, climate, and people. Together, they give a place its own character.

FOCUS ON READING
What do you know about environments?

Human-Environment Interaction

In addition to looking at the features of places, geographers examine how those features interact. In particular, they want to understand how people interact with their environment—how people and their physical environment affect each other. An area's **environment** includes its land, water, climate, plants, and animals.

People interact with their environment every day in all sorts of ways. They clear forests to plant crops, level fields to build cities, and dam rivers to prevent floods. At the same time, physical environments affect how people live. People in cold areas, for example, build houses with thick walls and wear heavy clothing to keep warm. People who live near oceans look for ways to protect themselves from storms.

14 CHAPTER 1

Movement

People are constantly moving. They move within cities, between cities, and between countries. Geographers want to know why and how people move. For example, they ask if people are moving to find work or to live in a more pleasant area. Geographers also study the roads and routes that make movement so common.

Regions

You have already learned how geographers divide the world into many regions to help the study of geography. Creating regions also makes it easier to compare places. Comparisons help geographers learn why each place has developed the way it has.

READING CHECK **Finding Main Ideas** What are the five themes of geography?

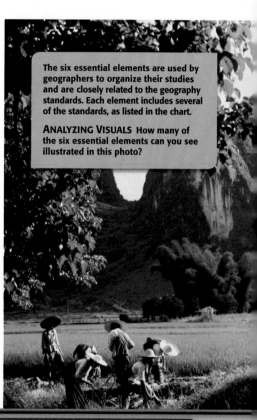

The six essential elements are used by geographers to organize their studies and are closely related to the geography standards. Each element includes several of the standards, as listed in the chart.

ANALYZING VISUALS How many of the six essential elements can you see illustrated in this photo?

Cross-Discipline Activity: English/Language Arts   At Level

Point of View   Standard English Mastery

1. Review with students the five themes of geography and the kind of information each theme helps you learn.

2. Ask students to imagine that they lived in your area several hundred years ago and have somehow ended up in that same spot today. Brainstorm with students about what might seem different.

3. Have each student use standard English to write a journal entry as if they were such a person, describing one day from start to finish. Journal entries should include observations related to each of the five

themes. Encourage students to describe what the person might feel, how he or she might try to make sense of the changes, and possible conflicts or funny situations.

4. Ask for volunteers to read their entries aloud. For each entry, discuss what information relates to each theme. As a class, discuss any necessary corrections to the sentences to align them with standard English usage.

LS Verbal/Linguistic

📖 Alternative Assessment Handbook, Rubric 39: Writing to Create

The Six Essential Elements

The five themes of geography are not the only system geographers use to study the world. They also use a system of standards and essential **elements**. Together, these standards and essential elements identify the most important ideas in the study of geography. These ideas are expressed in two lists.

The first list is the national geography standards. This is a list of 18 basic ideas that are central to the study of geography. These standards are listed in black type on the chart below.

The essential elements are based on the geography standards. Each element is a big idea that links several standards together. The six essential elements are The World in Spatial Terms, Places and Regions, Physical Systems, Human Systems, Environment and Society, and The Uses of Geography. On the chart, they are shown in purple.

Read through that list again. Do you see any similarities between geography's six essential elements and its five themes? You probably do. The two systems are very similar because the six essential elements build on the five themes.

ACADEMIC VOCABULARY
element part

The Essential Elements and Geography Standards

The World in Spatial Terms

- How to use maps and other geographic representations, tools, and technologies to acquire, process, and report information from a spatial perspective
- How to use mental maps to organize information about people, places, and environments in a spatial context
- How to analyze the spatial organization of people, places, and environments on Earth's surface

Places and Regions

- The physical and human characteristics of places
- How people create regions to interpret Earth's complexity
- How culture and experience influence people's perceptions of places and regions

Physical Systems

- The physical processes that shape the patterns of Earth's surface
- The characteristics and spatial distribution of ecosystems on Earth's surface

Human Systems

- The characteristics, distributions, and migration of human populations on Earth's surface
- The characteristics, distribution, and complexity of Earth's cultural mosaics
- The patterns and networks of economic interdependence on Earth's surface
- The processes, patterns, and functions of human settlement
- How the forces of cooperation and conflict among people influence the division and control of Earth's surface

Environment and Society

- How human actions modify the physical environment
- How physical systems affect human systems
- Changes that occur in the meaning, use, distribution, and importance of resources

The Uses of Geography

- How to apply geography to interpret the past
- How to apply geography to interpret the present and plan for the future

A GEOGRAPHER'S WORLD **15**

Direct Teach

Main Idea

❷ **The Six Essential Elements**

The six essential elements of geography highlight some of the subject's most important ideas.

List What are the six essential elements of geography? *world in spatial terms, places and regions, physical systems, human systems, environment and society, uses of geography*

Analyze How do the national geography standards and the six elements of geography relate to each other? *each element is a big idea that links several standards together*

Evaluate How useful do you think it is to identify themes and elements in the study of geography or another subject? *possible answer—very useful, since it lets people use one system to compare findings and to communicate results*

Collaborative Learning   At Level

Comparing Mental Maps

1. Discuss mental maps with students. Be sure they understand that these are people's internal map of their world and that they can include a variety of features a person notices.

2. Have each student list the features of his or her internal map for the route he or she takes to school. Encourage students to include all features, even those not commonly seen on a map.

3. Organize students in pairs or groups of three. Draw a two-circle and a three-circle Venn diagram on the board. Have each pair or group copy the appropriate diagram onto their own paper. Then have them list all the features from their mental maps in the appropriate spaces.

4. As a class, discuss which features were most common. Discuss whether people of other ages would have similar mental maps.
   LS Verbal/Linguistic, Visual/Spatial

   Alternative Assessment Handbook, Rubric 13: Graphic Organizers

Primary Source

Geography for Life

Recall Where were the six elements of geography first outlined? *in a book called* Geography for Life

Compare What are some ways that the six elements of geography build on the five themes? *The element Places and Regions combines the Place theme and the Regions theme; the element Environment and Society deals with similar issues as the Human-Environment Interaction theme.*

Analyze If a local committee were planning a new park, which theme or element of geography would apply most directly? *the element Uses of Geography*

● Review & Assess ●

Close

Have each student make a bookmark that lists the themes and elements of geography.

Review

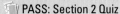 Online Quiz, Section 2

Assess

SE Section 2 Assessment

PASS: Section 2 Quiz

Alternative Assessment Handbook

Reteach/Classroom Intervention

Interactive Reader and Study Guide, Section 2

Interactive Skills Tutor CD-ROM

Answers

Analyzing Primary Sources *to find answers to questions about the world, make wiser decisions, solve issues at local and global levels*

Reading Check *world in spatial terms, places and regions, physical systems, human systems, environment and society, uses of geography*

16

Primary Source

BOOK

Geography for Life

The six essential elements were first outlined in a book called Geography for Life. *In that book, the authors—a diverse group of geographers and teachers from around the United States—explained why the study of geography is important.*

❝Geography *is* for life in every sense of that expression: lifelong, life-sustaining, and life-enhancing. Geography is a field of study that enables us to find answers to questions about the world around us—about where things are and how and why they got there.❞

❝Geography focuses attention on exciting and interesting things, on fascinating people and places, on things worth knowing because they are absorbing and because knowing about them lets humans make better-informed and, therefore, wiser decisions.❞

❝With a strong grasp of geography, people are better equipped to solve issues at not only the local level but also the global level.❞

–from *Geography for Life*, by the Geography Education Standards Project

ANALYSIS SKILL **ANALYZING PRIMARY SOURCES**
Why do the authors of these passages think that people should study geography?

For example, the element Places and Regions combines two of the five themes of geography—Place and Regions. Also, the element called Environment and Society deals with many of the same issues as the theme Human-Environment Interaction.

There are also some basic differences between the essential elements and the themes. For example, the last element, The Uses of Geography, deals with issues not covered in the five themes. This element examines how people can use geography to plan the landscapes in which they live.

Throughout this book, you will notice references to both the themes and the essential elements. As you read, use these themes and elements to help you organize your own study of geography.

READING CHECK **Summarizing** What are the six essential elements of geography?

SUMMARY AND PREVIEW You have just learned about the themes and elements of geography. Next, you will explore the branches into which the field is divided.

Section 2 Assessment

go.hrw.com
Online Quiz
KEYWORD: SK9 HP1

Reviewing Ideas, Terms, and Places

1. **a. Define** What is the difference between a place's **absolute location** and its **relative location**? Give one example of each type of location.
   b. Contrast How are the themes of Location and Place different?
   c. Elaborate How does using the five themes help geographers understand the places they study?
2. **a. Identify** Which of the five themes of geography is associated with airports, highways, and the migration of people from one place to another?
   b. Explain How are the geography standards and the six essential elements related?
   c. Compare How are the six essential elements similar to the five themes of geography?

Critical Thinking

3. **Categorizing** Draw a chart like the one below. Use your notes to list the five themes of geography, explain each of the themes, and list one feature of your city or town that relates to each.

Theme				
Explanation				
Feature				

FOCUS ON WRITING

4. **Including Themes and Essential Elements** The five themes and six essential elements are central to a geographer's job. How will you mention them in your job description? Write down some ideas.

16 CHAPTER 1

Section 2 Assessment Answers

1. **a.** Absolute location is a specific description, such as an address. A relative location describes one place by its relation to another. For example, the U.S. is south of Canada.
   b. location—description of where a point on Earth is; place—physical and human features that define an area/its character
   c. possible answer—It lets them study a place from many points of view and compare it to other places using the same system.

2. **a.** movement

   b. The elements build on the five themes but also expand upon them.
   c. Both are systems geographers use to study the world.

3. Students' charts will vary but should show that they can apply knowledge of each theme to their city or town's characteristics.

4. Student responses should reflect an understanding of each theme and element. Students may mention knowledge of maps and other geographers' tools.

Analyzing Satellite Images

Learn

In addition to maps and globes, satellite images are among the geographer's most valuable tools. Geographers use two basic types of these images. The first type is called true color. These images are like photographs taken from high above Earth's surface. The colors in these images are similar to what you would see from the ground. Vegetation, for example, appears green.

The other type of satellite image is called an infrared image. Infrared images are taken using a special type of light. These images are based on heat patterns, and so the colors on them are not what we might expect. Bodies of water appear black, for example, since they give off little heat.

Practice

Use the satellite images on this page to answer the following questions.

❶ On which image is vegetation red?

❷ Which image do you think probably looks more like Italy does from the ground?

Vegetation appears green.

Water appears blue.

True color satellite image of Italy

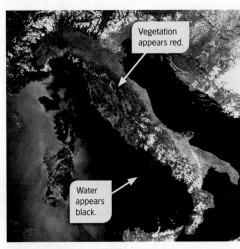

Vegetation appears red.

Water appears black.

Infrared satellite image of Italy

Apply

Search the Internet to find a satellite image of your state or region. Determine whether the image is true color or infrared. Then write three statements that describe what you see on the image.

A GEOGRAPHER'S WORLD **17**

17

Bellringer

If YOU lived there. . . Use the **Daily Bellringer Transparency** to help students answer the question.

🎲 Daily Bellringer Transparency, Section 3

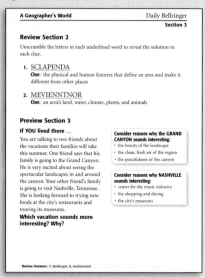

A Geographer's World   Daily Bellringer
                                              Section 3

Review Section 2
Unscramble the letters in each underlined word to reveal the solution to each clue.

1. SCLAPENDA
   Clue: the physical and human features that define an area and make it different from other places

2. MEVIENNTNOR
   Clue: an area's land, water, climate, plants, and animals

Preview Section 3

If YOU lived there ...
You are talking to two friends about the vacations their families will take this summer. One friend says that his family is going to the Grand Canyon. He is very excited about seeing the spectacular landscapes in and around the canyon. Your other friend's family is going to visit Nashville, Tennessee. She is looking forward to trying new foods at the city's restaurants and touring its museums.
Which vacation sounds more interesting? Why?

Consider reasons why the GRAND CANYON sounds interesting:
• the beauty of the landscape
• the clean, fresh air of the region
• the peacefulness of the canyon

Consider reasons why NASHVILLE sounds interesting:
• center for the music industry
• the shopping and dining
• the city's museums

Review Answers: 1. landscape; 2. environment

Key Terms

📑 **RF:** Vocabulary Builder, Section 3

Taking Notes

Have students copy the graphic organizer onto their own paper and then use it to take notes on the section. This activity will prepare students for the Section Assessment, in which they will complete a graphic organizer that builds on the information using the Critical Thinking Skill: Comparing and Contrasting.

The Branches of Geography

What You Will Learn...

Main Ideas

1. Physical geography is the study of landforms, water bodies, and other physical features.
2. Human geography focuses on people, their cultures, and the landscapes they create.
3. Other branches of geography examine specific aspects of the physical or human world.

The Big Idea

Geography is divided into two main branches—physical and human geography.

Key Terms

physical geography, *p. 18*
human geography, *p. 20*
cartography, *p. 21*
meteorology, *p. 22*

 TAKING NOTES Draw two large circles like the ones below in your notebook. As you read this section, take notes about one of the main branches of geography in each circle.

If YOU lived there...

You are talking to two friends about the vacations their families will take this summer. One friend says that his family is going to the Grand Canyon. He is very excited about seeing the spectacular landscapes in and around the canyon. Your other friend's family is going to visit Nashville, Tennessee. She is looking forward to trying new foods at the city's restaurants and touring its museums.

Which vacation sounds more interesting? Why?

BUILDING BACKGROUND Geography is the study of the world and its features. Some features are physical, like the Grand Canyon. Others are human, like restaurants and museums. The main branches of geography focus on these types of features.

Physical Geography

Think about a jigsaw puzzle. Seen as a whole, the puzzle shows a pretty or interesting picture. To see that picture, though, you have to put all the puzzle pieces together. Before you assemble them, the pieces do not give you a clear idea of what the puzzle will look like when it is assembled. After all, each piece contains only a tiny portion of the overall image.

In many ways, geography is like a huge puzzle. It is made up of many branches, or divisions. Each of these branches focuses on a single part of the world. Viewed separately, none of these branches shows us the whole world. Together, however, the many branches of geography improve our understanding of our planet and its people.

Geography's two main branches are physical geography and human geography. The first branch, **physical geography**, is the study of the world's physical features—its landforms, bodies of water, climates, soils, and plants. Every place in the world has its own unique combination of these features.

18 CHAPTER 1

Teach the Big Idea

The Branches of Geography

1. **Teach** Ask students the questions in the Main Idea boxes under Direct Teach.

2. **Apply** Have students draw or write a detailed depiction of a feature—physical or human—of the town or city where the school is located. Have each student show or read his or her work to the class.

3. **Review** As a class, create a collage of all the works. Decide on the collage design as a class. For example, you could arrange the pictures according to location.

4. **Practice/Homework** Have students write from an ant's eye view about a baseball field or other spot with physical and human features. Tell students to include details about how the ant puts the pieces of the "big picture" together as it travels over the area.
   LS Verbal/Linguistic, Visual/Spatial

   📑 Alternative Assessment Handbook, Rubrics 8: Collages; and 40: Writing to Describe

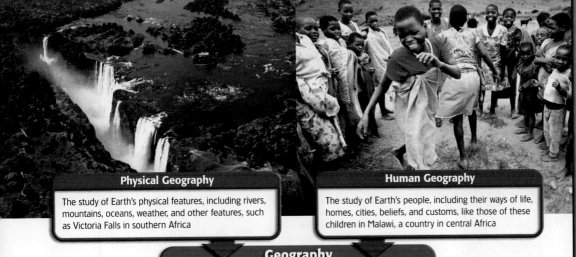

Physical Geography
The study of Earth's physical features, including rivers, mountains, oceans, weather, and other features, such as Victoria Falls in southern Africa

Human Geography
The study of Earth's people, including their ways of life, homes, cities, beliefs, and customs, like those of these children in Malawi, a country in central Africa

Geography
The study of Earth's physical and cultural features

The Physical World

What does it mean to say that physical geography is the study of physical features? Physical geographers want to know all about the different features found on our planet. They want to know where plains and mountain ranges are, how rivers flow across the landscape, and why different amounts of rain fall from place to place.

More importantly, however, physical geographers want to know what causes the different shapes on Earth. They want to know why mountain ranges rise up where they do and what causes rivers to flow in certain directions. They also want to know why various parts of the world have very different weather and climate patterns.

To answer these questions, physical geographers take detailed measurements. They study the heights of mountains and the temperatures of places. To track any changes that occur over time, physical geographers keep careful records of all the information they collect.

Uses of Physical Geography

Earth is made up of hundreds of types of physical features. Without a complete understanding of what these features are and the effect they have on the world's people and landscapes, we cannot fully understand our world. This is the major reason that geographers study the physical world—to learn how it works.

There are also other, more specific reasons for studying physical geography, though. Studying the changes that take place on our planet can help us prepare to live with those changes. For example, knowing what causes volcanoes to erupt can help us predict eruptions. Knowing what causes terrible storms can help us prepare for them. In this way, the work of physical geographers helps us adjust to the dangers and changes of our world.

READING CHECK **Analyzing** What are some features in your area that a physical geographer might study?

A GEOGRAPHER'S WORLD **19**

Main Idea

❶ Physical Geography
Physical geography is the study of landforms, water bodies, and other physical features.

Compare How is the study of geography similar to pieces of a jigsaw puzzle? *Viewed separately, no branch shows the whole world; viewed together, the different branches improve understanding of the planet and its people.*

Recall What might geographers measure to learn about the world? Name two elements or features. *mountain heights, temperatures*

Infer How could the study of physical geography help people who live in an area at risk for tsunamis? *understand what conditions may cause them, recognize the signs that one is coming, make changes and plans to minimize its effects*

📄 **RF:** Literature, *The Wind Makes Dust* by Carl Sagan

Did you know. . .

Victoria Falls, on the Zambezi River bordering Zambia and Zimbabwe, is one of the seven natural wonders of the world. It is the largest known "curtain of water." Here, the mild river, about 2 km (1.2 miles) wide, plummets into a narrow gorge about 100 m (328 feet) deep, causing a thunderous roar and a towering spray. In the 1850s, Scottish missionary and physician David Livingstone reported the falls to the outside world. He named them for Queen Victoria. The local people call the falls "Mosi-oa-Tunya" which means "smoke that thunders."

Differentiating Instruction

Below Level

English-Language Learners

1. Write the words *Who, What, Where, When, How,* and *Why* on the board.

2. Have students look at the picture of the children in Malawi. For each word on the board, have them write at least one question and answer about the picture, being as specific as possible (e.g., saying "boys and girls" instead of just "people" for "who is in the picture?").

3. Have students share their questions (you may want to start with all the *Who* questions first). Discuss possible answers or offer information students might need to answer the question.

4. Discuss ways in which the lives of young people in this picture might be different from and similar to your students' lives.
   LS Verbal/Linguistic, Visual/Spatial

📄 Alternative Assessment Handbook, Rubric 12: Drawing Conclusions

Answers

Reading Check *Answers will vary, but should include features related to land, soils or plants, weather or climate, and any bodies of water in your area.*

19

Main Idea

❷ Human Geography

Human geography focuses on people, their cultures, and the landscapes they create.

Recall What are some needs common to all people? *food, water, shelter, dealing with others*

Draw Conclusions Why do human geographers often specialize in a smaller area of study? *People's lives are so different that no one can study every aspect.*

 **RF: Biography, Ellen Churchill Semple**

 **RF: Primary Source, *The Travels of Marco Polo***

Linking to Today

Helping Others The work of Heifer International (www.heifer.org), an organization whose mission is to end hunger, is an example of human geography in practice. The organization donates animals so that people can work the land and improve their situation. "Heifer's Cornerstones" include: the community deciding together what animals and help they want, training people to feed and shelter the animals, and having people pass on offspring of animals so others can benefit.

Answers

Biography *He made many contributions to the field, including being the first to use the term* geography.

Reading Check *people, communities, and landscapes*

BIOGRAPHY

Eratosthenes
(c. 276–c. 194 BC)

Did you know that geography is over 2,000 years old? Actually, the study of the world is even older than that, but the first person ever to use the word *geography* lived then. His name was Eratosthenes (er-uh-TAHS-thuh-neez), and he was a Greek scientist and librarian. With no modern instruments of any kind, Eratosthenes figured out how large Earth is. He also drew a map that showed all of the lands that the Greeks knew about. Because of his many contributions to the field, Eratosthenes has been called the Father of Geography.

Generalizing Why is Eratosthenes called the Father of Geography?

Human Geography

The physical world is only one part of the puzzle of geography. People are also part of the world. **Human geography** is the study of the world's people, communities, and landscapes. It is the second major branch of geography.

The Human World

Put simply, human geographers study the world's people, past and present. They look at where people live and why. They ask why some parts of the world have more people than others, and why some places have almost no people at all.

Human geographers also study what people do. What jobs do people have? What crops do they grow? What makes them move from place to place? These are the types of questions that geographers ask about people around the world.

Because people's lives are so different around the world, no one can study every aspect of human geography. As a result, human geographers often specialize in a smaller area of study. Some may choose to study only the people and landscapes in a certain region. For example, a geographer may study only the lives of people who live in West Africa.

Other geographers choose not to limit their studies to one place. Instead, they may choose to examine only one aspect of people's lives. For example, a geographer could study only economics, politics, or city life. However, that geographer may compare economic patterns in various parts of the world to see how they differ.

Uses of Human Geography

Although every culture is different, people around the world have some common needs. All people need food and water. All people need shelter. All people need to deal with other people in order to survive.

Human geographers study how people in various places address their needs. They look at the foods people eat and the types of governments they form. The knowledge they gather can help us better understand people in other cultures. Sometimes this type of understanding can help people improve their landscapes and situations.

On a smaller scale, human geographers can help people design their cities and towns. By understanding where people go and what they need, geographers can help city planners place roads, shopping malls, and schools. Geographers also study the effect people have on the world. As a result, they often work with private groups and government agencies who want to protect the environment.

READING CHECK **Summarizing** What do human geographers study?

Differentiating Instruction

English-Language Learners
At Level
Standard English Mastery

1. Explain that studying what people eat can help us understand other people and cultures.

2. On the board, make four columns: *animal*, *vegetable*, *fruit*, and *grain*. Ask volunteers to tell one food they ate the day before and which category that food fits.

3. Have students use standard English to write two sentences explaining how the foods tell about their own cultures. **LS Verbal/Linguistic**

Alternative Assessment Handbook, Rubric 38: Writing to Classify

Advanced/Gifted and Talented
Above Level
Research Required

1. Have students do Internet or library research to learn how Eratosthenes determined Earth's size. Ask them to organize their findings about his process using a graphic organizer or chart.

2. Have students create a labeled poster or 3-D display to explain the process Eratosthenes used. **LS Logical/Mathematical, Verbal/Linguistic**

Alternative Assessment Handbook, Rubrics 28: Posters, and 30: Research

Other Fields of Geography

Physical geography and human geography are the two largest branches of the subject, but they are not the only ones. Many other fields of geography exist, each one devoted to studying one aspect of the world.

Most of these fields are smaller, more specialized areas of either physical or human geography. For example, economic geography—the study of how people make and spend money—is a branch of human geography. Another specialized branch of human geography is urban geography, the study of cities and how people live in them. Physical geography also includes many fields, such as the study of climates. Other fields of physical geography are the studies of soils and plants.

Cartography

One key field of geography is **cartography**, the science of making maps. You have already seen how important maps are to the study of geography. Without maps, geographers would not be able to study where things are in the world.

In the past, maps were always drawn by hand. Many were not very accurate. Today, though, most maps are made using computers and satellite images. Through advances in mapmaking, we can make accurate maps on almost any scale, from the whole world to a single neighborhood, and keep them up to date. These maps are not only used by geographers. For example, road maps are used by people who are planning long trips.

CONNECTING TO Technology

Computer Mapping

In the past, maps were drawn by hand. Making a map was a slow process. Even the simplest map took a long time to make. Today, however, cartographers have access to tools people in the past—even people who lived just 50 years ago—never imagined. The most important of these tools are computers.

Computers allow us to make maps quickly and easily. In addition, they let us make new types of maps that people could not make in the past.

The map shown here, for example, was drawn on a computer. It shows the number of computer users in the United States who were connected to the Internet on a particular day. Each of the lines that rises off of the map represents a city in which people were using the Internet. The color of the line indicates the number of computer users in that city. As you can see, this data resulted in a very complex map.

Making such a map required cartographers to sort through huge amounts of complex data. Such sorting would not have been possible without computers.

Contrasting How are today's maps different from those created in the past?

A GEOGRAPHER'S WORLD **21**

Direct Teach

Connect to History

The Telegraph The invention of the telegraph—a system of sending coded messages over wires using electricity—in the 19th century was important in the development of the field of meteorology. People had been observing and recording the weather long before the telegraph's invention (in daily farm journals, for example). But the telegraph enabled collecting, plotting, and analyzing weather observations from different places in a more timely manner. Today's computers have made this process even faster and more accurate, but the basic process is still the same—collecting weather data and analyzing it to make predictions.

Review & Assess

Close

Ask students to suggest a local example of each branch of geography discussed in this section.

Review

Online Quiz, Section 3

Assess

SE Section 3 Assessment

PASS: Section 3 Quiz

Alternative Assessment Handbook

Reteach/Classroom Intervention

Interactive Reader and Study Guide, Section 3

Interactive Skills Tutor CD-ROM

Meteorology is the study of weather. This meteorologist is using computers to follow and predict the movement of a powerful storm.

Hydrology

FOCUS ON READING
What do you already know about drinking water?

Another important branch of geography is hydrology, the study of water on Earth. Geographers in this field study the world's river systems and rainfall patterns. They study what causes droughts and floods and how people in cities can get safe drinking water. They also work to measure and protect the world's supply of water.

Meteorology

Have you ever seen the weather report on television? If so, you have seen the results of another branch of geography. This branch is called **meteorology**, the study of weather and what causes it.

Meteorologists study weather patterns in a particular area. Then they use the information to predict what the weather will be like in the coming days. Their work helps people plan what to wear and what to do on any given day. At the same time, their work can save lives by predicting the arrival of terrible storms. These predictions are among the most visible ways in which the work of geographers affects our lives every day.

READING CHECK Finding Main Ideas What are some major branches of geography?

SUMMARY AND PREVIEW In this section, you learned about two main branches of geography, physical and human. In the next chapter, you will learn more about the physical features that surround us and the processes that create them.

Section 3 Assessment

go.hrw.com
Online Quiz
KEYWORD: SK9 HP1

Reviewing Ideas, Terms, and Places

1. **a. Define** What is **physical geography**?
   b. Explain Why do we study physical geography?
2. **a. Identify** What are some things that people study as part of **human geography**?
   b. Summarize What are some ways in which the study of human geography can influence our lives?
   c. Evaluate Which do you think would be more interesting to study, physical geography or human geography? Why?
3. **a. Identify** What are two specialized fields of geography?
   b. Analyze How do cartographers contribute to the work of other geographers?

Critical Thinking

4. **Comparing and Contrasting** Draw a diagram like the one shown here. In the left circle, list three features of physical geography from your notes. In the right circle, list three features of human geography. Where the circles overlap, list one feature they share.

   Physical   Human

FOCUS ON WRITING

5. **Choosing a Branch** Your job description should point out to people that there are many branches of geography. How will you note that?

22 CHAPTER 1

Section 3 Assessment Answers

1. **a.** study of world's landforms, water bodies, other physical features
   b. to learn how physical world works, help us prepare for and adapt to changes
2. **a.** people past or present, where they live and why, their jobs/crops/movements
   b. better understand other cultures, improve landscapes, design cities and towns, protect environments
   c. possible response—physical, because you learn about why features are the way they are; human, because you understand people better

3. **a.** cartography, meteorology
   b. They make maps that other geographers use to study different aspects of the world.
4. possible response: physical—landforms, water, climate; human—people, communities, landscape; both—help us understand world better
5. Student responses should include a reasonable explanation, such as including some of the branches in the "areas of responsibilities" section of the job description.

Answers

Focus on Reading *Students' responses should reflect their understanding of the qualities that make water potable.*
Reading Check *The two main branches are physical and human, with some major branches including cartography, hydrology, and meteorology.*

Chapter Review

Geography's Impact
video series
Review the video to answer the closing question:
Why do you think it might be valuable to know the absolute location of a place?

Visual Summary

Use the visual summary below to help you review the main ideas of the chapter.

QUICK FACTS

Physical geography—the study of the world's physical features—is one main branch of geography.

Human geography—the study of the world's people and how they live—is the second main branch.

Geographers use many tools to study the world. The most valuable of these tools are maps.

Reviewing Vocabulary, Terms, and Places

Match the words in the columns with the correct definitions listed below.

1. geography
2. physical geography
3. human geography
4. element
5. meteorology

6. region
7. cartography
8. map
9. landscape
10. globe

a. a part of the world that has one or more common features that make it different from surrounding areas
b. a flat drawing of part of Earth's surface
c. a part
d. a spherical model of the planet
e. the study of the world's physical features
f. the study of weather and what causes it
g. the study of the world, its people, and the landscapes they create
h. the science of making maps
i. the physical and human features that define an area and make it different from other places
j. the study of people and communities

Comprehension and Critical Thinking

SECTION 1 *(Pages 6–11)*

11. **a. Identify** What are three levels at which a geographer might study the world? Which of these levels covers the largest area?

 b. Compare and Contrast How are maps and globes similar? How are they different?

 c. Elaborate How might satellite images and computers help geographers improve their knowledge of the world?

Answers

Visual Summary

Review and Inquiry Have students use the visual summary to discuss details related to the study of geography.

 Quick Facts Transparency: Visual Summary: A Geographer's World

Reviewing Vocabulary, Terms, and Places

1. g	**6.** a
2. e	**7.** h
3. j	**8.** b
4. c	**9.** i
5. f	**10.** d

Comprehension and Critical Thinking

11. **a.** levels—local, regional, global; largest—global

 b. possible response: similar—Both generally show what world looks like. different—Globes are round and show world as it really appears. Maps are flat but easier to work with and can show smaller areas, such as cities.

 c. possible response—They allow geographers to analyze more data at once and to get updates more often to track changes, so information is more accurate.

Review and Assessment Resources

Review and Reinforce

SE Chapter Review
 RF: Chapter Review
 Quick Facts Transparency: Visual Summary: A Geographer's World
 Spanish Chapter Summaries Audio CD Program
OSP Holt PuzzlePro; Quiz Show for ExamView
 Quiz Game CD-ROM

Assess

SE Standardized Test Practice
 PASS: Chapter Test, Forms A and B
 Alternative Assessment Handbook
OSP ExamView Test Generator, Chapter Test
 Differentiated Instruction Modified Worksheets and Tests CD-ROM: Chapter Test
HOAP Holt Online Assessment Program (in the Holt Interactive Online Edition)

Reteach/Intervene

 Interactive Reader and Study Guide
 Differentiated Instruction Teacher Management System: Lesson Plans
 Differentiated Instruction Modified Worksheets and Tests CD-ROM
 Interactive Skills Tutor CD-ROM

go.hrw.com
Online Resources
Chapter Resources:
KEYWORD: SK9 CH1

12. a. They mean the physical and human features that define an area and make it different from other places.

b. so people can use them to organize and guide their study of geography

c. possible response—as a study guide, helping to understand all aspects of places and people that are important to know

13. a. physical—landforms, bodies of water, other physical features; human—world's people and their cultures

b. It helps them make predictions and preparations.

c. possible response—because studying each part helps give a better understanding of Earth and its people

Using the Internet

14. Go to the HRW Web site and enter the keyword shown to access a rubric for this activity.

> KEYWORD: SK9 TEACHER

Social Studies Skills

15. true-color

16. light blue

17. to improve accuracy

Focus on Reading and Writing

18. Students' charts should clearly list prior knowledge, information learned in terms of the main ideas in each section, and questions or topics they would like to learn more about.

RF: Focus on Reading, Using Prior Knowledge

SECTION 2 *(Pages 12–16)*

12. a. Define What do geographers mean when they discuss an area's landscape?

b. Explain Why did geographers create the five themes and the six essential elements?

c. Predict How might the five themes and six essential elements help you in your study of geography?

SECTION 3 *(Pages 18–22)*

13. a. Identify What are the two main branches of geography? What does each include?

b. Summarize How can physical geography help people adjust to the dangers of the world?

c. Elaborate Why do geographers study both physical and human characteristics of places?

Using the Internet

14. Activity: Using Maps What does your town or community look like? What can be found there? Maps can help you understand your community and learn about its features. Enter the activity keyword to learn more about maps and how they can help you better understand your community. Then search the Internet to find a map of your community. Use the map to find the locations of at least five important features. For example, you might locate your school, the library, a park, or major highways. Be creative and find other places you think your classmates should be aware of.

Social Studies Skills

Analyzing Satellite Images *Use the satellite images of Italy from the Social Studies Skills lesson in this chapter to answer the following questions.*

15. On which image do forests appear more clearly, the true-color or the infrared image?

16. What color do you think represents mountains on the infrared satellite image?

17. Why might geographers use satellite images like these while making maps of Italy?

FOCUS ON READING AND WRITING

18. Using Prior Knowledge Create a chart with three columns. In the first column list what you knew about geography before you read the chapter. In the second column list what you learned in the chapter. In the third column list questions that you now have about geography.

19. Writing Your Job Description Review your notes on the different jobs geographers do. Then write your job description. You should begin your description by explaining why the job is important. Then identify the job's tasks and responsibilities. Finally, tell what kind of person might do well as a geographer.

Map Activity

20. Sketch Map Draw a map that shows your school and the surrounding neighborhood. Your map does not have to be complicated, but you should include major features like streets and buildings. Use the map shown here as an example.

---

19. Rubric Students' job descriptions should:

- give reasons why the job is important
- list the job's major tasks and responsibilities
- include characteristics needed to do the job well

RF: Focus on Writing, Writing a Job Description

Map Activity

20. Students' maps should clearly show where the school is and include major streets or roads and other features, such as stores.

Standardized Test Practice

DIRECTIONS (1–7): For each statement or question, write on a separate answer sheet the *number* of the word or expression that, of those given, best completes the statement or answers the question.

1 Which of the following subjects would a human geographer study the most?

(1) mountains

(2) populations

(3) rivers

(4) volcanoes

2 The study of weather is called

(1) meteorology.

(2) hydrology.

(3) social science.

(4) cartography.

3 A region is an area that has

(1) one or more common features.

(2) no people living in it.

(3) few physical features.

(4) set physical boundaries.

4 How many essential elements of geography have geographers identified?

(1) two

(2) four

(3) six

(4) eight

5 The physical and human characteristics that define an area are its

(1) landscape.

(2) location.

(3) region.

(4) science.

6 Which of the five themes of geography examines how people deal with their surroundings?

(1) movement

(2) location

(3) human-environment interaction

(4) landscape

7 The smallest level at which a geographer might study a place is

(1) microscopic.

(2) local.

(3) regional.

(4) global.

Base your answer to question 8 on the map below and on your knowledge of social studies.

The United States

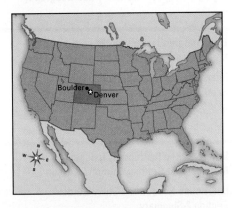

8 **Constructed-Response Question** Do you think this map is more likely to be used by a physical geographer or by a human geographer? Give two reasons for your answer. Then write two statements about what a geographer could find on this map.

A GEOGRAPHER'S WORLD **25**

1. 2
Break Down the Question This question requires students to eliminate answer choices a physical geographer would study.

2. 1
Break Down the Question This question requires students to recall factual information. Refer students who miss it to Section 3.

3. 1
Break Down the Question This question requires students to recall factual information. Refer students who miss it to Section 1.

4. 3
Break Down the Question Suggest that students try to picture the elements chart in their mind to recall the correct number. Refer students who miss it to Section 2.

5. 1
Break Down the Question This question requires students to recall factual information. Refer students who miss it to Section 1.

6. 3
Break Down the Question Students should recognize that the theme human-environment interaction is most appropriate.

7. 2
Break Down the Question Students can eliminate "microscopic" because it is not one of the three levels geographers use.

8. Constructed-Response Question
Possible response—by a physical geographer, because it can be used to understand the relative locations of two cities within Colorado and within the United States; A geographer could find the state boundaries of the United States and the capital of Colorado.

Reteach/Intervention Resources

Reproducible
- Interactive Reader and Study Guide
- Differentiated Instruction Teacher Management System: Lesson Plans

Technology
- Quick Facts Transparency: Visual Summary: A Geographer's World
- Differentiated Instruction Modified Worksheets and Tests CD-ROM
- Interactive Skills Tutor CD-ROM
- Quiz Game CD-ROM

Tips for Test Taking

Anticipate the Answers Give students this important tip: Before you read the answer choices, answer the question yourself. Then, read the choices. If the answer you gave is among the choices listed, it is probably correct!

Chapter 2 Planning Guide

The Eastern Hemisphere

Chapter Overview	Reproducible Resources	Technology Resources
CHAPTER 2 pp. 26–49 **Overview:** In this chapter, students will learn about how Earth's movements affect the energy we receive from the sun, the importance of water, and how Earth's landforms were made.	OSP **Differentiated Instruction Teacher Management System:*** • Instructional Pacing Guides • Lesson Plans for Differentiated Instruction **Interactive Reader and Study Guide:** Chapter Summary Graphic Organizer **Resource File*** • Chapter Review • Focus on Reading: Using Word Parts • Focus on Writing: Writing a Haiku • Social Studies Skills: Using a Physical Map **Experiencing World History and Geography**	OSP **Teacher's One-Stop Planner:** Calendar Planner **Power Presentations with Video CD-ROM** **Differentiated Instruction Modified Worksheets and Tests CD-ROM** **Interactive Skills Tutor CD-ROM** **Student Edition on Audio CD Program** **Music of the World Audio CD Program** **Geography's Impact Video Series (VHS/DVD):** Impact of Water on Earth* **World Outline Maps: Transparencies and Activities**
Section 1: **Location** **The Big Idea:** The Eastern Hemisphere lies east of the prime meridian and is home to a variety of countries and cultures.	OSP **Differentiated Instruction Teacher Management System:** Section 1 Lesson Plan* **Interactive Reader and Study Guide:** Section 1 Summary **Resource File*** • Vocabulary Builder: Section 1	**Daily Bellringer Transparency:** Section 1* **Map Zone Transparency:** The Eastern Hemisphere*
Section 2: **Water Features** **The Big Idea:** Water is a dominant feature on Earth's surface and is essential for life.	OSP **Differentiated Instruction Teacher Management System:** Section 2 Lesson Plan* **Interactive Reader and Study Guide:** Section 2 Summary **Resource File*** • Vocabulary Builder: Section 2 • Biography: Robert D. Ballard	**Daily Bellringer Transparency:** Section 2*
Section 3: **The Land** **The Big Idea:** Processes below and on Earth's surface shape the planet's physical features.	OSP **Differentiated Instruction Teacher Management System:** Section 3 Lesson Plan* **Interactive Reader and Study Guide:** Section 3 Summary **Resource File*** • Vocabulary Builder: Section 3 • Biography: Margaret Mead • Primary Source: Field Bulletin XIII from Samoa • Literature: *Cry, the Beloved Country* by Alan Paton	**Daily Bellringer Transparency:** Section 3* **Map Zone Transparency:** Earth's Plates* **Map Zone Transparency:** Ring of Fire* **Map Zone Transparency:** India: Physical* **Internet Activity:** Continental Drift in the Future

- **Quick Facts Transparency:** Visual Summary: The Eastern Hemisphere*
- **Spanish Chapter Summaries Audio CD Program**
- **Progress Assessment Support System (PASS):** Chapter Test*
- **Differentiated Instruction Modified Worksheets and Tests CD-ROM:** Modified Chapter Test
- **OSP Teacher's One-Stop Planner:** ExamView Test Generator (English/Spanish)
- **Alternative Assessment Handbook**
- **HOAP Holt Online Assessment Program (HOAP),** in the Holt Interactive Online Student Edition

- **PASS:** Section 1 Quiz*
- **Online Quiz:** Section 1
- **Alternative Assessment Handbook**

- **PASS:** Section 2 Quiz*
- **Online Quiz:** Section 2
- **Alternative Assessment Handbook**

- **PASS:** Section 3 Quiz*
- **Online Quiz:** Section 3
- **Alternative Assessment Handbook**

Power Presentations with Video CD-ROM

Power Presentations with Video are visual presentations of each chapter's main ideas. Presentations can be customized by including Quick Facts charts, images from the text, and video clips.

Holt Online Learning

go.hrw.com
Teacher Resources
KEYWORD: SK9 TEACHER

go.hrw.com
Student Resources
KEYWORD: SK9 CH2

- Interactive Multimedia Activities
- Current Events

- Chapter-based Internet Activities
- and more!

Holt Interactive
Online Student Edition

Complete online support for interactivity, assessment, and reporting

- Interactive Maps and Notebook
- Standardized Test Prep
- Homework Practice and Research Activities Online

Differentiating Instruction

How do I address the needs of varied learners?

The Target Resource acts as your primary strategy for differentiated instruction.

ENGLISH-LANGUAGE LEARNERS & STRUGGLING READERS

Interactive Reader and Study Guide

The activities in the Interactive Reader and Study Guide engage students with questions while presenting summaries of chapter content and provide opportunities for students to practice critical thinking skills.

Additional Resources

Differentiated Instruction Teacher Management System: Lesson Plans for Differentiated Instruction

Resource File:
- Vocabulary Builder Activities
- Social Studies Skills: Using a Physical Map

Quick Facts Transparency: Visual Summary: The Eastern Hemisphere

Student Edition on Audio CD Program

Spanish Chapter Summaries Audio CD Program

Teacher's One-Stop Planner:
- ExamView Test Generator, Spanish
- PuzzlePro, Spanish

English-Language Learner Strategies and Activities

SPECIAL NEEDS LEARNERS

Differentiated Instruction Teacher Management System

Lesson Plans for Differentiated Instruction provide teachers with strategies to help plan instruction for all learners.

Additional Resources

Differentiated Instruction Teacher Management System: Lesson Plans for Differentiated Instruction

Interactive Reader and Study Guide

Resource File: Social Studies Skills: Using a Physical Map

Student Edition on Audio CD Program

Interactive Skills Tutor CD-ROM

Graphic Organizer Transparencies with Support for Reading and Writing

ADVANCED/GIFTED AND TALENTED STUDENTS

Resource File

The Resource File activities allow students to extend their knowledge of chapter-related places and people and to practice geography skills.
- Focus on Reading: Using Word Parts
- Focus on Writing: Writing a Haiku
- Literature: *Cry, the Beloved Country* by Alan Paton

Additional Resources

Differentiated Instruction Teacher Management System: Lesson Plans for Differentiated Instruction

World History and Geography Document-Based Questions Activities

Geography, Science, and Cultures Activities

Experiencing World History and Geography

Differentiated Activities in the Teacher's Edition
- Writing a Letter about Water
- Learning from Visuals

Differentiated Activities in the Teacher's Edition
- Making a Landform Collage
- Writing a Persuasive Letter

Differentiated Activities in the Teacher's Edition
- Creating Water Diagrams
- Creating a Public Service Announcement
- Designing a Slide Show Presentation
- Observing the Effects of Erosion

HOLT Teacher's One-Stop Planner®

How can I manage the lesson plans and support materials for differentiated instruction?

With the Teacher's One-Stop Planner, you can easily organize and print lesson plans, planning guides, and instructional materials for all learners.

The Teacher's One-Stop Planner includes the following materials to help you differentiate instruction:
- Interactive Teacher's Edition
- Calendar Planner and pacing guides
- Editable lesson plans
- All reproducible ancillaries in Adobe Acrobat (PDF) format
- ExamView Test Generator (English & Spanish)
- Transparency and video previews

Professional Development

What teacher training resources are available to help me grow professionally?

- **In-service and staff development** as part of your Holt Social Studies product purchase
- **Quick Teacher Tutorial Lesson Presentation CD-ROM**
- Intensive tuition-based **Teacher Development Institute**
- **Convenient Holt Speaker Bureau** – face-to-face workshop options
- **24/7 Ask A Professional Development Expert** at http://www.hrw.com/prodev/

CHAPTER 2

The Eastern Hemisphere

FOCUS QUESTION

How did geography influence the development of the Eastern Hemisphere?

What You Will Learn...

In this chapter you will learn about the Eastern Hemisphere, which includes half of the planet. You will discover where the Eastern Hemisphere is located, how water affects life there, and how its various landforms were created.

FOCUS ON READING AND WRITING

Using Word Parts Sometimes you can figure out the meaning of a word by looking at its parts. A root is the base of the word. A prefix attaches to the beginning, and a suffix attaches to the ending. When you come across a word you don't know, check to see whether you recognize its parts. **See the lesson, Using Word Parts, on page S3.**

Writing a Haiku Join the poets who have celebrated our planet for centuries. Write a haiku, a short poem, about the Eastern Hemisphere. As you read the chapter, gather information about the hemisphere, its water supply, and shapes on the land. Then choose the most intriguing information to include in your haiku.

Cultures The variety of cultures and traditions in the Eastern Hemisphere are reflected in its buildings and ways of life.

Introduce the Chapter

At Level

Solar Energy, Water, and Land

1. Tell students that they are going to learn about the relationship between Earth and the sun and how it influences human activities, the part that water plays in sustaining life, and the variety of landforms on Earth and how they were shaped.

2. Explain that various regions have different climates and different landforms. Ask: Which parts of the Eastern Hemisphere are desert? Mountains? Plains? Where is it coldest and warmest? Where is the most water found?

3. Have students work in pairs to examine the chapter's photos, maps, and graphics. Encourage them to make a list of questions they would like to have answered as they read the chapter. **LS Visual/Spatial, Interpersonal**

📄 Alternative Assessment Handbook, Rubric 1: Acquiring Information

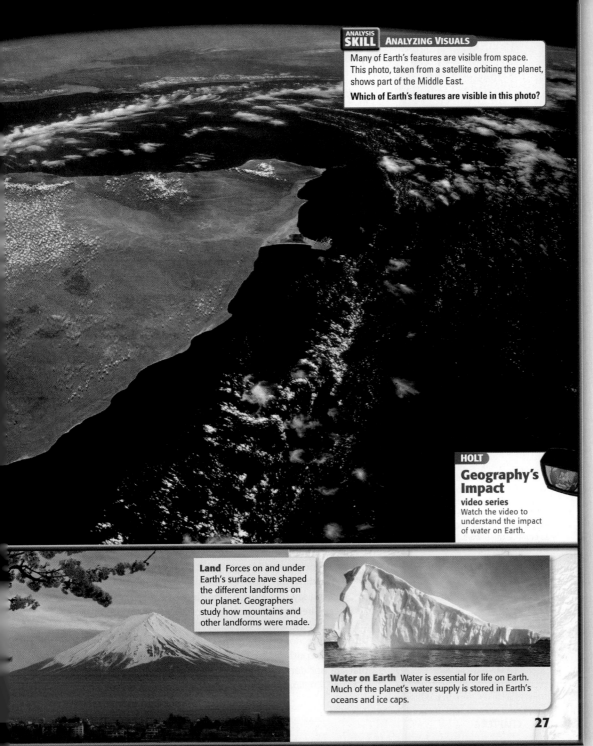

Many of Earth's features are visible from space. This photo, taken from a satellite orbiting the planet, shows part of the Middle East.

Which of Earth's features are visible in this photo?

HOLT
Geography's Impact
video series
Watch the video to understand the impact of water on Earth.

Land Forces on and under Earth's surface have shaped the different landforms on our planet. Geographers study how mountains and other landforms were made.

Water on Earth Water is essential for life on Earth. Much of the planet's water supply is stored in Earth's oceans and ice caps.

27

Cross-Discipline Activity: English/Language Arts

At Level

Writing a Poem

Standard English Mastery

1. Have students study the photographs in the chapter opener and throughout the chapter. Have them find additional photographs of Earth from space and of the planet's landforms, either on the Internet or in the library.

2. Have them list several words that describe each image. Suggest that they think of words that appeal to the senses of sight, sound, touch, hearing, and taste. Encourage students to use a thesaurus to find words that are interesting and descriptive.

3. Next, have students use standard English to write a poem from the point of view of a traveler approaching Earth for the first time. As the traveler comes closer to the surface of the planet, have students imagine his or her reaction and write a description of what the traveler might see.

4. Have volunteers read their poems aloud.
   LS Verbal/Linguistic, Visual/Spatial

   Alternative Assessment Handbook, Rubrics 26: Poems and Songs; and 39: Writing to Create

---

• Chapter Preview •

Explore the Pictures

Earth As the photograph shows, the planet is made up of land and water. Landforms and seasons vary greatly from one region to another.

Culture Ask students if they know the structure shown in the photograph and where it is located. *Taj Mahal, India* Taj Mahal represents the blending of several Eastern Hemisphere cultures, including Persian, Turkish, Indian, and Islamic. The main structure is a mausoleum. Construction was completed around 1648.

Land This photo is of Mt. Fuji in Japan. The landform is a dormant volcano that last erupted in the eighteenth century. It is surrounded by five lakes. Discuss with students how they think this landform was created. Ask them how it is different from other mountains they might have seen.

Water on Earth Icebergs are solid forms of water found near the poles. Ask students why they think the icebergs can stay solid.

HOLT
Geography's Impact
▶ video series
See the Video Teacher's Guide for strategies for using the chapter video to teach about the impact of water on Earth.

go.hrw.com
Online Resources
Chapter Resources:
KEYWORD: SK9 CH2
Teacher Resources:
KEYWORD: SK9 TEACHER

Answers
Analyzing Visuals *land, deserts, coast lines, ocean*

27

Preteach

Bellringer

If YOU lived there. . . Use the **Daily Bellringer Transparency** to help students answer the question.

📓 Daily Bellringer Transparency, Section 1

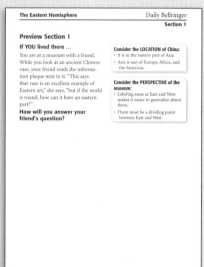

The Eastern Hemisphere	Daily Bellringer
	Section 1

Preview Section 1

If YOU lived there . . .
You are at a museum with a friend. While you look at an ancient Chinese vase, your friend reads the information plaque next to it. "This says that vase is an excellent example of Eastern art," she says, "but if the world is round, how can it have an eastern part?"
How will you answer your friend's question?

Consider the LOCATION of China:
• It is in the eastern part of Asia.
• Asia is east of Europe, Africa, and the Americas.

Consider the PERSPECTIVE of the museum:
• Labeling areas as East and West makes it easier to generalize about them.
• There must be a dividing point between East and West.

Academic Vocabulary

Review with students the high-use academic term in this section.

vary to be different (p. 30)

📓 RF: Vocabulary Builder, Section 1

Taking Notes

Have students copy the graphic organizer onto their own paper and then use it to take notes on the section. This activity will prepare students for the Section Assessment, in which they will complete a graphic organizer that builds on the information using the Critical Thinking Skill: Making Generalizations.

Location

What You Will Learn...

Main Ideas

1. Geographers use directions and longitude to define the Eastern Hemisphere.
2. The characteristics of the Eastern Hemisphere reflect its great diversity.

The Big Idea

The Eastern Hemisphere lies east of the prime meridian and is home to a variety of countries and cultures.

Key Terms

latitude, *p. 29*
longitude, *p. 29*
culture, *p. 30*
culture regions, *p. 31*
democracy, *p. 31*
developed countries, *p. 31*
developing countries, *p. 31*

 TAKING NOTES As you read, take notes about the location, definition, and characteristics of the Eastern Hemisphere. Use a diagram like the one shown below to organize your notes.

Location
Definition
Characteristics

If **YOU** lived there...

You are at a museum with a friend. While you look at an ancient Chinese vase, your friend reads the information plaque next to it. "This says that vase is an excellent example of Eastern art," she says, "but if the world is round, how can it have an eastern part?"

How will you answer your friend's question?

BUILDING BACKGROUND The world is a huge place. Instead of studying the whole world at once, geographers divide the world into smaller sections. One division they often use is called a hemisphere—half of the globe. Most commonly, geographers divide the world into Eastern and Western hemispheres.

Defining the Eastern Hemisphere

Imagine a globe. If you wanted to divide the globe into eastern and western halves, how would you decide where to do it? Any line drawn around the globe would divide it into two equal parts, so how could you determine which line would be best? Geographers face these issues when they divide the world into the East and the West.

Direction

To understand the hemispheres, you must know how to use directions to express location. The four cardinal, or main, directions are north, south, east, and west. North and south always point to the poles, the ends of the axis around which Earth turns. If you face north, east is to your right and west to your left.

The cardinal directions express general locations. For example, you can say that Europe is north of Africa and west of Asia. Yet these directions are not very specific. To be more precise, you need to use a different set of directions. Between the four cardinal directions are the intermediate directions: northeast, northwest, southeast, and southwest. These describe locations that are not due north, south, east, or west of each other. For example, England is northwest of France.

Teach the Big Idea

At Level

Location

1. **Teach** Ask students the questions in the Main Idea boxes under Direct Teach.

2. **Apply** Have students arrange their desks in a circle in the center of the room. State that the front of the classroom is North. Then ask students questions to reinforce the concepts of location. For example: Which students are in the Eastern Hemisphere? What would a line from Student A to Student B be called—a latitude line or a longitude line? Ask questions until students have mastered the concepts.

3. **Review** Tell students to close their books and take out a sheet of notebook paper. Have students write a definition of each of the section's key terms from memory.

4. **Practice/Homework** Instruct students to use the Atlas pages in the back of their books to write five factual statements using the concepts of location they learned in the section. 🅛🅢 **Visual/Spatial**

📓 Alternative Assessment Handbook, Rubrics 14: Group Activity; and 37: Writing Assignments

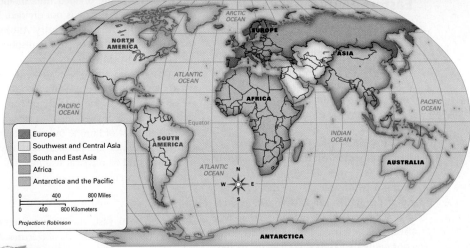

Europe
Southwest and Central Asia
South and East Asia
Africa
Antarctica and the Pacific

0   400   800 Miles
0   400   800 Kilometers

Projection: Robinson

map zone
Geography Skills

Location The prime meridian, the line at the center of this map on which the compass rose appears, divides the world into the Eastern and Western hemispheres.

1. **Use the Map** Through which continents does the prime meridian pass?
2. **Identify** Which continents are located mainly in the Eastern Hemisphere?

Latitude and Longitude

To identify the Eastern and Western hemispheres, we need a point of reference. What is the Eastern Hemisphere east of? For this reference, geographers use a set of imaginary lines drawn around the globe.

Look at the map on this page to see examples of these lines. You should notice that some of the lines run east to west. These lines measure **latitude**, a place's distance north or south of Earth's equator. The equator is the line halfway between the North and South poles.

Intersecting the lines of latitude are other lines that run north and south. These lines measure **longitude**, the distance east or west of the prime meridian. The prime meridian is a line of longitude that runs near London, England.

Latitude and longitude measure distance in degrees. A place's location can be expressed by numbers, called coordinates, that describe its distance north or south of the equator and east or west of the prime meridian. For example, Moscow, Russia, is 56 degrees north of the equator and 38 degrees east of the prime meridian. This location can be expressed as 56°N, 38°E.

Besides expressing location, the equator and the prime meridian divide the world into hemispheres. The equator divides the world into the Northern and Southern hemispheres. The prime meridian divides it into Eastern and Western hemispheres. In this course, you will focus your studies on the Eastern Hemisphere.

READING CHECK **Finding Main Ideas** What are the equator and prime meridian?

THE EASTERN HEMISPHERE **29**

Main Idea

① **Defining the Eastern Hemisphere**

Geographers use directions and longitude to define the Eastern Hemisphere.

Recall If you face north, which way is east and which way is west? *east to the right and west to the left*

Elaborate How are the intermediate directions useful? *They are more precise; can be used to describe locations that are not due north, south, east, or west*

Draw Conclusions What do you do when you specify a line of latitude and a line of longitude together, for example 56°N, 38°E? *You describe the location of a particular point on the surface of the Earth. For example, the city of Moscow, Russia is located at 56°N, 38°E.*

📖 Map Zone Transparency: The Eastern Hemisphere

Info to Know

The Prime Meridian Unlike the equator, the fixed location of which is exactly equidistant the Earth's poles, the location of the prime meridian is arbitrary. In fact, there have been many "prime meridians" throughout history. The line that today serves as the prime meridian was settled upon at a conference of nations held in 1884.

Hemispheres Maps   Prep Required

Materials Two outline maps of the world with latitude and longitude lines for each student; colored pencils

1. Distribute the outline maps to students. On one map, have students write the title *The Eastern and Western Hemispheres.* On the second map, have students write the title *The Northern and Southern Hemispheres.*

2. On both maps, have students highlight and clearly label the prime meridian and the equator, each with a different colored pencil.

3. Then, on the appropriate maps, have students label each of the hemispheres, and color each hemisphere in with a different color. Tell students to include legends on their maps.

4. On a separate sheet of paper, have students write a paragraph comparing and contrasting each of the hemispheres. **LS Visual/Spatial, Verbal/Linguistic**

📝 Alternative Assessment Handbook, Rubrics 20: Map Creation, and 40: Writing to Describe

Answers

Map Zone 1. *Europe, Africa, and Antarctica;* 2. *Europe, Africa, Asia, and Australia*

Reading Check *The equator is a line of latitude and the prime meridian is a line of longitude. The equator divides the world into Northern and Southern hemispheres and the prime meridian divides the world into Eastern and Western hemispheres.*

❷ Characteristics of the Eastern Hemisphere

The characteristics of the Eastern Hemisphere reflect its great diversity.

Recall What percentage of the world's land and people are in the Eastern Hemisphere? *60 percent of the land; 85 percent of the people*

Find Main Ideas Why is the Middle East considered a culture region? *The region is home to many cultures that have common traits such as religion and language.*

Draw Conclusions Is the United States a culture region? Why or why not? *possible answer—Yes. People from many cultures share common cultural traits, such as the English language and a tradition of democratic government.*

Did you know...

Food is typically an integral part of a people's culture. Certain fish eggs, called caviar, for example, have been a favorite in Russia for centuries, while in Japan, some types of raw fish, called sushi, have been popular for a long time. In France, geese were specially raised and overfed so their livers would taste a certain way. Today, all of these foods are enjoyed in the United States and many other parts of the world.

Answers

Contrasting *possible answer—Quality of life in Afghanistan would seem to be lower than in France. Afghanis make less money, live shorter lives, are less literate, and have limited access to medical care.*

Characteristics of the Eastern Hemisphere

The Eastern Hemisphere includes more than 60 percent of the world's land and more than 85 percent of its people. As a result, the Eastern Hemisphere is home to diverse societies. From Great Britain to South Africa to China, ways of life in the Eastern Hemisphere **vary** greatly.

ACADEMIC VOCABULARY
vary to be different

Continents and Countries

Four continents are located almost entirely within the Eastern Hemisphere. They are Africa, Asia, Australia, and Europe. Part of Antarctica lies in the Eastern Hemisphere as well, but no one lives there permanently because it is too cold. Surrounding these continents are vast bodies of water, including the Atlantic, Pacific, and Indian oceans. Some of the world's largest seas, such as the Mediterranean and Red seas, are located in the Eastern Hemisphere as well.

Three of the continents of the Eastern Hemisphere are divided into smaller countries. Only Australia is not divided. It is both a continent and a country. Among the countries of the Eastern Hemisphere are both the world's largest—Russia—and its smallest—Vatican City, located entirely within the city of Rome. Some countries are separated from one another by physical features. Italy, for example, is separated from the rest of Europe by mountains. Other boundaries are political and may not correspond to physical features. They often appear on maps as straight lines.

Cultures

Because it is so vast, the Eastern Hemisphere is home to thousands of cultures. A **culture** is a set of ideas, beliefs, values, and practices that a group of people have in common. Culture includes aspects of life, such as language and religion, that many people in a given area share.

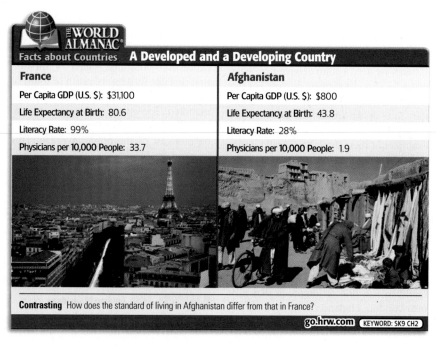

THE WORLD ALMANAC Facts about Countries **A Developed and a Developing Country**

France	Afghanistan
Per Capita GDP (U.S. $): $31,100	Per Capita GDP (U.S. $): $800
Life Expectancy at Birth: 80.6	Life Expectancy at Birth: 43.8
Literacy Rate: 99%	Literacy Rate: 28%
Physicians per 10,000 People: 33.7	Physicians per 10,000 People: 1.9

Contrasting How does the standard of living in Afghanistan differ from that in France?

go.hrw.com KEYWORD: SK9 CH2

Collaborative Learning

At Level

Developed and Developing Countries

Research Required

1. Organize the class into pairs. Provide each pair with an almanac or access to the Internet.

2. Assign each pair two countries (one developed and one developing). Each student will research one country, using either an almanac or an online resource such as the CIA World Factbook, to locate facts such as those found in the *World Almanac* feature on this page.

3. Ask pairs to report their findings and to classify each country as developed or developing. Ask students why they chose to classify each country as they did.

4. Draw a two-column chart on the board and list countries researched as developed or developing. Discuss the measurements students used to classify countries. Also discuss countries that were difficult to classify. **LS Logical/Mathematical**

📋 Alternative Assessment Handbook, Rubrics 11: Discussions; and 30: Research

All societies share some cultural features. For example, every society has some form of government, a plan for educating children, and art or music. However, the specific details of these cultural features vary widely from place to place.

Geographers use cultural features to divide the world into **culture regions**, or areas in which people have many shared culture traits. Some of these regions are very small. Others are large. For example, the Middle East is a huge culture region. It includes most of Southwest Asia as well as much of North Africa. Many people in the Middle East region share the same religion, Islam, and a single language, Arabic.

Government and Economy

Government and an economy are basic parts of any society. A government is needed to provide order and to regulate how people behave. An economy determines how people meet their basic needs, such as obtaining food and clothing. Although every country has both a government and an economy, their nature can vary widely.

Many governments in the Eastern Hemisphere, including those of Germany, South Africa, and Japan, are democracies. A **democracy** is a form of government in which people elect leaders and rule by majority. Not all countries, however, are democracies. Some, like Saudi Arabia, are monarchies, led by kings or queens. Others are dictatorships, led by single leaders who often restrict the people's rights. Under Saddam Hussein, Iraq was a dictatorship.

Economies also vary. Some countries, called **developed countries**, have strong economies and a high quality of life. People in these countries have relatively high incomes and can buy most of what they need. France is an example of a developed country. In poorer countries, such as Afghanistan, most people work as farmers or in low-paying jobs. These **developing countries** generally have less-productive economies and a lower quality of life.

One way to distinguish a country's level of development is to look at its gross domestic product (GDP). This figure is the value of all goods and services produced in a country in a single year. If you divide a country's GDP by its population, you learn its per capita GDP, also a useful indicator.

READING CHECK **Generalizing** What are some elements of Eastern culture?

SUMMARY AND PREVIEW In this section, you were introduced to the Eastern Hemisphere and its people. Next, you will learn about the region's water features and how they affect life there.

Section 1 Assessment

go.hrw.com
Online Quiz
KEYWORD: SK9 HP2

Reviewing Ideas, Terms, and Places

1. **a. Define** What are **latitude** and **longitude** used for?
   b. Explain Why are intermediate directions sometimes more useful than cardinal directions?
   c. Develop Why do you think geographers study the Eastern and Western hemispheres more often than the Northern and Southern hemispheres?

2. **a. Identify** What are some elements of your **culture**?
   b. Analyze Why do ways of life in the Eastern Hemisphere vary so greatly?
   c. Evaluate Would you prefer to live in a **developed country** or a **developing** one? Why?

Critical Thinking

3. **Making Generalizations** Use your notes to fill in the diagram with two statements about the Eastern Hemisphere.

   Eastern Hemisphere → [ ] [ ]

FOCUS ON WRITING

4. **Identifying Characteristics** What are some major characteristics of the Eastern Hemisphere? In your notebook, jot down a few notes about the region.

THE EASTERN HEMISPHERE **31**

Section 1 Assessment Answers

1. **a.** latitude—to measure distance north or south of the equator; longitude—to measure distance east or west of the prime meridian
   b. more precise; can describe locations that are not due north, south, east, or west
   c. possible answer—because the Eastern and Western hemispheres offer sharper contrasts than the Northern and Southern hemispheres

2. **a.** possible answer—language, religion, sports and recreation, music, food, holidays
   b. because the hemisphere is so large, containing 60 percent of the world's land and 85 percent of the world's people

   c. possible answer—a developed country; I would probably live longer and more comfortably.

3. possible answer—Most of the world's people live in the Eastern Hemisphere. In the Eastern Hemisphere there are many developed countries and also many developing countries.

4. possible answer—east of the prime meridian, a huge place with lots of people and land, home to thousands of cultures, many democracies

31

Bellringer

If YOU lived there. . . Use the **Daily Bellringer Transparency** to help students answer the question.

🖎 Daily Bellringer Transparency, Section 2

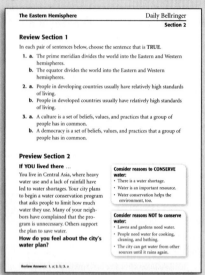

The Eastern Hemisphere · Daily Bellringer
Section 2

Review Section 1

In each pair of sentences below, choose the sentence that is TRUE.

1. a. The prime meridian divides the world into the Eastern and Western hemispheres.
b. The equator divides the world into the Eastern and Western hemispheres.

2. a. People in developing countries usually have relatively high standards of living.
b. People in developed countries usually have relatively high standards of living.

3. a. A culture is a set of beliefs, values, and practices that a group of people has in common.
b. A democracy is a set of beliefs, values, and practices that a group of people has in common.

Preview Section 2

If YOU lived there ...
You live in Central Asia, where heavy water use and a lack of rainfall have led to water shortages. Your city plans to begin a water conservation program that asks people to limit how much water they use. Many of your neighbors have complained that the program is unnecessary. Others support the plan to save water.
How do you feel about the city's water plan?

Consider reasons to CONSERVE water:
· There is a water shortage.
· Water is an important resource.
· Water conservation helps the environment, too.

Consider reasons NOT to conserve water:
· Lawns and gardens need water.
· People need water for cooking, cleaning, and bathing.
· The city can get water from other sources until it rains again.

Review Answers: 1. a; 2. b; 3. a.

Key Terms

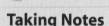 **RF:** Vocabulary Builder, Section 2

Taking Notes

Have students copy the graphic organizer onto their own paper and then use it to take notes on the section. This activity will prepare students for the Section Assessment, in which they will complete a graphic organizer that builds on the information using the Critical Thinking Skill: Sequencing.

Water Features

What You Will Learn...

Main Ideas

1. Salt water and freshwater make up Earth's water supply.
2. In the water cycle, water circulates from Earth's surface to the atmosphere and back again.
3. Water plays an important role in people's lives.

The Big Idea

Water is a dominant feature on Earth's surface and is essential for life.

Key Terms

freshwater, *p. 33*
glaciers, *p. 33*
surface water, *p. 33*
precipitation, *p. 33*
groundwater, *p. 34*
water vapor, *p. 34*
water cycle, *p. 35*

TAKING NOTES As you read, take notes about Earth's water, the water cycle, and how water affects our lives. Use a diagram like the one below to organize your notes.

Water on Earth
Water Supply → Water and People
→ Water Cycle

If **YOU** lived there...

You live in Central Asia, where heavy water use and a lack of rainfall have led to water shortages. Your city plans to begin a water conservation program that asks people to limit how much water they use. Many of your neighbors have complained that the program is unnecessary. Others support the plan to save water.

How do you feel about the city's water plan?

BUILDING BACKGROUND Although water covers much of Earth's surface, water shortages, like those in Central Asia, are common all over the planet. Because water is vital to the survival of all living things, geographers study Earth's water supply.

Earth's Water Supply

Think of the different uses for water. We use water to cook and clean, we drink it, and we grow crops with it. Water is used for recreation, to generate electricity, and even to travel from place to place. Water is perhaps the most important and abundant resource on Earth. In fact, water covers some two-thirds of the planet. Understanding Earth's water supply and how it affects our lives is an important part of geography.

Earth's Distribution of Water

Earth's water supply is divided into two main types—salt water and freshwater. Humans, plants, and animals rely on Earth's freshwater supply for survival.

Teach the Big Idea

At Level | Standard English Mastery

Water Features

1. **Teach** Ask students the questions in the Main Idea boxes under Direct Teach.

2. **Apply** Ask students to imagine that they will interview a geographer about water on Earth. Have them use standard English to write a list of interview questions about the material in the chapter. They should write at least three questions about the information under each main heading.

3. **Review** Have students take turns interviewing each other and answering the questions.

4. **Practice/Homework** Have students write the answers next to their interview questions. Then have students work together to come up with more questions.
   LS Verbal/Linguistic

   📑 Alternative Assessment Handbook, Rubrics 1: Acquiring Information; and 11: Discussions

Salt Water

Although water covers much of the planet, we cannot use most of it. About 97 percent of the Earth's water is salt water. Because salt water contains high levels of salt and other minerals, it is unsafe to drink.

In general, salt water is found in Earth's oceans. Oceans are vast bodies of water covering some 71 percent of the planet's surface. Earth's oceans are made up of smaller bodies of water such as seas, gulfs, bays, and straits. Altogether, Earth's oceans cover some 139 million square miles (360 million square km) of the planet's surface.

Some of Earth's lakes contain salt water. The Dead Sea near Israel, for example, is a saltwater lake. As salt and other minerals have collected in the lake, which has no outlet, the water has become salty.

Freshwater

Since the water in Earth's oceans is too salty to use, we must rely on other sources for freshwater. **Freshwater**, or water without salt, makes up only about 3 percent of our total water supply. Much of that freshwater is locked in Earth's **glaciers**, large areas of slow-moving ice, and in the ice of the Antarctic and Arctic regions. Most of the freshwater we use everyday is found in lakes, in rivers, and under Earth's surface.

One form of freshwater is surface water. **Surface water** is water that is found in Earth's streams, rivers, and lakes. It may seem that there is a great deal of water in our lakes and rivers, but only a tiny amount of Earth's water supply—less than 1 percent—comes from surface water.

Streams and rivers are a common source of surface water. Streams form when precipitation collects in a narrow channel and flows toward the ocean. **Precipitation** is water that falls to Earth's surface as rain, snow, sleet, or hail. In turn, streams join together to form rivers. Any smaller stream or river that flows into a larger stream or river is called a tributary. For example, the Ubangi River is a major tributary of Central Africa's Congo River.

Lakes are another important source of surface water. Some lakes were formed as rivers filled low-lying areas with water. Other lakes, like the lochs of Scotland, were formed when glaciers carved deep holes in Earth's surface and deposited water as they melted.

Most of Earth's available freshwater is stored underground. As precipitation falls to Earth, much of it is absorbed into the ground, filling spaces in the soil and rock.

Salt Water Earth's oceans contain some 97 percent of the planet's water supply. Unfortunately, this water is too salty to drink.

Freshwater Freshwater from lakes, rivers, and streams makes up only a fraction of Earth's water supply.

THE EASTERN HEMISPHERE **33**

Main Idea

❷ **The Water Cycle**

In the water cycle, water circulates from Earth's surface to the atmosphere and back again.

Recall What forms does water take? *solid (snow, ice), liquid (rain, oceans, rivers), gas (water vapor)*

Describe What happens to precipitation during the water cycle? *Some is absorbed into the soil as groundwater; runoff collects in streams, rivers, and oceans.*

Activity **Diagram** Have students make a poster with a detailed diagram of the water cycle. Students should write captions explaining each element of the diagram. **LS Visual/Spatial, Verbal/Linguistic**

📖 Alternative Assessment Handbook, Rubric 3: Artwork

Connect to Science

Recycling Water in Space Whether on a space shuttle or the International Space Station, astronauts need to recycle water. Using new technologies developed by NASA, astronauts' wastewater is collected, cleaned, and then reused. New recycling technologies are in development, including new ways of making water cleaner using bacteria. Perhaps more importantly, NASA's water recycling technologies may be useful elsewhere—on Earth.

Answers

Reading Check *Freshwater is suitable for drinking. It is locked in glaciers or stored as groundwater or surface water, whereas salt water is found in oceans and some lakes and is not suitable for drinking.*

Analyzing Visuals *Evaporation occurs when water turns from liquid to gas; precipitation is water that falls to Earth from condensed water vapor.*

Water found below Earth's surface is called **groundwater**. In some places on Earth, groundwater naturally bubbles from the ground as a spring. More often, however, people obtain groundwater by digging wells, or deep holes dug into the ground to reach the water.

READING CHECK **Contrasting** How is salt water different from freshwater?

⁕**Interactive** **Close-up**

The Water Cycle

Energy from the sun drives the water cycle. Surface water evaporates into Earth's atmosphere, where it condenses, then falls back to Earth as precipitation. This cycle repeats continuously, providing us with a fairly constant water supply.

go.**hrw**.com (KEYWORD: SK9 CH2)

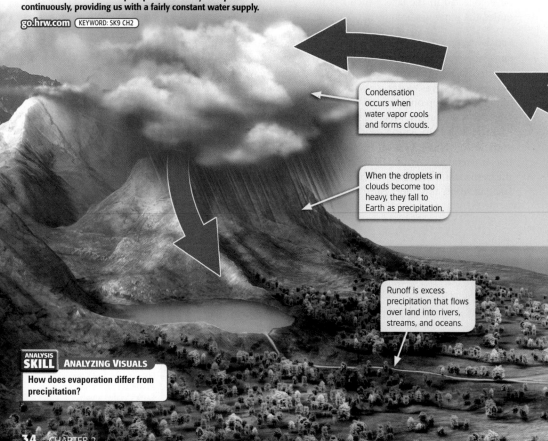

Condensation occurs when water vapor cools and forms clouds.

When the droplets in clouds become too heavy, they fall to Earth as precipitation.

Runoff is excess precipitation that flows over land into rivers, streams, and oceans.

ANALYSIS SKILL **ANALYZING VISUALS**
How does evaporation differ from precipitation?

34 CHAPTER 2

The Water Cycle

When you think of water, you probably visualize a liquid—a flowing stream, a glass of ice-cold water, or a wave hitting the beach. But did you know that water is the only substance on Earth that occurs naturally as a solid, a liquid, and a gas? We see water as a solid in snow and ice and as a liquid in oceans and rivers. Water also occurs in the air as an invisible gas called **water vapor**.

Water is always moving. As water heats up and cools down, it moves from the planet's surface to the atmosphere, or the mass of air that surrounds Earth. One of the most important processes in nature

Critical Thinking: Evaluating Information

Above Level

Creating a Public Service Announcement

Research Required

1. Have students write a script for a public service announcement about keeping groundwater free of pesticides.

2. Have students begin by exploring government or nonprofit Web sites. They should find out where pesticides come from, how they enter the water cycle, and how they affect the environment.

3. Before they begin writing, have students evaluate the information and draw conclusions. Some students might argue

that the benefits of pesticides outweigh any harmful effects. Students might write announcements expressing different opinions.

4. Have students read their announcements aloud to the class. Ask listeners to comment or ask questions about information that they found particularly interesting or surprising. **LS Verbal/Linguistic**

📖 Alternative Assessment Handbook, Rubrics 16: Judging Information; and 29: Presentations

is the water cycle. The **water cycle** is the movement of water from Earth's surface to the atmosphere and back.

The sun's energy drives the water cycle. As the sun heats water on Earth's surface, some of that water evaporates, or turns from liquid to gas, or water vapor. Water vapor then rises into the air. As the vapor rises, it cools. The cooling causes the water vapor to condense, or change from a vapor into tiny liquid droplets. These droplets join together to form clouds. If the droplets become heavy enough, precipitation occurs—that is, the water falls back to Earth as rain, snow, sleet, or hail.

When that precipitation falls back to Earth's surface, some of the water is absorbed into the soil as groundwater. Excess water, called runoff, flows over land and collects in streams, rivers, and oceans. Because the water cycle is constantly repeating, it allows us to maintain a fairly constant supply of water on Earth.

READING CHECK Finding Main Ideas What is the water cycle?

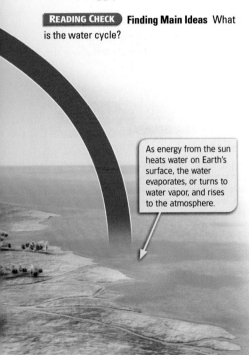

As energy from the sun heats water on Earth's surface, the water evaporates, or turns to water vapor, and rises to the atmosphere.

Water and People

How many times a day do you think about water? Many of us rarely give it a second thought, yet water is crucial for survival. Water problems such as the lack of water, polluted water, and flooding are concerns for people all around the world. Water also provides us with countless benefits, such as energy and recreation.

Water Problems

One of the greatest water problems people face is a lack of available freshwater. Many places face water shortages as a result of droughts, or long periods of lower-than-normal precipitation. Another cause of water shortages is overuse. In places like China, where the population has grown rapidly, the heavy demand for water has led to shortages.

Even where water is plentiful, it may not be clean enough to use. If chemicals and household wastes make their way into streams and rivers, they can contaminate the water supply. Polluted water can carry diseases. These diseases may harm humans, plants, and animals.

Flooding is another water problem that affects people around the world. Heavy rains often lead to flooding, which can damage property and threaten lives. One example of dangerous flooding occurred in Bangladesh in 2004. Floods there destroyed roads and schools and left some 25 million people homeless.

Water's Benefits

Water does more than just quench our thirst. It provides us with many benefits, such as food, power, and even recreation.

Water's most important benefit is that it provides us with food to eat. Everything we eat depends on water. For example, fruits and vegetables need water to grow.

THE EASTERN HEMISPHERE **35**

FOCUS ON READING

Look at the word *countless* in this paragraph. The suffix *-less* means unable to. What does *countless* mean?

Direct Teach

Main Idea

❸ Water and People

Water plays an important role in people's lives.

Explain Why is water necessary for survival? *People need water to drink and to produce food.*

Identify Cause and Effect What problems can be caused by too much or too little water? *too much—flooding; too little—drought*

Collaborative Learning

At Level

Making a Chart

Research Required

1. Organize the class into small groups. Have each group find out about your community's water supply. Ask them to brainstorm a list of questions they would like to have answered.

2. Next, have students look for answers by going to the library, using the Internet, or by contacting the local water department.

3. Have groups organize their findings in a chart, such as the one shown here.

Our Community's Water Supply

Question	Answer
Where does our water come from?	
How is drinking water treated?	
How much water does our community need?	

4. Have groups display their charts and discuss their findings. **LS** **Verbal/Linguistic, Visual/Spatial**

Alternative Assessment Handbook, Rubrics 7: Charts; and 30: Research

Answers

Reading Check *the circulation of water from Earth's surface to the atmosphere and back*

Focus on Reading *unable to be counted*

The Benefits of Water

Many people take advantage of the recreational and agricultural benefits that water provides.

Animals also need water to live and grow. As a result, we use water to farm and raise animals so that we will have food to eat.

Water is also an important source of energy. Using dams, we harness the power of moving water to produce electricity. Electricity provides power to air-condition or heat our homes, to run our washers and dryers, and to keep our food cold.

Water also provides us with recreation. Rivers, lakes, and oceans make it possible for us to swim, to fish, to surf, or to sail a boat. Although recreation is not critical for our survival, it does make our lives richer and more enjoyable.

READING CHECK **Summarizing** How does water affect people's lives?

SUMMARY AND PREVIEW In this section you learned that water is essential for life on Earth. Next, you will learn about the shapes on Earth's surface.

Section 2 Assessment

Reviewing Ideas, Terms, and Places

1. **a. Describe** Name and describe the different types of water that make up Earth's water supply.
   b. Analyze Why is only a small percentage of Earth's **freshwater** available to us?
   c. Elaborate In your opinion, which is more important—**surface water** or **groundwater**? Why?
2. **a. Recall** What drives the **water cycle**?
   b. Make Inferences From what bodies of water do you think most evaporation occurs? Why?
3. **a. Define** What is a drought?
   b. Analyze How does water support life on Earth?
   c. Evaluate What water problem do you think is most critical in your community? Why?

Critical Thinking

4. **Sequencing** Draw the graphic organizer at right. Then use your notes and the graphic organizer to identify the stages in Earth's water cycle.

FOCUS ON WRITING

5. **Learning about Water** Consider what you have learned about water in this section. How might you describe water in your haiku? What words might you use to describe Earth's water supply?

Heat from the sun evaporates water on Earth.
The water cycle repeats.

Section 2 Assessment Answers

1. **a.** freshwater—suitable for drinking, makes up 3 percent of Earth's water supply; salt water—unsafe to drink, makes up 97 percent of Earth's water supply, mainly found in oceans
   b. Most freshwater is stored underground or locked in glaciers.
   c. Answers will vary, but should reflect section content. surface water—more accessible; groundwater—abundant
2. **a.** evaporation and precipitation
   b. oceans and lakes because of size

3. **a.** a long period of lower-than-normal precipitation
   b. We depend on it for drinking, food, energy, and recreation.
   c. Answers will vary. Students may note pollution, lack of water, or flooding.
4. The water vapor cools and forms clouds. Droplets in the clouds become too heavy, causing precipitation. Runoff flows over land into rivers, streams, and oceans.
5. Students' word choices will vary but may include *precious, vital,* and *cool.*

The Land

If YOU lived there...

You live in southern Italy. All your life, you have looked out at the beautiful, cone-shaped peaks of nearby mountains. One of them is Mount Vesuvius, an active volcano. You know that in the year 79 it erupted violently, burying several nearby towns with thick layers of ash. Even today, scientists watch the mountain carefully.

How do you feel about living near a volcano?

> **BUILDING BACKGROUND** Over billions of years, many different forces have changed Earth's surface. Processes deep underground have built up landforms and even shifted the position of continents. Wind, water, and ice have also shaped the planet's landforms. Changes in Earth's surface continue to take place.

Landforms

Do you know the difference between a valley and a volcano? Can you tell a peninsula from a plateau? If you answered yes, then you are familiar with some of Earth's many landforms. **Landforms** are shapes on the planet's surface, such as hills or mountains. Landforms make up the landscapes that surround us, whether it's the rugged mountains of southern China or the flat plains of North Africa.

Earth's surface is covered with landforms of many different shapes and sizes. Some important landforms include:

- mountains, land that rises higher than 2,000 feet (610 m)
- valleys, areas of low land located between mountains or hills
- plains, stretches of mostly flat land
- islands, areas of land completely surrounded by water
- peninsulas, land surrounded by water on three sides

Because landforms play an important role in geography, many scientists study how landforms are made and how they affect human activity.

READING CHECK **Summarizing** What are some common landforms?

What You Will Learn...

Main Ideas

1. Earth's surface is covered by many different landforms.
2. Forces below Earth's surface build up our landforms.
3. Forces on the planet's surface shape Earth's landforms.
4. Landforms influence people's lives and culture.

The Big Idea

Processes below and on Earth's surface shape the planet's physical features.

Key Terms

landforms, *p. 37*
continents, *p. 38*
plate tectonics, *p. 38*
lava, *p. 39*
earthquakes, *p. 40*
weathering, *p. 41*
erosion, *p. 41*

TAKING NOTES As you read, use a diagram like the one below to take notes on Earth's landforms. In the circles, be sure to note how landforms are created, change, and affect people's lives.

Bellringer

If YOU lived there. . . Use the **Daily Bellringer Transparency** to help students answer the question.

Daily Bellringer Transparency, Section 3

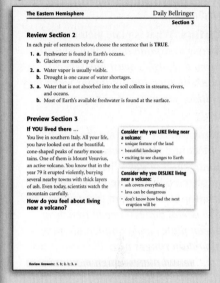

Academic Vocabulary

Review with students the high-use academic term in this section.

structure the way something is set up or organized (p. 38)

RF: Vocabulary Builder, Section 3

Taking Notes

Have students copy the graphic organizer onto their own paper and then use it to take notes on the section. This activity will prepare students for the Section Assessment, in which they will complete a graphic organizer that builds on the information using the Critical Thinking Skill: Analyzing.

Teach the Big Idea

At Level

The Land

1. **Teach** Ask students the questions in the Main Idea boxes under Direct Teach.

2. **Apply** Have each student create a KWL chart. Have students list what they know about landforms in the first column of the chart. In the second column, have students write questions about landforms. Finally, have students look through the chapter to see if they can find answers to their questions in the illustrations, captions, headings, and terms. Have them write the answers in the third column.

3. **Review** Have students quiz a partner by asking the questions in the second column and checking them against their answers in the third column.

4. **Practice/Homework** Have students create five multiple-choice questions about the section. Remind them to provide an answer key. **LS Verbal/Linguistic**

Alternative Assessment Handbook, Rubric 37: Writing Assignments

---

Main Idea

❶ **Landforms**

Earth's surface is covered by many different landforms.

Define What is a landform? *a shape on Earth's surface*

Answers

Reading Check *mountains, valleys, plains, islands, and peninsulas*

37

❷ Forces below Earth's Surface

Forces below Earth's surface build up our landforms.

Define What is plate tectonics? *A theory to explain how landforms are formed; Earth's crust has several plates that create landforms when they collide, separate, or slide past each other.*

Summarize What are the two types of tectonic plates? *ocean plates and continental plates* What three types of plate collisions are there, and what landforms result from these collisions? *two ocean plates—ocean trenches; ocean plates and continental plates—mountain ranges near the ocean; two continental plates—high mountains*

⬛ Map Zone Transparency: Earth's Plates

Did you know. . .

Alfred Wegener called the original "supercontinent" Pangaea, which in Greek means "all the land" or "all earth." A South African geologist named Alexander L. Du Toit suggested an alternative theory in 1937—that there were originally two continents: Gondwanaland in the south and Laurasia in the north.

Forces below Earth's Surface

Geographers often study how landforms are made. One explanation for how landforms have been shaped involves forces below Earth's surface.

Earth's Plates

ACADEMIC VOCABULARY
structure the way something is set up or organized

To understand how these forces work, we must examine Earth's **structure**. The planet is made up of three layers. A solid inner core is surrounded by a liquid layer, or mantle. The solid outer layer of Earth is called the crust. The planet's **continents**, or large landmasses, are part of Earth's crust.

Geographers use the theory of plate tectonics to explain how forces below Earth's surface have shaped our landforms. The theory of **plate tectonics** suggests that Earth's surface is divided into a dozen or so slow-moving plates, or pieces of Earth's crust. As you can see in the image below, some plates, like the Pacific plate, are quite large. Others, like the Indian plate, are much smaller. These plates cover Earth's entire surface. Some plates are under the ocean. These are known as ocean plates. Other plates, known as continental plates, are under Earth's continents.

Why do these plates move? Energy deep inside the planet puts pressure on Earth's crust. As this pressure builds up, it forces the plates to shift. Earth's tectonic plates all move. However, they move in different directions and at different speeds.

The Movement of Continents

Earth's tectonic plates move slowly—up to several inches per year. The continents, which are part of Earth's plates, shift as the plates move. If we could look back some 200 million years, we would see that the continents have traveled great distances. This idea is known as continental drift.

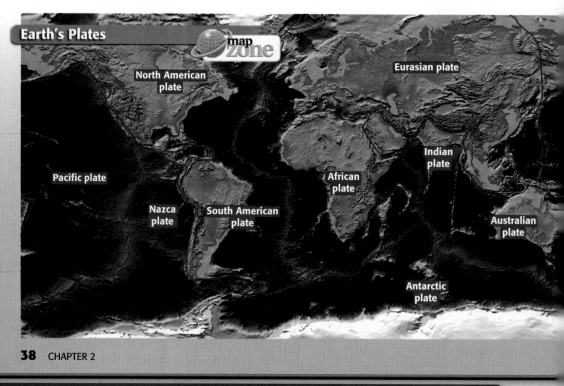

Earth's Plates

North American plate

Eurasian plate

Pacific plate

Indian plate

African plate

Nazca plate

South American plate

Australian plate

Antarctic plate

38 CHAPTER 2

Designing a Slide Show Presentation

1. Organize students in pairs or small groups. Ask them to imagine that they are park rangers at a national park in a region where landforms were formed by colliding continents.

2. Have students work together to design a slide show presentation about plate tectonics, to be shown to park visitors. They should include maps, photographs, and/or drawings to illustrate the information.

3. Have students write a commentary to accompany the slide show. Finally, have students present the slide show to the class, having one student show the images while another delivers the commentary. Encourage listeners to ask questions about the material.
LS Interpersonal, Verbal/Linguistic

📄 Alternative Assessment Handbook, Rubrics 14: Group Activity; and 22: Multimedia Presentations

The theory of continental drift, first developed by Alfred Wegener, states that the continents were once united in a single supercontinent. According to this theory, Earth's plates shifted over millions of years. As a result, the continents slowly separated and moved to their present positions.

Earth's continents are still moving. Some plates move toward each other and collide. Other plates separate and move apart. Still others slide past one another. Over time, colliding, separating, and sliding plates have shaped Earth's landforms.

Plates Collide

As plates collide, the energy created from their collision produces distinct landforms. The collision of different types of plates creates different shapes on Earth's surface. Ocean trenches and mountain ranges are two examples of landforms produced by the collision of tectonic plates.

BIOGRAPHY

Alfred Wegener
(1880–1930)

German scientist Alfred Wegener's fascination with the similarities between the western coast of Africa and the eastern coast of South America led to his theory of continental drift. Wegener argued that the two continents had once been joined together. Years of plate movement broke the continents apart and moved them to their current locations. It was only after Wegener's death that his ideas became a central part of the theory of plate tectonics.

The theory of plate tectonics suggests that the plates that make up Earth's crust are moving, usually only a few inches per year. As Earth's plates collide, separate, and slide past each other, they create forces great enough to shape many of Earth's landforms.

ANALYZING VISUALS Looking at the map, what evidence indicates that plates have collided or separated?

When two ocean plates collide, one plate pushes under the other. This process creates ocean trenches. Ocean trenches are deep valleys in the ocean floor. Near Japan, for example, the Pacific plate is slowly moving under other plates. This collision has created several deep ocean trenches, including the world's deepest trench, the Mariana Trench.

Ocean plates and continental plates can also collide. When this occurs, the ocean plate drops beneath the continental plate. This action forces the land above to crumple and form a mountain range. The islands of Japan, for example, are the peaks of mountains formed when the Pacific and Eurasian plates collided.

The collision of two continental plates also results in mountain-building. When continental plates collide, the land pushes up, sometimes to great heights. The world's highest mountain range, the Himalayas, formed when the Indian plate crashed into the Eurasian plate. In fact, the Himalayas are still growing as the two plates continue to crash into each other.

Plates Separate

A second type of plate movement causes plates to separate. As plates move apart, gaps between the plates allow magma, a liquid rock from the planet's interior, to rise to Earth's crust. **Lava**, or magma that reaches Earth's surface, emerges from the gap that has formed. As the lava cools, it builds a mid-ocean ridge, or underwater mountain. For example, the separation of the North American and Eurasian plates formed the largest underwater mountain, the Mid-Atlantic Ridge. If these mid-ocean ridges grow high enough, they can rise above the surface of the ocean, forming volcanic islands. Iceland, on the boundary of the Eurasian and North American plates, is an example of such an island.

FOCUS ON READING
The suffix *–sion* means the act of. What does the word *collision* mean?

Connect to Science

Deep Sea Life The deepest part of the Mariana Trench is more than 36,000 feet below sea level. (For comparison, Mount Everest is more than 29,000 feet above sea level.) Over the years, the variety of life found on the deepest sea floor has been astonishing. The creatures on the sea floor do not depend on the sun's energy for life. Instead, they use energy from the chemicals that rise from hydrothermal vents. Students may be interested in visiting the Web site of the American Museum of Natural History for more information about life on the sea floor. (www.amnh.org)

Info to Know

Underwater Mountains The Mid-Atlantic Ridge is an underwater mountain chain. About 10,000 miles long, it reaches from the Arctic Ocean to beyond the southern tip of Africa.

Answers

Analyzing Visuals *The plates of the Americas seem to fit, like pieces of a jigsaw puzzle, with the Eurasian and African plates, indicating that they were once joined and then were separated. Ocean ridges and mountains appear along many plate boundaries.*

Focus on Reading *the act of colliding, or coming together with impact*

Critical Thinking: Understanding Cause and Effect

At Level

Cause-and-Effect Chart

1. Have students reread the material under the Plates Collide heading on this page. Ask them if they can identify the main idea of each paragraph. Point out that the second, third, and fourth paragraphs each begin with a topic sentence that contains the main idea.

2. Ask students to identify the main ideas in the Plates Separate paragraphs and Plates Slide paragraphs on the following page. Help them see that each type of

plate movement results in a different kind of landform by making cause-and-effect charts to clarify this information.

Cause	Effect
colliding	ocean trenches
	mountains
separating	mid-ocean ridge
	(underwater mountains)
	volcanic islands
sliding	earthquakes

3. Ask volunteers to share their charts and get feedback. Have the class discuss examples of landforms they are familiar with that were caused by plate movement.

LS Visual/Spatial, Verbal/Linguistic

Alternative Assessment Handbook, Rubrics 6: Cause and Effect; and 7: Charts

Info to Know

Quake Force Powerful earthquakes have caused huge death tolls and devastation throughout the world. Of the nine most destructive earthquakes in the twentieth century, four occurred in China. In 1976 the town of Tangshan, China, was hit with an earthquake that killed approximately 240,000 people. About 500,000 were estimated to have been injured.

In the United States, the largest magnitude earthquakes have taken place in Alaska. On the mainland, most of the high-magnitude earthquakes have occurred in California. A number of earthquake faults, particularly in California, are closely watched by geologists. The San Andreas fault system runs about 800 miles north to south through the state. At its widest point, the fault is a few hundred feet wide.

Teaching Tip

Help students navigate this page by discussing each pair of visuals and captions separately. Explain that the illustration on the left of each pair of visuals shows the process, and the photograph on the right shows the result of the process. Have students reread the text about the separation of plates and the collision of continental plates.

Answers

Reading Check *Energy in Earth's core and mantle creates pressure against the crust. This pressure can force tectonic plates to move. When these plates collide or separate, they can form volcanoes, ocean trenches, mid-ocean ridges, and mountains. Sliding plates can also cause earthquakes and volcanic eruptions.*

Analyzing Visuals *mountains*

Plates Slide

Tectonic plates also slide past each other. As plates pass by one another, they sometimes grind together. This grinding produces **earthquakes**—sudden, violent movements of Earth's crust. Earthquakes often take place along faults, or breaks in Earth's crust where movement occurs. In Indonesia, for example, the Australian plate is sliding by the edge of the Eurasian plate. This has created the Great Sumatran Fault zone, an area where earthquakes are quite common.

The Great Sumatran Fault zone is one of many areas that lie along the boundaries of the Pacific plate. The frequent movement of this plate produces many earthquakes and volcanic eruptions along its edges. In fact, the region around the Pacific plate, called the Ring of Fire, is home to most of the world's earthquakes and volcanoes.

READING CHECK Finding Main Ideas What forces below Earth's surface shape landforms?

Plate Movement

The movement of tectonic plates has produced many of Earth's landforms. Volcanoes, islands, and mountains often result from the separation or collision of Earth's plates.

ANALYZING VISUALS What type of landform is created by the collision of two continental plates?

Plate A
magma
Plate B

The separation of plates can allow magma to rise up and create volcanic islands like Surtsey Island, near Iceland.

Plate A
Plate B

The Himalayas in South Asia resulted from the collision of two massive continental plates.

40 CHAPTER 2

Differentiating Instruction

Struggling Readers

To help struggling readers, have them study each photo and then match the text to the photo. Have students discuss what they see, and read the introduction and the captions aloud. Remind them to look for illustrations and captions throughout the book. **LS Visual/Spatial, Verbal/Linguistic**

📝 Alternative Assessment Handbook, Rubric 1: Acquiring Information

Special Needs Learners

Provide images of mountains and volcanoes from magazines and the Internet and have students make collages. Challenge them to distinguish volcanoes and other kinds of mountains. Point out that volcanoes are made when plates pull apart and that mountains are made when plates crash into each other. **LS Visual/Spatial**

📝 Alternative Assessment Handbook, Rubric 8: Collages

Forces on Earth's Surface

For millions of years, the movement of Earth's tectonic plates has been building up landforms on Earth's surface. At the same time, other forces are working to change those very same landforms.

Imagine a small pile of dirt and rock on a table. If you poured water on the pile, it would move the dirt and rock from one place to another. Likewise, if you were to blow at the pile, the rock and dirt would also move. The same process happens in nature. Weather, water, and other forces change Earth's landforms by wearing them away or reshaping them.

Weathering

One force that wears away landforms is weathering. **Weathering** is the process by which rock is broken down into smaller pieces. Several factors cause rock to break down. In desert areas, daytime heating and nighttime cooling can cause rocks to crack. Water may get into cracks in rocks and freeze. The ice then expands with a force great enough to break the rock. Even the roots of trees can pry rocks apart.

Regardless of which weathering process is at work, rocks eventually break down. These small pieces of rock are known as sediment. Once weathering has taken place, wind, ice, and water often move sediment from one place to another.

Erosion

Another force that changes landforms is the process of erosion. **Erosion** is the movement of sediment from one location to another. Erosion can wear away or build up landforms. Wind, ice, and water all cause erosion.

Powerful winds often cause erosion. Winds lift sediment into the air and carry it across great distances. On beaches and in deserts, wind can deposit large amounts of sand to form dunes. Blowing sand can also wear down rock. The sand acts like sandpaper to polish and wear away at rocks. As you can see in the photo below, wind can have a dramatic effect on landforms.

Earth's glaciers also have the power to cause massive erosion. Glaciers, or large, slow-moving sheets of ice, build up when winter snows do not melt the following summer. Glaciers can be huge. Glaciers in Asia and Antarctica, for example, are great sheets of ice up to two miles (3 km) thick. Some glaciers flow slowly downhill like rivers of ice. As they do so, they erode the land by carving large U-shaped valleys and sharp mountain peaks. As the ice flows downhill, it crushes rock into sediment and can move huge rocks long distances.

Glacial Erosion

Glaciers like this one in the Himalayas, a mountain range between India and China, carve deep valleys as they move slowly downhill.

THE EASTERN HEMISPHERE **41**

Main Idea

4 **Landforms Influence Life**

Landforms influence people's lives and culture.

Recall Where was the first civilization built? *in the valley of the Tigris and Euphrates rivers*

Explain How did the location help the civilization thrive? *People had plenty of water for crops and could use the rivers for trade.*

Analyze How do the landforms in your area influence your daily life? *Answers will vary. Students should identify the landforms in their region and tell how these landforms affect them.*

RF: *Cry, the Beloved Country* by Alan Paton

Water is the most common cause of erosion. Waves can wear away the shore, creating jagged coastlines, like those on the coast of Greece. Rivers also cause erosion. Over many years, the flowing water can cut through rock, forming canyons or gorges, narrow areas with steep walls. China's Three Gorges and Yarlung Tsangpo Canyon are examples of canyons created in this way.

Flowing water shapes other landforms as well. When water deposits sediment in new locations, it creates new landforms. For example, rivers create floodplains when they flood their banks and deposit sediment along the banks. Sediment that is carried by a river all the way out to sea creates a delta. The sediment settles to the bottom, where the river meets the sea. The Nile and Niger rivers have created two of the world's largest river deltas.

READING CHECK **Comparing** How are weathering and erosion similar?

Preventing Erosion

Wind and water wash away millions of acres of soil every year. This Chinese worker is burying a frame designed to help keep the soil in place.

42 CHAPTER 2

Landforms Influence Life

Why do you live where you do? Perhaps your family moved to the desert to avoid harsh winter weather. Or possibly one of your ancestors settled near a river delta because its fertile soil was ideal for growing crops. Maybe your family wanted to live near the ocean to start a fishing business. As these examples show, landforms exert a strong influence on people's lives. Earth's landforms affect our settlements and our culture. At the same time, we affect the landforms around us.

Earth's landforms can influence where people settle. People sometimes settle near certain landforms and avoid others. For example, many settlements are built near fertile river valleys or deltas. The earliest urban civilization, for example, was built in the valley between the Tigris and Euphrates rivers. Other times, landforms discourage people from settling in a certain place. Tall, rugged mountains, like the Himalayas, and harsh desert climates, like the Sahara, do not usually attract large settlements.

Landforms affect our culture in ways that we may not have noticed. Landforms often influence what jobs are available in a region. For example, rich mineral deposits in South Africa led to the development of a mining industry there. Landforms even affect language. On the island of New Guinea in Southeast Asia, rugged mountains have kept the people so isolated that more than 700 languages are spoken on the island today.

People sometimes change landforms to suit their needs. People may choose to modify landforms in order to improve their lives. For example, engineers built the Suez Canal to make travel from the Mediterranean Sea to the Red Sea easier. In Southeast Asia, people who farm on steep hillsides cut terraces into the slope

---

Critical Thinking: Drawing Conclusions

Below Level

Writing a Persuasive Letter

1. Ask students to imagine that they are moving to a country in the Eastern Hemisphere and that they are trying to find the best location to live. Have them explore the advantages and disadvantages of living in certain locations, based on the information in the section as well as their previous knowledge.

2. Have students write a persuasive letter to a friend or family member, urging them to move to the location they have chosen. In the letter, have students give reasons why

the location they have chosen is the best for their needs. If they wish, they can include a drawing of the location.

3. Have students share their letters and illustrations with the class and discuss which letters are most persuasive. **LS Verbal/Linguistic**

Alternate Assessment Handbook, Rubrics 9: Comparing and Contrasting; 25: Personal Letters; and 43: Writing to Persuade

---

Answers

Reading Check *similar—both cause rock to break up; water contributes to both*

Living with Landforms

The people of coastal Vietnam have learned to adapt to their country's low-lying, often flooded landscape.

ANALYZING VISUALS How have people in Vietnam adapted to their landscape?

Linking to Today

Erosion by the Beach Coastal erosion is a problem around the world. Floods, hurricanes, and heavy storms frequently erode beaches and shorelines. Human actions also cause erosion. The building of harbors and seawalls interferes with the transport of sediment. Leveling dunes to construct buildings takes away beaches' natural defense against erosion. The building of more houses and tourist facilities also contributes to erosion. Ironically, many of these buildings and developments are themselves damaged by erosion. Houses built too close to the sea can collapse. Roads can be destroyed.

to create more level space to grow their crops. People have even built huge dams along rivers to divert water for use in nearby towns or farms.

READING CHECK **Analyzing** What are some examples of humans adjusting to and changing landforms?

SUMMARY AND PREVIEW Landforms are created by actions deep within the planet's surface, and they are changed by forces on Earth's surface, like weathering and erosion. In the next chapter you will learn how other forces, like weather and climate, affect Earth's people.

● **Review & Assess** ●

Close

Discuss with students how landforms are made and how landforms affect people. Have them give examples.

Review

Online Quiz, Section 3

Assess

SE Section 3 Assessment

PASS: Section 3 Quiz

Alternative Assessment Handbook

Reteach/Classroom Intervention

Interactive Reader and Study Guide, Section 3

Interactive Skills Tutor CD-ROM

Section 3 Assessment

go.hrw.com
Online Quiz
KEYWORD: SK9 HP2

Reviewing Ideas, Terms, and Places

1. **a. Describe** What are some common **landforms**?
   b. Analyze Why do geographers study landforms?
2. **a. Identify** What is the theory of **plate tectonics**?
   b. Compare and Contrast How are the effects of colliding plates and separating plates similar and different?
   c. Predict How might Earth's surface change as tectonic plates continue to move?
3. **a. Recall** What is the process of **weathering**?
   b. Elaborate How does water affect sediment?
4. **a. Recall** How do landforms affect life on Earth?
   b. Predict How might people adapt to life in an area with steep mountains?

Critical Thinking

5. **Analyzing** Use your notes and the chart below to identify the different factors that alter Earth's landforms and the changes that they produce.

Factor	Change in Landform

FOCUS ON WRITING

6. **Writing about Earth's Land** Think of some vivid words you could use to describe Earth's landforms. As you think of them, add them to your notebook.

THE EASTERN HEMISPHERE **43**

Section 3 Assessment Answers

1. **a.** mountains, valleys, plains, islands
   b. to learn how they are made and how they affect human activity
2. **a.** It explains landforms through movement of pieces of Earth's crust, or plates.
   b. both form landforms; colliding—form ocean trenches, mountains; separating—form ocean ridges, volcanic islands
   c. create new landforms, change existing ones
3. **a.** breaking of rock into smaller pieces
   b. It moves sediment from one place to another, creating new landforms.

4. **a.** possible answer—People settle in certain areas because of landforms. Landforms also affect what kinds of jobs are available in an area.
   b. They might cut terraces to grow crops and build roads for transportation.
5. possible answer—movement of plates: creates ocean trenches and mountains; weathering: wears down landforms; erosion: moves sediment
6. Descriptions will vary, but may include *dramatic, spectacular,* and *weathered.*

Answers

Analyzing Visuals *possible answer—by building bridges to enable transportation across their low-lying landscape*

Reading Check *adjusting to—people living in delta areas can grow food on the fertile land; people living near the sea can trade and travel; people living in areas where rich mineral deposits can be mined; changing—building dams, drilling tunnels through mountains, farming on steep hillsides by building terraces.*

Info to Know

Anak Krakatau The eruption of Krakatau in 1883 destroyed most of the island volcano, leaving only about one-third of the original land mass above water. Following the 1883 eruption, Krakatau remained quiet for over four decades. In 1927, however, an undersea eruption was observed. Soon thereafter, a new island emerged from the sea. The new island volcano was given the name Anak Karakatau, which means "child of Krakatau." Since 1927, Anak Krakatau has erupted frequently, causing the island to grow in size, so that now it has a radius of over 5 miles and a high point of nearly 700 feet.

Map Zone Transparency: Ring of Fire

Did you know. . .

The origin of the name Krakatau is unclear. One theory is that the name is an imitation of the call of the cockatoos that formerly inhabited the island. Another theory is that the name comes from the Sanskrit word *karkataka,* which means "lobster" or "crab."

The Ring of Fire

Essential Elements

The World in Spatial Terms
Places and Regions
Physical Systems
Human Systems
Environment and Society
The Uses of Geography

Background Does "the Ring of Fire" sound like the title of a fantasy novel? It's actually the name of a region that circles the Pacific Ocean known for its fiery volcanoes and powerful earthquakes. The Ring of Fire stretches from the tip of South America all the way up to Alaska, and from Japan down to the islands east of Australia. Along this belt, the Pacific plate moves against several other tectonic plates. As a result, thousands of earthquakes occur there every year, and dozens of volcanoes erupt.

Eruption! One of the most violent volcanic eruptions—and one of the most destructive events of any kind—in recorded history took place in the Ring of Fire in 1883. Krakatau, a volcanic island in Indonesia, exploded with enough force to be heard 3,000 miles (5,000 km) away!

Though the explosion of Krakatau took place in August, the volcano had shown signs of erupting for months before. For several years, earthquakes had shaken places as far off as Australia, and steam had begun venting from Krakatau's peak as early as March. However, people were unprepared for the sheer power of the eruption, which left more than 36,000 people dead and 165 villages and towns destroyed.

Ring of Fire

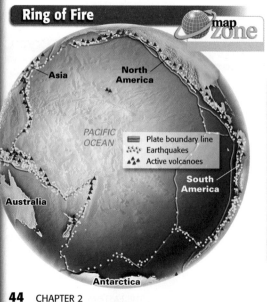

map zone

Asia
North America
PACIFIC OCEAN

— Plate boundary line
··· Earthquakes
▲▲ Active volcanoes

South America
Australia
Antarctica

THE WORLD ALMANAC Facts about the World **Major Eruptions in the Ring of Fire**

Volcano	Year
Tambora, Indonesia	1815
Krakatau, Indonesia	1883
Mount Saint Helens, United States	1980
Nevado del Ruiz, Colombia	1985
Mount Pinatubo, Philippines	1991

go.hrw.com KEYWORD: SK9 CH2

44 CHAPTER 2

Critical Thinking: Interpreting Maps

At Level

Making a Map of the Ring of Fire

Research Required

1. Have students use an atlas and other sources from the Internet or library to research the Ring of Fire. Have students draw maps showing the perimeter of the Ring of Fire, labeling continents and bodies of water. Then have students add symbols showing where volcanoes and earthquake faults can be found within the area covered by the map. Encourage students to annotate the maps with information about specific volcanoes, faults, and earthquakes.

2. Have students display their maps. Have them compare their maps with political maps of the region and note how close the earthquake faults and volcanoes are to centers of population. **LS Visual/Spatial**

Alternative Assessment Handbook, Rubric 20: Map Creation

Mount Pinatubo, 1991
The study of Krakatau by volcanologists helped them predict the eruption of Mount Pinatubo in 1991. Today, scientists study Pinatubo to learn more about predicting future eruptions.

Info to Know

The Mount Pinatubo Eruption Seismic activity early in 1991 made it clear to scientists that a major eruption of Mount Pinatubo was likely imminent. Evacuations of the area surrounding Pinatubo began in April and continued through June 15, the day that seismic activity at Pinatubo culminated in a massive volcanic explosion. The explosion began shortly after noon and lasted for nearly 12 hours. During the event, nearly 3 cubic miles of debris were ejected from Mount Pinatubo and nearly 1,000 feet were shaved off the mountain's elevation. About 300 lives were lost in the devastation—devastation made worse by a tropical typhoon that hit the area the same day!

The eruption of Krakatau had drastic effects even on distant places. The eruption triggered tsunamis recorded as far away as South America and injured thousands. Less destructive but no less dramatic, the volcano threw ash more than 50 miles in the air, where it was caught by prevailing winds and spread around the world. The presence of so much material in the atmosphere blocked much of the Sun's radiation from reaching Earth and caused average global temperatures to drop by more than 2 degrees Fahrenheit the next year.

What It Means The Krakatau eruption was one of the first to be studied with modern science. Within days of the eruption a Dutch geologist arrived at the mountain and began a systematic study of the eruption's causes and effects. His work was key in the formation of modern volcanology, the study of volcanoes.

Since the days of Krakatau, volcanology has improved considerably. Scientists now better understand how and why volcanoes act as they do. They can also sometimes predict volcanic activity in advance, which can help save lives and prevent damage. For example, the eruption of the Philippine volcano Mount Pinatubo in 1991, though the second largest in the 1900s, was far less deadly than other eruptions because scientists warned people in advance.

Geography for Life Activity

1. How did the eruption of Krakatau affect the surrounding area?

2. Why do scientists monitor volcanic activity?

3. **Investigating the Effects of Volcanoes** Some volcanic eruptions affect environmental conditions around the world. Research the eruption of either Krakatau or Mount Pinatubo to find out how its eruption affected the global environment.

THE EASTERN HEMISPHERE **45**

Cross-Discipline Activity: English/Language Arts
At Level

Writing a Story

1. Have students research and write an eyewitness account of the eruption of Krakatau, Mount Pinatubo, or another volcano on the Ring of Fire.

2. Ask students to imagine that they were living in or visiting the area near the volcano when it erupted. Using the information they gather as well as their imagination and prior knowledge, have students write a short story about the eruption and the events that preceded and followed the disaster.

Encourage students to include vivid images and details of the experience in their stories.

3. Finally, have students read their short stories aloud. Encourage class members to ask questions about the information.

LS Verbal/Linguistic

Alternative Assessment Handbook, Rubrics 1: Acquiring Information; and 40: Writing to Describe

Answers

Geography for Life 1. *36,000 people died and 165 villages and towns were destroyed. Tsunamis occurred as far away as South America. Global average temperatures dropped by two degrees farenheit.* **2.** *to try to predict when volcanoes might erupt so they can warn people;* **3.** *Students should find in their research that the amount of sulfur released into the atmosphere by the volcanic eruptions caused a decrease in worldwide temperatures.*

Using a Physical Map

Activity Plan a Trip **Prep Required**

Materials: a physical map of your region to print or copy for students

1. Provide students with a physical map of your region.

2. Tell students that they will use the map to plan a sightseeing tour of physical features in your area.

3. Have students identify places they would like to visit and mark them on the map.

4. Have students plan their route. They should label their start and end points and the routes they will take to get from one place to another.

5. When they have finished, have students share their plans with the class. They should tell whether they will be travelling by foot, bicycle, or another means of transportation. They should also use the scale of miles to estimate how long their trip will take.

LS Visual/Spatial, Verbal/Linguistic

📋 Alternative Assessment Handbook, Rubric 24: Oral Presentations

📄 **RF:** Social Studies Skills, Using a Physical Map

🖥 Map Zone Transparency: India: Physical

💿 Interactive Skills Tutor CD-ROM, Lesson 6: Interpret Maps, Graphs, Charts, Visuals, and Political Cartoons

Using a Physical Map

Learn

Physical maps show important physical features, like oceans and mountains, in a particular area. They also indicate an area's elevation, or the height of the land in relation to sea level.

When you use a physical map, there are important pieces of information you should always examine.

• Identify physical features. Natural features, such as mountains, rivers, and lakes, are labeled on physical maps. Read the labels carefully to identify what physical features are present.

• Read the legend. On physical maps, the legend indicates scale as well as elevation. The different colors in the elevation key indicate how far above or below sea level a place is.

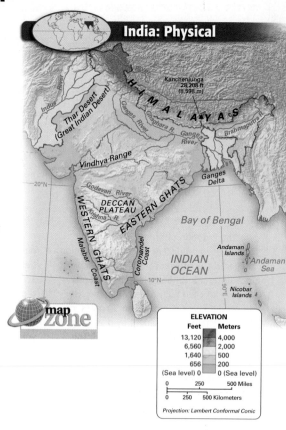

India: Physical

ELEVATION

Feet		Meters
13,120		4,000
6,560		2,000
1,640		500
656		200
(Sea level) 0		0 (Sea level)

0   250   500 Miles
0   250   500 Kilometers

Projection: Lambert Conformal Conic

Practice

Use the physical map of India at right to answer the questions below.

❶ What landforms and bodies of water are indicated on the map?

❷ What is the highest elevation in India? Where is it located?

Apply

Locate the physical map of Africa in the atlas in the back of the book. Use the map to answer the questions below.

1. Which region has the highest elevation?

2. What bodies of water surround Africa?

3. What large island is located off the east coast of Africa?

46 CHAPTER 2

Social Studies Skill Activity: Using a Physical Map   At Level

Describe Physical Features   Research Required

1. Divide students into small groups and assign each group a different region of the world.

2. Have students locate physical maps of their region using atlases or other library or Internet resources.

3. Students should use the maps to identify important physical features of their region. Then have them conduct further research to find out more about each feature.

4. When they have finished, have each group present their findings to the class.

LS Visual/Spatial, Verbal/Linguistic

📋 Alternative Assessment Handbook, Rubric 24: Oral Presentations

Answers

Practice 1. *mountain, desert, delta, plateau, river, bay, ocean, sea;* **2.** *28,208 ft, Himalayas*

Apply 1. *the eastern region, Mount Kilimanjaro, Tanzania;* **2.** *Indian Ocean, Atlantic Ocean, Red Sea, Mediterranean Sea;* **3.** *Madagascar*

Geography's Impact
video series
Review the video to answer the closing question:
What are some reasons for water shortages, and what can be done to solve this problem?

Visual Summary

Use the visual summary below to help you review the main ideas of the chapter.

QUICK FACTS

The countries of the Eastern Hemisphere have a wide variety of cultures, governments, and levels of development.

The Eastern Hemisphere's abundant water supply is stored in oceans, in lakes, and underground.

The hemisphere's various landforms are shaped by complex processes both under and on the planet's surface.

Reviewing Vocabulary, Terms, and Places

For each statement below, write T if it is true and F if it is false. If the statement is false, write the correct term that would make the sentence a true statement.

1. **Weathering** is the movement of sediment from one location to another.

2. Because high **latitude** areas receive indirect rays from the sun, they have cooler temperatures.

3. Most of our **groundwater** is stored in Earth's streams, rivers, and lakes.

4. It takes 365¼ days for Earth to complete one **rotation** around the sun.

5. Streams are formed when **precipitation** collects in narrow channels.

6. **Earthquakes** cause erosion as they flow downhill, carving valleys and mountain peaks.

7. The planet's tilt affects the amount of **erosion** Earth receives from the sun.

Comprehension and Critical Thinking

SECTION 1 *(Pages 28–31)*

8. **a. Identify** Which continents are located in the Eastern Hemisphere?

   b. Explain Why do geographers divide the world into hemispheres?

   c. Develop What factors have led to the development of different cultures in the countries of the Eastern Hemisphere?

SECTION 2 *(Pages 32–36)*

9. **a. Describe** What different sources of water are available on Earth?

   b. Draw Conclusions How does the water cycle keep Earth's water supply relatively constant?

   c. Elaborate What water problems affect people around the world? What solutions can you think of for one of those problems?

Answers

Visual Summary

Review and Inquiry Have students use the visual summary to discuss details related to the study of the Eastern Hemisphere.

 Quick Facts Transparency: Visual Summary: The Eastern Hemisphere

Reviewing Vocabulary, Terms, and Places

1. F; erosion   5. T

2. T   6. F; glaciers

3. F; surface water 7. F; solar energy

4. F; revolution

Comprehension and Critical Thinking

8. **a.** Africa, Asia, Australia, Europe, and part of Antarctica

   b. in order to study places in the world in more depth than they would if they just looked at the world as a whole

   c. vastness of the land area; variations in climate and physical geography; differences in language, religion, and government

9. **a.** salt water—oceans and seas; freshwater—streams, rivers, lakes, glaciers, underground

   b. Water is constantly evaporating from Earth's surfaces, rising up to the atmosphere, and falling back as precipitation.

   c. drought, overuse, pollution, flooding; possible answer—People could use water more wisely and reduce chemical use.

Review and Assessment Resources

Review and Reinforce

SE Chapter Review

 RF: Chapter Review

 Quick Facts Transparency: Visual Summary: The Eastern Hemisphere

 Spanish Chapter Summaries Audio CD Program

OSP Holt PuzzlePro; Quiz Show for ExamView

 Quiz Game CD-ROM

Assess

SE Standardized Test Practice

 PASS: Chapter Test, Forms A and B

 Alternative Assessment Handbook

OSP ExamView Test Generator, Chapter Test

 Differentiated Instruction Modified Worksheets and Tests CD-ROM: Chapter Test

HOAP Holt Online Assessment Program (in the Holt Interactive Online Student Edition)

Reteach/Intervene

 Interactive Reader and Study Guide

 Differentiated Instruction Teacher Management System: Lesson Plans

 Differentiated Instruction Modified Worksheets and Tests CD-ROM

 Interactive Skills Tutor CD-ROM

go.hrw.com
Online Resources
Chapter Resources
KEYWORD: SK9 CH2

10. a. a shape on a planet's surface; hills, mountains

b. because they rest on tectonic plates, which are moving

c. possible response—valleys, which are good for farming and raising livestock

Using the Internet

11. Go to the HRW Web site and enter the keyword shown to access a rubric for this activity.

> KEYWORD: SK9 TEACHER

Focus on Reading and Writing

12. -*ion*; *separate*; the act or process of keeping apart

13. not visible; not active

14. the action or process of moving

RF: Focus on Reading, Using Word Parts

15. Rubric Students' haikus should

- be short
- either be traditional with three lines and 17 syllables or have a nontraditional form
- use descriptive words
- describe an aspect of the Eastern Hemisphere

RF: Focus on Writing, Writing a Haiku

Social Studies Skills

16. Northern European Plain

17. Caucasus Mountains

18. Tiber River

Map Activity

19. C

20. A

21. B

22. F

23. E

24. D

SECTION 3 *(Pages 37–43)*

10. a. Define What is a landform? What are some common types of landforms?

b. Analyze Why are Earth's landforms still changing?

c. Elaborate What physical features dominate the landscape in your community? How do they affect life there?

Using the Internet

11. Activity: Researching Landscapes The Eastern Hemisphere includes a stunning variety of landscapes. Both the highest and lowest points of land are located there, as are the world's longest river, largest lake, and deepest cave. Enter the activity keyword to explore some of these landscapes. The use the interactive worksheet to answer some questions about what you learned.

FOCUS ON READING AND WRITING

Using Word Parts *Use what you learned about prefixes, suffixes, and word roots to answer the questions below.*

12. Examine the word *separation*. What is the suffix? What is the root? What does *separation* mean?

13. The prefix *in-* means not. What do the words *invisible* and *inactive* mean?

14. The suffix *-ment* means action or process. What does the word *movement* mean?

Writing a Haiku *Use your notes and the directions below to write a haiku.*

15. Look back through the notes you made about the Eastern Hemisphere. Choose one aspect of the region to describe in a haiku. Haikus are short, three-line poems. Traditional haikus consist of only 17 syllables—five in the first line, seven in the second line, and five in the third line. You may choose to write a traditional haiku, or you may choose to write a haiku with a different number of syllables. Be sure to use descriptive words to paint a picture of the Eastern Hemisphere.

Social Studies Skills

Using a Physical Map *Examine the physical map of Europe in the back of this book. Use it to answer the questions below.*

16. What low-elevation feature covers much of the northern part of the continent?

17. In what range is Europe's highest mountain located?

18. What river flows out of the Apennines?

Map Activity ✶Interactive

Physical Map *Use the map below to answer the questions that follow.*

19. Which letter indicates a river?

20. Which letter on the map indicates the highest elevation?

21. The lowest elevation on the map is indicated by which letter?

22. An island is indicated by which letter?

23. Which letter indicates a large body of water?

24. Which letter indicates an area of land between 1,640 feet and 6,560 feet above sea level?

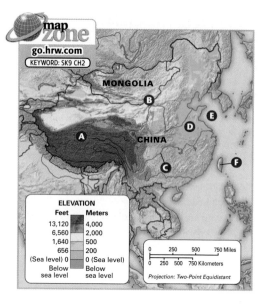

ELEVATION	
Feet	Meters
13,120	4,000
6,560	2,000
1,640	500
656	200
(Sea level) 0	0 (Sea level)
Below sea level	Below sea level

Projection: Two-Point Equidistant

Standardized Test Practice

DIRECTIONS (1–7): For each statement or question, write on a separate answer sheet the *number* of the word or expression that, of those given, best completes the statement or answers the question.

1 Which of these continents is *not* located in the Eastern Hemisphere?

(1) Asia
(2) South America
(3) Africa
(4) Europe

2 Most of Earth's water supply is made up of

(1) groundwater.
(2) water vapor.
(3) freshwater.
(4) salt water.

3 The theory of continental drift explains how

(1) Earth's continents have moved thousands of miles.
(2) Earth's axis has moved to its current position.
(3) mountains and valleys are formed.
(4) sediment moves from one place to another.

4 Which of the following is a cause of erosion?

(1) evaporation
(2) ice
(3) plate collisions
(4) Earth's tilt

5 Countries with advanced economies and high standards of living are called

(1) developing countries.
(2) transitional countries.
(3) independent countries.
(4) developed countries.

6 Which imaginary line divides the Eastern Hemisphere from the Western Hemisphere?

(1) prime meridian
(2) latitude line
(3) hemisphere line
(4) equator

7 Which of the following is *most likely* a cause of water pollution?

(1) River water is used to produce electricity.
(2) Heavy rainfall causes a river to overflow its banks.
(3) Chemicals from a factory seep into the local water supply.
(4) Groundwater is used faster than it can be replaced.

Base your answer to question 8 on the diagram below and on your knowledge of social studies.

The Water Cycle

8 Constructed-Response Question How does Earth's water cycle affect our water supply?

Reteach/Intervention Resources

Reproducible

📑 Interactive Reader and Study Guide
📑 Differentiated Instruction Teacher Management System: Lesson Plans

Technology

🖥 Quick Facts Transparency: Visual Summary: The Eastern Hemisphere
💿 Differentiated Instruction Modified Worksheets and Tests CD-ROM
💿 Interactive Skills Tutor CD-ROM

Tips for Test Taking

How Much Do I Write? Point out to students that if a writing question contains any of the following terms, they will need to write several sentences for a complete answer: *describe, justify, why, explain,* or *elaborate.* These are not the only words, however, that may indicate several sentences are required.

---

1. 2
Break Down the Question This question requires students to recall factual information. Refer students who miss it to Section 1.

2. 4
Break Down the Question Remind students not to confuse Earth's water supply, or the total water on the planet, with water available to people. Refer students who miss it to Section 2.

3. 1
Break Down the Question This question requires students to recall factual information. Refer students who miss it to Section 3.

4. 2
Break Down the Question Suggest that students try to recall the three causes of erosion. This will allow them to eliminate all choices except for number 2. Refer students who miss it to Section 3.

5. 4
Break Down the Question This question requires students to recall the definition of a key term. Refer students who miss it to Section 1.

6. 1
Break Down the Question The question requires students to recall factual information. Refer students who miss it to Section 1.

7. 3
Break Down the Question Remind students to focus on the term "most likely" to come up with the correct answer.

8. Constructed-Response Question Possible answer—Surface water evaporates into the atmosphere, condenses, then falls back to Earth as precipitation. This cycle helps keep the water supply fairly constant.

Climate and Resources of the Eastern Hemisphere

Chapter Overview	Reproducible Resources	Technology Resources
CHAPTER 3 pp. 50–73 **Overview:** In this chapter, students will learn about the weather, climate, and natural resources of the Eastern Hemisphere.	OSP **Differentiated Instruction Teacher Management System:*** • Instructional Pacing Guides • Lesson Plans for Differentiated Instruction **Interactive Reader and Study Guide:** Chapter Summary Graphic Organizer **Resource File*** • Chapter Review • Focus on Reading: Understanding Cause and Effect • Focus on Viewing: Presenting and Viewing a Weather Report • Social Studies Skills: Analyzing a Bar Graph **Experiencing World History and Geography**	OSP **Teacher's One-Stop Planner:** Calendar Planner **Power Presentations with Video CD-ROM** **Differentiated Instruction Modified Worksheets and Tests CD-ROM** **Interactive Skills Tutor CD-ROM** **Student Edition on Audio CD Program** **Music of the World Audio CD Program** **Geography's Impact Video Series (VHS/DVD):** Impact of Weather* **World Outline Maps: Transparencies and Activities**
Section 1: **Weather and Climate** **The Big Idea:** The sun, location, wind, water, and mountains affect weather and climate.	OSP **Differentiated Instruction Teacher Management System:** Section 1 Lesson Plan* **Interactive Reader and Study Guide:** Section 1 Summary **Resource File*** • Vocabulary Builder: Section 1 • Biography: Edward Lorenz	**Daily Bellringer Transparency:** Section 1* **Map Zone Transparency:** Major Ocean Currents* **Internet Activity:** Solar Energy **Internet Activity:** Experiencing Extremes
Section 2: **Climates of the Eastern Hemisphere** **The Big Idea:** Earth's five major climate zones are identified by temperature, precipitation, and plant life.	OSP **Differentiated Instruction Teacher Management System:** Section 2 Lesson Plan* **Interactive Reader and Study Guide:** Section 2 Summary **Resource File*** • Vocabulary Builder: Section 2 • Literature: "To Build a Fire" by Jack London	**Daily Bellringer Transparency:** Section 2* **Map Zone Transparency:** World Climate Regions*
Section 3: **Natural Resources** **The Big Idea:** Earth's natural resources have many valuable uses, and their availability affects people in many ways.	OSP **Differentiated Instruction Teacher Management System:** Section 3 Lesson Plan* **Interactive Reader and Study Guide:** Section 3 Summary **Resource File*** • Vocabulary Builder: Section 3 • Biography, Jane Goodall • Primary Source, Survivors of Krakatau • Interdisciplinary Project, Diagram an Ecosystem	**Daily Bellringer Transparency:** Section 3*

SE Student Edition	Print Resource	Audio CD
TE Teacher's Edition	Transparency	CD-ROM
go.hrw.com	**LS** Learning Styles	Video
OSP Teacher's One-Stop Planner	* also on One-Stop Planner	

Review, Assessment, Intervention

Quick Facts Transparency: Visual Summary: Climate and Resources of the Eastern Hemisphere*

Spanish Chapter Summaries Audio CD Program

Progress Assessment Support System (PASS): Chapter Test*

Differentiated Instruction Modified Worksheets and Tests CD-ROM: Modified Chapter Test

OSP Teacher's One-Stop Planner: ExamView Test Generator (English/Spanish)

Alternative Assessment Handbook

HOAP Holt Online Assessment Program (HOAP), in the Holt Interactive Online Student Edition

PASS: Section 1 Quiz*

Online Quiz: Section 1

Alternative Assessment Handbook

PASS: Section 2 Quiz*

Online Quiz: Section 2

Alternative Assessment Handbook

PASS: Section 3 Quiz*

Online Quiz: Section 3

Alternative Assessment Handbook

Power Presentations with Video CD-ROM

Power Presentations with Video are visual presentations of each chapter's main ideas. Presentations can be customized by including Quick Facts charts, images from the text, and video clips.

Holt Online Learning

go.hrw.com
Teacher Resources
KEYWORD: SK9 TEACHER

go.hrw.com
Student Resources
KEYWORD: SK9 CH3

• Interactive Multimedia Activities
• Current Events

• Chapter-based Internet Activities
• and more!

Holt Interactive
Online Student Edition

Complete online support for interactivity, assessment, and reporting

• Interactive Maps and Notebook
• Standardized Test Prep
• Homework Practice and Research Activities Online

CHAPTER 3 PLANNING GUIDE

Differentiating Instruction

How do I address the needs of varied learners?
The Target Resource acts as your primary strategy for differentiated instruction.

ENGLISH-LANGUAGE LEARNERS & STRUGGLING READERS

TARGET RESOURCE

Resource File

The Resource File activities allow students to extend their knowledge of chapter-related places and people and to practice geography skills.

- Vocabulary Builder Activities
- Social Studies Skills: Analyzing a Bar Graph

Additional Resources

Differentiated Instruction Teacher Management System: Lesson Plans for Differentiated Instruction

Quick Facts Transparency: Visual Summary: Climate and Resources of the Eastern Hemisphere

Student Edition on Audio CD Program

Interactive Skills Tutor CD-ROM

Spanish Chapter Summaries Audio CD Program

Teacher's One-Stop Planner:
- ExamView Test Generator, Spanish
- PuzzlePro, Spanish

English-Language Learner Strategies and Activities

SPECIAL NEEDS LEARNERS

TARGET RESOURCE

Differentiated Instruction Modified Worksheets and Tests CD-ROM

- Vocabulary Flash Cards
- Modified Vocabulary Builder Activities
- Modified Chapter Review Activity
- Modified Chapter Test

Additional Resources

Differentiated Instruction Teacher Management System: Lesson Plans for Differentiated Instruction

Interactive Reader and Study Guide

Resource File: Social Studies Skills: Analyzing a Bar Graph

Student Edition on Audio CD Program

Interactive Skills Tutor CD-ROM

Graphic Organizer Transparencies with Support for Reading and Writing

ADVANCED/GIFTED AND TALENTED STUDENTS

TARGET RESOURCE

Differentiated Instruction Teacher Management System

Lesson Plans for Differentiated Instruction provide teachers with strategies to help plan instruction for all learners.

Additional Resources

Resource File:
- Focus on Reading: Understanding Cause and Effect
- Focus on Viewing: Presenting and Viewing a Weather Report
- Literature: "To Build a Fire" by Jack London

World History and Geography Document-Based Questions Activities

Geography, Science, and Cultures Activities

Experiencing World History and Geography

Differentiated Activities in the Teacher's Edition
- Adapting to Climate
- *The Endless Steppe* Play

Differentiated Activities in the Teacher's Edition
- Analyzing Weather Map Symbols

Differentiated Activities in the Teacher's Edition
- Predicting Weather Fronts
- Making a Climate Graph for Your Community
- World Energy Consumption
- *The Endless Steppe* Play

HOLT Teacher's One-Stop Planner®

How can I manage the lesson plans and support materials for differentiated instruction?

With the Teacher's One-Stop Planner, you can easily organize and print lesson plans, planning guides, and instructional materials for all learners.

The Teacher's One-Stop Planner includes the following materials to help you differentiate instruction:
- Interactive Teacher's Edition
- Calendar Planner and pacing guides
- Editable lesson plans
- All reproducible ancillaries in Adobe Acrobat (PDF) format
- ExamView Test Generator (English & Spanish)

Professional Development

What teacher training resources are available to help me grow professionally?

- **In-service and staff development** as part of your Holt Social Studies product purchase
- **Quick Teacher Tutorial Lesson Presentation CD-ROM**
- Intensive tuition-based **Teacher Development Institute**
- **Convenient Holt Speaker Bureau** – face-to-face workshop options
- **24/7 Ask A Professional Development Expert** at http://www.hrw.com/prodev/

Chapter Big Ideas

Section 1 The sun, location, wind, water, and mountains affect weather and climate.

Section 2 Earth's five major climate zones are identified by temperature, precipitation, and plant life.

Section 3 Earth's natural resources have many valuable uses, and their availability affects people in many ways.

Focus on Reading and Viewing

Reading The Resource File provides a worksheet to help students practice understanding cause and effect.

RF: Focus on Reading, Understanding Cause and Effect

Viewing The Resource File provides a worksheet to help students create and view a weather report.

RF: Focus on Viewing, Creating and Viewing a Weather Report

Key to Differentiating Instruction

Below Level

Basic-level activities designed for all students encountering new material

At Level

Intermediate-level activities designed for average students

Above Level

Challenging activities designed for honors and gifted and talented students

Standard English Mastery

Activities designed to improve standard English usage

CHAPTER **3**

Climate and Resources of the Eastern Hemisphere

FOCUS QUESTION

How did geography influence the development of the Eastern Hemisphere?

What You Will Learn...

In this chapter you will learn about weather and climate. Climate is the weather conditions over a long period of time. You will also learn about the importance of Earth's natural resources.

FOCUS ON READING AND SPEAKING

Understanding Cause and Effect A cause makes something happen. An effect is the result of a cause. Words such as *because, result, since,* and *therefore* can signal causes or effects. As you read, look for causes and effects to understand how things relate. **See the lesson, Understanding Cause and Effect, on page S4.**

Presenting and Viewing a Weather Report You have likely seen a TV weather report, which tells the current weather conditions and predicts future conditions. After reading this chapter, prepare a weather report for a season and place of your choosing. Present your report to the class and then view your classmates' reports.

Climate Earth has many climates, such as the dry climate of the region shown here.

50 CHAPTER 3

Introduce the Chapter

At Level

The World Around Us

1. Draw three large bubbles on the board in a triangular pattern, and label them *Climate, Vegetation,* and *Resources.* Ask students to suggest words or short phrases that belong inside each bubble. Write down all appropriate suggestions, emphasizing words that also appear as key terms in the chapter. Help students write a definition for each term based as much as possible on the words or short phrases they originally suggested.

2. Ask students to look for connections from bubble to bubble. For example, *forest* under *Resources* could be connected to *rainfall* under *Climate* and *trees* under *Vegetation.*

3. After enough connections have been established, point out to students that almost everything in the world around us is connected to everything else. **LS Verbal/Linguistic, Visual/Spatial**

   Alternative Assessment Handbook, Rubrics 13: Graphic Organizers; and 14: Group Activity

ANALYSIS
SKILL ANALYZING VISUALS

This photo shows a severe thunderstorm. These storms produce violent weather, such as heavy rainfall and strong winds, which affects people's lives.

How do you think this storm might have affected the people who lived in this area?

HOLT
Geography's Impact
video series
Watch the video to understand the impact of weather.

Vegetation
Animals, such as this koala, depend on plants to survive.

Natural Resources Earth provides many valuable and useful natural resources, such as oil.

51

Explore the Picture

Severe Thunderstorms Violent storms often occur when hot and cold air masses come together. Often, temperatures drop dramatically after such storms pass. This type of storm can also produce a tornado. More tornadoes strike the United States than any other country.

Analyzing Visuals Ask students to name regions with dry climates. Have them describe what they think a dry climate is like. Then have them name other types of climates, where they occur, and what they might be like.

Have students think about how plants and animals survive in different environments. For example, koalas in eastern Australia depend on the eucalyptus trees there for food and shelter. Ask students to explain how other animals depend on their surroundings.

HOLT
Geography's Impact
▶ video series
See the Video Teacher's Guide for strategies for using the chapter video to teach about the impact of weather.

go.hrw.com
Online Resources

Chapter Resources:
KEYWORD: SK9 CH3
Teacher Resources:
KEYWORD: SK9 TEACHER

Collaborative Learning

At Level

Ways Resources Are Recycled

1. Divide students into four groups and assign each group one of the following: paper, glass, plastics, and metals. Have students use the Internet to identify ways each material is recycled.

2. Students should make a list of five ways their material can be reused or recycled. For example, a fleece garment can be made out of 12 two-liter plastic bottles. Students should also list three ways that their assigned material can be recycled at home or at school. For example, students can print only necessary pages when doing research.

3. Have students write their lists on a poster, then share their posters with the other three groups.

4. Display the posters around the school to teach others how resources are recycled.

LS Verbal/Linguistic

Alternative Assessment Handbook, Rubrics 30: Research; and 28: Posters

Answers

Analyzing Visuals *possible answer— People probably had to stop any outdoor activities and take shelter.*

Bellringer

If YOU lived there. . . Use the **Daily Bellringer Transparency** to help students answer the question.

🔲 Daily Bellringer Transparency, Section 1

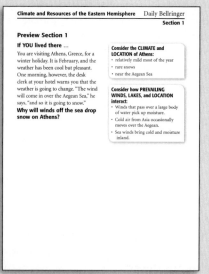

Key Terms

📓 **RF:** Vocabulary Builder, Section 1

Taking Notes

Have students copy the graphic organizer onto their own paper and then use it to take notes on the section. This activity will prepare students for the Section Assessment, in which they will complete a graphic organizer that builds on the information using the Critical Thinking Skill: Identifying Cause and Effect.

Answers

Reading Check *Weather is the short-term changes in the air, while climate is the long-term average weather conditions of a region.*

52

SECTION **1**

Weather and Climate

What You Will Learn...

Main Ideas

1. While weather is short term, climate is a region's average weather over a long period.
2. The amount of sun at a given location is affected by Earth's tilt, movement, and shape.
3. Wind and water move heat around Earth, affecting how warm or wet a place is.
4. Mountains influence temperature and precipitation.

The Big Idea

The sun, location, wind, water, and mountains affect weather and climate.

Key Terms

weather, *p. 52*
climate, *p. 52*
prevailing winds, *p. 53*
ocean currents, *p. 54*
front, *p. 55*

TAKING NOTES As you read, use a chart like the one here to take notes about the factors that affect weather and climate.

Sun and Location	Wind and Water	Mountains

52 CHAPTER 3

If YOU lived there...

You are visiting Athens, Greece, for a winter holiday. It is February, and the weather has been cool but pleasant. One morning, however, the desk clerk at your hotel warns you that the weather is going to change. "The wind will come in over the Aegean Sea," he says, "and so it is going to snow."

Why will winds off the sea drop snow on Athens?

BUILDING BACKGROUND All life on Earth depends on the sun's energy and on the cycle of water from the land to the air and back again. In addition, sun and water work with other forces, such as wind, to create global patterns of weather and climate.

Understanding Weather and Climate

"Climate is what you expect; weather is what you get."
—Robert Heinlein, from *Time Enough for Love*

What is it like outside right now where you live? Is it hot, sunny, wet, cold? Is this what it is usually like outside for this time of year? The first two questions are about **weather**, the short-term changes in the air for a given place and time. The last question is about **climate**, a region's average weather conditions over a long period.

Weather is the temperature and precipitation from hour to hour or day to day. "Today is sunny, but tomorrow it might rain" is a statement about weather. Climate is the expected weather for a place based on data and experience. "Summer here is usually hot and muggy" is a statement about climate. The factors that shape weather and climate include the sun, location on Earth, wind, water, and mountains.

READING CHECK Finding Main Ideas How are weather and climate different from each other?

Teach the Big Idea

At Level

Weather and Climate

1. **Teach** Ask students the questions in the Main Idea boxes under Direct Teach.

2. **Apply** Distribute one flashcard-sized strip of cardboard or paper to each student. Ask students to write one of these words or phrases on their strip: *altitude, large body of water, high pressure, low pressure, latitude, ocean current, westerly wind, doldrums, moisture, cold air mass, warm air mass, precipitation, desert, hurricane, rain shadow, front, wind, tornado, hurricane, moderate temperatures.*

Have a student hold up a card, and ask others to also hold up their cards if their term is related. Have them explain how their term is related.

3. **Review** Ask students to define their term and to tell if it applies to weather, climate, or both.

4. **Practice/Homework** Have students write ten true statements, each of which uses at least two of the terms in the list.
LS Verbal/Linguistic

📓 Alternative Assessment Handbook, Rubric 40, Writing to Describe

Sun and Location

Energy from the sun heats the planet. Different locations receive different amounts of sunlight, though. Thus, some locations are warmer than others. The differences are due to Earth's tilt, movement, and shape.

You have probably learned in science class that Earth is tilted on its axis. The part of Earth tilted toward the sun receives more solar energy than the part tilted away from the sun. As the Earth revolves around the sun, the part of Earth that is tilted toward the sun changes. This process creates the seasons. In general, temperatures in summer are warmer than in winter.

Earth's shape also affects the amount of sunlight different locations receive. Look at the diagram of Earth at right. You can see that Earth is a sphere, or wider in the middle. For this reason, the sun's rays directly strike the equator but only somewhat strike the poles.

As a result, areas near the equator, called the lower latitudes, are mainly hot year-round. Areas near the poles, called the higher latitudes, are cold year-round. Areas about halfway between the equator and poles have more seasonal change. In general, the farther from the equator, or the higher the latitude, the colder the climate.

READING CHECK Summarizing How does Earth's tilt on its axis affect climate?

Wind and Water

Heat from the sun moves across Earth's surface. The reason is that air and water warmed by the sun are constantly on the move. You might have seen a gust of wind or a stream of water carrying dust or dirt. In a similar way, wind and water carry heat from place to place. As a result, they make different areas of Earth warmer or cooler.

Global Wind Systems

Prevailing winds blow in circular belts across Earth. These belts occur at about every 30° of latitude.

ANALYZING VISUALS Which direction do the prevailing winds blow across the United States?

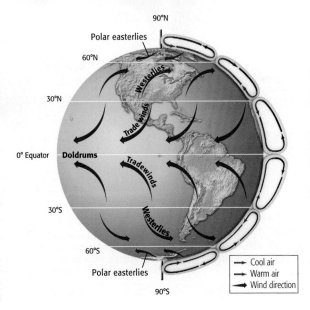

90°N
Polar easterlies
60°N
Westerlies
30°N
Trade winds
0° Equator   Doldrums
Tradewinds
30°S
Westerlies
60°S
Polar easterlies
90°S

→ Cool air
→ Warm air
→ Wind direction

Global Winds

Wind, or the sideways movement of air, blows in great streams around the planet. **Prevailing winds** are winds that blow in the same direction over large areas of Earth. The diagram above shows the patterns of Earth's prevailing winds.

To understand Earth's wind patterns, you need to think about the weight of air. Although you cannot feel it, air has weight. This weight changes with the temperature. Cold air is heavier than warm air. For this reason, when air cools, it gets heavier and sinks. When air warms, it gets lighter and rises. As warm air rises, cooler air moves in to take its place, creating wind.

CLIMATE AND RESOURCES OF THE EASTERN HEMISPHERE **53**

❸ Wind and Water

Wind and water move heat around Earth, affecting how warm or wet a place is.

Recall In which direction do the prevailing winds blow in the middle latitudes? *westerly*

Explain What effect does a large body of water have on a region or climate? *It helps to moderate temperatures.*

Draw Conclusions Why is it a good idea to check a weather forecast when a front moves through your area? *The front may bring severe weather.*

📄 Map Zone Transparency: Major Ocean Currents

Info to Know

Temperature Scales In the United States, most people use the Fahrenheit scale to measure temperature. Water freezes at 32°F and boils at 212°F.

Many people use the Celsius system. Water freezes at 0°C and boils at 100°C.

Here are some equivalent values:

Fahrenheit	Celsius
32	0
50	10
68	20
86	30
104	40
212	100

Answers

Map Zone 1. *warm;* **2.** *When warm water currents flow to colder areas, the air is heated above the currents, then the warmer air is blown by westerly winds.*

Focus on Reading *Prevailing winds curve east or west instead of in a straight line north or south.*

54

Major Ocean Currents

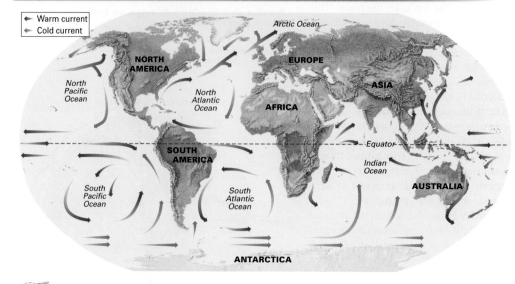

← Warm current
← Cold current

Geography Skills

Movement Ocean currents carry warm water from the equator toward the poles and cold water from the poles toward the equator. The currents affect temperature.

1. Use the Map Does a warm or cold ocean current flow along the northwest coast of Africa?
2. Explain How do ocean currents move heat between warmer and colder areas of Earth?

FOCUS ON READING

What is the effect of Earth's rotation on prevailing winds?

On a global scale, this rising, sinking, and flowing of air creates Earth's prevailing wind patterns. At the equator, hot air rises and flows toward the poles. At the poles, cold air sinks and flows toward the equator. Meanwhile, Earth is rotating. Earth's rotation causes prevailing winds to curve east or west.

Depending on their source, prevailing winds make a region warmer or colder. In addition, the source of the winds can make a region drier or wetter. Winds that form from warm air or pass over lots of water often carry moisture. In contrast, winds that form from cold air or pass over lots of land often are dry. Such areas can be prone to droughts, or long periods of little to no precipitation.

Ocean Currents

Like wind, **ocean currents** — large streams of surface seawater—move heat around Earth. Winds drive these currents. The map above shows how Earth's ocean currents carry warm or cool water to different areas. The water's temperature affects air temperature near it. Warm currents raise temperatures; cold currents lower them.

The Gulf Stream is a warm current that flows north along the U.S. East Coast. It then flows east across the Atlantic to become the North Atlantic Drift. As the warm current flows along northwestern Europe, it heats the air. Westerlies blow the warmed air across Europe. This process makes Europe warmer than it otherwise would be.

54 CHAPTER 3

Critical Thinking: Draw Conclusions   At Level

Oceans and Climate
                                                        Research Required

1. Using an almanac or the Internet, have students find the monthly average high and low temperatures for London and Moscow.

2. Have students draw a 2-column table and record the high and low temperatures for each city in the first four rows. Have them fill in the next two rows with the differences between the highs and lows for each month.

3. Remind students that London is near the ocean, and Moscow is located inland. Ask

students to explain the temperature patterns for each city. Call attention to the data for January and July.

4. Have students find monthly temperature data for other cities in the Eastern Hemisphere. Invite them to predict where these cities are located and then check their conclusions by finding the cities on a map. **LS** **Logical/Mathematical**

📄 Alternative Assessment Handbook, Rubrics 1: Acquiring Information; and 7: Charts

Large Bodies of Water

Large bodies of water, such as oceans or seas, also affect climate. Water heats and cools more slowly than land does. For this reason, large bodies of water make the temperature of the land nearby milder. Thus, coastal areas, such as the Italian coast, usually do not have as wide temperature ranges as inland areas. In contrast, the temperatures in inland areas can change drastically from season to season. For example, the country of Mongolia in the heart of Asia has very hot summers and very cold winters.

Wind, Water, and Storms

If you watch weather reports, you will hear about storms. Some storms are short-lived and only affect small areas. Others are huge and can last for days or weeks. Regardless of their size, all storms can be destructive. As you will see, some areas of the world have more storms than others do.

Most storms occur when two air masses collide. An air mass is a large body of air. The place where two air masses of different temperatures or moisture content meet is a **front**. Air masses frequently collide in regions where the westerlies meet the polar easterlies.

Fronts can produce rain or snow as well as severe weather such as thunderstorms and icy blizzards. Thunderstorms produce rain, lightning, and thunder. In temperate climates, they are most common in spring and summer. Blizzards produce strong winds and large amounts of snow and are most common during winter.

Thunderstorms and blizzards can also produce tornadoes, another type of severe storm. A tornado is a small, rapidly twisting funnel of air that touches the ground. Tornadoes usually affect a limited area and last only a few minutes. However, they can be highly destructive, uprooting trees and tossing large vehicles through the air.

Tornadoes can be extremely deadly as well. In 1989 a tornado that crossed central Bangladesh left some 1,300 people dead. It is the deadliest tornado on record.

The largest and most destructive storms, however, are hurricanes. These large, rotating storms form over tropical waters in the Atlantic Ocean, usually from late summer to fall. Did you know that hurricanes and typhoons are the same? Typhoons are just hurricanes that form in the Pacific Ocean.

Extreme Weather

Severe weather is often dangerous and destructive. In the top photo, Chinese workers rest in a riverbed left dry by a severe drought. Below, a tornado races across a wheat field.

55

Direct Teach

Connect to History

Columbus and the Sargasso Sea

Currents in the North Atlantic Ocean flow clockwise, roughly in a circle. In the center of this circle is an area of relatively calm water called the Sargasso Sea. The name comes from the Portuguese word for seaweed, which covers the calm water. Christopher Columbus thought he was close to land when he saw the Sargasso Sea, but in fact land was still hundreds of miles away.

Info to Know

Measuring Humidity Humidity can be measured by using the "wet bulb" method.

1. The bulb of an ordinary thermometer is covered in cloth, and the cloth is dipped in water.

2. The thermometer is whirled around in the air until the water on the cloth evaporates. The evaporation cools the thermometer, lowering its reading.

3. Results from the wet bulb reading are compared to a thermometer that has not been given the wet bulb treatment. The difference between the two readings is looked up on a chart that shows the humidity of the air.

Did you know. . .

Every year, the World Meteorological Association meets to decide what to call the hurricanes that will develop in the Atlantic Ocean in the coming season. Before 1979, hurricanes were given female names. Since then, male and female names have alternated. The name of the first storm begins with the letter A, then B, and so on. Names are chosen to reflect the Spanish, French, Dutch, and English languages spoken by the people affected by these seasonal storms.

Differentiating Instruction

Special Needs Learners   `Below Level`

Weather maps often use symbols to indicate weather conditions. Have students draw and label symbols for the following conditions: *sunny, rainy, snowy, cloudy, partly cloudy, hot, cold, windy, thunderstorms,* and *hurricane.*

Have students present their drawings with the labels covered and have the class guess which condition is represented. **LS** Visual/Spatial

📓 Alternative Assessment Handbook, Rubric 3: Artwork

Advanced/Gifted and Talented   `Above Level`

Explain to students that in Europe weather fronts generally follow the prevailing westerly winds. Find weather maps for several consecutive days. Show students the first two maps, pointing out how the air masses and fronts have moved. Have students draw their own maps predicting what the next day's map might look like. **LS** Visual/Spatial, Logical/Mathematical

📓 Alternative Assessment Handbook, Rubric 21: Map Reading

Direct Teach

Main Idea

❹ Mountains

Mountains influence temperature and precipitation.

Recall What part of a mountain is the coldest? *the top*

Cause and Effect What happens when warm, moist air blows against a mountainside? *The air rises and cools, clouds form, and precipitation falls.*

Draw Conclusions If the prevailing winds in a region are from the west, which side of a mountain in the region is less likely to receive rain? *the east side*

---

go.hrw.com
Online Resources

KEYWORD: SK9 CH3
ACTIVITY: Experiencing Extremes

Review & Assess

Close

Have students discuss what they think are the most important factors affecting climate and weather in their area.

Review

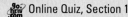 Online Quiz, Section 1

Assess

SE Section 1 Assessment

PASS: Section 1 Quiz

Alternative Assessment Handbook

Reteach/Classroom Intervention

Interactive Reader and Study Guide, Section 1

Interactive Skills Tutor CD-ROM

Answers

Reading Check (left) *Water heats and cools more slowly than land, making the temperatures of nearby land milder.*
Reading Check (right) *The temperature decreases as elevation increases.*

56

Rain Shadow Effect

Most of the moisture in the ocean air falls on the mountainside facing the wind. Little moisture remains to fall on the other side, creating a rain shadow.

Hurricanes produce drenching rain and strong winds that can reach speeds of 155 miles per hour (250 kph) or more. This is more than twice as fast as most people drive on highways. In addition, hurricanes form tall walls of water called storm surges. When a storm surge smashes into land, it can wipe out an entire coastal area.

READING CHECK **Analyzing** Why do coastal areas have milder climates than inland areas?

Mountains

Mountains can influence an area's climate by affecting both temperature and precipitation. Many high mountains are located in warm areas yet have snow at the top all year. How can this be? The reason is that temperature decreases with elevation—the height on Earth's surface above sea level.

Mountains also create wet and dry areas. Look at the diagram at left. A mountain forces air blowing against it to rise. As it rises, the air cools and precipitation falls as rain or snow. Thus, the side of the mountain facing the wind is often green and lush. However, little moisture remains for the other side. This effect creates a rain shadow, a dry area on the mountainside facing away from the direction of the wind.

READING CHECK **Finding Main Ideas** How does temperature change with elevation?

SUMMARY AND PREVIEW As you can see, the sun, location on Earth, wind, water, and mountains affect weather and climate. In the next section you will learn what the Eastern Hemisphere's different climate regions are like.

---

go.hrw.com
Online Quiz
KEYWORD: SK9 HP3

Section 1 Assessment

Reviewing Ideas, Terms, and Places

1. **a. Recall** What shapes **weather** and **climate**?
   b. Contrast How do weather and climate differ?
2. **a. Identify** What parts of Earth receive the most heat from the sun?
   b. Explain Why do the poles receive less solar energy than the equator does?
3. **a. Describe** What creates wind?
   b. Summarize How do **ocean currents** and large bodies of water affect climate?
4. **a. Define** What is a rain shadow?
   b. Explain Why might a mountaintop and a nearby valley have widely different temperatures?

Critical Thinking

5. **Identifying Cause and Effect** Draw a chart like this one. Use your notes to explain how each factor affects climate.

	Effect on Climate
Sun and Location	
Wind	
Water	
Mountains	

FOCUS ON SPEAKING

6. **Writing about Weather and Climate** Jot down information to include in your weather report. For example, you might want to include a term such as *fronts* or describe certain types of storms such as hurricanes or tornadoes.

56 CHAPTER 3

Section 1 Assessment Answers

1. **a.** the sun, location, wind, water, and mountains
   b. Weather is short-term changes; climate is long-term average weather conditions of a region.
2. **a.** the areas nearest the equator
   b. Because of Earth's rounded surface, solar rays nearer the poles are less direct and are spread over a larger region than at the equator, where solar rays are more direct and concentrated.
3. **a.** Warm air is lighter than cold air, so as warm air rises, cold air sinks to replace it, creating wind.
   b. Ocean currents carry cool or warm water to different areas. Because water heats and cools slower than land, air that is heated or cooled by water is blown by winds, bringing moderate temperatures to land near water.
4. **a.** a dry area on a mountainside that is away from the wind
   b. Temperatures decrease with elevation.
5. possible responses—Sun and location create seasons; Wind moves sun's heat; Water moves sun's heat; Mountains affect temperature and precipitation.
6. Students' notes will vary, but should include terms and details from this section.

Climates of the Eastern Hemisphere

If YOU lived there...

While visiting Tanzania, you decide to climb the famous Mount Kilimanjaro. Since it is July, it is hot in the campground in the valley. But your guide insists that you bring a heavy fleece jacket. By noon, you have climbed to 11,000 feet. You are surprised to see patches of snow in shady spots. Suddenly, you are very happy that you brought your jacket!

Why does it get colder as you climb higher?

BUILDING BACKGROUND While weather is the day-to-day changes in a certain area, climate is the average weather conditions over a long period. Climates depend on the sunlight a region receives and factors such as wind, water, and elevation.

Major Climate Zones

In January, how will you dress for the weekend? In some places, you might get dressed to go skiing. In other places, you might head out in a swimsuit to go to the beach. What the seasons are like where you live depends on climate.

The Eastern Hemisphere is a patchwork of climates. Geographers classify these climates by temperature, precipitation, and plant life. Using these items, we can divide the hemisphere into five general climate zones—tropical, temperate, polar, dry, and highland.

The first three climate zones relate to latitude. Tropical climates occur near the equator, in the low latitudes. Temperate climates occur about halfway between the equator and the poles, in the middle latitudes. Polar climates occur near the poles, in the high latitudes. The last two climate zones occur at many different latitudes. The chart and map on the next two pages describe these climate regions.

READING CHECK **Drawing Inferences** Why do you think geographers consider native plant life when categorizing climates?

What You Will Learn...

Main Ideas

1. Geographers use temperature, precipitation, and plant life to identify climate zones.
2. Tropical climates are wet and warm, while dry climates receive little or no rain.
3. Temperate climates have the most seasonal change.
4. Polar climates are cold and dry, while highland climates change with elevation.

The Big Idea

Earth's five major climate zones are identified by temperature, precipitation, and plant life.

Key Terms

monsoons, *p. 60*
savannas, *p. 60*
steppes, *p. 61*
permafrost, *p. 63*

TAKING NOTES As you read, use a chart like the one here to help you note the characteristics of Earth's major climate zones.

Climate Zone	Characteristics

57

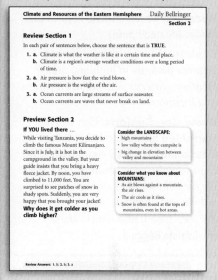
---

❶ Major Climate Zones

Geographers use temperature, precipitation, and plant life to identify climate zones.

Recall In which climate zone is the tundra located? *polar*

Explain Why are there different weather patterns in highland areas? *Weather patterns depend on elevation and location.*

Draw Conclusions Can native animal life be used to help identify climate zones? Explain your answer. *Yes. For example, some animals have thick fur for cold weather or can survive only in wet climates.*

 Map Zone Transparency: World Climate Regions

Info to Know

Ice Ages Many people in the United States live in areas that were covered by ice until about 10,000 years ago. Glaciers more than one mile thick extended across most of the northern United States. Water from the melting glaciers formed the Great Lakes.

Generally, ice ages have come about every 40,000 to 100,000 years. No one knows how or when another ice age will begin. But our knowledge of ice ages reminds us that climate zones can and do change over time.

★Interactive Map
World Climate Regions

To explore the world's climate regions, start with the chart below. After reading about each climate region, locate the places on the map that have that climate. As you locate climates, look for patterns. For example, places near the equator tend to have warmer climates than places near the poles. See if you can identify some other climate patterns.

Tropical climate

Climate		Where is it?	What is it like?	Plants
Tropical	HUMID TROPICAL	On and near the equator	Warm with high amounts of rain year-round; in a few places, monsoons create extreme wet seasons	Tropical rain forest
	TROPICAL SAVANNA	Higher latitudes in the tropics	Warm all year; distinct rainy and dry seasons; at least 20 inches (50 cm) of rain during the summer	Tall grasses and scattered trees
Dry	DESERT	Mainly center on 30° latitude; also in middle of continents, on west coasts, or in rain shadows	Sunny and dry; less than 10 inches (25 cm) of rain a year; hot in the tropics; cooler with wide daytime temperature ranges in middle latitudes	A few hardy plants, such as cacti
	STEPPE	Mainly bordering deserts and interiors of large continents	About 10–20 inches (25–50 cm) of precipitation a year; hot summers and cooler winters with wide temperature ranges during the day	Shorter grasses; some trees and shrubs by water
Temperate	MEDITERRANEAN	West coasts in middle latitudes	Dry, sunny, warm summers; mild, wetter winters; rain averages 15–20 inches (30–50 cm) a year	Scrub woodland and grassland
	HUMID SUBTROPICAL	East coasts in middle latitudes	Humid with hot summers and mild winters; rain year-round; in paths of hurricanes and typhoons	Mixed forest
	MARINE WEST COAST	West coasts in the upper-middle latitudes	Cloudy, mild summers and cool, rainy winters; strong ocean influence	Evergreen forests
	HUMID CONTINENTAL	East coasts and interiors of upper-middle latitudes	Four distinct seasons; long, cold winters and short, warm summers; average precipitation varies	Mixed forest

Collaborative Learning

At Level

Give a Weather Forecast

1. Have students work with a partner. Assign one of the climate regions to each pair.

2. Have each pair use the world climate regions map to find a place where their assigned climate region exists. Have them look on a political world map or globe and identify a city in that climate region.

3. Have students present a television news-style weather forecast for their city. Have them use the information in the climate region table to guide them as to what a reasonable forecast would be for the city they selected.

4. Encourage students to add visuals to their presentations such as weather maps, pictures of rain clouds, snowflakes, and so on.

LS Interpersonal, Logical/Mathematical

Alternative Assessment Handbook, Rubric 29: Presentations

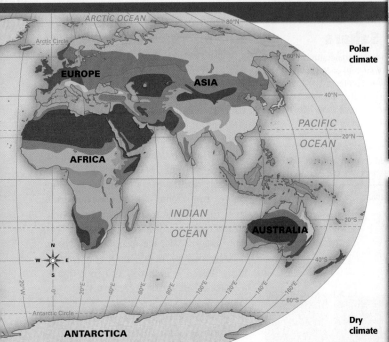

Polar climate

Dry climate

	Climate	Where is it?	What is it like?	Plants
Polar	SUBARCTIC	Higher latitudes of the interior and east coasts of continents	Extremes of temperature; long, cold winters and short, warm summers; little precipitation	Northern evergreen forests
Polar	TUNDRA	Coasts in high latitudes	Cold all year; very long, cold winters and very short, cool summers; little precipitation; permafrost	Moss, lichens, low shrubs
Polar	ICE CAP	Polar regions	Freezing cold; snow and ice; little precipitation	No vegetation
Highland	HIGHLAND	High mountain regions	Wide range of temperatures and precipitation amounts, depending on elevation and location	Ranges from forest to tundra

Geography Skills

Regions Note how Earth's climate regions relate to different locations.

1. Locate Which climates are found mainly in the Northern Hemisphere?

2. Identify What climate does most of northern Africa have?

3. Make Generalizations Where are many of the world's driest climates found on Earth?

4. Interpreting Charts Examine the chart. Which two climates have the least amount of vegetation?

go.hrw.com (KEYWORD: SK9 CH3)

CLIMATE AND RESOURCES OF THE EASTERN HEMISPHERE **59**

Direct Teach

World Climate Regions

Review the map with students. Ask the following questions:

Identify What climate is found in central Australia? *desert*

Explain Why is there no humid tropical climate in Europe? *None of Europe is in the tropics.*

Draw Conclusions In what kind of climate are trees mostly found? Why? *humid; Trees need a lot of water to grow.*

Info to Know

Extreme Weather Have you had any hot days recently where you live? Or have you complained about too much rain? Here are some all-time weather records, showing how bad weather can really get.

Highest Temperature: 136° Fahrenheit (El Azizia, Libya)

Lowest Temperature: −129° Fahrenheit (Vostok, Antarctica)

Highest Average Rainfall: 523.6 inches (Lloro, Colombia)

Lowest Average Rainfall: 0.03 inches (Arica, Chile)

Critical Thinking: Comparing and Contrasting   [At Level]

World Climate Regions

1. Ask students to study the table of world climate regions on these pages.

2. Copy the graphic organizer on the board, omitting the blue italicized text. Have students place each of the regions in the correct box.

3. Ask students to identify climates they didn't place in a box and explain why.
   LS Visual/Spatial

   Alternative Assessment Handbook, Rubric 9, Comparing and Contrasting

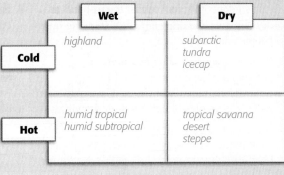

	Wet	Dry
Cold	*highland*	*subarctic tundra icecap*
Hot	*humid tropical humid subtropical*	*tropical savanna desert steppe*

Answers

Map Zone 1. *subarctic, tundra;*
2. *desert;* **3.** *mainly around 30° N and 30°S, bordering deserts, and interiors of continents;* **4.** *desert and ice cap*

59

Main Idea

❷ Tropical and Dry Climates

Tropical climates are wet and warm, while dry climates receive little or no rain.

Define What is a monsoon? *prevailing winds that change direction, creating wet and dry seasons*

Contrast How much rain falls in a desert compared to a humid tropical region? *desert: less than 10 inches per year; humid tropical regions: 70–450 inches per year*

Identify Cause and Effect What causes rapid cooling at night in the desert? *dry air and clear skies*

Info to Know

The Blooming Sahara? The Sahara in northern Africa is the world's largest desert, roughly the size of the entire United States. Like most places on Earth, the Sahara has had different climates at different times. As recently as about 5,000 years ago, the great Sahara Desert enjoyed a period of wetter climate, with far more vegetation than we see today.

Answers

Focus on Culture *They raise camels and wear veils to protect against windblown dust.*

60

The Tuareg of the Sahara

In the Sahara, the world's largest desert, temperatures can top 130°F (54°C). Yet the Tuareg (TWAH-reg) of North and West Africa call the Sahara home—and prefer it. The Tuareg have raised camels and other animals in the Sahara for more than 1,000 years. The animals graze on sparse desert plants. When the plants are gone, the Tuareg move on.

In camp, Tuareg families live in tents made from animal skins. Some wealthier Tuareg live in adobe homes. The men traditionally wear blue veils wrapped around their face and head. The veils help protect against windblown desert dust.

Summarizing How have the Tuareg adapted to life in a desert?

Tropical and Dry Climates

Are you the type of person who likes to go to extremes? Then tropical and dry climates might be for you. These climates include the wettest, driest, and hottest places on Earth.

Tropical Climates

Our tour of Earth's climates starts at the equator, in the heart of the tropics. This region extends from the Tropic of Cancer to the Tropic of Capricorn. Look back at the map to locate this region.

Humid Tropical Climate At the equator, the hot, damp air hangs like a thick, wet blanket. Sweat quickly coats your body.

60 CHAPTER 3

Welcome to the humid tropical climate. This climate is warm, muggy, and rainy year-round. Temperatures average about 80°F (26°C). Showers or storms occur almost daily, and rainfall ranges from 70 to more than 450 inches (180 to 1,140 cm) a year. In comparison, only a few parts of the United States average more than 70 inches (180 cm) of rain a year.

Some places with a humid tropical climate have **monsoons**, seasonal winds that bring either dry or moist air. During one part of the year, a moist ocean wind creates an extreme wet season. The winds then shift direction, and a dry land wind creates a dry season. Monsoons affect several parts of Asia. For example, the town of Mawsynram, India, receives on average more than 450 inches (1,140 cm) of rain a year—all in about six months! That is about 37 feet (11 m) of rain. As you can imagine, flooding during wet seasons is common and can be severe.

The humid tropical climate's warm temperatures and heavy rainfall support tropical rain forests. These lush forests contain more types of plants and animals than anywhere else on Earth. One of the world's largest rain forests is in the Congo River basin in Africa. There you can find more than 10,000 species, including rare trees, gorillas, elephants, and parrots.

Tropical Savanna Climate Moving north and south away from the equator, we find the tropical savanna climate. This climate has a long, hot, dry season followed by short periods of rain. Rainfall is much lower than at the equator but still high. Temperatures are hot in the summer, often as high as 90°F (32°C). Winters are cooler but rarely get cold.

This climate does not receive enough rainfall to support dense forests. Instead, it supports **savannas**—areas of tall grasses and scattered trees and shrubs.

Differentiating Instruction

Below Level | **Standard English Mastery**

Struggling Readers

1. Ask students to select one of the tropical or dry climates and draw a picture showing how people adapt to it.

2. Remind students that temperature, precipitation, and native plant life help geographers identify climates. Have students include examples of each in their drawings.

3. Have students use standard English to write a short paragraph on a separate sheet of paper identifying the type of climate and describing specifically what the people in the drawing are doing to adapt to it.

4. Have students present their drawings to the class and read their descriptive paragraphs. As a class, discuss any necessary corrections to the sentences to align them with standard English usage. **LS Visual/Spatial, Verbal/Linguistic**
📄 Alternative Assessment Handbook, Rubric 3: Artwork

Dry Climates

Leaving Earth's wettest places, we head to its driest. These climates are found in a number of locations on the planet.

Desert Climate Picture the sun baking down on a barren wasteland. This is the desert, Earth's hottest and driest climate. Deserts receive less than 10 inches (25 cm) of rain a year. Dry air and clear skies produce high daytime temperatures and rapid cooling at night. In some deserts, highs can top 130°F (54°C)! Under such conditions, only very hardy plants and animals can live. Many plants grow far apart so as not to compete for water. Others, such as cacti, store water in fleshy stems and leaves.

Steppe Climate Semidry grasslands or prairies—called **steppes** (STEPS)—often border deserts. Steppes receive slightly more rain than deserts do. Short grasses are the most common plants, but shrubs and trees grow along streams and rivers.

> **READING CHECK** **Contrasting** What are some ways in which tropical and dry climates differ?

Temperate Climates

If you enjoy hot, sunny days as much as chilly, rainy ones, then temperate climates are for you. *Temperate* means "moderate" or "mild." These mild climates tend to have four seasons, with warm or hot summers and cool or cold winters.

Temperate climates occur in the middle latitudes, the regions halfway between the equator and the poles. Air masses from the tropics and the poles often meet in these regions, which creates a number of different temperate climates. You very likely live in one, because most Americans do.

Mediterranean Climate Named for the region of the Mediterranean Sea, this sunny, pleasant climate is found in many popular vacation areas. In a Mediterranean climate, summers are hot, dry, and sunny. Winters are mild and somewhat wet. Plant life includes shrubs and short trees with scattered larger trees. The Mediterranean climate occurs mainly in coastal areas. In addition to the Mediterranean region, parts of South Africa have this climate.

Main Idea

❸ Temperate Climates

Temperate climates have the most seasonal change.

Compare What do humid subtropical climates and marine west coast climates have in common? *Both have mild winters, occur near coasts, have evergreen forests, and receive moisture from oceans.*

Recall Which climate has four distinct seasons? *humid continental*

Make Generalizations What is often the reason a climate is humid? *Winds are carrying moisture in from a nearby ocean.*

Info to Know

Temperate Caves Caves do not have much weather, but they do have varying temperatures. The temperature inside a cave tends to reflect the average temperature of the air outside. Earth's average temperature is about 60°F, and most caves are not much warmer or cooler than that. Caves in warm areas, of course, are warmer than caves in cool areas.

Why does this happen? The soil and rock surrounding a cave moderate its temperature, much like a large body of water affects the land nearby.

Mediterranean Climate

The climate graph shows average temperatures and precipitation for Nice (NEECE), France, which has a Mediterranean climate.

ANALYZING GRAPHS During which month is precipitation lowest?

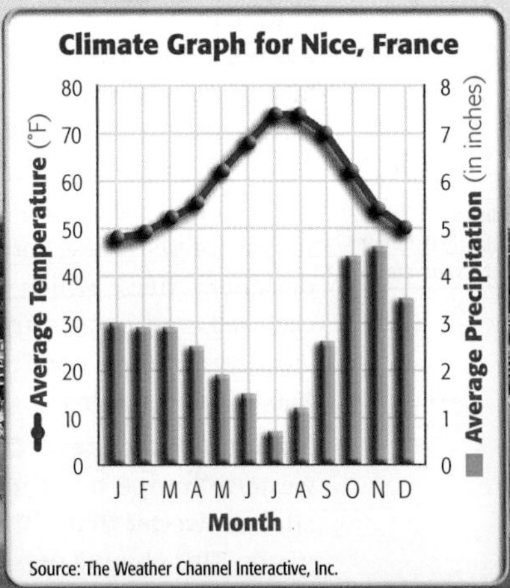

Climate Graph for Nice, France

Source: The Weather Channel Interactive, Inc.

Critical Thinking: Compare and Contrast

Above Level

Make a Climate Graph for Your Community

1. Review with students the Mediterranean climate graph of Nice, France. Make sure students understand that two types of data—average monthly temperatures and average monthly precipitation—are shown on the graph.

2. Help students collect monthly temperature and precipitation data for your community. Write the data on the board and have students create a climate graph using the data.

3. Ask students to compare the local climate graph to the graph for Nice, France. Have them make a table summarizing similarities and differences in climate.

LS Logical/Mathematical

Alternative Assessment Handbook, Rubric 9: Comparing and Contrasting

Answers

Reading Check *Tropical climates are usually wet; rain forests are found in the humid tropical climates. There is little rainfall in dry climates; deserts are found there.*

Analyzing Graphs *July*

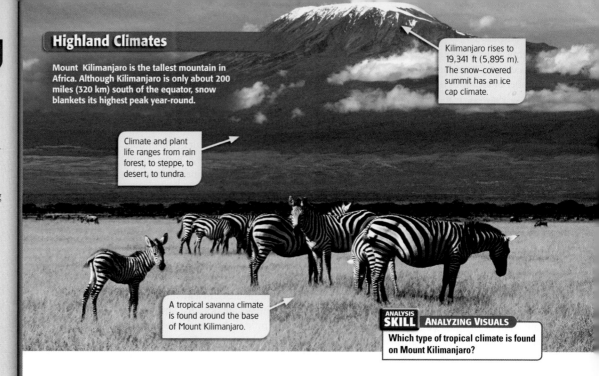

Highland Climates

Mount Kilimanjaro is the tallest mountain in Africa. Although Kilimanjaro is only about 200 miles (320 km) south of the equator, snow blankets its highest peak year-round.

Kilimanjaro rises to 19,341 ft (5,895 m). The snow-covered summit has an ice cap climate.

Climate and plant life ranges from rain forest, to steppe, to desert, to tundra.

A tropical savanna climate is found around the base of Mount Kilimanjaro.

ANALYSIS SKILL ANALYZING VISUALS
Which type of tropical climate is found on Mount Kilimanjaro?

Humid Subtropical Climate Eastern China and Japan are examples of the humid subtropical climate. This climate occurs along east coasts near the tropics. In these areas, warm, moist air blows in from the ocean. Summers are hot and muggy. Winters are mild, with occasional frost and snow. Storms occur year-round. In addition, hurricanes can strike, bringing violent winds, heavy rain, and high seas.

A humid subtropical climate supports mixed forests. These forests include both deciduous trees, which lose their leaves each fall, and coniferous trees, which are green year-round. Coniferous trees are also known as evergreens.

Marine West Coast Climate Most of western Europe has a marine west coast climate, wetter than other temperate climates. This climate occurs on west coasts where winds carry moisture in from the seas. The moist air keeps temperatures mild year-round. Winters are foggy, cloudy, and rainy, while summers can be warm and sunny. Dense evergreen forests thrive in this climate.

Humid Continental Climate Closer to the poles, in the upper–middle latitudes, many inland and east coast areas have a humid continental climate. This climate has four distinct seasons. Summers are short and hot. Spring and fall are mild, and winters are long, cold, and in general, snowy.

This climate's rainfall supports vast grasslands and forests. Grasses can grow very tall, such as in parts of Eastern Europe and Russia. Forests contain both deciduous and coniferous trees, with coniferous forests occurring in the colder areas.

READING CHECK Categorizing Which of the temperate climates is too dry to support forests?

ACADEMIC VOCABULARY

distinct
clearly different and separate

62 CHAPTER 3

Polar and Highland Climates

Get ready to feel the chill as we end our tour in the polar and highland climates. The three polar climates are found in the high latitudes near the poles. The varied highland climate is found on mountains.

Subarctic Climate The subarctic climate and the tundra climate described below occur mainly in the Northern Hemisphere south of the Arctic Ocean. In the subarctic climate, winters are long and bitterly cold. Summers are short and cool. Temperatures stay below freezing for about half the year. The climate's moderate rainfall supports vast evergreen forests called taiga (TY-guh).

Tundra Climate The tundra climate occurs in coastal areas along the Arctic Ocean. As in the subarctic climate, winters are long and bitterly cold. Temperatures rise above freezing only during the short summer. Rainfall is light, and only plants such as mosses, lichens, and small shrubs grow.

In parts of the tundra, soil layers stay frozen all year. Permanently frozen layers of soil are called **permafrost**. Frozen earth absorbs water poorly, which creates ponds and marshes in summer. This moisture causes plants to burst forth in bloom.

Ice Cap Climate The harshest places on Earth may be the North and South poles. These regions have an ice cap climate. Temperatures are bone-numbingly cold, and lows of more than –120°F (–84°C) have been recorded. Snow and ice remain year-round, but precipitation is light. Not surprisingly, no vegetation grows. However, mammals such as penguins and polar bears thrive.

Highland Climates The highland climate includes polar climates plus others. In fact, this mountain climate is actually several climates in one. As you go up a mountain, the climate changes. Temperatures drop, and plant life grows sparser. Going up a mountain can be like going from the tropics to the poles. On very tall mountains, ice coats the summit year-round.

FOCUS ON READING
What is the effect of elevation on climate?

READING CHECK **Comparing** How are polar and highland climates similar?

SUMMARY AND PREVIEW As you can see, the Eastern Hemisphere has many climates, which we identify based on temperature, precipitation, and native plant life. In the next section you will read about the various natural resources found in the same region.

Section 2 Assessment

go.hrw.com
Online Quiz
KEYWORD: SK9 HP3

Reviewing Ideas, Terms, and Places

1. **a. Recall** Which three major climate zones occur at certain latitudes?
   b. Summarize How do geographers categorize Earth's different climates?
2. **a. Define** What are **monsoons**?
   b. Make Inferences In which type of dry climate do you think the fewest people live, and why?
3. **a. Identify** What are the four temperate climates?
   b. Draw Conclusions Why are places with Mediterranean climates popular vacation spots?
4. **a. Describe** What are some effects of **permafrost**?
   b. Explain How are highland climates unique?

Critical Thinking

5. **Categorizing** Create a chart like the one below for each climate region. Then use your notes to describe each climate region's average temperatures, precipitation, and native plant life.

Climate Region	Temperature	Precipitation	Plant Life

FOCUS ON SPEAKING

6. **Discussing World Climates** Add information about the climate of the place you have selected, such as average temperature and precipitation.

CLIMATE AND RESOURCES OF THE EASTERN HEMISPHERE **63**

Bellringer

If YOU lived there. . . Use the **Daily Bellringer Transparency** to help students answer the question.

🗲 Daily Bellringer Transparency, Section 3

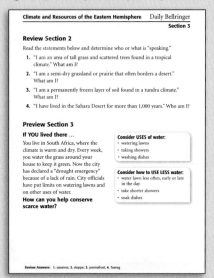

Climate and Resources of the Eastern Hemisphere	Daily Bellringer
	Section 3

Review Section 2

Read the statements below and determine who or what is "speaking."

1. "I am an area of tall grass and scattered trees found in a tropical climate." What am I?
2. "I am a semi-dry grassland or prairie that often borders a desert." What am I?
3. "I am a permanently frozen layer of soil found in a tundra climate." What am I?
4. "I have lived in the Sahara Desert for more than 1,000 years." Who am I?

Preview Section 3

If YOU lived there …
You live in South Africa, where the climate is warm and dry. Every week, you water the grass around your house to keep it green. Now the city has declared a "drought emergency" because of a lack of rain. City officials have put limits on watering lawns and on other uses of water. **How can you help conserve scarce water?**

Consider USES of water:
- watering lawns
- taking showers
- washing dishes

Consider how to USE LESS water:
- water lawn less often, early or late in the day
- take shorter showers
- soak dishes

Review Answers: 1. savanna; 2. steppe; 3. permafrost; 4. Tuareg

Key Terms

📓 **RF:** Vocabulary Builder, Section 3

Taking Notes

Have students copy the graphic organizer onto their own paper and then use it to take notes on the section. This activity will prepare students for the Section Assessment, in which they will complete a graphic organizer that builds on the information using the Critical Thinking Skill: Categorizing.

Natural Resources

What You Will Learn...

Main Ideas

1. Earth provides valuable resources for our use.
2. Energy resources provide fuel, heat, and electricity.
3. Mineral resources include metals, rocks, and salt.
4. Resources shape people's lives and countries' wealth.

The Big Idea

Earth's natural resources have many valuable uses, and their availability affects people in many ways.

Key Terms

natural resource, *p. 64*
renewable resources, *p. 65*
nonrenewable resources, *p. 65*
deforestation, *p. 65*
reforestation, *p. 65*
fossil fuels, *p. 65*
hydroelectric power, *p. 66*

 As you read, use a chart like this one to take notes on Earth's resources.

Earth's Valuable Resources →	
Energy Resources →	
Mineral Resources →	
Resources and People →	

If YOU lived there...

You live in South Africa, where the climate is warm and dry. Every week, you water the grass around your house to keep it green. Now the city has declared a "drought emergency" because of a lack of rain. City officials have put limits on watering lawns and on other uses of water.

How can you help conserve scarce water?

BUILDING BACKGROUND In addition to plant and animal life, other resources in the environment greatly influence people. In fact, certain vital resources, such as water, soils, and minerals, may determine whether people choose to live in a place or how wealthy people are.

Earth's Valuable Resources

Think about the materials in nature that you use. You have learned about the many ways we use sun, water, and land. They are just a start, though. Look at the human-made products around you. They all required the use of natural materials in some way. We use trees to make paper for books. We use petroleum, or oil, to make plastics for cell phones. We use metals to make machines, which we then use to make many items. Without these materials, our lives would change drastically.

Using Natural Resources

Trees, oil, and metals are all examples of natural resources. A **natural resource** is any material in nature that people use and value. Earth's most important natural resources include air, water, soils, forests, and minerals.

Understanding how and why people use natural resources is an important part of geography. We use some natural resources just as they are, such as wind. Usually, though, we change natural resources to make something new. For example, we change metals to make products such as bicycles and watches. Thus, most natural resources are raw materials for other products.

Teach the Big Idea

Natural Resources

1. **Teach** Ask students the questions in the Main Idea boxes under Direct Teach.

2. **Apply** Have students make a two-column table. Have them go through the entire section and list all of the resources mentioned in this section in the left column. Then have students list in the right column how often they use that resource.

3. **Review** Ask volunteers to share their ideas and write them on the board. If necessary,

have students explain the use of a resource (Example: Paper comes from the forest.)

4. **Practice/Homework** For homework, have students rank all the resources discussed in class in order of importance. Ask them to explain their rankings.

🅛🅢 **Verbal/Linguistic**

📓 Alternative Assessment Handbook, Rubric 42: Writing to Inform

---

Reforestation

Members of the Green Belt Movement plant trees in Kenya. Although trees are a renewable resource, some forests are being cut down faster than new trees can replace them. Reforestation helps protect Earth's valuable forestlands.

ANALYZING VISUALS How does reforestation help the environment?

Types of Natural Resources

We group natural resources into two types, those we can replace and those we cannot. **Renewable resources** are resources Earth replaces naturally. For example, when we cut down a tree, another tree can grow in its place. Renewable resources include water, soil, trees, plants, and animals. These resources can last forever if used wisely.

Other natural resources will run out one day. These **nonrenewable resources** are resources that cannot be replaced. For example, coal formed over millions of years. Once we use the coal up, it is gone.

Managing Natural Resources

People need to manage natural resources to protect them for the future. Consider how your life might change if we ran out of forests, for example. Although forests are renewable, we can cut down trees far faster than they can grow. The result is the clearing of trees, or **deforestation**.

By managing resources, however, we can repair and prevent resource loss. For example, some groups are engaged in **reforestation**, planting trees to replace lost forestland.

READING CHECK Contrasting How do renewable and nonrenewable resources differ?

BIOGRAPHY

Wangari Maathai
(1940–)

Can planting a tree improve people's lives? Wangari Maathai thinks so. Born in Kenya in East Africa, Maathai wanted to help people in her country, many of whom were poor. She asked herself what Kenyans could do to improve their lives. "Planting a tree was the best idea that I had," she says. In 1977 Maathai founded the Green Belt Movement to plant trees and protect forestland. The group has now planted more than 30 million trees across Kenya! These trees provide wood and prevent soil erosion. In 2004 Maathai was awarded the Nobel Peace Prize. She is the first African woman to receive this famous award.

Energy Resources

Every day you use plants and animals from the dinosaur age—in the form of energy resources. These resources power vehicles, produce heat, and generate electricity. They are some of our most important and valuable natural resources.

Nonrenewable Energy Resources

Most of the energy we use comes from **fossil fuels**, nonrenewable resources that formed from the remains of ancient plants and animals. The most important fossil fuels are coal, petroleum, and natural gas.

Coal has long been a reliable energy source for heat. However, burning coal causes some problems. It pollutes the air and can harm the land. For these reasons, people have used coal less as other fuel options became available.

Main Idea

❶ **Earth's Valuable Resources**

Earth provides valuable resources for our use.

Recall Is soil a renewable or nonrenewable resource? *renewable*

Explain What is reforestation? *planting new trees in places where forests have been lost*

Make Inferences Is it better to rely on renewable or nonrenewable resources? *Renewable resources, because nonrenewable resources will run out some day.*

📑 **RF:** Biography, Jane Goodall

📑 **RF:** Primary Source, Survivors of Krakatau

📑 **RF:** Interdisciplinary Project, Diagram an Ecosystem

Info to Know

Deforestation in China China's fast growing economy has caused environmental problems, such as rapid deforestation. Through much of the 1990s, Chinese loggers cut down forests at an unsustainable rate. By the end of the decade, forest land the size of Rhode Island had been entirely cleared of trees. Despite recent reforestation efforts and some restrictions on logging, some observers estimate that China continues to cut down forests at a rate of about 335 square miles per year.

Collaborative Learning

At Level

Local Resources

Research Required

1. Divide the class into four groups: air, water, soil, and forest. Have each group make a poster and present a report to the class after researching the topics outlined here.

2. Have the air team research air quality standards, including the substances measured and the amounts of each considered dangerous. Have them find out which, if any, pollutants have reached dangerous levels in their community.

3. Have the water team find out where their water comes from and have them research

water quality standards and how the community measures up.

4. Have the soil team research how soils are classified and what soil types are found in the area. They might also bring in a sample.

5. Have the forest team find out which trees grow in the area and where the closest state or national forest is. **LS Verbal/Linguistic**

📄 Alternative Assessment Handbook, Rubrics 1: Acquiring Information; and 24: Oral Presentations

Answers

Analyzing Visuals *possible answer— It prevents soil erosion.*

Reading Check *Renewable resources are replaced naturally, so they can last forever if used wisely. Nonrenewable resources cannot be replaced, so at some point, they will be gone forever.*

Main Idea

❷ **Energy Resources**

Energy resources provide fuel, heat, and electricity.

Recall What are some nonrenewable energy resources? *coal, natural gas, petroleum or oil, all of the fossil fuels*

Draw Conclusions What is a disadvantage of wind power? *When the wind does not blow, it provides no power.*

Contrast What are the advantages and disadvantages of coal? *Advantages—It can provide both heat and electricity; it is plentiful. Disadvantages—It creates pollution; it will run out some day.*

Info to Know

Future Energy Use Today all countries rely on energy from nonrenewable resources such as coal and oil. The more developed countries use huge amounts of these resources. As the world's population grows, the need for energy will grow. However, people will not be able to rely on these same resources. Their use causes pollution, and eventually nonrenewable resources will run out. More people around the world will have to develop cleaner, renewable sources of energy.

Answers

Focus on Reading *coal is plentiful; looking for cleaner ways to burn it*
Interpreting Graphs *North America*

66

FOCUS ON READING
In the second sentence on this page, what cause does the word *because* signal? What is the effect of this cause?

Today we use coal mainly to create electricity at power plants, not to heat single buildings. Because coal is plentiful, people are looking for cleaner ways to burn it.

Petroleum, or oil, is a dark liquid used to make fuels and other products. When first removed from the ground, petroleum is called crude oil. This oil is shipped or piped to refineries, factories that process the crude oil to make products. Fuels made from oil include gasoline, diesel fuel, and jet fuel. Oil is also used to make petrochemicals, which are processed to make products such as plastics and cosmetics.

As with coal, burning oil-based fuels can pollute the air and land. In addition, oil spills can harm wildlife. Because we are so dependent on oil for energy, however, it is an extremely valuable resource.

The cleanest-burning fossil fuel is natural gas. We use it mainly for heating and cooking. For example, your kitchen stove may use natural gas. Some vehicles run on natural gas as well. These vehicles cause less pollution than those that run on gasoline.

Renewable Energy Resources

Unlike fossil fuels, renewable energy resources will not run out. They also are generally better for the environment. On the other hand, they are not available everywhere and can be costly.

The main alternative to fossil fuels is **hydroelectric power**—the production of electricity from waterpower. We obtain energy from moving water by damming rivers. The dams harness the power of moving water to generate electricity.

Hydroelectric power has both pros and cons. On the positive side, it produces power without polluting and lessens our use of fossil fuels. On the negative side, dams create lakes that replace existing resources, such as farmland, and disrupt wildlife habitats.

Another renewable energy source is wind. People have long used wind to power windmills. Today we use wind to power wind turbines, a type of modern windmill. At wind farms, hundreds of turbines create electricity in windy places.

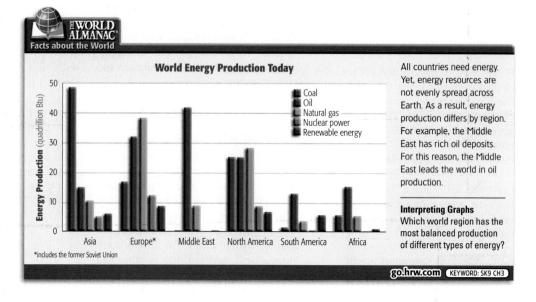

THE **WORLD ALMANAC** Facts about the World

World Energy Production Today

- Coal
- Oil
- Natural gas
- Nuclear power
- Renewable energy

Energy Production (quadrillion Btu)

Asia, Europe*, Middle East, North America, South America, Africa

*includes the former Soviet Union

All countries need energy. Yet, energy resources are not evenly spread across Earth. As a result, energy production differs by region. For example, the Middle East has rich oil deposits. For this reason, the Middle East leads the world in oil production.

Interpreting Graphs
Which world region has the most balanced production of different types of energy?

go.hrw.com KEYWORD: SK9 CH3

66 CHAPTER 3

Critical Thinking: Drawing Conclusions   Above Level

World Energy Consumption   Research Required

1. Review with students the World Energy Production chart above. Point out that an area might produce more energy than it uses and that some parts of the world use more energy than they produce.

2. Have students use an almanac or the Internet to find energy production and consumption data, by country. Ask them to make a chart of the top ten producers and the top ten consumers.

3. Have students find countries in each of three categories: those that consume more than they produce (example: Japan), those that produce more than they consume (example: Norway), those that consume about the same as they produce (example: United Kingdom).

4. Have students write a short essay exploring what impact a consumption/production imbalance might have on a country's economy as well as on the future spatial organization of Earth. **LS Verbal/Linguistic**

Alternative Assessment Handbook, Rubrics 30: Research; and 37: Writing Assignments

A third source of renewable energy is heat from the sun and Earth. We can use solar power, or power from the sun, to heat water or homes. Using special solar panels, we turn solar energy into electricity. We can also use geothermal energy, or heat from within Earth. Geothermal power plants use steam and hot water located within Earth to create electricity.

Nuclear Energy

A final energy source is nuclear energy. We obtain this energy by splitting atoms, small particles of matter. This process uses the metal uranium, so some people consider nuclear energy a nonrenewable resource. Nuclear power does not pollute the air, but it does produce dangerous wastes. These wastes must be stored for thousands of years before they are safe. In addition, an accident at a nuclear power plant can have terrible effects.

READING CHECK Drawing Inferences Why might people look for alternatives to fossil fuels?

Mineral Resources

Like energy resources, mineral resources can be quite valuable. These resources include metals, salt, rocks, and gemstones.

Minerals fulfill countless needs. Look around you to see a few. Your school building likely includes steel, made from iron. The outer walls might be granite or limestone. The window glass is made from quartz, a mineral in sand. From staples to jewelry to coins, metals are everywhere.

Minerals are nonrenewable, so we need to conserve them. Recycling items such as aluminum cans will make the supply of these valuable resources last longer.

READING CHECK Categorizing What are the major types of mineral resources?

From the Ground to the Air

The photo shows a bauxite mine. Bauxite is used to make aluminum. This metal is used in many products, such as jet planes. See how many other products made from aluminum you can name.

Resources and People

Natural resources vary from place to place. The resources available in a region can shape life and wealth for the people there.

Resources and Daily Life

The natural resources available to people affect their lifestyles and needs. In the United States we have many different kinds of natural resources. We can choose among many different ways to dress, eat, live, travel, and entertain ourselves. People in places with fewer natural resources will likely have fewer choices and different needs than those in other places.

For example, people who live in remote rain forests depend on forest resources for most of their needs. These people may craft containers by weaving plant fibers together. They may make canoes by hollowing out tree trunks. Instead of being concerned about money, they might be more concerned about food.

CLIMATE AND RESOURCES OF THE EASTERN HEMISPHERE **67**

68

Direct Teach

Main Idea

4 Resources and People

Resources shape people's lives and countries' wealth.

Explain What is the relationship between natural resources and wealth? *Natural resources generate wealth. Countries with many natural resources may grow wealthy from those resources.*

Draw Conclusions If people do not have a resource, what can they do? *Trade something else for it, find a substitute for it, or do without it.*

Review & Assess

Close

Have students discuss ways to conserve resources and why it is important.

Review

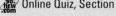 Online Quiz, Section 3

Assess

SE Section 3 Assessment

PASS: Section 3 Quiz

Alternative Assessment Handbook

Reteach/Classroom Intervention

Interactive Reader and Study Guide, Section 3

Interactive Skills Tutor CD-ROM

Answers

Analyzing Visuals *Responses should indicate students' understanding of the petroleum content in plastic, vinyl, synthetic fibers, adhesive, and other materials.*

Reading Check *Regions or countries with few natural resources often have weak economies and different concerns than regions or countries with abundant resources.*

Products from Petroleum

This family shows some common products made from petroleum, or oil.

ANALYZING VISUALS What petroleum-based products can you identify in this photo?

Resources and Wealth

The availability of natural resources affects countries' economies as well. For example, the many natural resources available in western Europe have helped it become one of the world's wealthiest regions. In contrast, countries with few natural resources often have weak economies.

Some countries have one or two valuable resources but few others. For example, Saudi Arabia is rich in oil but lacks water for growing food. As a result, Saudi Arabia must use its oil profits to import food.

READING CHECK **Identifying Cause and Effect** How can having few natural resources affect life and wealth in a region or country?

SUMMARY AND PREVIEW You can see that Earth's natural resources have many uses. In the next chapter you will read about how these resources helped bring about the beginnings of civilization in the Eastern Hemisphere.

Section 3 Assessment

go.hrw.com
Online Quiz
KEYWORD: SK9 HP3

Reviewing Ideas, Terms, and Places

1. **a. Define** What are **renewable resources** and **nonrenewable resources**?
   b. Explain Why is it important for people to manage Earth's natural resources?
   c. Develop What are some things you can do to help manage and conserve natural resources?
2. **a. Define** What are **fossil fuels**, and why are they significant?
   b. Summarize What are three examples of renewable energy resources?
   c. Predict How do you think life might change as we begin to run out of petroleum?
3. **a. Recall** What are the main types of mineral resources?
   b. Analyze What are some products that we get from mineral resources?

4. **a. Describe** How do resources affect people?
   b. Make Inferences How might a country with only one valuable resource develop its economy?

Critical Thinking

5. **Categorizing** Draw a chart like this one. Use your notes to identify and evaluate each energy resource.

Fossil Fuels	Renewable Energy	Nuclear Energy
Pros	Pros	Pros
Cons	Cons	Cons

FOCUS ON SPEAKING

6. **Noting Details about Natural Resources** What natural resources does the place you chose have? Note ways to refer to some of these resources (or the lack of them) in your weather report.

68 CHAPTER 3

Section 3 Assessment Answers

1. **a.** renewable—resources that are replaced naturally; nonrenewable—resources that cannot be replaced
   b. They could easily disappear in the future.
   c. Possible answers include recycling materials, turning lights off, and watering the lawn sparingly.
2. **a.** They are nonrenewable resources formed from remains of living things. They are energy resources.
   b. hydroelectric, wind, solar, geothermal, and nuclear power

   c. People will have to conserve energy and depend more on renewable energy sources.
3. **a.** metals, salt, rocks
   b. Possible answers include coins, glass, and cans.
4. **a.** They are the source of the energy and products people use.
   b. It could trade with other countries.
5. Charts should reflect details from the section.
6. Answers will vary depending on the places students chose.

from
The Endless Steppe

by Esther Hautzig

About the Reading *In* The Endless Steppe, *an autobiographical novel, Esther Hautzig writes about her own experiences as a teenage girl. In the novel, the girl Esther is from a wealthy Jewish family in Poland. In 1941 her family is deported to a labor camp in the frozen region of Siberia. In the excerpt below, Esther and her family are on the train to Siberia crossing Russia's vast steppes.*

AS YOU READ Think about what Esther feels as she watches the passing landscape. What ideas does she already have about life in Siberia?

The flatness of this land was awesome. There wasn't a hill in sight; it was an enormous, unrippled sea of parched and lifeless grass.

"Tata, why is the earth so flat here?"

"These must be steppes, Esther."

"Steppes? But steppes are in Siberia."

"This is Siberia," he said quietly.

If I had been told that I had been transported to the moon, I could not have been more stunned.

"Siberia?" My voice trembled. "But Siberia is full of snow."

"It will be," my father said. ❶

Siberia! Siberia was the end of the world, a point of no return. Siberia was for criminals and political enemies, where the punishment was unbelievably cruel, and where people died like flies. ❷ Summer or no summer—and who had ever talked about hot Siberia?—Siberia was the tundra and mountainous drifts of snow. Siberia was *wolves*.

GUIDED READING

WORD HELP

deported forced to leave a country

parched very thirsty

Tata Polish word that means "daddy" or "papa"

steppes vast, grassy plains in southern Russia

tundra in subarctic climates, an almost treeless plain with permanently frozen subsoil

❶ At the time of the train journey, it is summer.

❷ The labor camps in Siberia, called gulags, were harsh places to live. Many people died at the camps.

Connecting Literature to Geography

1. **Analyzing** What image does Esther have of Siberia's climate? What reaction does she have to her first glimpse of the region?

2. **Drawing Inferences** Why do you think Siberia was chosen as a place of exile? What made it a punishment to live there?

69

Differentiating Instruction

English-Language Learners
At Level

Organize students into groups of three, and have them rewrite the passage from *The Endless Steppe* as a short play. The three parts are Tata, Esther, and the narrator. Have selected groups perform their play for the rest of the class.
LS Verbal/Linguistic

Alternative Assessment Handbook, Rubric 33: Skits and Reader's Theater

Advanced/Gifted and Talented
Above Level

Tell students that Esther's father was separated from the rest of the family when they reached Siberia. Have students write a scene in a play about *The Endless Steppe*, this time depicting what they imagine would have happened when Tata was taken away.
LS Verbal/Linguistic

Alternative Assessment Handbook, Rubric 33: Skits and Reader's Theater

Literature

from *The Endless Steppe*

As You Read

As they read, ask students to pay attention to words or phrases that convey feelings of fear, loneliness, or desolation. Have them make note of these words or phrases, and ask volunteers to name the words they flagged when the reading is finished. Discuss with students. *possible answers—enormous, parched, lifeless, flat, stunned, trembled, end of the world, point of no return, unbelievably cruel, died like flies, mountainous drifts, wolves*

Info to Know

The Gulag Archipelago The Soviet Union's system of forced labor camps, called the Gulag, became well-known in western countries only after Alexandr Solzhenitsyn's *The Gulag Archipelago* was published in 1973. In this landmark book, Solzhenitsyn exposed the massive system of camps used to punish both criminal and political prisoners.

Meet the Writer

Esther Hautzig (1930–) Born Esther Rudomin in Vilna, Poland, Esther was the daughter of an engineer, Samuel Rudomin. In 1941 she was deported with her family to Siberia. Her father was separated from the rest of the family, but they were reunited after the war. Esther at first returned to Poland, but later lived in Sweden before settling in the United States. Esther married concert pianist Walter Hautzig in 1950. She wrote *The Endless Steppe* in 1968.

Answers

Connecting Literature to Geography 1. *possible answer— Esther has an image in her mind of Siberia being a "tundra" with "mountainous drifts of snow." Esther is stunned when she first arrives in Siberia to see an endless flat expanse of dry grass.* **2.** *possible answer—Siberia was a very difficult environment. It was probably difficult to escape. The cold, the tundra, the wolves, and the treatment of people made it difficult to live in Siberia.*

Social Studies Skills

Social Studies Skills

| Chart and Graph | Critical Thinking | Geography | Study |

Analyzing a Bar Graph

Activity Create and Compare Bar Graphs

Materials: Almanac (or Internet access), art paper, colored pencils

1. Tell students that they are going to use information from an almanac or an Online resource to create bar graphs.

2. Have students get together in groups of four, and use their almanacs or the Internet to find the highest elevation on each of the five continents (including Antarctica) of the Eastern Hemisphere.

3. Students should use their art supplies to create their bar graphs showing the highest elevation on each continent of the Eastern Hemisphere. Ask students to show the continents in alphabetical order across the bottom. Also help students to figure out which interval of feet works best along the left side. Encourage students to color each bar differently.

4. As a class, compare the bar graphs. Ask volunteers to rank the continents of the Eastern Hemisphere in order from the continent with highest high elevation to the continent with the lowest high elevation.
   LS Verbal/Linguistic

📄 Alternative Assessment Handbook, Rubric 7: Charts

💿 Interactive Skills Tutor CD-ROM, Lesson 6: Interpreting Graphs

📄 **RF:** Social Studies Skills, Analyzing a Bar Graph

Analyzing a Bar Graph

Learn

Bar graphs are drawings that use bars to show data in a clear, visual format. Use these guidelines to analyze bar graphs.

- Read the title to identify the graph's subject and purpose.

- Read the graph's other labels. Note what the graph is measuring and the units of measurement being used. For example, this bar graph is measuring precipitation by climate. The unit of measurement is inches. If the graph uses colors, note their purpose.

- Analyze and compare the data. As you do, note any increases or decreases and look for trends or changes over time.

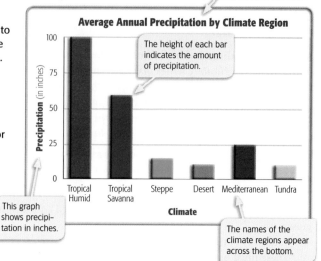

This bar graph compares the average annual precipitation of six climate regions.

The height of each bar indicates the amount of precipitation.

This graph shows precipitation in inches.

The names of the climate regions appear across the bottom.

Practice

❶ On the bar graph above, which climate region has the highest average annual precipitation?

❷ Which two climate regions have about the same amount?

❸ Which climate region receives an average of between 50 and 75 inches of precipitation each year?

Apply

Examine the World Energy Production Today bar graph in Section 3. Then use the graph to answer the following questions.

1. Which region produces the most oil?

2. Which three regions produce little or no nuclear power?

3. Based on the graph, what type of energy resource do most Asian countries likely use?

70 CHAPTER 3

Social Studies Skills Activity: Analyzing a Bar Graph **At Level**

Bar Graph Quiz

1. Have each student create a four-question quiz based on the bar graph on this page.

2. Allow students to make separate answer keys for their quizzes.

3. Invite pairs of students to exchange quizzes, then answer the questions before exchanging them back for grading.

4. Students should then summarize the information shown in the bar graph. Allow volunteers to read their summaries to the class. **LS Visual/Spatial**

📄 Alternative Assessment Handbook, Rubric 7: Charts

Answers

Practice 1. *tropical humid;* **2.** *tundra and desert;* **3.** *tropical savanna*

Apply 1. *Middle East;* **2.** *Africa, Middle East, and South America;* **3.** *coal*

Chapter Review

Geography's Impact
video series
Review the video to answer the closing question:
How are climate and weather different, and how does the influence they have differ?

Visual Summary

Use the visual summary below to help you review the main ideas of the chapter.

QUICK FACTS

Earth has a wide range of climates, which we identify by precipitation, temperature, and native plant life.

The people of the Eastern Hemisphere have adapted to the climates of the areas in which they live.

Earth's valuable natural resources, such as air, water, forests, and minerals, have many uses and affect people's lives.

Reviewing Vocabulary, Terms, and Places

Unscramble each group of letters below to spell a term that matches the given definition.

1. **rcstenur**—large streams of surface seawater
2. **tahrewe**—changes or conditions in the air at a certain time and place
3. **netorietfaosr**—planting trees where forests were
4. **cloeiyhrrtedc**—electric power produced from water
5. **estpep**—semidry grassland or prairie
6. **sifeticatorined**—spread of desertlike conditions
7. **laitemc**—an area's weather patterns over a long period of time
8. **arsmofrtpe**—permanently frozen layers of soil
9. **snonomo**—winds that change direction with the seasons and create wet and dry periods
10. **vansanas**—areas of tall grasses and scattered shrubs and trees

Comprehension and Critical Thinking

SECTION 1 *(Pages 52–56)*

11. **a. Identify** What are the five factors that affect climate?

    b. Analyze Is average annual precipitation an example of weather or climate?

    c. Evaluate Of the five factors that affect climate, which one do you think is the most important? Why?

SECTION 2 *(Pages 57–63)*

12. **a. Recall** What are the Eastern Hemisphere's five major climate zones?

    b. Explain In general, how does latitude relate to climate?

    c. Elaborate Why do you think the study of climate is important in geography?

CLIMATE AND RESOURCES OF THE EASTERN HEMISPHERE **71**

Answers

Visual Summary

Review and Inquiry Have students use the visual summary to provide details about Earth's climates, environments, and resources.

- Quick Facts Transparency: Visual Summary: Climate and Resources of the Eastern Hemisphere

Reviewing Vocabulary, Terms, and Places

1. currents
2. weather
3. reforestation
4. hydroelectric
5. steppe
6. desertification
7. climate
8. permafrost
9. monsoon
10. savanna

Comprehension and Critical Thinking

11. **a.** sun, location, wind, water, and mountains
    b. climate
    c. Students' responses will vary. Possible response—The sun is most important because its energy provides heat and light.

12. **a.** tropical, temperate, polar, dry, and highland
    b. Generally, the higher the latitude is, the colder the climate.
    c. possible answer—Climate affects all living things.

Review and Assessment Resources

Review and Reinforce

SE Chapter 3 Review

RF: Chapter Review

Quick Facts Transparency: Visual Summary: Climate and Resources of the Eastern Hemisphere

Spanish Chapter Summaries Audio CD Program

Teacher's One-Stop Planner

OSP Holt Puzzle Pro; Quiz Show for ExamView

Quiz Game CD-ROM

Assess

SE Standardized Test Practice

PASS: Chapter Test, Forms A and B

Alternative Assessment Handbook

OSP ExamView Test Generator, Chapter Test

Differentiated Instruction Modified Worksheets and Tests CD-ROM: Chapter Test

HOAP Holt Online Assessment Program (in the Holt Interactive Online Student Edition)

Reteach/Intervene

Interactive Reader and Study Guide

Differentiated Instruction Teacher Management System: Lesson Plans

Differentiated Instruction Modified Worksheets and Tests CD-ROM

Interactive Skills Tutor CD-ROM

go.hrw.com
Online Resources

Chapter Resources:
KEYWORD: SK9 CH3

Answers

13. a. Minerals are nonrenewable resources that come from Earth.

b. Nonrenewable resources cannot be replaced. Earth replaces renewable resources naturally.

c. It would require people to rely on fewer resources or to trade for the resources they need.

Using the Internet

14. Go to the HRW Web site and enter the keyword shown to access a rubric for this activity.

> **KEYWORD: SK9 TEACHER**

Focus on Reading and Viewing

15. erosion, growing the same crops over and over

16. Abundant resources can lead to a strong economy.

RF: Focus on Reading, Understanding Cause and Effect

17. Rubric Students' weather reports should:

- include a description of the current weather, as well as the extended forecast for the chosen area based on typical weather for the given season
- make a connection between the weather and the local environment or resources, if applicable

RF: Focus on Viewing, Creating and Viewing a Weather Report

Social Studies Skills

18. tropical humid

19. Mediterranean

20. 75 inches

SECTION 3 *(Pages 64–68)*

13. a. Define What are minerals?

b. Contrast How do nonrenewable resources and renewable resources differ?

c. Elaborate How might a scarcity of natural resources affect life in a region?

Using the Internet

> **go.hrw.com**
> **KEYWORD: SK9 CH3**

14. Activity: Experiencing Extremes Could you live in a place where for part of the year it is always dark and temperatures plummet to –104°F? What if you had to live in a place where it is always wet and stormy? Enter the activity keyword to learn more about some of the world's extreme climates. Then create a poster that describes some of those climates and the people, animals, and plants that live in them.

FOCUS ON READING AND SPEAKING

Understanding Cause and Effect *Answer the following questions about causes and effects.*

15. What causes desertification?

16. What are the effects of abundant natural resources on a country's economy?

Presenting and Viewing a Weather Report *Use your weather report notes to complete the activity below.*

17. Select a place and a season. Then write a script for a weather report for that place during that season. Describe the current weather and predict the upcoming weather. During your presentation, use a professional, friendly tone of voice and make frequent eye contact with your audience. Then view your classmates' weather reports. Be prepared to give feedback on the content and their presentation techniques.

Social Studies Skills

Analyzing a Bar Graph *Examine the bar graph titled Average Annual Precipitation by Climate Region in the Social Studies Skills for this chapter. Then use the bar graph to answer the following questions.*

18. Which climate region receives an average of 100 inches of precipitation a year?

19. Which climate region receives an average of 25 inches of precipitation a year?

20. What is the difference in average annual precipitation between tropical humid climates and Mediterranean climates?

Map Activity ★Interactive

21. Prevailing Winds On a separate sheet of paper, match the letters on the map with their correct labels.

equator	South Pole	westerly
North Pole	trade wind	

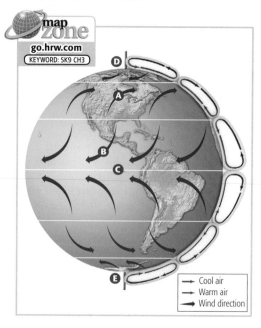

> **go.hrw.com**
> **KEYWORD: SK9 CH3**

→ Cool air
→ Warm air
➡ Wind direction

Map Activity

21. A. westerly

B. trade wind

C. equator

D. North Pole

E. South Pole

Standardized Test Practice

DIRECTIONS (1–7): For each statement or question, write on a separate answer sheet the *number* of the word or expression that, of those given, best completes the statement or answers the question.

1 The cold winds that flow away from the North and South poles are the
(1) doldrums.
(2) polar easterlies.
(3) trade winds.
(4) westerlies.

2 Which climate zone occurs only in the upper latitudes?
(1) highland
(2) temperate
(3) tropical
(4) polar

3 Where are the most diverse habitats in the Eastern Hemisphere found?
(1) steppe
(2) tropical rain forest
(3) tropical savanna
(4) tundra

4 What is the cleanest burning fossil fuel?
(1) coal
(2) natural gas
(3) oil
(4) petroleum

5 Which renewable energy source uses the heat of Earth's interior to generate power?
(1) geothermal energy
(2) hydroelectric energy
(3) nuclear energy
(4) solar energy

6 Which of the following form over tropical waters and are Earth's largest and most destructive storms?
(1) blizzards
(2) hurricanes
(3) thunderstorms
(4) tornadoes

7 Which seasonal winds bring heavy rain to some places?
(1) fronts
(2) steppes
(3) monsoons
(4) climates

Base your answer to question 8 on the graph below and on your knowledge of social studies.

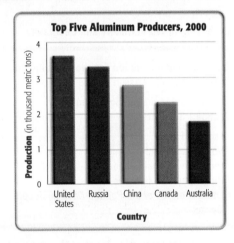

Top Five Aluminum Producers, 2000

Production (in thousand metric tons) vs. Country (United States, Russia, China, Canada, Australia)

8 Which country produced about 2,750 metric tons of aluminum in 2000?
(1) Australia
(2) China
(3) Russia
(4) United States

Reteach/Intervention Resources

Reproducible
- Interactive Reader and Study Guide
- Differentiated Instruction Teacher Management System: Lesson Plans

Technology
- Quick Facts Transparency: Visual Summary: Climate and Resources of the Eastern Hemisphere
- Differentiated Instruction Modified Worksheets and Tests CD-ROM
- Interactive Skills Tutor CD-ROM

Tips for Test Taking

When a question refers to a graph, such as Question 8 above, encourage students to first study the data plotted on the graph, as well as any headings and labels, before answering the question.

Standardized Test Practice

1. 3
Break Down the Question This question requires students to recall factual information. Refer students who miss it to Section 1.

2. 4
Break Down the Question This question requires students to recall factual information. Refer students who miss it to Section 2.

3. 2
Break Down the Question The steppe and tropical savanna have some shrubs, trees, and grasses, while the tundra has little vegetation.

4. 2
Break Down the Question This question requires students to recall factual information. Refer students who miss it to Section 4.

5. 1
Break Down the Question The prefix *geo* means "earth," and *thermal* refers to heat.

6. 2
Break Down the Question This question requires students to recall factual information. Refer students who miss it to Section 1.

7. 3
Break Down the Question This question requires students to recall factual information. Refer students who miss it to Section 2.

8. 2
Break Down the Question This question requires students to be able to read bar graphs. Refer students who miss it to the Social Studies Skills feature in this section.

Chapter 4 Planning Guide

Early Civilizations of the Eastern Hemisphere

Chapter Overview	Reproducible Resources	Technology Resources
CHAPTER 4 pp. 74–97 **Overview:** In this chapter, students will study our earliest ancestors and the beginnings of agriculture.	**Differentiated Instruction Teacher Management System:*** • Instructional Pacing Guides • Lesson Plans for Differentiated Instruction **Interactive Reader and Study Guide:** Chapter Summary Graphic Organizer* **Resource File:*** • Chapter Review • Focus on Reading: Understanding Main Ideas • Focus on Writing: Creating a Storyboard • Social Studies Skills: Understanding Chronological Terms **Experiencing World History and Geography**	**OSP Teacher's One-Stop Planner:** Calendar Planner **Power Presentations with Video CD-ROM** **Differentiated Instruction Modified Worksheets and Tests CD-ROM** **Interactive Skills Tutor CD-ROM** **Student Edition on Audio CD Program** **Music of the World Audio CD Program** **Geography's Impact Video Series (VHS/DVD):** Impact of Culture*
Section 1: **The First People** **The Big Idea:** Prehistoric people learned to adapt to their environment, to make simple tools, to use fire, and to use language.	**Differentiated Instruction Teacher Management System:** Section 1 Lesson Plan* **Interactive Reader and Study Guide:** Section 1 Summary* **Resource File:*** • Vocabulary Builder: Section 1 • Biography: Donald Johanson • Biography: The Leakeys • Literature: *Boy of the Painted Cave* by Justin Denzel	**Daily Bellringer Transparency:** Section 1* **Map Zone Transparency:** Early Hominid Sites* **Internet Activity:** Archaeology Article **Internet Activity:** Mary Leakey Sketch
Section 2: **Early Human Migration** **The Big Idea:** As people migrated around the world they learned to adapt to new environments.	**Differentiated Instruction Teacher Management System:** Section 2 Lesson Plan* **Interactive Reader and Study Guide:** Section 2 Summary* **Resource File:*** • Vocabulary Builder: Section 2	**Daily Bellringer Transparency:** Section 2* **Map Zone Transparency:** Early Human Migration*
Section 3: **Beginnings of Agriculture** **The Big Idea:** The development of agriculture brought great changes to human society	**Differentiated Instruction Teacher Management System:** Section 3 Lesson Plan* **Interactive Reader and Study Guide:** Section 3 Summary* **Resource File:*** • Vocabulary Builder: Section 3 • Primary Source: Objects from Çatal Hüyük	**Daily Bellringer Transparency:** Section 3* **Map Zone Transparency:** Early Domestication*

HOLT
Geography's Impact
Video Program

Impact of Culture
Suggested use: as a chapter introduction

Review, Assessment, Intervention

 Quick Facts Transparency: Visual Summary: Early Civilizations of the Eastern Hemisphere*

 Spanish Chapter Summaries Audio CD Program

 Progress Assessment Support System (PASS): Chapter Test*

 Differentiated Instruction Modified Worksheets and Tests CD-ROM: Modified Chapter Test

OSP Teacher's One-Stop Planner: ExamView Test Generator (English/Spanish)

 Alternative Assessment Handbook

HOAP Holt Online Assessment Program (HOAP), in the Holt Premier Online Student Edition

 PASS: Section 1 Quiz*

 Online Quiz: Section 1

 Alternative Assessment Handbook

 PASS: Section 2 Quiz*

 Online Quiz: Section 2

 Alternative Assessment Handbook

 PASS: Section 3 Quiz*

 Online Quiz: Section 3

 Alternative Assessment Handbook

Power Presentations with Video CD-ROM

Power Presentations with Video are visual presentations of each chapter's main ideas. Presentations can be customized by including Quick Facts charts, images from the text, and video clips.

Holt ●nline Learning

go.hrw.com
Teacher Resources
KEYWORD: SK9 TEACHER

go.hrw.com
Student Resources
KEYWORD: SK9 CH4

- Document-Based Questions
- Interactive Multimedia Activities

- Current Events
- Chapter-based Internet Activities
- and more!

Holt Premier
Online Student Edition

Complete online support for interactivity, assessment, and reporting
- Interactive Maps and Notebook
- Standardized Test Prep
- Homework Practice and Research Activities Online

CHAPTER 4 PLANNING GUIDE

Differentiating Instruction

How do I address the needs of varied learners?
The Target Resource acts as your primary strategy for differentiated instruction.

ENGLISH-LANGUAGE LEARNERS & STRUGGLING READERS

TARGET RESOURCE

Graphic Organizer Transparencies with Support for Reading and Writing

Spanish Resources

Spanish Chapter Summaries Audio CD

One-Stop Planner CD-ROM:
- ExamView Test Generator, Spanish
- PuzzlePro, Spanish

Additional Resources

Differentiated Instruction Teacher Management System: Lesson Plans for Differentiated Instruction

Resource File:
- Vocabulary Builder Activities
- Social Studies Skills: Understanding Chronological Terms

Quick Facts Transparency: Visual Summary: Early Civilizations of the Eastern Hemisphere

Student Edition on Audio CD Program

Interactive Skills Tutor CD-ROM

SPECIAL NEEDS LEARNERS

TARGET RESOURCE

Differentiated Instruction Modified Worksheets and Tests CD-ROM

- Vocabulary Flash Cards
- Modified Vocabulary Builder Activities
- Modified Chapter Review
- Modified Chapter Test

Additional Resources

Differentiated Instruction Teacher Management System: Lesson Plans for Differentiated Instruction

Interactive Reader and Study Guide

Resource File: Social Studies Skills: Understanding Chronological Terms

Student Edition on Audio CD Program

Interactive Skills Tutor CD-ROM

ADVANCED/GIFTED-AND-TALENTED STUDENTS

TARGET RESOURCE

Resource File

The Resource File activities allow students to extend their knowledge of chapter-related places and people and to practice geography skills.
- Focus on Reading: Understanding Main Ideas
- Focus on Writing: Creating a Storyboard
- Literature: *Boy of the Painted Cave* by Justin Denzel

Additional Resources

Differentiated Instruction Teacher Management System: Lesson Plans for Differentiated Instruction

World History and Geography Document-Based Questions Activities

Geography, Science, and Cultures Activities

Experiencing World History and Geography

Differentiated Activities in the Teacher's Edition

- Drawing Maps of Africa
- A Time Capsule
- Mural of Ancient Farm Community
- Understanding Maps
- Understanding Chronological Terms

HOLT Teacher's One-Stop Planner®

How can I manage the lesson plans and support materials for differentiated instruction?

With the Teacher's One-Stop Planner, you can easily organize and print lesson plans, planning guides, and instructional materials for all learners.

The Teacher's One-Stop Planner includes the following materials to help you differentiate instruction:

- Interactive Teacher's Edition
- Calendar Planner and pacing guides
- Editable lesson plans
- All reproducible ancillaries in Adobe Acrobat (PDF) format
- ExamView Test Generator (English & Spanish)
- Transparency and video previews

Differentiated Activities in the Teacher's Edition

- A Time Capsule
- Mural of Ancient Farm Community

Professional Development

What teacher training resources are available to help me grow professionally?

- **In-service and staff development** as part of your Holt Social Studies product purchase
- **Quick Teacher Tutorial Lesson Presentation CD-ROM**
- Intensive tuition-based **Teacher Development Institute**
- **Convenient Holt Speaker Bureau:** face-to-face workshop options
- **24/7 Ask A Professional Development Expert** at http://www.hrw.com/prodev/

Differentiated Activities in the Teacher's Edition

- Chance and Early People
- Researching Archaeological Sites
- Discussing Rivers
- Researching Online

DIFFERENTIATED INSTRUCTION PLANNING GUIDE

Chapter Big Ideas

Section 1 Prehistoric people learned to adapt to their environment, to make simple tools, to use fire, and to use language.

Section 2 As people migrated around the world they learned to adapt to new environments.

Section 3 The development of agriculture brought great changes to human society.

Focus on Reading and Writing

Reading The Resource File provides a worksheet to help students practice understanding main ideas.

RF: Focus on Reading, Understanding Main Ideas

Writing The Resource File provides a worksheet to help students organize and create their storyboards.

RF: Focus on Writing, Creating a Storyboard

Key to Differentiating Instruction

Below Level

Basic-level activities designed for all students encountering new material

At Level

Intermediate-level activities designed for average students

Above Level

Challenging activities designed for honors and gifted and talented students

Standard English Mastery

Activities designed to improve standard English usage

CHAPTER 4

Early Civilizations in the Eastern Hemisphere

FOCUS QUESTION

How did geography influence the development of the Eastern Hemisphere?

What You Will Learn...

In this chapter you will learn about the world's first people, from their origins in East Africa to the development of the world's first civilization. You will also learn about the factors that influenced where and when civilization began.

FOCUS ON READING AND WRITING

Understanding Main Ideas A main idea is the central idea around which a paragraph or passage is organized. As you read, ask yourself what each paragraph is about. Look for a sentence or two that summarizes the main point of the entire paragraph. **See the lesson, Understanding Main Ideas, on page S5.**

Creating a Storyboard Prehistoric humans did not write. However, they did carve and paint images on cave walls. In the spirit of these images, you will create a storyboard that uses images to tell the story of prehistoric humans. Remember that a storyboard tells a story with simple sketches and short captions.

The First People
The earliest ancestors of modern humans lived in Africa more than 1 million years ago.

74 CHAPTER 4

Introduce the Chapter

At Level

Focus on Early Civilizations

1. Ask students to describe ways in which early civilizations are depicted today in movies, comic strips, television programs, video games, or other media. List students' ideas on the board for the class to see.

2. Discuss whether these media show early peoples as stupid or smart, capable or clumsy, aggressive or peaceful.

3. Then challenge students to consider how well they would do if they faced the same challenges that the peoples of early civilizations faced.

4. Point out that in this chapter, students will learn that early people developed remarkable skills in order to survive. **LS** **Verbal/Linguistic**

Alternative Assessment Handbook, Rubric 11: Discussions

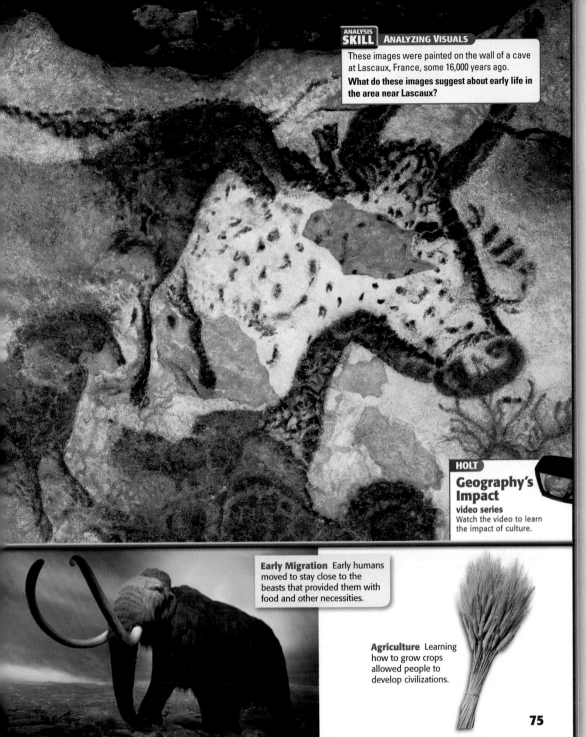

ANALYSIS SKILL **ANALYZING VISUALS**

These images were painted on the wall of a cave at Lascaux, France, some 16,000 years ago.

What do these images suggest about early life in the area near Lascaux?

HOLT

Geography's Impact

video series
Watch the video to learn the impact of culture.

Early Migration Early humans moved to stay close to the beasts that provided them with food and other necessities.

Agriculture Learning how to grow crops allowed people to develop civilizations.

75

• Chapter Preview •

Explore the Picture

Lascaux Cave Paintings The paintings shown at left are in a cave in France. They were created 17,000 to 15,000 years ago. Some 600 painted and drawn animals adorn the walls of this cave. Four teenage boys discovered the cave by accident in 1940, and the site was opened to the public in 1948. Because they were exposed to artificial lighting, damp air, and people, the paintings began to deteriorate. In 1963 the cave was closed to the public. A partial replica was created and made available to tourists.

Analyzing Visuals What details can you identify in the paintings of the animals? *possible answers—spots on the cow, horse's mane*

go.hrw.com

Online Resources

Chapter Resources:
KEYWORD: SK9 CH4
Teacher Resources:
KEYWORD: SK9 TEACHER

HOLT

Geography's Impact

▶ **video series**
See the Video Teacher's Guide for strategies for using the chapter video to teach about the impact of culture.

Did you know. . .

Archaeologists have discovered hearths, or fireplaces, along with the remains of hominids, or humanlike beings, who lived approximately 500,000 years ago. With the ability to control fire, they apparently started to cook their meat, making it easier to chew. As a result, the need for powerful jaws and large teeth eventually declined. The mastery of fire also allowed people to live in colder regions of the world.

Info to Know

Prehistoric Tools Scientists have little information on which to determine how the first hominids lived. Tools left behind by these early people leave scientists with clues as to how early people lived. These tools developed slowly over time from single, all-purpose tools to tools that were designed to serve a single purpose.

Make Inferences Why do we get most of our clues to the prehistoric period from tools? *because early tools were made of materials that would not decay such a stone and bone*

Answers

Analyzing Visuals *possible answer— Early life near Lascaux was probably dominated by the hunt for animals.*

75

Bellringer

If YOU were there . . . Use the **Daily Bellringer Transparency** to help students answer the question.

📖 Daily Bellringer Transparency, Section 1

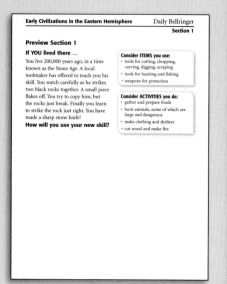

Early Civilizations in the Eastern Hemisphere	Daily Bellringer
	Section 1

Preview Section 1

If YOU lived there . . .

You live 200,000 years ago, in a time known as the Stone Age. A local toolmaker has offered to teach you his skill. You watch carefully as he strikes two black rocks together. A small piece flakes off. You try to copy him, but the rocks just break. Finally you learn to strike the rock just right. You have made a sharp stone knife!

How will you use your new skill?

Consider ITEMS you use:
- tools for cutting, chopping, carving, digging, scraping
- tools for hunting and fishing
- weapons for protection

Consider ACTIVITIES you do:
- gather and prepare foods
- hunt animals, some of which are large and dangerous
- make clothing and shelters
- cut wood and make fire

Academic Vocabulary

Review with students the high-use academic term in this section.

distribute to divide among a group of people (p. 81)

📝 RF: Vocabulary Builder, Section 1

Taking Notes

Have students copy the graphic organizer onto their own paper and then use it to take notes on the section. This activity will prepare students for the Section Assessment, in which they will complete a graphic organizer that builds on the information using the Critical Thinking Skill: Evaluating.

The First People

If YOU lived there...

You live 200,000 years ago, in a time known as the Stone Age. A local toolmaker has offered to teach you his skill. You watch carefully as he strikes two black rocks together. A small piece flakes off. You try to copy him, but the rocks just break. Finally you learn to strike the rock just right. You have made a sharp stone knife!

How will you use your new skill?

What You Will Learn...

Main Ideas

1. Scientists study the remains of early humans to learn about prehistory.
2. Hominids and early humans first appeared in East Africa millions of years ago.
3. Stone Age tools grew more complex as time passed.
4. Hunter-gatherer societies developed language, art, and religion.

The Big Idea

Prehistoric people learned to adapt to their environment, to make simple tools, to use fire, and to use language.

Key Terms

prehistory, p. 76
hominid, p. 76
ancestor, p. 76
tool, p. 78
Paleolithic Era, p. 79
society, p. 81
hunter-gatherers, p. 81

TAKING NOTES As you read, take notes on the advances made by prehistoric humans. Use a chart like this one to record your notes.

Advances

BUILDING BACKGROUND Over millions of years early people learned many new things. Making stone tools was one of the earliest and most valuable skills that they developed. Scientists who study early humans learn a lot about them from the tools and other objects that they made.

Scientists Study Remains

Although humans have lived on the earth for more than a million years, writing was not invented until about 5,000 years ago. Historians call the time before there was writing **prehistory**. To study prehistory, historians rely on the work of archaeologists and anthropologists.

One archaeologist who made important discoveries about prehistory was Mary Leakey. In 1959 she found bones in East Africa that were more than 1.5 million years old. She and her husband, Louis Leakey, believed that the bones belonged to an early **hominid** (HAH·muh-nuhd), an early ancestor of humans. An **ancestor** is a relative who lived in the past.

In fact, the bones belonged to an Australopithecus (aw-stray-loh-PI-thuh-kuhs), one of the earliest ancestors of humans. In 1974 anthropologist Donald Johanson (joh-HAN-suhn) found bones from another early ancestor. He described his discovery:

> “We reluctantly headed back toward camp . . . I glanced over my right shoulder. Light glinted off a bone. I knelt down for a closer look . . . Everywhere we looked on the slope around us we saw more bones lying on the surface.”
> –Donald Johanson, from *Ancestors: In Search of Human Origins*

Teach the Big Idea

The First People

1. **Teach** Ask students the questions in the Main Idea boxes under Direct Teach.

2. **Apply** Ask each student to choose a time period from the section and to imagine that he or she lived during that time. Have students create drawings to show what daily life was like. Students should include topics such as available tools, food, and activities in their drawings. 🔲 **Visual/Spatial**

3. **Review** Display and discuss the drawings.

4. **Practice/Homework** Ask students to imagine they are archaeologists who have discovered their drawings. Have each student write a paragraph about what an archaeologist might conclude about prehistoric life based on the drawings. Students should base the conclusions on the information in the section. 🔲 **Verbal/Linguistic**

📖 Alternative Assessment Handbook, Rubrics: 3: Artwork; and 40: Writing to Describe

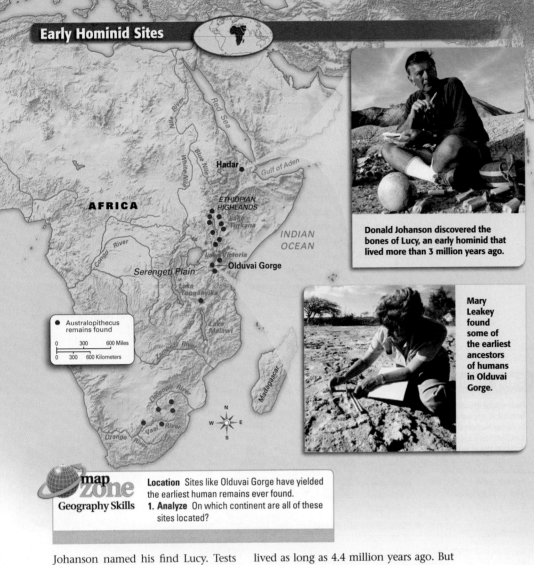

Early Hominid Sites

Hadar

ETHIOPIAN HIGHLANDS

Lake Turkana

AFRICA

Nile River

Red Sea

Gulf of Aden

Blue Nile

White Nile

INDIAN OCEAN

Congo River

Lake Victoria

Olduvai Gorge

Serengeti Plain

Lake Tanganyika

Lake Malawi

Madagascar

Zambezi River

Limpopo River

Orange River

Vaal River

● Australopithecus remains found

0   300   600 Miles

0   300   600 Kilometers

Donald Johanson discovered the bones of Lucy, an early hominid that lived more than 3 million years ago.

Mary Leakey found some of the earliest ancestors of humans in Olduvai Gorge.

map zone
Geography Skills

Location Sites like Olduvai Gorge have yielded the earliest human remains ever found.

1. Analyze On which continent are all of these sites located?

Johanson named his find Lucy. Tests showed that she lived more than 3 million years ago. Johanson could tell from her bones that she was small and had walked on two legs. The ability to walk on two legs was a key step in human development.

In 1994 anthropologist Tim White found even older remains. He believes that the hominid he found may have lived as long as 4.4 million years ago. But some scientists disagree with White's time estimate. Discoveries of ancient bones give us information about early humans and their ancestors, but not all scientists agree on the meaning of these discoveries.

READING CHECK **Drawing Inferences** What can ancient bones tell us about human ancestors?

Main Idea

❶ **Scientists Study Remains**

Scientists study the remains of early humans to learn about prehistory.

Recall What did Donald Johanson conclude by examining the bones of the hominid called Lucy? *that she was small and had walked on two legs*

Draw Conclusions What can the Leakeys' discoveries tell us about prehistory? *Hominids lived many years ago and were ancestors of humans.*

Make Judgments Why do you think some scientists do not agree that Tim White's discovery is 4.4 million years old? *It's difficult to determine the age of extremely old remains.*

📄 **RF:** Biography, Donald Johanson

🗺 Map Zone Transparency: Early Hominid Sites

go.hrw.com
Online Resources

KEYWORD: SK9 CH4
ACTIVITY: Archaeology Article

Linking to Today

A Family Tradition Mary and Louis Leakey's granddaughter, Louise, is also an anthropologist. In 1999 Louise and her mother, Meave Leakey, discovered a 3.5-million-year-old fossil skull at a site in Kenya. Some scholars believe this fossil may represent another early hominid group.

Differentiating Instruction

Below Level

English-Language Learners

1. Have students study the map shown on this page. Point out the map legend.

2. After students discuss the map, have them draw their own maps of Africa and create their own symbols for various features, such as bodies of water, mountain ranges, and early hominid sites. For example, students might draw a bone to represent a hominid site. In addition, students should provide a title and compass rose for their maps.

3. Call on volunteers to display their maps and explain their legends and symbols.

LS Visual/Spatial

📄 Alternative Assessment Handbook, Rubric 20: Map Creation

🗺 Map Zone Transparency: Early Hominid Sites

Answers

Map Zone *Africa*
Reading Check *They can teach us about human development and early human physical appearances.*

Main Idea

❷ Hominids and Early Humans

Hominids and early humans first appeared in East Africa millions of years ago.

Recall When do many scientists believe the first modern humans appeared? *about 200,000 years ago*

Compare What characteristic did *Homo erectus* have that modern humans also have? *the ability to walk upright*

Make Inferences How did fire help protect *Homo erectus* from wild animals? *Animals were probably afraid of fire, so* Homo erectus *could use fire to keep dangerous animals away.*

Activity **Early Human Time Line**
Have each student construct a time line showing when *Homo habilis*, *Homo erectus*, and *Homo sapiens* most likely first appeared.

📋 Alternative Assessment Handbook, Rubric 36: Time Lines

📋 **RF:** Biography, The Leakeys

---

go.hrw.com
Online Resources

KEYWORD: SK9 CH4
ACTIVITY: Mary Leakey
Sketch

Answers

Focus on Reading *by placing facts in chronological order*

Analyzing Visuals *Homo erectus*

Reading Check *Unlike Homo habilis, Homo erectus walked completely upright and could control fire.*

Hominids and Early Humans

FOCUS ON READING
How can dates in a text help you keep track of what you read?

Later groups of hominids appeared about 3 million years ago. As time passed they became more like modern humans.

In the early 1960s Louis Leakey found hominid remains that he called *Homo habilis*, or "handy man." Leakey and his son Richard believed that *Homo habilis* was more closely related to modern humans than Lucy and had a larger brain.

Scientists believe that another group of hominids appeared in Africa about 1.5 million years ago. This group is called *Homo erectus*, or "upright man." Scientists think these people walked completely upright like modern people do.

Scientists believe that *Homo erectus* knew how to control fire. Once fire was started by natural causes, such as lightning, people used it to cook food. Fire also gave them heat and protection against animals.

Eventually hominids developed characteristics of modern humans. Scientists are not sure exactly when or where the first modern humans lived. Many think that they first appeared in Africa about 200,000 years ago. Scientists call these people *Homo sapiens*, or "wise man." Every person alive today belongs to this group.

READING CHECK **Contrasting** How was *Homo erectus* different from *Homo habilis*?

Stone Age Tools

The first humans and their ancestors lived during a long period of time called the Stone Age. To help in their studies, archaeologists divide the Stone Age into three periods based on the kinds of tools used at the time. To archaeologists, a **tool** is any handheld object that has been modified to help a person accomplish a task.

Early Hominids

Four major groups of hominids appeared in Africa between 5 million and about 200,000 years ago. Each group was more advanced than the one before it and could use better tools.

ANALYZING VISUALS Which early hominid learned to control fire and use the hand ax?

Australopithecus

- Name means "southern ape"
- Appeared in Africa about 4–5 million years ago
- Stood upright and walked on two legs
- Brain was about one-third the size of modern humans

Homo habilis

- Name means "handy man"
- Appeared in Africa about 2.4 million years ago
- Used early stone tools for chopping and scraping
- Brain was about half the size of modern humans

An early Stone Age chopper

Critical Thinking: Drawing Inferences

Below Level

A Time Capsule

1. Review the definition of the word *tool*. Then discuss with students how discovering tools of our early ancestors helps us understand how early humans lived.

2. Ask students to propose three present-day tools that they would put in a time capsule to teach future generations about today's society. Discuss an example, such as a ballpoint pen, which tells later generations that we used writing.

3. Have students write short descriptions of what their items say about modern society.

4. Ask volunteers to read their lists and descriptions aloud. **LS Visual/Spatial**

📋 Alternative Assessment Handbook, Rubric 11: Discussions

The first part of the Stone Age is called the **Paleolithic** (pay-lee-uh-LI-thik) **Era**, or Old Stone Age. It lasted until about 10,000 years ago. During this time people used stone tools.

The First Tools

Scientists have found the oldest tools in Tanzania, a country in East Africa. These sharpened stones, about the size of an adult's fist, are about 2.6 million years old. Each stone had been struck with another rock to create a sharp, jagged edge along one side. This process left one unsharpened side that could be used as a handle.

Scientists think that these first tools were mostly used to process food. The sharp edge could be used to cut, chop, or scrape roots, bones, or meat. Tools like these, called choppers, were used for about 2 million years.

Later Tools

Over time people learned to make better tools. For example, they developed the hand ax. They often made this tool out of a mineral called flint. Flint is easy to shape, and tools made from it can be very sharp. People used hand axes to break tree limbs, to dig, and to cut animal hides.

People also learned to attach wooden handles to tools. By attaching a wooden shaft to a stone point, for example, they invented the spear. Because a spear could be thrown, hunters no longer had to stand close to animals they were hunting. As a result, people could hunt larger animals. Among the animals hunted by Stone Age people were deer, horses, bison, and elephantlike creatures called mammoths.

READING CHECK **Summarizing** How did tools improve during the Old Stone Age?

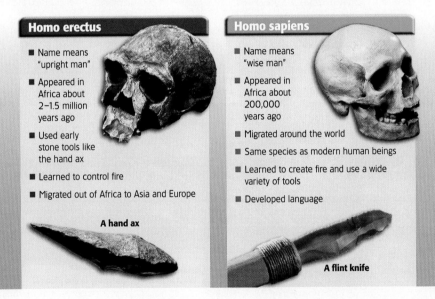

Homo erectus
- Name means "upright man"
- Appeared in Africa about 2–1.5 million years ago
- Used early stone tools like the hand ax
- Learned to control fire
- Migrated out of Africa to Asia and Europe

A hand ax

Homo sapiens
- Name means "wise man"
- Appeared in Africa about 200,000 years ago
- Migrated around the world
- Same species as modern human beings
- Learned to create fire and use a wide variety of tools
- Developed language

A flint knife

EARLY CIVILIZATIONS IN THE EASTERN HEMISPHERE **79**

Close-up
Hunter-Gatherers

1. Have students examine the images on this page. Discuss with students what life may have been like for the early hunter-gatherers.

2. Next, have students identify the various activities shown in the illustration. *hunting, painting on cave walls, cooking, gathering food, making tools*

3. Ask students to name some hardships that early hunter-gatherers faced, as suggested by the picture. *possible answers—limited protection from bad weather, limited food supply, had to rely on nearby resources since they only traveled on foot, dangerous animals* **LS** Visual/Spatial

Linking to Today
A New View of Hunter-Gatherers A site in central Texas now shows that some prehistoric people led a fairly settled life. At the 40-acre site, thick layers of earth blackened by cooking fires and countless stone flakes and tools indicate that people had settled there for thousands of years. Other evidence tells archaeologists that a wide range of plants and animals were available in the region. Because there was also a steady water supply along with the food sources, people could stay there for long periods of time instead of moving from place to place.

Close-up

Hunter-Gatherers

Early people were hunter-gatherers. They hunted animals and gathered wild plants to survive. Life for these hunter-gatherers was difficult and dangerous. Still, people learned how to make tools, use fire, and even create art.

Hunting
Most hunting was done by men. They worked together to bring down large animals.

Art
People painted herds of animals on cave walls.

Gathering
Most gathering was done by women. They gathered food like wild plants, seeds, fruits, and nuts.

Fire
People learned to use fire to cook their food.

Tools
Early people learned to make tools such as this spear for hunting.

ANALYSIS SKILL ANALYZING VISUALS
What tools are people using in this picture?

80 CHAPTER 4

Critical Thinking: Comparing and Contrasting   [At Level]

Creating a Venn Diagram

1. Have students examine the picture on this page, paying close attention to the roles that men and women may have played as hunter-gatherers.

2. Draw an example of a Venn diagram for students to see. Use the following labels: *Men's Chores, Women's Chores, Shared Chores.*

3. Next, have students copy the diagram and complete it by using the information shown in the illustration.

4. Review the answers students listed in their Venn diagrams as a class. **LS** Visual/Spatial, Logical/Mathematical

📝 Alternative Assessment Handbook, Rubric 13: Graphic Organizers

Answers
Analyzing Visuals *spears and bones*

Hunter-gatherer Societies

As early humans developed tools and new hunting techniques, they formed societies. A **society** is a community of people who share a common culture. These societies developed cultures with languages, religions, and art.

Society

Anthropologists believe that early humans lived in small groups. In bad weather they might have taken shelter in a cave if there was one nearby. When food or water became hard to find, groups of people would have to move to new areas.

The early humans of the Stone Age were **hunter-gatherers**—people who hunt animals and gather wild plants, seeds, fruits, and nuts to survive. Anthropologists believe that most Stone Age hunters were men. They hunted in groups, sometimes chasing entire herds of animals over cliffs. This method was both more productive and safer than hunting alone.

Women in hunter-gatherer societies probably took responsibility for collecting plants to eat. They likely stayed near camps and took care of children.

Language, Art, and Religion

The most important development of early Stone Age culture was language. Scientists have many theories about why language first developed. Some think it was to make hunting in groups easier. Others think it developed as a way for people to form relationships. Still others think language made it easier for people to resolve issues like how to **distribute** food.

Language wasn't the only way early people expressed themselves. They also created art. People carved figures out of stone, ivory, and bone. They painted and carved images of people and animals on cave walls. Scientists still aren't sure why people made art. Perhaps the cave paintings were used to teach people how to hunt, or maybe they had religious meanings.

ACADEMIC VOCABULARY

distribute to divide among a group of people

CONNECTING TO Technology

Stone Tools

Did you know that Stone Age people's tools weren't as primitive as we might think? They made knife blades and arrowheads—like the one shown below—out of volcanic glass called obsidian. The obsidian blades were very sharp. In fact, they could be 100 times sharper and smoother than the steel blades used for surgery in modern hospitals.

Today some doctors are going back to using these Stone Age materials. They have found that blades made from obsidian are more precise than modern scalpels. Some doctors use obsidian blades for delicate surgery on the face because the stone tools leave "nicer-looking" scars.

Drawing Conclusions How do you think modern obsidian blades are different from Stone Age ones?

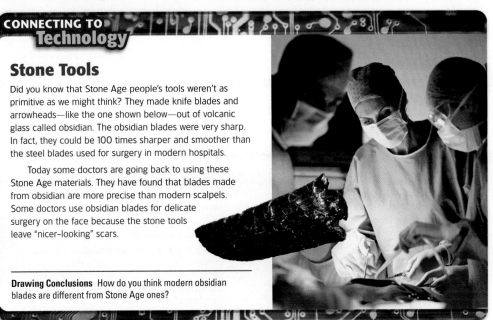

Main Idea

❹ Hunter-gatherer Societies

Hunter-gatherer societies developed language, art, and religion.

Define Who were hunter-gatherers? *early humans who hunted animals and gathered wild plants to survive*

Summarize How did early humans express themselves? *through language and art*

Draw Conclusions Why do you think hunting in groups was safer than hunting alone? *Groups offered protection against dangerous animals.*

📖 RF: Literature, *Boy of the Painted Cave*

Did you know . . .

Early humans used natural dyes from different colors of plants and berries to paint images on cave walls.

Checking for Understanding

True or False Answer each statement *T* if it is true or *F* if it is false. If false, explain why.

1. Historians use the term *prehistory* to refer to the time before there was writing. *T*
2. Scientists think the first tools were developed to use as weapons. *F; think they were developed to process food.*
3. An important development of *Homo erectus* was the ability to control fire. *T*

Collaborative Learning

At Level

Communicating Without Words

Materials: index cards

1. Discuss with students why language was so important to human development.

2. Organize students into pairs. Give one member of each pair a card with the sentence "I am thirsty." on it. Give the other student a card with the sentence "The rains washed away our food." Tell the students not to reveal what is written on their cards.

3. Have one member of each pair try to express what is on the card to the other

student without using words. Students can use drawings or body language to make themselves understood. Then have the other student try to express his or her statement.

4. After the activity, ask students to share how successful they were. What frustrations did they experience? Then lead a discussion about the ease or difficulty of communicating without words. **LS Interpersonal, Kinesthetic, Verbal/Linguistic**

📖 Alternative Assessment Handbook, Rubric 14: Group Activity

Answers

Connecting to Technology *They are more precise than modern scalpels and leave "nicer-looking" scars.*

Direct Teach

Info to Know

More Than a Pretty Picture Some cave paintings show not just animals that people hunted but also how predator animals hunted their own prey. For example, 32,000-year-old paintings in a Chauvet cave in France show now-extinct lions watching a herd of bison. The way the painter drew the lions with their heads down and their ears back shows that the artist had carefully observed the lions' behavior. In Africa today, lions pose the same way before rushing at their prey.

Review & Assess

Close

Have students summarize the important developments of hunter-gatherer societies covered in this section.

Review

Online Quiz, Section 1

Assess

SE Section 1 Assessment
PASS: Section 1 Quiz
Alternative Assessment Handbook

Reteach/Classroom Intervention

Interactive Reader and Study Guide, Section 1

Interactive Skills Tutor CD-ROM

Answers

Analyzing Visuals *shows animals that may have provided meat, hides, and other resources*

Reading Check *made it easier to hunt as a group, distribute food, and establish relationships*

82

Cave Paintings

Thousands of years ago, early people decorated cave walls with paintings like this one. No one knows for sure why people created cave paintings, but many historians think they were related to hunting.

ANALYZING VISUALS Why do you think this cave painting may be connected to hunting?

Scholars know little about the religious beliefs of early people. Archaeologists have found graves that included food and artifacts. Many scientists think these discoveries are proof that the first human religions developed during the Stone Age.

READING CHECK **Analyzing** What was one possible reason for the development of language?

SUMMARY AND PREVIEW Scientists have discovered and studied the remains of hominids and early humans who lived in East Africa millions of years ago. These Stone Age people were hunter-gatherers who used fire, stone tools, and language. In the next section you will learn how early humans moved out of Africa and populated the world.

Section 1 Assessment

go.hrw.com
Online Quiz
KEYWORD: SK9 HP4

Reviewing Ideas, Terms, and Places

1. **a. Identify** Who found the bones of Lucy?
   b. Explain Why do historians need archaeologists and anthropologists to study **prehistory**?
2. **a. Recall** What is the scientific name for modern humans?
   b. Make Inferences What might have been one advantage of walking completely upright?
3. **a. Recall** What kind of **tools** did people use during the **Paleolithic Era**?
   b. Design Design a stone and wood tool you could use to help you with your chores. Describe your tool in a sentence or two.
4. **a. Define** What is a **hunter-gatherer**?
   b. Rank In your opinion, what was the most important change brought by the development of language?

Critical Thinking

5. **Evaluate** Review the notes in your chart on the advances made by prehistoric humans. Using a graphic organizer like the one here, rank the three advances you think are most important. Next to your organizer, write a sentence explaining why you ranked the advances in that order.

FOCUS ON WRITING

6. **Listing Stone Age Achievements** Look back through this section and make a list of important Stone Age achievements. Which of these will you include on your storyboard? How will you illustrate them?

82 CHAPTER 4

Section 1 Assessment Answers

1. **a.** Donald Johanson
   b. because there are no written records from the earliest times of human development
2. **a.** *Homo sapiens*
   b. possible answers—Humans could use their hands, see farther, and perhaps travel faster.
3. **a.** stone choppers, axes, and spears
   b. Students' tools will vary, but descriptions should be logical.
4. **a.** a person who hunts animals and gathers wild plants, seeds, fruits, and nuts to survive
   b. possible answers—improved hunting; relationships formed; could more easily solve problems, such as how to distribute food
5. Rankings will vary, but students should justify their answers.
6. Lists and storyboards will vary, but students should support their selections.

The Iceman

Why was a Stone Age traveler in Europe's highest mountains?

The Iceman's dagger and the scabbard, or case, he carried it in

When did he live? about 5,300 years ago

Where did he live? The frozen body of the Iceman was discovered in the snowy Ötztal Alps of Italy in 1991. Scientists nicknamed him Ötzi after this location.

What did he do? That question has been debated ever since Ötzi's body was found. Apparently, he was traveling. At first scientists thought he had frozen to death in a storm. But an arrowhead found in his shoulder suggests that his death was not so peaceful. After he died, his body was covered by glaciers and preserved for thousands of years.

Why is he important? Ötzi is the oldest mummified human ever found in such good condition. His body, clothing, and tools were extremely well preserved, telling us a lot about life during the Stone Ages. His outfit was made of three types of animal skin stitched together. He wore leather shoes padded with grass, a grass cape, a fur hat, and a sort of backpack. He carried an ax with a copper blade as well as a bow and arrows.

Drawing Conclusions Why do you think the Iceman was in the Alps?

Scientists examine the Iceman's body in 1991, before it was removed from the glacier.

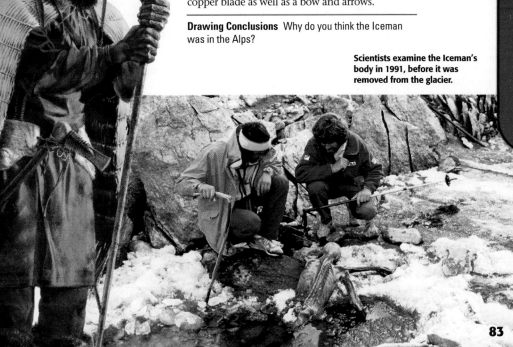

Reading Focus Question

Have students consider the basic needs of a person in the Stone Age, such as needs for food and shelter. Ask: What needs might this man have been trying to fill by climbing in the mountains? *possible answers—hunting, looking for materials to make clothing or shelter*

Did You Know . . .

The Iceman may have been hungry when he died. Scientists determined from studying a portion of the Iceman's intestine that he had not eaten within eight hours of his death.

About the Illustration

This illustration of the Iceman is an artist's conception based on available sources. However, historians are uncertain exactly what the Iceman looked like.

Answers

Drawing Conclusions *possible answers—He may have been hunting, escaping from the person or persons who may have killed him, or he could have been exiled from his people.*

Differentiating Instruction

Above Level

Advanced/Gifted and Talented

Research Required

1. Remind students that the Iceman's body was undiscovered for thousands of years. Only when surrounding ice had melted did climbers see the body.

2. Point out that archaeological sites both small and large are still being discovered. However, some sites are being destroyed. Warfare and rising waters from dam construction are two of the most common causes of this destruction.

3. Organize the class into two large groups—one to research recently discovered archaeological sites and the other to research sites that are being destroyed. Then have each group organize into smaller groups to conduct further research on individual sites within the two broad categories.

4. Ask each small group to prepare a presentation on its chosen site. Students should discuss what information the site may provide or has provided and its current condition. Encourage students to use visual aids to enhance their presentations.
LS Interpersonal, Verbal/Linguistic

Alternative Assessment Handbook, Rubrics 29: Presentations; and 30: Research

Bellringer

If YOU lived there . . . Use the **Daily Bellringer Transparency** to help students answer the question.

📦 Daily Bellringer Transparency, Section 2

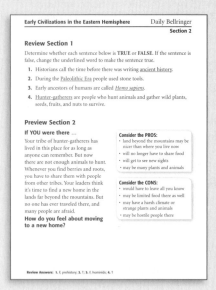

Key Terms

📖 RF: Vocabulary Builder, Section 2

Taking Notes

Have students copy the graphic organizer onto their own paper and then use it to take notes on the section. This activity will prepare students for the Section Assessment, in which they will complete a graphic organizer that builds on the information using the Critical Thinking Skill: Sequencing.

Early Human Migration

What You Will Learn...

Main Ideas

1. People moved out of Africa as the earth's climates changed.
2. People adapted to new environments by making clothing and new types of tools.

The Big Idea

As people migrated around the world they learned to adapt to new environments.

Key Terms

migrate, *p. 84*
ice ages, *p. 84*
land bridge, *p. 84*
Mesolithic Era, *p. 86*

TAKING NOTES As you read, take notes on the sequence and paths of migration of early humans. Record your notes in a graphic organizer like the one below. Add as many ovals as you need to record each stage of migration.

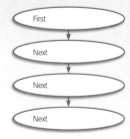

First
↓
Next
↓
Next
↓
Next

84

If **YOU** lived there...

Your tribe of hunter-gatherers has lived in this place for as long as anyone can remember. But now there are not enough animals to hunt. Whenever you find berries and roots, you have to share them with people from other tribes. Your leaders think it's time to find a new home in the lands far beyond the mountains. But no one has ever traveled there, and many people are afraid.

How do you feel about moving to a new home?

BUILDING BACKGROUND From their beginnings in East Africa, early humans moved in many directions. Eventually, they lived on almost every continent in the world. People probably had many reasons for moving. One reason was a change in the climate.

People Move Out of Africa

During the Old Stone Age, climate patterns around the world changed, transforming the earth's geography. In response to these changes, people began to **migrate**, or move, to new places.

The Ice Ages

Most scientists believe that about 1.6 million years ago, many places around the world began to experience long periods of freezing weather. These freezing times are called the **ice ages**. The ice ages ended about 10,000 years ago.

During the ice ages huge sheets of ice covered much of the earth's land. These ice sheets were formed from ocean water, leaving ocean levels lower than they are now. Many areas that are now underwater were dry land then. For example, a narrow body of water now separates Asia and North America. But scientists think that during the ice ages, the ocean level dropped and exposed a **land bridge**, a strip of land connecting two continents. Land bridges allowed Stone Age peoples to migrate around the world.

Teach the Big Idea   At Level

Early Human Migration

1. **Teach** Ask students the questions in the Main Idea boxes under Direct Teach.

2. **Apply** Organize students into small groups. Ask students to imagine that flooding has forced them to move from dwellings near a river to a colder, mountainous, and rocky environment. Have groups write down ways they could adapt to and survive in this new environment. **LS Interpersonal, Logical/ Mathematical**

3. **Review** Have volunteers from each group share their suggestions.

4. **Practice/Homework** Have each student write a short journal entry about this imaginary trek from one environment to another, including how people eventually settled in the new environment.
LS Verbal/Linguistic

📓 Alternative Assessment Handbook, Rubric 15: Journals

Early Human Migration

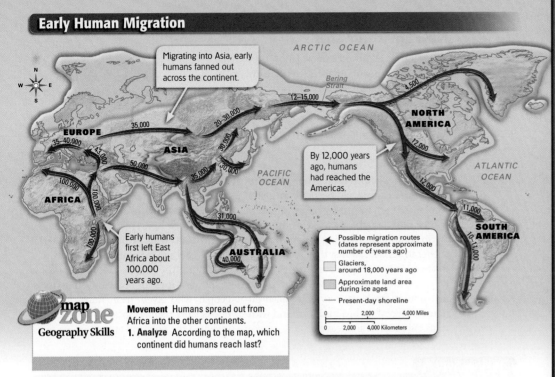

Migrating into Asia, early humans fanned out across the continent.

ARCTIC OCEAN

Bering Strait

4,500

12–15,000

NORTH AMERICA

35,000

20–30,000

30,000

EUROPE

35–40,000

43,000

50,000

ASIA

35,000

30,000

12,000

ATLANTIC OCEAN

PACIFIC OCEAN

By 12,000 years ago, humans had reached the Americas.

100,000

AFRICA

100,000

100,000

31,000

Early humans first left East Africa about 100,000 years ago.

AUSTRALIA

40,000

12,000

SOUTH AMERICA

11,000

10–11,000

Possible migration routes (dates represent approximate number of years ago)

Glaciers, around 18,000 years ago

Approximate land area during ice ages

Present-day shoreline

0   2,000   4,000 Miles

0   2,000   4,000 Kilometers

map zone

Geography Skills

Movement Humans spread out from Africa into the other continents.

1. Analyze According to the map, which continent did humans reach last?

Settling New Lands

Scientists agree that migration around the world took hundreds of thousands of years. Early hominids, the ancestors of modern humans, migrated from Africa to Asia as early as 2 million years ago. From there, they spread to Southeast Asia and Europe.

Later, humans also began to migrate around the world, and earlier hominids died out. Look at the map to see the dates and routes of early human migration.

Humans began to migrate from East Africa to southern Africa and southwestern Asia around 100,000 years ago. From there, people moved east across southern Asia. They could then migrate to Australia. Scientists are not sure exactly how the first people reached Australia. Even though ocean levels were lower then, there was always open sea between Asia and Australia.

From southwestern Asia, humans also migrated north into Europe. Geographic features such as high mountains and cold temperatures delayed migration northward into northern Asia. Eventually, however, people from both Europe and southern Asia moved into that region.

From northern Asia, people moved into North America. Scientists disagree on when and how the first people arrived in North America. Most scholars think people must have crossed a land bridge from Asia to North America. Once in North America, these people moved south, following herds of animals and settling South America. By 9000 BC, humans lived on all continents of the world except Antarctica.

READING CHECK **Analyzing** How did the ice ages influence human migration?

EARLY CIVILIZATIONS IN THE EASTERN HEMISPHERE **85**

❷ People Adapt to New Environments

People adapted to new environments by making clothing and new types of tools.

Explain Why did early humans build shelters? *because they migrated to colder climates*

Recall What types of shelters did early people use? *caves; when no caves available—pit houses, tents, or structures of wood, stone, clay, or other materials*

Elaborate How did new techniques change the daily lives of Middle Stone Age people? *Hooks, fishing spears, bows and arrows, canoes, and pottery enabled people to find new food sources, store various goods, and travel by water. Keeping dogs helped people hunt more efficiently and warned people of dangerous animals or intruders.*

Info to Know

A Third Theory Some archaeologists propose another origin for the first Americans—Europe. This theory says that early Europeans braved the North Atlantic in boats that may have been like those made by modern Arctic Inuit peoples. Similar spear points have been found in Europe and the Americas, which led some archaeologists to develop the new theory.

Answers

Analyzing Primary Sources *possible answer—New discoveries can provide new information and interpretations.*

People Adapt to New Environments

As early people moved to new lands, they found environments that differed greatly from those in East Africa. Many places were much colder and had strange plants and animals. Early people had to learn to adapt to their new environments.

Clothing and Shelter

Although fire helped keep people warm in very cold areas, people needed more protection. To keep warm, they learned to sew animal skins together to make clothing.

In addition to clothing, people needed shelter to survive. At first they took shelter in caves. When they moved to areas with no caves, they built their own shelters. The first human-made shelters were called pit houses. They were pits in the ground with roofs of branches and leaves.

Later, people began to build homes above the ground. Some lived in tents made of animal skins. Others built more permanent structures of wood, stone, clay, or other materials. Even bones from large animals such as mammoths were used in building shelters.

New Tools and Technologies

People also adapted to new environments with new types of tools. These tools were smaller and more complex than tools from the Old Stone Age. They defined the **Mesolithic** (me-zuh-LI-thik) **Era**, or the Middle Stone Age. This period began more than 10,000 years ago and lasted to about 5,000 years ago in some places.

During the Middle Stone Age, people found new uses for bone and stone tools. People who lived near water invented hooks and fishing spears. Other groups invented the bow and arrow.

Primary Source

POINTS OF VIEW
Views of Migration to the Americas

For many years scientists were fairly certain that the first Americans came from Asia, following big game through an ice-free path in the glaciers.

❝Doubtless it was a formidable [challenging] place . . . an ice-walled valley of frigid winds, fierce snows, and clinging fogs . . . yet grazing animals would have entered, and behind them would have come a rivulet [stream] of human hunters.❞

—Thomas Canby,
1979, quoted in *Kingdoms of Gold, Kingdoms of Jade* by Brian M. Fagan

New discoveries have challenged beliefs about the first Americans. Some scientists now are not so sure the first Americans came along an ice-free path in the glaciers.

❝There's no reason people couldn't have come along the coast, skirting [going around] the glaciers just the way recreational kayakers do today.❞

—James Dixon,
quoted in *National Geographic,*
December 2000

ANALYSIS SKILL **ANALYZING PRIMARY SOURCES**
Why might a scientist change his or her mind about a long-held belief?

86 CHAPTER 4

Critical Thinking: Drawing Conclusions   At Level

Views of Migration

1. Read aloud the quote by Thomas Canby. Ask students whether the journey he describes would have been difficult or easy. Ask students to pick out words or phrases from the quote that support their opinions.

2. Then display a map of the Western Hemisphere. Call on volunteers to point out the routes proposed by the two archaeologists in the feature—across land from northwestern Asia (Canby) and by boat from Asia along the Pacific coast (Dixon).

3. Have students write one to three paragraphs about which theory they think is more logical. Remind students to provide reasons to support their opinions.
LS Logical/Mathematical, Verbal/Linguistic

Alternative Assessment Handbook, Rubric 43: Writing to Persuade

A Mammoth House

Early people used whatever was available to make shelters. In Central Asia, where wood was scarce, some early people made their homes from mammoth bones.

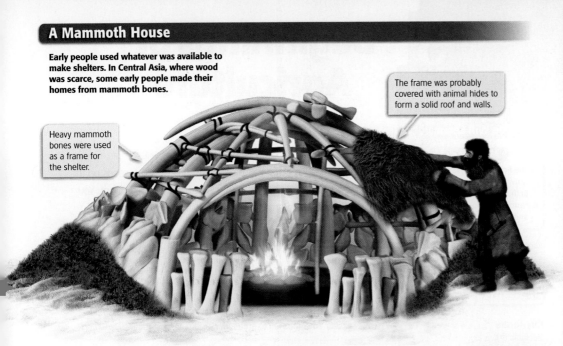

The frame was probably covered with animal hides to form a solid roof and walls.

Heavy mammoth bones were used as a frame for the shelter.

In addition to tools, people developed new technologies to improve their lives. For example, some learned to make canoes by hollowing out logs. They used the canoes to travel on rivers and lakes. They also began to make pottery. The first pets may also have appeared at this time. People kept dogs to help them hunt and for protection. Developments like these, in addition to clothing and shelter, allowed people to adapt to new environments.

READING CHECK Finding Main Ideas

What were two ways people adapted to new environments?

SUMMARY AND PREVIEW Early people adapted to new environments with new kinds of clothing, shelter, and tools. In Section 3 you will read about how Stone Age peoples developed farming.

Section 2 Assessment

go.hrw.com
Online Quiz
KEYWORD: SK9 HP4

Reviewing Ideas, Terms, and Places

1. **a. Define** What is a **land bridge**?
   b. Analyze Why did it take so long for early people to reach South America?
2. **a. Recall** What did people use to make tools in the **Mesolithic Era**?
   b. Summarize Why did people have to learn to make clothes and build shelters?

Critical Thinking

3. **Sequencing** Draw the organizer below. Use your notes and sequence chain to show the path of migration around the world.

FOCUS ON WRITING

4. **Illustrating** How will you illustrate early migration on your storyboard? Draw some sketches. How does this information relate to your ideas from Section 1?

EARLY CIVILIZATIONS IN THE EASTERN HEMISPHERE **87**

Bellringer

If YOU lived there . . . Use the **Daily Bellringer Transparency** to help students answer the question.

🖺 Daily Bellringer Transparency, Section 3

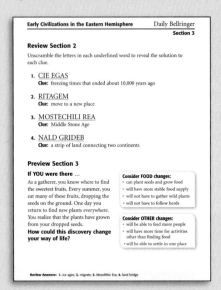

Academic Vocabulary

Review with students the high-use academic term in this section.

development creation (p. 90)

📝 **RF:** Vocabulary Builder, Section 3

Taking Notes

Have students copy the graphic organizer onto their own paper and then use it to take notes on the section. This activity will prepare students for the Section Assessment, in which they will complete a graphic organizer that builds on the information using the Critical Thinking Skill: Identifying Cause and Effect.

SECTION 3

Beginnings of Agriculture

What You Will Learn...

Main Ideas

1. The first farmers learned to grow plants and raise animals in the New Stone Age.
2. Farming changed societies and the way people lived.

The Big Idea

The development of agriculture brought great changes to human society.

Key Terms

Neolithic Era, *p. 89*
domestication, *p. 89*
agriculture, *p. 90*
megaliths, *p. 90*

TAKING NOTES As you read, take notes on the different changes related to the development of agriculture. Use a diagram like the one below to help organize your information.

Change in	Details
Climate	
Use of plants	
Use of animals	
Daily life	

If YOU lived there...

As a gatherer, you know where to find the sweetest fruits. Every summer, you eat many of these fruits, dropping the seeds on the ground. One day you return to find new plants everywhere. You realize that the plants have grown from your dropped seeds.

How could this discovery change your way of life?

BUILDING BACKGROUND The discovery that plants grew from seeds was one of the major advances of the late Stone Age. Other similar advances led to great changes in the way people lived.

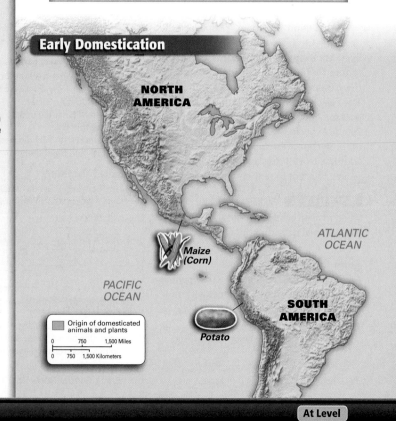

Early Domestication

NORTH AMERICA

ATLANTIC OCEAN

Maize (Corn)

PACIFIC OCEAN

SOUTH AMERICA

Potato

Origin of domesticated animals and plants

0   750   1,500 Miles
0 750 1,500 Kilometers

88

Teach the Big Idea

At Level

Beginnings of Agriculture

1. **Teach** Ask students the questions in the Main Idea boxes under Direct Teach.

2. **Apply** Draw a circle labeled *Beginnings of Agriculture* for students to see and copy. Call on students to identify basic changes in human societies caused by the development of agriculture. Add these suggestions to create an idea web. **LS Visual/Spatial**

3. **Review** Call on other volunteers to expand the web by suggesting further developments that could have been caused by the basic

changes. For example, building megaliths may have inspired new stonecutting techniques.

4. **Practice/Homework** Have students add to their idea webs by connecting elements already suggested and illustrating the webs. **LS Visual/Spatial**

📝 Alternative Assessment Handbook, Rubric 13: Graphic Organizers

The First Farmers

After the Middle Stone Age came a period of time that scientists call the **Neolithic** (nee·uh·LI·thik) **Era**, or New Stone Age. It began as early as 10,000 years ago in Southwest Asia. In other places, this era began much later and lasted much longer than it did there.

During the New Stone Age people learned to polish stones to make tools like saws and drills. People also learned how to make fire. Before, they could only use fire that had been started by natural causes such as lightning.

The New Stone Age ended in Egypt and Southwest Asia about 5,000 years ago, when toolmakers began to make tools out of metal. But tools weren't the only major change that occurred during the Neolithic Era. In fact, the biggest changes came in how people produced food.

Plants

After a warming trend brought an end to the ice ages, new plants began to grow in some areas. For example, wild barley and wheat plants started to spread throughout Southwest Asia. Over time, people came to depend on these wild plants for food. They began to settle where grains grew.

People soon learned that they could plant seeds themselves to grow their own crops. Historians call the shift from food gathering to food producing the Neolithic Revolution. Most experts believe that this revolution, or change, first occurred in the societies of Southwest Asia.

Eventually, people learned to change plants to make them more useful. They planted only the largest grains or the sweetest fruits. The process of changing plants or animals to make them more useful to humans is called **domestication**.

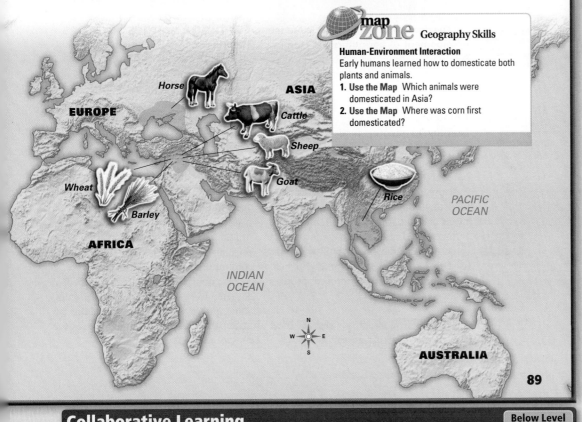

 **Geography Skills**

Human-Environment Interaction
Early humans learned how to domesticate both plants and animals.
1. **Use the Map** Which animals were domesticated in Asia?
2. **Use the Map** Where was corn first domesticated?

89

Direct Teach

Main Idea

❶ The First Farmers

The first farmers learned to grow plants and raise animals in the Stone Age.

Define What was the Neolithic Revolution? *the shift from food gathering to food producing*

Contrast What is the difference between the domestication of plants and simply planting seeds? *Domestication involves changing the plants to make them more useful.*

Rate Which do you think had more significant results—the domestication of plants or of animals? *possible answers—plants, because plants were more important food sources and people could still hunt; animals, because they helped with tasks besides farming, such as pulling loads of building materials.*

Map Zone Transparency: Early Domestication

Info to Know

Cats and People People domesticated cats not just for catching rats and mice, but also for companionship. In fact, the domestication of cats may have started some 9,500 years ago. This date comes from the earliest known burial of a cat with a human, found in 2004 in Cyprus. Archaeologists have concluded that the cat was the human's pet.

Answers

Map Zone 1. *cattle, sheep, goats, and rice* **2.** *southern part of North America*

Main Idea

❷ Farming Changes Societies

Farming changed societies and the way people lived.

Define What are megaliths? *huge stones used as monuments*

Identify What gods did people in the Neolithic Age probably believe in? *those associated with the four elements—air, water, fire, and earth—or with animals*

Draw Conclusions How did a change in the use of fire demonstrate human ingenuity? *People learned how to make fire, not just use fire that had been started by natural causes.*

📓 **RF:** Primary Source, Objects from Çatal Hüyük

Did you know...

Not all of the changes brought about by agriculture were positive. Although people in farming communities had more food, they did not eat the same variety of foods as hunter-gatherers did. In addition, the presence of animals in or near human communities brought new diseases.

Linking to Today

Major Megaliths A group of huge shaped stones was raised at Stonehenge in southern England starting in about 3100 BC. Neolithic people may have used Stonehenge for predicting the seasons and for religious ceremonies.

Answers

Reading Check *possible answers— People stopped moving around to find food, populations grew with better control of food production, and towns developed in some areas.*

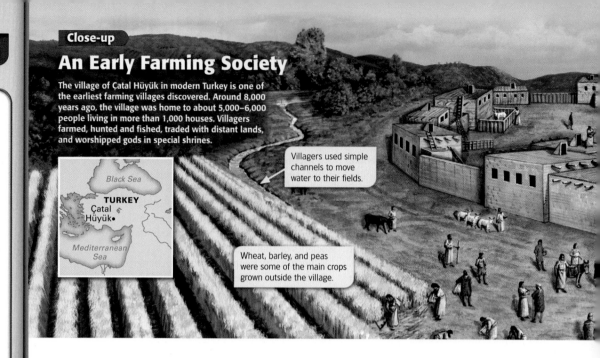

Close-up

An Early Farming Society

The village of Çatal Hüyük in modern Turkey is one of the earliest farming villages discovered. Around 8,000 years ago, the village was home to about 5,000–6,000 people living in more than 1,000 houses. Villagers farmed, hunted and fished, traded with distant lands, and worshipped gods in special shrines.

Black Sea
TURKEY
Çatal
Hüyük●
Mediterranean Sea

Villagers used simple channels to move water to their fields.

Wheat, barley, and peas were some of the main crops grown outside the village.

ACADEMIC VOCABULARY
development
creation

THE IMPACT TODAY
One famous megalith, Stonehenge in England, attracts millions of curious tourists and scholars each year.

The domestication of plants led to the **development** of **agriculture**, or farming. For the first time, people could produce their own food. This development changed human society forever.

Animals

Learning to produce food was a major accomplishment for early people. But learning how to use animals for their own purposes was almost equally important.

Hunters didn't have to follow wild herds anymore. Instead, farmers could keep sheep or goats for milk, food, and wool. Farmers could also use large animals like cattle to carry loads or to pull large tools used in farming. Using animals to help with farming greatly improved people's chances of surviving.

READING CHECK Identifying Cause and Effect
What was one effect of the switch to farming?

Farming Changes Societies

The Neolithic Revolution brought huge changes to people's lives. With survival more certain, people could focus on activities other than finding food.

Domestication of plants and animals enabled people to use plant fibers to make cloth. The domestication of animals made it possible to use wool from goats and sheep and skins from horses for clothes.

People also began to build permanent settlements. As they started raising crops and animals, they needed to stay in one place. Then, once people were able to control their own food production, the world's population grew. In some areas farming communities developed into towns.

As populations grew, groups of people gathered to perform religious ceremonies. Some put up megaliths. **Megaliths** are huge stones used as monuments or as the sites for religious gatherings.

90 CHAPTER 4

Critical Thinking: Summarizing

At Level | **Standard English Mastery**

A Day in the Life

1. Discuss with students how domestication of plants and animals changed how Neolithic people lived day-to-day.

2. Have each student write a journal entry describing a day in the life of a Neolithic farm family. Ask students to include such details as the crops and animals on the farm. Remind students to use standard English in their journal entries. Work with individual students as needed.

3. Ask volunteers to read their journal entries to the class.

4. **Extend** To extend the activity, ask students to add another journal entry in which the farmer reflects on stories he or she has heard about what daily life for the local people used to be like before farming. **L5 Verbal/Linguistic**

📓 Alternative Assessment Handbook, Rubric 15: Journals

Houses were made of wood covered with mud. Since they didn't have doors, people entered on ladders through rooftop openings.

Inside their houses, villagers made the earliest known wooden bowls and cups, pottery, and mirrors.

Some houses were built as shrines and had small statues of goddesses and large sculpted bulls' heads.

ANALYSIS SKILL **ANALYZING VISUALS**

How did farmers get water to their fields?

Early people probably believed in gods and goddesses associated with the four elements—air, water, fire, and earth—or with animals. For example, one European group honored a thunder god, while another group worshipped bulls. Some scholars also believe that prehistoric peoples also prayed to their ancestors. People in some societies today still hold many of these same beliefs.

READING CHECK Analyzing How did farming contribute to the growth of towns?

SUMMARY AND PREVIEW Stone Age peoples adapted to new environments by domesticating plants and animals. These changes led to the development of civilizations. In the next unit, you will learn about some early civilizations in the Eastern Hemisphere.

Section 3 Assessment

go.hrw.com
Online Quiz
KEYWORD: SK9 HP4

Reviewing Ideas, Terms, and Places

1. **a. Define** What is **domestication** of a plant or animal?
   b. Make Generalizations How did early people use domesticated animals?
2. **a. Describe** What were gods and goddesses probably associated with in prehistoric religion?
   b. Explain How did domestication of plants and animals lead to the development of towns?

Critical Thinking

3. **Identifying Cause and Effect** Copy the graphic organizer at right. Use it to show one cause and three effects of the development of agriculture.

Cause

↓

Development of agriculture

↓

Effects

FOCUS ON WRITING

4. **Beginnings of Agriculture** Now that you've read about the birth of agriculture, you're ready to plan your storyboard. Look back through your notes from previous sections and the text of this one. Make a list of the events and ideas you will include on your storyboard. Then plan how you will arrange these items.

EARLY CIVILIZATIONS IN THE EASTERN HEMISPHERE **91**

Section 3 Assessment Answers

1. **a.** changing a plant or animal to make it more useful to humans
   b. for milk, food, and/or wool; for carrying loads or pulling tools used in farming

2. **a.** earth, air, fire, and water or animals
   b. People settled in one place to grow crops and tend animals, and better control of food production enabled populations to grow.

3. cause—Warming trend after ice ages caused new plants to grow; effects—could produce own food, easier to farm, new kinds of clothing, populations grew, settlements became towns, religion more organized

4. Notes should include changes in climate, domestication of plants and animals, growth of populations and settlements, and the emergence of religious ceremonies.

91

Linking to Today

Aswan High Dam Egyptians lived by the flooding cycle of the Nile River for thousands of years. In 1970, however, Egypt built the Aswan High Dam. This dam is 364 feet (111 m.) high and more than two miles (3.2 km.) long at the top. The dam created Lake Nasser. The Aswan dam generates large amounts of electricity and provides irrigation to many parts of the Nile River Valley.

Activity **Cause-and-Effect Chart** Ask students to imagine that they are in a boat floating down either the Tigris or Euphrates River in ancient Mesopotamia. What might be some of the sights and activities they see on their trip? *Students might suggest farming, irrigation, and people in boats fishing or traveling like them.* Then have each student create a chart showing the causes and effects of settlement and farming in river valleys as shown along the river during their voyages. *causes— see introduction text at right; effects— see captions at right* **LS Verbal/Linguistic**

Alternative Assessment Handbook, Rubrics 6: Cause and Effect; and 7: Charts

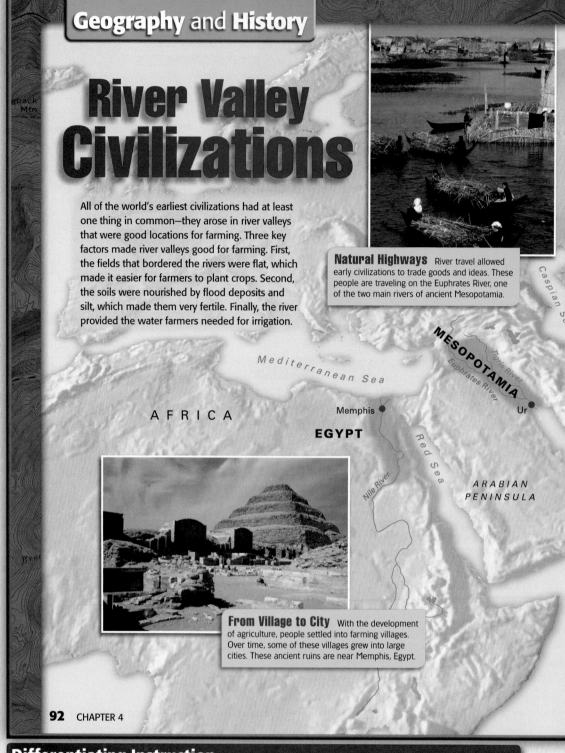

Geography and History

River Valley Civilizations

All of the world's earliest civilizations had at least one thing in common—they arose in river valleys that were good locations for farming. Three key factors made river valleys good for farming. First, the fields that bordered the rivers were flat, which made it easier for farmers to plant crops. Second, the soils were nourished by flood deposits and silt, which made them very fertile. Finally, the river provided the water farmers needed for irrigation.

Natural Highways River travel allowed early civilizations to trade goods and ideas. These people are traveling on the Euphrates River, one of the two main rivers of ancient Mesopotamia.

Caspian Sea

MESOPOTAMIA

Tigris River

Euphrates River

Mediterranean Sea

AFRICA

Memphis

EGYPT

Ur

Red Sea

Nile River

ARABIAN PENINSULA

From Village to City With the development of agriculture, people settled into farming villages. Over time, some of these villages grew into large cities. These ancient ruins are near Memphis, Egypt.

92 CHAPTER 4

Differentiating Instruction

Struggling Readers   Below Level

To help struggling readers, have them match the text to the images in the above feature. Read aloud the introduction and each caption. As you do, have students identify images and map elements that correspond to the text, such as cities and river highways. Remind students that this book has many illustrations that can help them learn.

LS Visual/Spatial

Alternative Assessment Handbook, Rubric 21: Map Reading

Advanced /Gifted and Talented   Above Level

Have students discuss how people rely on rivers today. Write students' responses for the class to see. If you have any rivers in your area, ask students if they know how these rivers are used. Then, encourage volunteers to share ways they have seen rivers being used. Remind students that people around the world are dependent on rivers.

LS Verbal/Linguistic

Alternative Assessment Handbook, Rubric 11: Discussions

Gifts of the River River water was key to farming in early civilizations. This farmer is using water from the Huang He (Yellow River) in China to water her crops.

ASIA

New Activities Food surpluses allowed people to pursue other activities, like crafts, art, and writing. This tile designer lives in the Indus Valley.

Harappa

H I M A L A Y A S

Indus River

Mohenjo Daro

INDUS VALLEY

Ganges River

CHINA

Huang He (Yellow River)

Chang Jiang (Yangzi River)

INDIA

Arabian Sea

Bay of Bengal

N W E S

River valley

0   500   1,000 Miles
0   500   1,000 Kilometers

INDIAN OCEAN

map zone Geography Skills

Human-Environment Interaction Four of the world's earliest civilizations arose on the banks of large rivers.
1. **Locate** Where were the four earliest river valley civilizations located?
2. **Explain** Why did the world's first civilizations all develop in river valleys?

EARLY CIVILIZATIONS IN THE EASTERN HEMISPHERE **93**

Social Studies Skills

Chart and Graph	Critical Thinking	Geography	Study

Understanding Chronological Terms

Learn

To learn about social studies, there are certain words and terms you need to know. Many of these terms deal with the passage of time. Study the terms listed in the table below. Knowing what these terms mean will help you make sense of what you read during this course.

Practice

Use the table below to answer the following questions.

❶ Were you born in a BC year or an AD year?

❷ Which is longer, a decade or a century? A century or a millennium?

❸ If you saw that an event happened c. AD 1000, what would that mean?

Chronological Terms

Terms to identify periods of time	Decade	A period of 10 years
	Century	A period of 100 years
	Millennium	A period of 1,000 years
	Age	A long period of time marked by a single cultural feature
	Era	A long period of time marked by great events, developments, or figures
	Ancient	Very old, or from a long time ago
Terms used with dates	circa, or c.	a word used to show that historians are not sure of an exact date; it means "about"
	BC	a term used to identify dates that occurred long ago, before the birth of Jesus Christ, the founder of Christianity; it means "before Christ." BC dates get smaller as time passes, so the larger the number the earlier the date.
	AD	a term used to identify dates that occurred after Jesus's birth; it comes from a Latin phrase that means "in the year of our Lord." Unlike BC dates, AD dates get larger as time passes, so the larger the number the later the date.
	BCE	another way to refer to BC dates; it stands for "before the common era"
	CE	another way to refer to AD dates; it stands for "common era"

Apply

Historians often refer to the decades or centuries by name. For example, the decade from 1960 to 1969 was the 1960s. The century that lasted from AD 1 to 100 was the first century, and the one that lasted from 1901 to 2000 was the twentieth century. Make a list of the year, decade, and century in which you were born.

94 CHAPTER 4

Social Studies Skills

Understanding Chronological
Activity Chronological Terms Narrative

1. Review the information in this Social Studies Skills feature with students. Be sure students understand each of the terms in the "Chronological Terms" table.

2. On notebook paper, have students write a short, one page or less narrative using each of the terms in the "Chronological Terms" table. Narratives can be fictional, but each of the terms should be used correctly.

3. When students have finished with their narratives, have volunteers share their narratives with the class. Correct any misuse of the chronological terms you may notice. Emphasize any particularly good usage of the chronological terms. **LS Visual/Spatial**

📖 Alternative Assessment Handbook, Rubric 37: Writing Assignments

📖 **RF:** Social Studies Skills, Understanding Chronological Terms

Answers

Practice 1. *an AD year;* **2.** *a century; a millennium;* **3.** *that the event happened approximately one millennium ago*

Apply *Students' answers will vary. possible answer—1995, the 1990s, the twentieth century*

94

Social Studies Skills Activity: Understanding Chronological Terms

Struggling Readers   [Below Level]

Have students close their textbooks. Then read the definition of one of the chronological terms at random. Call on students to supply the correct chronological term to match the definition. When all terms have been covered, repeat the process, but in reverse. Say one of the chronological terms aloud, and have students supply the definition. **LS Verbal/Linguistic**

📖 Alternative Assessment Handbook, Rubric 18: Listening

English-Language Learners   [At Level]

On a sheet of notebook paper, have students write one sentence for each chronological term. Sentences must include the chronological term and the term's definition. For example, "When I turned ten years old, I had been alive for exactly one decade." When students have finished, call on volunteers to share their sentences with the class. **LS Verbal/Linguistic**

📖 Alternative Assessment Handbook, Rubric 37: Writing Assignments

Chapter Review

Geography's Impact

video series
Review the video to answer the closing question:
Why do you think some peoples must work to preserve their culture in the modern world?

Visual Summary

Use the visual summary below to help you review the main ideas of the chapter.

QUICK FACTS

Scholars have discovered the earliest evidence of humans in Africa.

Humans migrated around the world, adapting to new environments.

Eventually, people learned how to farm and raise animals.

Reviewing Vocabulary, Terms, and Places

For each group of terms below, write a sentence that shows how all the terms in the group are related.

1. prehistory
   ancestor
   hominid

2. domestication
   Neolithic Era
   agriculture

3. Paleolithic Era
   tool
   hunter-gatherers
   develop

4. land bridge
   ice ages
   migrate

5. society
   megaliths
   Neolithic Era

Comprehension and Critical Thinking

SECTION 1 *(Pages 76–82)*

6. a. Recall What does *Homo sapiens* mean? When may *Homo sapiens* have first appeared in Africa?

b. Draw Conclusions If you were an archaeologist and found bead jewelry and stone chopping tools in an ancient woman's grave, what may you conclude?

c. Elaborate How did stone tools change over time? Why do you think these changes took place so slowly?

SECTION 2 *(Pages 84–87)*

7. a. Describe What new skills did people develop to help them survive?

b. Analyze How did global climate change affect the migration of early people?

c. Evaluate About 15,000 years ago, where do you think life would have been more difficult— in eastern Africa or northern Europe? Why?

EARLY CIVILIZATIONS IN THE EASTERN HEMISPHERE **95**

Answers

Visual Summary

Review and Inquiry Use the visual summary to review the chapter's main ideas. Ask students to provide details about what daily life may have been like in the early civilizations of the Eastern Hemisphere.

Quick Facts Transparency: Visual Summary: Early Civilizations in the Eastern Hemisphere

Reviewing Vocabulary, Terms, and Places

1. possible answer—Hominids, the ancestors of humans, lived during a time we call prehistory.

2. possible answer—During the Neolithic Era, the domestication of plants and animals led to agriculture.

3. possible answer—Hunter-gatherers developed stone tools during the Paleolithic Era.

4. possible answer—People might have migrated across a land bridge to get to North America during the ice ages.

5. possible answer—A Neolithic Era society might have used megaliths in religious ceremonies.

Comprehension and Critical Thinking

6. a. "wise man"; 200,000 years ago

b. possible answer—that the people who buried her had some form of religion

---

Review and Assessment Resources

Review and Reinforce

SE Chapter Review

RF: Chapter Review

Quick Facts Transparency: Visual Summary: Early Civilizations in the Eastern Hemisphere

Spanish Chapter Summaries Audio CD Program

OSP Holt PuzzlePro; Quiz Show for ExamView

Quiz Game CD-ROM

Assess

SE Standardized Test Practice

PASS: Chapter Test, Forms A and B

Alternative Assessment Handbook

OSP ExamView Test Generator, Chapter Test

Differentiated Instruction Modified Worksheets and Tests CD-ROM: Chapter Test

HOAP Holt Online Assessment Program (in the Premier Online Edition)

Reteach/Intervene

Interactive Reader and Study Guide

Differentiated Instruction Teacher Management System: Lesson Plans

Differentiated Instruction Modified Worksheets and Tests CD-ROM

Interactive Skills Tutor CD-ROM

go.hrw.com
Online Resources

Chapter Resources:
KEYWORD: SK9 CH4

c. went from choppers to using flint and having handles; possible answers—because the old tools worked well enough, better materials were not readily available, or early people couldn't communicate well enough to discuss improvements

7. a. how to make clothing, build shelters, make more complex tools, find new uses for tools, make canoes and pottery, tame dogs

b. created land bridge that allowed people to migrate from northern Asia to the Americas

c. possible answer—northern Europe, because the ice ages would have made survival there difficult

8. a. the shift from food gathering to food producing

b. allowed people to settle down and create towns

c. possible answers—Stone was readily available and long-lasting; large stone structures could be seen from far away; or building with stone required much labor but few tools.

Using the Internet

9. Go to the HRW Web site and enter the keyword shown to access a rubric for this activity.

KEYWORD: SK9 TEACHER

SECTION 3 *(Pages 88–91)*

8. a. **Define** What was the Neolithic Revolution?

b. **Make Inferences** How did domestication of plants and animals change early societies?

c. **Predict** Why do you think people of the Neolithic Era put up megaliths instead of some other kind of monuments?

Using the Internet
go.hrw.com
KEYWORD: SK9 CH4

9. **Activity: Creating a Skit** In the beginning of the Paleolithic Era, or the Old Stone Age, early humans used modified stones as tools. As the Stone Age progressed, plants and animals became materials for tools too. Enter the activity keyword and research the development of tools and the use of fire. Then create a skit that tells about an early human society discovering fire, creating a new tool, or developing a new way of doing a task.

FOCUS ON READING AND WRITING

Understanding Main Ideas *Read the paragraph below carefully, then write out the main idea of the paragraph.*

10. In addition to tools, people developed new technologies to improve their lives. For example, some learned to make canoes by hollowing out logs. They also began to make pottery. The first pets may also have appeared at this time.

Creating Your Storyboard *Use your notes and the instructions below to help you create a storyboard.*

11. What images will you include in each frame of the storyboard? How many frames will you need to tell the story a prehistoric people? How will you represent your ideas visually?

After you have sketched an outline for your storyboard, begin drawing it. Be sure to include all significant adaptations and developments made by prehistoric people, and don't worry if you can't draw that well. If you like, you might want to draw your storyboard in the simple style of prehistoric cave paintings. As the last frame in your storyboard, write a detailed summary to conclude your story.

Social Studies Skills

Understanding Chronological Terms *Use your knowledge of historical terms to answer the following questions.*

12. What is the term for a period of 100 years?

13. Put the following dates in order: AD 2000, 3100 BC, 15 BCE, AD 476, AD 2, CE 1215.

Map Activity

14. **Early Migration** Using the map below, list the following continents in the order in which they were first settled by humans.

Africa   Australia
Asia   Europe

go.hrw.com

Focus on Reading and Writing

10. People developed new technologies to improve their lives.

RF: Focus on Reading, Understanding Main Ideas

11. **Rubric** Students' storyboards should:

• include numbered panels.

• feature clear but simple sketches.

• end with a clear summary.

RF: Focus on Writing, Creating a Storyboard

Social Studies Skills

12. century

13. 3100 BC, 15 BCE, AD 2, AD 476, CE 1215, AD 2000

Map Activity

14. Africa, Asia, Europe, Australia

Answers

DIRECTIONS (1–7): For each statement or question, write on a separate answer sheet the *number* of the word or expression that, of those given, best completes the statement or answers the question.

1 The earliest humans lived
(1) by hunting and gathering their food.
(2) as herders of sheep and other livestock.
(3) alone or in pairs.
(4) in farming villages along rivers and streams.

2 The development of farming brought all of the following changes to the lives of early humans *except*
(1) the first human-made shelters.
(2) a larger supply of food.
(3) the construction of permanent settlements.
(4) new types of clothing.

3 The region of the world that was likely occupied *last* by early humans was
(1) northern Asia.
(2) southern Asia.
(3) North America.
(4) South America.

4 Hunter-gatherer societies in the Old Stone Age possessed all of the following *except*
(1) fire.
(2) art.
(3) bone tools.
(4) religious beliefs.

5 To learn about prehistory, historians would likely study all of the following *except*
(1) graves.
(2) journals.
(3) bones.
(4) art.

6 During the Paleolithic Era, people made tools out of
(1) bronze.
(2) stone.
(3) iron.
(4) gold.

7 What was one result of the domestication of plants?
(1) the end of the Ice Ages
(2) learning how to make fire
(3) increased migration
(4) the beginning of agriculture

Base your answer to question 8 on the map below and on your knowledge of social studies.

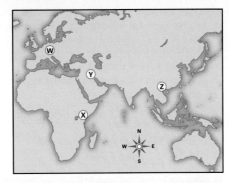

8 The region in which the first humans lived is shown on the map by the letter
(1) W.
(2) X.
(3) Y.
(4) Z.

EARLY CIVILIZATIONS IN THE EASTERN HEMISPHERE **97**

1. 1
Break Down the Question This question requires students to recall the chronology of human development.

2. 1
Break Down the Question Remind students that all but one of the answers describe changes to people's lives. Refer students who miss the question to the material titled "Clothing and Shelter" in Section 2.

3. 4
Break Down the Question This question requires students to recall information about the land bridge between Asia and the Americas. Refer students who missed the question to the map in Section 2.

4. 3
Break Down the Question This question requires that students recall factual information. Refer students who missed the question to the material on the Mesolithic Era in Section 2.

5. 2
Break Down the Question Students should recognize that of the answer options, only journals did not exist in the prehistoric era.

6. 2
Break Down the Question This question requires students to recall factual information. Refer students who miss it to Section 1.

7. 4
Students should understand that the domestication of plants allowed for the development of agriculture. Refer students who miss the question to Section 3.

8. 2
This question requires students to recall where the first humans are believed to have lived and to be able to pinpoint that location on a map. Refer students who miss the question to Section 1.

Reteach/Intervention Resources

Reproducible
Interactive Reader and Study Guide
Differentiated Instruction Teacher Management System: Lesson Plans

Technology
Quick Facts Transparency: Visual Summary: Early Civilizations in the Eastern Hemisphere
Differentiated Instruction Modified Worksheets and Tests CD-ROM
Interactive Skills Tutor CD-ROM
Quiz Game CD-ROM

Tips for Test Taking

Study the Directions In order to follow directions, students have to know what the directions are! Have students read all test directions as if they contain the key to lifetime happiness. Then they should read the directions again and study the answer sheet. How is it laid out?

Urge students to be sure they know what to do before they make the first mark.

Unit 1: The Uses of Geography

Word Help

utility usefulness
advantageously so as to cause benefit
conspicuous clear, obvious
proportion a balanced relationship

Biography

Strabo (c. 63 BC–c. AD 21) Greek historian and geographer Strabo (STRAY-bo) was born in northern Asia Minor in about 63 BC. While young, Strabo traveled to Rome with his family. There he received an education and remained until his thirties. Strabo traveled extensively in Europe, North Africa, and West Asia. He lived for many years at Alexandria and was a member of the Roman governor's inner circle there. Sometime around the turn of the first century AD, Strabo returned to Asia Minor to live out the rest of his life. Strabo's prominence came about only after his death.

Info to Know

Strabo's Geography The *Geography* is Strabo's only surviving work. The work is a compilation of Strabo's personal observations as well as those of others. It was mostly completed by 7 BC. The *Geography* consists of seventeen books: books 1–2 are introductory; books 3–10 discuss Europe; books 11–16 cover Asia; and book 17 is on Africa, mostly Egypt.

Answers

Document 1 1a. *by showing them the character and extent of the forest;* **1b.** *Disaster could result.*

Document 2 2a. *types of natural disasters common in the United States and where they occur;* **2b.** *to prepare for possible natural disasters*

The Uses of Geography

Part A: Short-Answer Questions

Directions: Read and examine the following documents. Then, on a separate sheet of paper, answer the questions using complete sentences.

DOCUMENT 1

Scholars have recognized the importance of geography for centuries. In the first century BC the Greek geographer Strabo wrote about its uses in the introduction to his *Geography*.

> The utility of geography in matters of small concern, also, is quite evident; for instance, in hunting. A hunter will be more successful in the chase if he knows the character and extent of the forest; and after, only one who knows a region can advantageously pitch camp there, or set an ambush, or direct a march. The utility of geography is more conspicuous, however, in great undertakings, in proportion as the prizes of knowledge and the disasters that result from ignorance are greater.
>
> —**Strabo**, *Geography* 1.17

1a. How does Strabo say geography will help hunters?

_____

1b. What does he say will happen if a person beginning a great undertaking does not understand geography?

_____

DOCUMENT 2

One of the most valuable skills geography teaches us is how to read maps. The map shown here is an example of the type of map you might encounter is a newspaper or on the Internet.

Natural Disasters in the United States

Earthquakes · Volcanoes · Wildfires · Tornadoes · Hurricanes · Tornado Risk · Flood areas · Moderate · High

2a. What information does this map show?

_____

2b. How might you use a map like this one in your daily life?

_____

Critical Thinking: Summarizing   At Level

Document Summaries

1. Have students read and examine the documents on these pages. Ask if students had any difficulty understanding the documents and answer any questions that may arise.

2. Tell students they will practice their summarizing skills. Be sure students understand that a summary covers the main points of a document in as few words as possible.

3. Model an effective summary for students by summarizing the first document on the board. Then have students write their own

summaries for Documents 3 and 4. Have volunteers share their summaries with the class. Critique the summaries and offer suggestions for how they could be improved.

4. Now tell students that visuals like maps and photos can be summarized, too. As a class, develop a summary for Document 2 and write it on the board. **LS Verbal/Linguistic**

Alternative Assessment Handbook, Rubric 37: Writing Assignments

DOCUMENT 3

The U.S. Geological Survey (USGS) is a branch of the Department of the Interior. The goal of the USGS is to study the natural environment using a variety of sciences. The following passage from the USGS Web site explains the significance of geography to the federal government.

> Governments depend on a common set of base information that describes the Earth's surface and locates features. They use this information as a tool for economic and community development, land and natural resource management, and health and safety services. Federal functions ranging from emergency management and defense to environmental protection rely on this information. Private industry, nongovernmental organizations, and individual citizens also use the same geographic data. Geographic information underpins an increasingly large part of the Nation's economy.
>
> —U.S. Geological Survey

3a. According to this passage, what are three areas in which the government uses geographic information as a tool?

_____

3b. Do you think the USGS would encourage people to study geography? Why or why not?

_____

DOCUMENT 4

A knowledge of geography and map reading is also essential when studying history. The document below was written by a professor of history to explain the importance of maps in his field.

> Maps are essential in the study of history. They can be used to show specific events, such as battles or wars. They can trace routes of trade, migration, or the diffusion of culture or diseases. They can show change in political alignments, territories, and boundaries. Maps show spatial relationships—where things are in relation to other things. If you want to know if one society is likely to be influenced by another, like Mexico by the United States, look at a map. Much of world history revolves around patterns of connection among regions, and maps help both to illustrate and explain these patterns.
>
> —**Dr. Peter Stearns,** "Using Maps to Understand History"

4a. What are three types of information historians can get from maps?

_____

4b. What does the author mean when he says maps help illustrate patterns of connection among regions?

_____

Part B: Essay

Historical Context: Throughout history, people have recognized the importance of geography and geographic information. From individuals to governments, everyone uses geography in some way.

TASK: Using information from the four documents and your knowledge of world history, write an essay in which you:

- identify one use to which geography can be put.
- explain how you can apply that use of geography in your daily life.

Word Help

base the most basic, fundamental
diffusion spread
alignments relationships
revolves to be centered or focused

Info to Know

Department of the Interior The U.S. Department of the Interior (DOI) was established in 1849 to handle the domestic affairs of the nation. The department's early responsibilities included exploring western lands, managing Native American affairs, and overseeing public lands. Today, the DOI consists of eight major bureaus and divisions, including the U.S. Geological Survey, the National Parks Service, and the Bureau of Land Management. The department employs over 67,000 individuals and boasts of having a corps of over 236,000 volunteers. The department operates on an annual budget of nearly $16 billion and raises nearly $13 billion from its operations.

Did you know . . .

U.S. Geological Survey scientists actively produce over 57,000 maps, some of which may be accessed at the USGS Web site—www.usgs.gov.

Collaborative Learning

At Level

The Uses of Geography Posters

Prep Required

Materials poster board, markers, nature and geography magazines, scissors, glue

1. Divide the class into groups of about four or five students each. Distribute the required materials to each of the groups.

2. Tell students they will be making "The Uses of Geography" posters. Posters should portray several of the uses of geography discussed in the documents on these pages. At least one use of geography from each document must be represented on students' posters.

3. Tell students they may use pictures and words for their posters, though final products should convey the uses of geography "at-a-glance." Encourage students to be creative in their representations of the uses of geography.

4. Have each group present its poster to the class. Offer feedback to groups. Select the best poster and award the group extra points on the assignment. **LS Visual/Spatial**

📖 Alternative Assessment Handbook, Rubric 28: Posters

Answers

Document 3 3a. *economic and community development; land and natural resource management; health and safety services;* **3b.** *possible answer—Yes. Geography is important to the nation's economy.*

Document 4 4a. *trade routes, political alignments, spatial relationships;* **4b.** *Maps show how and why regions are connected.*

Essay *Students' essays will vary but should thoroughly address all aspects of the task.*

Bellringer

Motivate Tell students that writing about how something works or how something is developed will help improve their critical thinking abilities. Encourage them to explain the steps in the process in a way that will clearly make sense to their readers.

Direct Teach

Prewrite

Organization Some students may struggle with organizing the information they have gathered. Offer them the following tips:

• Review the information and list the steps on a sheet of paper.
• Make sure the steps are in chronological order or order of importance. Redo the list if they are out of order.
• Review each step to determine what facts and details you need to explain that step.
• Find those facts and details in the information you have gathered and add them to the steps on your list.
• Use your list as an outline.

Practice & Apply

Editing

Activity **Practice Editing** Use portions of two or three students' papers (with student permission) to review editing. Using an overhead projector or computer presentation tool, work with students to revise the sections for content and style. You may also want to review standard editing marks.

Rubric

Students' explanations should

• start with an interesting fact or question.
• clearly identify the big idea.
• provide at least one paragraph for each point that supports the big idea with facts and details.
• follow an organization based on chronological order or order of importance.
• end with a paragraph that summarizes the steps in the process.
• use correct grammar, punctuation, spelling, and capitalization.

100

Explaining a Process

How does soil renewal work? How do cultures change? Often the first question we ask about something is how it works or what process it follows. One way we can answer these questions is by writing an explanation.

Assignment

Write a paper explaining one of these topics:

■ how water recycles on Earth
■ how agriculture developed

1. Prewrite

Choose a Process

■ Choose one of the topics above to write about.
■ Turn your topic into a big idea, or thesis. For example, your big idea might be "Water continually circulates from Earth's surface to the atmosphere and back."

> **TIP** **Organizing Information** Explanations should be in a logical order. You should arrange the steps in the process in chronological order, the order in which the steps take place.

Gather and Organize Information

■ Look for information about your topic in your textbook, in the library, or on the Internet.
■ Start a plan to organize support for your big idea. For example, look for the individual steps of the water cycle.

2. Write

Use a Writer's Framework

> **A Writer's Framework**
>
> **Introduction**
> ■ Start with an interesting fact or question.
> ■ Identify your big idea.
>
> **Body**
> ■ Create at least one paragraph for each point supporting the big idea. Add facts and details to explain each point.
> ■ Use chronological order or order of importance.
>
> **Conclusion**
> ■ Summarize your main points in your final paragraph.

3. Evaluate and Revise

Review and Improve Your Paper

■ Re-read your paper and make sure you have followed the framework.
■ Make the changes needed to improve your paper.

Evaluation Questions for an Explanation of a Process

❶ Do you begin with an interesting fact or question?
❷ Does your introduction identify your big idea? Does it provide any background information your readers might need?
❸ Do you have at least one paragraph for each point you are using to support the big idea?
❹ Do you include facts and details to explain and illustrate each point?
❺ Do you use chronological order or order of importance to organize your main points?

4. Proofread and Publish

Give Your Explanation the Finishing Touch

■ Make sure you have capitalized the first word in every sentence.
■ Check for punctuation at the end of every sentence.
■ Think of a way to share your explanation.

5. Practice and Apply

Use the steps and strategies outlined in this workshop to write your explanation. Share your paper with others and find out whether the explanation makes sense to them.

100

Below Level

Struggling Readers

Discuss chronological order and order of importance with students. Do the following activity with students to help them organize information.

1. Tell students that they are going to describe the process of making lunch. Ask the group to visualize the process of putting together a lunch to bring to school.

2 Have students contribute words that would be helpful in describing the process. Write the words on the board, e.g., *first, next, then, before, after, last, finally*. Ask students what

type of organization would work best to describe the process. *chronological*

3. Write sentences to describe the process. Ask individual students to write sentences on the board—with other students contributing ideas. Decide as a group whether the process is clearly explained and why. **LS** **Kinesthetic, Verbal/Linguistic**

📖 Alternative Assessment Handbook, Rubric 14: Group Activity

The Middle East

Unit Preview

Introduce the Unit

Share the information in the chapter overviews with students.

Chapter 5 The Middle East is noted for its dry climates and rich natural resources. The Eastern Mediterranean sits in the middle of three continents. The Arabian Peninsula, Iran, and Iraq are home to vast deserts. Central Asia is dry with rugged terrain.

Chapter 6 The world's oldest civilizations began in Mesopotamia. There, Sumerians and later peoples made advances in art, writing, astronomy, law, and science.

Chapter 7 Three major world religions—Judaism, Christianity, and Islam—began in the Middle East. The Hebrews formed a great kingdom in Israel and started Judaism. Christianity grew and spread under the Roman and Byzantine empires. Islam was founded on the Arabian Peninsula about AD 625.

Chapter 8 Over thousands of years, the countries of the Middle East have developed into modern, prosperous nations. Conflict continues to trouble many nations in the region.

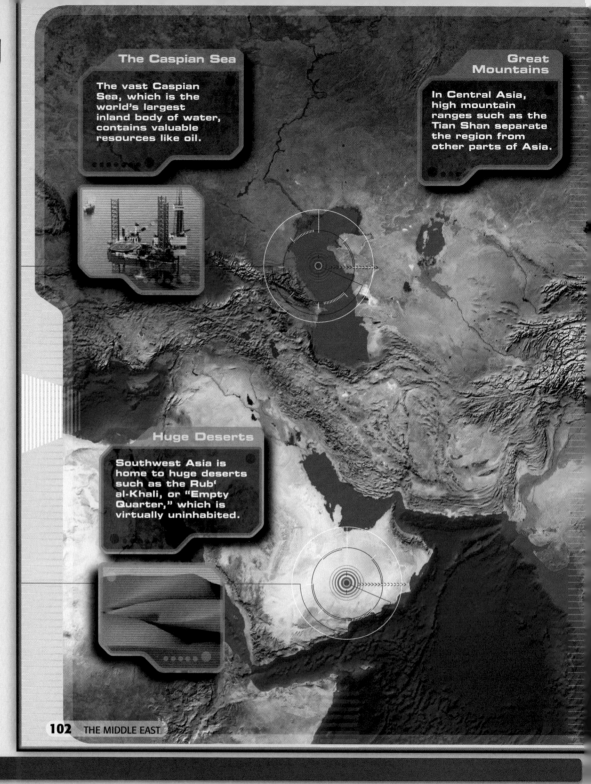

The Caspian Sea
The vast Caspian Sea, which is the world's largest inland body of water, contains valuable resources like oil.

Great Mountains
In Central Asia, high mountain ranges such as the Tian Shan separate the region from other parts of Asia.

Huge Deserts
Southwest Asia is home to huge deserts such as the Rub' al-Khali, or "Empty Quarter," which is virtually uninhabited.

102 THE MIDDLE EAST

Unit Resources

Planning

- Differentiated Instruction Teacher Management System: Pacing Guide
- OSP Teacher's One-Stop Planner: Calendar Planner
- Power Presentations with Video CD-ROM
- Virtual File Cabinet

Differentiating Instruction

- Differentiated Instruction Teacher Management System: Lesson Plans for Differentiated Instruction
- Differentiated Instruction Modified Worksheets and Tests CD-ROM

Enrichment

- **RF:** Interdisciplinary Project, News Report on the Palestinian-Israeli Conflict
- **RF:** Geography and History, The Growth of the Ottoman Empire
- Geography, Science, and Culture Activities with Answer Key

Assessment

- Progress Assessment Support System (PASS): Benchmark Test
- OSP ExamView Test Generator: Benchmark Test
- HOAP Holt Online Assessment Program, in the Premier Online Student Edition
- Alternative Assessment Handbook

The Middle East

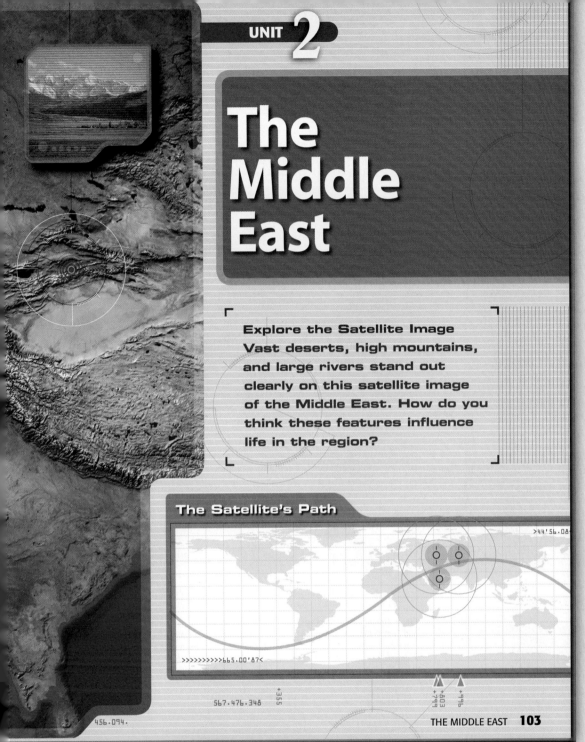

Explore the Satellite Image
Vast deserts, high mountains, and large rivers stand out clearly on this satellite image of the Middle East. How do you think these features influence life in the region?

The Satellite's Path

>44'56.08<

>>>>>>>>>665.00'87<

567.476.348

+355

809+
303
966+

456.094.

THE MIDDLE EAST **103**

Unit Preview

Connect to the Unit

Activity Role-Play Trading Partners Ask students to think about how trade—from the personal to the international level—impacts their daily lives. Have them identify goods and resources they use every day that came to them as a result of U.S. trade with another country.

During the study of the unit, ask students to examine three trade relationships: 1) between members of early Mesopotamian cultures; 2) between Arabic/Muslim traders and Central Asians; 3) and between modern oil-rich countries and their oil-dependent trading partners. Have them role-play interactions between these trading partners and discuss the common features of trade relationships. Lead a class discussion about how, in these examples and in general, trade can be beneficial but in some cases harmful to one or both of the parties if a trade imbalance exists. **LS Interpersonal**

Explore the Photographs

Have students examine the physical maps in the Atlas to identify the countries and land-forms connected to the photographs. Then ask how they think people in the Rub al-Khali, the Tian Shan, and the region around the Caspian Sea make their livings. *possible answers—The Rub al-Khali is inhospitable to settlement, but some people there might make their living as nomadic herders; the Tian Shan is also sparsely populated, and its people probably do some farming and herding; the oil-rich region of the Caspian Sea might have a large population supporting the oil industry.*

Critical Thinking: Analyzing Secondary Sources

At Level

Prep Required

Exploring Topics in Depth

1. Organize small groups, and distribute copies of news articles about the region, in as wide a coverage of topics as possible—religion, politics, natural resources, environment, war, ethnic conflicts, archaeological findings, and so on.

2. Have students read the articles and then discuss their content. Then have each group choose one topic and explore it in more detail. Suggest that they use Internet and library periodical resources to find more articles about the topic. Have them work as a group

to create a time line of events and write a summary of what they have learned. If they find secondary sources containing various opinions, have them refer to these opinions in their summaries as well.

3. Have groups share their time lines and summaries with the class. Elicit from students what they hope to learn more about as they read the unit. **LS Verbal/Linguistic, Interpersonal**

Alternative Assessment Handbook, Rubrics 23: Newspapers; and 36: Time Lines

Answers

Explore the Satellite Image *possible answer—These features influence decisions people make about where to live, what kinds of buildings to build, food to grow, clothes to wear, and other decisions about daily life.*

103

Direct Teach

Explore the Map

The Middle East: Physical As students examine the physical map on this page, tell them that this region of the world lacks certain physical resources that students have learned are very important in other places. Ask: What are these missing features? *major lakes and rivers* Which area in this region appears to be most severely affected by lack of water resources? *Arabian Peninsula* What suggestions do you have for residents living in these areas to increase their access to water? *possible answers—build desalinization plants to convert sea water to freshwater, build irrigation tunnels, dig wells*

Map Zone Transparency: The Middle East: Physical

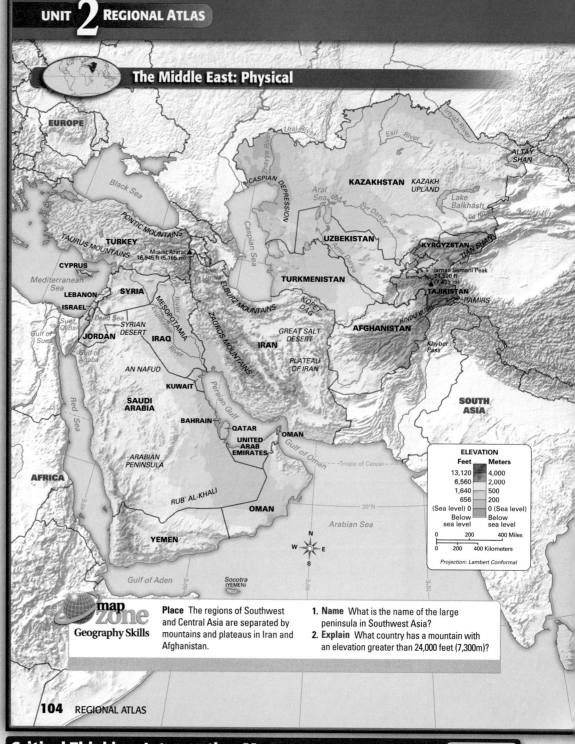

The Middle East: Physical

EUROPE

Black Sea

PONTIC MOUNTAINS

TAURUS MOUNTAINS

TURKEY

Mount Ararat 16,945 ft (5,165 m)

CYPRUS

Mediterranean Sea

LEBANON

ISRAEL

SYRIA

Dead Sea

Suez Canal

Gulf of Suez

JORDAN

SYRIAN DESERT

MESOPOTAMIA

Euphrates River

Tigris River

IRAQ

Gulf of Aqaba

AN NAFUD

Red Sea

SAUDI ARABIA

KUWAIT

BAHRAIN

QATAR

UNITED ARAB EMIRATES

Persian Gulf

ARABIAN PENINSULA

AFRICA

RUB' AL-KHALI

OMAN

Gulf of Oman

OMAN

YEMEN

Gulf of Aden

Socotra (YEMEN)

Arabian Sea

CASPIAN DEPRESSION

Zhayya River

Ural River

Aral Sea

Caspian Sea

Syr Darya

Amu Darya

ELBURZ MOUNTAINS

Lake Urmia

ZAGROS MOUNTAINS

GREAT SALT DESERT

IRAN

PLATEAU OF IRAN

KOPET DAG

KAZAKHSTAN

KAZAKH UPLAND

Esil River

Irtysh River

ALTAY SHAN

Lake Balkhash

Ile River

UZBEKISTAN

KYRGYZSTAN

TIAN SHAN

Ismail Semani Peak 24,590 ft (7,495 m)

TAJIKISTAN

PAMIRS

TURKMENISTAN

AFGHANISTAN

HINDU KUSH

Khyber Pass

SOUTH ASIA

Tropic of Cancer

20°N

N W E S

ELEVATION

Feet	Meters
13,120	4,000
6,560	2,000
1,640	500
656	200
(Sea level) 0	0 (Sea level)
Below sea level	Below sea level

0   200   400 Miles

0   200   400 Kilometers

Projection: Lambert Conformal

map zone

Geography Skills

Place The regions of Southwest and Central Asia are separated by mountains and plateaus in Iran and Afghanistan.

1. **Name** What is the name of the large peninsula in Southwest Asia?
2. **Explain** What country has a mountain with an elevation greater than 24,000 feet (7,300m)?

Critical Thinking: Interpreting Maps

At Level

Describe Location

1. As students look at the map on this page, point out some of the physical features they will learn about.

2. Have students choose five physical features on the map. Then have them write one sentence describing where each feature is located. (For example, "The Pontic Mountains are located near the Black Sea."

3. Ask students to read aloud their sentences. As they read, have volunteers take turns locating the physical feature being described on a large classroom map.

3. As a challenge, ask students reading their descriptions to say "This physical feature is located. . ." Then have students at the map locate and tell what physical feature is being described. **LS Visual/Spatial, Verbal/Linguistic**

Alternative Assessment Handbook, Rubrics 21: Map Reading; and 40: Writing to Describe

Answers

Map Zone 1. *Arabian Peninsula;*
2. *Tajikistan*

104

The Middle East

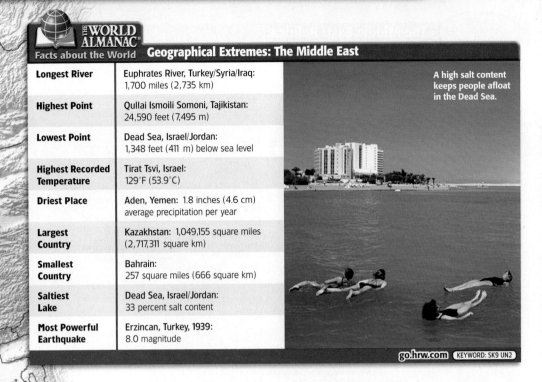

The World Almanac: Facts about the World

Geographical Extremes: The Middle East

Longest River	Euphrates River, Turkey/Syria/Iraq: 1,700 miles (2,735 km)
Highest Point	Qullai Ismoili Somoni, Tajikistan: 24,590 feet (7,495 m)
Lowest Point	Dead Sea, Israel/Jordan: 1,348 feet (411 m) below sea level
Highest Recorded Temperature	Tirat Tsvi, Israel: 129°F (53.9°C)
Driest Place	Aden, Yemen: 1.8 inches (4.6 cm) average precipitation per year
Largest Country	Kazakhstan: 1,049,155 square miles (2,717,311 square km)
Smallest Country	Bahrain: 257 square miles (666 square km)
Saltiest Lake	Dead Sea, Israel/Jordan: 33 percent salt content
Most Powerful Earthquake	Erzincan, Turkey, 1939: 8.0 magnitude

A high salt content keeps people afloat in the Dead Sea.

go.hrw.com   KEYWORD: SK9 UN2

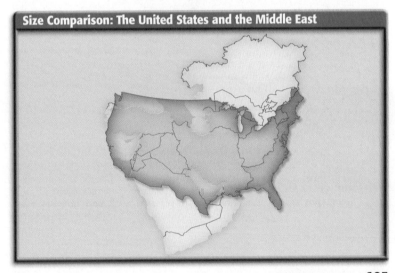

Size Comparison: The United States and the Middle East

The World Almanac: Facts about the World

Identify In what year did the most powerful earthquake in the region take place? *1939*

Analyze What three geographical extreme records does Israel hold? *lowest point: Dead Sea; highest recorded temperature: Tirat Tsvi; saltiest lake: Dead Sea*

Locate Refer to the political map of Southwest and Central Asia on the next page. Locate the smallest country in this region. *smallest—Bahrain*

🗝 Map Zone Transparency: Size Comparison: The United States and the Middle East

---

Differentiating Instruction

Struggling Readers   Below Level

1. Read each fact on the World Almanac chart out loud, beginning with the longest river. Have struggling readers read and repeat each fact after you.

2. Then have students pair up and repeat this activity, echoing each other while you listen.
   LS Auditory/Musical, Verbal/Linguistic
   📓 Alternative Assessment Handbook, Rubric 18: Listening

English-Language Learners   Below Level

1. Point out the suffix *-est* at the end of each word in the World Almanac chart. Discuss its meaning when added to the end of most adjectives.

2. Ask students to brainstorm a list of adjectives describing the Middle East. Have students convert these adjectives into words ending in *-est*. **LS Verbal/Linguistic**
   📓 Alternative Assessment Handbook, Rubric 37: Writing Assignments

Direct Teach

Explore the Map

The Middle East: Political As students examine the political map on this page, ask the following questions: Which three continents meet in the Middle East? *Europe, Asia, and Africa* How might this region's location have affected its history? *possible answers—trade routes, invasions, cultural diffusion* Which small countries border the Mediterranean Sea? *Syria, Lebanon, and Israel* What small country is landlocked? *Jordan*

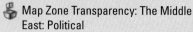 Map Zone Transparency: The Middle East: Political

Checking for Understanding

True or False Answer each statement *T* if it is true or *F* if it is false. If false, explain why.

1. The Aral Sea is located in Kazakhstan and Uzbekistan. *T*

2. The national capital of Iran is Baghdad. *F: Iran's capital is Tehran; the capital of Iraq is Baghdad.*

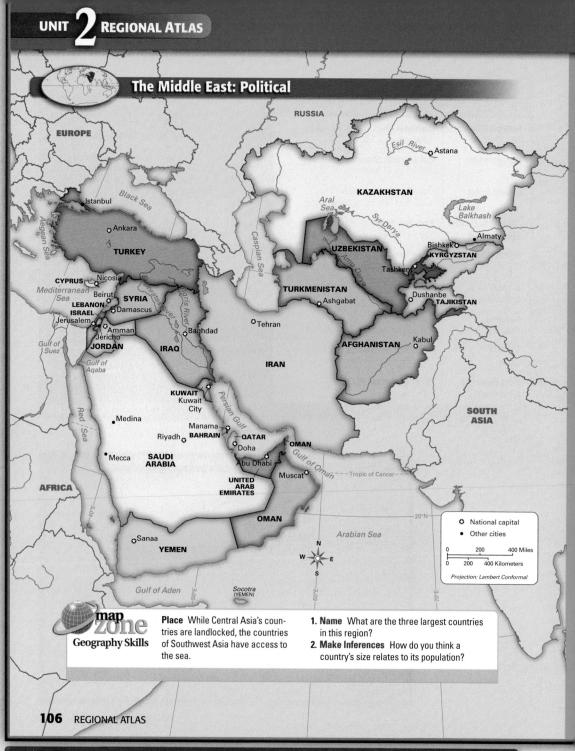

The Middle East: Political

map zone
Geography Skills

Place While Central Asia's countries are landlocked, the countries of Southwest Asia have access to the sea.

1. **Name** What are the three largest countries in this region?
2. **Make Inferences** How do you think a country's size relates to its population?

Answers

Map Zone 1. *Saudi Arabia, Iran, and Kazakhstan;* **2.** *possible answer—There is not always a clear relationship between a country's size and its population. Some large countries, such as Saudi Arabia, have huge areas that are almost uninhabitable. Poor countries that are large may not necessarily have large populations, although many do. Small, rich countries often have large urban populations. In both small and large countries, most population is concentrated in the cities.*

Differentiating Instruction

Below Level

Special Needs Learners

1. For students with visual impairments, make an enlarged copy of the political map on this page or allow students to use a classroom wall map to complete the map activity and answer the questions.

2. As students examine the political map, have them say aloud the name of each country featured on the map. If they have difficulty with pronunciation, have them repeat the country's name after you say it.

3. Have students share which countries they have heard mentioned in the news in recent years.

4. Lead a brief discussion about current U.S. involvement in the Middle East. **LS** Visual/Spatial, Verbal/Linguistic, Auditory/Musical

Alternative Assessment Handbook, Rubrics 11: Discussions; and 21: Map Reading

106

The Middle East

The Middle East: Resources

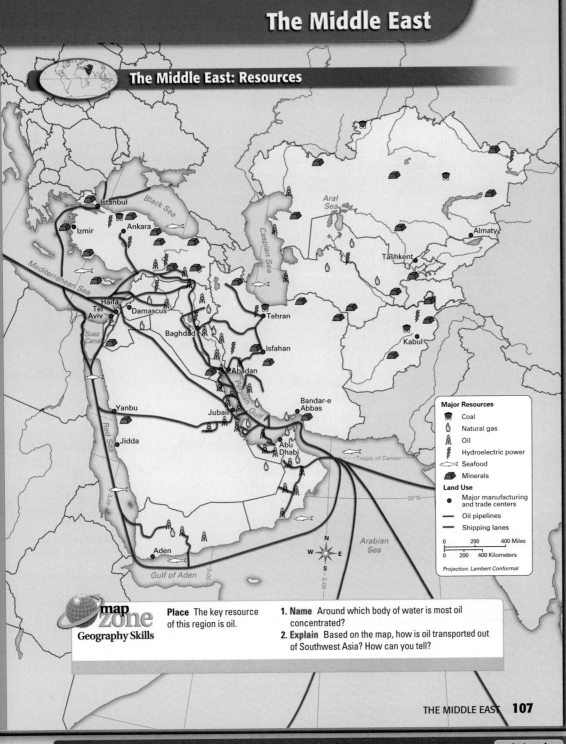

Major Resources
- Coal
- Natural gas
- Oil
- Hydroelectric power
- Seafood
- Minerals

Land Use
- Major manufacturing and trade centers
- Oil pipelines
- Shipping lanes

0 200 400 Miles
0 200 400 Kilometers

Projection: Lambert Conformal

map zone Geography Skills

Place The key resource of this region is oil.

1. **Name** Around which body of water is most oil concentrated?
2. **Explain** Based on the map, how is oil transported out of Southwest Asia? How can you tell?

THE MIDDLE EAST **107**

Explore the Map

The Middle East: Resources Focus students' attention on the resource map on this page. Then ask the following questions: What two resources are often found together in the region? *natural gas and oil* What major manufacturing and trade centers are located on the Persian Gulf? *Abadan, Jubail, Abu Dhabi, and Bandar-e Abbas*

🗺️ Map Zone Transparency: The Middle East: Land Use and Resources

Collaborative Learning

At Level

Locate Resources

1. Have students point out the symbols in the map key and discuss important resources in this region.

2. Divide students into small groups and assign each group one of the resources shown on the map. Give each group a blank transparency. Have them lay the transparency over the map and trace the political boundaries of the region.

3. Then have students mark the locations of their assigned resource. Students should work collaboratively to write a paragraph explaining how the location of their resources is related to the geography of the region.

4. Have each group present their findings on an overhead projector. As groups present, they can lay their transparency on top of the group's that presented before them.
LS Visual/Spatial, Verbal/Linguistic

📋 Alternative Assessment Handbook, Rubrics 14: Group Activity; and 21: Map Reading

Answers

Map Zone 1. *Persian Gulf;* **2.** *Most oil is transported out of Southwest Asia by ship. Ships go through the Persian Gulf to the Red Sea and Mediterranean or through the Persian Gulf to the Arabian Sea. Oil is also transported through pipelines. The map key and maps show the shipping routes and oil pipelines.*

107

Direct Teach

Explore the Map

The Middle East: Population Have students compare the population map on this page with the political map of the region. Ask: What is the most densely populated country in the region? *Israel* Which country in the region has the lowest population density? *Saudi Arabia*

🖥 Map Zone Transparency: The Middle East: Population

The Middle East: Population

RUSSIA

EUROPE

Black Sea

Istanbul

Izmir Ankara

Aegean Sea

Aral Sea

Lake Balkhash

Caspian Sea

Tashkent

Mediterranean Sea

Tel Aviv

Baghdad

Tehran

Gulf of Suez

Gulf of Aqaba

Persian Gulf

SOUTH ASIA

Red Sea

Riyadh

Gulf of Oman

Tropic of Cancer

Persons per square mile | **Persons per square km**

520	200
260	100
130	50
25	10
3	1
0	0

● Major cities over 2 million

0   200   400 Miles
0   200   400 Kilometers

Projection: Lambert Conformal

AFRICA

20°N

Arabian Sea

N W E S

Gulf of Aden

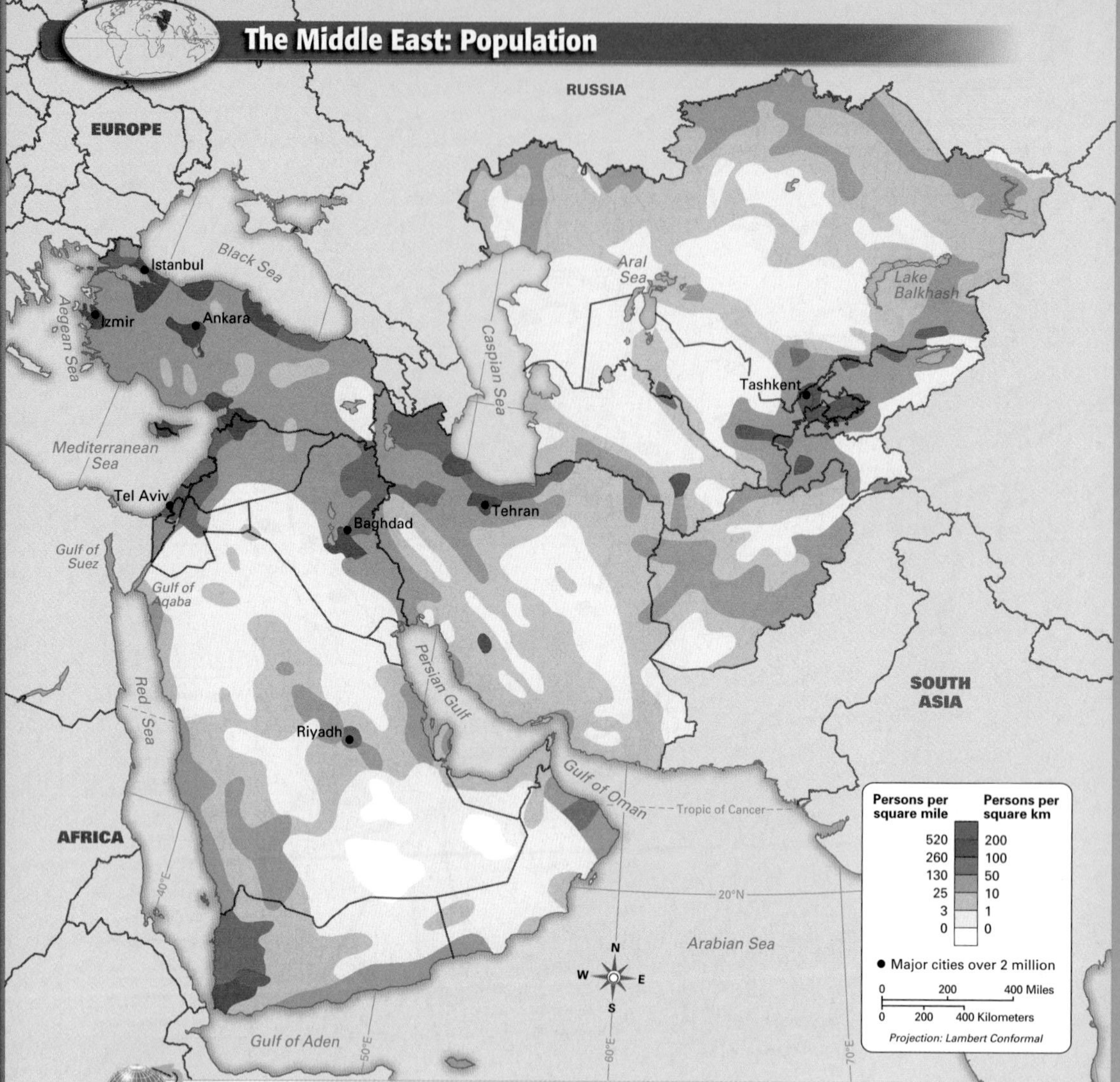

map zone

Geography Skills

Place In this region, most people live in plains and valleys.

1. **Name** Compare this map to the political map. Which country has three cities over 2 million?
2. **Compare** Compare this map to the physical map. How do physical features influence where people live in the region?

Differentiating Instruction

Above Level

Advanced/Gifted and Talented

1. Have students interpret the population statistics shown on the map and compare the data with a current almanac. Then have students create a computer-generated pie chart or bar graph displaying the population density for two countries in the region.

2. Students may wish to create a separate graphic for each country or combine the two countries' data into one chart or graph. Remind students to use accurate labeling for their charts. If computers are unavailable,

students can create the graphics using a ruler and a protractor. Have students display their completed graphs on a bulletin board.

LS Logical/Mathematical, Visual/Spatial

📄 Alternative Assessment Handbook, Rubrics 7: Charts; and 21: Map Reading

Answers

Map Zone 1. *Turkey;* **2.** *possible answer—Few people live in desert regions or at very high elevations; many people live along rivers and coastlines.*

108

The Middle East

EUROPE

Black Sea

Aegean Sea

Caspian Sea

Aral Sea

Lake Balkhash

Mediterranean Sea

Gulf of Suez

Gulf of Aqaba

Red Sea

Persian Gulf

Gulf of Oman

SOUTH ASIA

Tropic of Cancer

AFRICA

20°N

Arabian Sea

N W E S

Gulf of Aden

Climate Types

- Desert
- Steppe
- Mediterranean
- Humid subtropical
- Highland

0   150   300 Miles
0   150   300 Kilometers
Projection: Lambert Conformal

map zone
Geography Skills

Regions Hot and dry climates dominate Southwest and Central Asia.
1. Locate Which climates are found in this region?

2. Make Generalizations How do you think the region's climate influences people's daily lives?

THE MIDDLE EAST **109**

Direct Teach

Explore the Map

The Middle East: Climate After students examine the climate map on this page, ask them to list the climate types found in this region in order from least to greatest. *humid subtropical, highland, Mediterranean, steppe, desert* Have students compare the climate map to the political map of this region. Ask volunteers to share which country they would most like to live in based on climate. Have students support their answers. *Students may mention countries with a Mediterranean climate because these areas are mild and temperate year-round.*

Map Zone Transparency: The Middle East: Climate

Critical Thinking: Analyzing Visuals

At Level

Analyze Maps

1. Have students compare this map with the population map on the previous page.

2. Have students answer the following questions on notebook paper: In what climate regions do most people live? *steppe and Mediterranean* Why do you think this is? *possible answer—better growing areas, more comfortable for people*

3. Then ask students to compare the climate map with the political map of the same region. Ask: Which countries have predominantly a

desert climate? *Syria, Jordan, Iraq, Kuwait, Saudi Arabia, Yemen, Oman, United Arab Emirates, Uzbekistan, and Kazakhstan* What climate type is least common in this region? *humid subtropical* LS **Visual/Spatial, Verbal/Linguistic**

Alternative Assessment Handbook, Rubrics 21: Map Reading; and 37: Writing Assignments

Answers

Map Zone 1. *desert, steppe, Mediterranean, humid subtropical, and highland;* **2.** *possible answers—It probably influences how much and what kinds of food they can grow; in very hot areas, most work might take place during the cooler parts of the day; housing, clothing, and economic activity are also affected by a region's climate.*

109

The World Almanac: Facts about Countries

Analyze Ask students to identify the countries in the Middle East whose average life expectancy is 70 or higher. *Bahrain, Cyprus, Iran, Israel, Jordan, Kuwait, Lebanon, Oman, Qatar, Saudi Arabia, Syria, Turkey, United Arab Emirates*

Evaluate Lead a class discussion about what the number of TVs per 1,000 people can tell you about a country's population, economy, and culture. *Answers will vary but students should provide logical support for their opinions.*

THE WORLD ALMANAC® Facts about Countries

The Middle East

COUNTRY Capital	FLAG	POPULATION	AREA (sq mi)	PER CAPITA GDP (U.S. $)	LIFE EXPECTANCY AT BIRTH	TVS PER 1,000 PEOPLE
Afghanistan Kabul		31.9 million	250,001	$800	43.8	14
Bahrain Manama		708,600	257	$25,300	74.7	446
Cyprus Nicosia		788,500	3,571	$22,700	78.0	154
Iran Tehran		65.3 million	636,296	$8,900	70.6	154
Iraq Baghdad		27.5 million	168,754	$2,900	69.3	82
Israel Jerusalem		6.4 million	8,019	$26,200	79.6	328
Jordan Amman		6.0 million	35,637	$4,900	78.6	83
Kazakhstan Astana		15.3 million	1,049,155	$9,100	67.2	240
Kuwait Kuwait City		2.5 million	6,880	$21,600	77.4	480
Kyrgyzstan Bishkek		5.3 million	76,641	$2,000	68.8	49
Lebanon Beirut		3.9 million	4,015	$5,500	73.1	355
Oman Muscat		3.2 million	82,031	$14,100	73.6	575
Qatar Doha		907,200	4,416	$29,400	74.1	866
Saudi Arabia Riyadh		27.6 million	756,985	$13,800	75.9	263
Syria Damascus		19.3 million	71,498	$4,000	70.6	68
United States Washington, D.C.		301.1 million	3,718,711	$43,500	78.0	844

110 FACTS ABOUT COUNTRIES

Collaborative Learning

Make a Board Game

1. Have students work in small groups to create a board game that teaches information found on the World Almanac fact sheet.

2. Groups should work together to write, edit, and type a set of rules, including materials needed, purpose of game, set-up, game play, and how to win.

3. Students should also make a game board, playing pieces, dice, cards, and other materials required to play the game.

4. Have students play their own game, testing the rules and making sure the game is logical, educational, and fun. Students should make revisions as necessary following their practice game.

5. Then have students play each other's games. Afterward, lead a class discussion about their experiences. How did creating and playing the games help them learn about the countries of Southwest and Central Asia? **LS Interpersonal, Kinesthetic, Verbal/Linguistic**

Alternative Assessment Handbook, Rubric 14: Group Activity

Direct Teach

COUNTRY Capital	FLAG	POPULATION	AREA (sq mi)	PER CAPITA GDP (U.S. $)	LIFE EXPECTANCY AT BIRTH	TVS PER 1,000 PEOPLE
Tajikistan Dushanbe		7.1 million	55,251	$1,300	64.6	328
Turkey Ankara		71.2 million	301,384	$8,900	72.9	328
Turkmenistan Ashgabat		5.1 million	188,456	$8,900	62.3	198
United Arab Emirates Abu Dhabi		4.4 million	32,000	$49,700	75.7	309
Uzbekistan Tashkent		27.8 million	172,742	$2,000	65.0	280
Yemen Sanaa		22.2 million	203,850	$900	62.5	286
United States Washington, D.C.		301.1 million	3,718,711	$43,500	78.0	844

ANALYSIS SKILL ANALYZING TABLES

1. How does the per capita GDP of countries in this region compare to the per capita GDP of the United States?
2. Based on the table, which countries seem to have the highest standard of living?

Oil Giants

Interpret According to the bar graph, which two countries in the Middle East shown in the graph contain the least amount of oil reserves? *Kuwait and the United Arab Emirates* Which country has about 10% of the world's oil reserves? *Iran* What percentage of the world's oil does this entire region contain? *nearly 60 percent*

Predict Lead a class discussion about how oil affects this region's political and economic power because of the rest of the world's demand for oil. Ask students to predict what might happen to the region when the oil reserves are gone. *Answers will vary, but should include reasonable predictions about the future of the Middle East after its oil reserves have been used up.*

Oil Giants

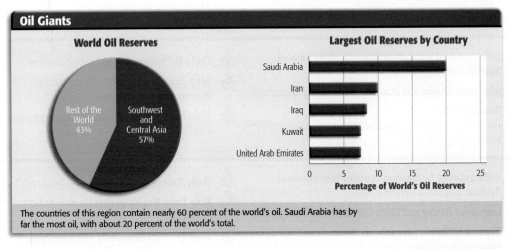

World Oil Reserves

Rest of the World 43%

Southwest and Central Asia 57%

Largest Oil Reserves by Country

Saudi Arabia, Iran, Iraq, Kuwait, United Arab Emirates

Percentage of World's Oil Reserves

The countries of this region contain nearly 60 percent of the world's oil. Saudi Arabia has by far the most oil, with about 20 percent of the world's total.

THE MIDDLE EAST **111**

Critical Thinking: Comparing and Contrasting   At Level

Write and Perform a Skit

1. Have students divide into two groups. Each group should select a country on the Fact Sheet to compare and contrast with the United States.

2. Using the data listed on the chart, have students write a skit comparing and contrasting information about the two countries.

3. Remind groups that every person in the group should participate in the writing process, as well as have a speaking part in the skit.

4. Allow students ample time to write, revise, and practice performing their skits. Then have each group perform their skit for the rest of the class. **LS Interpersonal, Kinesthetic, Verbal/Linguistic**

   Alternative Assessment Handbook, Rubrics 9: Comparing and Contrasting; and 33: Skits and Reader's Theater

Answers

Analyzing Tables 1. *The United Arab Emirates has a higher GDP than the United States; the region's other more prosperous countries have more than half of the United States's GDP; the rest have only a fraction.* **2.** *Bahrain, Cyprus, Israel, Kuwait, Oman, Qatar, Saudi Arabia, United Arab Emirates*

Chapter 5 Planning Guide

Physical Geography of the Middle East

Chapter Overview	Reproducible Resources	Technology Resources
CHAPTER 5 pp. 112–131 **Overview: In this chapter, students will study the physical geography of the Middle East, including the Eastern Mediterranean, the Arabian Peninsula, Iraq, Iran, and Central Asia.**	**Differentiated Instruction Teacher Management System:*** • Instructional Pacing Guides • Lesson Plans for Differentiated Instruction **Interactive Reader and Study Guide:** Chapter Summary Graphic Organizer* **Resource File:*** • Chapter Review • Focus on Reading: Re-reading • Focus on Writing: Writing a Description • Social Studies Skills: Analyzing Tables and Statistics	**OSP Teacher's One-Stop Planner:** Calendar Planner **Power Presentations with Video CD-ROM** **Differentiated Instruction Modified Worksheets and Tests CD-ROM** **Interactive Skills Tutor CD-ROM** **Student Edition on Audio CD Program** **Map Zone Transparency:** The Middle East: Physical* **Geography's Impact Video Program (VHS/DVD):** Impact of Oil on Southwest Asia*
Section 1: **The Eastern Mediterranean** **The Big Idea:** The Eastern Mediterranean, a region with a dry climate and valuable resources, sits in the middle of three continents.	**Differentiated Instruction Teacher Management System:** Section 1 Lesson Plan* **Interactive Reader and Study Guide:** Section 1 Summary* **Resource File:*** • Vocabulary Builder: Section 1	**Daily Bellringer Transparency:** Section 1* **Map Zone Transparency:** The Eastern Mediterranean: Physical* **Map Zone Transparency:** The Eastern Mediterranean: Climate* **Internet Activity:** The Dead Sea
Section 2: **The Arabian Peninsula, Iraq, and Iran** **The Big Idea:** The Arabian Peninsula, Iraq, and Iran make up a mostly desert region with very valuable oil resources.	**Differentiated Instruction Teacher Management System:** Section 2 Lesson Plan* **Interactive Reader and Study Guide:** Section 2 Summary* **Resource File:*** • Vocabulary Builder: Section 2 • Biography: Ibn Saud	**Daily Bellringer Transparency:** Section 2* **Map Zone Transparency:** The Arabian Peninsula, Iraq, and Iran: Physical* **Map Zone Transparency:** The Arabian Peninsula, Iraq, and Iran: Climate*
Section 3: **Central Asia** **The Big Idea:** Central Asia, a dry, rugged, landlocked region, has oil and other valuable mineral resources.	**Differentiated Instruction Teacher Management System:** Section 3 Lesson Plan* **Interactive Reader and Study Guide:** Section 3 Summary* **Resource File:*** • Vocabulary Builder: Section 3 • Biography: Al-Biruni • Primary Source: National Anthem of the Republic of Kazakhstan • Literature: *Manas*	**Daily Bellringer Transparency:** Section 3* **Map Zone Transparency:** Central Asia: Physical* **Map Zone Transparency:** Central Asia: Land Use and Resources* **Map Zone Transparency:** The Aral Sea

HOLT
Geography's Impact
Video Program
Impact of Oil on Southwest Asia
Suggested use: in Section 2

Review, Assessment, Intervention

 Quick Facts Transparency: Visual Summary: Physical Geography of the Middle East*

Spanish Chapter Summaries Audio CD Program

 Progress Assessment Support System (PASS): Chapter Test*

 Differentiated Instruction Modified Worksheets and Tests CD-ROM: Modified Chapter Test

OSP **Teacher's One-Stop Planner:** ExamView Test Generator (English/Spanish)

HOAP **Holt Online Assessment Program (HOAP),** in the Holt Interactive Online Student Edition

 PASS: Section 1 Quiz*

Online Quiz: Section 1

Alternative Assessment Handbook

 PASS: Section 2 Quiz*

Online Quiz: Section 2

Alternative Assessment Handbook

 PASS: Section 3 Quiz*

Online Quiz: Section 3

Alternative Assessment Handbook

Power Presentations with Video CD-ROM

Power Presentations with Video are visual presentations of each chapter's main ideas. Presentations can be customized by including Quick Facts charts, images from the text, and video clips.

Holt Online Learning

go.hrw.com
Teacher Resources
KEYWORD: SK9 TEACHER

go.hrw.com
Student Resources
KEYWORD: SK9 CH5

- Interactive Multimedia Activities
- Current Events

- Chapter-based Internet Activities
- and more!

Holt Interactive
Online Student Edition
Complete online support for interactivity, assessment, and reporting
- Interactive Maps and Notebook
- Standardized Test Prep
- Homework Practice and Research Activities Online

CHAPTER 5 PLANNING GUIDE

Differentiating Instruction

How do I address the needs of varied learners?
The Target Resource acts as your primary strategy for differentiated instruction.

ENGLISH-LANGUAGE LEARNERS & STRUGGLING READERS

TARGET RESOURCE

Spanish Resources

Spanish Chapter Summaries Audio CD Program

Teacher's One-Stop Planner:
- ExamView Test Generator, Spanish
- PuzzlePro, Spanish

English-Language Learner Strategies and Activities

Additional Resources

Differentiated Instruction Teacher Management System: Lesson Plans for Differentiated Instruction

Resource File:
- Vocabulary Builder Activities
- Social Studies Skills: Analyzing Tables and Statistics

Quick Facts Transparency:
- Visual Summary: Physical Geography of the Middle East

Student Edition on Audio CD Program

Interactive Skills Tutor CD-ROM

SPECIAL NEEDS LEARNERS

TARGET RESOURCE

Differentiated Instruction Modified Worksheets and Tests CD-ROM

- Vocabulary Flash Cards
- Modified Vocabulary Builder Activities
- Modified Chapter Review
- Modified Chapter Test

Additional Resources

Differentiated Instruction Teacher Management System: Lesson Plans for Differentiated Instruction

Interactive Reader and Study Guide

Resource File: Social Studies Skills: Analyzing Tables and Statistics

Student Edition on Audio CD Program

Interactive Skills Tutor CD-ROM

Graphic Organizer Transparencies with Support for Reading and Writing

ADVANCED/GIFTED AND TALENTED STUDENTS

TARGET RESOURCE

Resource File

The Resource File activities allow students to extend their knowledge of chapter-related places and people and to practice geography skills.
- Focus on Reading: Re-reading
- Focus on Writing: Writing a Description
- Primary Source: National Anthem of the Republic of Kazakhstan

Additional Resources

Differentiated Instruction Teacher Management System: Lesson Plans for Differentiated Instruction

World History and Geography Document-Based Questions Activities

Geography, Science, and Cultures Activities

Experiencing World History and Geography

Differentiated Activities in the Teacher's Edition

- Interpreting Maps
- Bodies of Water Web Diagram
- Describing Climate and Vegetation
- Identifying Countries in the Middle East
- Interpreting a Physical Map

Differentiated Activities in the Teacher's Edition

- Interpreting Maps
- Identifying Countries in the Middle East
- Answering Questions to Understand a Table

Differentiated Activities in the Teacher's Edition

- Researching Current Events
- Researching the Hindu Kush

HOLT Teacher's One-Stop Planner®

How can I manage the lesson plans and support materials for differentiated instruction?

With the Teacher's One-Stop Planner, you can easily organize and print lesson plans, planning guides, and instructional materials for all learners.

The Teacher's One-Stop Planner includes the following materials to help you differentiate instruction:

- · Interactive Teacher's Edition
- · Calendar Planner and pacing guides
- · Editable lesson plans
- · All reproducible ancillaries in Adobe Acrobat (PDF) format
- · ExamView Test Generator (English & Spanish)
- · Transparency and video previews

Professional Development

What teacher training resources are available to help me grow professionally?

- · **In-service and staff development** as part of your Holt Social Studies product purchase
- · **Quick Teacher Tutorial Lesson Presentation CD-ROM**
- · Intensive tuition-based **Teacher Development Institute**
- · **Convenient Holt Speaker Bureau** – face-to-face workshop options
- · **24/7 Ask A Professional Development Expert** at http://www.hrw.com/prodev/

Chapter Big Ideas

Section 1 The Eastern Mediterranean, a region with a dry climate and valuable resources, sits in the middle of three continents.

Section 2 The Arabian Peninsula, Iraq, and Iran make up a mostly desert region with very valuable oil resources.

Section 3 Central Asia, a dry, rugged, landlocked region, has oil and other valuable mineral resources.

Focus on Reading and Writing

Reading The Resource File provides a Focus on Reading worksheet to help students understand how to re-read.

RF: Focus on Reading, Re-reading

Writing The Resource File provides a Focus on Writing worksheet to help students plan and write a description.

RF: Focus on Writing, Writing a Description

112 CHAPTER 5

CHAPTER **5**

Physical Geography of the Middle East

FOCUS QUESTION

What forces had an impact on the development of the Middle East and why?

What You Will Learn...

The Middle East is also sometimes called Southwest Asia. The region is generally thought of as an arid desert, but some parts of the Middle East have much milder climates.

FOCUS ON READING AND WRITING

Re-reading Sometimes a single reading is not enough to fully understand a passage of text. If you feel like you do not fully understand something you have read, it may help to re-read the passage more slowly. **See the lesson, Re-Reading, on page S6.**

Writing a Description As you read this chapter, you will collect information about the lands of the Middle East. Later you will write a description of these lands. You will be writing for readers who have not read the chapter or visited the region.

112 CHAPTER 5

ELEVATION

Feet	Meters
13,120	4,000
6,560	2,000
1,640	500
656	200
(Sea level) 0	0 (Sea level)
Below sea level	Below sea level

0   200   400 Miles

0   200   400 Kilometers

Projection: Lambert Conformal

map zone

Geography Skills

Human-Environment Interaction Because so much of the Middle East is desert, water is a valuable resource there.
1. **Identify** What desert is north of the Plateau of Iran?
2. **Analyze** How many rivers cross the Arabian Peninsula?

Eastern Mediterranean The Jordan River valley in Israel has fertile soils for farming.

Introduce the Chapter

At Level

Physical Geography of the Middle East

1. Ask students to list the countries that make up the Middle East. Then ask students what they know of the physical geography of each of the countries on the list. Encourage students to use the map for help. Write students' responses for everyone to see.

2. Have each student select a different element of physical geography from the list. Then have students write a short paragraph in which they make predictions about how their selected feature might affect life in the Middle East. For example, students might predict that the Syrian Desert might make growing crops in the region difficult.

3. Ask students to share their predictions with the class. Lead a class discussion about the predictions. Point out to students how geography can have a significant impact on peoples' lives and on the development of a region. **LS Verbal/Linguistic**

Alternative Assessment Handbook, Rubric 11: Discussions

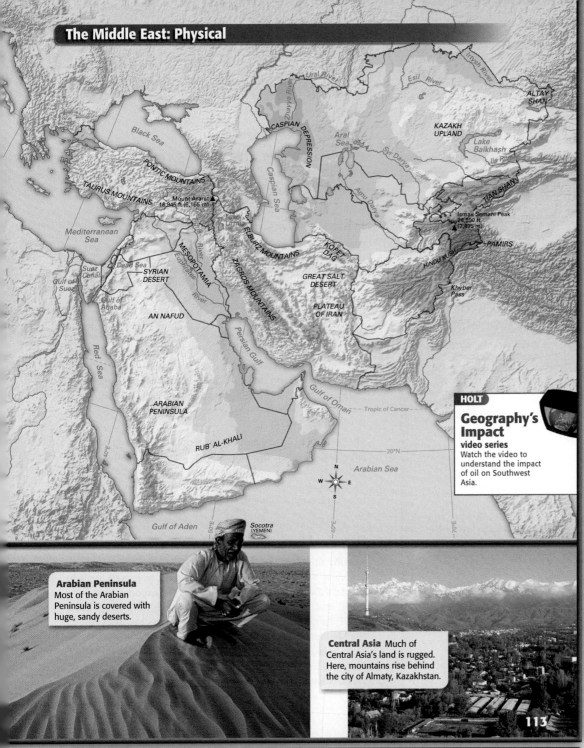

The Middle East: Physical

Explore the Map and Pictures

The Middle East: Physical Deserts dominate many areas in the Middle East. Iran's Great Salt Desert, known as Dasht-e Kavir, is about 500 miles long and 200 miles wide—almost the size of Colorado. Its name comes from the fact that more water evaporates there than is replaced by rain, leaving salt deposits on the land.

Map Zone Transparency: The Middle East: Physical

Analyzing Visuals Most of the Arabian Peninsula is covered in desert. In the summer, temperatures commonly reach 120 degrees or more. What might it be like to live in a desert climate? *possible answers—small populations and small settlements; difficult life; little farming*

go.hrw.com
Online Resources
Chapter Resources:
KEYWORD: SK9 CH5
Teacher Resources:
KEYWORD: SK9 TEACHER

HOLT
Geography's Impact
► video series
See the Video Teacher's Guide for strategies for using the chapter video to teach about the impact of oil on Southwest Asia.

HOLT
Geography's Impact
video series
Watch the video to understand the impact of oil on Southwest Asia.

Arabian Peninsula Most of the Arabian Peninsula is covered with huge, sandy deserts.

Central Asia Much of Central Asia's land is rugged. Here, mountains rise behind the city of Almaty, Kazakhstan.

113

Critical Thinking: Analyzing Visuals   At Level

Images of the Middle East

1. Have students examine the photographs on these two pages. Ask students what the photographs tell them about the physical geography of the Middle East. Point out to students that the Middle East is a large geographical area with a variety of physical features and climates.

2. Organize the class into small groups. Have each group create a scrapbook depicting the physical geography of the Middle East.

Instruct students to use their textbook and other sources for ideas of what kinds of illustrations to include in their scrapbook.

3. Instruct students to write a caption for each illustration in their scrapbook.

4. Have groups exchange scrapbooks and discuss the images selected. **LS Visual/Spatial, Interpersonal**

Alternative Assessment Handbook: Rubrics 11: Discussions; and 32: Scrapbooks

Answers
Map Zone 1. *Great Salt Desert;*
2. *none*

Bellringer

If YOU lived there. . . Use the **Daily Bellringer Transparency** to help students answer the question.

📦 Daily Bellringer Transparency, Section 1

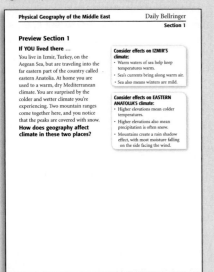

Physical Geography of the Middle East	Daily Bellringer
	Section 1

Preview Section 1

If YOU lived there ...
You live in Izmir, Turkey, on the Aegean Sea, but are traveling into the far eastern part of the country called eastern Anatolia. At home you are used to a warm, dry Mediterranean climate. You are surprised by the colder and wetter climate you're experiencing. Two mountain ranges come together here, and you notice that the peaks are covered with snow.
How does geography affect climate in these two places?

Consider effects on IZMIR'S climate:
• Warm waters of sea help keep temperatures warm.
• Sea's currents bring along warm air.
• Sea also means winters are mild.

Consider effects on EASTERN ANATOLIA's climate:
• Higher elevations mean colder temperatures.
• Higher elevations also mean precipitation is often snow.
• Mountains create a rain shadow effect, with most moisture falling on the side facing the wind.

Key Terms and Places

📋 **RF:** Vocabulary Builder, Section 1

Taking Notes

Have students copy the graphic organizer onto their own paper and then use it to take notes on the section. This activity will prepare students for the Section Assessment, in which they will complete a graphic organizer that builds on the information using the Critical Thinking Skill: Summarizing.

The Eastern Mediterranean

What You Will Learn...

Main Ideas

1. The Eastern Mediterranean's physical features include the Bosporus, the Dead Sea, rivers, mountains, deserts, and plains.
2. The region's climate is mostly dry with little vegetation.
3. Important natural resources in the Eastern Mediterranean include valuable minerals and the availability of water.

The Big Idea

The Eastern Mediterranean, a region with a dry climate and valuable resources, sits in the middle of three continents.

Key Terms and Places

Dardanelles, *p. 114*
Bosporus, *p. 114*
Sea of Marmara, *p. 114*
Jordan River, *p. 115*
Dead Sea, *p. 115*
Syrian Desert, *p. 116*

TAKING NOTES As you read, take notes on the physical features, climate and vegetation, and natural resources of the region.

Physical Features	Climate and Vegetation	Natural Resources

If **YOU** lived there...

You live in Izmir, Turkey, on the Aegean Sea, but are traveling into the far eastern part of the country called eastern Anatolia. At home you are used to a warm, dry Mediterranean climate. You are surprised by the colder and wetter climate you're experiencing. Two mountain ranges come together here, and you notice that the peaks are covered with snow.

How does geography affect climate in these two places?

BUILDING BACKGROUND The Eastern Mediterranean region lies at the crossroads of Europe, Africa, and Asia. In ancient times, Greek colonists settled here, and it was later part of the Roman Empire. Geographically, however, it is almost entirely in Southwest Asia.

The countries of the Eastern Mediterranean make up part of a larger region called the Middle East. Europeans first called the region the Middle East to distinguish it from the Far East, which included China and Japan. The region is also sometimes referred to as Southwest Asia because of its location.

Physical Features

As you can see on the physical map on the next page, a narrow waterway separates Europe from Asia. This waterway is made up of the **Dardanelles** (dahrd-uhn-ELZ), the **Bosporus** (BAHS-puh-ruhs), and the **Sea of Marmara** (MAHR-muh-ruh). Large ships travel through the waterway, which connects the Black Sea to the Mediterranean Sea. The Bosporus also splits the country of Turkey into two parts, a small part lies in Europe and the rest in Asia. The Asian part of Turkey includes the large peninsula called Anatolia (a-nuh-TOH-lee-uh).

114 CHAPTER 5

Teach the Big Idea

The Eastern Mediterranean

1. **Teach** Ask students the questions in the Main Idea boxes under Direct Teach.
2. **Apply** Ask students to choose one physical feature found in the Eastern Mediterranean that is different from any features in the region they live in. Have students look up information about this feature and how it might affect the daily lives of people living there. For example, people living in the Jordan River valley mainly make a living through farming. **LS Visual/Spatial**
3. **Review** Call on students to describe the feature they chose and how they think it might influence daily living.
4. **Practice/Homework** Have students write a paragraph further describing the significance of the physical feature they chose. **LS Verbal/Linguistic**

📋 Alternative Assessment Handbook, Rubrics 30: Research; and 42: Writing to Inform

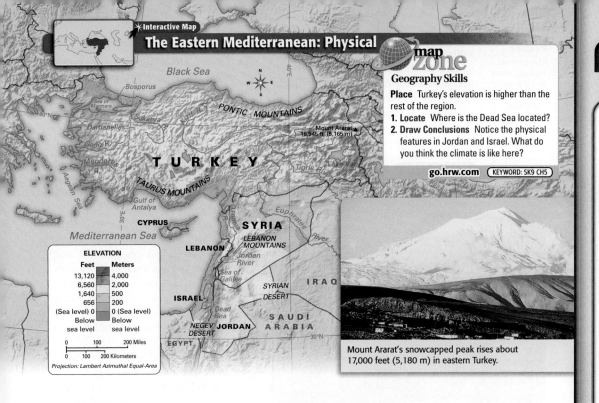

The Eastern Mediterranean: Physical

map zone

Geography Skills

Place Turkey's elevation is higher than the rest of the region.

1. **Locate** Where is the Dead Sea located?
2. **Draw Conclusions** Notice the physical features in Jordan and Israel. What do you think the climate is like here?

go.hrw.com   KEYWORD: SK9 CH5

ELEVATION

Feet	Meters
13,120	4,000
6,560	2,000
1,640	500
656	200
(Sea level) 0	0 (Sea level)
Below sea level	Below sea level

0   100   200 Miles
0   100   200 Kilometers
Projection: Lambert Azimuthal Equal-Area

Mount Ararat's snowcapped peak rises about 17,000 feet (5,180 m) in eastern Turkey.

Rivers and Lakes

The **Jordan River** begins in Syria and flows south through Israel and Jordan. The river finally empties into a large lake called the **Dead Sea**. As its name suggests, the Dead Sea contains little life. Only bacteria lives in the lake's extremely salty water. The world's saltiest lake, its surface is 1,312 feet (400 m) below sea level—the lowest point on any continent.

Mountains and Plains

As you can see on the map, two mountain systems stretch across Turkey. The Pontic Mountains run east–west along the northern edge. The Taurus Mountains run east–west along the southern edge.

Heading south from Turkey and into Syria lies a narrow plain. The Euphrates River flows southeast from Turkey through the plains to Syria and beyond.

Dead Sea

Because of its high salt content, swimmers do not sink in the Dead Sea.

ANALYZING VISUALS
What appears on the shore of the Dead Sea?

115

Main Idea

❷ Climate and Vegetation

The region's climate is mostly dry with little vegetation.

Recall Which areas have a Mediterranean climate? *Turkey's Black Sea coast and the Mediterranean coast all the way to northern Israel* Which areas have a desert climate? *much of Syria and Jordan, as well as southern Israel*

Identify Name two deserts found in this region. *Syrian Desert and Negev Desert*

Compare and Contrast How are the Syrian Desert and the Negev Desert alike and different? *alike— region's driest areas; only scattered shrubs grow there; Syrian—rock and gravel; less than 5 inches of rain per year; Negev—in southern Israel; temperatures as high as 114°F; in some areas barely 2 inches of rainfall*

FOCUS ON READING

After you read each paragraph on this page, re-read it and focus on the main ideas.

Farther inland lies plateaus, hills, and valleys. A rift valley that begins in Africa extends northward into Syria. Hills rise on both sides of the rift. Two main mountain ridges run north–south. One runs from southwestern Syria through western Jordan. The other, closer to the coast, runs through Lebanon and Israel.

READING CHECK Summarizing What are the region's main physical features?

Satellite View

The Bosporus is a strait that divides the city of Istanbul, Turkey.

Istanbul and the Bosporus

Throughout history, geography has almost always determined the location of a city. Istanbul, Turkey, which sits between Europe and Asia, is no exception. In this satellite image the city of Istanbul appears light brown and white. The body of water that cuts through the city is a strait called the Bosporus. It separates the Sea of Marmara in the south with the Black Sea in the north. Historically, the Bosporus has served as a prized area for empires that have controlled the city. Today, the strait is a major shipping route.

Drawing Conclusions Why do you think the Bosporus was seen as a strategic location?

Climate and Vegetation

The Eastern Mediterranean is a mostly dry region. However, there are important variations. As you can see on the map on the next page, Turkey's Black Sea coast and the Mediterranean coast all the way to northern Israel have a Mediterranean climate. Much of interior Turkey experiences a steppe climate. Central Syria and lands farther south have a desert climate. A small area of northeastern Turkey has a humid subtropical climate.

The region's driest areas are its deserts. Much of Syria and Jordan is covered by the **Syrian Desert**. This desert of rock and gravel usually receives less than five inches (12.7 cm) of rainfall a year. Another desert, the Negev (NE-gev), lies in southern Israel. Here the temperatures can reach as high as 114°F (46°C), and annual rainfall totals barely two inches.

In such dry conditions, only shrubs grow scattered throughout the region's deserts. However, in other areas vegetation is plentiful. In Israel, more than 2,800 species of plants thrive throughout the country's various environments.

READING CHECK Generalizing What are climates like in the Eastern Mediterranean?

Natural Resources

Because the Eastern Mediterranean is so dry, water is a valuable resource. The people of this region are mostly farmers. The region lacks oil resources, but does have valuable minerals.

Land and Water

In this dry region the limited availability of water limits how land is used. Commercial farms can only grow crops where rain or irrigation provides enough water.

Collaborative Learning

At Level

Climate Maps

1. Have students work in pairs to create their own maps of the region using a key to show the climates of each country. Students can use the map on the next page as a guide.

2. Have teams discuss where they think the best areas on the map are for farming, business, and trade. Remind students to consider climate, the location of rivers, lakes, and oceans, and the location of major cities when deciding where to put things. Have them make a map key to show the locations of their farms, businesses, and centers of trade.

3. Ask for student volunteers to present their maps to the class. **LS Verbal/Linguistic, Visual/Spatial**

   Alternative Assessment Handbook, Rubrics 20: Map Creation; and 14: Group Activity

---

Answers

Reading Check (left) *plateaus, highlands, rivers, and mountains*

Satellite View *because it connects the Black Sea with the Sea of Marmara and the Mediterranean Sea, which would make it ideal for trading and transportation*

Reading Check *mostly desert, Mediterranean, and steppe climates*

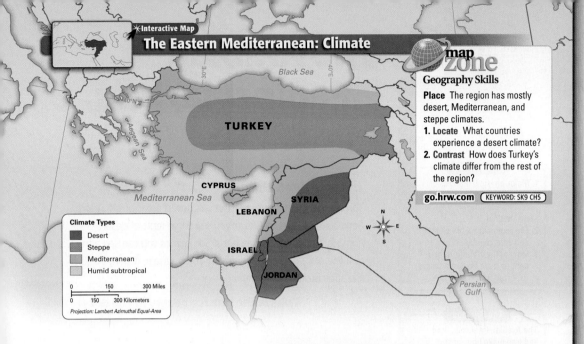

Interactive Map
The Eastern Mediterranean: Climate

Black Sea

TURKEY

Aegean Sea

CYPRUS

Mediterranean Sea

LEBANON

SYRIA

ISRAEL

JORDAN

Persian Gulf

Climate Types
- Desert
- Steppe
- Mediterranean
- Humid subtropical

0   150   300 Miles
0   150   300 Kilometers
Projection: Lambert Azimuthal Equal-Area

map zone
Geography Skills

Place The region has mostly desert, Mediterranean, and steppe climates.
1. **Locate** What countries experience a desert climate?
2. **Contrast** How does Turkey's climate differ from the rest of the region?

go.hrw.com   KEYWORD: SK9 CH5

In drier areas, subsistence farming and livestock herding are common. In the desert areas, available water supports a few nomadic herders, but no farming.

Mineral Resources

The region's resources include many minerals, including sulfur, mercury, and copper. Syria, Jordan, and Israel all produce phosphates—mineral salts that contain the element phosphorus. Phosphates are used to make fertilizers. This region also produces asphalt—the dark tarlike material used to pave streets.

READING CHECK **Drawing Conclusions** How do people use the region's mineral resources?

SUMMARY AND PREVIEW In this section you learned about the geography of the Eastern Mediterranean. Next, you will learn about the Arabian Peninsula.

Section 1 Assessment

go.hrw.com
Online Quiz
KEYWORD: SK9 HP5

Reviewing Ideas, Terms, and Places
1. **a. Describe** What makes the **Dead Sea** unusual?
   b. Explain What physical features separate Europe and Asia?
2. **a. Recall** What desert covers much of Syria and Jordan?
   b. Make Generalizations What is the climate of the Eastern Mediterranean like?
3. **a. Identify** What mineral resource is produced by Syria, Jordan, and Israel?
   b. Draw Conclusions Why must farmers in the region rely on irrigation?

Critical Thinking
4. **Summarizing** Using your notes, summarize the physical geography of Israel and Turkey. Use this chart to organize your notes.

Physical Features	
Turkey	Israel

FOCUS ON WRITING
5. **Describing the Physical Geography** What physical features of this region would you include in your description? How would you describe the climate? Note your ideas.

PHYSICAL GEOGRAPHY OF THE MIDDLE EAST **117**

Bellringer

If YOU lived there. . . Use the **Daily Bellringer Transparency** to help students answer the question.

Daily Bellringer Transparency, Section 2

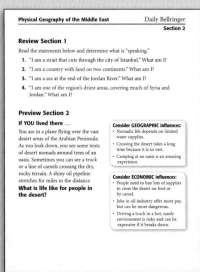

Physical Geography of the Middle East	Daily Bellringer
	Section 2

Review Section 1

Read the statements below and determine what is "speaking."

1. "I am a strait that cuts through the city of Istanbul." What am I?
2. "I am a country with land on two continents." What am I?
3. "I am a sea at the end of the Jordan River." What am I?
4. "I am one of the region's driest areas, covering much of Syria and Jordan." What am I?

Preview Section 2

If YOU lived there . . .

You are in a plane flying over the vast desert areas of the Arabian Peninsula. As you look down, you see some tents of desert nomads around trees of an oasis. Sometimes you can see a truck or a line of camels crossing the dry, rocky terrain. A shiny oil pipeline stretches for miles in the distance. **What is life like for people in the desert?**

Consider GEOGRAPHIC influences:
- Nomadic life depends on limited water supplies.
- Crossing the desert takes a long time because it is so vast.
- Camping at an oasis is an amazing experience.

Consider ECONOMIC influences:
- People need to buy lots of supplies to cross the desert on foot or by camel.
- Jobs in oil industry offer more pay, but can be more dangerous.
- Driving a truck in a hot, sandy environment is risky and can be expensive if it breaks down.

Academic Vocabulary

Review with students the high-use academic term in this section.

factor cause (p. 120)

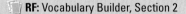 **RF:** Vocabulary Builder, Section 2

Taking Notes

Have students copy the graphic organizer onto their own paper and then use it to take notes on the section. This activity will prepare students for the Section Assessment, in which they will complete a graphic organizer that builds on the information using the Critical Thinking Skill: Comparing and Contrasting.

What You Will Learn...

Main Ideas

1. Major physical features of the Arabian Peninsula, Iraq, and Iran are desert plains and mountains.
2. The region has a dry climate and little vegetation.
3. Most of the world is dependent on oil, a resource that is exported from this region.

The Big Idea

The Arabian Peninsula, Iraq, and Iran make up a mostly desert region with very valuable oil resources.

Key Terms and Places

Arabian Peninsula, *p. 118*
Persian Gulf, *p. 118*
Tigris River, *p. 118*
Euphrates River, *p. 118*
oasis, *p. 120*
wadis, *p. 121*
fossil water, *p. 121*

TAKING NOTES As you read, use a chart like the one below to help organize your notes on the region's physical geography.

Physical Features	Climate and Vegetation	Resources

The Arabian Peninsula, Iraq, and Iran

If YOU lived there...

You are in a plane flying over the vast desert areas of the Arabian Peninsula. As you look down, you see some tents of desert nomads around trees of an oasis. Sometimes you can see a truck or a line of camels crossing the dry, rocky terrain. A shiny oil pipeline stretches for miles in the distance.

What is life like for people in the desert?

BUILDING BACKGROUND Iran, Iraq, and the countries of the Arabian Peninsula lie at the intersection of Africa, Asia, and Europe. Much of the region is dry and rugged.

Physical Features

Did you know that not all deserts are made of sand? The **Arabian Peninsula** has the largest sand desert in the world. But it also has huge expanses of desert covered with bare rock or gravel. These wide desert plains are a common landscape in the region that includes the Arabian Peninsula, Iraq, and Iran.

The countries of this region appear on the map in sort of a semicircle, with the **Persian Gulf** in the center. The Arabian Peninsula is also bounded by the Gulf of Oman, the Arabian Sea, and the Red Sea. The Caspian Sea borders Iran to the north.

The region contains four main landforms: rivers, plains, plateaus, and mountains. The **Tigris** (TY-gruhs) and **Euphrates** (yooh-FRAY-teez) rivers flow across a low, flat plain in Iraq. They join together before they reach the Persian Gulf. The Tigris and Euphrates are what are known as exotic rivers, or rivers that begin in humid regions and then flow through dry areas. The Arabian Peninsula has no permanent rivers.

Teach the Big Idea

The Arabian Peninsula, Iraq, and Iran

1. **Teach** Ask students the questions in the Main Idea boxes under Direct Teach.

2. **Apply** Have students create a map and legend illustrating the section's main ideas. On a sheet of art paper, have students draw a black outline of the region and use different colors to draw outlines of political boundaries, elevation areas, and climate regions. Ask students to indicate the location of oil fields on their map by creating a symbol for oil and drawing their

symbols in the appropriate locations. Tell students to draw these symbols in pencil in case they want to revise their maps as they see other illustrations. **LS Visual/Spatial**

3. **Review** Have each student share his or her map with the class.

4. **Practice/Homework** Have each student write an explanation of what his or her map shows. **LS Verbal/Linguistic**

Alternative Assessment Handbook, Rubrics 20: Map Creation; and 21: Map Reading

The vast, dry expanse of the Arabian Peninsula is covered by plains in the east. The peninsula's desert plains are covered with sand in the south and volcanic rock in the north. As you can see on the map, the surface of the peninsula rises gradually from the Persian Gulf to the Red Sea. Near the Red Sea the landscape becomes one of plateaus and mountains, with almost no coastal plain. The highest point on the peninsula is in the mountains of Yemen.

Plateaus and mountains also cover most of Iran. In fact, Iran is one of the world's most mountainous countries. In the west, the land climbs sharply to form the Zagros Mountains. The Elburz Mountains and the Kopet-Dag lie in the north. Historically, this mountainous landscape has kept towns there isolated from each other.

FOCUS ON READING After you read this paragraph, re-read it to make sure you understand Iran's landscape.

READING CHECK Summarizing What are the major physical features of this area?

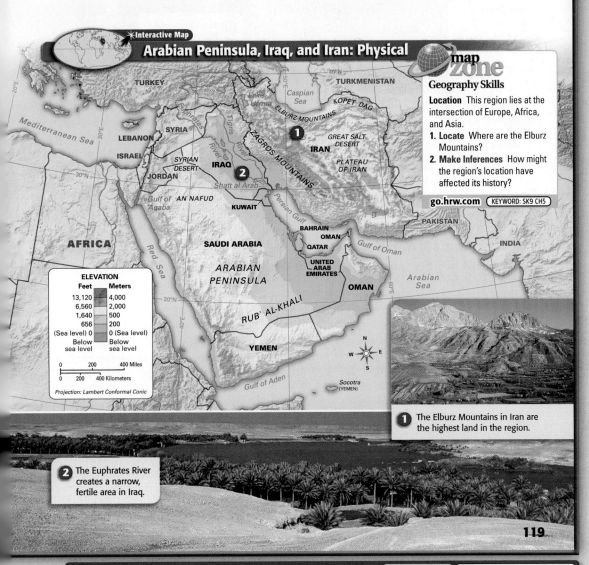

Interactive Map

Arabian Peninsula, Iraq, and Iran: Physical

map zone

Geography Skills

Location This region lies at the intersection of Europe, Africa, and Asia.

1. **Locate** Where are the Elburz Mountains?
2. **Make Inferences** How might the region's location have affected its history?

go.hrw.com KEYWORD: SK9 CH5

ELEVATION

Feet	Meters
13,120	4,000
6,560	2,000
1,640	500
656	200
(Sea level) 0	0 (Sea level)
Below sea level	Below sea level

0 — 200 — 400 Miles
0 — 200 — 400 Kilometers
Projection: Lambert Conformal Conic

1 The Elburz Mountains in Iran are the highest land in the region.

2 The Euphrates River creates a narrow, fertile area in Iraq.

119

Direct Teach

Main Idea

1 Physical Features

Major physical features of the Arabian Peninsula, Iraq, and Iran are desert plains and mountains.

Recall What bodies of water surround the Arabian Peninsula? *Persian Gulf, Gulf of Oman, Arabian Sea, Red Sea, Gulf of Aden*

Define What are exotic rivers? *rivers that begin in humid regions and then flow through dry areas*

Contrast How do the Arabian Peninsula's desert plains differ in the south and north? *covered with sand in south, volcanic rock in north*

🗝 Map Zone Transparency: Arabian Peninsula, Iraq, and Iran: Physical

📄 RF: Biography, Ibn Saud

Did you know. . .

Iran's Great Salt Desert (Dasht-e Kavir) is about 500 miles long and 200 miles wide—almost the size of Colorado. Its name comes from the fact that more water evaporates there than is replaced by rain, leaving salt deposits on the land.

go.hrw.com

Online Resources

KEYWORD: SK9 CH5
ACTIVITY: Importance of Camels

Differentiating Instruction

At Level	Standard English Mastery

Struggling Readers

1. Draw a graphic organizer like this for students to copy. Omit the blue type, and copy only the black type in the appropriate circles.

2. Have students look up *river*, *gulf*, and *sea*, and write the definitions in the appropriate circles.

3. Have students label the blank circles with the names of the appropriate bodies of water.

LS Visual/Spatial, Verbal/Linguistic

📄 Alternative Assessment Handbook, Rubrics 13: Graphic Organizers; and 21: Map Reading

Answers

Reading Check *mainly desert plains and mountains*

Map Zone 1. *in northern Iran near the Caspian Sea;* **2.** *possible answer—The region's culture and civilizations influenced and were influenced by those in the neighboring continents.*

119

❷ Climate and Vegetation

The region has a dry climate and little vegetation.

Explain What does "Rub' al-Khali" mean, and why is it called that? *"Empty Quarter," because there is not much life there*

Identify Cause and Effect Why do mountain areas in this region have trees? *because there is enough rainfall to support their growth*

Draw Conclusions If you saw a plant growing in the desert, what would you conclude about the way its roots grow? *that they grow either deep or spread out far*

🔖 Map Zone Transparency: The Arabian Peninsula, Iraq, and Iran: Climate

Connect to Literature

Desert Poem Have students look at the picture and caption of Rub' al-Khali on this page. Have them create a list of adjectives describing the picture. Have students write a poem with the first and last line "Rub' al-Khali," with several lines that use the adjectives to create an image and feeling for the reader.

Answers

Map Zone 1. *Kuwait, Bahrain, Qatar, United Arab Emirates;* **2.** *possible answer—The plateau and mountain areas get winter rains and snow which gives those areas a semiarid steppe climate.*

Reading Check *desert*

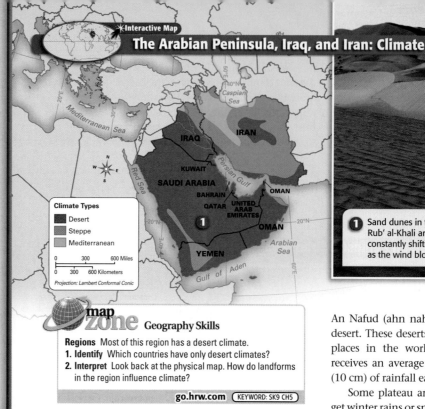

★Interactive Map

The Arabian Peninsula, Iraq, and Iran: Climate

Climate Types
- Desert
- Steppe
- Mediterranean

0   300   600 Miles
0   300   600 Kilometers
Projection: Lambert Conformal Conic

❶ Sand dunes in the Rub' al-Khali are constantly shifting as the wind blows.

map zone — Geography Skills

Regions Most of this region has a desert climate.
1. **Identify** Which countries have only desert climates?
2. **Interpret** Look back at the physical map. How do landforms in the region influence climate?

go.hrw.com   KEYWORD: SK9 CH5

ACADEMIC VOCABULARY

factor cause

Climate and Vegetation

As you have already read, most of this region has a desert climate. The desert can be both very hot and very cold. In the summer, afternoon temperatures regularly climb to over 100°F (38°C). During the night, however, the temperature may drop quickly. Nighttime temperatures in the winter sometimes dip below freezing.

The world's largest sand desert, the Rub' al-Khali (ROOB ahl-KAH-lee), covers much of southern Saudi Arabia. *Rub' al-Khali* means "Empty Quarter," a name given to the area because there is so little life there. Sand dunes in the desert can rise to 800 feet (245 m) high and stretch for nearly 200 miles! In northern Saudi Arabia is the An Nafud (ahn nah-FOOD), another large desert. These deserts are among the driest places in the world. The Rub' al-Khali receives an average of less than 4 inches (10 cm) of rainfall each year.

Some plateau and mountain areas do get winter rains or snow. These higher areas generally have semiarid steppe climates. Some mountain peaks receive more than 50 inches (130 cm) of rain per year.

Rainfall is a major **factor** in determining what vegetation grows in the region. Trees are common in mountain regions and in desert oases. An **oasis** is a wet, fertile area in a desert that forms where underground water bubbles to the surface. Most desert plants have adapted to survive without much rain. The shrubs and grasses that grow in deserts have roots that either grow deep or spread out far to capture as much water as possible. Still, some places in the region are too dry or too salty to support any vegetation.

READING CHECK Finding the Main Idea
What climate dominates this region?

120 CHAPTER 5

Differentiating Instruction

English-Language Learners   At Level

1. Read the "Climate and Vegetation" information out loud as students listen. Then ask them to share words they heard that describe the region's climate. Write these words on the board.

2. Have students use three to five of these words in a paragraph describing the region's climate.
   LS **Auditory/Musical, Verbal/Linguistic**
   📖 Alternative Assessment Handbook, Rubrics 18: Listening; and 40: Writing to Describe

Struggling Readers   Below Level / Prep Required

1. Give each student a blank outline map of the region. Have them copy the name of each country from the map in the text, using a different color for each. Have students use that same color to outline the country's boundary.

2. Have each student name a country and describe its relative location.
   LS **Verbal/Linguistic, Visual/Spatial**
   📖 Alternative Assessment Handbook, Rubric 21: Map Reading

Resources

Water is one of the region's two most valuable resources. However, this resource is very scarce. In some places in the desert, springs provide water. At other places, water can come from wells dug into dry streambeds called **wadis**. Modern wells can reach water deep underground, but the groundwater in these wells is often fossil water. **Fossil water** is water that is not being replaced by rainfall. Wells that pump fossil water will eventually run dry.

While water is scarce, the region's other important resource, oil, is plentiful. Oil exports bring great wealth to the countries that have oil fields. Most of the oil fields are located near the shores of the Persian Gulf. However, although oil is plentiful now, it cannot be replaced once it is taken from Earth. Too much drilling for oil now may cause problems in the future because most countries of the region are not rich in other resources. Iran is an exception with its many mineral deposits.

READING CHECK **Summarizing** What are the region's important resources?

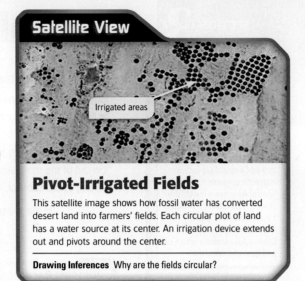

Satellite View

Irrigated areas

Pivot-Irrigated Fields

This satellite image shows how fossil water has converted desert land into farmers' fields. Each circular plot of land has a water source at its center. An irrigation device extends out and pivots around the center.

Drawing Inferences Why are the fields circular?

SUMMARY AND PREVIEW The Arabian Peninsula, Iraq, and Iran form a desert region with significant oil resources. Next, you will learn about the physical features of Central Asia.

Section 2 Assessment

go.hrw.com
Online Quiz
KEYWORD: SK9 CH5

Reviewing Ideas, Terms, and Places

1. **a. Describe** Where was Mesopotamia?
   b. Explain Where are the region's mountains?
   c. Elaborate Why do you think the **Tigris** and **Euphrates** rivers were so important in history?
2. **a. Recall** What parts of the region receive the most rainfall?
   b. Explain How have desert plants adapted to their environment?
3. **a. Define** What is **fossil water**?
   b. Make Inferences How do you think resources in the region influence where people live?
   c. Predict What might happen to the oil-rich countries if their oil was used up or if people found a new energy source to replace oil?

Critical Thinking

4. **Comparing and Contrasting** Using your notes and a graphic organizer like the one here, note physical characteristics unique to each area. Then list characteristics shared by all three areas.

Arabian Peninsula	Iraq	Iran
All		

FOCUS ON WRITING

5. **Choosing Descriptive Details** What details about the Arabian Peninsula, Iraq, and Iran would you include in a description of the region? Write down some ideas.

PHYSICAL GEOGRAPHY OF THE MIDDLE EAST **121**

Section 2 Assessment Answers

1. **a.** between the Tigris and Euphrates rivers
   b. near the Red Sea, in most of Iran, and in Oman near the Gulf of Oman
   c. Fertile land allowed early people to plant crops and settle there.
2. **a.** plateau and mountain areas
   b. Roots grow deep or spread out far.
3. **a.** water that is not replaced by rainfall
   b. possible answer—People live near sources of water needed for survival and near oil fields that provide jobs.

   c. possible answer—Population would decrease because people would need to move where they could get jobs.
4. possible answers—Arabian Peninsula: desert; Iraq: rivers; Iran: many areas covered by mountains; all: plains, desert climate, oil
5. possible answers—desert plains and mountains dominate the region; there is a dry climate and little vegetation; oil is a valuable resource

If YOU lived there... Use the **Daily Bellringer Transparency** to help students answer the question.

📖 Daily Bellringer Transparency, Section 3

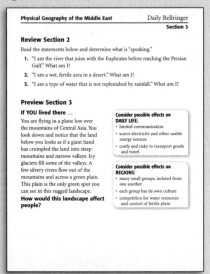

Key Terms and Places

📖 **RF:** Vocabulary Builder, Section 3

Taking Notes

Have students copy the graphic organizer onto their own paper and then use it to take notes on the section. This activity will prepare students for the Section Assessment, in which they will complete a graphic organizer that builds on the information using the Critical Thinking Skill: Finding Main Ideas.

Central Asia

What You Will Learn...

Main Ideas

1. Key physical features of land-locked Central Asia include rugged mountains.
2. Central Asia has a harsh, dry climate that makes it difficult for vegetation to grow.
3. Key natural resources in Central Asia include water, oil and gas, and minerals.

The Big Idea

Central Asia, a dry, rugged, landlocked region, has oil and other valuable mineral resources.

Key Terms and Places

landlocked, p. 122
Pamirs, p. 122
Fergana Valley, p. 123
Kara-Kum, p. 124
Kyzyl Kum, p. 124
Aral Sea, p. 125

 TAKING NOTES As you read, use a chart like the one below to help you organize your notes on the physical geography of Central Asia.

Physical Features	
Climate and Vegetation	
Natural Resources	

If YOU lived there...

You are flying in a plane low over the mountains of Central Asia. You look down and notice that the area below you looks as if a giant hand has crumpled the land into steep mountains and narrow valleys. Icy glaciers fill some of the valleys. A few silvery rivers flow out of the mountains and across a green plain. This plain is the only green spot you can see in this rugged landscape.

How would this landscape affect people?

BUILDING BACKGROUND The physical geography of Central Asia affects the lives of the people who live there. This region has been shaped throughout its history by its isolated location, high mountains, dry plains, and limited resources.

Physical Features

As the name suggests, Central Asia lies in the middle of Asia. All of the countries in this region are landlocked. **Landlocked** means completely surrounded by land with no direct access to the ocean. This isolated location is just one challenge presented by the physical features of the region.

Mountains

Much of Central Asia has a rugged landscape. In the south, many high mountain ranges, such as the Hindu Kush, stretch through Afghanistan. Tajikistan and Kyrgyzstan are also very mountainous. Large glaciers are common in high mountains such as the **Pamirs**.

Like its landlocked location, Central Asia's rugged terrain presents a challenge for the region. Throughout history, the mountains have made travel and communication difficult and have contributed to the region's isolation. Only a few high passes allow access to the region, and travel through these passes is difficult. In addition, tectonic activity causes frequent earthquakes there.

Teach the Big Idea

At Level

Central Asia

1. **Teach** Ask students the questions in the Main Idea boxes under Direct Teach.

2. **Apply** Have students imagine they are an explorer who has discovered Central Asia. Have them create an explorer's log noting something about the physical features, climate conditions, and natural resources this section discusses. The log should be written in the first-person. Encourage students to use vivid language and to describe feelings, such as being very hot or cold, tired, or in awe from climbing high mountains. **LS** Verbal/Linguistic

3. **Review** Have volunteers share their logs with the class.

4. **Practice/Homework** Have students expand on one entry, describing it using each of the five senses. **LS** Verbal/Linguistic

📖 Alternative Assessment Handbook, Rubric 40: Writing to Describe

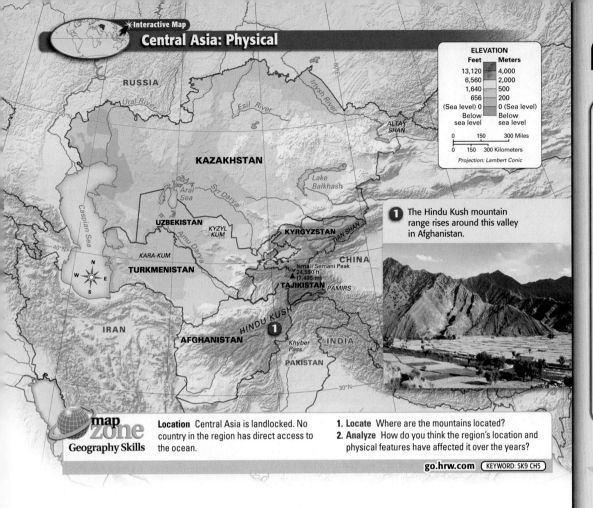

Central Asia: Physical

ELEVATION

Feet	Meters
13,120	4,000
6,560	2,000
1,640	500
656	200
(Sea level) 0	0 (Sea level)
Below sea level	Below sea level

0   150   300 Miles

0   150   300 Kilometers

Projection: Lambert Conic

RUSSIA

Ural River

Esil River

Irtysh River

KAZAKHSTAN

ALTAY SHAN

Lake Balkhash

Aral Sea

Syr Darya

UZBEKISTAN

KYZYL KUM

KYRGYZSTAN

TIAN SHAN

CHINA

Caspian Sea

KARA-KUM

Amu Darya

Ismail Semani Peak
24,590 ft
(7,495 m)

TURKMENISTAN

TAJIKISTAN

PAMIRS

HINDU KUSH

IRAN

AFGHANISTAN

Khyber Pass

INDIA

PAKISTAN

1 The Hindu Kush mountain range rises around this valley in Afghanistan.

map zone
Geography Skills

Location Central Asia is landlocked. No country in the region has direct access to the ocean.

1. **Locate** Where are the mountains located?
2. **Analyze** How do you think the region's location and physical features have affected it over the years?

go.hrw.com KEYWORD: SK9 CH5

Plains and Plateaus

From the mountains in the east, the land gradually slopes toward the west. There, near the Caspian Sea, the land is as low as 95 feet (29 m) below sea level. The central part of the region, between the mountains and the Caspian Sea, is covered with plains and low plateaus.

The plains region is the site of the fertile **Fergana Valley**. This large valley has been a major center of farming in the region for thousands of years.

Rivers and Lakes

The Fergana Valley is fertile because of two rivers that flow through it—the Syr Darya (sir duhr-YAH) and the Amu Darya (uh-MOO duhr-YAH). These rivers flow from eastern mountains into the Aral Sea, which is really a large lake. Another important lake, Lake Balkhash, has freshwater at one end and salty water at the other end.

READING CHECK **Generalizing** What challenges do the mountains present to this region?

PHYSICAL GEOGRAPHY OF THE MIDDLE EAST **123**

123

Main Idea

❷ Climate and Vegetation

Central Asia has a harsh, dry climate that makes it difficult for vegetation to grow.

Explain Why are the mountain areas of Central Asia not suitable for vegetation? *High peaks are too cold, dry, and windy for vegetation.*

Identify What part of Central Asia has a milder climate than most of the region? *the far north*

Draw a Conclusion Where in the Kara-Kum and Kyzyl Kum deserts would people most likely live? *near rivers*

Activity Doing Business in **Central Asia** Have students pick a major resource from the map legend and imagine they are in that business. Have them state which country in Central Asia they would want to do business with and why. **LS** Verbal/Linguistic

📝 Alternative Assessment Handbook, Rubric 12: Drawing Conclusions

💻 Map Zone Transparency: Central Asia: Land Use and Resources

Info to Know

Human-Environment Interaction
People have built two major structures to help them live in or cross the Kara-Kum Desert. One is the Kara Kum Canal, the largest irrigation canal in the world. The other is the Trans-Caspian Railroad, a major transportation route in Central Asia.

Answers

Map Zone 1. *Kazakhstan, Turkmenistan, and Uzbekistan;* **2.** *water for irrigation, milder climate, and rainfall*

Reading Check *extreme temperature ranges and limited rainfall*

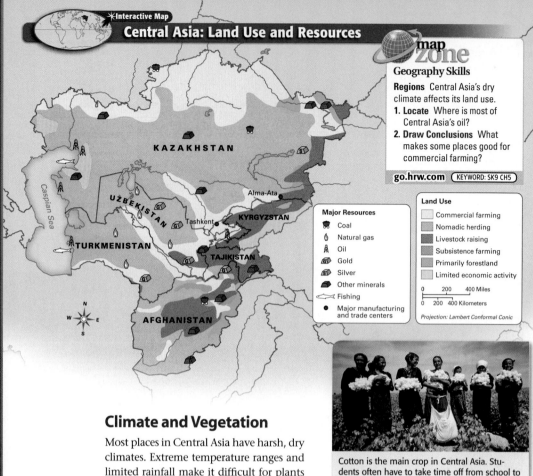

★Interactive Map
Central Asia: Land Use and Resources

map Zone

Geography Skills

Regions Central Asia's dry climate affects its land use.
1. **Locate** Where is most of Central Asia's oil?
2. **Draw Conclusions** What makes some places good for commercial farming?

go.hrw.com KEYWORD: SK9 CH5

Major Resources
- 🪨 Coal
- 🔥 Natural gas
- ⛏ Oil
- 💰 Gold
- 🪙 Silver
- 🪨 Other minerals
- 🐟 Fishing
- ● Major manufacturing and trade centers

Land Use
- ☐ Commercial farming
- Nomadic herding
- Livestock raising
- Subsistence farming
- Primarily forestland
- Limited economic activity

0 200 400 Miles
0 200 400 Kilometers
Projection: Lambert Conformal Conic

KAZAKHSTAN
Caspian Sea
UZBEKISTAN
Alma-Ata
Tashkent
KYRGYZSTAN
TURKMENISTAN
TAJIKISTAN
AFGHANISTAN

Cotton is the main crop in Central Asia. Students often have to take time off from school to help harvest the cotton.

Climate and Vegetation

Most places in Central Asia have harsh, dry climates. Extreme temperature ranges and limited rainfall make it difficult for plants to grow there.

One area with harsh climates in the region is the mountain area in the east. The high peaks in this area are too cold, dry, and windy for vegetation.

West of the mountains and east of the Caspian Sea is another harsh region. Two deserts—the **Kara-Kum** (kahr-uh-KOOM) in Turkmenistan and the **Kyzyl Kum** (ki-ZIL KOOM) in Uzbekistan and Kazakhstan—have extremely high temperatures in the summer. Rainfall is limited, though both deserts contain several settlements. Rivers crossing this dry region make settlements

possible, because they provide water for irrigation. Irrigation is a way of supplying water to an area of land.

The only part of Central Asia with a milder climate is the far north. There, temperature ranges are not so extreme and rainfall is heavy enough for grasses and trees to grow.

READING CHECK Generalizing Why is it hard for plants to grow in much of Central Asia?

124 CHAPTER 5

Critical Thinking: Interpreting Charts   At Level

Natural Resources Chart

1. Have students complete a chart like the one below, based on the Land Use and Resources map.

2. Have a class discussion, comparing and

contrasting each country's resources.
LS Visual/Spatial, Verbal/Linguistic

📝 Alternative Assessment Handbook, Rubrics 13: Graphic Organizers; and 21: Map Reading

COUNTRY	COAL	NATURAL GAS	OIL	GOLD	SILVER	OTHER MINERALS	FISHING
Afghanistan	X			X		X	
Kazakhstan	X		X		X	X	X
Kyrgyzstan							
Tajikistan			X	X		X	
Turkmenistan		X	X	X			X
Uzbekistan		X		X		X	

Natural Resources

In this dry region, water is one of the most valuable resources. Although water is scarce, or limited, the countries of Central Asia do have oil and other resources.

Water

The main water sources in southern Central Asia are the Syr Darya and Amu Darya rivers. Since water is so scarce there, different ideas over how to use the water from these rivers have led to conflict between Uzbekistan and Turkmenistan.

Today farmers use river water mostly to irrigate cotton fields. Cotton grows well in Central Asia's sunny climate, but it requires a lot of water. Irrigation has taken so much water from the rivers that almost no water actually reaches the **Aral Sea** today. The effect of this irrigation has been devastating to the Aral Sea. It has lost more than 75 percent of its water since 1960. Large areas of seafloor are now exposed.

In addition to water for irrigation, Central Asia's rivers supply power. Some countries have built large dams on the rivers to generate hydroelectricity.

Oil and Other Resources

The resources that present the best economic opportunities for Central Asia are oil and gas. Uzbekistan, Kazakhstan, and Turkmenistan all have huge reserves of oil and natural gas.

However, these oil and gas reserves cannot benefit the countries of Central Asia unless they can be exported. Since no country in the region has an ocean port, the only way to transport the oil and gas efficiently is through pipelines. But the rugged mountains, along with economic and political turmoil in some surrounding countries, make building and maintaining pipelines difficult.

In addition to oil and gas, some parts of Central Asia are rich in other minerals. They have deposits of gold, silver, copper, zinc, uranium, and lead. Kazakhstan, in particular, has many mines with these minerals. It also has large amounts of coal.

FOCUS ON READING
What context clues give you a restatement of the term *scarce*?

READING CHECK **Categorizing** What are three types of natural resources in Central Asia?

SUMMARY AND PREVIEW In this section you learned about the Middle East's rugged terrain, dry climate, and limited resources. In the next chapter you will learn about the first civilizations to develop there in the region of Mesopotamia.

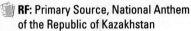

Section 3 Assessment

Reviewing Ideas, Terms, and Places

1. **a. Identify** What fertile area has been a center of farming in Central Asia for many years?
   b. Make Inferences How does Central Asia's terrain affect life there?
2. **a. Describe** Where do people find water in the deserts?
   b. Make Generalizations What is the climate like in most of Central Asia?
3. **a. Recall** What mineral resources does Central Asia have?
   b. Explain How have human activities affected the **Aral Sea**?
   c. Elaborate What kinds of situations would make it easier for countries of Central Asia to export oil and gas?

Critical Thinking

4. **Finding Main Ideas** Look at your notes on this section. Then, using a chart like the one here, write a main idea statement about each topic.

	Main Idea
Physical Features	
Climate and Vegetation	
Natural Resources	

FOCUS ON WRITING

5. **Describing Central Asia** Note information about physical features, climates, and resources of this region. Highlight information to include in your description.

PHYSICAL GEOGRAPHY OF THE MIDDLE EAST **125**

Section 3 Assessment Answers

1. **a.** Fergana Valley
   b. makes travel, communication, and growing crops difficult
2. **a.** rivers that run through the deserts
   b. harsh and dry, with extreme temperatures and limited rainfall
3. **a.** gold, silver, copper, zinc, uranium, lead, and coal
   b. Irrigation from rivers has caused it to lose more than 75 percent of its water.
   c. better technology and political cooperation to build pipelines

4. Charts should include one clear main idea for each topic.
5. Highlighting should show that students have selected key points from the section to include in their presentations.

Did you know...

There are reports of serious leaks in the Soviet-era canals of Central Asia. Some reports say that half or more of the water from the Kara-Kum Canal leaks into the desert.

Linking to Today

Moynaq, Uzbekistan Moynaq was once one of two major fishing ports on the Aral Sea. Today, the town is about 25 miles from the water. The remains of its fishing fleet lie rusting in the sand. Without the presence of the sea, winters and summers are more extreme, and dust storms and the polluted seabed harm people's health.

Activity **Letter from a Fisher**
Have students imagine being a fisher who once lived at the shore of the Aral Sea but is now farther from it. Have students write a letter from the fisher to a family member who moved away many years before, describing how the sea has changed, and how the changes have affected his or her life.
LS Verbal/Linguistic
Alternative Assessment Handbook, Rubric 25: Personal Letters

Geography and History

The Aral Sea

In 1960 the Aral Sea was the world's fourth-largest lake. However, human activities over the years have caused the Aral Sea to shrink drastically. The lake's former seafloor is now a desert of sand and salt. Also, towns that once benefited from their lakeside location are now left without access to the water. Area governments have built dams to control the flow of water into the lake, but so far their efforts have been unsuccessful.

Cause
Farmers have taken water from the Amu Darya and the Syr Darya to irrigate cotton fields. Now, less water flows into the sea than evaporates from it.

Effect
Stranded boats are a reminder of the fishing industry once based near the Aral Sea. The fishing industry is dying with the sea.

126 CHAPTER 5

Critical Thinking: Understanding Cause and Effect   At Level

Cause-and-Effect Charts

1. Have students examine the images and text to identify cause(s) and effect(s) related to the shrinking of the Aral Sea. They may also want to review other parts of the chapter that discuss this issue.

2. Have students design and complete a chart on large art paper that presents this information. Remind them that the format they choose should clearly show a relationship between cause and effect.

3. Have students illustrate their charts in a way that adds to the impact of the information.

4. Ask volunteers to share their charts and explain why they chose to present the information in the form they did.
LS Verbal/Linguistic, Visual/Spatial
Alternative Assessment Handbook, Rubrics 6: Cause and Effect; and 7: Charts

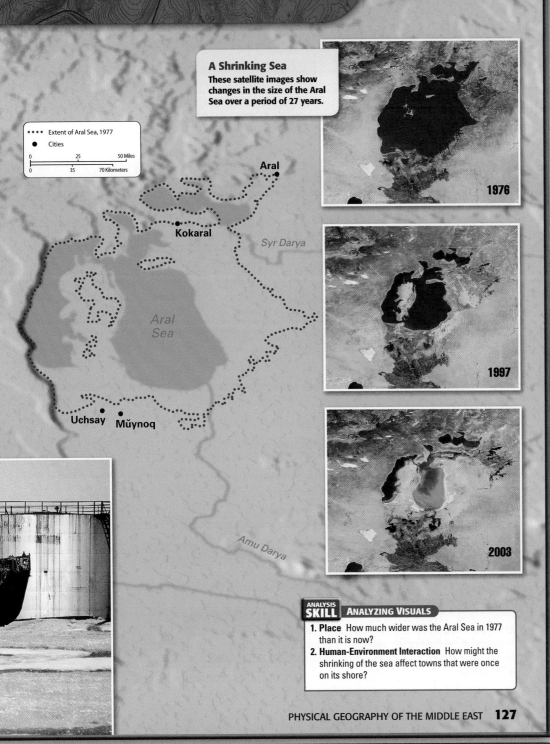

A Shrinking Sea
These satellite images show changes in the size of the Aral Sea over a period of 27 years.

•••• Extent of Aral Sea, 1977
• Cities

0   25   50 Miles
0   35   70 Kilometers

Aral

Kokaral

Syr Darya

Aral Sea

Uchsay   Mŭynoq

Amu Darya

1976

1997

2003

ANALYSIS SKILL ANALYZING VISUALS

1. **Place** How much wider was the Aral Sea in 1977 than it is now?
2. **Human-Environment Interaction** How might the shrinking of the sea affect towns that were once on its shore?

Geography and History

Info to Know

Satellite Images Students can view images of the Aral Sea and other areas of environmental change at the USGS Earthshots Web site: http://earthshots.usgs.gov

Did you know. . .

The salt concentration of the Aral Sea is now over 23 percent. This has lowered crop production in fields irrigated by its water. Wind also deposits salt from the dry seabed on cultivated land. The drinking water in the region now contains four times more salt per liter than the limit recommended by the World Health Organization.

Activity **Line Plot** Have each student create a line plot showing the change in size of the Aral Sea, using the map and satellite images.
LS Logical/Mathematical

Alternative Assessment Handbook, Rubrics 7: Charts; and 21: Map Reading

Map Zone Transparency: The Aral Sea

Collaborative Learning   At Level

The Great Aral Sea Debate

1. Have students work in small groups. Assign each group one of these two viewpoints in a debate about the Aral Sea: any activities that are shrinking the sea must be stopped immediately; solutions to save the sea must not affect current activities, such as irrigating crops.

2. Have each group come up with reasons supporting its point of view. Also have them anticipate the other team's arguments and prepare rebuttals.

3. Have the groups assign different pieces of information to each member, so each will have a turn to speak.

4. Have teams debate each other, giving each team a chance to present and to make a rebuttal. After each debate, discuss as a class what went well and what improvements could be made. **LS Verbal/Linguistic, Interpersonal**

Alternative Assessment Handbook, Rubrics 10: Debates; and 14: Group Activity

Answers

Analyzing Visuals 1. *about 200 miles;* **2.** *Answers will vary but should include mention of changes in how people interact with their environment because of this landscape change.*

127

Analyzing Tables and Statistics

Activity Table of Favorite Musical Groups

1. Using this table as a model, have the class create a chart showing the favorite musical groups of female and male students. Have the class brainstorm favorite groups. Write the list on the board. Help the class decide which groups to include in the table.

2. Have a volunteer draw the table. Guide the class to agreement on a title and labels and write these in.

3. Take hand counts to tabulate votes for each group, counting boys and girls separately. Ask for volunteers to enter the raw data. Then work with the class to change the numbers to percentages and have volunteers write these in.

4. Discuss what the data shows about the popularity of various groups.

LS Logical/Mathematical, Verbal/Linguistic

Alternative Assessment Handbook, Rubrics 14: Group Activity; and 11: Discussions

Interactive Skills Tutor CD-ROM, Lesson 6: Interpret Maps, Graphs, Charts, Visuals, and Political Cartoons

RF: Social Studies Skills, Analyzing Tables and Statistics

Social Studies Skills

| Chart and Graph | Critical Thinking | Geography | Study |

Analyzing Tables and Statistics

Learn

Tables provide an organized way of presenting statistics, or data. The data are usually listed side by side for easy reference and comparison. Use the following guidelines to analyze a table:

- Read the table's title to determine its subject.
- Note the headings and labels of the table's columns and rows. This will tell you how the data are organized.
- Locate statistics where rows and columns intersect by reading across rows and down columns.
- Use critical thinking skills to compare and contrast data, identify relationships, and note trends.

Arable Land in the Middle East			
Country	Total Area (sq mi)	Arable Area (sq mi)	Percent Arable
Afghanistan	250,001	30,325	12%
Iran	636,296	61,530	10%
Kazakhstan	1,049,155	86,870	8%
Saudi Arabia	756,985	12,642	2%
Turkey	301,384	89,843	30%
Yemen	203,850	5,932	3%

Source: Central Intelligence Agency, *World Factbook 2008*

Practice

Use the table here to answer the following questions.

1. Which country on this table has the highest total area? Which country has the lowest?

2. In which country is the smallest percentage of the land arable? Which country actually has the least arable land?

3. What inference, or educated guess, can you make about climate in these countries?

Apply

Using the Internet, an encyclopedia, or an almanac, locate information on the highest and lowest points in each country listed in the table above. Then create your own table to show this information.

Social Studies Skills Activity: Analyzing Tables and Statistics

Answering Questions to Understand a Table

Below Level

1. Ask students these questions to ensure they understand the table and how to read it:

- What is the title, and what does it mean?

- Which are the columns, and which are the rows?

- What is the heading for all the columns, and what does it tell you?

- What are the column labels?

- What does this table tell you?

LS Verbal/Linguistic, Visual/Spatial

Alternative Assessment Handbook, Rubric 7: Charts

Answers

Practice 1. *highest: Kazakhstan; lowest: Yemen;* **2.** *smallest percentage—Saudi Arabia; least—Yemen;* **3.** *possible answer—For the most part, these countries have very dry climates.*

Apply *Students' tables will vary depending on the source used, but should include information on the highest and lowest points in each country.*

Chapter Review

Geography's Impact
video series
Review the video to answer the closing question:
Why is it important for countries to prepare for possible oil shortages?

Visual Summary

Use the visual summary below to help you review the main ideas of the chapter.

QUICK FACTS

Rugged mountains cover parts of the Middle East, but plains are more common in the region.

Only a few rivers cross the dry landscapes of the Middle East. Water is scarce through much of the region.

The Middle East is mostly a desert region. Much of the area receives almost no rain.

Reviewing Vocabulary, Terms, and Places

Match the words in the columns with the correct definitions listed below.

1. wadis
2. landlocked
3. Dead Sea
4. Persian Gulf
5. fossil water
6. factor
7. Fergana Valley
8. oasis

a. a wet, fertile area in a desert
b. dry streambeds
c. fertile center of farming in Central Asia
d. large body of water northeast of the Arabian Peninsula
e. water that is not being replaced by rainfall
f. cause
g. completely surrounded by land with no direct access to the ocean
h. the world's saltiest lake

Comprehension and Critical Thinking

SECTION 1 *(Pages 114–117)*

9. a. **Describe** How is the Eastern Mediterranean considered a part of the Middle East?

   b. **Draw Conclusions** How would the region's dry climates affect where people lived?

   c. **Predict** What would happen if the region's people did not have access to water?

SECTION 2 *(Pages 118–121)*

10. a. **Identify** Through what country do the Tigris and Euphrates rivers flow?

    b. **Analyze** Based on the landforms and climate, where do you think would be the best place in the Arabian Peninsula to live? Why?

    c. **Evaluate** Do you think oil or water is a more important resource in the Arabia Peninsula? Explain your answer.

PHYSICAL GEOGRAPHY OF THE MIDDLE EAST **129**

Answers

Visual Summary

Review and Inquiry Have students write each section's Big Idea on a separate piece of self-stick note paper and then stick each note under the most relevant picture.

- Quick Facts Transparency: Visual Summary: Physical Geography of the Middle East

Reviewing Vocabulary, Terms, and Places

1. b   5. e
2. g   6. f
3. h   7. c
4. d   8. a

Comprehension and Critical Thinking

9. a. located at crossroads between Europe and the Far East (area farther east located on the Pacific Ocean)

   b. People need to live in areas where they can use irrigation for crops if water is scarce.

   c. They would not be able to farm or have drinking water and they would have to leave the area.

10. a. Iraq

    b. possible answer—between the Tigris and Euphrates Rivers where there is more vegetation and it is possible to grow food

    c. possible answer—Water is more important because without water, no one can survive.

Review and Assessment Resources

Review and Reinforce

SE Chapter Review

RF: Chapter Review

Quick Facts Transparency: Visual Summary: Physical Geography of the Middle East

Spanish Chapter Summaries Audio CD Program

OSP Holt PuzzlePro; Quiz Show for ExamView

Quiz Game CD-ROM

Assess

SE Standardized Test Practice

PASS: Chapter Test, Forms A and B

Alternative Assessment Handbook

OSP ExamView Test Generator, Chapter Test

Differentiated Instruction Modified Worksheets and Tests CD-ROM: Modified Chapter Test

HOAP Holt Online Assessment Program (in the Holt Interactive Online Student Edition)

Reteach/Intervene

Interactive Reader and Study Guide

Differentiated Instruction Teacher Management System: Lesson Plans

Differentiated Instruction Modified Worksheets and Tests CD-ROM

Interactive Skills Tutor CD-ROM

go.hrw.com
Online Resources

Chapter Resources:
KEYWORD: SK7 CH5

11. a. dryland farming, irrigation

b. no ocean ports, rugged mountains, political turmoil

c. possible answers: mountains—make travel and communication difficult; locations—no access to sea

Focus on Reading and Writing

12. Students should identify at least one new piece of information that they learned from re-reading the passage and add it to their lists of main ideas.

📖 **RF:** Focus on Reading, Re-Reading

13. Rubric Students' descriptions should

- give details about physical features of the country
- include information about the climate of the country
- describe the resources of the country
- provide a variety of sensory details that help readers picture the country

📖 **RF:** Focus on Writing, Writing a Description

Social Studies Skills

14. 27.5 million

15. Bahrain

16. 866

Using the Internet

17. Go to the HRW Web site and enter the keyword shown to access a rubric for this activity.

> KEYWORD: SK9 TEACHER

Map Activity

18. A. Rub' al-Khali
   B. Arabian Peninsula
   C. Tigris River
   D. Persian Gulf
   E. Euphrates River
   F. Elburz Mountains

SECTION 3 *(Pages 122–125)*

11. a. Describe How are farmers able to grow crops in Central Asia's dry landscapes?

b. Analyze What factors make it difficult for the countries of Central Asia to export their oil and gas resources?

c. Evaluate Do you think Central Asia's location or its mountains do more to keep the region isolated? Explain your answer.

FOCUS ON READING AND WRITING

12. Re-Reading Read the passage titled Resources in Section 2. After you read, write down the main ideas of the passage. Then go back and re-read the passage carefully. Identify at least one thing you learned from the passage when you re-read it and add the new information to your list of main ideas.

13. Writing a Description Look over your notes and choose one Middle Eastern country to describe. Organize your notes by topic—physical features, climate, resources. Then, write a one- to two-paragraph description of the country. Include information you think would be interesting to someone who knows nothing about the country. Add details that will help your readers picture the country.

Social Studies Skills

Analyzing Tables and Statistics *Use the Facts about Countries table at the beginning of the unit to answer the following questions.*

14. What is the population of Iraq?

15. What country is the smallest?

16. How many TVs per thousand people are there in Qatar?

Using the Internet

17. Activity: Writing Home For thousands of years, nomads have traveled the plains of Central Asia. They move their herds to several different pasture areas as the seasons change. Enter the activity keyword and join a caravan of nomads. Find out what it is like to pack up your house, clothes, and all you own as you move from place to place. Then create a postcard to share your adventures with friends and family back home in the United States.

Map Activity ★Interactive

18. The Arabian Peninsula, Iraq, and Iran On a separate sheet of paper, match the letters on the map with their correct labels.

Rub' al-Khali	Elburz Mountains
Persian Gulf	Arabian Peninsula
Tigris River	Euphrates River

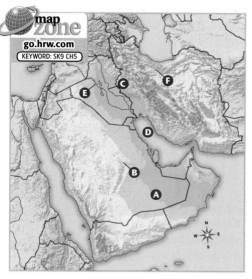

go.hrw.com
KEYWORD: SK9 CH5

Standardized Test Practice

DIRECTIONS (1–7): For each statement or question, write on a separate answer sheet the *number* of the word or expression that, of those given, best completes the statement or answers the question.

1 Dry streambeds in the desert are known as
  (1) wadis.
  (2) salty rivers.
  (3) exotic rivers.
  (4) disappearing rivers.

2 What is the most valuable resources of the Arabian Peninsula?
  (1) lead
  (2) gold
  (3) oil
  (4) copper

3 Where does most of the water used for growing crops in Central Asia come from?
  (1) rainfall
  (2) wells
  (3) irrigation
  (4) runoff

4 The climate of most of Israel, Jordan, and Syria is
  (1) desert.
  (2) steppe.
  (3) humid subtropical.
  (4) Mediterranean.

5 The world's largest sand desert is called the
  (1) Euphrates.
  (2) Elburz.
  (3) Dead Sea.
  (4) Rub' al-Khali.

6 The waterway that separates Europe from Asia is made up of the Sea of Marmara, the Dardanelles, and the
  (1) Bosporus.
  (2) Jordan River.
  (3) Tigris.
  (4) Dead Sea.

7 Which of the following descriptions *best* describes the landscapes of Central Asia?
  (1) dry and rugged
  (2) dry and flat
  (3) humid and landlocked
  (4) humid and cold

Base your answer to question 8 on the graph below and on your knowledge of social studies.

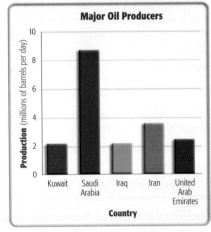

Major Oil Producers

Source: Central Intelligence Agency, *The World Factbook 2005*

8 Based on the graph above, about how many barrels of oil per day does Saudi Arabia produce?
  (1) 9
  (2) 9 thousand
  (3) 9 million
  (4) 9 billion

PHYSICAL GEOGRAPHY OF THE MIDDLE EAST **131**

1. 1
Break Down the Question This question requires students to recall factual information. Refer students who miss it to Section 2.

2. 3
Break Down the Question This question requires students to recall factual information. Refer students who missed it to Section 2.

3. 3
Break Down the Question This question requires students to recall factual information. Refer students who miss it to Section 3.

4. 1
Break Down the Question This question requires students to recall factual information. Refer students who miss it to Section 1.

5. 4
Break Down the Question Suggest that students first eliminate any answer they know is wrong based on their general knowledge of the region.

6. 1
Break Down the Question This question requires students to recall factual information. Refer students who miss it to Section 1.

7. 1
Break Down the Question Remind students to make sure the whole answer is correct before choosing it. Point out that in choice 2, *dry* describes the region, but *flat* does not, and in choice 3, *landlocked* describes the region but *humid* does not.

8. 3
Break Down the Question Point out to students that they will need to estimate and examine the units indicated in the label.

Reteach/Intervention Resources

Reproducible
- Interactive Reader and Study Guide
- Differentiated Instruction Teacher Management System: Lesson Plans

Technology
- Quick Facts Transparency: Visual Summary: Physical Geography of the Middle East
- Differentiated Instruction Modified Worksheets and Tests CD-ROM
- Interactive Skills Tutor CD-ROM

Tips for Test Taking

Use the 50/50 Strategy Tell students that if they have no idea about an answer, they can make an educated guess. They should first read all the choices carefully and eliminate any that are obviously wrong (for example because they are too broad or narrow or not relevant). They should next eliminate the least likely choice, then the next. If two choices seem equally correct, they should make their best guess and choose one.

Ancient Civilizations of the Middle East—Mesopotamia

Chapter Overview	Reproducible Resources	Technology Resources
CHAPTER 6 pp. 132–157 **Overview: In this chapter, students will learn about the world's oldest civilizations, which developed in the Mesopotamian region of the Fertile Crescent.**	**Differentiated Instruction Teacher Management System:*** • Instructional Pacing Guides • Lesson Plans for Differentiated Instruction **Interactive Reader and Study Guide:*** Chapter Summary Graphic Organizer **Resource File:*** • Chapter Review • Focus on Reading: Paraphrasing • Focus on Writing: Creating a Poster • Social Studies Skills: Sequencing and Using Time Lines **Experiencing World History and Geography**	**OSP Teacher's One-Stop Planner:** Calendar Planner **Power Presentations with Video CD-ROM** **Differentiated Instruction Modified Worksheets and Tests CD-ROM** **Interactive Skills Tutor CD-ROM** **Student Edition on Audio CD Program** **Map Zone Transparency:** The Fertile Crescent, 7000–500 BC* **Geography's Impact Video Program (VHS/DVD):** Impact of a System of Laws* **World Outline Maps: Transparencies and Activities**
Section 1: **The Fertile Crescent** **The Big Idea:** The valleys of the Tigris and Euphrates rivers were the site of the world's first civilizations.	**Differentiated Instruction Teacher Management System:** Section 1 Lesson Plan* **Interactive Reader and Study Guide:** Section 1 Summary* **Resource File:*** • Vocabulary Builder: Section 1	**Daily Bellringer Transparency:** Section 1* **Map Zone Transparency:** The Fertile Crescent*
Section 2: **The Rise of Sumer** **The Big Idea:** The Sumerians developed the first civilization in Mesopotamia.	**Differentiated Instruction Teacher Management System:** Section 2 Lesson Plan* **Interactive Reader and Study Guide:** Section 2 Summary* **Resource File:*** • Vocabulary Builder: Section 2 • Primary Source: Sumerian Flood Story • Biography: Enheduanna	**Daily Bellringer Transparency:** Section 2* **Map Zone Transparency:** Sargon's Empire, c. 2330 BC* **Internet Activity:** Drawing of a City-State **Internet Activity:** Sumerian Gods and Goddesses
Section 3: **Sumerian Achievements** **The Big Idea:** The Sumerians made many advances that helped their society develop.	**Differentiated Instruction Teacher Management System:** Section 3 Lesson Plan* **Interactive Reader and Study Guide:** Section 3 Summary* **Resource File:*** • Vocabulary Builder: Section 3 • Literature: *The Epic of Gilgamesh*	**Daily Bellringer Transparency:** Section 3*
Section 4: **Later Peoples of the Fertile Crescent** **The Big Idea:** After the Sumerians, many cultures ruled parts of the Fertile Crescent.	**Differentiated Instruction Teacher Management System:** Section 4 Lesson Plan* **Interactive Reader and Study Guide:** Section 4 Summary* **Resource File:*** • Vocabulary Builder: Section 4 • Biography: Hammurabi	**Daily Bellringer Transparency:** Section 4* **Map Zone Transparency:** Babylonian and Assyrian Empires* **Map Zone Transparency:** Phoenicia, c. 800 BC*

SE Student Edition	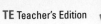 Print Resource	Audio CD
TE Teacher's Edition	Transparency	CD-ROM
go.hrw.com	**LS** Learning Styles	Video
OSP Teacher's One-Stop Planner	* also on One-Stop Planner	

HOLT
Geography's Impact
Video Program
Impact of a System of Laws
Suggested use: in Section 4

Review, Assessment, Intervention

 Quick Facts Transparencies: Visual Summary: Ancient Civilizations of the Middle East—Mesopotamia*

 Spanish Chapter Summaries Audio CD Program

 Progress Assessment Support System (PASS): Chapter Test*

 Differentiated Instruction Modified Worksheets and Tests CD-ROM: Modified Chapter Test

OSP Teacher's One-Stop Planner: ExamView Test Generator (English/Spanish)

 Alternative Assessment Handbook

HOAP Holt Online Assessment Program (HOAP), in the Holt Interactive Online Student Edition

---

 PASS: Section 1 Quiz*

 Online Quiz: Section 1

 Alternative Assessment Handbook

 PASS: Section 2 Quiz*

 Online Quiz: Section 2

 Alternative Assessment Handbook

 PASS: Section 3 Quiz*

 Online Quiz: Section 3

 Alternative Assessment Handbook

 PASS: Section 4 Quiz*

 Online Quiz: Section 4

 Alternative Assessment Handbook

Power Presentations with Video CD-ROM

Power Presentations with Video are visual presentations of each chapter's main ideas. Presentations can be customized by including Quick Facts charts, images from the text, and video clips.

Holt Online Learning

go.hrw.com
Teacher Resources
KEYWORD: SK9 TEACHER

go.hrw.com
Student Resources
KEYWORD: SK9 CH6

- Interactive Multimedia Activities
- Current Events

- Chapter-based Internet Activities
- and more!

Holt Interactive
Online Student Edition

Complete online support for interactivity, assessment, and reporting
- Interactive Maps and Notebook
- Standardized Test Prep
- Homework Practice and Research Activities Online

CHAPTER 6 PLANNING GUIDE

ANCIENT CIVILIZATIONS OF THE MIDDLE EAST—MESOPOTAMIA   **131b**

Differentiating Instruction

How do I address the needs of varied learners?
The Target Resource acts as your primary strategy for differentiated instruction.

ENGLISH-LANGUAGE LEARNERS & STRUGGLING READERS

TARGET RESOURCE

Resource File

The Resource File activities allow students to extend their knowledge of chapter-related places and people and to practice geography skills.

- Vocabulary Builder Activities
- Social Studies Skills: Sequencing and Using Time Lines

Additional Resources

Differentiated Instruction Teacher Management System: Lesson Plans for Differentiated Instruction

Quick Facts Transparency: Visual Summary: Ancient Civilizations of the Middle East—Mesopotamia

Student Edition on Audio CD Program

Interactive Skills Tutor CD-ROM

Spanish Chapter Summaries Audio CD Program

Teacher's One-Stop Planner:
- ExamView Test Generator, Spanish
- PuzzlePro, Spanish

English-Language Learner Strategies and Activities

SPECIAL NEEDS LEARNERS

TARGET RESOURCE

Differentiated Instruction Modified Worksheets and Tests CD-ROM

- Vocabulary Flash Cards
- Modified Vocabulary Builder Activities
- Modified Chapter Review
- Modified Chapter Test

Additional Resources

Differentiated Instruction Teacher Management System: Lesson Plans for Differentiated Instruction

Interactive Reader and Study Guide

Resource File: Social Studies Skills: Sequencing and Using Time Lines

Student Edition on Audio CD Program

Interactive Skills Tutor CD-ROM

Graphic Organizer Transparencies with Support for Reading and Writing

ADVANCED/GIFTED AND TALENTED STUDENTS

TARGET RESOURCE

Differentiated Instruction Teacher Management System

Lesson Plans for Differentiated Instruction provide teachers with strategies to help plan instruction for all learners.

Additional Resources

Resource File:
- Focus on Reading: Paraphrasing
- Focus on Writing: Creating a Poster
- Literature: *The Epic of Gilgamesh*

World History and Geography Document-Based Questions Activities

Geography, Science, and Cultures Activities

Experiencing World History and Geography

Differentiated Activities in the Teacher's Edition
- Examining the Rise of Sumer
- Creating Pictographs
- Writing a Letter
- Calculating Dates on a Time Line
- Creating a Human Time Line

HOLT Teacher's One-Stop Planner®

How can I manage the lesson plans and support materials for differentiated instruction?

With the Teacher's One-Stop Planner, you can easily organize and print lesson plans, planning guides, and instructional materials for all learners.

The Teacher's One-Stop Planner includes the following materials to help you differentiate instruction:
- Interactive Teacher's Edition
- Calendar Planner and pacing guides
- Editable lesson plans
- All reproducible ancillaries in Adobe Acrobat (PDF) format
- ExamView Test Generator (English & Spanish)
- Transparency and video previews

Differentiated Activities in the Teacher's Edition
- Cause and Effect Posters
- Creating a Farming Community
- Creating a Collage of Sumerian Inventions

Professional Development

HOLT Professional Development

What teacher training resources are available to help me grow professionally?

- **In-service and staff development** as part of your Holt Social Studies product purchase
- **Quick Teacher Tutorial Lesson Presentation CD-ROM**
- Intensive tuition-based **Teacher Development Institute**
- **Convenient Holt Speaker Bureau:** face-to-face workshop options
- **24/7 Ask A Professional Development Expert** at http://www.hrw.com/prodev/

Differentiated Activities in the Teacher's Edition
- Writing in Sumerian Numerals
- Writing a Story about Laws

DIFFERENTIATED INSTRUCTION PLANNING GUIDE

Chapter Big Ideas

Section 1 The valleys of the Tigris and Euphrates rivers were the site of the world's first civilizations.

Section 2 The Sumerians developed the first civilization in Mesopotamia.

Section 3 The Sumerians made many advances that helped their society develop.

Section 4 After the Sumerians, many cultures ruled parts of the Fertile Crescent.

Focus on Reading and Writing

Reading The Resource File provides a Focus on Reading worksheet to help students understand a passage of text by paraphrasing it.

📝 **RF:** Focus on Reading, Paraphrasing

Writing The Resource File provides a Focus on Writing worksheet to help students organize and create their posters.

📝 **RF:** Focus on Writing, Creating a Poster

CHAPTER **6**

Ancient Civilizations of the Middle East— Mesopotamia

FOCUS QUESTION

How did ancient civilizations contribute to the development of the Eastern Hemisphere?

What You Will Learn...

In this chapter you will learn about the world's oldest civilizations. These civilizations developed in the region of Mesopotamia, part of a larger area known as the Fertile Crescent.

FOCUS ON READING AND WRITING

Paraphrasing One way to be sure you understand a passage of text is to paraphrase it, or restate it in your own words. Practice paraphrasing sentences and whole paragraphs as you read this chapter. **See the lesson, Paraphrasing, on page S7.**

Creating a Poster Most elementary students have not read or heard much about ancient Mesopotamia. As you read this chapter, you can gather information about that land. Then you can create a colorful poster to share some of what you have learned with a young child.

132 CHAPTER 6

Mediterranean Sea

Phoenician trading ship

Empires The world's first empires were formed in the Fertile Crescent. Soldiers from these empires wore bronze helmets like this one.

Introduce the Chapter | At Level

The Development of Cities

1. Ask students to imagine that they are living in a large farming community in ancient times. Remind students that early farming villages were not technologically advanced. As the communities grew more food, their settlements grew in size. Have students discuss what inventions, technology, or organizations would be needed in the community as it grows. Ask students to explain why each item or idea is needed. What might it take to create these advances?

2. Explain to students that they are going to learn about the world's first civilization, Mesopotamia, and how it grew from small farming communities to a civilization with advanced technology and large cities.

3. Ask students to keep track of the new ideas that were developed in Mesopotamia and the impact those new ideas would have on the world. **LS Verbal/Linguistic, Interpersonal**

📝 Alternative Assessment Handbook, Rubric 11: Discussions

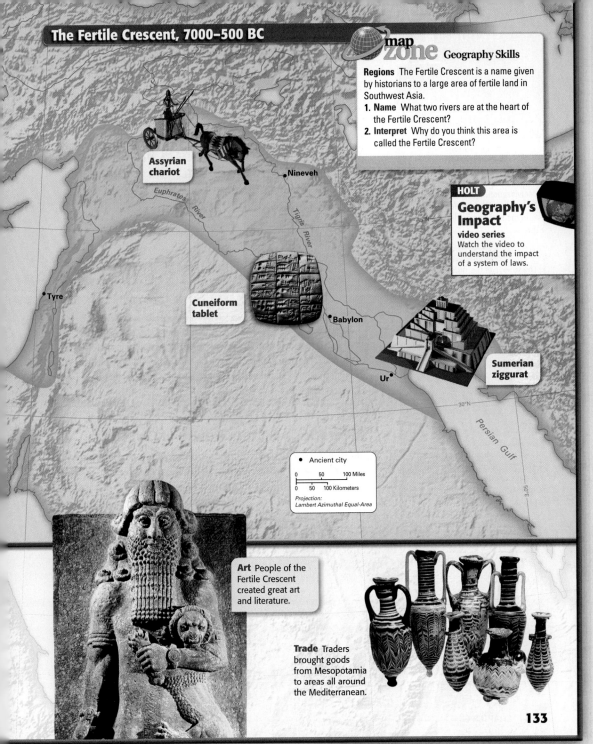

The Fertile Crescent, 7000–500 BC

map zone Geography Skills

Regions The Fertile Crescent is a name given by historians to a large area of fertile land in Southwest Asia.

1. **Name** What two rivers are at the heart of the Fertile Crescent?
2. **Interpret** Why do you think this area is called the Fertile Crescent?

Assyrian chariot

Nineveh

Euphrates River

Tigris River

Tyre

Cuneiform tablet

Babylon

Ur

Sumerian ziggurat

Persian Gulf

- ● Ancient city

0   50   100 Miles
0   50   100 Kilometers
Projection: Lambert Azimuthal Equal-Area

HOLT
Geography's Impact
video series
Watch the video to understand the impact of a system of laws.

Art People of the Fertile Crescent created great art and literature.

Trade Traders brought goods from Mesopotamia to areas all around the Mediterranean.

133

Info to Know

Chariot Racing Invented in Mesopotamia, ancient peoples of the Fertile Crescent used chariots not only as transportation, but for competition. Chariot racing became a popular sport in the ancient Olympic Games held in Greece. It was also the main sport at the games that took place in Rome's Circus Maximus coliseum. These chariots were drawn by up to three pairs of horses. Between four and six chariots raced around the arena seven times. The racing chariots were light and crashed easily, often injuring or killing the drivers.

Info to Know

Purple Cloth The Phoenicians were famous for trading purple cloth, a color used to signify royalty or wealth. The purple dye came from a type of mollusk called a murex. When the murex died, it secreted a liquid that turned violet when applied to white cloth. Depending on how long the murex had been dead and the amount of exposure to the sun, the dye ranged from pink to deep purple. Murex were once quite common along the Phoenician coast, but they gradually disappeared due to such high demand.

● **Chapter Preview** ●

Explore the Map and Pictures

The Fertile Crescent, 7000–500 BC
Have students locate the Fertile Crescent region on a map or globe, using the Persian Gulf as an aid. Ask students which countries currently make up the region of the Fertile Crescent. *Israel, Jordan, Syria, Iraq, and Kuwait*

Analyzing Visuals What type of material was readily available to early Mesopotamians for use in creating art and literature? *clay* How can you tell? *The statues, pottery, and cuneiform tablet are all made from clay.* What might be the purpose of a Sumerian ziggurat? possible answers—*place of worship, place to bury the dead, home for the king or ruler*

Map Zone Transparency: The Fertile Crescent, 7000–500 BC

go.hrw.com
Online Resources

Chapter Resources:
KEYWORD: SK9 CH6
Teacher Resources:
KEYWORD: SK9 TEACHER

HOLT
Geography's Impact
▶ video series
See the Video Teacher's Guide for strategies for using the chapter video to teach about the impact of a system of laws.

Answers

Map Zone 1. *Tigris and Euphrates;*
2. *The land is curved in a crescent shape, and the soil must be good for agriculture because of the rivers.*

Bellringer

If YOU lived there. . . Use the **Daily Bellringer Transparency** to help students answer the question.

📖 Daily Bellringer Transparency, Section 1

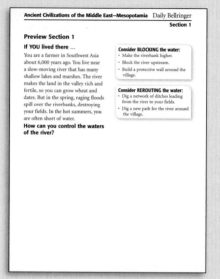

Ancient Civilizations of the Middle East—Mesopotamia   Daily Bellringer
Section 1

Preview Section 1

If YOU lived there ...

You are a farmer in Southwest Asia about 6,000 years ago. You live near a slow-moving river that has many shallow lakes and marshes. The river makes the land in the valley rich and fertile, so you can grow wheat and dates. But in the spring, raging floods spill over the riverbanks, destroying your fields. In the hot summers, you are often short of water.

How can you control the waters of the river?

Consider BLOCKING the water:
• Make the riverbank higher.
• Block the river upstream.
• Build a protective wall around the village.

Consider REROUTING the water:
• Dig a network of ditches leading from the river to your fields.
• Dig a new path for the river around the village.

Key Terms

📖 **RF:** Vocabulary Builder, Section 1

Taking Notes

Have students copy the graphic organizer onto their own paper and then use it to take notes on the section. This activity will prepare students for the Section Assessment, in which they will complete a graphic organizer that builds on the information using the Critical Thinking Skill: Identifying Cause and Effect.

The Fertile Crescent

What You Will Learn...

Main Ideas

1. The rivers of Southwest Asia supported the growth of civilization.
2. New farming techniques led to the growth of cities.

The Big Idea

The valleys of the Tigris and Euphrates rivers were the site of the world's first civilizations.

Key Terms

Fertile Crescent, *p. 135*
silt, *p. 135*
irrigation, *p. 136*
canals, *p. 136*
surplus, *p. 136*
division of labor, *p. 136*

TAKING NOTES As you read, take notes on the cause-and-effect relationship between river valleys and the civilizations that developed around it. Use a graphic organizer like this one to list causes and effects.

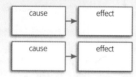

| cause | → | effect |
| cause | → | effect |

If **YOU** lived there...

You are a farmer in Southwest Asia about 6,000 years ago. You live near a slow-moving river that has many shallow lakes and marshes. The river makes the land in the valley rich and fertile, so you can grow wheat and dates. But in the spring, raging floods spill over the riverbanks, destroying your fields. In the hot summers, you are often short of water.

How can you control the waters of the river?

BUILDING BACKGROUND The region known today as the Middle East was the home of the world's first civilizations. Centuries before the first cities appeared in India and China, people in this region had formed complex societies and made remarkable achievements in many fields.

Rivers Support the Growth of Civilization

Early peoples settled where crops would grow. Crops usually grew well near rivers, where water was available and regular floods made the soil rich. One region in Southwest Asia was especially well suited for farming. It lay between two rivers.

Teach the Big Idea

The Fertile Crescent

1. **Teach** Ask students the questions in the Main Idea boxes under Direct Teach.

2. **Apply** Have each student create a proposal to the United Nations requesting a memorial or historical marker for Mesopotamia. Have students explain why they believe there should be a memorial and what significance Mesopotamia has to history. Remind students to cite specific accomplishments from the section and to use persuasive language in their proposals.
LS Verbal/Linguistic

3. **Review** Ask students to exchange their completed proposals with one another as a review of the section.

4. **Practice/Homework** Have students draw sketches of what their proposed memorials or markers might look like and describe where they could be located. **LS Visual/Spatial**

📖 Alternative Assessment Handbook, Rubrics 3: Artwork; and 43: Writing to Persuade

The Land between the Rivers

The Tigris and Euphrates rivers are the most important physical features of the region sometimes known as Mesopotamia (mes-uh-puh-TAY-mee-uh). Mesopotamia means "between the rivers" in Greek.

As you can see on the map, the region called Mesopotamia lies between Asia Minor and the Persian Gulf. The region is part of the **Fertile Crescent**, a large arc of rich, or fertile, farmland. As you can see on the map, the Fertile Crescent extends from the Persian Gulf to the Mediterranean Sea.

In ancient times, Mesopotamia was made of two parts. Northern Mesopotamia was a plateau bordered on the north and the east by mountains. The southern part of Mesopotamia was a flat plain. The Tigris and Euphrates rivers flowed down from the hills into this low-lying plain.

The Rise of Civilization

Hunter-gatherer groups first settled in Mesopotamia more than 12,000 years ago. Over time, these people learned how to plant crops to grow their own food. Every year, floods on the Tigris and Euphrates rivers brought **silt**, a mixture of rich soil and tiny rocks, to the land. The fertile silt made the land ideal for farming.

The first farm settlements were formed in Mesopotamia as early as 7000 BC. There, farmers grew wheat, barley, and other types of grain. Livestock, birds, and fish were also good sources of food. Plentiful food led to population growth, and villages formed. Eventually, these early villages developed into the world's first civilization.

READING CHECK Summarizing What made civilization possible in Mesopotamia?

FOCUS ON READING
Make sure you understand this paragraph by restating it in your own words.

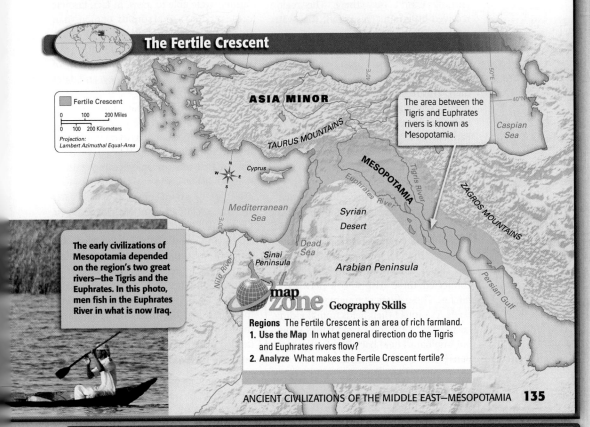

The Fertile Crescent

The early civilizations of Mesopotamia depended on the region's two great rivers—the Tigris and the Euphrates. In this photo, men fish in the Euphrates River in what is now Iraq.

Fertile Crescent

0   100   200 Miles
0   100   200 Kilometers

Projection:
Lambert Azimuthal Equal-Area

ASIA MINOR
TAURUS MOUNTAINS
Cyprus
Mediterranean Sea
MESOPOTAMIA
Euphrates River
Tigris River
Caspian Sea
ZAGROS MOUNTAINS
Syrian Desert
Dead Sea
Sinai Peninsula
Nile River
Arabian Peninsula
Persian Gulf

The area between the Tigris and Euphrates rivers is known as Mesopotamia.

map zone Geography Skills

Regions The Fertile Crescent is an area of rich farmland.
1. **Use the Map** In what general direction do the Tigris and Euphrates rivers flow?
2. **Analyze** What makes the Fertile Crescent fertile?

ANCIENT CIVILIZATIONS OF THE MIDDLE EAST—MESOPOTAMIA **135**

❷ Farming and Cities

New farming techniques led to the growth of cities.

Explain How did irrigation help farmers? *It provided a way of supplying water to fields and storing water for times of need.*

Analyze What effects did irrigation have on farming settlements? *It made farmers more productive, which led to a food surplus and less need for people to farm; these in turn led to a division of labor.*

Make Inferences How might big construction projects like the building of canals and large buildings lead to laws and government? *To keep workers organized and following the construction plan, structure and rules were needed, and these would lead to governments and laws.*

Info to Know

Raw Materials The people of Mesopotamia survived on resources provided by the Tigris and Euphrates rivers and the flat plains along the rivers. Wood, stone, and metal were almost nonexistent in the region. Without wood, buildings had to be made of clay bricks. Without stone, roads were difficult to maintain. However, by carefully using their water resources, people had enough vegetables, grains, fish, and livestock.

Irrigation and Civilization

Early farmers faced the challenge of learning how to control the flow of river water to their fields in both rainy and dry seasons.

1 Early settlements in Mesopotamia were located near rivers. Water was not controlled, and flooding was a continual problem.

2 Later, people built canals to protect houses from flooding and to move water to their fields.

Farming and Cities

Although Mesopotamia had fertile soil, farming wasn't easy there. The region received little rain. This meant that water levels in the Tigris and Euphrates rivers depended on rainfall in eastern Asia Minor where the two rivers began. When a great amount of rain fell, water levels got very high. This flooding destroyed crops, killed livestock, and washed away homes. When water levels were too low, crops dried up. Farmers knew that they needed to develop a way to control the rivers' flow.

Controlling Water

THE IMPACT TODAY

People still build dikes, or earthen walls along rivers or shorelines, to hold back water.

To solve their problems, Mesopotamians used **irrigation**, a way of supplying water to an area of land. To irrigate their land, they dug out large storage basins to catch rainwater that fell to the north. Then they dug **canals**, human-made waterways, that connected these basins to a network of ditches. These ditches brought water to the fields. To protect their fields from flooding, farmers built up the rivers' banks. These built-up banks held back floodwaters even when river levels were high.

Food Surpluses

Irrigation increased the amount of food farmers were able to grow. In fact, farmers could produce a food **surplus**, or more than they needed. Farmers also used irrigation to water grazing areas for cattle and sheep. As a result, Mesopotamians ate a variety of foods. Fish, meat, wheat, barley, and dates were plentiful.

Because irrigation made farmers more productive, fewer people needed to farm. Some people became free to do other jobs. As a result, new occupations developed. For the first time, people became crafters, religious leaders, and government workers. The type of arrangement in which each worker specializes in a particular task or job is called a **division of labor**.

Having people available to work on different jobs meant that society could accomplish more. Large projects, such as raising buildings and digging irrigation systems, required specialized workers, managers, and organization. To complete these types of projects, the Mesopotamians needed structure and rules. These could be provided by laws and government.

Collaborative Learning

Below Level

Creating a Farming Community

1. Organize the class into small groups. On a sheet of paper, have each group sketch a small farming community in its early stages. Students may use icons for houses, water, and other features.

2. Have groups introduce irrigation to their community. Ask students what adjustments they need to make to their village. Inform students that their village now has a food surplus. Ask groups how the village might change as a result. Have them add the changes to their drawings.

3. Remind students that one result of a food surplus is the division of labor. Have groups decide how their community will develop as a result and revise their drawings.

4. Drawings should gradually get larger, and students should see that their small community is becoming a city. Ask students what features they think are necessary for their city.

LS Visual/Spatial, Logical/Mathematical

Alternative Assessment Handbook, Rubric 14: Group Activity

3 With irrigation, the people of Mesopotamia were able to grow more food.

4 Food surpluses allowed some people to stop farming and concentrate on other jobs, like making clay pots or tools.

Linking to Today

Irrigation Irrigation is still a necessary part of farming. In fact, over 50 percent of all farmers today use some form of irrigation for their crops. While many farmers still use canals to direct water onto their fields, they use many other methods as well. Sprinkler irrigation and drip irrigation are two forms widely used in the United States.

Appearance of Cities

Over time, Mesopotamian settlements grew both in size and complexity. They gradually developed into cities between 4000 and 3000 BC.

Despite the growth of cities, society in Mesopotamia was still based on agriculture. Most people still worked in farming jobs. However, cities were becoming important places. People traded goods there, and cities provided leaders with power bases.

Cities were the political, religious, cultural, and economic centers of civilization.

READING CHECK **Analyzing** Why did the Mesopotamians create irrigation systems?

SUMMARY AND PREVIEW Mesopotamia's rich, fertile lands supported productive farming, which led to the development of cities. In Section 2 you will learn about some of the first city builders.

• Review & Assess •

Close

Discuss with students the role that water, and the control of it, played in the development of Mesopotamian civilizations.

Review

Online Quiz Section 1

Assess

SE Section 1 Assessment
PASS: Section 1 Quiz
Alternative Assessment Handbook

Reteach/Classroom Intervention

Interactive Reader and Study Guide, Section 1
Interactive Skills Tutor CD-ROM

Section 1 Assessment

go.hrw.com
Online Quiz
KEYWORD: SK9 HP6

Reviewing Ideas, Terms, and Places

1. a. Identify Where was Mesopotamia?
b. Explain How did the **Fertile Crescent** get its name?
c. Evaluate What was the most important factor in making Mesopotamia's farmland fertile?
2. a. Describe Why did farmers need to develop a system to control their water supply?
b. Explain In what ways did a **division of labor** contribute to the growth of the Mesopotamian civilization?
c. Elaborate How might managing large projects prepare people for running a government?

Critical Thinking

3. Identifying Cause and Effect Farmers who used the rivers for irrigation were part of a cause-effect chain. Use a chart like this one to show that chain.

River levels were uneven. → [ ] → [ ] → People enjoy many foods.

FOCUS ON WRITING

4. Understanding Geography Think of the images you might use on your poster. Would you want to show an image of the canals or rivers? Can you find pictures to show important features?

ANCIENT CIVILIZATIONS OF THE MIDDLE EAST—MESOPOTAMIA **137**

Section 1 Assessment Answers

1. a. in Southwest Asia, between the Tigris and Euphrates rivers
b. It came from the arc of fertile land from the Mediterranean Sea to the Persian Gulf.
c. annual flooding of the Tigris and Euphrates

2. a. When the rivers flooded, crops, livestock, and homes were destroyed. Too little water ruined crops. Farmers needed a stable water supply for farming and raising livestock.
b. People developed expertise outside of farming; large-scale projects were com-

pleted, and laws and government needed to carry out such projects were developed.
c. Both require specialized workers, organization, planning, and rules.

3. possible answers—build up riverbanks to hold back floodwaters; dig basins to hold excess water; build canals to connect basins to ditches; dig ditches to bring water to fields; use irrigation to water grazing areas

4. Students should consider images that best reflect the geography of ancient Mesopotamia.

Answers

Reading Check *to protect against damage from too much or too little water and to ensure a stable supply of water for crops and livestock*

Bellringer

If YOU lived there. . . Use the **Daily Bellringer Transparency** to help students answer the question.

🖎 Daily Bellringer Transparency, Section 2

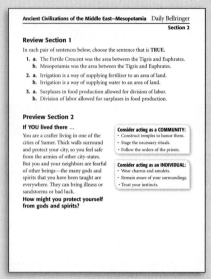

Academic Vocabulary

Review with students the high-use academic terms in this section.

role a part or function (p. 140)

interpret to explain the meaning of something (p. 141)

📖 RF: Vocabulary Builder, Section 2

Taking Notes

Have students copy the graphic organizer onto their own paper and then use it to take notes on the section. This activity will prepare students for the Section Assessment, in which they will complete a graphic organizer that builds on the information using the Critical Thinking Skill: Summarizing.

SECTION 2

The Rise of Sumer

What You Will Learn...

Main Ideas

1. The Sumerians created the world's first advanced society.
2. Religion played a major role in Sumerian society.

The Big Idea

The Sumerians developed the first civilization in Mesopotamia.

Key Terms and Places

Sumer, *p. 138*
city-state, *p. 138*
empire, *p. 139*
polytheism, *p. 140*
priests, *p. 141*
social hierarchy, *p. 141*

TAKING NOTES As you read, use a chart like the one below to take notes on the Sumerian civilization.

Characteristics	Notes
Cities	
Government	
Religion	
Society	

If YOU lived there...

You are a crafter living in one of the cities of Sumer. Thick walls surround and protect your city, so you feel safe from the armies of other city-states. But you and your neighbors are fearful of other beings—the many gods and spirits that you have been taught are everywhere. They can bring illness or sandstorms or bad luck.

How might you protect yourself from gods and spirits?

BUILDING BACKGROUND As civilizations developed along rivers, their societies and governments became more advanced. Religion became a main characteristic of these ancient cultures. Kings claimed to rule with the approval of the gods, and ordinary people wore charms and performed rituals to avoid bad luck.

An Advanced Society

In southern Mesopotamia, a people known as the Sumerians (soo-MER-ee-unz) developed the world's first civilization. No one knows where they came from or when they moved into the region. All we know is that by 3000 BC, several hundred thousand Sumerians had settled in Mesopotamia, in a land they called **Sumer** (soo-muhr). There they built an advanced society.

City-States of Sumer

Most people in Sumer were farmers. They lived mainly in rural, or countryside, areas. The centers of Sumerian society, however, were the urban, or city, areas. The first cities in Sumer had about 10,000 residents. Over time, the cities grew. Historians think that by 2000 BC, some of Sumer's largest cities had more than 100,000 residents.

As a result, the basic political unit of Sumer combined the two parts. This unit was the city-state. A **city-state** consisted of a central city and all the countryside around it. The amount of farmland controlled by a city-state depended on its military strength. Stronger city-states controlled larger areas.

Teach the Big Idea

At Level

The Rise of Sumer

1. **Teach** Ask students the questions in the Main Idea boxes under Direct Teach.

2. **Apply** Have students create a three-column chart on their own paper. In the first column ask students to write down any headings, subheadings, or important terms from the section. In the second column, have students create as many questions about each term or heading in the first column as they can. Lastly, have students write the answers to their questions in the third column.
🖎 **Verbal/Linguistic**

3. **Review** Have students cover the answer column with a sheet of blank paper as they review the answers to the questions from the section. Students may also quiz a partner.

4. **Practice/Homework** Have students use their charts to create five multiple-choice questions about the section. Remind students to provide an answer key and an explanation of why each answer is correct.
🖎 **Verbal/Linguistic**

📝 Alternative Assessment Handbook, Rubric 37: Writing Assignments

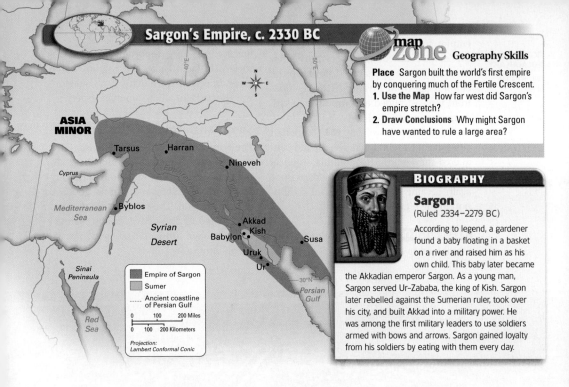

Sargon's Empire, c. 2330 BC

ASIA MINOR

Tarsus
Harran
Nineveh
Cyprus
Mediterranean Sea
Byblos
Syrian Desert
Akkad
Babylon
Kish
Uruk
Susa
Ur
Persian Gulf
Sinai Peninsula
Red Sea

Empire of Sargon
Sumer
Ancient coastline of Persian Gulf

0   100   200 Miles
0   100   200 Kilometers

Projection: Lambert Conformal Conic

map zone Geography Skills

Place Sargon built the world's first empire by conquering much of the Fertile Crescent.
1. **Use the Map** How far west did Sargon's empire stretch?
2. **Draw Conclusions** Why might Sargon have wanted to rule a large area?

BIOGRAPHY

Sargon
(Ruled 2334–2279 BC)
According to legend, a gardener found a baby floating in a basket on a river and raised him as his own child. This baby later became the Akkadian emperor Sargon. As a young man, Sargon served Ur-Zababa, the king of Kish. Sargon later rebelled against the Sumerian ruler, took over his city, and built Akkad into a military power. He was among the first military leaders to use soldiers armed with bows and arrows. Sargon gained loyalty from his soldiers by eating with them every day.

City-states in Sumer fought each other to gain more farmland. As a result of these conflicts, the city-states built up strong armies. Sumerians also built strong, thick walls around their cities for protection.

Individual city-states gained and lost power over time. By 3500 BC, a city-state known as Kish had become quite powerful. Over the next 1,000 years, the city-states of Uruk and Ur fought for dominance. One of Uruk's kings, known as Gilgamesh, became a legendary figure in Sumerian literature.

Rise of the Akkadian Empire
In time, another society developed along the Tigris and Euphrates. This society was built by the Akkadians (uh-KAY-dee-uhns). They lived just north of Sumer, but they were not Sumerians. They even spoke a different language than the Sumerians.

In spite of their differences, however, the Akkadians and the Sumerians lived in peace for many years.

That peace was broken in the 2300s BC when Sargon sought to extend Akkadian territory. He built a new capital, Akkad (A-kad), on the Euphrates River, near what is now the city of Baghdad. Sargon was the first ruler to have a permanent army. He used that army to launch a series of wars against neighboring kingdoms.

Sargon's soldiers defeated all the city-states of Sumer. They also conquered northern Mesopotamia, finally bringing the entire region under his rule. With these conquests, Sargon established the world's first **empire**, or land with different territories and peoples under a single rule. Sargon's huge empire stretched from the Persian Gulf to the Mediterranean Sea.

ANCIENT CIVILIZATIONS OF THE MIDDLE EAST—MESOPOTAMIA **139**

Cross-Discipline Activity: Literature   At Level

Writing an Autobiography

1. Review with students the information regarding Sargon of Akkad, including the biography feature above.

2. Ask each student to imagine that he or she is Sargon of Akkad and that Sargon has been asked to write an autobiography. Have students choose an event or accomplishment from Sargon's life.

3. Have each student write about the event or accomplishment they chose from Sargon's point of view. Students should include what

they imagine Sargon might have thought about the event or accomplishment. Ask students to use vivid descriptions and details.

4. Ask volunteers to share their autobiographies with the class. **LS** **Verbal/Linguistic**

Alternative Assessment Handbook, Rubric 41: Writing to Express

Main Idea

❷ Religion Shapes Society

Religion played a major role in Sumerian society.

Identify What is polytheism? *the worship of many gods*

Explain What powers did Sumerians believe their gods possessed? *power over harvests, floods, illness, health, and wealth*

Make Inferences Why did priests gain high status in Sumer? *because the people believed the priests gained the gods' favor*

📖 **RF:** Primary Source, The Sumerian Flood Story

Info to Know

Religion and Government Each city-state in Sumer had a city god and goddess. People built houses for the gods. As the city developed, these houses became large temples, or ziggurats. According to tradition, the ruler of the city, called an *ensi*, was in charge of the temple to the city's god. The ruler's wife was in charge of the temple to the city's goddess. The people of Sumer believed that the well-being of the city-state depended on the way they treated the gods.

Answers

Reading Check *He was a very capable military leader and used a permanent army to defeat all the city-states of Sumer.*

140

ACADEMIC VOCABULARY
role a part or function

Sargon was emperor, or ruler of his empire, for more than 50 years. However, the empire lasted only a century after his death. Later rulers could not keep the empire safe from invaders. Hostile tribes from the east raided and captured Akkad. A century of chaos followed.

Eventually, however, the Sumerian city-state of Ur rebuilt its strength and conquered the rest of Mesopotamia. Political stability was restored. The Sumerians once again became the most powerful civilization in the region.

READING CHECK **Summarizing** How did Sargon build an empire?

Religion Shapes Society

Religion was very important in Sumerian society. In fact, it played a **role** in nearly every aspect of life. In many ways, religion was the basis for all of Sumerian society.

Sumerian Religion

The Sumerians practiced **polytheism**, the worship of many gods. Among the gods they worshipped were Enlil, lord of the air; Enki, god of wisdom; and Inanna, goddess of love and war. The sun and moon were represented by the gods Utu and Nanna. Each city-state considered one god to be its special protector.

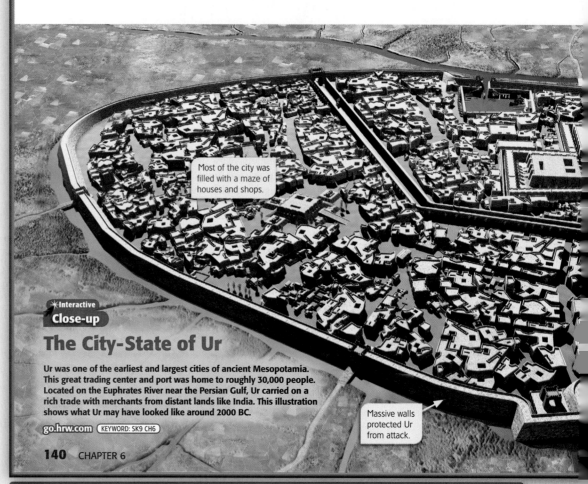

Most of the city was filled with a maze of houses and shops.

⭐Interactive
Close-up

The City-State of Ur

Ur was one of the earliest and largest cities of ancient Mesopotamia. This great trading center and port was home to roughly 30,000 people. Located on the Euphrates River near the Persian Gulf, Ur carried on a rich trade with merchants from distant lands like India. This illustration shows what Ur may have looked like around 2000 BC.

go.hrw.com KEYWORD: SK9 CH6

140 CHAPTER 6

Massive walls protected Ur from attack.

Differentiating Instruction

Below Level

Struggling Readers

1. To help students learn the major characteristics of Sumer, draw the graphic organizer for students to see. Omit the blue, italicized answers.

2. Have each student copy and complete the graphic organizer. When students are finished, review the answers with the class.
   LS Verbal/Linguistic, Visual/Spatial

The Rise of Sumer		
Government	**Religion**	**Society**
• originally organized into city-states	• polytheistic	• kings
	• each city had a god as protector	• priests
• large empire created by Sargon	• gods have enormous power	• skilled crafters, merchants, and traders
• first permanent army	• priests interpret wishes of gods	• laborers and farmers
	• everyone must serve and worship gods	• slaves

The Sumerians believed that their gods had enormous powers. Gods could bring good harvests or disastrous floods. They could bring illness, or they could bring good health and wealth. The Sumerians believed that success in life depended on pleasing the gods. Every Sumerian had to serve and worship the gods.

Priests, people who performed or led religious ceremonies, had great status in Sumer. People relied on them to help gain the gods' favor. Priests <u>interpreted</u> the wishes of the gods and made offerings to them. These offerings were made in temples, special buildings where priests performed their religious ceremonies.

Sumerian Social Order

Because of their status, priests occupied a high level in Sumer's **social hierarchy**, the division of society by rank or class. In fact, priests were just below kings. The kings of Sumer claimed that they had been chosen by the gods to rule.

Below the priests were Sumer's skilled craftspeople, merchants, and traders. Trade had a great impact on Sumerian society. Traders traveled to faraway places and exchanged grain for gold, silver, copper, lumber, and precious stones.

Below traders, farmers and laborers made up the large working class. Slaves were at the bottom of the social order.

ACADEMIC VOCABULARY

interpret to explain the meaning of something

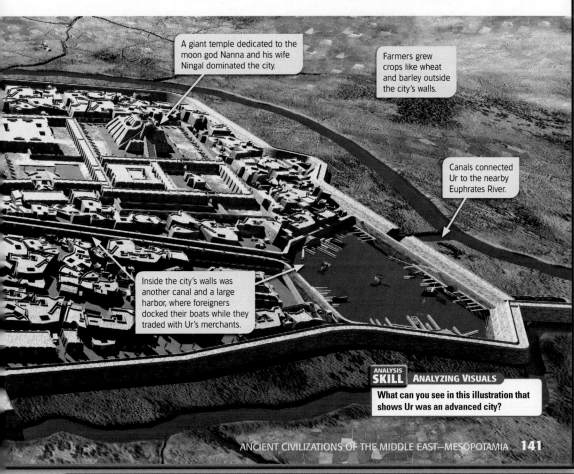

A giant temple dedicated to the moon god Nanna and his wife Ningal dominated the city.

Farmers grew crops like wheat and barley outside the city's walls.

Canals connected Ur to the nearby Euphrates River.

Inside the city's walls was another canal and a large harbor, where foreigners docked their boats while they traded with Ur's merchants.

ANALYSIS SKILL **ANALYZING VISUALS**

What can you see in this illustration that shows Ur was an advanced city?

ANCIENT CIVILIZATIONS OF THE MIDDLE EAST—MESOPOTAMIA **141**

Direct Teach

Close-up

The City-State of Ur Review the illustration of Ur with students. Ask the following questions:

Recall What purpose did the wall around the city serve? *protected the city from attack*

Make Inferences Where did the merchants of Ur probably live? *in the city, possibly near their shops or the market*

Elaborate Why do you think the temple is the largest building in Ur? *possible answers—because religion was very important, because many people visited the temple*

Info to Know

The Discovery of Ur The ruins of Ur were not discovered until the 1800s. Until that time, people thought references to the city of Ur were mere legend. Excavations in the 1920s indicated that the city was established around 4000 BC. In the 1950s archaeologists found the oldest known written laws at Ur. They dated back to about 2050 BC. Over the years great riches have been found in the ruins, including beautiful gold jewelry, golden weapons, and precious stones.

Critical Thinking: Summarizing

At Level

Illustrated Social Hierarchy

1. Review with students the meaning of the term *social hierarchy*. Ask students to look up the word *hierarchy* in a dictionary. Help students understand that a hierarchy is a ranking of things.

2. Have each student create a list of the social classes in ancient Sumer, along with the jobs or responsibilities of members in each social class. Ask students which classes they think would have more people. Why? Which classes would have fewer people?

3. Then have each student create an illustration that reflects the social classes of Sumer as well as the primary responsibilities of each. One example might be a triangle with a crown in the top level to represent the king.

4. Have students display their social hierarchy illustrations for the class to see.
   LS **Visual/Spatial, Verbal/Linguistic**

   Alternative Assessment Handbook, Rubric 3: Artwork

Answers

Analyzing Visuals *massive walls, elaborate buildings, system of canals and harbors*

141

Main Idea

Religion Shapes Society, *continued*

Explain Who made up the middle ranks of society? *craftspeople, merchants, and traders*

Make Inferences Why might Enheduanna have had an easier time than other women in becoming a writer? *possible answers—because she was Sargon's daughter and therefore had privileges* What hurdles might she still have faced? *still faced ridicule or hostility from men who held powerful positions in society*

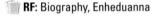 **RF:** Biography, Enheduanna

● Review & Assess ●

Close

Have students write a short paragraph summarizing the government, religion, and society of Sumer.

Review

 Online Quiz Section 2

Assess

SE Section 2 Assessment
PASS: Section 2 Quiz
Alternative Assessment Handbook

Reteach/Classroom Intervention

Interactive Reader and Study Guide, Section 2

Interactive Skills Tutor CD-ROM

Answers

Reading Check *It brought important goods like copper and lumber to Sumer and led to greater wealth.*

142

Sumerian Society

Sumerian society was divided into different groups. This ancient artifact shows Sumerian leaders celebrating a military victory while a musician plays an instrument.

Men and Women in Sumer

Sumerian men and women had different roles. In general, men held political power and made laws while women took care of the home and children. Education was usually reserved for men, but some upper-class women were educated as well.

Some educated women were priestesses in Sumer's temples. They helped shape Sumerian culture. One, Enheduanna, the daughter of Sargon, wrote hymns to the goddess Inanna. The first known female writer in history, she wrote these verses:

" My Queen,
[all] the Anunna, the great gods,
Fled before you like fluttering bats,
Could not stand before your awesome face, "
–Enheduanna, from *Adoration of Inanna of Ur*

READING CHECK **Analyzing** How did trade affect Sumerian society?

SUMMARY AND PREVIEW In this section you learned about Sumerian city-states, religion, and society. In Section 3, you will read about Sumerian achievements.

Section 2 Assessment

go.hrw.com
Online Quiz
KEYWORD: SK9 HP6

Reviewing Ideas, Terms, and Places

1. **a. Recall** What was the basic political unit of Sumer?
   b. Explain What steps did Sumerian **city-states** take to protect themselves from their rivals?
   c. Elaborate How do you think that Sargon's creation of an **empire** changed the later history of Mesopotamia? Defend your answer.
2. **a. Identify** What is **polytheism**?
   b. Draw Conclusions Why do you think **priests** were so influential in ancient Sumerian society?
   c. Elaborate Why would rulers benefit if they claimed to be chosen by the gods?

Critical Thinking

3. **Summarizing** In the right column of your note-taking chart, write a summary sentence for each of the four characteristics. Then add a box at the bottom of the chart and write a sentence summarizing the Sumerian civilization.

Characteristics	Notes
Cities	
Government	
Religion	
Society	

Summary Sentence:

FOCUS ON WRITING

4. **Gathering Information about Sumer** You will need some pictures of Sumerian society on your poster. Note two or three things to add.

142 CHAPTER 6

Section 2 Assessment Answers

1. **a.** the city-state
   b. built up strong armies and constructed walls around their cities
   c. possible answers—reduced conflicts between city-states, created better chance for civilization to develop in peacetime
2. **a.** the worship of many gods
   b. because people relied on them to gain the gods' favor

   c. People would do what the rulers said because they did not want to offend the gods by disobeying the rulers.
3. Students' summary sentences should accurately reflect what they read about Sumer.
4. possible answers—Sumerians worshipping gods, traders exchanging grain for gold, priestess writing a hymn

Sumerian Achievements

If **YOU** lived there...

You are a student at a school for scribes in Sumer. Learning all the symbols for writing is very hard. Your teacher assigns you lessons to write on your clay tablet, but you can't help making mistakes. Then you have to smooth out the surface and try again. Still, being a scribe can lead to important jobs for the king. You could make your family proud.

Why would you want to be a scribe?

BUILDING BACKGROUND Sumerian society was advanced in terms of religion and government organization. The Sumerians were responsible for many other achievements, which were passed down to later civilizations.

Invention of Writing

The Sumerians made one of the greatest cultural advances in history. They developed **cuneiform** (kyoo-NEE-uh-fohrm), the world's first system of writing. The Sumerians did not have pens, pencils, or paper, though. Instead, they used sharp tools called styluses to make wedge-shaped symbols on clay tablets.

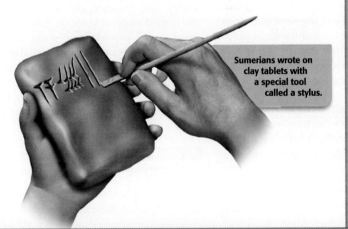

Sumerians wrote on clay tablets with a special tool called a stylus.

What You Will Learn...

Main Ideas

1. The Sumerians invented the world's first writing system.
2. Advances and inventions changed Sumerian lives.
3. Many types of art developed in Sumer.

The Big Idea

The Sumerians made many advances that helped their society develop.

Key Terms

cuneiform, *p. 143*
pictographs, *p. 144*
scribe, *p. 144*
epics, *p. 144*
architecture, *p. 146*
ziggurat, *p. 146*

TAKING NOTES Create a chart like the one below. As you read, list the achievements and advances made by the Sumerians.

Sumerian Advances and Achievements

143

Preteach

Bellringer

If YOU lived there. . . Use the **Daily Bellringer Transparency** to help students answer the question.

Daily Bellringer Transparency, Section 3

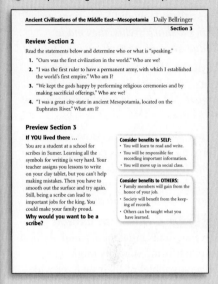

Ancient Civilizations of the Middle East—Mesopotamia Daily Bellringer
Section 3

Review Section 2

Read the statements below and determine who or what is "speaking."

1. "Ours was the first civilization in the world." Who are we?
2. "I was the first ruler to have a permanent army, with which I established the world's first empire." Who am I?
3. "We kept the gods happy by performing religious ceremonies and by making sacrificial offerings." Who are we?
4. "I was a great city-state in ancient Mesopotamia, located on the Euphrates River." What am I?

Preview Section 3

If YOU lived there ...

You are a student at a school for scribes in Sumer. Learning all the symbols for writing is very hard. Your teacher assigns you lessons to write on your clay tablet, but you can't help making mistakes. Then you have to smooth out the surface and try again. Still, being a scribe can lead to important jobs for the king. You could make your family proud.
Why would you want to be a scribe?

Consider benefits to SELF:
• You will learn to read and write.
• You will be responsible for recording important information.
• You will move up in social class.

Consider benefits to OTHERS:
• Family members will gain from the honor of your job.
• Society will benefit from the keeping of records.
• Others can be taught what you have learned.

Academic Vocabulary

Review with students the high-use academic term in this section.

complex difficult, not simple (p. 144)
RF: Vocabulary Builder, Section 3

Taking Notes

Have students copy the graphic organizer onto their own paper and then use it to take notes on the section. This activity will prepare students for the Section Assessment, in which they will complete a graphic organizer that builds on the information using the Critical Thinking Skill: Identifying Effects.

Teach the Big Idea

At Level

Sumerian Achievements

1. **Teach** Ask students the questions in the Main Idea boxes under Direct Teach.

2. **Apply** Tell students to draw a table with two long columns. As they read through the chapter, have them list in one column the different Sumerian achievements, such as those in writing, technology, and art. Once they have finished the section, have them fill in the other column, explaining whether we use each achievement in today's world and, if so, how. **LS Visual/Spatial**

3. **Review** As you review the section's main ideas, have students discuss some of the specific achievements, how they were used at the time, and how they are used today.

4. **Practice/Homework** Have students write down five inventions that have been made in the last 20 years and predict whether or not those inventions might still be used 5,000 years from now. **LS Verbal/Linguistic**

   Alternative Assessment Handbook, Rubrics 7: Charts; and 37: Writing Assignments

Main Idea

❶ Invention of Writing

The Sumerians invented the world's first writing system.

Describe How did Sumerians write? *Using a sharp stylus, they made wedge-shaped symbols on clay tablets.*

Explain Why were scribes important? *They kept track of items people traded and records for the government or temples.*

Draw Conclusions How was cuneiform used to express complex ideas? *Cuneiform used symbols to represent syllables and could combine syllables to express complex ideas.*

Activity **Cuneiform Exhibit**
Have students create a museum exhibit on cuneiform. Students might create a clay tablet of their own, provide information about cuneiform, or show images of actual cuneiform writing.
LS Visual/Spatial, Verbal/Linguistic
📄 RF: Literature, *The Epic of Gilgamesh*

Did you know...

Sumerian scribes wrote their symbols on wet clay tablets, which were then dried in the sun or in ovens. Though these clay tablets were the standard writing surface in Mesopotamia, wood, metal, and even stone were used occasionally. The more durable of these materials have lasted thousands of years!

Answers

Reading Check *for keeping business records*

144

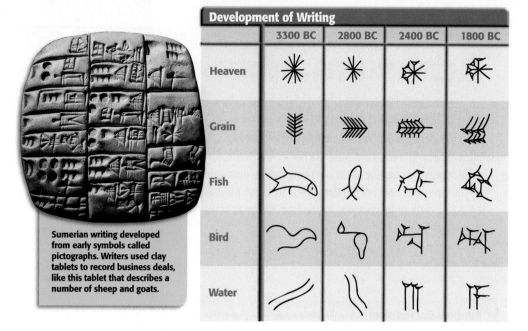

Development of Writing				
	3300 BC	**2800 BC**	**2400 BC**	**1800 BC**
Heaven				
Grain				
Fish				
Bird				
Water				

Sumerian writing developed from early symbols called pictographs. Writers used clay tablets to record business deals, like this tablet that describes a number of sheep and goats.

ACADEMIC VOCABULARY
complex
difficult, not simple

Earlier written communication had used **pictographs**, or picture symbols. Each pictograph represented an object, such as a tree or an animal. In cuneiform, symbols could also represent syllables, or basic parts of words. As a result, Sumerian writers could combine multiple symbols to express more **complex** ideas such as "joy" or "powerful."

Sumerians first used cuneiform to keep business records. A **scribe**, or writer, would be hired to keep track of the items people traded. Government officials and temples also hired scribes to keep their records. Becoming a scribe was a way to move up in social class.

Sumerian students went to school to learn to read and write. Like today, though, some students did not want to study. A Sumerian story tells of a father who urged his son to do his schoolwork:

❝Go to school, stand before your 'school-father,' recite your assignment, open your schoolbag, write your tablet ...After you have finished your assignment and reported to your monitor [teacher], come to me, and do not wander about in the street.❞
–Sumerian essay quoted in *History Begins at Sumer*, by Samuel Noah Kramer

In time, Sumerians put their writing skills to new uses. They wrote works on history, law, grammar, and math. They also created works of literature. Sumerians wrote stories, proverbs, and songs. They wrote poems about the gods and about military victories. Some of these were **epics**, long poems that tell the stories of heroes. Later, people used some of these poems to create *The Epic of Gilgamesh*, the story of a legendary Sumerian king.

READING CHECK **Generalizing** How was cuneiform first used in Sumer?

144 CHAPTER 6

Differentiating Instruction

At Level

English-Language Learners

1. Review with students the chart on the development of writing. Discuss how pictographs in 3300 BC resembled the objects they expressed. Have students create ten pictographs for everyday objects or ideas. Ask students to write the English translation next to each pictograph.

2. Remind students that pictographs were only the beginning of the development of writing. Symbols became simpler as people wrote more and more. Have students simplify their pictographs into symbols like those in the chart above.

3. Lastly, have students write only their symbols on a blank sheet of paper. Organize the class into pairs and have students try to guess the meanings of each other's symbols.
LS Visual/Spatial
📄 Alternative Assessment Handbook, Rubric 3: Artwork

Advances and Inventions

Writing was not the only great Sumerian invention. These early people made many other advances and discoveries.

Technical Advances

One of the Sumerians' most important developments was the wheel. They were the world's first people to build wheeled vehicles, such as carts. Using the wheel, Sumerians invented a device that spins clay as a craftsperson shapes it into bowls. This device is called a potter's wheel.

The plow was another important Sumerian invention. Pulled by oxen, plows broke through the hard clay soil of Sumer to prepare it for planting. This technique greatly increased farm production. The Sumerians also invented a clock that used falling water to measure time.

Sumerian advances improved daily life. Sumerians built sewers under city streets. They used bronze to make strong tools and weapons. They even produced makeup and glass jewelry.

Math and Science

Another area in which Sumerians excelled was math. In fact, they developed a math system based on the number 60. Based on this system, they divided a circle into 360 degrees. Dividing a year into 12 months—a factor of 60—was another Sumerian idea. Sumerians also calculated the areas of rectangles and triangles.

Sumerian scholars studied science, too. They wrote long lists to record their study of the natural world. These tablets included the names of thousands of animals, plants, and minerals.

The Sumerians also made advances in medicine. Using ingredients from animals, plants, and minerals, they produced many healing drugs. Among the items used in these medicines were milk, turtle shells, figs, and salt. The Sumerians catalogued their medical knowledge, listing treatments according to symptoms and body parts.

THE IMPACT TODAY We still use a base-60 system when we talk about 60 seconds in a minute and 60 minutes in an hour.

READING CHECK Categorizing What areas of life were improved by Sumerian inventions?

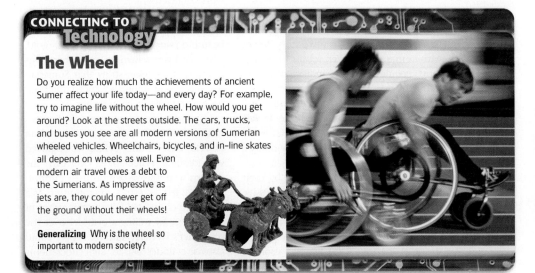

CONNECTING TO Technology

The Wheel

Do you realize how much the achievements of ancient Sumer affect your life today—and every day? For example, try to imagine life without the wheel. How would you get around? Look at the streets outside. The cars, trucks, and buses you see are all modern versions of Sumerian wheeled vehicles. Wheelchairs, bicycles, and in-line skates all depend on wheels as well. Even modern air travel owes a debt to the Sumerians. As impressive as jets are, they could never get off the ground without their wheels!

Generalizing Why is the wheel so important to modern society?

Main Idea

❸ The Arts of Sumer

Many types of art developed in Sumer.

Recall What was at the center of most Sumerian cities? *the temple, or ziggurat*

Compare and Contrast How were the homes of rich Sumerians similar to and different from those of most Sumerians? *rich—lived in large, two-story homes with many rooms; most Sumerians—smaller, one-story homes, fewer rooms; both—made of mud bricks, built side-by-side on narrow unpaved streets*

Summarize What different types of art did the Sumerians create? *sculpture, pottery, jewelry, cylinder seals, music, and dance*

Linking to Today

Lost Art Hundreds of thousands of ancient Mesopotamian works of art were housed in the National Museum of Iraq in Baghdad. When the 2003 Iraqi war broke out, museum workers stored many artifacts to protect them from damage. Unfortunately, thousands of pieces were damaged or stolen when thieves looted the museum. In the months following the war, some items were returned, although many priceless items are still missing today.

Answers

Focus on Reading *a small stone cylinder with engraved designs that, when rolled onto clay, would leave a unique imprint*

146

Sumerian Achievements

The Sumerians' artistic achievements included beautiful works of gold, wood, and stone.

Cylinder seals like this one were carved into round stones and then rolled over clay to leave their mark.

This stringed musical instrument is called a lyre. It features a cow's head and is made of silver decorated with shell and stone.

The Arts of Sumer

The Sumerians' skills in the fields of art, metalwork, and **architecture**—the science of building—are well known to us. The ruins of great buildings and fine works of art have provided us with many examples of the Sumerians' creativity.

Architecture

Most Sumerian rulers lived in large palaces. Other rich Sumerians had two-story homes with as many as a dozen rooms. However, most people lived in smaller, one-story houses. These homes had six or seven rooms arranged around a small courtyard. Large and small houses stood side by side along the narrow, unpaved streets of the city. Bricks made of mud were the houses' main building blocks.

FOCUS ON READING
What was a cylinder seal? Describe one in your own words.

City centers were dominated by their temples, the largest and most impressive buildings in Sumer. A **ziggurat**, a pyramid-shaped temple, rose high above each city. Outdoor staircases led to a platform and a shrine at the top. Some temples also had columns to make them more attractive.

The Arts

Sumerian sculptors produced many fine works. Among them are the statues of gods created for temples. Sumerian artists also sculpted small objects out of ivory and rare woods. Sumerian pottery is better known for its quantity than its quality. Potters turned out many items, but few were works of beauty.

Jewelry was a popular item in Sumer. The jewelers of the region made many beautiful works out of imported gold, silver, and gems. Earrings and other items found in the region show that Sumerian jewelers knew rather advanced methods for putting gold pieces together.

Cylinder seals are perhaps Sumer's most famous works of art. These small objects were stone cylinders engraved with designs. When rolled over clay, the designs would leave behind their imprint. Each seal left its own distinct imprint. As a result, a person could show ownership of a container by rolling a cylinder over the container's wet clay surface. People could also use cylinder seals to "sign" documents or to decorate other clay objects.

Collaborative Learning

At Level

Creating a Television Commercial

1. Organize the class into small groups. Ask students to imagine that they are the curators of a museum that has a new exhibit titled "Sumerian Achievements."

2. Have each group create a television commercial that promotes the museum exhibit. Commercials should highlight Sumerian achievements discussed in this section and convince people to visit the museum exhibit.

3. Have each group record their commercial or perform it live for the class. **LS Interpersonal, Visual/Spatial**

   Alternative Assessment Handbook, Rubrics 2: Advertisements; and 29: Presentations

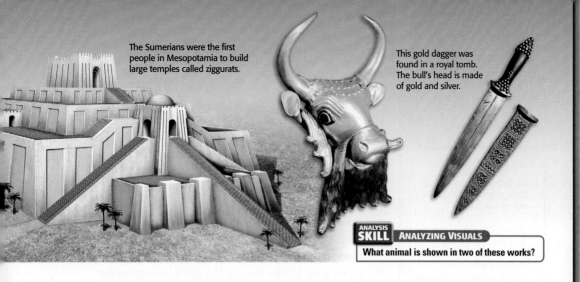

The Sumerians were the first people in Mesopotamia to build large temples called ziggurats.

This gold dagger was found in a royal tomb. The bull's head is made of gold and silver.

ANALYSIS SKILL **ANALYZING VISUALS**

What animal is shown in two of these works?

Some cylinder seals showed battle scenes. Others displayed worship rituals. Some were highly decorative, covered with hundreds of carefully cut gems.

The Sumerians also enjoyed music. Kings and temples hired musicians to play on special occasions. Sumerian musicians played reed pipes, drums, tambourines, and harplike stringed instruments called lyres. Children learned songs in school. People sang hymns to gods and kings.

Music and dance provided entertainment in marketplaces and homes.

READING CHECK **Drawing Inferences** What might historians learn from cylinder seals?

SUMMARY AND PREVIEW The Sumerians greatly enriched their society. Next, you will learn about the later peoples who lived in Mesopotamia.

Section 3 Assessment

go.hrw.com
Online Quiz
KEYWORD: SK9 HP6

Reviewing Ideas, Terms, and Places

1. **a. Identify** What is **cuneiform**?
   b. Analyze Why do you think writing is one of history's most important cultural advances?
   c. Elaborate What current leader would you choose to write an **epic** about, and why?
2. **a. Recall** What were two early uses of the wheel?
   b. Explain Why do you think the invention of the plow was so important to the Sumerians?
3. **a. Describe** What was the basic Sumerian building material?
   b. Make Inferences Why do you think cylinder seals developed into works of art?

Critical Thinking

4. **Identifying Effects** In a chart like this one, identify the effect of each Sumerian advance you listed in your notes.

Advance/Achievement	Effect

FOCUS ON WRITING

5. **Evaluating Information** What will you include on your poster to show Sumerian achievements? A ziggurat? A piece of jewelry? A musical instrument? Make a list of the pictures you think would be most interesting to elementary students.

ANCIENT CIVILIZATIONS OF THE MIDDLE EAST—MESOPOTAMIA **147**

Bellringer

If YOU lived there. . . Use the **Daily Bellringer Transparency** to help students answer the question.

🖐 Daily Bellringer Transparency, Section 4

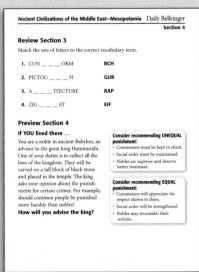

Ancient Civilizations of the Middle East—Mesopotamia   Daily Bellringer
Section 4

Review Section 3
Match the sets of letters to the correct vocabulary term.

1. CUN _ _ _ ORM   RCH
2. PICTOG _ _ _ H   GUR
3. A _ _ _ ITECTURE   RAP
4. ZIG _ _ _ AT   EIF

Preview Section 4

If YOU lived there ...
You are a noble in ancient Babylon, an advisor to the great king Hammurabi. One of your duties is to collect all the laws of the kingdom. They will be carved on a tall block of black stone and placed in the temple. The king asks your opinion about the punishments for certain crimes. For example, should common people be punished more harshly than nobles?
How will you advise the king?

Consider recommending UNEQUAL punishment:
• Commoners must be kept in check.
• Social order must be maintained.
• Nobles are superior and deserve better treatment.

Consider recommending EQUAL punishment:
• Commoners will appreciate the respect shown to them.
• Social order will be strengthened.
• Nobles may reconsider their actions.

Key Terms and Places

📋 RF: Vocabulary Builder, Section 4

Taking Notes

Have students copy the graphic organizer onto their own paper and then use it to take notes on the section. This activity will prepare students for the Section Assessment, in which they will complete a graphic organizer that builds on the information using the Critical Thinking Skill: Categorizing.

SECTION 4

Later Peoples of the Fertile Crescent

What You Will Learn...

Main Ideas

1. The Babylonians conquered Mesopotamia and created a code of law.
2. Invasions of Mesopotamia changed the region's culture.
3. The Phoenicians built a trading society in the eastern Mediterranean region.

The Big Idea

After the Sumerians, many cultures ruled parts of the Fertile Crescent.

Key Terms and Places

Babylon, *p. 148*
Hammurabi's Code, *p. 149*
chariot, *p. 150*
alphabet, *p. 153*

TAKING NOTES As you read, use a diagram like the one below to keep track of the later empires of the Fertile Crescent.

Fertile Crescent Empires

If **YOU** lived there...

You are a noble in ancient Babylon, an adviser to the great king Hammurabi. One of your duties is to collect all the laws of the kingdom. They will be carved on a tall block of black stone and placed in the temple. The king asks your opinion about the punishments for certain crimes. For example, should common people be punished more harshly than nobles?

How will you advise the king?

BUILDING BACKGROUND Many peoples invaded Mesopotamia. A series of kings conquered the lands between the rivers. Each new culture inherited the earlier achievements of the Sumerians. Some of the later invasions of the region also introduced new skills and ideas that still influence civilization today, such as a written law code.

The Babylonians Conquer Mesopotamia

Although Ur rose to glory after the death of Sargon, repeated foreign attacks drained its strength. By 2000 BC, Ur lay in ruins. With Ur's power gone, several waves of invaders battled to gain control of Mesopotamia.

Rise of Babylon

Babylon was home to one such group. That city was located on the Euphrates near what is now Baghdad, Iraq. Babylon had once been a Sumerian town. By 1800 BC, however, it was home to a powerful government of its own. In 1792 BC, Hammurabi (ham-uh-RAHB-ee) became Babylon's king. He would become the city's greatest ruler.

Teach the Big Idea   At Level

Later Peoples of the Fertile Crescent

1. **Teach** Ask students the questions in the Main Idea boxes under Direct Teach.

2. **Apply** Have students draw a time line that includes the later empires and kingdoms that developed in Mesopotamia. Students should also include a short note about why each civilization was important. Encourage students to share their time lines with the class. **LS Visual/Spatial**

3. **Review** As a review of the section, have students create seven multiple-choice questions. Then have students quiz each other with the questions they have created.

4. **Practice/Homework** Have students use their time lines to help them create at least one illustration for every empire or people mentioned in the section. **LS Visual/Spatial**

   📄 Alternative Assessment Handbook, Rubrics 3: Artwork; and 36: Time Lines

Hammurabi's Code

Hammurabi was a brilliant war leader. His armies fought many battles to expand his power. Eventually, Hammurabi brought all of Mesopotamia into his empire, called the Babylonian Empire after his capital city.

Hammurabi was not only skilled on the battlefield, though. He was also an able ruler who could govern a huge empire. He used tax money to pay for building and irrigation projects. He also brought wealth through increased trade. Hammurabi is best known, however, for his code of laws.

Hammurabi's Code was a set of 282 laws that dealt with almost every part of daily life. There were laws on everything from trade, loans, and theft to marriage, injury, and murder. It contained some ideas that are still found in laws today.

Under Hammurabi's Code, each crime brought a specific penalty. However, social class did matter. For example, injuring a rich man brought a greater penalty than injuring a poor man.

Hammurabi's Code was important not only for how thorough it was but also because it was written down for all to see. People all over the empire could read exactly what was against the law.

Hammurabi ruled for 42 years. During his reign, Babylon became the major city in Mesopotamia. However, after his death, Babylonian power declined. The kings that followed faced invasions from the people Hammurabi had conquered. Before long, the Babylonian Empire came to an end.

READING CHECK **Analyzing** What was Hammurabi's most important accomplishment?

Primary Source

HISTORIC DOCUMENT
Hammurabi's Code

The Babylonian ruler Hammurabi is credited with putting together the earliest known written collection of laws. The code set down rules for both criminal and civil law and informed citizens about what was expected of them.

196. If a man put out the eye of another man, his eye shall be put out.

197. If he break another man's bone, his bone shall be broken.

198. If he put out the eye of a freed man, or break the bone of a freed man, he shall pay one gold mina.

199. If he put out the eye of a man's slave, or break the bone of a man's slave, he shall pay one-half of its value.

221. If a physican heal the broken bone or diseased soft part of a man, the patient shall pay the physician five shekels in money.

222. If he were a freed man he shall pay three shekels.

223. If he were a slave his owner shall pay the physician two shekels.

–Hammurabi, from *The Code of Hammurabi*, translated by L. W. King

 ANALYSIS SKILL **ANALYZING PRIMARY SOURCES**
How do you think Hammurabi's code of laws affected citizens of that time?

149

149

Main Idea

❷ Invasions of Mesopotamia

Invasions of Mesopotamia changed the region's culture.

Recall Why did the Hittite Kingdom come to an end? *Their king was assassinated, and the kingdom was overrun by the Kassites.*

Identify What military advantages did the Assyrians have? *iron weapons, chariots, and good organization*

Draw Conclusions How do you think the use of chariots by Hittites affected the opposing army's foot soldiers? *possible answer—increased their fear and reduced their effectiveness, because they could not predict from where the enemy would appear next, and the chariots were moving targets*

 Map Zone Transparency: Babylonian and Assyrian Empires

Info to Know

The Assyrian Army The Assyrian military was impressive, even by today's standards. Assyrian field armies consisted of 50,000 men, the equal of five modern U.S. divisions. When taking the field for a battle, the army would stretch about a mile and a half across and 100 yards deep! The Assyrian military was also known for its innovations—cavalry, battering rams, and boots for their soldiers.

Invasions of Mesopotamia

Several other civilizations developed in and around the Fertile Crescent. As their armies battled for land, control of the region passed from one empire to another.

Hittites and Kassites

FOCUS ON READING
Make sure you understand this paragraph by restating it in your own words.

A people known as the Hittites built a strong kingdom in Asia Minor, in what is today Turkey. Their success came, in part, from two key military advantages they had over rivals. First, the Hittites were among the first people to master ironworking. This meant they could make stronger weapons than their foes. Second, the Hittite army skillfully used the **chariot**, a wheeled, horse-drawn cart used in battle. Chariots allowed Hittite soldiers to move quickly around a battlefield. Archers riding in the chariots fired arrows at the enemy.

Using these advantages, Hittite forces captured Babylon around 1595 BC. Hittite rule did not last long, however. Soon after taking Babylon, the Hittite king was killed by an assassin. The kingdom plunged into chaos. The Kassites, a people who lived north of Babylon, captured the city and ruled for almost 400 years.

Assyrians

Later, in the 1200s BC, a group called the Assyrians (uh-SIR-ee-unz) from northern Mesopotamia briefly gained control of Babylon. However, their empire was soon overrun by invaders. After this defeat, the Assyrians took about 300 years to recover their strength. Then, starting about 900 BC, they began to conquer all of the Fertile Crescent. They even took over parts of Asia Minor and Egypt.

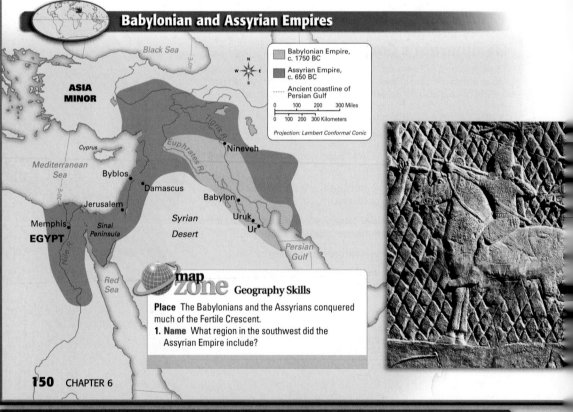

Babylonian and Assyrian Empires

Babylonian Empire, c. 1750 BC
Assyrian Empire, c. 650 BC
Ancient coastline of Persian Gulf

0   100   200   300 Miles
0 100 200 300 Kilometers
Projection: Lambert Conformal Conic

Black Sea
ASIA MINOR
Cyprus
Mediterranean Sea
Byblos
Damascus
Jerusalem
Memphis
EGYPT
Sinai Peninsula
Nile R.
Red Sea
Nineveh
Euphrates R.
Tigris R.
Babylon
Uruk
Ur
Syrian Desert
Persian Gulf

map zone Geography Skills

Place The Babylonians and the Assyrians conquered much of the Fertile Crescent.
1. Name What region in the southwest did the Assyrian Empire include?

150 CHAPTER 6

Differentiating Instruction

Below Level | Standard English Mastery

Struggling Readers

1. Have students use standard English to write a letter from the Hittite king to the leader of Babylon explaining why the Babylonians should surrender. You may wish to pair a student who has good writing skills with a struggling reader to complete this activity.

2. Have students include details about the superiority of the Hittite military and what consequences might result from the Babylonians' refusal to surrender.

3. Ask for volunteers to read their letters to the class. As a class, discuss any necessary corrections to the letters to align them with standard English usage. **LS Verbal/Linguistic**

Alternative Assessment Handbook, Rubric 37: Writing Assignments

Answers

Map Zone 1. *Egypt*
Focus on Reading *Students should paraphrase the paragraph in an accurate and readable manner.*

The key to the Assyrians' success was their strong army. Like the Hittites, the Assyrians used iron weapons and chariots. The army was very well organized, and every soldier knew his role.

The Assyrians were fierce in battle. Before attacking, they spread terror by looting villages and burning crops. Anyone who still dared to resist them was killed.

After conquering the Fertile Crescent, the Assyrians ruled from their capital city, Nineveh (NI-nuh-vuh). They demanded heavy taxes from across the empire. Areas that resisted the Assyrians' demands were harshly punished.

Assyrian kings ruled their large empire through local leaders. Each governed a small area, collected taxes, enforced laws, and raised troops for the army. Roads were built to link distant parts of the empire. Messengers on horseback were sent to deliver orders to faraway officials.

Chaldeans

In 652 BC a series of wars broke out in the Assyrian Empire over who should rule. These wars greatly weakened the empire.

Sensing this weakness, the Chaldeans (kal-DEE-unz), a group from the Syrian Desert, led other peoples in an attack on the Assyrians. In 612 BC, they destroyed Nineveh and the Assyrian Empire.

In its place, the Chaldeans set up a new empire of their own. Nebuchadnezzar (neb-uh-kuhd-NEZ-uhr), the most famous Chaldean king, rebuilt Babylon into a beautiful city. According to legend, his grand palace featured the famous Hanging Gardens. Trees and flowers grew on its terraces and roofs. From the ground the gardens seemed to hang in the air.

The Chaldeans greatly admired the ideas and culture of the Sumerians. They studied the Sumerian language and built temples to Sumerian gods.

At the same time, Babylon became a center for astronomy. Chaldeans charted the positions of the stars and kept track of economic, political, and weather events. They also created a calendar and solved complex problems of geometry.

READING CHECK **Sequencing** List in order the peoples who ruled Mesopotamia.

The Assyrian Army

The Assyrian army was the most powerful fighting force the world had ever seen. Large and well organized, it featured iron weapons, war chariots, and giant war machines used to knock down city walls.

ANALYZING VISUALS What kinds of weapons can you see in this carving?

151

Phoenicia, c. 800 BC

ATLANTIC
OCEAN

SPAIN

Strait of
Gibraltar

ATLAS MOUNTAINS

The Phoenicians sailed throughout the Mediterranean, seeking trade goods and founding new cities.

Main Idea

❸ The Phoenicians

The Phoenicians built a trading society in the eastern Mediterranean region.

Identify Where did Phoenician ships sail? *They sailed around the Mediterranean to Egypt, Greece, Italy, Sicily, and Spain, and through the Strait of Gibraltar into the Atlantic Ocean.*

Explain Why was the Phoenician alphabet an important development? *It made writing much easier and has had a major impact on other languages, including English.*

Draw Conclusions What led the Phoenicians to create a successful sea trade? *Mountains and hostile neighbors blocked overland trade routes, so in order to trade they had to go to sea.*

Map Zone Transparency: Phoenicia, c. 800 BC

Info to Know

The Cedars of Lebanon The famous trees are so closely tied to the history of Lebanon that a cedar is featured in the middle of the Lebanese flag. However, because people have been cutting down the big trees for centuries, few traces of the old forests remain. Reforestation efforts are currently underway.

The Phoenicians

At the western end of the Fertile Crescent, along the Mediterranean Sea, was a land known as Phoenicia (fi-NI-shuh). It was not home to a great military power and was often ruled by foreign governments. Nevertheless, the Phoenicians created a wealthy trading society.

Geography of Phoenicia

Today the nation of Lebanon occupies most of what was Phoenicia. Mountains border the region to the north and east. To the west lies the Mediterranean.

The Phoenicians were largely an urban people. Among their chief cities were Tyre, Sidon, and Byblos. These three cities, like many Phoenician cities, still exist today.

Phoenicia had few resources. One thing it did have, however, was cedar. Cedar trees were prized for their timber, a valuable trade item. But Phoenicia's overland trade routes were blocked by mountains and hostile neighbors. Phoenicians had to look to the sea for a way to trade.

 THE IMPACT TODAY

Because so many cedar trees have been cut down in Lebanon's forests over the years, very few trees remain.

Expansion of Trade

Motivated by a desire for trade, the people of Phoenicia became expert sailors. They built one of the world's finest harbors at the city of Tyre. Fleets of fast Phoenician trading ships sailed to ports all around the Mediterranean Sea. Traders traveled to Egypt, Greece, Italy, Sicily, and Spain. They even passed through the Strait of Gibraltar to reach the Atlantic Ocean.

The Phoenicians founded several new colonies along their trade routes. Carthage (KAHR-thij), located on the northern coast of Africa, was the most famous of these. It later became one of the most powerful cities on the Mediterranean.

Phoenicia grew wealthy from its trade. Besides lumber, the Phoenicians traded silverwork, ivory carvings, and slaves. They also made and sold beautiful glass items. In addition, the Phoenicians made purple dye from a type of shellfish. They then traded cloth that had been dyed with this purple color. Phoenician purple fabric was very popular with rich people all around the Mediterranean.

152 CHAPTER 6

Critical Thinking: Analyzing

At Level

Phoenician Exports

1. Tell students that a nation's exports are the goods and products it sells to other nations.

2. To help students identify the exports of the Phoenicians, copy the graphic organizer for students to see. Omit the blue, italicized answers. Have students copy and complete the graphic organizer on their own paper.
   🅛 Visual/Spatial, Verbal/Linguistic

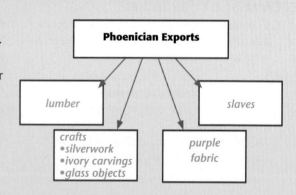

Phoenician Exports

lumber

slaves

crafts
• *silverwork*
• *ivory carvings*
• *glass objects*

purple fabric

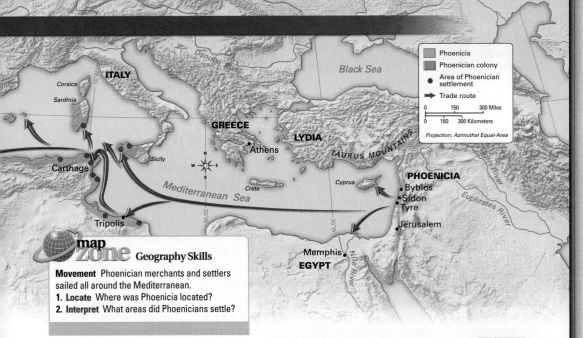

Phonecia
Phoenician colony
● Area of Phoenician settlement
→ Trade route

0   150   300 Miles
0   150   300 Kilometers
Projection: Azimuthal Equal-Area

 map Zone **Geography Skills**

Movement Phoenician merchants and settlers sailed all around the Mediterranean.
1. **Locate** Where was Phoenicia located?
2. **Interpret** What areas did Phoenicians settle?

The Phoenicians' most important achievement, however, wasn't a trade good. To record their activities, Phoenician traders developed one of the world's first alphabets. An **alphabet** is a set of letters that can be combined to form words. This development made writing much easier. It had a major impact on the ancient world and on our own. In fact, the alphabet we use today is based on the Phoenicians'.

READING CHECK Finding Main Ideas What were the Phoenicians' main achievements?

SUMMARY AND PREVIEW Many peoples ruled in the Fertile Crescent after the Sumerians. Some made contributions that are still valued today. Next, you will learn about three religions that developed in the region and are still alive today—Judaism, Christianity, and Islam.

Section 4 Assessment

go.hrw.com **Online Quiz** KEYWORD: SK9 HP6

Reviewing Ideas, Terms, and Places
1. **a. Identify** Where was **Babylon** located?
   b. Analyze What does **Hammurabi's Code** reveal about Babylonian society?
2. **a. Describe** What two advantages did Hittite soldiers have over their opponents?
   b. Rank Which empire discussed in this section do you feel contributed the most to modern-day society? Why?
3. **a. Identify** For what trade goods were the Phoenicians known? For what else were they known?
   b. Analyze How did Phoenicia grow wealthy?

Critical Thinking
4. **Categorizing** Use your note-taking diagram with the names of the empires. List at least one advance or achievement made by each empire.

Fertile Crescent Empires

FOCUS ON WRITING
5. **Gathering Information about Later Peoples** Several different peoples contributed to civilization in the Fertile Crescent after the Sumerians. Which ones, if any, will you include on your poster? What will you show?

153

Section 4 Assessment Answers

1. **a.** on the Euphrates near what is today Baghdad, Iraq
   b. It was based on social hierarchy and showed the importance of class distinctions. It also reveals the significance of business, trade, and family in the Babylonian Empire.

2. **a.** iron weapons and chariots
   b. possible answers: Babylonians—Hammurabi's laws; Chaldeans—restored Sumerian customs, studies in math and astronomy; Phoenicians—an alphabet

3. **a.** lumber, silverwork, ivory carvings, slaves, beautiful glass objects, and purple cloth; development of an alphabet
   b. Phoenicians were expert sailors with a fast fleet of trading ships and had valuable items to trade.

4. Babylonian; Hittite; Assyrian; Chaldean; Phoenician; advances or achievements listed will vary.

5. Students may choose to include information about the Babylonians, Hittites, Kassites, Assyrians, Chaldeans, or Phoenicians.

Answers

Map Zone 1. *at the eastern end of the Mediterranean Sea;* **2.** *Spain, Sardinia, Sicily, and Northern Africa*

Reading Check *They were expert sailors with fast ships, built outstanding harbors and a vast trade network, and developed an alphabet.*

Social Studies Skills

Chart and Graph | Critical Thinking | Geography | Study

Sequencing and Using Time Lines

Activity Making an Illustrated Time Line

Materials: large paper, rulers, markers, photos that students have brought from home (optional)

1. Have students create a time line using one-year increments from the year they were born to the present.

2. Students should write important dates and events from their lives in the appropriate place on the time lines. Examples might be moving into a new house, getting a pet, starting school, birthdates of younger siblings, and other memorable events.

3. Ask students to bring photos from home that illustrate each event on their time line. If photos are unavailable, have students create original artwork for each event.

LS Visual/Spatial

Alternative Assessment Handbook, Rubric 36: Time Lines

Interactive Skills Tutor CD-ROM, Lesson 3: Interpret and Create a Time Line and Sequence Events

RF: Social Studies Skills, Sequencing and Using Time Lines

Sequencing and Using Time Lines

Learn

When you are reading about events in the past, it is important to learn their sequence, or the order in which the events occurred. If you do not know the sequence in which events happen, history will not make any sense.

One way to examine the sequence of events is to construct a time line. A time line is a visual display showing events in the order in which they happened. Events on the left side of the time line occurred first. Events farther to the right occurred later.

Practice

Use the time line below to answer the following questions.

1. Around what year did Hammurabi issue his code of laws?

2. Which happened earlier, the formation of Sargon's empire or the beginning of Phoenician trade?

3. About how many years after Hammurabi issued his law code did the Assyrians conquer Babylon?

Major Events in the Fertile Crescent

| 2500 BC | 2000 BC | 1500 BC | 1000 BC | 500 BC |

c. 2350 BC
Sargon of Akkad conquers Mesopotamia and forms the world's first empire.

c. 1770 BC
Hammurabi of Babylon issues a written code of laws.

c. 1200 BC
Assyrians take over Babylon.

c. 1000 BC
Phoenicians trade all around the Mediterranean.

Apply

Think about a typical school day. What time do you wake up? What classes do you have? When do you get home? Make a list of events that occur on a typical day. Once you have made your list, rearrange it so that the events are listed in sequence. Then use your list to draw a time line of your day.

154 CHAPTER 6

Social Studies Skills Activity: Sequencing and Using Time Lines

Struggling Readers   **Below Level**

Write two dates and events from the chapter on the board. Have students determine which event occurred first. Then have students calculate how many years separate the two events.

LS Logical/Mathematical

Alternative Assessment Handbook, Rubric 36: Time Lines

English-Language Learners   **At Level**

Have students create a human time line. Assign each student one event from the chapter. Students should write the date and event in large letters on paper and tape it to the front of their shirts. Have students arrange themselves in chronological order across the room.

LS Kinesthetic, Verbal/Linguistic

Alternative Assessment Handbook, Rubric 36: Time Lines

Answers

Practice **1.** *1770 BC;* **2.** *the formation of Sargon's empire;* **3.** *about 570 years*

Apply *Students' time lines should show events in sequence, such as "7:00 AM: woke up"; "7:15 AM: ate breakfast"; "7:45 AM: went to school"; and so on.*

Chapter Review

Geography's Impact
video series
Review the video to answer the closing question:
What would life in America be like today without a written code of laws?

Visual Summary

Use the visual summary below to help you review the main ideas of the chapter.

QUICK FACTS

The early Mesopotamians developed irrigation to grow food. As a result, they were able to form cities.

Sumerian advances included ziggurats, the wheel, and the world's first writing system, cuneiform.

Later peoples created the first written laws and the first empires. They also formed great trading networks.

Reviewing Vocabulary, Terms, and Places

Using your own paper, complete the sentences below by providing the correct term for each blank.

1. Mesopotamian farmers built _____ to irrigate their fields.

2. The art and science of building is known as _____.

3. The people of Sumer practiced _____, the worship of many gods.

4. Instead of using pictographs, Sumerians developed a type of writing called _____.

5. Horse-drawn _____ gave the Hittites an advantage during battle.

6. _____ was Hammurabi's capital and one of Mesopotamia's greatest cities.

7. _____ ideas are not simple.

8. Sumerian society was organized in _____, which consisted of a city and the surrounding lands.

Comprehension and Critical Thinking

SECTION 1 *(Pages 134–137)*

9. **a. Describe** Where was Mesopotamia, and what does the name mean?

   b. Analyze How did Mesopotamian irrigation systems allow civilization to develop?

   c. Elaborate Do you think a division of labor is necessary for civilization to develop? Why or why not?

SECTION 2 *(Pages 138–142)*

10. **a. Identify** Who built the world's first empire, and what land did that empire include?

    b. Analyze Politically, how was early Sumerian society organized? How did that organization affect society?

    c. Elaborate Why did the Sumerians consider it everyone's responsibility to keep the gods happy?

ANCIENT CIVILIZATIONS OF THE MIDDLE EAST—MESOPOTAMIA **155**

Answers

Visual Summary

Review and Inquiry Have students use the visual summary to write a brief paragraph summarizing the important themes depicted in the illustration.

🖙 Quick Facts Transparency: Visual Summary: Ancient Civilizations of the Middle East—Mesopotamia

Reviewing Vocabulary, Terms, and Places

1. canals	5. chariots
2. architecture	6. Babylon
3. polytheism	7. complex
4. cuneiform	8. city-states

Comprehension and Critical Thinking

9. **a.** It was located between the Tigris and Euphrates rivers, and the name means " between the rivers" in Greek.
   b. They allowed the people to control the flow of the rivers and produce a surplus of food, which freed people to create a civilization.
   c. possible answer—yes, because it allows people to focus on building a civilization rather than just surviving

10. **a.** Sargon; the area between the Tigris and Euphrates rivers and much of Mesopotamia
    b. Kings and priests made up the upper class, while the middle class was craftspeople, merchants, and traders and the working class consisted of farmers and laborers. Slaves were at the bottom. Priests and the wealthy ruled society, while the working class supported them.

Review and Assessment Resources

Review and Reinforce

📄 Chapter Review

📄 **RF:** Chapter Review

🖙 Quick Facts Transparency: Visual Summary: Ancient Civilizations of the Middle East— Mesopotamia

🔊 Spanish Chapter Summaries Audio CD Program

OSP Holt PuzzlePro; Quiz Show

💿 Quiz Game CD-ROM

Assess

SE Standardized Test Practice

📄 PASS: Chapter Test, Forms A and B

📄 Alternative Assessment Handbook

OSP ExamView Test Generator, Chapter Test

💿 Differentiated Instruction Modified Worksheets and Tests CD-ROM: Modified Chapter Test

HOAP Holt Online Assessment Program (in the Holt Interactive Online Student Edition)

Reteach/Intervene

📄 Interactive Reader and Study Guide

📄 Differentiated Instruction Teacher Management System: Lesson Plans

💿 Differentiated Instruction Modified Worksheets and Tests CD-ROM

💿 Interactive Skills Tutor CD-ROM

go.hrw.com
Online Resources

Chapter Resources:
KEYWORD: SK9 CH6

10. c. The gods had great powers, and in order for the people to lead happy and prosperous lives, everyone had to do their part in keeping the gods happy.

11. a. cuneiform; because it is the world's first system of writing
b. similar—Students went to school to learn to read and write; they produced makeup and jewelry; they enjoyed music; different—Their writing was cuneiform, and they wrote on clay tablets.
c. Answers will vary but should display knowledge of the two inventions and their significance.

12. a. possible answers—purple dye, founded Carthage, developed an alphabet
b. possible answer—Separately they stood no chance of victory but by banding together they were able to make an impact.
c. Answers will vary but should be supported by facts from the text.

Focus on Reading and Writing

13. Students should paraphrase the main ideas in the paragraph using their own words. An example might be: The Sumerians were the first of many ancient civilizations to settle in the Mesopotamian region. Some of their achievements include inventing the wheel and coming up with a writing system.

RF: Focus on Reading, Paraphrasing

14. Rubric Students' posters should

- show mindfulness of the intended audience
- include an informative title
- include 5 or 6 images
- be colorful
- include a one- or two-sentence introduction
- include labels or captions for each image

RF: Focus on Writing, Creating a Poster

SECTION 3 (Pages 143–147)

11. a. Identify What was the Sumerian writing system called, and why is it so significant?
b. Compare and Contrast What were two ways in which Sumerian society was similar to our society today? What were two ways in which it was different?
c. Evaluate Other than writing and the wheel, which Sumerian invention do you think is most important? Why?

SECTION 4 (Pages 148–153)

12. a. Describe What were two developments of the Phoenicians?
b. Draw Conclusions Why do you think several peoples banded together to fight the Assyrians?
c. Evaluate Do you think Hammurabi was more effective as a ruler or as a military leader? Why?

FOCUS ON READING AND WRITING

Paraphrasing *Read the paragraph below carefully. Then rewrite the paragraph in your own words, taking care to include all the main ideas.*

13. Mesopotamia was the home of many ancient civilizations. The first of these civilizations was the Sumerians. They lived in Mesopotamia by 3000 BC. There they built cities, created a system of writing, and invented the wheel.

Creating a Poster *Use your notes and the instructions below to help you create a poster.*

14. Using a large poster board, create a poster on the Fertile Crescent. From your list, select 5 or 6 pictures to show. Remember that your audience is young children and think about what would interest them.
　　Begin by collecting pictures or drawings from magazines or the Internet. Then make a plan for your poster. Decide where you will place each picture and what you will say about each. After you have arranged the pictures, create a title for the poster and center it at the top. Write a one- or two-sentence introduction for your poster. You will also have to create a label or short caption for each picture.

Social Studies Skills

15. Sequencing and Using Time Lines Create a time line that shows the various people who ruled the Fertile Crescent. Remember that the people should appear on your time line in order.

Using the Internet

16. Activity: Looking at Writing The Sumerians made one of the greatest cultural advances in history by developing the world's first system of writing. Enter the activity keyword and research the evolution of language and its written forms. Look at one of the newest methods of writing: text messaging. Then write a paragraph explaining why writing is important using abbreviations and symbols used in text messaging.

Map Activity ★Interactive

17. The Fertile Crescent On a separate sheet of paper, match the letters on the map with their correct labels.

Babylon	Euphrates River
Phoenicia	Tigris River
Sumer	

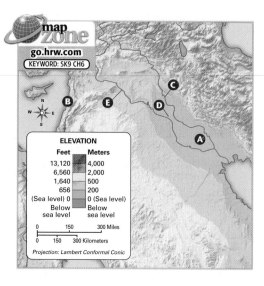

map zone
go.hrw.com
KEYWORD: SK9 CH6

ELEVATION

Feet	Meters
13,120	4,000
6,560	2,000
1,640	500
656	200
(Sea level) 0	0 (Sea level)
Below sea level	Below sea level

0　　150　　300 Miles
0　　150　　300 Kilometers
Projection: Lambert Conformal Conic

Social Studies Skills

15. Students' time lines should include the following:
3000 BC—Sumerians;
2300s BC—Sargon;
1800 BC—Babylonians;
c. 1595 BC—Hittites;
1500s BC—Kassites;
1200s BC—Assyrians;
612 BC—Chaldeans

Using the Internet

16. Go to the HRW Web site and enter the keyword shown to access a rubric for this activity.

KEYWORD: SK9 CH6

Map Activity

17. A. Sumer
B. Phoenicia
C. Tigris River
D. Babylon
E. Euphrates River

Standardized Test Practice

DIRECTIONS (1–7): For each statement or question, write on a separate answer sheet the *number* of the word or expression that, of those given, best completes the statement or answers the question.

1 The first people to develop a civilization in Mesopotamia were the
(1) Akkadians.
(2) Babylonians.
(3) Egyptians.
(4) Sumerians.

2 Which of the following statements about the first writing system is false?
(1) It was developed by the Babylonians.
(2) It began with the use of pictures to represent syllables and objects.
(3) It was recorded on tablets made of clay.
(4) It was first used to keep business records.

3 In Sumerian society, people's social class or rank depended on their wealth and their
(1) appearance.
(2) religion.
(3) location.
(4) occupation.

4 Which of the following was the subject of a great Sumerian epic?
(1) Cuneiform
(2) Ziggurat
(3) Gilgamesh
(4) Babylon

5 What was the most important contribution of the Phoenicians to our civilization?
(1) purple dye
(2) their alphabet
(3) founding of Carthage
(4) sailing ships

6 A professional writer in ancient Sumer was called a
(1) ziggurat.
(2) pictograph.
(3) scribe.
(4) priest.

7 Hammurabi's Code is important in world history because it was an early
(1) form of writing that could be used to record important events.
(2) written list of laws that controlled people's daily life and behavior.
(3) record-keeping system that enabled the Phoenicians to become great traders.
(4) set of symbols that allowed the Sumerians to communicate with other peoples.

Base your answer to question 8 on the image below and on your knowledge of social studies.

Mesopotamia

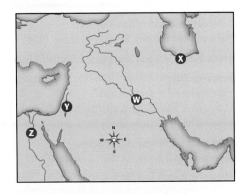

8 The region known as Mesopotamia is indicated on the map above by the letter
(1) W.
(2) X.
(3) Y.
(4) Z.

1. 4
Break Down the Question Remind students that they need to choose the civilization that came before all the others.

2. 1
Break Down the Question Remind students that the word *false* in this question signals that they should identify the answer choice that is not true.

3. 4
Break Down the Question This question requires students to recall factual information from Section 2.

4. 3
Break Down the Question This question requires students to recall factual information from Section 2.

5. 2
Break Down the Question Point out to students that the most lasting contribution from the Phoenicians to our world has been the alphabet.

6. 3
Break Down the Question This question requires students to recall factual information from Section 3.

7. 2
Break Down the Question This question requires students to recall factual information from Section 4.

8. 1
Break Down the Question Point out that the region labeled Y is part of the Fertile Crescent, but not Mesopotamia. Have students who miss the question review the map in Section 1.

Intervention Resources

Reproducible
y Interactive Reader and Study Guide
y Differentiated Instruction Teacher Management System: Lesson Plans

Technology
Quick Facts Transparency: Visual Summary: Ancient Civilizations of the Middle East—Mesopotamia
Differentiated Instruction Modified Worksheets and Tests CD-ROM
Interactive Skills Tutor CD-ROM

Tips for Test Taking

I'm Stuck! Give students these tips for when they get stuck on a standardized test. If you come across a question that stumps you, don't get frustrated. First master the question to make sure you understand what is being asked. Then work through the strategies you have already learned. If you are still stuck, circle the question and go on to others. Come back to it later. What if you still have no idea? Practice the 50/50 strategy and make an educated guess.

Religions of the Ancient Middle East— Judaism, Christianity, and Islam

Chapter Overview	Reproducible Resources	Technology Resources
CHAPTER 7 pp. 158–193 **Overview:** In this chapter, students will study the origins of three major world religions, each of which began in the Middle East.	**Differentiated Instruction Teacher Management System:*** • Instructional Pacing Guides • Lesson Plans for Differentiated Instruction **Interactive Reader and Study Guide:** Chapter Summary Graphic Organizer* **Resource File:*** • Chapter Review • Focus on Reading: Understanding Implied Main Ideas • Focus on Writing: Writing a Letter • Social Studies Skills: Interpreting a Route Map	OSP **Teacher's One-Stop Planner:** Calendar Planner **Power Presentations with Video CD-ROM** **Differentiated Instruction Modified Worksheets and Tests CD-ROM** **Student Edition on Audio CD Program** **Music of the World Audio CD Program** **Map Zone Transparency:** Judaism, Christianity, and Islam, 500 BC–AD 1000* **Geography's Impact Video Program (VHS/DVD):** Impact of Mecca on Islam*
Section 1: **Origins of Judaism** **The Big Idea:** The Hebrews formed a great kingdom in Israel and started a religion called Judaism.	**Differentiated Instruction Teacher Management System:** Section 1 Lesson Plan* **Interactive Reader and Study Guide:** Section 1 Summary* **Resource File:*** • Vocabulary Builder: Section 1 • Literature: *The Chosen*, by Chaim Potok	**Daily Bellringer Transparency:** Section 1* **Map Zone Transparency:** Jewish Migration after AD 70* **Map Zone Transparency:** Possible Routes of the Exodus* **Internet Activity:** Jewish Holy Days
Section 2: **Origins of Christianity** **The Big Idea:** Christianity, a religion based on the life and teachings of Jesus of Nazareth, spread throughout the Roman Empire.	**Differentiated Instruction Teacher Management System:** Section 2 Lesson Plan* **Interactive Reader and Study Guide:** Section 2 Summary* **Resource File:*** • Vocabulary Builder: Section 2 • Biography: Kathleen Kenyon	**Daily Bellringer Transparency:** Section 2* **Map Zone Transparency:** Paul's Journeys* **Map Zone Transparency:** The Spread of Christianity, 300–400* **Internet Activity:** Examples of Opposition
Section 3: **Origins of Islam** **The Big Idea:** In the harsh desert climate of Arabia, Muhammad, a merchant from Mecca, introduced a major world religion called Islam.	**Differentiated Instruction Teacher Management System:** Section 3 Lesson Plan* **Resource File:*** • Vocabulary Builder: Section 3 • Biography: Khadijah • Primary Source: Reading from the Qur'an	**Daily Bellringer Transparency:** Section 3*
Section 4: **Islamic Beliefs and Practices** **The Big Idea:** Sacred texts called the Qur'an and the Sunnah guide Muslims in their religion, daily life, and laws.	**Differentiated Instruction Teacher Management System:** Section 4 Lesson Plan* **Interactive Reader and Study Guide:** Section 4 Summary* **Resource File:*** • Vocabulary Builder: Section 4	**Daily Bellringer Transparency:** Section 4* **Internet Activity:** Islamic Beliefs and Practices Presentation
Section 5: **Cultural Achievements** **The Big Idea:** Jewish, Christian, and Muslim scholars and artists made important contributions to science, art, and literature.	**Differentiated Instruction Teacher Management System:** Section 5 Lesson Plan* **Interactive Reader and Study Guide:** Section 5 Summary* **Resource File:*** • Vocabulary Builder: Section 5	**Daily Bellringer Transparency:** Section 5*

SE Student Edition

 Print Resource

 Audio CD

TE Teacher's Edition

 Transparency

 CD-ROM

 go.hrw.com

LS Learning Styles

Video

OSP Teacher's One-Stop Planner   * also on One-Stop Planner

Review, Assessment, Intervention

 Quick Facts Transparencies: Visual Summary: Religions of the Ancient Middle East—Judaism, Christianity, and Islam*

 Spanish Chapter Summaries Audio CD Program

 Progress Assessment Support System (PASS): Chapter Test*

Differentiated Instruction Modified Worksheets and Tests CD-ROM: Modified Chapter Test

OSP Teacher's One-Stop Planner: ExamView Test Generator (English/Spanish)

HOAP Holt Online Assessment Program (HOAP), in the Holt Interactive Online Student Edition

 PASS: Section 1 Quiz*

 Online Quiz: Section 1

 Alternative Assessment Handbook

 PASS: Section 2 Quiz*

 Online Quiz: Section 2

 Alternative Assessment Handbook

 PASS: Section 3 Quiz*

 Online Quiz: Section 3

 Alternative Assessment Handbook

 PASS: Section 4 Quiz*

 Online Quiz: Section 4

 Alternative Assessment Handbook

 PASS: Section 5 Quiz*

 Online Quiz: Section 5

 Alternative Assessment Handbook

HOLT
Geography's Impact
Video Program

Impact of Mecca on Islam
Suggested use: in Section 4

Power Presentations with Video CD-ROM

Power Presentations with Video are visual presentations of each chapter's main ideas. Presentations can be customized by including Quick Facts charts, images from the text, and video clips.

Holt Online Learning

go.hrw.com
Teacher Resources
KEYWORD: SK9 TEACHER

go.hrw.com
Student Resources
KEYWORD: SK9 CH7

- Interactive Multimedia Activities
- Current Events

- Chapter-based Internet Activities
- and more!

Holt Interactive
Online Student Edition

Complete online support for interactivity, assessment, and reporting

- Interactive Maps and Notebook
- Standardized Test Prep
- Homework Practice and Research Activities Online

CHAPTER 7 PLANNING GUIDE

Differentiating Instruction

How do I address the needs of varied learners?
The Target Resource acts as your primary strategy for differentiated instruction.

ENGLISH-LANGUAGE LEARNERS & STRUGGLING READERS

TARGET RESOURCE

Interactive Skills Tutor CD-ROM

The Interactive Skills Tutor CD-ROM contains lessons that provide additional practice for 20 different critical thinking skills.

Additional Resources

Differentiated Instruction Teacher Management System: Lesson Plans for Differentiated Instruction

Resource File:
- Vocabulary Builder Activities
- Social Studies Skills: Interpreting a Route Map

Student Edition on Audio CD Program

Spanish Chapter Summaries Audio CD Program

Teacher's One Stop Planner:
- ExamView Test Generator, Spanish
- PuzzlePro, Spanish

English-Language Learner Strategies and Activities

SPECIAL NEEDS LEARNERS

TARGET RESOURCE

Resource File

The Resource File activities allow students to extend their knowledge of chapter-related places and people and to practice geography skills.
- Vocabulary Builder Activities
- Social Studies Skills: Interpreting a Route Map

Additional Resources

Differentiated Instruction Teacher Management System: Lesson Plans for Differentiated Instruction

Interactive Reader and Study Guide

Student Edition on Audio CD Program

Interactive Skills Tutor CD-ROM

Differentiated Instruction Modified Worksheets and Tests CD-ROM

Graphic Organizer Transparencies with Support for Reading and Writing

ADVANCED/GIFTED AND TALENTED STUDENTS

TARGET RESOURCE

Differentiated Instruction Teacher Management System

Lesson Plans for Differentiated Instruction provide teachers with strategies to help plan instruction for all learners.

Additional Resources

Resource File:
- Focus on Reading: Understanding Implied Main Ideas
- Focus on Writing: Writing a Letter
- Literature, *The Chosen* by Chaim Potok
- Primary Source: Reading from the Qur'an

World History and Geography Document-Based Questions Activities

Geography, Science, and Cultures Activities

Experiencing World History and Geography

Differentiated Activities in the Teacher's Edition

- Jewish Migration Graphic Organizer
- Interpreting Visuals
- Identifying New Vocabulary
- Christianity Cluster Diagram
- Understanding Vocabulary
- Illustrated Time Line of Persian Empire
- Persian Road System Poster
- Persian Culture and Achievements Chart

Differentiated Activities in the Teacher's Edition

- Choosing the Best Route
- Christianity Cluster Diagram
- Learning about the Qur'an

Differentiated Activities in the Teacher's Edition

- Researching Hebrew Proverbs
- Creating a Web Log
- Writing a Narrative Poem
- Analyzing the Edict of Milan
- Comparing Religions
- Examining Muslim Architecture
- Satrap Résumés
- Persian Culture Presentations

HOLT Teacher's One-Stop Planner®

How can I manage the lesson plans and support materials for differentiated instruction?

With the Teacher's One-Stop Planner, you can easily organize and print lesson plans, planning guides, and instructional materials for all learners.

The Teacher's One-Stop Planner includes the following materials to help you differentiate instruction:

· **Interactive Teacher's Edition**
· **Calendar Planner and pacing guides**
· **Editable lesson plans**
· **All reproducible ancillaries in Adobe Acrobat (PDF) format**
· **ExamView Test Generator (English & Spanish)**
· **Transparency and video previews**

Professional Development

What teacher training resources are available to help me grow professionally?

· **In-service and staff development** as part of your Holt Social Studies product purchase
· **Quick Teacher Tutorial Lesson Presentation CD-ROM**
· Intensive tuition-based **Teacher Development Institute**
· **Convenient Holt Speaker Bureau:** face-to-face workshop options
· **24/7 Ask A Professional Development Expert** at http://www.hrw.com/prodev/

Chapter Big Ideas

Section 1 The Hebrews formed a great kingdom in Israel and started a religion called Judaism.

Section 2 Christianity, a religion based on the life and teachings of Jesus of Nazareth, spread throughout the Roman Empire.

Section 3 In the harsh desert climate of Arabia, Muhammad, a merchant from Mecca, introduced a major world religion called Islam.

Section 4 Sacred texts called the Qur'an and the Sunnah guide Muslims in their religion, daily life, and laws.

Section 5 Jewish, Christian, and Muslim scholars and artists made important contributions to science, art, and literature.

Focus on Reading and Writing

Reading The Resource File provides a Focus on Reading worksheet to help students understand how to identify implied main ideas.

RF: Focus on Reading, Understanding Implied Main Ideas

Writing The Resource File provides a Focus on Writing worksheet to help students plan, organize, and write a letter.

RF: Focus on Writing, Writing a Letter

158   CHAPTER 7

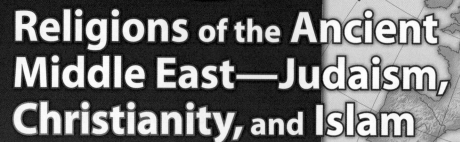

CHAPTER 7

Religions of the Ancient Middle East—Judaism, Christianity, and Islam

FOCUS QUESTION

How did ancient civilizations contribute to the development of the Eastern Hemisphere?

What You Will Learn...

In this chapter you will learn about three major religions that developed in the Middle East: Judaism, Christianity, and Islam.

FOCUS ON READING AND WRITING

Understanding Implied Main Ideas Sometimes the main idea of a paragraph or passage is not directly stated; instead it is implied, or suggested. **See the lesson, Understanding Implied Main Ideas, on page S8.**

Writing a Letter After you read this chapter, you will write a letter to describe one of the events described in it, as though you were an eyewitness to that event.

158 CHAPTER 7

Córdoba

Muslim scholars

Judaism Jews pray at the Western Wall in Jerusalem. The wall is part of the Second Temple, which was built by ancient Hebrews.

ATLANTIC OCEAN

Introduce the Chapter   At Level

Religions of the Ancient Middle East

1. Ask students to name the religions that began in the Middle East. Remind students that Judaism, Christianity, and Islam are three major world religions that began there.

2. Have students discuss what they already know about each religion. Then have students preview the chapter by looking at main headings, maps, and images. Have each student draw a three-column chart on his or her own paper. Instruct students to title the columns "Judaism," "Christianity," and

"Islam." As students preview the chapter, they should write down information they find significant in the appropriate column. Have students share their findings with the class.

3. Have students use their charts to keep track of other important information on the three religions as they study the chapter. Encourage students to use their charts as a review for the chapter test. **LS Verbal/Linguistic**

Alternative Assessment Handbook, Rubric 13: Graphic Organizers

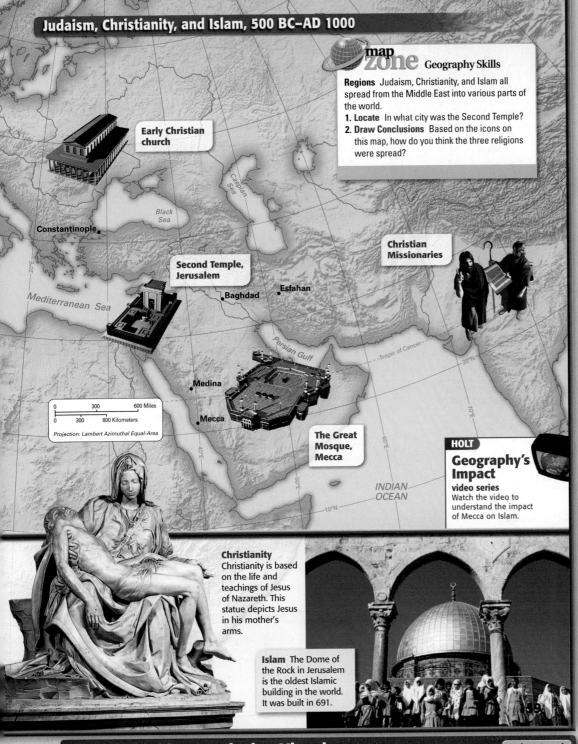

Judaism, Christianity, and Islam, 500 BC–AD 1000

map Zone Geography Skills

Regions Judaism, Christianity, and Islam all spread from the Middle East into various parts of the world.
1. **Locate** In what city was the Second Temple?
2. **Draw Conclusions** Based on the icons on this map, how do you think the three religions were spread?

Early Christian church

Constantinople

Black Sea

Caspian Sea

Second Temple, Jerusalem

Baghdad

Esfahan

Mediterranean Sea

Christian Missionaries

Persian Gulf

~Tropic of Cancer~

Medina

Mecca

The Great Mosque, Mecca

0   300   600 Miles
0   300   600 Kilometers
Projection: Lambert Azimuthal Equal-Area

INDIAN OCEAN

HOLT
Geography's Impact
video series
Watch the video to understand the impact of Mecca on Islam.

Christianity
Christianity is based on the life and teachings of Jesus of Nazareth. This statue depicts Jesus in his mother's arms.

Islam The Dome of the Rock in Jerusalem is the oldest Islamic building in the world. It was built in 691.

Critical Thinking: Analyzing Visuals

Below Level

Examining Religious Symbols

1. Point out the photograph of the sculpture on this page. Explain that the sculpture, by Michelangelo, is called the Pieta. Next, point out the photograph of the Western Wall. Tell students that the Western Wall is located in the Old City of Jerusalem. The Hebrew King David is believed to have had the wall built. Lastly, point out the photograph of the mosque on this page. Tell students that this mosque is located in Jerusalem on the site where Muhammad is believed to have ascended to Heaven.

2. Have students write a short paragraph comparing and contrasting these important symbols of the three religions.

3. Have students examine the icons on the map. Then lead a class discussion about the photographs and icons and what they tell us about the three religions. Ask students to name other symbols of the three religions with which they are familiar.
LS Visual/Spatial, Verbal/Linguistic
Alternative Assessment Handbook, Rubric 11: Discussions

• Chapter Preview •

Explore the Map and Pictures

Judaism, Christianity, and Islam, 500 BC–AD 1000 Have students research the locations where each of the three religions began. Then have students note those locations on the map.
Judaism—Jerusalem;
Christianity—near Jerusalem;
Islam—near Mecca

Map Zone Transparency: Judaism, Christianity, and Islam, 500 BC–AD 1000

Analyzing Visuals Have students examine the images on these two pages. Ask students to briefly describe each image. Write students' responses for everyone to see. For each image in the class list, have students make inferences on how that image relates to one or more of the major religions. Have students share their inferences with the class.

go.hrw.com
Online Resources

Chapter Resources:
KEYWORD: SK9 CH7
Teacher Resources:
KEYWORD: SK9 TEACHER

HOLT
Geography's Impact
▶ video series
See the Video Teacher's Guide for strategies for using the chapter video to teach about the impact of Mecca on Islam.

Answers

Map Zone 1. *Jerusalem;*
2. *with the help of missionaries and scholars*

159

Origins of Judaism

Bellringer

If YOU lived there. . . Use the **Daily Bellringer Transparency** to help students answer the question.

Daily Bellringer Transparency, Section 1

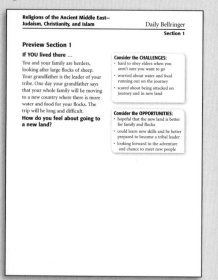

Religions of the Ancient Middle East—
Judaism, Christianity, and Islam

Daily Bellringer
Section 1

Preview Section 1

If YOU lived there . . .
You and your family are herders, looking after large flocks of sheep. Your grandfather is the leader of your tribe. One day your grandfather says that your whole family will be moving to a new country where there is more water and food for your flocks. The trip will be long and difficult.

How do you feel about going to a new land?

Consider the CHALLENGES:
- hard to obey elders when you aren't sure you want to go
- worried about water and food running out on the journey
- scared about being attacked on journey and in new land

Consider the OPPORTUNITIES:
- hopeful that the new land is better for family and flocks
- could learn new skills and be better prepared to become a tribal leader
- looking forward to the adventure and chance to meet new people

Academic Vocabulary

Review with students the high-use academic term in this section.

principle basic belief, rule, or law (p. 164)

RF: Vocabulary Builder, Section 1

Taking Notes

Have students copy the graphic organizer onto their own paper and then use it to take notes on the section. This activity will prepare students for the Section Assessment, in which they will complete a graphic organizer that builds on the information using the Critical Thinking Skill: Sequencing.

What You Will Learn...

Main Ideas

1. The Hebrews' early history began in Canaan and ended when the Romans forced them out of Israel.
2. Jewish beliefs in God, justice, and law anchor their society.
3. Jewish sacred texts describe the laws and principles of Judaism.
4. Traditions and holy days celebrate the history and religion of the Jewish people.

The Big Idea

The Hebrews formed a great kingdom in Israel and started a religion called Judaism.

Key Terms and Places

Judaism, *p. 160*
Canaan, *p. 161*
Exodus, *p. 161*
monotheism, *p. 163*
Torah, *p. 164*
rabbis, *p. 165*

TAKING NOTES As you read, use a graphic organizer like this one to organize your notes on the origins of Judaism.

History | Beliefs
Holidays | Texts

If YOU were there...

You and your family are herders, looking after large flocks of sheep. Your grandfather is the leader of your tribe. One day your grandfather says that your whole family will be moving to a new country where there is more water and food for your flocks. The trip will be long and difficult.

How do you feel about going to a new land?

BUILDING BACKGROUND Like the family described above, the early Hebrews moved to new lands in ancient times. According to Hebrew tradition, their history began when God told an early Hebrew leader to travel west to a new land.

Early History

Sometime between 2000 and 1500 BC a new people appeared in Southwest Asia. They were the Hebrews (HEE-brooz). Most of what is known about early Hebrew history comes from the work of archaeologists and from accounts written by Hebrew scribes. These accounts describe the Hebrews' early history and the laws of **Judaism** (JOO-dee-i-zuhm), the Hebrews' religion. In time these accounts became the Hebrew Bible.

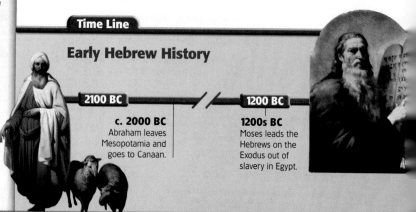

Time Line

Early Hebrew History

2100 BC

c. 2000 BC
Abraham leaves Mesopotamia and goes to Canaan.

1200 BC

1200s BC
Moses leads the Hebrews on the Exodus out of slavery in Egypt.

Teach the Big Idea

At Level

Origins of Judaism

1. **Teach** Ask students the questions in the Main Idea boxes under Direct Teach.

2. **Apply** Ask students to write a dialogue between modern Jews and ancient Hebrews. Have them discuss their shared history, their sacred texts, and their beliefs and traditions. If they wish, students may structure the dialogue as an interview, or even invent characters for a story.

3. **Review** Have students share their dialogues with a partner and take turns reading them aloud.

4. **Practice/Homework** Have students write two or three paragraphs summarizing the text of their dialogues. **LS** Verbal/Linguistic

Alternative Assessment Handbook, Rubric 40: Writing to Describe

Beginnings in Canaan and Egypt

The Bible traces the Hebrews back to a man named Abraham. One day, the Bible says, God told Abraham to leave his home in Mesopotamia. He was to take his family on a long journey to the west. God promised to lead Abraham to a new land and make his descendants into a mighty nation.

Abraham left Mesopotamia and settled in **Canaan** (KAY-nuhn) on the Mediterranean Sea. His descendants—the Hebrews—lived in Canaan for many years. Later, however, some Hebrews moved to Egypt, perhaps because of famine in Canaan.

The Hebrews lived well in Egypt, and their population grew. This growth worried Egypt's ruler, the pharaoh. He feared that the Hebrews might soon become too powerful. To stop this from happening, the pharaoh made the Hebrews slaves.

The Exodus

According to the Hebrew Bible, a leader named Moses appeared among the Hebrews in Egypt. In the 1200s BC, God told Moses to lead the Hebrews out of Egypt. Moses went to the pharaoh and demanded that he free the Hebrews. The pharaoh refused. Soon afterward a series of terrible plagues, or disasters, struck Egypt.

The plagues frightened the pharaoh so much that he agreed to free the Hebrews. Overjoyed with the news of their release, Moses led his people out of Egypt in a journey called the **Exodus**. To the Hebrews, the release from slavery proved that God was protecting and watching over them.

For years after their release, the Hebrews wandered through the desert, trying to return to Canaan. On their journey, they reached a mountain called Sinai. The Hebrew Bible says that while Moses was on the mountain, God gave him two stone tablets. On the tablets was written a code of moral laws known as the Ten Commandments. These laws shaped Hebrew society.

Once the Hebrews reached Canaan, they had to fight to gain control of the land. After they conquered Canaan and settled down on the land, the Hebrews became known as the Israelites.

A Series of Invasions

The Israelites soon faced more threats to their land. Invaders swept through the region in the mid-1000s BC. For a while, strong kings kept Israel together. Israel even grew rich through trade and expanded its territory. With their riches, the Israelites built a great temple to God in Jerusalem.

Some years later when one king died, the Israelites could not agree on who would be the next king. This conflict caused Israel to split into two kingdoms, one called Israel and one called Judah (JOO-duh). The people of Judah became known as Jews.

FOCUS ON READING
What is the main idea of this paragraph? Is it clearly stated or implied?

● **Direct Teach** ●

Main Idea

❶ **Early History**

The Hebrews' early history began in Canaan and ended when the Romans forced them out of Israel.

Identify Who was Abraham? *according to the Bible, a man told by God to lead his people from Mesopotamia to Canaan on the Mediterranean Sea*

Summarize What happened to the Hebrews during the Exodus? *Led by Moses, they left Egypt and wandered through the desert. On Mount Sinai, Moses found the Ten Commandments, laws that have shaped Hebrew society ever since.*

Understand Cause and Effect Why did Egypt's pharaoh make the Hebrews slaves? *As their population grew, he worried that that they might take over Egypt.*

About the Illustrations
These illustrations are artists' conceptions based on available sources. However, historians are uncertain exactly what these people looked like.

---

c. 1000 BC
David becomes king of Israel.

c. 965 BC
David's son Solomon becomes king of Israel. Solomon builds a great temple in Jerusalem.

| 1000 BC | 900 BC | 800 BC |

ANALYSIS SKILL **READING TIME LINES**
About how many years after Abraham settled in Canaan did David become the king of Israel?

161

Critical Thinking: Evaluating Information   At Level

Writing Headlines

1. Have students imagine that they are reporters for local newspapers in Canaan and Egypt. Ask them to write a series of headlines and introductory paragraphs of newspaper articles about Abraham's arrival in Canaan, the movement of some Hebrews to Egypt, and then the Exodus from Egypt.

2. As they write their headlines and plan their articles, have students prepare a list of questions they would like to ask Abraham and Moses.

3. Encourage students to research answers to their questions with Internet or library sources. Then have them invent and incorporate quotes in their articles based on the information they have found.

4. Ask volunteers to read their headlines and introductory paragraphs. **LS Verbal/Linguistic**
   Alternative Assessment Handbook, Rubric 23: Newspapers

Answers

Reading Time Lines *about 1,000 years*
Focus on Reading *Despite many threats, the Israelites stayed together and thrived; implied*

161

Main Idea

❶ Early History, continued

Describe What happened during the Diaspora? *The Jews were scattered outside of Israel and Judah.*

Explain Into what two kingdoms were the Israelites split? Which people became known as the Jews? *Israel and Judah; the people of Judah*

Understand Cause and Effect How were the Jews in Jerusalem affected by the Roman conquest? *They were killed or enslaved; the survivors were forced to flee Jerusalem.*

🗂 Map Zone Transparency: Jewish Migration after AD 70

Linking to Today

The Diaspora For much of their history, the majority of Jews have lived far from Jerusalem. Today the worldwide Jewish population is about 14 million. Of these, only about 4 million live in Israel. About 4.5 million live in the United States. More than 2 million Jews live in Russia and other former Soviet republics, and the rest are scattered around the world.

Connect to Music

Reggae Spiritual The song "By the Rivers of Babylon" refers to the Jews' exile in Babylon. Based on Psalm 137, the song has been recorded by several musicians, including the Reggae artist Bob Marley.

Answers

Reading Check *At first, strong kings kept Israel together. Later, Israel was split into two kingdoms. Invaders sent the Jews out of Jerusalem; some of them returned, but others were scattered outside of Israel.*

Map Zone 1. *Jerusalem;* **2.** *possible answer—settlements already existed in these areas; opportunities for trade*

The two new kingdoms lasted for a few centuries. Israel eventually fell to invaders about 722 BC. Judah lasted until 586 BC, when invaders captured Jerusalem and destroyed Solomon's temple. They sent the Jews out of Jerusalem as slaves. When these invaders were themselves conquered, some Jews returned home. Others moved to other places in Southwest Asia. Scholars call the scattering of Jews outside of Israel and Judah the Diaspora (dy-AS-pruh).

The Jews who returned to Jerusalem ruled themselves for about 100 years. They even rebuilt Solomon's temple. Eventually, however, they were conquered by the Romans. The Jews revolted against the Romans, but most gave up after the Romans destroyed their temple. As punishment for the rebellion, the Romans killed or enslaved much of Jerusalem's population. Thousands of Jews fled Jerusalem. Over the next centuries, Jews moved all around the world. Often they were forced to move by other religious groups who discriminated against them.

READING CHECK **Identifying Cause and Effect** How did invasions affect the Hebrews?

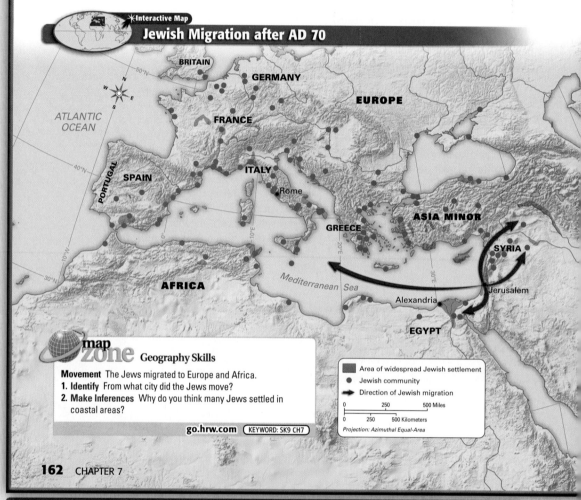

✴Interactive Map
Jewish Migration after AD 70

map zone Geography Skills

Movement The Jews migrated to Europe and Africa.
1. **Identify** From what city did the Jews move?
2. **Make Inferences** Why do you think many Jews settled in coastal areas?

go.hrw.com **KEYWORD: SK9 CH7**

■ Area of widespread Jewish settlement
● Jewish community
➔ Direction of Jewish migration

0   250   500 Miles
0   250   500 Kilometers
Projection: Azimuthal Equal-Area

162 CHAPTER 7

Struggling Readers

1. Pair struggling readers with more proficient readers and have them work together to create and complete a chart summarizing where Jews settled after AD 70, based on the map on this page. The parts of the chart, corresponding to the key, should be labeled *Area of Widespread Jewish Settlement, Jewish Community,* and *Direction of Jewish Migration.*

2. Ask students to write three main idea statements based on the chart. 🅛 **Visual/Spatial**

📖 Alternative Assessment Handbook, Rubrics 7: Charts; and 21: Map Reading

Jewish Migration after AD 70		
Areas of Widespread Jewish Settlement	Jewish Community	Direction of Jewish Migration

Jewish Beliefs

Wherever Jews live around the world, their religion is the foundation upon which they base their whole society. In fact, much of Jewish culture is based directly on Jewish beliefs. The central beliefs of Judaism are belief in one God, in justice and righteousness, and in law.

Belief in One God

Most importantly, Jews believe in one God. The belief in one and only one God is called **monotheism**. Many people believe that Judaism was the world's first monotheistic religion.

In the ancient world where most people worshipped many gods, the Jews' worship of only one God set them apart. This worship shaped Jewish society. The Jews believed they were God's chosen people. They believed that God had guided their history through relationships with Abraham, Moses, and other leaders.

Belief in Justice and Righteousness

Also central to the Jews' religion are the ideas of justice and righteousness. To Jews, justice means kindness and fairness in dealing with other people. Everyone deserves justice, even strangers and criminals. Jews are expected to give aid to those who need it, including the poor, the sick, and orphans. Jews are also expected to be fair in business dealings.

Righteousness refers to doing what is proper. Jews are supposed to behave properly, even if others around them do not. For the Jews, righteous behavior is more important than rituals, or ceremonies.

Belief in Law

Closely related to the ideas of justice and righteousness is obedience to the law. Jews believe that God gave them religious and moral laws to follow. The most important Jewish laws are the Ten Commandments. The commandments require that Jews worship only one God. They also do not allow Jews to do bad things like murder, steal, or lie.

The commandments are only one part of Jewish law. Jews believe that Moses recorded a system of laws, now called Mosaic law, that God had set down for them. Mosaic laws guide many areas of Jews' daily lives, such as how people pray and observe holy days.

READING CHECK Generalizing What are the most important beliefs of Judaism?

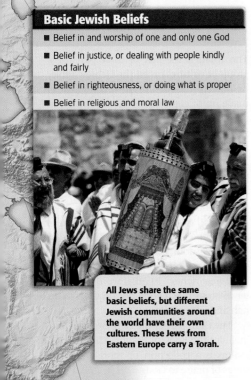

Basic Jewish Beliefs

- Belief in and worship of one and only one God
- Belief in justice, or dealing with people kindly and fairly
- Belief in righteousness, or doing what is proper
- Belief in religious and moral law

All Jews share the same basic beliefs, but different Jewish communities around the world have their own cultures. These Jews from Eastern Europe carry a Torah.

RELIGIONS OF THE ANCIENT MIDDLE EAST—JUDAISM, CHRISTIANITY, AND ISLAM **163**

❸ Jewish Texts

Jewish sacred texts describe the laws and principles of Judaism.

Describe What is the Torah? *a sacred text, part of the Hebrew Bible, containing laws and a history of the Jewish people*

Elaborate What other kinds of religious teachers are there, in addition to rabbis? *possible answers—priests, ministers, imams*

RF: Literature: *The Chosen* by Chaim Potok

Info to Know

The Torah The Torah is handwritten on parchment and rolled on two wooden staves. Readers follow the text with a pointer called a *yad*, which is shaped like a hand with a pointing finger. When Jewish children reach the age of 13, they read the Torah for the first time at a synagogue ceremony called a bar mitzvah (for a boy) or a bat mitzvah (for a girl). Some practice is required in order to read the Torah aloud because the text does not include any vowels or musical notations.

Linking to Today

Female Rabbis The first female rabbi was ordained from a Reform seminary in 1972. Orthodox congregations do not officially support the ordination of women, although a few Orthodox women have become rabbis.

Answers

Analyzing Visuals *The Torah is a scroll, while the Hebrew Bible and the commentaries are books.*

164

Jewish Texts

The Torah
Using a special pointer called a *yad*, this girl is reading aloud from the Torah. The Torah is the most sacred of Hebrew texts. It plays a central role in many Jewish ceremonies.

ANALYSIS SKILL ANALYZING VISUALS
How does the Torah look different from the Hebrew Bible and the commentaries?

ACADEMIC VOCABULARY
principle basic belief, rule, or law

Jewish Texts

The laws and **principles** of Judaism are described in several sacred texts. Among the main texts are the Torah, the Hebrew Bible, and the commentaries.

The Torah

The ancient Jews recorded most of their laws in five books. Together, these books are called the Torah. The **Torah** is the most sacred text of Judaism. In addition to laws, it includes a history of the Jewish people until the death of Moses. Jews believe the contents of the Torah were revealed to Moses by God.

Readings from the Torah are central to Jewish religious services today. Nearly every synagogue (SI-nuh-gawg), or Jewish house of worship, has at least one Torah. Out of respect for the Torah, readers do not touch it. They use special pointers to mark their places in the text.

The Hebrew Bible

The Torah is the first of three parts of a group of writings called the Hebrew Bible, or Tanach (tah-NAHK). The second part is made up of eight books that describe the messages of Hebrew prophets. Prophets are people who are said to receive messages from God to be taught to others.

The final part of the Hebrew Bible is 11 books of poetry, songs, stories, lessons, and history. Many of these stories are told by Jews to show the power of faith.

Also in the final part of the Hebrew Bible are the Proverbs, short expressions of Hebrew wisdom. For example, one Proverb says, "A good name is to be chosen rather than great riches." In other words, it is better to be seen as a good person than to be rich and not respected.

The third part of the Hebrew Bible also includes the Book of Psalms. The Book of Psalms is a collection of short and long songs of praise to God.

Differentiating Instruction

English-Language Learners | Below Level | Standard English Mastery

Pair students with more proficient writers and ask them to use standard English to write three brief paragraphs linking the visuals on this page to the text. Have them begin by describing the visual (for example, "The girl is reading the Torah."). Following sentences should include more information as well as questions. Encourage students to use a dictionary or the thesaurus as necessary. **LS Verbal/Linguistic**

Alternative Assessment Handbook, Rubric 40: Writing to Describe

Advanced/Gifted and Talented | Above Level

Have students research proverbs from the Hebrew Bible as well as other sources. Have them choose their favorite proverbs and then compose five of their own. Ask them to collect the proverbs in a booklet. Then invite them to share these proverbs with a partner and discuss how they might use them as a guide to ethical behavior. **LS Verbal/Linguistic**

Alternative Assessment Handbook, Rubric 39: Writing to Create

The Hebrew Bible
These beautifully decorated pages are from a Hebrew Bible. The Hebrew Bible, sometimes called the Tanach, includes the Torah and other ancient writings.

The Commentaries
The Talmud is a collection of commentaries and discussions about the Torah and the Hebrew Bible. The Talmud is a rich source of information for discussion and debate. Religious scholars like these young men study the Talmud to learn about Jewish history and laws.

The Commentaries

For centuries **rabbis**, or religious teachers, and scholars have studied the Torah and Jewish laws. Because some laws are hard to understand, scholars write commentaries to explain them. Many explanations can be found in the Talmud (TAHL-moohd), a set of commentaries and lessons for everyday life. The writings of the Talmud were produced between AD 200 and 600. Many Jews consider them second only to the Hebrew Bible in significance to Judaism.

READING CHECK Analyzing What texts do Jews consider sacred?

Traditions and Holy Days

Jews feel that understanding their history will help them better follow the Jewish teachings. Their traditions and holy days help Jews connect with their past and celebrate their history.

Hanukkah

One Jewish tradition is celebrated by Hanukkah, which falls in December. It honors a historical event. The ancient Jews wanted to celebrate a victory that had convinced their rulers to let them keep their religion. According to legend, though, the Jews did not have enough lamp oil to celebrate at the temple. Miraculously, the oil they had—enough for only one day—burned for eight full days.

Today Jews celebrate this event by lighting candles in a special candleholder called a menorah (muh-NOHR-uh). Its eight branches represent the eight days through which the oil burned. Many Jews also exchange gifts on each of the eight nights.

Passover

More important to Jews than Hanukkah, Passover is celebrated in March or April. During Passover Jews honor the Exodus, the journey of the Hebrews out of slavery.

RELIGIONS OF THE ANCIENT MIDDLE EAST—JUDAISM, CHRISTIANITY, AND ISLAM **165**

165

Info to Know

Dead Sea Scrolls In 1947 Bedouin goat herders found several jars in a cave along the edge of the Dead Sea, just 13 miles east of Jerusalem. The jars contained scrolls of manuscripts, which have since come to be known as the Dead Sea Scrolls. Remnants of more than 800 manuscripts, dating from about 200 BC to AD 68, have since been discovered in other caves. Most of the manuscripts are written in Hebrew, and a few are written in Aramaic. Scholars think that the Dead Sea Scrolls are the library of a Jewish sect, which hid them for protection during the advance of the Roman army in AD 66–70.

Review & Assess

Close

Use the section's vocabulary to review important information about early Hebrew history and the practice of Judaism today.

Review

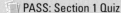 Online Quiz, Section 1

Assess

SE Section 1 Assessment

PASS: Section 1 Quiz

Alternative Assessment Handbook

Reteach/Classroom Intervention

Interactive Reader and Study Guide, Section 1

Interactive Skills Tutor CD-ROM

A Passover Meal

During a special Passover meal called a seder, participants reflect on the events of the Exodus.

ANALYZING VISUALS How can you tell this is a special meal?

High Holy Days

The two most sacred of all Jewish holidays are the High Holy Days. They take place in September or October. The first two days of celebration, Rosh Hashanah (rahsh uh-SHAH-nuh), celebrate the start of a new year in the Jewish calendar.

On Yom Kippur (yohm ki-POOHR), which falls soon afterward, Jews ask God to forgive their sins. Jews consider Yom Kippur to be the holiest day of the entire year. Because it is so holy, Jews do not eat or drink anything all day. They also perform ancient ceremonies that help many Jews feel more connected with their past.

READING CHECK Finding Main Ideas What are the two most important Jewish holidays?

According to Jewish tradition, the Hebrews left Egypt so quickly that bakers did not have time to let their bread rise. Therefore, during Passover Jews eat only matzo, a flat, unrisen bread. They also celebrate the holiday with ceremonies.

SUMMARY AND PREVIEW Judaism was the world's first monotheistic religion. Jewish culture and traditions are rooted in the history of the Hebrew people. Next, you will read about a religion that is related to Judaism—Christianity.

---

go.hrw.com
Online Quiz
KEYWORD: SK9 HP7

Section 1 Assessment

Reviewing Ideas, Terms, and Places

1. **a. Identify** Who first led the Jews to **Canaan**?
   b. Evaluate Why was the **Exodus** a significant event in Hebrew history?
2. **a. Define** What is **monotheism**?
   b. Explain What is the Jewish view of justice and righteousness?
3. **a. Identify** What are the main sacred texts of Judaism?
   b. Elaborate Why do you think the Commentaries are so significant to many Jews?
4. **a. Identify** What event in Hebrew history does Passover celebrate?
   b. Elaborate How do you think celebrating traditions and holy days helps Jews connect to their past?

Critical Thinking

5. **Sequencing** Review your notes on Hebrew history. Then draw a diagram like this one and fill in important events from Hebrew history in the order they occurred. You may add as many boxes as you need for the information.

Abraham settles in Canaan. → ☐ → ☐ → ☐

FOCUS ON WRITING

6. **Noting Main Events in the Origins of Judaism** Look back over this section and imagine what it would have been like to witness some of these events. Identify one or two events that you might describe in your letter.

166 CHAPTER 7

Section 1 Assessment Answers

1. **a.** Abraham
   b. The Jews, freed from slavery in Egypt, wandered for years until settling in Canaan, present-day Israel. According to the Torah, Moses received the Ten Commandments during the Exodus.
2. **a.** belief in only one god
   b. justice—kindness and fairness toward all; righteousness—proper behavior
3. **a.** the Hebrew bible (Tanach) which includes the Torah, the Commentaries (Talmud)
   b. possible answer—because they help Jews today understand ancient Jewish laws

4. **a.** the Exodus
   b. possible answer—They remind Jews of their history.
5. Sequence charts should include important events from Hebrew history, such as the Exodus, invasions, the fall of Israel and Judah, the Diaspora, the Roman conquest of Jerusalem.
6. Students may mention the Exodus, the destruction of Solomon's temple, or the Diaspora.

Answers

Analyzing Visuals *possible answers—People are wearing nice clothes; the food and booklets hint at a special ritual.*

Reading Check *possible answers—Rosh Hashanah, Yom Kippur (High Holy Days)*

Chart and Graph	Critical Thinking	Geography	Study

Interpreting a Route Map

Learn

A route map shows movement from one place to another. Usually, different routes are shown with different colored arrows. Look at the legend to see what the different arrows represent.

Practice

Use the map of Possible Routes of the Exodus to answer the following questions.

1 How many possible Exodus routes does the map show?

2 Where did the Exodus begin?

3 Which possible route would have been the longest?

4 Which route would have passed closest to the Mediterranean Sea?

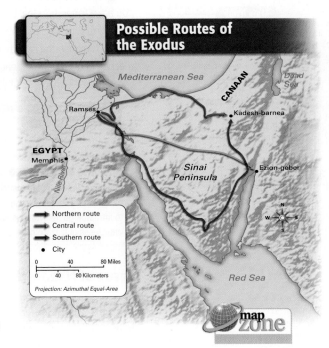

Possible Routes of the Exodus

- → Northern route
- → Central route
- → Southern route
- • City

0   40   80 Miles
0   40   80 Kilometers
Projection: Azimuthal Equal-Area

map zone

Apply

Find a map of your city either in an atlas or on the Internet. You will need to draw on the map, so either print it, copy it, or draw a map on your own paper using the information. On the city map, draw the route you take from your home to school. Then draw another route you could take to get to school. Be sure to create a legend to show what your route lines mean.

167

Interpreting a Route Map

Activity Planning a Route

Materials: copies of contemporary maps of Jerusalem

1. Distribute maps to students. Tell students that they are going to plan a trip to Jerusalem in order to learn more about the people and events discussed in this chapter.

2. Have students examine the maps, deciding which parts of the city they would most like to visit, and in what order. Tell them they have three days to visit the various sights in Jerusalem. Then have them trace the route they would like to take on each day. Suggest that they mark each route with a different color or a different design and create a descriptive legend.

3. When they have finished drawing their routes, have them exchange the maps with another student and compare the different routes they have selected. Have students discuss why they chose one route over another. **LS Visual/Spatial**

   - Alternative Assessment Handbook, Rubric 21: Map Reading
   - Interactive Skills Tutor CD-ROM, Lesson 6: Interpret Maps, Graphs, Charts, Visuals, and Political Cartoons
   - **RF:** Social Studies Skills, Interpreting a Route Map
   - Map Zone Transparency: Possible Routes of the Exodus

Social Studies Skills Activity: Interpreting a Route Map   `Below Level`

Choosing the Best Route

1. Distribute one or more maps to pairs of students. Maps can include subway maps, bus maps, tourist maps, building directories, and so on. Each map should have a legend. Tell students that they are going to practice interpreting these route maps and then create a route map of their own.

2. Have students decide where they want to go, and then work together to find the best route. Have them identify several alternate routes that they can take to arrive at the same location.

3. Finally, have students work together to create maps of the school and mark the route they take each day. Have them give each other feedback about how clearly the route has been marked. **LS Visual/Spatial**

   - Alternative Assessment Handbook, Rubric 21: Map Reading

Answers

Practice 1. *3;* **2.** *Ramses, Egypt;* **3.** *the southern route;* **4.** *the northern route*

Apply *Make sure that students have drawn both regular and alternate routes on the map and that they have created a legend.*

Bellringer

If YOU lived there. . . Use the **Daily Bellringer Transparency** to help students answer the question.

🗃 Daily Bellringer Transparency, Section 2

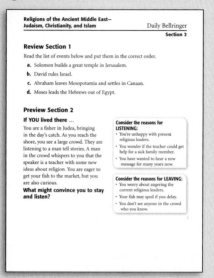

Academic Vocabulary

Review with students the high-use academic term in this section.

ideals ideas or goals that people try to live up to (p. 172)

📝 **RF:** Vocabulary Builder, Section 2

Taking Notes

Have students copy the graphic organizer onto their own paper and then use it to take notes on the section. This activity will prepare students for the Section Assessment, in which they will complete a graphic organizer that builds on the information using the Critical Thinking Skill: Making Generalizations.

Origins of Christianity

What You Will Learn...

Main Ideas

1. The life and death of Jesus of Nazareth inspired a new religion called Christianity.
2. Christians believe that Jesus's acts and teachings focused on love and salvation.
3. Jesus's followers taught others about Jesus's life and teachings.
4. Christianity spread throughout the Roman Empire by 400.

The Big Idea

Christianity, a religion based on the life and teachings of Jesus of Nazareth, spread throughout the Roman Empire.

Key Terms and Places

Messiah, *p. 168*
Christianity, *p. 168*
Bible, *p. 168*
Bethlehem, *p. 168*
Resurrection, *p. 169*
disciples, *p. 169*
saint, *p. 172*

TAKING NOTES As you read, use a graphic organizer like this one to take notes on Jesus and the spread of Christianity.

Life and Death	
Acts and Teachings	
Jesus's Followers	
Spread of Christianity	

168 CHAPTER 7

If YOU lived there...

You are a fisher in Judea, bringing in the day's catch. As you reach the shore, you see a large crowd. They are listening to a man tell stories. A man in the crowd whispers to you that the speaker is a teacher with some new ideas about religion. You are eager to get your fish to the market, but you are also curious.

What might convince you to stay and listen?

BUILDING BACKGROUND In the first century AD, Roman soldiers occupied Judea, but the Jews living there held firmly to their own beliefs and customs. During that time, one religious teacher began to attract large followings among the people of Judea. That teacher was Jesus of Nazareth.

Jesus of Nazareth

Jesus of Nazareth was the man many people believed was the **Messiah**—a great leader the ancient Jews predicted would come to restore the greatness of Israel. Jesus was a great leader and one of the most influential figures in world history. Jesus's life and teachings form the basis of a religion called **Christianity**. However, we know relatively little about his life. Everything we do know is contained in the **Bible**, the holy book of Christianity.

The Christian Bible is made up of two parts. The first part, the Old Testament, is largely the same as the Hebrew Bible. The second part, the New Testament, is an account of the life and teachings of Jesus and of the early history of Christianity.

The Birth of Jesus

According to the Bible, Jesus was born in a small town called **Bethlehem** (BETH-li-hem) at the end of the first century BC. Jesus's mother, Mary, was married to a carpenter named Joseph. But Christians believe God, not Joseph, was Jesus's father.

Teach the Big Idea

At Level

Origins of Christianity

1. **Teach** Ask students the questions in the Main Idea boxes under Direct Teach.

2. **Apply** Have students make a sequence chart such as the one below to show the events that led to the spread of Christianity. As they read, have them fill in the boxes.

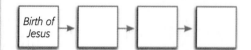

3. **Review** Have students compare their sequence charts.

4. **Practice/Homework** Have students write a paragraph summarizing the information in their sequence charts, using transitional words and phrases to make the sequence clear. **LS** Verbal/Linguistic, Visual/Spatial

🗂 Alternative Assessment Handbook, Rubric 13: Graphic Organizers

---

As a young man Jesus lived in the town of Nazareth and probably studied with Joseph to become a carpenter. Like many young Jewish men of the time, Jesus also studied the laws and teachings of Judaism. By the time he was about 30, Jesus had begun to travel and teach. Stories of his teachings and actions from this time make up the beginning of the New Testament.

The Crucifixion

As a teacher, Jesus drew many followers with his ideas. But at the same time, his teachings challenged the authority of political and religious leaders. According to the Bible, they arrested Jesus while he was in Jerusalem in or around AD 30.

Shortly after his arrest, Jesus was tried and executed. He was killed by crucifixion (kroo-suh-FIK-shuhn), a type of execution in which a person was nailed to a cross. In fact, the word *crucifixion* comes from the Latin word for "cross." After he died, Jesus's followers buried him.

The Resurrection

According to Christian beliefs, Jesus rose from the dead and vanished from his tomb three days after he was crucified. Now Christians refer to Jesus's rise from the dead as the **Resurrection** (re-suh-REK-shuhn).

Christians further believe that after the Resurrection, Jesus appeared to some groups of his **disciples** (di-SY-puhls), or followers. Jesus stayed with these disciples for the next 40 days, teaching them and giving them instructions about how to pass on his teachings. Then Jesus rose up into heaven.

Early Christians believed that the Resurrection was a sign that Jesus was the Messiah and the son of God. Some people began to call him Jesus Christ, from the Greek word for Messiah, *Christos*. It is from this word that the words *Christian* and *Christianity* eventually developed.

READING CHECK **Summarizing** What do Christians believe happened after Jesus died?

Jesus of Nazareth

The Bible says that Jesus was born in Bethlehem but grew up in Nazareth. The famous artist Giotto (1266–1336) painted this scene from Jesus's childhood.

ANALYZING VISUALS How does the artist imply that Jesus was important?

169

Differentiating Instruction

| At Level | Standard English Mastery |

English-Language Learners

1. Explain that some English words are spelled the same but have multiple meanings. Examples are words like *file*, *steer*, and *bear*. Discuss the meanings of these words with students. Point out the words with multiple meanings on this page: *cross*, *rose*, and *pass*.

2. Pair English learners with more proficient readers and have them work together to write sentences in standard English using the different meanings of the words. Encourage students to write sentences that are linked thematically.
LS Verbal/Linguistic

Term	Meaning	Other Meaning(s)
cross	a shape	annoyed, prevent
rose	went up	a flower, a shade of pink
pass	convey	permit, succeed

📖 *Alternative Assessment Handbook, Rubric 7: Charts*

Direct Teach

Main Idea

❶ Jesus of Nazareth
The life and death of Jesus of Nazareth inspired a new religion called Christianity.

Define Who were Jesus's disciples? *his followers*

Analyze Why did people think that Jesus of Nazareth was the Messiah? *He was a great leader who they thought would fulfill the ancient predictions and restore the greatness of Israel.*

Summarize What was the Resurrection? *according to Jesus's followers, his rising from the dead*

Linking to Today

Population of Bethlehem Today the population of Bethlehem is predominantly Christian and Muslim. Nazareth is the largest Arab city in Israel. Both cities are destinations for pilgrims and tourists from around the world.

Teaching Tip

Point out the halos worn by Jesus, his mother, and the angels depicted in the painting. Explain that painters, like writers, sometimes use symbols to represent a belief—in this case, the holiness of Jesus and his family.

About the Illustration

This illustration is an artist's conception based on available sources. However, historians are uncertain exactly what this scene looked like.

Answers

Reading Check *They believe he rose from the dead.*

Analyzing Visuals *possible answer— He is at the center of the painting; he wears a halo, most of the figures are facing in his direction.*

169

❷ Jesus's Acts and Teachings

Christians believe that Jesus's acts and teachings focused on love and salvation.

Explain Which rules did Jesus emphasize that were also in the Torah? *to love God and love other people*

Analyze How did Jesus use parables in his teachings? *to link his beliefs and teachings to his listeners' everyday lives*

Understand Cause and Effect According to the New Testament, why were people drawn to Jesus, and why did they follow him? *They saw him perform miracles, which convinced them that he was the son of God.*

📄 **RF: Biography, Kathleen Kenyon**

FOCUS ON CULTURE

Christian Holidays

For centuries, Christians have honored key events in Jesus's life. Some of these events inspired holidays that Christians celebrate today.

The most sacred holiday for Christians is Easter, which is celebrated each spring. Easter is a celebration of the Resurrection. On Easter Christians usually attend church services. Many people also celebrate by dyeing eggs because eggs are seen as a symbol of new life.

Another major Christian holiday is Christmas. It honors Jesus's birth and is celebrated every December 25. Although no one knows on what date Jesus was actually born, Christians have placed Christmas in December since the 200s. Today people celebrate with church services and the exchange of gifts. Some people reenact scenes of Jesus's birth.

Drawing Conclusions Why do you think people celebrate events in Jesus's life?

Jesus's Acts and Teachings

During his lifetime, Jesus traveled from village to village spreading his message among the Jewish people. As he traveled, he attracted many followers. These early followers later became the first Christians.

Miracles

According to the New Testament, many people became Jesus's followers after they saw him perform miracles. A miracle is an event that cannot normally be performed by a human. For example, the books of the New Testament tell of times when Jesus healed people who were sick or injured. One passage also describes how Jesus once fed an entire crowd with just a few loaves of bread and a few fish. Although there should not have been enough food for everyone, people ate their fill and even had food to spare.

Parables

The Bible says that miracles drew followers to Jesus and convinced them that he was the son of God. Once Jesus had attracted followers, he began to teach them. One way he taught was through parables, or stories that teach lessons about how people should live. Parables are similar to fables, but they usually teach religious lessons. The New Testament includes many of Jesus's parables.

Through his parables, Jesus linked his beliefs and teachings to people's everyday lives. The parables explained complicated ideas in ways that most people could understand. For example, in one parable, Jesus compared people who lived sinfully to a son who had left his home and his family. Just as the son's father would joyfully welcome him home, Jesus said, God would forgive sinners when they turned away from sin.

Differentiating Instruction

Below Level

Struggling Readers

1. Based on the information in the section, have students complete a cluster diagram about Christianity. Create a diagram like the one at right and help students fill in the ovals. Place the word *Christianity* in a center oval. Then fill in the remaining ovals with details about Jesus's life and teachings, Christian beliefs, and other facts related to the religion.

2. Have students write one or two paragraphs summarizing the details in the diagram.
   🅛🅢 **Visual/Spatial**

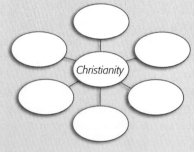

📄 Alternative Assessment Handbook, Rubric 13: Graphic Organizers

---

Answer

Focus on Culture *possible answer—to remember the events in his life and to participate in traditional celebrations with others*

In another parable, Jesus compared society to a wheat field. In this story, a farmer plants wheat seed, but an enemy comes and plants weeds among the wheat. The farmer lets the weeds and wheat grow in the field together. At harvest time, he gathers the wheat in his barn, but he burns the weeds. Jesus explained this parable by comparing the wheat and weeds to good people and evil people who must live together. However, in the end, Jesus said, the good people would be rewarded and the evil people would be punished.

Jesus's Message

Much of Jesus's message was rooted in older Jewish traditions. For example, he emphasized two rules that were also in the Torah: love God and love other people.

Jesus expected his followers to love all people, not just friends and family. He encouraged his followers to be generous to the poor and the sick. He told people that they should even love their enemies. The way people treated others, Jesus said, showed how much they loved God.

Another important theme in Jesus's teachings was salvation, or the rescue of people from sin. Jesus taught that people who were saved from sin would enter the Kingdom of God when they died. Many of his teachings dealt with how people could reach God's kingdom.

Over the many centuries since Jesus lived, people have interpreted his teachings in different ways. As a result, many different denominations of Christians have developed. A denomination is a group of people who hold mostly the same beliefs. Despite their differences, however, Christians around the world share many basic beliefs about Jesus.

READING CHECK Summarizing What were the main ideas in Jesus's message?

The Sermon on the Mount

The Bible says that Jesus attracted many followers. One day he led his followers onto a mountainside to give a religious speech. In this speech, called the Sermon on the Mount, Jesus said that people who love God will be blessed. An excerpt of this sermon appears below.

When Jesus saw the crowds, he went up the mountain; and after he sat down, his disciples came to him. Then he began to speak, and taught them, saying:

"Blessed are the poor in spirit, for theirs is the kingdom of heaven.

"Blessed are those who mourn, for they will be comforted.

"Blessed are the meek, for they will inherit the earth.

"Blessed are those who hunger and thirst for righteousness, for they will be filled.

"Blessed are the merciful, for they will receive mercy.

"Blessed are the pure in heart, for they will see God.

"Blessed are the peacemakers, for they will be called children of God.

"Blessed are those who are persecuted for righteousness' sake, for theirs is the kingdom of heaven.

"Blessed are you when people revile you and persecute you and utter all kinds of evil against you falsely on my account. Rejoice and be glad, for your reward is great in heaven, for in the same way they persecuted the prophets who were before you."

—Matthew 5:1–12, New Revised Standard Version

Scholars believe this location was the site of Jesus's Sermon on the Mount.

ANALYSIS SKILL ANALYZING INFORMATION
What kinds of qualities does Jesus say will be rewarded?

RELIGIONS OF THE ANCIENT MIDDLE EAST—JUDAISM, CHRISTIANITY, AND ISLAM **171**

The Last Supper

This famous painting by Italian artist Leonardo da Vinci shows Jesus and his Apostles sharing their last meal before Jesus was arrested.

ANALYZING VISUALS What kind of mood do people appear to be in?

Jesus's Followers

Shortly after the Resurrection, the Bible says, Jesus's followers traveled throughout the Roman world telling about Jesus and his teachings. Among the people to pass on Jesus's teachings were 12 chosen disciples called Apostles (uh-PAHS-uhlz) and a man called Paul.

The Apostles

The Apostles were 12 men whom Jesus chose to receive special teaching. During Jesus's lifetime they were among his closest followers and knew him very well. Jesus frequently sent the Apostles to spread his teachings. After the Resurrection, the Apostles continued this task.

ACADEMIC VOCABULARY
ideals ideas or goals that people try to live up to

One of the Apostles, Peter, became the leader of the group after Jesus died. Peter traveled to a few Roman cities and taught about Jesus in the Jewish communities there. Eventually, he went to live in Rome, where he had much authority among Jesus's followers. In later years after the Christian Church was more organized, many people looked back to Peter as its first leader.

The Gospels

Some of Jesus's disciples wrote accounts of his life and teachings. These accounts are called the Gospels. Four Gospels are found in the New Testament of the Bible.

The Gospels were written by men known as Matthew, Mark, Luke, and John. All the men's accounts differ slightly from one another, but together they make up the best source we have on Jesus's life. Historians and religious scholars depend on these stories for information about Jesus's life and teachings. The Gospels tell of miracles Jesus performed. They also contain the parables he told.

Paul

Probably the most important person in the spread of Christianity after Jesus's death was Paul of Tarsus. Although he had never met Jesus, Paul did more to spread Christian beliefs and **ideals** than anyone else. He had so much influence that many people think of him as another Apostle. After Paul died, he was named a **saint**, a person known and admired for his or her holiness.

172 CHAPTER 7

Like most of Jesus's early followers, Paul was born Jewish. At first he did not like Jesus's ideas, which he considered a threat to Judaism. For a time, Paul even worked to prevent followers of Jesus from spreading their message.

According to the Bible, though, something happened to Paul one day as he traveled on the road to Damascus. He saw a blinding light and heard the voice of Jesus calling out to him. Soon after that event, Paul became a Christian.

After his conversion, Paul traveled widely, spreading Christian teachings. As you can see on the map, he visited many of the major cities along the eastern coast of the Mediterranean. In addition, he wrote long letters to communities throughout the Roman world. These letters helped explain and elaborate on Jesus's teachings.

In his letters Paul wrote at length about the Christian belief in the Resurrection and about salvation. He also mentioned the idea of the Trinity. The Trinity is a central Christian belief that God is made up of three persons. They are God the Father, Jesus the Son, and the Holy Spirit. This belief holds that, even though there are three persons, there is still only one God.

Paul's teachings attracted both Jews and non-Jews to Christianity in many areas around the Mediterranean. In time, this growing number of Christians helped the Christian Church break away from its Jewish roots. People began to recognize Christianity as a separate religion.

READING CHECK Finding Main Ideas
What did Jesus's followers do to help spread Christianity?

Direct Teach

MISCONCEPTION ALERT

Jesus's Religion Many people forget that Jesus was a Jew, and that his followers also were Jewish. Christianity did not exist until many years after the death of Jesus.

Checking for Understanding

Ask students the following questions to make sure that they understand the concepts in this section.
1. What were the Gospels? *four disciples' accounts of Jesus's life and teachings*
2. Who was Peter? *Apostles' leader*
3. What might have happened if Paul had preached only to Jews? *possible answer—Christianity might have stayed closer to its Jewish roots*

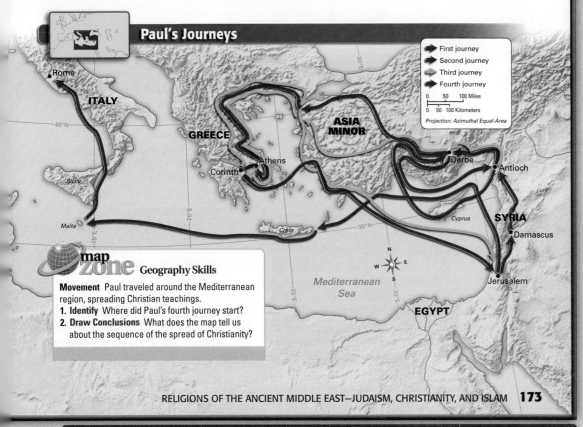

Paul's Journeys

Rome
ITALY
Sicily
Malta
GREECE
Athens
Corinth
Crete
ASIA MINOR
Derbe
Antioch
Cyprus
SYRIA
Damascus
Jerusalem
EGYPT
Mediterranean Sea

First journey
Second journey
Third journey
Fourth journey

0   50   100 Miles
0   50   100 Kilometers
Projection: Azimuthal Equal-Area

map zone Geography Skills

Movement Paul traveled around the Mediterranean region, spreading Christian teachings.
1. **Identify** Where did Paul's fourth journey start?
2. **Draw Conclusions** What does the map tell us about the sequence of the spread of Christianity?

RELIGIONS OF THE ANCIENT MIDDLE EAST—JUDAISM, CHRISTIANITY, AND ISLAM **173**

Cross-Discipline Activity: English/Language Arts

Above Level

Writing a Narrative Poem

Prep Required

1. Have students write a narrative poem describing the experiences of Paul.
2. Begin by reading aloud excerpts from some narrative poems, such as "Rime of the Ancient Mariner" (Coleridge) and "Spoon River Anthology" (Robinson). Point out that these poems tell a chronological story, and that the subjects of the stories often speak in the poems.
3. Before they begin writing, encourage students to find more information about Paul. Then have them create an outline of the poem. Have students try to write a refrain that captures the central ideas of the poem.
4. Ask volunteers to read all or part of their poems aloud. **Verbal/Linguistic**

    Alternative Assessment Handbook, Rubric 26: Poems and Songs

Answers

Reading Check *They traveled from place to place spreading Jesus's teachings; Jesus's disciples wrote accounts of Jesus's life and teachings in the Gospels; Paul preached and wrote letters.*

Map Zone 1. *Jerusalem;* **2.** *that it began in Asia Minor, then spread to Greece, then much farther west to Italy*

❹ The Spread of Christianity

Christianity spread throughout the Roman Empire by 400.

Describe Who were the leaders of the early church? *bishops, or local Christian leaders; the pope*

Summarize How were Christians treated by Roman leaders? *They were persecuted; many Christians were arrested and killed. Some emperors tolerated Christian worship but later banned Christianity.*

Understand Cause and Effect What was the ultimate effect of Constantine's conversion? *the acceptance of Christianity in the Roman Empire*

🔲 Map Zone Transparency: The Spread of Christianity, 300–400

Did you know. . .

Early Christians in the Roman Empire had to worship in secret in order to avoid persecution. To mark their gathering places, they sometimes used the symbol of a fish. The symbol appeared on the homes of some believers, and also on Christian gravestones and jewelry. Many of Jesus's followers were fishermen, and some of the stories in the New Testament have to do with fish and fishing.

Answers

Map Zone 1. *Toledo, Rome, Carthage, Constantinople, Antioch, Jerusalem, Alexandria;* **2.** *Christianity arose in the region, and Asia Minor would have been widely traveled by Jesus's followers.*

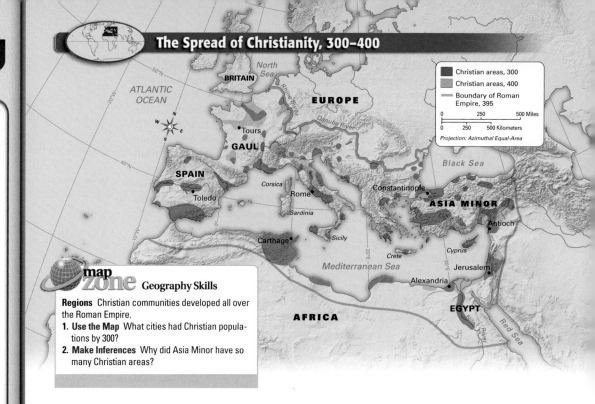

The Spread of Christianity, 300–400

■	Christian areas, 300
■	Christian areas, 400
—	Boundary of Roman Empire, 395

0   250   500 Miles
0   250   500 Kilometers
Projection: Azimuthal Equal-Area

map zone Geography Skills

Regions Christian communities developed all over the Roman Empire.
1. **Use the Map** What cities had Christian populations by 300?
2. **Make Inferences** Why did Asia Minor have so many Christian areas?

The Spread of Christianity

Early Christians like Paul wanted to share their message about Jesus with the world. To do that, Christians began to write down parts of Jesus's message, including the Gospels. They distributed copies of the Gospels and other writings to strengthen people's faith. Because of their efforts, Christianity spread quickly in Roman communities.

Persecution

As Christianity became more popular, some Roman leaders became concerned. They looked for ways to put an end to this new religion. Sometimes local officals challenged the Christians trying to spread their beliefs. Some of these officials even arrested and killed Christians who refused to worship the gods of Rome. Many of the leaders of the early Christians, including Peter and Paul, were killed for their efforts in spreading Christian teachings.

Most of Rome's emperors let Christians worship as they pleased. However, a few emperors in the 200s and 300s feared that the Christians could cause unrest in the empire. To prevent such unrest, these emperors banned Christianity. Christians were often forced to meet in secret.

Growth of the Church

Because the early church usually had to meet in secret, it did not have any single leader to govern it. Instead, bishops, or local Christian leaders, led each Christian community. Most of these early bishops lived in cities.

174 CHAPTER 7

Critical Thinking: Analyzing Primary Sources   Above Level

Analyzing the Edict of Milan

Materials: photocopies of the Edict of Milan

1. Distribute copies of Constantine's Edict of Milan, in which he articulated a policy of religious toleration in the empire. Find an English translation of this edict on the Internet.

2. Review or preteach difficult vocabulary. Have students work in pairs to summarize the edict's main points. Then have them write a newspaper editorial describing the edict and responding to it. Have them predict what

effect the edict will have on Christians and others in the empire and how it might be enforced.

3. Have students "publish" their editorials by reading them aloud. Lead a discussion about the main points brought up by students.
LS Verbal/Linguistic

📓 Alternative Assessment Handbook, Rubrics 23: Newspapers; and 41: Writing to Express

By the late 100s Christians were looking to the bishops of large cities for guidance. These bishops had great influence, even over other bishops. The most honored of all the empire's bishops was the bishop of Rome, or the pope. Gradually, the pope's influence grew and many people in the West came to see him as the head of the whole Christian Church. As the church grew, so did the influence of the pope.

Acceptance of Christianity

As the pope's influence grew, Christianity continued to spread throughout Rome even though it was banned. Then an event changed things for Christians in Rome. The emperor himself became a Christian.

The emperor who became a Christian was Constantine (KAHN-stuhn-teen). According to legend, Constantine was preparing for battle against a rival when he saw a cross in the sky. He thought that this vision meant he would win the battle if he converted to Christianity. Constantine did convert, and he won the battle. As a result of his victory, he became the new emperor of Rome.

As emperor, Constantine removed bans against the practice of Christianity. He also called together a council of Christian leaders from around the empire to try to clarify Christian teachings. Almost 60 years after Constantine died, another emperor banned all non-Christian religious practices in the empire. Christianity eventually spread from Rome all around the world.

FOCUS ON READING
What is the main idea of this paragraph?

READING CHECK **Analyzing** What difficulties did early Christians face in practicing and spreading their religion?

SUMMARY AND PREVIEW The life and teachings of Jesus of Nazareth inspired a new religion among the Jews. This religion was Christianity. Next, you will learn about a religion inspired by the message of the prophet Muhammad. That religion was Islam.

Section 2 Assessment

go.hrw.com
Online Quiz
KEYWORD: SK9 HP7

Reviewing Ideas, Terms, and Places

1. **a. Define** In Christian teachings, what was the **Resurrection**?
   b. Elaborate Why do you think Christians use the cross as a symbol of their religion?
2. **a. Identify** What did Jesus mean by salvation?
   b. Explain How have differing interpretations of Jesus's teachings affected Christianity?
3. **a. Define** What is a **saint**?
   b. Summarize How did Paul influence early Christianity?
4. **a. Recall** What was the role of bishops in the early Christian Church?
   b. Explain Why were some Roman leaders worried about the growing popularity of Christianity?
   c. Predict What do you think might have happened to Christianity if Constantine had not become a Christian?

Critical Thinking

5. **Making Generalizations** Review your notes on Jesus's acts and teachings. Then make generalizations about the topics shown in the graphic organizer.

Acts and Teachings of Jesus of Nazareth

| Miracles | Parables | Message |

FOCUS ON WRITING

6. **Identifying Events Related to Christianity** What events from this time can you imagine witnessing? Identify at least one or two events that you might describe in your letter.

RELIGIONS OF THE ANCIENT MIDDLE EAST—JUDAISM, CHRISTIANITY, AND ISLAM **175**

Section 2 Assessment Answers

1. **a.** the rising of Jesus from the dead
   b. Jesus was crucified—killed on a cross
2. **a.** the rescue of people from sin so that they could enter the Kingdom of God when they died
   b. They have led to the development of different denominations.
3. **a.** a person known and admired for holiness
   b. Through his travels and his letters, Paul attracted many converts. His letters explained Jesus's teachings and Christian beliefs, such as the Resurrection and the Trinity.
4. **a.** They were local Christian leaders; bishops in large cities had more influence than other bishops. The pope (bishop of Rome) had the most influence.
   b. They worried that the Christians would cause unrest.
   c. possible answer—It might have continued to struggle for influence; it might not have spread around the world.
5. Generalizations will vary.
6. Students should identify at least one event and explain its significance.

175

Bellringer

If YOU lived there. . . Use the **Daily Bellringer Transparency** to help students answer the question.

🔖 Daily Bellringer Transparency, Section 3

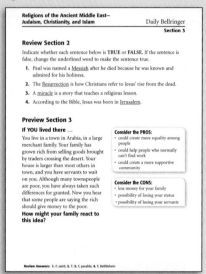

Religions of the Ancient Middle East—
Judaism, Christianity, and Islam
Daily Bellringer
Section 3

Review Section 2

Indicate whether each sentence below is **TRUE** or **FALSE**. If the sentence is false, change the underlined word to make the sentence true.

1. Paul was named a <u>Messiah</u> after he died because he was known and admired for his holiness.
2. The <u>Resurrection</u> is how Christians refer to Jesus' rise from the dead.
3. A <u>miracle</u> is a story that teaches a religious lesson.
4. According to the Bible, Jesus was born in <u>Jerusalem</u>.

Preview Section 3

If YOU lived there ...
You live in a town in Arabia, in a large merchant family. Your family has grown rich from selling goods brought by traders crossing the desert. Your house is larger than most others in town, and you have servants to wait on you. Although many townspeople are poor, you have always taken such differences for granted. Now you hear that some people are saying the rich should give money to the poor.
How might your family react to this idea?

Consider the PROS:
• could create more equality among people
• could help people who normally can't find work
• could create a more supportive community

Consider the CONS:
• less money for your family
• possibility of losing your status
• possibility of losing your servants

Review Answers: 1. F, saint; 2. T; 3. F, parable; 4. F, Bethlehem

Key Terms and Places

📄 **RF:** Vocabulary Builder, Section 3

Taking Notes

Have students copy the graphic organizer onto their own paper and then use it to take notes on the section. This activity will prepare students for the Section Assessment, in which they will complete a graphic organizer that builds on the information using the Critical Thinking Skill: Sequencing.

What You Will Learn...

Main Ideas

1. Arabia is mostly a desert land, where two ways of life, nomadic and sedentary, developed.
2. A new religion called Islam, founded by the prophet Muhammad, spread throughout Arabia in the 600s.

The Big Idea

In the harsh desert climate of Arabia, Muhammad, a merchant from Mecca, introduced a major world religion called Islam.

Key Terms and Places

Mecca, *p. 178*
Islam, *p. 178*
Muslim, *p. 178*
Qur'an, *p. 178*
Medina, *p. 179*
mosque, *p. 179*

TAKING NOTES As you read, take notes on key places, people, and events in the origins of Islam. Organize your notes in a series of boxes like the ones below.

| Places | People | Events |

Origins of Islam

If **YOU** lived there...

You live in a town in Arabia, in a large merchant family. Your family has grown rich from selling goods brought by traders crossing the desert. Your house is larger than most others in town, and you have servants to wait on you. Although many townspeople are poor, you have always taken such differences for granted. Now you hear that some people are saying the rich should give money to the poor.

How might your family react to this idea?

BUILDING BACKGROUND For thousands of years, traders have crossed the deserts of Arabia to bring goods to market. Scorching temperatures and lack of water have made the journey difficult. However, Arabia not only developed into a thriving trade center, it also became the birthplace of a new religion.

Life in a Desert Land

The Arabian Peninsula, or Arabia, is located in the southwest corner of Asia. It lies near the intersection of Africa, Europe, and Asia. For thousands of years Arabia's location, physical features, and climate have shaped life in the region.

Physical Features and Climate

Arabia lies in a region with hot and dry air. With a blazing sun and clear skies, summer temperatures in the interior parts of the peninsula reach 100°F (38°C) daily. This climate has created a band of deserts across Arabia and northern Africa. Sand dunes, or hills of sand shaped by the wind, can rise to 800 feet (240 m) high and stretch across hundreds of miles!

Arabia's deserts have a very limited amount of water. What water there is exists mainly in scattered oases. An oasis is a wet, fertile area in a desert. Oases have long been key stops along Arabia's overland trade routes.

Teach the Big Idea
At Level

The Origins of Islam

1. **Teach** Ask students the questions in the Main Idea boxes under Direct Teach.

2. **Apply** Have students write each of the red titles in the section on a piece of paper. Ask students to review the material under each title. Have students write one sentence that expresses the main idea of the information under each title.

3. **Review** Have students share the main idea statements they created for each heading. Ask students to list supporting details for

each main idea. Have students add the details below their main ideas.

4. **Practice/Homework** Ask students to imagine they are nomads, craftspeople, or traders. Have each student write a letter describing that lifestyle to a friend.
LS Verbal/Linguistic

📄 Alternative Assessment Handbook, Rubric 25: Personal Letters

Two Ways of Life

To live in Arabia's harsh deserts, people developed two main ways of life. Nomads lived in tents and raised herds of sheep, goats, and camels. The animals provided milk, meat, wool, and leather. The camels also carried heavy loads. Nomads traveled with their herds across the desert in search of food and water for their animals.

Among the nomads, water and land belonged to tribes. Membership in a tribe, a group of related people, offered safety from desert dangers.

While nomads moved around, other Arabs lived a more settled life. They made their homes in oases where they could farm. These settlements, particularly the ones along trade routes, became towns.

Towns became centers of trade. There, nomads traded animal products and herbs for goods like cooking supplies and clothes. Merchants sold spices, gold, leather, and other goods brought by caravans.

READING CHECK Categorizing What two ways of life were common in Arabia?

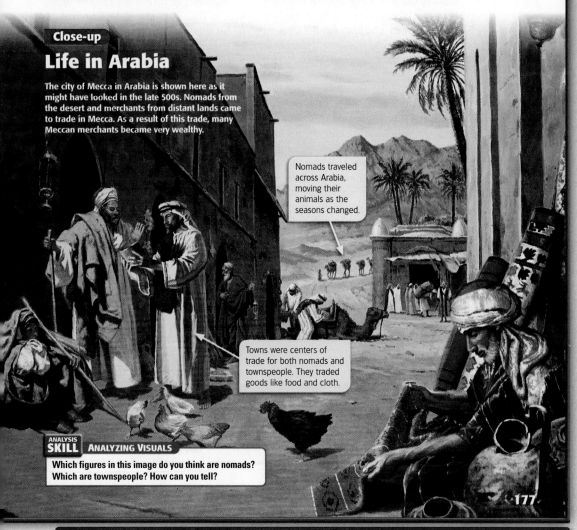

Close-up
Life in Arabia

The city of Mecca in Arabia is shown here as it might have looked in the late 500s. Nomads from the desert and merchants from distant lands came to trade in Mecca. As a result of this trade, many Meccan merchants became very wealthy.

Nomads traveled across Arabia, moving their animals as the seasons changed.

Towns were centers of trade for both nomads and townspeople. They traded goods like food and cloth.

ANALYSIS SKILL ANALYZING VISUALS

Which figures in this image do you think are nomads? Which are townspeople? How can you tell?

177

177

Main Idea

❷ A New Religion

A new religion called Islam, founded by the prophet Muhammad, spread throughout Arabia in the 600s.

Recall In what business was Muhammad involved? *caravan trade*

Explain What is the difference between the terms *Islam* and *Muslim*? *Islam is a religion, while a Muslim is a follower of Islam.*

Draw Conclusions Why do you think Muhammad did not tell people right away that an angel had spoken to him? *He may have been afraid that no one would believe him or that his message would make people angry.*

📄 **RF:** Biography, Khadijah

📄 **RF:** Primary Source, Reading from the Qur'an

Reading Time Lines

Activity **Illustrated Time Line**
Ask students to examine the time line titled "Beginnings of Islam." Have each student create an illustrated version of the time line with one illustration for each entry. **LS** Visual/Spatial

📄 Alternative Assessment Handbook, Rubric 36: Time Lines

Answers

Focus on Reading *Muhammad created a monotheistic religion that emphasized a belief in one god.*

Reading Time Lines *19 years (from 613 to 632)*

A New Religion

In early times, Arabs worshipped many gods. That changed, however, when a man named Muhammad brought a new religion to Arabia. Historians know little about Muhammad. What they do know comes from religious writings.

Muhammad Becomes a Prophet

Muhammad was born into an important family in the city of **Mecca** around 570. As a small child, he traveled with his uncle's caravans. Once he was grown, he managed a caravan business owned by a wealthy woman named Khadijah (ka-DEE-jah). At age 25, Muhammad married Khadijah.

The caravan trade made Mecca a rich city, but most of the wealth belonged to just a few people. Traditionally, wealthy people in Mecca had helped the poor. As Muhammad was growing up, though, many rich merchants ignored the needy.

Concerned about these changes, Muhammad often went to the hills to pray and meditate. One day, when he was about 40 years old, he went to meditate in a cave. According to religious writings, an angel spoke to Muhammad, telling him to "Recite! Recite!" Muhammad asked what he should recite. The angel answered:

FOCUS ON READING
How would you state the main idea of the last paragraph on this page?

> "Recite in the name of your Lord who created, created man from clots of blood!
> Recite! Your Lord is the Most Bountiful One,
> Who by the pen taught man what he did not know."
>
> —From *The Koran*, translated by N. J. Dawood

Muslims believe that God had spoken to Muhammad through the angel and had made him a prophet, a person who tells of messages from God. The messages that Muhammad received form the basis of the religion called **Islam**. In Arabic, the word *Islam* means "to submit to God."

Muslims, or people who follow Islam, believe that God chose Muhammad to be his messenger to the world. They also believe that Muhammad continued to receive messages from God for the rest of his life. Eventually, these messages were collected in the **Qur'an** (kuh-RAN), the holy book of Islam.

Muhammad's Teachings

In 613 Muhammad began to talk about his messages. He taught that there was only one God, Allah, which means "the God" in Arabic. Like Judaism and Christianity, Islam is monotheistic, or based on the belief in one God. Although people of all three religions believe in one God, their beliefs about God are not the same.

Time Line

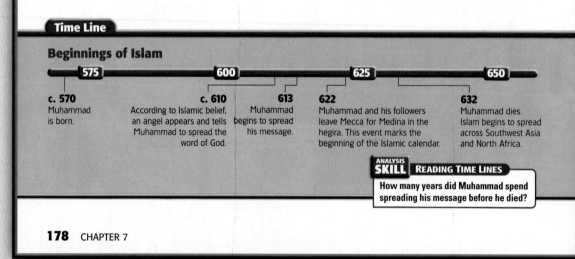

Beginnings of Islam

| 575 | 600 | 625 | 650 |

c. 570 Muhammad is born.

c. 610 According to Islamic belief, an angel appears and tells Muhammad to spread the word of God.

613 Muhammad begins to spread his message.

622 Muhammad and his followers leave Mecca for Medina in the hegira. This event marks the beginning of the Islamic calendar.

632 Muhammad dies. Islam begins to spread across Southwest Asia and North Africa.

ANALYSIS SKILL **READING TIME LINES**
How many years did Muhammad spend spreading his message before he died?

Differentiating Instruction

Above Level

Advanced/Gifted and Talented

Research Required

1. Review with students the similarities among Christianity, Judaism, and Islam.

2. Have students conduct research in a library, on the Internet, or in other resources to find more similarities among these three major religions.

3. Have students create a graphic organizer that shows the similarities that exist among the three religions. Ask students to be creative in the design of their graphic organizers and to respect the beliefs and practices of each religion.

4. Ask volunteers to share their comparisons with the class. Write the similarities for the entire class to see.
LS Verbal/Linguistic, Visual/Spatial

📄 Alternative Assessment Handbook, Rubric 13: Graphic Organizers

Muhammad's teachings also dealt with how people should live. He taught that all people who believed in Allah were bound together like members of a family. As a result, he said, people should help those who are less fortunate. For example, he thought that people who had money should use that money to help the poor.

Islam Spreads in Arabia

At first Muhammad had few followers. Slowly, more people began to listen to his ideas. As Islam spread, Mecca's rulers grew worried. They threatened Muhammad and even planned to kill him.

A group of people living north of Mecca invited Muhammad to move to their city. So in 622 Muhammad and many of his followers went to **Medina** (muh-DEE-nuh). The name *Medina* means "the Prophet's city" in Arabic. Muhammad's departure from Mecca is called the hegira (hi-JY-ruh), or journey. It is so important a date in the history of Islam that Muslims made 622 the first year of the Islamic calendar.

Muhammad became a spiritual and political leader in Medina. His house became the first **mosque** (MAHSK), or building for Muslim prayer.

As the Muslim community in Medina grew stronger, other Arab tribes began to accept Islam. Conflict with the Meccans, however, increased. In 630, after several years of fighting, the people of Mecca gave in. They accepted Islam as their religion.

Before long, most people in Arabia had accepted Muhammad as their spiritual and political leader and become Muslims. Muhammad died in 632, but the religion he taught would soon spread far beyond the Arabian Peninsula.

READING CHECK **Summarizing** How did Islam spread in Arabia?

Over many centuries, Islam spread from Arabia into other parts of the world. These Muslim children in the African country of Nigeria are studying the Qur'an.

SUMMARY AND PREVIEW In the early 600s Islam was introduced to Arabia by Muhammad. In the next section, you will learn more about the main Islamic teachings and beliefs.

go.hrw.com
Online Quiz
KEYWORD: SK9 HP7

Section 3 Assessment

Reviewing Ideas, Terms, and Places

1. **a. Define** What is an oasis?
   b. Make Generalizations Where did towns develop? Why?
   c. Predict Do you think life would have been better for nomads or townspeople in early Arabia? Explain.
2. **a. Identify** What is the **Qur'an**?
   b. Explain According to Islamic belief, what was the source of Islamic teachings?
   c. Elaborate Why did Muhammad move from **Mecca** to **Medina**? What did he accomplish there?

Critical Thinking

3. **Sequencing** Draw a time line like the one below. Using your notes on Muhammad, identify the key dates in his life.

   ⟵———┼———┼———┼———┼———⟶

FOCUS ON WRITING

4. **Thinking about Muhammad and Islam** In this section you read about Muhammad and the beginnings of Islam. What events from this period might you describe in your letter? Write down some notes.

179

Direct Teach

Info to Know

The Qur'an Muhammad continued to receive messages for the rest of his life. These revelations make up Islam's Qur'an, or Koran. While Muhammad himself did not write down the messages, it is likely that he dictated them to others. The Qur'an was collected and organized about 644, about 12 years after Muhammad's death.

Review & Assess

Close

Have students work in pairs to write one-paragraph summaries of the geography of Arabia. Then have students discuss the origins of Islam as well as early reactions to Muhammad and his teachings.

Review

Online Quiz, Section 3

Assess

SE Section 3 Assessment
PASS: Section 3 Quiz
Alternative Assessment Handbook

Reteach/Classroom Intervention

Interactive Reader and Study Guide, Section 3
Interactive Skills Tutor CD-ROM

Section 3 Assessment Answers

1. **a.** a wet, fertile area in a desert
   b. in oases, especially along trade routes, so people could farm and trade
   c. Answers will vary, but students should show an understanding that sedentary lifestyles were safer and more convenient, while nomads led more adventurous lifestyles.
2. **a.** the holy book of Islam
   b. an angel who told Muhammad to spread the word of God
   c. It was easier for Muhammad to convert people in a safer environment like Medina.

People there accepted his ideas. Eventually he gained enough support to spread his message to Mecca and beyond.

3. c. 570, Muhammad is born; c. 595, marries Khadijah; c. 610, he hears the voice of an angel in a cave; 613, he begins spreading his message; 622, he leaves Mecca for Medina; 630, people of Mecca accept Islam; 632, he dies.

4. Notes will vary but might include the birth of Muhammad, Muhammad's new teachings, the hegira, Mecca's acceptance of Islam, and Muhammad's death.

Answers

Reading Check *It spread with Muhammad's move to Medina and became popular with Arab tribes.*

179

Bellringer

If YOU lived there. . . Use the **Daily Bellringer Transparency** to help students answer the question.

🖐 Daily Bellringer Transparency, Section 4

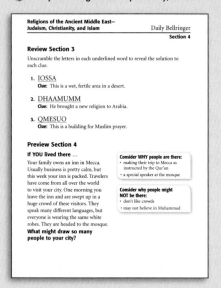

Academic Vocabulary

Review with students the high-use academic terms in this section.

explicit fully revealed without vagueness (p. 181)

implicit understood though not clearly put into words (p. 181)

📒 RF: Vocabulary Builder, Section 4

Taking Notes

Have students copy the graphic organizer onto their own paper and then use it to take notes on the section. This activity will prepare students for the Section Assessment, in which they will complete a graphic organizer that builds on the information using the Critical Thinking Skill: Categorizing.

Islamic Beliefs and Practices

What You Will Learn...

Main Ideas

1. The Qur'an guides Muslims' lives.
2. The Sunnah tells Muslims of important duties expected of them.
3. Islamic law is based on the Qur'an and the Sunnah.

The Big Idea

Sacred texts called the Qur'an and the Sunnah guide Muslims in their religion, daily life, and laws.

Key Terms

jihad, *p. 181*
Sunnah, *p. 181*
Five Pillars of Islam, *p. 182*

 TAKING NOTES As you read, take notes on the most important beliefs and practices of Islam. You can organize your notes in a table like this one.

Religious beliefs	Daily life	Laws

If YOU lived there...

Your family owns an inn in Mecca. Usually business is pretty calm, but this week your inn is packed. Travelers have come from all over the world to visit your city. One morning you leave the inn and are swept up in a huge crowd of these visitors. They speak many different languages, but everyone is wearing the same white robes. They are headed to the mosque.

What might draw so many people to your city?

BUILDING BACKGROUND One basic Islamic belief is that everyone who can must make a trip to Mecca sometime during his or her lifetime. More Islamic teachings can be found in Islam's holy books—the Qur'an and the Sunnah.

The Qur'an

During Muhammad's life, his followers memorized his messages and his words and deeds. After Muhammad's death, they collected and his teachings and wrote them down to form the book known as the Qur'an. Muslims believe the Qur'an to be the exact word of God as it was told to Muhammad.

Beliefs

The central teaching in the Qur'an is that there is only one God—Allah—and that Muhammad is his prophet. The Qur'an says people must obey Allah's commands. Muslims learned of these commands from Muhammad.

Islam teaches that the world had a definite beginning and will end one day. Muhammad said that on the final day God will judge all people. Those who have obeyed his orders will be granted life in paradise. According to the Qur'an, paradise is a beautiful garden full of fine food and drink. People who have not obeyed God, however, will suffer.

180 CHAPTER 7

Teach the Big Idea

At Level

Islamic Beliefs and Practices

Materials: poster board, art supplies

1. **Teach** Ask students the questions in the Main Idea boxes under Direct Teach.

2. **Apply** Have each student create a poster that lists the important beliefs, guidelines, and practices of Islam. Students should decorate their posters to look like an official set of rules. Remind students to include the Five Pillars of Islam and guidelines for behavior. 🔲 **Verbal/Linguistic, Visual/Spatial**

3. **Review** Ask each student to write two questions that cover guidelines or practices from his or her poster. Go around the room and have students ask one another their questions. Discuss the answers with the class.

4. **Practice/Homework** Have students write a short paragraph to explain the importance of the Qur'an, the Sunnah, and Shariah. 🔲 **Verbal/Linguistic**

📒 Alternative Assessment Handbook, Rubrics 28: Posters; and 42: Writing to Inform

Studying the Qur'an

The Qur'an, pictured below, plays a central role in the lives of many Muslims. Both children and adults study and memorize verses from the Qur'an at home, at Islamic schools, and in mosques.

ANALYZING VISUALS Where do you think these children are studying the Qur'an?

Guidelines for Behavior

Like holy books of other religions, the Qur'an describes Muslim acts of worship, guidelines for moral behavior, and rules for social life.

Some of these guidelines for life are stated **explicitly**. For example, the Qur'an clearly describes how a person should prepare for worship. Muslims must wash themselves before praying so they will be pure before Allah. The Qur'an also tells Muslims what they should not eat or drink. Muslims are not allowed to eat pork or drink alcohol.

Other guidelines for behavior are not stated directly but are **implicit** in the Qur'an. Even though they are not written directly, many of these ideas altered early Arabian society. For example, the Qur'an does not expressly forbid the practice of slavery, which was common in early Arabia. It does, however, imply that slavery should be abolished. Based on this implication, many Muslim slaveholders chose to free their slaves.

Another important subject in the Qur'an has to do with **jihad** (ji-HAHD), which means "to make an effort, or to struggle." Jihad refers to the inner struggle people go through in their effort to obey God and behave according to Islamic ways. Jihad can also mean the struggle to defend the Muslim community, or, historically, to convert people to Islam. The word has also been translated as "holy war."

ACADEMIC VOCABULARY
explicit fully revealed without vagueness

READING CHECK Analyzing Why is the Qur'an important to Muslims?

The Sunnah

The Qur'an is not the only source for the teachings of Islam. Muslims also study the hadith (huh-DEETH), the written record of Muhammad's words and actions. It is also the basis for the Sunnah. The **Sunnah** (SOOH-nuh) refers to the way Muhammad lived, which provides a model for the duties and the way of life expected of Muslims. The Sunnah guides Muslims' behavior.

ACADEMIC VOCABULARY
implicit understood though not clearly put into words

Main Idea

❷ The Sunnah

The Sunnah tells Muslims of important duties expected of them.

Define What is the Sunnah? *It is the record of the way Muhammad lived; it serves as a model for the expected duties and way of life of Muslims.*

Identify List the Five Pillars of Islam. *statement of faith, daily prayer, yearly donation to charity, fasting during Ramadan, pilgrimage to Mecca*

Draw Conclusions How does the Sunnah affect the daily lives of Muslims? *It sets forth the Five Pillars of Islam and forms the basis of rules regarding business, government, and personal relations.*

go.hrw.com
Online Resources
Chapter Resources:
KEYWORD: SK9 CH7
ACTIVITY: Islamic Beliefs and Practices Presentation

Info to Know

Ramadan Muslims mark the end of Ramadan with a three-day celebration known as the ʻ*Eid ul-Fitr*, or the Festival of Fast-Breaking. Muslims celebrate with services at the mosque, gatherings with family and friends, and carnivals. Gifts for children and special sweets are often handed out during this holiday.

Answers

Analyzing Visuals *the third pillar, giving to the poor and needy*

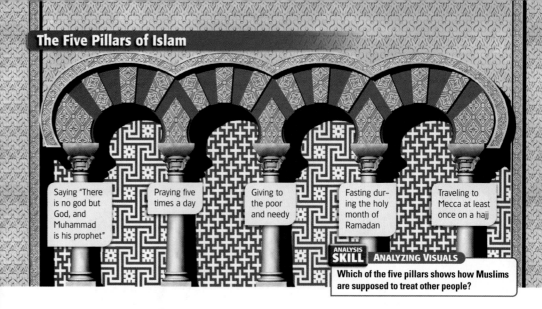

The Five Pillars of Islam

Saying "There is no god but God, and Muhammad is his prophet"

Praying five times a day

Giving to the poor and needy

Fasting during the holy month of Ramadan

Traveling to Mecca at least once on a hajj

ANALYSIS SKILL **ANALYZING VISUALS**
Which of the five pillars shows how Muslims are supposed to treat other people?

The Five Pillars of Islam

The first duties of a Muslim are known as the **Five Pillars of Islam**, which are five acts of worship required of all Muslims. The first pillar is a statement of faith. At least once in their lives, Muslims must state their faith by saying, "There is no god but God, and Muhammad is his prophet." Muslims say this when they accept Islam. They also say it in their daily prayers.

The second pillar of Islam is daily prayer. Muslims must pray five times a day: before sunrise, at midday, in late afternoon, right after sunset, and before going to bed. At each of these times, a call goes out from a mosque, inviting Muslims to come pray. Muslims try to pray together at a mosque. They believe prayer is proof that someone has accepted Allah.

The third pillar of Islam is a yearly donation to charity. Muslims must pay part of their wealth to a religious official. This money is used to help the poor, build mosques, or pay debts. Helping and caring for others is important in Islam.

The fourth pillar of Islam is fasting—going without food and drink. Muslims fast during the holy month of Ramadan (RAH-muh-dahn). The Qur'an says Allah began his revelations to Muhammad in this month. Throughout Ramadan, most Muslims will not eat or drink anything between dawn and sunset. Muslims believe fasting is a way to show that God is more important than one's own body. Fasting also reminds Muslims of people in the world who struggle to get enough food.

The fifth pillar of Islam is the hajj (HAJ), a pilgrimage to Mecca. All Muslims must travel to Mecca at least once in their lives if they can. The Kaaba, in Mecca, is Islam's most sacred place.

The Sunnah and Daily Life

Besides the five pillars, the Sunnah has other examples of Muhammad's actions and teachings. These form the basis for rules about how to treat others. According to Muhammad's example, people should treat guests with generosity.

182 CHAPTER 7

Critical Thinking: Summarizing
At Level

The Five Pillars of Islam Book Jacket

1. Explain to students what a book jacket looks like and its purpose. You might want to provide a sample book jacket.

2. Point out to students that book jackets include a picture or illustration and the title on the front cover; a brief summary of the book's contents on the inside flaps; the title, author, and publisher on the spine; and comments about the book on the back cover.

3. Have students prepare a book jacket for a book titled The Five Pillars of Islam. Draw

a sample layout of the elements of a book jacket for students to follow.

4. Ask volunteers to share their finished book jackets with the class.
LS Verbal/Linguistic, Visual/Spatial

Alternative Assessment Handbook, Rubrics 3: Artwork; and 37: Writing Assignments

The Sunnah also provides guidelines for how people should conduct their relations in business and government. For example, one Sunnah rule says that it is bad to owe someone money. Another rule says that people should obey their leaders.

READING CHECK **Generalizing** What do Muslims learn from the Sunnah?

Islamic Law

Together, the Qur'an and the Sunnah are important guides for how Muslims should live. They also form the basis of Islamic law, or Shariah (shuh-REE-uh). Shariah uses both Islamic sources and human reason to judge the rightness of actions a person or community might take. All actions fall on a scale ranging from required to accepted to disapproved to forbidden. Islamic law makes no distinction between religious beliefs and daily life, so Islam affects all aspects of Muslims' lives.

Shariah sets rewards for good behavior and punishments for crimes. It also describes limits of authority. It was the basis for law in Muslim countries until modern times.

Today, though, most Muslim countries blend Islamic law with legal systems like those in the United States or western Europe.

Islamic law is not found in one book. Instead, it is a set of opinions and writings that have changed over the centuries. As a result, different ideas about Islamic law are found in different Muslim regions.

READING CHECK **Finding Main Ideas** What is the purpose of Islamic law?

SUMMARY AND PREVIEW The Qur'an, the Sunnah, and Shariah teach Muslims how to live. In the next section, you will learn about how Muslims from various parts of Asia, Africa, and Europe made advances in many fields.

Sources of Islamic Beliefs		
Qur'an	**Sunnah**	**Shariah**
Holy book that includes all the messages Muhammad received from God	Muhammad's example for the duties and way of life expected of Muslims	Islamic law, based on interpretations of the Qur'an and Sunnah

Section 4 Assessment

go.hrw.com
Online Quiz
KEYWORD: SK9 HP7

Reviewing Ideas, Terms, and Places

1. **a. Recall** What is the central teaching of the Qur'an?
   b. Explain How does the Qur'an help Muslims obey God?
2. **a. Recall** What are the **Five Pillars of Islam**?
   b. Make Generalizations Why do Muslims fast during Ramadan?
3. **a. Identify** What is Islamic law called?
   b. Make Inferences How is Islamic law different from law in the United States?
   c. Elaborate What is one possible reason that opinions and writings about Islamic law have changed over the centuries?

Critical Thinking

4. **Categorizing** Draw a chart like the one to the right. Use your notes to list three key teachings from the Qur'an and three teachings from the Sunnah.

Qur'an	Sunnah

FOCUS ON WRITING

5. **Describing Islam** What information would you include in your letter about the beliefs and practices of Islam? Note how you might describe these beliefs and practices to your friend.

RELIGIONS OF THE ANCIENT MIDDLE EAST—JUDAISM, CHRISTIANITY, AND ISLAM **183**

Info to Know

More Than One Billion Muslims Most of the world's more than one billion Muslims live in Africa and the Middle East. However, the country with the largest number of Muslims is Indonesia, an island nation located between Australia and Southeast Asia. Here are the countries with the largest number of Muslims (estimated) and the percentage of the population that practices the Muslim religion.

Country	Muslims (in millions)	Percent of Population
Indonesia	210	88
Pakistan	155	97
India	145	13
China	140	11
Bangladesh	120	83

Did you know. . .

Every year, more people want to make the Hajj than can be accommodated by the city of Mecca. To help with this problem, the government of Saudi Arabia has set up restrictions by limiting the number of Hajj visas, favoring people who have never made the journey before. A special Hajj Commission has been established to help visitors and establish policies.

Geography and History

The Hajj

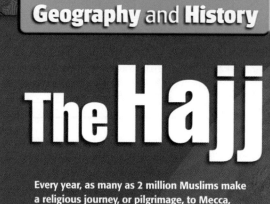

Every year, as many as 2 million Muslims make a religious journey, or pilgrimage, to Mecca, Saudi Arabia. This journey, called the hajj, is one of the Five Pillars of Islam—all Muslims are expected to make the journey at least once in their lifetime if they can.

Mecca is the place where Muhammad lived and taught more than 1,300 years ago. As a result, it is the holiest city in Islam. The pilgrims who travel to Mecca each year serve as a living reminder of the connection between history and geography.

Europe and the Americas Many countries in Europe and the Americas have a Muslim population. These pilgrims are from Germany.

On the Road to Mecca

- Before entering Mecca, pilgrims undergo a ritual cleansing and put on special white garments.
- At Mecca, guides help pilgrims through religious rituals.
- One important ritual is the "Standing" on Mount Arafat, near Mecca. Pilgrims stand for hours, praying, at a place where Muhammad is said to have held his last sermon.
- Pilgrims then participate in a three-day ritual of "Stoning," in which they throw pebbles at three pillars.
- Finally, pilgrims complete their journey by returning to the Grand Mosque in Mecca, where a great feast is held.

Africa Pilgrims also come from Africa. These pilgrims are from Nigeria, just one of the African countries that is home to a large Muslim population.

184 CHAPTER 7

Differentiating Instruction

Below Level

Struggling Readers

1. Have students read the box titled "On the Road to Mecca," and ask them to make a list of all words they do not know.

2. Read the box aloud, pausing after each sentence to ask students if it contains any of the words from their list. Define or discuss the words so that students understand them. Where possible, find illustrations or photographs in the chapter that help clarify the meaning of the words.

3. Pay particular attention to these words: *undergo, ritual, cleansing, garments, pillars,* and *feast*. Guide students to see how context clues in this box and in other text on this spread might help them understand the meaning of these words. **LS Verbal/Linguistic**

Alternative Assessment Handbook, Rubric 11: Discussions

Southeast Asia These pilgrims are from Indonesia, in Southeast Asia. Like all pilgrims, they wear simple white garments that symbolize the equality and unity of all Muslims.

Persian Gulf

MECCA

SAUDI ARABIA

Red Sea

Southwest Asia Pilgrims from Southwest Asia live closest to Mecca. Because of their close relative location, some are able to make the hajj more than once.

Arabian Sea

GEOGRAPHY SKILLS INTERPRETING MAPS

1. **Movement** What are some of the places from which Muslims begin their journey to Mecca?
2. **Place** Why is Mecca the holiest city in Islam?

Info to Know

The Kaaba Part of the Hajj ritual is to walk seven times around the Kaaba, a structure about 50 feet high, 35 feet wide, and 40 feet long. Inside the Kaaba is the Hajar al Aswad, a black stone, which pilgrims try to touch as they walk by. The stone is probably a meteorite, and is known to have been an object of reverence even in pre-Islamic Arabia.

Did you know. . .

With millions of pilgrims coming together at one time, the Hajj has been the scene of more than one deadly tragedy. The most deadly occurred in 1990 when 1,426 Hajj pilgrims were trampled to death inside a tunnel leading into the shrine.

Collaborative Learning

At Level

Researching the Hajj

Research Required

1. Organize students into groups and have them report on one aspect of the Hajj. Topics can be chosen by the group or selected from the following list:
   - Arrangements that need to be made to go on the Hajj
   - Fatal incidents that have occurred, and precautions that are being taken to prevent future tragedies
   - The significance of Medina to Islamic history and religious practice
   - The Kaaba and the black stone contained within it
   - A short biography of Muhammad

2. Have the groups present their results to the class. They may write research papers, make posters, or use some other presentation method. **LS Verbal/Linguistic**

   Alternative Assessment Handbook, Rubrics 30: Research; and 40: Writing to Describe

Answers

Interpreting Maps 1. *Africa, Europe, the Americas, Southeast Asia, Southwest Asia;* **2.** *Mecca is the place where Muhammad lived and taught more than 1,300 years ago.*

Bellringer

If YOU lived there. . . Use the **Daily Bellringer Transparency** to help students answer the question.

📄 Daily Bellringer Transparency, Section 5

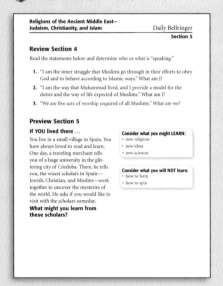

> **Religions of the Ancient Middle East—**
> **Judaism, Christianity, and Islam**
> Daily Bellringer
> **Section 5**
>
> **Review Section 4**
> Read the statements below and determine who or what is "speaking."
>
> 1. "I am the inner struggle that Muslims go through in their efforts to obey God and to behave according to Islamic ways." What am I?
> 2. "I am the way that Muhammad lived, and I provide a model for the duties and the way of life expected of Muslims." What am I?
> 3. "We are five acts of worship required of all Muslims." What are we?
>
> **Preview Section 5**
> **If YOU lived there …**
> You live in a small village in Spain. You have always loved to read and learn. One day, a traveling merchant tells you of a huge university in the glittering city of Córdoba. There, he tells you, the wisest scholars in Spain— Jewish, Christian, and Muslim—work together to uncover the mysteries of the world. He asks if you would like to visit with the scholars someday. **What might you learn from these scholars?**
>
> **Consider what you might LEARN:**
> • new religions
> • new ideas
> • new sciences
>
> **Consider what you will NOT learn:**
> • how to farm
> • how to spin

Academic Vocabulary

Review with students the high-use academic term in this section.

classical referring to the cultures of ancient Greece or Rome (p. 187)

📄 **RF:** Vocabulary Builder, Section 5

Taking Notes

Have students copy the graphic organizer onto their own paper and then use it to take notes on the section. This activity will prepare students for the Section Assessment, in which they will complete a graphic organizer that builds on the information using the Critical Thinking Skill: Analyzing.

Cultural Achievements

What You Will Learn...

Main Ideas

1. Jewish, Christian, and Muslim scholars made lasting contributions to the fields of science and philosophy.
2. Jews, Christians, and Muslims all made great contributions to the visual and literary arts.

The Big Idea

Jewish, Christian, and Muslim scholars and artists made important contributions to science, art, and literature.

Key Terms

alchemy, *p. 187*
synagogues, *p. 189*
cathedrals, *p. 189*
minarets, *p. 189*
calligraphy, *p. 189*

TAKING NOTES As you read, take notes on the achievements and advances made in various fields. In each outer circle of this word web, describe one achievement or advance. You may need to add more circles.

Achievements and Advances

If **YOU** lived there...

You live in a small village in Spain. You have always loved to read and learn. One day, a traveling merchant tells you of a huge university in the glittering city of Córdoba. There, he tells you, the wisest scholars in Spain—Jewish, Christian, and Muslim—work together to uncover the mysteries of the world. He asks if you would like to visit with the scholars someday.

What might you learn from these scholars?

BUILDING BACKGROUND By the year 1000 Judaism, Christianity, and Islam were well established. As members of these religions settled in cities, they became interested in learning and science. Their efforts led to great advances in many fields.

Science and Philosophy

The rise and spread of three major religions led to great changes in parts of Asia, Africa, and Europe. As these religions spread, they brought people into contact with each other. With this contact came new ideas and inspirations. By the 1000s, these ideas had led to great advances in science and philosophy.

Cultural Achievements

Jewish Philosophy
Jewish scholars like Moses Maimonides combined their faith with ancient Greek logic to explain the world.

Teach the Big Idea   At Level

Cultural Achievements

1. **Teach** Ask students the questions in the Main Idea boxes under Direct Teach.

2. **Apply** Organize the students into small groups. Assign each group an achievement or figure discussed in the section, such as alchemy, Moses Maimonides, or Omar Khayyám. Each group is to take notes on its assigned scholar or achievement. Have representatives share information about their group's scholar or achievement. Compile a class list. 🗪 **Interpersonal, Verbal/Linguistic**

3. **Review** As you review the section have students discuss the class list of scholars and achievements. Ask students to evaluate the list and select the scholar and the achievement they think are most significant.

4. **Practice/Homework** Have each student create illustrations related to a scholar or achievement he or she thinks is most significant. Illustrations might include art, maps, and inventions. 🗪 **Visual/Spatial**

📄 Alternative Assessment Handbook, Rubrics 3: Artwork; and 14: Group Activity

Science

Judaism, Christianity, and Islam all taught that God had created the world. Inspired by their beliefs, many people wanted to know more about what God had created for them. As a result, they began to take a closer look at the natural world. Over time, these closer looks led to dramatic advances in their understanding of science.

In Europe, these advances were the result of an early form of chemistry known as **alchemy**. Christian alchemists wanted to improve the world. Some tried to find medicines that would cure any sickness. Others wanted to find a way to turn worthless metals like lead into gold. Their experiments helped shape the later development of modern science.

While alchemists were trying to change the world, Muslim scientists had more practical goals. Many of these goals dealt with medicine. Muslim scientists had learned basic medical skills from ancient Greek and Indian works, but they also added many discoveries of their own. Muslim doctors started the world's first pharmacy school to teach people how to make medicine. They built hospitals and learned to cure many serious diseases, such as smallpox. A Muslim doctor known in the West as Avicenna recorded medical knowledge in an encyclopedia. It was used in Europe until the 1600s.

Philosophy

In addition to science, Jewish, Christian, and Muslim thinkers made great contributions to philosophy. Many of these contributions came out of Córdoba, Spain. Although Córdoba was mostly a Muslim city, it was also home to many Jews and Christians. Because they lived and worked together peacefully, people of all three religions prospered.

Among those who prospered was the Jewish philosopher Moses Maimonides (my-MAHN-uh-deez). Maimonides studied **classical** writings and, like the ancient Greeks, believed in the importance of reason. Many of his writings deal with the nature of faith.

Muslim scholars in Córdoba were interested in ancient Greek and Roman writings. Among them was Ibn-Rushd, also known as Averroes. He was particularly interested in Greek ideas about logic.

Philosophers like Maimonides and Ibn-Rushd influenced thinking for many years to come. For example, their works shaped the ideas of Thomas Aquinas, whom many consider to be the greatest Christian philosopher of the Middle Ages. Inspired by these earlier thinkers, Aquinas worked to blend Christian faith with Greek logic.

ACADEMIC VOCABULARY
classical referring to the cultures of ancient Greece or Rome

READING CHECK Drawing Conclusions
How did cooperation among faiths lead to developments in philosophy?

Christian Science
Christian alchemists conducted experiments to learn about and change the world. They hoped to improve people's lives through their work.

Muslim Medicine
Muslim doctors made medicines from plants like this mandrake plant, which was used to treat pain and illnesses. They developed better ways to prevent, diagnose, and treat many diseases.

RELIGIONS OF THE ANCIENT MIDDLE EAST—JUDAISM, CHRISTIANITY, AND ISLAM **187**

Direct Teach

Main Idea

❶ Science and Philosophy

Jewish, Christian, and Muslim scholars made lasting contributions to the fields of science and philosophy.

Recall What was one Christian achievement in science or philosophy? *possible answers—alchemy, Aquinas's blend of Christian faith and Greek logic*

Compare and Contrast How did Christian and Muslim science differ? *Christian alchemists wanted to improve the world while Muslim scientists were more practical.*

Evaluate What do you think was the most important advance made by Jews, Muslims, and Christians in the field of science? Why? *Answers will vary, but students should select one of the advances mentioned and provide reasons to support their choice.*

Connect to Science

Muslim Hospitals Among the most significant of Muslim medical advances is the idea of the hospital. Although treatment facilities existed in other cultures and in earlier times, Muslim hospitals provided a much wider range of functions. They served as treatment and recovery facilities as well as homes for the elderly, disabled, and mentally ill. Most Muslim hospitals treated both Muslims and non-Muslims, rich and poor alike.

Answers

Reading Check *Cooperation in Cordoba led to a sharing of ideas, especially Greek and Roman writings which philosophers of all three religions relied upon.*

187

Critical Thinking: Finding Main Ideas   At Level

Cultural Achievements: Museum Exhibits

Materials: art supplies

1. Ask students to imagine that they work in a museum as an exhibit planner. The museum will host an exhibit on the cultural achievements of early Jews, Christians, and Muslims.

2. Have each student create a plan for a museum exhibit that illustrates the achievements of these three groups in science and philosophy. Tell students to focus on specific individuals and concepts.

3. Have students write a proposal that explains in detail their plans for the exhibit. The proposal should attempt to persuade the reader to fund the exhibit.

4. Have volunteers share their proposal with the class. If time permits, have students create and display their planned exhibit. **LS Verbal/Linguistic, Visual/Spatial**

   Alternative Assessment Handbook, Rubric 43: Writing to Persuade

Close-up
The Blue Mosque

The Blue Mosque was built to rival Hagia Sophia, which stands nearby. The Mosque can hold some 10,000 worshippers at a time. The large dome soars 140 feet above the ground, and four pillars, each about 16 feet in diameter, support the roof.

According to one legend, the Blue Mosque's six minarets were a mistake. The story goes that the sultan had asked for minarets of gold, which is *altin* in Turkish. But the architect thought the sultan had said *alti,* which means "six." So he built six minarets, and the sultan decided he liked the results.

Did you know...

Most Muslim prayer rugs also have an image of a mihrab at one end. The prayer rug must be placed on the floor so that this mihrab, or arch-shaped design, points toward Mecca.

Activity **Comparing Places of Worship** Have students use the library, Internet, or other sources to examine photos of Christian churches, Jewish synagogues, and Muslim mosques. Have students write a short essay comparing and contrasting the three different types of places of worship.
LS Visual/Spatial

Answers

Analyzing Visuals *possible answers—The patrons wanted the mosque to be impressive as a sign of their wealth and status; the elaborate decorations are a way for Muslims to glorify God.*

Close-up
The Blue Mosque

The Blue Mosque in Istanbul is an example of Muslim architecture from the 1600s. Like most religious architecture, it was designed to honor God and inspire religious followers.

Domes are a common feature of Islamic architecture. Huge columns support the center of this dome, and more than 250 windows let light into the mosque.

The mosque gets its name from its beautiful blue Iznik tiles.

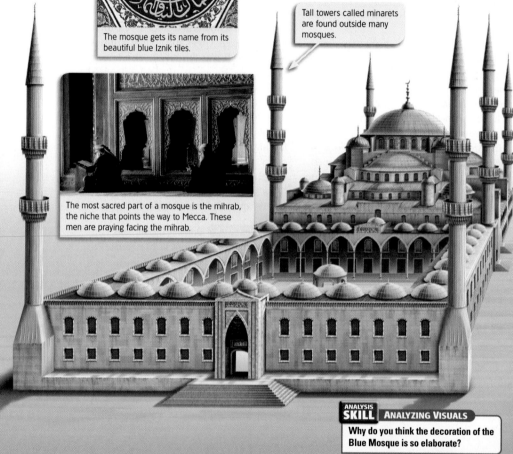

Tall towers called minarets are found outside many mosques.

The most sacred part of a mosque is the mihrab, the niche that points the way to Mecca. These men are praying facing the mihrab.

ANALYSIS SKILL **ANALYZING VISUALS**
Why do you think the decoration of the Blue Mosque is so elaborate?

188 CHAPTER 7

Cross-Discipline Activity: Arts and the Humanities   At Level

Mosque Web Site   Research Required

1. Have students study this page closely. Ask students what interests them most about the Blue Mosque. Have students share and discuss their answers.

2. Then organize students into small groups and have each group conduct research on mosques.

3. Have each group use its findings to create a design for a Web site about mosques. The Web site should include information about the architectural and religious features of

mosques and identify some of the famous mosques that exist today. Tell students that their Web site design should include a home, or main, page as well as links to supporting pages on specific topics.
LS Interpersonal, Verbal/Linguistic

📄 Alternative Assessment Handbook, Rubrics 30: Research; and 42: Writing to Inform

Art and Literature

In addition to scientific and philosophical achievements, Jews, Christians, and Muslims made great advances in the arts. Some of these artistic advances can be seen in the visual arts and literature.

Visual Arts

Of the advances in the visual arts, those in architecture were the most visible. Members of all three religions built houses of worship as symbols of their faith. As they moved through the Mediterranean, for example, Jews built ornate **synagogues**—Jewish houses of worship—in many cities. These synagogues were often located near large Christian churches called **cathedrals.** These cathedrals were often ornately decorated with statues and paintings of religious figures. Muslims likewise built beautiful mosques built to honor God and inspire religious followers. Many mosques feature large domes and graceful **minarets,** tall towers from which Muslims are called to prayer.

Unlike Christians, Jews and Muslims did not show people in their art, because they thought only God could create the human image. To decorate their mosques, therefore, Muslim artists created complex geometric patterns. Muslim artists also turned to **calligraphy,** or the art of decorative writing. They made sayings from the Qur'an into works of art.

Literature

Religious beliefs also inspired great works of literature. For example, devout followers of all three religions wrote poetry in which they expressed their love for God. Many Jewish and Christian poems were written by holy men and women who lived apart from society. The Christian poet Hildegard of Bingen was a nun. She lived in an isolated convent, where she wrote

beautiful religious poems and songs. In contrast, Muslim poets were often active in society. One of the most famous was Omar Khayyám (oh-mahr ky-AHM). In a book of poems known as the *Rubáiyát*, he wrote about faith, hope, and other emotions.

READING CHECK **Generalizing** How were Jewish, Christian, and Muslim literature similar?

SUMMARY AND PREVIEW The Jews, Christians, and Muslims made great advances in science and art. In the next chapter, you'll learn about another people that made lasting advances in many fields, the Persians.

Section 5 Assessment

go.hrw.com
Online Quiz
KEYWORD: SK9 HP7

Reviewing Ideas, Terms, and Places

1. **a. Identify** Who was Moses Maimonides, and what was his major achievement?
   b. Explain How did alchemy help bring about the development of modern science?
   c. Rank In your opinion, what was the most important scientific achievement of this era? Why?
2. **a. Describe** What function do **minarets** serve in mosques?
   b. Explain What was the purpose behind most religious literature?

Critical Thinking

3. **Analyzing** Using your notes, complete a chart like the one below. For each category in the first column, list one important achievement or advance the Muslims made.

Category	Achievement or Advance
Science	
Philosophy	
Architecture	
Art	
Literature	

FOCUS ON WRITING

4. **Describing Religious Achievements and Advances** Review your notes on key achievements and advances in science, philosophy, literature, and the arts. Now decide what information about each of these topics you will include in your letter.

189

Section 5 Assessment Answers

1. **a.** a Jewish philosopher; examined classical writings and wrote about the nature of faith and how religious people should behave
   b. the use of experiments helped shape modern science
   c. Students' responses will vary, but might include alchemy, curing sickness, medicines, hospitals. Students should provide support for their answers.

2. **a.** provide a place from which calls to prayer are made
   b. to express love for God

3. science—developed medicines and opened hospitals; philosophy—Ibn-Rushd studied Greek logic; architecture—built elaborate mosques; art—used calligraphy; literature—Omar Khayyam wrote beautiful poems

4. Students should include in their letters information about key Jewish, Christian, and Muslim achievements and advances.

Outlining

Activity **Materials:** a copy for each student of a long newspaper article

1. Distribute copies of the article to the class. Tell students that the class will create an outline of the article.

2. Point out to students that sometimes newspaper articles have main ideas toward the end and begin with a detail to grab the reader's attention.

3. Read the newspaper article aloud and write the title of the article on the board. Below it, write the Roman numeral I and capital letters A and B. Point out to students that an outline's main ideas must have at least two supporting details, or none at all.

4. Have students name the article's main ideas. Write their answers on the outline.

5. Call on students to name the supporting details, if any, for each main idea; write them in the appropriate place on the outline.

6. When the outline is complete, check that students understand that an outline lists main ideas with Roman numerals and supporting details with capital letters. **LS** **Verbal/Linguistic**

🖥 Interactive Skills Tutor CD-ROM, Lesson 14: Identify Main Ideas and Supporting Details

Answers

Practice **1.** *Visual Arts, Literature; with Roman numerals;* **2.** *Jewish synagogues, Christian cathedrals, Muslim mosques;* **3.** *They follow the same order.*

Apply *possible outline: I. Science, A. Christians studied alchemy, B. Muslims studied medicine, C. Muslims; I. Science, A. Christian alchemy, 1. medicines to cure sicknesses, 2. turn metals into gold; B. Muslim science, 1. medical skills, 2. pharmacy schools, 3. hospitals; II. Philosophy, A. Cordoba was home to many achievements; B. Moses Maimonides studied classical writings; B. Ibn-Rashd studied Greek logic; C. Thomas Aquinas blended Christian faith with Greek logic*

190

Outlining

Learn

The chapters in your textbooks are full of facts and ideas. Sometimes keeping track of all the information that you read can be overwhelming. At these times, it may help you to construct an outline of what you are reading.

An outline lists the main ideas of a chapter and the details that support those main ideas. The most important ideas are labeled with Roman numerals (I, II, III, and so on). Supporting ideas are listed below the main ideas, indented and labeled with capital letters (A, B, C, and so on). Less important details are indented farther and labeled with numbers (1, 2, 3) and lowercase letters (a, b, c). By arranging the ideas in an outline, you can see which are most important and how various ideas are related.

Practice

To the right is a partial outline of the discussion titled Art and Literature in Section 5 of this chapter. Study the outline and then answer the following questions.

❶ What are the major ideas on this outline? How are they marked?

❷ What details were listed to support the first main idea?

❸ How are the heads on the outline related to the heads in the text of the discussion?

> Art and Literature
> I. Visual Arts
>   A. Architecture
>   1. Jewish synagogues
>   2. Christian cathedrals
>   3. Muslim mosques
>   a. Large domes
>   b. Minarets
>   B. Art
>   1. No people in Jewish or Muslim art
>   2. Calligraphy
> II. Literature
>   A. Hildegard of Bingen
>   B. Omar Khayyám

Apply

Read back over the discussion titled Science and Philosophy in Section 5 of this chapter. Create an outline of this discussion. Before you write your outline, decide what you will use as your main heads. Then fill in the details below each of the heads.

190 CHAPTER 7

Social Studies Skills Activity: Outlining

At Level

Call to Order

Materials: slips of paper, copies of outline

1. Prepare an outline for the discussion of the Qur'an in Section 4, using the main ideas "Beliefs" and "Guidelines for Behavior." Transfer the main ideas and their supporting details onto separate slips of paper.

2. Read the discussion of the Qur'an aloud with students. Tell students that they are going to create a living outline of this discussion.

3. Give students the slips of paper. If there are not enough slips for each student, give them to pairs of students.

Prep Required

4. Have students mingle to match their slip of paper to related slips. Tell students to stand together once they have made their match.

5. Give students a copy of the outline you prepared. Compare how your outline matches up with the groups they formed. **LS** **Verbal/Linguistic, Kinesthetic**

📝 Alternative Assessment Handbook, Rubric 14: Group Activity

Chapter Review

Geography's Impact
video series
Review the video to answer the closing question:
Why might the pilgrimage to Mecca mean so much to the pilgrims who go there?

Answers

Visual Summary

Visual Summary *Use the visual summary below to help you review the main ideas of the chapter.*

QUICK FACTS

Jews read the Torah to learn about Jewish history and traditions.

Christianity is based on the life and teachings of Jesus of Nazareth.

The teachings of Islam are found in the Qur'an and the Sunnah.

Reviewing Vocabulary, Terms, and People

Match each "I" statement with the person, place, or thing that might have made the statement.

a. Bible   **e.** Mecca
b. rabbi   **f.** monotheism
c. Bethlehem   **g.** Torah
d. Qur'an

1. "I am the town where Jesus of Nazareth was born."
2. "I am the holy city of Islam."
3. "I am the holy book of Christianity."
4. "I am Islam's sacred book."
5. "I am the most sacred text of Judaism."
6. "I am a Jewish religious teacher."
7. "I am the belief in only one God."

Comprehension and Critical Thinking

SECTION 1 *(Pages 160–166)*

8. a. Identify What are the basic beliefs of Judaism?

b. Analyze What do the various sacred Jewish texts contribute to Judaism?

c. Elaborate How are Jewish ideas reflected in modern western society today?

SECTION 2 *(Pages 168–175)*

9. a. Describe According to the Bible, what were the crucifixion and Resurrection?

b. Analyze Why do you think Jesus's teachings appealed to many people in the Roman Empire?

c. Evaluate Why do you think Paul is considered one of the most important people in the history of Christianity?

Visual Summary

Review and Inquiry Recalling what they have learned about the early history of Judaism, Christianity, and Islam, students should write a hypothetical conversation among members of each religion. Have each student write a dialogue and share it with the class.

Quick Facts Transparency: Visual Summary: Religions of the Ancient Middle East—Judaism, Christianity, and Islam

Reviewing Vocabulary, Terms, and People

1. c	**5.** g
2. e	**6.** b
3. a	**7.** f
4. d	

Comprehension and Critical Thinking

8. a. belief in only one god (monotheism), justice, righteousness, and law

b. The texts contain the laws and principles of Judaism as well as its early history.

c. through traditions such as Hanukkah and Passover and holy days such as Rosh Hashanah and Yom Kippur; through religious services

9. a. crucifixion—Jesus's death upon a cross; Resurrection—Jesus's rising from the dead

b. possible answers—They thought Jesus was the Messiah they had been looking for; he urged people to love each other and to care for the poor and sick; his teachings were linked to the lives of everyday people.

RELIGIONS OF THE ANCIENT MIDDLE EAST—JUDAISM, CHRISTIANITY, AND ISLAM **191**

Review and Assessment Resources

Review and Reinforce

SE Chapter Review

RF: Chapter Review

Quick Facts Transparency: Visual Summary: Religions of the Ancient Middle East—Judaism, Christianity, and Islam

Spanish Chapter Summaries Audio CD Program

OSP Holt Puzzle Pro; Quiz Show for ExamView

Quiz Game CD-ROM

Assess

SE Standardized Test Practice

PASS: Chapter Test, Forms A and B

Alternative Assessment Handbook

OSP ExamView Test Generator, Chapter Test

Differentiated Instruction Modified Worksheets and Tests CD-ROM: Modified Chapter Test

HOAP Holt Online Assessment Program (in the Holt Interactive Online Student Edition)

Reteach/Intervene

Interactive Reader and Study Guide

Differentiated Instruction Teacher Management System: Lesson Plans

Differentiated Instruction Modified Worksheets and Tests CD-ROM

Interactive Skills Tutor CD-ROM

go.hrw.com
Online Resources

Chapter Resources
KEYWORD: SK9 CH7

Answers

9. c. possible answer—He worked against Christianity but later converted. He traveled throughout the Mediterranean and Asia Minor, spreading Christian teachings. His letters elaborated on ideas about the Resurrection, salvation, and the Trinity. Because of Paul, Christianity became a widespread religion.

10. a. One day while Muhammad was meditating God spoke to Muhammad through an angel.
b. He taught that all people who believe in Allah are bound together and are equal. People should help those who are less fortunate.

11. a. a pilgrimage to Mecca that Muslims should make at least once in their lives
b. The Qur'an is a collection of Muhammad's teachings and the exact word of God as told to Muhammad. The Sunnah is the way in which Muhammad lived and an example for behavior for all Muslims.

12. a. minarets and domes
b. They could more easily share ideas and inspirations.
c. possible answer—to honor and show devotion to God

Using the Internet

13. Go to the HRW Web site and enter the keyword shown to access a rubric for this activity.

KEYWORD: SK9 TEACHER

Social Studies Skills

14. four

15. Antioch

16. second and third

17. Rome

SECTION 3 (Pages 176–179)

10. a. Recall According to Muslim belief, how was Islam revealed to Muhammad?
b. Analyze How did Muhammad encourage people to treat each other?

SECTION 4 (Pages 180–183)

11. a. Define What is the hajj?
b. Contrast How do the Qur'an and the Sunnah differ?

SECTION 5 (Pages 186–189)

12. a. Describe What are two elements often found in Muslim architecture?
b. Draw Conclusions How did having a common language help scholars in the Muslim world?
c. Elaborate Why might a ruler have wanted to use his or her money to build a mosque?

Using the Internet

13. Activity: Creating Maps Within 400 years of Jesus's death, Christianity had grown from a small group of Jesus's disciples into the only religion practiced in the Roman Empire. What explains the rapid growth of Christianity? Enter the activity keyword. Then research the key figures, events, and factors in the spread of Christianity. Use what you learn to create an illustrated and annotated map.

Social Studies Skills

Interpreting Route Maps *Use the map of Paul's Journeys in Section 2 to answer the following questions.*

14. How many journeys did Paul take?
15. From where did he start his third journey?
16. On which journeys did Paul visit the cities of Corinth and Athens?
17. What was the last city Paul traveled to?

---

18. Understanding Implied Main Ideas Look back at the beginning of Section 5 of this chapter. For each paragraph under the heading "Science," write a statement that you think is the main idea of the paragraph. Identify each as a stated or implied main idea.

19. Writing a Letter Your letter is from an eyewitness to the event to a good friend. Look back over your notes and choose one important event for your letter. Your letter should answer the Who? What? Where? How? questions about the event. Write the letter as though you are writing to a good friend and are excited about having seen this event.

Map Activity ★Interactive

20. Jewish, Christian, and Muslim Worlds On a separate sheet of paper, match the letters on the map with their correct labels.

Rome   Istanbul

Jerusalem

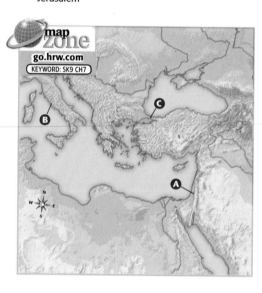

go.hrw.com
KEYWORD: SK9 CH7

Focus on Reading and Writing

18. The idea of learning more about God inspired people to examine the world. Christians in Europe examined the world through alchemy. Muslim scientists studied the world through medicine and other practical sciences.

📖 **RF:** Focus on Reading, Understanding Implied Main Ideas

19. Rubric Students' letters should

• be in letter format
• tell about one important event
• describe the setting
• explain who was involved
• tell the significance of the event

📖 **RF:** Focus on Writing, Writing a Letter

Map Activity

20. A. Jerusalem
     B. Rome
     C. Istanbul

Standardized Test Practice

Answers

DIRECTIONS (1–6): For each statement or question, write on a separate answer sheet the *number* of the word or expression that, of those given, best completes the statement or answers the question.

1 The Jewish holiday that celebrates the start of a new year in the Jewish calendar is
(1) Hanukkah.
(2) Passover.
(3) Rosh Hashanah.
(4) Yom Kippur.

2 Many people believe that the Hebrews were the first people to practice
(1) monotheism.
(2) rituals.
(3) religion.
(4) law.

3 Which of the following statements about Jesus is false?
(1) Some people believed Jesus was the Messiah that Jewish prophets had predicted.
(2) Some Jewish and Roman leaders viewed Jesus as a threat to their power.
(3) Jesus fought in a rebellion of the Jews against the Romans.
(4) Jesus taught people to love God and to be kind to each other.

4 Muslim scholars are credited with developing
(1) geometry.
(2) algebra.
(3) calculus.
(4) physics.

5 During the month of Ramadan, Muslims
(1) fast.
(2) do not pray.
(3) travel to Medina.
(4) hold feasts.

6 Which of Jesus's followers knew Jesus well and received special teaching?
(1) Paul
(2) Constantine
(3) the Gospels
(4) the Apostles

Base your answer to question 7 on the text excerpt below and on your knowledge of social studies.

> "Honor your father and mother, that you may long endure on the land that the Lord your God is assigning to you.
>
> You shall not murder.
>
> You shall not commit adultery.
>
> You shall not steal.
>
> You shall not bear false witness against your neighbor.
>
> You shall not covet your neighbor's house. "
>
> —Exodus 20:12–14

7 Constructed-Response Question The Ten Commandments from which this passage was drawn are important in both Judaism and Christianity. List two ideas or beliefs that are held by members of both groups. Then explain why the two religions share some ideas and beliefs.

RELIGIONS OF THE ANCIENT MIDDLE EAST—JUDAISM, CHRISTIANITY, AND ISLAM **193**

Standardized Test Practice

1. 3
Break Down the Question This question requires students to recall factual information. Refer students who miss it to Section 1.

2. 1
Break Down the Question Option 1 is the only correct answer; the other choices are too general, describing activities practiced by many people.

3. 3
Break Down the Question Answer 3 is a false statement, because the rebellion of the Jews against the Romans took place long before Jesus's lifetime. 1, 2, and 4 are true statements.

4. 2
Break Down the Question This question requires students to recall factual information. Refer students who miss it to Section 5.

5. 1
Break Down the Question This question requires students to recall factual information. Refer students who miss it to Section 4.

6. 4
Break Down the Question Neither Paul nor Constantine lived during Jesus's lifetime, so choices 1 and 2 are incorrect. The Gospels are books, not people. Option 4 is the only correct answer.

7. Constructed-Response Question possible answer—There are many ideas shared by Jews and Christians. Both believe in one God. This is called monotheism. Both believe in justice and law. The Ten Commandments express these ideas. These two religions may share similar beliefs because Christianity grew out of Jewish traditions.

Reteach/Intervention Resources

Reproducible
- Interactive Reader and Study Guide
- Differentiated Instruction Teacher Management System: Lesson Plans

Technology
- Quick Facts Transparency: Visual Summary: Religions of the Ancient Middle East—Judaism, Christianity, and Islam
- Differentiated Instruction Modified Worksheets and Tests CD-ROM
- Interactive Skills CD-ROM Tutor

Tips for Test Taking

Master the Question Multiple choice questions have two forms: open and closed. In an open multiple choice question, you have to finish the sentence so that it is correct. In a closed multiple choice question, you must answer the question posed. Whether answering an open or closed question, always make sure you read and think about each possible answer. If there are four possible answers, make sure you have eliminated three answers before you make your selection.

The Persians

History

In the 500s BC a new power arose in the Middle East. That new power was the Persian Empire. Within 100 years, the Persians had expanded their empire to rule most of Southwest Asia, including both Mesopotamia and Egypt.

The Persian Empire was established about 550 BC by a ruler known as Cyrus the Great. Born in what is now Iran, Cyrus built a powerful army and defeated several neighboring peoples to gain control of the entire Plateau of Iran.

From Iran, Cyrus set out to expand his empire. He led his army west to Asia Minor, defeating the wealthy kingdom of Lydia. From there he moved south to Mesopotamia and conquered Babylon, which had been the most powerful city of that time. In Babylon, Cyrus found thousands of Jews enslaved in the city. Cyrus freed the Jews and allowed them to return to Jerusalem. By the time Cyrus died in about 529 BC, his empire stretched from Asia Minor to central Asia.

The rulers who followed Cyrus learned from his successes. His son, for example, led Persian forces into Egypt and conquered it. The empire reached its largest size under the next ruler, Darius I, who gained power over the entire Indus Valley in India. He also tried to expand the Persian Empire into Europe. However, he soon ran into problems.

The ruins of Persepolis, one of the capitals of ancient Persia, stand proudly in central Iran. Built by Darius I, it was one of the most spectacular cities of the ancient world.

194 CASE STUDY

Preteach

Bellringer

Motivate Have students spend a few minutes previewing the Case Study. Ask students to examine the images and maps and to read each caption. Then have students make predictions about the history and culture of the Persians. Write students' responses for everyone to see. As the class reviews the Case Study examine which predictions proved accurate and which were inaccurate.

Key Terms

Preteach the following terms:

satraps local governors who ruled the provinces in the name of the Persian emperor (p. 196)

Zoroastrianism Persian religion that taught that good and evil are fighting for control of the universe (p. 198)

Did you know . . .

The term *Persians* refers to the people that live primarily in what is today the country of Iran. The name *Persia* was originally applied to the people of this region by ancient Greek scholars.

Teach the Case Study

At Level

The Persians

1. **Teach** Ask students the questions in the Main Idea boxes under Direct Teach.

2. **Apply** Have students preview the Case Study and write down the names of key events and people they find important. Write the list for everyone to see. Then have each student write a headline for each main event and person in the list. Model the activity by doing the first headline for students.

3. **Review** As you review the Case Study, have students share their related headlines with the class.

4. **Practice/Homework** Select one headline and have each student write an article or draw a political cartoon to accompany the headline. **LS Verbal/Linguistic, Visual/Spatial**

   Alternative Assessment Handbook, Rubrics 23: Newspapers; and 27: Political Cartoons

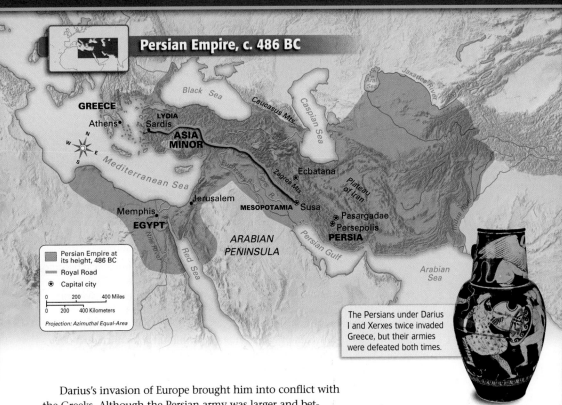

Persian Empire, c. 486 BC

GREECE
Athens
LYDIA
Sardis
ASIA MINOR
Black Sea
Caucasus Mts.
Aral Sea
Jaxartes River
Caspian Sea
Mediterranean Sea
Euphrates R.
Tigris R.
Zagros Mts.
Ecbatana
Plateau of Iran
MESOPOTAMIA Susa
Jerusalem
Memphis
EGYPT
Nile River
Red Sea
ARABIAN PENINSULA
Pasargadae
Persepolis
PERSIA
Persian Gulf
Indus River
Arabian Sea

Persian Empire at its height, 486 BC
Royal Road
Capital city

0   200   400 Miles
0   200   400 Kilometers
Projection: Azimuthal Equal-Area

Direct Teach

Main Idea

History

Identify Who were Cyrus and Darius? *Cyrus established the Persian Empire by gaining control of the Plateau of Iran and conquering Mesopotamia. Darius succeeded Cyrus as emperor of Persia and conquered the entire Indus Valley.*

Analyze How did Darius come into conflict with the Greeks? *He attempted to expand the Persian Empire into Europe and soon found himself at war with the Greeks.*

Evaluate Who do you think was the most successful emperor—Cyrus, Darius, or Xerxes? Explain. *possible answer—Cyrus, because he established the empire and conquered Iran and Mesopotamia.*

Map Zone Transparency: Persian Empire, c. 486 BC

The Persians under Darius I and Xerxes twice invaded Greece, but their armies were defeated both times.

Darius's invasion of Europe brought him into conflict with the Greeks. Although the Persian army was larger and better trained than that of the Greeks, the Greeks nonetheless defeated the Persians. Darius's son Xerxes (ZURKH-seez) tried to invade Greece again 10 years later, but his efforts failed as well.

The Persians never fully recovered from their defeat by the Greeks. In the 330s BC, the Persian Empire was invaded by the army of Alexander the Great. The Persians fought Alexander for three years, but they could not hold him off. Persia collapsed and became part of Alexander's empire.

The last emperor of Persia, Darius III, was defeated by Alexander the Great in 332 BC.

Case Study Assessment

1. What role did Cyrus the Great play in Persian history?

2. What happened when the Persians invaded Greece?

3. **Activity** Design a monument to honor the accomplishments of one of Persia's kings. Include a sketch of the monument and any text you would include on it.

THE PERSIANS **195**

Differentiating Instruction

Below Level

Struggling Readers

1. Review the history of the Persian Empire with the class. Ask students to point out key events from the reading. Write students' responses for everyone to see.

2. Have students write the list of events in the correct chronological order on their own paper. Instruct students to create an illustrated time line of the events from Persian history.

3. Remind students to list the events in the correct order in their time lines and to create

an illustration or symbol that represents each event. For example, students may choose to draw an illustration of Cyrus and his army to represent the conquest of Babylon.

4. Have students display their completed time lines for everyone to see. **LS Visual/Spatial**

Alternative Assessment Handbook, Rubrics 3: Artwork; and 36: Time Lines

Answers

Case Study Assessment 1. *He established the empire by creating a powerful army, defeating the people of the Plateau of Iran, and expanding the empire into Mesopotamia.* **2.** *Although the Persians had a larger army, the Greeks defeated them.* **3.** *Students' responses will vary. See Rubrics 3: Artwork and 41: Writing to Express, in the Alternative Assessment Handbook.*

Main Idea

Society and Daily Life

Define What was a satrap? *a governor appointed by the emperor to rule a province in the name of the emperor*

Make Inferences Why do you think Persian men competed with one another to have many sons? *It was a matter of pride and it would ensure that their family name carried on to the next generation.*

Evaluate In your opinion, was the Persian education system good or bad? Explain your answer. *possible answer—good, because it trained young boys to be good soldiers and to be honest*

 Quick Facts Transparency: Persian Society

Info to Know

Succeeding Cyrus Cyrus the Great died in 530 BC while fighting in Central Asia. At the time of his death, he ruled the largest empire in the world. After Cyrus died, his son Cambyses II became emperor. Building on a plan devised by his father, Cambyses invaded Egypt and added it to the empire. Unlike Cyrus, who was admired for his tolerance, Cambyses was described as a tyrant and a madman. While in Egypt, he received word of a rebellion in Persia. On his way back home to crush the rebellion, however, Cambyses died.

Society and Daily Life

Although the ancient Persians built a huge empire, they left behind few written records. Most of what we know about this society comes from writings by other people, especially the ancient Greeks.

Government

The Persian government was headed by a king. The king was all-powerful: He was called the Great King or the King of Kings. The Persians created special rules to demonstrate their kings' power and glory. The kings wore elaborately decorated robes and golden jewelry covered with gems. Anyone who came into the king's presence had to bow low to the ground. No one was allowed to look directly at him.

By the time Darius I came to power, the empire had become too large for one person to rule alone. As a result, Darius organized the empire into 20 provinces. Then he chose governors called satraps (SAY-traps) to rule the provinces for him. The satraps collected taxes, served as judges, and put down rebellions. Satraps had great power within their provinces, but Darius remained the empire's real ruler. His officials visited each province to make sure the satraps were loyal to the king.

Persian Society

Persian society was rigidly organized. Everyone in the empire had to answer to the king. To demonstrate the king's power, the walls of the royal palace at Persepolis were carved with figures like the ones shown to the right. These figures represent people from all levels of Persian society who had come to honor the king.

The King, Darius himself, sits on a throne, ready to be honored by his subjects.

Nobles traveled to and from the capital in horse-drawn chariots.

196

Differentiating Instruction

Above Level

Advanced/Gifted and Talented

Materials: photocopies of a sample résumé

1. Tell students that a résumé is a record of a person's qualifications and experience. People often must submit a résumé to apply for a job.

2. Instruct students to create a résumé for a hypothetical candidate for satrap. Provide students with photocopies of a résumé to use as an example.

3. Students' résumés should provide information about the candidate's qualifications for the

position of satrap and communicate to the emperor why their candidate would be good for the position.

4. Conclude by discussing with the class what qualifications would have made a person a successful satrap. **LS Verbal/Linguistic**

Alternative Assessment Handbook, Rubric 31: Résumés

Daily Life

Most of what we know about daily life in the Persian Empire comes from the writings of the Greek historian Herodotus. As a child, he had lived in a city ruled by the Persians and so had become familiar with many of their customs.

According to Herodotus, Persian men often had several wives. The men also considered it a mark of pride to have many sons. In fact, Herodotus says, Persian men often competed with one another to see who could have the most sons.

When children were born, they went to live with their mothers. Fathers were not allowed to see the children until they were five years old. Once boys reached age five, they began their education. This education focused on three areas: horseback riding, archery, and telling the truth. The Persians considered lying among the worst things a person could do.

Case Study Assessment

1. How was power distributed in Persia?

2. What was the Persian education system?

3. **Activity** Imagine you were the ruler of Persia. Write a letter to your satraps in which you outline how you expect them to behave.

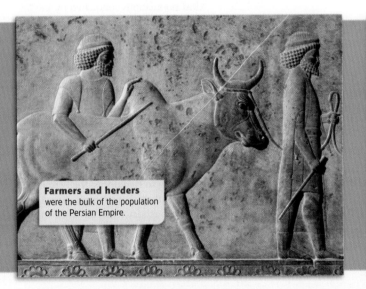

Farmers and herders were the bulk of the population of the Persian Empire.

Persian women were not allowed in positions of authority. Some worked as servants in the royal palace.

THE PERSIANS **197**

Checking for Understanding

True or False Answer each statement *T* if it is true or *F* if it is false. If false, explain why.

1. Persian emperors were often called the King of kings. *T*

2. Satraps held the real power in the Persian Empire, while the emperor was simply a figurehead. *F; They ruled in the name of the emperor, who retained the real power.*

3. Satraps were military leaders appointed by the emperor to guard the empire's borders. *F; They were governors who collected taxes, served as judges, and put down rebellions.*

4. Persian men often had more than one wife. *T*

5. Most of what we know about life in the Persian Empire comes from the writings of Darius I. *F; the writings of the Greek historian Herdotus*

Info to Know

Emperor Darius I In addition to organizing the government and conquering new lands, Darius made many other valuable contributions to the Persian Empire. Under his rule, the first coins ever minted in Persia were issued. To make trade easier, Darius implemented a standardized system of weights and measures for the empire. He also encouraged trade by building roads throughout the empire and establishing naval routes.

Critical Thinking: Supporting Points of View   At Level

Honoring Darius I

1. Have students examine the photos of Persian society on these two pages. Explain to students that Darius I often had carvings like these created to honor his many accomplishments.

2. Instruct students to plan a wall carving similar to those shown here. Students should create a sketch of their final plan. Remind students that the purpose of the illustration is to demonstrate the greatness of Darius I.

3. Instruct students to select an achievement of Darius. Then have students illustrate that

achievement in a manner similar to the Persian wall carvings. Have students write a description of the achievement for a plaque that might have accompanied the wall carving.

4. Ask for volunteers to display their wall carving ideas to the class. **LS Visual/Spatial, Verbal/Linguistic**

Alternative Assessment Handbook, Rubric 3: Artwork

Answers

Case Study Assessment 1. *The emperor held the most power. Satraps served as provincial governors who carried out the emperor's decisions.* **2.** *Persian boys began their education at the age of five. Their education consisted of archery, horseback riding, and telling the truth.* **3.** *Students' responses may vary, but should include the expectations of loyalty, honesty, and good leadership. See Rubric 5: Business Letters, in the Alternative Assessment Handbook.*

525 BC
The Persians conquer Egypt.

c. 515 BC
Darius I orders the construction of a new capital at Persepolis.

480 BC
Xerxes invades Greece during the Persian Wars.

c. 550 BC
Cyrus the Great establishes the Persian Empire.

Persian goblet from the 500s BC

Culture and Achievements

The Persian Empire was far-reaching and long-lasting. It included people from many different backgrounds who had many different experiences. Persian rulers encouraged people to share ideas with their neighbors and welcomed the spread of various customs. As a result, Persian culture blended elements borrowed from many different civilizations.

Culture

In building their empire, the Persians triumphed over many people. Unlike some other conquerors, however, the Persians did not force the people they had defeated to adopt Persian ways of life. Instead, they let each group they conquered keep its own customs.

This policy had two main effects in Persia. First, it kept the conquered people from becoming angry with the Persians and rebelling. Second, it led to cultural diversity in the empire. For example, people in Persian cities often wore many different styles of clothing. Among the people from whom the Persians borrowed clothing styles or other customs were the Mesopotamians, the Egyptians, and the Greeks.

Most populations conquered by the Persians retained their own languages. However, many also spoke Aramaic, a language that first developed in the eastern Mediterranean region. Aramaic was used as the official language for government and business.

Probably the most popular religion in Persia was Zoroastrianism. This religion taught that there were two forces, one good and one evil, fighting for control of the universe.

According to Herodotus, the Persians loved celebrations. For example, they threw huge birthday feasts at which they served beef, camel, horse, and donkey. They were also very fond of desserts.

BIOGRAPHY

Zoroaster
c. 628–c. 551 BC

Zoroaster, the founder of Zoroastrianism, was one of the most influential people in ancient Persia. However, historians know very little about his life. They are not even sure when he lived. Ancient writings suggest that he was born in a rural village in what is now Iran and that he grew up to be a priest. The same sources say that he received a vision from the god Ahura Mazda—the source of all good in the universe—at age 30. In this vision, the god revealed the teachings that Zoroaster was to share with the world, the teachings that developed into Zoroastrianism. Zoroaster later recorded those teachings in writings that became the Avesta, the religion's sacred book.

198 CASE STUDY

---

334 BC–327 BC
In a series of battles, Alexander the Great overpowers Persia.

Achievements

The Persians accomplished much during their empire. In large part, they were able to achieve so much because their empire was peaceful. Very seldom did people within the empire fight among themselves.

One area in which the Persians excelled was communication. Kings like Darius I had roads built to connect various parts of the empire. One road, called the Royal Road, was more than 1,700 miles long. Soldiers and messengers alike used these roads to travel quickly throughout Persia. These Persian messengers made up one of the world's first postal systems. Mounted on horses, they could deliver a message from one end of the empire to the other in just a few days.

The Persians were also skilled artists. Persian artists created delicate items out of gold and gems, many of them decorated with animals. Many of these items were used by the king and his family in their capital, Persepolis.

The city of Persepolis itself was an artistic feat. Built to reflect the glory of Persia's kings, It was filled with beautiful works of art. More than 3,000 carvings lined the city's walls, and its buildings were decorated with statues of gold, silver, and jewels. At the center of the city was a huge palace, the largest in the ancient Middle East. All that remains of Persepolis today is ruins. Much of the city was burned by Alexander the Great's army.

Case Study Assessment

1. Why was Persian culture so diverse?

2. What were some key Persian achievements?

3. **Activity** If you had been a Persian noble, would you have supported Cyrus's tolerance policy? Write a speech to express your views.

Persian Roads

The Persian road network helped keep the vast empire running smoothly. Both soldiers and messengers used the roads. Persian soldiers like the ones pictured below could march quickly along the roads to put down uprisings. By changing horses often, royal messengers could ride all the way across the empire in a few days.

"Nothing mortal travels so fast as these Persian messengers . . . these men will not be hindered from accomplishing at their best speed the distance which they have to go, either by snow, or rain, or heat, or by the darkness of night."

—Herodotus, from *History of the Persian Wars*

THE PERSIANS **199**

• Review & Assess •

Close

Instruct students to create a three-column chart summarizing what they know of Persian history, society, and culture.

Assess

📋 Alternative Assessment Handbook

Reteach/Classroom Intervention

💿 Interactive Skills Tutor CD-ROM

Answers

Case Study Assessment 1. *because conquered people were allowed to maintain their own culture, which added great diversity to the empire*
2. *a vast road system, a postal system, skilled artists, beautiful architecture*
3. *Students' responses will vary. See Rubric 41: Writing to Express, in the Alternative Assessment Handbook.*

Differentiating Instruction

Struggling Readers   `Below Level`

1. Organize the class into two groups. Assign one group to examine the text under the heading "Culture" and the other the text under the heading "Achievements."

2. Have each group read their assigned text. Then have group members work together to write the main idea of each paragraph.

3. Ask each group to share its main ideas with the class. **LS Verbal/Linguistic**

📋 Alternative Assessment Handbook, Rubric 37: Writing Assignments

English-Language Learners   `Below Level`

1. Review with students the road system created by the Persians.

2. Have each student create a poster that illustrates the benefits of Persian roads.

3. Ask for volunteers to share their posters with the class. **LS Visual/Spatial**

📋 Alternative Assessment Handbook, Rubric 28: Posters

Advanced/Gifted and Talented   `Above Level`   `Research Required`

1. Organize the class into pairs. Instruct students to select some aspect of Persian culture, for example language, religion, or art.

2. Have each pair research and prepare a five minute multimedia presentation on the aspect of Persian culture they selected. Have students make the presentations to the class. **LS Verbal/Linguistic**

📋 Alternative Assessment Handbook, Rubric 22: Multimedia Presentations

THE PERSIANS **199**

Chapter 8 Planning Guide

Growth and Development of the Middle East

Chapter Overview	Reproducible Resources	Technology Resources

CHAPTER 8
pp. 200–225
Overview: In this chapter, students will study the growth and development of the Middle East from the 600s to today.

Differentiated Instruction Teacher Management System:*
- Instructional Pacing Guides
- Lesson Plans for Differentiated Instruction

Interactive Reader and Study Guide:
Chapter Summary Graphic Organizer*

Resource File:*
- Chapter Review
- Focus on Reading: Sequencing
- Focus on Writing: Creating a Web Site
- Social Studies Skills: Locating Information

Experiencing World History and Geography

OSP Teacher's One-Stop Planner:
Calendar Planner

Power Presentations with Video CD-ROM

Differentiated Instruction Modified Worksheets and Tests CD-ROM

Student Edition on Audio CD Program

Music of the World Audio CD Program

Map Zone Transparency: The Middle East, AD 550–Today*

Geography's Impact Video Program (VHS/DVD): Impact of Cooperation and Conflict in Jerusalem*

World Outline Maps: Transparencies and Activities

Section 1:

Muslim Empires

The Big Idea: After the early spread of Islam, large Muslim empires formed—the Ottoman and Safavid empires.

Differentiated Instruction Teacher Management System: Section 1 Lesson Plan*

Interactive Reader and Study Guide: Section 1 Summary

Resource File:*
- Vocabulary Builder: Section 1
- Geography and History: Growth of the Ottoman Empire

Daily Bellringer Transparency: Section 1*

Map Zone Transparency: The Ottoman Empire*

Map Zone Transparency: The Safavid Empire*

Internet Activity: The Ottoman Empire

Section 2:

Development of the Modern Middle East

The Big Idea: Life in the Middle East since 1900 has been dominated by political change, conflict, and the oil industry.

Differentiated Instruction Teacher Management System: Section 2 Lesson Plan*

Interactive Reader and Study Guide: Section 2 Summary

Resource File:*
- Vocabulary Builder: Section 2
- Biography: Golda Meir
- Biography: Masumeh Ebtekar
- Primary Source: Atatürk's Address to Turkish Youth
- Interdisciplinary Project: Palestinian-Israeli Conflict

Daily Bellringer Transparency: Section 2*

Map Zone Transparency: Saudi Arabia's Oil Fields*

Section 3:

History and Culture of Central Asia

The Big Idea: The countries of Central Asia share similar histories and traditions, but particular ethnic groups give each country a unique culture.

Differentiated Instruction Teacher Management System: Section 3 Lesson Plan*

Interactive Reader and Study Guide: Section 3 Summary

Resource File:*
- Vocabulary Builder: Section 3
- Literature: "Friendship" by Kahlil Gibran

Daily Bellringer Transparency: Section 3*

Map Zone Transparency: Languages of Central Asia*

Internet Activity: Cyrillic Alphabet

HOLT

Geography's Impact
Video Program

Impact of Cooperation and Conflict in Jerusalem
Suggested use: in Section 2

Review, Assessment, Intervention

 Quick Facts Transparency: Visual Summary: Growth and Development of the Middle East*

 Spanish Chapter Summaries Audio CD Program

 Progress Assessment Support System (PASS): Chapter Test*

 Differentiated Instruction Modified Worksheets and Tests CD-ROM: Modified Chapter Test

OSP **Teacher's One-Stop Planner:** ExamView Test Generator (English/Spanish)

HOAP **Holt Online Assessment Program (HOAP),** in the Holt Interactive Online Student Edition

 PASS: Section 1 Quiz*
 Online Quiz: Section 1
 Alternative Assessment Handbook

 PASS: Section 2 Quiz*
 Online Quiz: Section 2
 Alternative Assessment Handbook

 PASS: Section 3 Quiz*
 Online Quiz: Section 3
 Alternative Assessment Handbook

Power Presentations with Video CD-ROM

Power Presentations with Video are visual presentations of each chapter's main ideas. Presentations can be customized by including Quick Facts charts, images from the text, and video clips.

 **Holt Online Learning**

go.hrw.com
Teacher Resources
KEYWORD: SK9 TEACHER

go.hrw.com
Student Resources
KEYWORD: SK9 CH8

- Interactive Multimedia Activities
- Current Events

- Chapter-based Internet Activities
- and more!

Holt Interactive
Online Student Edition

Complete online support for interactivity, assessment, and reporting

- Interactive Maps and Notebook
- Standardized Test Prep
- Homework Practice and Research Activities Online

CHAPTER 8 PLANNING GUIDE

Differentiating Instruction

How do I address the needs of varied learners?
The Target Resource acts as your primary strategy for differentiated instruction.

ENGLISH-LANGUAGE LEARNERS & STRUGGLING READERS

Interactive Skills Tutor CD-ROM

The Interactive Skills Tutor CD-ROM contains lessons that provide additional practice for 20 different critical thinking skills.

Additional Resources

Differentiated Instruction Teacher Management System: Lesson Plans for Differentiated Instruction

Resource File:
- Vocabulary Builder Activities
- Social Studies Skills: Locating Information

Quick Facts Transparency: Visual Summary: Growth and Development of the Middle East

Student Edition on Audio CD Program

Spanish Chapter Summaries Audio CD Program

Teacher's One Stop Planner:
- ExamView Test Generator, Spanish
- PuzzlePro, Spanish

English-Language Learner Strategies and Activities

SPECIAL NEEDS LEARNERS

Resource File

The Resource File activities allow students to extend their knowledge of chapter-related places and people and to practice geography skills.
- Vocabulary Builder Activities
- Social Studies Skills: Locating Information

Additional Resources

Differentiated Instruction Teacher Management System: Lesson Plans for Differentiated Instruction

Interactive Reader and Study Guide

Student Edition on Audio CD Program

Interactive Skills Tutor CD-ROM

Differentiated Instruction Modified Worksheets and Tests CD-ROM

Graphic Organizer Transparencies with Support for Reading and Writing

ADVANCED/GIFTED AND TALENTED STUDENTS

Differentiated Instruction Teacher Management System

Lesson Plans for Differentiated Instruction provide teachers with strategies to help plan instruction for all learners.

Additional Resources

Resource File:
- Focus on Reading: Sequencing
- Focus on Writing: Creating a Web Site
- Primary Source: Atatürk's Address to Turkish Youth
- Interdisciplinary Project: Palestinian-Israeli Conflict

World History and Geography Document-Based Questions Activities

Geography, Science, and Cultures Activities

Experiencing World History and Geography

HOLT Teacher's One-Stop Planner®

How can I manage the lesson plans and support materials for differentiated instruction?

With the Teacher's One-Stop Planner, you can easily organize and print lesson plans, planning guides, and instructional materials for all learners.

The Teacher's One-Stop Planner includes the following materials to help you differentiate instruction:

· **Interactive Teacher's Edition**
· **Calendar Planner and pacing guides**
· **Editable lesson plans**
· **All reproducible ancillaries in Adobe Acrobat (PDF) format**
· **ExamView Test Generator (English & Spanish)**
· **Transparency and video previews**

Professional Development

What teacher training resources are available to help me grow professionally?

· **In-service and staff development** as part of your Holt Social Studies product purchase
· **Quick Teacher Tutorial Lesson Presentation CD-ROM**
· Intensive tuition-based **Teacher Development Institute**
· **Convenient Holt Speaker Bureau:** face-to-face workshop options
· **24/7 Ask A Professional Development Expert** at http://www.hrw.com/prodev/

Chapter Big Ideas

Section 1 After the early spread of Islam, large Muslim empires formed—the Ottoman and Safavid empires.

Section 2 Life in the Middle East since 1900 has been dominated by political change, conflict, and the oil industry.

Section 3 The countries of Central Asia share similar histories and traditions, but particular ethnic groups give each country a unique culture.

Focus on Reading and Writing

Reading The Resource File provides a Focus on Reading worksheet to help students understand how to keep track of sequence.

📖 **RF:** Focus on Reading, Sequencing

Writing The Resource File provides a Focus on Writing worksheet to help students plan and design a Web site.

📖 **RF:** Focus on Writing, Designing a Web Site

CHAPTER **8**

Growth and Development of the Middle East

FOCUS QUESTION

What forces had an impact on the development of the Middle East and why?

What You Will Learn...

The Middle East is a land of contrasts. It is a region shaped both by ancient traditions and modern economics. Throughout the centuries, various forces have influenced life in the region.

FOCUS ON READING AND WRITING

Sequencing When you read, it is important to keep track of the sequence, or order, in which events happen. Look for dates and other clues to help you figure out the proper sequence. **See the lesson, Sequencing, on page S9.**

Designing a Web Site You have been asked to design a Web site about the modern Middle East. As you read this chapter, you will collect information about events and ideas that have shaped life in the region. Then you will use that information to design your Web site.

ATLANTIC OCEAN

• Córdoba

| 0 | 300 | 600 Miles |
| 0 | 300 | 600 Kilometers |

Projection: Lambert Azimuthal Equal-Area

A Muslim trader

Muslim Empires The Muslim Empire of the 600s and 700s included many centers of learning, such as Córdoba, Spain.

Introduce the Chapter

At Level

Growth and Development of the Middle East

1. Instruct each student to copy the chapter focus question on his or her own sheet of paper. Ask students what they think the question means. Help students understand that the question will focus on key events, individuals, and issues that have shaped the Middle East since the 600s.

2. Have students examine the map on the opposite page for clues as to what forces shaped the development of the Middle East. Instruct students to predict how each force they identify might have influenced the people and countries of the Middle East.

3. Then have students skim the chapter, identifying other forces that have shaped the development of the countries of the Middle East.

4. Have students work in small groups to create a poster titled "Forces that Shaped Middle Eastern Development." Encourage students to update their posters as they study the chapter.
📋 **Visual/Spatial, Verbal/Linguistic**

📖 Alternative Assessment Handbook, Rubric 28: Posters

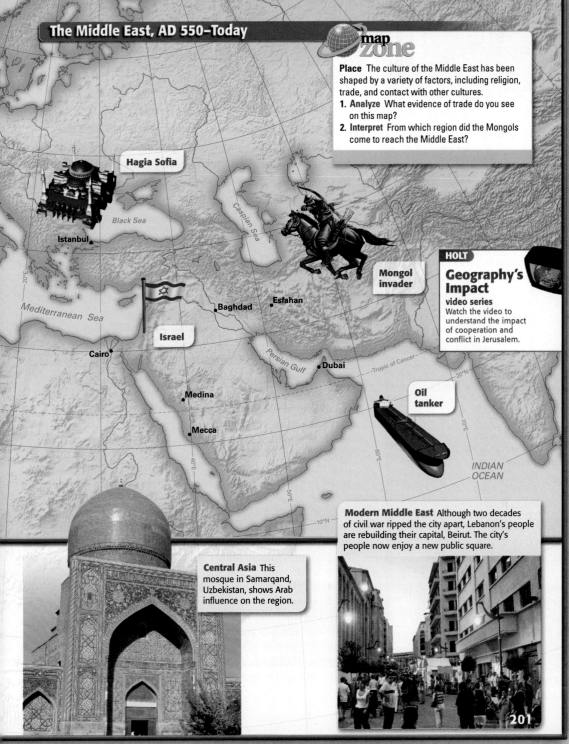

map Zone

Place The culture of the Middle East has been shaped by a variety of factors, including religion, trade, and contact with other cultures.

1. **Analyze** What evidence of trade do you see on this map?
2. **Interpret** From which region did the Mongols come to reach the Middle East?

Hagia Sofia

Black Sea

Istanbul

Caspian Sea

Mongol invader

Baghdad

Esfahan

Mediterranean Sea

Israel

Cairo

Persian Gulf

Dubai

Tropic of Cancer

Medina

Mecca

Oil tanker

INDIAN OCEAN

HOLT

Geography's Impact
video series
Watch the video to understand the impact of cooperation and conflict in Jerusalem.

Central Asia This mosque in Samarqand, Uzbekistan, shows Arab influence on the region.

Modern Middle East Although two decades of civil war ripped the city apart, Lebanon's people are rebuilding their capital, Beirut. The city's people now enjoy a new public square.

201

• Chapter Preview •

Explore the Map and Pictures

The Middle East, AD 550–Today Instruct students to study the map on this page. Ask students to identify what each icon on the map might mean. *Muslim trader—spread of Muslim trade and religion to Africa; Hagia Sofia—religion and culture in the Eastern Mediterranean; Israeli flag—the creation of Israel; oil tanker—the significance of oil in Middle Eastern economics; Mongol invader—Mongol influence in Central Asia*

Map Zone Transparency, The Middle East, AD 550–Today

Analyzing Visuals What topics do the photographs indicate? *education, religion, and modern development*

HOLT

Geography's Impact

▶ **video series**
See the Video Teacher's Guide for strategies for using the chapter video to teach about the impact of cooperation and conflict in Jerusalem.

Critical Thinking: Analyzing Visuals

At Level

Studying Maps

1. Discuss with students what they can learn and understand about a region by looking closely at a map.

2. Ask students to look at the map carefully. Have students call out facts such as the location of bodies of water, physical features, or other elements that define the Middle East. Write students' responses for everyone to see.

3. Tell students that some of these facts may be useful in understanding events involving different groups of people in the Middle East.

Have students locate on the map the areas related to the following events: the founding of Islam—*Mecca*; the nationalization of the Suez Canal—*near Cairo*; the creation of Israel—*the Eastern Mediterranean*; the fall of Saddam Hussein—*Baghdad*.

4. Ask students to use the map and their knowledge of the Middle East to identify shared characteristics within this region.
LS Verbal/Linguistic, Visual/Spatial

Alternative Assessment Handbook: Rubric 21: Map Reading

Answers

Map Zone 1. *the Muslim trader, the oil tanker;* **2.** *from Asia*

Bellringer

If YOU lived there. . . Use the **Daily Bellringer Transparency** to help students answer the question.

🔖 Daily Bellringer Transparency, Section 1

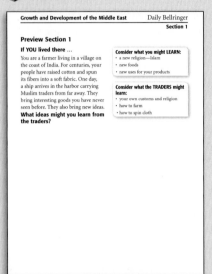

Growth and Development of the Middle East	Daily Bellringer
	Section 1

Preview Section 1

If YOU lived there . . .
You are a farmer living in a village on the coast of India. For centuries, your people have raised cotton and spun its fibers into a soft fabric. One day, a ship arrives in the harbor carrying Muslim traders from far away. They bring interesting goods you have never seen before. They also bring new ideas. **What ideas might you learn from the traders?**

Consider what you might LEARN:
• a new religion—Islam
• new foods
• new uses for your products

Consider what the TRADERS might learn:
• your own customs and religion
• how to farm
• how to spin cloth

Key Terms and Places

🔖 **RF:** Vocabulary Builder, Section 1

Taking Notes

Have students copy the graphic organizer onto their own paper and then use it to take notes on the section. This activity will prepare students for the Section Assessment, in which they will complete a graphic organizer that builds on the information using the Critical Thinking Skill: Comparing and Contrasting.

Muslim Empires

What You Will Learn...

Main Ideas

1. Muslim armies conquered many lands into which Islam slowly spread.
2. Trade helped Islam spread into new areas.
3. Muslim empires controlled much of Europe, Asia, and Africa from the 1400s to the 1800s.

The Big Idea

After the early spread of Islam, large Muslim empires formed—the Ottoman and Safavid empires.

Key Terms and Places

caliph, *p. 202*
tolerance, *p. 204*
Baghdad, *p. 204*
Córdoba, *p. 204*
janissaries, *p. 204*
Istanbul, *p. 204*
harem, *p. 205*
Esfahan, *p. 207*

 TAKING NOTES As you read, take notes on the spread of Islam and large Muslim empires. Organize your notes in a chart like the one below.

Spread of Islam	Muslim Empires

If YOU lived there...

You are a farmer living in a village on the coast of India. For centuries, your people have raised cotton and spun its fibers into a soft fabric. One day, a ship arrives in the harbor carrying Muslim traders from far away. They bring interesting goods you have never seen before. They also bring new ideas.

What ideas might you learn from the traders?

BUILDING BACKGROUND For years traders traveled from Arabia to markets far away. As they traveled, they picked up new goods and ideas, and they introduced these to the people they met. Some of the new ideas the traders spread were Islamic ideas.

Muslim Armies Conquer Many Lands

After Muhammad's death his followers quickly chose Abu Bakr (uh-boo BAK-uhr), one of Muhammad's first converts, to be the next leader of Islam. He was the first **caliph** (KAY-luhf), a title that Muslims use for the highest leader of Islam. In Arabic, the word *caliph* means "successor." As Muhammad's successors, the caliphs had to follow the prophet's example. This meant that they had to rule according to the Qur'an. Unlike Muhammad, however, the early caliphs were not religious leaders.

Beginnings of an Empire

Abu Bakr directed a series of battles to unite Arabia. By his death in 634, he had made Arabia into a unified Muslim state. With Arabia united, Muslim leaders turned their attention elsewhere. Their armies, strong after their battles in Arabia, won many stunning victories. They defeated the Persian and Byzantine empires, which were weak from many years of fighting.

When the Muslims conquered lands, they set certain rules for non-Muslims living there. For example, some non-Muslims could not build churches in Muslim cities or dress like Muslims. However, Christians and Jews could continue to practice their own religion. They were not forced to convert to Islam.

Teach the Big Idea

Muslim Empires

1. **Teach** Ask students the questions in the Main Idea boxes under Direct Teach.

2. **Apply** Help students identify cause and effect in the spread of Islam after Muhammad's death. Have students list major events in the history of Islam's expansion. Write the list for students to see. Then have students identify different causes and effects of these events.
   📗 **Verbal/Linguistic**

3. **Review** As you review the section's main ideas, have students share the causes and effects that they identified.

4. **Practice/Homework** Have each student create a flowchart that illustrates some of the developments in the early spread of Islam. Each development should be connected with arrows. *Flowcharts may include military conquest, moving the capital, increased trade, new cities, spread of ideas through trade, and blending of cultures.*
   📗 **Visual/Spatial**

   📗 Alternative Assessment Handbook, Rubric 7: Charts

Growth of the Empire

Many early caliphs came from one family, the Umayyad (oom-EYE-yuhd) family. The Umayyads moved the capital to Damascus, in Muslim-conquered Syria, and continued to expand the empire. They took over lands in Central Asia and in northern India. The Umayyads also gained control of trade in the eastern Mediterranean and conquered parts of North Africa.

The Berbers, the native people of North Africa, resisted Muslim rule at first. After years of fighting, however, many Berbers converted to Islam.

In 711 a combined Arab and Berber army invaded Spain and quickly conquered it. Next, the army moved into what is now France, but it was stopped by a Christian army near the city of Tours (TOOR). Despite this defeat, Muslims called Moors ruled parts of Spain for the next 700 years.

A new Islamic dynasty, the Abbasids (uh-BAS-idz), came to power in 749. They reorganized the government to make it easier to rule such a large region.

READING CHECK **Analyzing** What role did armies play in spreading Islam?

Trade Helps Islam Spread

Islam gradually spread through areas the Muslims conquered. Trade also helped spread Islam. Along with their goods, Arab merchants took Islamic beliefs to India, Africa, and Southeast Asia. Though Indian kingdoms remained Hindu, coastal trading cities soon had large Muslim communities. In Africa, many leaders converted to Islam. As a result, societies often had both African and Muslim customs. Between 1200 and 1600, Muslim traders carried Islam even farther east. Muslim communities grew up in what are now Malaysia and Indonesia.

Trade also brought new products to Muslim lands. For example, Arabs learned from the Chinese how to make paper and use gunpowder. New crops such as cotton, rice, and oranges arrived from India, China, and Southeast Asia.

Many Muslim merchants traveled to African market towns, too. They wanted African products such as ivory, cloves, and slaves. In return they offered fine white pottery called porcelain from China, cloth goods from India, and iron from Europe and Southwest Asia. Arab traders grew wealthy from trade between regions.

FOCUS ON READING

As you read this page, look for words that give clues to the sequence of events.

THE IMPACT TODAY

Indonesia now has the world's largest Muslim population.

The City of Córdoba

By the early 900s, Córdoba, Spain, was one of the wealthiest cities in Europe and a center of Islamic learning. Rich examples of Islamic architecture can still be seen in the city.

203

❸ Later Muslim Empires

Three Muslim empires controlled much of Europe, Asia, and Africa from the 1400s to the 1800s.

Identify What city became the Ottoman capital? *Constantinople, renamed Istanbul*

Describe How was Mehmed II able to conquer Constantinople? *fierce warriors, huge cannons, gunpowder*

Analyze How did the conquest of Constantinople help the Ottoman Empire expand? *Its location made expanding into Europe much easier.*

📄 **RF:** Geography and History, Growth of the Ottoman Empire

---

Info to Know. . .

Baghdad The city of Baghdad was one of the largest cities in the world in the 800s. More than 300,000 residents lived in Baghdad and enjoyed its markets, zoos, and horse races. Baghdad also had many public buildings. These buildings included hospitals, libraries, and public baths. The House of Wisdom, an institution of learning, was a gathering place for scholars whose work contributed much to civilization.

Answers

Reading Check *As Arab merchants traveled, they shared their faith with the people they met.*

A Mix of Cultures

As Islam spread, Arabs came into contact with people who had different beliefs and lifestyles than they did. Muslims generally practiced **tolerance**, or acceptance, with regard to the people they conquered. For example, Muslims did not ban all other religions in their lands. Because they shared some beliefs with Muslims, Christians and Jews in particular kept many of their rights. They did, however, have to pay a special tax. Christians and Jews were also forbidden from converting anyone to their religions.

Many people conquered by the Arabs converted to Islam. These people often adopted other parts of Arabic culture, including the Arabic language. The Arabs, in turn, adopted some customs from the people they conquered. This cultural blending changed Islam from a mostly Arab religion into a religion that included many other cultures. However, the Arabic language and shared religion helped unify the different groups of the Islamic world.

Growth of Cities

The growing cities of the Muslim world reflected the blending of cultures. Trade had brought people together and created wealth, which supported great cultural development in Muslim cities.

Baghdad, in what is now Iraq, became the capital of the Islamic Empire in 762. Trade and farming made Baghdad one of the world's richest cities. The caliphs there supported science and the arts. The city was a center of culture and learning.

Córdoba (KAWR-doh-bah), a great city in Spain, became another showplace of Muslim civilization. By the early 900s Córdoba was the largest and most advanced city in western Europe.

> **READING CHECK** **Finding the Main Idea** How did trade affect the spread of Islam?

Later Muslim Empires

The great era of Arab Muslim expansion lasted until the 1100s. Afterward, non-Arab Muslim groups built large, powerful empires that took control of much of Europe, Asia, and Africa.

The Ottoman Empire

In the mid-1200s Muslim Turkish warriors known as Ottomans began to take territory from the Christian Byzantine Empire. They eventually ruled land from eastern Europe to North Africa and Arabia.

The key to the empire's expansion was the Ottoman army. The Ottomans trained Christian boys from conquered towns to be soldiers. These slave soldiers, called **janissaries**, converted to Islam and became fiercely loyal warriors. The Ottomans also benefitted from their use of new weapons, especially gunpowder.

In 1453 Ottomans led by Mehmed II used huge cannons to conquer the city of Constantinople. With the city's capture, Mehmed defeated the Byzantine Empire. He became known as the Conqueror. Mehmed made Constantinople, which the Ottomans called **Istanbul**, his capital. He also turned the Byzantines' great church, Hagia Sophia, into a mosque.

After Mehmed's death, another ruler, or sultan, continued his conquests. This sultan expanded the empire to the east through the rest of Anatolia, another name for Asia Minor. His armies also conquered Syria and Egypt. The holy cities of Mecca and Medina then accepted Ottoman rule.

The Ottoman Empire reached its height under Suleyman I (soo-lay-MAHN), "the Magnificent." During his rule from 1520 to 1566, the Ottomans took control of the eastern Mediterranean and pushed farther into Europe, areas they would control until the early 1800s.

Critical Thinking: Comparing and Contrasting   At Level

Explaining Trading Goods and Ideas

1. Discuss with students how ideas and cultures can be shared just as material goods can be shared.

2. Ask students to think about what "cultural blending" means. Have students list some items they use or have come into contact with that are from other cultures. Food, music, and holidays are examples most students may be familiar with. For non-native students, ask them what American customs they have adopted or come to enjoy.

(Use your discretion; not all students will be comfortable with this activity.)

3. Have students share, compare, and contrast their lists. Then relate the activity to the blending of Arabic and other cultures as Islam spread.

4. Close by guiding students in a discussion of how their lives are richer as a result of the mixing of cultures. **LS Interpersonal**

📄 Alternative Assessment Handbook, Rubric 11: Discussions

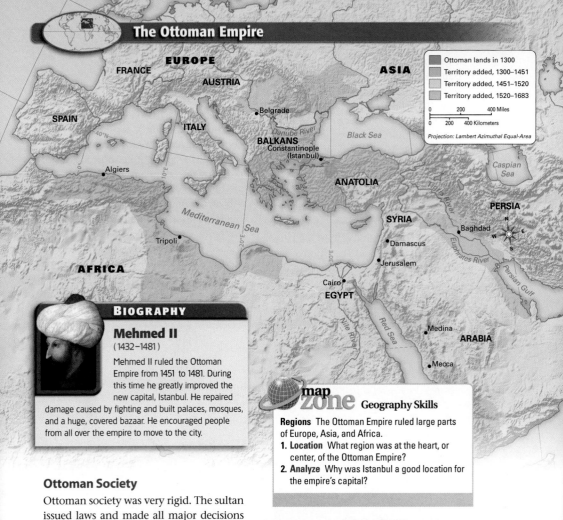

The Ottoman Empire

FRANCE
EUROPE
ASIA
AUSTRIA
SPAIN
ITALY
BALKANS
Belgrade
Danube River
Black Sea
Constantinople
(Istanbul)
Caspian
Sea
Algiers
ANATOLIA
Mediterranean Sea
PERSIA
SYRIA
Baghdad
Tripoli
Damascus
Euphrates River
Jerusalem
AFRICA
Cairo
EGYPT
Persian Gulf
Nile River
Red Sea
Medina
ARABIA
Mecca

| Ottoman lands in 1300 |
| Territory added, 1300–1451 |
| Territory added, 1451–1520 |
| Territory added, 1520–1683 |

0   200   400 Miles
0   200   400 Kilometers
Projection: Lambert Azimuthal Equal-Area

BIOGRAPHY

Mehmed II
(1432–1481)

Mehmed II ruled the Ottoman Empire from 1451 to 1481. During this time he greatly improved the new capital, Istanbul. He repaired damage caused by fighting and built palaces, mosques, and a huge, covered bazaar. He encouraged people from all over the empire to move to the city.

map Zone — Geography Skills

Regions The Ottoman Empire ruled large parts of Europe, Asia, and Africa.
1. **Location** What region was at the heart, or center, of the Ottoman Empire?
2. **Analyze** Why was Istanbul a good location for the empire's capital?

Ottoman Society

Ottoman society was very rigid. The sultan issued laws and made all major decisions in the empire. Most Ottoman law was based on Shariah, or Islamic law, but sultans also made laws of their own. Sultans were advised by a ruling class. Members of the ruling class had to be loyal to the sultan, practice Islam, and know Ottoman customs.

People who didn't fit these requirements made up the lower classes. Many of them were Christians or Jews from lands the Ottomans had conquered. Christians

and Jews formed religious communities, or millets, within the empire. Each millet had its own leaders and religious laws.

Ottoman society limited the rights of women, especially women of the ruling class. Many women had to live apart from men in an area of a household called a **harem**. By separating women from men, harems kept women out of public life. However, wealthy women could still own property or businesses.

GROWTH AND DEVELOPMENT OF THE MIDDLE EAST **205**

Main Idea

Later Muslim Empires,
continued

Identify What two cultural traditions did the Safavid Empire blend? *Persian and Muslim*

Contrast How do the Sunnis and Shia differ? *Sunnis were part of the Ottoman Empire and did not believe that caliphs had to be related to Muhammad; Shias were part of the Safavid Empire and thought that only Muhammad's descendants could be caliphs.*

⬛ Map Zone Transparency: The Safavid Empire

Did you know. . .

Tell students that the two major branches of Islam—Sunni and Shia—are found throughout the world today. The Sunni form the majority of the world's Muslims. Countries with large populations of Shia include Iran, Iraq, and Yemen. Shia populations are also found in East Africa, India, Lebanon, Pakistan, and Syria.

Linking to Today

Iran Much of what was the Safavid Empire is now part of the nation of Iran. Today more than 69 million people live in Iran. Some 89 percent are Shia Muslims. In addition, Shia religious leaders have run Iran's government since 1979.

Answers

Map Zone 1. *Ottomans and Uzbeks*
2. *Their advance from west to east threatened to cut off the Safavids, who were advancing southward from Tabriz.*

The Safavid Empire

As the Ottoman Empire reached its height, a group of Persian Muslims, the Safavids (sah-FAH-vuhds), was gaining power to the east, in the area of present-day Iran. Before long, the Safavids came into conflict with the Ottomans and other Muslims.

The conflict arose from an old dispute among Muslims about who should be caliph. In the mid-600s, Islam split into two groups. The two groups were the Shia (SHEE-ah) and the Sunni (SOO-nee). Shia Muslims thought only Muhammad's descendants could become caliphs. The Sunni did not think caliphs had to be related to Muhammad. The Ottomans were Sunni, and the Safavid leaders were Shia.

THE IMPACT TODAY
Most Muslims today belong to the Sunni branch of Islam.

The Safavid Empire began in 1501 when a strong Safavid leader named Esma'il (is-mah-EEL) conquered Persia. He took the ancient Persian title of shah, or king.

Esma'il made Shiism—the beliefs of the Shia—the official religion of the empire. But he wanted to spread Shiism farther. He tried to gain more Muslim lands and convert more Muslims to Shiism. He fought the Uzbek people, but he suffered a major defeat by the Ottomans in 1514.

In 1588 the greatest Safavid leader, 'Abbas, became shah. He strengthened the military and gave his soldiers gunpowder weapons. Copying the Ottomans, 'Abbas trained foreign slave boys to be soldiers. Under 'Abbas's rule the Safavids defeated

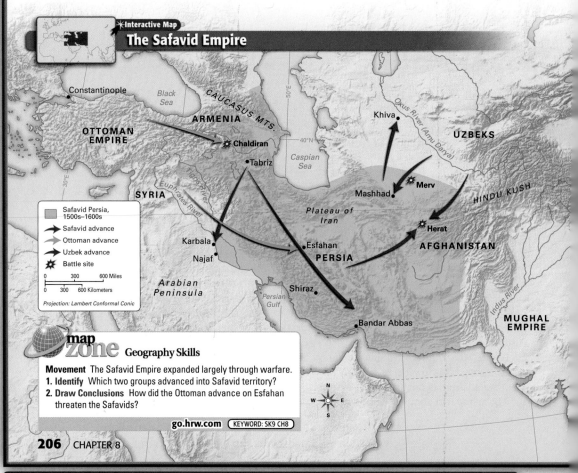

⊕ **Interactive Map**

The Safavid Empire

map zone Geography Skills

Movement The Safavid Empire expanded largely through warfare.
1. **Identify** Which two groups advanced into Safavid territory?
2. **Draw Conclusions** How did the Ottoman advance on Esfahan threaten the Safavids?

go.hrw.com KEYWORD: SK9 CH8

206 CHAPTER 8

Differentiating Instruction

Below Level

English-Language Learners

1. To help students understand the richness of Safavid culture, draw the graphic organizer here for students to see.

2. Have students copy the graphic organizer. As you discuss the accomplishments of Safavid culture, have students fill in the circles of the graphic organizer. *Circles should mention strengthening of military, conquest of Uzbeks, regaining of land lost to Ottomans, building of mosques, and trade.* **LS** Visual/Spatial

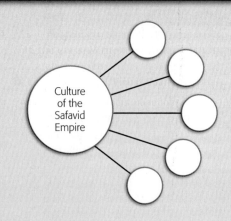

the Uzbeks and took back land that had been lost to the Ottomans.

The Safavids blended Persian and Muslim traditions. They built beautiful mosques in their capital, **Esfahan** (es-fah-HAHN). Esfahan was considered one of the most magnificent cities in the 1600s.

The Safavid economy was based on trade. 'Abbas encouraged the sale of traditional products, such as handwoven carpets, silk, and velvet. In addition, the Safavids were admired for ceramics and steel goods. Trade brought wealth to the empire and helped make it a major Islamic civilization. It lasted until the mid-1700s.

READING CHECK **Analyzing** How did the Ottomans gain land for their empire?

SUMMARY AND PREVIEW Islam spread beyond Arabia through warfare and trade. The Ottomans and Safavids built empires and continued the spread of Islam. In the next section you will learn how the Middle East changed after the collapse of these empires.

Esfahan

The Safavid capital of Esfahan was one of the most magnificent cities of the 1500s. Travelers from all over Asia admired the colorful tiles and huge domes of structures like the shah's mosque, built for 'Abbas.

ANALYZING VISUALS What evidence of Esfahan's magnificence can you see in this photo?

Section 1 Assessment

go.hrw.com
Online Quiz
KEYWORD: SK9 HP8

Reviewing Ideas, Terms, and Places

1. **a. Define** What is a **caliph**?
   b. Evaluate Do you think the rules that Muslims made for conquered non-Muslims were fair? Why or why not?
2. **a. Identify** Name three places Islam spread to through trade.
   b. Explain How did trade help spread Islam?
   c. Elaborate What was life in **Córdoba** like?
3. **a. Recall** Who were the **janissaries**?
   b. Contrast How did Sunni and Shia beliefs about caliphs differ?
   c. Evaluate Which of the Muslim empires do you think made the greater achievements? Why?

Critical Thinking

4. **Comparing and Contrasting** Draw a chart like the one below. Use your notes to compare and contrast the Ottoman and Safavid empires.

	Ottomans	Safavids
Leaders		
Location		
Religious policy		

FOCUS ON WRITING

5. **Collecting Information about Empires** You will need one Web page on Muslim empires. Note one or two points you will make about each empire.

GROWTH AND DEVELOPMENT OF THE MIDDLE EAST **207**

Section 1 Assessment Answers

1. **a.** Muslim title for highest leader of Islam
   b. fair—conquered people could practice their religion; unfair—conquered people didn't have the same rights

2. **a.** possible answers—Africa, India, Southeast Asia
   b. As they traveled, Muslim merchants shared their beliefs with other people.
   c. possible answer—People in Córdoba probably lived a comfortable life, as the city was wealthy and a center of culture and learning.

3. **a.** Christian boys the Ottomans captured, converted to Islam, and used as slave troops
   b. Sunnis didn't think caliphs had to be related to Muhammad. The Shia thought caliphs had to be members of Muhammad's family.
   c. Students' answers will vary but should include examples from the text.

4. Students' charts should reflect an understanding of what they read in the section.

5. Student answers will vary but should include information about each empire.

Review & Assess

Close

Briefly review the ways in which Islam spread throughout the Ottoman and Safavid empires. Point out that by the end of the 1600s, Islam was the dominant religion in the region.

Review

Online Quiz, Section 1

Assess

SE Section 1 Assessment

PASS: Section 1 Quiz

Alternative Assessment Handbook

Reteach/Classroom Intervention

Interactive Reader and Study Guide Section 1

Interactive Skills Tutor CD-ROM

Answers

Reading Check *The Ottomans trained Christian boys from conquered towns to be fierce soldiers and take territory from the Byzantine Empire; they used new gunpowder weapons and huge cannons.*

207

Bellringer

If YOU lived there... Use the **Daily Bellringer Transparency** to help students answer the question.

📖 Daily Bellringer Transparency, Section 2

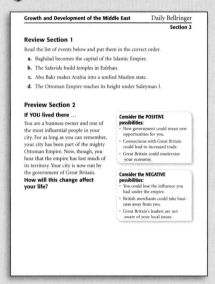

Key Terms

📖 **RF:** Vocabulary Builder, Section 2

Taking Notes

Have students copy the graphic organizer onto their own paper and then use it to take notes on the section. This activity will prepare students for the Section Assessment, in which they will complete a graphic organizer that builds on the information using the Critical Thinking Skill: Sequencing.

SECTION 2

Development of the Modern Middle East

What You Will Learn...

Main Ideas

1. New governments in the Middle East after World War I brought about major political changes.
2. Conflict has challenged many countries in the Middle East.
3. The oil industry has been a major influence in the region.

The Big Idea

Life in the Middle East since 1900 has been dominated by political change, conflict, and the oil industry.

Key Terms

shah, *p. 209*
embargo, *p. 211*
Taliban, *p. 212*
OPEC, *p. 213*

TAKING NOTES As you read, take notes on political changes, conflict, and oil in the Middle East using a graphic organizer like the one below.

Change	Conflict	Oil

If YOU were there...

You are a business owner and one of the most influential people in your city. For as long as you can remember, your city has been part of the mighty Ottoman Empire. Now, though, you hear that the empire has lost much of its territory. Your city is now run by the government of Great Britain.

How will this change affect your life?

BUILDING BACKGROUND Under the Ottoman Empire, many places in the Middle East did not grow or develop. Their economies changed very little, and the people had little say in the government. With the fall of the empire, many people saw a chance for change.

Political Changes

For centuries most of the Middle East had been dominated by the Muslim Ottoman Empire. During World War I, however, the Ottomans fought on the losing side. When the war ended, they lost most of their territory. Before long, many countries in the region had experienced sweeping political changes.

Turkey

Turkey had been the heart of the Ottoman Empire. When the empire collapsed after World War I, military officers took over the government. They were led by a war hero named Mustafa Kemal. He later adopted the name Kemal Atatürk, which means Father of Turks. Atatürk made Turkey a democracy and moved the capital to Ankara. He removed all elements of Islam from the government and closed Islamic schools. He also encouraged people to adopt Western-style clothing and names.

208 CHAPTER 8

Teach the Big Idea

At Level

Development of the Modern Middle East

Standard English Mastery

1. **Teach** Ask students the questions in the Main Idea boxes under Direct Teach.

2. **Apply** Have students use the information in this section to develop a list of 10 to 15 "Frequently Asked Questions" and answers about the development of the modern Middle East.

3. **Review** As you review the section, ask volunteers to share their questions. Have a student answer each question, then have the

student who wrote it read his or her answer to see how the two answers compare.

4. **Practice/Homework** Have students copy their questions and answers, revising if desired, to make an attractive and readable list for display. Remind students to use standard English as they write and revise their questions and answers. **LS** Verbal/Linguistic

📄 Alternative Assessment Handbook, Rubric 37: Writing Assignments

Egypt

Egypt had been a British colony during World War I. It was granted independence shortly afterward. However, the king who ruled the newly independent Egypt maintained close ties with the British. Many Egyptians were unhappy with his rule.

In 1952 a military coup abolished the monarchy and left Egypt in the hands of Gamal Abdel Nasser. To raise money for his government, Nasser tried to take control of the Suez Canal from the British and French. The British and French sent troops into Egypt, but the United States persuaded them to leave. Egypt kept control of the canal. His defiance of the Europeans made Nasser a hero to many Arabs.

Iran

In 1921 an Iranian military officer took power and encouraged change in Iran's government. He claimed the old Persian title of **shah**, or king. In 1941 the shah's son Muhammad Reza Pahlavi took control. This new shah became an ally of the United States and Great Britain and tried to modernize Iran. However, his programs were unpopular with many Iranians.

Palestine and Israel

After World War I the region of Palestine was made a British colony. The region was inhabited mostly by Muslim Arabs. For almost a century, however, Jews in Europe and other regions had been calling for a state in Palestine, their ancient homeland.

In 1947 the United Nations voted to divide Palestine into Jewish and Arab states. Whle Arab countries rejected this plan, the Jews accepted it, and a year later created the State of Israel.

READING CHECK Finding Main Ideas What political changes took place in the Middle East?

Political Change in the Middle East

In the early part of the 1900s, new leaders in the Middle East worked to change their countries. Their goal was to bring the region into the modern world.

Kemal Atatürk

- Took control of Turkey after World War I
- Created a democratic government
- Removed Islam from the government and closed Islamic schools
- Encouraged people to adopt Western customs

Turkish rally to honor Atatürk's policies, 2008

Gamel Abdel Nasser

- Seized power in Egypt in 1952
- Tried to take control of the Suez Canal
- Defied the French and British who owned the canal
- Became a hero to many Arabs

Nasser after the British withdrawal from Egypt, 1956

Muhammad Reza Pahlavi

- Became shah, or king, of Iran in 1941
- Became an ally of the United States and Great Britain
- Tried to modernize Iran
- Angered many Iranians with his programs

The shah on his throne, 1967

GROWTH AND DEVELOPMENT OF THE MIDDLE EAST **209**

209

Main Idea

❷ Conflict in the Middle East

Conflict has challenged many countries in the Middle East.

Recall What were the results of the Six-Day War? *Israel gained territories in Gaza, the West Bank, and East Jerusalem.*

Explain What was the cause of the civil war in Lebanon? *Muslim and Christian populations came into conflict.*

Draw Conclusions Why is control of Jerusalem a sensitive issue? *Jerusalem is home to Jewish, Christian, and Muslim holy sites, therefore it is often an emotional issue*

Make Inferences Why did Israel cede territory back to the Palestinians beginning in the 1990s? *possible answer—to improve relations and ease conflict with Palestinians*

📝 **RF:** Biography: Golda Meir

📝 **RF:** Interdisciplinary Project: Palestinian-Israeli Conflict

Info to Know

Arab-Israeli Wars Since 1948 Israel and several Arab countries have been involved in a series of wars. The first war, sometimes known as the 1948 War, took place when a union of Arab forces invaded Israel. The second war, the Suez Crisis, broke out in 1956 when Israel invaded Egypt's Sinai Peninsula. In 1967 the Six-Day War erupted when Syria attacked Israel. Another war took place in 1974 when Egypt and Syria invaded Israel in the Yom Kippur War.

Did you know. . .

The first Arab-Israeli war caused a massive refugee problem. By the end of the war, around 700,000 Palestinian Arabs had become refugees when they fled or were expelled from areas that Israel took over.

Conflict in the Middle East

In some cases, the political changes that swept through the Middle East led to conflict between or within countries. In some places cultural and religious differences also led to conflict.

Conflict in Israel

Many Arab states were not happy about the founding of Israel. They felt that the United Nations had taken away land that was rightfully theirs. Much of their unhappiness dealt with control of Jerusalem. Now the capital of Israel, Jerusalem has sites that are considered holy by Jews, Christians, and Muslims. Control of the city is a difficult and emotional issue for members of all three religions.

Within a year of the founding of Israel, Arab armies had invaded. In a very short war, the Israelis defeated the Arabs. Many Palestinians fled to neighboring Arab countries. Another short war broke out in 1967. During this so-called Six-Day War, Israel captured areas from Jordan and Egypt inhabited by Palestinian Arabs. These captured areas included Gaza, the West Bank, and East Jerusalem.

Since then, tens of thousands of Jews have moved into settlements there. However, the Palestinians consider the Jewish settlements an invasion of their land. This conflict over land has caused great tension between Arabs and Israelis.

In the 1990s Israel agreed to turn over parts of the territories to the Palestinians. In return, the Palestinians agreed to recognize Israel's existence. In 2005 Israel transferred Gaza to the Palestinians.

Civil War in Lebanon

In the 1970s a civil war broke out in Lebanon between the country's Muslim and Christian populations. Before long, Syria, Israel, and other countries had become involved in the conflict. During the fighting, many people died and the capital, Beirut, was badly damaged. Warfare lasted until 1990.

After 1990, Syria continued to maintain a strong influence in Lebanon. In fact, Syrian troops stayed in Lebanon until they were pressured to leave in 2005. In 2006, cross-border attacks by Lebanese guerillas against Israel led to fighting between the two countries.

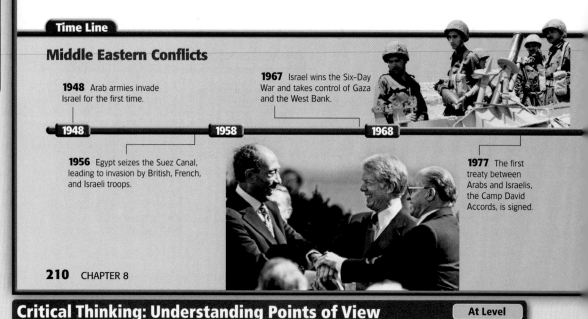

Time Line

Middle Eastern Conflicts

1948 Arab armies invade Israel for the first time.

1956 Egypt seizes the Suez Canal, leading to invasion by British, French, and Israeli troops.

1967 Israel wins the Six-Day War and takes control of Gaza and the West Bank.

1977 The first treaty between Arabs and Israelis, the Camp David Accords, is signed.

1948 — 1958 — 1968

210 CHAPTER 8

Critical Thinking: Understanding Points of View   At Level

Palestine and Israel

Research Required

1. Review with students the information about the creation of Israel and the subsequent Arab-Israeli wars. Remind students that both Palestine and Israel have legitimate claims to land in the Middle East.

2. Have students conduct outside research to find one article about the conflict from the Arab point of view and one from the Israeli point of view. Tell students to look for scholarly, historical articles that are sensitive to the needs and claims of both groups.

3. Have students answer the questions who, what, why, when, and how about each of their articles. Then have students analyze the articles for language that shows bias.

4. Have students present their research findings to the class. **LS Verbal/Linguistic**

📝 Alternative Assessment Handbook, Rubrics 24: Oral Presentations; and 30: Research

The Iranian Revolution

Fighting also broke out in Iran in the 1970s. A revolution began in that country in 1978. By 1979, Iranians led by the Ayatollah Khomeini, a religious leader, overthrew the shah and set up an Islamic republic. This type of government follows strict Islamic law.

Soon after Iran's Islamic Revolution began, relations with the United States broke down. A mob of students attacked the U.S. Embassy in Iran's capital, Tehran. With the approval of Iran's government, the students took Americans working at the embassy hostage. More than 50 Americans were held by force for over a year.

Iraqi Aggression

In 1968 Saddam Hussein became Iraq's president. Saddam Hussein was a harsh ruler. He controlled Iraq's media, restricted personal freedoms, and killed an unknown number of political enemies.

Under Saddam's leadership, Iraq invaded Iran in 1980. The Iranians fought back, and the Iran-Iraq War dragged on until 1988. Both countries' economies were seriously damaged, and many people died.

In 1990 Iraq invaded Kuwait, its oil-rich neighbor to the south. This event shocked and worried many world leaders. They were concerned that Iraq might gain control of the region's oil. In addition, they worried about Iraq's supply of weapons of mass destruction, including chemical and biological weapons.

In 1991 an alliance of countries led by the United States forced the Iraqis out of Kuwait. This six-week event was called the Persian Gulf War. Saddam, who remained in power after the war, would not accept the peace terms recommended by the United Nations (UN). In response, the UN placed an **embargo**, or limit on trade, on Iraq. As a result, Iraq's economy suffered.

Soon after the Persian Gulf War ended, Saddam faced two rebellions from Shia Muslims and Kurds. He brutally put down these uprisings. In response, the UN forced Iraq to end all military activity. The UN also requested that Iraq allow inspectors into the country. They also wanted to make sure that the Iraqi government had destroyed its weapons of mass destruction. Iraq later refused to cooperate completely with the UN.

Direct Teach

Main Idea

2 Conflict in the Middle East, *continued*

Recall What type of government did Iranians establish as a result of the 1978 revolution? *an Islamic republic*

Sequence List in order the conflicts in which Iraq was involved under Saddam Hussein's leadership. *Iran-Iraq War; invasion of Kuwait; Persian Gulf War; two internal rebellions; overthrow of Hussein regime*

Elaborate What did the UN hope to accomplish by placing an embargo on Iraq following the Persian Gulf War? *possible answers—to oust Hussein from power; to force Iraq to accept the peace terms*

Did you know. . .

U.S. President Jimmy Carter was president while Americans were held hostage in Iran. Carter was also a key figure in the Camp David Accords that created a lasting peace between Egypt and Israel. In 2002 Carter won the Nobel Peace Prize, in part "for his decades of untiring effort to find peaceful solutions to international conflicts."

1979 The Iranians overthrow the shah and create an Islamic republic.

2003 Saddam Hussein is removed from power in Iraq.

1978   1988   1998   2008

1990 Iraq invades Kuwait, beginning the Persian Gulf War.

ANALYSIS SKILL | **READING TIME LINES**

How many years passed between Iraq's invasion of Kuwait and Saddam Hussein's removal?

211

Differentiating Instruction

At Level

English-Language Learners

Standard English Mastery

1. Review with students the key conflicts that have taken place in the Middle East. Then have students examine the time line on the pages above.

2. Have students write a paragraph summarizing Middle Eastern conflicts in their own words. Instruct students to begin their paragraph with a main idea sentence and to present the conflicts in correct chronological order.

Remind students to write their paragraph using standard English.

3. When students are finished, ask for volunteers to read their paragraphs aloud to the class.
LS Verbal/Linguistic

Alternative Assessment Handbook, Rubric 37: Writing Assignments

Answers

Reading Time Lines *13 years*

❷ Conflict in the Middle East, *continued*

Identify Who are the Taliban? *a radical Muslim group that rose to power in Afghanistan in the mid-1990s*

Identify Cause and Effect What led to increased tensions between the United States and Iraq after 2001? *the belief on the part of many U.S. officials that Iraq had aided terrorists*

Elaborate Why have Kurds been the target of mistreatment by several governments? *possible answers—because they are different than the majority; because some Kurds have attempted to rebel*

📑 **RF:** Biography: Masumeh Ebtekar

FOCUS ON CULTURE

The Kurds

Traditionally a nomadic people, the Kurds have never had a country of their own. Scholars estimate that more than 20 million Kurds live throughout the Middle East and Central Asia. The exact number is difficult to determine.

The Kurds are mostly Muslim. They speak their own language, which is related to the Farsi language spoken in Iran. People have traditionally lived in independent tribes, each headed by a sheik. Most Kurds have historically lived as herders, tending sheep and goats. In recent years, however, many Kurds have moved to cities.

Drawing Conclusions Why do you think many Kurds want their own country?

Afghanistan and the War on Terror

In the mid-1990s a radical Muslim group known as the **Taliban** rose to power in Afghanistan. The Taliban used a strict interpretation of Islamic teachings to rule Afghanistan. It also supported terrorist organizations that shared its strict beliefs. Among those groups was the al Qaeda network. This network, headed by Osama bin Laden, was responsible for the September 11, 2001, terrorist attacks on New York City and Washington, D.C.

After the attacks, U.S. and British forces attacked Taliban and al Qaeda targets and toppled the Taliban government. Since then Afghanistan has created a new government headed by an elected president.

The terrorist attacks of September 11 also led to increased tensions between the United States and Iraq. Many U.S. government officials believed that Iraq had aided the terrorists. In March 2003, President George W. Bush ordered U.S. forces to attack Iraqi targets. Within a few weeks the Iraqi army was defeated and Saddam's government was crushed. Saddam went into hiding, but U.S. soldiers later found him in an underground hole in Iraq. Saddam was arrested, tried, and executed for his crimes.

Ethnic Conflict

Throughout the twentieth century, political change has also led to ethnic conflict in some parts of the Middle East. As power shifted within countries and new government were formed, some people felt their rights have been denied. In many cases, these feelings have led to conflict.

Among the groups who have come into conflict with the government are the Kurds. The region in which they live includes parts of eastern Turkey, northern Iraq, and western Iran. This area is unofficially called Kurdistan. For decades, many Kurds have wanted Kurdistan to become an independent country. Some have risen up in rebellion. Both Turkey and Iraq have put down Kurdish revolts, and both governments treated the Kurds very harshly afterward. Millions of Kurds were forced to leave their homes.

Religious differences can also lead to conflict between ethnic groups. In Iraq, for example, some ethnic groups are mostly Sunni Muslims while others are Shia. Since the collapse of Saddam's government, Sunni and Shia groups have fought each other bitterly for control of the country.

READING CHECK Making Generalizations What has led to violence in the Middle East?

Critical Thinking: Comparing and Contrasting [At Level]

Conflicts in the Middle East

1. Organize the class into small, mixed-ability groups. Have each student copy a graphic organizer like the one here. Then have students use their textbooks to complete the graphic organizer.

2. When students have finished, create a large class chart. Have students add their notes to the class chart.

3. Have students use the chart as a study tool.
   LS Visual/Spatial, Verbal/Linguistic

   📝 Alternative Assessment Handbook, Rubrics 6: Cause and Effect; and 14: Graphic Organizers

Conflicts in the Middle East

Causes	Conflicts	Effects

Answers

Focus on Culture *possible answer— because they want to rule themselves*

Reading Check *conflict over territory and resources and terrorism*

Oil in the Middle East

Other than religion and politics, nothing has shaped life in the Middle East more than the oil industry. The first oil in the region was found in Persia—now Iran—in 1908. Soon afterward, huge reserves were discovered below much of the region.

The production of oil is now the backbone of many Middle Eastern economies. Many countries there are members of the Organization of Petroleum Exporting Countries, or OPEC. Founded in 1960, **OPEC** is an international organization whose members work to influence the price of oil on world markets by controlling the supply. Oil has brought tremendous wealth to the region.

Oil money has allowed Middle Eastern countries to improve their citizens' lives. Some provide free health care and education to all citizens, for example. However, many people worry what will happen to the region's economy when oil supplies finally run dry.

READING CHECK Drawing Conclusions How did oil change life in the Middle East?

Oil Wealth

The skyline of the city of Dubai in the United Arab Emirates is a symbol of the wealth oil has brought to the region.

ANALYZING VISUALS How does this picture show both traditional and modern Middle Eastern culture?

SUMMARY AND PREVIEW After World War I, new governments and new countries were formed in the Middle East. However, conflicts arose between and within some countries. Next, you will learn how the countries of Central Asia changed during the same period.

Section 2 Assessment

go.hrw.com
Online Quiz
KEYWORD: SK9 HP8

Reviewing Ideas, Terms, and Places

1. **a. Identify** Which leader worked to modernize Turkey? Iran?
   b. Explain Why was Palestine divided into two countries?
2. **a. Recall** What led to the Persian Gulf War?
   b. Summarize How did Iran change after the Iranian Revolution?
   c. Elaborate How have religious and political differences contributed to conflict in the Middle East?
3. **a. Describe** What is **OPEC**'s purpose?
   b. Develop How will life in the Middle East change if the oil supply runs out?

Critical Thinking

4. **Sequencing** Using your notes, create a time line of the major conflicts that have occurred in the Middle East since World War II.

   ←—|———|———|———|———|———|→

FOCUS ON WRITING

5. **Choosing Topics** How will you describe the creation of the modern Middle East on your Web site? Which topics will you include? Write some notes down in your notebook.

GROWTH AND DEVELOPMENT OF THE MIDDLE EAST **213**

Section 2 Assessment Answers

1. **a.** Turkey—Kemal Atatürk; Iran—Muhammad Reza Pahlavi
   b. the UN voted to give Jews a homeland in the Middle East
2. **a.** Iraq invaded Kuwait
   b. became an Islamic republic
   c. religious—civil war in Lebanon; political—conflict between Arabs and Israelis; Iran-Iraq War; Persian Gulf War
3. **a.** to influence world oil prices
   b. possible answer—The economies will suffer.

4. Turkey becomes a democracy; Muhammad Reza Pahlavi modernizes Iran; UN creates Israel; Arabs invade Israel; Nasser takes control of Suez Canal; Six-Day War; civil war in Lebanon; Iranian Revolution; Iran-Iraq War; Persian Gulf War; war in Afghanistan and Iraq
5. Students' notes might include a description of political changes in Turkey, Egypt, Iran, and Israel, conflict in the Middle East, and the importance of oil in the Middle East.

Direct Teach

Main Idea

❸ Oil in the Middle East

The oil industry has been a major influence in the region.

Recall How does oil influence the economies of the Middle East? *For many countries oil is the basis of their economies.*

Analyze How does OPEC influence world oil prices? *by controlling the supply of oil*

Evaluate How has oil benefited the countries of the Middle East? *improving citizens' lives and providing money for free health care and education*

Review & Assess

Close

Lead a class discussion on the impact that political change, conflict, and oil have had on the development of the Middle East.

Review

Online Quiz, Section 2

Assess

SE Section 2 Assessment
PASS: Section 2 Quiz
Alternative Assessment Handbook

Reteach/Classroom Intervention

Interactive Reader and Study Guide, Section 2
Interactive Skills Tutor CD-ROM

Answers

Analyzing Visuals *traditional clothing; modern skyscrapers and technology*

Reading Check *It brought great wealth to the region and improved the lives of the people there.*

213

Connect to Science

Crude Oil Oil taken directly from the ground is called crude oil or petroleum. It is a hydrocarbon—made up of molecules that contain hydrogen and carbon. Because it is highly flammable, crude oil is an excellent source of fuel, but it must be refined first, to form useful products such as gasoline. Its chemical makeup also means crude oil can be refined into many other forms, from asphalt to detergents and from fertilizers to synthetic fibers and rubbers.

Connect to Math

The Price of Oil One barrel of oil holds 42 gallons. Have students use this information to compute the following:

• the price of a gallon of oil when a barrel costs $53.00 *about $1.28*

• the highest number of gallons of oil produced per day, based on information in the Oil Production chart in their textbook *about 4,200,000 gallons*

⬡ Map Zone Transparency: Saudi Arabia's Oil Fields

The Middle East's Oil Reserves

Essential Elements
The World in Spatial Terms
Places and Regions
Physical Systems
Human Systems
Environment and Society
The Uses of Geography

Background Try to imagine your life without oil. You would probably walk or ride a horse to school. You would heat your home with coal or wood. You would never fly in a plane, walk in rubber-soled shoes, or even drink out of a plastic cup.

Our society depends on oil. However, oil is a nonrenewable resource. This means that supplies are limited, and we may one day run out of oil. In fact, the United States no longer produces enough oil to satisfy its own needs. We now depend on foreign suppliers, such as the countries of the Middle East, for oil.

Oil in the Middle East

Most of the world's standard crude oil is located in reserves deep below the Middle East. According to recent estimates, the region has two thirds of all the known oil in the world. Saudi Arabia alone has nearly a quarter of the world's known oil supplies. Other Middle Eastern countries with huge oil reserves include Iran, Iraq, Kuwait, the United Arab Emirates, and Qatar.

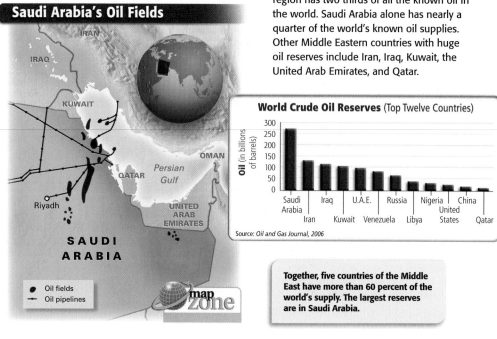

Saudi Arabia's Oil Fields

• Oil fields
← Oil pipelines

World Crude Oil Reserves (Top Twelve Countries)

Source: *Oil and Gas Journal, 2006*

Together, five countries of the Middle East have more than 60 percent of the world's supply. The largest reserves are in Saudi Arabia.

214 CHAPTER 8

Critical Thinking: Analyzing

At Level

Oil in the Middle East Poster

Materials: poster board, drawing supplies

1. Have students create a poster entitled "Oil in the Middle East" with text and illustrations that provide information for each of the essential elements of geography. To make their posters, have students divide the poster into sections, one for each essential element. Instruct students to write in the name and definition of each element.

2. Have students analyze the reading to determine what information applies to each

element, and then add the information in text and illustrations.

3. Have students share their posters, explaining why they chose certain information for each element. **LS Verbal/Linguistic, Visual/Spatial**

📝 Alternative Assessment Handbook, Rubrics 3: Artwork; and 38: Writing to Classify

Oil from the Middle East is pumped through pipelines to tankers that ship the oil around the world. The oil industry has made the region very rich.

World Crude Oil Reserves
(by Percentage)

- ■ World's Top 5
- ■ Rest of Top 12
- ■ Rest of World

23.7%
55.4%
20.9%

Source: *Oil and Gas Journal, 2006*

Info to Know

OPEC The Organization of the Petroleum Exporting Countries, or OPEC was created at the Baghdad Conference in September 1960. The five founding members were Iran, Iraq, Kuwait, Saudi Arabia, and Venezuela. Its headquarters started in Geneva, Switzerland, and are now in Vienna, Austria. Along with its original five members, OPEC now includes Algeria, Indonesia, Libya, Nigeria, Qatar, and the United Arab Emirates. OPEC describes as one of its primary missions the achievement of stable oil prices that are fair and reasonable both for oil producers and consumers.

Connect to Economics

Other Industries Some other key industries in the Middle East include textiles, cement, construction, and food processing.

Because the region has such huge oil reserves, the oil industry has become the backbone of the Middle Eastern economy. The sale of crude oil to other countries around the world brings billions of dollars to the region each year. Most of the oil exported from the Middle East is unrefined. Only a portion of the region's oil is actually processed locally. What little refining does take place in the region is done by foreign companies. However, most refining is done elsewhere in Asia, Europe, or the United States.

In recent years, many Middle Eastern governments have examined the rate at which they produce oil. These governments have to decide what is best for their countries. Should they produce more oil to sell now, hoping to increase their total income? Or should they limit production to drive up the price of each unit of oil and to preserve their supply of oil for the future? With the support of OPEC, most countries have chosen to limit their production. As a result, world oil prices have steadily increased.

What It Means Oil has brought a lot of money to the Middle East. However, since the world's oil supplies are limited, the region's economy may be at risk in the future. Many countries are beginning to research other types of energy that can one day be used in place of oil. In addition, political disputes have led many countries to limit their dealings with the Middle East and to seek alternative energy sources. However, for now, the many countries buying oil from the Middle East will continue to pump wealth into the region.

Geography for Life Activity

1. Why is oil so central to the Middle Eastern economy?

2. How do the countries of the Middle East use their oil resources to influence world affairs?

3. **The Problem of an Oil Economy** How has dependence on oil caused problems for the Middle East? What challenges might this dependence cause in the future?

GROWTH AND DEVELOPMENT OF THE MIDDLE EAST **215**

Collaborative Learning

At Level | Standard English Mastery

Collaborate on a Script

1. Have students work in pairs or groups of four. Have them carefully examine each of the four visuals on these pages, discussing the information each one shows.

2. Ask students to imagine they are preparing a presentation with these visuals to an audience who knows nothing about the role of oil in the Middle East. Have students use standard English to write the script for the presentation, agreeing on who will write (and later present) each part. The group should agree on a title and on how they will introduce and conclude the presentation.

3. Have groups give their presentations. After each presentation, discuss as a class what went well and where any improvements might be made.

LS Interpersonal, Verbal/Linguistic, Visual/Spatial

Alternative Assessment Handbook, Rubrics 14: Group Activity; and 24: Oral Presentations

Answers

Geography for Life 1. *possible answers—increased wealth and modernized society; revenue used to make improvements in housing, education, and transportation systems;* **2.** *They make decisions regarding how much oil to produce that affect oil prices around the world.* **3.** *As a result of oil dependence, the supply of oil is diminishing. This means that Middle Eastern countries have to make important decisions about whether to produce oil now or preserve their oil supply for the future. In the future, Middle Eastern countries will have to find alternative resources to replace oil.*

Red Brocade

As You Read Ask students to think about hospitality. Have them list ways that they welcome people into their homes. Ask if students have different ways to greet friends and strangers. After students have read the poem, ask them to compare the way Arab people in Southwest Asia greet strangers at their door with how many people in the United States greet strangers.

Meet the Writer

Naomi Shihab Nye This poet and writer is a Palestinian American. She was born in Missouri in 1952 to an American mother and a Palestinian father. She now lives in San Antonio, Texas, with her family. She writes about the details of life, often from a Palestinian American perspective.

MISCONCEPTION //// ALERT \\\\

Saying No Many people know that one custom in some Arab homes is for the host to offer to give something to a guest that she or he has admired. Fewer people know that it is customary to refuse to take the item.

Drinking tea with guests is a traditional Arab custom.

GUIDED READING

WORD HELP

pine nuts a small sweet edible seed of some pine trees

brocade a heavy fabric of silk, cotton, or wool woven with a raised design, often using metallic threads

mint a plant with aromatic leaves that grows in northern temperate regions and is often used for flavoring

❶ Arabs are a cultural group that speak Arabic. They live mostly in Southwest Asia and North Africa.

❷ When entertaining, Arabs often sit on pillows on the floor.

---

from Red Brocade

by Naomi Shihab Nye

About the Poem *In "Red Brocade," Arab-American writer Naomi Shihab Nye tells about an Arab custom. As a part of this custom, strangers are given a special welcome by those who meet them at the door. Since the poet is Arab-American, she is suggesting that we go "back to that" way of accepting new people.*

AS YOU READ Identify the special way that Arab people in the Middle East greet strangers at their door.

The Arabs ❶ used to say,
When a stranger appears at your
   door,
feed him for three days
before asking who he is,
where he's come from,
where he's headed.
That way, he'll have strength
enough to answer.
Or, by then you'll be
such good friends
you don't care.

Let's go back to that.
Rice? Pine nuts?

Here, take the red brocade
   pillow. ❷
My child will serve water
to your horse.

No, I was not busy when you
   came!
I was not preparing to be busy.
That's the armor everyone put
   on to pretend they had a purpose
in the world.

I refuse to be claimed.
Your plate is waiting.
We will snip fresh mint
into your tea.

Connecting Literature to Geography

1. Describing What details in the second verse show us that the Arab speaker is extending a warm welcome to the stranger?

2. Comparing and Contrasting Do you think this poem about greeting a stranger at the door would be different if it had taken place in another region of the world? Explain your answer.

216

Differentiating Instruction

English-Language Learners   At Level

Create small, mixed-ability groups of students. Ask each group to read the poem and determine who is speaking in each verse of the poem. Ask: Is the speaker the same in the first verse and the second and third verses? *No, a narrator is speaking in the first verse, but the focus shifts to someone greeting a stranger in the second and third verses.* **LS** **Verbal/Linguistic**

Alternative Assessment Handbook, Rubric 26: Poems and Songs

Advanced/Gifted and Talented   Above Level

Place students in small groups. Have students interpret the meaning of the poem through discussion. Encourage students to analyze how this poem might relate to the Palestinian and Israeli conflict. Ask each group to write a short summary of their ideas to present to the class. Remind the class that when sharing and giving opinions, it is important to listen to and respect each other's ideas. **LS** **Verbal/Linguistic**

Alternative Assessment Handbook, Rubrics 14: Group Activity; and 26: Poems and Songs

---

Answers

Connecting Literature to Geography 1. *offering rice, pine nuts, and a pillow; giving water to the horse;* **2.** *Answers will vary. Students should explain why they think hospitality is or is not different in other parts of the world.*

Locating Information

Learn

Your teacher has asked you to find information about Israel. Where should you go? What should you do? The best place to start your search for information is in the library. The chart at right includes some library resources you may find helpful.

Practice

Determine which of the sources described here you would most likely use to locate the information in the questions that follow.

❶ Which different sources could you use to find information about Israeli culture?

❷ In which source would you most likely find maps of Jewish migration routes to Israel?

❸ Where might you look to find videos about Israeli culture and daily life?

❹ Which resource would be best for locating information about the current population of Israel?

Library Resources

almanac	a collection of current statistics and general information usually published annually
atlas	a collection of maps and charts
electronic database	a collection of information you can access and search by computer
encyclopedias	books or computer software with short articles on a variety of subjects, usually arranged in alphabetical order
magazine and newspaper indexes	listings of recent and past articles from newspapers and magazines
online catalog	a computerized listing of books, videos, and other library resources; you search for resources by title, author, keyword, or subject
World Wide Web	a collection of information on the Internet; if you use a Web site, be sure to carefully examine its reliability, or trustworthiness

Apply

Use resources from a local library to answer the questions below.

1. About how many Jews moved to Israel when it was first created?

2. What different subtopics can you find on Israel in the library catalog?

3. Write a list of important facts about Israel.

217

Social Studies Skills Activity: Locating Information

At Level

Using the Library to Locate Information

Research Required

1. Organize students into pairs. Assign each pair a topic on the growth and development of the Middle East. Topics might include the creation of Israel, the oil in the Middle East, the Palestinian-Israeli conflict, or OPEC.

2. Tell students that they will research and write a news article summarizing their topic.

3. Have students begin by identifying which of the library resources listed in the table above will be useful for their research. Instruct students to use at least four of the seven types of resources.

4. Have students conduct library research. Encourage them to take notes on their findings.

5. Have students use their notes to write newspaper articles explaining the who, what, when, where, why, and how of their topic.

6. Lead a discussion of the research process. What resources did students find most useful? Which were least useful?

LS Verbal/Linguistic, Interpersonal

Alternative Assessment Handbook, Rubrics 23: Newspapers; and 30: Research

Social Studies Skills

Locating Information

Activity Advertisements

1. Organize the class into seven groups to conduct research and write a persuasive advertisement about using a library resource. Assign each group one of the library resources listed in this Social Studies Skills feature.

2. Have each group choose a Middle Eastern country from the chapter to find information about, using their assigned library resources. They should look for three facts or resources that might only be found using their assigned library resource.

3. Then have each group prepare a a two-part oral presentation. One part should report each group's findings about their selected Middle Eastern country. The other part should be an advertisement for the library resource each group was assigned. In the advertisements, students should tell what type of information can be found using that resource, why that resource is unique, how easy that resource is to access and use, and why students should use that resource when researching in the future. **LS Verbal/Linguistic, Interpersonal**

Alternative Assessment Handbook, Rubrics 2: Advertisements; 14: Group Activity; 24: Oral Presentations; and 43: Writing to Persuade

RF: Social Studies Skills, Locating Information

Answers

Practice 1. *encyclopedias, electronic database, magazine and newspaper indexes, World Wide Web;* **2.** *atlas;* **3.** *online catalog;* **4.** *almanac*

Apply 1. *almost 1 million;* **2.** *possible answers—culture, religion, history;* **3.** *Students' lists of facts about Israel will vary, but should be accurate.*

217

Bellringer

If YOU lived there. . . Use the **Daily Bellringer Transparency** to help students answer the question.

 Daily Bellringer Transparency, Section 3

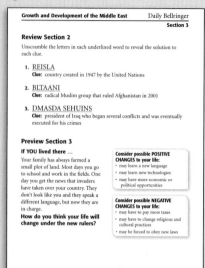

Growth and Development of the Middle East	Daily Bellringer
	Section 3

Review Section 2

Unscramble the letters in each underlined word to reveal the solution to each clue.

1. REISLA
   Clue: country created in 1947 by the United Nations
2. BLTAANI
   Clue: radical Muslim group that ruled Afghanistan in 2001
3. DMASDA SEHUINS
   Clue: president of Iraq who began several conflicts and was eventually executed for his crimes

Preview Section 3

If YOU lived there ...
Your family has always farmed a small plot of land. Most days you go to school and work in the fields. One day you get the news that invaders have taken over your country. They don't look like you and they speak a different language, but now they are in charge.
How do you think your life will change under the new rulers?

Consider possible POSITIVE CHANGES to your life:
• may learn a new language
• may learn new technologies
• may have more economic or political opportunities

Consider possible NEGATIVE CHANGES to your life:
• may have to pay more taxes
• may have to change religious and cultural practices
• may be forced to obey new laws

Academic Vocabulary

Review with students the high-use academic term in this section.

implemented put in place (p. 221)

📝 **RF:** Vocabulary Builder, Section 3

Taking Notes

Have students copy the graphic organizer onto their own paper and then use it to take notes on the section. This activity will prepare students for the Section Assessment, in which they will complete a graphic organizer that builds on the information using the Critical Thinking Skill: Sequencing.

SECTION 3

History and Culture of Central Asia

What You Will Learn...

Main Ideas

1. Throughout history, many different groups have conquered Central Asia.
2. Many different ethnic groups and their traditions influence culture in Central Asia.

The Big Idea

The countries of Central Asia share similar histories and traditions, but particular ethnic groups give each country a unique culture.

Key Terms and Places

Samarqand, *p. 218*
nomads, *p. 220*
yurt, *p. 220*

TAKING NOTES As you read, use a chart like the one here to organize your notes on the history and culture of Central Asia. Be sure to pay attention to the different peoples that influenced the region.

History	Culture

218 CHAPTER 8

If **YOU** lived there...

Your family has always farmed a small plot of land. Most days you go to school and work in the fields. One day you get news that invaders have taken over your country. They don't look like you and they speak a different language, but now they are in charge.

How do you think your life will change under the new rulers?

BUILDING BACKGROUND You may have noticed that the names of the countries in Central Asia all end with *stan*. In the language of the region, *stan* means "land of." So, for example, Kazakhstan means "land of the Kazakhs." However, throughout history many different groups have ruled these lands.

History

Central Asia has been somewhat of a crossroads for traders and invaders for hundreds of years. As these different peoples have passed through Central Asia, they have each left their own unique and lasting influences on the region.

Trade

At one time, the best trade route between Europe and India ran through Afghanistan. The best route between Europe and China ran through the rest of Central Asia. Beginning in about 100 BC, merchants traveled along the China route to trade European gold and wool for Chinese spices and silk. As a result, this route came to be called the Silk Road. Cities along the road, such as **Samarqand** and Bukhara, grew rich from the trade.

By 1500 the situation in Central Asia had changed, however. When Europeans discovered they could sail to East Asia through the Indian Ocean, trade through Central Asia declined. The region became more isolated and poor.

Teach the Big Idea

At Level

History and Culture of Central Asia

1. **Teach** Ask students the questions in the Main Idea boxes under Direct Teach.

2. **Apply** Have students create pairs of cards, one with a statement of information and one with the answer (for example, *this route connected Europe and China* and *Silk Road*). 🅛🅢 **Verbal/Linguistic**

3. **Review** Have pairs of students combine their cards and play the game. With the cards face down, players must turn over

matching pairs. Players get another turn if they match a pair. The player with the most pairs wins.

4. **Practice/Homework** Have students illustrate their cards based on images and designs in their textbook chapter.
   🅛🅢 **Verbal/Linguistic, Visual/Spatial, Kinesthetic**

   📋 Alternative Assessment Handbook, Rubrics 1: Acquiring Information; and 14: Group Activity

Invasions

Because of its location on the Silk Road, many groups of people were interested in Central Asia. Group after group swarmed into the region. Among the first people to establish a lasting influence in the region were Turkic-speaking nomads who came from northern Asia in AD 500.

In the 700s Arab armies took over much of the region. They brought a new religion—Islam—to Central Asia. Many of the beautiful mosques in Central Asian cities date from the time of the Arabs.

Arabs, followed by other invaders, ruled Central Asia until the 1200s. Then, Mongol armies conquered Central Asia, destroying many cities with their violent attacks. Eventually, their empire crumbled. With the fall of the Mongols, various tribes of peoples, such as the Uzbeks, Kazakhs, and Turkmens moved into parts of the region.

Russian and Soviet Rule

In the mid-1800s the Russians became the next major group to conquer Central Asia. Although the Russians built railroads and expanded cotton and oil production, people began to resent their rule.

After the Russian Revolution in 1917, the new Soviet government wanted to weaken resistance to its rule. The new Soviet leaders did this by dividing the land into republics. The Soviets encouraged ethnic Russians to move to these areas and made other people settle on government-owned farms. The Soviets also built huge irrigation projects to improve cotton production.

The Soviet Union collapsed in 1991. As the Soviet government and economy fell apart, it could no longer control its huge territory. The Central Asian republics finally became independent countries.

READING CHECK Generalizing What groups of people influenced Central Asia?

Influences on Central Asia

The Arabs, Mongols, and Soviets all had a major influence on Central Asia.

Arab Influence

- The Arabs ruled Central Asia in the 700s and 800s.
- They introduced Islam and built beautiful mosques.
- They influenced styles of art and architecture in the region.

Mongol Influence

- The Mongols ruled from 1220 to the mid-1300s.
- They destroyed cities and irrigation systems.
- Eventually, they supported literature and the arts at Samarqand.

Soviet Influence

- The Soviet Union controlled Central Asia from 1917 to 1991.
- The Soviets separated ethnic groups and banned religious practices.
- They began growing cotton and constructed many useful but stark buildings.

GROWTH AND DEVELOPMENT OF THE MIDDLE EAST **219**

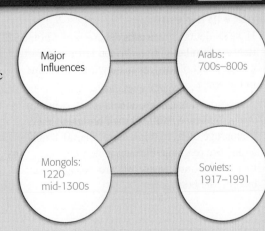

❷ Culture

Many different ethnic groups and their traditions influence culture in Central Asia.

Explain How did the people who came through Central Asia influence its culture? *brought new religions and new languages, new ways of life mixed with traditional ways*

Contrast What is the difference between the Cyrillic and Latin alphabets? *Cyrillic used for Russian language; Latin used for English*

Evaluate What do you think it would be like to live in a yurt in the area where you live? *Answers will vary but should mention features of a yurt.*

MISCONCEPTION
**//// ALERT **

Nomads in Modern Times People may think that a nomadic lifestyle means using only ancient ways. In fact, nomadic peoples of today may use technology such as cars, electricity, and boom boxes.

Close-Up

Inside a Yurt

Activity Describing a Yurt
Have students write a paragraph that describes the yurt shown in their textbook. Ask for volunteers to share paragraphs, then discuss the differences and similarities students noticed.

LS **Verbal/Linguistic**

📖 Alternative Assessment Handbook, Rubric 40: Writing to Describe

Answers

Analyzing Visuals *Felt mats and the frame are probably light to carry and easy to take apart and set back up.*

220

Culture

The people who came through Central Asia influenced culture in the region. They brought new languages, religions, and ways of life that mixed with traditional ways of life in Central Asia.

Traditional Lives

For centuries, Central Asians have made a living by raising horses, cattle, sheep, and goats. Many herders live as **nomads**, people who move often from place to place. The nomads move their herds from mountain pastures in the summer to lowland pastures in the winter. Today most people in Central Asia live in more permanent settlements, but many others still live as nomads. The nomadic lifestyle is especially common in Kyrgyzstan.

Unique homes, called yurts, make moving with the herds possible. A **yurt** is a movable round house made of wool felt mats hung over a wood frame. Today the yurt is a symbol of the region's nomadic heritage. Even people who live in cities may put up yurts for special events such as weddings and funerals.

Close-up

Inside a Yurt

Historically, the nomadic life required that all possessions be portable—even houses. Nomads moved their yurts with them from place to place.

A hole at the top allows smoke from a fire to escape.

Nomads roll up part of the felt mat to create a door.

Traditional carpets provide decoration and warmth and are a yurt's main furniture.

ANALYSIS SKILL **ANALYZING VISUALS**
Why would a yurt be easier to move than another type of house?

220 CHAPTER 8

Critical Thinking: Comparing and Contrasting   [At Level]

What's in a Home?

1. Have students draw a cross-section of a home they are familar with in the top left quarter of a large sheet of art paper, showing the rooms in the home.

2. After they finish, ask students what rooms are in the home and how they are used. Encourage them to think about intended and actual use (e.g., the kitchen table may also be used for homework). List rooms and their uses on the board.

3. Discuss with the class how these homes are different from and similar to a yurt.

4. Have students draw the yurt from their textbook on the bottom left quarter of the art paper. Then have them create and complete two columns on the right, one labeled *same* and one labeled *different*. **LS** **Visual/Spatial, Verbal/Linguistic**

📖 Alternative Assessment Handbook, Rubrics 3: Artwork; 9: Comparing and Contrasting; and 11: Discussions

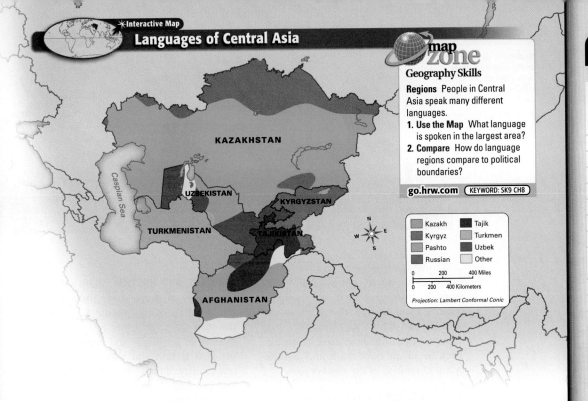

KAZAKHSTAN

Caspian Sea

UZBEKISTAN

KYRGYZSTAN

TURKMENISTAN

TAJIKISTAN

AFGHANISTAN

map zone

Geography Skills

Regions People in Central Asia speak many different languages.

1. **Use the Map** What language is spoken in the largest area?
2. **Compare** How do language regions compare to political boundaries?

go.hrw.com KEYWORD: SK9 CH8

Kazakh		Tajik
Kyrgyz		Turkmen
Pashto		Uzbek
Russian		Other

0   200   400 Miles
0   200   400 Kilometers

Projection: Lambert Conformal Conic

People, Languages, and Religion

Most people in Central Asia today belong to one of several ethnic groups that are part of a larger ethnic group called Turkic. Some of these ethnic groups are Kazakh (kuh-ZAHK), Kyrgyz (KIR-giz), Turkmen, and Uzbek (OOZ-bek). Another group, ethnic Russians, came to Central Asia when Russia conquered the region. They still live in every Central Asian country.

Each ethnic group speaks its own language. Look at the map above to see where a particular language is the primary language. In most countries in the region, more than one language is spoken.

When the Russians conquered Central Asia, they **implemented** a policy that made Russian the official language for business and government. It is still an official language in some Central Asian countries. The Russians also introduced the Cyrillic alphabet, the alphabet used to write the Russian language. Most countries in Central Asia now use the Latin alphabet, however, which is the one used to write English. Afghanistan also has its own alphabet. It is used for writing Pashto, one of that country's official languages.

Just as people in the region are of many ethnic groups and speak different languages, they also practice different religions. Traders and conquerors brought their religious beliefs and practices to the region. Islam, brought by the Arabs, is the main religion in Central Asia. Some people there also practice Christianity. Most of the region's Christians belong to the Russian Orthodox Church.

ACADEMIC VOCABULARY

implement to put in place

Direct Teach

Checking for Understanding

True or False Answer each statement *T* if it is true or *F* if it is false. If false, explain why.

1. Most people in Central Asia today are ethnic Russians. *F; Most people are part of a Turkic ethnic group.*
2. Afghanistan has its own alphabet. *T*
3. Christianity is the main religion of Central Asia. *F; Islam is the major religion in this region.*

Interpreting Maps

Languages of Central Asia

Russian Language What is the main area where Russian is spoken, and why is it concentrated there? *in the north of Kazakhstan, because that area is along the Russian border*

Map Zone Transparency: Languages of Central Asia

go.hrw.com
Online Resources

KEYWORD: SK9 CH8
ACTIVITY: Cyrillic Alphabet

Collaborative Learning

At Level

Creating a Map-Based Quiz

Standard English Mastery

1. Have students work in pairs to brainstorm questions based on the information in the Languages of Central Asia map. Questions should be worded so that "What country am I?" can follow. Each student should use standard English to write five questions and answers.

2. Change the pairs, so that each student has a new partner. Have each partner quiz the other. Be sure both partners agree on what the correct answers are for each question.

3. Ask students to share some of the questions. As a class, discuss any necessary corrections to the sentences to align them with standard English usage.

LS Verbal/Linguistic, Visual/Spatial, Kinesthetic

Alternative Assessment Handbook, Rubrics 14: Group Activity; and 21: Map Reading

Answers

Map Zone 1. *Kazakh;* **2.** *possible answers—In some places, they match closely, but in others they are not the same; there are more language regions.*

222

Ethnic Groups of Central Asia

Traditional clothing, such as the hats men wear, distinguishes members of different ethnic groups in Central Asia.

ANALYZING VISUALS
Why do you think men wear different hats?

Uzbek

Kyrgyz

Turkmen

Did you know. . .

The Cyrillic alphabet has 33 letters, 7 more than the Latin alphabet. Two of these are silent. They change the sound of the consonant that comes before it in a word.

Info to Know

Mosque Discovery Archaeological discoveries continue to shed light on Central Asian culture and history. One example is the discovery of a ninth-century, nine-domed mosque found near Balkh, Afghanistan.

Review & Assess

Close

Ask students to explain how the different ethnic groups in Central Asia influence its culture.

Review

Online Quiz, Section 3

Assess

SE Section 3 Assessment

PASS: Section 3 Quiz

Alternative Assessment Handbook

Reteach/Classroom Intervention

Interactive Reader and Study Guide, Section 3

Interactive Skills Tutor CD-ROM

During the Soviet era, the government closed or destroyed more than 35,000 religious buildings, such as mosques, churches, and Islamic schools. However, since the end of the Soviet Union in 1991, many religious buildings have reopened. They are in use once again and are also beautiful symbols of the region's past.

READING CHECK **Summarizing** How did Russian and Soviet rule influence culture in Central Asia?

SUMMARY AND PREVIEW Many different groups of people have influenced the countries of the Middle East over the years. As a result, the region has a mixture of languages and religions. In the next section you will learn about one country of the region, Saudi Arabia. You will learn how religious traditions shape life there as well as how economic changes have brought both prosperity and new challenges.

Section 3 Assessment

go.hrw.com
Online Quiz
KEYWORD: SK9 HP8

Reviewing Ideas, Terms, and Places

1. **a. Identify** What people brought Islam to Central Asia?
   b. Analyze What impact did the Silk Road have on Central Asia?
   c. Elaborate How might Central Asia's history have been different without the influence of the Silk Road?
2. **a. Define** What is a **yurt**?
   b. Analyze What are some of the benefits of nomadic life, and what are some of the challenges of this lifestyle?
   c. Elaborate How might the mix of ethnic groups, languages, and religions in Central Asian countries affect life there today?

Critical Thinking

3. **Sequencing** Review your notes on the history of Central Asia. Then organize your information using a time line like the one below. You may add more dates if you need to.

100 BC   1991

FOCUS ON WRITING

4. **Taking Notes on History and Culture** What information about the history and culture of Central Asia should you include on your Web site? What sites might visitors be interested in learning more about? Jot down a few notes.

222 CHAPTER 8

Section 3 Assessment Answers

1. **a.** Arabs
   b. brought many traders and invading armies, mixing new languages, religions, and ways of life with the existing traditions
   c. possible answer—It might have remained more isolated, with little or no mixing cultures.
2. **a.** movable, round house made of wool felt mats over a round frame
   b. possible answers: benefits—move livestock to best pastures during the year; challenges—hard to grow crops or have as many

comforts as permanent homes do, such as running water and electricity
   c. possible answer—could cause conflicts or increase diversity as people get to know and interact with people in other culture groups
3. Time lines should show accurate chronology of the groups that conquered the area.
4. Notes should reflect information in the section and should provide information about Central Asia.

Answers

Analyzing Visuals *possible answers—tradition of their ethnic group; useful for the climate*

Reading Check *established Russian as official language, introduced Cyrillic alphabet, closed or destroyed many religious buildings*

222

Chapter Review

Geography's Impact
video series
Review the video to answer the closing question:
Why do you think the conflict in Jerusalem today is difficult to solve?

Answers

Visual Summary

Use the visual summary below to help you review the main ideas of the chapter.

QUICK FACTS

From Arabia, Islam spread into many parts of the world. Muslims ruled great empires in Asia, Europe, and Africa.

After World War I, the Ottoman Empire fell apart. New political leaders worked to reform and modernize their countries.

The discovery of huge oil reserves beneath the Middle East changed the economy and brought great wealth to the region.

Reviewing Vocabulary, Terms, and Places

For each statement below, write T if it is true and F if it is false. If the statement is false, write the correct term that would make the sentence a true statement.

1. **Baghdad**, a great city in Spain, was center of learning and culture.
2. The United Nations placed a **tolerance**, or limit on trade, on Iraq in the 1990s.
3. Iran's rulers took the title **shah** from the ancient Persian word for a king.
4. The Ottomans renamed Constantinople **Istanbul**.
5. The Safavid capital, **Esfehan**, was a magnificent city.
6. Many Central Asians live as **yurts**, people who move from place to place.
7. **Janissaries** converted to Islam and became fierce warriors in the Ottoman army.
8. **OPEC** is an international organization whose members work to influence the price of oil on world markets.

Comprehension and Critical Thinking

SECTION 1 *(pages 202–207)*

9. a. **Identify** Who was Abu Bakr, and why is he important in the history of Islam?
   b. **Analyze** Why did the Safavids come into conflict with the Ottomans?
   c. **Evaluate** In your opinion, was conquest or trade more effective in spreading Islam? Why?

SECTION 2 *(pages 208–213)*

10. a. **Identify** In which country did the Ayatollah Khomeini lead a revolution?
    b. **Explain** Why did the creation of the state of Israel lead to conflict in the Middle East?
    c. **Elaborate** What role does OPEC play in world affairs? How might that affect politics in the Middle East?

GROWTH AND DEVELOPMENT OF THE MIDDLE EAST **223**

Visual Summary

Review and Inquiry Have students use the visual summary to review main events, belief systems, and achievements of the Islamic World and the time of Muhammad to the late 1660s.

Quick Facts Transparency: Visual Summary: History of the Islamic World

Reviewing Vocabulary, Terms, and Places

1. F, Córdoba   5. T
2. F; sanction   6. F; nomads
3. T   7. T
4. T   8. T

Comprehension and Critical Thinking

9. a. Abu Bakr was the first caliph. He made Arabia into a unified Muslim state.

   b. because of a conflict concerning how to decide who should become caliph

   c. Answers will vary, but students should provide a logical answer supported with information from the text.

10. a. Iran
    b. It forced Palestinians out of territory that had long been their home.
    c. OPEC helps determine oil prices and supply; possible answer—it gives OPEC countries a great deal of influence, which non-OPEC Middle Eastern countries might resent.

Review and Assessment Resources

Review and Reinforce

SE Chapter Review

RF: Chapter Review

Quick Facts Transparency: Visual Summary: Growth and Development of the Middle East

Spanish Chapter Summaries Audio CD Program

OSP Holt Puzzle Pro; Quiz Show for ExamView

Quiz Game CD-ROM

Assess

SE Standardized Test Practice

PASS: Chapter Test, Forms A and B

Alternative Assessment Handbook

OSP ExamView Test Generator, Chapter Test

Differentiating Instruction Modified Worksheets and Tests CD-ROM: Modified Chapter Test

HOAP Holt Online Assessment Program (in the Holt Interactive Online Student Edition)

Reteach/Intervene

Interactive Reader and Study Guide

Differentiating Instruction Teacher Management System: Lesson Plans

Differentiating Instruction Modified Worksheets and Tests CD-ROM

Interactive Skills Tutor CD-ROM

go.hrw.com
Online Resources
Chapter Resources:
KEYWORD: SK9 CH8

11. a. The Soviets expanded railroads, cotton and oil production, and built many buildings. Land and ethnic groups divided into republics and ethnic Russians moved in. Russian became the official language. Many religious buildings closed.

b. continuing nomadic life, use of yurts for special events in city life, ethnic languages, traditional religions and clothing

c. possible answer—Some people may prefer jobs in the city and comforts in a permanent home. Others may prefer living on the land with fewer people nearby.

Social Studies Skills

12. magazine or newspaper indexes or the World Wide Web

13. online catalog

14. electronic database, online catalog, or World Wide Web

Focus on Reading and Writing

15. Students' paragraphs should reflect an understanding of "Iraqi Aggression" in Section 2. Correct order of events:

- Saddam Hussein takes control of Iraq.
- Iraq invades Kuwait.
- The Persian Gulf War is fought.
- Saddam Hussein is removed from power.

RF: Focus on Reading: Sequencing

16. Rubric Students' Web sites should

- include one home page and one Web page for each topic
- include four or five sentences of text on each page
- make sure the text is easy enough for children to read
- give accurate, interesting information
- catch the audience's attention with color and/or images.

RF: Focus on Writing, Creating a Web Site

SECTION 3 (pages 218–222)

11. a. Describe How did life in Central Asia change under Russian and Soviet rule?

b. Analyze In what ways do the people of Central Asia show their pride in their past and their culture?

c. Evaluate Why do you think many former nomads now live in cities? Why do you think other people still choose to live as nomads?

Social Studies Skills

Locating Information *Use your knowledge about locating information to answer the questions below.*

12. Where might you look to find information about recent conflicts in the Middle East?

13. What types of sources might you use to find books about early governments in the Middle East?

14. What sources could you use to find electronic resources about Central Asia?

FOCUS ON READING AND WRITING

15. Sequencing Arrange the following list of events in the order in which they happened. Then write a brief paragraph describing the events, using clue words such as *after*, *then*, and *later* to show the proper sequence.

- Saddam Hussein is removed from power.
- Saddam Hussein takes control of Iraq.
- Iraq invades Kuwait.
- The Persian Gulf War is fought.

16. Creating Your Web Site You have now collected information on the growth and development of the Middle East. Create a home page and one Web page on each of these topics. You can write about your topics in paragraph form or in a list of bullet points. You may design the pages either online or on sheets of paper. Remember that your audience is children, so you should keep your sentences simple.

Using the Internet

17. Activity: Charting Democracy Some countries face challenges as they work to promote a more democratic form of government. Iraq, for example, has struggled as it has begun to develop its own form of democracy. How does democracy in the Middle East differ from democracy in the United States? Enter the activity keyword. Then create a chart or diagram that compares democratic life in the United States with democratic life in Iraq and other countries of the Middle East.

Map Activity ★Interactive

18. The Middle East On a separate sheet of paper, match the letters on the map with their correct labels.

Mecca   Medina   Red Sea

Persian Gulf   Arabian Sea

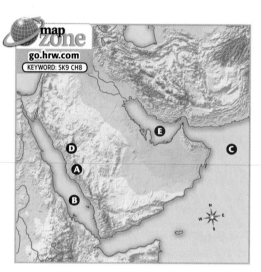

Using the Internet

17. Go to the HRW Web site and enter the keyword shown to access a rubric for this activity.

KEYWORD: SK9 TEACHER

Map Activity

18. A. Mecca
B. Red Sea
C. Arabian Sea
D. Medina
E. Persian Gulf

Standardized Test Practice

DIRECTIONS (1–6): For each statement or question, write on a separate answer sheet the *number* of the word or expression that, of those given, best completes the statement or answers the question.

1 Which Muslim empire had a capital at Istanbul and ruled much of Europe, Asia, and Africa?

(1) Ottoman Empire
(2) Baghdad Empire
(3) Constantinople Empire
(4) Safavid Empire

2 Which country was created as a homeland for the Jewish people?

(1) Iran
(2) Israel
(3) Iraq
(4) Lebanon

3 How did the Arabs influence Central Asia in the 700s and 800s?

(1) separated ethnic groups
(2) destroyed cities and irrigation systems
(3) built railroads and expanded oil production
(4) introduced Islam

4 Which of the following statements about the nomadic lifestyle is false?

(1) Nomads move their herds depending on the season.
(2) Nomads decorate their yurts with carpets.
(3) It is a symbol of the region's heritage.
(4) Nomads often move from one dwelling to another.

5 What country did the Taliban rule?

(1) Kazakhstan
(2) Afghanistan
(3) Kyrgyzstan
(4) Uzbekistan

6 Which of the following statements about conflict in the Middle East is true?

(1) All conflict is based on religious differences.
(2) Iraq has not been involved in any conflicts.
(3) Conflicts have been caused by religious and ethnic differences.
(4) Conflict in the region was all resolved before 1970.

Base your answer to question 7 on the map below and on your knowledge of social studies.

Farmland in Central Asia

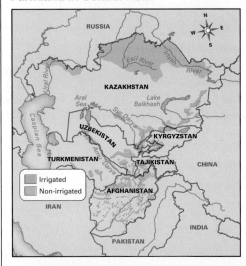

7 Based on the map above, what country has the most non-irrigated farmland?

(1) Kazakhstan
(2) Tajikistan
(3) Turkmenistan
(4) Uzbekistan

GROWTH AND DEVELOPMENT OF THE MIDDLE EAST **225**

1. 3
Break Down the Question This question requires students to recall factual information. Refer students who miss it to Section 1.

2. 2
Break Down the Question This question requires students to recall factual information. Refer students who miss it to Section 2.

3. 4
Break Down the Question Remind students that they can rely on general knowledge during tests—in this case, that Arab people often belong to Islam.

4. 4
Break Down the Question Remind students to read each answer carefully. Point out that while option 4 mentions houses, an important point from the reading, it is false because it says nomads moved to different houses rather than stating that they moved their houses with them.

5. 2
Break Down the Question This question requires students to recall factual information. Refer students who miss it to Section 3.

6. 1
Break Down the Question Refer students who miss this question to Section 2.

7. 1
Break Down the Question Remind students to carefully examine the map text and labels before choosing an answer.

Reteach/Intervention Resources

Reproducible

- Interactive Reader and Study Guide
- Differentiated Instruction Teacher Management System: Lesson Plans

Technology

- Quick Facts Transparency: Visual Summary: Growth and Development of the Middle East
- Differentiated Instruction Modified Worksheets and Tests CD-ROM
- Interactive Skills Tutor CD-ROM

Tips for Test Taking

Master the Question Multiple choice questions may be open, requiring you to finish a sentence, or closed, requiring you to choose an answer. For either type, always make sure you read and think about each possible answer. If there are four possible answers, try to eliminate three before you answer. If you can't decide between two, make your best guess.

Motivate Explain to students that looking carefully at pictures can tell us a lot about a place. Have students look at the pictures in this chapter and think about this question: What evidence do these pictures give that this region has both very traditional and very modern elements? Ask volunteers to share their answers. Then ask students to write a short paragraph describing what they expect to learn about the culture of Saudi Arabia in this Case Study. Have volunteers read their paragraphs to the class.

Key Terms

Preteach the following terms:

hajj a pilgrimage that Muslims are expected to make at least once in their lives (p. 227)

nomads people who move often from place to place (p. 228)

Wahhabism a strict form of Islam practiced in Saudi Arabia (p. 228)

Shariah Islamic law (p. 230)

desalinization the process of removing salt from seawater (p. 231)

Case Study

 # Saudi Arabia

Geography

Facts About QUICK FACTS

Saudi Arabia

Official Name: Kingdom of Saudi Arabia

Capital: Riyadh

Area: 756,985 square miles (slightly smaller than the United States west of the Rockies)

Population: 27.6 million (33 people/square mile)

Average Life Expectancy: 76 years

Official Language: Arabic

Major Religion: Islam

Unit of Currency: Riyal

The nation of Saudi Arabia occupies most of the Arabian Peninsula in the Middle East. Like the rest of the peninsula, Saudi Arabia is a harsh, dry land. It has no permanent rivers, lakes, or other bodies of water. Rain is rare. Few places in Saudi Arabia see more than three inches of rain per year, and some places might go as long as 10 years with no rain at all.

Saudi Arabia's land is generally highest in the west and lowest in the east. A narrow coastal plain along the Red Sea gives way suddenly to steep mountains, the highest in Saudi Arabia. East of the mountains is a vast plateau called the Nejd, or "uplands." The plateau gradually slopes downward to the east. Near the Persian Gulf, the land is mostly a rocky plain.

The Southern part of the country is covered by the Rub' al-Khali, or "Empty Quarter," one of the largest sandy regions in the world. Huge dunes, some more than 1,000 feet (330 m) high, shift constantly in the wind. Temperatures in the Rub' al-Khali regularly climb to more than 130°F (55°C) during the summer. As a result, few people live or travel much in the area.

Because southern Saudi Arabia is so harsh, most people live further north. The country's largest city is the capital, Riyadh (ree-YAHD), the historic home of the royal family. In addition to being the center of the government, it is also a commercial and transportation center. Modern skyscrapers dominate the skyline. The city is also home to more than 4,200 mosques.

1 The **An Nafud** is a vast desert area in northern Saudi Arabia. Huge dunes dominate the landscapes of Saudi Arabia's many deserts.

226 CASE STUDY

Teach the Case Study
At Level

Saudi Arabia

1. **Teach** Ask students the questions in the Main Idea boxes under Direct Teach.

2. **Apply** Instruct students to preview the Case Study by examining the photographs, captions, and main headings. Have students imagine that they are on a trip to Saudi Arabia. Have students write a travelogue describing the geography, history, and culture of Saudi Arabia. Encourage students to use vivid language to describe what they see and hear.

3. **Review** As you review the Case Study, have students share their travelogues with the class.

4. **Practice/Homework** Have students expand on one travelogue, describing it using each of the five senses.
   LS Verbal/Linguistic
   Alternative Assessment Handbook, Rubric 40: Writing to Describe

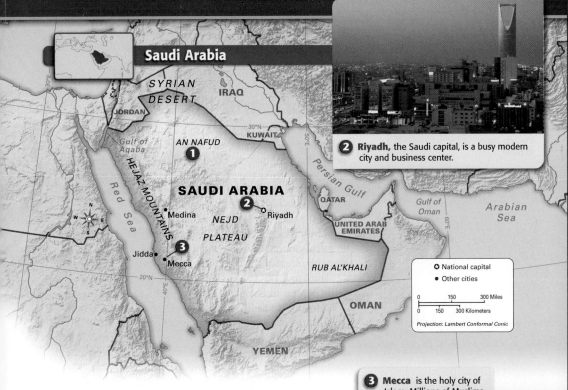

Saudi Arabia

SYRIAN DESERT

IRAQ

JORDAN

Gulf of Aqaba

AN NAFUD ①

KUWAIT

30°N

50°E

HEJAZ MOUNTAINS

Red Sea

SAUDI ARABIA ②

Medina

NEJD PLATEAU

Riyadh ✪

Persian Gulf

QATAR

UNITED ARAB EMIRATES

Gulf of Oman

Arabian Sea

60°E

Jidda • ③
Mecca •

RUB AL'KHALI

20°N

40°E

OMAN

YEMEN

② Riyadh, the Saudi capital, is a busy modern city and business center.

✪ National capital
● Other cities

0   150   300 Miles
0   150   300 Kilometers

Projection: Lambert Conformal Conic

③ Mecca is the holy city of Islam. Millions of Muslims visit the city each year.

Riyadh is Saudi Arabia's capital, but Mecca and Medina are its spiritual heart. Mecca is the most sacred city in Islam, the site of the Grand Mosque and the Kaaba. Muslims around the world turn to face the Kaaba each time they pray. Mecca is the destination of the hajj, the pilgrimage that all able Muslims are expected to make at least once during their lifetime. Some 2 million Muslims visit Mecca on hajj each year. No non-Muslims are allowed to enter the city at any time.

Case Study Assessment

1. Why do few people live in Saudi Arabia's interior?

2. Why is Mecca visited by so many people?

3. **Activity** Plan a desert survival kit. Imagine that you will be traveling for three days in the Saudi desert. Make a list of what you will need to bring with you to survive.

SAUDI ARABIA **227**

600 ● 1500 ●

622
Muhammad leaves Mecca for Medina. The Muslim calendar begins with this date.

The Qur'an, the holy book of Islam

1517
The Ottoman Empire takes control of Mecca.

Ottoman scimitar

Main Idea

History and Culture

Identify In 1932 who united much of the Arabian Peninsula under the Kingdom of Saudi Arabia? *Abdul Aziz Ibn Saud*

Explain Describe the early towns and villages of what is today Saudi Arabia. *They were centers of trade where people settled; they were parts of small kingdoms.*

Draw Conclusions What elements of Wahhabism are present in modern Saudi culture? *modest clothing for men, coverings for women, alcohol and pork are illegal, laws and customs that limit women's activities*

Info to Know

Wahhabism Wahhabism, a strict form of Islam, was founded in the Arabian Peninsula in the 1700s. Around 1744 the Saud family adopted Wahhabism, and it eventually grew to become the dominant faith in what is today Saudi Arabia. Adherents of Wahhabism promote a return to the original teachings of the Qur'an and the Hadith, the traditions of Muhammad.

History and Culture

The land we now call Saudi Arabia was once the home of a number of small kingdoms. Within these kingdoms, many people lived as nomads. Others preferred to settle down and form towns. These towns often became centers of trade, welcoming merchants from as far away as Ethiopia and Persia. One of these early trading cities was Mecca.

In the late 570s Muhammad, the prophet of Islam, was born in Mecca. By the time he died in 632, Islam had grown to be the dominant religion in all of Arabia. As Islam spread through much of the world, Mecca was its spiritual capital.

From the 700s to the 1800s Saudi Arabia was part of a series of Muslim empires. However, in the early 1700s a new alliance arose in Saudi Arabia. The members of the alliance were followers of a strict form of Islam called Wahhabism. The Wahhabis wanted to remove what they saw as modern corruptions of Islam. For more than a century, the Wahhabis fought against the Ottoman Empire, which then ruled Arabia. The result of their fight was the creation in 1932 of the Kingdom of Saudi Arabia. Its first king was Abdul Aziz Ibn Saud.

Experiencing Saudi Culture

Saudi culture is heavily influenced by tradition, particularly by Islamic teachings. At the same time, the oil industry has brought modern influences to the country.

Saudi Muslims like these in Medina pray five times a day.

Because Islam emphasizes modesty, many Saudi men wear long shirts and headdresses.

Saudi women have few rights. They are usually required to cover themselves completely in public.

228 CASE STUDY

Collaborative Learning

At Level

Saudi Culture

Research Required

1. Organize the class into small groups. Ask each group to select a cultural practice or tradition common in Saudi Arabia. Have students research the details about their choice. Students may wish to select religious traditions, clothing styles, foods, music, or family life as their topic.

2. Have each group work collaboratively to write one to two paragraphs describing their subject.

3. Have each group make a poster that focuses on their selected topic. Instruct students to

include the description of the topic on their poster and decorate the poster with drawings and words that illustrate their paragraph. For example, if students choose a popular Saudi food, they should include their description of the food, drawings of the ingredients, and other interesting visuals.

4. Have each group present its poster to the class. **LS Verbal/Linguistic, Interpersonal**

Alternative Assessment Handbook, Rubric 28: Posters

c. 1740
Wahhabism develops
in Saudi Arabia.

**Abdul Aziz
Ibn Saud**

1932
Abdul Aziz Ibn Saud
becomes the first king
of Saudi Arabia.

2005

2005
King Abdullah, a son of Ibn
Saud, becomes the sixth
king of Saudi Arabia.

In some ways, Saudi Arabia has not changed much since it became independent. For example, the kingdom is still ruled by the Saud family. In other ways, however, life today is very different. The discovery of oil in Saudi Arabia in the 1930s led to major economic changes. Later, the presence of oil workers from other parts of the world led to social changes as well.

Nearly all Saudis are Arabs and speak Arabic. Their culture is strongly influenced by Islam, especially the Sunni branch of Islam. About 85 percent of Saudi Muslims are Sunni. Wahhabism remains the official religion of the royal family.

Islam influences Saudi Arabia's culture in many ways. For example, Islam forbids the eating of pork and the drinking of alcohol, so those products are illegal in Saudi Arabia. In part because Islam requires modesty, Saudi clothing keeps arms and legs covered. Men usually wear a long, loose shirt. They also often wear a cotton headdress held in place with a cord. Saudi women traditionally wear a black cloak and veil in public, although some now wear Western-style clothing.

Saudi laws and customs limit women's activities. For example, a woman rarely appears in public without her husband or a male relative. Also, women are not allowed to drive cars. However, women can own and run businesses in Saudi Arabia.

Outside of the city, some Saudi Arabians continue to live as nomads. Among these nomads are the Bedouins. Traditionally, Bedouin families have wandered the region's deserts tending flocks of camels, sheep, or goats. Since the 1950s, however, many Bedouins have given up their traditional ways for the higher standard of living of the city.

A Saudi prince flies home from France on his luxurious private jet. Oil has brought tremendous wealth to some Saudi leaders.

Case Study Assessment

1. Which groups have ruled Saudi Arabia over time?

2. How does Islam influence Saudi life?

3. **Activity** Create a comic book to teach Saudi history. Choose one event from the country's history and illustrate it in comic book style.

SAUDI ARABIA **229**

Main Idea

Culture and Achievements

Recall What type of government does Saudi Arabia have? *an absolute monarchy*

Summarize How has oil changed Saudi society? *led to higher incomes and more money to spend on goods; opening of new stores, restaurants, and schools; increased education and literacy rates; better healthcare*

Evaluate What advantages and disadvantages could the type of government practiced in Saudi Arabia pose? *possible answers: advantages—ease of making decisions, less bureaucracy, keeps long Saudi tradition; disadvantages—only a few people have a say in government, the king can remove ministers with whom he disagrees, only members of the royal family have a say in government*

Info to Know

Saudi Government Although Saudi Arabia has an absolute monarchy, the king's power is not unlimited. Because the king must obey the Qur'an and Islamic law, known as Sharia, his powers are not absolute. In addition, a Council of Ministers advises the king on foreign and domestic policies and a consultative assembly, known as the Shura Council, advises the king on a variety of other matters. Members of these councils, however, are not elected; they are appointed by the king. In addition to appointed officials, the king also seeks advice on government decisions from members of the royal family and business and religious leaders.

Structure of the Saudi Arabian Government

Saudi Arabia is a monarchy. Under Saudi law, no one but a descendant of Ibn Saud can rule the country.

The King
The king of Saudi Arabia is an absolute monarch. He makes all government decisions. However, he is required to follow Islamic law.

Council of Ministers
A council of ministers advises the king and makes suggestions for laws, though he must approve all of their actions. The council is largely made up of members of the royal family.

Saudi Arabia Today

Government

Saudi Arabia today is an absolute monarchy. Members of the Saud family—the sons and grandsons of the first king—have ruled the kingdom since it became independent in 1932. The king makes all decisions in the country, and his word is law. However, the king cannot issue any laws that would be against the Qur'an or Shariah (Islamic law).

Since 1953 the king has been advised by a Council of Ministers. This council is made up of about 20 members, most of whom are relatives of the king. They are appointed by the king and can be removed by him at any time. They may advise the king on a variety of issues, but he is not obligated to accept their advice. In addition, the king may ask Islamic scholars and tribal leaders for advice on decisions. The country has no elected legislature.

Economics

Saudi Arabia's economy is based on oil. In fact, Saudi Arabia has the world's largest reserves, or supply, of oil and is the world's leading oil exporter. Because it controls so much oil, Saudi Arabia is an influential member of OPEC. As a result, it influences the price of oil on the world market. Countries around the world want to have good relations with Saudi Arabia because of its vast oil reserves.

Oil has brought great wealth to Saudi Arabia. Income from oil exports has given the government money to invest in improvements such as new apartments, communications systems, airports, oil pipelines, and roads. For example, in 1960 Saudi Arabia had only about 1,000 miles (1,600 km) of roads. By 2005 it had over 94,000 miles (152,000 km) of roads. These improvements have helped modernize the economy.

Oil exports have also affected Saudi society. Rising incomes have given many Saudis more money to spend on consumer goods. New stores and restaurants have opened, and new schools have been built throughout the country. Education is now available to all citizens. Increased education means the literacy rate has increased as well—from about 3 percent when oil was discovered to about 79 percent today. Health care there has also improved.

Differentiating Instruction

Special Needs Learners

1. Copy the graphic organizer below for everyone to see. Have students copy the diagram on their own sheet of paper.

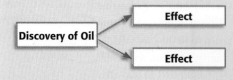

2. Discuss with the class one of the effects of the discovery of oil in Saudi Arabia. Then have students complete the graphic organizer by identifying other effects. Students may need to add more boxes as necessary.

3. Have students share their completed diagrams with the class. **LS Verbal/Linguistic**

   Alternative Assessment Handbook, Rubric 13: Graphic Organizers

Issues

Although oil has made Saudi Arabia very rich, the country still faces economic challenges. For example, it must import much of its food because fresh water needed for farming is scarce. Efforts to increase food production have resulted in larger crop harvests, but these efforts have also severely drained the country's water supply. The country uses desalinization plants to remove salt from seawater, but this requires an extremely expensive procedure.

Another economic challenge for Saudi Arabia is its high unemployment rate. One reason for the lack of jobs is the high population growth rate. More than 40 percent of Saudis are younger than 15. Another reason for unemployment is that many young Saudis choose to study religion instead of the technical subjects their economy requires. As a result, many of the people employed in Saudi Arabia's oil industry are foreign workers. In fact, non-Saudis make up nearly 20 percent of the country's population today.

Saudi Arabia's Economy

3% 17% 45% 35%

- ■ Petroleum Industry
- ■ Services
- ■ Agriculture
- ■ Other Industries

Source: CIA, *The World Factbook 2008*

Case Study Assessment

1. Why is oil a major industry in Saudi Arabia?
2. What are two issues that face the country?
3. **Activity** Compare the Saudi government to the U.S. government. Create a chart that lists similarities and differences between the two.

Saudi Arabia's desert climate makes agriculture a challenge. In recent years, the government has encouraged farmers to use intensive irrigation to increase their crop production.

Saudi Arabian Food Imports vs. Production

1984
Production 34%
Imports 66%

1995
Imports 26%
Production 74%

Source: The Trade and Environment Database

SAUDI ARABIA **231**

Critical Thinking: Solving Problems

At Level

Planning for Saudi Arabia's Future

Research Required

1. Review with students the issues that face Saudi Arabia today, including the need to improve food production, high unemployment, and the future of the country's oil reserves. Discuss with students the potential problems that could result from each issue.

2. Organize the class into pairs and have each pair select one issue. Have students use the library, the Internet, and other sources to research the background and potential problems related to their selected issue.

3. After students have completed their research, have each pair develop possible solutions for how to deal with problems related to their topic. For example, students concentrating on Saudi Arabia's water supply might recommend the construction of more desalinization plants.

4. Have each pair select the solution that they believe works best. Then have each pair present their solution to the class.

LS Verbal/Linguistic, Interpersonal

Alternative Assessment Handbook, Rubric 35: Solving Problems

Document-Based Question

Unit 2: Peace in the Middle East

Word Help

coexistence to live together in peace
escalating increasing in amount or volume
brink the edge of something

Info to Know

Camp David Accords By 1978 Egypt and Israel had been at war for decades. In 1948, shortly after the creation of Israel, several Arab states—including Egypt—went to war against Israel. In a subsequent war in 1967, Israel took over Egyptian territory in the Sinai Peninsula. Although the UN called for an Israeli withdrawal from this and other territory, Israel refused. When Israeli and Egyptian leaders expressed an interest in ending the hostilities between the two countries, U.S. President Jimmy Carter arranged a private meeting between himself, Egyptian President Anwar Sadat, and Israeli Prime Minister Menachem Begin. The successful meetings at Camp David led to peace between Egypt and Israel and won Begin and Sadat the Nobel Peace Prize for 1978. In 2002 Jimmy Carter was awarded the Nobel Peace Prize for his efforts to promote international peace.

Peace in the Middle East

Part A: Short-Answer Questions

Directions: Read and examine the following documents. Then, on a separate sheet of paper, answer the questions using complete sentences.

DOCUMENT 1

In 1978 President Jimmy Carter of the United States, President Anwar Sadat of Egypt, and Prime Minister Menachim Begin of Israel met at Camp David, the U.S. president's private retreat. The result of their meeting was the Camp David Accords, the first peace treaty between Israel and an Arab country. An excerpt appears below.

> After four wars during 30 years, despite intensive human efforts, the Middle East, which is the cradle of civilization and the birthplace of three great religions, does not enjoy the blessings of peace. The people of the Middle East yearn for peace so that the vast human and natural resources of the region can be turned to the pursuits of peace and so that this area can become a model for coexistence and cooperation among nations.
>
> —**Camp David Accords**

1a. How long were Egypt and Israel at war before the Camp David Accords?

1b. What benefit does the document say peace will bring to the region?

DOCUMENT 2

The Camp David Accords did not lead to lasting peace in the Middle East. Violence once again plagues the region. In 2008 Secretary General Kofi Annan of the United Nations expressed his concern about the ongoing violence in the region.

> I am deeply concerned at the possibility of the violence escalating. I have offered our strong support for all efforts to bring about an end to the violence and a period of calm. I call on all parties to step back from the brink of even deeper and more deadly clashes.
>
> —**Kofi Annan,** March 1, 2008

2a. What does the speaker ask leaders in the Middle East to do?

2b. How might the United Nations help resolve conflict in the region?

Answers

Document 1 1a. *30 years;* **1b.** *The area will become a model of coexistence and cooperation.*
Document 2 2a. *make efforts to bring an end to escalating violence;*
2b. *possible answers—promoting efforts at peace, holding peace talks between the different sides*

Critical Thinking: Sequencing

At Level

Middle East Peace Talks Time Line

Research Required

1. Organize the class into small groups. Have each group create a time line depicting key events in the efforts to bring peace to the Middle East.

2. Have students use the library, the Internet, and other sources to find information about major steps in the peace process in the Middle East. Remind students to also include events that have derailed or delayed the peace process.

3. Remind students to identify the year of each event in order to place the events on a time line in correct chronological order.

4. Have students share their time lines with the class. **LS Visual/Spatial, Verbal/Linguistic**

   Alternative Assessment Handbook, Rubrics 14: Group Activity; and 36: Time Lines

DOCUMENT 3

As the department responsible for international relations, the U.S. State Department is deeply concerned about conflict in the Middle East. In 2003 the department issued a plan that it called a roadmap to a solution for the conflict. A key portion of this roadmap was the creation of two states, one Israeli and one Palestinian.

> A two-state solution to the Israeli–Palestinian conflict will only be achieved through an end to violence and terrorism, when the Palestinian people have a leadership acting decisively against terror and willing and able to build a practicing democracy based on tolerance and liberty, and through Israel's readiness to do what is necessary for a democratic Palestinian state to be established, and a clear, unambiguous acceptance by both parties of the goal of a negotiated settlement.
>
> —U.S. Department of State, "A Performance-Based Roadmap to a Permanent Two-State Solution to the Israeli-Palestinian Conflict," 2003

3a. What does the State Department say the Palestinians must do to achieve peace?

_____

3b. What does the State Department say the Israelis must do to achieve peace?

_____

DOCUMENT 4

The idea of a roadmap to peace in the Middle East has been met with both optimism and scorn in other parts of the world. One observer's opinion of the idea is expressed in the political cartoon below. It first appeared in the Indian newspaper *National Herald*.

4a. Based on this cartoon, what do you think is the cartoonist's opinion about peace in the Middle East?

_____

4b. What evidence from the cartoon supports your position?

_____

Part B: Essay

Historical Context: The Middle East has been the site of violent conflict for decades. Leaders from the region as well as interested parties from around the world have sought to resolve the conflict, but so far no permanent solution has been found.

TASK: Using information from the four documents and your knowledge of social studies, write an essay in which you:

> • identify the reasons for bringing peace to the region.
> • analyze solutions that have been proposed to the conflict.

THE MIDDLE EAST **233**

Word Help

tolerance willingness to respect the beliefs of others
unambiguous not vague; clear

Info to Know

Middle East Peace Process Numerous attempts have been made to help Israel and Palestinian leaders negotiate a successful peace in their decades-long conflict. The United States has often played a key role in the peace process, bringing representatives from both sides to the negotiating table. In 1991 President George H. W. Bush co-sponsored the Madrid Conference, in an attempt to bring peace to the Middle East. Bill Clinton in 1993 oversaw the Oslo Accords which laid the framework for future peace settlements. In 2003 President George W. Bush helped establish the so-called Road Map to Peace between Israel and Palestine.

Critical Thinking: Supporting a Point of View   `At Level`

Preparing for the Essay

1. Review with students the directions for writing the essay. Point out to students that their essay responses should include two key parts—the reasons for bringing peace to the Middle East, and solutions that have been proposed to reach a peace.

2. Instruct students to use the documents on these pages to develop a list of the reasons for peace, with solutions to accomplish peace.

3. Have students consider how each item on their lists has helped bring about better relations.

4. Have students create a thesis statement that summarizes their key points. Then have students plan their essay around the thesis statement they created. **LS Verbal/Linguistic**

📖 Alternative Assessment Handbook, Rubric 40: Writing to Describe

Answers

Document 3 3a. *practice democracy and tolerance and support a government that does not condone terrorism*
3b. *do what is necessary to establish a democratic government in Palestine*
Document 4 4a. *possible answers— It is confusing and hard to solve; it is extremely complicated.* **4b.** *many puzzle peaces, oddly-shaped puzzle pieces that appear to be difficult to fit together; the sweat of those working on the puzzle*
Essay *Students' essays will vary but should thoroughly address all aspects of the task.*

Motivate Discuss the things students do in their own lives that involve comparing and contrasting (buying anything new, deciding what movie or TV show to view). Ask: In what way do these activities involve comparing and contrasting?

Direct Teach

Prewrite

Organizing Information Explain the options students have for organizing the information in their papers:

- **Block Style 1** Discuss one country first and then the other.
- **Block Style 2** Discuss the similarities of the two countries first and then the differences.
- **Point-by-Point Style** Discuss the similarities and differences one aspect at a time, devoting separate paragraphs to physical geography, government, and/or culture.

Practice & Apply

Revising and Proofreading

Activity Working in Groups
Allow time for students to share first drafts with partners. Peer feedback is especially helpful during the revising and proofreading stages of writing. Partners/groups can point out details that need clarification, material to add or delete, and errors in grammar, punctuation, and spelling.

Rubric

Students' papers should

- start with an interesting fact or question relating to both countries.
- clearly identify the big idea and provide background information.
- write at least one paragraph for each country or each point.
- discuss at least three similarities and differences.
- include facts and details to help explain each point.
- summarize the main similarities and differences in the final paragraph.
- use correct grammar, punctuation, spelling, and capitalization.

Unit 2 Writing Workshop

Compare and Contrast

How are two countries alike? How are they different? Comparing the similarities and contrasting the differences between countries can teach us more than we can learn by studying them separately.

Assignment

Write a paper comparing and contrasting two countries from this unit. Consider physical geography, government, and/or culture.

1. Prewrite

Choose a Topic
- Choose two countries to write about.
- Create a big idea, or thesis, about the two countries. For example, your big idea might be "Iran and Iraq both have oil-based economies, but they also have many differences."

> **TIP** **Organizing Information** A Venn diagram (two overlapping circles) can help you plan your paper. Write similarities in the overlapping area and differences in the areas that do not overlap.

Gather and Organize Information
- Identify at least three similarities or differences between the countries.
- Decide whether to write about each country one at a time or to discuss each point of similarity or difference one at a time.

2. Write

Use a Writer's Framework

> **A Writer's Framework**
>
> **Introduction**
> - Start with a fact or question relating to both countries.
> - Identify your big idea.
>
> **Body**
> - Write at least one paragraph for each country or each point of similarity or difference. Include facts and details to help explain each point.
> - Use block style or point-by-point style.
>
> **Conclusion**
> - Summarize the process in your final paragraph.

3. Evaluate And Revise

Review and Improve Your Paper
- Re-read your draft, then ask yourself the questions below to see if you have followed the framework.
- Make any changes needed to improve your comparison and contrast paper.

Evaluation Questions for a Compare and Contrast Paper
1. Do you begin with an interesting fact or question that relates to both countries?
2. Does your first paragraph clearly state your big idea and provide background information?
3. Do you discuss at least three similarities and differences between the countries?
4. Do you include facts and details to explain each similarity or difference?
5. Is your paper clearly organized by country or by similarities and differences?

4. Proofread And Publish

Give Your Explanation the Finishing Touch
- Make sure you have capitalized the names of countries and cities.
- Check for punctuation around transitional words and phrases like and, but, or similarly.
- Share your compare-and-contrast paper by reading it aloud in class or in small groups.

5. Practice And Apply

Use the steps outlined in this workshop to write a compare-and-contrast paper. Compare and contrast your paper to those of your classmates.

234

Differentiating Instruction

Advanced/Gifted and Talented

Encourage students to supplement the information they find in the text with some library research. Have them do a detailed comparison and contrast of a single aspect of both countries. Give them the following choices or allow them to create their own topics with your approval.

- Compare and contrast the physical geography of the countries, focusing on how the land, water, climate, and resources affect the lives of the people.

- Compare and contrast the histories of the countries, including early inhabitants, the influence of foreign powers, important conflicts, and recent events of significance.

- Compare and contrast one aspect of culture (for example, art, music, architecture, traditions, or celebrations), focusing on qualities unique to each country. **LS Verbal/Linguistic**

Alternative Assessment Handbook, Rubrics 9: Comparing and Contrasting, and 30: Research

Africa

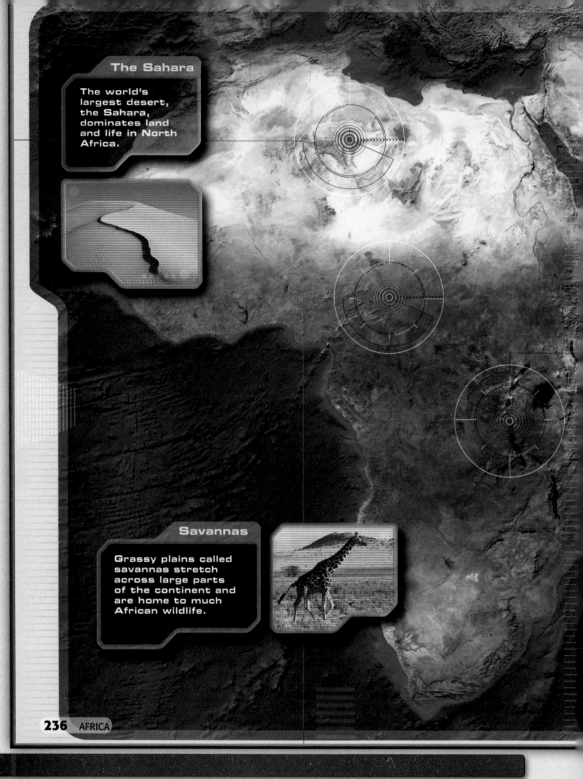

Direct Teach

Introduce the Unit

Share the information in the chapter overviews with students.

Chapter 9 Africa's physical geography varies greatly from place to place. The five geographical regions have different climates, physical features, and resources.

Chapter 10 The civilization of ancient Egypt grew up along the Nile River. The Egyptians made achievements in writing, agriculture, and art.

Chapter 11 Powerful and wealthy trading kingdoms developed in North and West Africa and played a great role in influencing the culture of those regions.

Chapter 12 Modern Africa has been shaped by years of outside influences, colonization, and the struggle for independence. Today, African countries continue to face many changes and challenges.

The Sahara

The world's largest desert, the Sahara, dominates land and life in North Africa.

Savannas

Grassy plains called savannas stretch across large parts of the continent and are home to much African wildlife.

Unit Resources

Planning

- Differentiated Instruction Teacher Management System: Pacing Guide
- OSP One-Stop Planner CD-ROM with Test Generator: Calendar Planner
- Power Presentations with Video CD-ROM
- Virtual File Cabinet

Differentiating Instruction

- Differentiated Instruction Teacher Management System: Lesson Plans for Differentiated Instruction
- Differentiated Instruction Modified Worksheets and Tests CD-ROM

Enrichment

- RF: Interdisciplinary Projects, Irrigation, Simple Machines, and the Nile
- RF: Geography and History, Major Cities of North Africa
- Geography, Science, and Culture Activities with Answer Key

Assessment

- PASS: Benchmark Test
- OSP ExamView Test Generator: Benchmark Test
- HOAP Holt Online Assessment Program, in the Premier Online Student Edition
- Alternative Assessment Handbook

Africa

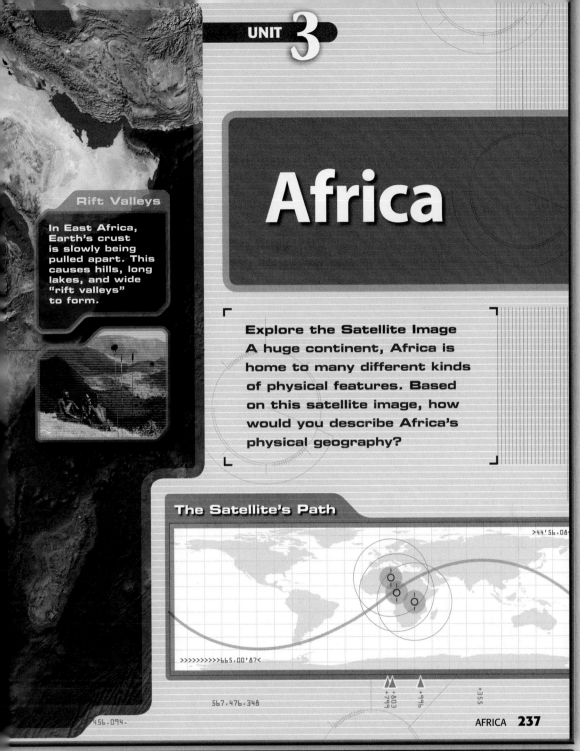

Rift Valleys

In East Africa, Earth's crust is slowly being pulled apart. This causes hills, long lakes, and wide "rift valleys" to form.

Explore the Satellite Image
A huge continent, Africa is home to many different kinds of physical features. Based on this satellite image, how would you describe Africa's physical geography?

The Satellite's Path

>44'56.08<

>>>>>>>>>665.00'87<

567.476.348

456.094.

+803
+799

+996

+355

AFRICA **237**

Connect to the Unit

Activity Write a Commercial
Have small groups write scripts for radio or television commercials encouraging people to visit various regions in Africa. Have them decide whether their commercials will rely more on visual or verbal content. Commercials should include at least two specific and relevant details to support or illustrate its message. Finally, challenge students to create a slogan for each region and to use that slogan in the commercial.

During their study of the unit, have students look for more details they can add to their commercials.
LS Interpersonal

Alternative Assessment Handbook, Rubrics 2: Advertisements; and 34: Slogans and Banners

Explore the Pictures

Point out the photograph and satellite images of the Sahara. Tell students that ancient traders from West Africa crossed the Sahara to trade with Arab and Mediterranean peoples. Ask them what these traders would have had to bring with them in order to survive. *possible answer—plenty of water and food, appropriate clothing* Point out the photograph of the giraffe and ask students what the photograph reveals about the features of the savanna. *dry, flat, limited vegetation* Ask students what other African wildlife might live on the savanna. *possible answers— lions, gazelles, elephants, leopards, hyenas, zebras*

Map Zone Transparency: Africa

Collaborative Learning

At Level

Research Ethnic Groups

Prep Required **Research Required**

1. Provide students with a list of ethnic groups from various parts of Africa. Encourage them to look through the unit to find information about the ethnic groups. Then have students work with a partner to choose a group and write a report about the group's origin, history, and traditions.

2. Encourage students to augment their reports with photographs, literary excerpts, and so on.

3. Invite volunteers to share their reports. Discuss the similarities and differences

among ethnic groups. Lead a discussion about conflicts that might develop between ethnic groups within a country that has limited resources. Discuss the ways in which an ethnic group could be threatened or weakened by an outside influence, such as colonizers or environmental problems such as drought.
LS Verbal/Linguistic

Alternative Assessment Handbook, Rubric 42: Writing to Inform

Answers

Explore the Satellite Image
Africa's physical geography is diverse, ranging from deserts to plains, and highlands to rain forests.

Explore the Map

Africa: Physical As students look at the physical map on this page, point out that Africa is the second-largest continent after Asia.

Place Which African country has the largest region of land over 6,560 feet? *Ethiopia*

Location What are four major geographical features located in Tanzania and Kenya? *Lake Victoria, Mount Kilimanjaro, Serengeti Plain, and Lake Tanganyika*

Region Which region of Africa might have tropical rain forests? Why? *Congo Basin area; possible answer—because it has a low elevation and probably gets plenty of water from the Congo River*

Map Zone Transparency: Africa: Physical

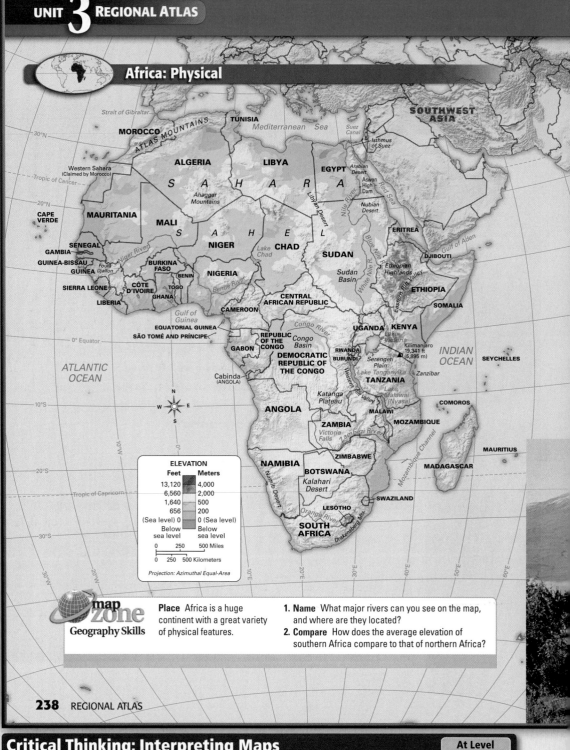

Africa: Physical

ELEVATION

Feet		Meters
13,120		4,000
6,560		2,000
1,640		500
656		200
(Sea level) 0		0 (Sea level)
Below sea level		Below sea level

0   250   500 Miles
0   250   500 Kilometers

Projection: Azimuthal Equal-Area

map Zone
Geography Skills

Place Africa is a huge continent with a great variety of physical features.

1. **Name** What major rivers can you see on the map, and where are they located?
2. **Compare** How does the average elevation of southern Africa compare to that of northern Africa?

Critical Thinking: Interpreting Maps

At Level

Write Africa Facts from A to Z

1. Have students use the physical map on this page to write 26 facts about Africa.

2. Students should write one fact beginning with each letter of the alphabet. Encourage students to preview the information about Africa in their textbooks or use outside sources to locate additional facts and details.

3. Remind students, however, that most of their facts should come from the physical map and World Almanac chart on these two pages.

4. Have students write their facts neatly on a piece of poster board. They should also include 3–5 pictures to make their posters more interesting.

5. Have volunteers present their completed posters to the rest of the class.

LS Verbal/Linguistic, Visual/Spatial

Alternative Assessment Handbook, Rubrics 28: Posters; and 37: Writing Assignments

Answers

Map Zone 1. *Nile, Blue Nile, White Nile (North Africa); Niger, Benue (West Africa); Congo (Central Africa); Orange, Zambezi (southern Africa);* **2.** *The average elevation of southern Africa is higher than that of northern Africa; much of it is above 1,640 feet (500 meters).*

Africa

THE WORLD ALMANAC®
Facts about the World

Geographical Extremes: Africa

Longest River	Nile River, Egypt: 4,160 miles (6,693 km)	**Driest Place**	Wadi Halfa, Sudan: .1 inches (.3 cm) average precipitation per year
Highest Point	Mount Kilimanjaro, Tanzania: 19,340 feet (5,895 m)	**Largest Country**	Sudan: 967,498 square miles (2,505,820 square km)
Lowest Point	Lake Assal, Djibouti: 512 feet (156 m) below sea level	**Smallest Country**	Seychelles: 176 square miles (456 square km)
Highest Recorded Temperature	El Azizia, Libya: 136°F (57.8°C)	**Largest Desert**	Sahara: 3,500,000 square miles (9,065,000 square km)
Lowest Recorded Temperature	Ifrane, Morocco: –11°F (–23.9°C)	**Largest Island**	Madagascar: 226,658 square miles (587,044 square km)
Wettest Place	Debundscha, Cameroon: 405 inches (1,028.7 cm) average precipitation per year	**Highest Waterfall**	Tugela, South Africa: 2,014 feet (614 m)

go.hrw.com KEYWORD: SK9 UN3

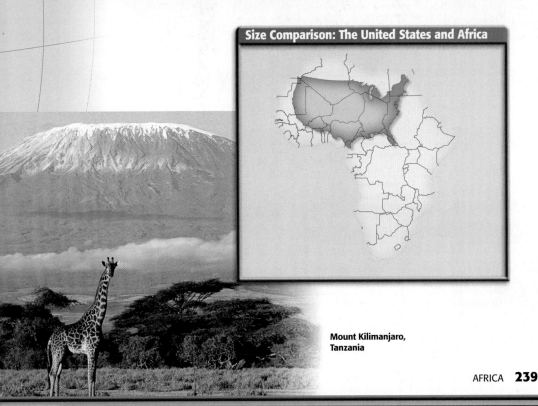

Size Comparison: The United States and Africa

Mount Kilimanjaro, Tanzania

AFRICA **239**

Direct Teach

Africa

Activity **Write a Personal Letter**   Divide students into two groups. Tell one group to imagine that they live on Mount Kilimanjaro with a view of the Serengeti Plain. Tell the other group to imagine that they live on the Serengeti Plain with a view of Mount Kilimanjaro. Have each student write a letter to a classmate in the other group describing their environment and the view from their house. Then have students exchange letters.

Lead a class discussion about the varied physical geography of Africa, as well as people's perspective and different points of view. Ask volunteers to read their letters out loud.

LS **Verbal/Linguistic, Intrapersonal, Interpersonal**

▢ Alternative Assessment Handbook, Rubrics 11: Discussions; 25: Personal Letters; and 40: Writing to Describe

▢ Interactive Skills Tutor CD-ROM, Lesson 18: Identify Point of View and Frame of Reference

▢ Map Zone Transparency: Size Comparison: The United States and Africa

---

Differentiating Instruction

English-Language Learners
At Level
Standard English Mastery

1. Have students draw a three-circle Venn Diagram, labeling the circles Nile River, Congo River, and Zambezi River.

2. Students should use standard English to write details in their Venn diagrams comparing and contrasting the three rivers. Challenge students to list at least five facts in each section. **LS** **Verbal/Linguistic, Visual/Spatial**

▢ Alternative Assessment Handbook, Rubrics 9: Comparing and Contrasting; and 21: Map Reading

Special Needs Learners
Below Level

1. Give each student about 20 inches of string or yarn and an enlarged copy of the physical map of Africa. Have each student tape string along the rivers in Africa. Have them cover the lakes in the region with string, as well.

2. Lead a class discussion about the importance of fresh water in Africa. Remind students that both people and animals rely on this precious resource for survival.

LS **Visual/Spatial, Kinesthetic**

▢ Alternative Assessment Handbook, Rubrics 11: Discussions; and 21: Map Reading

AFRICA **239**

Explore the Map

Africa: Political As students examine the map on this page, point out the straight national boundaries in nothern and southern Africa. Explain that one reason the borders may have been drawn this way is because the regions are dry, sparsely populated areas where there are no rivers or other physical features to serve as natural boundaries.

Place What country is completely surrounded by another country? *Lesotho* What country surrounds it? *South Africa*

Location What country lies mostly on the mainland, but its capital is located on an island? *Equatorial Guinea*

Region What country claims Western Sahara? *Morocco* What country controls the Cabinda region? *Angola*

🗺 Map Zone Transparency: Africa: Political

Answers

Map Zone 1. *Madagascar, Mauritius, Seychelles, São Tomé and Príncipe, Comoros, Cape Verde;* **2.** *possible answer—The capitals are located along the Mediterranean coast. They are north of the harsh desert climate of the Sahara.*

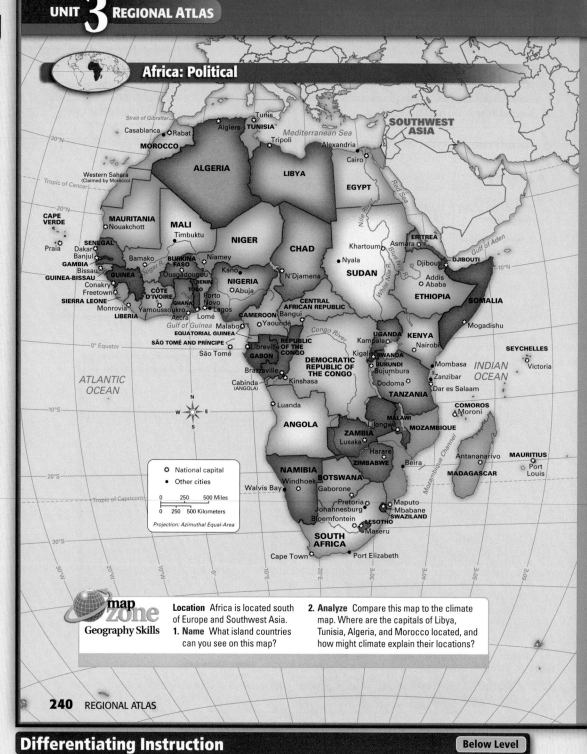

Africa: Political

Location Africa is located south of Europe and Southwest Asia.
1. Name What island countries can you see on this map?

2. Analyze Compare this map to the climate map. Where are the capitals of Libya, Tunisia, Algeria, and Morocco located, and how might climate explain their locations?

Differentiating Instruction

Below Level

Struggling Readers

1. Give struggling readers a blank outline map of Africa.

2. Have students lightly shade the mainland countries that have a seacoast with a blue colored pencil and label them. Have them shade the landlocked countries with an orange colored pencil and label them. Students should use a green pencil to shade Africa's island nations and label them.

3. Instruct students to use black marker to draw an "L" on Africa's largest country (Sudan), an "E" on the easternmost mainland country

(Somalia), and an "S" on the southernmost mainland country (South Africa).

4. Have students compare their maps with the physical map of Africa. Then tell them to draw slanted lines on the countries with access to lakes and rivers.

5. Finally, tell students to draw black dots on the five countries that border the Mediterranean Sea. **LS** Visual/Spatial, Auditory/Musical

Alternative Assessment Handbook, Rubrics **18:** Listening; **20:** Map Creation; and **21:** Map Reading

Africa

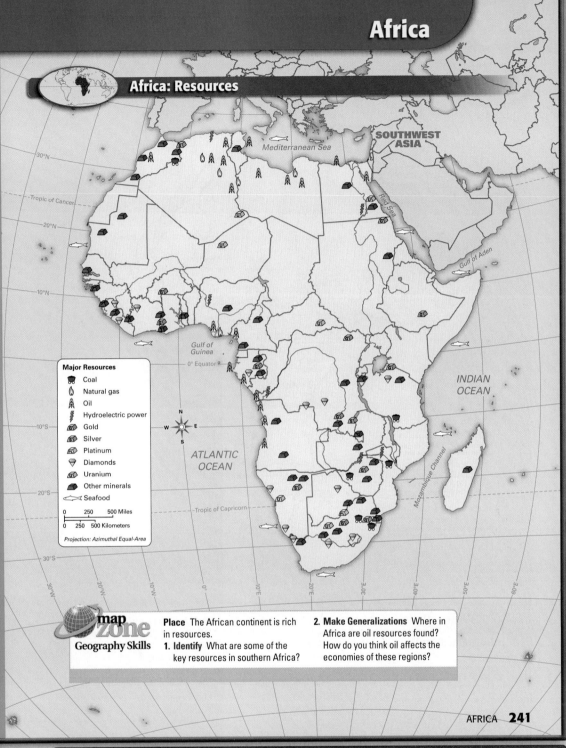

SOUTHWEST ASIA

Mediterranean Sea

Tropic of Cancer

Red Sea

Gulf of Aden

Gulf of Guinea

0° Equator

INDIAN OCEAN

ATLANTIC OCEAN

Mozambique Channel

Tropic of Capricorn

Major Resources

- Coal
- Natural gas
- Oil
- Hydroelectric power
- Gold
- Silver
- Platinum
- Diamonds
- Uranium
- Other minerals
- Seafood

0   250   500 Miles
0   250   500 Kilometers
Projection: Azimuthal Equal-Area

map zone
Geography Skills

Place The African continent is rich in resources.
1. Identify What are some of the key resources in southern Africa?

2. Make Generalizations Where in Africa are oil resources found? How do you think oil affects the economies of these regions?

AFRICA **241**

Direct Teach

Explore the Map

Africa: Resources As students examine the resource map on this page, point out the uneven distribution of resources in Africa: most of the oil and gas is found in northern Africa, while some countries have few or no major resources.

Human/Environment Interaction Compare this map to the physical and political maps of Africa. What countries use water resources to produce hydroelectric power? *Egypt, Algeria, Nigeria, Zambia, Mozambique, and Zimbabwe*

Region Compare this map to the political map of Africa. What mainland countries have no major resources? *Mali, Chad, Eritrea, Djibouti, Somalia, Uganda, Malawi* What economic activities do you think these countries depend on instead of manufacturing or mining? *possible answers—farming, raising livestock*

Place What resources are found on Madagascar? *other minerals*

Map Zone Transparency: Africa: Land Use and Resources

Differentiating Instruction

Above Level

Advanced/Gifted and Talented Students

Research Required

1. Have students use the resource map on this page to identify the African countries where seafood is a major resource.

2. Then have students conduct research to learn what types of fish and seafood are prominent in each region of Africa. Have students find out which types of seafood are more valued economically.

3. Students should create a graphic to illustrate their findings. The chart should compare and contrast the types of fish and seafood found

around the various coasts of Africa and give their values.

4. Then have students write a report about their findings using this prompt: Imagine you are a fisher in Africa. In what country would you want to live in order to run a successful business? Give reasons based on research to support your answer.

LS **Verbal/Linguistic, Logical/Mathematical**

Alternative Assessment Handbook, Rubrics 7: Charts; 30: Research; and 37: Writing Assignments

---

Answers

Map Zone 1. *seafood, diamonds, coal, uranium, platinum, silver, gold, and other minerals;* **2.** *possible answer—Most oil is located along the west-central coast and in northern Africa; those countries might have strong economies because they can export so much oil.*

241

Explore the Map

Africa: Population Have students compare the population map on this page with the physical map of Africa. Discuss reasons why the eastern part of southern Africa is more densely populated than the western part. *Namib and Kalahari deserts cover much of western Africa; eastern part has water from the Zambezi River and lakes.*

Place Which country has the most cities with more than 2 million inhabitants? *Egypt*

Location What are the three largest African cities located south of the equator? *Kinshasa, Nairobi, and Johannesburg*

Map Zone Transparency: Africa: Population

Africa: Population

Strait of Gibraltar

Algiers

Mediterranean Sea

SOUTHWEST ASIA

Alexandria

Cairo

Nile River

30°N

Tropic of Cancer

20°N

Red Sea

Khartoum

Gulf of Aden

10°N

Niger River

Kano

Abidjan

Lagos

Gulf of Guinea

0° Equator

Nairobi

INDIAN OCEAN

ATLANTIC OCEAN

N W E S

Kinshasa

10°S

Persons per square mile	**Persons per square km**
520	200
260	100
130	50
25	10
3	1
0	0

Mozambique Channel

20°S

Tropic of Capricorn

Johannesburg

● Major cities over 2 million

0   125   250 Miles
0   125   250 Kilometers

Projection: Azimuthal Equal-Area

30°S

30°W 20°W 10°W 0° 10°E 20°E 30°E 40°E 50°E 60°E

map zone

Geography Skills

Regions Many areas of Africa have a relatively even population density.
1. **Name** What river in North Africa has a very high population density along its course?

2. **Analyze** Compare this map to the climate map. How does climate seem to influence population patterns in Africa?

Collaborative Learning

At Level

Identify Population Regions

1. Have students name the relative locations of the most highly-populated regions in Africa. List these on the board. *possible answers— around Gulf of Guinea, northeast corner, upper northwest, near lake in East Africa, southeast corner*

2. Then have students compare this map with the political map of Africa. Ask them to identify countries in each of these regions. Have volunteers locate each country on a large classroom map.

3. Lead a class discussion giving possible reasons why these countries are more highly populated than the rest of Africa. *climate, natural resources, physical features, access to the coast* Encourage students to compare this map with other maps of Africa in the Regional Atlas to aid in the discussion.

LS Visual/Spatial, Verbal/Linguistic

Alternative Assessment Handbook, Rubrics 11: Discussions; and 21: Map Reading

Answers

Map Zone 1. *Nile River;* **2.** *possible answer—Most people live in the Mediterranean, steppe, and tropical savanna climate regions; the desert regions are sparsely populated, if at all.*

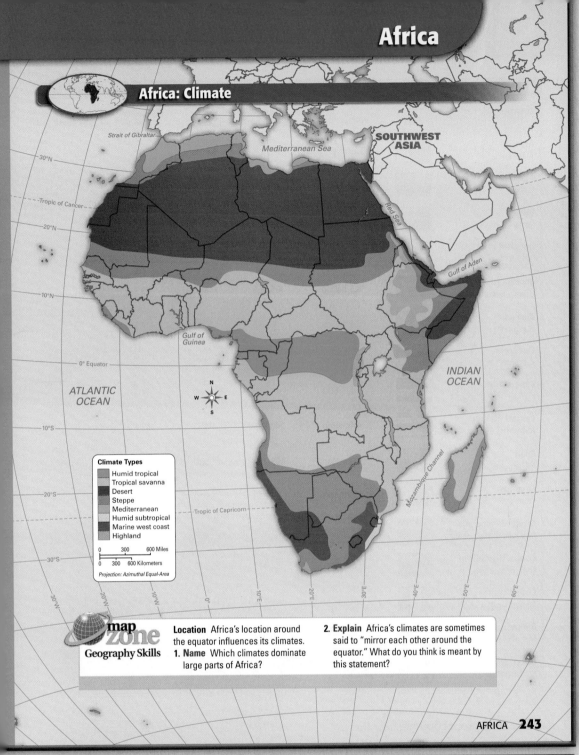

Africa: Climate

SOUTHWEST ASIA

Strait of Gibraltar

Mediterranean Sea

Red Sea

Gulf of Aden

Tropic of Cancer

30°N

20°N

10°N

0° Equator

Gulf of Guinea

ATLANTIC OCEAN

INDIAN OCEAN

10°S

20°S

Tropic of Capricorn

Mozambique Channel

30°S

Climate Types
- Humid tropical
- Tropical savanna
- Desert
- Steppe
- Mediterranean
- Humid subtropical
- Marine west coast
- Highland

0 300 600 Miles
0 300 600 Kilometers

Projection: Azimuthal Equal-Area

map zone
Geography Skills

Location Africa's location around the equator influences its climates.
1. Name Which climates dominate large parts of Africa?

2. Explain Africa's climates are sometimes said to "mirror each other around the equator." What do you think is meant by this statement?

Explore the Map

Africa: Climate Have students compare the climate map on this page with the population map of Africa. Discuss ways that climate affects population in Africa. Point out that both the humid tropical climate region in central Africa and the desert regions in the north and south are areas of lower population density.

Region What climate type dominates most of northern Africa? *desert*

Place What climate type is least common in Africa? *humid subtropical* Where is this climate found? *in the southeast corner of Africa*

Location Compare this map with the political map of Africa. What countries have a highland climate? *Sudan, Eritrea, Ethiopia, Uganda, Kenya, Rwanda, Democratic Republic of the Congo, Burundi, Tanzania*

Map Zone Transparency: Africa: Climate

Differentiating Instruction

Below Level

Special Needs Learners

Prep Required

Materials: sandpaper, green felt, straw or hay, tiny pebbles, blue ribbon, scissors, glue

1. Have students use the climate map on this page to create a textured map of Africa.

2. Give each student an outline map of Africa. Students should use sandpaper to cover areas with a desert climate, straw or hay for steppe and tropical savanna climates, green felt for humid tropical climate, small pebbles for highland climate, and blue ribbon for marine west coast climate.

3. On the board, help students create a textured map legend to write on their maps.

4. Have students compare their textured maps to a political map of Africa. Then have students ask each other questions such as, "What type of climate does Egypt have?" or "What climate type does the green felt represent?"

LS Visual/Spatial, Kinesthetic

Alternative Assessment Handbook, Rubric 20: Map Creation

Answers

Map Zone 1. *desert and tropical savanna;* **2.** *possible answer—Moving either north or south from the equator, a traveler would experience similar climate conditions. A humid tropical climate exists at the equator. A savanna climate is found north and south of the humid tropical zone. Steppe and desert climates are found north and south of the savanna zone.*

THE WORLD ALMANAC® Facts about Countries

World Almanac: Facts about Countries

Identify Which African countries have the highest and lowest life expectancy at birth? *highest—Libya, lowest—Swaziland*

Contrast Based on the number of TVs per every 1,000 people, how does daily life differ in Chad and Gabon? *Most people in Chad do not own TVs, so they spend their free time doing other activities; In Gabon one out of every four people owns a TV so they probably spend some of their free time watching TV for entertainment and for news.*

Evaluate Do you think other countries should provide economic aid to countries with low life expectancies? Why or why not? *Students' answers will vary, but they should provide logical reasons for their opinions.*

Africa

COUNTRY Capital	FLAG	POPULATION	AREA (sq mi)	PER CAPITA GDP (U.S. $)	LIFE EXPECTANCY AT BIRTH	TVS PER 1,000 PEOPLE
Algeria Algiers		33.3 million	919,595	$7,700	73.5	107
Angola Luanda		12.2 million	481,354	$4,300	37.6	15
Benin Porto-Novo		8.1 million	43,483	$1,100	53.4	44
Botswana Gaborone		1.8 million	231,804	$11,400	33.7	21
Burkina Faso Ouagadougou		14.3 million	105,869	$1,300	49.2	11
Burundi Bujumbura		8.4 million	10,745	$700	51.3	15
Cameroon Yaoundé		18.1 million	183,568	$2,400	52.9	34
Cape Verde Praia		423,600	1,557	$6,000	71.0	5
Central African Republic; Bangui		4.4 million	240,535	$1,100	43.7	6
Chad N'Djamena		9.9 million	495,755	$1,500	47.9	1
Comoros Moroni		711,400	838	$600	62.7	4
Congo, Democratic Republic of the; Kinshasa		65.8 million	905,568	$700	51.9	2
Congo, Republic of the; Brazzaville		3.8 million	132,047	$1,300	53.3	13
Côte d'Ivoire Yamoussoukro		18 million	124,503	$1,600	49.0	65
Djibouti Djibouti		496,400	8,880	$1,000	43.3	48
United States Washington, D.C.		301.1 million	3,718,711	$43,500	78.0	844

Cross-Discipline Activity: Mathematics

At Level

Calculate Mean, Median, and Mode

1. Divide the class into five groups and assign each group a region of Africa to analyze statistics: northern, southern, west, east, or central Africa.

2. Using the data on the World Almanac chart, have students calculate the mean (average), median (middle figure), and mode (most common figure) for the countries in their assigned region's population, area, per capita GDP, and life expectancy at birth.

3. Each student should calculate the figures individually, then group members should compare answers for accuracy.

4. Each group should create a fact sheet displaying the mean, median, and mode for their region's categories. Have groups present general summaries of their findings.

LS Logical/Mathematical, Verbal/Linguistic

Alternative Assessment Handbook, Rubrics 14: Group Activity; 28: Posters; 29: Presentations; and 35: Solving Problems

COUNTRY Capital	FLAG	POPULATION	AREA (sq mi)	PER CAPITA GDP (U.S. $)	LIFE EXPECTANCY AT BIRTH	TVS PER 1,000 PEOPLE
Egypt Cairo		80.3 million	386,662	$4,200	71.6	170
Equatorial Guinea Malabo		551,200	10,831	$50,200	49.5	116
Eritrea Asmara		4.9 million	46,842	$1,000	59.6	16
Ethiopia Addis Ababa		76.5 million	435,186	$1,000	49.2	5
Gabon Libreville		1.5 million	103,347	$7,200	54.0	251
Gambia Banjul		1.7 million	4,363	$2,000	54.5	3
Ghana Accra		22.9 million	92,456	$2,600	59.1	115
Guinea Conakry		9.9 million	94,926	$2,000	49.7	47
Guinea-Bissau Bissau		1.5 million	13,946	$900	47.2	43
Kenya Nairobi		36.9 million	224,962	$1,200	55.3	22
Lesotho Maseru		2.1 million	11,720	$2,600	34.5	16
Liberia Monrovia		3.2 million	43,000	$1,000	40.4	26
Libya Tripoli		6 million	679,362	$12,700	76.9	139
Madagascar Antananarivo		19.4 million	226,657	$900	62.1	23
Malawi Lilongwe		13.6 million	45,745	$600	43.0	3
United States Washington, D.C.		301.1 million	3,718,711	$43,500	78.0	844

AFRICA **245**

Direct Teach

World Almanac: Facts about Countries

Checking for Understanding

True or False Answer each statement *T* if it is true or *F* if it is false. If false, explain why.

1. The population of the Democratic Republic of the Congo is more than 15 times the population of the Republic of the Congo. *T*

2. Equatorial Guinea in Africa has a higher per capita GDP than the United States. *T*

Cross Discipline Activity: Arts and the Humanities

At Level

Make a Collage

Research Required

1. Have students use the information in the World Almanac chart on these pages to create a collage about an African country of their choice. Students should also conduct outside research to find additional information and images for their collages.

2. Students' collages should be in the shape of each student's selected country. Students should first create and cut out an enlarged shape of their country on heavy art paper.

3. Students should then divide their country into three sections. For each section, students

should use a different material. The first section could be words—headlines or letters cut out of magazines and newspapers using words that describe their country. A second section could be images of their country's physical and human features. Students should think creatively and use materials besides words and pictures to fill the third section.

4. Have volunteers share their completed collages with the rest of the class.

LS Visual/Spatial, Verbal/Linguistic, Kinesthetic

Alternative Assessment Handbook, Rubrics 3: Artwork; and 30: Research

AFRICA 245

Direct Teach

World Almanac: Facts about Countries

Activity **Write a Biography** Have students conduct research and choose a famous African about whom to write a biography. (You may wish to prepare a list of biography subjects ahead of time and have each student select a person from the list.) Students' biographies should include the following:

- brief summary of the person's life
- list of characteristics or qualities describing the person
- three or more positive achievements
- time line listing dates and major events from the person's life
- brief summary explaining the impact the person had on others
- image (photo or painting) of the person, if possible

Have students use a variety of sources to conduct research about the person they selected, including primary and secondary sources, interviews, Internet news articles, television features, encyclopedias, books, magazines, and newspapers. Remind students to create a bibliography as they find information to include in their biographies.

Students may choose how to present their biographies. They may create a poster, multimedia presentation, oral presentation, written report, or other teacher-approved method of sharing their information. **LS Verbal/Linguistic**

📑 Alternative Assessment Handbook, Rubrics 29: Presentations; 30: Research; 36: Time Lines; and 42: Writing to Inform

💿 Interactive Skills Tutor CD-ROM, Lesson 4: Use a Variety of Sources to Gather Information

THE WORLD ALMANAC Facts about Countries

COUNTRY Capital	FLAG	POPULATION	AREA (sq mi)	PER CAPITA GDP (U.S. $)	LIFE EXPECTANCY AT BIRTH	TVS PER 1,000 PEOPLE
Mali Bamako		11.9 million	478,767	$1,200	49.5	13
Mauritania Nouakchott		3.3 million	397,955	$2,600	53.5	95
Mauritius Port Louis		1.3 million	788	$13,500	72.9	248
Morocco Rabat		33.8 million	172,414	$4,400	71.2	165
Mozambique Maputo		20.9 million	309,496	$1,500	40.9	5
Namibia Windhoek		2.1 million	318,696	$7,400	43.1	38
Niger Niamey		13 million	489,191	$1,000	44.0	15
Nigeria Abuja		135 million	356,669	$1,400	47.4	69
Rwanda Kigali		9.9 million	10,169	$1,600	49.0	0.09
São Tomé and Príncipe; São Tomé		199,600	386	$1,200	67.6	229
Senegal Dakar		12.5 million	75,749	$1,800	56.7	41
Seychelles Victoria		81,900	176	$7,800	72.3	214
Sierra Leone Freetown		6.1 million	27,699	$900	40.6	13
Somalia Mogadishu		9.1 million	246,201	$600	48.8	14
United States Washington, D.C.		301.1 million	3,718,711	$43,500	78.0	844

246 FACTS ABOUT COUNTRIES

Cross Discipline Activity: Government | At Level

Compare Governments in Africa | Research Required

1. Have students use current almanacs to research information about types of government in Africa.

2. Give each student an outline map of Africa with each country labeled. Students should then shade each country on the map according to its type of government. Remind students to create a map legend explaining what type of government each color represents. Students should title their maps as well.

3. Instruct students to compare their government maps with the data on the World Almanac chart on these pages. Have them look for relationships between government and countries with high per capita GDPs. Lead a class discussion about what effect(s) a form of government might have on a country's per capita GDP. **LS Visual/Spatial, Verbal/Linguistic**

📑 Alternative Assessment Handbook, Rubrics 11: Discussions; 20: Map Creation; and 30: Research

COUNTRY Capital	FLAG	POPULATION	AREA (sq mi)	PER CAPITA GDP (U.S. $)	LIFE EXPECTANCY AT BIRTH	TVS PER 1,000 PEOPLE
South Africa; Pretoria, Cape Town, Bloemfontein		44 million	471,010	$13,000	42.5	138
Sudan Khartoum		39.4 million	967,498	$2,300	59.3	173
Swaziland Mbabane		1.2 million	6,704	$5,500	32.2	112
Tanzania Dar es Salaam, Dodoma		39.4 million	364,900	$800	46.1	21
Togo Lomé		5.7 million	21,925	$1,700	57.9	22
Tunisia Tunis		10.3 million	63,170	$8,600	75.3	190
Uganda Kampala		30.3 million	91,136	$1,800	51.8	28
Zambia Lusaka		11.5 million	290,586	$1,000	38.4	145
Zimbabwe Harare		12.3 million	150,804	$2,000	39.5	35
United States Washington, D.C.		301.1 million	3,718,711	$43,500	78.0	844

Africa's Growing Population

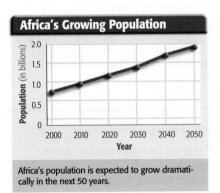

Africa's population is expected to grow dramatically in the next 50 years.

Africa and the World

	Average Age	Life Expectancy at Birth	Per Capita GDP (in U.S. $)
Africa	19.3 years	51.9	$2,800
Rest of the World	28.0 years	65.7	$10,000

Compared to the rest of the world, Africa's population is younger, has a shorter life expectancy, and has less money.

ANALYSIS SKILL ANALYZING INFORMATION

1. Based on the information above, what do you think are some key challenges in Africa today?

AFRICA **247**

247

Chapter 9 Planning Guide

Physical Geography of Africa

Chapter Overview	Reproducible Resources	Technology Resources
CHAPTER 9 pp. 248–275 **Overview:** In this chapter, students will study the physical geography of the Africa's five different regions.	**Differentiated Instruction Teacher Management System:*** • Instructional Pacing Guides • Lesson Plans for Differentiated Instruction **Interactive Reader and Study Guide:** Chapter Summary Graphic Organizer* **Resource File:*** • Chapter Review • Focus on Reading: Understanding Comparison-Contrast • Focus on Writing: Writing a Letter Home • Social Studies Skills: Analyzing a Precipitation Map	**OSP Teacher's One-Stop Planner:** Calendar Planner **Power Presentations with Video CD-ROM** **Differentiated Instruction Modified Worksheets and Tests CD-ROM** **Student Edition on Audio CD Program** **Map Zone Transparency:** Africa: Physical* **Geography's Impact Video Program (VHS/DVD):** Impact of Desertification **World Outline Maps: Transparencies and Activities**
Section 1: **North Africa** **The Big Idea:** North Africa is a dry region with limited water resources.	**Differentiated Instruction Teacher Management System:** Section 1 Lesson Plan* **Interactive Reader and Study Guide:** Section 1 Summary **Resource File:*** • Vocabulary Builder: Section 1 • Geography and History: Major Cities of North Africa	**Daily Bellringer Transparency:** Section 1* **Map Zone Transparency:** North Africa: Physical*
Section 2: **West Africa** **The Big Idea:** West Africa, which is mostly a region of plains, has climates ranging from arid to tropical and has important resources.	**Differentiated Instruction Teacher Management System:** Section 2 Lesson Plan* **Interactive Reader and Study Guide:** Section 2 Summary **Resource File:*** • Vocabulary Builder: Section 2 • Literature: *Knowing Robs Us* by Chinua Achebe	**Daily Bellringer Transparency:** Section 2* **Map Zone Transparency:** West Africa: Physical* **Map Zone Transparency:** West Africa: Climate* **Internet Activity:** Baobab Trees
Section 3: **East Africa** **The Big Idea:** East Africa is a region of diverse physical features, climates, and vegetation.	**Differentiated Instruction Teacher Management System:** Section 3 Lesson Plan* **Interactive Reader and Study Guide:** Section 3 Summary **Resource File:*** • Vocabulary Builder: Section 3 • Biography: Florence Wambugu	**Daily Bellringer Transparency:** Section 3* **Map Zone Transparency:** East Africa: Physical* **Internet Activity:** Drought in East Africa
Section 4: **Central Africa** **The Big Idea:** The Congo River, tropical forests, and mineral resources are important features of Central Africa's physical geography.	**Differentiated Instruction Teacher Management System:** Section 4 Lesson Plan* **Interactive Reader and Study Guide:** Section 4 Summary **Resource File:*** • Vocabulary Builder: Section 4	**Daily Bellringer Transparency:** Section 4* **Map Zone Transparency:** Central Africa: Physical* **Map Zone Transparency:** Central Africa's National Parks* **Map Zone Transparency:** Michael Fay's Route* **Internet Activity:** Central African Wildlife
Section 5: **Southern Africa** **The Big Idea:** Southern Africa's physical geography includes a high, mostly dry plateau, grassy plains and rivers, and valuable mineral resources.	**Differentiated Instruction Teacher Management System:** Section 5 Lesson Plan* **Interactive Reader and Study Guide:** Section 5 Summary **Resource File:*** • Vocabulary Builder: Section 5	**Daily Bellringer Transparency:** Section 5* **Map Zone Transparency:** Southern Africa: Physical* **Map Zone Transparency:** Southern Africa: Vegetation*

SE Student Edition   Print Resource   Audio CD

TE Teacher's Edition   Transparency CD-ROM

 go.hrw.com   Learning Styles Video

OSP Teacher's One-Stop Planner * also on One-Stop Planner

HOLT
Geography's Impact
Video Program

Impact of Desertification
Suggested use: in Section 1

Review, Assessment, Intervention

 Quick Facts Transparency: Visual Summary: Physical Geography of Africa*

 Spanish Chapter Summaries Audio CD Program

 Progress Assessment Support System (PASS): Chapter Test*

 Differentiated Instruction Modified Worksheets and Tests CD-ROM: Modified Chapter Test

OSP Teacher's One-Stop Planner: ExamView Test Generator (English/Spanish)

HOAP Holt Online Assessment Program (HOAP), in the Holt Interactive Online Student Edition

---

 PASS: Section 1 Quiz*

 Online Quiz: Section 1

 Alternative Assessment Handbook

 PASS: Section 2 Quiz*

 Online Quiz: Section 2

 Alternative Assessment Handbook

 PASS: Section 3 Quiz*

 Online Quiz: Section 3

 Alternative Assessment Handbook

 PASS: Section 4 Quiz*

 Online Quiz: Section 4

 Alternative Assessment Handbook

 PASS: Section 5 Quiz*

 Online Quiz: Section 5

 Alternative Assessment Handbook

Power Presentations with Video CD-ROM

Power Presentations with Video are visual presentations of each chapter's main ideas. Presentations can be customized by including Quick Facts charts, images from the text, and video clips.

Holt Online Learning

go.hrw.com
Teacher Resources
KEYWORD: SK9 TEACHER

go.hrw.com
Student Resources
KEYWORD: SK9 CH9

- Interactive Multimedia Activities
- Current Events

- Chapter-based Internet Activities
- and more!

Holt Interactive
Online Student Edition
Complete online support for interactivity, assessment, and reporting
- Interactive Maps and Notebook
- Standardized Test Prep
- Homework Practice and Research Activities Online

CHAPTER 9 PLANNING GUIDE

Differentiating Instruction

How do I address the needs of varied learners?
The Target Resource acts as your primary strategy for differentiated instruction.

ENGLISH-LANGUAGE LEARNERS & STRUGGLING READERS

TARGET RESOURCE

Spanish Resources

Spanish Chapter Summaries Audio CD Program

Teacher's One-Stop Planner:
- ExamView Test Generator, Spanish
- PuzzlePro, Spanish

English-Language Learner Strategies and Activities

Additional Resources

Differentiated Instruction Teacher Management System: Lesson Plans for Differentiated Instruction

Resource File:
- Vocabulary Builder Activities
- Social Studies Skills: Analyzing a Precipitation Map

Quick Facts Transparency: Visual Summary: Physical Geography of Africa

Student Edition on Audio CD Program

Interactive Skills Tutor CD-ROM

SPECIAL NEEDS LEARNERS

TARGET RESOURCE

Interactive Skills Tutor CD-ROM

The Interactive Skills Tutor CD-ROM contains lessons that provide additional practice for 20 different critical thinking skills.

Additional Resources

Differentiated Instruction Teacher Management System: Lesson Plans for Differentiated Instruction

Interactive Reader and Study Guide

Resource File: Social Studies Skills: Analyzing a Precipitation Map

Student Edition on Audio CD Program

Graphic Organizer Transparencies with Support for Reading and Writing

ADVANCED/GIFTED AND TALENTED STUDENTS

TARGET RESOURCE

Resource File

The Resource File activities allow students to extend their knowledge of chapter-related places and people and to practice geography skills.
- Focus on Reading: Understanding Comparison-Contrast
- Focus on Writing: Writing a Letter
- Literature: *Knowing Robs Us*

Additional Resources

Differentiated Instruction Teacher Management System: Lesson Plans for Differentiated Instruction

World History and Geography Document-Based Questions Activities

Geography, Science, and Cultures Activities

Experiencing World History and Geography

Differentiated Activities in the Teacher's Edition

- Understanding a Delta
- Examining East Africa's Physical Features
- Writing a Postcard Home
- Reading Maps

Differentiated Activities in the Teacher's Edition

- Understanding a Delta
- Understanding Low Latitudes

Differentiated Activities in the Teacher's Edition

- Researching Africa's Deltas
- East Africa Board Game
- Creating a Chronology
- Researching Southern Africa

HOLT Teacher's One-Stop Planner®

How can I manage the lesson plans and support materials for differentiated instruction?

With the Teacher's One-Stop Planner, you can easily organize and print lesson plans, planning guides, and instructional materials for all learners.

The Teacher's One-Stop Planner includes the following materials to help you differentiate instruction:

- Interactive Teacher's Edition
- Calendar Planner and pacing guides
- Editable lesson plans
- All reproducible ancillaries in Adobe Acrobat (PDF) format
- ExamView Test Generator (English & Spanish)
- Transparency and video previews

Professional Development

What teacher training resources are available to help me grow professionally?

- **In-service and staff development** as part of your Holt Social Studies product purchase
- **Quick Teacher Tutorial Lesson Presentation CD-ROM**
- Intensive tuition-based **Teacher Development Institute**
- **Convenient Holt Speaker Bureau:** face-to-face workshop options
- **24/7 Ask A Professional Development Expert** at http://www.hrw.com/prodev/

Chapter Big Ideas

Section 1 North Africa is a dry region with limited water resources.

Section 2 West Africa, which is mostly a region of plains, has climates ranging from arid to tropical and has important resources.

Section 3 East Africa is a region of diverse physical features, climates, and vegetation.

Section 4 The Congo River, tropical forests, and mineral resources are important features of Central Africa's physical geography.

Section 5 Southern Africa's physical geography includes a high, mostly dry plateau, grassy plains and rivers, and valuable mineral resources.

Focus on Reading and Writing

Reading The Resource File provides a Focus on Reading worksheet to help students understand how to identify comparison and contrast.

　RF: Focus on Reading, Understanding Comparison-Contrast

Writing The Resource File provides a Focus on Writing worksheet to help students plan, organize, and write a letter.

　RF: Focus on Writing, Writing a Letter Home

Key to Differentiating Instruction

Below Level

Basic-level activities designed for all students encountering new material

At Level

Intermediate-level activities designed for average students

Above Level

Challenging activities designed for honors and gifted and talented students

Standard English Mastery

Activities designed to improve standard English usage

248　CHAPTER 9

CHAPTER 9

Physical Geography of Africa

FOCUS QUESTION

What forces had an impact on the development of Africa and why?

ELEVATION

Feet		Meters
13,120		4,000
6,560		2,000
1,640		500
656		200
(Sea level) 0		0 (Sea level)
Below sea level		Below sea level

0　　250　　500 Miles
0　　250　　500 Kilometers
Projection: Azimuthal Equal-Area

Tropic of Cancer

What You Will Learn...

Africa is one of the largest continents and one of the most diverse. Its landscapes range from harsh deserts in the north and south to lush tropical rain forests near the equator.

FOCUS ON READING AND WRITING

Understanding Comparison-Contrast Comparing and contrasting, or looking for similiarities and differences, can help you more fully understand the subject you are studying. **See the lesson, Understanding Comparison-Contrast, on page S12.**

Writing a Letter Home Imagine that you are spending your summer vacation visiting the countries of Africa. You want to write a letter home to a friend in the United States describing the land that you see. As you read this chapter, you will gather information that you can include in your letter.

248　CHAPTER 9

East Africa The plains surrounding Mount Kilimanjaro are rich in wildlife. Millions of tourists come to visit this part of East Africa each year.

North Africa Most of North Africa is covered by the world's largest desert—the Sahara.

Introduce the Chapter

At Level

Physical Geography of Africa

Materials: outline map of Africa

1. Distribute photocopies of a blank outline map of Africa to the class. Instruct students to use the map on this page to identify the main geographic regions of Africa on their outline map. Ask students to explain why they divided their regions the way they did.

2. Have students scan the chapter, looking at the regions identified in each section. Ask students how their regions differ from those identified in the chapter.

3. List the five geographic regions of Africa for students to see. Instruct students to create a chart listing the five regions.

4. Have students use their charts to make note of important information about each region as they study the chapter. Encourage students to use their charts as a review for the chapter test.
　LS Visual/Spatial, Verbal/Linguistic

　Alternative Assessment Handbook, Rubrics 7: Charts; 20: Map Creation

---

248　**CHAPTER 9**

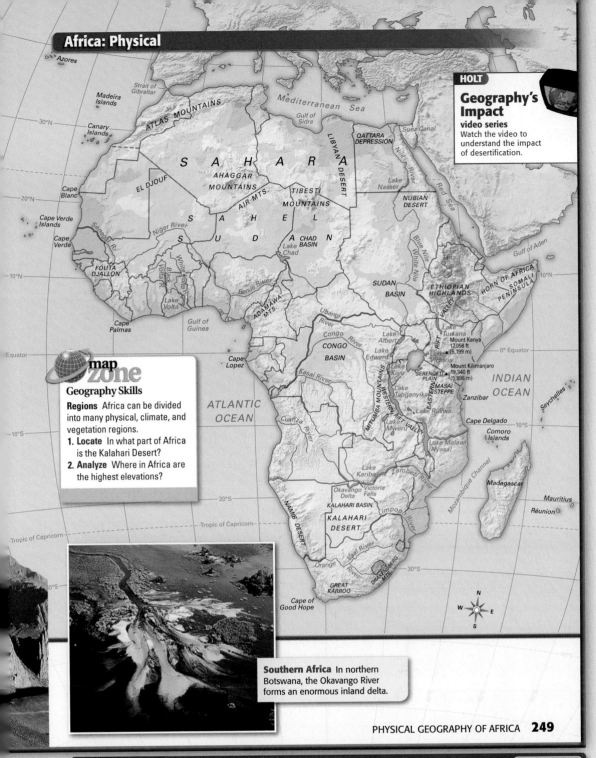

Africa: Physical

Azores
Strait of Gibraltar
Madeira Islands
ATLAS MOUNTAINS
Mediterranean Sea
Gulf of Sidra
Suez Canal

Canary Islands
S A H A R A
AHAGGAR MOUNTAINS
LIBYAN DESERT
QATTARA DEPRESSION

Cape Blanc
EL DJOUF
AIR MTS.
TIBESTI MOUNTAINS
Lake Nasser
NUBIAN DESERT
Red Sea

Cape Verde Islands
S A H E L
Niger River
CHAD BASIN
Lake Chad

Cape Verde
S U D A N
FOUTA DJALLON
Senegal R.
White Volta
Black Volta
Benue River
Lake Volta
SUDAN BASIN
Blue Nile
White Nile
Lake Tana
ETHIOPIAN HIGHLANDS
HORN OF AFRICA
SOMALI PENINSULA
Gulf of Aden

Cape Palmas
Gulf of Guinea
ADAMAWA MTS.
Ubangi River
Congo River
CONGO BASIN
Lake Albert
Lake Edward
RIFT VALLEY
Lake Turkana
Mount Kenya 17,058 ft (5,199 m)

Cape Lopez
Kasai River
Lake Kivu
Lake Victoria
SERENGETI PLAIN
Mount Kilimanjaro 19,340 ft (5,895 m)
INDIAN OCEAN

ATLANTIC OCEAN
Cuanza River
MITUMBA MOUNTAINS
WESTERN RIFT VALLEY
Lake Tanganyika
MASAI STEPPE
Zanzibar
Seychelles

Lake Mweru
EASTERN RIFT VALLEY
Lake Rukwa
Cape Delgado
Comoro Islands

Lake Malawi (Nyasa)
Madagascar
Mauritius

Lake Kariba
Zambezi River
Réunion

Okavango Delta
Victoria Falls
NAMIB DESERT
KALAHARI BASIN
Limpopo River
Mozambique Channel

KALAHARI DESERT
Vaal River
Orange River
DRAKENSBERG MTS.
Tropic of Capricorn

GREAT KARROO
Cape of Good Hope

N
W E
S

HOLT
Geography's Impact
video series
Watch the video to understand the impact of desertification.

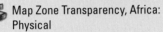

map zone
Geography Skills

Regions Africa can be divided into many physical, climate, and vegetation regions.

1. **Locate** In what part of Africa is the Kalahari Desert?
2. **Analyze** Where in Africa are the highest elevations?

Southern Africa In northern Botswana, the Okavango River forms an enormous inland delta.

PHYSICAL GEOGRAPHY OF AFRICA **249**

Chapter Preview

Explore the Map and Pictures

Africa: Physical Have students name the physical features they see on the map of Africa on this page. Make a list of students' responses for everyone to see. Have students use the list of physical features and the map of Africa to make inferences about the physical geography of Africa. Then have students write one to two paragraphs describing what they think Africa's geography is like. Have students refer back to their descriptions as they study the chapter to see if their inferences were correct. **LS Verbal/Linguistic**

Alternative Assessment Handbook: Rubric 37: Writing Assignments

Map Zone Transparency, Africa: Physical

go.hrw.com
Online Resources

Chapter Resources:
KEYWORD: SK9 CH9
Teacher Resources:
KEYWORD: SK9 TEACHER

HOLT
Geography's Impact
▶ **video series**
See the Video Teacher's Guide for strategies for using the chapter video to teach about the impact of desertification.

Critical Thinking: Analyzing Visuals

At Level

Writing Poems

1. Instruct students to examine the photographs on these two pages. Have students express their feelings about each photograph. Encourage students to write down their thoughts about each photograph.

2. Instruct students to use their notes to write a poem for each photograph. Remind students to use descriptive and expressive language to explain the photographs or to express their emotions toward the photographs.

3. Encourage students to share their poems with the class. **LS Visual/Spatial, Verbal/Linguistic**

Alternative Assessment Handbook, Rubrics 11: Discussions; and 26: Poems and Songs

Answers

Map Zone 1. *Southern Africa;*
2. *Ethiopian Highlands and the Atlas and Tibesti mountains*

249

Bellringer

If YOU lived there. . . Use the **Daily Bellringer Transparency** to help students answer the question.

📄 Daily Bellringer Transparency, Section 1

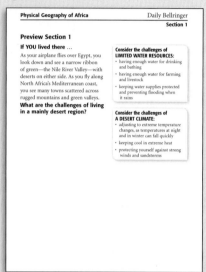

Physical Geography of Africa   Daily Bellringer
Section 1

Preview Section 1

If YOU lived there ...

As your airplane flies over Egypt, you look down and see a narrow ribbon of green—the Nile River Valley—with deserts on either side. As you fly along North Africa's Mediterranean coast, you see many towns scattered across rugged mountains and green valleys. **What are the challenges of living in a mainly desert region?**

Consider the challenges of LIMITED WATER RESOURCES:
· having enough water for drinking and bathing
· having enough water for farming and livestock
· keeping water supplies protected and preventing flooding when it rains

Consider the challenges of A DESERT CLIMATE:
· adjusting to extreme temperature changes, as temperatures at night and in winter can fall quickly
· keeping cool in extreme heat
· protecting yourself against strong winds and sandstorms

Academic Vocabulary

Review with students the high-use academic term in this section.

impact effect, result (p. 252)

📄 **RF:** Vocabulary Builder, Section 1

Taking Notes

Have students copy the graphic organizer onto their own paper and then use it to take notes on the section. This activity will prepare students for the Section Assessment, in which they will complete a graphic organizer that builds on the information using the Critical Thinking Skill: Categorizing.

North Africa

What You Will Learn...

Main Ideas

1. Major physical features of North Africa include the Nile River, the Sahara, and the Atlas Mountains.
2. The climate of North Africa is hot and dry, and water is the region's most important resource.

The Big Idea

North Africa is a dry region with limited water resources.

Key Terms and Places

Sahara, *p. 250*
Nile River, *p. 250*
silt, *p. 250*
Suez Canal, *p. 251*
oasis, *p. 252*
Atlas Mountains, *p. 252*

TAKING NOTES As you read, take notes on the physical geography of North Africa. Use the chart below to organize your notes.

Physical Features	
Climate	
Resources	

If YOU lived there...

As your airplane flies over Egypt, you look down and see a narrow ribbon of green—the Nile River. On either side of the green valley, sunlight glints off of bright sands that stretch as far as the eye can see. As you fly along North Africa's Mediterranean coast, you see many towns scattered across rugged mountains and green valleys.

What are the challenges of living in a mainly desert region?

BUILDING BACKGROUND Even though much of North Africa is covered by rugged mountains and huge areas of deserts, the region is not a bare wasteland. Areas of water include wet, fertile land with date palms and almond trees.

Physical Features

The region of North Africa includes Morocco, Algeria, Tunisia, Libya, and Egypt. From east to west the region stretches from the Atlantic Ocean to the Red Sea. Off the northern coast is the Mediterranean Sea. In the south lies the **Sahara** (suh-HAR-uh), a vast desert. Both the desert sands and bodies of water have helped shape the cultures of North Africa.

The Nile

The **Nile River** is the world's longest river. It is formed by the union of two rivers, the Blue Nile and the White Nile. Flowing northward through the eastern Sahara for about 4,000 miles, the Nile finally empties into the Mediterranean Sea.

For centuries, rain far to the south caused floods along the northern Nile, leaving rich silt in surrounding fields. **Silt** is finely ground fertile soil that is good for growing crops.

The Nile River Valley is like a long oasis in the desert. Farmers use water from the Nile to irrigate their fields. The Nile fans out near the Mediterranean Sea, forming a large delta. A delta

---

Teach the Big Idea   **At Level**

North Africa

1. **Teach** Ask students the questions in the Main Idea boxes under Direct Teach.

2. **Apply** Have students make a list of the reasons why North Africa is a dry region with limited water resources. Have them use details from the section to support their ideas. Allow students time to discuss their ideas in mixed-ability groups.
   LS Verbal/Linguistic

3. **Review** Have students use the Taking Notes charts they created for the section to review their notes with the class.

4. **Practice/Homework** Have students discuss their charts with family members, describing important details.
   LS Verbal/Linguistic, Interpersonal
   📄 Alternative Assessment Handbook, Rubrics 7: Charts; and 14: Group Activity

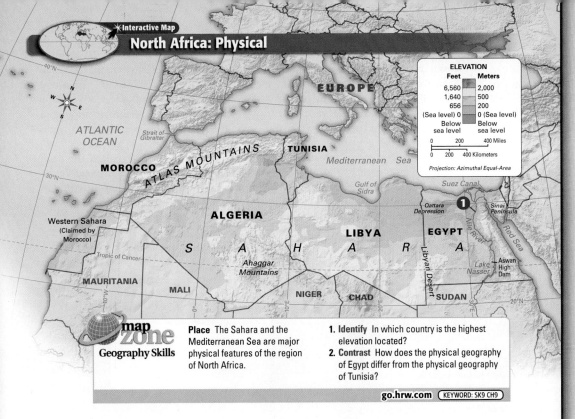

Interactive Map
North Africa: Physical

ELEVATION

Feet	Meters
6,560	2,000
1,640	500
656	200
(Sea level) 0	0 (Sea level)
Below sea level	Below sea level

0   200   400 Miles
0   200   400 Kilometers

Projection: Azimuthal Equal-Area

map zone
Geography Skills

Place The Sahara and the Mediterranean Sea are major physical features of the region of North Africa.

1. **Identify** In which country is the highest elevation located?
2. **Contrast** How does the physical geography of Egypt differ from the physical geography of Tunisia?

go.hrw.com **KEYWORD: SK9 CH9**

is a landform at the mouth of a river that is created by the deposit of sediment. The sediment in the Nile delta makes the area extremely fertile.

The Aswan High Dam controls flooding along the Nile. However, the dam also traps silt, preventing it from being carried downriver. Today some of Egypt's farmers must use fertilizers to enrich the soil.

The Sinai and the Suez Canal

East of the Nile is the triangular Sinai Peninsula. Barren, rocky mountains and desert cover the Sinai. Between the Sinai and the rest of Egypt is the **Suez Canal**. The French built the canal in the 1860s. It is a narrow waterway that connects the Mediterranean Sea with the Red Sea. Large cargo ships carry oil and goods through the canal.

1 Flowing for 4,132 miles, the Nile is the longest river in the world.

Critical Thinking Skill: Interpreting Maps   At Level

Important Physical Features of North Africa

1. Use the physical map of North Africa to point out the Mediterranean Sea, the Sahara Desert, and the Nile River. Ask: How many North African countries have coastlines on the Mediterranean? *five* How might the Mediterranean influence North African life? *provides North Africa with water access to Europe*

2. Ask: How large is the Sahara? *covers most of North Africa—parts of all five countries* Remind students of the photo of the Sahara.

How might the Sahara influence life in North Africa? *Much of the Sahara is uninhabitable.*

3. Have students locate the Nile on the map and review information about it in the text. Ask: Why do you think almost all of the people of Egypt live near the Nile? *supports farming*
LS Verbal/Linguistic, Visual/Spatial

Alternative Assessment Handbook, Rubrics 11: Discussions; and 21: Map Reading

251

Connect to Science

Sahara Oases The springs that supply water to an oasis are fed by rainfall or melting snow from higher elevations. After seeping into the ground, the water travels through underground rocks until it reaches a low place in the desert where it resurfaces, forming a spring. A few (under 100) large oases in the Sahara include settlements of farmers who grow crops such as dates, barley, and wheat. Many small oases have only enough resources to sustain a single family or two. Paved roads connect some of the larger oases, but the camel remains the main form of transportation in the Sahara.

Info to Know

Tuareg Culture The Tuareg people of North Africa, illustrated on this page, are Muslims who are related to the Berbers. They move from place to place in the desert, primarily in Algeria, living in tents. They have been called "the Blue Men of the Desert" because their indigo-dyed robes stain their skins. They wear turbans wrapped around their heads and faces to shield them from sandstorms and the sun. The Tuareg raise camels, sheep, cattle, and goats. They rely on seasonal rainfall to nourish the pastures. A severe drought in the late 1960s and early 1970s was responsible for the deaths of thousands of Tuareg people and their animals.

About the Illustration

This illustration is an artist's conception of a typical scene at a small oasis in the Sahara. It does not depict an actual location in the Sahara.

Answers

Reading Check *the Sahara, Nile River, Mediterranean Sea, Sinai Peninsula, Red Sea, Ahaggar Mountains, Atlas Mountains*

252

The Sahara

ACADEMIC VOCABULARY

impact effect, result

The Sahara, the largest desert in the world, covers most of North Africa. The name Sahara comes from the Arabic word for "desert." It has an enormous **impact** on the landscapes of North Africa.

One impact of the very dry Sahara is that few people live there. Small settlements are located near a water source such as an oasis. An **oasis** is a wet, fertile area in a desert where a natural spring or well provides water.

In addition to broad, windswept gravel plains, sand dunes cover much of the Sahara. Dry streambeds are also common.

Mountains

Do you think of deserts as flat regions? You may be surprised to learn that the Sahara is far from flat. Some sand dunes and ridges rise as high as 1,000 feet (305 m). The Sahara also has spectacular mountain ranges. For example, a mountain range in southern Algeria rises to a height of 9,800 feet (3,000 m). Another range, the **Atlas Mountains** on the northwestern side of the Sahara near the Mediterranean coast, rises even higher, to 13,600 feet (4,160 m).

READING CHECK **Summarizing** What are the major physical features of North Africa?

Close-up

A Sahara Oasis

The largest desert in the world, the Sahara, spans almost 4 million square miles across North Africa. From ancient times to today, traders crossing the Sahara have relied on the desert's oases. These oases provide water and shade.

Date palms thrive on the banks of this natural spring, which provides water to travelers and irrigated fields.

By carrying supplies, camels help the nomadic Tuareg people travel from oasis to oasis.

252 CHAPTER 9

Critical Thinking: Analyzing Visuals

At Level

Analyzing an Illustration

1. After reviewing the information about climate and resources, focus attention on the Close-up feature to emphasize the importance of oases in the dry Sahara environment. Use the notes in the side column to provide students with additional information to analyze the illustration.

2. Direct attention to the dunes in the distance, the vegetation near the water, the camels, the travelers' clothes, and the shelter.

3. Ask: What purpose do the robes and the turbans serve? *protection from sandstorms and sun* What benefits do the date palms provide? *shade and food* Why are camels included in the picture? *They are the primary form of transportation in the desert.* Why are shelters shown? *They provide a place for travelers to rest.* **LS** **Verbal/Linguistic, Visual/Spatial**

📝 Alternative Assessment Handbook, Rubric 12: Drawing Conclusions

Climate and Resources

North Africa is very dry. However, rare storms can cause flooding. In some areas these floods as well as high winds have carved bare rock surfaces out of the land.

North Africa has three main climates. A desert climate covers most of the region. Temperatures range from mild to very hot. How hot can it get? Temperatures as high as 136°F (58°C) have been recorded in Libya. However, the humidity is very low. As a result, temperatures can drop quickly after sunset. In winter temperatures can fall below freezing at night.

The second climate type in the region is a Mediterranean climate. Much of the northern coast west of Egypt has this type of climate. Winters there are mild and moist. Summers are hot and dry. Areas between the coast and the Sahara have a steppe climate.

Oil and gas are important resources, particularly for Libya, Algeria, and Egypt. Morocco mines iron ore and minerals used to make fertilizers. The Sahara has natural resources such as coal, oil, and natural gas.

READING CHECK **Generalizing** What are North Africa's major resources?

SUMMARY AND PREVIEW In this section, you learned about the physical geography of North Africa. Next, you will learn about a very different region to the south—West Africa.

FOCUS ON READING
How are summers and winters different in a Mediterranean climate?

Section 1 Assessment

go.hrw.com
Online Quiz
KEYWORD: SK9 HP9

Reviewing Ideas, Terms, and Places

1. **a. Define** What is an **oasis**?
   b. Explain Why is the **Suez Canal** an important waterway?
   c. Elaborate Would it be possible to farm in Egypt if the **Nile River** did not exist? Explain your answer.
2. **a. Recall** What is the climate of most of North Africa?
   b. Draw Conclusions What resources of North Africa are the most valuable?

Critical Thinking

3. **Categorizing** Draw a diagram like the one shown here. Use your notes to list two facts about each physical feature of North Africa.

Physical Features
- Nile
- Sinai and Suez Canal
- Sahara
- Mountains

FOCUS ON WRITING

4. **Noting Interesting Details** What physical feature of North Africa do you think your friend back home would find interesting? Write down some notes about what you could mention in your letter.

PHYSICAL GEOGRAPHY OF AFRICA **253**

Direct Teach

Main Idea

❷ Climate and Resources

The climate of North Africa is hot and dry, and water is the region's most important resource.

Recall Describe the desert climate of much of North Africa. *It is mostly hot and dry. At night it can get cold. There is little rain, but flooding can occur.*

Draw Conclusions Why is water an important resource in North Africa? *It supports crop growth.*

📄 **RF:** Geography and History, Major Cities of North Africa

📄 **RF:** Interdisciplinary Project: Irrigation, Simple Machines, and the Nile

---

Review & Assess

Close

Ask students to summarize the ways in which the Sahara and the Nile River influence life in North Africa.

Review

🖥 Online Quiz, Section 1

Assess

SE Section 1 Assessment
📄 PASS: Section 1 Quiz
📄 Alternative Assessment Handbook

Reteach/Classroom Intervention

📄 Interactive Reader and Study Guide, Section 1

💿 Interactive Skills Tutor CD-ROM

Section 1 Assessment Answers

1. **a.** a wet, fertile area in the desert with a natural spring or well that supplies water
   b. It connects the Mediterranean Sea with the Red Sea.
   c. It would be unlikely or impossible except for small areas by oases or near the Mediterranean, with its mild and moist winters. The rest of Egypt is desert.

2. **a.** desert—hot, dry, with little rain
   b. water, oil, and gas

3. possible answers: Nile—world's longest river, provides fertile farmland; Sahara—largest desert in the world, few people live there; Sinai—peninsula with barren, rocky mountains and desert; Suez Canal—French-built waterway connecting Red Sea and Mediterranean Sea; Mountains—Atlas in northwestern side of the Sahara, Ahaggar in southeastern Algeria

4. Answers will vary, but students may choose the Sahara. Students may mention that it covers most of North Africa, is very dry, has oases, large sand dunes, and broad, wind-swept gravel plains.

Answers

Analyzing Visuals *An oasis provides water, food, shade, and a place to rest.*

Focus on Reading *Winters are mild and moist, while summers are hot and dry.*

Reading Check *iron ore, oil, gas, coal, and minerals*

253

Preteach

Bellringer

If YOU lived there. . . Use the **Daily Bellringer Transparency** to help students answer the question.

📖 Daily Bellringer Transparency, Section 2

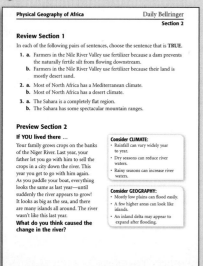

Key Terms and Places

📄 RF: Vocabulary Builder, Section 2

Taking Notes

Have students copy the graphic organizer onto their own paper and then use it to take notes on the section. This activity will prepare students for the Section Assessment, in which they will complete a graphic organizer that builds on the information using the Critical Thinking Skill: Identifying Cause and Effect.

SECTION 2

West Africa

If YOU lived there...

Your family grows crops on the banks of the Niger River. Last year, your father let you go with him to sell the crops in a city down the river. This year you get to go with him again. As you paddle your boat, everything looks the same as last year—until suddenly the river appears to grow! It looks as big as the sea, and there are many islands all around. The river wasn't like this last year.

What do you think caused the change in the river?

BUILDING BACKGROUND The Niger River is one of West Africa's most important physical features. It brings precious water to the region's dry plains. Much of the interior of West Africa experiences desertlike conditions, but the region's rivers and lakes help to support life there.

Physical Features

The region we call West Africa stretches from the Sahara in the north to the coasts of the Atlantic Ocean and the Gulf of Guinea in the west and south. While West Africa's climate changes quite a bit from north to south, the region does not have a wide variety of landforms. Throughout all of West Africa, the main physical features are plains and rivers.

Plains and Highlands

Plains, flat areas of land, cover most of West Africa. The coastal plain along the Gulf of Guinea is home to most of the region's cities. The interior plains provide land where people can raise a few crops or animals.

West Africa's plains are vast, interrupted only by a few highland areas. One area in the southwest has plateaus and cliffs. People have built houses directly into the sides of these cliffs for many hundreds of years. The region's only high mountains are the Tibesti Mountains in the northeast.

What You Will Learn...

Main Ideas

1. West Africa's key physical features include plains and the Niger River.
2. West Africa has distinct climate and vegetation zones that go from arid in the north to tropical in the south.
3. West Africa has good agricultural and mineral resources that may one day help the economies in the region.

The Big Idea

West Africa, which is mostly a region of plains, has climates ranging from arid to tropical and has important resources.

Key Terms and Places

Niger River, *p. 255*
zonal, *p. 256*
Sahel, *p. 256*
desertification, *p. 256*
savanna, *p. 256*

 TAKING NOTES As you read, use a chart like the one below to help you organize your notes on the physical geography of West Africa.

Physical features	
Climate and vegetation	
Resources	

254 CHAPTER 9

Teach the Big Idea

At Level

West Africa

1. **Teach** Ask students the questions in the Main Idea boxes under Direct Teach.

2. **Apply** Draw three columns on the board with the following headings: *Physical Features*, *Climate and Vegetation*, *Resources*. Have students scan the text and take turns writing details under each column that describe West Africa. For each detail listed, ask students to explain how it affects life in the region. **LS Verbal/Linguistic**

3. **Review** Ask students to review the climate photos in Section 2. Then have students

guess where each photo might have been taken. Call on students to explain their answers, including why they think the photo was taken in that specific location (i.e., southern Niger, northern Burkina Faso, etc.).

4. **Practice/Homework** Ask students to select one country in West Africa and write a few sentences describing its physical features, climate, vegetation, and resources. **LS Verbal/Linguistic**

📄 Alternative Assessment Handbook, Rubric 37: Writing Assignments

The Niger River

As you can see on the map below, many rivers flow across West Africa's plains. The most important river is the Niger (NY-juhr). The **Niger River** starts in some low mountains not too far from the Atlantic Ocean. From there, it flows 2,600 miles (4,185 km) into the interior of the region before emptying into the Gulf of Guinea.

The Niger brings life-giving water to West Africa. Many people farm along its banks or fish in its waters. It is also an important transportation route, especially during the rainy season. At that time, the river floods and water flows smoothly over its rapids.

Part of the way along its route the river divides into a network of channels, swamps, and lakes. This watery network is called the inland delta. Although it looks much like the delta where a river flows into the sea, this one is actually hundreds of miles from the coast in Mali.

FOCUS ON READING

The word *although* signals contrast in this paragraph. What is being contrasted?

READING CHECK Summarizing Why is the Niger River important to West Africa?

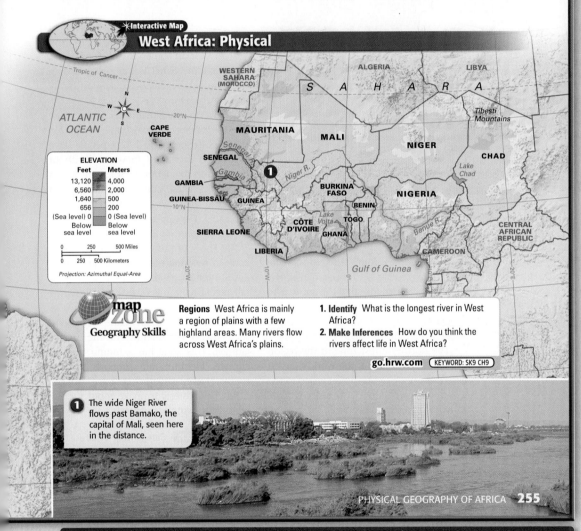

West Africa: Physical

ELEVATION

Feet	Meters
13,120	4,000
6,560	2,000
1,640	500
656	200
(Sea level) 0	0 (Sea level)
Below sea level	Below sea level

Projection: Azimuthal Equal-Area

map zone
Geography Skills

Regions West Africa is mainly a region of plains with a few highland areas. Many rivers flow across West Africa's plains.

1. **Identify** What is the longest river in West Africa?
2. **Make Inferences** How do you think the rivers affect life in West Africa?

go.hrw.com **KEYWORD: SK9 CH9**

1. The wide Niger River flows past Bamako, the capital of Mali, seen here in the distance.

PHYSICAL GEOGRAPHY OF AFRICA **255**

Differentiating Instruction

Advanced/Gifted and Talented
Above Level
Research Required

1. Note that the Niger River has one delta inland and one at its mouth in the Gulf of Guinea.

2. Assign individuals or a group to research the deltas of other major rivers such as the Nile, Amazon, and Mississippi. Students should use a chart to compare width, climate, etc.

3. Ask the group or an individual to display their chart and discuss differences and similarities.

LS Verbal/Linguistic

Alternative Assessment Handbook, Rubric 7: Charts

English-Language Learners
At Level

1. Explain that delta is the fourth letter of the Greek alphabet and draw a picture of its symbol (Δ). Ask students why people might have used this name for the area at the mouth of rivers.

2. Ask students for examples of other objects that have a "delta" shape, (e.g., highway signs, aircraft wings, triangles).

LS Verbal/Linguistic

Alternative Assessment Handbook, Rubric 1: Acquiring Information

● **Direct Teach** ●

Main Idea

❶ Physical Features

West Africa's key physical features include plains and the Niger River.

Contrast How is the inland delta of the Niger River different from other deltas? *It is hundreds of miles from the coast.*

Make an Inference Why do many people live along the Niger River? *It provides water for drinking, farming, fishing, and transportation.*

Map Zone Transparency: West Africa: Physical

RF: Literature, *Knowing Robs Us* by Chinua Achebe

Info to Know

Kainji Dam Dams have been built along the Niger River for irrigation and hydroelectricity. The Kainji Dam was completed in 1968 in western Nigeria. It formed Kainji Lake, which is about 80 miles long and 20 miles wide. The dam should provide about one-sixth of Nigeria's electricity, but the supply is unpredictable—partially because drought sometimes makes the water levels too low.

Connect to Science

Oil Industry The Niger Delta is the center of Nigeria's large oil industry. Environmental groups claim oil production has had a detrimental effect on the water, air, and soil there because of oil spills, burning excess gas, and clearing forests for exploration and development. However, oil companies, government officials, and some studies say that the oil industry is only one of the causes of environmental damage. An increasing population and sewage are among the other contributors to environmental problems.

Answers

Reading Check *It brings life-giving water for farming and fishing and allows transportation and settlements.*

Focus on Reading *the Niger inland delta and other river deltas*

Map Zone 1. *Niger River;* **2.** *They enable farming, fishing, and transportation and encourage settlements near them.*

255

Main Idea

❷ Climate and Vegetation

West Africa has distinct climate and vegetation zones that go from arid in the north to tropical in the south.

Identify Which climate zone is the farthest north? *desert*

Summarize How does climate vary from north to south? *Climate varies in zones from arid desert in the north to semiarid steppe to wetter savanna and humid tropical zones in the south.*

Identify Cause and Effect How is climate related to the vegetation from north to south? *Desert and steppe climates get the least rain and have the least vegetation; the tropical savanna and humid tropical climates get more rainfall and have much more vegetation.*

🔲 Map Zone Transparency: West Africa: Climate

📑 RF: Biography, Leo Africanus

Connect to Civics

Politics and Desertification

Mauritania and Senegal became independent countries in 1960. Before that time, the nomadic people were allowed to move freely with their animal herds throughout the region. During a drought, nomadic groups would move to the south into areas of Senegal where conditions weren't so severe. After independence created strong borders between the two countries, nomads were no longer allowed to migrate south. They were forced to stay in the Sahel and continue grazing animals there to produce food. This overgrazing began the process of desertification in Mauritania.

go.hrw.com
Online Resources
KEYWORD: SK9 CH9
ACTIVITY: Baobab Trees

Answers

Map Zone 1. *Mauritania, Mali, Niger, Chad;* **2.** *areas with a humid tropical climate along the coast*

Reading Check *humid tropical, tropical savanna, steppe, desert*

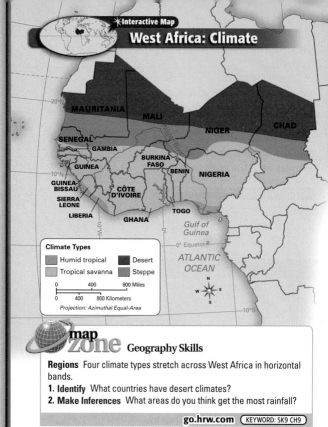

★Interactive Map
West Africa: Climate

Climate Types
- Humid tropical
- Tropical savanna
- Desert
- Steppe

0   400   800 Miles
0   400   800 Kilometers
Projection: Azimuthal Equal-Area

map zone Geography Skills

Regions Four climate types stretch across West Africa in horizontal bands.
1. **Identify** What countries have desert climates?
2. **Make Inferences** What areas do you think get the most rainfall?

go.hrw.com KEYWORD: SK9 CH9

Sahel Vegetation in the semiarid Sahel is limited, but it does support some grazing animals.

Climate and Vegetation

West Africa has four different climate regions. As you can see on the map above, these climate regions stretch from east to west in bands or zones. Because of this, geographers say the region's climates are **zonal**, which means "organized by zone."

The northernmost zone of the region lies within the Sahara, the world's largest desert. Hardly any vegetation grows in the desert, and large areas of this dry climate zone have few or no people.

South of the Sahara is the semiarid **Sahel** (SAH-hel), a strip of land that divides the desert from wetter areas. It has a steppe climate. Rainfall there varies greatly from year to year. In some years it never rains. Although the Sahel is quite dry, it does have enough vegetation to support hardy grazing animals.

However, the Sahel is becoming more like the Sahara. Animals have overgrazed the land in some areas. Also, people have cut down trees for firewood. Without these plants to anchor the soil, wind blows soil away. These conditions, along with drought, are causing desertification in the Sahel. **Desertification** is the spread of desertlike conditions.

To the south of the Sahel is a savanna zone. A **savanna** is an area of tall grasses and scattered trees and shrubs. When rains fall regularly, farmers can do well in this region of West Africa.

The fourth climate zone lies along the coasts of the Atlantic and the Gulf of Guinea. This zone has a humid tropical climate. Plentiful rain supports tropical forests. However, many trees have been cut from these forests to make room for the region's growing populations.

READING CHECK **Categorizing** What are the region's four climate zones?

256 CHAPTER 9

Cross-Discipline Activity: Science

At Level

The Dust Bowl

Research Required

1. Divide the class into small groups. Explain that the Dust Bowl is a common name for a large area of the southern Great Plains in the United States that suffered greatly from wind erosion and desertification during the 1930s.

2. Assign each group one of the following topics to research about the Dust Bowl: Areas Affected, Causes, Effects, Prevention Strategies. Each group should create a poster or chart which illustrates its findings.

3. Have each group display its poster or chart, explain the information, and answer questions. **⬡ Verbal/Linguistic, Visual Spatial, Interpersonal**

📑 Alternative Assessment Handbook, Rubrics 14: Group Activity; and 28: Posters

Savanna Grasses and scattered trees grow on the savanna. This region can be good for farming.

Tropical Forest Thick forests are found along the coasts of West Africa. The tall trees provide homes for many animals.

Resources

West Africa has a variety of resources. These resources include agricultural products, oil, and minerals.

The climate in parts of West Africa is good for agriculture. For example, Ghana is the world's leading producer of cacao, which is used to make chocolate. Coffee, coconuts, and peanuts are also among the region's main exports.

Oil, which is found off the coast of Nigeria, is the region's most valuable resource. Nigeria is a major exporter of oil. West Africa also has mineral riches, such as diamonds, gold, iron ore, and bauxite. Bauxite is the main source of aluminum.

READING CHECK **Summarizing** What are some of the region's resources?

SUMMARY AND PREVIEW West Africa is mostly covered with plains. Across these plains stretch four different climate zones, most of which are dry. In spite of the harsh climate, West Africa has some valuable resources. Next, you will learn about similar features in East Africa.

Section 2 Assessment

go.hrw.com **Online Quiz** KEYWORD: SK9 CH9

Reviewing Ideas, Terms, and Places

1. **a. Describe** What is the inland delta on the **Niger River** like?
   b. Summarize What is the physical geography of West Africa like?
   c. Elaborate Why do you think most of West Africa's cities are located on the coastal plain?
2. **a. Recall** Why do geographers say West Africa's climates are **zonal**?
   b. Compare and Contrast What is one similarity and one difference between the **Sahel** and the **savanna**?
   c. Evaluate How do you think **desertification** affects people's lives in West Africa?
3. **a. Identify** What is the most valuable resource in West Africa?
   b. Make Inferences Where do you think most of the crops in West Africa are grown?

Critical Thinking

4. **Identifying Cause and Effect**
   Review your notes on climate. Using a graphic organizer like the one here, identify the causes and effects of desertification.

   | Causes | → | Desertification | → | Effects |

   FOCUS ON WRITING

5. **Comparing Landscapes** The landscapes you see in West Africa are very different from those you encountered in the North. How will you explain these differences to your friend? Write down some ideas.

PHYSICAL GEOGRAPHY OF AFRICA **257**

Section 2 Assessment Answers

1. **a.** a network of channels, swamps, and lakes
   b. mostly plains with a few highlands, including high mountains in the northeast
   c. It is an area with plenty of rainfall and water for farming and transportation.

2. **a.** They stretch east to west in bands or zones.
   b. Both support some agriculture with enough rainfall; savanna is farther south and has tall grasses, unlike the Sahel.
   c. It takes away land that could be used for farming and cattle grazing.

3. **a.** oil
   b. in the tropical savanna climate region

4. causes—overgrazing, too many trees cut down, soil loss, drought; effects—Sahara expanding southward, loss of farmland, people must move from area

5. Answers will vary, but should examine the differences between North and West Africa, such as deserts in North African and mountains and rivers in West Africa.

Direct Teach

Main Idea

3 Resources

West Africa has good agricultural and mineral resources that may one day help the economies in the region.

Recall What is a major crop in Ghana, and what is it used for? *Cacao is used to make chocolate.*

Make an Inference Why do you think Nigeria is an important country to the United States and other industrial countries? *It is a major exporter of oil, which industrial countries need.*

Did you know. . .

Several countries in West Africa are among the world's leaders in cacao production and exports, while the United States is the world leader in cacao imports.

Review & Assess

Close

Lead a class discussion about the physical features, climates and vegetation, and resources of West Africa.

Review

Online Quiz, Section 2

Assess

SE Section 2 Assessment
PASS: Section 2 Quiz
Alternative Assessment Handbook

Reteach/Classroom Intervention

Interactive Reader and Study Guide, Section 2
Interactive Skills Tutor CD-ROM

Answers

Reading Check *agricultural products, oil, and minerals*

257

Bellringer

If YOU lived there. . . Use the **Daily Bellringer Transparency** to help students answer the question.

🔖 Daily Bellringer Transparency, Section 3

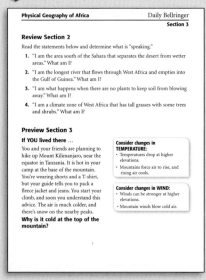

Key Terms and Places

📕 **RF:** Vocabulary Builder, Section 3

Taking Notes

Have students copy the graphic organizer onto their own paper and then use it to take notes on the section. This activity will prepare students for the Section Assessment, in which they will complete a graphic organizer that builds on the information using the Critical Thinking Skill: Categorizing.

SECTION 3

East Africa

What You Will Learn...

Main Ideas

1. East Africa's physical features range from rift valleys to plains.
2. East Africa's climate is influenced by its location and elevation, and the region's vegetation includes savannas and forests.

The Big Idea

East Africa is a region of diverse physical features, climates, and vegetation.

Key Terms and Places

rift valleys, *p. 258*
Great Rift Valley, *p. 258*
Mount Kilimanjaro, *p. 259*
Serengeti Plain, *p. 259*
Lake Victoria, *p. 260*
droughts, *p. 260*

TAKING NOTES As you read, use the chart below to take notes on East Africa's physical features and climate and vegetation.

Physical Features	
Climate and Vegetation	

If YOU lived there...

You and your friends are planning to hike up Mount Kilimanjaro, near the equator in Tanzania. It is hot in your camp at the base of the mountain. You're wearing shorts and a T-shirt, but your guide tells you to pack a fleece jacket and jeans. It is so hot outside that you think the idea is silly, but you take his advice. You start your climb, and soon you understand this advice. The air is much colder, and there's snow on the nearby peaks.

Why is it cold at the top of the mountain?

BUILDING BACKGROUND The landscapes of East Africa have been shaped by powerful forces. The movement of tectonic plates has stretched the Earth's surface here, creating steep-sided valleys and huge lakes.

Physical Features

East Africa is a region of spectacular landscapes and wildlife. Vast plains and plateaus stretch throughout the region. In the north lie huge deserts and dry grasslands. In the southwest, large lakes dot the plateaus. In the east, sandy beaches and colorful coral reefs run along the coast.

The Rift Valleys

Look at the map on the next page. As you can see, East Africa's rift valleys cut from north to south across the region. **Rift valleys** are places on Earth's surface where the crust stretches until it breaks. Rift valleys form when Earth's tectonic plates move away from each other. This movement causes the land to arch and split along the rift valleys. As the land splits open, volcanoes erupt and deposit layers of rock in the region.

Seen from the air, the **Great Rift Valley** looks like a giant scar. The Great Rift Valley is the largest rift on Earth and is made up of two rifts—the eastern rift and the western rift.

258 CHAPTER 9

Teach the Big Idea

At Level

East Africa

1. **Teach** Ask students the questions in the Main Idea boxes under Direct Teach.

2. **Apply** Ask students to imagine that they will have an opportunity to visit East Africa. Have them work with a partner to create an itinerary, including details about the landforms, rivers, and lakes they will see as well as the vegetation and climate they will encounter during their travels. Have students refer to the physical map of East Africa on the facing page for information.
   LS Verbal/Linguistic, Visual/Spatial

3. **Review** Have students compare their itineraries and discuss their choice of destinations.

4. **Practice/Homework** Have students make a packing list for the trip based on the information in the chapter.
   LS Verbal/Linguistic
   📄 Alternative Assessment Handbook, Rubric 40: Writing to Describe

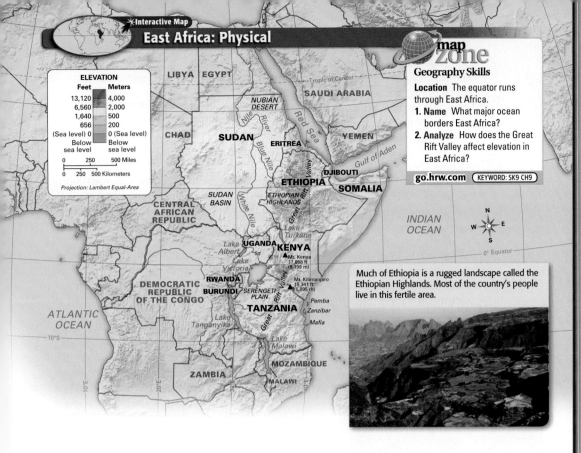

East Africa: Physical

ELEVATION

Feet	Meters
13,120	4,000
6,560	2,000
1,640	500
656	200
(Sea level) 0	0 (Sea level)
Below sea level	Below sea level

0   250   500 Miles

0   250   500 Kilometers

Projection: Lambert Equal-Area

Geography Skills

Location The equator runs through East Africa.

1. **Name** What major ocean borders East Africa?
2. **Analyze** How does the Great Rift Valley affect elevation in East Africa?

go.hrw.com   **KEYWORD: SK9 CH9**

Much of Ethiopia is a rugged landscape called the Ethiopian Highlands. Most of the country's people live in this fertile area.

The rift walls are usually a series of steep cliffs. These cliffs rise as much as 6,000 feet (2,000 m).

Mountains and Highlands

The landscape of East Africa has many high volcanic mountains. The highest mountain in Africa, **Mount Kilimanjaro** (ki-luh-muhn-JAHR-oh), rises to 19,340 feet (5,895 m). Despite Kilimanjaro's location near the equator, the mountain's peak has long been covered in snow. This much colder climate is caused by Kilimanjaro's high elevation.

Other areas of high elevation in East Africa include the Ethiopian Highlands.

These highlands, which lie mostly in Ethiopia, are very rugged. Deep river valleys cut through this landscape.

Plains

Even though much of East Africa lies at high elevations, some areas are flat. For example, plains stretch as far as the eye can see along the eastern rift in Tanzania and Kenya. Tanzania's **Serengeti Plain** is one of the largest plains. It is here that an abundance of wildlife thrives. The plain's grasses, trees, and water provide nutrition for wildlife that includes elephants, giraffes, lions, and zebras. To protect this wildlife, Tanzania established a national park.

PHYSICAL GEOGRAPHY OF AFRICA **259**

Direct Teach

Main Idea

❶ **Physical Features**

East Africa's physical features range from rift valleys to plains.

Explain How are rift valleys formed? *Earth's tectonic plates move away from each other, causing the land to arch and split.*

Make Inferences What is unusual about Mount Kilimanjaro? *It is located near the equator, a hot region, but its peak is covered in snow and ice because of its high elevation.*

Draw Conclusions Why does wildlife thrive on the Serengeti Plain? *Grasses, trees, and water provide nutrition.*

🗄 Map Zone Transparency: East Africa: Physical

Connect to Science

Melting Ice The area of the ice pack on Mount Kilimanjaro has shrunk about 80 percent in the 1900s. In 1912 the ice pack measured 4.6 square miles. By 2000 it had shrunk to just one square mile. At this rate, scientists worry that the tropical glacier will melt away completely in the next 20 years. Some scientists think that global warming is one cause, but global warming alone cannot explain the rapid change. This shrinkage of the ice pack will threaten tourism, the supply of drinking water, irrigation, and the production of hydroelectric power.

Differentiating Instruction

Struggling Readers   Below Level

To help struggling readers, have them match the information in the text to details shown on the map. Read aloud each paragraph in "Physical Features." As you do, have students identify map elements that correspond to the text, including elevation, landforms, rivers, lakes, and so on.

LS Verbal/Linguistic, Visual/Spatial

📒 Alternative Assessment Handbook, Rubric 21: Map Reading

Advanced/Gifted and Talented   Above Level

Have students work in small groups or with a partner to design a board game. The game's purpose should be to test players' knowledge of East African geography. Encourage students to research interesting facts about the region. Students must create the game's objectives, rules, board, and game pieces. Have groups play each other's games. **LS Interpersonal, Visual/Spatial**

📒 Alternative Assessment Handbook, Rubrics 3: Artwork; and 14: Group Activity

Answers

Map Zone 1. *Indian Ocean;* **2.** *It has created areas of high elevation, such as volcanic mountains and highlands.*

259

❷ Climate and Vegetation

East Africa's climate is influenced by its location and elevation, and the region's vegetation includes savannas and forests.

Describe Where do the Blue Nile and the White Nile begin? Where do they meet? *Blue Nile—Ethiopia's highlands; White Nile—Lake Victoria; Khartoum, Sudan*

Activity **Evaluate** Ask students to imagine they are space travelers visiting Earth for the first time. Have them write a description of their initial impressions, based on the satellite image found on this page. **LS Verbal/Linguistic**

📄 Alternative Assessment Handbook, Rubric 39: Writing to Describe

📄 **RF:** Biography, Florence Wambugu

📄 **RF:** Primary Source, Tinga Tinga Style of Art

Info to Know

Satellite Mapping In East Africa, satellite and computer technology, including Global Positioning System (GPS) and Geographic Information System (GIS), is being used to monitor and map existing resources and environmental conditions. Countries can use the detailed information gathered with this technology to assess and manage environmental problems and resource shortages.

Answers

Satellite View *When the tectonic plates moved apart, they created valleys into which water collected.*

Reading Check *Nile; Farmers in the desert depend on it for irrigation.*

Rivers and Lakes

East Africa also has a number of rivers and large lakes. The world's longest river, the Nile, begins in East Africa and flows north to the Mediterranean Sea. The Nile is formed by the meeting of the Blue Nile and the White Nile at Khartoum, Sudan. The White Nile is formed by the water that flows into Africa's largest lake, **Lake Victoria**. The Blue Nile is formed from waters that run down from Ethiopia's highlands. As the Nile meanders through Sudan, it provides a narrow, fertile lifeline to farmers in the desert.

The region has a number of great lakes in addition to Lake Victoria. One group of lakes forms a chain in the western rift valleys. There are also lakes along the drier eastern rift valleys. Near the eastern rift, heat from the Earth's interior makes some lakes so hot that no human can swim in them. In addition, some lakes are extremely salty. However, some of these rift lakes provide algae for the region's flamingos.

READING CHECK **Evaluating** What river is the most important in this region? Why?

Climate and Vegetation

When you think of Africa, do you think of it as being a hot or cold place? Most people usually think all of Africa is hot. However, they are mistaken. Some areas of East Africa have a cool climate.

East Africa's location on the equator and differences in elevation influence the climates and types of vegetation in East Africa. For example, areas near the equator receive the greatest amount of rainfall. Areas farther from the equator are much drier and seasonal droughts are common. **Droughts** are periods when little rain falls, and crops are damaged. During a drought, crops and the grasses for cattle die and people begin to starve. Several times in recent decades droughts have affected the people of East Africa.

Further south of the equator the climate changes to tropical savanna. Tall grasses and scattered trees make up the savanna landscape. Here the greatest climate changes occur along the sides of the rift valleys. The rift floors are dry with grasslands and thorn shrubs.

North of the equator, areas of plateaus and mountains have a highland climate and dense forests. Temperatures in the highlands are much cooler than temperatures on the savanna. The highlands experience heavy rainfall because of its high elevation, but the valleys are drier. This mild climate makes farming possible. As a result, most of the region's population lives in the highlands.

Satellite View

Great Rift Valley

This satellite image of part of the Great Rift Valley in Ethiopia was created by using both infrared light and true color. The bright blue dots are some of the smaller lakes that were created by the rifts. Once active volcanoes, some of these lakes are very deep. Vegetation appears as areas of green. Bare, rocky land appears pink and gray.

Analyzing How were the lakes in the Great Rift Valley created?

260 CHAPTER 9

Critical Thinking: Analyzing Information   Above Level

Creating a Chronology

1. Have students research the history of the search for the source of the Blue Nile. Explain that the source of the Nile was a compelling mystery to the ancient Greeks and others in the Mediterranean world. Many attempted to find the source, but failed. It wasn't until the 17th century that westerners resumed the search.

2. Have students create a detailed chronology of expeditions searching for the source of the Nile since the 17th century, from that of the Spanish missionary Pedro Paez in 1618 to the National Geographic expedition of 1999. Encourage them to add details about members of the expeditions and the obstacles they faced.

3. Have students discuss what they have learned and describe the expedition that they find most compelling. Have them discuss contemporary expeditions for scientific, geographical, and astronomical knowledge and explore what these have in common. **LS Verbal/Linguistic**

📄 Alternative Assessment Handbook, Rubrics 30: Research; and 40: Writing to Describe

Ancient volcanoes surround Uganda's Lake Mutanda. Here villagers rely on the lake's plentiful supply of fish.

Areas east of the highlands and on the Indian Ocean coast are at a much lower elevation. These areas have desert and steppe climates. Vegetation is limited to shrubs and hardy grasses that are adapted to water shortages.

READING CHECK **Categorizing** What are some of East Africa's climate types?

SUMMARY AND PREVIEW In this section you learned about East Africa's rift valleys, mountains, highlands, plains, rivers, and lakes. You also learned that the region's location and elevation affect its climate and vegetation. In the next section you will learn about the geography of Central Africa.

Section 3 Assessment

go.hrw.com
Online Quiz
KEYWORD: SK9 HP9

Reviewing Ideas, Terms, and Places

1. **a. Define** What are **rift valleys**?
   b. Explain Why is there snow on **Mount Kilimanjaro**?
   c. Elaborate What are some unusual characteristics of the lakes in the **Great Rift Valley**?
2. **a. Recall** What is the climate of the highlands in East Africa like?
   b. Draw Conclusions What are some effects of **drought** in the region?
   c. Develop How are the climates of some areas of East Africa affected by elevation?

Critical Thinking

3. **Categorizing** Using your notes and this chart, place details about East Africa's physical features into different categories.

Physical Features			
Rift Valleys	Mountains and Highlands	Plains	Rivers and Lakes

FOCUS ON WRITING

4. **Describing the Physical Geography** Note the physical features of East Africa that you can describe in your letter. How do these features compare to the features where you live?

PHYSICAL GEOGRAPHY OF AFRICA **261**

Section 3 Assessment Answers

1. **a.** places where Earth's tectonic plates are moving away from each other, causing the crust to stretch and break
   b. because of the mountain's high elevation
   c. Some are hot, and others are salty.
2. **a.** mild and rainy
   b. Crops are damaged; dying grass causes cattle to die; people starve.
   c. Climates in low elevations, such as the rift floors, are hot and dry; climates in higher elevations, such as the highlands, are cooler with heavy rainfall.

3. possible answer—Rift Valleys: caused by tectonic plate movement, volcanoes, high cliffs; Mountains and Highlands: Mount Kilimanjaro snow covered, highlands in Ethiopia; Plains: Serengeti, lions, giraffes, elephants, and zebras; Rivers and Lakes: White and Blue Nile, Lake Victoria, some Rift Valley lakes are hot or salty.

4. Answers will vary. Students should accurately compare physical features of East Africa to the features where they live.

• **Direct Teach** •

Main Idea

Climate and Vegetation, *continued*

Describe Why does most of the region's population live in the highlands? *because of the mild climate, which makes farming possible*

Define What is a drought? *a period when little rain falls and crops are damaged*

go.hrw.com
Online Resources
KEYWORD: SK9 CH9
ACTIVITY: Drought in East Africa

• Review & Assess •

Close

Use the section's vocabulary to review important information about the physical geography of East Africa.

Review

Online Quiz, Section 3

Assess

SE Section 3 Assessment
PASS: Section 3 Quiz
Alternative Assessment Handbook

Reteach/Classroom Intervention

Interactive Reader and Study Guide, Section 3
Interactive Skills Tutor CD-ROM

Answers

Reading Check *desert, steppe, tropical savanna, highland*

261

Bellringer

If YOU lived there. . . Use the **Daily Bellringer Transparency** to help students answer the question.

📚 Daily Bellringer Transparency, Section 4

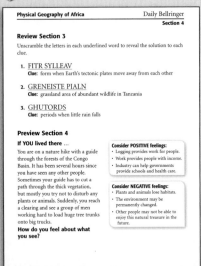

Key Terms and Places

📖 RF: Vocabulary Builder, Section 4

Taking Notes

Have students copy the graphic organizer onto their own paper and then use it to take notes on the section. This activity will prepare students for the Section Assessment, in which they will complete a graphic organizer that builds on the information using the Critical Thinking Skill: Contrasting.

Central Africa

What You Will Learn...

Main Ideas

1. Central Africa's major physical features include the Congo Basin and plateaus surrounding the basin.
2. Central Africa has a humid tropical climate and dense forest vegetation.
3. Central Africa's resources include forest products and valuable minerals such as diamonds and copper.

The Big Idea

The Congo River, tropical forests, and mineral resources are important features of Central Africa's physical geography.

Key Terms and Places

Congo Basin, *p. 262*
basin, *p. 262*
Congo River, *p. 263*
Zambezi River, *p. 263*
periodic market, *p. 265*
copper belt, *p. 265*

TAKING NOTES As you read, use a chart like the one here to note characteristics of Central Africa's physical geography.

Physical features	
Climate and vegetation	
Resources	

If **YOU** lived there...

You are on a nature hike with a guide through the forests of the Congo Basin. It has been several hours since you have seen any other people. Sometimes your guide has to use a heavy machete to cut a path through the thick vegetation, but mostly you try not to disturb any plants or animals. Suddenly, you reach a clearing and see a group of men working hard to load huge tree trunks onto big trucks.

How do you feel about what you see?

BUILDING BACKGROUND Much of Central Africa, particularly in the Congo Basin, is covered with thick, tropical forests. The forests provide valuable resources, but people have different ideas about how the forests should be used. Forests are just one of the many types of landscapes in Central Africa.

Physical Features

Central Africa is bordered by the Atlantic Ocean in the west. In the east, it is bordered by a huge valley called the Western Rift Valley. The land in between has some of the highest mountains and biggest rivers in Africa.

Landforms

You can think of the region as a big soup bowl with a wide rim. Near the middle of the bowl is the **Congo Basin**. In geography, a **basin** is a generally flat region surrounded by higher land such as mountains and plateaus.

Plateaus and low hills surround the Congo Basin. The highest mountains in Central Africa lie farther away from the basin, along the Western Rift Valley. Some of these snowcapped mountains rise to more than 16,700 feet (5,090 m). Two lakes also lie along the rift—Lake Nyasa and Lake Tanganyika (tan-guhn-YEE-kuh). Lake Nyasa is also called Lake Malawi.

Teach the Big Idea

At Level

Central Africa

1. **Teach** Ask students the questions in the Main Idea boxes under Direct Teach.

2. **Apply** Read the names of the countries in Central Africa aloud. Have individual students come up and point to each country on a wall map. Discuss things that these countries may have in common based on location. How might proximity to the equator affect climate and vegetation in these countries? **LS Visual/Spatial**

3. **Review** After completing the section, have students discuss and answer each of these questions again.

4. **Practice/Homework** Have each student write three true/false questions about the physical geography of Central Africa to share with the class. **LS Verbal/Linguistic**

📝 Alternative Assessment Handbook, Rubrics 11: Discussions; and 37: Writing Assignments

Rivers

The huge **Congo River** is fed by hundreds of smaller rivers. They drain the swampy Congo Basin and flow into the river as it runs toward the Atlantic. Many rapids and waterfalls lie along its route, especially near its mouth. These obstacles make it impossible for ships to travel from the interior of Central Africa all the way to the Atlantic. The Congo provides an important transportation route in the interior, however.

In the southern part of the region, the **Zambezi** (zam-BEE-zee) **River** flows eastward toward the Indian Ocean. Many rivers in Angola and Zambia, as well as water from Lake Nyasa, flow into the Zambezi. The Zambezi also has many waterfalls along its route, the most famous of which are the spectacular Victoria Falls.

READING CHECK Finding Main Ideas Where is the highest land in Central Africa?

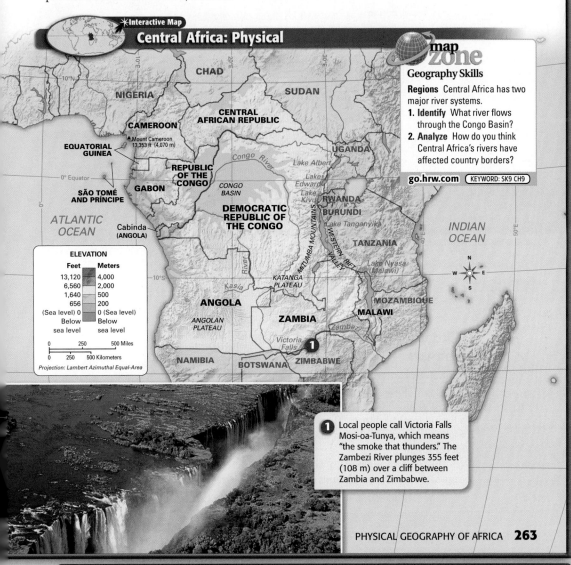

Central Africa: Physical

★ Interactive Map

map Zone

Geography Skills

Regions Central Africa has two major river systems.
1. **Identify** What river flows through the Congo Basin?
2. **Analyze** How do you think Central Africa's rivers have affected country borders?

go.hrw.com | KEYWORD: SK9 CH9

ELEVATION

Feet	Meters
13,120	4,000
6,560	2,000
1,640	500
656	200
(Sea level) 0	0 (Sea level)
Below sea level	Below sea level

0   250   500 Miles
0   250   500 Kilometers
Projection: Lambert Azimuthal Equal-Area

Mount Cameroon 13,353 ft (4,070 m)

1 Local people call Victoria Falls Mosi-oa-Tunya, which means "the smoke that thunders." The Zambezi River plunges 355 feet (108 m) over a cliff between Zambia and Zimbabwe.

PHYSICAL GEOGRAPHY OF AFRICA **263**

Direct Teach

Main Idea

1 Physical Features

Central Africa's major physical features include the Congo Basin and plateaus surrounding the basin.

Identify What is the Congo Basin? *a generally flat region in Central Africa surrounded by higher land including low hills and plateaus*

Describe Where are the major lakes and mountains in Central Africa located? *Western Rift Valley*

Make Inferences What prevents the Congo and Zambezi rivers from being more useful for trade and transportation? *Rapids and waterfalls reduce navigability and limit the rivers' usefulness for trade and transportation.*

Map Zone Transparency: Central Africa: Physical

Info to Know

Congo River The Congo River is the fifth-longest river in the world. It is Africa's second-longest river. Only the Nile is longer. The Congo's many tributaries form close to 9,000 miles of navigable water. The river begins just south of Lake Tanganyika and passes through a long stretch of rapids until it gets to Stanley Falls. Then it is navigable for about 1,000 miles until close to Kinshasa, the capital of the Democratic Republic of the Congo. The river has 32 waterfalls and crosses the equator twice.

Collaborative Learning

Managing the Congo River

At Level

Research Required

1. Explain that while the Congo River is an important transportation route, several problems prevent it from providing even more of the region's needs for energy and transportation. Among these problems are rapids and waterfalls, poorly maintained roads and ports, lack of bridges, and poorly functioning government water management agencies.

2. Divide students into small groups. Ask each group to research one problem and suggest ways in which it might be solved. For example, a railroad connecting Kinshasa with the city of Matadi on the coast has overcome the limitations of the rapids.

3. Have each group prepare a proposal describing the problem, the causes of the problem, how it might be solved, and equipment or resources needed.

4. Have a member of each group present its proposal to the class. Have the class decide which solutions seem most practical.

LS Verbal/Linguistic

Alternative Assessment Handbook, Rubric 35: Solving Problems

Answers

Reading Check *along the Western Rift Valley*

Map Zone 1. *Congo River;* **2.** *possible answer—Rivers are the borders or partial borders of several nations in the region.*

263

Main Idea

❷ Climate, Vegetation, and Animals

Central Africa has a humid tropical climate and dense forest vegetation.

Recall What kind of vegetation and climate does the Atlantic coast have? *dense tropical forest, humid tropical climate*

Explain How is the climate and vegetation in areas north and south of the Congo Basin different than those in the Congo Basin? *These areas have a tropical savanna climate with distinct dry and wet seasons. The vegetation to the north and south includes shrubs, grasslands, and scattered trees.*

Cause and Effect What economic effects might clearing tropical forests have? *Farming and logging provide food or income for some, but loss of habitat for animals might mean loss of homes or food for people living near forests.*

 Map Zone Transparency: Central Africa's National Parks

Connect to Science

Transpiration Tropical forests have an influence on climate. Trees and other plants are an important part of the water cycle. By taking in water and giving off water vapor through transpiration, the trees in a tropical forest return huge amounts of water to the atmosphere, increasing humidity and rainfall and cooling the air. Tropical forests also renew the air by taking in carbon dioxide and giving off oxygen.

Answers

Map Zone 1. *Angola, Republic of Congo, Gabon, Cameroon;* **2.** *possible answers—to preserve habitats of animals and plants that would otherwise disappear; to increase biodiversity; to promote tourism; to provide enjoyment, educational, and recreational opportunities for people*

264

Central Africa's National Parks

National parks in Central Africa protect the habitat of gorillas (above), which are endangered, and okapis (below).

map zone Geography Skills

Human-Environment Interaction People have created national parks in Central Africa to try to protect the region's landscapes and animals.
1. **Use the Map** What Central African countries have national parks in coastal areas?
2. **Explain** Why do people want to protect natural environments?

Climate, Vegetation, and Animals

Central Africa lies along the equator and in the low latitudes. Therefore, the Congo Basin and much of the Atlantic coast have a humid tropical climate. These areas have warm temperatures all year and receive a lot of rainfall.

This climate supports a large, dense tropical forest. The many kinds of tall trees in the forest form a complete canopy. The canopy is the uppermost layer of the trees where the limbs spread out. Canopy leaves block sunlight to the ground below.

Such animals as gorillas, elephants, wild boars, and okapis live in the forest. The okapi is a short-necked relative of the giraffe. However, since little sunlight shines through the canopy, only a few animals live on the forest floor. Some animals, such as birds, monkeys, bats, and snakes, live in the trees. Many insects also live in Central Africa's forest.

264 CHAPTER 9

Differentiating Instruction

Below Level

Special Needs Learners

1. Use a globe or large wall map of the world to review the terms *low latitudes* and *tropical climate*. Have students find the equator on the map or globe. Ask why the area around the equator is known as the *low* latitudes.

2. Have students name countries in the low latitudes and define the word *humid*. Ask students if their area is humid at any time during the year.

3. Next discuss the term *tropical*. Explain that it describes weather or climate that is hot and humid. Have students describe the weather in the tropics in April, July, and December.

4. Discuss differences between the words *tropical* and *tropics* and how the terms are related. Give students additional practice by having them explain what the phrases "tropical weather," "tropical islands," and "tropical fruit" mean. **LS Verbal/Linguistic**

Alternative Assessment Handbook, Rubrics 21: Map Reading; and 28: Presentations

The animals in Central Africa's tropical forests, as well as the forests themselves, are in danger. Large areas of forest are being cleared rapidly for farming and logging. Also, people hunt the large animals in the forests to get food. To promote protection of forests and other natural environments, governments have set up national park areas in their countries.

North and south of the Congo Basin are large areas with a tropical savanna climate. Those areas are warm all year, but they have distinct dry and wet seasons. There are grasslands, scattered trees, and shrubs. The high mountains in the east have a highland climate. Dry steppe and even desert climates are found in the far southern part of the region.

READING CHECK Summarizing What are the climate and vegetation like in the Congo Basin?

Resources

The tropical environment of Central Africa is good for growing crops. Most people in the region are subsistence farmers. However, many farmers are now beginning to grow crops for sale. Common crops are coffee, bananas, and corn. In rural areas, people trade agricultural and other products in periodic markets. A **periodic market** is an open-air trading market that is set up once or twice a week.

Central Africa is rich in other natural resources as well. The large tropical forest provides timber, while the rivers provide a way to travel and to trade. Dams on the rivers produce hydroelectricity, an important energy resource. Other energy resources in the region include oil, natural gas, and coal.

Central Africa also has many valuable minerals, including copper, uranium, tin, zinc, diamonds, gold, and cobalt. Of these, copper is the most important. Most of

Africa's copper is found in an area called the **copper belt**. The copper belt stretches through northern Zambia and southern Democratic Republic of the Congo. However, poor transportation systems and political problems have kept the region's resources from being fully developed.

READING CHECK Analyzing Why are Central Africa's rivers an important natural resource?

SUMMARY AND PREVIEW Mighty rivers, the tropical forest of the Congo Basin, and mineral resources characterize the physical geography of Central Africa. These landscapes have influenced the region's history. Next, you will move south to study Southern Africa.

Section 4 Assessment

go.hrw.com
Online Quiz
KEYWORD: SK9 HP9

Reviewing Ideas, Terms, and Places
1. **a. Describe** What is the **Congo Basin**?
   b. Elaborate How do you think the **Congo River**'s rapids and waterfalls affect the economy of the region?
2. **a. Recall** What part of Central Africa has a highland climate?
   b. Explain Why have governments in the region set up national parks?
   c. Evaluate Is it more important to use the forest's resources or to protect the natural environment? Why?
3. **a. Define** What is a **periodic market**?
   b. Elaborate What kinds of political problems might keep mineral resources from being fully developed?

Critical Thinking
4. **Contrasting** Use your notes and a graphic organizer like this one to list differences between the Congo Basin and the areas surrounding it in Central Africa.

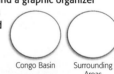

Congo Basin   Surrounding Areas

FOCUS ON WRITING
5. **Sharing Details** What details about Central Africa will you include in your letter? Will you describe the animals you have seen and the weather you have experienced? Take some notes.

PHYSICAL GEOGRAPHY OF AFRICA **265**

Section 4 Assessment Answers

1. **a.** generally flat region of Central Africa surrounded by plateaus and low hills
   b. hurt it by reducing travel; help it by promoting tourism and production of electricity
2. **a.** high mountains in east
   b. to protect tropical forests from being cleared for farming and logging, protect endangered animals, and promote tourism
   c. Students' answers will vary but should include reasons and supporting details.
3. **a.** open-air trading market set up once or twice a week

b. political instability, collapse of governments, wars and other conflicts, corruption of government officials

4. Congo Basin—humid tropical climate, large dense tropical forests; Surrounding areas—varied climates: north and south of basin tropical savanna climate with grasslands; in east highland climate in high mountains; dry steppe and desert climates in far southern area

5. Answers will vary, but should mention topics such as the physical geography, climate, vegetation, animals, and resources of Central Africa.

Direct Teach

Main Idea

❸ **Resources**

Central Africa's resources include forest products and valuable minerals such as diamonds and copper.

Recall What mineral resources does this region have? *copper, tin, uranium, zinc, diamonds, gold, cobalt*

Analyze What kinds of transportation problems might make it hard to develop natural resources? *poorly built or maintained roads, absence of any roads or railroads, lack of alternative routes for roads in areas with waterfalls and rapids*

Review & Assess

Close

Ask students to describe Central Africa's landforms, climates, vegetation, and resources.

Review

Online Quiz, Section 4

Assess

SE Section 4 Assessment

PASS: Section 4 Quiz

Alternative Assessment Handbook

Reteach/Classroom Intervention

Interactive Reader and Study Guide, Section 4

Interactive Skills Tutor CD-ROM

Answers

Reading Check (left) *humid tropical climate with warm temperatures year-round and plentiful rain; large, dense tropical forests*

Reading Check (right) *They are used for travel, trade, and the production of hydroelectricity.*

265

Activity **Plan a Walk** Divide students into groups. Designate a one-mile walk in a nearby area that is safe for walking. Arrange to have parent volunteers accompany each group on its walk. If possible, the routes should feature a variety of scenery such as residential neighborhoods, businesses, offices, parks, golf courses, rivers, or lakes and waterfront areas. Before taking the walk, students should decide their group's purpose for the walk. Point out that some of Fay's goals were to measure the effects of human activities on the environment and help geographers plan for the future use of land. Students should take notes as they walk. Have each group decide what types of data they want to gather, such as the number of people on sidewalks, animals, traffic lights, cars, bicycles, parking spaces, trash disposal containers, or types of buildings. Once data is gathered, have groups use their field notes to draw conclusions on what they have observed. Lead the class in comparing the data gathered by the groups.

Linking to Today

National Parks In 2002 the campaign by Michael Fay to help preserve Gabon's tropical forests succeeded. Gabon's president responded to the efforts of Fay and other conservationists as well as international organizations like the World Wildlife Fund by creating the country's first national parks. One of the new parks is Loango National Park on Gabon's Atlantic coast. Visitors to Loango can see elephants, buffalo, hippos, gorillas, and leopards. Along Loango's coast, tourists can observe large numbers of humpback and killer whales. Loango Park is one of 12 national parks or wildlife reserves planned for Gabon.

go.hrw.com
Online Resources
KEYWORD: SK9 CH9
ACTIVITY: Central African Wildlife

Eye on Earth

Mapping Central Africa's Forests

Essential Elements
The World in Spatial Terms
Places and Regions
Physical Systems
Human Systems
Environment and Society
The Uses of Geography

Background Imagine taking a walk along a street in your neighborhood. Your purpose is to see the street in spatial terms and gather information to help you make a map. While you walk, you ask the kinds of questions geographers ask. How many houses, apartment buildings, or businesses are on the street? What kinds of animals or trees do you see? Your walk ends, and you organize your data. Now imagine that you are going to gather data on another walk. This walk will be 2,000 miles long.

A 2,000-Mile Walk In September 1999, an American scientist named Michael Fay began a 465-day, 2,000-mile walk through Central Africa's forests. He and his team followed elephant trails through thick vegetation. They waded through creeks and mucky swamps.

On the walk, Fay gathered data on the number and kinds of animals he saw. He counted elephant dung, chimpanzee nests, leopard tracks, and gorillas. He counted the types of trees and other plants along his

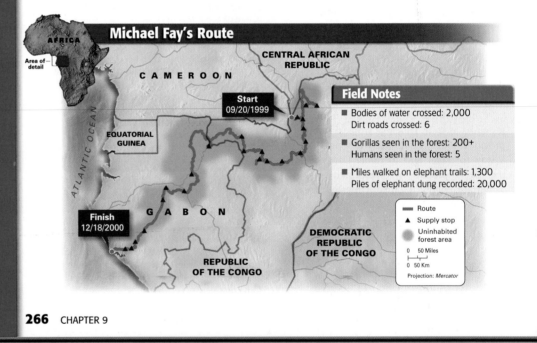

Michael Fay's Route

AFRICA
Area of detail

CENTRAL AFRICAN REPUBLIC
CAMEROON
EQUATORIAL GUINEA
ATLANTIC OCEAN
GABON
REPUBLIC OF THE CONGO
DEMOCRATIC REPUBLIC OF THE CONGO

Start 09/20/1999
Finish 12/18/2000

Field Notes
■ Bodies of water crossed: 2,000
Dirt roads crossed: 6
■ Gorillas seen in the forest: 200+
Humans seen in the forest: 5
■ Miles walked on elephant trails: 1,300
Piles of elephant dung recorded: 20,000

— Route
▲ Supply stop
● Uninhabited forest area
0   50 Miles
0   50 Km
Projection: *Mercator*

266 CHAPTER 9

Differentiating Instruction

Below Level   **Standard English Mastery**

Struggling Readers

1. Have students study the photographs on the next page as you read aloud the caption. Write the word *clearing* on the board. Have students find the root word in a dictionary and use context clues to decode this word. Ask them to describe what Fay and the elephants are doing in these pictures. Based on what they have read about Fay's walk, what animals and plants might they see on a visit to a forest in Central Africa?

2. Have students imagine they are sending a postcard of a photograph from this chapter to a friend after visiting a national park in Central Africa. Have students write two or three sentences using standard English to describe what they have seen or draw a picture of animals they might see. Encourage students to use a thesaurus to find words that are descriptive. **LS** **Visual/Spatial, Verbal/Linguistic**

Alternative Assessment Handbook, Rubric 40: Writing to Describe

Michael Fay (above) and his team had to chop their way through thick forest vegetation. In a clearing, they spotted this group of elephants.

Biography

Michael Fay After graduating from college in Arizona, Michael Fay spent six years in the Peace Corps working as a botanist in national parks in Tunisia and the savannas of the Central African Republic. He first spent time in the forests of Central Africa when he was working on his doctorate. He did his doctoral work on western lowland gorillas. In the 1990s, he helped to create and manage the Dzanga-Sangha and Nouabale-Ndoki parks in the Central African Republic and Congo. His flights in a small plane over the forests of Congo and Gabon drew his attention to the vast forested area and led in 1999 to his 2,000-mile walk and campaign for forest preservation.

🗺 Map Zone Transparency: Michael Fay's Route

route. He also counted human settlements and determined the effect of human activities on the environment.

Fay used a variety of tools to record the data he gathered on his walk. He wrote down what he observed in waterproof notebooks. He shot events and scenes with video and still cameras. To measure the distance he and his team walked each day, he used a tool called a Fieldranger. He also kept track of his exact position in the forest by using a GPS, or global positioning system.

What It Means Michael Fay explained the purpose of his long walk. "The whole idea behind this is to be able to use the data we've collected as a tool." Other geographers can compare Fay's data with their own. Their comparison may help them create more accurate maps. These maps will show where plants, animals, and humans are located in Central Africa's forests.

Fay's data can also help scientists plan the future use of land or resources in a region. For example, Fay has used his data to convince government officials in Gabon to set aside 10 percent of its land to create 13 national parks. The parks will be protected from future logging and farming. They also will preserve many of the plants and animals that Fay and his team observed on their long walk.

Geography for Life Activity

1. Why did Michael Fay walk 2,000 miles?
2. In what practical way has Michael Fay used his data?
3. **Read More about Fay's Walk** Read the three-part article on Michael Fay's walk in *National Geographic* October 2000, March 2001, and August 2001. After you read the article, explain why Fay called his walk a "megatransect."

PHYSICAL GEOGRAPHY OF AFRICA **267**

Critical Thinking: Identifying Points of View   `At Level`

Preserving Gabon's Natural Resources

1. Display the following quote from Michael Fay about his walk: "It makes you wake up to the fact that human beings even in the 21st century, still don't regard natural resources as something precious. Because if they did, there would be a worldwide effort to preserve these places rather than extract wood out of them as quickly as possibly with zero regard for ecosystems . . ."

2. Have students restate this quote in their own words. Identify any unfamiliar words or expressions.

3. Tell students that Fay describes himself as a conservationist. Have students identify how this quote reflects his point of view. Have them describe Fay's concerns about the natural resources in Gabon. Then discuss other views about this issue.

4. Ask students to write an opinion piece expressing their own views about Fay's concerns about natural resources.

LS Verbal/Linguistic

📖 Alternative Assessment Handbook, Rubric 41, Writing to Express

267

Bellringer

If YOU lived there. . . Use the **Daily Bellringer Transparency** to help students answer the question.

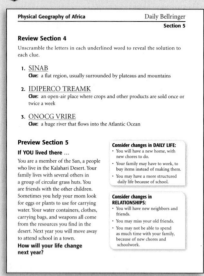 Daily Bellringer Transparency, Section 5

Physical Geography of Africa	Daily Bellringer
	Section 5

Review Section 4

Unscramble the letters in each underlined word to reveal the solution to each clue.

1. SINAB
   Clue: a flat region, usually surrounded by plateaus and mountains
2. IDIPERCO TREAMK
   Clue: an open-air place where crops and other products are sold once or twice a week
3. ONOCG VRIRE
   Clue: a huge river that flows into the Atlantic Ocean

Preview Section 5

If YOU lived there ...

You are a member of the San, a people who live in the Kalahari Desert. Your family lives with several others in a group of circular grass huts. You are friends with the other children. Sometimes you help your mom look for eggs or plants to use for carrying water. Your water containers, clothes, carrying bags, and weapons all come from the resources you find in the desert. Next year you will move away to attend school in a town. **How will your life change next year?**

Consider changes in DAILY LIFE:
- You will have a new home, with new chores to do.
- Your family may have to work, to buy items instead of making them.
- You may have a more structured daily life because of school.

Consider changes in RELATIONSHIPS:
- You will have new neighbors and friends.
- You may miss your old friends.
- You may not be able to spend as much time with your family, because of new chores and schoolwork.

Key Terms and Places

 RF: Vocabulary Builder, Section 5

Taking Notes

Have students copy the graphic organizer onto their own paper and then use it to take notes on the section. This activity will prepare students for the Section Assessment, in which they will complete a graphic organizer that builds on the information using the Critical Thinking Skill: Categorizing.

Southern Africa

What You Will Learn...

Main Ideas

1. Southern Africa's main physical feature is a large plateau with plains, rivers, and mountains.
2. The climate and vegetation of Southern Africa is mostly savanna and desert.
3. Southern Africa has valuable mineral resources.

The Big Idea

Southern Africa's physical geography includes a high, mostly dry plateau, grassy plains and rivers, and valuable mineral resources.

Key Terms and Places

escarpment, *p. 268*
veld, *p. 270*
Namib Desert, *p. 270*
pans, *p. 270*

TAKING NOTES As you read, take notes on the physical geography of Southern Africa. Use a chart like this one to organize your notes.

Physical Features	
Climate and Vegetation	
Resources	

If YOU lived there...

You are a member of the San, a people who live in the Kalahari Desert. Your family lives with several others in a group of circular grass huts. You are friends with the other children. Sometimes you help your mom look for eggs or plants to use for carrying water. You also helped make all your water containers, clothes, carrying bags, and weapons, all of which come from the resources you find in the desert. Next year you will move away to attend school in a town.

How will your life change next year?

BUILDING BACKGROUND Parts of Southern Africa have a desert climate. Little vegetation grows in these areas, but some people do live there. Most of Southern Africa's people live in cooler and wetter areas, such as on the high, grassy plains in the south and east.

Physical Features

Southern Africa has some amazing scenery. On a visit to the region, you might see grassy plains, steamy swamps, mighty rivers, rocky waterfalls, and steep mountains and plateaus.

Plateaus and Mountains

Most of the land in Southern Africa lies on a large plateau. Parts of this plateau reach more than 4,000 feet (1,220 m) above sea level. To form the plateau, the land rises sharply from a narrow coastal plain. The steep face at the edge of a plateau or other raised area is called an **escarpment**.

In eastern South Africa, part of the escarpment is made up of a mountain range called the Drakensberg (DRAH-kuhnz-buhrk). The steep peaks rise as high as 11,425 feet (3,482 m). Farther north, another mountain range, the Inyanga (in-YANG-guh) Mountains, separates Zimbabwe and Mozambique. Southern Africa also has mountains along its western coast.

268 CHAPTER 9

Teach the Big Idea

At Level

Southern Africa

1. **Teach** Ask students the questions in the Main Idea boxes under Direct Teach.

2. **Apply** Have each student write the names of the countries located in Southern Africa on a piece of paper, using the map on the opposite page as a guide. Next to each name, have students write three facts about the country, based on what they see on the map. For example, "Mozambique borders the Indian Ocean." **LS Visual/Spatial**

3. **Review** Ask students to read their facts aloud to the class. Have students write down any additional facts they learn, but had not listed.

4. **Practice/Homework** Have students write out one generalization about each country based on the facts they now know.
   LS Verbal/Linguistic
   Alternative Assessment Handbook, Rubric 21: Map Reading

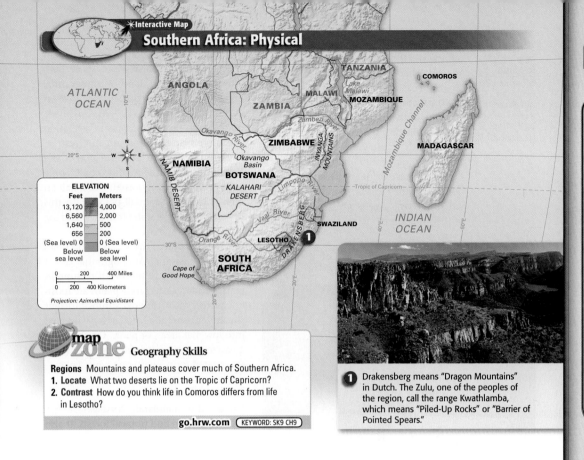

Southern Africa: Physical

ATLANTIC OCEAN

ANGOLA

ZAMBIA

TANZANIA

Lake Malawi

MALAWI

MOZAMBIQUE

COMOROS

NAMIBIA

ZIMBABWE

Okavango River

Okavango Basin

BOTSWANA

KALAHARI DESERT

NAMIB DESERT

Zambezi River

INYANGA MOUNTAINS

Limpopo River

Mozambique Channel

MADAGASCAR

Tropic of Capricorn

INDIAN OCEAN

Vaal River

Orange River

SWAZILAND

LESOTHO ❶

SOUTH AFRICA

DRAKENSBERG

Cape of Good Hope

ELEVATION

Feet	Meters
13,120	4,000
6,560	2,000
1,640	500
656	200
(Sea level) 0	0 (Sea level)
Below sea level	Below sea level

0   200   400 Miles
0   200   400 Kilometers

Projection: Azimuthal Equidistant

map Zone Geography Skills

Regions Mountains and plateaus cover much of Southern Africa.
1. **Locate** What two deserts lie on the Tropic of Capricorn?
2. **Contrast** How do you think life in Comoros differs from life in Lesotho?

go.hrw.com (KEYWORD: SK9 CH9)

❶ Drakensberg means "Dragon Mountains" in Dutch. The Zulu, one of the peoples of the region, call the range Kwathlamba, which means "Piled-Up Rocks" or "Barrier of Pointed Spears."

Plains and Rivers

Southern Africa's narrow coastal plain and the wide plateau are covered with grassy plains. These flat plains are home to animals such as lions, leopards, elephants, baboons, and antelope.

Several large rivers cross Southern Africa's plains. The Okavango River flows from Angola into a huge basin in Botswana. This river's water never reaches the ocean. Instead it forms a swampy inland delta that is home to crocodiles, zebras, hippos, and other animals. Many tourists travel to Botswana to see these wild animals in their natural habitat.

The Orange River passes through the rocky Augrabies (oh-KRAH-bees) Falls as it flows to the Atlantic Ocean. When the water in the river is at its highest, the falls are several miles wide. The water tumbles down 19 separate waterfalls. The Limpopo River is another of the region's major rivers. It flows into the Indian Ocean. Features such as waterfalls and other obstacles block ships from sailing up these rivers. However, the rivers do allow irrigation for farmland in an otherwise dry area.

ACADEMIC VOCABULARY

features characteristics

READING CHECK **Generalizing** What are Southern Africa's main physical features?

PHYSICAL GEOGRAPHY OF AFRICA **269**

Direct Teach

Main Idea

❶ Physical Features

Southern Africa's main physical feature is a large plateau with plains, rivers, and mountains.

Identify Name the countries that do not share a border with South Africa. *Comoros, Madagascar*

Define What is an escarpment? *the steep face at the edge of a plateau or other raised area* What is the veld? *open grassland areas of South Africa*

Recall Which two mountain ranges form the eastern escarpment of Southern Africa? *the Drakensberg and the Inyanga Mountains*

📦 Map Zone Transparency: Southern Africa: Physical

Connect to Arts and the Humanities

Mountain Gallery The Drakensberg is South Africa's highest mountain range. Its mountain tops have a layer of basalt, with sandstone underneath. This creates steep-sided blocks and peaks—with many caves found in the sandstone. In some of these caves, thousands of images of rock art can be found. The art was created by the indigenous San people who lived in the mountains for about 4,000 years.

Differentiating Instruction

Struggling Readers   Below Level

1. To help struggling readers, point to each label on the map and help them read the names out loud.

2. Ask which labels are countries, rivers, deserts, and mountains, or point these out as necessary. Remind students that their textbook has many illustrations that can help them learn. **LS Verbal/Linguistic, Visual/Spatial**

📓 Alternative Assessment Handbook, Rubric 21: Map Reading

Advanced/Gifted and Talented   Above Level   Research Required

1. Have students research and write a report on one of the major rivers of Southern Africa. Have students include information about waterfalls and other features, plant and animal life on or near the river, and any threats to the river's environment.

2. Ask for volunteers to present their reports to the class. **LS Verbal/Linguistic**

📓 Alternative Assessment Handbook, Rubrics 29: Presentations; and 30: Research

Answers

Map Zone 1. *the Namib Desert and the Kalahari Desert;* **2.** *possible answer— Because Comoros is an island country while Lesotho is landlocked, its people likely rely on the sea, not the land, for food and jobs.*

Reading Check *Physical features include a large plateau, the Drakensberg mountain range, the Inyanga Mountains, grasslands, many rivers, waterfalls, swamps, and deserts.*

2 Climate and Vegetation

The climate and vegetation of Southern Africa is mostly savanna and desert.

Recall What is the driest area in the region? *the Namib Desert*

Describe What are pans? *low, flat areas where ancient streams have drained* Why do they have a glittering white layer? *The minerals left behind when the water evaporated created a glittering white layer.*

Explain Why have many of the animals on Madagascar become endangered? *because of the destruction of the forests*

Activity Research Required

Life in the Namib Desert Divide the class into groups of three or four. Have each group choose a desert animal to research. Have students create a poster illustrating the animal and how it survives in the desert. The poster should include captions for important information, such as what food the animal eats, and how it gets water. Have each group present their poster to the class. **LS Verbal/Linguistic, Visual/Spatial**

📖 Alternative Assessment Handbook, Rubric 28: Posters

Climate and Vegetation

FOCUS ON READING
What phrase tells you that the eastern and western parts of Southern Africa are different?

Southern Africa's climates vary from east to west. The wettest place in the region is the east coast of the island of Madagascar. On the mainland, winds carrying moisture blow in from the Indian Ocean. Because the Drakensberg's high elevation causes these winds to blow upward, the eastern slopes of these mountains are rainy.

In contrast to the eastern part of the continent, the west is very dry. From the Atlantic coast, deserts give way to plains with semiarid and steppe climates.

Satellite View

Namib Desert

One of the world's most unusual deserts, the Namib lies on the Atlantic coast in Namibia. As this satellite image shows, the land there is extremely dry. Some of the world's highest sand dunes stretch for miles along the coast.

In spite of its harsh conditions, some insects have adapted to life in the desert. They can survive there because at night a fog rolls in from the ocean. The insects use the fog as a source of water.

Drawing Conclusions How have some insects adapted to living in the Namib Desert?

Savanna and Deserts

A large savanna region covers much of Southern Africa. Shrubs and short trees grow on the grassy plains of the savanna. In South Africa, these open grassland areas are known as the **veld** (VELT). As you can see on the map on the next page, vegetation gets more sparse in the south and west.

The driest place in the region is the **Namib Desert** on the Atlantic coast. Some parts of the Namib get as little as a half an inch (13 mm) of rainfall per year. In this dry area, plants get water from dew and fog rather than from rain.

Another desert, the Kalahari, occupies most of Botswana. Although this desert gets enough rain in the north to support grasses and trees, its sandy plains are mostly covered with scattered shrubs. Ancient streams crossing the Kalahari have drained into low, flat areas, or **pans**. On these flat areas, minerals left behind when the water evaporated form a glittering white layer.

Tropical Forests

Unlike the mainland, Madagascar has lush vegetation and tropical forests. It also has many animals found nowhere else. For example, some 50 species of lemurs, relatives of apes, live only on this island. However, the destruction of Madagascar's forests has endangered many of the island's animals.

READING CHECK **Summarizing** What is the climate and vegetation like in Southern Africa?

Resources

Southern Africa is rich in natural resources. Madagascar's forests provide timber. The region's rivers supply hydroelectricity and water for irrigation. Where rain is plentiful or irrigation is possible, farmers can grow a wide range of crops.

Collaborative Learning

At Level

Mapping Climates

1. Organize the class into pairs or small groups.

2. Using a large piece of paper, have students draw a map of Southern Africa, outlining the borders of each country. Students should label each country, and fill in the locations of mountains, rivers, and deserts.

3. Then, have students create a "climate key" and map out the climates of the region.

4. Based on the climate maps, have a class discussion about which areas students think would be best for farming, most comfortable for living, and most difficult for living. Encourage them to give reasons to support their responses. **LS Verbal/Linguistic, Visual/Spatial**

📖 Alternative Assessment Handbook, Rubrics 11: Discussions; and 20: Map Creation

Answers

Focus on Reading *"climates vary from east to west"*

Reading Check *The climate is diverse. The eastern slopes are rainy, but it's drier inland and westward. The central and western parts of the region include two deserts. Vegetation in most of Southern Africa includes shrubs, grassland areas, and some areas with trees. Madagascar has lush vegetation and tropical forests.*

Satellite View *by drinking the dew created by the fog*

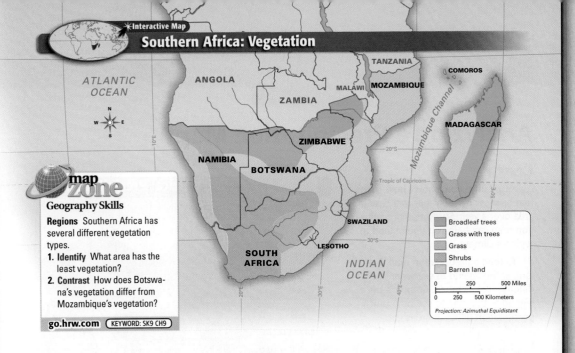

Interactive Map

Southern Africa: Vegetation

ATLANTIC OCEAN

ANGOLA

ZAMBIA

TANZANIA

MALAWI MOZAMBIQUE

COMOROS

MADAGASCAR

ZIMBABWE

NAMIBIA

BOTSWANA

Mozambique Channel

SWAZILAND

LESOTHO

SOUTH AFRICA

INDIAN OCEAN

Tropic of Capricorn

map Zone

Geography Skills

Regions Southern Africa has several different vegetation types.

1. **Identify** What area has the least vegetation?
2. **Contrast** How does Botswana's vegetation differ from Mozambique's vegetation?

go.hrw.com KEYWORD: SK9 CH9

- Broadleaf trees
- Grass with trees
- Grass
- Shrubs
- Barren land

0   250   500 Miles
0   250   500 Kilometers

Projection: Azimuthal Equidistant

The region's most valuable resources, however, are minerals. Mines in South Africa produce most of the world's gold. In addition, South Africa, Botswana, and Namibia have productive diamond mines. Other mineral resources in Southern Africa include coal, platinum, copper, uranium, and iron ore. Although mining is very important to the economy of the region, the mines can have damaging effects on the surrounding natural environments.

READING CHECK Finding Main Ideas What are the main resources of Southern Africa?

SUMMARY AND PREVIEW Africa is a huge continent with a variety of landforms, water features, and climates. In the next chapters, you will learn how landforms and climate affected one of Africa's earliest civilizations, ancient Egypt.

Section 5 Assessment

go.hrw.com
Online Quiz
KEYWORD: SK9 HP9

Reviewing Ideas, Terms, and Places

1. **a. Define** What is an **escarpment**?
   b. Elaborate How is the Okavango River different from most other rivers you have studied?
2. **a. Recall** Where in Southern Africa is the driest climate?
   b. Explain What caused minerals to collect in **pans** in the Kalahari Desert?
3. **a. Identify** What are Southern Africa's most valuable resources?
   b. Elaborate How do you think the gold and diamond mines have affected South Africa's economy?

Critical Thinking

4. **Categorizing** Review your notes and use a graphic organizer like this one to sort characteristics by location.

	East	West
Physical Features		
Climate and Vegetation		

FOCUS ON WRITING

5. **Planning Your Letter** Now that you have finished your tour of Africa you can plan exactly what you will include in your letter home. Write a short outline of the topics you will include.

PHYSICAL GEOGRAPHY OF AFRICA **271**

Direct Teach

Main Idea

❸ Resources

Southern Africa has valuable mineral resources.

Recall What are Southern Africa's valuable minerals? *gold, diamonds, coal, platinum, copper, uranium, iron ore*

Map Zone Transparency: Southern Africa: Vegetation

Interpreting Maps

Have students study the map, then answer the following questions.
Place Which countries have the most broadleaf trees? *Botswana, Zimbabwe, Madagascar, Namibia*
Location What oceans border Southern Africa? *Atlantic and Indian*
Location Which country in the region reaches farthest north? *Mozambique*

Review & Assess

Close

Discuss with students the diverse physical features, climate, vegetation, and natural resources of Southern Africa.

Review

Online Quiz, Section 5

Assess

SE Section 5 Assessment
PASS: Section 5 Quiz
Alternative Assessment Handbook

Reteach/Classroom Intervention

Interactive Reader and Study Guide, Section 5
Interactive Skills Tutor CD-ROM

Section 5 Assessment Answers

1. **a.** the steep face at the edge of a plateau or other raised area
   b. Instead of flowing into the ocean, its waters form a swampy inland delta.

2. **a.** the Namib Desert
   b. The minerals were left behind when the water from ancient rivers evaporated.

3. **a.** minerals—gold, diamonds, coal, platinum, copper, uranium, and iron ore; also water and timber
   b. possible answer—The mines have helped the economy, but potential environmental damage may be costly to fix.

4. Students' graphic organizers will vary but should reflect characteristics accurately sorted by location. For example, students may note that Madagascar differs from mainland Southern Africa in that it has lush vegetation, tropical forests, and unique animals.

5. Answers will vary. Students should provide details about the aspects of Africa's physical geography that they found most interesting.

Answers

Map Zone 1. *western Southern Africa;* **2.** *Botswana has broadleaf trees, shrubs, and grass with trees while Mozambique has mostly only grass with trees.*

Reading Check *timber, water, and minerals, especially gold and diamonds*

271

Social Studies Skills

Chart and Graph	Critical Thinking	Geography	Reading and Studying

Analyzing a Precipitation Map

Materials: a precipitation map of the United States

1. Ask students to locate their community on a U.S. map and determine their region's average annual precipitation.

2. Have students refer to the precipitation map on this page and identify an area in West Africa that receives about the same amount of precipitation as their community. If there is not an exact match, find the area that is the closest.

3. Ask students to describe the type of vegetation they think grows in that area of West Africa. Refer students to the climate map in Section 2 of the textbook chapter to see if they are correct. Ask what factors make the areas similar or different.
LS Visual/Spatial

- Alternative Assessment Handbook, Rubrics 9: Comparing and Contrasting; and 21: Map Reading

- Interactive Skills Tutor CD-ROM, Lesson 6: Interpret Maps, Graphs, Charts, Visuals, and Political Cartoons

- **RF:** Social Studies Skills, Analyzing a Precipitation Map

Analyzing a Precipitation Map

Learn

A precipitation map shows how much rain or snow typically falls in a certain area over a year. Studying a precipitation map can help you understand a region's climate.

To read a precipitation map, first look at the legend to see what the different colors mean. Compare the legend to the map to see how much precipitation different areas get.

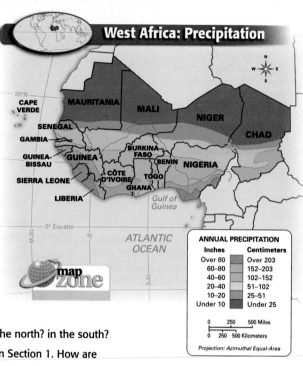

West Africa: Precipitation

ANNUAL PRECIPITATION

Inches	Centimeters
Over 80	Over 203
60–80	152–203
40–60	102–152
20–40	51–102
10–20	25–51
Under 10	Under 25

0   250   500 Miles
0   250   500 Kilometers

Projection: Azimuthal Equal-Area

Practice

Use the map on this page to answer the following questions.

1. What countries have areas that get over 80 inches of rain every year?

2. In what part of the region does the least amount of rain fall?

3. What do you think vegetation is like in the north? in the south?

4. Compare this map to the climate map in Section 1. How are the two maps similar?

Apply

Using an atlas or the Internet, find a precipitation map of all of Africa. Use that map to answer the following questions.

1. What area of the continent gets the most precipitation?

2. What area of the continent gets the least precipitation?

3. How much annual precipitation does Madagascar get?

Social Studies Skills: Analyzing a Precipitation Map   `Below Level`

Special Needs Learners

Materials: paper, colored markers

1. Explain that the colors on a precipitation map have no meaning in themselves but are only connected to the map legend. For example, areas with over 80 inches of precipitation might be shown in white, black, or any other color, as long as it matches the legend.

2. Ask students to draw a map of a fictional country, give the country a name, and then color in the map with at least four different precipitation ranges. Remind students to create a legend to match.

3. When maps are complete, ask volunteers to display their maps and point out the legend and amounts of precipitation indicated.

4. Ask students to predict what the climate and vegetation might be like in the regions of their country. **LS Logical/Mathematical, Visual/Spatial**

- Alternative Assessment Handbook, Rubric 20: Map Creation

Answers

Practice 1. *Guinea, tiny bit in Guinea-Bissau, Sierra Leone, Liberia, Nigeria;* **2.** *North;* **3.** *North—very sparse; South—much thicker;* **4.** *The climate and precipitation zones form similar bands running east to west.*

Apply 1. *South;* **2.** *Midwest and Southwest;* **3.** *about 12 inches, but answers will vary depending on the precipitation map*

Chapter Review

Geography's Impact
video series
Review the video to answer the closing question:
What are some of the ways desertification can be slowed, stopped, or even reversed?

Answers

Visual Summary

Use the visual summary below to help you review the main ideas of the chapter.

QUICK FACTS

Africa has a few highland areas, but most of the continent is covered by plains and plateaus.

Several major rivers, including the Nile, Congo, Niger, and Zambezi, flow through Africa.

Africa's climates and vegetation range from harsh deserts to lush tropical rain forest to temperate savannas.

Visual Summary

Review and Inquiry Have students use the visual summary to discuss details related to the physical geography of Africa. Ask what is pictured in each photograph and for details relating to each picture.

🗝 Quick Facts Transparency: Visual Summary: Physical Geography of Africa

Reviewing Vocabulary, Terms, and Places

1. F; zonal   5. F; silt
2. T   6. T
3. F; basin   7. T
4. T   8. T

Reviewing Vocabulary, Terms, and Places

For each statement below, write T if it is true and F if it is false. If the statement is false, write the correct term that would make the sentence a true statement.

1. West Africa's climate is described as <u>savanna</u> because it is organized by zone.
2. The <u>Nile River</u> is the longest river in the world.
3. A <u>copper belt</u> is a generally flat region surrounded by higher land such as mountains or plateaus.
4. <u>Rift valleys</u> are places on Earth's surface where the crust stretches until it breaks.
5. Finely ground fertile soil that is good for growing crops is called <u>oasis</u>.
6. The <u>Niger River</u> flows through many countries in West Africa and empties into the Gulf of Guinea.
7. The open grasslands of South Africa are called the <u>veld</u>.
8. Some animals can graze in the <u>Sahel</u>.

Comprehension and Critical Thinking

SECTION 1 *(Pages 250–253)*

9. **a. Describe** What is the Nile River Valley like?
   b. Draw Conclusions Why are oases important to people traveling through the Sahara?
   c. Elaborate Why do you think few people live in the Sahara?

SECTION 2 *(Pages 254–257)*

10. **a. Identify** What are the four climate zones of West Africa?
    b. Make Inferences What are some problems caused by desertification?
    c. Elaborate Why do you think resources such as gold and diamonds have not made West Africa a rich region?

SECTION 3 *(Pages 258–261)*

11. **a. Identify** What is the Great Rift Valley?
    b. Draw Conclusions Why is the Nile necessary for farming in the desert?

Comprehension and Critical Thinking

9. **a.** a long oasis in the desert; farmers rely on water from the Nile for irrigation
   b. They provide travelers with a much-needed source of water and shade.
   c. because the Sahara is so dry

10. **a.** desert, steppe, tropical savanna, humid tropical
    b. Soil blows away, leaving less land for grazing and agriculture.
    c. possible answer—Colonizers and internal conflicts have prevented the region's economies from developing.

11. **a.** Earth's largest rift, a place on Earth's surface where the crust has stretched until it broke
    b. It provides farmers with irrigation and water for their crops.

PHYSICAL GEOGRAPHY OF AFRICA **273**

Review and Assessment Resources

Review and Reinforce

SE Chapter Review
📄 **RF:** Chapter Review
🗝 Quick Facts Transparency: Visual Summary: Physical Geography of Africa
🔊 Spanish Chapter Summaries Audio CD Program
OSP Holt Puzzle Pro; Quiz Show for ExamView
💿 Quiz Game CD-ROM

Assess

SE Standardized Test Practice
📄 PASS: Chapter Test, Forms A and B
📄 Alternative Assessment Handbook
OSP ExamView Test Generator, Chapter Test
💿 Differentiated Instruction Modified Worksheets and Tests CD-ROM: Modified Chapter Test
HOAP Holt Online Assessment Program (in the Holt Interactive Online Student Edition)

Reteach/Intervene

📄 Interactive Reader and Study Guide
📄 Differentiated Instruction Teacher Management System: Lesson Plans
💿 Differentiated Instruction Modified Worksheets and Tests CD-ROM
💿 Interactive Skills Tutor CD-ROM

go.hrw.com
Online Resources

Chapter Resources:
KEYWORD: SK9 CH9

c. possible answers—by conserving water; by developing ways of storing water for use during droughts

12. a. basin, mountains, plateaus

b. few grocery stores in rural areas, goods in periodic markets may be less costly and easier to get

c. Land set aside for national parks cannot be used for farming and logging, but helps protect the environment

13. a. Kalahari, Namib

b. The wettest part of the region is the east coast and the island of Madagascar, while the western part of the region is very dry.

c. possible answer—People have tended to settle in places that have good water resources and good land for farming or raising livestock.

Using the Internet

14. Go to the HRW Web site and enter the keyword shown to access a rubric for this activity.

> KEYWORD: SK9 TEACHER

Social Studies Skills

15. Mauritania, Mali, Niger, Chad

16. along the southern and southwestern coasts

17. It increases from north to south.

Focus on Reading and Writing

18. Both are dry with sparse vegetation, and support few people.

19. The Sahara supports almost no plants or farming and gets very little rain; the Sahel supports some plants and grazing and gets uneven rainfall.

20. Both support some vegetation and get some rain; both support farming.

RF: Focus on Reading, Understanding Comparison-Contrast

21. Rubric Students' letters should

• describe the land, climate, and vegetation of Africa's different regions

• include a heading, greeting, introduction, body, closure, and signature

RF: Focus on Writing, Writing a Letter Home

SECTION 3 *(continued)*

c. Predict How do you think the effects of drought can be avoided in the future?

SECTION 4 *(Pages 262–265)*

12. a. Describe What are the main landforms in Central Africa?

b. Make Inferences Why would people in rural areas be more likely to shop at periodic markets than at grocery stores?

c. Elaborate How does the development of national parks affect Central Africa?

SECTION 5 *(Pages 268–271)*

13. a. Identify What are the two main deserts in Southern Africa?

b. Contrast How is the eastern part of Southern Africa different from the western part?

c. Elaborate How do you think the geography of Southern Africa has affected settlement patterns there?

Using the Internet

14. Activity: Creating a Postcard Come and learn about the mighty baobab tree. This unique tree looks as if it has been plucked from the ground and turned upside down. These trees are known not only for their unique look but also for their great size. Some are so big that a chain of 30 people is needed to surround one tree trunk! Enter the activity keyword to visit Web sites about baobab trees in Africa. Then create a postcard about this strange wonder of nature.

Social Studies Skills

Analyzing a Precipitation Map *Use the precipitation map in the Social Studies Skills lesson to answer the following questions.*

15. What countries have areas that receive under 10 inches of rain every year?

16. Where in West Africa does the most rain typically fall?

17. How would you describe annual precipitation in Chad?

Understanding Comparison-Contrast *Look over your notes or re-read Section 2. Use the information on climate and vegetation to answer the following questions.*

18. How are the Sahara and the Sahel similar?

19. How are the Sahara and the Sahel different?

20. Compare the Sahel and the savanna zone. How are they similar?

21. Writing a Letter Now that you have information about all of Africa, you need to organize it. Think about your audience, a friend at home, and what would feel natural if you had been traveling. Would you organize by topics like landforms and climate? Or would you organize by region? After you organize your information, write a one-page letter.

Map Activity ★Interactive

22. East Africa On a separate sheet of paper, match the letters on the map with their correct labels.

Great Rift Valley	Mount Kilimanjaro
Lake Victoria	Nile River
Indian Ocean	

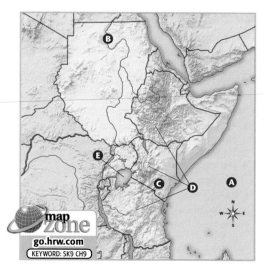

go.hrw.com
KEYWORD: SK9 CH9

Map Activity

22. A. Indian Ocean

B. Nile River

C. Mount Kilimanjaro

D. Great Rift Valley

E. Lake Victoria

Standardized Test Practice

DIRECTIONS (1–7): For each statement or question, write on a separate answer sheet the *number* of the word or expression that, of those given, best completes the statement or answers the question.

1 What physical feature of East Africa is usually covered with snow and ice?

(1) Serengeti Plain
(2) Mount Kilimanjaro
(3) Great Rift Valley
(4) Mount Kenya

2 Which of the following is not a major river in Africa?

(1) Niger
(2) Kilimanjaro
(3) Congo
(4) Nile

3 The Great Rift Valley is located in

(1) North Africa.
(2) West Africa.
(3) East Africa.
(4) Southern Africa.

4 The climate zone just south of the Sahara is called the

(1) desert.
(2) savanna.
(3) Sahel.
(4) tropical forest.

5 The Nile empties into the

(1) Red Sea.
(2) Gulf of Guinea.
(3) Indian Ocean.
(4) Mediterranean Sea.

6 Most of the land in Southern Africa lies on a

(1) mountain range.
(2) coastal plain.
(3) plateau.
(4) delta.

7 What do ships use to avoid sailing around Southern Africa?

(1) the Nile
(2) the Suez Canal
(3) the Aswan High Dam
(4) the Strait of Gibraltar

Base your answer to question 8 on the passage below and on your knowledge of social studies.

"Then they were over the first hills and the wildebeeste were trailing up them, and then they were over the mountains with sudden depths of green-rising forest and solid bamboo slopes, and then the heavy forest again, sculptured into peaks and hollows until they crossed, and hills sloped down and then another plain, hot now, and purple brown, bumpy with heat..."

—Ernest Hemingway, "The Snows of Kilimanjaro"

8 Which of these conclusions about Africa's geography could you draw from this passage?

(1) Africa is covered with desert.
(2) Parts of Africa have hills, mountains, and forests.
(3) Lions and elephants live in Africa's forests.
(4) It is never cold in Africa.

Answers

1. 2
Break Down the Question This question requires students to recall factual information. Refer students who miss it to Section 3.

2. 2
Break Down the Question This question requires students to recall factual information. Remind students who missed this question that Kilimanjaro is a mountain in East Africa.

3. 3
Break Down the Question This question requires students to recall factual information. Refer students who miss it to Section 3.

4. 3
Break Down the Question This question requires students to recall factual information. Refer students who miss it to Section 2.

5. 4
Break Down the Question This question requires students to recall factual information. Refer students who miss it to Section 1.

6. 3
Break Down the Question This question requires students to recall factual information. Refer students who miss it to Section 5.

7. 2
Break Down the Question This question requires students to recall factual information. Refer students who miss it to Section 1.

8. 2
Break Down the Question Students should note that the passage describes hills, mountains, forests, and plains.

Intervention Resources

Reproducible
- Interactive Reader and Study Guide
- Differentiated Instruction Teacher Management System: Lesson Plans

Technology
- Quick Facts Transparency: Visual Summary: Physical Geography of Africa
- Differentiated Instruction Modified Worksheets and Tests CD-ROM
- Interactive Skills Tutor CD-ROM

Tips for Test Taking

Read and Re-Read If students are taking a reading comprehension text, they should read the selection, master all the questions, and then re-read the selection. The answers will probably stand out during the second reading. Students should remember that the purpose of the test is not to trick them; its purpose is to test their knowledge and thinking skills.

Ancient Civilizations of Africa—Egypt

Chapter Overview	Reproducible Resources	Technology Resources
CHAPTER 10 pp. 276–307 **Overview:** In this chapter, students learn about the history, culture, and achievements of ancient Egypt.	**Differentiated Instruction Teacher Management System:*** • Instructional Pacing Guides • Lesson Plans for Differentiated Instruction **Interactive Reader and Study Guide:*** Chapter Summary Graphic Organizer **Resource File:*** • Chapter Review • Focus on Reading: Categorizing • Focus on Writing: Writing a Riddle • Social Studies Skills: Analyzing Primary and Secondary Sources **Experiencing World History and Geography**	**OSP Teacher's One-Stop Planner:** Calendar Planner **Power Presentations with Video CD-ROM** **Differentiated Instruction Modified Worksheets and Tests CD-ROM** **Interactive Skills Tutor CD-ROM** **Student Edition on Audio CD Program** **Map Zone Transparency:** Ancient Egypt, 4500–500 BC* **Geography's Impact: Video Program (VHS/DVD):** Impact of the Egyptian Pyramids*
Section 1: **Geography and Early Egypt** **The Big Idea:** The water and fertile soils of the Nile Valley enabled a great civilization to develop in Egypt.	**Differentiated Instruction Teacher Management System:** Section 1 Lesson Plan* **Interactive Reader and Study Guide:** Section 1 Summary* **Resource File:*** • Vocabulary Builder: Section 1	**Daily Bellringer Transparency:** Section 1* **Map Zone Transparency:** Ancient Egypt*
Section 2: **The Old Kingdom** **The Big Idea:** Egyptian government and religion were closely connected during the Old Kingdom.	**Differentiated Instruction Teacher Management System:** Section 2 Lesson Plan* **Interactive Reader and Study Guide:** Section 2 Summary* **Resource File:*** • Vocabulary Builder: Section 2 • Biography: Khufu	**Daily Bellringer Transparency:** Section 2* **go.hrw.com Internet Activity:** Pyramids
Section 3: **The Middle and New Kingdoms** **The Big Idea:** During the Middle and New Kingdoms, order and greatness were restored in Egypt.	**Differentiated Instruction Teacher Management System:** Section 3 Lesson Plan* **Interactive Reader and Study Guide:** Section 3 Summary* **Resource File:*** • Vocabulary Builder: Section 3 • Biography: Nefertiti	**Daily Bellringer Transparency:** Section 3* **Map Zone Transparency:** Egyptian Trade, c. 1400 BC*
Section 4: **Egyptian Achievements** **The Big Idea:** The Egyptians made lasting achievements in writing, art, and architecture.	**Differentiated Instruction Teacher Management System:** Section 4 Lesson Plan* **Interactive Reader and Study Guide:** Section 4 Summary* **Resource File:*** • Vocabulary Builder: Section 4 • Literature: *The Book of the Dead* • Primary Source: Tomb Paintings	**Daily Bellringer Transparency:** Section 4* **go.hrw.com Internet Activity:** Hieroglyphics

HOLT
Geography's Impact
Video Program

Impact of the Egyptian Pyramids
Suggested use: as a chapter introduction

Review, Assessment, Intervention

🖼️ **Map Zone Transparency:** Visual Summary: Ancient Civilizations of Africa—Egypt*

🔊 **Spanish Chapter Summaries Audio CD Program**

📄 **Progress Assessment Support System (PASS):** Chapter Test*

💿 **Differentiated Instruction Modified Worksheets and Tests CD-ROM:** Modified Chapter Test

OSP **Teacher's One-Stop Planner:** ExamView Test Generator (English/Spanish)

📄 **Alternative Assessment Handbook**

HOAP **Holt Online Assessment Program (HOAP),** in the Holt Interactive Online Student Edition

---

📄 **PASS:** Section 1 Quiz*

📶 **Online Quiz:** Section 1

📄 **Alternative Assessment Handbook**

📄 **PASS:** Section 2 Quiz*

📶 **Online Quiz:** Section 2

📄 **Alternative Assessment Handbook**

📄 **PASS:** Section 3 Quiz*

📶 **Online Quiz:** Section 3

📄 **Alternative Assessment Handbook**

📄 **PASS:** Section 4 Quiz*

📶 **Online Quiz:** Section 4

📄 **Alternative Assessment Handbook**

Power Presentations with Video CD-ROM

Power Presentations with Video are visual presentations of each chapter's main ideas. Presentations can be customized by including Quick Facts charts, images from the text, and video clips.

Holt Online Learning

go.hrw.com
Teacher Resources
KEYWORD: SK9 TEACHER

go.hrw.com
Student Resources
KEYWORD: SK9 CH10

- Interactive Multimedia Activities
- Current Events
- Chapter-based Internet Activities
- and more!

Holt Interactive
Online Student Edition

Complete online support for interactivity, assessment, and reporting

- Interactive Maps and Notebook
- Standardized Test Prep
- Homework Practice and Research Activities Online

CHAPTER 10 PLANNING GUIDE

Differentiating Instruction

How do I address the needs of varied learners?
The Target Resource acts as your primary strategy for differentiated instruction.

ENGLISH-LANGUAGE LEARNERS & STRUGGLING READERS

TARGET RESOURCE

Graphic Organizer Transparencies with Support for Reading and Writing

Spanish Resources

Spanish Chapter Summaries Audio CD

Teacher's One-Stop Planner:
- ExamView Test Generator, Spanish
- PuzzlePro, Spanish

English-Language Learner Strategies and Activities

Additional Resources

Differentiated Instruction Teacher Management System: Lesson Plans for Differentiated Instruction

Resource File:
- Vocabulary Builder Activities
- Social Studies Skills: Analyzing Primary and Secondary Sources

Map Zone Transparency: Visual Summary: Ancient Civilizations of Africa—Egypt

Student Edition on Audio CD Program

SPECIAL NEEDS LEARNERS

TARGET RESOURCE

Differentiated Instruction Modified Worksheets and Tests CD-ROM

- Vocabulary Flash Cards
- Modified Vocabulary Builder Activities
- Modified Chapter Review
- Modified Chapter Test

Additional Resources

Differentiated Instruction Teacher Management System: Lesson Plans for Differentiated Instruction

Interactive Reader and Study Guide

Resource File: Social Studies Skills: Analyzing Primary and Secondary Sources

Student Edition on Audio CD Program

Interactive Skills Tutor CD-ROM

Graphic Organizer Transparencies with Support for Reading and Writing

ADVANCED/GIFTED AND TALENTED STUDENTS

TARGET RESOURCE

Resource File

The Resource File activities allow students to extend their knowledge of chapter-related places and people, and to practice geography skills.

- Focus on Reading: Categorizing
- Focus on Writing: Writing a Riddle
- Literature: *The Book of the Dead*

Additional Resources

Differentiated Instruction Teacher Management System: Lesson Plans for Differentiated Instruction

World History and Geography Document-Based Questions Activities

Geography, Science, and Cultures Activities

Experiencing World History and Geography

Differentiated Activities in the Teacher's Edition
- The Nile Graphic Organizer
- Drawing Egyptians at Work
- Writing a Rosetta Stone Summary

Differentiated Activities in the Teacher's Edition
- Two New Kingdom Rulers

Differentiated Activities in the Teacher's Edition
- Creating Storyboards
- The Geography of Pyramids
- Writing Journal Entries
- Measuring a Temple

HOLT Teacher's One-Stop Planner®

How can I manage the lesson plans and support materials for differentiated instruction?

With the Teacher's One-Stop Planner, you can easily organize and print lesson plans, planning guides, and instructional materials for all learners.

The Teacher's One-Stop Planner includes the following materials to help you differentiate instruction:
- Interactive Teacher's Edition
- Calendar Planner and pacing guides
- Editable lesson plans
- All reproducible ancillaries in Adobe Acrobat (PDF) format
- ExamView Test Generator (English & Spanish)
- Transparency and video previews

Professional Development

HOLT Professional Development

What teacher training resources are available to help me grow professionally?

- **In-service and staff development** as part of your Holt Social Studies product purchase
- **Quick Teacher Tutorial Lesson Presentation CD-ROM**
- Intensive tuition-based **Teacher Development Institute**
- **Convenient Holt Speaker Bureau:** face-to-face workshop options
- **24/7 Ask A Professional Development Expert** at http://www.hrw.com/prodev/

Chapter Big Ideas

Section 1 The water and fertile soils of the Nile Valley enabled a great civilization to develop in Egypt.

Section 2 Egyptian government and religion were closely connected during the Old Kingdom.

Section 3 During the Middle and New Kingdoms, order and greatness were restored in Egypt.

Section 4 The Egyptians made lasting achievements in writing, art, and architecture.

Focus on Reading and Writing

Reading The Resource File provides a worksheet to help students look for ways to categorize facts and details when reading.

📝 **RF:** Focus on Reading, Categorizing

Writing The Resource File provides a worksheet to help students write their riddles.

📝 **RF:** Focus on Writing, Writing a Riddle

CHAPTER 10
Ancient Civilizations of Africa—Egypt

FOCUS QUESTION

How did ancient civilizations contribute to the development of the Eastern Hemisphere?

What You Will Learn...

In this chapter you will learn about the fascinating civilization of ancient Egypt and how it developed along the Nile River.

FOCUS ON READING AND WRITING

Categorizing A good way to make sense of what you read is to separate facts and details into groups called categories. For example, you could sort facts about ancient Egypt into categories like geography, history, and culture. As you read this chapter, look for ways to categorize the information you are learning. **See the lesson, Categorizing, on page S13.**

Writing a Riddle In this chapter you will read about the civilization of the ancient Egyptians. In ancient times a sphinx, an imaginary creature like the sculpture in Egypt shown on the next page, was supposed to have demanded the answer to a riddle. People died if they did not answer the riddle correctly. After you read this chapter, you will write a riddle. The answer to your riddle should be "Egypt."

map zone

Geography Skills

Location The civilization of ancient Egypt developed along the fertile Nile River.
1. **Name** What other bodies of water are near Egypt?
2. **Make Inferences** Based on the land around ancient Egypt, why do you think the Nile was so important to life?

~~Tropic of Cancer~~

20°N

20°E

| 0 | 75 | 150 Miles |
| 0 | 75 | 150 Kilometers |

Projection: Lambert Equal-Area

The Gift of the Nile The fertile land along the Nile River drew early people to the region. Cities are still found along the Nile today.

Introduce the Chapter

At Level

Impressions of Egypt

1. Ask students what they already know about ancient Egypt. What books or articles have they read? What photos or movies have they seen? Do they have or have they seen any jewelry that has Egyptian designs? Write responses for students to see.

2. Tell students that some things portrayed in popular culture and in the media are true and some are not. For example, workers on the pyramids have often been portrayed as slaves, but most Egyptologists now think these workers were mostly common people, such as free farmers. Tell students that in their research they may see the term *Egyptologist*, which refers to a person who studies Egyptian antiquities.

3. Tell students that in this chapter they will see how accurately their current knowledge about Egypt reflects ancient Egyptian life.
LS Verbal/Linguistic

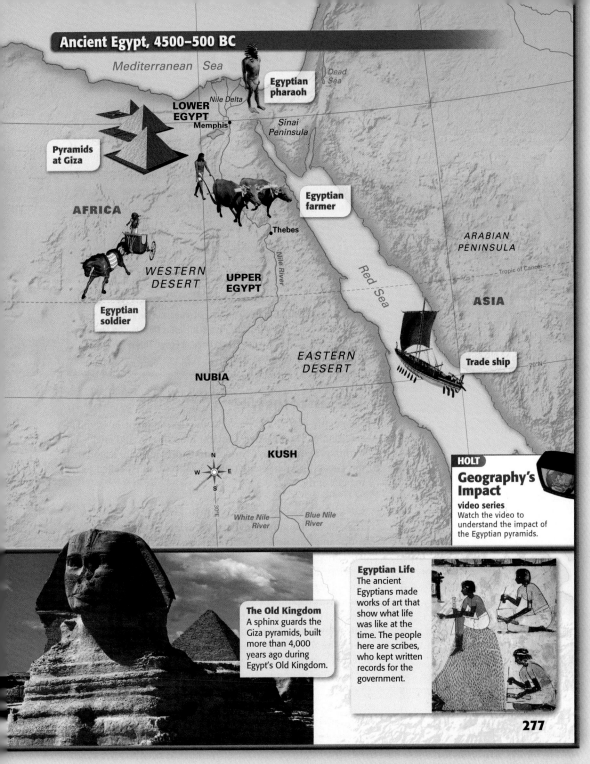

Ancient Egypt, 4500–500 BC

Mediterranean Sea

Egyptian pharaoh

Dead Sea

Nile Delta

LOWER EGYPT

Memphis

Sinai Peninsula

Pyramids at Giza

AFRICA

Egyptian farmer

Thebes

ARABIAN PENINSULA

Nile River

Red Sea

Tropic of Cancer

WESTERN DESERT

UPPER EGYPT

ASIA

Egyptian soldier

EASTERN DESERT

Trade ship

20°N

NUBIA

N
W   E
S

KUSH

30°E

White Nile River

Blue Nile River

HOLT
Geography's Impact
video series
Watch the video to understand the impact of the Egyptian pyramids.

The Old Kingdom
A sphinx guards the Giza pyramids, built more than 4,000 years ago during Egypt's Old Kingdom.

Egyptian Life
The ancient Egyptians made works of art that show what life was like at the time. The people here are scribes, who kept written records for the government.

277

Explore the Map and Pictures

Ancient Egypt, 4500–500 BC The Nile River brought northern Africa to life by providing much-needed water in an otherwise arid region. While the annual flooding of the Nile was viewed as a gift to ancient Egyptians, in modern times people sought to control the unpredictable Nile. In 1952 planning for the High Aswan Dam began, to allow its waters to be used for hydroelectricity and to store valuable water in times of drought. One of the negative effects of the dam, however, was that the region of Nubia flooded, displacing its residents and forcing them to move and attempt to reestablish their original way of life elsewhere.

Analyzing Visuals What do you think the scribe on the left is sitting on in the Egyptian Life photo? *a pile of sand* What part of the Nile is probably best for agriculture? *the Nile Delta*

Map Zone Transparency: Ancient Egypt, 4500–500 BC

HOLT
Geography's Impact
▶ video series
See the Video Teacher's Guide for strategies for using the chapter video to teach about the impact of the Egyptian pyramids.

Info to Know

Riddle of the Sphinx Historians date the construction of the Great Sphinx around 2500 BC. Some 240 feet long and 66 feet high, the Sphinx has the body of a lion and the head of a man. The lion symbolizes strength and power, while the head symbolizes intelligence. The sphinx is often associated with Greek mythology in which a sphinx destroyed those who could not answer its riddle: "What creature walks on four legs in the morning, two legs at noon, and three legs in the evening?" The Greek hero Oedipus solved the riddle. Can you? *man*

Connect to Science

Why Is It Called the Dead Sea? The Dead Sea is so named because no plants or animals of any kind can survive in its salty water, which is 6 to 10 times saltier than ocean water. The Dead Sea is, however, rich in mineral deposits. It is also a very popular tourist destination. The Dead Sea is beautiful, with beaches and salt formations. Visitors can even swim in the Dead Sea. The extreme saltiness of the water causes everything and everyone to float! The mineral-rich waters and mud are also used for spa and beauty treatments.

Answers

Map Zone 1. *Mediterranean Sea, Red Sea, Dead Sea;* **2.** *Much of the region is desert so people had to rely on the Nile for drinking water and for growing crops.*

277

Bellringer

If YOU lived there. . . Use the **Daily Bellringer Transparency** to help students answer the question.

🗄 Daily Bellringer Transparency, Section 1

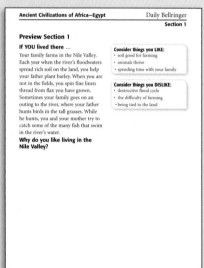

Ancient Civilizations of Africa—Egypt

Daily Bellringer
Section 1

Preview Section 1

If YOU lived there ...

Your family farms in the Nile Valley. Each year when the river's floodwaters spread rich soil on the land, you help your father plant barley. When you are not in the fields, you spin fine linen thread from flax you have grown. Sometimes your family goes on an outing to the river, where your father hunts birds in the tall grasses. While he hunts, you and your mother try to catch some of the many fish that swim in the river's water.

Why do you like living in the Nile Valley?

Consider things you LIKE:
• soil good for farming
• animals thrive
• spending time with your family

Consider things you DISLIKE:
• destructive flood cycle
• the difficulty of farming
• being tied to the land

Key Terms and Places

📖 RF: Vocabulary Builder, Section 1

Taking Notes

Have students copy the graphic organizer onto their own paper and then use it to take notes on the section. This activity will prepare students for the Section Assessment, in which they will complete a graphic organizer that builds on the information using the Critical Thinking Skill: Categorizing.

Early Egypt

What You Will Learn...

Main Ideas

1. Egypt was called the gift of the Nile because the Nile River was so important.
2. Civilization developed after people began farming along the Nile River.
3. Strong kings unified all of ancient Egypt.

The Big Idea

The water and fertile soils of the Nile Valley enabled a great civilization to develop in Egypt.

Key Terms and Places

Nile River, *p. 278*
Upper Egypt, *p. 278*
Lower Egypt, *p. 278*
cataracts, *p. 279*
delta, *p. 279*
pharaoh, *p. 281*
dynasty, *p. 281*

 TAKING NOTES As you read, take notes on the characteristics of the Nile River and on the way in which it affected Egypt. Use a chart like this one to organize your notes.

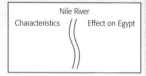

Nile River

Characteristics / Effect on Egypt

If YOU lived there...

Your family farms in the Nile Valley. Each year when the river's floodwaters spread rich soil on the land, you help your father plant barley. When you are not in the fields, you spin fine linen thread from flax you have grown. Sometimes your family goes on an outing to the river, where your father hunts birds in the tall grasses. While he hunts, you and your mother try to catch some of the many fish that swim in the river's water.

Why do you like living in the Nile Valley?

BUILDING BACKGROUND In ancient times, the fertile land in the Nile River Valley drew people to live in the area. Over time, a farming civilization developed that became ancient Egypt. This civilization would be stable and long-lasting.

The Gift of the Nile

Geography played a key role in the development of Egyptian civilization. The **Nile River** brought life to Egypt and enabled it to thrive. The river was so important to people in this region that the Greek historian Herodotus (hi-RAHD-uh-tuhs) called Egypt the gift of the Nile.

Location and Physical Features

The Nile is the longest river in the world. It begins in central Africa and runs north through Egypt to the Mediterranean Sea, a distance of over 4,000 miles. The civilization of ancient Egypt developed along a 750-mile stretch of the Nile.

Ancient Egypt included two regions, a southern region and a northern region. The southern region was called **Upper Egypt**. It was so named because it was located upriver in relation to the Nile's flow. **Lower Egypt**, the northern region, was located downriver. The Nile sliced through the desert of Upper Egypt. There, it created a fertile river valley about 13 miles wide. On either side of the Nile lay hundreds of miles of bleak desert sands.

Teach the Big Idea

At Level

Geography and Early Egypt

1. **Teach** Ask students the questions in the Main Idea boxes under Direct Teach.

2. **Apply** Organize the class into pairs. Have each pair write a verse for a national anthem that Menes may have commissioned to celebrate the unification of Upper and Lower Egypt. Verses may focus on any aspect of early Egyptian history as reflected in the section. **LS Auditory/Musical, Verbal/Linguistic**

3. **Review** Call on volunteers to read their verses. Adventuresome students may want to sing their verses to the tune of a popular song. Discuss any section topics not covered by the verses.

4. **Practice/Homework** Have each student write another verse for his or her anthem.
   LS Auditory/Musical, Verbal/Linguistic

   📝 Alternative Assessment Handbook, Rubric 26: Poems and Songs

As you can see on the map, the Nile flowed through rocky, hilly land to the south of Egypt. At several points, this rough terrain caused **cataracts**, or rapids, to form. The first cataract was located 720 miles south of the Mediterranean Sea. This cataract, shown by a red bar on the map, marked the southern border of Upper Egypt. Five more cataracts lay farther south. These cataracts made sailing on that portion of the Nile very difficult.

In Lower Egypt, the Nile divided into several branches that fanned out and flowed into the Mediterranean Sea. These branches formed a **delta**, a triangle-shaped area of land made from soil deposited by a river. At the time of ancient Egypt, swamps and marshes covered much of the Nile Delta. Some two-thirds of Egypt's fertile farmland was located in the Nile Delta.

The Floods of the Nile

Because little rain fell in the region, most of Egypt was desert. Each year, however, rain fell far to the south of Egypt in the high-lands of East Africa. This rainfall caused the Nile River to flood. Almost every year, the Nile flooded Upper Egypt in mid-summer and Lower Egypt in the fall.

The Nile's flooding coated the land around it with a rich silt. This silt made the soil ideal for farming. The silt also made the land a dark color. That is why Egyptians called their country the black land. They called the dry, lifeless desert beyond the river valley the red land.

Each year, Egyptians eagerly awaited the flooding of the Nile River. For them, the river's floods were a life-giving miracle. Without the Nile's regular flooding, people never could have farmed in Egypt. The Nile truly was a gift to Egypt.

READING CHECK Finding Main Ideas Why was Egypt called the gift of the Nile?

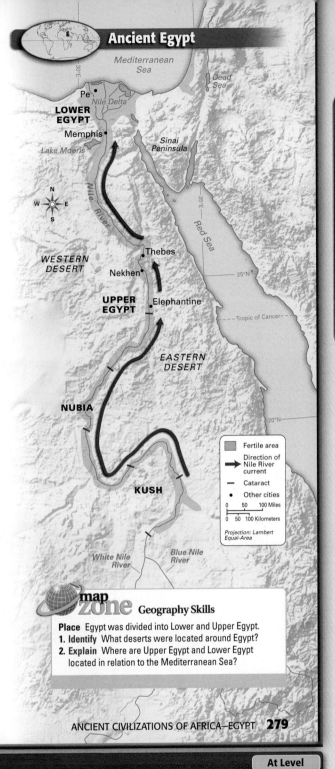

Ancient Egypt

Mediterranean Sea

Dead Sea

Pe
Nile Delta
LOWER EGYPT
Memphis
Sinai Peninsula
Lake Moeris

Nile River

Red Sea

WESTERN DESERT
Thebes
Nekhen
Tropic of Cancer
UPPER EGYPT
Elephantine

EASTERN DESERT

NUBIA
20°N

KUSH

Fertile area
Direction of Nile River current
Cataract
Other cities

0   50   100 Miles
0   50   100 Kilometers
Projection: Lambert Equal-Area

White Nile River
Blue Nile River

map zone Geography Skills

Place Egypt was divided into Lower and Upper Egypt.
1. **Identify** What deserts were located around Egypt?
2. **Explain** Where are Upper Egypt and Lower Egypt located in relation to the Mediterranean Sea?

ANCIENT CIVILIZATIONS OF AFRICA—EGYPT **279**

279

Main Idea

❷ Civilization Develops in Egypt

Civilization developed after people began farming along the Nile River.

Recall How did farmers use the Nile to grow their crops? *They built canals to direct the Nile's water to the fields.*

Predict Why might the ruins of early Egyptian settlements lack evidence of protective walls? *because the desert, bodies of water, and Nile cataracts provided natural protection from many enemies*

Linking to Today

Damming the Nile The Aswan High Dam on the Nile was completed in 1970 and officially inaugurated in 1971. It was built to generate electricity and make water available year-round to farmers. Although the dam fulfilled these goals, it has caused other problems. Because the Nile no longer drops silt on the fields, Egyptian farmers now have to use millions of tons of expensive chemical fertilizers. In addition, because less silt is deposited there, the Mediterranean coastline is eroding more rapidly.

Connect to Art

Farming in Egypt Ask students what this artwork reveals about farming in ancient Egypt. *possible answers— Farmers did some work by hand and had simple tools; both men and women worked in the fields.*

Civilization Develops in Egypt

The Nile provided both water and fertile soil for farming. Over time, scattered farms grew into villages and cities. Eventually, an Egyptian civilization developed.

Increased Food Production

Hunter-gatherers first moved into the Nile Valley more than 12,000 years ago. They found plants, wild animals, and fish there to eat. In time, these people learned how to farm, and they settled along the Nile. By 4500 BC, farmers living in small villages grew wheat and barley.

Over time, farmers in Egypt developed an irrigation system. This system consisted of a series of canals that directed the Nile's flow and carried water to the fields.

The Nile provided Egyptian farmers with an abundance of food. Farmers in Egypt grew wheat, barley, fruits, and vegetables. They also raised cattle and sheep. The river provided many types of fish, and hunters trapped wild geese and ducks along its banks. With these many sources of food, the Egyptians enjoyed a varied diet.

Two Kingdoms

In addition to a stable food supply, Egypt's location offered another advantage. It had natural barriers, which made it hard to invade Egypt. To the west, the desert was too big and harsh to cross. To the north, the Mediterranean Sea kept many enemies away. To the east, more desert and the Red Sea provided protection. Finally, to the south, cataracts in the Nile made it difficult for invaders to sail into Egypt that way.

Farming in Egypt

280 CHAPTER 10

Differentiating Instruction

Below Level

English-Language Learners

1. Draw the diagram shown here for students to see, omitting the answers in blue. Have students copy the diagram.

2. Instruct students to fill in the diagram. Below *The Nile provides life*, they should add at least two ways the Nile helped civilization grow. Below *Natural barriers provide protection*, they should add at least three different types of natural barriers that discouraged invaders.

3. Call on students to discuss their graphic organizers to ensure that they have been completed correctly. 🖼 **Visual/Spatial**

📓 Alternative Assessment Handbook, Rubric 13: Graphic Organizers

The Nile provides life.
• fertile soil for crops
• water for people, animals, and irrigation

Natural barriers provide protection.
• deserts
• cataracts along the Nile
• bodies of water

Growth of Ancient Egypt

Protected from invaders, the villages of Egypt grew. Wealthy farmers emerged as village leaders. In time, strong leaders gained control over several villages. By 3200 BC, villages had grown and banded together to create two kingdoms—Lower Egypt and Upper Egypt.

Each kingdom had its own capital city where its ruler was based. The capital city of Lower Egypt was Pe, located in the Nile Delta. There, wearing a red crown, the king of Lower Egypt ruled. The capital city of Upper Egypt was Nekhen, located on the Nile's west bank. In this southern kingdom, the king wore a cone-shaped white crown. For centuries, Egyptians referred to their country as the two lands.

READING CHECK **Summarizing** What attracted early settlers to the Nile Valley?

Farmers in ancient Egypt learned how to grow wheat and barley. The tomb painting at left shows a couple harvesting their crop. As the photo above shows, people in Egypt still farm along the Nile.

ANALYZING VISUALS Based on the above photo, what methods do Egyptian farmers use today?

Kings Unify Egypt

According to tradition, around 3100 BC Menes (MEE-neez) rose to power in Upper Egypt. Some historians think Menes is a myth and that his accomplishments were really those of other ancient kings named Aha, Scorpion, or Narmer.

Menes wanted to unify the kingdoms of Upper and Lower Egypt. He had his armies invade Lower Egypt and take control of it. Menes then married a princess from Lower Egypt to strengthen his control over the newly unified country.

Menes wore both the white crown of Upper Egypt and the red crown of Lower Egypt to symbolize his leadership over the two kingdoms. Later, he combined the two crowns into a double crown, as you can see on the next page.

Many historians consider Menes to be Egypt's first **pharaoh** (FEHR-oh), the title used by the rulers of ancient Egypt. The title *pharaoh* means "great house." Menes also founded Egypt's first **dynasty**, or series of rulers from the same family.

Menes built a new capital city at the southern tip of the Nile Delta. The city was later named Memphis. It was near where Lower Egypt met Upper Egypt, close to what is now Cairo, Egypt. For centuries, Memphis was the political and cultural center of Egypt. Many government offices were located there, and the city bustled with artistic activity.

Egypt's First Dynasty was a theocracy that lasted for about 200 years. A theocracy is a government ruled by religious leaders such as priests or a monarch thought to be divine.

Over time, Egypt's rulers extended Egyptian territory southward along the Nile River and into Southwest Asia. They also improved irrigation and trade, making Egypt wealthier.

FOCUS ON READING
Identify two or three categories that you could use to organize the information under Kings Unify Egypt.

Main Idea

❸ Kings Unify Egypt
Strong kings unified all of ancient Egypt.

Explain How did the pharaoh's crown display the unification of Egypt? *The pharaoh combined the white crown of Upper Egypt and the red crown of Lower Egypt to symbolize his rule over both lands.*

Analyze Do you think Menes made a good choice in building his capital city at Memphis? Why or why not? *possible answer—yes; because it was in a fertile region, but still had the protection of being inland*

Make Judgments Which part of Egypt—Upper or Lower—do you think was more valuable to a ruler? Why? *possible answer—Lower Egypt, because it had the extremely fertile delta and access to the Mediterranean*

Biography

Menes (lived c. 3100 BC) Menes placed his capital on an island in the Nile, probably to protect the city from invaders and to help him control the Nile Delta. The location not protect him from other threats, however. Menes died at age 63, killed either by wild dogs and crocodiles or by a hippopotamus.

Critical Thinking: Analyzing Information | At Level |

The Double Crown of Menes

1. Discuss with students the significance of symbols for people in authority.

2. Ask students to name symbols of authority with which they are familiar, from the past and the present. Write down suggestions for students to see. *examples—crowns, badges, uniforms, jewels, weapons*

3. Discuss how these symbols are similar and different. What is their purpose—to inspire fear, trust, or awe, or to send some other message?

4. Lead a discussion about the message Menes sent by wearing both the white crown and the red crown and then combining the two. What effect might his use of the double crown have had on Egyptians living in a newly unified country? **LS** **Verbal/Linguistic**

   Alternative Assessment Handbook, Rubric 11: Discussions

Answers

Reading Check *plants, wild animals, and fish to eat; natural protection from invasion*

Analyzing Visuals *possible answer— similar methods as used in the past, relying on animal and human labor and simple tools as opposed to machines*

Focus on Reading *possible answers—Menes; new capital city of Memphis; later First Dynasty rulers*

281

Main Idea

Kings Unify Egypt, *continued*

Define What is a pharaoh, and what does the title *pharaoh* mean? *ruler of ancient Egypt; "great house"*

Explain Where did the First Dynasty extend its power? How did the First Dynasty end? *extended Egyptian territory southward along the Nile and into southwest Asia; challengers took over Egypt and established the Second Dynasty*

• **Review & Assess** •

Close

Call on volunteers to compose additional questions about the illustrations in this section.

Review

 Online Quiz, Section 1

Assess

SE Section 1 Assessment

PASS: Section 1 Quiz

Alternative Assessment Handbook

Reteach/Classroom Intervention

Interactive Reader and Study Guide, Section 1

Interactive Skills Tutor CD-ROM

Answers

Reading Check *Ruling over both kingdoms brought him and Egypt greater wealth, status, and power.*

282

Crown of United Egypt

The pharaoh Menes combined the white crown of Upper Egypt and the red crown of Lower Egypt as a symbol of his rule of a united Egypt.

Eventually, however, rivals arose to challenge Egypt's First Dynasty for power. These challengers took over Egypt and established the Second Dynasty. In time, some 30 dynasties would rule ancient Egypt over a span of more than 2,500 years.

READING CHECK **Drawing Inferences** Why do you think Menes wanted to rule over both kingdoms of Egypt?

SUMMARY AND PREVIEW As you have read, ancient Egypt began in the fertile Nile River Valley. Two kingdoms developed in this region. The two kingdoms were later united under one ruler, and Egyptian territory grew. In the next section you will learn how Egypt continued to grow and change under later rulers in a period known as the Old Kingdom.

Section 1 Assessment

go.hrw.com
Online Quiz
KEYWORD: SK9 HP10

Reviewing Ideas, Terms, and Places

1. **a. Identify** Where was the Egyptian kingdom of **Lower Egypt** located?
   b. Analyze Why was the **delta** of the **Nile River** well suited for settlement?
   c. Predict How might the Nile's **cataracts** have both helped and hurt Egypt?
2. **a. Describe** What foods did the Egyptians eat?
   b. Analyze What role did the Nile play in supplying Egyptians with the foods they ate?
   c. Elaborate How did the desert on both sides of the Nile help ancient Egypt?
3. **a. Identify** Who was the first **pharaoh** of Egypt?
   b. Draw Conclusions Why did the pharaohs of the First Dynasty wear a double crown?

Critical Thinking

4. **Categorizing** Create a chart like the one shown here. Use your notes to provide information for each category in the chart.

Development along Nile	Two Kingdoms	United Kingdoms

FOCUS ON WRITING

5. **Thinking about Geography and Early History** In your riddle, what clues could you include related to Egypt's geography and early history? For example, you might include the Nile River or pharaohs as clues. Add some ideas to your notes.

282 CHAPTER 10

Section 1 Assessment Answers

1. **a.** south of the Mediterranean and along the Nile River in northern Egypt
   b. possible answer—provided fertile soil and abundant wildlife, was near the sea
   c. provided protection against invasion, but made travel on the river difficult

2. **a.** wheat, barley, fruits, vegetables, beef, lamb, fish, goose, and duck
   b. essential role—provided water for crops and animals, fish, homes for wild geese and ducks
   c. provided natural barriers against invasion

3. **a.** Menes
   b. to symbolize the unification of Lower and Upper Egypt

4. possible answers: Development along Nile— river coated land with silt, allowing for farming; Two Kingdoms—Lower Egypt and Upper Egypt each had its own capital and ruler; United Kingdoms—Menes brought kingdoms together and built new capital city, later called Memphis

5. Answers will vary but should be accurately based on what students learned in this section.

The Old Kingdom

If YOU lived there...

You are a farmer in ancient Egypt. To you, the pharaoh is the god Horus as well as your ruler. You depend on his strength and wisdom. For part of the year, you are busy planting crops in your fields. But at other times of the year, you work for the pharaoh. You are helping to build a great tomb so that your pharaoh will be comfortable in the afterlife.

How do you feel about working for the pharaoh?

BUILDING BACKGROUND As in other ancient cultures, Egyptian society was based on a strict order of social classes. A small group of royalty and nobles ruled Egypt. They depended on the rest of the population to supply food, crafts, and labor. Few people questioned this arrangement of society.

Life in the Old Kingdom

The First and Second Dynasties ruled ancient Egypt for about four centuries. Around 2700 BC, though, a new dynasty rose to power in Egypt. Called the Third Dynasty, its rule began a period in Egyptian history known as the Old Kingdom.

Early Pharaohs

The **Old Kingdom** was a period in Egyptian history that lasted for about 500 years, from about 2700 to 2200 BC. During this time, the Egyptians continued to develop their political system. The system they developed was based on the belief that Egypt's pharaoh, or ruler, was both a king and a god.

The ancient Egyptians believed that Egypt belonged to the gods. The Egyptians believed the pharaoh had come to Earth in order to manage Egypt for the rest of the gods. As a result, he had absolute power over all the land and people in Egypt.

But the pharaoh's status as both king and god came with many responsibilities. People blamed him if crops did not grow well or if disease struck. They also demanded that the pharaoh make trade profitable and prevent wars.

What You Will Learn...

Main Ideas

1. Life in the Old Kingdom was influenced by pharaohs, roles in society, and trade.
2. Religion shaped Egyptian life.
3. The pyramids were built as tombs for Egypt's pharaohs.

The Big Idea

Egyptian government and religion were closely connected during the Old Kingdom.

Key Terms

Old Kingdom, *p. 283*
nobles, *p. 284*
afterlife, *p. 286*
mummies, *p. 286*
elite, *p. 287*
pyramids, *p. 288*
engineering, *p. 288*

TAKING NOTES  As you read, take notes on government and religion during Egypt's Old Kingdom. Use a chart like the one below to record your notes.

Government	Religion

283

Preteach

Bellringer

If YOU lived there. . . Use the **Daily Bellringer Transparency** to help students answer the question.

Daily Bellringer Transparency, Section 2

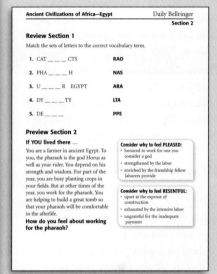

Academic Vocabulary

Review with students the high-use academic terms in this section.

acquire to get (p. 284)

method a way of doing something (p. 286)

RF: Vocabulary Builder, Section 2

Taking Notes

Have students copy the graphic organizer onto their own paper and then use it to take notes on the section. This activity will prepare students for the Section Assessment, in which they will complete a graphic organizer that builds on the information using the Critical Thinking Skill: Generalizing.

Teach the Big Idea

The Old Kingdom

1. **Teach** Ask students the questions in the Main Idea boxes under Direct Teach.

2. **Apply** Ask students to imagine that they have been asked by the government of Egypt to design a stamp commemorating the 4,700th anniversary of the Old Kingdom's beginning. Organize the class into three groups—one for each subsection. Then have each student choose a subtopic within that subsection and draw a stamp to illustrate that topic. **LS Visual/Spatial**

3. **Review** Display the stamps and call on volunteers to describe their illustrations.

4. **Practice/Homework** Have students write summaries of how the topics they illustrated were related to other aspects of the Old Kingdom. **LS Verbal/Linguistic**

   Alternative Assessment Handbook, Rubric 42: Writing to Inform

❶ Life in the Old Kingdom

Life in the Old Kingdom was influenced by pharaohs, roles in society, and trade.

Recall How long did the Old Kingdom last? *about 500 years, from about 2700 to 2200 BC*

Draw Conclusions What responsibilities did the pharaoh have that balanced his high status? *according to ancient Egyptian belief, make crops grow, keep people healthy, make trade profitable, prevent wars*

Make Judgments What may be some advantages and disadvantages of such a large segment of the population being farmers, servants, and slaves? *possible answers—advantages: plenty of food and labor; disadvantages: potential for unrest and rebellion*

📄 RF: Biography, Khufu

Primary Source

A Father's Career Advice In an ancient text, an Egyptian scribe named Duaf gives advice to his son Khety, who is training to be a scribe. Duaf writes, "I will make you love writing more than your mother, I will show its beauties to you; Now, it is greater than any trade, There is not one like it in the land." Duaf goes on to describe the miseries of the metalworker, carpenter, jeweler, and barber. Ask: Do you think Duaf exaggerated the hardships of the other trades? Why or why not? *possible answers: yes, to make being a scribe sound better; no, because being a scribe really was a better trade*

Answers

Analyzing Visuals *nobles*

Reading Check *pharaoh at the top; nobles; scribes and craftspeople; farmers, servants, and slaves at the bottom*

Egyptian Society

Pharaoh
The pharaoh ruled Egypt as a god.

Nobles
Officials and priests helped run the government and temples.

Scribes and Craftspeople
Scribes and craftspeople wrote and produced goods.

Farmers, Servants, and Slaves
Most Egyptians were farmers, servants, or slaves.

ANALYSIS SKILL **ANALYZING VISUALS**
Which group helped run the government and temples?

The most famous pharaoh of the Old Kingdom was Khufu (KOO-foo), who ruled in the 2500s BC. Even though he is famous, we know relatively little about Khufu's life. Egyptian legend says that he was cruel, but historical records tell us that the people who worked for him were well fed. Khufu is best known for the monuments that were built to him.

Society and Trade

ACADEMIC VOCABULARY
acquire (uh-KWYR) to get

By the end of the Old Kingdom, Egypt had about 2 million people. As the population grew, social classes appeared. The Egyptians believed that a well-ordered society would keep their kingdom strong.

At the top of Egyptian society was the pharaoh. Just below him were the upper classes, which included priests and key government officials. Many of these priests and officials were **nobles**, or people from rich and powerful families.

Next in society was the middle class. This class included lesser government officials, scribes, and a few rich craftspeople.

The people in Egypt's lower class, more than 80 percent of the population, were mostly farmers. During flood season, when they could not work in the fields, farmers worked on the pharaoh's building projects. Servants and slaves also worked hard.

As society developed during the Old Kingdom, Egypt traded with some of its neighbors. Traders traveled south along the Nile to Nubia to **acquire** gold, copper, ivory, slaves, and stone for building. Trade with Syria provided Egypt with wood for building and for fire.

Egyptian society grew more complex during this time. It continued to be organized, disciplined, and highly religious.

READING CHECK **Generalizing** How was society structured in the Old Kingdom?

Critical Thinking: Evaluating

At Level

Being Pharaoh

1. Ask students what advantages pharaohs seemed to have in Egyptian society. Write responses for students to see. *possible responses—believed to be a god, wealth and easy life, monuments honored him*

2. Then ask what disadvantages there were to being a pharaoh. Write these next to the advantages. *possible answers—blamed for natural disasters, hardships, and invasions*

3. Organize students into pairs. Have partners discuss whether they would want to be a pharaoh and give specific reasons for their responses.

4. Call on volunteers to share their reasoning with the class. **LS** **Interpersonal, Logical/Mathematical**

📄 Alternative Assessment Handbook, Rubric 11: Discussions

Religion and Egyptian Life

Worshipping the gods was a part of daily life in Egypt. But the Egyptian focus on religion extended beyond people's lives. Many customs focused on what happened after people died.

The Gods of Egypt

The Egyptians practiced polytheism. Before the First Dynasty, each village worshipped its own gods. During the Old Kingdom, however, Egyptian officials expected everyone to worship the same gods, though how people worshipped the gods might differ from place to place.

The Egyptians built temples to the gods all over the kingdom. Temples collected payments from both worshippers and the government. These payments enabled the temples to grow more influential.

Over time, certain cities became centers for the worship of certain gods. In the city of Memphis, for example, people prayed to Ptah, the creator of the world.

The Egyptians worshipped many gods besides Ptah. They had gods for nearly everything, including the sun, the sky, and Earth. Many gods blended human and animal forms. For example, Anubis, the god of the dead, had a human body but a jackal's head. Other major gods included

- Re, or Amon-Re, the sun god
- Osiris, the god of the underworld
- Isis, the goddess of magic
- Horus, a sky god; god of the pharaohs
- Thoth, the god of wisdom
- Geb, the Earth god

Egyptian families also worshipped household gods at shrines in their homes.

FOCUS ON READING

How is the text under the heading Religion and Egyptian Life categorized?

Egyptian Gods

Re, or Amon-Re, the sun god

Osiris, the god of the underworld

Isis, the goddess of magic

Horus, a sky god and the god of the pharaohs

285

Differentiating Instruction

Above Level

Advanced/Gifted and Talented

Research Required

1. Tell students that there are many stories about the Egyptian gods, their duties, and their interactions.

2. Organize students into small groups. Have each group conduct research on two or three Egyptian gods. Have students look for specific characteristics and stories about the gods. Then have each group create a storyboard about each god the group researched.

3. Have groups present their storyboards to the class.

4. Then lead a discussion about how these stories might have affected the ancient Egyptians' lives or behavior. **LS Interpersonal, Visual/Spatial**

   Alternative Assessment Handbook, Rubric 3: Artwork

Direct Teach

Main Idea

❷ Religion and Egyptian Life

Religion shaped Egyptian life.

Identify Who was the Egyptian sun god? What else did the main Egyptian gods represent? *Re, or Amon-Re; underworld, magic, sky, wisdom, Earth*

Analyze How is the portrayal of Horus connected to the god's function in Egyptian mythology? *He is pictured with the head of a bird, which is appropriate for a sky god.*

Evaluate Why might the ways in which Egyptians worshipped the gods have differed from place to place? *possible answer—Different groups or villages might have emphasized gods that were important to them. For example, scribes might place more emphasis on Thoth, the god of wisdom.*

Teaching Tip

Polytheism Remind students that the word polytheism means "the worship of more than one god."

Info to Know

Egyptian Gods Horus, the Egyptian god of the sky and of the pharaohs, was often depicted as a falcon or as a man wearing a falcon headdress. Egyptians believed that the eyes of Horus were the sun and the moon. Ask students why the Egyptians may have formed this connection between the falcon, the sun, and the moon. *possible answer—because falcons have keen eyesight*

Answers

Focus on Reading *possible answers—gods, afterlife, burial practices*

285

Main Idea

Religion and Egyptian Life, continued

Describe How did the Egyptians see the afterlife? *as an ideal world where all the people are young, healthy, and happy*

Contrast How was the *ka* different from the body? *The ka was not a physical entity, but rather a person's life force. It left the physical body at death.*

Predict How would you expect a pharaoh to be drawn on the walls of his tomb? *possible answer—He would be drawn as young, powerful, happy, and doing the things he enjoyed doing while alive.*

Info to Know

Ancient Absences Builders of pyramids were closely supervised. In Deir el-Medina—a village built especially for tomb builders—records show that scribes kept track of the workers' attendance and their reasons for being absent. Those excuses included an eye ailment, having to embalm the laborer's mother, and having to take a donkey to the veterinarian.

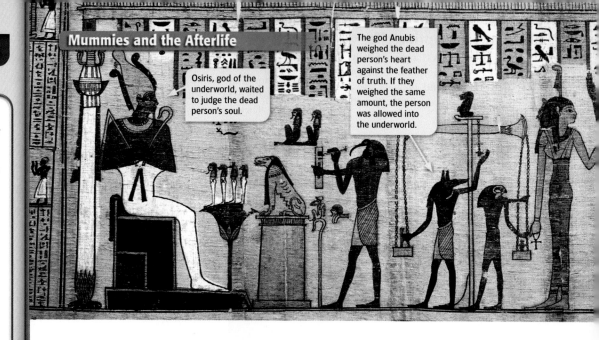

Mummies and the Afterlife

Osiris, god of the underworld, waited to judge the dead person's soul.

The god Anubis weighed the dead person's heart against the feather of truth. If they weighed the same amount, the person was allowed into the underworld.

Emphasis on the Afterlife

Much of Egyptian religion focused on the **afterlife**, or life after death. The Egyptians believed that the afterlife was a happy place. Paintings from Egyptian tombs show the afterlife as an ideal world where all the people are young and healthy.

The Egyptian belief in the afterlife stemmed from their idea of *ka* (KAH), or a person's life force. When a person died, his or her *ka* left the body and became a spirit. The *ka* remained linked to the body and could not leave its burial site. However, it had all the same needs that the person had when he or she was living. It needed to eat, sleep, and be entertained.

To fulfill the *ka's* needs, people filled tombs with objects for the afterlife. These objects included furniture, clothing, tools, jewelry, and weapons. Relatives of the dead were expected to bring food and beverages to their loved ones' tombs so the *ka* would not be hungry or thirsty.

ACADEMIC VOCABULARY
method a way of doing something

Burial Practices

Egyptian ideas about the afterlife shaped their burial practices. For example, the Egyptians believed that a body had to be prepared for the afterlife before it could be placed in a tomb. This meant the body had to be preserved. If the body decayed, its spirit could not recognize it. That would break the link between the body and spirit. The *ka* would then be unable to receive the food and drink it needed.

To help the *ka*, Egyptians developed a **method** called embalming to preserve bodies and to keep them from decaying. Egyptians preserved bodies as **mummies**, specially treated bodies wrapped in cloth. Embalming preserves a body for many, many years. A body that was not embalmed decayed far more quickly.

Embalming was a complex process that took several weeks to complete. In the first step, embalmers cut open the body and removed all organs except for the heart.

286 CHAPTER 10

Collaborative Learning

| At Level |

Egyptian Game Show

Prep Required | Research Required

1. Prepare a series of 20 to 30 questions on Egyptian gods, beliefs about the afterlife, and burial practices.

2. Organize students into two teams. Each team may want to assign one of the three subtopics to each team member. Provide basic research materials, and challenge students to learn as much as they can about their topics in approximately 30 minutes.

3. Tell students they will now play a game show on the topics they have been reading about.

4. Conduct the game show, awarding a point for each correct answer. Award a prize to the winning team. **LS Interpersonal, Kinesthetic**

   Alternative Assessment Handbook, Rubric 14: Group Activity

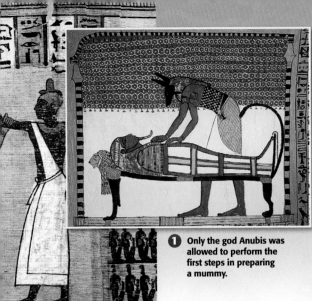

① Only the god Anubis was allowed to perform the first steps in preparing a mummy.

② The body's organs were preserved in special jars and kept next to the mummy.

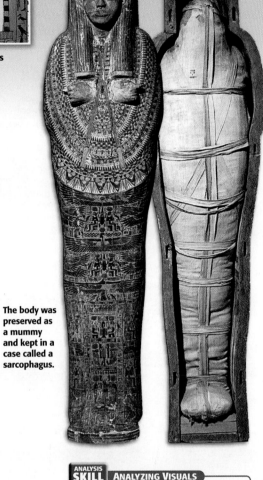

③ The body was preserved as a mummy and kept in a case called a sarcophagus.

Embalmers stored the removed organs in special jars. Next, the embalmers used a special substance to dry out the body. They later applied some special oils. The embalmers then wrapped the dried-out body with linen cloths and bandages, often placing special charms inside the cloth wrappings.

Wrapping the body was the last step in the mummy-making process. Once it was completely wrapped, a mummy was placed in a coffin called a sarcophagus, such as the one shown at right.

Only royalty and other members of Egypt's **elite** (AY-leet), or people of wealth and power, could afford to have mummies made. Peasant families did not need the process. They buried their dead in shallow graves at the edge of the desert. The hot, dry sand preserved the bodies naturally.

READING CHECK Analyzing How did religious beliefs affect Egyptian burial practices?

ANALYSIS SKILL **ANALYZING VISUALS**

How did gods participate in the afterlife?

ANCIENT CIVILIZATIONS OF AFRICA—EGYPT **287**

Main Idea

❸ The Pyramids

The pyramids were built as tombs for Egypt's pharaohs.

Recall How many limestone blocks did the Great Pyramid require? *more than 2 million*

Describe What is the shape of a pyramid? *four triangle-shaped walls that meet in a point on top*

Predict How would the invention of large animal-drawn wheeled vehicles have affected pyramid construction? *possible answer—made transporting the blocks of stone much easier, reducing labor needs and construction time considerably*

Did you know...

In 1954, archaeologists made an astonishing discovery. Buried at the base of the Great Pyramid was a 144-foot-long wooden boat. The boat may have carried Khufu's body across the Nile to his tomb. Or, it may have been placed there to symbolically carry Khufu into the afterlife.

Linking to Today

Pyramids and Pollution Even though the pyramids have stood for thousands of years, they are not safe from harm. In fact, the stone shows signs of deterioration. Pollution from nearby Cairo and damage done by tourists may be to blame for the problems.

Close-up

The Great Sphinx has undergone many restorations, including one by pharaoh Tuthmosis IV in about 1400 BC. The pharaoh dreamed that the sphinx asked him to clear the sand from around it in return for giving the pharaoh power over both Upper and Lower Egypt.

The Pyramids

The Egyptians believed that burial sites, especially royal tombs, were very important. For this reason, they built spectacular monuments in which to bury their rulers. The most spectacular were the **pyramids**—huge, stone tombs with four triangle-shaped sides that met in a point on top.

The Egyptians built the first pyramids during the Old Kingdom. Some of the largest pyramids were built during that time.

Many of these huge Egyptian pyramids are still standing. The largest is the Great Pyramid of Khufu near the town of Giza. It covers more than 13 acres at its base and stands 481 feet (146 m) high. This one pyramid took thousands of workers and more than 2 million limestone blocks to build. Like all the pyramids, it is an amazing example of Egyptian **engineering**, the application of scientific knowledge for practical purposes.

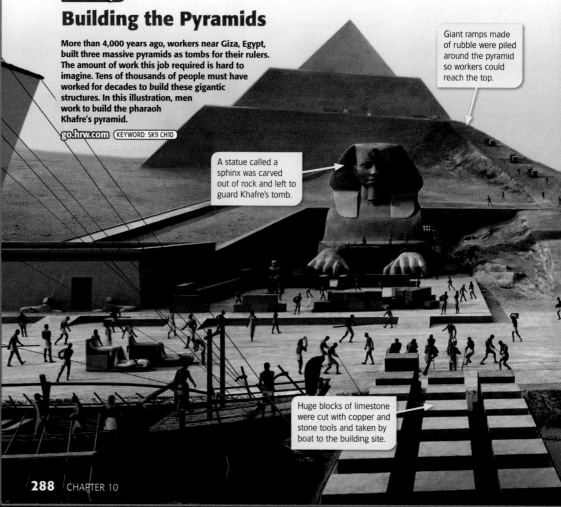

✳Interactive Close-up

Building the Pyramids

More than 4,000 years ago, workers near Giza, Egypt, built three massive pyramids as tombs for their rulers. The amount of work this job required is hard to imagine. Tens of thousands of people must have worked for decades to build these gigantic structures. In this illustration, men work to build the pharaoh Khafre's pyramid.

go.hrw.com (KEYWORD: SK9 CH10)

Giant ramps made of rubble were piled around the pyramid so workers could reach the top.

A statue called a sphinx was carved out of rock and left to guard Khafre's tomb.

Huge blocks of limestone were cut with copper and stone tools and taken by boat to the building site.

288 CHAPTER 10

Cross-Discipline Activity: Math

Above Level

The Geometry of Pyramids

Research Required

Materials: heavy paper or cardboard, glue or tape

1. Explain to students that the Egyptians would not have been able to build the pyramids without a clear understanding of geometry. To construct a pyramid, each side had to slope upward and inward at exactly the same angle. Builders checked their work often, because even a tiny error in the early stages could mean a big error later.

2. Have students use the Internet and other resources to conduct research on the geometry of pyramid building.

3. Have students build and label models to demonstrate their findings.

🔲 **Logical/Mathematical, Verbal/Linguistic**

📃 Alternative Assessment Handbook, Rubric 30: Research

Building the Pyramids

The earliest pyramids did not have the smooth sides we usually imagine when we think of pyramids. The Egyptians began building the smooth-sided pyramids we usually see around 2700 BC. The steps of these pyramids were filled and covered with limestone. The burial chamber was located deep inside the pyramid. After the pharaoh's burial, workers sealed the passages to this room with large blocks.

Historians do not know for certain how the ancient Egyptians built the pyramids. What is certain is that such massive projects required a huge labor force. As many as 100,000 workers may have been needed to build just one pyramid. The government paid the people working on the pyramids.

Inside the Great Pyramid, tunnels led to the pharaoh's burial chamber, which was sealed off with rocks.

Teams of workers dragged the stones on wooden sleds to the pyramid.

ANALYSIS SKILL **ANALYZING VISUALS**

How did workers get their stone blocks to the pyramids?

Main Idea

The Pyramids, continued

Explain Why did the Egyptians want the pyramids to be spectacular? *because they believed the pharaoh controlled everyone's afterlife, their own fate in the afterlife depended on the pharaoh's happiness in the afterlife*

Make Judgments Do you think the Egyptians were gloomy and obsessed by death? Why or why not? *possible answer—No, they were more interested in living forever because they loved life.*

● Review & Assess ●

Close

Ask students to imagine what went through the workers' minds as they built the pyramids.

Review

🔲 Online Quiz, Section 2

Assess

SE Section 2 Assessment

📋 PASS: Section 2 Quiz

📋 Alternative Assessment Handbook

Reteach/Classroom Intervention

📋 Interactive Reader and Study Guide, Section 2

💿 Interactive Skills Tutor CD-ROM

Answers

Reading Check *because the Egyptians believed that their own afterlife was linked to the eternal life of the pharaoh buried in the pyramid*

290

Wages for working on construction projects were paid in goods such as grain instead of money, however.

For years, scholars have debated how the Egyptians moved the massive stones used to build the pyramids. Some scholars think that during the Nile's flooding, builders floated the stones downstream directly to the construction site. Most historians believe that workers used brick ramps and strong wooden sleds to drag the stones up the pyramid once at the building site.

Significance of the Pyramids

Burial in a pyramid showed a pharaoh's importance. Both the size and shape of the pyramid were symbolic. Pointing to the sky above, the pyramid symbolized the pharaoh's journey to the afterlife. The Egyptians wanted the pyramids to be spectacular because they believed the pharaoh, as their link to the gods, controlled everyone's afterlife. Making the pharaoh's spirit happy was a way of ensuring happiness in one's own afterlife.

To ensure that the pharaohs remained safe after death, the Egyptians sometimes wrote magical spells and hymns on tombs.

Together, these spells and hymns are called Pyramid Texts. The first such text, addressed to Re, the sun god, was carved into the pyramid of King Unas (OO-nuhs). He was a pharaoh of the Old Kingdom.

" Re, this Unas comes to you,
A spirit indestructible . . .
Your son comes to you, this Unas . . .
May you cross the sky united in the dark,
May you rise in lightland, [where] you shine! "
–from Pyramid Text, Utterance 217

The builders of Unas's pyramid wanted the god Re to look after their leader's spirit. Even after death, the Egyptians' pharaoh was important to them.

READING CHECK **Identifying Points of View** Why were pyramids important to the ancient Egyptians?

SUMMARY AND PREVIEW As you have read, during the Old Kingdom, new political and social orders were created in Egypt. Religion was important, and many pyramids were built for pharaohs. In the next section you will learn about Egypt's Middle and New Kingdoms.

Section 2 Assessment

go.hrw.com
Online Quiz
KEYWORD: SK9 HP10

Reviewing Ideas, Terms, and Places

1. **a. Define** To what Egyptian period does the phrase **Old Kingdom** refer?
   b. Analyze Why did Egyptians never question the pharaoh's authority?
   c. Elaborate Why do you think pharaohs might have wanted the support of **nobles**?
2. **a. Define** What did Egyptians mean by the **afterlife**?
   b. Analyze Why was embalming important to Egyptians?
3. **a. Describe** What is **engineering**?
   b. Elaborate What does the building of the **pyramids** tell us about Egyptian society?

Critical Thinking

4. **Generalizing** Using your notes, complete this graphic organizer by listing three facts about the relationship between government and religion in the Old Kingdom.

   Government and Religion
   1.
   2.
   3.

FOCUS ON WRITING

5. **Noting Characteristics of the Old Kingdom** The Old Kingdom has special characteristics of government, society, and religion. Write down details about any of those characteristics that you might want to include as one of the clues in your Egypt riddle.

290 CHAPTER 10

Section 2 Assessment Answers

1. **a.** the 500-year period in Egyptian history from 2700 to 2200 BC
   b. The Egyptians thought of him as a god.
   c. possible answer—needed help running the government, may have needed rich and powerful supporters if problems such as disease or invasion occurred
2. **a.** life after death
   b. If a body was allowed to decay, the spirit would not recognize it in the afterlife.
3. **a.** the application of scientific knowledge for practical purposes

b. possible answer—that Egyptian society was capable of the complex skills, organization, and discipline required to build the pyramids

4. possible answers—pharaoh was both king and god; officials expected everyone to worship the same gods; temples collected payments from government

5. Answers will vary, but details should be based on information learned in Section 2.

The Middle and New Kingdoms

If YOU lived there...

You are a servant to Hatshepsut, the ruler of Egypt. You admire her, but some people think a woman should not rule. She calls herself king and dresses like a pharaoh—even wearing a fake beard. That was your idea! But you want to help more.

What could Hatshepsut do to show her authority?

BUILDING BACKGROUND The power of the pharaohs expanded during the Old Kingdom. Society was orderly, based on great differences between social classes. But rulers and dynasties changed, and Egypt changed with them. In time, these changes led to new eras in Egyptian history, eras called the Middle and New Kingdoms.

The Middle Kingdom

At the end of the Old Kingdom, the wealth and power of the pharaohs declined. Building and maintaining pyramids cost a lot of money. Pharaohs could not collect enough taxes to keep up with their expenses. At the same time, ambitious nobles used their government positions to take power from pharaohs.

In time, nobles gained enough power to challenge Egypt's pharaohs. By about 2200 BC the Old Kingdom had fallen. For the next 160 years, local nobles ruled much of Egypt. During this period, the kingdom had no central ruler.

Time Line

Periods of Egyptian History

3000 BC	2000 BC	1000 BC
c. 2700–2200 BC Old Kingdom	c. 2050–1750 BC Middle Kingdom	c. 1550–1050 BC New Kingdom

What You Will Learn...

Main Ideas

1. The Middle Kingdom was a period of stable government between periods of disorder.
2. The New Kingdom was the peak of Egyptian trade and military power, but its greatness did not last.
3. Work and daily life differed among Egypt's social classes.

The Big Idea

During the Middle and New Kingdoms, order and greatness were restored in Egypt.

Key Terms

Middle Kingdom, *p. 292*
New Kingdom, *p. 292*
trade routes, *p. 293*

TAKING NOTES As you read, use a chart like the one here to take notes on the Middle and New Kingdoms and on work and life in ancient Egypt.

Middle Kingdom	New Kingdom	Work and Life

291

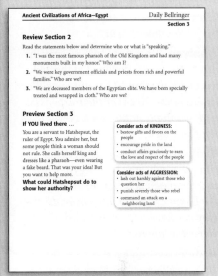

Main Idea

❶ The Middle Kingdom

The Middle Kingdom was a period of stable government between periods of disorder.

Identify Where were the Hyksos from? *Southwest Asia*

Analyze What were two reasons the pharaohs' power declined at the end of the Old Kingdom? *They did not collect enough taxes to cover their expenses, and ambitious nobles took power from the pharaohs.*

Evaluate What may the Hyksos conquest indicate about Egypt's level of technological advance? *Although the Egyptians had built pyramids, they may not have had chariots or advanced weapons.*

About the Illustration

This illustration of Hatshepsut is an artist's conception based on available sources. However, historians are uncertain exactly what Hatshepsut looked like.

Info to Know

A Mysterious Death Thutmose III became pharaoh after Hatshepsut's death. The sources are unclear about how she died. According to some historians, Thutmose had her murdered so he could succeed her as pharaoh.

Answers

Biography *possible answer—objections to a woman ruling, her desire to make her role as pharaoh more acceptable to the Egyptian people*

Reading Check *the Hyksos invasion and eventual conquest of Lower Egypt*

292

Finally, around 2050 BC, a powerful pharaoh defeated his rivals. Once again all of Egypt was united. His rule began the **Middle Kingdom**, a period of order and stability that lasted to about 1750 BC. Toward the end of the Middle Kingdom, however, Egypt began to fall into disorder once again.

Around 1750 BC, a group from Southwest Asia called the Hyksos (HIK-sohs) invaded. The Hyksos used horses, chariots, and advanced weapons to conquer Lower Egypt. The Hyksos then ruled the region as pharaohs for 200 years.

The Egyptians eventually fought back. In the mid-1500s BC, Ahmose (AHM-ohs) of Thebes declared himself king and drove the Hyksos out of Egypt. Ahmose then ruled all of Egypt.

READING CHECK **Summarizing** What caused the end of the Middle Kingdom?

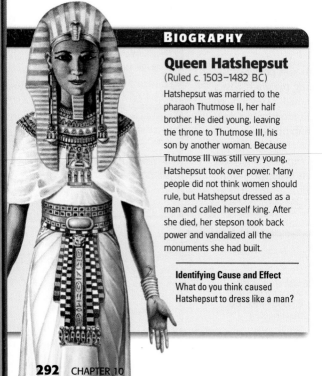

BIOGRAPHY

Queen Hatshepsut
(Ruled c. 1503–1482 BC)

Hatshepsut was married to the pharaoh Thutmose II, her half brother. He died young, leaving the throne to Thutmose III, his son by another woman. Because Thutmose III was still very young, Hatshepsut took over power. Many people did not think women should rule, but Hatshepsut dressed as a man and called herself king. After she died, her stepson took back power and vandalized all the monuments she had built.

Identifying Cause and Effect
What do you think caused Hatshepsut to dress like a man?

292 CHAPTER 10

The New Kingdom

Ahmose's rise to power marked the start of Egypt's eighteenth dynasty. More importantly, it was the start of the **New Kingdom**, the period during which Egypt reached the height of its power and glory. During the New Kingdom, which lasted from about 1550 to 1050 BC, conquest and trade brought wealth to the pharaohs.

Building an Empire

After battling the Hyksos, Egypt's leaders feared future invasions. To prevent such invasions from occurring, they decided to take control of all possible invasion routes into the kingdom. In the process, these leaders turned Egypt into an empire.

Egypt's first target was the homeland of the Hyksos. After taking over that area, the army continued north and conquered Syria. As you can see from the map, Egypt took over the entire eastern shore of the Mediterranean and the kingdom of Kush, south of Egypt. By the 1400s BC, Egypt was the leading military power in the region. Its empire extended from the Euphrates River to southern Nubia.

Military conquests made Egypt rich as well as powerful. The kingdoms that Egypt conquered regularly sent gifts and treasure to their Egyptian conquerors. For example, the kingdom of Kush in Nubia sent yearly payments of gold, precious stones, and leopard skins to the pharaohs. In addition, Assyrian, Babylonian, and Hittite kings sent expensive gifts to Egypt in an effort to maintain good relations.

Growth and Effects of Trade

As Egypt's empire expanded, so did its trade. Conquest brought Egyptian traders into contact with more distant lands. Many of these lands had valuable resources for trade. The Sinai Peninsula is one example.

Critical Thinking: Interpreting Maps

At Level

Trade Routes of Ancient Egypt

1. Have students examine the map on the opposite page.

2. Lead a class discussion about the following questions: Which of these routes do you think would have been easier to follow? Which would have been more difficult? Why might particular routes have developed? For example, why does the southernmost route loop southward from the Nile and then back north to Elephantine?

3. Ask students to describe the different routes and the challenges traders would have faced

along them. Call on volunteers to propose how trade changed the lives of both the Egyptians and the people with whom they traded.

4. Complete the discussion by asking how the Egyptians may have used the products listed in the map legend. **LS Visual/Spatial, Auditory/Musical**

🗐 Alternative Assessment Handbook, Rubrics 11: Discussions; and 21: Map Reading

It had valuable supplies of turquoise and copper. Profitable **trade routes**, or paths followed by traders, developed from Egypt to these lands, as the map shows.

One of Egypt's rulers who worked to increase trade was Queen Hatshepsut. She sent Egyptian traders south to trade with the kingdom of Punt on the Red Sea and north to trade with people in Asia Minor and Greece.

Hatshepsut and later pharaohs used the money they gained from trade to support the arts and architecture. Hatshepsut in particular is remembered for the many impressive monuments and temples built during her reign. The best known of these structures was a magnificent temple built for her near the city of Thebes.

Invasions of Egypt

Despite its military might, Egypt still faced threats to its power. In the 1200s BC the pharaoh Ramses (RAM-seez) II, or Ramses the Great, fought the Hittites, who came from Asia Minor. The two powers fought fiercely for years, but neither one could defeat the other.

Egypt faced threats in other parts of its empire as well. To the west, a people known as the Tehenu invaded the Nile Delta. Ramses fought them off and built a series of forts to strengthen the western frontier. This proved to be a wise decision because the Tehenu invaded again a century later. Faced with Egypt's strengthened defenses, the Tehenu were defeated once again.

Soon after Ramses the Great died, invaders called the Sea Peoples sailed into Southwest Asia. Little is known about these people. Historians are not even sure who they were. All we know is that they were strong warriors who had crushed the Hittites and destroyed cities in Southwest Asia. Only after 50 years of fighting were the Egyptians able to turn them back.

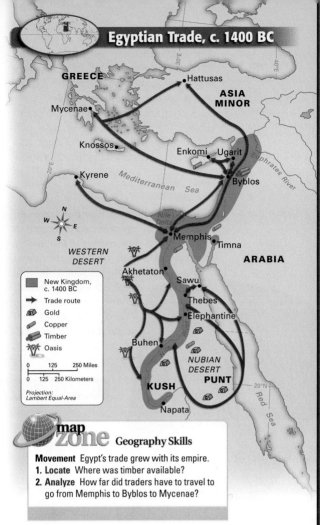

Egyptian Trade, c. 1400 BC

map zone Geography Skills

Movement Egypt's trade grew with its empire.
1. **Locate** Where was timber available?
2. **Analyze** How far did traders have to travel to go from Memphis to Byblos to Mycenae?

Egypt survived, but its empire in Asia was gone. Shortly after the invasions of the Hittites and the Sea Peoples, the New Kingdom came to an end. Ancient Egypt fell into a period of violence and disorder. Egypt would never regain its power.

READING CHECK Identifying Cause and Effect
What caused Egypt's growth of trade during the New Kingdom?

ANCIENT CIVILIZATIONS OF AFRICA—EGYPT **293**

293

❸ Work and Daily Life

Work and daily life differed among Egypt's social classes.

Describe What kinds of writing did scribes do? *kept records and accounts for the state and temples, wrote and copied religious and literary texts*

Analyze Why did the pharaohs value talented architects? *Having well-designed pyramids and temples made the pharaoh powerful and, according to Egyptian religion, ensured a happy afterlife.*

Make Judgments Which of these jobs would you have preferred: scribe, artisan, artist, or architect? Why? *Answers will vary.*

📖 RF: Biography, Nefertiti

Did you know. . .

Some Egyptians slept on their backs, with their heads placed in wooden head-rests to keep their hairstyles neat.

Teaching Tip

Ask students to explain the difference between an artist and an artisan. If they are uncertain, ask a student to look up the terms in a dictionary and report to the class.

Connect to Art

Queen Nefertiti The painted limestone statue of Nefertiti shown on this page is one of the most famous works of Egyptian art. Ask: Do you think this is exactly what Queen Nefertiti looked like? *probably not, because few Egyptian portraits are very realistic* Why is the statue usually shown in profile? *because the eye on one side is damaged*

Answers

Focus on Reading *possible answers—scribes, artisans, artists, architects, merchants, traders, soldiers, farmers, peasants*

294

Work and Daily Life

FOCUS ON READING
What categories of jobs made up the society of ancient Egypt?

Although Egyptian dynasties rose and fell, daily life for Egyptians did not change very much. But as the population grew, Egypt's society became even more complex.

A complex society requires people to take on different jobs. In Egypt, these jobs were often passed on within families. At a young age, boys started to learn their future jobs from their fathers.

Scribes

After the priests and government officials, scribes were the most respected people in ancient Egypt. As members of the middle class, scribes worked for the government and the temples. This work involved keeping records and accounts. Scribes also wrote and copied religious and literary texts.

Because of their respected position, scribes did not have to pay taxes. For this reason, many scribes became wealthy.

Artisans, Artists, and Architects

Another group in society was made up of artisans whose jobs required advanced skills. Among the artisans who worked in Egypt were sculptors, builders, carpenters, jewelers, metalworkers, and leatherworkers. Artisans made items such as statues, furniture, jewelry, pottery, and shoes. Most artisans worked for the government or for temples. Egypt's artisans were admired and often paid fairly well.

Architects and artists were admired in Egypt as well. Architects designed the temples and royal tombs for which Egypt is famous. Talented architects could rise to become high government officials. Artists often worked for the state or for temples.

Daily Life in Egypt

Most Egyptians spent their days in the fields, plowing and harvesting their crops.

Queen Nefertiti, shown here, and other Egyptian queens wore makeup, jewelry, and perfume.

294 CHAPTER 10

Differentiating Instruction

Below Level

Struggling Readers

Materials: art supplies

1. Lead a discussion comparing each group in Egyptian society with a similar group of people today. For example, compare the work and daily life of ancient Egyptian farmers to those of farmers in the present-day United States.

2. Then have students draw Egyptians at work from at least three of the following groups: government officials, priests, scribes, artists and artisans, architects, merchants and

traders, soldiers, and farmers. Pictures should be as detailed as possible.

3. Have students display and explain their work.
   LS Visual/Spatial

📖 Alternative Assessment Handbook, Rubric 3, Artwork

Egyptian artists produced many different types of works. Many artists worked in the deep burial chambers of the pharaohs' tombs painting detailed pictures.

Merchants and Traders

Although trade was important to Egypt, only a small group of Egyptians became merchants and traders. Some traveled long distances to buy and sell goods. On their journeys, merchants were usually accompanied by soldiers, scribes, and laborers.

Soldiers

After the wars of the Middle Kingdom, Egypt established a professional army. The military offered people a chance to rise in social status. Soldiers received land as payment and could also keep any treasure they captured in war. Soldiers who excelled could be promoted to officer positions.

Farmers and Other Peasants

As in the society of the Old Kingdom, Egyptian farmers and other peasants were toward the bottom of Egypt's social scale. These hardworking people made up the vast majority of Egypt's population.

Egyptian farmers grew crops to support their families. These farmers depended on the Nile's regular floods to grow their crops. Farmers used wooden hoes or plows pulled by cows to prepare the land before the flood. After the floodwaters had drained away, farmers planted seeds for crops such as wheat and barley. At the end of the growing season, Egypt's farmers worked together to gather the harvest.

Farmers had to give some of their crops to the pharaoh as taxes. These taxes were intended to pay the pharaoh for use of the land. Under Egyptian law, the pharaoh controlled all land in the kingdom.

This jar probably held perfume, a valuable trade item.

Servants worked for Egypt's rulers and nobles and did many jobs, like preparing food.

ANALYSIS SKILL **ANALYZING VISUALS**
What were some luxury goods used by Egypt's queens and rulers?

ANCIENT CIVILIZATIONS OF AFRICA—EGYPT **295**

Direct Teach

Main Idea

Work and Daily Life,
continued

Identify Who made up the majority of Egypt's population? *farmers and other peasants*

Explain What special challenge do you think artists who painted a pharaoh's burial chamber faced? *No natural light reached the burial chamber, so artists had to work by torchlight or candlelight.*

Predict What might have happened if large numbers of peasants had refused to take part in special duties, such as working on the pyramids, mining gold, and fighting in the military? *possible answer—rebellion crushed by the pharaoh, or his power threatened*

Did you know. . .
Since wood was rare in Egypt, the common people built their houses out of sun-baked bricks. Because summers were hot, Egyptians often slept on the roofs of their houses.

Info to Know
Precious Perfumes Perfume was not only a valuable Egyptian trade item, but also was used extensively in religious ceremonies. At one temple, perfume recipes were engraved on walls leading to a small laboratory.

Differentiating Instruction

Above Level

Advanced/Gifted and Talented

Research Required

1. Ask students to imagine that they are traders in ancient Egypt. Have them conduct research to learn more about Egyptian trade, such as methods of travel over land and sea.

2. Then have students write journal entries about their journeys, what they sold, and what they bought. Each journal entry should include a map to show the trader's routes.

3. Encourage students to make their journals as interesting and specific as they can.

4. Ask for volunteers to read their journal entries to the class. **LS Verbal/Linguistic**

Alternative Assessment Handbook; Rubrics 15: Journals; and 30: Research

Answers
Analyzing Visuals *makeup, jewelry, perfume*

295

Work and Daily Life,
continued

Describe How did some people come to be enslaved in Egypt? *convicted criminals or prisoners captured in war*

Make Inferences How might we have learned about Egyptian toys and games? *artifacts, art showing the toys and games in use*

● **Review & Assess** ●

Close

Point out that Egyptian children played versions of tug-of-war, leap-frog, and checkers. Ask how life in ancient Egypt was similar to and differed from life today.

Review

Online Quiz, Section 3

Assess

SE Section 3 Assessment

PASS: Section 3 Quiz

Alternative Assessment Handbook

Reteach/Classroom Intervention

Interactive Reader and Study Guide, Section 3

Interactive Skills Tutor CD-ROM

Answers

Reading Check *priests, government officials, scribes, artisans, artists, architects, merchants, traders, soldiers, farmers, peasants*

296

ACADEMIC
VOCABULARY
contracts binding legal agreements

All peasants, including farmers, were also subject to special duty. Under Egyptian law, the pharaoh could demand at any time that people work on projects, such as building pyramids, mining gold, or fighting in the army. The government paid the workers in grain.

Slaves

The few slaves in Egyptian society were considered lower than farmers. Many slaves were convicted criminals or prisoners captured in war. These slaves worked on farms, on building projects, in workshops, and in private households. Unlike most slaves in history, however, slaves in Egypt had some legal rights. Also, in some cases, they could earn their freedom.

Family Life in Egypt

Family life was very important in Egyptian society. Most Egyptian families lived in their own homes. Sometimes unmarried female relatives lived with them, but men were expected to marry young so that they could start having children.

Most Egyptian women were devoted to their homes and families. Some women, however, did have jobs outside the home.

A few women served as priestesses, and some worked as royal officials, administrators, or artisans. Unlike most women in ancient times, Egyptian women had a number of legal rights. They could own property, make **contracts**, and divorce their husbands. They could even keep their property after a divorce.

Children's lives were not as structured as adults' lives were. Children played with toys such as dolls, tops, and clay animal figurines. Children also played ballgames and hunted. Most children, boys and girls, received some education. At school they learned morals, writing, math, and sports. At age 14 most boys left school to enter their father's profession. At that time, they took their place in Egypt's social structure.

READING CHECK **Categorizing** What types of jobs existed in ancient Egypt?

SUMMARY AND PREVIEW Pharaohs faced many challenges to their rule. After the defeat of the Hyksos, Egypt grew in land and wealth. People in Egypt worked at many jobs. In the next section you will learn about Egyptian achievements.

---

go.hrw.com
Online Quiz
KEYWORD: SK9 HP10

Section 3 Assessment

Reviewing Ideas, Terms, and Places

1. **a. Define** What was the **Middle Kingdom**?
   b. Analyze How did Ahmose manage to become king of all Egypt?
2. **a. Recall** What two things brought wealth to the pharaohs during the **New Kingdom**?
   b. Explain What did Hatshepsut do as pharaoh of Egypt?
3. **a. Identify** What job employed the majority of the people in Egypt?
   b. Analyze What rights did Egyptian women have?
   c. Elaborate Why do you think scribes were so honored in Egyptian society?

Critical Thinking

4. **Categorizing** Draw pyramids like the ones shown. Using your notes, fill in the pyramids with the political and military factors that led to the rise and fall of the Middle and New Kingdoms.

Rise / Fall / Rise / Fall — Middle Kingdom / New Kingdom

FOCUS ON WRITING

5. **Developing Ideas from the Middle and New Kingdoms** Your riddle should contain information about these periods. Decide which key ideas you should include and add them to your list.

Section 3 Assessment Answers

1. **a.** a period of order and stability from about 2050 to 1750 BC that began after a powerful pharaoh defeated his rivals
   b. by driving the Hyksos out of Egypt
2. **a.** conquest and trade
   b. increased trade, built many impressive temples and monuments
3. **a.** farming
   b. the ability to own property, make contracts, and divorce their husbands
   c. possible answer—because they were involved in religious procedures, which were

very important to the Egyptians, and because they portrayed history to later generations

4. possible answers—Middle Kingdom: Rise—powerful pharaoh defeats his rivals; Fall—Hyksos invade Egypt; New Kingdom: Rise—Ahmose defeats the Hyksos, Egypt becomes an empire through military conquest, trade expands; Fall—invasions by various peoples

5. Students' key ideas will vary, but should reflect an understanding of the text.

BIOGRAPHY

Ramses the Great

How could a ruler achieve fame that would last 3,000 years?

When did he live? late 1300s and early 1200s BC

Where did he live? As pharaoh, Ramses lived in a city he built on the Nile Delta. The city's name, Pi-Ramesse, means the "house of Ramses."

What did he do? From a young age, Ramses was trained as a ruler and a fighter. Made an army captain at age 10, he began military campaigns even before he became pharaoh. During his reign, Ramses greatly increased the size of his kingdom.

Why is he important? Many people consider Ramses the last great Egyptian pharaoh. He accomplished great things, but the pharaohs who followed could not maintain them. Both a great warrior and a great builder, he is known largely for the massive monuments he built. The temples at Karnak, Luxor, and Abu Simbel stand as 3,000-year-old symbols of the great pharaoh's power.

Drawing Conclusions Why do you think Ramses built monuments all over Egypt?

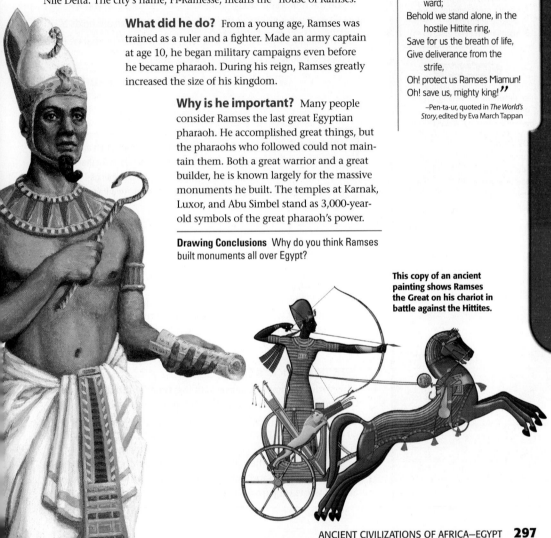

This copy of an ancient painting shows Ramses the Great on his chariot in battle against the Hittites.

KEY IDEAS

Ramses had a poem praising him carved into the walls of five temples, including Karnak. One verse of the poem praises Ramses as a great warrior and the defender of Egypt.

" Gracious lord and bravest king, savior–guard
Of Egypt in the battle, be our ward;
Behold we stand alone, in the hostile Hittite ring,
Save for us the breath of life,
Give deliverance from the strife,
Oh! protect us Ramses Miamun!
Oh! save us, mighty king! "

–Pen-ta-ur, quoted in *The World's Story*, edited by Eva March Tappan

---

Critical Thinking: Solving Problems

Above Level

Saving Abu Simbel

Research Required

1. Explain to students that in the 1950s and 1960s Egypt's leaders decided to control the Nile's annual flood by building the Aswan High Dam. Unfortunately, the lake created—Lake Nasser—would flood many Egyptian antiquities, including the temple of Ramses at Abu Simbel. Many organizations worked together to save the Abu Simbel temple.

2. Have students work in pairs to conduct research on this engineering feat and report on their findings.

3. Reports should explain some of the engineering problems that the project presented and how they were solved. Reports may take any form.

4. Challenge students to suggest alternative solutions to the engineering hurdles.
   LS Interpersonal, Kinesthetic
   Alternative Assessment Handbook, Rubrics 30: Research; and 35: Solving Problems

---

Biography

Ramses the Great
Achievements of Leaders Point out that Ramses was known not just for wartime accomplishments but also for peacetime achievements. Challenge students to name more recent leaders who have achieved lasting fame in both areas. *possible answers—George Washington, Winston Churchill*

Info to Know

Ramses the Warrior At one point in a famous battle against the Hittites, Ramses and a few of his charioteers appeared to be doomed when they were completely surrounded by Hittite forces. Fortunately, reinforcements arrived in time to save them. Ramses was extremely proud of his stand against the larger Hittite force. A long poem was written about the battle, and scenes from it were carved into several temple walls.

Did you know. . .

The reign of Ramses II was the second-longest in Egyptian history. Ramses II was so popular that nine pharaohs of the 20th dynasty used his name.

Connect to Art

Egyptian Warfare What does this painting tell about Egyptian warfare during the time of Ramses the Great? *that the Egyptians used bows and arrows and fought in two-wheeled chariots with spoked wheels drawn by two horses*

About the Illustration

This illustration of Ramses the Great is an artist's conception based on available sources. However, historians are uncertain exactly what Ramses the Great looked like.

Answers

Biography *possible answer—to impress possible invaders or rebels with his power, to make sure his fame lasted a long time*

297

Bellringer

If YOU lived there. . . Use the **Daily Bellringer Transparency** to help students answer the question.

📖 Daily Bellringer Transparency, Section 4

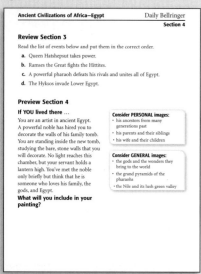

Ancient Civilizations of Africa—Egypt   Daily Bellringer
Section 4

Review Section 3

Read the list of events below and put them in the correct order.

a. Queen Hatshepsut takes power.

b. Ramses the Great fights the Hittites.

c. A powerful pharaoh defeats his rivals and unites all of Egypt.

d. The Hyksos invade Lower Egypt.

Preview Section 4

If YOU lived there …

You are an artist in ancient Egypt. A powerful noble has hired you to decorate the walls of his family tomb. You are standing inside the new tomb, studying the bare, stone walls that you will decorate. No light reaches this chamber, but your servant holds a lantern high. You've met the noble only briefly but think that he is someone who loves his family, the gods, and Egypt.

What will you include in your painting?

Consider PERSONAL images:
• his ancestors from many generations past
• his parents and their siblings
• his wife and their children

Consider GENERAL images:
• the gods and the wonders they bring to the world
• the grand pyramids of the pharaohs
• the Nile and its lush green valley

Key Terms

📝 **RF:** Vocabulary Builder, Section 4

Taking Notes

Have students copy the graphic organizer onto their own paper and then use it to take notes on the section. This activity will prepare students for the Section Assessment, in which they will complete a graphic organizer that builds on the information using the Critical Thinking Skill: Summarizing.

Egyptian Achievements

What You Will Learn...

Main Ideas

1. Egyptian writing used symbols called hieroglyphics.
2. Egypt's great temples were lavishly decorated.
3. Egyptian art filled tombs.

The Big Idea

The Egyptians made lasting achievements in writing, art, and architecture.

Key Terms

hieroglyphics, *p. 298*
papyrus, *p. 298*
Rosetta Stone, *p. 299*
sphinxes, *p. 300*
obelisk, *p. 300*

TAKING NOTES As you read, use a chart like this one to take notes on the achievements of the ancient Egyptians. In each column, identify Egyptian achievements in the appropriate field.

Writing	Architecture	Art

If **YOU** lived there...

You are an artist in ancient Egypt. A powerful noble has hired you to decorate the walls of his family tomb. You are standing inside the new tomb, studying the bare, stone walls that you will decorate. No light reaches this chamber, but your servant holds a lantern high. You've met the noble only briefly but think that he is someone who loves his family, the gods, and Egypt.

What will you include in your painting?

BUILDING BACKGROUND The ancient Egyptians had a rich and varied history. Today, though, most people remember them for their cultural achievements. Egyptian art, such as the tomb paintings mentioned above, and Egypt's unique writing system are admired by millions of tourists in museums around the world.

Egyptian Writing

If you were reading a book and saw pictures of folded cloth, a leg, a star, a bird, and a man holding a stick, would you know what it meant? You would if you were an ancient Egyptian. In the Egyptian writing system, or **hieroglyphics** (hy-ruh-GLIH-fiks), those five symbols together meant "to teach." Egyptian hieroglyphics were one of the world's first writing systems.

Writing in Ancient Egypt

The earliest known examples of Egyptian writing are from around 3300 BC. These early Egyptian writings were carved in stone or on other hard materials. Later, Egyptians learned how to make **papyrus** (puh-PY-ruhs), a long-lasting, paperlike material made from reeds. The Egyptians made papyrus by pressing layers of reeds together and pounding them into sheets. These sheets were tough and durable, yet could be rolled into scrolls. Scribes wrote on papyrus using brushes and ink.

Teach the Big Idea

At Level

Egyptian Achievements

1. **Teach** Ask students the questions in the Main Idea boxes under Direct Teach.

2. **Apply** Ask students to imagine that they are Egyptians who contributed to the civilization's achievements. For example, a student may imagine herself as the inventor of papyrus or as a temple painter. Have students create book jackets for autobiographies of their chosen characters. The books' titles should be *My Life as ___* , filling in the chosen role. 🄻 **Visual/Spatial**

3. **Review** Call on students to display and explain their book jackets until all the major achievements have been discussed.

4. **Practice/Homework** Have students write the introductory paragraphs for the blurbs inside their book jackets. 🄻 **Verbal/Linguistic**

📝 Alternative Assessment Handbook, Rubrics 3: Artwork; and 37: Writing Assignments

Egyptian Writing

Egyptian hieroglyphics used picture symbols to represent sounds.

	Sound	Meaning
	Imn	Amon
	Tut	Image
	Ankh	Living

Translation—"Living image of Amon"

	Heka	Ruler
	Iunu	Heliopolis
	Resy	Southern

Translation—"Ruler of Southern Heliopolis"

ANALYSIS SKILL · ANALYZING VISUALS

What does the symbol for ruler look like?

The hieroglyphic writing system used more than 600 symbols, mostly pictures of objects. Each symbol represented one or more sounds in the Egyptian language. For example, a picture of an owl represented the same sound as our letter M.

Hieroglyphics could be written either horizontally or vertically. They could be written from right to left or from left to right. These options made hieroglyphics flexible to write but difficult to read. The only way to tell which way a text is written is to look at individual symbols.

The Rosetta Stone

Historians and archaeologists have known about hieroglyphics for centuries. For a long time, though, historians did not know how to read them. In fact, it was not until 1799 that a lucky discovery by a French soldier gave historians the key they needed to read ancient Egyptian writing.

That key was the **Rosetta Stone**, a huge, stone slab inscribed with hieroglyphics. In addition to the hieroglyphics, the Rosetta Stone had text in Greek and a later form of Egyptian. Because the message in all three languages was the same, scholars who knew Greek were able to figure out what the hieroglyphics said.

Egyptian Texts

Because papyrus did not decay in Egypt's dry climate, many ancient Egyptian texts still survive. These texts include government records, historical records, science texts, and medical manuals. In addition, many literary works have survived. Some of them, such as *The Book of the Dead,* tell about the afterlife. Others tell stories about gods and kings.

READING CHECK **Comparing** How is our writing system similar to hieroglyphics?

THE IMPACT TODAY

An object that helps solve a difficult mystery is sometimes now called a Rosetta Stone.

ANCIENT CIVILIZATIONS OF AFRICA—EGYPT **299**

299

Main Idea

❷ Egypt's Great Temples

Egypt's great temples were lavishly decorated.

Identify What is a sphinx? *imaginary creature with the body of a lion and the head of another animal or a human*

Recall What are the two types of large structures created by the Egyptian architects? *pyramids and temples*

Analyze Why do you think builders placed obelisks at the gates of temples? *possible answer—because they pointed to the sky, leading the way to the afterlife*

Info to Know

Obelisks Most obelisks were carved from red granite. Their pyramid-shaped tops were usually sheathed in electrum, an alloy of gold and silver. Some obelisks weighed more than 100 tons. Because some obelisks have been taken out of Egypt, genuine Egyptian obelisks now stand in London, Rome, and New York City.

Linking to Today

Tourism in Egypt Revenue from tourism accounts for about 25 percent of Egypt's foreign exchange income. The pyramids and temples are major attractions in Egypt. More than 5 million tourists visit Egypt each year.

Answers

Analyzing Visuals *columns covered by paintings and hieroglyphics, high windows*

Reading Check *sphinxes, obelisks, statues, a sanctuary, stone columns, paintings and hieroglyphic carvings*

Egypt's Great Temples

In addition to their writing system, the ancient Egyptians are famous for their magnificent architecture. You have already read about the Egyptians' most famous structures, the pyramids. But the Egyptians also built massive temples. Those that survive are among the most spectacular sites in Egypt today.

The Egyptians believed that temples were the homes of the gods. People visited the temples to worship, offer the gods gifts, and ask for favors.

Many Egyptian temples shared some similar features. Rows of stone **sphinxes**—imaginary creatures with the bodies of lions and the heads of other animals or humans—lined the path leading to the entrance. That entrance itself was a huge, thick gate. On either side of the gate might stand an **obelisk** (AH-buh-lisk), a tall, four-sided pillar that is pointed on top.

THE IMPACT TODAY
The Washington Monument, in Washington, D.C., is an obelisk.

Inside, Egyptian temples were lavishly decorated, as you can see in the drawing of the Temple of Karnak. Huge columns supported the temple's roof. These columns were often covered with paintings and hieroglyphics, as were the temple walls. Statues of gods and pharaohs often stood along the walls as well. The sanctuary, the most sacred part of the building, was at the far end of the temple.

The Temple of Karnak is only one of Egypt's great temples. Other temples were built by Ramses the Great at Abu Simbel and Luxor. The temple at Abu Simbel is especially known for the huge statues that stand next to its entrance. The 66-foot-tall statues are carved out of sandstone cliffs and show Ramses the Great as pharaoh. Nearby are smaller statues of his family.

READING CHECK Generalizing What were some features of ancient Egyptian temples?

Close-up

The Temple of Karnak

The Temple of Karnak was Egypt's largest temple. Built mainly to honor Amon-Re, the sun god, Karnak was one of Egypt's major religious centers for centuries. Over the years, pharaohs added to the temple's many buildings. This illustration shows how Karnak's great hall might have looked during an ancient festival.

Karnak's interior columns and walls were painted brilliant colors.

ANALYSIS SKILL ANALYZING VISUALS
What features of Egyptian architecture can you see in this illustration?

Cross-Discipline Activity: Math
Above Level

Measuring a Temple

1. Organize students into small groups.

2. Have students calculate various dimensions of the interior of the illustrated Temple of Karnak. Students should use the priests in the foreground as a basic ruler and estimate that the men were about 5'5" tall.

3. To add interest to the activity, challenge groups to race in making their calculations.

4. Lead a discussion about how the Egyptians built and decorated temples with such stupendous dimensions.

LS Interpersonal, Logical/Mathematical

Alternative Assessment Handbook, Rubric 14: Group Activity

Massive columns, some more than 80 feet high, supported the temple's high roof.

High windows let light and air into the temple.

In the annual Opet festival, priests carried statues of the gods and sacred boats from the temple to the Nile River.

Only the pharaoh and priests were allowed inside the temple, which was considered the home of the gods.

Main Idea

Egypt's Great Temples, continued

Identify What was the most sacred part of a temple? *the sanctuary*

Analyze Why do you think many Egyptian temples had rows of sphinxes leading to the entrance? *possible answer—as symbolic protection for the temple*

Close-up

Analyzing Visuals Many elements of Egyptian art reflected the Egyptians' close connection to nature. What examples of this do you see in the illustration? *possible answers—tops and bottoms of columns painted like flower buds, bird wings and snake heads over door, animals and birds incorporated into hieroglyphics*

Cross-Discipline Activity: Arts and the Humanities   At Level

The Opet Festival
Materials: art supplies

Research Required

1. Have students conduct research on the Opet festival, including its purpose and what kinds of ceremonies took place during that time.

2. Have students paint a picture of an event that might have taken place during Opet. They should not simply copy an existing painting, but create an original one based on what they have learned in their research.

3. Encourage students to include as much detail as possible, showing, for example, the kinds of garments and jewelry people would have worn. People should be drawn in the Egyptian style.

4. Display students' paintings. **LS Visual/Spatial**

   Alternative Assessment Handbook, Rubrics 3: Artwork; and 30: Research

Direct Teach

Main Idea

❸ Egyptian Art

Egyptian art filled tombs.

Recall Give examples of two common subjects of Egyptian paintings. *events such as the crowning of kings and founding of temples, religious rituals, and scenes from everyday life*

Analyze Why was the discovery of King Tutankhamen's tomb so important? *It had never been disturbed by tomb robbers.*

Elaborate Why do you suppose the Egyptians drew animals realistically but drew people with their heads and legs from the side and their upper bodies and shoulders straight on? *Answers will vary but should be consistent with text information.*

📓 **RF:** Primary Source, Egyptian Tomb Paintings

Linking to Today

How Did Tut Die? Tutankhamen was a minor ruler, but because his tomb was discovered intact, he is one of the most famous pharaohs. He took the throne when he was about nine years old but ruled briefly before his death at about 18. Because the skull of Tut's mummy displays damage, some Egyptologists think Tutankhamen was murdered. In 2004 archaeologists announced plans to move the mummy for the first time from Luxor to Cairo. In 2005 the mummy went through CAT X-rays and a radio scan to determine the cause of death. Results were inconclusive, so the mystery remains.

History Humor

What did the young King Tut say when he got scared? *I want my mummy!*

Answers

Focus on Reading *possible answer—paintings, carvings, jewelry*

302

Treasures of King Tut's Tomb

In 1922 the archaeologist Howard Carter discovered the tomb of King Tut. Unlike most Egyptian tombs, it had never been robbed and was still filled with treasures, some of which are shown here.

Howard Carter examining King Tut's coffin in 1922

Egyptian Art

FOCUS ON READING
What categories could you use to organize the information under Egyptian Art?

One reason Egypt's temples are so popular with tourists is the art they contain. The ancient Egyptians were masterful artists. Many of their greatest works were created to fill the tombs of pharaohs and other nobles. The Egyptians took great care in making these items because they believed the dead could enjoy them in the afterlife.

Paintings

Egyptian art was filled with lively, colorful scenes. Detailed works covered the walls of temples and tombs. Artists also painted on canvas, papyrus, pottery, plaster, and wood. Most Egyptians never saw these paintings, however. Only kings, priests, and important people could enter temples and tombs, and even they rarely entered the tombs.

The subjects of Egyptian paintings vary widely. Some of the paintings show important historical events, such as the crowning of a new king or the founding of a temple.

Others show major religious rituals. Still other paintings show scenes from everyday life, such as farming or hunting.

Egyptian painting has a distinctive style. People, for example, are drawn in a certain way. In Egyptian paintings, people's heads and legs are always seen from the side, but their upper bodies and shoulders are shown straight on. In addition, people do not all appear the same size. Important figures such as pharaohs appear huge in comparison to others, especially servants or conquered people. In contrast, Egyptian animals were usually drawn realistically.

Carvings and Jewelry

Painting was not the only art form Egyptians practiced. The Egyptians were also skilled stoneworkers. Many tombs included huge statues and detailed carvings.

In addition, the Egyptians made lovely objects out of gold and precious stones. They made jewelry for both men and women.

302 CHAPTER 10

Collaborative Learning

At Level

King Tut's Tomb

Research Required

1. Tell students that many pharaohs were buried not in pyramids but in tombs hidden deep in the Valley of the Kings—the same area where Howard Carter found King Tut's tomb.

2. Organize students in pairs to prepare for an interview of Howard Carter for a television talk show. Have the partners conduct research to compose questions and their replies.

3. Encourage students to use their imaginations to make the interview interesting. For example, the interview might include

information about the conditions under which the team lived and worked.

4. Each pair should decide which student will be Carter and which will be the interviewer. Have students present their interviews to the class. **LS Interpersonal, Verbal/Linguistic**

📓 Alternative Assessment Handbook, Rubrics 30: Research; and 33: Skits and Reader's Theater

The back of King Tut's chair was decorated with this image of the pharaoh and his wife.

Gold mask

ANALYSIS SKILL   ANALYZING VISUALS

What might archaeologists learn about ancient Egypt from these artifacts?

This jewelry included necklaces, bracelets, and collars. The Egyptians also used gold to make burial items for their pharaohs.

Over the years, treasure hunters emptied many pharaohs' tombs. At least one tomb, however, was not disturbed. In 1922 some archaeologists found the tomb of King Tutankhamen (too-tang-KAHM-uhn), or King Tut. The tomb was filled with many treasures, including boxes of jewelry, robes, a burial mask, and ivory statues. King Tut's treasures have taught us much about Egyptian burial practices and beliefs.

READING CHECK   Summarizing What types of artwork were contained in Egyptian tombs?

SUMMARY AND PREVIEW The Egyptians made advances that shaped life for centuries. Next, you will learn about several civilizations that developed in Africa after Egypt and grew wealthy from trade.

Section 4 Assessment

go.hrw.com
Online Quiz
KEYWORD: SK9 HP10

Reviewing Ideas, Terms, and Places

1. **a. Define** What are **hieroglyphics**?
   b. Contrast How was hieroglyphic writing different from our writing today?
   c. Evaluate Why was the **Rosetta Stone** important?
2. **a. Describe** What were two ways the Egyptians decorated their temples?
   b. Evaluate Why do you think pharaohs like Ramses the Great built huge temples?
3. **Recall** Why did Egyptians fill tombs with art, jewelry, and other treasures?

Critical Thinking

4. **Summarizing** Draw a chart like the one below. In each column, write a statement that summarizes Egyptian achievements in the listed category.

Writing	Architecture	Art

FOCUS ON WRITING

5. **Considering Egyptian Achievements** For your riddle, note some Egyptian achievements in writing, architecture, and art that make Egypt different from other places.

Section 4 Assessment Answers

1. **a.** the Egyptian writing system
   b. had more than 600 symbols, rather than the 26 in our alphabet; could be written horizontally or vertically, left to right, or right to left
   c. enabled scholars to decipher hieroglyphics
2. **a.** possible answers—columns, obelisks, paintings, hieroglyphics, and statues
   b. possible answers—to worship the gods, to display the pharaoh's power and wealth
3. The Egyptians believed that the dead enjoyed these items in the afterlife.

4. possible answers: Writing—hieroglyphics, with more than 600 symbols, wrote on papyrus; Architecture—temples covered in hieroglyphics, many buildings were built for religious purposes; Art—people drawn in a distinctive style, animals drawn realistically
5. Students' notes will vary, but should reflect section content, including answers given above for question 4.

Answers

Analyzing Visuals *possible answer—clothing, jewelry, and furniture styles; artistic techniques; religious ceremonies*

Reading Check *paintings, carvings, statues, jewelry, clothing, burial masks*

303

Analyzing Primary and Secondary Sources

Social Studies Skills

Chart and Graph | Critical Thinking | Geography | Study

Analyzing Primary and Secondary Sources

Learn

Primary sources are materials created by people who lived during the times they describe. Examples include letters, diaries, and photographs. *Secondary sources* are accounts written later by someone who was not present. They often teach about or discuss a historical topic. This chapter is an example of a secondary source.

By studying both types, you can get a better picture of a historical period or event. However, not all sources are accurate or reliable. Use these checklists to judge which sources are reliable.

Checklist for Primary Sources

• Who is the author? Is he or she trustworthy?

• Was the author present at the event described in the source? Might the author have based his or her writing on rumor, gossip, or hearsay?

• How soon after the event occurred was the source written? The more time that passed, the greater the chance for error.

• What is the purpose? Authors can have reasons to exaggerate—or even lie—to suit their own purposes. Look for evidence of emotion, opinion, or bias in the source. They can affect the accuracy.

• Can the information in the source be verified in other primary or secondary sources?

Checklist for Secondary Sources

• Who is the author? What are his or her qualifications? Is he or she an authority on the subject?

• Where did the author get his or her information? Good historians always tell you where they got their information.

• Has the author drawn valid conclusions?

Practice

"The Egyptians quickly extended their military and commercial influence over an extensive [wide] region that included the rich provinces of Syria ... and the numbers of Egyptian slaves grew swiftly."

–C. Warren Hollister, from *Roots of the Western Tradition*

"Let me tell you how the soldier fares ... how he goes to Syria, and how he marches over the mountains. His bread and water are borne [carried] upon his shoulders like the load of [a donkey]; ... and the joints of his back are bowed [bent] ... When he reaches the enemy, ... he has no strength in his limbs."

–from *Wings of the Falcon: Life and Thought of Ancient Egypt*, translated by Joseph Kaster

❶ Which of the above passages is a primary source, and which is a secondary source?

❷ Is there evidence of opinion, emotion, or bias in the second passage? Why, or why not?

❸ Which passage would be better for learning about what life was like for Egyptian soldiers, and why?

Apply

Refer to the Ramses the Great biography in this chapter to answer the following questions.

1. Identify the primary source in the biography.

2. What biases or other issues might affect the reliability or accuracy of this primary source?

304 CHAPTER 10

Social Studies Skills: Analyzing Primary and Secondary Sources   At Level

Applying the Skill

1. Have students look at the Egyptian tomb painting in Section 1, which shows a couple harvesting their crop. Ask students to look closely at the image and write two questions about Egypt that could be answered from the image.

2. Then have students write two questions about Egypt that would best be answered by a secondary source, such as a history book about Egypt.

3. Have volunteers discuss their questions with the class. Continue the exercise by having

students suggest other questions about Egypt that could best be answered by a primary source or a secondary source.

4. Extend Have students create a poster that lists the guidelines for analyzing primary and secondary sources and provides an image to illustrate each guideline.

LS Logical/Mathematical, Visual Spatial

Alternative Assessment Handbook, Rubrics 11: Discussions; and 28: Posters

---

Social Studies Skills

Analyzing Primary and Secondary Sources

Activity Graphic Organizer Have students consider the following scenario: They missed the last football game at their school. They asked several of their friends who attended to describe the game. The students then asked other friends who played in the game to discuss it. The students also read a local newspaper article about the game. Have students discuss how each of these accounts of the game might differ. How might some of the accounts be biased or inaccurate? Why might students want to hear or read all of these accounts? How might the accounts combine to form a more complete picture of the game? Encourage student discussion.

Next, have students discuss the importance of primary and secondary sources in the study of history. Then have each student create a graphic organizer of his or her choosing that illustrates what primary and secondary sources are, the problems with each (such as bias), and how they combine to provide a better picture of history.

LS Verbal/Linguistic, Visual/Spatial

Alternative Assessment Handbook, Rubric 13: Graphic Organizers

Interactive Skills Tutor CD-ROM, Lesson 2: Identify Primary and Secondary Sources; Lesson 17: Interpret Primary Sources

RF: Social Studies Skills, Analyzing Primary and Secondary Sources

Answers

Practice 1. *Hollister quote—secondary; Wings of the Falcon quote—primary;* **2.** *yes, emotion and opinion, as the author describes the hardships soldiers face;* **3.** *secondary, to provide an objective overall view of the period, but primary to illustrate how some soldiers of the time thought and felt about events*

Apply 1. *It is a poem carved into a temple wall in praise of Ramses.* **2.** *Ramses had the temple built, so he may have dictated the poem. Workers might have wanted to please Ramses.*

Geography's Impact
video series
Review the video to answer the closing question:
What do the pyramids of ancient Egypt tell you about the people of that civilization?

Visual Summary

Use the visual summary below to help you review the main ideas of the chapter.

QUICK FACTS

Egyptian civilization developed along the Nile River, which provided water and fertile soil for farming.

Egypt's kings were considered gods, and Egyptians made golden burial masks and pyramids in their honor.

Egyptian cultural achievements included beautiful art and the development of a hieroglyphic writing system.

Reviewing Vocabulary, Terms, and Places

Imagine these terms are answers to items in a crossword puzzle. Write the clues for the answers. Then make the puzzle with answers down and across.

1. cataract
2. Nile River
3. pharaoh
4. nobles
5. mummy
6. acquire
7. contract
8. pyramids
9. hieroglyphics
10. sphinxes

Comprehension and Critical Thinking

SECTION 1 *(Pages 278–282)*

11. **a. Identify** Where was most of Egypt's fertile land located?

b. Make Inferences Why did Memphis become a political and social center of Egypt?

c. Predict How might history have been different if the Nile had not flooded every year?

SECTION 2 *(Pages 283–290)*

12. **a. Describe** Who were the pharaohs, and what responsibilities did they have?

b. Analyze How were beliefs about the afterlife linked to items placed in tombs?

c. Elaborate What challenges, in addition to moving stone blocks, do you think the pyramid builders faced?

SECTION 3 *(Pages 291–296)*

13. **a. Describe** What did a scribe do, and what benefits did a scribe receive?

b. Analyze When was the period of the New Kingdom, and what two factors contributed to Egypt's wealth during that period?

c. Evaluate Ramses the Great was a powerful pharaoh. Do you think his military successes or his building projects are more important to evaluating his greatness? Why?

ANCIENT CIVILIZATIONS OF AFRICA—EGYPT **305**

12.
a. Pharaohs were rulers who Egyptians believed were both kings and gods; they were responsible for ensuring that crops grew, keeping away diseases, making trade profitable, and preventing wars.

b. Items were placed in tombs to fulfill the needs of the buried person's *ka*.

c. possible answers—cutting the stones, organizing and feeding the workers, keeping the dimensions of the pyramids correct

13.
a. Scribes kept records and accounts for the state and wrote and copied religious and literary texts. They did not have to pay taxes, so many became wealthy.

b. 1550–1050 BC; conquest and trade

c. Answers will vary, but students should be familiar with both his military successes and his building projects as described in this section.

14.
a. as a surface for writing

b. Hieroglyphics had more than 600 symbols, rather than the 26 in our alphabet. Hieroglyphics could also be written horizontally or vertically, left to right, or right to left. Our writing is horizontal and left to right.

c. The larger size of the pharaohs versus that of the servants reflected the Egyptian social hierarchy.

Social Studies Skills

15. a, primary source—most likely to give first-hand account of beliefs

16. b, secondary source—most likely to provide accurate explanation

17. a, primary source—most likely to list actual goods traded

18. b, primary source—most likely to provide accurate details

Internet Activity

19. Go to the HRW Web site and enter the keyword shown to access a rubric for this activity.

KEYWORD: SK9 TEACHER

SECTION 4 *(Pages 298–303)*

14. a. Describe For what was papyrus used?

b. Contrast How are the symbols in Egyptian hieroglyphics different from the symbols used in our writing system?

c. Elaborate How does the Egyptian style of painting people reflect their society?

Social Studies Skills

Analyzing Primary and Secondary Sources *Each of the questions below lists two sources that a historian might consult to answer a question about ancient Egypt. For each question, decide which source is likely to be more accurate or reliable and why. Then indicate whether that source is a primary or secondary source.*

15. What were Egyptian beliefs about the afterlife?

a. Egyptian tomb inscriptions

b. writings by a priest who visited Egypt in 1934

16. Why did the Nile flood every year?

a. songs of praise to the Nile River written by Egyptian priests

b. a book about the rivers of Africa written by a modern geographer

17. What kinds of goods did the Egyptians trade?

a. ancient Egyptian trade records

b. an ancient Egyptian story about a trader

18. What kind of warrior was Ramses the Great?

a. a poem in praise of Ramses

b. a description of a battle in which Ramses fought, written by an impartial observer

Using the Internet

19. Activity: Creating Egyptian Art The Egyptians excelled in the arts. Egyptian artwork included beautiful paintings, carvings, and jewelry. Egyptian architecture included huge pyramids and temples. Enter the activity keyword and research Egyptian art and architecture. Then imagine you are an Egyptian. Create a work of art for the pharaoh's tomb. Provide hieroglyphics telling the pharaoh about your art.

---

20. Categorizing Create a chart with three columns. Title the chart "Egyptian Pharaohs." Label the three chart columns "Position and Power," "Responsibilities," and "Famous Pharaohs." Then list facts and details from the chapter under each category in the chart.

21. Writing a Riddle Choose five details about Egypt. Then write a sentence about each detail. Each sentence of your riddle should be a statement ending with "me." For example, if you were writing about the United States, you might say, "People come from all over the world to join me." After you have written your five sentences, end your riddle with "Who am I?" The answer to your riddle must be "Egypt."

Map Activity ★Interactive

22. Ancient Egypt On a separate sheet of paper, match the letters on the map with their correct labels.

Lower Egypt
Mediterranean Sea
Nile River

Red Sea
Sinai Peninsula
Upper Egypt

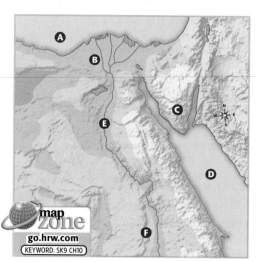

map zone
go.hrw.com
KEYWORD: SK9 CH10

Focus on Reading and Writing

20. Information in students' charts should relate to or support the category heading in which it is placed.

RF: Focus on Reading, Categorizing

21. **Rubric** Students' riddles should:

• have five sentences, each ending with "me"

• end with "Who am I?"

• explain something about the civilization of ancient Egypt

• use correct grammar, punctuation, spelling, and capitalization

RF: Focus on Writing, Writing a Riddle

Map Activity

22. **A.** Mediterranean Sea
B. Lower Egypt
C. Sinai Peninsula
D. Red Sea
E. Nile River
F. Upper Egypt

DIRECTIONS (1–7): For each statement or question, write on a separate answer sheet the *number* of the word or expression that, of those given, best completes the statement or answers the question.

1 Which statement about how the Nile helped civilization develop in Egypt is false?

(1) It provided a source of food and water.

(2) It enabled farming in the area.

(3) Its flooding enriched the soil along its banks.

(4) It protected against invasion from the west.

2 The most fertile soil in Egypt was located in the

(1) Nile Delta.

(2) deserts.

(3) cataracts.

(4) far south.

3 The high position that priests held in Egyptian society shows that

(1) the pharaoh was a descendant of a god.

(2) government was large and powerful.

(3) religion was important in Egyptian life.

(4) the early Egyptians worshipped many gods.

4 The Egyptians are probably *best* known for building

(1) pyramids.

(2) irrigation canals.

(3) cataracts.

(4) deltas.

5 During which period did ancient Egypt reach the height of its power and glory?

(1) First Dynasty

(2) Old Kingdom

(3) Middle Kingdom

(4) New Kingdom

6 Who was considered the first ruler of unified Egypt?

(1) Menes

(2) Ramses the Great

(3) King Tutankhamen

(4) Queen Hatshepsut

7 What discovery gave historians the key they needed to read Egyptian hieroglyphics?

(1) obelisk

(2) papyrus

(3) Rosetta Stone

(4) sphinx

Base your answer to question 8 on the text excerpt below and on your knowledge of social studies.

> Oh great god and ruler, the gift of Amon-Re,
>   god of the Sun.
> Oh great protector of Egypt and its people.
> Great one who saved us from the Tehenu.
> You, who have fortified our western border
>   to protect us from our enemies.
> You, who honored the gods with mighty
> temples at Abu Simbel and Luxor.
> We bless you, oh great one.
> We worship and honor you, oh great and
>   mighty pharaoh.

8 Constructed-Response Question **The passage above was written to honor Ramses the Great. What are two achievements for which the author was praising Ramses?**

Answers

1. 4

Break Down the Question Refer students who miss this question to the map in Section 1 and to the fact that desert protected against invasion from the west.

2. 1

Break Down the Question This question requires students to recall factual information. Refer students who miss it to Section 1.

3. 3

Break Down the Question Although the other choices contain true statements or beliefs, only option 3 fulfills the cause-and-effect requirement.

4. 1

Break Down the Question The Egyptians built irrigation canals but were not known for these. Cataracts and deltas are natural formations.

5. 4

Break Down the Question This question requires students to recall factual information. Refer students who miss it to Section 3.

6. 1

Break Down the Question This question requires students to recall the notable features of four pharaohs' reigns. Refer students who miss it to Section 3.

7. 3

Break Down the Question Remind students who missed the question that the Rosetta Stone has the same text in three different languages inscribed on it.

8. 2

Break Down the Question This question requires students to recall factual information. Refer students who miss it to Section 3.

9. Constructed-Response Question The writer is praising Ramses the Great for providing protection for Egypt from the Tehenu, fortifying the western border, and building great temples at Abu Simbel and Luxor to honor the gods.

Intervention Resources

Reproducible

📖 Interactive Reader and Study Guide

📖 Differentiated Instruction Teacher Management System: Lesson Plans

Technology

💻 Quick Facts Transparency: Visual Summary: Ancient Civilizations of Africa—Egypt

💿 Differentiated Instruction Modified Worksheets and Tests CD-ROM

💿 Interactive Skills Tutor CD-ROM

Tips for Test Taking

Search for Skips and Smudges Remind students that to avoid losing points on a machine-graded test they should be sure they did not skip any answers, gave only one answer for each question, made the marks dark and within the lines, and erased any smudges. Students should also make sure there are no stray pencil marks, such as from pencil tapping. They should cleanly erase places where they changed their minds.

Ancient Civilizations of Africa—Trading Kingdoms

Chapter Overview	Reproducible Resources	Technology Resources
CHAPTER 11 pp. 308–341 **Overview:** In this chapter students will learn about four great trading kingdoms of ancient Africa.	**Differentiated Instruction Teacher Management System:*** • Instructional Pacing Guides • Lesson Plans for Differentiated Instruction **Interactive Reader and Study Guide:** Chapter Summary Graphic Organizer* **Resource File:*** • Chapter Review • Focus on Reading: Understanding Cause and Effect • Focus on Writing: Writing a Journal Enry • Social Studies Skills: Making Decisions	**OSP Teacher's One-Stop Planner:** Calendar Planner **Power Presentations with Video CD-ROM** **Differentiated Instruction Modified Worksheets and Tests CD-ROM** **Student Edition on Audio CD Program** **Map Zone Transparency:** Ancient African Civilizations, 2000 BC–AD 1650* **Geography's Impact Video Program (VHS/DVD):** Impact of the Salt Trade*
Section 1: **Ancient Kush** **The Big Idea:** The kingdom of Kush, in the region of Nubia, was first conquered by Egypt but later conquered and ruled Egypt.	**Differentiated Instruction Teacher Management System:** Section 1 Lesson Plan* **Interactive Reader and Study Guide:** Section 1 Summary* **Resource File:*** • Vocabulary Builder: Section 1	**Daily Bellringer Transparency:** Section 1* **Map Zone Transparency:** Ancient Kush* **Internet Activity:** Time Travel to Ancient Kush
Section 2: **Later Kush** **The Big Idea:** Although Kush developed an advanced civilization, it eventually declined.	**Differentiated Instruction Teacher Management System:** Section 2 Lesson Plan* **Resource File:*** • Vocabulary Builder: Section 2 • Biography: Queen Amanirenas • Literature: *The Fall of Meroë*	**Daily Bellringer Transparency:** Section 2* **Internet Activity:** Iron Industry of Kush
Section 3: **Empire of Ghana** **The Big Idea:** The rulers of Ghana built an empire by controlling the salt and gold trade.	**Interactive Reader and Study Guide:** Section 3 Summary* **Resource File:*** • Vocabulary Builder: Section 3	**Daily Bellringer Transparency:** Section 3* **Map Zone Transparency:** Ghana Empire, c. 1050* **Internet Activity:** Trading Groups*
Section 4: **Mali and Songhai** **The Big Idea:** Between 1000 and 1500 the empires of Mali and Songhai developed in West Africa.	**Differentiated Instruction Teacher Management System:** Section 4 Lesson Plan* **Resource File:*** • Vocabulary Builder: Section 4 • Biography: Sundiata • Primary Source: Descriptions of Emperors of Mali	**Daily Bellringer Transparency:** Section 4* **Map Zone Transparency:** Mali and Songhai* **Internet Activity:** Askia Time Line
Section 5: **Historical and Artistic Traditions of West Africa** **The Big Idea:** West African culture has been passed down through oral history, writings by other people, and the arts.	**Differentiated Instruction Teacher Management System:** Section 5 Lesson Plan* **Interactive Reader and Study Guide:** Section 5 Summary* **Resource File:*** • Vocabulary Builder: Section 5	**Daily Bellringer Transparency:** Section 5*

HOLT
Geography's Impact
Video Program (VHS/DVD)
Impact of the Salt Trade
Suggested use: in Section 3

Review, Assessment, Intervention

 Quick Facts Transparencies: Visual Summary: Ancient Civilizations of Africa—Trading Kingdoms*

 Spanish Chapter Summaries Audio CD Program

 Progress Assessment Support System (PASS): Chapter Test*

 Differentiated Instruction Modified Worksheets and Tests CD-ROM: Modified Chapter Test

OSP **Teacher's One-Stop Planner:** ExamView Test Generator (English/Spanish)

HOAP **Holt Online Assessment Program (HOAP),** in the Holt Interactive Online Student Edition

---

 PASS: Section 1 Quiz*

 Online Quiz: Section 1

 Alternative Assessment Handbook

 PASS: Section 2 Quiz*

 Online Quiz: Section 2

 Alternative Assessment Handbook

 PASS: Section 3 Quiz*

 Online Quiz: Section 3

 Alternative Assessment Handbook

 PASS: Section 4 Quiz*

 Online Quiz: Section 4

 Alternative Assessment Handbook

 PASS: Section 5 Quiz*

 Online Quiz: Section 5

 Alternative Assessment Handbook

Power Presentations with Video CD-ROM

Power Presentations with Video are visual presentations of each chapter's main ideas. Presentations can be customized by including Quick Facts charts, images from the text, and video clips.

Holt Online Learning

go.hrw.com
Teacher Resources
KEYWORD: SK9 TEACHER

go.hrw.com
Student Resources
KEYWORD: SK9 CH11

- Interactive Multimedia Activities
- Current Events

- Chapter-based Internet Activities
- and more!

Holt Interactive
Online Student Edition
Complete online support for interactivity, assessment, and reporting

- Interactive Maps and Notebook
- Standardized Test Prep
- Homework Practice and Research Activities Online

CHAPTER 11 PLANNING GUIDE

Differentiating Instruction

How do I address the needs of varied learners?
The Target Resource acts as your primary strategy for differentiated instruction.

ENGLISH-LANGUAGE LEARNERS & STRUGGLING READERS

TARGET RESOURCE

Graphic Organizer Transparencies with Support for Reading and Writing

Spanish Resources

Spanish Chapter Summaries Audio CD

Teacher's One-Stop Planner:
- ExamView Test Generator, Spanish
- PuzzlePro, Spanish

English-Language Learner Strategies and Activities

Additional Resources

Differentiated Instruction Teacher Management System: Lesson Plans for Differentiated Instruction

Resource File:
- Vocabulary Builder Activities
- Social Studies Skills, Making Decisions

Quick Facts Transparency: Visual Summary: Ancient Civilizations of Africa—Trading Kingdoms

Student Edition on Audio CD Program

Interactive Skills Tutor CD-ROM

SPECIAL NEEDS LEARNERS

TARGET RESOURCE

Differentiated Instruction Modified Worksheets and Tests CD-ROM

- Vocabulary Flash Cards
- Vocabulary Builder Activities
- Modified Chapter Review
- Modified Chapter Test

Additional Resources

Differentiated Instruction Teacher Management System: Lesson Plans for Differentiated Instruction

Interactive Reader and Study Guide

Resource File: Social Studies Skills, Making Decisions

Student Edition on Audio CD Program

Interactive Skills Tutor CD-ROM

Graphic Organizer Transparencies with Support for Reading and Writing

ADVANCED/GIFTED AND TALENTED STUDENTS

TARGET RESOURCE

Resource File

The Resource File activities allow students to extend their knowledge of chapter-related places and people, and to practice geography skills.

Additional Resources

Differentiated Instruction Teacher Management System: Lesson Plans for Differentiated Instruction

World History and Geography Document-Based Questions Activities

Geography, Science, and Cultures Activities

Experiencing World History and Geography

Differentiated Activities in the Teacher's Edition

- Cultural Borrowing Venn Diagrams
- Understanding Tribute
- Askia the Great Graphic Organizers
- Writing and Performing Oral Histories
- Writing Descriptions of the Niger
- Murals Honoring Benin

Differentiated Activities in the Teacher's Edition

- Charting Natural Resources
- Kush Stone Carvings
- Edo Culture Posters

Differentiated Activities in the Teacher's Edition

- Ancient Kush Elevation Profiles
- Iron-Making Skits
- Creating a Web Page
- Researching Trade Restrictions
- Long Distance Trade Then and Now
- Researching Edo Culture

HOLT Teacher's One-Stop Planner®

How can I manage the lesson plans and support materials for differentiated instruction?

With the Teacher's One-Stop Planner, you can easily organize and print lesson plans, planning guides, and instructional materials for all learners.

The Teacher's One-Stop Planner includes the following materials to help you differentiate instruction:
- Interactive Teacher's Edition
- Calendar Planner and pacing guides
- Editable lesson plans
- All reproducible ancillaries in Adobe Acrobat (PDF) format
- ExamView Test Generator (English & Spanish)
- Transparency and video previews

Professional Development

What teacher training resources are available to help me grow professionally?

- **In-service and staff development** as part of your Holt Social Studies product purchase
- **Quick Teacher Tutorial Lesson Presentation CD-ROM**
- Intensive tuition-based **Teacher Development Institute**
- **Convenient Holt Speaker Bureau:** face-to-face workshop options
- **24/7 Ask A Professional Development Expert** at http://www.hrw.com/prodev/

• Chapter Preview •

Chapter Big Ideas

Section 1 The kingdom of Kush, in the region of Nubia, was first conquered by Egypt but later conquered and ruled Egypt.

Section 2 Although Kush developed an advanced civilization, it eventually declined.

Section 3 The rulers of Ghana built an empire by controlling the salt and gold trade.

Section 4 Between 1000 and 1500 the empires of Mali and Songhai developed in West Africa.

Section 5 West African culture has been passed down through oral history, writings by other people, and the arts.

Focus on Reading and Writing

Reading The Resource File provides a worksheet to help students recognize causes and effects.

📓 **RF:** Focus on Reading, Understanding Cause and Effect

Writing The Resource File provides a worksheet to help students write their journal entries.

📓 **RF:** Focus on Writing, Writing a Journal Entry

Ancient Civilizations of Africa—Trading Kingdoms

FOCUS QUESTION

How did ancient civilizations contribute to the development of the Eastern Hemisphere?

What You Will Learn...

In this chapter you will learn about several early African civilizations that grew rich from trade, including Kush and the trading empires of West Africa.

FOCUS ON READING AND WRITING

Understanding Cause and Effect When you read about history, it is important to recognize causes and effects. A cause is an action or event that makes something else happen. An effect is the result of a cause. **See the lesson, Understanding Cause and Effect, on page S14.**

A Journal Entry Many people feel that keeping journals helps them to understand their own experiences. Writing a journal entry from someone else's point of view can help you to understand what that person's life was like. As you read this chapter, you will imagine a character and write a journal entry from his or her point of view.

308 CHAPTER 11

Kush The culture of Kush was heavily influenced by its northern neighbor, Egypt. These Kushite pyramids reflect that influence.

Key to Differentiating Instruction

Below Level

Basic-level activities designed for all students encountering new material

At Level

Intermediate-level activities designed for average students

Above Level

Challenging activities designed for honors and gifted and talented students

Standard English Mastery

Activities designed to improve standard English usage

308 CHAPTER 11

Introduce the Chapter

At Level

Ancient Civilizations of Africa

1. Ask students what life might have been like in Africa more than 1,000 years ago. Remind them that many places in Africa are hot and dry most of the year. Then ask why gold and salt would become important trade items in a hot, dry climate. *possible answer—Salt and gold aren't affected by weather; people need to replace salt in their bodies.*

2. Explain to students that they are going to learn about ancient African empires. Discuss with students that they will learn about four different civilizations and the various economic and geographic factors that affected them all.

3. Have students take notes on all four civilizations using maps and time lines in this chapter. 📓 **Visual/Spatial, Verbal/Linguistic**

📓 Alternative Assessment Handbook, Rubric 1: Acquiring Information

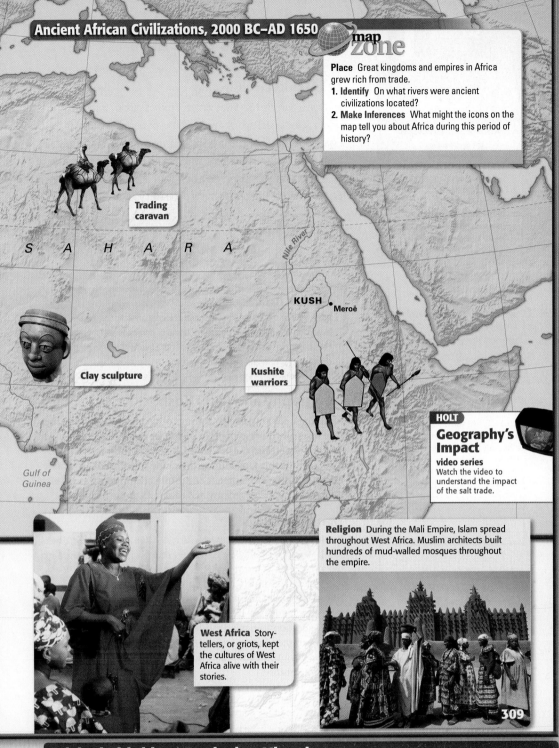

Ancient African Civilizations, 2000 BC–AD 1650

map Zone

Place Great kingdoms and empires in Africa grew rich from trade.

1. **Identify** On what rivers were ancient civilizations located?
2. **Make Inferences** What might the icons on the map tell you about Africa during this period of history?

Trading caravan

S A H A R A

Nile River

KUSH • Meroë

Clay sculpture

Kushite warriors

Gulf of Guinea

HOLT
Geography's Impact
video series
Watch the video to understand the impact of the salt trade.

Religion During the Mali Empire, Islam spread throughout West Africa. Muslim architects built hundreds of mud-walled mosques throughout the empire.

West Africa Storytellers, or griots, kept the cultures of West Africa alive with their stories.

309

• Chapter Preview •

Explore the Map and Pictures

Ancient African Civilizations, 2000 BC–AD 1650 Africa was home to great civilizations with rich cultures during this time. Their wealth allowed the development of great cities and markets, as well as contact with other cultures through trade. Ask students: what river flowed through the kingdom of Kush? *the Nile River;* Islam grew as an important religion in Africa as traders brought it from the East. Ask students why it may have been difficult for these traders to travel to Africa. *The Sahara Desert was difficult to traverse.*

Analyzing Visuals Ask students to compare the photos of griots with the people in front of the mosque. What do these two photos tell about traditional clothing in the region? *It is loose and flowing; cloth includes bright colors and patterns.*

HOLT
Geography's Impact
▶ Video Series
See the Video Teacher's Guide for strategies for using the chapter video to teach about the impact of the salt trade.

go.hrw.com
Online Resources
Chapter Resources:
KEYWORD: SK9 CH11
Teacher Resources:
KEYWORD: SK9 TEACHER

Critical Thinking: Analyzing Visuals

Mud-Walled Mosques

1. Ask students to review the photo labeled "Religion" and study the building in the background. It is the famous Djenné Mosque. Originally constructed in the thirteenth century, the present structure dates from about 1906. It is the largest mud structure in the world. Discuss the appearance of the mosque as a class.

2. Ask students why mosques might have been built from mud rather than wood or stone. *Little wood is available because there are few forests; stone was not available, either.*

3. Have students talk about what they know about the Sahara Desert and how it influences life in the area. What effect does the Sahara have on the economy? *Farming is very hard; nomadic herding is more common.* Why are important cities located near rivers? *Water allows farming and permanent settlements.*

LS Verbal/Linguistic

Alternative Assessment Handbook, Rubric 11: Discussions

Answers

Map Zone 1. *the Niger and Nile rivers;* **2.** *Trade was important and involved gold; Islam was important; art, architecture, and engineering flourished*

309

Bellringer

If YOU lived there. . . Use the **Daily Bellringer Transparency** to help students answer the question.

📖 Daily Bellringer Transparency, Section 1

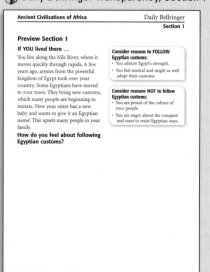

Key Terms and Places

📄 **RF:** Vocabulary Builder, Section 1

Taking Notes

Have students copy the graphic organizer onto their own paper and then use it to take notes on the section. This activity will prepare students for the Section Assessment, in which they will complete a graphic organizer that builds on the information using the Critical Thinking Skill: Sequencing.

Ancient Kush

If YOU lived there...

You live along the Nile River, where it moves quickly through rapids. A few years ago, armies from the powerful kingdom of Egypt took over your country. Some Egyptians have moved to your town. They bring new customs, which many people are beginning to imitate. Now your sister has a new baby and wants to give it an Egyptian name! This upsets many people in your family.

How do you feel about following Egyptian customs?

What You Will Learn...

Main Ideas

1. Geography helped early Kush civilization develop in Nubia.
2. Egypt controlled Kush for about 450 years.
3. After winning its independence, Kush ruled Egypt and set up a new dynasty there.

The Big Idea

The kingdom of Kush, in the region of Nubia, was first conquered by Egypt but later conquered and ruled Egypt.

Key Terms and Places

Nubia, *p. 310*
ebony, *p. 312*
ivory, *p. 312*

TAKING NOTES As you read, take notes on the important events in the early history of the kingdom of Kush. Use a chart like the one below to identify significant events, their dates, and their importance.

Event	Date	Importance

BUILDING BACKGROUND The Nile River valley was home to one of the ancient world's oldest and greatest civilizations. Nearly everyone is familiar with Egypt, the home of pyramids and mummies. Fewer people, however, know much about Egypt's southern neighbor Kush, itself a rich and powerful kingdom.

Geography and Early Kush

More than 6,000 years ago a group of people settled along the Nile River south of Egypt in the region we now call Nubia. These Africans established the first large kingdom in the interior of Africa. We know this kingdom by the name the ancient Egyptians gave it—Kush. Development of Kushite civilization was greatly influenced by the geography and resources of the region.

The Land of Nubia

Nubia is a region in northeast Africa. It lies on the Nile River south of Egypt. Today desert covers much of Nubia, located in the present-day country of Sudan. In ancient times, however, the region was much more fertile. Heavy rainfall flooded the Nile every year. These floods provided a rich layer of fertile soil to nearby lands. The kingdom of Kush developed in this area.

In addition to having fertile soil, ancient Nubia was rich in valuable minerals such as gold, copper, and stone. These natural resources contributed to the region's wealth and played a major role in its history.

Teach the Big Idea
At Level

Ancient Kush

1. **Teach** Ask students the questions in the Main Idea boxes under Direct Teach.

2. **Apply** Help students locate and describe ancient Kush and summarize its relations with Egypt. To do so, have each student plan a billboard advertisement with words and pictures for one of the following purposes: to draw new settlers to Kush, to join the Egyptian army in the conquest of Kush, or to join the Kushite army in the fight for independence from Egypt. Organize the

class into three groups to ensure all topics are covered. 📘 **Verbal/Linguistic, Visual/Spatial**

3. **Review** As you review the section's main ideas, have students discuss the information contained or implied in their billboard ads.

4. **Practice/Homework** Have each student create an ad for one of the other two topics. 📘 **Verbal/Linguistic, Visual/Spatial**

📄 Alternative Assessment Handbook, Rubric 2: Advertisements

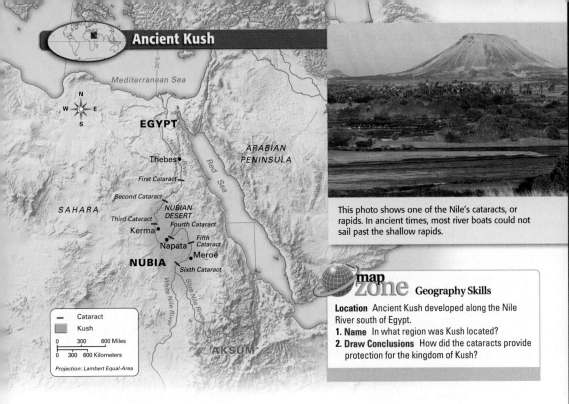

EGYPT

Mediterranean Sea

ARABIAN PENINSULA

Thebes

First Cataract

Second Cataract

SAHARA

NUBIAN DESERT

Third Cataract   Fourth Cataract

Kerma

Fifth Cataract

Napata

Meroë

NUBIA

Sixth Cataract

AKSUM

Cataract

Kush

0   300   600 Miles

0   300   600 Kilometers

Projection: Lambert Equal-Area

This photo shows one of the Nile's cataracts, or rapids. In ancient times, most river boats could not sail past the shallow rapids.

map zone — Geography Skills

Location Ancient Kush developed along the Nile River south of Egypt.

1. Name In what region was Kush located?

2. Draw Conclusions How did the cataracts provide protection for the kingdom of Kush?

Early Civilization in Nubia

Like all early civilizations, the people of Nubia depended on agriculture for their food. Fortunately for them, the Nile's floods allowed the Nubians to plant both summer and winter crops. Among the crops they grew were wheat, barley, and other grains. In addition to farmland, the banks of the river provided grazing land for cattle and other livestock. As a result, farming villages thrived all along the Nile by about 3500 BC.

Over time some farmers became richer and more successful than others. These farmers became leaders of their villages. Sometime around 2000 BC, one of these leaders took control of other villages and made himself king of the region. His new kingdom was called Kush.

The early kings of Kush ruled from their capital at Kerma (KAR-muh). This city was located on the Nile just south of a cataract, or stretch of rapids. Cataracts made travel through some parts of the Nile extremely difficult. As a result, the cataracts were natural barriers against invaders. For many years the cataracts kept Kush safe from the powerful Egyptian kingdom to the north.

As time passed, Kushite society grew more complex. In addition to farmers and herders, some people of Kush became priests or artisans. Early on, civilizations to the south greatly influenced the kingdom of Kush. Later, however, Egypt played a greater role in the kingdom's history.

FOCUS ON READING
What was one effect of Kush's location?

READING CHECK Finding Main Ideas How did geography help civilization grow in Nubia?

Direct Teach

Main Idea

❶ Geography and Early Kush

Geography helped early Kush civilization develop in Nubia.

Identify What resources did the kingdom of Kush have? *fertile soil, gold, copper, stone*

Compare How was the geography of ancient Kush similar to that of ancient Egypt and Mesopotamia? *All three civilizations developed in valleys where the rivers flooded, providing fertile soil.*

Map Zone Transparency: Ancient Kush

go.hrw.com
Online Resources

KEYWORD: SK9 CH11
ACTIVITY: Time Travel to Ancient Kush

Analyzing Maps
Ancient Kush
Movement What was probably the main north-south travel route in Kush? *the Nile River*

Differentiating Instruction   Above Level

Advanced/Gifted and Talented

1. Display the Map Zone Transparency titled "Ancient Kush" for students to see.

2. Using a washable marker, draw three horizontal parallel lines across Nubia—near its northern edge, near its southern edge, and at its center. The lines should be parallel to the top of the page.

3. Instruct students to use these lines to draw elevation profiles. An elevation profile is like a cross-sectional or cutaway view of a region.

4. Have each student use the transparency and the above map to create three elevation profiles of Nubia.

5. After students have drawn their elevation profiles, lead a discussion about how the profiles show mountains to the east, the Nile valley, and the river itself. **LS** Visual/Spatial

Alternative Assessment Handbook, Rubric 21: Map Reading

Map Zone Transprency: Ancient Kush

Answers

Map Zone 1. *Nubia;* **2.** *They were natural barriers against invaders.*

Focus on Reading *Kush was protected from invaders.*

Reading Check *The flooding Nile provided fertile agricultural land; the land had gold, copper, and stone; and the river's cataracts served as barriers to invaders.*

311

❷ Egypt Controls Kush

Egypt controlled Kush for about 450 years.

Recall What raw materials did Kush sell to Egypt? *gold, copper, stone, ebony, ivory*

Analyze Why did the Egyptians attack Kush? *They feared Kush was getting too powerful and could even attack Egypt.*

Identify Cause and Effect Egypt ruled Kush for about 450 years. How did Egyptian rule affect the people of Kush? *Egyptian language, styles, and religion became widespread in Kush.*

Checking for Understanding

True or False Answer each statement *T* if it is true or *F* if it is false. If false, explain why.

1. After their invasion of Kush, Egyptian leaders respected Kushite buildings and religion. *F; The Egyptians destroyed the Kushite palace at Kerma and built temples in what had been Kushite territory.*

2. Kush remained under Egyptian control for 2,000 years. *F; Kush became independent again after about 450 years.*

Answers

Reading Check *The Kushite people began speaking Egyptian, using Egyptian names, wearing Egyptian-style clothing, and adopting Egyptian religious practices.*

312

Egypt Controls Kush

Kush and Egypt were neighbors. At times the neighbors lived in peace with each other and helped each other prosper. For example, Kush became a supplier of slaves and raw materials to Egypt. The Kushites sent materials such as gold, copper, and stone to Egypt. The Kushites also sent the Egyptians **ebony**, a type of dark, heavy wood, and **ivory**, a white material taken from elephant tusks.

Egypt's Conquest of Kush

Relations between Kush and Egypt were not always peaceful. As Kush grew wealthy from trade, its army grew stronger as well. Egypt's rulers soon feared that Kush would grow even stronger. They were afraid that a powerful Kush might attack Egypt.

To prevent such an attack, the pharaoh Thutmose I sent an army to take control of Kush around 1500 BC. The pharaoh's army conquered all of Nubia north of the Fifth Cataract. As a result, the kingdom of Kush became part of Egypt.

After his army's victory, the pharaoh destroyed the Kushite palace at Kerma. Later pharaohs—including Ramses the Great—built huge temples in what had been Kushite territory.

Effects of the Conquest

Kush remained an Egyptian territory for about 450 years. During that time, Egypt's influence over Kush grew tremendously. Many Egyptians settled in Kush. Egyptian became the language of the region. Many Kushites used Egyptian names and wore Egyptian-style clothing. They also adopted Egyptian religious practices.

A Change in Power

In the mid-1000s BC the New Kingdom in Egypt was ending. As the power of Egypt's pharaohs declined, Kushite leaders regained control of Kush. Kush once again became independent.

READING CHECK Identifying Cause and Effect How did Egyptian rule change Kush?

Kush and Egypt

Early in its history, Egypt dominated Kush, forcing Kushites to give tribute to Egypt.

312 CHAPTER 11

Critical Thinking: Analyzing Information   Below Level

Charting Natural Resources

1. To promote understanding of Kush's trade in raw materials, copy the chart at right for students to see. Omit the blue, italicized answers.

2. Have students copy the chart and complete it by using what they know, by looking at the section's visuals, and by making predictions. Students should also refer back to the chapter on Egypt for ideas. **LS** **Visual/Spatial**

   Alternative Assessment Handbook, Rubric 13: Graphic Organizers

Kush's Exports	
Natural Resources	How Might Have Been Used
gold	coins, jewelry
copper	coins, pots, tools
stone	pyramids, temples, statues
ebony	furniture, decorative items
ivory	small statues, jewelry, decorative items

Kush Rules Egypt

We know almost nothing about the history of the Kushites for about 200 years after they regained independence from Egypt. Kush is not mentioned in any historical records until the 700s BC, when armies from Kush swept into Egypt and conquered it.

The Conquest of Egypt

By around 850 BC, Kush had regained its strength. It was once again as strong as it had been before it was conquered by Egypt. Because the Egyptians had captured the old capital at Kerma, the kings of Kush ruled from the city of Napata. Napata was located on the Nile, about 100 miles southeast of Kerma.

As Kush was growing stronger, Egypt was losing power. A series of weak pharaohs left Egypt open to attack. In the 700s BC a Kushite king, Kashta, took advantage of Egypt's weakness. Kashta attacked Egypt. By about 751 BC he had conquered Upper Egypt. He then established relations with Lower Egypt.

BIOGRAPHY

Piankhi
(c. 751–716 BC)

Also known as Piye, Piankhi was among Kush's most successful military leaders. A fierce warrior on the battlefield, the king was also deeply religious. Piankhi's belief that he had the support of the gods fueled his passion for war against Egypt. His courage inspired his troops on the battlefield. Piankhi loved his horses and was buried with eight of them.

Drawing Conclusions How did Piankhi's belief that he was supported by the gods help him in the war against Egypt?

After Kashta died, his son Piankhi (PYANG-kee) continued to attack Egypt. The armies of Kush captured many cities, including Egypt's ancient capital. Piankhi fought the Egyptians because he believed that the gods wanted him to rule all of Egypt. By the time he died in about 716 BC, Piankhi had accomplished this task. His kingdom extended north from Napata all the way to the Nile Delta.

Later, as Kush's power increased, its warriors invaded and conquered Egypt. This photo shows Kushite and Egyptian warriors.

After conquering Egypt, Kush established a new dynasty. This sculpture shows one of Kush's pharaohs kneeling before an Egyptian god.

ANALYSIS SKILL | ANALYZING VISUALS

What did Kushites give to Egypt as tribute?

ANCIENT CIVILIZATIONS OF AFRICA—TRADING KINGDOMS **313**

Info to Know

Chariots in the Ancient World The use of chariots, such as the one in the photo, probably began in Mesopotamia about 3000 BC. Horses had not been introduced to the region at that time, so the first chariots were drawn by oxen or donkeys. Eventually, chariots contributed to victories not just in Mesopotamia and Egypt but also in Anatolia, India, Greece, China, and western Europe. Each culture developed somewhat different designs. Assyrians were the first warriors to equip the wheels with long blades, which functioned as weapons.

● Review & Assess ●

Close

Call on volunteers to pose new questions about the images in this section and for other students to suggest answers.

Review

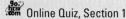 Online Quiz, Section 1

Assess

SE Section 1 Assessment

PASS: Section 1 Quiz

Alternative Assessment Handbook

Reteach/Classroom Intervention

Interactive Reader and Study Guide, Section 1

Interactive Skills Tutor CD-ROM

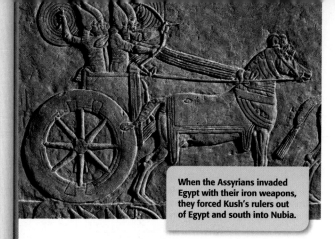

When the Assyrians invaded Egypt with their iron weapons, they forced Kush's rulers out of Egypt and south into Nubia.

The Kushite rulers of Egypt built new temples to Egyptian gods and restored old ones. They also worked to preserve many Egyptian writings. As a result, Egyptian culture thrived during the Kushite dynasty.

The End of Kushite Rule in Egypt

The Kushite dynasty remained strong in Egypt for about 40 years. In the 670s BC, however, the powerful army of the Assyrians from Mesopotamia invaded Egypt. The Assyrians' iron weapons were better than the Kushites' bronze weapons, and the Kushites were slowly pushed out of Egypt. In just 10 years the Assyrians had driven the Kushite forces completely out of Egypt.

The Kushite Dynasty

After Piankhi died, his brother Shabaka (SHAB-uh-kuh) took control of the kingdom and declared himself pharaoh. His declaration marked the beginning of Egypt's Twenty-fifth, or Kushite, Dynasty.

Shabaka and later rulers of his dynasty tried to restore many old Egyptian cultural practices. Some of these practices had died out during Egypt's period of weakness. For example, Shabaka was buried in a pyramid. The Egyptians had stopped building pyramids for their rulers centuries earlier.

READING CHECK **Sequencing** How did the leaders of Kush gain control over Egypt?

SUMMARY AND PREVIEW Kush was conquered by Egypt, but later the Kushites controlled Egypt. In the next section, you will learn how the civilization of Kush developed after the Kushites were forced out of Egypt by the Assyrians.

Section 1 Assessment

go.hrw.com
Online Quiz
KEYWORD: SK9 HP11

Reviewing Ideas, Terms, and Places

1. **a. Identify** On which river did Kush develop?
   b. Analyze How did **Nubia**'s natural resources influence the early history of Kush?
2. **a. Describe** What is **ivory**?
   b. Explain How did Egypt's conquest of Kush affect the people of Kush?
   c. Evaluate Why do you think Thutmose I destroyed the Kushite palace at Kerma?
3. **a. Describe** What territory did Piankhi conquer?
   b. Make Inferences Why is the Twenty-fifth Dynasty significant in the history of Egypt?
   c. Predict What might have happened in Kush and Egypt if Kush had developed iron weapons earlier?

Critical Thinking

4. **Sequencing** Use a time line like the one below to show the sequence and dates of important events in the early history of the kingdom of Kush.

   2000 BC   680 BC

FOCUS ON WRITING

5. **Noting People and Events** Who will be the subject of your journal? What events will it mention? Make a chart with two columns. In the first column, list key figures from Kush's history. In the second column, list some key events.

314 CHAPTER 11

Section 1 Assessment Answers

1. **a.** the Nile
   b. Nubia's natural resources were in demand in Egypt, so they helped Kush grow in wealth and power.

2. **a.** a white material made from elephant tusks
   b. The Kushites adopted Egyptian language, clothing, religion, and names.
   c. possible answer—to eliminate a symbol of Kushite independence

3. **a.** north from Napata to the Nile Delta
   b. possible answer—because Kushite leaders ruled and restored many ancient Egyptian cultural practices and traditions

c. They might have fought off the Assyrians.

4. possible answers: 2000 BC—village leader becomes king of new kingdom of Kush; 1500 BC—Egyptian pharaoh Thutmose I conquers Kush; mid-1000s BC—Kush becomes independent again; 751 BC—Kashta, king of Kush, conquers Upper Egypt; 716 BC—kingdom of Kush rules all of Egypt; 670s BC—Assyrians invade Egypt, driving Kushites from region.

5. Charts will vary but should reflect section content and mention key people and events.

Answers

Reading Check *Kashta, a Kushite king, attacked a weakened Egypt, conquering Upper Egypt and establishing relations with Lower Egypt. His son Piankhi continued attacks on Egypt, eventually conquering the rest of the kingdom.*

314

Later Kush

If **YOU** lived there...

You live in Meroë, the capital of Kush, in 250 BC. Your father is a skilled ironworker. From him you've learned to shape iron tools and weapons. Everyone expects that you will carry on his work. If you do become an ironworker, you will likely make a good living. But you are restless. You'd like to travel down the Nile to see Egypt and the great sea beyond it. Now a neighbor who is a trader has asked you to join his next trading voyage.

Will you leave Meroë to travel? Why or why not?

BUILDING BACKGROUND The Assyrians drove the Kushites out of Egypt in the 600s BC, partly through their use of iron weapons. Although the Kushites lost control of Egypt, their kingdom did not disappear. In fact, they built up another empire in the African interior, based on trade and their own iron industry.

Kush's Economy Grows

After they lost control of Egypt, the people of Kush devoted themselves to improving agriculture and trade. They hoped to make their country rich again. Within a few centuries, Kush had indeed become a rich and powerful kingdom once more.

Kushite Metalwork

Kush's craftspeople made iron spearheads and gold jewelry like you see here.

PHOTOGRAPH © 2004
MUSEUM OF FINE ARTS, BOSTON

What You Will Learn...

Main Ideas

1. Kush's economy grew because of its iron industry and trade network.
2. Some elements of Kushite society and culture were borrowed from other cultures while others were unique to Kush.
3. The decline and defeat of Kush was caused by both internal and external factors.

The Big Idea

Although Kush developed an advanced civilization, it eventually declined.

Key Terms and Places

Meroë, *p. 316*
trade network, *p. 316*
merchants, *p. 316*
exports, *p. 316*
imports, *p. 316*

TAKING NOTES As you read, take notes about the civilization of Kush and how it finally declined. Organize your notes in a diagram like the one below.

Kush	
Economy	Society

↓

Decline

315

Teach the Big Idea

Later Kush

1. **Teach** Ask students the questions in the Main Idea boxes under Direct Teach.

2. **Apply** Have each student create a one-page magazine article about the Kush civilization. Students' articles should address one of the following magazine sections: news, business, technology, architecture, religion, fashion, people, or the environment. More than one student may choose the same subject, but be certain all subjects are covered.
LS Verbal/Linguistic

3. **Review** As you review the section's main ideas, have volunteers present their articles to the class.

4. **Practice/Homework** Have each student create another article for a different section of the magazine. **LS Verbal/Linguistic**

Alternative Assessment Handbook, Rubric 19: Magazines

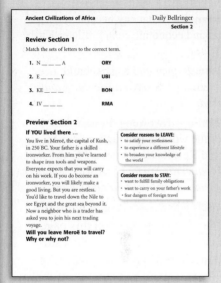

Main Idea

❶ Kush's Economy Grows

Kush's economy grew because of its iron industry and trade network.

Identify What city became the capital and economic center of later Kush? *Meroë*

Recall How did Kush rebuild its economy? *through agriculture and trade*

Make Inferences In what parts of the world might archaeologists find Kushite export items? *Egypt, the Mediterranean and Red seas, southern Africa, possibly India and China*

Activity Kush's Trade Network
Photocopy the map on this page and provide a copy for each student. Supply art materials. Have students draw and cut out symbols for the various products that were traded along the network. Ask students to put the symbols in their places of origin and then to move them along the trade route to their destinations.

LS Kinesthetic, Visual/Spatial

Alternative Assessment Handbook, Rubric 21: Map Reading

Answers

Analyzing Visuals *leopard skins, ostrich eggs, iron tools and weapons, jewelry, silk, glass*

Reading Check *the availability of resources such as wood and iron ore*

316

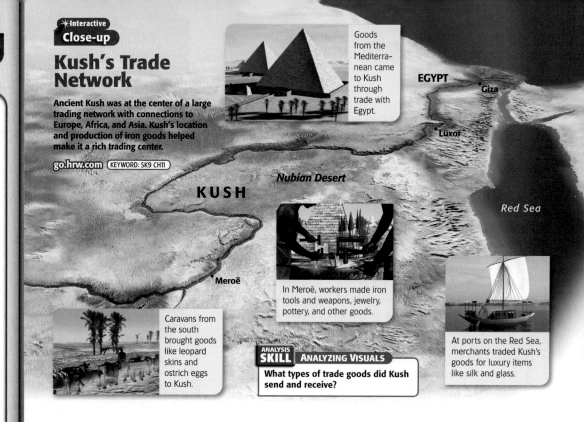

Interactive
Close-up

Kush's Trade Network

Ancient Kush was at the center of a large trading network with connections to Europe, Africa, and Asia. Kush's location and production of iron goods helped make it a rich trading center.

go.hrw.com KEYWORD: SK9 CH11

EGYPT
Giza
Luxor

Nubian Desert

KUSH

Red Sea

Meroë

Goods from the Mediterranean came to Kush through trade with Egypt.

In Meroë, workers made iron tools and weapons, jewelry, pottery, and other goods.

Caravans from the south brought goods like leopard skins and ostrich eggs to Kush.

At ports on the Red Sea, merchants traded Kush's goods for luxury items like silk and glass.

ANALYSIS SKILL | **ANALYZING VISUALS**
What types of trade goods did Kush send and receive?

Kush's Iron Industry

During this period, the economic center of Kush was **Meroë** (MER-oh-wee), the new Kushite capital. Meroë's location on the east bank of the Nile helped Kush's economy. Gold could be found nearby, as could forests of ebony and other wood. More importantly, the area around Meroë was rich in deposits of iron ore.

In this location the Kushites developed an iron industry. Because resources such as iron ore and wood for furnaces were easily available, the industry grew quickly.

Expansion of Trade

In time, Meroë became the center of a large **trade network**, a system of people in different lands who trade goods back and forth.

The Kushites sent goods down the Nile to Egypt. From there, Egyptian and Greek **merchants**, or traders, carried goods to ports on the Mediterranean and Red seas and to southern Africa. These goods may have eventually reached India and China.

Kush's **exports**—items sent to other regions for trade—included gold, pottery, iron tools, slaves, and ivory. Merchants from Kush also exported leopard skins, ostrich feathers, and elephants. In return, Kushites received **imports**—goods brought in from other regions—such as jewelry and other luxury items from Egypt, Asia, and lands around the Mediterranean Sea.

READING CHECK **Drawing Inferences** What helped Kush's iron industry grow?

Differentiating Instruction

Above Level

Advanced/Gifted and Talented

Research Required

1. Have students conduct research into how ancient peoples made iron. Then organize students into groups of four and have students choose a role from among the following: wood cutter, miner, bellows operator, and blacksmith.

2. Ask each group to write a short skit that explains how iron is made. Skits should be suitable for presentation to elementary school students, as if they were on a field trip to a Kushite iron-making workshop.

3. Have the students perform their skits for the class. Discuss the skits to make sure that students understand the iron-making process.

LS Interpersonal, Kinesthetic

Alternative Assessment Handbook, Rubrics 30: Research; and 33: Skits and Reader's Theater

Society and Culture

As Kushite trade grew, merchants came into contact with people from many other cultures. As a result, the people of Kush combined customs from other cultures with their own unique culture.

Kushite Culture

The most obvious influence on the culture of Kush was Egypt. Many buildings in Meroë, especially temples, resembled those in Egypt. Many people in Kush worshipped Egyptian gods and wore Egyptian clothing. Like Egyptian rulers, Kush's rulers used the title *pharaoh* and were buried in pyramids.

Many elements of Kushite culture were unique and not borrowed from anywhere else. For example, Kushite daily life and houses were different from those in other places. One Greek geographer noted some of these differences.

" The houses in the cities are formed by inter-weaving split pieces of palm wood or of bricks . . . They hunt elephants, lions, and panthers. There are also serpents, which encounter elephants, and there are many other kinds of wild animals. "

–Strabo, from *Geography*

In addition to Egyptian gods, Kushites worshipped their own gods. For example, their most important god was the lion-headed god Apedemek. The people of Kush also developed their own written language, known today as Meroitic. Unfortunately, historians have not yet been able to interpret the Meroitic language.

Women in Kushite Society

Unlike women in other early societies, Kushite women were expected to be active in their society. Like Kushite men, women worked long hours in the fields. They also raised children, cooked, and performed other household tasks. During times of war, many women fought alongside men.

Some Kushite women rose to positions of **authority**, especially religious authority. For example, King Piankhi made his sister a powerful priestess. Later rulers followed his example and made other princesses priestesses as well. Other women from royal families led the ceremonies in which new kings were crowned.

Some Kushite women had even more power. These women served as co-rulers with their husbands or sons. A few Kushite women, such as Queen Shanakhdakheto (shah-nahk-dah-KEE-toh), even ruled the empire alone. Several other queens ruled Kush later, helping increase the strength and wealth of the kingdom. Throughout most of its history, however, Kush was ruled by kings.

READING CHECK **Analyzing** In what ways were the society and culture of Kush unique?

ACADEMIC VOCABULARY
authority power or influence

THE IMPACT TODAY
More than 50 ancient Kushite pyramids still stand near the ruins of Meroë in present-day Sudan.

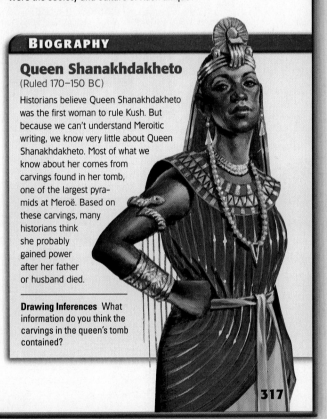

BIOGRAPHY

Queen Shanakhdakheto
(Ruled 170–150 BC)

Historians believe Queen Shanakhdakheto was the first woman to rule Kush. But because we can't understand Meroitic writing, we know very little about Queen Shanakhdakheto. Most of what we know about her comes from carvings found in her tomb, one of the largest pyramids at Meroë. Based on these carvings, many historians think she probably gained power after her father or husband died.

Drawing Inferences What information do you think the carvings in the queen's tomb contained?

317

Direct Teach

Main Idea

❷ **Society and Culture**

Society and culture in Kush had elements borrowed from other cultures and elements unique to Kush.

Identify What Kushite customs were borrowed from other cultures? *Egyptian-style temples, religion, clothing, and pyramids*

Compare and Contrast How were the roles of Kushite women similar and different from women's roles in other cultures? *Like women in other cultures, Kushite women worked in the fields, raised children, cooked, and performed other household tasks. Unlike most ancient cultures, Kushite women sometimes fought alongside men in battle. Some Kushite women rose to high positions in religion and government.*

RF: Biography: Queen Amanirenas

Did you know . . .

As early as 4000 BC, people discovered how to make iron objects from meteorites. Centuries later, people mastered smelting—heating iron ore in a furnace along with charcoal.

About the Illustration

This illustration of Kushite queen Shanakhdakheto is an artist's conception based on available sources. However, historians are uncertain exactly what Queen Shanakhdakheto looked like.

Differentiating Instruction

Below Level

English-Language Learners

1. To help students understand cultural borrowing in Kush, draw the Venn diagram at right for students to see. Omit the blue answers.

2. Have students copy the Venn diagram. As you discuss the connections between Egypt and Kush, have students fill in the Venn diagram with words or pictures. **LS Visual/Spatial**

Alternative Assessment Handbook, Rubric 13: Graphic Organizers

Kushite Culture
houses of palm wood and brick; hunted elephants, lions, and panthers; worshiped both their own gods and Egyptian gods; their own written language; women worked and fought in wars

Both Cultures
depended on the Nile; Egyptian-style temples; Egyptian gods; Egyptian-style clothing; title of pharaoh; pyramids; women raised children, cooked, and did household tasks; some women became queens

Egyptian Culture
houses of mud and brick; Egyptian gods; hieroglyphics for written language

Answers

Biography *possible answers—information about the death of her father or husband, her own accomplishments*

Reading Check *Their houses were made of palm wood or bricks; they hunted elephants, lions, and panthers; and the women played an active role in society, including working in fields, fighting in wars and rising to positions of power.*

Close-up
Rulers of Kush

Activity Ask students these questions to highlight similarities and differences between Kushite and Egyptian culture.

1. Which culture believed their rulers to be gods? *both*

2. How were Kushite pyramids different from Egyptian pyramids? *smaller, different style*

3. How were Kushite queens viewed compared to Egyptian queens? *seem to have been more important*

4. Why did the Kushites and Egyptians carve on stone? *to commemorate important buildings and events*

Linking to Today

Collections of Kushite Artifacts Some of the finest collections of Kushite artifacts are here in the United States. These collections are on display at Boston's Museum of Fine Arts, Philadelphia's University Museum, and Chicago's Oriental Institute Museum. These museums have all participated in archaeological digs in Nubia.

Answers

Analyzing Visuals *pyramids, wigs, clothing and jewelry styles, stone carvings*

318

Close-up
Rulers of Kush

Like the Egyptians, the people of Kush considered their rulers to be gods. Kush's culture was similar to Egypt's, but there were also important differences.

Like the Egyptians, Kush's rulers built pyramids. Kushite pyramids, however, were much smaller and the style was different.

Kush was at times ruled by powerful queens. Queens seem to have been more important in Kush than in Egypt.

Stone carvings were made to commemorate important buildings and events, just like in Egypt. Kush's writing system was similar to Egyptian hieroglyphics, but scholars have been unable to understand most of it.

ANALYSIS SKILL **ANALYZING VISUALS**
What can you see in the illustration that is similar to Egyptian culture?

318 CHAPTER 11

Differentiating Instruction

Below Level

Special Needs Learners
Materials: art supplies

1. Discuss with students what they have learned about ancient Kush and its relations with Egypt.

2. Have each student identify two pieces of information they know about ancient Kush.

3. Have students study the stone carving on this page. Tell students to draw on paper a stone carving that uses pictures to relate their two pieces of information about ancient Kush. Have volunteers share their stone carvings with the class. Ask students to decipher what each stone carving means. **LS Visual/Spatial**

Alternative Assessment Handbook, Rubric 3: Artwork

Decline and Defeat

The Kushite kingdom centered at Meroë reached its height in the first century BC. Four centuries later, Kush had collapsed. Developments both inside and outside the empire led to its downfall.

Loss of Resources

A series of problems within Kush weakened its economic power. One possible problem was that farmers allowed their cattle to overgraze the land. When the cows ate all the grass, there was nothing to hold the soil down. As a result, wind blew the soil away. Without this soil, farmers could not produce enough food for Kush's people.

In addition, ironmakers probably used up the forests near Meroë. As wood became scarce, furnaces shut down. Kush could no longer produce enough weapons or trade goods. As a result, Kush's military and economic power declined.

Trade Rivals

Kush was also weakened by a loss of trade. Foreign merchants set up new trade routes that went around Kush. For example, a new trade route bypassed Kush in favor of a nearby kingdom, Aksum (AHK-soom).

Rise of Aksum

Aksum was located southeast of Kush on the Red Sea, in present-day Ethiopia and Eritrea. In the first two centuries AD, Aksum grew wealthy from trade. But Aksum's wealth and power came at the expense of Kush. As Kush's power declined, Aksum became the most powerful state in the region.

By the AD 300s, Kush had lost much of its wealth and military might. Seeing that the Kushites were weak, the king of Aksum sent an army to conquer his former trade rival. In about AD 350, the army of Aksum's King Ezana (AY-zah-nah) destroyed Meroë and took over the kingdom of Kush.

In the late 300s, the rulers of Aksum became Christian. Their new religion reshaped culture throughout Nubia, and the last influences of Kush disappeared.

READING CHECK **Summarizing** What internal problems caused Kush's power to decline?

SUMMARY AND PREVIEW In this section you learned about the rise and fall of a powerful Kushite kingdom centered in Meroë. Next, you will learn about the rise of strong empires in West Africa.

THE IMPACT TODAY
Much of the population of Ethiopia, which includes what used to be Aksum, is still Christian.

Section 2 Assessment

go.hrw.com
Online Quiz
KEYWORD: SK9 HP11

Reviewing Ideas, Terms, and Places

1. **a. Recall** What were some of Kush's **exports**?
   b. Analyze Why was **Meroë** in a good location?
2. **a. Identify** Who was Queen Shanakhdakheto?
   b. Compare How were Kushite and Egyptian cultures similar?
   c. Elaborate How does our inability to understand Meroitic affect our knowledge of Kush's culture?
3. **a. Identify** What kingdom conquered Kush in about AD 350?
   b. Summarize What was the impact of new trade routes on Kush?

Critical Thinking

4. **Identifying Causes** Review your notes to identify causes of the rise and the fall of the Kushite kingdom centered at Meroë. Use a chart like this one to record the causes.

Causes of rise	Causes of fall

FOCUS ON WRITING

5. **Adding Details** Which famous Kushites could you choose for your journal entry? Make a list of major figures from Kush and list important details about each.

ANCIENT CIVILIZATIONS OF AFRICA—TRADING KINGDOMS **319**

Section 2 Assessment Answers

1. **a.** gold, pottery, iron tools, slaves, ivory, leopard skins, ostrich feathers, and elephants
   b. nearby gold, ebony and other wood, iron ore deposits
2. **a.** possibly the first woman to rule Kush
   b. had similar clothing and building styles, used title pharaoh, worshiped some similar gods, had some female rulers
   c. We can read only what non-Meroitic writers have recorded, so many details are missing, and we may have misinterpreted some information.
3. **a.** Aksum
   b. Kush was weakened by loss of trade.
4. Causes of rise—fertile soil, valuable natural resources, iron industry, trade; Causes of fall—overgrazing that led to loss of fertile soil, forests used up so iron weapons and trade goods no longer produced, new trade routes that bypassed Kush, weakness of Kush
5. Lists will vary, but students should list key figures from Kush and provide details about their lives.

Direct Teach

Main Idea

❸ **Decline and Defeat**

The decline and defeat of Kush was caused by both internal and external factors.

Describe Why did agriculture and ironmaking decline in Kush? *Cows ate the grass, and the soil blew away; ironmakers cut down the forests.*

Analyze How did shifts in trade routes affect Kush? *New trade routes that went around Kush weakened Kush and its economy further.*

RF: Literature: *The Fall of Meroë*

Review & Assess

Close

Review the reasons that a large trading network was important to Kush.

Review

Online Quiz, Section 2

Assess

SE Section 2 Assessment
PASS: Section 2 Quiz
Alternative Assessment Handbook

Reteach/Classroom Intervention

Interactive Reader and Study Guide, Section 2
Interactive Skills Tutor CD-ROM

Answers

Reading Check *Overgrazing by cows led to the loss of fertile soil, and the using up of forests caused furnaces for iron to be shut down. With the loss of these resources, Kush's military and economic power declined.*

319

Bellringer

If YOU lived there. . . Use the **Daily Bellringer Transparency** to help students answer the question.

📦 Daily Bellringer Transparency, Section 3

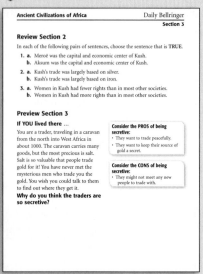

Academic Vocabulary

Review with students the high-use academic term in this section.

procedure the way a task is accomplished (p. 322)

📝 **RF:** Vocabulary Builder, Section 3

Taking Notes

Have students copy the graphic organizer onto their own paper and then use it to take notes on the section. This activity will prepare students for the Section Assessment, in which they will complete a graphic organizer that builds on the information using the Critical Thinking Skill: Identifying Causes.

SECTION 3

Empire of Ghana

What You Will Learn...

Main Ideas

1. Ghana controlled trade and became wealthy.
2. Through its control of trade, Ghana built an empire.
3. Attacking invaders, overgrazing, and the loss of trade caused Ghana's decline.

The Big Idea

The rulers of Ghana built an empire by controlling the salt and gold trade.

Key Terms

silent barter, *p. 322*

 TAKING NOTES As you read, make a list of important events from the beginning to the end of the empire of Ghana. Keep track of these events using a diagram like this one.

> Empire of Ghana
> ↓
> Event
> ↓
> Event
> ↓
> Event

If YOU lived there...

You are a trader, traveling in a caravan from the north into West Africa in about 1000. The caravan carries many goods, but the most precious is salt. Salt is so valuable that people trade gold for it! You have never met the mysterious men who trade you the gold. You wish you could talk to them to find out where they get it.

Why do you think the traders are so secretive?

BUILDING BACKGROUND The various regions of Africa provide people with different resources. West Africa, for example, was rich in both fertile soils and minerals, especially gold and iron. Other regions had plentiful supplies of other resources, such as salt. Over time, trade developed between regions with different resources. This trade led to the growth of the first great empire in West Africa.

Ghana Controls Trade

For hundreds of years, trade routes crisscrossed West Africa. For most of that time, West Africans did not profit much from the Saharan trade because the routes were run by Berbers from northern Africa. Eventually, that situation changed. Ghana (GAH-nuh), an empire in West Africa, gained control of the valuable routes. As a result, Ghana became a powerful state.

As you can see on the map on the following page, the empire of Ghana lay between the Niger and Senegal rivers. This location was north and west of the location of the modern nation that bears the name Ghana.

Ghana's Beginnings

Archaeology provides some clues to Ghana's early history, but we do not know much about its earliest days. Historians think the first people in Ghana were farmers. Sometime after 300 these farmers, the Soninke (soh-NING-kee), were threatened by nomadic herders. The herders wanted to take the farmers' water and pastures. For protection, groups of Soninke families began to band together. This banding together was the beginning of Ghana.

Teach the Big Idea

At Level

Empire of Ghana

1. **Teach** Ask students the questions in the Main Idea boxes under Direct Teach.

2. **Apply** Have students write each of the blue headings in the section on a piece of paper. Tell students to leave space between each heading. Have students use the main ideas from this page and identify which one corresponds with each blue heading. Then have students review the material under each heading and write three to five specific details that support the main idea.
   LS Verbal/Linguistic

3. **Review** To review the section, have volunteers share their supporting details with the class. Then have the class discuss the section's big idea.

4. **Practice/Homework** Have students write a one-paragraph summary of this section that uses the supporting details they have identified. **LS Verbal/Linguistic**

   📝 Alternative Assessment Handbook, Rubric 42: Writing to Inform

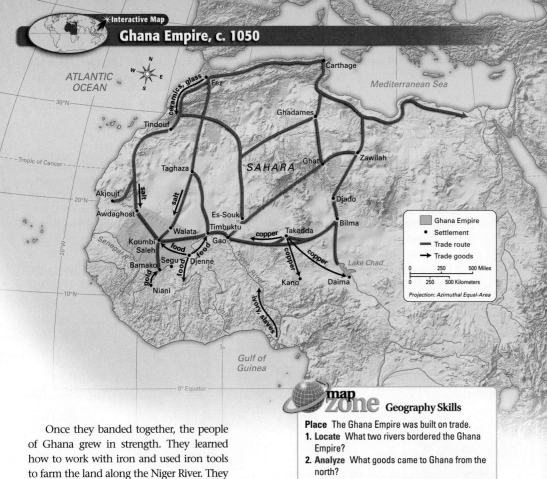

ATLANTIC OCEAN

Mediterranean Sea

SAHARA

Carthage

Fez

Ghadames

Tindouf

Ghat

Zawilah

Taghaza

Akjoujt

Awdaghost

Es-Souk

Djado

Walata   Timbuktu

Bilma

Koumbi Saleh   Gao

Takedda

copper

copper

Segou   Djenné

copper

Bamako

Kano

Daima

Lake Chad

Niani

Senegal

Niger River

Gulf of Guinea

Tropic of Cancer

Equator

	Ghana Empire
•	Settlement
▬	Trade route
→	Trade goods

0   250   500 Miles
0   250   500 Kilometers

Projection: Azimuthal Equal-Area

map Zone Geography Skills

Place The Ghana Empire was built on trade.
1. **Locate** What two rivers bordered the Ghana Empire?
2. **Analyze** What goods came to Ghana from the north?

go.hrw.com KEYWORD: SK9 CH11

Once they banded together, the people of Ghana grew in strength. They learned how to work with iron and used iron tools to farm the land along the Niger River. They also herded cattle for meat and milk. Because these farmers and herders could produce plenty of food, the population of Ghana increased. Towns and villages grew.

Besides farm tools, iron was also useful for making weapons. Other armies in the area had weapons made of bone, wood, and stone. These were no match for the iron spear points and blades used by Ghana's army.

Trade in Valuable Goods

Ghana lay between the vast Sahara Desert and deep forests. In this location, they were in a good position to trade in the region's most valuable resources—gold and salt. Gold came from the south, from mines near the Gulf of Guinea and along the Niger. Salt came from the Sahara in the north.

People wanted gold for its beauty. But they needed salt in their diets to survive. Salt, which could be used to preserve food, also made bland food tasty. These qualities made salt very valuable. In fact, Africans sometimes cut up slabs of salt and used the pieces as money.

ANCIENT CIVILIZATIONS OF AFRICA—TRADING KINGDOMS   **321**

Differentiating Instruction

Above Level

Advanced/Gifted and Talented

1. Have students study the map on this page. Guide students in a discussion of where various resources, such as salt and gold, are located on the map. Ask students to describe the geography of the region around Ghana.

2. Ask students to imagine a Web site that would give information about the ancient empire of Ghana. Tell students that their assignment is to plan a Web page about the effect of Ghana's geography on its economy.

3. Suggest that students make a sketch on paper of images and text they could include on their

Web page. Encourage students to be creative and use drawings and symbols for their sites. To help students get started, show them examples of interesting, informative, and visually appealing Web sites.

4. Ask volunteers to show and explain their Web page plans to the class. Encourage the students to ask questions about the information or construction of the Web page. **LS** Visual/Spatial

Alternative Assessment Handbook, Rubric 22: Multimedia Presentations

---

Direct Teach

Main Idea

❶ Ghana Controls Trade

Ghana controlled trade and became wealthy.

Recall Where was the ancient empire of Ghana located? *in West Africa between the Niger and Senegal Rivers; between the Sahara Desert to the north and the forests of the south*

Explain How did early Soninke farmers create a strong state? *They banded together against nomadic herders, grew in strength, used iron tools to produce more food, and formed villages and towns.*

Summarize What was the silent barter of gold and salt? *the process in which people trade without any direct contact; in Ghana it provided for peaceful exchange of salt for gold and kept the location of gold mines secret*

Activity Trade Advertisements
Have students look closely at the map on this page. Ask students to identify the trade goods exchanged in Africa. Then have students create an advertisement for one of the trade goods. **LS** Visual/Spatial

Alternative Assessment Handbook, Rubric 2: Advertisements

Map Zone Transparency: Ghana Empire, c. 1050

Did you know...

The Iron Age took a long time to catch on. Iron was being used in the Middle East by 1000 BC. By around 500 BC, the use of iron had spread throughout most of Europe. When people in Ghana began using it several hundred years later, they learned how effective it could be. The use of iron tools allowed farmers to grow much more food than before. Soldiers also appreciated their new iron weapons, which made the soldiers far superior to their neighbors without iron.

Answers

Map Zone 1. *Senegal and Niger;*
2. *salt, ceramics, and glass*

321

Did you know. . .

The English word "salary" means a fixed payment for a job on a regular schedule. The word comes from the Latin word salarium which was a part of Roman soldiers' pay to allow them to purchase salt.

Connect to Math

The Purity of Gold Discuss how metals can be mixed with other metals to form alloys and how the purity of gold is measured (in karats; 1 karat equals 1/24th of total weight). Discuss the common purities of gold jewelry (18k and 24k). Ask which has more gold (24k) and how much gold is in 18k expressed as a fraction or percent (3/4 or 75%).

Connect to Economics

Gold and the Law of Supply and Demand Discuss reasons that gold has always been a valuable metal (its beauty combined with its scarcity). Ask students to role-play a market or auction in which there is one gold bracelet available for each student in the class. How much would each be worth and how much would students be willing to pay? Then change the situation to one where there is only one available for the entire class. Why does the bracelet become more valuable? Discuss this concept in relation to the way Ghana was able to build wealth through access to gold as well as why rulers would not allow people to own gold nuggets.

go.hrw.com
Online Resources
KEYWORD: SK9 CH11
ACTIVITY: Trading Groups

ACADEMIC VOCABULARY
procedure the way a task is accomplished

The exchange of gold and salt sometimes followed a **procedure** called silent barter. **Silent barter** is a process in which people exchange goods without ever contacting each other directly. The method made sure that the traders did business peacefully. It also kept the exact location of the gold mines secret from the salt traders.

In the silent barter process, salt traders went to a riverbank near gold fields. There they left slabs of salt in rows and beat a drum to tell the gold miners that trading had begun. Then the salt traders moved back several miles from the riverbank.

Soon afterward, the gold miners arrived by boat. They left what they considered a fair amount of gold in exchange for the salt. Then the gold miners also moved back several miles so the salt traders could return. If they were happy with the amount of gold left there, the salt traders beat the drum again, took the gold, and left. The gold miners then returned and picked up their salt. Trading continued until both sides were happy with the exchange.

Growth of Trade

As the trade in gold and salt increased, Ghana's rulers gained power. Over time, their military strength grew as well. With their armies they began to take control of this trade from the merchants who had once controlled it. Merchants from the north and south met to exchange goods in Ghana. As a result of their control of trade routes, the rulers of Ghana became wealthy.

Salt and Gold

Collaborative Learning

At Level

Using the Barter System

Materials: colored chips, cards, or other types of markers to represent different types of goods

1. Discuss the reasons silent barter was used in Ghana. Also note that Koumbi Saleh was the site of a trading market for many other items such as sheep, cattle, honey, cloth, and so on. Then divide the class into three small groups.

2. Select one group to be gold traders and another to be salt traders. The third group will be local traders who will offer goods like those listed. Work with the class to establish some value system for the markers (for example, one

marker is equal to a slab of salt; ten slabs of salt are worth one gold bracelet, and so on.)

3. Have the gold and salt traders enact a silent barter first, noting that the barter isn't complete until both sides are satisfied. Then have all three groups gather at a market to exchange goods they need and want.

4. After a period of bartering, discuss how the system worked. **LS Logical/Mathematical, Interpersonal**

Alternative Assessment Handbook, Rubric 14: Group Activity

Additional sources of wealth and trade were developed to add to Ghana's wealth. Wheat came from the north. Sheep, cattle, and honey came from the south. Local products, including leather and cloth, were also traded for wealth. Among the prized special local products were tassels made from golden thread.

As trade increased, Ghana's capital grew as well. The largest city in West Africa, Koumbi Saleh (KOOM-bee SAHL-uh) was an oasis for travelers. These travelers could find all the region's goods for sale in its markets. As a result, Koumbi Saleh gained a reputation as a great trading center.

READING CHECK **Generalizing** How did trade help Ghana develop?

Ghana's rulers became rich by controlling the trade in salt and gold. Salt came from the north in large slabs like the ones shown at left. Gold, like the woman above is wearing, came from the south.

Ghana Builds an Empire

By 800 Ghana was firmly in control of West Africa's trade routes. Nearly all trade between northern and southern Africa passed through Ghana. Traders were protected by Ghana's army, which kept trade routes free from bandits. As a result, trade became safer. Knowing they would be protected, traders were not scared to travel to Ghana. Trade increased, and Ghana's influence grew as well.

Taxes and Gold

With so many traders passing through their lands, Ghana's rulers looked for ways to make money from them. One way they raised money was by forcing traders to pay taxes. Every trader who entered Ghana had to pay a special tax on the goods he carried. Then he had to pay another tax on any goods he took with him when he left.

Traders were not the only people who had to pay taxes. The people of Ghana also had to pay taxes. In addition, Ghana conquered many small neighboring tribes, then forced them to pay tribute. Rulers used the money from taxes and tribute to support Ghana's growing army.

Not all of Ghana's wealth came from taxes and tribute. Ghana's rich mines produced huge amounts of gold. Some of this gold was carried by traders to lands as far away as England, but not all of Ghana's gold was traded. Ghana's kings kept huge stores of gold for themselves. In fact, all the gold produced in Ghana was officially the property of the king.

Knowing that rare materials are worth far more than common ones, the rulers banned anyone else in Ghana from owning gold nuggets. Common people could own only gold dust, which they used as money. This ensured that the king was richer than his subjects.

ANCIENT CIVILIZATIONS OF AFRICA—TRADING KINGDOMS **323**

❸ **Ghana's Decline**

Attacking invaders, overgrazing, and the loss of trade caused Ghana's decline.

Recall What group attacked Ghana in the 1060s, and what effect did the attack have? *Almoravids greatly weakened Ghana's trade empire.*

Draw Conclusions What was the significance of overgrazing? *The Almoravids overgrazed the lands in Ghana, leaving the soil worthless for farming or herding. This greatly hurt Ghana's economy and society and caused many farmers to leave.*

Make Judgments Why do you think people rebelled in about 1200? *possible answer—They were angry that they had been conquered by Ghana.*

Activity **Living under Tunka Manin** Ask students to imagine that they live in a village in Ghana that Tunka Manin has just visited. Have students write a journal entry in the voice of a villager, describing what it was like to talk to the king. Entries should include details about the king and his visit to the village.
LS Verbal/Linguistic, Intrapersonal

📝 Alternative Assessment Handbook, Rubric 15: Journals

Expansion of the Empire

Ghana's kings used their great wealth to build a powerful army. With this army the kings of Ghana conquered many of their neighbors. Many of these conquered areas were centers of trade. Taking over these areas made Ghana's kings even richer.

Ghana's kings didn't think that they could rule all the territory they conquered by themselves. Their empire was quite large, and travel and communication in West Africa could be difficult. To keep order in their empire, they allowed conquered kings to retain much of their power. These kings acted as governors of their territories, answering only to the king.

The empire of Ghana reached its peak under Tunka Manin (TOOHN-kah MAH-nin). This king had a splendid court where he displayed the vast wealth of the empire. A Spanish writer noted the court's splendor.

FOCUS ON READING
How is this quotation an example of the effects of the king's wealth?

" The king adorns himself . . . round his neck and his forearms, and he puts on a high cap decorated with gold and wrapped in a turban of fine cotton. Behind the king stand ten pages holding shields and swords decorated with gold. "
–al-Bakri, from *The Book of Routes and Kingdoms*

READING CHECK **Summarizing** How did the rulers of Ghana control trade?

BIOGRAPHY

Tunka Manin
(Ruled around 1068)

All we know about Tunka Manin comes from the writings of a Muslim geographer who wrote about Ghana. From his writings, we know that Tunka Manin was the nephew of the previous king, a man named Basi. Kingship and property in Ghana did not pass from father to son, but from uncle to nephew. Only the king's sister's son could inherit the throne. Once he did become king, Tunka Manin surrounded himself with finery and many luxuries.

Contrasting How was inheritance in Ghana different from inheritance in other societies you have studied?

Ghana's Decline

In the mid-1000s Ghana was rich and powerful, but by the end of the 1200s, the empire had collapsed. Three major factors contributed to its end.

Invasion

The first factor that helped bring about Ghana's end was invasion. A Muslim group called the Almoravids (al-moh-RAH-vidz) attacked Ghana in the 1060s in an effort to force its leaders to convert to Islam.

The people of Ghana fought hard against the Almoravid army. For 14 years they kept the invaders at bay. In the end, however, the Almoravids won. They destroyed the city of Koumbi Saleh.

The Almoravids didn't control Ghana for long, but they certainly weakened the empire. They cut off many trade routes through Ghana and formed new trading partnerships with Muslim leaders instead. Without this trade Ghana could no longer support its empire.

Overgrazing

A second factor in Ghana's decline was a result of the Almoravid conquest. When the Almoravids moved into Ghana, they brought herds of animals with them. These animals ate all the grass in many pastures, leaving the soil exposed to hot desert winds. These winds blew away the soil, leaving the land worthless for farming or herding. Unable to grow crops, many farmers had to leave in search of new homes.

Internal Rebellion

A third factor also helped bring about the decline of Ghana's empire. In about 1200 the people of a country that Ghana had conquered rose up in rebellion. Within a few years the rebels had taken over the entire empire of Ghana.

324 CHAPTER 11

Critical Thinking: Sequencing

Illustrated Time Line

1. Review with the class the events that led to the decline of the empire of Ghana. Then tell students that they will create an illustrated time line of the rise and fall of Ghana.

2. Have each student make a list of four to five important events during the history of the empire of Ghana. Next to each event, have students indicate why the event was significant or what impact it had on the people of Ghana.

3. Have each student create an illustrated time line using the events he or she developed. Remind students to place the events in the order in which they occurred, and to include a picture that illustrates the importance of the event.

4. Ask students to post their time lines for the class to see. **LS** Verbal/Linguistic, Visual/Spatial

📝 Alternative Assessment Handbook, Rubric 36: Time Lines

Answers

Focus on Reading *It describes the valuable gold and cloth the king wears and the gold used in decorations for the king's servants.*

Reading Check *They taxed traders coming to and leaving from Ghana, and they used their armies to protect trade routes.*

Biography *Inheritance was handed down to the king's nephew, rather than to the king's son.*

Overgrazing
Too many animals grazing in one area can lead to problems, such as the loss of farmland that occurred in West Africa.

1 Animals are allowed to graze in areas with lots of grass.

2 With too many animals grazing, however, the grass disappears, leaving the soil below exposed to the wind.

3 The wind blows the soil away, turning what was once grassland into desert.

Once in control, however, the rebels found that they could not keep order in Ghana. Weakened, Ghana was attacked and defeated by one of its neighbors. The empire fell apart.

READING CHECK **Identifying Cause and Effect** Why did Ghana decline in the 1000s?

SUMMARY AND PREVIEW The empire of Ghana in West Africa grew rich and powerful through its control of trade routes. The empire lasted for centuries, but eventually Ghana fell. In the next section you will learn that it was replaced by a new empire, Mali.

Section 3 Assessment

go.hrw.com
Online Quiz
KEYWORD: SK9 HP11

Reviewing Ideas, Terms, and Places

1. a. Identify What were the two most valuable resources traded in Ghana?
b. Explain How did the **silent barter** system work?
2. a. Identify Who was Tunka Manin?
b. Generalize What did Ghana's kings do with the money they raised from taxes?
c. Elaborate Why did the rulers of Ghana not want everyone to have gold?
3. a. Identify What group invaded Ghana in the late 1000s?
b. Summarize How did overgrazing help cause the fall of Ghana?

Critical Thinking

4. Identifying Causes Draw a diagram like the one shown here. Use it to identify factors that caused Ghana's trade growth and those that caused its decline.

Growth → Ghana's Trade → Decline

FOCUS ON WRITING

5. Gathering Information Think about what it would have been like to live in Ghana. Whose journal would you create? Would you choose the powerful Tunka Manin? a trader? Jot down some ideas.

Section 3 Assessment Answers

1. a. gold and salt
b. Traders exchanged goods without contacting each other directly, and business was peacefully conducted.

2. a. a king of Ghana who ruled around 1068
b. The rulers built a powerful army.
c. to ensure the king was richer than his subjects

3. a. the Almoravids
b. Overgrazing left the soil exposed to hot desert winds, which blew it away, making it worthless for farmers.

4. Growth—location, silent barter from the north and south, control of trade routes; Decline—invasion, overgrazing, internal rebellion

5. possible answer—It might be interesting to create a journal of a trader, because trade is what helped turn Ghana into an empire.

Linking to Today
Desertification in West Africa
Overgrazing, along with drought and cutting too much wood continues today in areas south of the Sahara Desert. The desert area is increasing and usable farmland and grazing land is decreasing. Without farmland, some of the countries south of the Sahara have suffered severe famines and remain some of the poorest countries in the world.

Review & Assess

Close
Ask students to imagine what life was like in Ghana at the height of its empire about 800. Discuss the peace and prosperity of the empire. Ask students to imagine what life was like around 1200, when the empire began to fall apart.

Review
Online Quiz, Section 3

Assess
SE Section 3 Assessment
PASS: Section 3 Quiz
Alternative Assessment Handbook

Reteach/Classroom Intervention
Interactive Reader and Study Guide, Section 3
Interactive Skills Tutor CD-ROM

Answers
Reading Check *invasion, overgrazing, and internal rebellion*

Geography and History

Activity **A Saharan Mural** Discuss with students items that were traded across the Sahara. Then have students work together to draw a mural of a Saharan caravan on a long piece of butcher paper. Suggest that students include camels and different trade items discussed in this feature. Display the mural in the classroom. **LS Visual/Spatial**

📝 Alternative Assessment Handbook: Rubric 3: Artwork

Did you know. . .

Although conditions are harsh, people do live in the Sahara. A people called the Tuareg live in or near the desert and roam the southern Sahara from the south of Algeria into Libya, Niger, and Mali. The Tuareg wear blue robes that reduce harmful UVB radiation from the sun. Their dark clothing and the veils that protect their faces earned the Tuareg the nicknames "Blue Men" and "Veiled Men of the Sahara."

Teaching Tip

Comparing Distances To help students understand the distances involved in Saharan trade, refer them to the physical and political maps of Africa in the atlas at the back of this book. Challenge students to match features on those maps to features on the "Crossing the Sahara" map on these pages and to use the scale in the atlas to calculate sample distances on this map.

Crossing the Sahara

Crossing the Sahara has never been easy. Bigger than the entire continent of Australia, the Sahara is one of the hottest, driest, and most barren places on earth. Yet for centuries, people have crossed the Sahara's gravel-covered plains and vast seas of sand. Long ago, West Africans crossed the desert regularly to carry on a rich trade.

Salt, used to preserve and flavor food, was available in the Sahara. Traders from the north took salt south. Camel caravans carried huge slabs of salt weighing hundreds of pounds.

In exchange for salt, people in West Africa offered other valuable trade goods, especially gold. Gold dust was measured with special spoons and stored in boxes. Ivory, from the tusks of elephants, was carved into jewelry.

Tindouf

Akjoujt

Taghaza

Koumbi Saleh

Walata

Timbuktu

Es-Souk

Gao

Takedda

A F R I C A

Gulf of Guinea

326 CHAPTER 11

Critical Thinking: Comparing

Above Level

Long-Distance Trade Then and Now

Materials: business sections of newspapers or magazines

1. To help students compare the ancient Saharan trade with international trade today, first distribute the business pages from newspapers or magazines. The print material does not have to be current or local.

2. Call on students to make generalizations about what they read in the newspapers or magazines about long-distance trade. *possible*

answers—security concerns, differences in resources among countries, high costs of transport

3. Then lead a discussion about how these same topics also concerned traders in the Sahara. Challenge students to make direct comparisons. **LS Verbal/Linguistic, Logical/Mathematical**

📝 Alternative Assessment Handbook, Rubric 11: Discussions

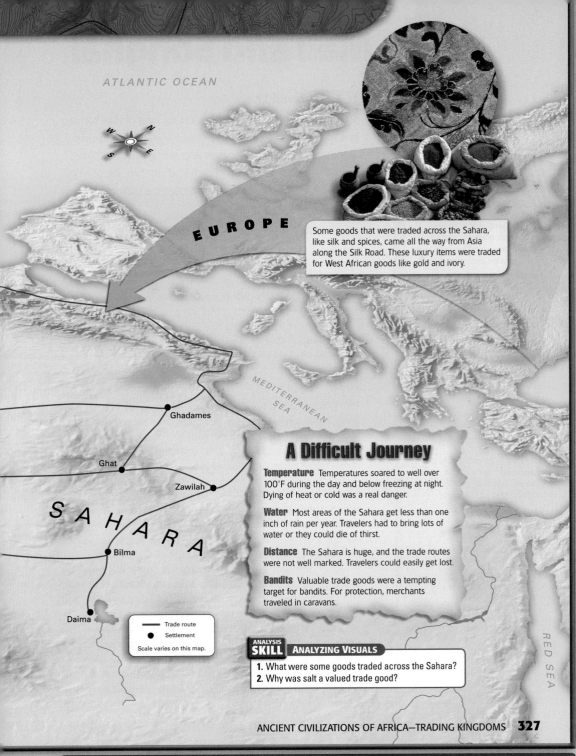

ATLANTIC OCEAN

EUROPE

Some goods that were traded across the Sahara, like silk and spices, came all the way from Asia along the Silk Road. These luxury items were traded for West African goods like gold and ivory.

MEDITERRANEAN SEA

Ghadames

Ghat

Zawilah

S A H A R A

Bilma

Daima

RED SEA

A Difficult Journey

Temperature Temperatures soared to well over 100°F during the day and below freezing at night. Dying of heat or cold was a real danger.

Water Most areas of the Sahara get less than one inch of rain per year. Travelers had to bring lots of water or they could die of thirst.

Distance The Sahara is huge, and the trade routes were not well marked. Travelers could easily get lost.

Bandits Valuable trade goods were a tempting target for bandits. For protection, merchants traveled in caravans.

—— Trade route
● Settlement
Scale varies on this map.

ANALYSIS SKILL ANALYZING VISUALS

1. What were some goods traded across the Sahara?
2. Why was salt a valued trade good?

ANCIENT CIVILIZATIONS OF AFRICA—TRADING KINGDOMS **327**

Geography and History

Activity **A Desert Travelogue** A travelogue is an illustrated account of a journey. There is a long history of travelogues for both entertainment and education. Have students imagine they have traveled with a caravan across the Sahara. Instruct them to write and illustrate a descriptive one-page travelogue about the experience. Tell them to include details that they have learned in this feature, "Crossing the Sahara."

LS Verbal/Linguistic

Alternative Assessment Handbook, Rubric 40: Writing to Describe

Connect to Science

Desert Plant Survival The Rose of Jericho is a plant that grows in the Sahara. How does it survive and reproduce in the harsh desert climate? It sheds its leaves during its last few hours before it dies. Then the bare stem and branches dry up and become a lightweight ball that is easily tumbled along by the wind. As the dead Rose of Jericho rolls, it scatters its seeds, which will remain dormant until a desert rainfall. Then the seeds will quickly sprout to begin the next generation of the Rose of Jericho.

Collaborative Learning

At Level

Loading a Caravan

1. Discuss with students the necessities and limitations of loading a caravan. Ask students to suggest items travelers would need as they traveled in a caravan. Write a list of these items for students to see.

2. Remind students that travelers would not only be carrying food and water, but they would also need protection from the daytime heat and nighttime cold of a desert climate.

Students should consider the type of clothing needed and the kinds of food that could be transported in a caravan.

3. Have students copy the list. Instruct them to write a sentence for each listed item that explains why the item is necessary.

LS Verbal/Linguistic

Alternative Assessment Handbook, Rubric 38: Writing to Classify

Answers

Analyzing Visuals 1. *gold, salt, ivory, silk, spices;* **2.** *Salt was used to preserve and flavor food.*

327

Bellringer

If YOU lived there. . . Use the **Daily Bellringer Transparency** to help students answer the question.

📔 Daily Bellringer Transparency, Section 4

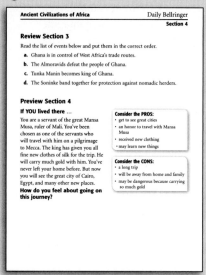

Key Terms and Places

📑 **RF:** Vocabulary Builder, Section 4

Taking Notes

Have students copy the graphic organizer onto their own paper and then use it to take notes on the section. This activity will prepare students for the Section Assessment, in which they will complete a graphic organizer that builds on the information using the Critical Thinking Skill: Finding Main Ideas.

SECTION 4

Mali and Songhai

What You Will Learn...

Main Ideas

1. The empire of Mali reached its height under the ruler Mansa Musa, but the empire fell to invaders in the 1400s.
2. The Songhai built a new Islamic empire in West Africa, conquering many of the lands that were once part of Mali.

The Big Idea

Between 1000 and 1500 the empires of Mali and Songhai developed in West Africa.

Key Terms and Places

Niger River, *p. 328*
Timbuktu, *p. 329*
mosque, *p. 331*
Gao, *p. 331*
Djenné, *p. 332*

 TAKING NOTES As you read, take notes about life in the cultures that developed in West Africa—Mali and Songhai.

West Africa

328 CHAPTER 11

If YOU lived there...

You are a servant of the great Mansa Musa, ruler of Mali. You've been chosen as one of the servants who will travel with him on a pilgrimage to Mecca. The king has given you all fine new clothes of silk for the trip. He will carry much gold with him. You've never left your home before. But now you will see the great city of Cairo, Egypt, and many other new places.

How do you feel about going on this journey?

BUILDING BACKGROUND Mansa Musa was one of Africa's greatest rulers, and his empire, Mali, was one of the largest in African history. Rising from the ruins of Ghana, Mali took over the trade routes of West Africa and grew into a powerful state.

Mali

Like Ghana, Mali (MAH-lee) lay along the upper **Niger River**. This area's fertile soil helped Mali grow. Mali's location on the Niger also allowed its people to control trade on the river. As a result, the empire grew rich and powerful. According to legend, Mali's rise to power began under a ruler named Sundiata (soohn-JAHT-ah).

Sundiata Makes Mali an Empire

When Sundiata was a boy, a harsh ruler conquered Mali. But as an adult, Sundiata built up an army and won back his country's independence. He then conquered nearby kingdoms, including Ghana, in the 1230s.

After Sundiata conquered Ghana, he took over the salt and gold trades. He also worked to improve agriculture in Mali. Sundiata had new farmlands cleared for beans, onions, rice, and other crops. Sundiata even introduced a new crop—cotton. People made clothing from the cotton fibers that was comfortable in the warm climate. They also sold cotton to other people.

To keep order in his prosperous kingdom, Sundiata took power away from local leaders. Each of these local leaders had the title mansa (MAHN-sah), a title Sundiata now took

---

Teach the Big Idea

At Level

Mali and Songhai

1. **Teach** Ask students the questions in the Main Idea boxes under Direct Teach.

2. **Apply** Review with students the history of Mali and Songhai, including the rule of Sundiata, Mansa Musa, and Askia the Great, and the decline of the empires. Have students work with a partner to create a children's book that briefly outlines the history of Mali or of Songhai and provides illustrations to support the story. Encourage students to create an outline for their story before they begin to write. Remind students

to include important events and people in their history. 🔲 **Visual/Spatial, Verbal/Linguistic**

3. **Review** Have students exchange and read each other's children's books as a review of the information from the section.

4. **Practice/Homework** Have each student write a book review of another group's book. 🔲 **Verbal/Linguistic**

📔 Alternative Assessment Handbook, Rubrics 3: Artwork; and 42: Writing to Inform

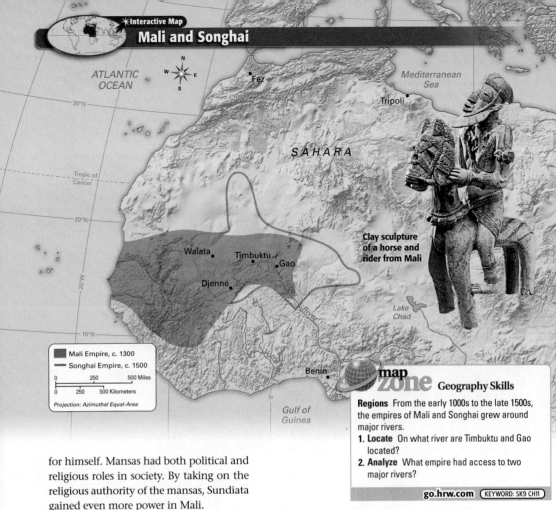

Interactive Map
Mali and Songhai

ATLANTIC OCEAN

Fez

Mediterranean Sea

Tripoli

SAHARA

Walata

Timbuktu

Gao

Djenné

Clay sculpture of a horse and rider from Mali

Lake Chad

Benin

Gulf of Guinea

Mali Empire, c. 1300
Songhai Empire, c. 1500

0   250   500 Miles
0   250   500 Kilometers

Projection: Azimuthal Equal-Area

map Zone
Geography Skills

Regions From the early 1000s to the late 1500s, the empires of Mali and Songhai grew around major rivers.

1. **Locate** On what river are Timbuktu and Gao located?
2. **Analyze** What empire had access to two major rivers?

go.hrw.com KEYWORD: SK9 CH11

for himself. Mansas had both political and religious roles in society. By taking on the religious authority of the mansas, Sundiata gained even more power in Mali.

Sundiata died in 1255. Later rulers of Mali took the title of mansa. Unlike Sundiata, most of these rulers were Muslims.

Mansa Musa

Mali's most famous ruler was a Muslim named Mansa Musa (MAHN-sah moo-SAH). Under his skillful leadership, Mali reached the height of its wealth, power, and fame in the 1300s. Because of Mansa Musa's influence, Islam spread through a large part of West Africa, gaining many new believers.

Mansa Musa ruled Mali for about 25 years, from 1312 to 1337. During that time, Mali added many important trade cities to its empire, including **Timbuktu** (tim-buhk-TOO).

Religion was very important to Mansa Musa. In 1324 he left Mali on a pilgrimage to Mecca. Through his journey, Mansa Musa introduced his empire to the Islamic world. He spread Mali's fame far and wide.

Mansa Musa also supported education. He sent many scholars to study in Morocco.

ANCIENT CIVILIZATIONS OF AFRICA—TRADING KINGDOMS **329**

Critical Thinking: Comparing and Contrasting   At Level

The Empires of West Africa

Materials: map pencils or markers, blank outline map of Africa

1. Review with students the locations of the Ghana, Mali, and Songhai Empires.

2. Using the maps of Ghana (from Section 1), and Mali and Songhai (above), have students indicate the area of all three West African empires on a blank outline map of Africa. Remind students to use a different color or pattern for each empire and to label each

empire and the approximate time period represented by the map.

3. Ask students to make a graphic organizer to compare and contrast the three empires. Discuss with the class the similarities and differences between the empires in terms of size, location, and time periods of the empires. **LS** Visual/Spatial, Verbal/Linguistic

Alternative Assessment Handbook, Rubrics 11: Discussions; and 20: Map Creation

---

Direct Teach

Main Idea

❶ Mali

The empire of Mali reached its height under the ruler Mansa Musa, but the empire fell to invaders in the 1400s.

Identify After conquering nearby kingdoms, on what did Sundiata focus? *improving agriculture and taking over the salt and gold trade*

Explain How did Sundiata consolidate political and religious power? *by taking power away from local leaders; by taking on the religious authority of local mansas*

Make Inferences Why do you think it was important for the ruler of Mali to take away power from local leaders? *Taking power from local leaders meant they could not rise up against the ruler.*

📄 **RF:** Primary Source, Two Descriptions of Emperors of Mali

📄 **RF:** Biography, Sundiata

📠 Map Zone Transparency: Mali and Songhai

Biography

Sundiata (c. 1210–c.1255) Born Mari Diata, Sundiata was the son of the king of the small kingdom of Kangaba. When his father's kingdom was overtaken by King Sumanguru of the Soso Empire, Mari Diata was forced to live in exile. Eventually, however, he returned to defeat Sumanguru in the Battle of Kirina. After the battle, he took the name Sundiata, which means the "lion prince," and went on to establish one of the greatest empires in African history.

Answers

Map Zone 1. *Niger River;* 2. *Mali*

329

Direct Teach

Close-up

Timbuktu

Ask students these questions based on the illustration of Timbuktu.

Identify What kinds of structures existed in Timbuktu? *round huts, shaded marketplaces, buildings and walls made of dried mud, mosques*

Analyze What was one advantage of the location of Timbuktu along a river? *possible answer—traders could reach the city by boat.*

Drawing Conclusions Why do you think the people of Timbuktu were dressed the way they were? *possible answer—Because there were few trees, people needed to protect themselves from the sun.*

Did you know. . .

European explorers did not reach Timbuktu until the 1820s. One reason for this was because Timbuktu was extremely difficult to reach; the terrain of the nearby Sahara Desert kept explorers from being able to make the journey to Timbuktu. Partly because of this, Timbuktu was seen as a mysterious and exotic city. Some people even believed that the entire city was made of gold.

Linking to Today

Timbuktu Today The city of Timbuktu still exists, but as a much smaller community, and the Sahara Desert actually threatens its existence. The shifting sands of the Sahara, caused by the dry winds in the area, threaten to eventually cover the city. In 1990, Timbuktu was added to the World Heritage List in Danger, and efforts are being made to save the city.

About the Illustration

This illustration of Timbuktu is an artist's conception based on available sources. However, historians are uncertain exactly what ancient Timbuktu looked like.

Answers

Analyzing Visuals *by camel caravans*

Close-up

Timbuktu

Timbuktu became a major trading city at the height of Mali's power under Mansa Musa. Traders came to Timbuktu from the north and south to trade for salt, gold, metals, shells, and many other goods.

Mansa Musa and later rulers built several large mosques in the city, which became a center of Islamic learning.

Winter floods allowed boats to reach Timbuktu from the Niger River.

Timbuktu's walls and buildings were mostly built with bricks made of dried mud. Heavy rains can soften the bricks and destroy buildings.

At crowded market stalls, people traded for goods like sugar, kola nuts, and glass beads.

Camel caravans from the north brought goods like salt, cloth, books, and slaves to trade at Timbuktu.

ANALYSIS SKILL **ANALYZING VISUALS**

How did traders from the north bring their goods to Timbuktu?

330 CHAPTER 11

Critical Thinking: Categorizing [At Level]

The Rule of Mansa Musa

1. Review the description of Mansa Musa's reign.

2. To help students understand the influence of Mansa Musa, copy the graphic organizer for students. Omit the blue answers.

3. Have students copy and complete the graphic organizer. Review the answers with the class.

4. Discuss with students why they feel Mansa Musa was significant. Then have each student create a report card in which they evaluate the rule of Mansa Musa. Cards should list contributions of Mansa Musa, a grade for each, and why it was assigned that grade.

LS **Verbal/Linguistic, Visual/Spatial**

Trade	Religion	Education
• captured important trade city of Timbuktu	• encouraged study of Islam • built mosques • encouraged study of Arabic for the study of the Qur'an	• built schools • sent scholars to study in Morocco, who later set up schools

Alternative Assessment Handbook, Rubric 13: Graphic Organziers

These scholars later set up schools in Mali. Mansa Musa stressed the importance of learning to read the Arabic language so that Muslims in his empire could read the Qur'an. To spread Islam in West Africa, Mansa Musa hired Muslim architects to build mosques. A **mosque** (mahsk) is a building for Muslim prayer.

The Fall of Mali

When Mansa Musa died, his son Maghan (MAH-gan) took the throne. Maghan was a weak ruler. When raiders from the southeast poured into Mali, he couldn't stop them. The raiders set fire to Timbuktu's great schools and mosques. Mali never fully recovered from this terrible blow. The empire continued to weaken and decline.

In 1431 the Tuareg (TWAH-reg), nomads from the Sahara, seized Timbuktu. By 1500 nearly all of the lands the empire had once ruled were lost. Only a small area of Mali remained.

READING CHECK Sequencing What steps did Sundiata take to turn Mali into an empire?

Songhai

Even as the empire of Mali was reaching its height, a rival power was growing in the area. That rival was the Songhai (SAHNG-hy) kingdom. From their capital at **Gao**, the Songhai participated in the same trade that had made Ghana and Mali so rich.

The Building of an Empire

In the 1300s Mansa Musa conquered the Songhai, adding their lands to his empire. But as the Mali Empire weakened in the 1400s, the people of Songhai rebelled and regained their freedom.

The Songhai leaders were Muslims. So too were many of the North African Berbers who traded in West Africa. Because of this shared religion, the Berbers were willing to trade with the Songhai, who grew richer.

As the Songhai gained in wealth, they expanded their territory and built an empire. Songhai's expansion was led by Sunni Ali (SOOH-nee ah-LEE), who became ruler of the Songhai in 1464. Before he took over, the Songhai state had been disorganized and poorly run. As ruler, Sunni Ali worked to unify, strengthen, and enlarge his empire. Much of the land that he added to Songhai had been part of Mali.

As king, Sunni Ali encouraged everyone in his empire to work together. To build religious harmony, he participated in both Muslim and local religions. As a result, he brought stability to Songhai.

Askia the Great

Sunni Ali died in 1492. He was followed as king by his son Sunni Baru, who was not a Muslim. The Songhai people feared that if Sunni Baru didn't support Islam, they

THE IMPACT TODAY
Some of the mosques built by Mansa Musa can still be seen in West Africa today.

BIOGRAPHY

Askia the Great
(c. 1443–1538)

Askia the Great became the ruler of Songhai when he was nearly 50 years old. He ruled Songhai for about 35 years. During his reign the cities of Songhai gained power over the countryside.

When he was in his 80s, Askia went blind. His son Musa forced him to leave the throne. Askia was sent to live on an island. He lived there for nine years until another of his sons brought him back to the capital, where he died. His tomb is still one of the most honored places in all of West Africa.

Drawing Inferences Why do you think Askia the Great's tomb is still considered an honored place?

ANCIENT CIVILIZATIONS OF AFRICA—TRADING KINGDOMS **331**

331

Info to Know

The Fall of Songhai Even before attacks by Moroccan armies, the Songhai Empire had begun to decline. A civil war in the 1580s weakened the empire, and Songhai control of trade routes had diminished. In fact, Songhai gold supplies had declined as a great deal of gold was used to trade with Europeans who had arrived on the coast of West Africa in the late 1400s.

● Review & Assess ●

Close

Have students create a time line of the key events in the history of the empires of Mali and Songhai.

Review

🖥 Online Quiz, Section 4

Assess

SE Section 4 Assessment

📝 PASS: Section 4 Quiz

📝 Alternative Assessment Handbook

Reteach/Classroom Intervention

📝 Interactive Reader and Study Guide, Section 4

📝 Interactive Skills Tutor CD-ROM

Answers

Focus on Reading *possible answers—Morocco wanted to control Songhai's salt mines, so they invaded Songhai; changes in trade patterns caused trade to diminish in the region.*

Reading Check *possible answer—his support of education, because it increased learning throughout the Songhai Empire*

FOCUS ON READING

As you read Songhai Falls to Morocco, identify two causes of Songhai's fall.

would lose their trade with Muslim lands. They rebelled against the king.

The leader of that rebellion was a general named Muhammad Ture (moo-HAH-muhd too-RAY). After overthrowing Sunni Baru, Muhammad Ture chose the title *askia*, a title of high military rank. Eventually, he became known as Askia the Great.

Askia supported education and learning. Under his rule, Timbuktu flourished, drawing thousands to its universities, schools, libraries, and mosques. The city was especially known for the University of Sankore (san-KOH-rah). People arrived there from North Africa and other places to study math, science, medicine, grammar, and law. **Djenné** was another city that became a center of learning.

Most of Songhai's traders were Muslim, and as they gained influence in the empire so did Islam. Askia, himself a devout Muslim, encouraged the growth of Islamic influence. He made many laws similar to those in other Muslim nations.

To help maintain order, Askia set up five provinces within Songhai. He appointed governors who were loyal to him. Askia also created a professional army and specialized departments to oversee tasks.

Songhai Falls to Morocco

A northern rival of Songhai, Morocco, wanted to gain control of Songhai's salt mines. So the Moroccan army set out for the heart of Songhai in 1591. Moroccan soldiers carried advanced weapons, including the terrible arquebus (AHR-kwih-buhs). The arquebus was an early form of a gun.

The swords, spears, and bows used by Songhai's warriors were no match for the Moroccans' guns and cannons. The invaders destroyed Timbuktu and Gao.

Changes in trade patterns completed Songhai's fall. Overland trade declined as port cities on the Atlantic coast became more important. Africans south of Songhai and European merchants both preferred trading at Atlantic ports to dealing with Muslim traders. Slowly, the period of great West African empires came to an end.

READING CHECK **Evaluating** What do you think was Askia's greatest accomplishment?

SUMMARY AND PREVIEW Mali was a large empire famous for its wealth and centers of learning. Songhai similarly thrived. Next, you will learn about historical and artistic traditions of West Africa.

Section 4 Assessment

go.hrw.com
Online Quiz
KEYWORD: SK9 HP11

Reviewing Ideas, Terms, and Places

1. **a. Identify** Who was Sundiata?
   b. Explain What major river was important to the people of Mali? Why?
   c. Elaborate What effects did the rule of Mansa Musa have on Mali and West Africa?
2. **a. Identify** Who led the expansion of Songhai in the 1400s?
   b. Explain How did Askia the Great's support of education affect **Timbuktu**?
   c. Elaborate What were two reasons why Songhai fell to the Moroccans?

Critical Thinking

3. **Finding Main Ideas** Use your notes to help you list three major accomplishments of Sundiata and Askia.

Sundiata	Askia

FOCUS ON WRITING

4. **Comparing and Contrasting** Whose journal could you write from the empires of Mali and Songhai? Would you create a journal for an important person, like Mansa Musa or Askia the Great? Or would you create a journal for someone who has a different role in one of the empires? List your ideas.

Section 4 Assessment Answers

1. **a.** ruler of the empire of Mali
   b. Niger; its fertile soil helped Mali grow; people could control trade along the river.
   c. He spread Islam and supported education.
2. **a.** Sunni Ali
   b. Timbuktu flourished, with universities, schools, libraries, and mosques.
   c. Morocco invaded Songhai with advanced weapons to take control of the salt mines; changes in trade patterns diminished trade in the region.

3. Sundiata—won back Mali's independence; conquered Ghana and took over salt and gold trades; improved agriculture in Mali; Askia—supported education and learning; encouraged growth of Islamic influence; set up five provinces in Songhai

4. possible answer—A journal for Mansa Musa might be a good choice, as he was Mali's most famous ruler and helped the empire reach its peak.

Mansa Musa

How could one man's travels become a major historic event?

When did he live? the late 1200s and early 1300s

Where did he live? Mali

What did he do? Mansa Musa, the ruler of Mali, was one of the Muslim kings of West Africa. He became a major figure in African and world history largely because of a pilgrimage he made to the city of Mecca.

Why is he important? Mansa Musa's spectacular journey attracted the attention of the Muslim world and of Europe. For the first time, other people's eyes turned to West Africa. During his travels, Mansa Musa gave out huge amounts of gold. His spending made people eager to find the source of such wealth. Within 200 years, European explorers would arrive on the shores of western Africa.

Identifying Points of View How do you think Mansa Musa changed people's views of West Africa?

THE GRANGER COLLECTION, NEW YORK

This Spanish map from the 1300s shows Mansa Musa sitting on his throne.

KEY FACTS

According to chroniclers of the time, Mansa Musa was accompanied on his journey to Mecca by some 60,000 people. Of those people

- **12,000** were servants to attend to the king.

- **500** were servants to attend to his wife.

- **14,000** more were slaves wearing rich fabrics such as silk.

- **500** carried staffs heavily decorated with gold. Historians have estimated that the gold Mansa Musa gave away on his trip would be worth more than $100 million today.

ANCIENT CIVILIZATIONS OF AFRICA—TRADING KINGDOMS **333**

Info to Know

Mansa Musa's Journey On his famous pilgrimage to Mecca, Mansa Musa passed through several kingdoms in North Africa. From his capital of Niani, on the Upper Niger River, Mansa Musa and his entourage of thousands traveled north to Walata, to Tuat in modern-day Algeria, then to Cairo, Egypt. From Egypt, Mansa Musa traveled to Mecca in Arabia.

Linking to Today

The Hajj A pilgrimage or journey, the hajj, is still an important ritual for Muslims today. Every year, millions of Muslims travel to Mecca for the annual hajj. During the pilgrimage, which lasts six days, pilgrims perform special rites, including circling the Kaaba, a sacred shrine, seven times. Making the hajj is one of five duties expected of every Muslim who is physically and financially able.

About the Illustration

The illustration on this page is from a fourteenth century map by Spanish mapmaker, Abraham Cresques. Mansa Musa is depicted at the bottom right of the map sitting in a throne and holding a gold scepter. This illustration of Mansa Musa is an artist's conception based on available sources. However, historians are uncertain exactly what Mansa Musa looked like.

Critical Thinking: Summarizing

At Level

Writing a Eulogy

1. Review with students the biography of Mansa Musa. Tell students that they will write a eulogy that could have been read at Mansa Musa's funeral. A eulogy is a speech given to honor someone who has died.

2. Ask students to include details found in this section in the eulogy. Encourage students to include one or two short accounts of interesting events from the life of Mansa Musa. Remind students to consider the purpose of the eulogy and their audience when choosing what to write about Mansa Musa.

3. Ask for volunteers to deliver their eulogies to the class. Discuss with students the important contributions or accomplishments of Mansa Musa. **LS Verbal/Linguistic**

   Alternative Assessment Handbook, Rubric 41: Writing to Express

---

Answers

Biography *possible answers—Mansa Musa spread new knowledge that West Africa had great wealth. This caused European and African interest in West Africa, which brought new trade and even more wealth for Mali.*

333

Bellringer

If YOU lived there. . . Use the **Daily Bellringer Transparency** to help students answer the question.

📋 Daily Bellringer Transparency, Section 5

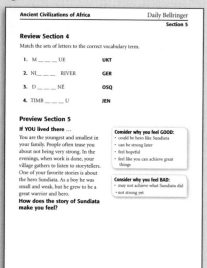

Key Terms

📖 **RF:** Vocabulary Builder, Section 5

Taking Notes

Have students copy the graphic organizer onto their own paper and then use it to take notes on the section. This activity will prepare students for the Section Assessment, in which they will complete a graphic organizer that builds on the information using the Critical Thinking Skill: Summarizing.

What You Will Learn...

Main Ideas

1. West Africans have preserved their history through storytelling and the written accounts of visitors.
2. Through art, music, and dance, West Africans have expressed their creativity and kept alive their cultural traditions.

The Big Idea

West African culture has been passed down through oral history, writings by other people, and the arts.

Key Terms

oral history, *p. 334*
griots, *p. 334*
proverbs, *p. 335*
kente, *p. 337*

TAKING NOTES As you read, take notes on West African historical and artistic traditions. Write your notes in a diagram like the one below.

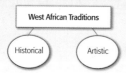

West African Traditions → Historical / Artistic

Historical and Artistic Traditions of West Africa

If YOU lived there...

You are the youngest and smallest in your family. People often tease you about not being very strong. In the evenings, when work is done, your village gathers to listen to storytellers. One of your favorite stories is about the hero Sundiata. As a boy he was small and weak, but he grew to be a great warrior and hero.

How does the story of Sundiata make you feel?

BUILDING BACKGROUND Although trading empires rose and fell in West Africa, many traditions continued through the centuries. In every town and village, storytellers passed on the people's histories, legends, and wise sayings. These were at the heart of West Africa's arts and cultural traditions.

Preserving History

Writing was never very common in West Africa. In fact, none of the major early civilizations of West Africa developed a written language. Arabic was the only written language they used. The lack of a native written language does not mean that the people of West Africa didn't know their history, though. They passed along information through oral histories. An **oral history** is a spoken record of past events. The task of remembering and telling West Africa's history was entrusted to storytellers.

The Griots

The storytellers of early West Africa were called **griots** (GREE-ohz). They were highly respected in their communities because the people of West Africa were very interested in the deeds of their ancestors. Griots helped keep this history alive for each new generation.

Teach the Big Idea

Historical and Artistic Traditions of West Africa

1. **Teach** Ask students the questions in the Main Idea boxes under Direct Teach.

2. **Apply** Have students create a two-columned chart, labeling the columns *Historical Traditions* and *Artistic Traditions*. In one column, have students list how we have learned about West Africa's past. In the other column, have students identify art forms from West Africa. Then ask: What problems might result from keeping history only in oral form? *Facts might be forgotten or distorted.* What West African artistic

traditions influence our world? *styles of music such as jazz, blues, and rock; sculpture; and traditional dances*
   LS Verbal/Linguistic

3. **Review** Have students exchange charts and discuss the answers to the questions.

4. **Practice/Homework** Have students create a collage that depicts the historical and artistic traditions of West Africa.
   LS Visual/Spatial
   📋 Alternative Assessment Handbook, Rubrics 8: Collages; and 13: Graphic Organizers

The griots' stories were both entertaining and informative. They told of important past events and of the accomplishments of distant ancestors. For example, some stories explained the rise and fall of the West African empires. Other stories described the actions of powerful kings and warriors. Some griots made their stories more lively by acting out the events like scenes in a play.

In addition to stories, the griots recited **proverbs**, or short sayings of wisdom or truth. They used proverbs to teach lessons to the people. For example, one West African proverb warns, "Talking doesn't fill the basket in the farm." This proverb reminds people that they must work to accomplish things. It is not enough for people just to talk about what they want to do.

In order to tell their stories and proverbs, the griots memorized hundreds of names and events. Through this process the griots passed on West African history from generation to generation. However, some griots confused names and events in their heads. When this happened, the facts of some historical events became distorted. Still, the griots' stories tell us a great deal about life in the West African empires.

West African Epics

Some of the griot poems are epics—long poems about kingdoms and heroes. Many of these epic poems are collected in the *Dausi* (DAW-zee) and the *Sundiata*.

The *Dausi* tells the history of Ghana. Intertwined with historical events, though, are myths and legends. One story is about a seven-headed snake god named Bida. This god promised that Ghana would prosper if the people sacrificed a young woman to him every year. One year a mighty warrior killed Bida. As the god died, he cursed Ghana. The griots say that this curse caused the empire of Ghana to fall.

The *Sundiata* is about Mali's great ruler. According to the epic, when Sundiata was still a boy, a conqueror captured Mali and killed Sundiata's father and 11 brothers.

Oral Traditions

West African storytellers called griots had the job of remembering and passing on their people's history. Here, people gather to perform traditional dances and to listen to the stories of a griot.

ANCIENT CIVILIZATIONS OF AFRICA—TRADING KINGDOMS **335**

Direct Teach

Main Idea

❶ Preserving History

West Africans have preserved their history through storytelling and the written accounts of visitors.

Recall What are proverbs, and what are they intended to do? *short sayings of wisdom or truth; to teach a lesson or provide a warning*

Identify Name two West African epic poems and the subject of each. Dausi—*the history of Ghana; tells the story of the killing of the god, Bida, and of the decline of Ghana;* Sundiata—*tells the story of Mali's first great ruler; how Sundiata overthrew the ruler and became king*

Make Judgments Why do you think griots were so valued in West African society? *because their stories were both informative and entertaining*

Activity **Epic Poem Illustrations** Ask students to select a scene from one of the epic poems discussed in this section. Then have each student create an illustration that depicts that scene. **LS Visual/Spatial**
Alternative Assessment Handbook, Rubric 3: Artwork

Linking to Today

Griots of Mali Griots are alive and active in Mali today. They still sing and tell stories in villages across the country. In fact, some wealthy nobles in modern Mali even employ their own personal griot to remind them of their family's past. Several griots have achieved international fame. Singers such as Salif Keita and Ali Farke Toure continue the griot tradition by touring the world and selling recordings of their music.

Differentiating Instruction

At Level

English-Language Learners

1. Review with the class the use of oral histories in West Africa.

2. Organize the class into small groups of mixed-ability levels. Instruct group members to create oral histories that describe a story they know well. Each group should have a different story. To help students think of stories, suggest well-known stories like the first Thanksgiving, Christopher Columbus's voyage to the Americas, or an event from a recent unit of study.

3. Group members should discuss details of the story. Remind students that oral histories often try to teach a lesson. Encourage students to memorize their oral history and to try to use language that will entertain their listeners.

4. Have each group perform its oral history for the rest of the class. Encourage students to set their oral history to music, if they wish. **LS Auditory/Musical, Interpersonal**
Alternative Assessment Handbook, Rubrics 14: Group Activity; and 24: Oral Presentations

Preserving History,
continued

West Africans have preserved their history through storytelling and the written accounts of visitors.

Explain How do we know the history of early West Africa if the people of West Africa left no written histories? *from oral histories and the writings of travelers and scholars from Muslim lands*

Identify What is included in Ibn Battutah's account of his journey to West Africa? *details of the political and cultural lives of West Africans*

Linking to Today

Pop Music Western pop music has influenced African music over the past several decades. Pop music, in particular, has become a part of modern African life. African musicians borrow ideas freely from Western music while adding their own unique sounds. The result of this blending process is called Afro-pop. This vibrant music, which one can hear everywhere in African cities, now influences Western pop artists in return.

Answers

Focus on Reading *possible answer—People today are able to learn about the history of West Africa.*

Reading Check *They were the only forms of recording or remembering West African history.*

CONNECTING TO the Arts

Music from Mali to Memphis

Did you know that the music you listen to today may have begun with the griots? From the 1600s to the 1800s, many people from West Africa were brought to America as slaves. In America, these slaves continued to sing the way they had in Africa. They also continued to play traditional instruments such as the *kora* played by Senegalese musician Soriba Kouyaté (right), the son of a griot. Over time, this music developed into a style called the blues, made popular by such artists as B. B. King (left). In turn, the blues shaped other styles of music, including jazz and rock. So, the next time you hear a Memphis blues track or a cool jazz tune, listen for its ancient African roots!

He didn't kill Sundiata, however, because the boy was sick and didn't seem like a threat. But Sundiata grew up to be an expert warrior. Eventually he overthrew the conqueror and became king.

Visitors' Written Accounts

FOCUS ON READING
What is one effect of visitors' written accounts of West Africa?

In addition to the oral histories told about West Africa, visitors wrote about the region. In fact, much of what we know about early West Africa comes from the writings of travelers and scholars from Muslim lands such as Spain and Arabia.

Ibn Battutah was the most famous Muslim visitor to write about West Africa. From 1353 to 1354 he traveled through the region. Ibn Battutah's account of this journey describes the political and cultural lives of West Africans in great detail.

READING CHECK **Drawing Conclusions** Why were oral traditions important in West Africa?

Art, Music, and Dance

Like most peoples, West Africans valued the arts. They expressed themselves creatively through sculpture, mask-making, cloth-making, music, and dance.

Sculpture

Of all the visual art forms, the sculpture of West Africa is probably the best known. West Africans made ornate statues and carvings out of wood, brass, clay, ivory, stone, and other materials.

Most statues from West Africa are of people—often the sculptor's ancestors. Usually these statues were made for religious rituals, to ask for the ancestors' blessings. Sculptors made other statues as gifts for the gods. These sculptures were kept in holy places. They were never meant to be seen by people.

Because their statues were used in religious rituals, many African artists were

---

Critical Thinking: Analyzing Visuals | **At Level**

Art Appreciation

Research Required

1. Review with the class the importance of art to West African life. Ask students to recall the various artistic traditions of West Africa.

2. Ask students to think about pieces of art they may have seen in pictures or museums and what they may reveal about the artist's culture or heritage. To help students understand, show them a painting or sculpture with which they may be familiar.

3. Have students use the library, Internet, or other resources to research different types of African art. Have students select two

images to analyze. Ask students to note any background information that gives clues about the artist's society, culture, or heritage.

4. Have students write a brief analysis for each image they select. They should explain how each artwork reflects the culture in which it was created. **LS Verbal/Linguistic, Visual/Spatial**

Alternative Assessment Handbook, Rubric 37: Writing Assignments

deeply respected. People thought artists had been blessed by the gods.

Long after the decline of Ghana, Mali, and Songhai, West African art is still admired. Museums around the world display African art. In addition, African sculpture inspired some European artists of the 1900s, including Henri Matisse and Pablo Picasso.

Masks and Clothing

In addition to statues, the artists of West Africa carved elaborate masks. Made of wood, these masks bore the faces of animals such as hyenas, lions, monkeys, and antelopes. Artists often painted the masks after carving them. People wore the masks during rituals as they danced around fires. The way firelight reflected off the masks made them look fierce and lifelike.

Many African societies were famous for the cloth they wove. The most famous of these cloths is called kente (ken-TAY). **Kente** is a hand-woven, brightly colored fabric. The cloth was woven in narrow strips that were then sewn together. Kings and queens in West Africa wore garments made of kente for special occasions.

Music and Dance

In many West African societies, music and dance were as important as the visual arts. Singing, drumming, and dancing were great entertainment, but they also helped people honor their history and mark special occasions. For example, music was played when a ruler entered a room.

Dance has long been a central part of African society. Many West African cultures used dance to celebrate specific events or ceremonies. For example, they may have performed one dance for weddings and another for funerals. In some parts of West Africa, people still perform dances similar to those performed hundreds of years ago.

READING CHECK **Summarizing** Summarize how traditions were preserved in West Africa.

SUMMARY AND PREVIEW The societies of West Africa did not have written languages but preserved their histories and cultures through storytelling and the arts. Next, you will learn about one kingdom whose history has been passed on through such traditions, Benin.

go.hrw.com
Online Quiz
KEYWORD: SK9 HP11

Section 5 Assessment

Reviewing Ideas, Terms, and Places

1. **a. Define** What is **oral history**?
   b. Make Generalizations Why were **griots** and their stories important in West African society?
   c. Evaluate Why may an oral history provide different information than a written account of the same event?
2. **a. Identify** What were two forms of visual art popular in West Africa?
   b. Make Inferences Why do you think that the sculptures made as gifts for the gods were not meant to be seen by people?
   c. Elaborate What role did music and dance play in West African society?

Critical Thinking

3. **Summarizing** Use a chart like this one and your notes to summarize the importance of each tradition in West Africa.

Tradition	Importance
Storytelling	
Epics	
Sculpture	

FOCUS ON WRITING

4. **Identifying West African Traditions** Think about the arts and how they affected people who lived in the West African empires. Would you create a journal of one of these artists? Or would you create a journal of someone who is affected by the arts or artists?

Section 5 Assessment Answers

1. **a.** a spoken record of past events
   b. The griots helped keep history alive for each new generation.
   c. possible answer—because people sometimes confuse and embellish facts
2. **a.** sculpture, masks, cloth
   b. possible answer—Statues were personalized and holy gifts to the gods.
   c. Music and dance were used to honor and celebrate people and events.

3. Storytelling—griots helped preserve history and traditions through oral history; Epics—*Dausi* tells the history of Ghana and *Sundiata* tells the story of Mali's first great ruler; Sculpture—has lasted through the ages and has influenced contemporary artists

4. Answers will vary, but students should explain why they picked either an artist or someone affected by the arts or artists.

Direct Teach

Main Idea

❷ **Art, Music, and Dance**
Through art, music, and dance, West Africans have expressed their creativity and kept alive their cultural traditions.

Identify What is the best known visual art form of West Africa? *sculpture*

Recall How were masks used in West African culture? *Dancers wore the masks during rituals.*

Analyze Why were singing and dancing so important in West Africa? *Besides being forms of entertainment, they were creative expressions and they helped people honor their history and most special occasions.*

Review & Assess

Close

Have students discuss the elements of historical and artistic traditions that have had a lasting effect on West Africa. Ask students to identify elements that still exist today.

Review

Online Quiz, Section 5

Assess

SE Section 5 Assessment
PASS: Section 5 Quiz
Alternative Assessment Handbook

Reteach/Classroom Intervention

Interactive Reader and Study Guide, Section 5
Interactive Skills Tutor CD-ROM

Answers

Reading Check *through the arts, such as sculpture, the making of masks and cloth, music, and dance*

Making Decisions

1. Ask students to take a few minutes and identify a decision they have made recently or one they need to make in the near future. These might include things like trying out for a school activity or sport, choosing school classes, spending or saving money, and so on.

2. Ask students to draw a graphic organizer like the one shown to detail the process of making the decision. They should list at least one positive consequence and one negative consequence for each option.

3. Ask volunteer to share their decisions and graphic organizers with the class. Encourage students to ask questions and suggest possible additions to negative and positive consequences listed. **LS Intrapersonal, Visual/Spatial**

📑 Alternative Assessment Handbook, Rubric 13: Graphic Organizers

💿 Interactive Skills Tutor CD-ROM, Lesson 16: Identify Possible Solutions and Predict Consequences

📑 RF: Social Studies Skills, Making Decisions

Answers

Practice 1. *possible answers: positive—fun, companionship; negative—work to care for pet, expense; possible damage to house;* **2.** *possible answers: positive—more money for other things, less work to care for pet; negative—less fun, companionship* **3.** *possible answer—yes; it is worth the cost and effort; no, there are too many problems associated with getting a pet*

Apply *Answers will vary, but students' paragraphs should include the understanding and weighing of positive and negative consequences. Students' paragraphs should reflect a thoughtful decision.*

338

Making Decisions

Learn

You make decisions every day. Some decisions are very easy to make and take little time. Others are much harder. Regardless of how easy or hard a decision is, it will have consequences, or results. These consequences can be either positive or negative.

Before you make a decision, consider all your possible options. Think about the possible consequences of each option and decide which will be best for you. Thinking about the consequences of your decision beforehand will allow you to make a better, more thoughtful decision.

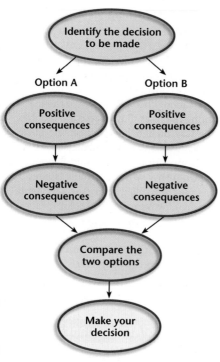

Practice

Imagine your parents have given you the option of getting a new pet. Use a graphic organizer like the one on this page to help you decide whether to get one.

❶ What are the consequences of getting a pet? Which of these consequences are positive? Which are negative?

❷ What are the consequences of not getting a pet? Which of them are positive? Which are negative?

❸ Compare your two options. Look at the positive and negative consequences of each option. Based on these consequences, do you think you should get a pet?

Apply

Imagine that your school has just received money to build either a new art studio or a new track. School officials have asked students to vote on which of these new facilities they would prefer, and you have to decide which option you think would be better for the school. Use a graphic organizer like the one above to consider the consequences of each option. Compare your lists, and then make your decision. Write a short paragraph to explain your decision.

338 CHAPTER 11

Social Studies Skills Activity: Making Decisions   [At Level]

Weighing Consequences

1. Identify a personal, local, national, or international decision that has been made recently or one that needs to be made in the near future. These might include buying a new or different car, a local law or bylaw such as a teen curfew, national spending priorities, going to war, and so on.

2. Draw a graphic organizer on the board or ask a student volunteer to do it. Label the decision and options.

3. Guide students through a group discussion and listing of consequences. Allow them to brainstorm to come up with ideas.

4. Ask individual students to compare the two options and weigh positives and negatives. Assist them in giving weight to different issues.

5. Ask each student to write a sentence or two with their personal choice as well as an explanation of which factor (consequence) was most important to them. **LS Interpersonal, Intrapersonal**

📑 Alternative Assessment Handbook, Rubric 41: Writing to Express

Geography's Impact
video series
Review the video to answer the closing question:
Why was the salt trade important to African civilizations before the 1600s?

Answers

Visual Summary

Use the visual summary below to help you review the main ideas of the chapter.

QUICK
FACTS

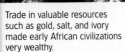
Trade in valuable resources such as gold, salt, and ivory made early African civilizations very wealthy.

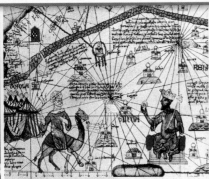
Kush, Ghana, Mali, and Songhai built powerful kingdoms through trade and conquest.

The history of West Africa has been preserved through story-telling, visitors' accounts, art, music, and dance.

Reviewing Vocabulary, Terms, and Places

Choose the letter of the answer that best completes each statement below.

1. One of Kush's most valuable exports was a dark wood called
   a. ebony.   c. gold.
   b. ivory.   d. salt.

2. Mali's rise to power began under a ruler named
   a. Tunka Manin.   c. Ibn Battutah.
   b. Sunni Ali.   d. Sundiata.

3. A spoken record of the past is
   a. a Soninke.   c. a Gao.
   b. an oral history. d. an age-set proverb.

4. A West African storyteller is
   a. an Almoravid.   c. an arquebus.
   b. a griot.   d. a rift.

Comprehension and Critical Thinking

SECTION 1 *(pages 310–314)*

5. **a. Describe** How did the physical geography of Nubia affect civilization in the region?

   b. Analyze Why did the relationship between Kush and Egypt change more than once?

   c. Predict If an archaeologist found an artifact near the Fourth Cataract, why might he or she have difficulty deciding how to display it in a museum?

SECTION 2 *(pages 315–319)*

6. **a. Identify** Who was Queen Shanakhdakheto? Why don't we know more about her?

   b. Compare and Contrast What are some features that Kushite and Egyptian cultures had in common? How were they different?

   c. Evaluate What do you think was the most important cause of Kush's decline? Why?

Visual Summary

Review and Inquiry Have students use the visual summary to explain the history of Africa's trading kingdoms.

🔲 Quick Facts Transparency: Visual Summary: Ancient Civilizations of Africa—Trading Kingdoms

Reviewing Vocabulary, Terms, and Places

1. a   **3.** b
2. d   **4.** b

Comprehension and Critical Thinking

5. **a.** The Nile's flooding allowed farmers to plant both summer and winter crops, which allowed farming villages to thrive. Cataracts on the Nile provided protection from invasion.
   b. Egypt conquered and ruled Kush and later Kush conquered Egypt.
   c. because Egypt conquered Kush above the fifth cataract, which would make it hard to determine whether the artifact was Kushite or Egyptian; also because Kush and Egypt shared styles

6. **a.** probably the first woman to rule Kush; because historians cannot read Meroitic writing
   b. similar—building styles, clothing styles, some gods, title of pharaoh, pyramids; different—housing styles, written languages, some unique gods, women had more power in Kush

---

Review and Assessment Resources

Review and Reinforce

SE Chapter Review
📄 **RF:** Chapter Review
🔲 Quick Facts Transparency: Visual Summary: Ancient Civilizations of Africa—Trading Kingdoms
🔊 Spanish Chapter Summaries Audio CD Program
OSP Holt PuzzlePro; Quiz Show for ExamView
💽 Quiz Game CD-ROM

Assess

SE Standardized Test Practice
📄 PASS: Chapter Test, Forms A and B
📄 Alternative Assessment Handbook
OSP ExamView Test Generator, Chapter Test
💽 Differentiated Instruction Modified Worksheets and Tests CD-ROM: Modified Chapter Test
HOAP Holt Online Assessment Program (in the Holt Interactive Online Student Edition)

Reteach/Intervene

📄 Interactive Reader and Study Guide
📄 Differentiated Instruction Teacher Management System: Lesson Plans
💽 Differentiated Instruction Modified Worksheets and Tests CD-ROM
💽 Interactive Skills Tutor CD-ROM

go.hrw.com
Online Resources

Chapter Resources:
KEYWORD: SK9 CH11

c. Students' answers may vary but should include support for their answer. Possible causes include overgrazing, lack of wood, and decline in iron production.

7. a. Gold and salt

b. possible answers—because the traders might mine the gold for themselves; Ghana would lose its position of power and control

c. possible answers: Ghana—they rebelled in about 1200, weakening the country; outsiders—Invaders called Almoravids attacked and weakened Ghana and overgrazed their lands.

8. a. Arabic became a major language; many mosques were built; schools were built to teach Muslims to read the Qur'an.

b. similar—Both were great rulers; both increased the wealth of the country. different—Mansa Musa was Muslim and he stressed Islam and learning; his death began the decline of the Mali empire. Sundiata was not Muslim; his rule marked the beginning of Mali's power.

c. warriors—The warriors kept peace; traders—They helped keep the nation's economy strong.

9. a. history and the deeds of people's ancestors

b. Visitors, such as Ibn Battutah, describe in their writings the political and cultural lives of Africans; unlike oral histories, writings are not open to changes over time.

c. possible answer—music and dance, which helped people celebrate their history and were central to many religious celebrations

Social Studies Skills

10. Students' responses will vary, but should include lists of the consequences of trading either item and a final decision about which item they would trade.

Focus on Reading and Writing

11. trade between regions with different resources, such as gold and salt

12. Mali became wealthy and powerful under his leadership, and Islam began to spread through West Africa.

SECTION 3 (pages 320–325)

7. a. Identify What were the two major trade goods that made Ghana rich?

b. Make Inferences Why did merchants in Ghana not want other traders to know where their gold came from?

c. Evaluate Who do you think was more responsible for the collapse of Ghana, the people of Ghana or outsiders? Why?

SECTION 4 (pages 328–332)

8. a. Describe How did Islam influence society in Mali?

b. Compare and Contrast How were Sundiata and Mansa Musa similar? How were they different?

c. Evaluate Which group do you think played a larger role in Songhai, warriors or traders?

SECTION 5 (pages 334–337)

9. a. Recall What different types of information did griots pass on to their listeners?

b. Analyze Why are the writings of visitors to West Africa so important?

c. Evaluate Which of the various arts of West Africa do you think is most important? Why?

Social Studies Skills

10. Making Decisions You are a young trader in Kush and must decide which good you would prefer to trade, pottery or iron. List the consequences that might result from trading each of them. Then make a decision.

FOCUS ON READING AND WRITING

Understanding Cause and Effect *Answer the following questions about causes and effects.*

11. What caused the empire of Ghana to grow?

12. What were some effects of Mansa Musa's rule?

Writing Your Journal Entry *Use your notes and the instructions below to help you create your news report.*

13. Review your notes on possible subjects for your journal entry. Choose one, and think about an experience that person might write about in his or her journal. Write a journal entry of a paragraph or two.

Using the Internet

14. Activity: Writing a Proverb Does the early bird get the worm? If you go outside at sunrise to check, you missed the fact that this is a proverb that means "The one that gets there first can earn something good." Griots created many proverbs that expressed wisdom or truth. Enter the activity keyword. Then use the Internet resources to write three proverbs that might have been said by griots during the time of the great West African empires. Make sure your proverbs are written from the point of view of a West African person living during those centuries.

Map Activity ★Interactive

15. West Africa On a separate sheet of paper, match the letters on the map with their correct labels.

Senegal River   Timbuktu
Lake Chad   Niger River
Gulf of Guinea

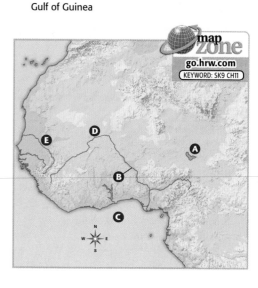

Using the Internet

14. Go to the HRW Web site and enter the keyword shown to access a rubric for this activity.

KEYWORD: SK9 TEACHER

Map Activity

15. A. Lake Chad
B. Niger River
C. Gulf of Guinea
D. Timbuktu
E. Senegal River

Education also became more important, and many mosques were built.

📄 **RF:** Focus on Reading: Understanding Cause and Effect

13. Rubric Students' journal entries should:

- mention sights, sounds, and activities that are appropriate to the time and place
- tell how the character feels about his or her experiences
- place the character within the larger organizations and events of the time
- use plenty of sensory details

📄 **RF:** Focus on Writing: Writing a Journal Entry

Standardized Test Practice

Standardized Test Practice

DIRECTIONS (1–6): For each statement or question, write on a separate answer sheet the *number* of the word or expression that, of those given, best completes the statement or answers the question.

1 The wealth of Ghana, Mali, and Songhai was based on

(1) raiding other tribes.

(2) the gold and salt trade.

(3) trade in ostriches and elephant tusks.

(4) making iron tools and weapons.

2 The two rulers who were most responsible for spreading Islam in West Africa were

(1) Sunni Ali and Mansa Musa.

(2) Sundiata and Sunni Ali.

(3) Ibn Battutah and Tunka Manin.

(4) Mansa Musa and Askia the Great.

3 Which of the following statements regarding women in ancient Kush is true?

(1) Some Kushite women served as religious and political leaders.

(2) Kushite women had more rights and opportunities than Kushite men.

(3) Kushite women were forbidden to leave their homes.

(4) Many Kushite women were wealthy merchants.

4 Griots contributed to West African societies by

(1) fighting battles.

(2) collecting taxes.

(3) preserving oral history.

(4) trading with the Berbers.

5 Which of the following rivers helped the development of Ghana and Mali?

(1) Niger

(2) Congo

(3) Nile

(4) Zambezi

6 How did cataracts on the Nile River benefit Kush?

(1) They allowed Kushite farmers to plant both summer and winter crops.

(2) Because they were highly prized by the Egyptians, Kush gained wealth from trade.

(3) Because they were difficult to pass through, they provided protection against invaders.

(4) They allowed the Kushites to build a powerful army.

Base your answer to question 7 on the text excerpt below and on your knowledge of social studies.

> "Well placed for the caravan trade, it was badly situated to defend itself from the Tuareg raiders of the Sahara. These restless nomads were repeatedly hammering at the gates of Timbuktu, and often enough they burst them open with disastrous results for the inhabitants. Life here was never quite safe enough to recommend it as the centre [center] of a big state."
>
> —Basil Davidson, from *A History of West Africa*

7 Constructed-Response Question The location of the city of Timbuktu had both advantages and drawbacks. List one positive and one negative effect of the city's location.

1. 2

Break Down the Question Refer students to the section on Trade in Valuable Goods in Section 3. Point out that Mali and Songhai participated in the same trade as Ghana.

2. 4

Break Down the Question This question requires students to recall factual information from Section 2.

3. 1

Break Down the Question Remind students who miss the question that Kushite women were expected to take on active roles in the kingdom's society.

4. 3

Break Down the Question This question requires students to recall factual information from Section 5.

5. 1

Break Down the Question Students should recall from their reading that the Niger River was important to the development of Ghana and Mali.

6. 3

Break Down the Question Remind students that cataracts, or a stretch of rapids in a river, can make it difficult to travel by boat.

7. Constructed-Response Question positive—well placed for the caravan trade; negative—badly situated to defend against the Tuareg raiders of the Sahara

Intervention Resources

Reproducible

📄 Interactive Reader and Study Guide

📄 Differentiated Instruction Teacher Management System: Lesson Plans

Technology

💾 Quick Facts Transparency: Visual Summary: Ancient Civilizations of Africa—Trading Kingdoms

💿 Differentiated Instruction Modified Worksheets and Tests CD-ROM

💿 Interactive Skills Tutor CD-ROM

Tips for Test Taking

Look All Around If the test item asks for vocabulary knowledge, look at the surrounding sentences, or context, to see which definition fits. To identify the best definition of an underlined word as it is used in the **context,** consider the surrounding words and phrases.

The Kingdom of Benin

This ivory mask pendant was worn by the *oba*, or king, of Benin.

History

Although the trading empires of Ghana, Mali, and Songhai were the largest states in West Africa, they were not the only ones. Farther south, a number of kingdoms grew up in the forests that lined the Niger River. Among them was the kingdom of Benin (buh-NEEN), which reached its height in the 1400s. (Although the two share a name, the kingdom was not in the same location as the modern country of Benin. The kingdom was farther east, in what is now Nigeria.)

According to legend, the first people of Benin—the Edo—were ruled by the Kings of the Sky. Over time, the Edo grew unhappy with these kings. In the late 1100s the Edo invited the prince of a nearby kingdom to be their new ruler. The prince ruled Benin until his first son was born, after which he returned home. His son became the first *oba*, or king, of Benin.

Perhaps Benin's most famed *oba* was Ewuare (e-WOO-AH-reh), who ruled from about 1440 to about 1470. He was a great military leader who added new lands to the kingdom. Ewuare was also a skilled administrator. He reorganized Benin's political system and expanded the capital, Benin City.

Shortly after Ewuare's death, Portuguese sailors arrived in Benin. Because Benin had been at war for many years, its people had many captives they could sell to the Portuguese as slaves. The slave trade between Benin and Portugal continued for many years. Benin also traded goods such as pepper, ivory, and cotton. In the mid-1500s the English arrived in Benin, wanting to trade. They were particularly interested in palm oil from Benin's palm trees. Palm oil soon became Benin's main export.

Soldiers guard the palace of the *oba* in this bronze plaque from ancient Benin.

342 CASE STUDY

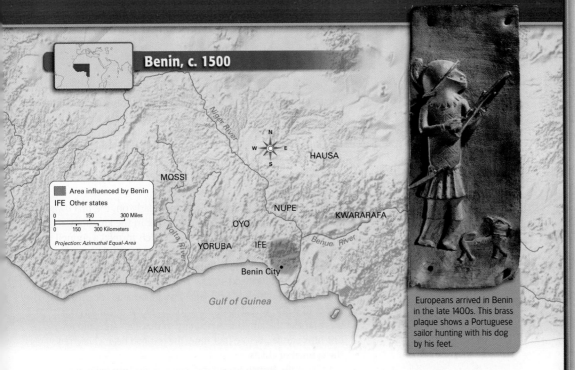

Benin, c. 1500

Area influenced by Benin
IFE Other states

MOSSI
HAUSA
NUPE
KWARARAFA
OYO
YORUBA   IFE
AKAN   Benin City
Benue River
Niger River
Volta River
Gulf of Guinea

0   150   300 Miles
0   150   300 Kilometers
Projection: Azimuthal Equal-Area

Europeans arrived in Benin in the late 1400s. This brass plaque shows a Portuguese sailor hunting with his dog by his feet.

Trade between Benin and Europeans continued for many years. In the late 1800s, British officials proposed a treaty that would have made Benin into a colony, but the *oba* rejected it. The British sent troops toward Benin City to force the treaty. Fearing a British attack, some royal guards ambushed and killed the troops. In response, the British army attacked Benin City in force in 1897. They looted the city, burned it to the ground, and forced the reigning *oba* into exile. This attack marked the end of the kingdom of Benin.

Case Study Assessment

1. According to legend, how did the first *oba* come to power in Benin?

2. Why did the British attack Benin City?

3. **Activity** Ancient rulers often gave gifts to show their kingdoms' wealth or power. Plan a gift that the *oba* might have sent to impress the king of Portugal.

Leopards were a symbol of royal authority in Benin. These bronze leopards were made in the 1500s.

THE KINGDOM OF BENIN **343**

Society and Daily Life

Explain How do we know what we know about ancient Benin? *oral history; because people of the region have passed down stories over many generations*

Describe How did the power of the *obas* change over time? *The first obas did not have much real power. Real power rested with a council of chiefs. Later* obas *increased their power over the chiefs until their power became absolute. Later still,* obas *lost nearly all power when the British took over the region.*

Make Judgments If you had lived in the kingdom of Benin, would you have preferred to live in Benin City or the countryside? Explain your answer. *possible answer—Benin City, because life in the kingdom centered around the capital, and the city was safe from attack because it was surrounded by a wall and a moat*

Quick Facts Transparency: Modern Edo Society

Society and Daily Life

Very little remains of ancient Benin. The destruction of Benin City by the British made later study of the culture much more difficult. As a result, much of what we know today about ancient Benin comes from oral history. Inhabitants of the region have passed down stories about the kingdom and its people over many generations.

Government

Although Benin was ruled by *obas* from early on, the first *obas* did not have much power. Instead, power in the kingdom rested mostly with local chiefs. These chiefs formed a council that was supposed to advise the *oba* about decisions. In truth, however, members of the council made most decisions.

In the late 1200s and 1300s, *obas* began to increase their power over the chiefs. By the time Ewuare became *oba*, his power in Benin was absolute. One of his major actions as *oba* was to make the kingship hereditary so that his son could follow him as ruler. Before that time, the *oba* had been chosen by the council of chiefs.

When the British forced the reigning *oba* into exile in 1897, he lost most of his authority. However, he did not abandon his title. In fact, Benin still has an *oba*. The current holder

Modern Edo Society

QUICK FACTS

Although the kingdom of Benin is long gone, the Edo live on in Nigeria. Many elements of modern Edo culture resemble those of the ancient kingdom.

■ An *oba* still serves as the symbolic leader of the Edo people. He has little power himself, but the *oba* advises political officials in southern Nigeria.

■ Most of the Edo live in villages and towns. These can range in size from a few dozen people to several thousand. Many Edo also live in modern Benin City.

■ Within Edo villages, coucils of elders have great authority. These councils make decisions about village responsibilities and religious matters. They also handle relations between the village and the Nigerian government.

■ Most Edo today are farmers. They grow crops such as yams, corn, plantains, and cassava. Some Edo are herders, raising goats, sheep, and chickens.

■ Today many Edo are Christians or Muslims.

Oba Erediauwa leads a thanksgiving festival, an annual ceremony to celebrate the end of the year.

344 CASE STUDY

Critical Thinking: Predicting

At Level

Writing a Letter to the *Oba*

1. Review the information about the arrival of the Portuguese and the British in Benin with students. Ask students to consider the positive and negative effects of contact between Europeans and the Edo people. How might increased trade have benefited the Edo? How might foreign interference have hurt the Edo?

2. Have each student make a list of the possible outcomes of increased contact between Europeans and the people of Benin in the period from the sixteenth to the nineteenth

centuries. Have students categorize the possible outcomes as positive and negative.

3. Then have students write a letter to the *oba* of Benin to inform him of the predictions they have made about contact with Europeans. Encourage students to make suggestions for how the *oba* could prepare for each result.

4. Have volunteers share their letters with the class. **LS** **Verbal/Linguistic**

Alternative Assessment Handbook, Rubrics 37: Writing Assignments

Benin City

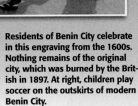

Residents of Benin City celebrate in this engraving from the 1600s. Nothing remains of the original city, which was burned by the British in 1897. At right, children play soccer on the outskirts of modern Benin City.

of the title, Erediauwa I, became *oba* in 1979. Although he has no official power, Oba Erediauwa has great influence on politics in southern Nigeria, the area that was once the kingdom of Benin.

Daily Life

Life in the kingdom of Benin centered around the capital, Benin City. The city was immense. Despite its huge size, the entire city was surrounded by a wall and a moat.

European visitors to Benin City in the 1600s were amazed by its size and splendor, comparing it favorably to some of Europe's major cities. The largest structure in town was the royal palace. Surrounded by courtyards, the palace took up about a fifth of the city. Its walls were covered with brass plaques that showed images of great *obas* from the past. On the roof, bronze and brass birds posed as if about to take flight. Surrounding the royal palace were smaller palaces and houses for Benin's nobles. Like the royal palace, these houses were lavishly decorated with brass, bronze, and ivory.

Case Study Assessment

1. What powers did Benin's *obas* have?
2. Why were Europeans impressed by Benin City?
3. **Activity** Imagine that you are a European sailor who has just arrived in Benin City. Write a letter to your family, describing what you see as you explore the city.

THE KINGDOM OF BENIN **345**

Checking for Understanding

True or False Answer each statement *T* if it is true or *F* if it is false. If false, explain why.

1. Written records provide historians with most of what is known about ancient Benin. *F; Most of what is known about ancient Benin comes from oral history.*

2. *Obas* first had absolute power, then later were forced to share power with a council of chiefs. *F; Obas at first shared power with a council of chiefs, then later had absolute power.*

3. There is no *oba* of Benin today. *F; There is an oba of Benin today—Oba Erediauwa.*

4. Benin City was comparable in size and splendor to some major European cities. *T*

5. Beninese art was typically made of clay, iron, or wood. *F; brass, bronze, or ivory*

Critical Thinking: Identifying Points of View [At Level]

The Destruction of Benin City

1. Have students review the information about Benin City and the feud between the British and the Edo that led to the city's destruction. You may wish to have students conduct additional research about the topic.

2. Then have students write two journal entries. The first entry should present the events related to the destruction of Benin City from the point of view of a native resident of the city. The second journal entry should describe the same events from the point of view of a soldier in the British army.

3. Each account should be written in the first person and begin with a description of the author. Encourage students to be as descriptive in their journal entries as possible.

4. Ask for volunteers to share their journal entries with the class. **LS Verbal/Linguistic**

📖 Alternative Assessment Handbook, Rubric 15: Journals

Answers

Case Study Assessment 1. *At first, Benin's obas had little power. Later the power of obas was absolute.* **2.** *because the city was large and splendid and comparable to European cities;* **3.** *Students' letters will vary. See Rubric 25: Personal Letters in the Alternative Assessment Handbook.*

345

1150

1180
According to legend, the first *oba* comes to power in Benin.

Brass statue of an *oba*

c. 1300
Powerful *obas* increase their control over the kingdom's nobles.

1440
Ewuare becomes *oba* and begins a policy of expansion.

1485
Portuguese sailors visit Benin City.

Direct Teach

Main Idea

Culture and Achievements

Identify Where do most of the descendants of Benin's founders now live? *in southern Nigeria, especially the Edo region*

Summarize Which elements of Beninese culture have been maintained and which have vanished? *maintained—language, and forms of music and dance; vanished—religion involving worship of many gods, goddesses, and nature spirits*

Identify Points of View How do you think the people of Benin felt about European greed for their art? *possible answer—Maybe the people of Benin were proud that their art was so desired, but also saddened and angry that so much of it was taken from them without their permission.*

Culture and Achievements

Although the kingdom of Benin is gone, many elements of its culture remain in West Africa. Descendants of the Edo who founded Benin still live in southern Nigeria, especially in the Edo region, and they have kept many elements of traditional Edo culture. The Edo language is still spoken. About 5 million people in Nigeria today speak it as their first language. In addition, the people of the Edo region have maintained many customs, including traditional forms of music and dance, that were practiced in ancient Benin.

Other customs from Benin have largely vanished. The ancient religion of Benin, for example, is not widely practiced. This religion involved the worship of many gods, goddesses, and nature spirits. When the Portuguese arrived in Benin in the 1400s, they introduced Christianity to the region. Today most of the Edo in West Africa are either Christian or Muslim.

The ancient kingdom of Benin is now best remembered for its art. The artists of Benin made intricately detailed works from brass, bronze, and ivory. For example, they used bronze to make statues of their *obas*. In addition, artists made brass plaques

Music and Dance

Music and dance have always been central to life in West Africa, and Benin was no exception. Music and dance were important elements of celebrations and religious ceremonies alike. The descendants of the people of Benin, including the Bini of Nigeria, have maintained many styles of music practiced centuries ago.

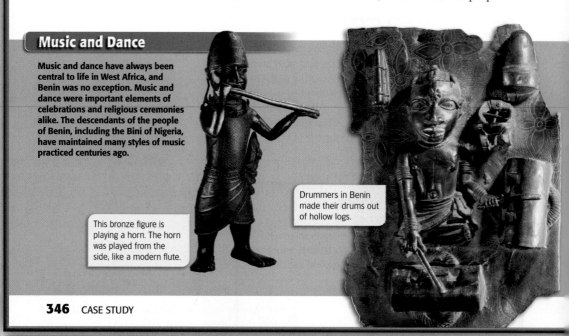

This bronze figure is playing a horn. The horn was played from the side, like a modern flute.

Drummers in Benin made their drums out of hollow logs.

346 CASE STUDY

Differentiating Instruction

Below Level

English-Language Learners

Materials: butcher paper, art supplies

Prep Required

1. Ask students to imagine that they are Edo artists during the reign of Oba Ewuare and that the *oba* has asked them to create a mural highlighting the culture and achievements of the kingdom of Benin.

2. Organize students into small groups and distribute the art supplies. If possible, place students who are proficient in English in the groups with English-language learners.

3. Have students examine the examples of Edo artwork in the section and study the material about the culture and achievements of Benin, including the "Music and Dance" feature.

4. Have each group create a mural depicting the highlights of the culture and achievements of Benin. When groups have finished, have them explain their murals to the class.
   LS Interpersonal, Visual/Spatial

   Alternative Assessment Handbook, Rubrics 3: Artwork; and 14: Group Activity

1553
The British arrive in what is now southern Nigeria.

European gun from the 1600s

1897
The British take over Benin, burning Benin City and exiling the *oba*.

1900

to celebrate great events of the past. As you have read, these plaques were used to decorate the royal palace and other buildings throughout Benin City.

European visitors to Benin were greatly impressed with the kingdom's art. In fact, many Europeans asked Benin's artists to create works for them to take home to Europe. As a result, Benin's brass plaques, bronze statues, and ivory containers were introduced to Europe. These items led to a demand for African art among Europe's wealthy. Unfortunately, this demand led to greed. When the British took over Benin in the 1800s, they carried as much art as they could back to Europe.

Case Study Assessment

1. What customs from Benin are still followed today?

2. How did art from Benin become popular in Europe?

3. **Activity** The art of Benin often portrayed great rulers or major events. Design a plaque that an artist from Benin might have created to illustrate one such event.

Traditional music in West Africa reflects the influence of ancient kingdoms like Benin.

THE KINGDOM OF BENIN **347**

Direct Teach

Primary Source

Oba Erediauwa Comments on an Exhibition of Beninese Art When British soldiers destroyed Benin City in 1897, they first looted the city of its prized art. In 2007 an exhibition of that art opened at the Museum of Ethnology in Vienna, Austria. The present Beninese king, Oba Erediauwa, was invited to write the introduction to the catalog that accompanied the exhibition. In his comments Oba Erediauwa reminded museum visitors that they were viewing objects stolen from his great grandfather's palace. He asked visitors to note that the objects "were not meant to be mere museum pieces . . . for art lovers to admire. [Rather] they were objects with religious and archival value to my people." Oba Erediauwa ended his comments with a plea to the Austrian government for a return of at least some of the stolen art.

Review & Assess

Close

Guide students in a discussion of the impact of the arrival of Europeans on the kingdom on Benin.

Assess

Alternative Assessment Handbook

Reteach/Classroom Intervention

Interactive Skills Tutor CD-ROM

Differentiating Instruction

Special Needs Learners
Below Level

1. Ask students to imagine that they are modern-day residents of the Edo region of Nigeria.

2. Have each student create a poster that encourages their fellow Edo to be proud of their cultural heritage.

3. Ask for volunteers to share their posters with the class. **LS Visual/Spatial**

Alternative Assessment Handbook, Rubric 28: Posters

Advanced/Gifted and Talented
Above Level
Research Required

1. Remind students that while the kingdom of Benin no longer exists, Edo culture is still alive and well in Nigeria.

2. Have students research and prepare a five minute multimedia presentation on modern Edo culture. Allow students time to make their presentations. **LS Verbal/Linguistic**

Alternative Assessment Handbook: Rubric 22: Multimedia Presentations

Answers
Case Study Assessment
1. *language, music, and dance;*
2. *European visitors to Benin brought art home with them.* 3. *Students' plaques will vary. See Rubric 3: Artwork in the Alternative Assessment Handbook.*

347

Chapter 12 Planning Guide

Growth and Development of Africa

Chapter Overview	Reproducible Resources	Technology Resources
CHAPTER 12 pp. 348–381 **Overview:** In this chapter, students will study the growth and development of Africa from the 1400s to today.	**Differentiated Instruction Teacher Management System:*** • Instructional Pacing Guides • Lesson Plans for Differentiated Instruction **Interactive Reader and Study Guide:** Chapter Summary Graphic Organizer* **Resource File:*** • Chapter Review • Focus on Reading: Identifying Supporting Details • Focus on Speaking: Presenting a TV News Report • Social Studies Skills: Interpreting a Population Pyramid	**OSP Teacher's One-Stop Planner:** Calendar Planner **Power Presentations with Video CD-ROM** **Differentiated Instruction Modified Worksheets and Tests CD-ROM** **Student Edition on Audio CD-ROM** **Map Zone Transparency:** Africa, 1400–Today* **Geography's Impact Video Program (VHS/DVD):** Impact of Apartheid*
Section 1: **Contact with Other Cultures** **The Big Idea:** African contact with other cultures led to major cultural changes, particularly the spread of Christianity and Islam.	**Differentiated Instruction Teacher Management System:** Section 1 Lesson Plan* **Interactive Reader and Study Guide:** Section 1 Summary* **Resource File:*** • Vocabulary Builder: Section 1	**Daily Bellringer Transparency:** Section 1* **Internet Activity:** East African Music
Section 2: **European Colonization** **The Big Idea:** Europeans established colonies in Africa to take advantage of trade in gold, ivory, slaves, and other items.	**Differentiated Instruction Teacher Management System:** Section 2 Lesson Plan* **Interactive Reader and Study Guide:** Section 2 Summary* **Resource File:*** • Vocabulary Builder: Section 2	**Daily Bellringer Transparency:** Section 2* **Internet Activity:** History of the Slave Trade
Section 3: **Imperialism in Africa** **The Big Idea:** In the late 1800s Europeans once again created colonies in Africa and became involved in African politics and economics.	**Differentiated Instruction Teacher Management System:** Section 3 Lesson Plan* **Interactive Reader and Study Guide:** Section 3 Summary* **Resource File:*** • Vocabulary Builder: Section 3 • Primary Source: Colonialism in Africa • Literature: *Western Civilization* by Agostinho Neto	**Daily Bellringer Transparency:** Section 3* **Map Zone Transparency:** Imperialism in Africa, 1914* **Internet Activity:** Suez Canal
Section 4: **Revolution and Freedom** **The Big Idea:** African colonies began to call for independence after World War II, eventually gaining their freedom.	**Differentiated Instruction Teacher Management System:** Section 4 Lesson Plan* **Interactive Reader and Study Guide:** Section 4 Summary* **Resource File:*** • Vocabulary Builder: Section 4 • Biography: Kwame Nkrumah	**Daily Bellringer Transparency:** Section 4* **Map Zone Transparency:** Independence in Africa*
Section 5: **Africa since Independence** **The Big Idea:** The people of Africa have faced both changes and challenges since they won their independence.	**Differentiated Instruction Teacher Management System:** Section 5 Lesson Plan* **Interactive Reader and Study Guide:** Section 5 Summary* **Resource File:*** • Vocabulary Builder: Section 5 • Biography: Assia Djebar	**Daily Bellringer Transparency:** Section 5* **Internet Activity:** Researching Apartheid **Internet Activity:** The African Union

SE Student Edition   Print Resource Audio CD

TE Teacher's Edition   Transparency   CD-ROM

 go.hrw.com **LS** Learning Styles   Video

OSP Teacher's One-Stop Planner   * also on One-Stop Planner

HOLT

Geography's Impact
Video Program (VHS/DVD)

Impact of Apartheid
Suggested use: in Section 5

Review, Assessment, Intervention

 Quick Facts Transparency: Visual Summary: Growth and Development of Africa*

 Spanish Chapter Summaries Audio CD Program

 Progress Assessment Support System (PASS): Chapter Test*

 Differentiated Instruction Modified Worksheets and Tests CD-ROM: Modified Chapter Test

OSP **Teacher's One-Stop Planner:** ExamView Test Generator (English/Spanish)

HOAP **Holt Online Assessment Program (HOAP),** in the Holt Interactive Online Student Edition

---

 PASS: Section 1 Quiz*

 Online Quiz: Section 1

 Alternative Assessment Handbook

 PASS: Section 2 Quiz*

 Online Quiz: Section 2

 Alternative Assessment Handbook

 PASS: Section 3 Quiz*

 Online Quiz: Section 3

 Alternative Assessment Handbook

 PASS: Section 4 Quiz*

 Online Quiz: Section 4

 Alternative Assessment Handbook

 PASS: Section 5 Quiz*

 Online Quiz: Section 5

 Alternative Assessment Handbook

Power Presentations with Video CD-ROM

Power Presentations with Video are visual presentations of each chapter's main ideas. Presentations can be customized by including Quick Facts charts, images from the text, and video clips.

Holt Online Learning

go.hrw.com
Teacher Resources
KEYWORD: SK9 TEACHER

go.hrw.com
Student Resources
KEYWORD: SK9 CH12

- Interactive Multimedia Activities
- Current Events
- Chapter-based Internet Activities
- and more!

Holt Interactive
Online Student Edition

Complete online support for interactivity, assessment, and reporting

- Interactive Maps and Notebook
- Standardized Test Prep
- Homework Practice and Research Activities Online

CHAPTER 12 PLANNING GUIDE

Differentiating Instruction

How do I address the needs of varied learners?
The Target Resource acts as your primary strategy for differentiated instruction.

ENGLISH-LANGUAGE LEARNERS & STRUGGLING READERS

Spanish Resources

Spanish Chapter Summaries Audio CD Program

Teacher's One-Stop Planner:
- ExamView Test Generator, Spanish
- PuzzlePro, Spanish

English Language Learner Strategies and Activities

Additional Resources

Differentiated Instruction Teacher Management System: Lesson Plans for Differentiated Instruction

Resource File:
- Vocabulary Builder Activities
- Social Studies Skills: Interpreting a Population Pyramid

Quick Facts Transparency: Visual Summary: Growth and Development of Africa

Student Edition on Audio CD Program

Interactive Skills Tutor CD-ROM

SPECIAL NEEDS LEARNERS

Interactive Reader and Study Guide

The activities in the Interactive Reader and Study Guide engage students with questions while presenting summaries of chapter content and provide opportunities for students to practice critical thinking skills.

Additional Resources

Differentiated Instruction Teacher Management System: Lesson Plans for Differentiated Instruction

Resource File: Social Studies Skills: Interpreting a Population Pyramid

Student Edition on Audio CD Program

Interactive Skills Tutor CD-ROM

Graphic Organizer Transparencies with Support for Reading and Writing

ADVANCED/GIFTED AND TALENTED STUDENTS

Resource File

The Resource File activities allow students to extend their knowledge of chapter-related places and people and to practice geography skills.
- Focus on Reading: Identifying Supporting Details
- Focus on Speaking: Presenting a TV News Report
- Literature: *Western Civilization*

Additional Resources

Differentiated Instruction Teacher Management System: Lesson Plans for Differentiated Instruction

World History and Geography Document-Based Questions Activities

Geography, Science, and Cultures Activities

Experiencing World History and Geography

Differentiated Activities in the Teacher's Edition

- Mapping Trade Routes
- Sharing Images of the Atlantic Slave Trade
- Describing Mansa Musa's Caravan
- Analyzing Motives for Colonizing Africa
- Analyzing a Quote
- Interpreting a Population Pyramid
- Studying Nigeria's Geography

Differentiated Activities in the Teacher's Edition

- Understanding Chronology
- Sharing Images of the Atlantic Slave Trade
- Analyzing a Quote
- African Independence Chart

Differentiated Activities in the Teacher's Edition

- Researching Ethiopia and Aksum
- Presenting Information about Kwanzaa
- Writing a Biography of an Independence Leader
- Researching Military Dictatorships
- Addressing Nigeria's Challenges

HOLT Teacher's One-Stop Planner®

How can I manage the lesson plans and support materials for differentiated instruction?

With the Teacher's One-Stop Planner, you can easily organize and print lesson plans, planning guides, and instructional materials for all learners.

The Teacher's One-Stop Planner includes the following materials to help you differentiate instruction:

- · Interactive Teacher's Edition
- · Calendar Planner and pacing guides
- · Editable lesson plans
- · All reproducible ancillaries in Adobe Acrobat (PDF) format
- · ExamView Test Generator (English & Spanish)
- · Transparency and video previews

Professional Development

What teacher training resources are available to help me grow professionally?

- · **In-service and staff development** as part of your Holt Social Studies product purchase
- · **Quick Teacher Tutorial Lesson Presentation CD-ROM**
- · Intensive tuition-based **Teacher Development Institute**
- · **Convenient Holt Speaker Bureau:** face-to-face workshop options
- · **24/7 Ask A Professional Development Expert** at http://www.hrw.com/prodev/

DIFFERENTIATED INSTRUCTION PLANNING GUIDE

Chapter Big Ideas

Section 1 African contact with other cultures led to major cultural changes, particularly the spread of Christianity and Islam.

Section 2 Europeans established colonies in Africa to take advantage of trade in gold, ivory, slaves, and other items.

Section 3 In the late 1800s Europeans once again created colonies in Africa and became involved in African politics and economics.

Section 4 African colonies began to call for independence after World War II, eventually gaining their freedom.

Section 5 The people of Africa have faced both changes and challenges since they won their independence.

Focus on Reading and Speaking

Reading The Resource File provides a Focus on Reading worksheet to help students understand how to identify supporting details.

📝 **RF:** Focus on Reading, Identifying Supporting Details

Speaking The Resource File provides a Focus on Speaking worksheet to help students plan, write, and present a television news report.

📝 **RF:** Focus on Speaking, Presenting a TV News Report

Key to Differentiating Instruction

Below Level

Basic-level activities designed for all students encountering new material

At Level

Intermediate-level activities designed for average students

Above Level

Challenging activities designed for honors and gifted and talented students

Standard English Mastery

Activities designed to improve standard English usage

348   **CHAPTER 12**

CHAPTER 12

Growth and Development of Africa

FOCUS QUESTION

What forces had an impact on the development of Africa and why?

Explorer's ship

ATLANTIC OCEAN

What You Will Learn...

In this chapter you will learn about the many influences that have shaped African culture. Both traditional cultures and outside forces have played roles in creating modern Africa.

FOCUS ON READING AND SPEAKING

Identifying Supporting Details Supporting details are the facts and examples that provide information to support a main idea. As you read this chapter, look for the details that support each section's main ideas. **See the lesson, Identifying Supporting Details, on page S15.**

Presenting a TV News Report You are a journalist assigned to create a brief TV news report on a person or event in Africa. As you read this chapter, you will collect information about Africa's history and plan your report. Later, you will present your report to the class.

348 CHAPTER 12

Europeans in Africa Europeans became involved in African affairs in order to make money for themselves.

COMPLETE INDEPENDENCE 1961

Independence Tanzanians celebrate their independence from Great Britain in 1961.

Introduce the Chapter

At Level

Growth and Development of Africa

1. Instruct each student to copy the chapter focus question on his or her own sheet of paper. Ask students what they think the question means. Help students understand that the question will focus on key events, individuals, and issues that have shaped Africa since the 1400s.

2. Have students start by examining the map on the opposite page for clues as to what forces shaped African development. Instruct students to predict how each force might have influenced the people and countries of Africa.

3. Then have students skim the chapter, identifying other forces that have shaped the development of Africa.

4. Have students work in small groups to create a poster titled "Forces that Shaped African Development." Encourage students to update their posters as they study the chapter.

LS **Visual/Spatial, Verbal/Linguistic**

📝 Alternative Assessment Handbook, Rubric 28: Posters

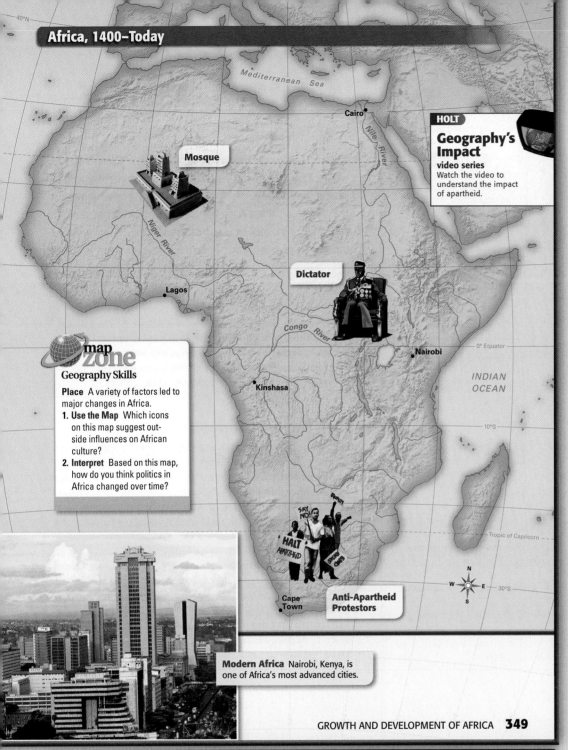

Africa, 1400–Today

Mediterranean Sea

Cairo

Mosque

HOLT

Geography's Impact
video series
Watch the video to
understand the impact
of apartheid.

Niger River

Lagos

Dictator

Congo River

0° Equator

Nairobi

**INDIAN
OCEAN**

Kinshasa

10°S

map zone

Geography Skills

Place A variety of factors led to
major changes in Africa.
1. **Use the Map** Which icons
   on this map suggest outside influences on African
   culture?
2. **Interpret** Based on this map,
   how do you think politics in
   Africa changed over time?

SAY NO!
HALT APARTHEID

Tropic of Capricorn

N
W   E
S

Cape
Town

**Anti-Apartheid
Protestors**

30°S

Modern Africa Nairobi, Kenya, is
one of Africa's most advanced cities.

GROWTH AND DEVELOPMENT OF AFRICA **349**

Chapter Preview

Explore the Map and Pictures

Africa, 1400–Today Instruct students to
study the map on this page. Ask students
to identify what each icon on the map
might mean. *explorer's ship—arrival of
Europeans; mosque—spread of Islam;
dictator—harsh, authoritarian governments after independence; anti-apartheid
protests—end of apartheid in South Africa*

Map Zone Transparency, Africa,
1400–Today

Analyzing Visuals What do the
photographs on these pages indicate
about the growth and development of
Africa? *Europeans in Africa—imperialism; independence—the independence
movement that took place after World
War II; modern Africa—the technological and economic development of
African countries*

go.hrw.com
Online Resources

Chapter Resources:
KEYWORD: SK9 CH12
Teacher Resources:
KEYWORD: SK9 TEACHER

HOLT

Geography's Impact

▶ **video series**
See the Video Teacher's Guide
for strategies for using the chapter video to teach about the
impact of apartheid.

Introduce the Chapter

At Level

Info to Know

Tanzanian Independence Originally a German
colony, Tanzania was turned over to British
control as a result of World War I. Following
World War II, the British government handed
over mainland Tanzania, known as Tanganyika,
to the UN as a trusteeship. On December 9,
1961, Tanganyika gained its complete independence from both the United Kingdom and the
UN trusteeship. Julius Nyerere, pictured above,
became the first prime minister. In 1964 Tanganyika united with the island of Zanzibar to create
the United Republic of Tanzania.

Info to Know

Nairobi, Kenya The city of Nairobi is the capital
and largest city in Kenya. Founded in the 1890s,
the city was originally a colonial railroad settlement. Around 1900 a small Indian market was
created at the settlement. From that first market,
Nairobi eventually became the trading center of
Kenya. Today Nairobi serves as the industrial
heart of the country. Transportation, manufacturing, and tourism are among the chief industries
focused in Nairobi. Pictured above is the Nairobi skyline, featuring the Times Tower, Kenya's
tallest building.

Answers

Map Zone 1. *the explorer's ship and
the mosque;* **2.** *possible answer—some
African countries were once ruled by
dictators*

349

Contact with Other Cultures

Bellringer

If YOU lived there. . . Use the **Daily Bellringer Transparency** to help students answer the question.

📖 Daily Bellringer Transparency, Section 1

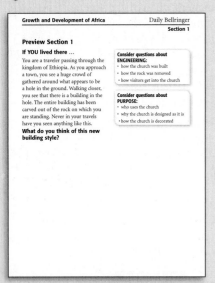

Growth and Development of Africa	Daily Bellringer
	Section 1

Preview Section 1

If YOU lived there ...
You are a traveler passing through the kingdom of Ethiopia. As you approach a town, you see a huge crowd of gathered around what appears to be a hole in the ground. Walking closer, you see that there is a building in the hole. The entire building has been carved out of the rock on which you are standing. Never in your travels have you seen anything like this.
What do you think of this new building style?

Consider questions about ENGINEERING:
• how the church was built
• how the rock was removed
• how visitors get into the church

Consider questions about PURPOSE:
• who uses the church
• why the church is designed as it is
• how the church is decorated

Key Terms and Places

📄 **RF:** Vocabulary Builder, Section 1

Taking Notes

Have students copy the graphic organizer onto their own paper and then use it to take notes on the section. This activity will prepare students for the Section Assessment, in which they will complete a graphic organizer that builds on the information using the Critical Thinking Skill: Analyzing Information.

What You Will Learn...

Main Ideas

1. Christianity arrived in North Africa by the 300s and became a major influence.
2. Trade and military conquest led to the spread of Islam through Africa.

The Big Idea

African contact with other cultures led to major cultural changes, particularly the spread of Christianity and Islam.

Key Terms and Places

Aksum, *p. 350*
Ethiopia, *p. 351*
Coptic Christianity, *p. 352*
Djenné, *p. 352*
Swahili, *p. 353*

TAKING NOTES As you read, use a diagram like this one to take notes on the influences of Christianity and Islam on the cultures of Africa.

If YOU lived there...

You are a traveler passing through the kingdom of Ethiopia. As you approach a town, you see a huge crowd of gathered around what appears to be a hole in the ground. Walking closer, you see that there is a building in the hole. The entire building has been carved out of the rock on which you are standing. Never in your travels have you seen anything like this.

What do you think of this new building style?

BUILDING BACKGROUND By the AD 600s several powerful kingdoms had arisen in various parts of Africa, each with its own distinct culture. However, the arrival of people from other cultures with their own ideas and religions led to significant changes in Africa.

Christianity in North Africa

During the days of the Roman Empire, parts of northern Africa had been closely tied to Europe. From Morocco to Egypt, the Mediterranean coast of Africa had been part of the Roman Empire. After that Empire fell apart, however, the ties between Europe and Africa disappeared. Africa's earliest civilizations were replaced by new ones that had little knowledge of Europeans.

Aksum

One of the new civilizations that developed in Africa was **Aksum** (AHK-soom). This powerful kingdom was located near the Red Sea in northeast Africa. This location made it easy to transport goods over water, and Aksum became a major trading power as a result. Traders from inland Africa brought goods like gold and ivory to Aksum. From there, the items were shipped to markets as far away as India. In return for their goods, the people of Aksum received cloth, spices, and other products.

Teach the Big Idea

Contact with Other Cultures

1. **Teach** Ask students the questions in the Main Idea boxes under Direct Teach.

2. **Apply** Instruct students to draw a simple T-chart on their own paper. Have students label one side of the chart Christianity and the other side Islam. Ask students what they know about the influence of both religions on the development of Africa.

3. **Review** As you review the section, have students complete the T-chart by taking

notes on the ways in which each religion influenced Africa and African culture.

4. **Practice/Homework** Have students write a short paragraph comparing and contrasting the impact that Christianity and Islam had on Africa. **LS Verbal/Linguistic, Visual/Spatial**

📄 Alternative Assessment Handbook, Rubrics 9: Comparing and Contrasting; and 13: Graphic Organizers

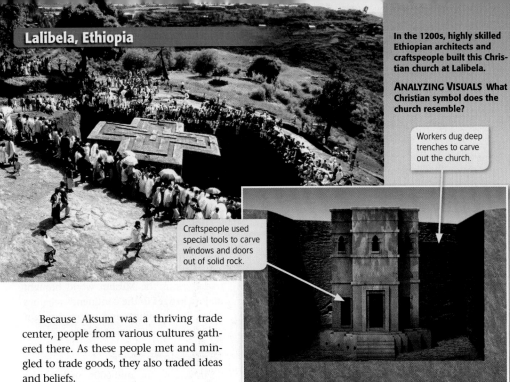

Lalibela, Ethiopia

In the 1200s, highly skilled Ethiopian architects and craftspeople built this Christian church at Lalibela.

ANALYZING VISUALS What Christian symbol does the church resemble?

Workers dug deep trenches to carve out the church.

Craftspeople used special tools to carve windows and doors out of solid rock.

Because Aksum was a thriving trade center, people from various cultures gathered there. As these people met and mingled to trade goods, they also traded ideas and beliefs.

One of the beliefs that was brought to Aksum by traders was Christianity. Christian teachings quickly took hold in Aksum, and many people converted. In the late 300s, Aksum's most famous ruler, King Ezana (AY-zah-nah), made Christianity the kingdom's official religion.

As a Christian kingdom, Aksum developed ties with other Christian states. For example, it was an ally of the Byzantine Empire. However, contact with these allies was cut off in the 600s and 700s, when Muslim armies from Southwest Asia conquered most of North Africa.

Although Aksum itself was never conquered, its major ports were taken by the Muslims. As a result, the kingdom became isolated from other lands. Cut off from their allies and their trade, the people of Aksum retreated to the mountains of northern Ethiopia.

Ethiopia

In time, the descendants of the people of Aksum formed a new kingdom, **Ethiopia**. By about 1150 Ethiopia had become one of Africa's most powerful kingdoms.

The most famous of Ethiopia's rulers was King Lalibela, who ruled in the 1200s. He is famous for the 11 Christian churches he built, many of which still stand. One of these churches is pictured above. The churches of Lalibela were carved into solid rock, many of them set into the ground. Worshippers had to walk down long flights of steps to get to them. Impressive feats of engineering, these churches also show the Ethiopians' devotion to Christianity. This devotion to Christianity set the Ethiopians apart from their neighbors, most of whom were Muslim.

❷ The Spread of Islam

Trade and military conquest led to the spread of Islam through Africa.

Identify What North African cities became centers of learning under Muslim rule? *Cairo, Egypt, Fés, Morocco, and Djenné, Mali*

Explain How did Islam spread into North Africa? *Arab armies swept across Southwest Asia into Egypt and the rest of North Africa, spreading their religion along the way.*

Elaborate What effects did Islam have on North Africa? *conquered lands became part of the Muslim empire; religion and Arabic language were introduced; schools and universities were opened*

Shared beliefs helped unify Ethiopians, but their isolation from other Christians led to some changes in their beliefs. Over time, some local African customs blended with Christian teachings. This resulted in a new form of Christianity in Africa called **Coptic Christianity**. The name *Coptic* comes from an Arabic word for "Egyptian." Most Christians who live in North Africa today—including many Ethiopians—belong to Coptic churches.

FOCUS ON CULTURE

The Architecture of Djenné

Stone and wood are rare in the Sahara Desert. Therefore, when the Muslims of Djenné decided to build a mosque, they looked to a material that was widely available: mud. They dried mud into bricks to build the Great Mosque, shown below. They then covered the bricks with a plaster, also made of mud, to give the building a smooth finish.

First built in the 1200s, the Great Mosque of Djenné was demolished in 1834. The city's ruler at that time thought the mosque was too ornate. However, it was rebuilt in 1907 and has stood ever since. Today, the citizens of Djenné gather yearly to repair damage from rain or extreme heat, either of which can harm the fragile mud bricks.

Drawing Conclusions Why are mud bricks a suitable building material in the Sahara Desert?

Although most people in Ethiopia were Christian, not everyone was. For example, a Jewish group known as the Beta Israel lived there. Though some Christian rulers tried to force the Beta Israel to give up their religion and adopt Christianity, they were not successful. Ethiopia's Jewish population remained active for centuries.

READING CHECK **Sequencing** How did Christianity take hold in parts of Africa?

The Spread of Islam

By the 600s and 700s Christianity had taken firm hold in parts of northeastern Africa. However, the arrival of soldiers and traders from the Muslim world brought major changes to the continent's religious map. These soldiers and traders brought with them a new religion, Islam.

Muslim North Africa

Beginning in the mid-600s, Arab armies from Southwest Asia swept across North Africa. Led by strong and clever generals, these armies quickly took over Egypt and the Nile Valley. From there they headed west, eventually conquering all of Africa's Mediterranean coast. These conquered lands became part of a Muslim empire that stretched from Persia all the way to Spain.

The Muslims introduced Islam and the Arabic language into North Africa. They also established schools and universities. Students there studied not only religion but also science, medicine, astronomy, and other subjects. Scholars from all over the Muslim world moved to North Africa to study and teach.

As a result of Muslim rule, many cities in North Africa grew and became centers of learning. Among the cities that developed in this way were Cairo in Egypt, Fès in Morocco, and **Djenné** in Mali.

Differentiating Instruction

Special Needs Learners

Materials: photocopies of physical map of North Africa, colored markers

1. Review with the students the spread of Islam into North Africa.

2. Ask students to locate the paragraph in the text above that explains how Islam spread throughout North Africa. *first paragraph under head Muslim North Africa*

3. Have students list the events detailing the spread of Islam in correct chronological order. Instruct students to number each event.

4. Distribute the photocopies of the maps and the markers. Have students use their list to identify how Islam spread through North Africa. Encourage students to use different colors for each stage in the spread of Islam.
LS Verbal/Linguistic, Visual/Spatial

Alternative Assessment Handbook, Rubric 20: Map Creation

Answers

Reading Check *traders introduced Christianity to Aksum; people converted to the new religion; King Ezana made it the official religion; Christianity was passed down to the people of Ethiopia; a new form of Christianity, Coptic Christianity, emerged.*

Focus on Culture *possible answers— Mud is plentiful in the desert; it can withstand the heat better than other materials.*

Trade in the East

While Islam came to North Africa through conquest, the religion's arrival in East Africa was less violent. Located on the Indian Ocean, East Africa had been a destination for traders from Asia for centuries. Among these traders were Muslims from India, Persia, and Arabia. They came to Africa in search of African goods and new markets for products from their homelands, but they also gave Africa a new culture.

To make trade easy and profitable, the Muslim traders and African locals built cities all along the coast. By 1100, East African cities like Mogadishu, Mombasa, Kilwa, and Sofala had become trade centers.

Muslim traders from Arabia and Persia settled down in many of these coastal trading cities. As a result, the cities developed large Muslim communities. Africans, Arabs, and Persians lived near each other and worked together. One result of this closeness was the spread of Islam through East Africa. People at all levels of society, from workers to rulers, adopted Islam. As a result, mosques appeared in cities and towns throughout the region.

The contact between cultures also led to other changes in East Africa. For example, the architecture of the region changed. People began to build houses that mixed **traditional** materials, such as coral and mangrove trees, with Arab designs, such as arched windows and carved doors.

As the cultures grew closer, their speech began to reflect their new relationship. Some Africans, who spoke mostly Bantu languages, adopted many Arabic and Persian words. In time, the languages blended into a new language, Swahili (swah-HEE-lee). The term **Swahili** refers to the blended African-Arab culture that had become common in East Africa.

READING CHECK Summarizing How did Islam change African society?

SUMMARY AND PREVIEW In this section, you learned about early contact between African societies and people from other regions. Next, you will learn how the arrival of European traders in Africa led to significant changes.

ACADEMIC VOCABULARY
traditional customary, time-honored

---

go.hrw.com
Online Quiz
KEYWORD: SK9 HP12

Section 1 Assessment

Reviewing Ideas, Terms, and Places

1. **a. Identify** What was the first kingdom in Africa to become Christian after the fall of Rome? Which ruler was responsible for its conversion?
   b. Identify Cause and Effect What led to the creation of **Coptic Christianity** in Africa?
   c. Develop Why did Christianity serve as a unifying factor for the people of **Ethiopia**?

2. **a. Define** What does **Swahili** mean?
   b. Contrast How did the arrival of Islam in North Africa differ from its arrival in East Africa?
   c. Predict How might life in East Africa have been different if the people there had not accepted the presence of Muslim traders?

Critical Thinking

3. **Analyzing Information** Use your notes and the graphic organizer to examine how the arrival of Christianity and Islam in Africa influenced local culture and led to changes in the two religions.

FOCUS ON SPEAKING

4. **Describing Cultural Influences** Your TV news report might mention the influence of various religions on Africa. What details from this section might you include in your report?

GROWTH AND DEVELOPMENT OF AFRICA **353**

353

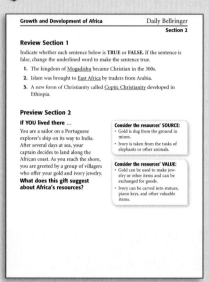

Preteach

Bellringer

If YOU lived there. . . Use the **Daily Bellringer Transparency** to help students answer the question.

📖 Daily Bellringer Transparency, Section 2

Key Terms and Places

📄 **RF:** Vocabulary Builder, Section 2

Taking Notes

Have students copy the graphic organizer onto their own paper and then use it to take notes on the section. This activity will prepare students for the Section Assessment, in which they will complete a graphic organizer that builds on the information using the Critical Thinking Skill: Sequencing.

About the Illustration

This illustration is an artist's conception based on available sources. Historians, however, are uncertain exactly what this scene looked like.

SECTION 2

European Colonization

What You Will Learn...

Main Ideas

1. Europeans arrived in Africa in search of valuable trade goods.
2. The slave trade had terrible effects in Africa.
3. Many European countries established colonies in Africa.

The Big Idea

Europeans established colonies in Africa to take advantage of trade in gold, ivory, slaves, and other items.

Key Terms and Places

Middle Passage, *p. 356*
Gold Coast, *p. 357*

 TAKING NOTES As you read, use a graphic organizer like this one to take notes on the arrival of Europeans in Africa, the African slave trade, and European colonies.

```
┌──────────┐
│  Arrival │
└──────────┘
      │
┌──────────────┐
│  Slave Trade │
└──────────────┘
      │
┌──────────┐
│ Colonies │
└──────────┘
```

If **YOU** lived there...

You are a sailor on a Portuguese explorer's ship on its way to India. After several days at sea, your captain decides to land along the African coast. As you reach the shore, you are greeted by a group of villagers who offer you gold and ivory jewelry.

What does this gift suggest about Africa's resources?

BUILDING BACKGROUND Before the 1300s, few people in Europe knew much about Africa. Ancient Greek writers had described parts of the continent, but most people knew little about Africa as it actually existed. After European explorers landed in Africa in the 1400s, however, the continent drew the attention of traders and colonists.

✳Interactive Close-up

Mansa Musa's Pilgrimage

Mansa Musa's pilgrimage to Mecca in 1324 brought the wealth of Mali to the attention of the Muslim world and Europe. Based on historical accounts, Mansa Musa's impressive caravan included more than 60,000 people.

 go.hrw.com (KEYWORD: SK9 CH12)

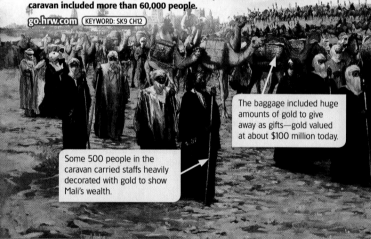

The baggage included huge amounts of gold to give away as gifts—gold valued at about $100 million today.

Some 500 people in the caravan carried staffs heavily decorated with gold to show Mali's wealth.

Teach the Big Idea   **At Level**

European Colonization

1. **Teach** Ask students the questions in the Main Idea boxes under Direct Teach.

2. **Apply** Organize the class into small groups. Assign each group one of the following topics: The Arrival of Europeans, The Slave Trade, or European Colonies in Africa. Instruct each group to skim the text under the heading that matches their assigned topic. Have students make a list of key events or people.

3. **Review** As you review the section, have each group share its list of events and people with the class.

4. **Practice/Homework** Have each student create a cause-and-effect graphic organizer for the section. **LS** Verbal/Linguistic, Visual/Spatial

   📄 Alternative Assessment Handbook, Rubrics 6: Cause and Effect; and 14: Group Activity

The Arrival of Europeans

In the late 1400s explorers set sail from ports around Europe. Many of these explorers hoped to find new trade routes to places like India and China. There, they could find goods that would sell for high prices in Europe and make them wealthy.

As part of their quest, some Portuguese explorers set out to sail around Africa. During their journeys, many landed at spots along the African coast. Some of these explorers soon found that they could get rich without ever reaching India or China.

Rumors of Gold

For centuries, Europeans had heard rumors of golden kingdoms in Africa. Those rumors began in the 1300s when Mansa Musa, the ruler of Mali, set out on his famous hajj, or Muslim pilgrimage, to Mecca. He was accompanied by thousands of attendants and slaves. As they traveled, the pilgrims gave away lavish gifts of gold to the rulers of lands through which they passed.

For years after Mansa Musa's hajj, stories of his wealth passed from Southwest Asia into Europe. However, most Europeans did not believe they could find gold in Africa. When the Portuguese reached the coasts of West Africa, however, they learned that the stories had been true. Africa did have gold, and the Europeans wanted it.

Trade Goods

Gold was the first item to bring European attention to Africa, but it was not the only valuable product to be found there. Another was ivory. Europeans used ivory to make furniture, jewelry, statues, piano keys, and other expensive items.

At first, the Portuguese had little interest in products other than gold and ivory. Before long, however, they found that they could make more profit from something else the Africans were willing to sell them—slaves.

READING CHECK Summarizing Why did some Europeans become interested in Africa?

Mansa Musa rode near the front. During his journey, he gained fame for his generosity.

Called "ships of the desert," camels could go for long periods without water and could withstand heat better than horses or donkeys.

ANALYSIS SKILL **ANALYZING VISUALS**
Why do you think people were impressed by stories about Mansa Musa's pilgrimage?

355

Direct Teach

Main Idea

① The Arrival of Europeans

Europeans arrived in Africa in search of valuable trade goods.

Recall Why did Europeans first set sail around Africa? *They were searching for a trade route to India and China.*

Summarize What rumors encouraged some Europeans to explore Africa? *Tales of Mansa Musa's hajj told of great wealth belonging to the African king.*

Make Judgments Do you think you would have believed the tales of the wealth of Mansa Musa? Explain. *Students' responses will vary, but should include support for their answers.*

Info to Know

Mansa Musa's Pilgrimage The 1324 pilgrimage of Mansa Musa created quite a stir in the Muslim world. Arab writers of the time described the caravan in great detail. According to Arab sources, the caravan consisted of some 60,000 people, all dressed in fine cloths such as brocade and silk. Mansa Musa himself is said to have ridden on horseback behind some 500 slaves, each carrying a golden staff.

Differentiating Instruction

At Level

English-Language Learners

Standard English Mastery

1. Instruct students to examine the illustration of Mansa Musa's pilgrimage. Have students look for details of the people, the architecture, and signs of wealth in the image. Lead a class discussion in which you ask students to describe what they see in the illustration.

2. Organize the students into pairs. Have students imagine that they witnessed Mansa Musa's caravan. Have each pair work together to write a letter to a friend describing what

Mansa Musa's caravan looked like as it passed through their town. Instruct students to use descriptive language to paint a picture of what the caravan was like. Remind students to use standard English in their letters.

3. Encourage volunteers to share their letters with the class. **LS Visual/Spatial, Verbal/Linguistic**
   Alternative Assessment Handbook, Rubrics 25: Personal Letters; and 40: Writing to Describe

Answers

Reading Check *They were searching for a new trade route to India and China; they heard rumors of great wealth in Africa.*

Analyzing Visuals *There were tens of thousands of people and great wealth associated with the pilgrimage.*

355

❷ The Slave Trade

The slave trade had terrible effects in Africa.

Recall Approximately how many Africans were shipped to the Americas as slaves? *15 to 20 million*

Draw Conclusions Why were slaves needed to work in the Americas? *because Europeans needed labor for the plantations there*

Elaborate What effects did the slave trade have on Africa? *decrease in population, increased warfare, years of mistrust between African peoples*

Info to Know

Ivory Trade The slave trade and the ivory trade both expanded in the second half of the 1700s. Slaves were used as porters to carry huge elephant tusks from the interior to the coast. Some were so heavy that it took four people to carry a single tusk.

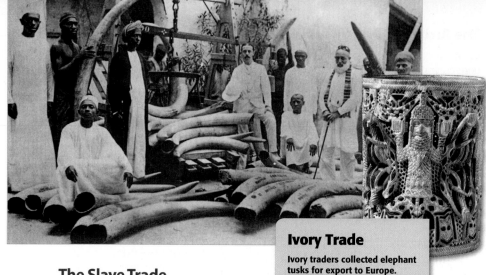

Ivory Trade

Ivory traders collected elephant tusks for export to Europe.

ANALYZING VISUALS Who was involved in the ivory trade?

The Slave Trade

Slavery was nothing new in Africa. For centuries, societies within Africa had kept slaves. Most of these slaves were prisoners captured in battle or as the result of raids on rival villages or kingdoms.

The European Slave Trade

Slavery had existed for centuries in Africa, but the arrival of Europeans in West Africa led to a drastic increase in the demand for slaves. Europeans wanted slaves to put to work on plantations, or large farms, in the Americas. Slave traders made deals with many rulers in West and Central Africa to buy the slaves they captured in battle. These slaves were then put in chains and loaded onto ships. These ships carried the slaves on a grueling trip across the Atlantic called the **Middle Passage**.

The slave trade continued for more than 300 years. Though some Europeans argued against slavery, calling it an evil institution that should be stopped, slave traders considered the practice too profitable to stop. It was not until the 1800s that European governments stepped in and finally banned the trading of slaves.

Effects of the Slave Trade

The European slave trade in Africa had devastating consequences. It led to a drastic decrease in Africa's population. Millions of young African men were forced to move away from their homes to lands far away, and thousands of them died. Historians estimate that 15 to 20 million African slaves were shipped to the Americas against their will. Millions more were sent to Europe, Asia, and the Middle East.

The slave trade had terrible effects on those who remained in Africa as well. The efforts of some kingdoms to capture slaves from their rivals led to decades of warfare on the continent. This warfare further reduced Africa's population and weakened many societies. It also caused caused years of resentment and mistrust between many African peoples.

READING CHECK Identifying Cause and Effect What were the results of the slave trade?

Differentiating Instruction

Special Needs Learners

1. Review with the students the slave trade in Africa that resulted from the arrival of Europeans. Draw a graphic organizer like this one for everyone to see. Omit the blue, italicized answers.

2. Instruct students to copy the graphic organizer on their own paper and use the their textbooks to complete it.

3. When students are finished, review the answers as a class. **LS** Verbal/Linguistic, Visual/Spatial

   Alternative Assessment Handbook, Rubrics 6: Cause and Effect; and 13: Graphic Organizers

Causes

1. *Europeans arrive*
2. *Need for slave labor in the Americas*

→ **European Slave Trade** →

Effects

1. *population decreases dramatically*
2. *warfare and mistrust between African kingdoms*

Answers

Analyzing Visuals *Europeans and people from Central African kingdoms*

Reading Check *Millions of Africans were sent to the Americas, Europe, Asia, and the Middle East as slaves.*

356

European Colonies in Africa

Trade in gold, ivory, and slaves made many Portuguese merchants very rich. Envious of this wealth, other European countries rushed to grab part of the trade. The result was a struggle among several countries to establish colonies along the African coast.

Colonies in West Africa

The first European colony in West Africa was the **Gold Coast**, established by the Portuguese in 1482. It was located in the area now occupied by the country of Ghana. Most colonies in West Africa were named after the products traded there. In addition to the Gold Coast, the region had colonies called Ivory Coast and Slave Coast.

To keep order in their colonies, Europeans built forts along West Africa's coast. These forts served both as trading centers and military outposts.

Over time, the colonies of West Africa merged. For example, the Portuguese gave their colony to the Dutch in the mid-1600s. Eventually, the entire Gold Coast came under the control of the British, who kept the colony there until the 1950s.

The Portuguese in East Africa

While several countries had colonies in West Africa, only the Portuguese were interested in East Africa. They knew that trade on the Indian Ocean was very profitable, and they wanted to control that trade.

The Portuguese knew they could not take over East Africa as long as strong African kingdoms ruled the region. To weaken those kingdoms, they encouraged rulers to go to war with each other. The Portuguese then made alliances with the winners.

However, Portuguese influence in East Africa was weakened when Muslims arrived. The Muslims forced the Portuguese almost completely out of the region. Although the Portuguese kept a colony in Mozambique, their influence was almost gone.

READING CHECK Identifying Cause and Effect Why did Europeans establish colonies in Africa?

SUMMARY AND PREVIEW Europeans arrived in Africa in the 1500s and built a number of colonies. Next, you will learn about another period of European involvement in Africa during the 1800s.

Section 2 Assessment

go.hrw.com
Online Quiz
KEYWORD: SK9 HP12

Reviewing Ideas, Terms, and Places

1. **a. Identify** What trade goods did Europeans find available in Africa?
   b. Analyze How did Mansa Musa's pilgrimage affect European views toward Africa?
2. **a. Define** What was the **Middle Passage**?
   b. Summarize Why did Europeans want slaves?
   c. Evaluate In your opinion, what was the worst result of the slave trade? Explain your answer.
3. **a. Recall** Why did Europeans want to form colonies in West Africa?
   b. Develop What do names like **Gold Coast** suggest about Europeans' views toward their African colonies?

Critical Thinking

4. **Sequencing** Use your notes and a diagram like the one below to list the major steps in the formation of European colonies in Africa. You may add more boxes to the diagram if necessary.

FOCUS ON SPEAKING

5. **Describing Colonies** Will your news report mention the arrival of Europeans in Africa and the formation of colonies? Write down some notes about topics you might include in your report.

GROWTH AND DEVELOPMENT OF AFRICA **357**

Info to Know

History of African Slave Trading

European powers transported as many as 12 million slaves to the Americas in less than 400 years. The practice of capturing and selling slaves in Africa began when early African kingdoms as well as Arab Muslims began capturing Africans around 700 AD and transporting them north across the Sahara to be sold. During the period between 700 and 1900, it is estimated that as many as 8 to 12 million Africans were captured and sold this way. Central African groups captured slaves and took them east to the Indian Ocean, where they were sold to Middle Eastern and Asian traders.

In many cases, white Europeans purchased slaves from Africans who captured other Africans and offered them for sale. Slave trading was the main economic activity for some groups in West Africa. Some of these slave traders grew wealthy and established themselves as powerful leaders in their communities.

go.hrw.com
Online Resources

ACTIVITY: History of the Slave Trade
KEYWORD: SK9 CH12

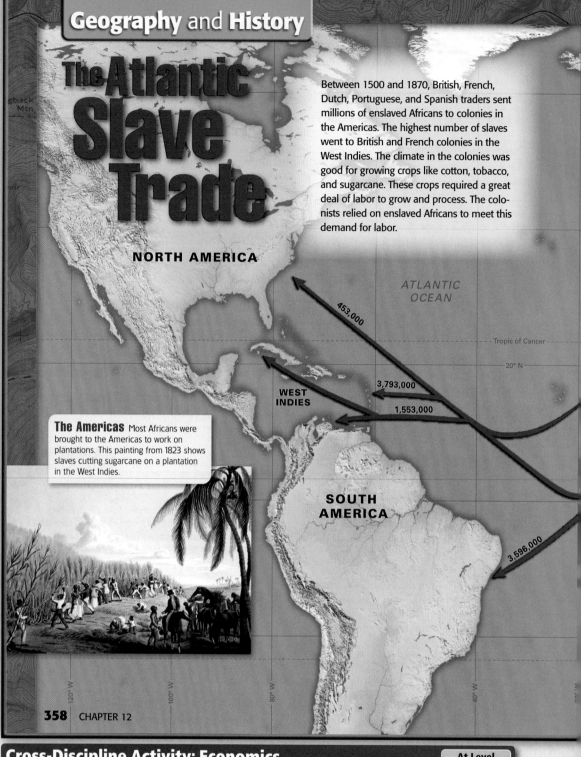

Geography and History

The Atlantic Slave Trade

NORTH AMERICA

Between 1500 and 1870, British, French, Dutch, Portuguese, and Spanish traders sent millions of enslaved Africans to colonies in the Americas. The highest number of slaves went to British and French colonies in the West Indies. The climate in the colonies was good for growing crops like cotton, tobacco, and sugarcane. These crops required a great deal of labor to grow and process. The colonists relied on enslaved Africans to meet this demand for labor.

ATLANTIC OCEAN

Tropic of Cancer

20° N

453,000

3,793,000

1,553,000

WEST INDIES

The Americas Most Africans were brought to the Americas to work on plantations. This painting from 1823 shows slaves cutting sugarcane on a plantation in the West Indies.

SOUTH AMERICA

3,596,000

120° W 100° W 80° W 40° W

358 CHAPTER 12

Cross-Discipline Activity: Economics [At Level]

Triangle Trade

1. Note that the Atlantic slave trade generated great wealth for those involved with buying and selling.

2. Illustrate the other two sides of the triangle— the Americas to Europe and Europe to Africa. Point out that improved sailing ships made this route much safer and more dependable than years before.

3. Discuss the resources available in the Americas and Europe at the time and ask students to predict what might be acquired on each leg of the trip (raw materials such as

sugar and molasses, cotton, and tobacco in the Americas; manufactured goods and goods from Asian colonies in Europe).

4. Discuss reasons that each point on the triangle needed what was provided from the previous point. *Africa needed manufactured goods and imported items; the Americas needed slaves for plantations; Europe needed raw materials to use in manufacture.* **LS Verbal/Linguistic**

Alternative Assessment Handbook, Rubric 11: Discussions

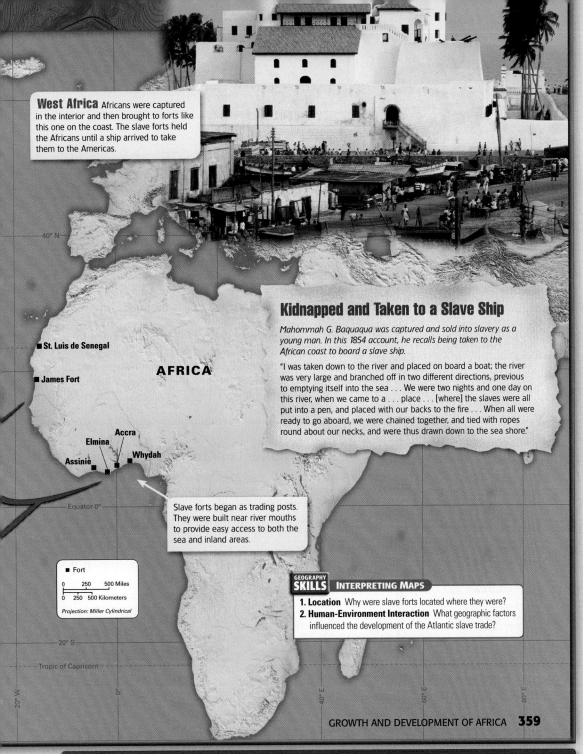

West Africa Africans were captured in the interior and then brought to forts like this one on the coast. The slave forts held the Africans until a ship arrived to take them to the Americas.

AFRICA

■ St. Luis de Senegal

■ James Fort

Accra
Elmina
Assinie Whydah

Equator 0°

Kidnapped and Taken to a Slave Ship

Mahommah G. Baquaqua was captured and sold into slavery as a young man. In this 1854 account, he recalls being taken to the African coast to board a slave ship.

"I was taken down to the river and placed on board a boat; the river was very large and branched off in two different directions, previous to emptying itself into the sea . . . We were two nights and one day on this river, when we came to a . . . place . . . [where] the slaves were all put into a pen, and placed with our backs to the fire . . . When all were ready to go aboard, we were chained together, and tied with ropes round about our necks, and were thus drawn down to the sea shore."

Slave forts began as trading posts. They were built near river mouths to provide easy access to both the sea and inland areas.

■ Fort

0   250   500 Miles
0 250 500 Kilometers

Projection: Miller Cylindrical

20° S

Tropic of Capricorn

GEOGRAPHY SKILLS INTERPRETING MAPS

1. **Location** Why were slave forts located where they were?
2. **Human-Environment Interaction** What geographic factors influenced the development of the Atlantic slave trade?

Geography and History

Biography

Alex Haley (1921–1992) Haley traced his family back through generations of slavery to a West African village. His book, *Roots: The Saga of an American Family,* was published in 1976. Millions of people read it, and it was translated into more than 30 languages. It dramatized the brutality of the Atlantic slave trade through a mixture of fact and fiction. When it was shown as a miniseries on television in 1977, 130 million people saw at least part of it. It provided a reference point for many African Americans who could not trace their ancestry and was a dramatic story for those who knew little of the slave trade.

MISCONCEPTION ALERT

Slave Destinations Between 1441 and 1888 an estimated 12 million slaves were taken from Africa. Only about 4.5 percent of the slaves entered what is now the United States. Other slaves went to the Caribbean, Brazil, and other South American countries. However, slaves in North America tended to live much longer because working conditions were not as harsh, and there were fewer tropical diseases. For this reason, the number of people of African descent in North America grew even after the import of slaves was stopped in the early 1800s.

Differentiating Instruction

Advanced/Gifted and Talented   **Above Level**   **Research Required**

1. Assign individuals or small groups to research Kwanzaa. They should note its history and its connection to African words, symbols, and African American culture.

2. Students should give an oral report, including visual aids, and explain the connection of Kwanzaa to African culture.
   LS Verbal/Linguistic, Visual/Spatial
   Alternative Assessment Handbook, Rubric 24: Oral Presentations

Struggling Readers   **At Level**   **Research Required**

1. Assign individuals to do research on the Atlantic slave trade and slavery in the United States. Have students find an image (painting, drawing, photo, etc.) that portrays some part of the slave trade and make a copy of it.

2. Students will share their images with the class, explain what part of the slave trade the image depicts, and answer audience questions. **LS Visual/Spatial, Verbal/Linguistic**
   Alternative Assessment Handbook, Rubric 29: Presentations

Answers

Interpreting Maps 1. *to provide easy access to the sea and inland areas;* **2.** *Climates in the Americas favored crops that required a great deal of labor; Europeans had access to West Africa, and transportation directly across the Atlantic was relatively easy.*

Bellringer

If YOU lived there. . . Use the **Daily Bellringer Transparency** to help students answer the question.

📦 Daily Bellringer Transparency, Section 3

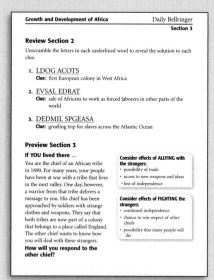

| Growth and Development of Africa | Daily Bellringer |
| | Section 3 |

Review Section 2

Unscramble the letters in each underlined word to reveal the solution to each clue.

1. LDOG ACOTS
   Clue: first European colony in West Africa

2. EVSAL EDRAT
   Clue: sale of Africans to work as forced laborers in other parts of the world

3. DEDMIL SPGEASA
   Clue: grueling trip for slaves across the Atlantic Ocean

Preview Section 3

If YOU lived there ...
You are the chief of an African tribe in 1890. For many years, your people have been at war with a tribe that lives in the next valley. One day, however, a warrior from that tribe delivers a message to you. His chief has been approached by soldiers with strange clothes and weapons. They say that both tribes are now part of a colony that belongs to a place called England. The other chief wants to know how you will deal with these strangers. **How will you respond to the other chief?**

Consider effects of ALLYING with the strangers:
• possibility of trade
• access to new weapons and ideas
• loss of independence

Consider effects of FIGHTING the strangers:
• continued independence
• chance to win respect of other chiefs
• possibility that many people will die

Academic Vocabulary

Review with students the high-use academic term in this section.

values ideas that people hold dear and try to live by (p. 361)

📝 **RF:** Vocabulary Builder, Section 3

Taking Notes

Have students copy the graphic organizer onto their own paper and then use it to take notes on the section. This activity will prepare students for the Section Assessment, in which they will complete a graphic organizer that builds on the information using the Critical Thinking Skill: Identifying Cause and Effect.

Imperialism in Africa

What You Will Learn...

Main Ideas

1. The search for raw materials led to a new wave of European involvement in Africa.
2. The Scramble for Africa was a race by Europeans to form colonies there.
3. Some Africans resisted rule by Europeans.

The Big Idea

In the late 1800s Europeans once again created colonies in Africa and became involved in African politics and economics.

Key Terms and Places

entrepreneurs, *p. 361*
imperialism, *p. 361*
Suez Canal, *p. 362*
Berlin Conference, *p. 362*
Boers, *p. 364*

 TAKING NOTES As you read, use a graphic organizer like this one to take notes on various aspects of European imperialism in Africa in the 1800s.

New Involvement → European Imperialism → Berlin Conference / African Resistance

360 CHAPTER 12

If YOU lived there...

You are the chief of an African tribe in 1890. For many years, your people have been at war with a tribe that lives in the next valley. One day, however, a warrior from that tribe delivers a message to you. His chief has been approached by soldiers with strange clothes and weapons. They say that both tribes are now part of a colony that belongs to a place called England. The other chief wants to know how you will deal with these strangers.

How will you respond to the other chief?

BUILDING BACKGROUND Europeans had formed colonies in Africa as early as the 1400s, but they actually controlled only a small percentage of the continent. During the late 1800s, though, European attitudes toward Africa changed, and they soon fought to control as much of the continent as they could.

New Involvement in Africa

When Europeans first arrived in Africa in the 1400s, they hoped to get rich through trade. For centuries, controlling the trade of rare products from distant lands had been the surest road to wealth in Europe. The merchants who brought spices, silks, and other goods from Asia had been among the richest people on the continent.

With the beginning of the Industrial Revolution in the 1700s, however, a new road to riches emerged. Europeans found that they could become rich by building factories and making products that other people wanted, such as cheap cloth, tools, or steel. In order to make products, business owners needed raw materials. However, Europe did not have sufficient resources to supply all the factories that were opening. Where were these resources to come from?

Teach the Big Idea

At Level

Imperialism in Africa

1. **Teach** Ask students the questions in the Main Idea boxes under Direct Teach.

2. **Apply** Have students work in pairs to make graphic organizers showing which European countries controlled which regions of Africa.

3. **Review** Review students' graphic organizers as a class. Guide students in a discussion of the reasons Europeans felt entitled to take control of Africa.

4. **Practice/Homework** Have students write a letter to the editor from the point of view of an African, explaining why Europeans should not colonize their country. 🔲 **Verbal/Linguistic**

📝 Alternative Assessment Handbook, Rubrics 13: Graphic Organizers; and 17: Letters to Editors

---

The Quest for Raw Materials

By the 1880s Europeans decided that the best way to get resources was to create new colonies. They wanted these colonies to be located in places that had abundant resources not available in Europe.

One such place was Africa. Since the slave trade had ended in the early 1800s, few Europeans had paid much attention to Africa. Unless they could make a huge fortune in Africa, most people did not care what happened there. As factory owners looked for new sources of raw materials, though, some people took another look at Africa. For the first time, they noticed its huge open spaces and its mineral wealth.

Once again, Europeans rushed to Africa to establish colonies. Most of these new colonists who headed to Africa in the 1800s were **entrepreneurs**, or independent businesspeople. In Africa they built mines, plantations, and trade routes with the dream of growing rich.

Cultural Interference

Though they were in Africa to get rich, the European entrepreneurs who moved there frequently became involved in local affairs. Often, they became involved because they thought their ideas about government and culture were better than native African ways. As a result, they often tried to impose their own ideas on the local people. This sort of attempt to dominate a country's government, trade, or culture is called **imperialism.**

European imperialists justified their behavior by claiming that they were improving the lives of Africans. In fact, many Europeans saw it as their duty to introduce their customs and **values** to what they saw as a backward land. They forced Africans to assimilate, or adopt, many elements of European culture. As a result, thousands of Africans became Christian and learned to speak European languages.

ACADEMIC VOCABULARY
values ideas that people hold dear and try to live by

CONNECTING TO Economics

Diamond Mining

Among the resources that caught the eye of European entrepreneurs in Africa were diamonds. First discovered in South Africa in 1867, diamonds were extremely profitable. South Africa soon became the world's leading diamond producer. Nearly all of that production was done by one company, the De Beers Consolidated Mine Company, owned by English business leader Cecil Rhodes. De Beers mines like the one shown here at Kimberley poured the gems into the world market.

South Africa is still one of the world's leading diamond producers, and De Beers is one of the leading companies. By controlling the supply of diamonds available to the public, the company can command higher prices for its gems.

Analyze How can a company control the supply of a product?

GROWTH AND DEVELOPMENT OF AFRICA **361**

❶ New Involvement in Africa, *continued*

Identify Who was Cecil Rhodes? *a British business owner who believed it was the duty of Europeans to share their culture with Africans*

Analyze What role did rivalries in Europe play in the control of African colonies? *European countries often took over colonies simply to prevent their rivals from gaining that territory; it lead France, Britain, Germany, and Italy to establish African colonies.*

go.hrw.com
Online Resources
KEYWORD: SK9 CH12
ACTIVITY: Suez Canal

One firm believer in imperialism was English business owner Cecil Rhodes. He believed that British culture was superior to all others and that it was his duty to share it with the people of Africa. To that end, he planned to build a long railroad between Britain's colonies in Egypt and South Africa. He thought that this railroad would bring what he saw as the benefits of British civilization to all Africans. However, his railroad was never completed.

FOCUS ON READING
What details support the main idea that European governments became involved in African affairs?

Government Involvement

Though the early imperialists in Africa were entrepreneurs, national governments soon became involved as well. Their involvement was largely the result of rivalries between countries. Each country wanted to control more land and more colonies than its rivals did. As a result, countries tried to create as many colonies as they could and to block others from creating colonies.

For example, France began to form colonies in West Africa in the late 1800s. Seeing this, the British hurried to the area to form colonies of their own. Before long, Germany and Italy also sought to control land in West Africa. They did not want to be seen as less powerful than either France or Britain.

The English government also got involved in Africa for other reasons. The British wanted to protect the **Suez Canal,** a waterway built in Egypt in the 1860s to connect the Mediterranean and Red Seas. The British used the canal as a fast route to their colonies in India. In the 1880s, however, instability in Egypt's government made the British fear they would lose access to the canal. As a result, the British moved into Egypt and took partial control of the country to protect their shipping routes.

READING CHECK Categorizing What were three reasons Europeans went to Africa?

The Scramble for Africa

Desperate to have more power in Africa than their rivals, European countries rushed to claim as much land there as they could. Historians refer to this rush to claim land as the Scramble for Africa. The Europeans moved so quickly to snap up land that by 1914 most of African had been made into European colonies. As you can see on the map on the next page, only Ethiopia and Liberia remained independent.

The Berlin Conference

For many years Europeans competed aggressively for land in Africa. Conflicts sometimes arose when multiple countries tried to claim the same area. To prevent these conflicts from developing into wars, Europe's leaders agreed to meet and devise a plan to maintain order in Africa. They hoped this meeting would settle disputes and prevent future conflicts.

The meeting these European leaders held was called the **Berlin Conference.** Begun in 1884, it led to the division of Africa among various European powers. As the map shows, the conference left Africa a patchwork of European colonies.

When they were dividing Africa among themselves, Europe's leaders paid little attention to the people who lived there. As a result, the boundaries they drew for their colonies often divided kingdoms, clans, and families.

Separating people with common backgrounds was bad, but so was forcing people to live together who did not want to. Some European colonies grouped together peoples with different customs, languages, and religions. This forced contact between peoples often led to conflict and war. In time, the Europeans' disregard for Africans led to significant problems for Europeans and Africans alike.

Differentiating Instruction

Below Level

Struggling Readers

1. Organize students into mixed-ability pairs.

2. Write the following categories for everyone to see: Economic, Cultural, and Political. Instruct students to create a graphic organizer using the three categories as main headings.

3. Then have each pair identify the economic, cultural, and political motives that Europeans had for colonizing Africa.

4. When students have completed their graphic organizers, have them create a poster with the same information.

5. Display completed posters for the class to see.
   LS Verbal/Linguistic, Visual/Spatial

   Alternative Assessment Handbook, Rubrics 14: Graphic Organizers; and 28: Posters

---

Answers

Focus on Reading *Involvement was the result of rivalries; as countries created colonies, they could block their rivals from creating their own colonies.*

Reading Check *raw materials; to spread culture; to prevent rivals from gaining colonies*

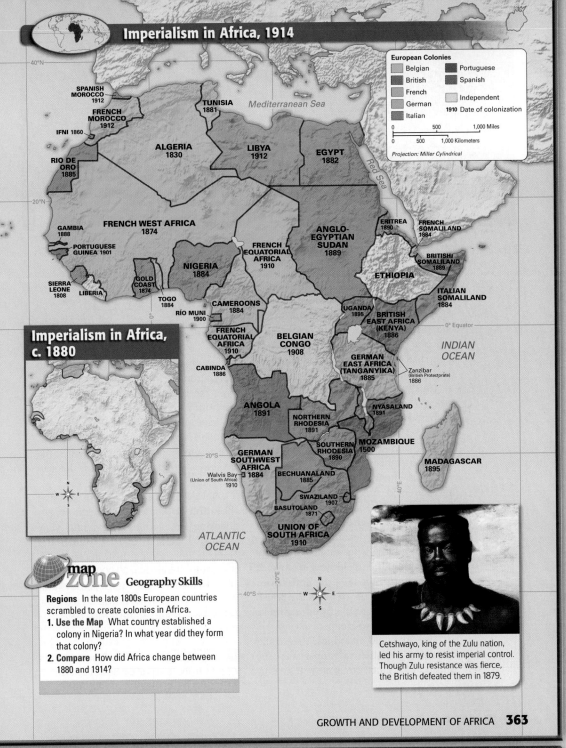

Imperialism in Africa, 1914

European Colonies

Belgian	Portuguese
British	Spanish
French	Independent
German	
Italian	**1910** Date of colonization

0   500   1,000 Miles
0   500   1,000 Kilometers

Projection: Miller Cylindrical

SPANISH MOROCCO
FRENCH MOROCCO 1912
IFNI 1860
RIO DE ORO 1885
TUNISIA 1881
Mediterranean Sea
ALGERIA 1830
LIBYA 1912
EGYPT 1882
Red Sea
GAMBIA 1888
FRENCH WEST AFRICA 1874
PORTUGUESE GUINEA 1901
SIERRA LEONE 1808
LIBERIA
GOLD COAST 1874
TOGO 1884
RÍO MUNI 1900
NIGERIA 1884
FRENCH EQUATORIAL AFRICA 1910
CAMEROONS 1884
ANGLO-EGYPTIAN SUDAN 1889
ERITREA 1890
FRENCH SOMALILAND 1884
BRITISH SOMALILAND 1889
ETHIOPIA
ITALIAN SOMALILAND 1884
FRENCH EQUATORIAL AFRICA 1910
BELGIAN CONGO 1908
UGANDA 1895
BRITISH EAST AFRICA (KENYA) 1886
0° Equator
CABINDA 1886
GERMAN EAST AFRICA (TANGANYIKA) 1885
Zanzibar (British Protectorate) 1886
INDIAN OCEAN
ANGOLA 1891
NYASALAND 1891
NORTHERN RHODESIA 1891
MOZAMBIQUE 1500
GERMAN SOUTHWEST AFRICA 1884
SOUTHERN RHODESIA 1890
MADAGASCAR 1895
Walvis Bay (Union of South Africa) 1910
BECHUANALAND 1885
SWAZILAND 1907
BASUTOLAND 1871
UNION OF SOUTH AFRICA 1910
ATLANTIC OCEAN

Imperialism in Africa, c. 1880

map zone Geography Skills

Regions In the late 1800s European countries scrambled to create colonies in Africa.
1. **Use the Map** What country established a colony in Nigeria? In what year did they form that colony?
2. **Compare** How did Africa change between 1880 and 1914?

Cetshwayo, king of the Zulu nation, led his army to resist imperial control. Though Zulu resistance was fierce, the British defeated them in 1879.

GROWTH AND DEVELOPMENT OF AFRICA **363**

Main Idea

❷ The Scramble for Africa, *continued*

Identify Who were the Boers? *Dutch farmers in South Africa*

Summarize What led to the Boer War? *The discovery of gold in South Africa encouraged Great Britain to try to take over South Africa and push out the Boers.*

Identify Cause and Effect What effect did the use of guerilla warfare tactics have? *At first it led to several victories for the Boers, but ultimately it angered the British, who took Boer women and children prisoner.*

Info to Know

Boer War The Boer War, also known as the South African War, lasted from 1899 to 1902. The war was triggered when Boer officials refused to grant political rights to British settlers. From the beginning the Boers were vastly outnumbered by British forces. The British had nearly 500,000 troops to about 88,000 Boer troops. The Boers resorted to guerilla tactics as a result of early losses to the British. In response to the sneak attacks of the Boers, the British used a scorched-earth policy, destroying the farms of Boers and Africans alike.

Battle of Adwa

This painting of the Battle of Adwa was created years after the battle. The battle kept Ethiopia from becoming an Italian colony and is still celebrated today.

ANALYZING VISUALS Why might Ethiopians celebrate their victory at Adwa?

The Boer War

The Berlin Conference was intended to prevent conflicts over African territory, but it was not completely successful. In the late 1890s war broke out in South Africa between British and Dutch settlers. Each group had claimed the land and wanted to drive the other out.

Dutch farmers called **Boers** had arrived in South Africa in the 1600s. There they had established two independent republics. For about 200 years the Boers lived mainly as farmers. During that time they met with little interference from other Europeans.

Things changed in the 1800s, though. In 1886 gold was discovered near the Orange River in South Africa. Suddenly, the land on which the Boers had been living became highly desired.

Among those who wanted to control South Africa after gold was discovered were the British. In 1899 the British tried to make the Boers' land part of the British Empire. The Boers resisted, and war broke out between the two groups.

The Boers did not think they could defeat the British in a regular war. The British had a much larger army than they did, especially once the British brought in troops from their various colonies. In addition, the British troops had much better weapons than the Boers had.

Instead, the Boers decided to wage a guerilla war, one based on sneak attacks and ambushes. Through these tactics, the Boers quickly defeated several British forces and gained an advantage in the war.

However, these guerilla tactics angered the British. To punish the Boers, they began attacking and burning Boer farms. They captured thousands of Boer women and children, imprisoning them in concentration camps. More than 20,000 women and children died in these camps, mostly from disease. In the end, the British defeated the Boers. As a result, South Africa became a British colony.

READING CHECK Identifying Cause and Effect What were the results of the Berlin Conference?

Critical Thinking: Summarizing

At Level

African Resistance

1. Assign each student to one of the following nationalities: Zulu, Ethiopian, French West African, or German East African.

2. Instruct students to use the library, the Internet, and other sources to research ways in which their assigned group resisted colonization by Europeans.

3. Have students use the information they find to write a news article focusing on attempts to resist colonization.

4. Encourage volunteers to share their news articles with the class. **LS Verbal/Linguistic**

    Alternative Assessment Handbook, Rubric 42: Writing to Inform

Answers

Analyzing Visuals *It was a key victory that allowed Ethiopia to remain independent.*

Reading Check *Most of Africa was divided among the various European powers.*

African Resistance

The Europeans thought that the Berlin Conference and the Boer War would put an end to conflict in Africa. Once again, however, they had overlooked the African people. Many African people did not want to be ruled by Europeans. They refused to peacefully give up their own cultures and adopt European ways.

As a result, the Europeans who entered African territory often met with resistance from local rulers and peoples. Europeans were able to end most of these rebellions quickly with their superior weapons. However, two well-organized peoples, the Zulu and the Ethiopians, caused more problems for the Europeans.

Zulu Resistance

One of the most famous groups to resist the Europeans were the Zulu of southern Africa. In the early 1800s a Zulu leader named Shaka had brought various tribes together into a single nation. This nation was so strong that the Europeans were hesitant to enter Zulu territory.

After Shaka's death, however, the Zulu nation weakened. Even without Shaka's leadership, the fierce Zulu army successfully fought off the British for more than 50 years. In the end, however, the superior weapons of the British helped them defeat the Zulu. Their lands were made into a new British colony.

Ethiopian Resistance

Although most resistance to European imperialism was ended, one kingdom managed to remain free from European control. That kingom was Ethiopia. It is the only country in Africa to never be a European colony. Its success in fighting the Europeans was largely due to the efforts of one man, Emperor Menelik II.

Menelik had seen that the strength of European armies was based on their modern weapons. He therefore decided that he would create an equally powerful army with equally modern weapons bought from Europe. As a result, when the Italians invaded Ethiopia in 1895, the Ethiopian army was able to defeat the invaders. This victory in the Battle of Adwa is celebrated as a high point in Ethiopian history.

READING CHECK Drawing Conclusions Why did many Africans resist European imperialism?

SUMMARY AND PREVIEW In the 1800s Europeans divided Africa into dozens of colonies. In the next section, you will learn how these colonies eventually broke free from European control to become independent countries.

Section 3 Assessment

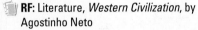
go.hrw.com
Online Quiz
KEYWORD: SK9 HP12

Reviewing Ideas, Terms, and Places

1. **a. Describe** What role did **entrepreneurs** play in European **imperialism** in Africa?
   b. Explain Why did European governments want to form colonies in Africa?

2. **a. Summarize** What happened at the **Berlin Conference**?
   b. Predict What problems do you think the Berlin Conference caused in Africa after the Europeans left?

3. **a. Identify** Which African country never became a colony?
   b. Make Inferences Why did most African resistance fail?

Critical Thinking

4. **Identifying Cause and Effect** Use your notes and the diagram to the right to identify the causes and effects of European imperialism in Africa.

Causes		Effects
	Imperialism	

FOCUS ON SPEAKING

5. **Analyzing Imperialism** Jot down some notes about the effects of imperialism you could mention in your report.

GROWTH AND DEVELOPMENT OF AFRICA **365**

Section 3 Assessment Answers

1. **a.** They built mines and plantations and established trade routes in order to gain wealth from African resources.
   b. to prevent their rivals from gaining colonies

2. **a.** European powers divided Africa among themselves.
   b. possible answer—It created tensions between people of differing cultures who had been forced to live together under European rule.

3. **a.** Ethiopia
   b. Africans lacked the powerful weapons that Europeans had.

4. causes—Industrial Revolution creates demand for raw materials; European governments want to prevent rival nations from gaining colonies; Europeans believe it is their duty to bring Western culture to Africa; effects—Africa is divided by Berlin Conference; some Africans resist colonization

5. Students' notes will vary, but may include African resistance and the division of African kingdoms and families.

Bellringer

If YOU lived there. . . Use the **Daily Bellringer Transparency** to help students answer the question.

🗄 Daily Bellringer Transparency, Section 4

Growth and Development of Africa — Daily Bellringer Section 4

Review Section 3

Read the statements below and determine who or what is "speaking."

1. "I am an attempt by one country to dominate the government, trade, or culture of another country." What am I?
2. "I was a meeting of European leaders to divide Africa into colonies." What was I?
3. "I am a waterway built in Egypt to connect the Mediterranean and Red Seas." What am I?
4. "We were Dutch farmers who arrived in South Africa in the 1600s and later fought the British." Who were we?

Preview Section 4

If YOU lived there ...
You are a soldier from the French colony of Morocco. For the last year, you have fought alongside soldiers from France to defeat the German army. Now, the war is over and you are being sent home. You had hoped that you would be rewarded for your service, but your commander sent you off without even saying thanks. **How does this lack of gratitude make you feel?**

Consider your ACHIEVEMENTS:
• helped defeat the Germans
• returned home safely
• were paid for your service during the war

Consider your SACRIFICES:
• left home for a year
• risked your life in combat
• were separated from friends and family

Academic Vocabulary

Review with students the high-use academic term in this section.

rebel to fight against authority (p. 370)

📑 **RF:** Vocabulary Builder, Section 4

Taking Notes

Have students copy the graphic organizer onto their own paper and then use it to take notes on the section. This activity will prepare students for the Section Assessment, in which they will complete a graphic organizer that builds on the information using the Critical Thinking Skill: Summarizing.

Revolution and Freedom

What You Will Learn...

Main Ideas

1. Unhappiness with European rule led to a call for independence in Africa.
2. British colonies were some of the first to become free.
3. French colonies followed two paths to independence.
4. Belgian and Portuguese colonies had to fight for their freedom.

The Big Idea

African colonies began to call for independence after World War II, eventually gaining their freedom.

Key Terms and Places

Ghana, *p. 367*
Kenya, *p. 367*
Mau Mau, *p. 368*
Belgian Congo, *p. 370*

TAKING NOTES As you read, take notes in a chart like this one about the call for independence in Africa and how that goal was achieved in various colonies.

```
          Call for
        Independence
    ┌────────┴────────┐
 British          French
 Colonies         Colonies

 Belgian          Portuguese
 Colonies         Colonies
```

366 CHAPTER 12

If YOU lived there...

You are a soldier from the French colony of Morocco. For the last year, you have fought alongside soldiers from France to defeat the German army. Now, the war is over and you are being sent home. You had hoped that you would be rewarded for your service, but your commander sent you off without even saying thanks.

How does this lack of gratitude make you feel?

BUILDING BACKGROUND For years, Africa was governed by European imperialists. However, events of the early 1900s, especially the two world wars, led to significant social and political changes and, eventually, to African independence.

The Call for Independence

Many Africans were understandably unhappy with European control of their homeland. For centuries, they had ruled their own kingdoms and societies. Now, they were forced to accept outsiders as their leaders. After several rebellions against the Europeans had been put down, however, people across Africa resigned themselves to life in European colonies. Their attitudes began to change, though, after the two world wars.

World War I

After World War I broke out in Europe in 1914, fighting spread to European colonies as well. Among the areas in which violence broke out was Africa. The Allies, including England and France, attacked German colonies in Africa. They hoped that taking Germany's colonies would weaken the country financially.

Much of the fighting in Africa was done by the people of English and French colonies. Hundreds of thousands of Africans were recruited to assist European armies. Tens of thousands of these recruits died in combat.

Teach the Big Idea

Revolution and Freedom

1. **Teach** Ask students the questions in the Main Idea boxes under Direct Teach.

2. **Apply** Organize the class into small groups. Assign each group one of the main headings in this section: The Call for Independence, British Colonies, French Colonies, Belgian and Portuguese Colonies. Have each group read and take notes on their portion of the section.

3. **Review** As you review the section, have each group teach the class what they learned

in their portion of the section. Remind each group to focus on main ideas and supporting details from the reading.

4. **Practice/Homework** Instruct students to create a poster that highlights the main ideas of their reading. Remind students to include text, visuals, and captions that reflect their topic. **LS** Verbal/Linguistic, Visual/Spatial

📑 Alternative Assessment Handbook, Rubrics 11: Discussions; 28: Posters

When the war ended, the African soldiers returning home thought they would be thanked for their efforts. Instead, they were largely ignored. As a result of this snub, resentment toward Europeans increased in parts of Africa.

World War II

In the late 1930s, war once again broke out in Europe. As before, Africans were called upon to help Europeans fight. Some half a million African troops fought alongside the British, the French, and their allies.

When the war ended, the Africans were once again not suitably thanked for their contributions. Angry leaders began calling for political change in Africa. They wanted their independence.

READING CHECK Summarizing How did the two world wars lead to calls for independence?

British Colonies

Among the colonies most loudly calling for independence were those belonging to Great Britain. Their demands only increased in 1947 when Britain granted independence to India. If India could be free, many Africans asked, why couldn't they? Before long, several British colonies in Africa, including Ghana and Kenya, had won their freedom.

Ghana

That first British colony to win its freedom was **Ghana**, formerly called the Gold Coast. Its fight for freedom was led by Kwame Nkrumah (KWAHM-eh en-KROO-muh). In 1947 Nkrumah organized strikes and demonstrations against the British. The British responded by arresting him.

Even from prison, however, Nkrumah called for independence. Inspired by his courage, many people joined his struggle.

Largely because of Nkrumah's actions, the British granted the Gold Coast its independence in 1957. Nkrumah became the first prime minister. As its leader, he renamed the country Ghana after the ancient empire of West Africa.

Kenya

Other British colonies did not find the road to independence as smooth as Ghana did. For example, the East African colony of **Kenya** only became independent after a long and violent struggle.

When the British arrived in Kenya, they claimed land that had once been lived on by the Kikuyu people. They used that land to grow valuable crops, such as coffee. Therefore they did not want to give the land up. The Kikuyu, however, wanted independence, and they wanted their former lands back.

GROWTH AND DEVELOPMENT OF AFRICA **367**

❸ French Colonies

French colonies followed two paths to independence.

Recall Which French colonies had a smooth transition to independence? *the West African colonies*

Contrast How did the road to independence differ in Algeria? *The French sent the military to Algeria to keep order and did not grant Algerians independence until 1962. In Tunisia and Morocco, they negotiated for independence.*

Elaborate What problems do you think may have resulted in Algeria as a result of the violence associated with gaining independence? *possible answers: poor relations with French government; economic difficulties; resentment on the part of Algerian Muslims*

Answers

Reading Check *In Ghana the independence movement was peaceful, but in Kenya it was quite violent.*

Focus on Reading *In West Africa the transition was smooth; in North Africa the change was rough and violent.*

Reading Check *West Africa—France offered colonial leaders a larger role in government; France gave colonies a choice between independence and the French Community; France granted colonies independence; North Africa— Colonists demanded independence; France sent army to prevent violence; negotiations eventually led to independence.*

To retake their land, Kikuyu farmers formed a violent movement called the Mau Mau. Its goal was to rid Kenya of white settlers. Between 1952 and 1960 the Mau Mau terrorized the British in Kenya. Its members attacked and killed anyone they suspected of opposing their goals. They even attacked Africans who cooperated with the British.

The British responded by arresting and torturing any members of the Mau Mau they could find. Nevertheless, the British eventually realized that they would have to grant Kenya's independence. In 1963 they made Kenya a free country. Its first prime minister was Jomo Kenyatta, who had been one of the first people to call for Kenyan freedom.

READING CHECK **Contrasting** How were the paths to independence taken by Ghana and Kenya different?

French Colonies

Like the British, the French began to grant independence to their colonies after World War II. For some colonies, particularly those in West Africa, the transition to independence was smooth. In North Africa, however, the change was rough and violent.

West Africa

France's attitude toward its colonies in West Africa had always been different from Britain's. While the British saw their colonies as backward societies that needed guidance, the French wanted to make their colonies part of France. After World War II, France's leaders offered Africans more of a role in the colonial government. Largely because they had already been given a role in the government, many African leaders in French colonies did not want to break away from France completely.

In 1958, the French government gave its West African colonies a choice. They could become completely independent, or they could join a new organization called the French Community with political and economic ties to France. Most chose to become part of the Community. A few years later, France granted most of the former colonies full independence anyway.

North Africa

Although French colonies in West Africa were willing to work peacefully with the French to gain independence, the colonies of Morocco, Tunisia, and Algeria were not. In all three colonies, protestors calling for independence staged strikes, demonstrations, and attacks. Observers thought that guerilla wars seemed likely.

The French government decided that it could not fight wars in all three colonies. Because Algeria had the largest French population, the French sent their army there. They thought their people would need the army's protection.

With the army in Algeria, the French sent diplomats to Morocco and Tunisia to negotiate. As a result, both countries became independent in 1956.

Meanwhile, violence continued in Algeria. Political groups there attacked French leaders and citizens. In response, the French attacked Algerian Muslims. Finally, France's prime minister suggested a compromise, offering the Algerians some self-government. However, neither the French nor the Algerians were happy with this compromise, and conflict threatened to break out again. Realizing that they could not maintain order in Algeria, the French granted the country its independence in 1962.

READING CHECK **Sequencing** What steps did France's colonies take to become free?

Differentiating Instruction

Special Needs Learners

1. Review with students the ways in which British and French colonies gained their independence.

2. Instruct students to create a four-column chart with the heads Ghana, Kenya, West Africa, and North Africa. Have students use their textbooks to help them take notes on how each region or country gained its independence, when they gained their independence, and what European country gave them independence.

3. Review students' answers as a class.

4. Lead a class discussion on the similarities and differences between independence movements in British and French colonies.
LS Verbal/Linguistic

⬜ Alternative Assessment Handbook, Rubrics 7: Charts; and 11: Discussions

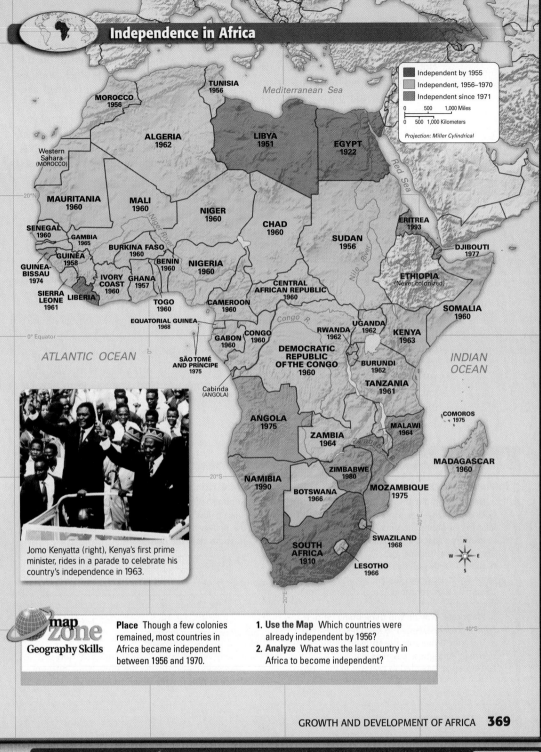

Independence in Africa

Legend:
- Independent by 1955
- Independent, 1956–1970
- Independent since 1971

0   500   1,000 Miles
0   500   1,000 Kilometers

Projection: Miller Cylindrical

Mediterranean Sea

TUNISIA 1956
MOROCCO 1956
ALGERIA 1962
LIBYA 1951
EGYPT 1922
Western Sahara (MOROCCO)
MAURITANIA 1960
MALI 1960
NIGER 1960
CHAD 1960
SUDAN 1956
ERITREA 1993
SENEGAL 1960
GAMBIA 1965
BURKINA FASO 1960
GUINEA 1958
BENIN 1960
NIGERIA 1960
DJIBOUTI 1977
GUINEA-BISSAU 1974
IVORY COAST 1960
GHANA 1957
CENTRAL AFRICAN REPUBLIC 1960
ETHIOPIA (Never colonized)
SIERRA LEONE 1961
LIBERIA
TOGO 1960
CAMEROON 1960
EQUATORIAL GUINEA 1968
SÃO TOMÉ AND PRÍNCIPE 1975
GABON 1960
CONGO 1960
DEMOCRATIC REPUBLIC OF THE CONGO 1960
RWANDA 1962
UGANDA 1962
KENYA 1963
SOMALIA 1960
BURUNDI 1962
TANZANIA 1961
Cabinda (ANGOLA)
ANGOLA 1975
ZAMBIA 1964
MALAWI 1964
COMOROS 1975
MADAGASCAR 1960
NAMIBIA 1990
ZIMBABWE 1980
BOTSWANA 1966
MOZAMBIQUE 1975
SWAZILAND 1968
SOUTH AFRICA 1910
LESOTHO 1966

ATLANTIC OCEAN
INDIAN OCEAN
Red Sea
Nile River
Niger River
Congo R.
Zambezi R.

Jomo Kenyatta (right), Kenya's first prime minister, rides in a parade to celebrate his country's independence in 1963.

map zone
Geography Skills

Place Though a few colonies remained, most countries in Africa became independent between 1956 and 1970.

1. **Use the Map** Which countries were already independent by 1956?
2. **Analyze** What was the last country in Africa to become independent?

GROWTH AND DEVELOPMENT OF AFRICA **369**

Main Idea

❹ Belgian and Portuguese Colonies

Belgian and Portuguese colonies had to fight for their freedom.

Identify What African colony did Belgium control? What colonies did Portugal control in Africa? *Belgium—the Belgian Congo; Portugal—Angola, Guinea, Mozambique*

Make Inferences Why do you think the Belgian and Portuguese governments were so unwilling to let go of their African colonies? *possible answer—They had become dependent on African raw materials.*

● Review & Assess ●

Close

Have students discuss the various ways in which African countries gained their independence from European rule.

Review

 Online Quiz, Section 4

Assess

SE Section 4 Assessment

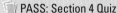 PASS: Section 4 Quiz

Alternative Assessment Handbook

Reteach/Classroom Intervention

Interactive Reader and Study Guide, Section 4

Interactive Skills Tutor CD-ROM

Answers

Reading Check *because Belgium and Portugal fought to keep control of their colonies*

370

Belgian and Portuguese Colonies

Not all European countries were willing to set their colonies free. The Belgians and the Portuguese in particular fought to keep their colonies. Neither country willingly gave up its claims in Africa.

ACADEMIC VOCABULARY
rebel to fight against authority

The Belgian Congo

Belgium controlled only one major colony in Africa—the **Belgian Congo**. After World War II, the Belgians granted some freedoms to the colony's people. Wanting full indendence, however, the Congolese people rose up. Various Congolese groups staged riots and even held elections. However, not all of these groups shared the same goals and conflict between groups was common.

The Belgians refused to recognize the colonists' rights for many years. In 1960, though, they suddenly changed their position. They withdrew from the Congo and the colony became independent. Shortly afterward, civil war broke out between various groups who wanted to run the newly independent Congo.

Portuguese Colonies

Unlike the Belgians, the Portuguese held several colonies in Africa, mostly in the south and east. Even as the other countries of Europe were setting their colonies free, the Portuguese fought to keep theirs.

Eventually, however, the people of Portugal's colonies **rebelled** against them. In Angola, Guinea, and Mozambique, rebels attacked Portuguese troops. These attacks began decades of bloody war.

In 1974 Portugal's military government was overthrown and replaced with a democracy. Shortly afterward, the Portuguese gave up any claim to their colonies and withdrew from Africa completely.

READING CHECK Identifying Cause and Effect Why were the Belgian and Portuguese colonies among the last to become free?

SUMMARY AND PREVIEW By 1970 most colonies in Africa had won their independence. Next, you will learn how life in Africa changed after independence.

Section 4 Assessment

go.hrw.com
Online Quiz
KEYWORD: SK9 HP12

Reviewing Ideas, Terms, and Places

1. **a. Recall** What did Africans do in World War I?
   b. Draw Conclusions How did the world wars lead to resentment in Africa?
2. **a. Identify** What was the first British colony to become independent?
   b. Explain Why was the **Mau Mau** formed?
3. **a. Contrast** How was the French attitude toward its West African colonies different from the British?
   b. Elaborate Why do you think many former French colonies wanted to keep ties to France?
4. **a. Describe** What was the struggle for independence in Portuguese colonies like?
   b. Sequence What led to civil war in the Congo?

Critical Thinking

5. **Summarizing** Using your notes, complete the chart below with one statement that summarizes the path each country's colonies took to win their freedom from the Europeans.

Country	Colonies' path to independence
Great Britain	
France	
Belgium	
Portugal	

FOCUS ON SPEAKING

6. **Examining the Role of Independence** How will your news report discuss the struggle for independence in Africa? Write down some ideas.

Section 4 Assessment Answers

1. **a.** They helped European nations fight.
   b. Africans were resentful that they were not granted independence in return for their efforts in the world wars.
2. **a.** Ghana
   b. to rid Kenya of white settlers
3. **a.** The French wanted to make their colonies part of France.
   b. possible answer—The French were more welcoming of the colonists.
4. **a.** Portugal refused to grant its colonies independence, so the colonists rebelled, leading to bloody wars.

   b. arguments over what group would rule the independent country
5. British colonies—used both demonstrations and violence to gain independence; French colonies—used negotiations and violence to gain independence; Belgian colonies—used warfare; Portuguese colonies—used warfare to gain independence
6. Students' responses may vary, but should accurately reflect the ways in which African countries gained their independence.

Literature

from
AKÉ: The Years of Childhood

by Wole Soyinka

About the Reading *In this excerpt from his childhood memoir, Nigerian-born Wole Soyinka describes life in Nigeria before independence. His later works discussed, often critically, the political changes in the country after it became free.*

AS YOU READ Notice the variety of goods the traders brought to the author's house.

It was a strange procedure, one which made little sense to me. ❶ They spread their wares in front of the house and I had to be prised off them. There were brass figures, horses, camels, trays, bowls, ornaments. Human figures spun on a podium, balanced by weights at the end of curved light metal rods. We spun them round and round, yet they never fell off their narrow perch. The smell of fresh leather filled the house as pouffs, handbags, slippers and worked scabbards were unpacked. There were bottles encased in leather, with leather stoppers, . . . scrolls, glass beads, bottles of scent with exotic names—I never forgot, from the first moment I read it on the label—Bint el Sudan, with its picture of a turbanned warrior by a kneeling camel. A veiled maiden offered him a bowl of fruits. They looked unlike anything in the orchard and Essay said they were called dates. ❷ I did not believe him; dates were figures which appeared on a calendar on the wall, so I took it as one of his jokes.

Merchants from North Africa sometimes traded brass objects in West Africa.

GUIDED READING

WORD HELP

wares goods
prised taken by force
pouff fluffy clothing or accessory
scabbard a case to hold a knife
turbanned wearing a turban, or wrapped cloth, on the head

❶ The author is describing a visit by the Hausa traders who came from northwestern Africa.

❷ Essay is the author's father.

Connecting Literature to Geography

1. **Drawing Inferences** The author describes many unusual things. What descriptions or comments lead you to believe that the trader traveled to Aké from far away?

2. **Analyzing** Think about the way the author described the goods. What senses did the author use as a child to discover the goods the traders brought?

371

Literature

from *AKÉ: The Years of Childhood* by Wole Soyinka

As You Read
Describing People from a Different Region Ask students to imagine that they have a house guest from a different region of the United States. Have them think about hints, such as dialect, that reveal that the person is visiting from a different region.

Meet the Writer
Wole Soyinka Born in Nigeria, Soyinka attended college there as well as in Great Britain. Upon returning home in 1960, he began to write and produce plays. He was arrested and jailed for his political beliefs during the Nigerian civil war (1967–1970) and was then forced into exile from 1994 to 1998. In 1986 he became the first African writer to win the Nobel Prize for Literature.

Collaborative Learning

At Level

Charting Sense Details

1. Review the five senses—sight, sound, smell, taste, and touch. Discuss how the things we sense are related to geography. For example, a person living on a mountain might see and smell different things than a person living in a valley.

2. Divide the class into small groups. Have each group create a chart of the five senses. For each sense, students should list details from the literature that describe the sense.

3. Have each group decide which senses are not represented in the text. *(sound, taste)* Each group should then write sentences describing details that represent the senses not used in the text. Encourage students to write their sentences from Wole Soyinka's point of view.

4. As a class, discuss and share information from the sense charts. Ask each group to share their additional detail sentences.
LS Interpersonal, Verbal/Linguistic
Alternative Assessment Handbook, Rubric 14: Group Activity

Answers
Connecting Literature to Geography **1.** *"They looked unlike anything in the orchard. . ."* **2.** *sight, touch, smell*

Bellringer

If YOU lived there. . . Use the **Daily Bellringer Transparency** to help students answer the question.

📦 Daily Bellringer Transparency, Section 5

Growth and Development of Africa	Daily Bellringer
	Section 5

Review Section 4

Match the sets of letters below to the correct term.

1. Kwame N _ _ _ mah   **HAN**
2. Ki _ _ _ _ u   **KRU**
3. G _ _ _ _ a   **LGI**
4. Be _ _ _ _ an Congo   **KUY**

Preview Section 5

If YOU lived there ...

You live in South Africa. One day, you and some friends join a protest against certain unfair government policies. Although the protest is peaceful, a large number of police officers show up and arrest its organizer. As they handcuff him and drag him off to prison, many people are angry. **How do you feel about this event?**

Consider the CROWD'S point of view:
- The protest was peaceful.
- No one was hurt or put in danger.
- People should have the right to protest government policies.

Consider the POLICE'S point of view:
- Large crowds can turn violent.
- It is the government's job to create policies.
- No one was physically hurt by the arrest.

Key Terms and Places

📄 RF: Vocabulary Builder, Section 5

Taking Notes

Have students copy the graphic organizer onto their own paper and then use it to take notes on the section. This activity will prepare students for the Section Assessment, in which they will complete a graphic organizer that builds on the information using the Critical Thinking Skill: Categorizing.

Africa since Independence

What You Will Learn...

Main Ideas

1. People in South Africa faced social struggles related to racial equality.
2. Many African countries saw political challenges after they became independent.
3. The economy and the environment affect life in Africa.
4. African culture blends traditional and European elements.

The Big Idea

The people of Africa have faced both changes and challenges since they won their independence.

Key Terms and Places

apartheid, *p. 373*
townships, *p. 373*
sanctions, *p. 373*
Darfur, *p. 375*
Lagos, *p. 376*
Kinshasa, *p. 376*

TAKING NOTES As you read, take notes about changes that have occurred in Africa since independence. Use a chart like the one below to organize your notes.

Changes in Africa

If YOU lived there...

You live in South Africa. One day, you and some friends join a protest against certain unfair government policies. Although the protest is peaceful, a large number of police officers show up and arrest its organizer. As they handcuff him and drag him off to prison, many people are angry.

How do you feel about this event?

BUILDING BACKGROUND Though most African countries won their independence between the 1950s and the 1970s, they faced unexpected challenges with their newfound freedom. Military rule and civil war were common problems that plagued Africa into the 1990s.

Social Struggles in South Africa

Many Africans suffered during the imperial period. They felt that their lives would improve once they were free. With independence, many found that their lives were indeed better. At the same time, though, a new set of problems developed.

One example of these new problems could be seen in South Africa. The country gained independence in 1910, much earlier than most African countries. However, racial tensions there led to the creation of an official policy of discrimination.

Apartheid

In the early 1900s South Africa's government was largely controlled by the white descendants of early Dutch, French, and German settlers. Many of these white residents believed that they should have all the power and that black South Africans should have no voice in the government. Understandably, black South Africans opposed this plan. To defend their rights, they formed the African National Congress (ANC) in 1912.

Teach the Big Idea

At Level

Africa since Independence

1. **Teach** Ask students the questions in the Main Idea boxes under Direct Teach.

2. **Apply** Organize the class into seven groups. Assign each group one of the following topics: apartheid, military dictatorships, ethnic conflict and civil war, democracy in Africa, struggling economies, environmental challenges, and African culture. Have each group read the text in the section that addresses their topic. Then have each group create a poster summarizing the main ideas and supporting details of their section.

3. **Review** As you review the section, have students keep a list of challenges and accomplishments of African nations today.

4. **Practice/Homework** Have students create a political cartoon on a topic from the section. **LS Verbal/Linguistic, Visual/Spatial**

📄 Alternative Assessment Handbook, Rubrics 27: Political Cartoons; and 28: Posters

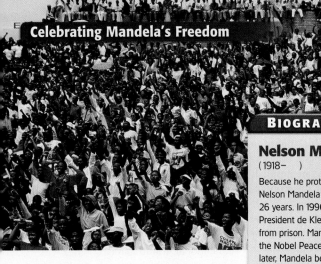

Celebrating Mandela's Freedom

South Africans in Soweto warmly welcomed Nelson Mandela after he was released from prison in 1990.

Despite protests by the ANC, South Africa's government set up a policy of separation of races, or **apartheid** (uh-PAHR-tayt), which means "apartness." This policy divided people into four groups: whites, blacks, Coloureds, and Asians. Coloureds were people of mixed ancestry.

Under apartheid, only white South Africans could vote or hold political office. Blacks, who made up nearly 75 percent of the population, were not citizens. They could only work certain jobs and made very little money. They were only allowed to live in certain areas. In cities, black residents had to live in specially designated **townships**, which were often crowded clusters of tiny homes. Only certain types of businesses were allowed in the townships, which ensured that people living there would stay poor. In the 1950s, South Africa's government created "homelands" for various black African tribes. However, these homelands generally did not include good farmland or resources, which were owned by the whites. Coloured and Asian citizens also had restricted rights, though they had more rights than blacks.

BIOGRAPHY

Nelson Mandela
(1918–)

Because he protested against apartheid, Nelson Mandela was imprisoned for 26 years. In 1990, however, South Africa's President de Klerk released Mandela from prison. Mandela and de Klerk shared the Nobel Peace Prize in 1993. One year later, Mandela became South Africa's first black president. He wrote a new constitution and worked to improve the living conditions of all black South Africans.

Summarizing What did Nelson Mandela accomplish when he was South Africa's president?

The End of Apartheid

By the 1940s many South Africans, especially members of the ANC, were protesting loudly against apartheid. Among the leaders of these protests was a young lawyer named Nelson Mandela. He urged black South Africans to fight apartheid.

In 1960 the South African government banned the ANC and put Mandela in jail. Even with their leader in jail, however, people continued to protest apartheid. The protests were not limited to South Africa, either. People around the world called for an end to apartheid. Other governments placed **sanctions**—economic or political penalties imposed by one country on another to force a policy change—against South Africa.

GROWTH AND DEVELOPMENT OF AFRICA **373**

373

❷ Political Challenges

Many African countries saw political challenges after they became independent.

Recall How did African military dictators stay in control? *by refusing to allow others to run for office; by banning political organizations that did not support the government*

Draw Conclusions Why might many African countries have changed the country name after independence? *possible answers—to show that they were no longer under European control; to replace European names with traditional African names*

Elaborate What might citizens of Zaire have thought of Mobutu's rule? *possible answer—They were angered by his corruption and use of violence.*

Biography

Idi Amin (1924 or 1925–2003) Like many African dictators, Ugandan dictator, Idi Amin, rose to power through the military. Amin, who originally joined the British army in Uganda in 1946 and served as a cook, rose quickly through the ranks. After Uganda's independence, Amin was one of only a few native-born officers. By 1966 Amin was head of the Ugandan army and air force. From his position of power, Amin staged a coup in 1971. Amin's rule was marked by economic problems and violence. In 1978, after attacking neighboring Tanzania, Amin's opponents joined with Tanzanian troops to defeat the Ugandan military. Amin eventually fled Uganda and lived the remainder of his life in exile in Saudi Arabia.

Answers

Reading Check *They were opposed to discrimination against black South Africans.*

374

Faced with this pressure from inside and outside, the South African government finally began to move away from apartheid in the late 1980s. In 1990 it released Mandela from prison. Soon afterward, South Africans of all races were given the right to vote. In 1994 Mandela was elected South Africa's first black president.

Today all races have equal rights in South Africa. Public schools and universities are open to all people, as are hospitals and transportation. However, full economic equality has come more slowly. White South Africans are still wealthier than the majority of blacks. Still, South Africans now have better opportunities for the future.

READING CHECK **Making Inferences** Why did people around the world protest apartheid?

Political Challenges

South Africa was not the only country to face political challenges after winning independence. Across Africa, people suffered under harsh military dictatorships and long civil wars.

Military Dictatorships

By the late 1960s most of Africa was independent. In most of the newly free countries, the government was run by military dictators. These dictators kept power by not allowing anyone else to run for office. As a result, the dictator remained in charge. In most countries with military dictatorships, all political organizations that did not support the government were banned.

Perhaps the best example of a military dictator in Africa was Joseph Mobutu. He rose to power in the Congo in 1965 after the Belgians left. To show his power, he changed the name of the country to Zaire, a traditional African name.

As dictator, Mobutu took over foreign-owned industries. He borrowed money from other countries to try to improve the country's industry. However, most farmers suffered during Mobutu's rule. In addition, many government and business leaders were corrupt. While the country's economy collapsed, Mobutu become one of the richest people in the world. Anyone who dared to challenge his authority was met with violence.

Political Change in Africa

The countries of Africa underwent many political changes after they became independent. In many countries those change led to corrupt governments and violent conflicts. Eventually, most countries formed democratic governments.

Dictators
Military dictators like Uganda's Idi Amin seized power in many countries.

374

Differentiating Instruction

Advanced/Gifted and Talented

1. Lead a class discussion about the rise of military dictatorships in Africa following independence.

2. Organize the students into pairs, and have each group conduct research to identify one African military dictator. Encourage each pair to select a different dictator.

3. Have students use the library, the Internet, and other sources to research the military dictator they select. Have students identify how the dictator came to power, what

strategies the dicatator used to stay in power, and how the different social and ethnic groups in that country fared under the dictator's rule.

4. Have each pair create and present a five-slide multimedia presentation on its dictator.

5. After each pair has presented, lead a class discussion on the similarities and differences among the various dictators. **⑤ Verbal/Linguistic**

📝 Alternative Assessment Handbook, Rubrics 22: Multimedia Presentations; and 30: Research

Ethnic Conflict and Civil War

Many Africans were not happy with these military dictators and took steps to replace them. Mobutu, for example, was overthrown after a civil war in 1997. The new government renamed the country the Democratic Republic of the Congo. Similar civil wars were fought in many countries.

Political disagreement was only one factor that has led to violence in Africa. Ethnic conflict is also common. As you recall, when the leaders of Europe divided Africa among themselves, they paid little attention to the people who lived there. As a result, colonies often included people from many ethnic groups. In some cases, these groups did not get along at all.

When colonies became independent years later, these ethnic groups sometimes fought each other for control. Their fighting often led to long, bloody civil wars. In Rwanda, for example, the Hutu and Tutsi ethnic groups went to war in 1994. The government, run by the Hutu, began killing all the Tutsi in the country. About 1 million Tutsi civilians were killed in the conflict. Many more fled the country.

Similar conflict has plagued Sudan for decades. Muslims and Christians have fought each other for years. More recently, a genocide has occurred in the region of **Darfur.** Ethnic conflict there has resulted in tens of thousands of black Sudanese being killed by an Arab militia group. Millions more have fled Darfur. Those who fled are now scattered throughout northern and eastern Africa as refugees.

Democracy in Africa

Dictatorships and civil wars were common in Africa through the late 1900s. As the year 2000 approached, however, political changes swept through Africa. People began to demand more democratic forms of government. They wanted to choose their own leaders.

By 2005 more than 30 countries in Africa had abandoned dictatorships and held elections. Though some of these elections were rigged to keep corrupt governments in place, others resulted in true democratic governments coming to power.

READING CHECK **Describing** What political challenges have African nations faced?

Civil War and Ethnic Conflict
Ethnic conflict in Darfur, Sudan, has forced millions of people to flee the country as refugees. Some receive food and aid at camps like this one.

Democracy
Like many African nations, Nigeria is a democracy. Its citizens elected a new president in 2007.

375

• Direct Teach •

Main Idea

❷ Political Challenges, *continued*

Recall What was sometimes the result of ethnic conflicts within African countries? *civil war*

Explain What was the source of the conflict that emerged in Darfur? *ethnic and religious disagreements*

Elaborate What led to a movement toward democracy in some parts of Africa? *People began to demand the right to choose their own leaders.*

Info to Know

Conflict in Nigeria Ethnic conflict in Nigeria led to a bloody civil war. In 1967 the Igbo-speaking people of eastern Nigeria proclaimed their own independent country, the Republic of Biafra. The Nigerian leaders, however, were unwilling to let them remain independent. As a result, a bloody civil war erupted. About 2 million Nigerians died from fighting and just as many died of starvation. After Biafra collapsed, the territory rejoined Nigeria.

Critical Thinking: Summarizing

At Level

Political Change Collage

1. Review with students the political changes that took place in Africa in the years after countries there earned their independence.

2. Have students make a list of the changes discussed on these pages. Then have students identify images that might represent each of the changes they identified.

3. Have students create a collage of images and words or phrases that represent the political changes in Africa since independence.

4. Have students use old magazines and newspapers, the Internet, and other sources to locate images for their collages.

5. Have students display their completed collages for everyone to see. **LS Visual/Spatial, Verbal/Linguistic**

   Alternative Assessment Handbook, Rubric 8: Collages

Answers

Reading Check *military dictatorships, violence, ethnic conflict, and civil war*

375

Main Idea

❸ Economy and Environment

The economy and the environment affect life in Africa.

Recall Why did many African countries have weak economies after they became independent? *They had not industrialized.*

Explain What environmental challenges do African countries face? *diseases, such as malaria and AIDS, and drought*

Elaborate How might African countries improve their struggling economies? *Students' responses may vary, but should suggest reasonable solutions.*

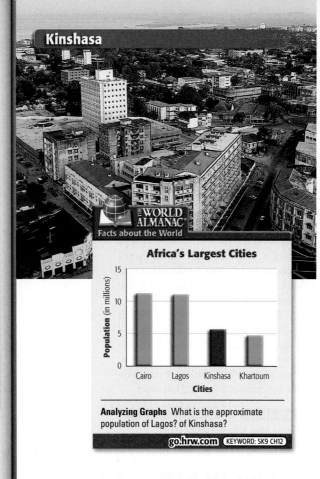

Kinshasa

THE WORLD ALMANAC® Facts about the World

Africa's Largest Cities

[Bar graph: "Population (in millions)" on y-axis from 0 to 15. Cities on x-axis: Cairo (~11), Lagos (~11), Kinshasa (~6), Khartoum (~5).]

Analyzing Graphs What is the approximate population of Lagos? of Kinshasa?

go.hrw.com KEYWORD: SK9 CH12

Economy and Environment

Political challenges were not the only ones faced by Africa's countries. Many countries faced economic challenges as well. At the same time, Africans had to fight environmental issues, including deadly diseases.

Struggling Economies

After they became independent, many African countries had weak economies. Most countries had not industrialized and depended mainly on farming or mining. For example, Ghana earned most of its income from cocoa, and Nigeria from oil.

Since independence, however, many countries have found new economic opportunities. As a result, their economies are stronger than ever. Among the countries with Africa's strongest economies are South Africa, Nigeria, and many countries in North Africa. However, some other countries still have huge debts and little infrastructure and must depend on aid from other countries.

As Africa's economies grow, so do its cities. These cities offer more jobs and higher standards of living than rural areas. Each year millions of people move there. As a result, already-large cities like Cairo, Egypt; **Lagos**, Nigeria; and **Kinshasa**, Democratic Republic of the Congo, are growing even larger. Rapid growth has led to crowding and high unemployment in some cities.

Environmental Challenges

Economic development in Africa has been slow in part because people have to deal with environmental challenges, including disease. For example, malaria, a disease spread by mosquitoes, is one of the leading causes of death in many parts of Africa. Even more deadly than malaria is AIDS. This disease that weakens the immune system is widespread in Africa. In some countries, more than one fourth of the entire population is infected with AIDS.

Other environmental challenges also make survival difficult. Much of the continent suffered terrible droughts in the 1980s. These droughts left farmers unable to grow crops, and terrible famines swept through Africa. Famines are made worse by desertification, the spread of desertlike conditions. In parts of Africa, especially West Africa, farmers must take care to prevent fertile soil from disappearing.

READING CHECK **Identifying** What are two challenges people in Africa have faced?

376 CHAPTER 12

Critical Thinking: Identifying Problem and Solution   At Level

Confronting Environmental Challenges in Africa

1. Review with the class some of the environmental challenges that African countries face. Ask students to explain how each challenge might affect the people and governments of Africa.

2. Organize the class into small groups. Have each group select one of the challenges mentioned in the text or during the class discussion.

3. Have each group prepare a plan for how to combat the effects that their selected

challenge may have on Africa. For example, students may suggest a solution for combating malaria. Remind students to carefully consider several options before deciding on a final plan.

4. Instruct each group to present its plan to the class. Then have the class discuss the pros and cons of each plan.

📝 Alternative Assessment Handbook, Rubric 35: Solving Problems

Answers

Analyzing Graphs *Lagos—approximately 11 million; Kinshasa—approximately 6 million*

Reading Check *possible answers—struggling economies; high debt; a lack of infrastructure; disease; drought; famine*

African Culture

After they became independent, many African countries underwent identity crises. As colonies, they were forced to adopt many elements of European culture. At the same time, however, African peoples had their own cultures that stretched back through centuries. How would people deal with these mixed cultures?

People reacted in different ways. Many elements of European culture can still be seen in Africa. For example, many people in West Africa still speak French or English in their daily lives.

At the same time, many Africans have rejected European culture and sought to reclaim their own traditional cultures. Writers and musicians draw on traditional themes from African folklore in their works, often written in Swahili or other African languages. Artists create masks, musical instruments, and sculptures from wood and bronze, just as their ancestors did centuries ago.

READING CHECK **Analyzing** How does African culture reflect African and European ideas?

African Music

Artists like the Mahotella Queens singing group have brought African culture to a worldwide audience.

SUMMARY AND PREVIEW In this section, you learned how African countries have grown and changed since they became independent. Next, you will read in more detail about life and society in one of those countries, Nigeria.

Section 5 Assessment

go.hrw.com
Online Quiz
KEYWORD: SK9 HP12

Reviewing Ideas, Terms, and Places

1. **a. Define** What was **apartheid**?
   b. Elaborate How did international protests help end apartheid?
2. **a. Describe** What problems did military dictators cause in some African countries?
   b. Explain What led to violence in parts of Africa?
3. **a. Recall** What issues do cities like **Lagos** and **Kinshasa** face today?
   b. Develop How might environmental challenges lead to economic issues?
4. **a. Identify** What is one element of European culture present in Africa today?

b. Draw Conclusions Why did many Africans want to reclaim their traditional culture?

Critical Thinking

5. **Categorizing**
   Review your notes. Then complete the chart by listing political, economic, and social changes in Africa.

Changes in Africa		
Political	Economic	Social

FOCUS ON SPEAKING

6. **Choosing Your Topic** Now that you have studied modern Africa, you can choose the topic for your news report. What will you discuss?

GROWTH AND DEVELOPMENT OF AFRICA **377**

Section 5 Assessment Answers

1. **a.** the South African policy of separating the races
   b. They attracted attention to apartheid and pressured the government to change.
2. **a.** corruption, economic problems, and violence
   b. ethnic and religious conflict
3. **a.** overcrowding, rapid growth, and high unemployment
   b. possible answer—Problems like disease and famine may put a strain on government resources, leading to economic troubles.

4. **a.** English and French language
   b. to eliminate European influences
5. political—end of apartheid, rise of military dictatorships, spread of democracy, economic—lack of industrialization, huge debt, unemployment, famine; social—rich culture, renewal of African traditional culture
6. Students' responses may vary, but might include political, economic, environmental, and cultural changes.

• **Direct Teach** •

Main Idea

❹ **African Culture**

African culture blends traditional and European elements.

Describe How have Africans sought to reclaim their traditional culture? *by drawing on traditional themes from folklore and writing in traditional languages*

Evaluate Do you think that African culture has become richer since independence? Explain your answer. *Students' responses may vary, but should include sufficient support for their stances.*

RF: Biography: Assia Djebar

• Review & Assess •

Close

Have students write a news article summarizing the changes and challenges African countries have faced since independence.

Review

Online Quiz, Section 5

Assess

SE Section 5 Assessment
PASS: Section 5 Quiz
Alternative Assessment Handbook

Reteach/Classroom Intervention

Interactive Reader and Study Guide, Section 5
Interactive Skills Tutor CD-ROM

Answers

Reading Check *It includes a mix of both cultures, such as European languages and traditional African customs.*

377

Social Studies Skills

Interpreting a Population Pyramid

Learn

A population pyramid shows the percentages of males and females by age group in a country's population. The pyramids are split into two sides. Each bar on the left shows the percentage of a country's population that is male and of a certain age. The bars on the right show the same information for females.

Population pyramids help us understand population trends in countries. Countries that have large percentages of young people have populations that are growing rapidly. Countries with more older people are growing slowly or not at all.

Practice

Use the population pyramid of Angola to answer the following questions.

❶ What age group is the largest?

❷ What percent of Angola's population is made up of 15- to 19-year-old males?

❸ What does this population pyramid tell you about the population trend in Angola?

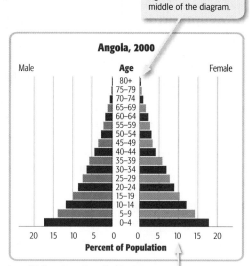

Ages are listed down the middle of the diagram.

Angola, 2000

Male Age Female

Source: U.S. Census Bureau, International Data Base

Percentages are labeled across the bottom of the diagram.

Apply

Do research at the library or on the Internet to find age and population data for the United States. Use that information to answer the following questions.

1. What age group is the largest?

2. Are there more males or females over age 80?

3. How would you describe the shape of the population pyramid?

378 CHAPTER 12

Social Studies Skills

Interpreting a Population Pyramid

Activity Comparing Population Pyramids Numerous Internet sites including the U.S. Census Bureau provide population pyramids for every country in the world. Bring to class or have students search the Internet for population pyramids of Yemen, Niger, or the Democratic Republic of the Congo. These three countries have populations that are among the top five youngest in the world. Students can also search for population pyramids for the three countries with the oldest populations: Italy, Greece, and Germany. Organize students into groups. Give each group a population pyramid and have the groups compare their country's pyramid with the one for Angola.

Conclude by having each group predict what the future needs of its country will be for primary schools, doctors, hospitals, senior care, and other facilities or services. **LS** Logical/Mathematical, Verbal/Linguistic

- Alternative Assessment Handbook, Rubric 12: Drawing Conclusions
- Interactive Skills Tutor CD-ROM, Lesson 6: Interpret Maps, Graphs, Charts, Visuals, and Political Cartoons
- RF: Social Studies Skills, Interpreting a Population Pyramid

Social Studies Skills Activity: Interpreting a Population Pyramid

Struggling Readers

Below Level **Prep Required**

1. Make enlarged copies of the population pyramid on this page or project a population pyramid on an overhead. Have students take turns explaining what type of data each part of the pyramid provides. Make sure students understand that the center vertical line divides the bars by gender.

2. Check understanding by having students find their own age group and identify the percentage for each gender.

3. Then have students put a blank sheet of paper over all but the two lowest bars and tell what percentage of boys and girls are in the youngest age category. Repeat this process for the highest bars on the pyramid.

4. Conclude by discussing why governments collect this kind of data and how it might be used to plan for the future.
   LS Visual/Spatial, Linguistic/Verbal

- Alternative Assessment Handbook, Rubric 7: Charts

Answers

Practice 1. *0–4;* **2.** *approximately 10%;* **3.** *Angola has a very young population with few people aged 40 and over. It seems likely this trend will continue.*

Apply *Answers will vary based on data used by students. Answers here based on 2000 census.* **1.** *ages 35–44;* **2.** *females;* **3.** *possible answer—a modified pyramid that looks like a pagoda*

378

Chapter Review

Geography's Impact
video series
Review the video to answer the closing question:
What are some ways South Africans could continue working together?

Visual Summary

Use the visual summary below to help you review the main ideas of the chapter.

QUICK FACTS

Valuable trade goods like ivory and gold lured many Europeans to Africa and led to the creation of colonies.

Between the 1950s and the 1970s many African countries won their independence from Europe.

Many African cities have grown tremendously. People move to the cities for economic opportunity.

Reviewing Vocabulary, Terms, and Places

Match the words with their definitions.

1. Swahili
2. sanctions
3. apartheid
4. Middle Passage
5. entrepreneurs
6. Mau Mau
7. Gold Coast
8. imperialism

a. policy of separation of races
b. grueling trip endured by slaves across the Atlantic Ocean
c. attempt to dominate a country's government, trade, or culture
d. economic or political penalties
e. colony established by the British in West Africa
f. violent movement intended to rid Kenya of white settlers
g. blended African-Arab culture of East Africa
h. independent business owners

Comprehension and Critical Thinking

SECTION 1 *(Pages 350–353)*

9. **a. Recall** What brought Islam to East Africa?
   b. Compare and Contrast How did Coptic Christianity differ from other forms?
   c. Elaborate How do you think the arrival of new religions changed life in Africa?

SECTION 2 *(Pages 354–357)*

10. **a. Identify** Which European country was the first to trade in Africa?
    b. Draw Conclusions Why do you think early European activity in Africa was limited mostly to West Africa?
    c. Develop How did the slave trade weaken African society?

SECTION 3 *(Pages 360–365)*

11. **a. Define** What is imperialism, and what led to European imperialism in Africa?

Answers

Visual Summary

Review and Inquiry Have students write each section's Big Idea on a separate sheet of self-stick note paper and stick each note under the most relevant picture. Have students illustrate any remaining ideas on a separate sheet and then put the corresponding note under their illustration.

Quick Facts Transparency: Visual Summary: Growth and Development of Africa

Reviewing Vocabulary, Terms, and Places

1. g   5. h
2. d   6. f
3. a   7. e
4. b   8. c

Comprehension and Critical Thinking

9. **a.** Muslim traders and settlers
   b. It includes a blend of Christianity and traditional African customs.
   c. Many Africans converted to the new religions, thus weakening traditional African religions.

10. **a.** Portugal
    b. possible answers—because it was difficult to travel to the interior; it was the first area in African that Europeans explored
    c. It greatly decreased African populations by taking millions of people, mostly young men.

Review and Assessment Resources

Review and Reinforce

SE Chapter Review
RF: Chapter Review
Quick Facts Transparency: Visual Summary: Growth and Development of Africa
Spanish Chapter Summaries Audio CD Program
OSP Holt Puzzle Pro; Quiz Show for ExamView
Quiz Game CD-ROM

Assess

SE Standardized Test Practice
PASS: Chapter Test, Forms A and B
Alternative Assessment Handbook
OSP ExamView Test Generator, Chapter Test
Differentiated Instruction Modified Worksheets and Tests CD-ROM: Modified Chapter Test
HOAP Holt Online Assessment Program (in the Premier Online Edition)

Reteach/Intervene

Interactive Reader and Study Guide
Differentiated Instruction Teacher Management System: Lesson Plans
Differentiated Instruction Modified Worksheets and Tests CD-ROM
Interactive Skills Tutor CD-ROM

go.hrw.com
Online Resources
Chapter Resources:
KEYWORD: SK9 CH12

11. a. the attempt to dominate a country's government, trade or culture; the need for raw materials

b. The British attempted to make the Boers' land part of the British Empire.

c. They did not have the military might to match the Europeans.

12. a. Kenya, Algeria, Belgian Congo, Angola, Guinea, and Mozambique

b. campaign of strikes and boycotts against the British

c. possible answer—Those that had the easiest road to independence.

13. a. a South African who fought against apartheid, was imprisoned by the South African government, and the first black president of South Africa

b. Dictators often were corrupt and resorted to violence.

c. Students' responses may vary, but should include reasonable and logical predictions about the future of African countries.

Using the Internet

14. Go to the HRW Web site and enter the keyword shown to access a rubric for this activity.

KEYWORD: SK9 TEACHER

Social Studies Skills

15. 80+

16. many more young people than old people, especially people under the age of 30

Focus on Reading and Speaking

17. Africans did not want to be ruled by Europeans; Africans refused to peacefully give up their own cultures and adopt European ways; the Zulu of southern Africa united to oppose European rule; Ethiopia managed to remain free from European rule.

SECTION 3 *(continued)*

b. Sequence What led to the Boer War?

c. Elaborate Why do you think few groups were successful in resisting European imperialism?

SECTION 4 *(Pages 366–370)*

12. a. Identify What were two colonies in which Africans had to fight for their freedom?

b. Summarize How did Ghana win its freedom?

c. Evaluate Which new countries do you think had the best relations with Europe? Why?

SECTION 5 *(Pages 372–377)*

13. a. Identify Who is Nelson Mandela? For what is he most famous?

b. Make Inferences Why were many Africans unhappy with military dictatorships?

c. Predict How do you think African governments will change in the future? Why?

Using the Internet
go.hrw.com
KEYWORD: SK9 CH12

14. Activity: Understanding Cultures Modern Africa is home to thousands of ethnic groups, each with its own culture, traditions, and customs. For many Africans, independence came with a renewed pride in their own cultures. Enter the activity keyword. Discover some African ethnic groups as you visit Web sites about their cultures. Then create a graphic organizer or chart that compares African ethnic groups. It might include comparisons of their language, beliefs, traditions, foods, and more. It might also show how each of the groups was affected by European imperialism.

Social Studies Skills

Interpreting a Population Pyramid *Use the population pyramid in the Social Studies Skills lesson to answer the following questions.*

15. What age group is the smallest?

16. How would you describe the current population in Angola?

---

17. Identifying Supporting Details Look back over the paragraphs under the African Resistance heading in Section 3. Then make a list of details you find to support the section's main ideas.

18. Presenting a TV News Report Review your notes and decide on a topic for your report. Next, identify the point you want to make about your topic—your purpose. Your purpose may be to share interesting information—about an interesting figure from the past, for example. Or your purpose may be more serious—perhaps to show the effects of poverty on Africa. Decide what images you will show and what you will say to make your point to your listeners.

Create a script identifying visuals and voiceover. Present your report to the class using visuals as though you were on the TV news.

Map Activity

19. Growth and Development of Africa On a separate sheet of paper, match the letters on the map with the correct labels.

Cairo

South Africa

Ethiopia

Ghana

Congo River

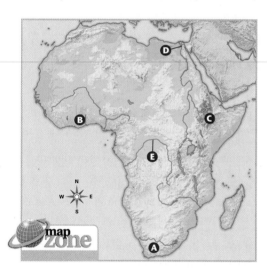

---

18. Rubric Students presentations should

- include a clear purpose
- include relevant images
- use specific facts and details that support the purpose of the report

📄 **RF:** Focus on Speaking, Presenting a TV News Report

Map Activity

19. A. South Africa

B. Ghana

C. Ethiopia

D. Cairo

E. Congo River

DIRECTIONS (1–7): **For each statement or question, write on a separate answer sheet the** *number* **of the word or expression that, of those given, best completes the statement or answers the question.**

1 What was the only country in Africa never to be a European colony?
(1) Ghana
(2) South Africa
(3) Algeria
(4) Ethiopia

2 The Suez Canal is located in
(1) Nigeria.
(2) Egypt.
(3) Tanzania.
(4) Morocco.

3 Which of the following is *not* a challenge that African countries have faced since they became independent?
(1) poverty
(2) ethnic conflict
(3) overeducation
(4) racial tension

4 South Africa's most famous leader in the fight against apartheid was
(1) Nelson Mandela.
(2) Jomo Kenyatta.
(3) Kwame Nkrumah.
(4) Joseph Mobutu.

5 Which of the following statements about military dictators is true?
(1) They never rose to power in Africa.
(2) They held free elections.
(3) They were often corrupt.
(4) They were all fair and just rulers.

6 Which colony had to fight for independence?
(1) South Africa
(2) Belgian Congo
(3) Ethiopia
(4) Ghana

7 The language known as Swahili developed in
(1) North Africa.
(2) South Africa.
(3) West Africa.
(4) East Africa.

Base your answer to question 8 on the diagram below and on your knowledge of social studies.

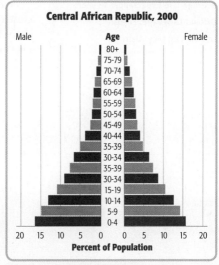

Central African Republic, 2000

Male | Age | Female

80+
75-79
70-74
65-69
60-64
55-59
50-54
45-49
40-44
35-39
30-34
35-39
30-34
15-19
10-14
5-9
0-4

20 15 10 5 0   0 5 10 15 20
Percent of Population

Source: U.S. Census Bureau, International Data Base

8 **Constructed-Response Question** **What generalizations can you make about the population of the Central African Republic?**

GROWTH AND DEVELOPMENT OF AFRICA **381**

1. 4
Break Down the Question This question requires students to recall factual information. Refer students who miss the question to Section 4.

2. 2
Break Down the Question This question requires students to recall factual information. Refer students who miss the question to Section 3.

3. 3
Break Down the Question Remind students to eliminate the answers they know are not correct. This should help them eliminate choices 1, 2, and 4.

4. 1
Break Down the Question This question requires students to recall factual information. Refer students who miss the question to Section 5.

5. 3
Break Down the Question Students should recall that one common complaint about African dictatorships was that the governments were often corrupt.

6. 2
Break Down the Question Remind students that South Africa and Ghana gained their independence through negotiation and protest, while Ethiopia never lost its independence.

7. 4
Break Down the Question This question requires students to recall factual information. Refer students who miss the question to Section 1.

8. Constructed-Response Question
Possible answer—The vast majority of the population in the Central African Republic is made up of very young people. The population there will likely continue to grow as members of the young population start families.

Reteach/Intervention Resources

Reproducible
📖 Interactive Reader and Study Guide
📖 Differentiated Instruction Teacher Management System: Lesson Plans

Technology
💾 Quick Facts Transparency: Visual Summary: Growth and Development of Africa
💿 Differentiated Instruction Modified Worksheets and Tests CD-ROM
💿 Interactive Skills Tutor CD-ROM

Tips for Test Taking

Main Idea Tell students that they will get more out of their studying time if they make sure they understand the main ideas of what they are reading or studying. One way to do this is to be sure that they have understood the main idea of a passage before moving on to the next one. Suggest that while reading, students stop after every few paragraphs or after every heading and identify that passage's main idea. This will help students become active readers and retain more of what they read.

Motivate Before beginning the Case Study, instruct students to examine the photograph on this page. Ask students to identify what they see in the photo. *young men fishing with a net; smoke stacks in the distance* What might the different elements in the photograph indicate about the country of Nigeria? *fishing with a net—traditional culture, underdevelopment; smoke stacks—modernization, industrialization, pollution* Ask students to list the characteristics they expect to learn about Nigeria. Write students' responses for everyone to see. As you review the Case Study, have students refer back to the list to see if their expectations proved true or false.

🖋 Quick Facts Transparency: Facts about Nigeria

Key Terms

Preteach the following terms:

confluence point where two rivers meet or intersect (p. 382)

delta a landform at the mouth of a river created by sediment deposits (p. 382)

secede to break away from the main country (p. 384)

Shariah Muslim law (p. 387)

Case Study

🇳🇬 Nigeria

Geography

Facts About **QUICK FACTS**

Nigeria

Official Name: Federal Republic of Nigeria

Capital: Abuja

Area: 356,669 square miles (slightly larger than Texas and Oklahoma)

Population: 135 million (384 people/ square mile)

Average Life Expectancy: 48 years

Official Language: English

Unit of Currency: Naira

Though it is not Africa's largest country by area, Nigeria is the most populous country on the continent. More than 130 million people live within its borders.

The landscape of Nigeria is mostly river plains. Two major rivers, the Niger and the Benue, come together in central Nigeria. At the confluence, or point where the two rivers meet, the Niger is more than three-fourths of a mile wide, and the Benue more than a mile. South of the confluence, the river is more than two miles wide. Farther south, the river narrows as it flows through a hilly region.

Where the Niger flows into the Gulf of Guinea, it has created the largest delta in the world. A delta is a triangle-shaped deposit of silt that builds up at the mouth of a river. Like most deltas, the Niger Delta is very fertile. It is a swampy area filled with mangrove trees and various animals. Much of the delta's natural vegetation has been cleared to make room for homes and farms. Today the delta is one of the most densely populated regions in Nigeria. In addition, oil companies have built drilling platforms and refineries to take advantage of the delta's huge oil deposits.

To the west of the Niger Delta is Nigeria's largest city, Lagos. Home to more than 11 million people, Lagos is one of the largest cities in Africa, and the fastest growing. Millions of people move to the city each year in search of opportunity because it is Nigeria's main financial and economic center. However, overcrowding and unemployment are severe problems in the city.

1 The **Niger Delta** is home to about a fifth of Nigeria's people and the bulk of its oil and gas reserves.

382 CASE STUDY

Teach the Case Study

At Level

Nigeria

1. **Teach** Ask students the questions in the Main Idea boxes under Direct Teach.

2. **Apply** Organize students into small groups. Assign each group one of the following topics from the Case Study: geography, history, culture, economics, government, and issues. Have each group create a collage that focuses on characteristics of their assigned feature in Nigeria.

3. **Review** As you review the Case Study, have each group present and explain its collage to the class.

4. **Practice/Homework** Have students write a letter to a friend explaining what life is like in Nigeria today. Have students address at least three of the topics addressed by the group collages. **LS Interpersonal, Visual/Spatial**

📝 Alternative Assessment Handbook, Rubrics 8: Collages; and 25: Personal Letters

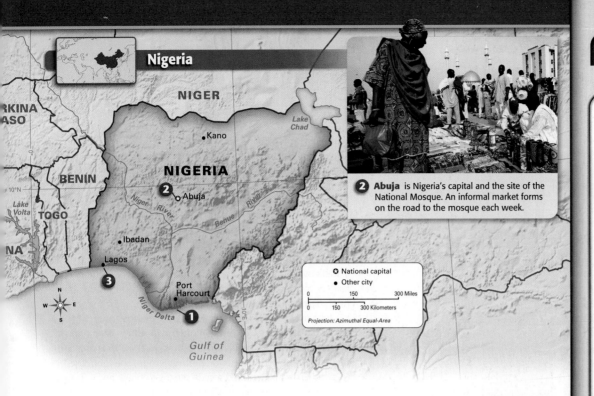

Nigeria

NIGER

Kano

NIGERIA

② Abuja

Ibadan

Lagos

Port
Harcourt

Niger Delta ①

Gulf of
Guinea

BENIN

BURKINA
FASO

TOGO

Lake
Volta

Lake
Chad

○ National capital
● Other city

0   150   300 Miles
0   150   300 Kilometers
Projection: Azimuthal Equal-Area

② **Abuja** is Nigeria's capital and the site of the National Mosque. An informal market forms on the road to the mosque each week.

Lagos was once Nigeria's capital. However, many people were not happy with that location. People in northern Nigeria feared that southerners would have more influence in the government if the capital remained in the south. As a result, the nation's leaders moved the capital in the 1990s. For their new capital, they chose Abuja. Centrally located, Abuja is in a less densely populated region of Nigeria. Leaders hoped that fewer people would cause fewer ethnic conflicts in the new capital.

③ **Lagos** is Nigeria's largest city, one of the largest in Africa.

Case Study Assessment

1. What is the Niger Delta like?
2. Why did Nigeria's capital move to Abuja?
3. **Activity** Design a Nigeria diorama. Choose one region of Nigeria and create a diorama to present its major physical or cultural features.

NIGERIA **383**

383

c. 1200–1400
The Yoruba and Benin kingdoms rule what is now Nigeria.

c. 1471
Portuguese sailors reach the Niger River.

c. 1820
British traders arrive in Nigeria.

Artists from Nigeria's Yoruba culture made beautiful items like this cup from ivory.

History and Culture

For many centuries, Nigeria was home to a number of small kingdoms. Among these kingdoms were Benin, the Yoruba states, and the Hausa states. These kingdoms traded among themselves and with other cultures. Many were famous for their work with brass, bronze, and ivory.

British traders arrived in Nigeria in the late 1800s. Before long they made Nigeria a British colony. It remained a colony until 1960, when it was granted independence under a newly elected government. Within a few years, however, military leaders overthrew the government and took over. Military leaders continued to rule Nigeria until the late 1990s. At that time, democracy was restored in Nigeria.

Like many other former colonies, Nigeria has many different ethnic groups within its borders. Conflicts have often taken place among these ethnic groups. In the 1960s one conflict became so serious that one ethnic group, the Igbo, tried to secede from Nigeria. To secede means to break away from a country. This action led to a bloody civil war, which the Igbo eventually lost.

Nigerian Culture

Nigeria is home to more than 250 ethnic groups, each with its own history, customs, and values. These groups are proud of their cultures and work to keep their heritage alive. As a result, many elements of Nigerian culture today, such as clothing and music, reflect traditional ways of life.

Clothing Traditional Nigerian clothing includes flowing garments in bright colors.

384 CASE STUDY

Direct Teach

Main Idea

History and Culture

Identify Which European empire colonized Nigeria? *Great Britain*

Sequence List in chronological order the types of governments that have ruled Nigeria. *ancient kingdoms, colony of Great Britain, democracy, military rule, democracy*

Make Inferences What is the cause of the conflict between the various ethnic groups? *possible answer—They each want to control government or society and are unhappy when another group exerts more influence.*

Did you know . . .

In the late 1960s tensions between the Hausa-Fulani and the Ibo people in northern Nigeria led to violence. In May 1967 a group of Ibo broke away from Nigeria to form the Republic of Biafra. The Nigerian government, however, refused to recognize their independence and sent troops to reclaim the region. In January 1970 Biafra surrendered to Nigeria and the nation was reunited.

Collaborative Learning

At Level

History Detectives

Research Required

1. Organize the class into groups of three or four. Have each group select a major event from Nigerian history. For example, students might select the independence of Nigeria or the civil war that took place in the 1960s.

2. Have each group work together to research the event. Have students use the library, the Internet, or other sources to research more about their selected event. Have members of each group research different aspects of their event, including its causes and effects.

3. Have each group plan a presentation for the class describing their selected event. Encourage students to use visual aids to enhance their presentations.

4. Have groups give their presentations to the class. Encourage other students to offer their feedback after each presentation.

LS Verbal/Linguistic, Interpersonal

Alternative Assessment Handbook, Rubrics 14: Group Activity; and 24: Oral Presentations

1884
Nigeria becomes
a British colony.

2010

1960
Nigeria becomes
independent.

1999
Free elections in
Nigeria mark the end
of military rule.

**Nigerians celebrate their newfound
independence in 1960.**

Because the country has so many ethnic groups, Nigeria's culture is rich and complex. Many people continue to practice traditional arts, including sculpture, music, dance, and story-telling. In addition, many Nigerians still wear traditional styles of clothing, either in white or in bright colors. At the same time, however, European influences remain strong. English is commonly spoken, and soccer is the most popular sport.

Two other influences in Nigeria are Christianity and Islam. Christianity is common in the south, where most Europeans lived during the colonial period. Islam is more common in the north, where contact with North Africa is more prevalent.

Case Study Assessment

1. Why is Nigerian culture so diverse?
2. Which religions influence Nigerian culture?
3. **Activity** Plan a documentary about Nigerian culture. What topics would you choose to discuss? What images would you include?

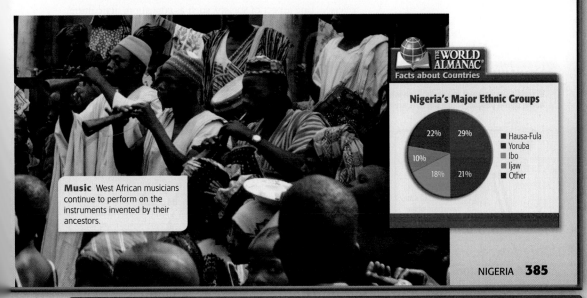

Music West African musicians continue to perform on the instruments invented by their ancestors.

THE WORLD ALMANAC
Facts about Countries

Nigeria's Major Ethnic Groups

- 29% Hausa-Fula
- 22%
- 10%
- 18%
- 21% Yoruba
- Ibo
- Ijaw
- Other

NIGERIA **385**

Nigeria Today

Identify What type of government does Nigeria have? *a democracy*

Understanding Cause and Effect How has a large supply of oil affected Nigeria? *It has brought more wealth to the country and allowed the building of good roads and railroads for transportation.*

Analyze Why does Nigeria still suffer from extreme poverty despite its rich natural resources? *A rapidly growing population means that the country cannot produce enough food to feed everyone; corrupt governments in the past took money away from the people.*

Did you know . . .

Nigeria is the fifth-largest importer of oil to the United States. Among its other imports to the United States are rubber, cocoa, nuts, and coffee.

Info to Know

Nigerian Constitution In 1999 Nigerians adopted a new constitution that established the Federal Republic of Nigeria. Modeled after the U.S. Constitution, the Nigerian constitution organizes the government into executive, legislative, and judicial branches. The constitution calls for freedom of the press, freedom of religion, and an end to government corruption. The constitution also organizes Nigeria into 36 states and the federal capital territory of Abuja.

Nigerian laborers work in a Chinese oil refinery in the Niger Delta. Much of the income from Nigeria's oil industry goes to other countries.

Nigeria Today

Economics

Nigeria has some of Africa's richest natural resources. Major oil fields, the country's most important resource, are located in the Niger River delta and just off the coast. Oil accounts for 95 percent of the country's export earnings. Income from oil exports has allowed Nigeria to build good roads and railroads for transporting oil. The oil industry is centered around Lagos.

Although Nigeria is rich in resources, many Nigerians are poor. One cause of the poverty there is the high birthrate. Nigeria cannot produce enough food for its growing population. Another cause of Nigeria's poverty is a history of bad government. Corrupt officials have often used their positions to enrich themselves while their people suffered.

Government

Although Nigeria has officially been a democracy since it became independent, people have had little say in the government for most of that time. Instead, military leaders have fought each other for power. In 1999, however, free elections led to a new president and a return to democracy in Nigeria.

Nigeria's president serves as the head of the executive branch of the government. This branch is responsible for carrying out the country's laws. The president is assisted in his duties by a executive council of ministers. Each minister oversees one aspect of society, such as education, agriculture, sports, or tourism.

Structure of the Nigerian Government

Nigeria's government is a republic in which elected officials govern in the name of the people. Those officials are organized into three branches.

Executive Branch
As in the United States, Nigeria's president is both the head of state and head of the government.

Legislative Branch
The Senate and the House of Representatives work together to make laws.

Judicial Branch
Made up of 14 justices, the Supreme Court is Nigeria's highest judicial body.

386 CASE STUDY

Differentiating Instruction

Below Level

Struggling Readers

1. Use the graphic above titled Structure of the Nigerian Government to help students understand the basics of Nigeria's government.

2. Point out to students that the Nigerian government is made up of three branches, executive, legislative, and judicial. Ask students to use the illustrations and the captions to identify what the major responsibilities are of each branch.

3. Have students review the text under the heading Government for more clues as to the responsibilities of each branch. Then have students create a simple chart that identifies each branch and its duties.

4. Ask for volunteers to share their charts with the class. **LS Verbal/Linguistic, Visual/Spatial**

📝 Alternative Assessment Handbook, Rubric 7: Charts

The other two branches of Nigeria's government are the legislative and judicial branches. The legislative branch makes the country's laws. It includes a two-house legislature called the National Assembly. The judicial branch includes all of the country's courts and is headed by the Supreme Court.

Issues

Nigeria's diversity enriches the country's culture. However, it has also led to problems within the country. As you have read, members of various ethnic groups have fought for power in the past, even to the point of civil war. Today, the government moves very carefully to avoid favoring any one group.

Religious differences have also lead to issues in Nigeria. The majority of northern Nigeria's population is Muslim. Many northern states have adopted Shariah, or Muslim law, into their legal codes. However, most of southern Nigeria is not Muslim and does not want to live under Shariah. As a result, some southern lawmakers have argued that Shariah should not have any official recognition in Nigeria. Their protests have sparked fierce debate over the role of religion in the country.

Economic issues have also led to conflict in Nigeria. As mentioned on the previous page, most of Nigeria's population lives in poverty. At the same time, however, many foreign companies are profiting from Nigerian oil. Recently, angry residents of the Niger Delta have protested what they see as the exploitation of Nigeria's land and people.

Case Study Assessment

1. What is the main industry in Nigeria?
2. What duties does Nigeria's president have?
3. **Activity** Stage a debate about a current issue in Nigeria. Choose one issue. Divide the class into two groups to argue the two sides of the issue.

Religious Differences

Debates over religion and its role in society have led to political controversy in Nigeria. Northern Nigeria is mostly Muslim, the south is largely Christian. In recent years, lawmakers have clashed over the influence of religious law in Nigeria.

Mosque, Kano

Christian church, Abuja

THE WORLD ALMANAC® Facts about Countries

Nigeria's Major Religions

- Islam 50%
- Christianity 40%
- Traditional religions 10%

NIGERIA **387**

Nigeria Today

Define What is Shariah, and where is it practiced in Nigeria? *Muslim law; in many northern states*

Analyze Why has the production of oil led to protests? *Some people have protested the use of Nigeria's resources and people for the benefit of foreign oil companies.*

Rank Of the issues mentioned, which do you think is the most pressing for the Nigerian government? Why? *Students' responses may vary, but should include an explanation of why that issue is pressing.*

Review & Assess

Close

Have students write a summary of the geography, history, and culture of Nigeria.

Assess

Alternative Assessment Handbook

Reteach/Classroom Intervention

Interactive Skills Tutor CD-ROM

Differentiating Instruction

Above Level

Advanced/Gifted and Talented

1. Review with students the issues discussed in the text. Ask students to discuss how each issue might pose potential problems for the people of Nigeria.

2. Have each student select an issue mentioned in the text. Instruct students to consider the potential problems and solutions to the issue they selected.

3. Then have students write a policy brief for the president of Nigeria. Their briefs should include a description of the issue, potential problems related to the issue, and suggestions for how to prevent these problems.

4. Encourage students to present their policy briefs to the class. **LS Verbal/Linguistic**

Alternative Assessment Handbook: Rubric 42: Writing to Inform

Answers

Case Study Assessment 1. *oil;* **2.** *head of the executive branch and carries out the laws;* **3.** *Students' responses will vary. See Rubric 10: Debates, in the* Alternative Assessment Handbook.

387

Unit 3: The Future of Africa

Word Help

marginalisation the act of treating something as unimportant or trivial
intervention anything designed to alter the course of events
accountability the state of being responsible for one's actions
prerequisite something necessary in order to carry out a function or action

Did you know . . .

NEPAD, or the New Partnership for Africa's Development, was founded in 2001 by the Organisation of African Unity (OAU). NEPAD's primary goals are to eliminate poverty, help place African countries on a path to sustainable development and growth, and help African countries more fully enter the global economy.

The Future of Africa

Part A: Short-Answer Questions

Directions: Read and examine the following documents. Then, on a separate sheet of paper, answer the questions using complete sentences.

DOCUMENT 1

Many members of the United Nations want to bring about changes in Africa. They worry that Africa has been marginalized, or treated as unimportant, by many world leaders. To help fix this problem, the United Nations created the New Partnership for Africa's Development, or NEPAD.

> What is the need for NEPAD?
>
> NEPAD is designed to address the current challenges facing the African continent. Issues such as the escalating poverty levels, underdevelopment and the continued marginalisation of Africa needed a new radical intervention, spearheaded by African leaders, to develop a new Vision that would guarantee Africa's Renewal.

1a. What challenges does NEPAD think face the people of Africa?

1b. Who does this document say should lead the efforts to change Africa?

DOCUMENT 2

One issue that has plagued Africa in the past has been bad government. Military dictatorship and corruption have prevented growth and development. In recent years, however, democracy has taken root in many parts of Africa.

> Africa does not suffer a democracy deficit. More than two-thirds of sub-Saharan African countries have had democratic elections since 2000. Power has changed hands in a number of nations, from Senegal to Tanzania, and from Ghana to Zambia. So, elections have been a success. Over the next two to three years, the goal is to move beyond elections as the measure of freedom, and toward supporting African efforts to fortify government accountability. Good governance is an essential prerequisite for any other social changes.
>
> —U.S. Department of State, Bureau of African Affairs

2a. According to this document, how has government in Africa changed?

2b. What challenges does the Bureau see in Africa's future?

Differentiating Instruction

Above Level

Advanced/Gifted and Talented

1. Lead a class discussion about the issues facing the countries of Africa, including the spread of democracy, curbing government corruption, and expanding opportunities for education.

2. Organize the class into small groups. Have each group select one issue of importance in determining the future of Africa. Have students use the library, the Internet, and other sources to find more information about their selected issue.

3. Stage a panel discussion titled "Planning for Africa's Future." Have at least one member from each group participate on the panel. Assign one or two students to serve as moderators. Have each member of the panel give an opening statement that explains the issue his or her group studied. Have the rest of the class serve as the audience, asking questions that pertain to each topic. **Verbal/Linguistic**

Alternative Assessment Handbook, Rubrics 11: Discussions; and 14: Group Activity

---

Answers

Document 1 1a. *escalating poverty levels, underdevelopment, and marginalization of African countries;* **1b.** *African leaders*

Document 2 2a. *it has become more democratic in many countries;* **2b.** *the challenge of ensuring that governments are accountable to the people*

DOCUMENT 3

One key factor in improving the lives of people is education. The graph below shows how many students were enrolled in schools in Africa from 1999 to 2005.

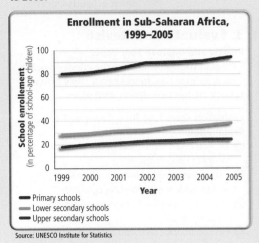

Enrollment in Sub-Saharan Africa, 1999–2005

School enrollment (in percentage of school-age children)

- Primary schools
- Lower secondary schools
- Upper secondary schools

Source: UNESCO Institute for Statistics

3a. How has school enrollment in Africa changed over time?

3b. At which level are the most African students enrolled?

DOCUMENT 4

To help promote growth, African countries have banded together in the African Union (AU), an organization modeled after the European Union. The AU has not yet achieved the level of unity enjoyed by its European counterpart, but it has worked to resolve conflicts in Africa. Some of the AU's objectives are listed below.

- To promote peace, security, and stability on the continent;
- To promote and protect human and peoples' rights in accordance with the African Charter on Human and Peoples' Rights and other relevant human rights instruments;
- To promote sustainable development at the economic, social and cultural levels as well as the integration of African economies;
- To promote co-operation in all fields of human activity to raise the living standards of African peoples;
- To advance the development of the continent by promoting research in all fields, in particular in science and technology

—from "The Objectives of the AU"

4a. What is one economic goal of the AU?

4b. How does the AU propose improving the lives of Africans?

Part B: Essay

Historical Context: Since independence, many African countries have been plagued by political challenges and slow economic development. In recent years, people in Africa and around the world have devoted their efforts to securing a better future for the African people.

TASK: Using information from the four documents and your knowledge of social studies, write an essay in which you:

- describe steps people have taken to improve Africa's future.
- explain how each step will lead to positive change in Africa.

AFRICA **389**

Word Help

sustainable able to be continued indefinitely

Did you know . . .

Sustainable development refers to the ability to meet human needs now and in the future. According to some economists, sustainable development would allow countries to meet the needs of their people today without endangering the ability of future generations to meet their needs.

Critical Thinking: Supporting a Point of View

At Level

Preparing for the Essay

1. Review with students the directions for writing the essay. Point out to students that their essay responses should include two key parts—the steps people have taken to improve Africa's future and how each step will lead to positive change.

2. Instruct students to use the documents on these pages to develop a list of the steps people have taken to improve conditions in Africa.

3. Have students consider how each item on their lists has helped to bring about positive change in Africa.

4. Have students create a thesis statement that summarizes their key points. Then have students plan their essay around the thesis statement they created. **LS Verbal/Linguistic**

📖 Alternative Assessment Handbook, Rubric 40: Writing to Describe

Answers

Document 3 3a. *It has gradually increased at all levels since 1999.*
3b. *the primary school level*

Document 4 4a. *promote sustainable development, integrate African economies into the world economy, raise standards of living;* **4b.** *promoting security, protecting human rights, raising standards of living, and advancing scientific and technological research*

Essay *Students' essays will vary but should thoroughly address all aspects of the task.*

Preteach

Bellringer

Motivate Have students explain "cause" and "effect" in their own words to be sure they understand each term. Remind students that "causes" help explain why something happened. "Effects" help explain what resulted from an event.

Direct Teach

Prewrite

Organizing Information Suggest these tips:

• When explaining causes, remind students not to be too general in what they say about the effect(s). Students' essays should identify which specific economic problems West Africa faces as a result of the three causes.

• When explaining effects, remind students not to spend too much time on explaining the causes. Their focus should be on clearly explaining the results, or effects, of colonization in Southern Africa, not its causes.

Practice & Apply

Publish

Activity **Current Affairs Magazine** Have students collect their papers (revised for accuracy) in a magazine. They can enter them in a computer, order them by country, add a title and table of contents, and print out copies. They can use the magazine to help study for the unit test on Africa.

Rubric

Students' cause/effect papers should

• start with an interesting fact or question related to their big idea.
• clearly identify their big idea and provide background information.
• include one paragraph for each cause or effect.
• include facts and details that support each cause or effect.
• summarize the causes or effects in the final paragraph.
• use correct grammar, punctuation, spelling, and capitalization.

Explaining Cause or Effect

"Why did it happen?" "What were the results?" Questions like these help us identify causes and effects. This, in turn, helps us understand the relationships among physical geography, history, and culture.

Assignment

Write a paper about one of these topics:

■ causes of desertification in West Africa
■ effects of European colonization in South Africa

1. Prewrite

Choose a Topic

■ Choose one of the topics above to write about.
■ Turn that topic into a big idea, or thesis. For example, "Three main factors cause most of the desertification in West Africa."

> **TIP** **What Relationships?** Transitional words like *as a result, because, since,* and *so* can help make connections between causes and effects.

Gather and Organize Information

■ Depending on the topic you have chosen, identify at least three causes or three effects. Use your textbook, the library, or the Internet.
■ Organize causes or effects in their order of importance. To have the most impact on your readers, put the most important cause or effect last.

2. Write

Use a Writer's Framework

> **A Writer's Framework**
>
> **Introduction**
> ■ Start with an interesting fact or question related to your big idea, or thesis.
> ■ State your big idea and provide background information.
>
> **Body**
> ■ Write at least one paragraph, including supporting facts and examples, for each cause or effect.
> ■ Organize your causes or effects by order of importance.
>
> **Conclusion**
> ■ Summarize the causes or effects.
> ■ Restate your big idea.

3. Evaluate and Revise

Review and Improve Your Paper

■ Re-read your paper and use the questions below to determine how to make your paper better.
■ Make changes to improve your paper.

Evaluation Questions for a Cause and Effect Explanation

❶ Do you begin with a fact or question related to your big idea, or thesis?
❷ Does your introduction identify your big idea and provide any needed background?
❸ Do you have at least one paragraph for each cause or effect?
❹ Do you include facts and details to support the connections between causes and effects?
❺ Do you explain the causes or effects in order of importance?
❻ Do you summarize the causes or effects and restate your big idea?

4. Proofread and Publish

Give Your Explanation the Finishing Touch

■ Make sure transitional words and phrases connect causes and effects as clearly as possible.
■ Check for capitalization of proper nouns, such as the names of countries and regions.
■ Have someone else read your paper.

5. Practice and Apply

Use the steps and strategies outlined in this workshop to write your cause-and-effect paper. Share your paper with other students who wrote on the same topic. Compare your lists of causes or effects.

Differentiating Instruction

Struggling Readers   `Below Level`

Students might benefit from simplifying the assignment.

• Have them focus on one cause or one effect. Tell them to write a brief introduction that identifies the cause or effect, one paragraph that describes the cause or explains the effect, and a closing paragraph that briefly summarizes the cause or effect. **LS Verbal/Linguistic**

Alternative Assessment Handbook, Rubrics 6: Cause and Effect; and 37: Writing Assignments

Advanced/Gifted and Talented   `Above Level`

Some students might enjoy the challenge of expanding the assignment in either or both of the following ways:

• Focus on other possible causes (such as land features or climate, resources) or on both positive and negative effects.
• Present the paper orally, accompanying it with pictures or other items to illustrate the causes or effects. **LS Verbal/Linguistic**

Alternative Assessment Handbook, Rubrics 6: Cause and Effect; 24: Oral Presentations; and 37: Writing Assignments

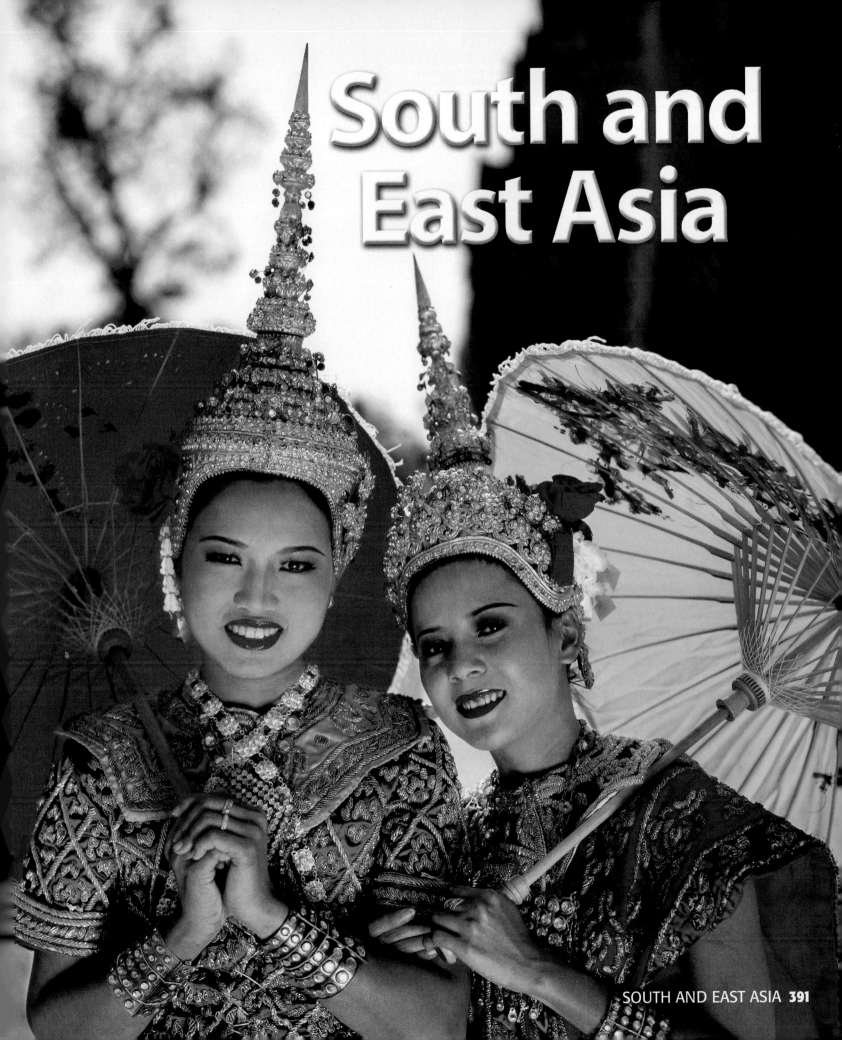

South and East Asia

Unit Preview

Introduce the Unit

Share the information in the chapter overviews with students.

Chapter 13 The physical geography of South and East Asia features unique physical features and a variety of climates and resources.

Chapter 14 Ancient India was the birthplace of two major world religions—Hinduism and Buddhism. Indians made major achievements in art and science.

Chapter 15 China, one of the world's early centers of civilization, was shaped by powerful dynasties and cultural traditions.

Chapter 16 People and ideas from Asia, Europe, and elsewhere have shaped the the growth and development of South and East Asia.

Himalayas

The highest mountain range in the world, the Himalayas, separates the Indian Subcontinent from the rest of Asia.

The Mekong

Southeast Asia's largest river, the Mekong floods often, covering much of the region with water.

392 SOUTH AND EAST ASIA

Unit Resources

Planning

- Differentiated Instruction Teacher Management System: Pacing Guide
- OSP One-Stop Planner CD-ROM with Test Generator: Calendar Planner
- Power Presentations with Video CD-ROM
- Virtual File Cabinet

Differentiating Instruction

- Differentiated Instruction Teacher Management System: Lesson Plans for Differentiated Instruction
- Differentiated Instruction Modified Worksheets and Tests CD-ROM

Enrichment

- **RF:** Interdisciplinary Project, Dynasty Triptych
- **RF:** Geography and History, Dinosaurs of the Gobi
- Geography, Science, and Culture Activities with Answer Key

Assessment

- PASS: Benchmark Test
- OSP ExamView Test Generator: Benchmark Test
- HOAP Holt Online Assessment Program, in the Premier Online Student Edition
- Alternative Assessment Handbook

UNIT 4

South and East Asia

Rain Forest

The rich green color of Southeast Asia is caused by tropical rain forests. They are home to rare animals like the orangutan, found only in this region.

Explore the Satellite Image

Towering mountains, dense rain forests, and dry plains are all features of this large region in Asia. What other physical features can you see in this satellite image?

The Satellite's Path

>44'56.08

>>>>>>>>665.00'87<

+355

+799
E03+
966+

567.476.348

456.094.

SOUTH AND EAST ASIA **393**

Collaborative Learning

At Level

Research Explorers and Settlers

1. Have students research explorers or settlers in South and East Asia. Explorers might include Sir Francis Drake or Ernest Shackleton. Settlers might include British colonists in India or Chinese traders in Japan and Korea.

2. Have students brainstorm ideas with a partner to develop a documentary film about this individual's or group's experiences. Suggest that they consider the various elements of documentary filmmaking, such as interviews,

still photography, news footage, excerpts from letters, and so on.

3. Have students present their ideas and get feedback from other students. Encourage interested students to continue developing their films. **LS Verbal/Linguistic, Visual/Spatial**

   Alternative Assessment Handbook, Rubric 22: Multimedia Presentations

Unit Preview

Connect to the Unit

Activity **Investigate Current Events** Ask students to think about what they already know about the region's geography, people, and history from books, television, and movies. Divide the class into small groups and assign each group one sub-region. Sub-regions are China, Mongolia, and Taiwan; the Indian Subcontinent; Southeast Asia; or Japan and the Koreas. Have each group research newsworthy events in the last 6–12 months—events that already have had or most likely will have a worldwide impact. Have each group create a poster with visuals or write a report. Then have groups share their findings with the class. Lead a discussion to generate questions about these events.

During their study of the unit, have students think about how events in South and East Asia affect their own lives.

LS Interpersonal

Alternative Assessment Handbook, Rubrics 1: Acquiring Information; and 14: Group Activity

Explore the Pictures

Point out the variety of landforms and climate regions shown in the photographs. Help students locate the places on the satellite image that correspond with the photographs. Ask: Where do most Chinese probably live? Why? *possible answer—along major rivers and the coast, away from the Himalayas, because those areas would be best for large-scale settlement* Why might some animals in Southeast Asia be found only in limited areas? *possible answer—because it was difficult to spread from island to island*

Map Zone Transparency: South and East Asia

Answers

Explore the Satellite Image
possible answer—rivers, lakes, deserts,

393

Direct Teach

Explore the Map

South and East Asia: Physical As students examine the map on this page, point out the variety of physical features found in this world region.

Place What natural barrier separates China and India? *Himalayas*

Movement Which of the region's physical features could make travel and trade difficult? *large expanses of water, high mountains, vast deserts*

Location What small island nation is located off China's east coast? *Taiwan*

Map Zone Transparency: South and East Asia: Physical

South and East Asia: Physical

ELEVATION

Feet		Meters
13,120		4,000
6,560		2,000
1,640		500
656		200
(Sea level) 0		0 (Sea level)
Below sea level		Below sea level

0   250   500   750 Miles

0   250   500   750 Kilometers

Projection: Two-Point Equidistant

map zone
Geography Skills

Regions South and East Asia includes many major rivers, long coastal plains, and large islands.

1. **Identify** What major rivers can you see in China and India?
2. **Make Inferences** How do you think rivers influence where people live in this region?

394 REGIONAL ATLAS

Answers

Map Zone 1. *China—Huang He (Yellow River), Chang Jiang (Yangzi River), Xi River; India—Ganges River, Krishna River, Godavari River;* **2.** *possible answer—Rivers provide water for irrigation and drinking and can facilitate trade; as a result, many people settle near rivers.*

394

Collaborative Learning

[At Level]

Make a Ring of Fire Scrapbook

1. Tell students that the Philippines, Japan, and Indonesia are part of the Pacific Ring of Fire. Have students learn more about the volcanic activity in this world region.

2. In three groups—one group per region listed in Step 1—have students conduct research looking for names and locations of active volcanoes, dates of volcanic eruptions, and effects of these eruptions.

3. Groups should organize their information in a scrapbook format. Scrapbooks should contain photos, captions, a time line of eruptions, and descriptions.

4. Encourage students to use creative techniques to decorate their scrapbooks and make them attractive and artistic.

5. When complete, have each group share their scrapbook with the rest of the class. Then put the scrapbooks on a display table, inviting others to learn about the Pacific Ring of Fire.

LS Verbal/Linguistic, Visual/Spatial, Interpersonal

Alternative Assessment Handbook, Rubrics 30: Research; and 32: Scrapbooks

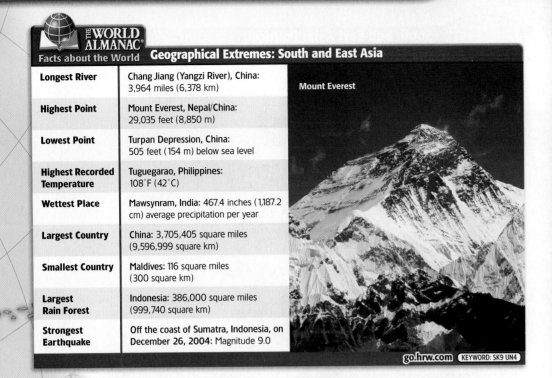

THE WORLD ALMANAC®
Facts about the World
Geographical Extremes: South and East Asia

Longest River	Chang Jiang (Yangzi River), China: 3,964 miles (6,378 km)
Highest Point	Mount Everest, Nepal/China: 29,035 feet (8,850 m)
Lowest Point	Turpan Depression, China: 505 feet (154 m) below sea level
Highest Recorded Temperature	Tuguegarao, Philippines: 108°F (42°C)
Wettest Place	Mawsynram, India: 467.4 inches (1,187.2 cm) average precipitation per year
Largest Country	China: 3,705,405 square miles (9,596,999 square km)
Smallest Country	Maldives: 116 square miles (300 square km)
Largest Rain Forest	Indonesia: 386,000 square miles (999,740 square km)
Strongest Earthquake	Off the coast of Sumatra, Indonesia, on December 26, 2004: Magnitude 9.0

Mount Everest

go.hrw.com KEYWORD: SK9 UN4

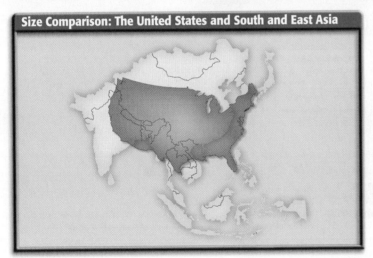

Size Comparison: The United States and South and East Asia

Checking for Understanding

True or False Answer each statement T if it is true or F if it is false. If false, explain why.

1. According to the comparison map, China is roughly the same size as the United States. *T*

2. The smallest country in the region, Maldives, covers only 300 square miles. *F: Maldives covers 116 square miles (300 square km).*

Map Zone Transparency: Size Comparison: The United States and South and East Asia

---

Differentiating Instruction

English-Language Learners
Below Level
Standard English Mastery

1. Read and discuss the information on the World Almanac chart as a class. Focus students' attention on the photo of Mount Everest on this page. Discuss the positive and negative aspects of living on or near the world's highest mountain.

2. Have students use standard English to write a poem about Mount Everest. When complete, ask volunteers to share their poems with the class. **LS Verbal/Linguistic**

Alternative Assessment Handbook, Rubric 26: Poems and Songs

Struggling Readers
Below Level
Research Required

1. Form small mixed-ability groups to learn more about one of the physical features listed on the World Almanac chart on this page.

2. Have each student in the group find one interesting fact about the physical feature they chose to research. Ask groups to read their facts aloud to the rest of the class. Challenge classmates to guess which physical feature is being described. **LS Verbal/Linguistic**

Alternative Assessment Handbook, Rubric 1: Acquiring Information

Direct Teach

Explore the Map

South and East Asia: Political As students look at the map on this page, point out that physical features such as the Himalayas and the Mekong River form both natural and political borders in this region. Have students compare this map to the physical map on the previous page to look for more examples.

Location What are the landlocked countries in south and east Asia? *Mongolia, Laos, Nepal, and Bhutan*

Region Are there more mainland countries or island countries in this world region? *mainland*

Map Zone Transparency: South and East Asia: Political

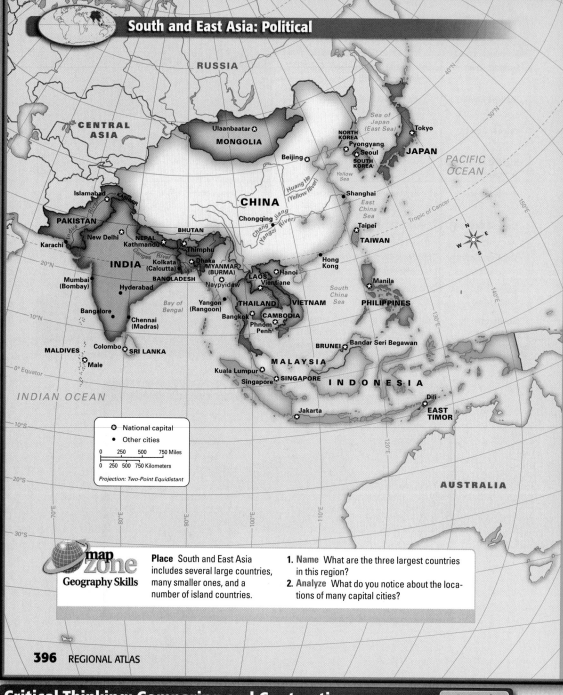

South and East Asia: Political

map zone
Geography Skills

Place South and East Asia includes several large countries, many smaller ones, and a number of island countries.

1. **Name** What are the three largest countries in this region?
2. **Analyze** What do you notice about the locations of many capital cities?

Critical Thinking: Comparing and Contrasting   At Level

Analyze Maps

1. Have students study the political map on this page in order to compare and contrast the countries with one another.

2. Ask students to set up a graphic organizer on a separate sheet of paper to record their findings. It can be a three-column chart, a series of Venn diagrams, a cluster chart, or another style of graphic organizer.

3. Students should write the name of each country, then list one way that country is similar to the other countries in the region, and one way that the country is unique.

4. When complete, draw a graphic organizer on the board and have students take turns adding details about the countries in south and east Asia. **LS Verbal/Linguistic, Visual/Spatial**

   Alternative Assessment Handbook, Rubrics 9: Comparing and Contrasting; and 13: Graphic Organizers

Answers

Map Zone 1. *India, China, Indonesia;* **2.** *possible answer—Most capital cities are located on or near the coast.*

396

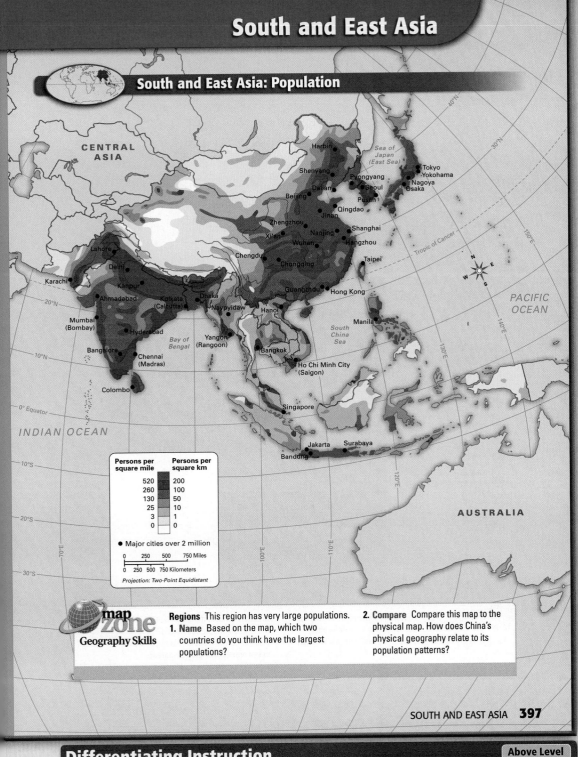

South and East Asia

South and East Asia: Population

CENTRAL ASIA

Sea of Japan (East Sea)

Harbin

Shenyang

Pyongyang
Tokyo
Yokohama
Nagoya
Osaka

Dalian
Seoul
Beijing
Pusan

Jinan
Qingdao

Zhengzhou
Nanjing
Shanghai

Xi'an
Wuhan
Hangzhou

Chengdu
Chongqing

Taipei

Lahore

Delhi

Karachi

Kanpur

Ahmadabad
Kolkata (Calcutta)
Dhaka
Naypyidaw
Hanoi

Guangzhou
Hong Kong

PACIFIC OCEAN

Mumbai (Bombay)

Hyderabad

Bangalore

Chennai (Madras)

Bay of Bengal

Yangon (Rangoon)

Bangkok

Manila

South China Sea

Ho Chi Minh City (Saigon)

Colombo

INDIAN OCEAN

Singapore

Jakarta   Surabaya

Bandung

AUSTRALIA

Persons per square mile	Persons per square km
520	200
260	100
130	50
25	10
3	1
0	0

● Major cities over 2 million

0 250 500 750 Miles
0 250 500 750 Kilometers
Projection: Two-Point Equidistant

map zone
Geography Skills

Regions This region has very large populations.
1. Name Based on the map, which two countries do you think have the largest populations?

2. Compare Compare this map to the physical map. How does China's physical geography relate to its population patterns?

SOUTH AND EAST ASIA **397**

Differentiating Instruction

Above Level

Advanced/Gifted and Talented

Research Required

1. Have students use almanacs or the Internet to research population statistics in China from the past ten years. Then have them display their findings in a bar graph or chart.

2. Using the information they find in their research, have students make a second graph or chart, predicting China's population for each of the next ten years. Students should analyze the data and look for patterns. Students' predictions should be based on the growth rate they find in their research.

3. Ask students to write a summary of the data in their charts and to include a list of potential problems that China may face as a result of overpopulation.

LS Logical/Mathematical, Verbal/Linguistic

Alternative Assessment Handbook, Rubrics 7: Charts; and 37: Writing Assignments

---

Direct Teach

Explore the Map

South and East Asia: Population
As students examine the population map on this page, point out the area of China with the highest concentration of densely populated cities. Explain that because of agricultural and urban runoff, the Yellow Sea is at risk for pollution.

Region Which four countries have no metropolitan areas with more than 2 million residents? *Brunei, Bhutan, Cambodia, Laos, Mongolia, and Nepal*

Place How many metropolitan areas in China have more than 2 million inhabitants? *16*

Map Zone Transparency: South and East Asia: Population

Answers

Map Zone 1. *India and China;*
2. *Most Chinese live in the eastern part of the country, on the North China Plain. This region has low elevation and major rivers.*

397

Direct Teach

Explore the Map

South and East Asia: Climate As students study the climate map on this page, point out that the region stretches from nearly 50° north of the equator to 10° south. Explain that this wide range of latitude is one reason the region has different climates.

Place What climate type does most of Mongolia have? *steppe*

Location How does climate differ in the countries south of the equator compared to those located in northern latitudes? *Climates are cooler and drier in northern latitudes.*

Map Zone Transparency: South and East Asia: Climate

South and East Asia: Climate

Climate Types
- Humid tropical
- Tropical savanna
- Desert
- Steppe
- Humid subtropical
- Humid continental
- Subarctic
- Highland

0   250   500 Miles
0   250   500 Kilometers

Projection: Two-Point Equidistant

map zone
Geography Skills

Location Climates in South and East Asia are very different depending on an area's location.

1. **Identify** What is the main climate in the islands of Southeast Asia?
2. **Analyze** Does most of this region have warm climates or cold climates?

Differentiating Instruction

English-Language Learners
Below Level
Standard English Mastery

1. Have students create a list describing climate. Students should list each country from north to south. Then have them use the map to list each climate type found in that country.

2. Students should use standard English to write a one-sentence summary about each country's climate. Ask volunteers to read their summary sentences aloud.

LS Visual/Spatial, Verbal/Linguistic

Alternative Assessment Handbook, Rubrics 7: Charts; and 21: Map Reading

Struggling Readers
Below Level

1. Using the climate map on this page, have students select three countries—each with a different climate type.

2. Students should then write a quatraine (a four-lined, rhyming poem) about the climate in each of the countries they selected. Have volunteers read their quatraines aloud.

LS Visual/Spatial, Verbal/Linguistic

Alternative Assessment Handbook, Rubrics 21: Map Reading; and 26: Poems and Songs

Answers

Map Zone 1. *humid tropical;* 2. *warm climates*

398

South and East Asia

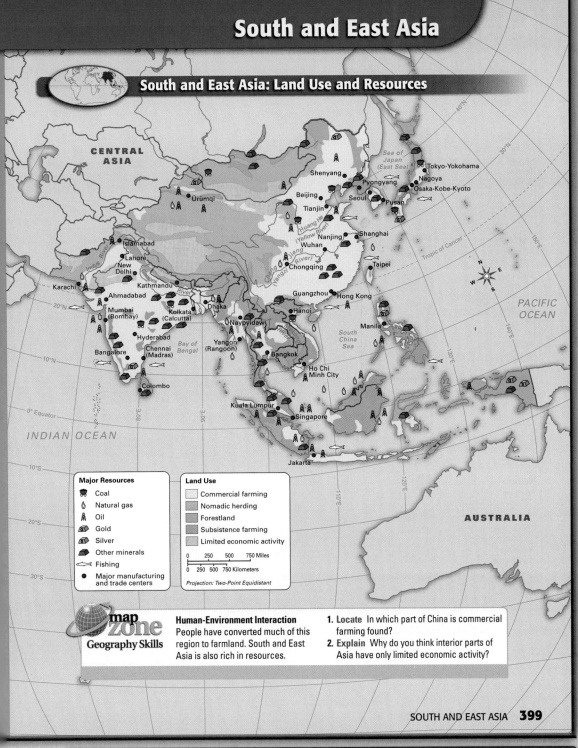

South and East Asia: Land Use and Resources

CENTRAL ASIA

Ürümqi

Shenyang
Beijing
Pyongyang
Seoul
Pusan
Tianjin
Huang He (Yellow River)
Nanjing
Wuhan
Shanghai
Chongqing
Chang Jiang (Yangzi River)
Taipei

Tokyo-Yokohama
Nagoya
Osaka-Kobe-Kyoto
Sea of Japan (East Sea)

Islamabad
Lahore
New Delhi
Karachi
Kathmandu
Ahmadabad
Mumbai (Bombay)
Kolkata (Calcutta)
Dhaka
Hyderabad
Bangalore
Chennai (Madras)
Bay of Bengal
Yangon (Rangoon)
Naypyidaw
Bangkok

Guangzhou
Hong Kong
Hanoi
Manila
South China Sea
Ho Chi Minh City
Kuala Lumpur
Singapore
Jakarta
Colombo

PACIFIC OCEAN

INDIAN OCEAN

AUSTRALIA

Tropic of Cancer
Equator

Major Resources
- Coal
- Natural gas
- Oil
- Gold
- Silver
- Other minerals
- Fishing
- Major manufacturing and trade centers

Land Use
- Commercial farming
- Nomadic herding
- Forestland
- Subsistence farming
- Limited economic activity

0 250 500 750 Miles
0 250 500 750 Kilometers

Projection: Two-Point Equidistant

map zone Geography Skills

Human-Environment Interaction People have converted much of this region to farmland. South and East Asia is also rich in resources.

1. **Locate** In which part of China is commercial farming found?
2. **Explain** Why do you think interior parts of Asia have only limited economic activity?

Explore the Map

South and East Asia: Land Use and Resources As students examine the land use and resources map on this page, point out that farming and nomadic herding are found in large areas of China.

Place In what countries is gold a resource? *Indonesia, Japan, India, China, and the Philippines* What is the only country to mine silver? *Indonesia*

Location Near what geographical feature are most major manufacturing and trade centers located? *bodies of water—rivers or oceans*

Map Zone Transparency: South and East Asia: Land Use and Resources

---

Differentiating Instruction

Below Level

Special Needs Learners

1. Make enlarged copies of an outline map of south and east Asia. Have students paste maps to a piece of cardstock or poster board.

2. Using the climate map on this page as a guide, have students use colored pencils to shade each climate area. Remind students to make a map key showing what climate type each color represents.

3. Have students use a black marker to neatly label each country on their maps.

4. Then have students turn their maps over and draw a puzzle pattern on the back. Have them cut out the pieces and practice putting their maps back together.

5. Have students trade maps and assemble each other's puzzles. Have volunteers share which was more challenging: creating the climate map or assembling the puzzle.

LS Visual/Spatial, Kinesthetic

Alternative Assessment Handbook, Rubrics 20: Map Creation; and 35: Solving Problems

Answers

Map Zone 1. *eastern China;*
2. *possible answer—Deserts and high mountains mean lower population and limited economic activity.*

399

Checking for Understanding

True or False Answer each statement *T* if it is true or *F* if it is false. If false, explain why.

1. According to the statistics on the chart, Bangladesh has only about 7 television sets in the entire country. *F: There are 7 television sets for every 1,000 people in Bangladesh, or approximately 150,400 television sets.*

2. The national flags of Japan and Vietnam are identical. *F: Vietnam's flag is orange with a yellow star in the middle, while Japan's is white with a red circle in the middle.*

THE WORLD ALMANAC® Facts about Countries

South and East Asia

COUNTRY Capital	FLAG	POPULATION	AREA (sq mi)	PER CAPITA GDP (U.S. $)	LIFE EXPECTANCY AT BIRTH	TVS PER 1,000 PEOPLE
Bangladesh Dhaka		150.4 million	55,599	$2,200	62.8	7
Bhutan Thimphu		2.3 million	18,147	$1,400	55.2	6
Brunei Bandar Seri Begawan		374,600	2,228	$25,600	75.2	637
Cambodia Phnom Penh		14 million	69,900	$2,600	59.7	9
China Beijing		1,322 million	3,705,407	$7,600	72.9	291
East Timor Dili		1.1 million	5,794	$800	66.6	NA
India New Delhi		1,129.8 million	1,269,346	$3,700	68.6	75
Indonesia Jakarta		234.7 million	741,100	$3,800	70.2	143
Japan Tokyo		127.4 million	145,883	$33,100	81.4	719
Laos Vientiane		6.5 million	91,429	$2,100	55.9	10
Malaysia Kuala Lumpur		24.8 million	127,317	$12,700	72.8	174
Maldives Male		369,000	116	$3,900	64.8	38
Mongolia Ulaanbaatar		2.9 million	603,909	$2,000	65.3	58
United States Washington, D.C.		301.1 million	3,718,711	$43,500	78.0	844

Cross Discipline Activity: Science

At Level

Classify Life in the Indonesian Islands

Research Required

1. Have students conduct research about the many different kinds of life in the Indonesian Islands.

2. Then come together as a class and create a master list of plants and animals that live in the islands.

3. Have each student develop their own classification system to organize the living things on the master list.

4. Students may need to do further research about an animal in order to classify it. For example, if a student decided to classify animals according to what they eat, he or she might need to read more about an animal's dietary habits.

5. Have students write a summary of their classification system. They should explain what criteria they used and why they set up the categories the way they did.

LS Verbal/Linguistic

Alternative Assessment Handbook, Rubrics 30: Research; and 38: Writing to Classify

COUNTRY Capital	FLAG	POPULATION	AREA (sq mi)	PER CAPITA GDP (U.S. $)	LIFE EXPECTANCY AT BIRTH	TVS PER 1,000 PEOPLE
Myanmar (Burma); Yangon (Rangoon) Naypyidaw		47.4 million	261,970	$1,800	62.5	7
Nepal Kathmandu		28.9 million	54,363	$1,500	60.6	6
North Korea Pyongyang		23.3 million	46,541	$1,800	71.9	55
Pakistan Islamabad		164.7 million	310,403	$2,600	63.8	105
Papua New Guinea Port Moresby		5.8 million	178,704	$2,700	65.6	13
Philippines Manila		91.1 million	115,831	$5,000	70.5	110
Singapore Singapore		4.6 million	268	$30,900	81.8	341
South Korea Seoul		49 million	38,023	$24,200	77.2	364
Sri Lanka Colombo		20.9 million	25,332	$4,600	74.8	102
Taiwan Taipei		22.8 million	13,892	$29,000	77.6	327
Thailand Bangkok		65.1 million	198,457	$9,100	72.6	274
Vietnam Hanoi		85.3 million	127,244	$3,100	71.1	184
United States Washington, D.C.		301.1 million	3,718,711	$43,500	78.0	844

ANALYSIS SKILL ANALYZING TABLES

1. Which five countries in this region have the highest per capita GDPs? How do they compare to the per capita GDP of the United States?
2. Compare the life expectancy and number of TVs per 1,000 people in Japan and Laos. What might this comparison indicate about life in the two countries?

SOUTH AND EAST ASIA **401**

Critical Thinking: Distinguishing Facts from Opinions At Level

Deliver a News Report

1. Have students use the World Almanac chart to write a brief news report about the countries of South and East Asia.
2. Tell students that they will report facts and opinions about the region in their reports. However, they should try to disguise their opinion statements within their news reports. Each report should include five facts and at least one opinion.
3. As students listen to each report, they should listen carefully for facts and opinions. When

they hear an opinion statement they should quickly jot down a few notes or the opinion statement on scrap paper.

4. When each news report is over, collect papers to see who identified the opinion statement correctly. Give students a point for each opinion they identified.

LS Auditory/Musical, Verbal/Linguistic

Alternative Assessment Handbook, Rubrics 16: Judging Information; 18: Listening; and 24: Oral Presentations

Direct Teach

World Almanac: Facts about Countries

Activity Create an Annotated Time Line Ask each student to choose a country in South and East Asia and generate an annotated time line of that country's history.

Students should use a variety of resources and materials to research major historical events, including the birth of the nation, wars or conflicts, significant changes in government, disasters, and important achievements.

Have students tape 8.5" x 11" sheets of paper end-to-end to ensure ample space for their time lines. Ask students to type their annotations for each event and place them on the time line in the correct sequence.

Time lines should include at least ten events. Annotations should list the date of the event, the event that took place, and the location (if appropriate). Then students should write a one-sentence summary describing the event's cause, effect, outcome, or other detail.

Have students present their time lines to the rest of the class, describing each event and summarizing their country's history.

LS Verbal/Linguistic, Visual/Spatial, Logical/Mathematical

Alternative Assessment Handbook, Rubrics 30: Research; and 36: Time Lines

Interactive Skills Tutor CD-ROM, Lesson 3: Interpret and Create a Time Line and Sequence Events

Answers

Analyzing Tables 1. *Japan, Singapore, Taiwan, Brunei, South Korea; the highest per capita GDP–$33,100 for Japan–is $10,400 lower than the per capita GDP of the United States, which is $43,500.*
2. *Japan: life expectancy—81.4, number of TVs—719; Laos: life expectancy—55.9, number of TVs—10; possible answer— The standard of living is higher in Japan than in Laos.*

401

World Almanac: Facts about Countries

Activity **Apply for a Government Position** Ask each student to choose a country in the region. Have students imagine that they are applying for a government position as a United States ambassador to a nation in South and East Asia or the Pacific. Ask students to write a cover letter and resumé.

In small groups, have students discuss the kinds of skills a U.S. ambassador would need to do the job well. Ask them to talk about the kinds of character traits the government might be looking for in its applicants.

Share sample cover letters and resumés with the students to use as models for their writing. In their cover letters, students should list several countries in which they would like to be assigned, as well as the reasons why they want the job.

Students may use a combination of real and fictional information to include on their resumés. For example, students may say that they speak several different languages or that they have multiple college degrees.

LS Verbal/Linguistic, Intrapersonal

Alternative Assessment Handbook, Rubrics 5: Business Letters; and 31: Resumés

Interactive Skills Tutor CD-ROM, Lesson 8: Create Written, Visual, Oral Presentations

THE WORLD ALMANAC® Facts about Countries

Economic Powers

Japan	China
■ World's third-largest economy	■ World's second-largest economy
■ $590.3 billion in exports	■ $974 billion in exports
■ Per capita GDP of $33,100	■ GDP growth rate of 10.5%
■ Major exports: transportation equipment, cars, semiconductors, electronics	■ Major exports: machinery and electronics, clothing, plastics, furniture, toys

Japan is one of the most technologically advanced countries and is a leading producer of hi-tech goods.

China is an emerging economic powerhouse with a huge population and a fast growing economy.

402

Collaborative Learning

At Level

Gather and Analyze Statistics

Research Required

1. Have students use current almanacs to research additional statistics about the countries of South and East Asia.

2. As a class, decide on 3–5 categories to add to the World Almanac chart on this page. (Sample categories include type of government, number of cars, percentage of youth population, number of Internet users, type of currency, chief religion, etc.)

3. Either in small groups or individually, assign students a group of countries to gather the information selected in Step 2. Students should record their statistics on notebook paper first, double check the data for accuracy, then transfer the information to a class chart on the board.

4. Lead a class discussion looking for patterns, generalizations, and comparisons in the data.

LS Verbal/Linguistic

Alternative Assessment Handbook, Rubrics 9: Comparing and Contrasting; and 11: Discussions

Population Giants

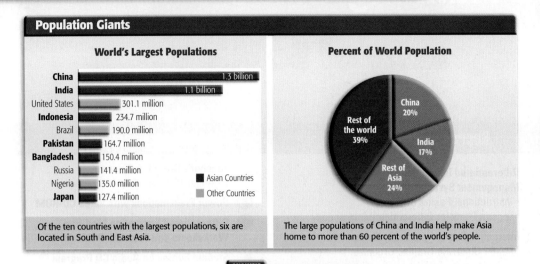

World's Largest Populations

Country	Population
China	1.3 billion
India	1.1 billion
United States	301.1 million
Indonesia	234.7 million
Brazil	190.0 million
Pakistan	164.7 million
Bangladesh	150.4 million
Russia	141.4 million
Nigeria	135.0 million
Japan	127.4 million

■ Asian Countries
▨ Other Countries

Percent of World Population

China 20%
India 17%
Rest of Asia 24%
Rest of the world 39%

Of the ten countries with the largest populations, six are located in South and East Asia.

The large populations of China and India help make Asia home to more than 60 percent of the world's people.

Nanjing Road, Shanghai, China

ANALYSIS SKILL | ANALYZING VISUALS

1. Which two countries have the largest populations?
2. What kinds of exports help make Japan and China economic powers?

SOUTH AND EAST ASIA 403

Population Giants and Economic Powers

Identify What is the population of the United States? *301.1 million people.*

Draw a Conclusion How might China and India's large populations affect the countries' manufacturing and exports? *possible answer—There are many people to work in factories and make more products to increase exports.*

Cross-Discipline Activity: Art

`At Level`

Paint a Watercolor Landscape

1. Have students select a country in South and East Asia whose landscape they will capture in a watercolor painting.

2. Students should use the Internet, travel magazines, and books to locate images of the country they selected. Encourage students to look at a variety of images to understand the contrast in their country's landscape. (e.g., urban vs. rural, water vs. land, mountains vs. plains, etc.)

3. If necessary, provide students with art paper and watercolors. Instruct students to create

a painting of their country's landscape. Students can recreate an image, or they may paint an original image based on their research.

4. Have students add frames to their dried watercolors, title them, and write a brief summary explaining background of the painting for a placard. **LS** Visual/Spatial

Alternative Assessment Handbook, Rubric 1: Acquiring Information; and 3: Artwork

Answers

Analyzing Visuals 1. *China and India;* **2.** *Japan—transportation equipment, cars, semiconductors, electronics; China—machinery and electronics, clothing, plastics, furniture, toys*

403

Chapter 13 Planning Guide

Physical Geography of South and East Asia

Chapter Overview	Reproducible Resources	Technology Resources
CHAPTER 13 pp. 404–427 **Overview:** In this chapter students will learn about the physical geography of the countries that make up South and East Asia.	**Differentiated Instruction Teacher Management System:*** • Instructional Pacing Guides • Lesson Plans for Differentiated Instruction **Interactive Reader and Study Guide:** Chapter Summary Graphic Organizer* **Resource File:*** • Chapter Review • Focus on Reading: Understanding Fact and Opinion • Focus on Speaking: Presenting a Travelogue • Social Studies Skills: Using a Topographic Map	**OSP Teacher's One-Stop Planner:** Calendar Planner **Power Presentations with Video CD-ROM** **Differentiated Instruction Modified Worksheets and Tests CD-ROM** **Student Edition on Audio CD Program** **Map Zone Transparency:** South and East Asia: Physical* **Geography's Impact Video Program (VHS/DVD):** Impact of Natural Hazards
Section 1: **The Indian Subcontinent** **The Big Idea:** The physical geography of the Indian Subcontinent features unique physical features and a variety of climates and resources.	**Differentiated Instruction Teacher Management System:** Section 1 Lesson Plan* **Interactive Reader and Study Guide:** Section 1 Summary* **Resource File:*** • Vocabulary Builder: Section 1	**Daily Bellringer Transparency:** Section 1* **Map Zone Transparency:** Indian Subcontinent: Physical* **Map Zone Transparency:** Indian Subcontinent: Precipitation* **Internet Activity:** Indus River
Section 2: **China, Mongolia, and Taiwan** **The Big Idea:** Physical features, climate, and resources vary across China, Mongolia, and Taiwan.	**Differentiated Instruction Teacher Management System:** Section 2 Lesson Plan* **Interactive Reader and Study Guide:** Section 2 Summary* **Resource File:*** • Vocabulary Builder: Section 2 • Biography: Shi Huangdi • Biography: Genghis Khan • Geography and History: Dinosaurs of the Gobi	**Daily Bellringer Transparency:** Section 2* **Map Zone Transparency:** China, Mongolia, and Taiwan: Physical* **Map Zone Transparency:** China, Mongolia, and Taiwan: Precipitation*
Section 3: **Japan and the Koreas** **The Big Idea:** Japan and Korea are both rugged, mountainous areas surrounded by water.	**Differentiated Instruction Teacher Management System:** Section 3 Lesson Plan* **Interactive Reader and Study Guide:** Section 3 Summary* **Resource File:*** • Vocabulary Builder: Section 3 • Literature: *Haiku*	**Daily Bellringer Transparency:** Section 3* **Map Zone Transparency:** Japan and the Koreas: Physical* **Map Zone Transparency:** Japan and the Koreas: Volcanoes and Earthquakes* **Internet Activity:** Volcanoes and Earthquakes
Section 4: **Southeast Asia** **The Big Idea:** Southeast Asia is a tropical region of peninsulas, islands, and waterways with diverse plants, animals, and resources.	**Differentiated Instruction Teacher Management System:** Section 4 Lesson Plan* **Resource File:*** • Vocabulary Builder: Section 4 • Primary Source: Stranger in the Forest: On Foot across Borneo	**Daily Bellringer Transparency:** Section 4* **Map Zone Transparency:** Southeast Asia: Physical* **Map Zone Transparency:** Southeast Asia: Climate* **Map Zone Transparency:** Indian Ocean Tsunami

SE Student Edition	Print Resource
TE Teacher's Edition	Transparency
go.hrw.com	**LS** Learning Styles

SE Student Edition	Print Resource	Audio CD
TE Teacher's Edition	Transparency	CD-ROM
go.hrw.com	**LS** Learning Styles	**Video** Video

OSP Teacher's One-Stop Planner   * also on One-Stop Planner

HOLT
Geography's Impact
Video Program
Impact of Natural Hazards
Suggested use: in Section 2

Review, Assessment, Intervention

 Quick Facts Transparencies: Visual Summary: Physical Geography of South and East Asia*

 Spanish Chapter Summaries Audio CD Program

 Progress Assessment Support System (PASS): Chapter Test*

 Differentiated Instruction Modified Worksheets and Tests CD-ROM: Modified Chapter Test

OSP **Teacher's One-Stop Planner:** ExamView Test Generator (English/Spanish)

HOAP **Holt Online Assessment Program (HOAP),** in the Holt Interactive Online Student Edition

 PASS: Section 1 Quiz*

 Online Quiz: Section 1

 Alternative Assessment Handbook

 PASS: Section 2 Quiz*

 Online Quiz: Section 2

 Alternative Assessment Handbook

 PASS: Section 3 Quiz*

 Online Quiz: Section 3

 Alternative Assessment Handbook

 PASS: Section 4 Quiz*

 Online Quiz: Section 4

 Alternative Assessment Handbook

Power Presentations with Video CD-ROM

Power Presentations with Video are visual presentations of each chapter's main ideas. Presentations can be customized by including Quick Facts charts, images from the text, and video clips.

Holt Online Learning

go.hrw.com
Teacher Resources
KEYWORD: SK9 TEACHER

go.hrw.com
Student Resources
KEYWORD: SK9 CH13

- Interactive Multimedia Activities
- Current Events
- Chapter-based Internet Activities
- and more!

Holt Interactive
Online Student Edition
Complete online support for interactivity, assessment, and reporting

- Interactive Maps and Notebook
- Standardized Test Prep
- Homework Practice and Research Activities Online

CHAPTER 13 PLANNING GUIDE

Differentiating Instruction

How do I address the needs of varied learners?

The Target Resource acts as your primary strategy for differentiated instruction.

ENGLISH-LANGUAGE LEARNERS & STRUGGLING READERS

TARGET RESOURCE

Interactive Skills Tutor CD-ROM

The Interactive Skills Tutor CD-ROM contains lessons that provide additional practice for 20 different critical thinking skills.

Additional Resources

Differentiated Instruction Teacher Management System: Lesson Plans for Differentiated Instruction

Resource File:
- Vocabulary Builder Activities
- Social Studies Skills: Using a Topographic Map

Quick Facts Transparency: Visual Summary: Physical Geography of South and East Asia

Student Edition on Audio CD Program

Spanish Chapter Summaries Audio CD

Teacher's One-Stop Planner:
- ExamView Test Generator, Spanish
- PuzzlePro, Spanish

English-Language Learner Strategies and Activities

SPECIAL NEEDS LEARNERS

TARGET RESOURCE

Differentiated Instruction Modified Worksheets and Tests CD-ROM

- Vocabulary Flash Cards
- Modified Vocabulary Builder Activities
- Modified Chapter Review
- Modified Chapter Test

Additional Resources

Differentiated Instruction Teacher Management System: Lesson Plans for Differentiated Instruction

Interactive Reader and Study Guide

Resource File: Social Studies Skills: Using a Topographic Map

Student Edition on Audio CD Program

Interactive Skills Tutor CD-ROM

Graphic Organizer Transparencies with Support for Reading and Writing

ADVANCED/GIFTED AND TALENTED STUDENTS

TARGET RESOURCE

Resource File

The Resource File activities allow students to extend their knowledge of chapter-related places and people and to practice geography skills.
- Focus on Reading: Understanding Fact and Opinion
- Focus on Speaking: Presenting a Travelogue
- Literature: *Haiku*

Additional Resources

Differentiated Instruction Teacher Management System: Lesson Plans for Differentiated Instruction

World History and Geography Document-Based Questions Activities

Geography, Science, and Cultures Activities

Experiencing World History and Geography

Differentiated Activities in the Teacher's Edition

- Classifying the Countries of South and East Asia
- Making an Elevation Graph
- Japan and the Koreas Charts
- Southeast Asia Questions

Differentiated Activities in the Teacher's Edition

- Comparing and Contrasting Landforms
- Locating Physical Features of Southeast Asia
- Creating a 3-D Topographic Map

Differentiated Activities in the Teacher's Edition

- Planning a Documentary

HOLT Teacher's One-Stop Planner®

How can I manage the lesson plans and support materials for differentiated instruction?

With the Teacher's One-Stop Planner, you can easily organize and print lesson plans, planning guides, and instructional materials for all learners.

The Teacher's One-Stop Planner includes the following materials to help you differentiate instruction:

- **Interactive Teacher's Edition**
- **Calendar Planner and pacing guides**
- **Editable lesson plans**
- **All reproducible ancillaries in Adobe Acrobat (PDF) format**
- **ExamView Test Generator (English & Spanish)**
- **Transparency and video previews**

Professional Development

What teacher training resources are available to help me grow professionally?

- **In-service and staff development** as part of your Holt Social Studies product purchase
- **Quick Teacher Tutorial Lesson Presentation CD-ROM**
- Intensive tuition-based **Teacher Development Institute**
- **Convenient Holt Speaker Bureau:** face-to-face workshop options
- **24/7 Ask A Professional Development Expert** at http://www.hrw.com/prodev/

• Chapter Preview •

Chapter Big Ideas

Section 1 The physical geography of the Indian Subcontinent features unique physical features and a variety of climates and resources.

Section 2 Physical features, climate, and resources vary across China, Mongolia, and Taiwan.

Section 3 Japan and Korea are both rugged, mountainous areas surrounded by water.

Section 4 Southeast Asia is a tropical region of peninsulas, islands, and waterways with diverse plants, animals, and resources.

Focus on Reading and Speaking

Reading The Resource File provides a worksheet to help students understand facts and opinions.

📓 **RF:** Focus on Reading, Understanding Fact and Opinion

Speaking The Resource File provides a worksheet to help students present a travelogue.

📓 **RF:** Focus on Speaking, Presenting a Travelogue

404 CHAPTER 13

CHAPTER **13**

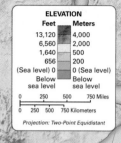

Physical Geography of South and East Asia

FOCUS QUESTION

What forces had an impact on the development of Asia and why?

What You Will Learn...

South and East Asia contain both the world's highest mountains and of some of its most often flooded rivers. The diversity of the land shapes how people live in the region.

FOCUS ON READING AND WRITING

Understanding Fact and Opinion A fact is a statement that can be proved true. An opinion is someone's belief about something. When you read a textbook, you need to recognize the difference between facts and opinions. **See the lesson, Understanding Fact and Opinion, on page S16.**

Presenting a Travelogue You are journeying through Asia, noting the sights and sounds of this beautiful region. As you read this chapter you will gather details about the region's landscapes. Then you will create an oral presentation of a travelogue, or traveler's journal.

404 CHAPTER 13

ELEVATION

Feet	Meters
13,120	4,000
6,560	2,000
1,640	500
656	200
(Sea level) 0	0 (Sea level)
Below sea level	Below sea level

0   250   500   750 Miles

0 250 500 750 Kilometers

Projection: Two-Point Equidistant

map zone

Geography Skills

Place The physical features of South and East Asia vary widely within the region.

1. Identify Which large islands are located in the region?

2. Interpret Where are the highest mountains in South and East Asia found?

Mountains The Indian Subcontinent is home to some of the world's highest mountains, including Pakistan's K2.

Introduce the Chapter

At Level

A Trip to South and East Asia

1. Ask students to imagine that they are planning a trip to South and East Asia. Tell students that their itinerary will include India, China, South Korea, Japan, and the Philippines. Have students make a quick list of things they want to know and preparations they should make as visitors to get the most out of this trip.

2. Call on students to read their lists aloud. Students' lists should include practical tourist concerns such as climate, languages spoken, availability and quality of transportation, and sights to visit.

3. As a class, look over the maps, photos, and captions in the chapter. Encourage students to ask questions. Tell them that this chapter will help them become informed visitors to South and East Asia. 🅻🆂 **Verbal/Linguistic**

📓 Alternative Assessment Handbook, Rubric 11: Discussions

South and East Asia: Physical

Plains The plains of Mongolia allowed people to live as nomadic herders.

Water Features A woman carries sea salt across the salt pans in Doc Let Beach in Vietnam.

405

Explore the Maps and Pictures

South and East Asia: Physical
Have students note the variety of geographical features in South and East Asia. Draw students' attention to the label for Mount Everest. Tell students that at 29,035 feet, Mount Everest is the tallest mountain in the world. Its peak is over five miles above sea level. Then draw students' attention to the label for the North China Plain. Tell students that the North China Plain is about the size of the state of California and that most of it is less than 160 feet above sea level. It is also one the most densely populated regions in the world and is one of China's main agricultural areas.

🖳 Map Zone Transparency: South and East Asia: Physical

Analyzing Visuals Have students examine the two photographs on page 553. Ask students to speculate about the differences between life in Mongolia and life in Vietnam. *possible answers— Mongolia is dry and mountainous. People live nomadic lifestyles. Vietnam is close to the water, and life there involves close interaction with water.*

Differentiating Instruction

Below Level

Special Needs Learners

1. Tell students that they are going to classify the different countries in South and East Asia according to general geographic characteristics that they share. Have students draw a three column-chart with the following headings: *Low Land, Mountains, Islands.*

2. Ask students to look at the map and identify the countries that make up the bulk of the low land in the region (India, Bangladesh, Cambodia, Thailand, Malaysia), those in the mountains (Nepal, Bhutan, China), and those that are islands (Indonesia, the Philippines, Japan). Have students write the country names in the corresponding columns.

3. Explain to students that this classification makes it easier to remember the locations of the countries and the geographical features in the region. **LS Visual/Spatial**

📄 Alternative Assessment Handbook, Rubric 21: Map Reading

Answers

Map Zone 1. *Borneo, Sumatra, New Guinea;* **2.** *in western China, the Himalayas*

Preteach

Bellringer

If YOU lived there. . . Use the **Daily Bellringer Transparency** to help students answer the question.

Daily Bellringer Transparency, Section 1

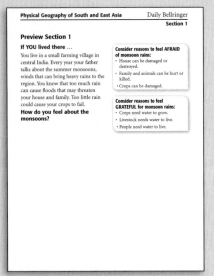

| Physical Geography of South and East Asia | Daily Bellringer Section 1 |

Preview Section 1

If YOU lived there ...
You live in a small farming village in central India. Every year your father talks about the summer monsoons, winds that can bring heavy rains to the region. You know that too much rain can cause floods that may threaten your house and family. Too little rain could cause your crops to fail.
How do you feel about the monsoons?

Consider reasons to feel AFRAID of monsoon rains:
• House can be damaged or destroyed.
• Family and animals can be hurt or killed.
• Crops can be damaged.

Consider reasons to feel GRATEFUL for monsoon rains:
• Crops need water to grow.
• Livestock needs water to live.
• People need water to live.

Key Terms and Places

RF: Vocabulary Builder, Section 1

Taking Notes

Have students copy the graphic organizer onto their own paper and then use it to take notes on the section. This activity will prepare students for the Section Assessment, in which they will complete a graphic organizer that builds on the information using the Critical Thinking Skill: Drawing Inferences.

The Indian Subcontinent

What You Will Learn...

Main Ideas

1. Towering mountains, large rivers, and broad plains are the key physical features of the Indian Subcontinent.
2. The Indian Subcontinent has a great variety of climate regions and resources.

The Big Idea

The physical geography of the Indian Subcontinent features unique physical features and a variety of climates and resources.

Key Terms and Places

subcontinent, *p. 406*
Mount Everest, *p. 407*
Ganges River, *p. 407*
delta, *p. 407*
Indus River, *p. 408*
monsoons, *p. 409*

 TAKING NOTES As you read, take notes on the physical features, climates, and resources of the Indian Subcontinent. Use a diagram like the one below to organize your notes.

If YOU lived there...

You live in a small farming village in central India. Every year your father talks about the summer monsoons, winds that can bring heavy rains to the region. You know that too much rain can cause floods that may threaten your house and family. Too little rain could cause your crops to fail.

How do you feel about the monsoons?

BUILDING BACKGROUND Weather in the Indian Subcontinent, a region in southern Asia, is greatly affected by monsoon winds. Monsoons are just one of the many unique features of the physical geography of the Indian Subcontinent.

Physical Features

Locate Asia on a map of the world. Notice that the southern-most portion of Asia creates a triangular wedge of land that dips into the Indian Ocean. The piece of land jutting out from the rest of Asia is the Indian Subcontinent. A **subcontinent** is a large landmass that is smaller than a continent.

The Indian Subcontinent, also called South Asia, consists of seven countries—Bangladesh, Bhutan, India, Maldives, Nepal, Pakistan, and Sri Lanka. Together these countries make up one of the most unique geographic regions in the world. Soaring mountains, powerful rivers, and fertile plains are some of the region's dominant features.

Mountains

Huge mountain ranges separate the Indian Subcontinent from the rest of Asia. The rugged Hindu Kush mountains in the north-west divide the subcontinent from Central Asia. For thousands of years, peoples from Asia and Europe have entered the Indian Subcontinent through mountain passes in the Hindu Kush.

Teach the Big Idea

At Level

The Indian Subcontinent

1. **Teach** Ask students the questions in the Main Idea boxes under Direct Teach.

2. **Apply** Divide the class into groups. Have each group create a brochure on the physical geography of the Indian Subcontinent. The brochure will have three sections: Physical Features, Climate Regions, and Resources. Have students write information for each section of their brochure and draw pictures or maps to illustrate that information. **LS Verbal/Linguistic, Visual/Spatial**

3. **Review** Discuss the physical geography of the Indian Subcontinent, asking students to tell what they or their group found most interesting about it. Display the brochures in the classroom.

4. **Practice/Homework** Have students choose a dominant feature of the physical geography of the Indian Subcontinent and write a sensory description of it so that the reader can visualize it. **LS Verbal/Linguistic, Visual/Spatial**

   Alternative Assessment Handbook, Rubrics 14: Group Activity; and 40: Writing to Describe

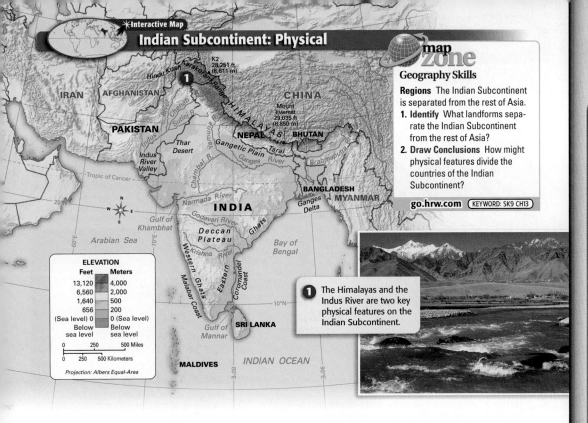

★Interactive Map

Indian Subcontinent: Physical

map Zone

Geography Skills

Regions The Indian Subcontinent is separated from the rest of Asia.

1. **Identify** What landforms separate the Indian Subcontinent from the rest of Asia?
2. **Draw Conclusions** How might physical features divide the countries of the Indian Subcontinent?

go.hrw.com KEYWORD: SK9 CH13

ELEVATION

Feet	Meters
13,120	4,000
6,560	2,000
1,640	500
656	200
(Sea level) 0	0 (Sea level)
Below sea level	Below sea level

0 — 250 — 500 Miles
0 — 250 — 500 Kilometers

Projection: Albers Equal-Area

1 The Himalayas and the Indus River are two key physical features on the Indian Subcontinent.

Two smaller mountain ranges stretch down India's coasts. The Eastern and Western Ghats (GAWTS) are low mountains that separate India's east and west coasts from the country's interior.

Perhaps the most impressive physical features in the subcontinent, however, are the Himalayas. These enormous mountains stretch about 1,500 miles (2,415 km) along the northern border of the Indian Subcontinent. Formed by the collision of two massive tectonic plates, the Himalayas are home to the world's highest mountains. On the border between Nepal and China is **Mount Everest**, the highest mountain on the planet. It measures some 29,035 feet (8,850 m). K2 in northern Pakistan is the world's second highest peak.

Rivers and Plains

Deep in the Himalayas are the sources of some of Asia's mightiest rivers. Two major river systems—the Ganges (GAN-jeez) and the Indus—originate in the Himalayas. Each carries massive amounts of water from the mountains' melting snow and glaciers. For thousands of years, these rivers have flooded the surrounding land, leaving rich soil deposits and fertile plains.

India's most important river is the Ganges. The **Ganges River** flows across northern India and into Bangladesh. There, the Ganges joins with other rivers and creates a huge delta. A **delta** is a landform at the mouth of a river created by sediment deposits. Along the length of the Ganges is a vast area of rich soil and fertile farmland.

FOCUS ON READING

Are the sentences in this paragraph facts or opinions? How can you tell?

PHYSICAL GEOGRAPHY OF SOUTH AND EAST ASIA **407**

Direct Teach

Main Idea

1 Physical Features

Towering mountains, large rivers, and broad plains are the key physical features of the Indian Subcontinent.

Recall What is the most populous area in Pakistan? *Indus River Valley*

Describe What is the Ganges Plain? *a vast area of rich soil and fertile farmland near the Ganges River in Northern India*

Draw Conclusions Why would people from Asia enter the Indian Subcontinent through the Hindu Kush rather than the Himalayas? *the Himalayas are higher, and harder to cross while the Hindu Kush has mountain passes*

🖳 Map Zone Transparency: Indian Subcontinent: Physical

Info to Know

Continental Drift 180 million years ago the land that is now India was located far to the south, and was part of a supercontinent called Gondwana. Antarctica, South America, Africa, and Australia were also part of Gondwana, which was clustered around the South Pole. About 160 million years ago Africa broke off from South America, and India broke off from Africa about 125 million years ago. India continued drifting north, a few inches or feet per year, until it slammed into the southern edge of Asia about 40 million years ago. The collision immediately began pushing up the Himalayas.

Differentiating Instruction

Below Level

Struggling Readers

1. Remind students that Mount Everest is the highest point on Earth, and is on the continent of Asia. Have students research the names and elevations of the highest points on the other continents and record the information in a table.

2. Have students use elevation data to make a bar graph comparing each continent's highest points. Pictograms may be used instead of bars. Suggest a range of 0 to 30,000 feet at intervals of 5,000 feet for the vertical axis.

3. Students may also research other mountains and peaks, such as the highest point in their home state, or famous mountains such as K2, Pike's Peak, Mount Rushmore, or Mount Fuji.

4. Have students locate each peak or mountain on a globe or world map.

LS Visual/Spatial, Logical/Mathematical

📄 Alternative Assessment Handbook, Rubrics 7: Charts; and 30: Research

Answers

Map Zone 1. *Himalayas, Hindu Kush;* **2.** *Rivers, deserts, plateaus, and mountains all form natural barriers that can separate groups of people.*

Focus on Reading *facts; Each sentence could be verified by consulting trusted reference resources.*

Welcome Rains The summer monsoons that sweep over the Indian Subcontinent sometimes bring great destruction, but they are vital to the life of the region. Farmers in India and Bangladesh depend on the rains for irrigation for their crops. The monsoons are also the source of almost 90 percent of India's water supply, and, indirectly, its electricity—the force of rain-swollen rivers is harnessed in hydroelectric plants to generate much of the country's electricity.

MISCONCEPTION ///ALERT\\\

Other Monsoons The Indian Subcontinent is not the only place in the world where monsoons take place. Smaller monsoons also affect equatorial Africa, northern Australia, and, to a lesser degree, the southwestern United States. The southwest U.S. monsoon season is in August, when thunderstorms from Mexico come up and bring heavy rains across the southwest and even as far north as Idaho, Montana, and Wyoming.

go.hrw.com
Online Resources
KEYWORD: SK9 CH13
ACTIVITY: Indus River

 Map Zone Transparency: Indian Subcontinent: Precipitation

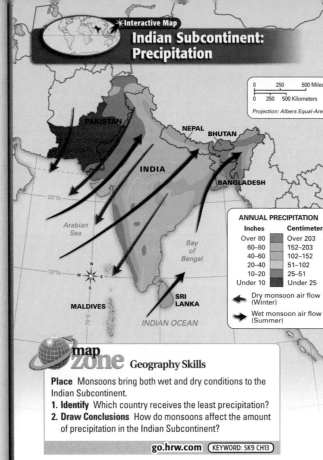

★Interactive Map
Indian Subcontinent: Precipitation

| | 0 | 250 | 500 Miles |
| | 0 | 250 | 500 Kilometers |

Projection: Albers Equal-Area

PAKISTAN
NEPAL
BHUTAN
INDIA
BANGLADESH
20°N
Arabian Sea
Bay of Bengal
10°N
MALDIVES
SRI LANKA
INDIAN OCEAN

ANNUAL PRECIPITATION

Inches	Centimeters
Over 80	Over 203
60–80	152–203
40–60	102–152
20–40	51–102
10–20	25–51
Under 10	Under 25

→ Dry monsoon air flow (Winter)
→ Wet monsoon air flow (Summer)

Summer monsoons often bring heavy rains and fertile growing conditions to many places in the Indian Subcontinent.

During the winter, monsoons change direction, bringing dry air from the north to the subcontinent. Little rain falls during this time of year.

map zone Geography Skills

Place Monsoons bring both wet and dry conditions to the Indian Subcontinent.
1. **Identify** Which country receives the least precipitation?
2. **Draw Conclusions** How do monsoons affect the amount of precipitation in the Indian Subcontinent?

go.hrw.com (KEYWORD: SK9 CH13)

Known as the Ganges Plain, this region is India's farming heartland.

Likewise, Pakistan's **Indus River** also creates a fertile plain known as the Indus River Valley. This valley was once home to the earliest Indian civilizations. Today, it is Pakistan's most densely populated region.

Other Features
Other geographic features are scattered throughout the subcontinent. South of the Ganges Plain, for example, is a large, hilly plateau called the Deccan. East of the Indus Valley is the Thar (TAHR), or Great Indian Desert. Marked by rolling sand dunes, parts of this desert receive as little as 4 inches (100 mm) of rain per year. Still another geographic region is the Tarai (tuh-RY) in southern Nepal. It has fertile farmland and tropical jungles.

READING CHECK Summarizing What are the physical features of the Indian Subcontinent?

Climates and Resources
Just as the physical features of the Indian Subcontinent differ, so do its climates and resources. A variety of climates and natural resources exist throughout the region.

408 CHAPTER 13

Map Zone 1. *Pakistan;* **2.** *They bring heavy rains in summer and dry air in winter.*

Reading Check *mountains, rivers, fertile plains, a delta, a plateau, a desert*

408

Cross-Discipline Activity: English/Language Arts   At Level

Writing the River
Research Required

1. Guide the class in a discussion of rivers as an inspiration for writers. Focus on the ways that rivers appeal to all the senses—sight, smell, hearing, touch, and taste. Discuss themes that might be expressed with river imagery, such as change, cleansing, new beginnings, or eternity.

2. Tell students that they will be writing a story or poem about the Ganges River or Indus River. Explain that their writing will be creative, but must also reflect research about the river—for example, students may learn

about a traditional legend about the river and write a retelling of it, or find an interesting fact and write creatively about it.

3. Have students research one of these rivers and write their story or poem reflecting the information they learn. Encourage students to attach illustrations or photos to their writing.

4. Ask volunteers to share their stories or poems and any accompanying visuals with the class.

LS Intrapersonal, Verbal/Linguistic

Alternative Assessment Handbook, Rubric 39: Writing to Create

Climate Regions

From the Himalayas' snow-covered peaks to the dry Thar Desert, the climates of the Indian Subcontinent differ widely. In the Himalayas, a highland climate brings cool temperatures to much of Nepal and Bhutan. The plains south of the Himalayas have a humid subtropical climate. Hot, humid summers with plenty of rainfall are common in this important farming region.

Tropical climates dominate much of the subcontinent. The tropical savanna climate in central India and Sri Lanka keeps temperatures there warm all year long. This region experiences wet and dry seasons during the year. A humid tropical climate brings warm temperatures and heavy rains to parts of southwest India, Sri Lanka, Maldives, and Bangladesh.

The remainder of the subcontinent has dry climates. Desert and steppe climates extend throughout southern and western India and most of Pakistan.

Monsoons have a huge influence on the weather and climates in the subcontinent. **Monsoons** are seasonal winds that bring either moist or dry air to an area. From June to October, summer monsoons bring moist air up from the Indian Ocean, causing heavy rains. Flooding often accompanies these summer monsoons. In 2005, for example, the city of Mumbai (Bombay), India received some 37 inches (94 cm) of rain in just 24 hours. However, in winter the monsoons change direction, bringing dry air from the north. Because of this, little rain falls from November to January.

Natural Resources

A wide variety of resources are found on the Indian Subcontinent. Agricultural and mineral resources are the most plentiful.

Perhaps the most important resource is the region's fertile soil. Farms produce many different crops, such as tea, rice, nuts, and jute, a plant used for making rope. Timber and livestock are also key resources in the subcontinent, particularly in Nepal and Bhutan.

The Indian Subcontinent also has an abundance of mineral resources. Large deposits of iron ore and coal are found in India. Pakistan has natural gas reserves, while Sri Lankans mine many gemstones.

READING CHECK Summarizing What climates and resources are located in this region?

SUMMARY AND PREVIEW In this section you learned about the wide variety of physical features, climates, and resources in the Indian Subcontinent. Next, you will cross the Himalayas to study China, Mongolia, and Taiwan.

Section 1 Assessment

go.hrw.com
Online Quiz
KEYWORD: SK9 HP13

Reviewing Ideas, Terms, and Places

1. **a. Define** What is a **subcontinent**?
   b. Make Inferences Why do you think the **Indus River** Valley is so heavily populated?
   c. Rank Which physical features in the Indian Subcontinent would you most want to visit? Why?
2. **a. Identify** What natural resources are found in the Indian Subcontinent?
   b. Analyze What are some of the benefits and drawbacks of **monsoons**?

Critical Thinking

3. **Drawing Inferences** Draw a chart like the one shown here. Using your notes, write a sentence explaining how each aspect affects life on the Indian Subcontinent.

	Effect on Life
Physical Features	
Climates	
Natural Resources	

FOCUS ON SPEAKING

4. **Telling about Physical Geography** What information and images of India's physical geography might you include in your travelogue? Jot down some ideas.

Section 1 Assessment Answers

1. **a.** a large landmass that is smaller than a continent
   b. The river creates a vast plain of rich soil and fertile farmland.
   c. Answers will vary, but should be consistent with text content.

2. **a.** a variety of resources, with agricultural and mineral resources being the most plentiful
   b. possible answers: benefits—rain allows for farming and drinking water; drawbacks—floods can kill people and destroy property

3. possible answers: Physical Features—The geographical features that separate this region and its peoples from the rest of Asia make it a unique place. Climates—The wide variety of climates affect daily life with many people dependent on summer rains for farming. Natural Resources—With lots of fertile soil, the region's farmers produce many different crops, including tea, rice, nuts, and jute.

4. Students' answers will vary, but should reflect an understanding of the unique aspects of the Indian Subcontinent's physical geography.

409

Bellringer

If YOU lived there. . . Use the **Daily Bellringer Transparency** to help students answer the question.

Daily Bellringer Transparency, Section 2

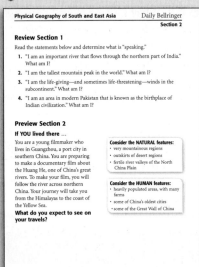

Key Terms and Places

RF: Vocabulary Builder, Section 2

Taking Notes

Have students copy the graphic organizer onto their own paper and then use it to take notes on the section. This activity will prepare students for the Section Assessment, in which they will complete a graphic organizer that builds on the information using the Critical Thinking Skill: Categorizing.

China, Mongolia, and Taiwan

What You Will Learn...

Main Ideas

1. Physical features of China, Mongolia, and Taiwan include mountains, plateaus and basins, plains, and rivers.
2. China, Mongolia, and Taiwan have a range of climates and natural resources.

The Big Idea

Physical features, climate, and resources vary across China, Mongolia, and Taiwan.

Key Terms and Places

Himalayas, *p. 410*
Plateau of Tibet, *p. 411*
Gobi, *p. 411*
North China Plain, *p. 412*
Huang He, *p. 412*
loess, *p. 412*
Chang Jiang, *p. 412*

 TAKING NOTES As you read, use a chart like the one below to take notes on the physical features, climate, and resources of China, Mongolia, and Taiwan.

Mountains	
Other Landforms	
Rivers	
Climate and Resources	

If YOU lived there...

You are a young filmmaker who lives in Guangzhou, a port city in southern China. You are preparing to make a documentary film about the Huang He, one of China's great rivers. To make your film, you will follow the river across northern China. Your journey will take you from the Himalayas to the coast of the Yellow Sea.

What do you expect to see on your travels?

BUILDING BACKGROUND China, Mongolia, and Taiwan make up a large part of East Asia. They include a range of physical features and climates—dry plateaus, rugged mountains, fertile plains. This physical geography has greatly influenced life in each country.

Physical Features

Have you seen the view from the top of the world? At 29,035 feet (8,850 m), Mount Everest in the **Himalayas** is the world's highest mountain. From atop Everest, look east. Through misty clouds, icy peaks stretch out before you, fading to land far below. This is China. About the size of the United States, China has a range of physical features. They include not only the world's tallest peaks but also some of its driest deserts and longest rivers.

Two other areas are closely linked to China. To the north lies Mongolia (mahn-GOHL-yuh). This landlocked country is dry and rugged, with vast grasslands and desert. In contrast, Taiwan (TY-WAHN), off the coast of mainland China, is a green tropical island. Look at the map to see the whole region's landforms.

Mountains

Much of the large region, including Taiwan, is mountainous. In southwest China, the Himalayas run along the border. They are Earth's tallest mountain range. Locate on the map the region's other ranges. As a tip, the Chinese word *shan* means "mountain."

Teach the Big Idea

At Level | Standard English Mastery

China, Mongolia, and Taiwan

1. **Teach** Ask students the questions in the Main Idea boxes under Direct Teach.

2. **Apply** Have students create a chart with three columns. Have them label the columns *China, Mongolia,* and *Taiwan*. As they read the section, have them list details about each country's physical geography.
 Verbal/Linguistic

3. **Review** Have each student create five True/False questions about the information. Then have them take turns quizzing each

other. When students identify false items, have them explain why they are false.

4. **Practice/Homework** Have students use Standard English to write three paragraphs in which they explain the effect that physical geography has on human life in these countries. In their paragraphs, have students include at least one dictionary definition and three words they found in a thesaurus. Have them underline these items. **Verbal/Linguistic**

Alternative Assessment Handbook, Rubrics 7: Charts; and 37: Writing Assignments

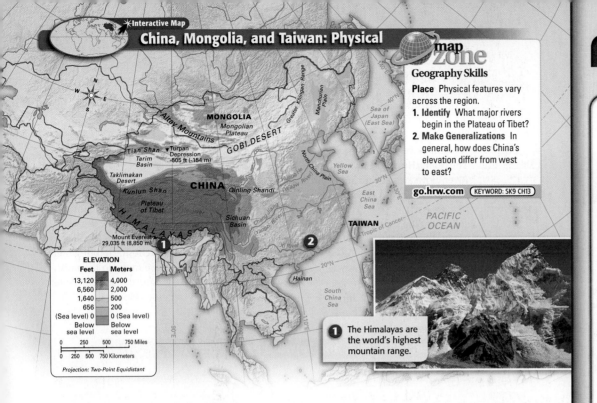

Interactive Map
China, Mongolia, and Taiwan: Physical

map zone
Geography Skills

Place Physical features vary across the region.

1. **Identify** What major rivers begin in the Plateau of Tibet?
2. **Make Generalizations** In general, how does China's elevation differ from west to east?

go.hrw.com | KEYWORD: SK9 CH13

ELEVATION

Feet	Meters
13,120	4,000
6,560	2,000
1,640	500
656	200
(Sea level) 0	0 (Sea level)
Below sea level	Below sea level

0   250   500   750 Miles
0   250   500   750 Kilometers

Projection: Two-Point Equidistant

1 The Himalayas are the world's highest mountain range.

Other Landforms

Many of the mountain ranges are separated by plateaus, basins, and deserts. In southwest China, the **Plateau of Tibet** lies north of the Himalayas. The world's highest plateau, it is called the Roof of the World.

Moving north, we find a low, dry area. A large part of this area is the Taklimakan (tah-kluh-muh-KAHN) Desert, a barren land of sand dunes and blinding sandstorms.

In fact, sandstorms are so common that the desert's Turkish name, Taklimakan, has come to mean "Enter and you will not come out." To the northeast, the Turpan (toohr-PAHN) Depression is China's lowest point, at 505 feet (154 m) below sea level.

Continuing northeast, in Mongolia we find the **Gobi**. This harsh area of gravel and rock is the world's coldest desert. Temperatures can drop to below –40°F (–40°C).

2 Hills that are called karst towers line the Li River in southeast China. These dramatic hills formed over time as rainwater eroded limestone.

PHYSICAL GEOGRAPHY OF SOUTH AND EAST ASIA **411**

Direct Teach

Main Idea

① Physical Features

Physical features of China, Mongolia, and Taiwan include mountains, plateaus and basins, plains, and rivers.

Describe Where are the Himalayas and the Plateau of Tibet located? *in southwest China*

Identify What are two major deserts in the region? *the Taklimakan in western China and the Gobi in Mongolia*

Draw Conclusions How might the fact that Mongolia is a landlocked country affect its culture? *possible answers—fewer opportunities for trade and cultural exchange; traditional ways might flourish*

📓 Map Zone Transparency: China, Mongolia, and Taiwan: Physical

📄 **RF:** Geography and History: Dinosaurs of the Gobi

Did you know...

American Erik Weihenmayer reached the summit of the Himalayas' Mount Everest in 2001. Many people have climbed Mount Everest. However, Weihenmayer is blind. He has also climbed Mount McKinley and Kilimanjaro.

Info to Know

Mongolia's Geography Mongolia has over 3,000 lakes, many of which are salty. More than 200 extinct volcanoes are located in the eastern part of the country.

Critical Thinking: Interpreting Maps

Below Level

Comparing and Contrasting Landforms

1. Have students compare and contrast the landforms in the region.

2. Begin by pointing out the photographs on the page, and then have students find the location of the Himalayas and southeast China on the map.

3. Next, have students find photographs of other landforms in the region, either in the textbook or by using Internet or library sources. Suggest that they look for a variety of landforms, such as extinct volcanoes in Mongolia, Tian Shan, the region's deserts, and the North China Plain.

4. Have students use these images to create posters showing the variety of landforms in the region. Have students label the images and note the elevation of each landform.
   LS Visual/Spatial
   📄 Alternative Assessment Handbook, Rubric 28: Posters

Answers

Map Zone 1. *Chang Jiang (Yangzi River), Huang He (Yellow River), Nu, and Brahmaputra;* **2.** *higher in the west and lower in the east*

411

❷ Climate and Resources

China, Mongolia, and Taiwan have a range of climates and natural resources.

Describe Where do most typhoons occur in the region? *in the southeast*

Compare and Contrast Which resource do China and Taiwan have that is not plentiful in Mongolia? *farmland*

📑 **RF:** Biography: Shi Huangdi

📑 **RF:** Biography: Genghis Khan

Connect to Science

Fossil Hunting from Space Buried under the deep sands of the Gobi Desert in Mongolia, researchers discovered a rich fossil site in 1993. For years, they have gone back to the Gobi in search of more fossils. However, these trips were very expensive and dangerous. Today, these scientists are using satellites to find new fossil sites. The Global Positioning System (GPS) uses satellites to determine exact locations—a much more efficient process than walking in one of the world's biggest deserts.

🗺 Map Zone Transparency: China, Mongolia, and Taiwan: Precipitation

Answers

Focus on Reading *The paragraph expresses facts, not the author's opinion. All of the sentences could be verified.*

Reading Check *mountains, plateaus, deserts, plains, rivers, and basins*

Map Zone 1. *40–60 inches (102–152 cm) per year;* **2.** *Compared to Taiwan, Mongolia has very low annual precipitation; most of the country has less than 10 inches (25 cm) per year. More than half of Taiwan has 60–80 inches (152–203 cm) per year.*

412

In east China, the land levels out into low plains and river valleys. These fertile plains, such as the **North China Plain**, are China's main population centers and farmlands. On Taiwan, a plain on the west coast is the island's main population center.

Rivers

FOCUS ON READING
Does this paragraph express the author's opinion? How can you tell?

In China, two great rivers run west to east. The **Huang He** (HWAHNG HEE), or the Yellow River, flows across northern China. Along its course, this river picks up large amounts of **loess** (LES), or fertile, yellowish soil. The soil colors the river and gives it its name.

In summer, the Huang He often floods. The floods spread layers of loess, enriching the soil for farming. However, such floods have killed millions of people. For this reason, the river is called China's Sorrow.

The mighty **Chang** (CHAHNG) **Jiang**, or the Yangzi (YAHNG-zee) River, flows across central China. It is Asia's longest river and a major transportation route.

READING CHECK Summarizing What are the main physical features found in this region?

Climate and Resources

Climate varies widely across the region. The tropical southeast is warm to hot, and monsoons bring heavy rains in summer. In addition, typhoons can strike the southeast coast in summer and fall. Similar to hurricanes, these violent storms bring high winds and rain. As we move to the northeast, the climate is drier and colder. Winter temperatures can drop below 0°F (–18°C).

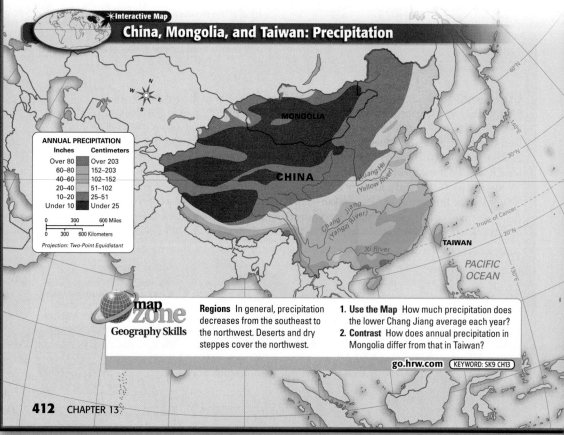

★ **Interactive Map**

China, Mongolia, and Taiwan: Precipitation

ANNUAL PRECIPITATION

Inches	Centimeters
Over 80	Over 203
60–80	152–203
40–60	102–152
20–40	51–102
10–20	25–51
Under 10	Under 25

0   300   600 Miles
0 300 600 Kilometers
Projection: Two-Point Equidistant

mapZone Geography Skills

Regions In general, precipitation decreases from the southeast to the northwest. Deserts and dry steppes cover the northwest.

1. **Use the Map** How much precipitation does the lower Chang Jiang average each year?
2. **Contrast** How does annual precipitation in Mongolia differ from that in Taiwan?

go.hrw.com KEYWORD: SK9 CH13

412 CHAPTER 13

Differentiating Instruction

Above Level

Advanced/Gifted and Talented

Research Required

1. Divide the class into small groups. Have each group plan a documentary about flooding in the region. Have them begin by researching the history of flooding along the Huang He. Suggest that they gather photographs, write interview questions for flood survivors, and in very broad terms examine human-made causes for the floods and actions that might be taken to prevent future flooding.

2. Next, have students create a storyboard for the documentary, sketching out a rough sequence for both text and visuals.

3. Have students display their storyboards and discuss what they have learned.

LS Interpersonal, Visual/Spatial

📑 Alternative Assessment Handbook, Rubrics 14: Group Activity; and 22: Multimedia Presentations

Satellite View

Flooding in China

China's rivers and lakes often flood during the summer rainy season. The satellite images here show Lake Dongting Hu in southern China. The lake appears blue, and the land appears red. Soon after the Before image was taken, heavy rains led to flooding. The After image shows the results. Compare the two images to see the extent of the flood, which killed more than 3,000 people and destroyed some 5 million homes.

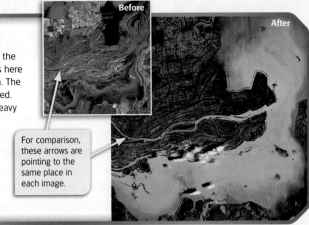

For comparison, these arrows are pointing to the same place in each image.

Drawing Inferences Why might people continue to live in areas that often flood?

In the north and west, the climate is mainly dry. Temperatures vary across the area and can get both very hot and cold.

Like the climate, the region's natural resources cover a wide range. China has a wealth of natural resources. The country is rich in mineral resources and is a leading producer of coal, lead, tin, and tungsten. China produces many other minerals and metals as well. China's forestland and farmland are also valuable resources.

Mongolia's natural resources include minerals such as coal, iron, and tin as well as livestock. Taiwan's major natural resource is its farmland. Important crops include sugarcane, tea, and bananas.

READING CHECK **Contrasting** Which of these three countries has the most natural resources?

SUMMARY AND PREVIEW As you have read, China, Mongolia, and Taiwan have a range of physical features, climate, and resources. Next, you will study the features of Japan and the Koreas.

Section 2 Assessment

go.hrw.com
Online Quiz
KEYWORD: SK9 HP13

Reviewing Ideas, Terms, and Places

1. **a. Identify** What two major rivers run through China?
   b. Explain How does the **Huang He** both benefit and hurt China's people?
   c. Elaborate Why do you think many people in China live on the **North China Plain**?
2. **a. Define** What is a typhoon?
   b. Contrast What are some differences between the climates of southeast and northwest China?
   c. Rate Based on the different climates in this region, which part of the region would you prefer to live in? Why?

Critical Thinking

3. **Categorizing** Look back over your notes for this section. Then use a chart like the one shown here to organize, identify, and describe the main physical features of China, Mongolia, and Taiwan.

FOCUS ON SPEAKING

4. **Describing China's Landforms** Which of China's landforms will you describe in your travelogue? Write down some ideas. Features to consider include mountains, plateaus, and deserts.

PHYSICAL GEOGRAPHY OF SOUTH AND EAST ASIA **413**

Section 2 Assessment Answers

1. **a.** Huang He (Yellow River) and Chang Jiang (Yangzi River)
   b. It benefits China by enriching the soil for farming. It hurts China by flooding.
   c. possible answer—More food can be grown in this area to support a larger population.

2. **a.** similar to a hurricane, a violent storm that brings heavy wind and rain
   b. in the southeast—warm to hot, with heavy rains brought by monsoons; in the north and west—mainly dry, with temperatures ranging from cold to hot

   c. Answers will vary, but students should support their opinions with information from the section.

3. Mountains—Himalayas; Plateaus, basins, deserts—Plateau of Tibet, Taklimakan Desert, Gobi Desert, Turpan Depression; Plains and river valleys—North China Plain; Rivers—Huang He, Chang Jiang

4. Students' should include some features of China's physical geography in their notes.

Direct Teach

Teaching Tip

Understanding Climate Remind students that temperature and precipitation are influenced not only by latitude but also by elevation.

Review & Assess

Close

Briefly review with students the physical features, climates, and resources of the region.

Review

Online Quiz, Section 2

Assess

SE Section 2 Assessment
PASS: Section 2 Quiz
Alternative Assessment Handbook

Reteach/Classroom Intervention

Interactive Reader and Study Guide, Section 2
Interactive Skills Tutor CD-ROM

Answers

Satellite View *because the soil is fertile for growing crops*
Reading Check *China*

413

Bellringer

If YOU lived there. . . Use the **Daily Bellringer Transparency** to help students answer the question.

🖥 Daily Bellringer Transparency, Section 3

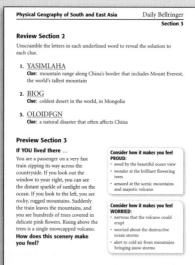

Key Terms and Places

📑 **RF:** Vocabulary Builder, Section 3

Taking Notes

Have students copy the graphic organizer onto their own paper and then use it to take notes on the section. This activity will prepare students for the Section Assessment, in which they will complete a graphic organizer that builds on the information using the Critical Thinking Skill: Categorizing.

SECTION 3

Japan and the Koreas

What You Will Learn...

Main Ideas

1. The main physical features of Japan and the Koreas are rugged mountains.
2. The climates and resources of Japan and the Koreas vary from north to south.

The Big Idea

Japan and Korea are both rugged, mountainous areas surrounded by water.

Key Terms and Places

Fuji, *p. 415*
Korean Peninsula, *p. 415*
tsunamis, *p. 416*
fishery, *p. 417*

TAKING NOTES Draw a table like the one below. As you read, take notes about the physical geography of Japan in one column and about the Korean Peninsula in the other column.

Physical Geography	
Japan	Korean Peninsula

If YOU lived there...

You are a passenger on a very fast train zipping its way across the countryside. If you look out the window to your right, you can see the distant sparkle of sunlight on the ocean. If you look to the left, you see rocky, rugged mountains. Suddenly the train leaves the mountains, and you see hundreds of trees covered in delicate pink flowers. Rising above the trees is a single snowcapped volcano.

How does this scenery make you feel?

BUILDING BACKGROUND The train described above is one of the many that cross the islands of Japan every day. Japan's mountains, trees, and water features give the islands a unique character. Not far away, the Korean Peninsula also has a distinctive landscape.

Physical Features

Japan, North Korea, and South Korea are on the eastern edge of the Asian continent, just east of China. Separated from each other only by a narrow strait, Japan and the Koreas share many common landscape features.

Physical Features of Japan

Japan is an island country. It is made up of four large islands and more than 3,000 smaller islands. These islands are arranged in a long chain more than 1,500 miles (2,400 km) long. This is about the same length as the eastern coast of the United States, from southern Florida to northern Maine. All together, however, Japan's land area is slightly smaller than the state of California.

About 95 percent of Japan's land area is made up of four large islands. From north to south, these major islands are Hokkaido (hoh-KY-doh), Honshu (HAWN-shoo), Shikoku (shee-KOH-koo), and Kyushu (KYOO-shoo). Together they are called the home islands. Most of Japan's people live there.

Teach the Big Idea

At Level

Japan and the Koreas

1. **Teach** Ask students the questions in the Main Idea boxes under Direct Teach.

2. **Apply** Draw this chart for students to copy and complete using details from the text.

	Japan	Korean Peninsula
Mountains/Volcanoes		
Plains		
Rivers		
Oceans		

3. **Review** Ask students to contribute information from their charts to complete the chart you drew.

4. **Practice/Homework** Have students choose a country—Japan, North Korea, or South Korea—and write a geographical profile of it. Encourage students to use transitional phrases so that their profiles are not just disconnected pieces of information.

🔵 **Verbal/Linguistic**

📑 Alternative Assessment Handbook, Rubric 13: Graphic Organizers

Rugged, tree-covered mountains are a common sight in Japan. In fact, mountains cover some 75 percent of the country. For the most part, Japan's mountains are very steep and rocky. As a result, the country's largest mountain range, the Japanese Alps, is popular with climbers and skiers.

Japan's highest mountain, **Fuji**, is not part of the Alps. In fact, it is not part of any mountain range. A volcano, Mount Fuji rises high above a relatively flat area in eastern Honshu. The mountain's cone-shaped peak has become a symbol of Japan. In addition, many Japanese consider Fuji a sacred place. As a result, many shrines have been built at its foot and summit.

Physical Features of Korea

Jutting south from the Asian mainland, the **Korean Peninsula** includes both North Korea and South Korea. Like the islands of Japan, much of the peninsula is covered with rugged mountains. These mountains form long ranges that run along Korea's eastern coast. The peninsula's highest mountains are in the north.

Unlike Japan, Korea also has some large plains. These plains are found mainly along the peninsula's western coast and in river valleys. Korea also has more rivers than Japan does. Most of these rivers flow westward across the peninsula and pour into the Yellow Sea.

FOCUS ON
READING
How might the facts in these paragraphs shape your opinion of Japan or Korea?

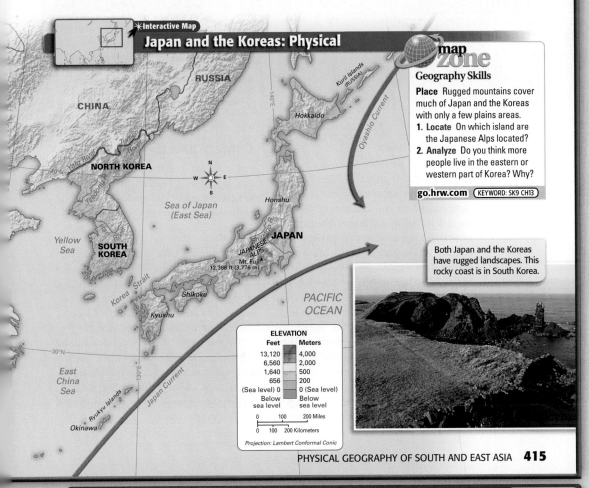

Interactive Map

Japan and the Koreas: Physical

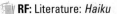

Geography Skills

Place Rugged mountains cover much of Japan and the Koreas with only a few plains areas.

1. **Locate** On which island are the Japanese Alps located?
2. **Analyze** Do you think more people live in the eastern or western part of Korea? Why?

go.hrw.com **KEYWORD: SK9 CH13**

Both Japan and the Koreas have rugged landscapes. This rocky coast is in South Korea.

ELEVATION

Feet		Meters
13,120		4,000
6,560		2,000
1,640		500
656		200
(Sea level) 0		0 (Sea level)
Below sea level		Below sea level

0   100   200 Miles
0   100   200 Kilometers

Projection: Lambert Conformal Conic

PHYSICAL GEOGRAPHY OF SOUTH AND EAST ASIA **415**

Direct Teach

Direct Teach

Main Idea

❶ Physical Features

The main physical features of Japan and the Koreas are rugged mountains.

Identify What physical feature is considered a symbol of Japan? *Mount Fuji*

Define What is a **tsunami**? *destructive waves caused by large underwater earthquakes*

Analyze Give one reason for the fact that the Koreas have fewer earthquakes than Japan. *possible answer—Korea is not located along the boundaries of tectonic plates, like Japan is.*

▪ Map Zone Transparency: Japan and the Koreas: Physical

▪ RF: Literature: *Haiku*

Info to Know

Climbing Mount Fuji, Past and Present The beautifully symmetrical, snow-capped top of Mount Fuji, rising 12,389 feet in central Honshu, Japan, has traditionally been the goal of Japanese religious pilgrims, who consider the mountain sacred. Legend claims that the first person to climb Mount Fuji was a monk in 663. Women were forbidden to climb it until the Meiji Era (1868–1912), when Japan began to modernize from its feudalistic society. Today, thousands of people from all over the world climb Mount Fuji, especially during the official climbing season in July and August.

Differentiating Instruction

Below Level

English-Language Learners

1. Draw a chart like the one shown below.

Land	Water

2. Read with students the information about the physical features of Japan and Korea, and have them note words that might go in the columns. Tell students to include verbs as well as nouns, such as *flow* and *pour*.

3. Review the words on the chart with students. Discuss their definitions. Point out synonyms (*rugged/rocky*) and antonyms (*steep/flat*). You might also ask for synonyms and antonyms of given words. **LS Verbal/Linguistic**

▪ Alternative Assessment Handbook, Rubric 7: Charts

Answers

Focus on Reading *possible answer— by enabling me to develop a mental picture of the region*

Map Zone 1. *Honshu;* **2.** *western, because there is more flat land there for building and farming*

415

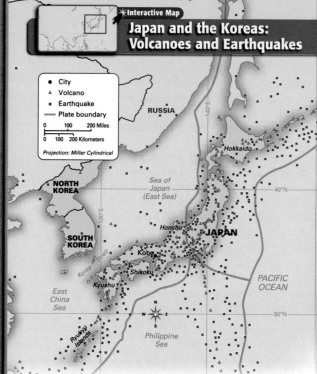

★Interactive Map
Japan and the Koreas: Volcanoes and Earthquakes

map **zone** Geography Skills

Human-Environment Interaction More than 1,000 earthquakes hit Japan every year. Most are minor, but some cause huge amounts of damage.
1. **Locate** On which large island did the 1995 Kobe earthquake occur?
2. **Compare** How does volcanic activity in Korea compare to activity in Japan?

go.hrw.com   KEYWORD: SK9 CH13

Direct Teach

Main Idea

❷ Climate and Resources

The climates and resources of Japan and the Koreas vary from north to south.

Recall Which country in the region has large deposits of coal? *North Korea*

Make Inferences Which is more important to the Japanese economy: fisheries or mining? Why? *possible answer—fisheries, because there are few mineral resources available in Japan, and fisheries are found close by*

🗺 Map Zone Transparency: Japan and the Koreas: Volcanoes and Earthquakes

Connect to Science

Earthquakes in Japan Four tectonic plates—the Eurasian, North American, Philippine, and Pacific plates—come together in Japan, making the country especially vulnerable to earthquakes. Twenty percent of the world's most powerful earthquakes take place there. In May 2005 Japanese geologist Shinji Toda announced the discovery of a new tectonic plate under Tokyo. The new tectonic plate was thought to be part of the Philippine plate under the region, but Toda's analysis of data on quakes in the region led him to conclude that it was a separate plate.

go.hrw.com
Online Resources

KEYWORD: SK9 CH13
ACTIVITY: Volcanoes and Earthquakes

A devastating earthquake struck Kobe (KOH-bay), Japan, in 1995. It caused more than $100 billion in damages and left thousands homeless.

Natural Disasters

Because of its location, Japan is subject to many sorts of natural disasters. Among these disasters are volcanic eruptions and earthquakes. As you can see on the map, these disasters are common in Japan. They can cause huge amounts of damage in the country. In addition, large underwater earthquakes sometimes cause destructive waves called **tsunamis** (sooh-NAH-mees).

Korea does not have many volcanoes or earthquakes. From time to time, though, huge storms called typhoons sweep over the peninsula from the Pacific. These storms cause great damage in both the Korean Peninsula and Japan.

READING CHECK **Contrasting** How are the physical features of Japan and Korea different?

Climate and Resources

Just as Japan and the Koreas have many similar physical features, they also have similar climates. The resources found in each country, however, differ greatly.

Climate

The climates of Japan and the Koreas vary from north to south. The northern parts of the region have a humid continental climate. This means that summers are cool, but winters are long and cold. In addition, the area has a short growing season.

To the south, the region has a humid subtropical climate with mild winters and hot, humid summers. These areas see heavy rains and typhoons in the summer. Some places receive up to 80 inches (200 cm) of rain each year.

Answers

Map Zone 1. *Honshu;* **2.** *Korea has much less volcanic activity.*

Reading Check *Korea is a peninsula, and Japan is made up of islands; Korea has more plains and rivers than Japan.*

416

Cross-Discipline Activity.: Science

At Level

Preparing for Disaster

Research Required

1. Divide the class into three groups. Have each group research technology the Japanese government uses to prepare for natural disasters common to the region.

2. Assign volcano eruptions to one group, earthquakes to another, and typhoons to the third. Have groups use the library, Internet, or other resources to research warning technology (for example, the NEC Earth Simulator in Yokohama used for typhoon prediction). Ask groups to gather the following

information about their natural disaster: most recent disaster in Japan of that kind; worst disaster in Japanese history of that kind.

3. Have groups create a presentation for the class. Remind them to use maps, charts, and photographs in their presentation.
LS Verbal/Linguistic, Visual/Spatial

📝 Alternative Assessment Handbook, Rubrics 14: Group Activity; and 29: Presentations

Resources

Resources are not evenly distributed among Japan and the Koreas. Neither Japan nor South Korea, for example, is very rich in mineral resources. North Korea, on the other hand, has large deposits of coal, iron, and other minerals.

Although most of the region does not have many mineral resources, it does have other resources. For example, the people of the Koreas have used their land's features to generate electricity. The peninsula's rocky terrain and rapidly flowing rivers make it an excellent location for creating hydroelectric power.

In addition, Japan has one of the world's strongest fishing economies. The islands lie near one of the world's most productive fisheries. A **fishery** is a place where lots of fish and other seafood can be caught. Swift ocean currents near Japan carry countless fish to the islands. Fishers then use huge nets to catch the fish and bring them to Japan's many bustling fish markets. These fish markets are among the busiest in the world.

READING CHECK Analyzing What are some resources found in Japan and the Koreas?

This fish market in Tokyo, Japan, is the busiest in the world. People gather here every morning to buy freshly caught fish.

SUMMARY AND PREVIEW The islands of Japan and the Korean Peninsula share many common features. In the next section, you will see similar features in the region of Southeast Asia and learn how those features affect life in that region.

Section 3 Assessment

go.hrw.com
Online Quiz
KEYWORD: SK9 HP13

Reviewing Ideas, Terms, and Places

1. **a. Identify** What types of landforms cover Japan and the **Korean Peninsula**?
   b. Compare and Contrast How are the physical features of Japan and Korea similar? How are they different?
   c. Predict How do you think natural disasters affect life in Japan and Korea?
2. **a. Describe** What kind of climate is found in the northern parts of the region? What kind of climate is found in the southern parts?
   b. Draw Conclusions Why are **fisheries** important to Japan's economy?

Critical Thinking

3. **Categorizing** Draw a chart like this one. In each row, describe the region's landforms, climate, and resources.

	Japan	Korean Peninsula
Landforms		
Climate		
Resources		

FOCUS ON SPEAKING

4. **Thinking about Nature** Nature is central to the art and culture of both Japan and Korea. How will you describe the natural environments of this region in your travelogue? Jot down some ideas.

PHYSICAL GEOGRAPHY OF SOUTH AND EAST ASIA **417**

Section 3 Assessment Answers

1. **a.** rugged mountains (Japan and Korean Peninsula); plains (Korean Peninsula)
   b. similar—rugged mountains; different—Koreas are on a peninsula, and Japan is made up of islands; Koreas have more plains and rivers than Japan.
   c. possible answers—Earthquakes and tsunamis cause damage and kill people; people plan carefully for natural disasters.

2. **a.** northern—humid continental; southern—humid subtropical
   b. They are an important source of food and business.

3. Landforms: Japan—rugged mountains, Korean Peninsula—rugged mountains and plains; Climate: Japan and Korean Peninsula—humid continental in the north and humid subtropical in the south; Resources: Japan—fisheries, Korean Peninsula—coal, iron, hydroelectric power

4. Answers will vary. Students may note the high mountains, rushing water, the seas, or the plains.

Direct Teach

Did you know . . .
The Korean Peninsula is surrounded by different bodies of water and edged with islands, inlets, and reefs. It has some of the best fishing waters in the world. Sea life is plentiful and varied, attracted by the presence of both warm and cold water currents and the different environments along the long coastline. Because of this abundance, seafood is basic in the Korean diet. Seaweed soups are fed to babies and are part of traditional birthday celebrations, and other kinds of seafood are eaten every day as snacks or meals.

Review & Assess

Close
Have students identify two ways that Japan's geography is different from the Korean Peninsula.

Review
Online Quiz, Section 3

Assess
SE Section 3 Assessment
PASS: Section 3 Quiz
Alternative Assessment Handbook

Reteach/Classroom Intervention
Interactive Reader and Study Guide, Section 3
Interactive Skills Tutor CD-ROM

Answers
Reading Check Japan—fisheries; the Koreas—coal, iron, hydroelectric power

417

Bellringer

If YOU lived there. . . Use the **Daily Bellringer Transparency** to help students answer the question.

🔹 Daily Bellringer Transparency, Section 4

Academic Vocabulary

Review with students the high-use academic term in this section.

circumstances conditions that influence an event or activity (p. 420)

📖 **RF:** Vocabulary Builder, Section 4

Taking Notes

Have students copy the graphic organizer onto their own paper and then use it to take notes on the section. This activity will prepare students for the Section Assessment, in which they will complete a graphic organizer that builds on the information using the Critical Thinking Skill: Summarizing.

SECTION 4

Southeast Asia

What You Will Learn...

Main Ideas

1. Southeast Asia's physical features include peninsulas, islands, rivers, and many seas, straits, and gulfs.
2. The tropical climate of Southeast Asia supports a wide range of plants and animals.
3. Southeast Asia is rich in natural resources such as wood, rubber, and fossil fuels.

The Big Idea

Southeast Asia is a tropical region of peninsulas, islands, and waterways with diverse plants, animals, and resources.

Key Terms and Places

Indochina Peninsula, *p. 418*
Malay Peninsula, *p. 418*
Malay Archipelago, *p. 418*
archipelago, *p. 418*
New Guinea, *p. 419*
Borneo, *p. 419*
Mekong River, *p. 419*

TAKING NOTES As you read, use a chart like this one to help you take notes on the physical geography of Southeast Asia.

Physical Features	
Climate, Plants, Animals	
Natural Resources	

If YOU lived there...

Your family lives on a houseboat on a branch of the great Mekong River in Cambodia. You catch fish in cages under the boat. Your home is part of a floating village of houseboats and houses built on stilts in the water. Local merchants paddle their boats loaded with fruits and vegetables from house to house. Even your school is on a nearby boat.

How does water shape life in your village?

BUILDING BACKGROUND Waterways, such as rivers, canals, seas, and oceans, are important to life in Southeast Asia. Waterways are both "highways" and sources of food. Where rivers empty into the sea, they form deltas, areas of rich soil good for farming.

Physical Features

Where can you find a flower that grows up to 3 feet across and smells like rotting garbage? How about a lizard that can grow up to 10 feet long and weigh up to 300 pounds? These amazing sights as well as some of the world's most beautiful tropical paradises are all in Southeast Asia.

The region of Southeast Asia is made up of two peninsulas and two large island groups. The **Indochina Peninsula** and the **Malay** (muh-LAY) **Peninsula** extend from the Asian mainland. We call this part of the region Mainland Southeast Asia. The two island groups are the Philippines and the **Malay Archipelago**. An **archipelago** (ahr-kuh-PE-luh-goh) is a large group of islands. We call this part of the region Island Southeast Asia.

Landforms

In Mainland Southeast Asia, rugged mountains fan out across the countries of Myanmar (MYAHN-mahr), Thailand (TY-land), Laos (LOWS), and Vietnam (vee-ET-NAHM). Between these mountains are low plateaus and river floodplains.

Teach the Big Idea

At Level

Southeast Asia

1. **Teach** Ask students the questions in the Main Idea boxes under Direct Teach.

2. **Apply** Have each student create a poster titled "Southeast Asia: Physical Geography." Below the title, have them write *tropical region, waterways, plants, animals,* and *resources* each in a different color. Have them use information from the chapter to illustrate one aspect of each category. **LS Visual/Spatial**

3. **Review** Have volunteers share their posters.

4. **Practice/Homework** Have students add at least three details in writing under each category, using information from the chapter. Students may also choose to illustrate these details. Ask volunteers to share their posters and explain their choices of details. **LS Verbal/Linguistic, Visual/Spatial**

   📖 Alternative Assessment Handbook, Rubric 28: Posters

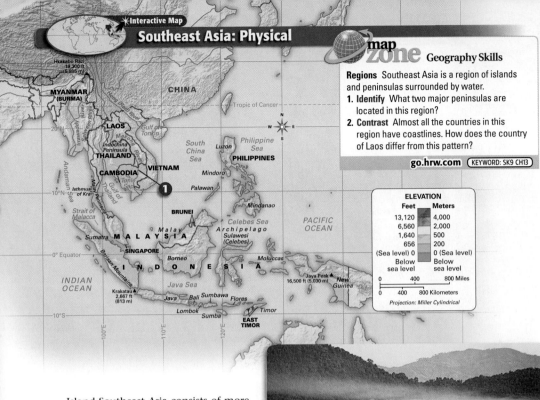

Southeast Asia: Physical

map **Zone** Geography Skills

Regions Southeast Asia is a region of islands and peninsulas surrounded by water.
1. **Identify** What two major peninsulas are located in this region?
2. **Contrast** Almost all the countries in this region have coastlines. How does the country of Laos differ from this pattern?

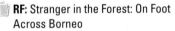

go.hrw.com KEYWORD: SK9 CH13

ELEVATION

Feet	Meters
13,120	4,000
6,560	2,000
1,640	500
656	200
(Sea level) 0	0 (Sea level)
Below sea level	Below sea level

0   400   800 Miles
0   400   800 Kilometers
Projection: Miller Cylindrical

Island Southeast Asia consists of more than 20,000 islands, some of them among the world's largest. **New Guinea** is Earth's second largest island, and **Borneo** its third largest. Many of the area's larger islands have high mountains. A few peaks are high enough to have snow and glaciers.

Island Southeast Asia is a part of the Ring of Fire as well. As a result, earthquakes and volcanic eruptions often rock the area. When such events occur underwater, they can cause tsunamis, or giant series of waves. In 2004 a tsunami in the Indian Ocean killed hundreds of thousands of people, many in Southeast Asia.

Bodies of Water

Water is a central part of Southeast Asia. Look at the map to identify the many seas, straits, and gulfs in this region.

① Mist hovers over the Mekong River as it flows through the forested mountains of northern Thailand.

In addition, several major rivers drain the mainland's peninsulas. Of these rivers, the mighty **Mekong** (MAY-KAWNG) **River** is the most important. The mainland's fertile river valleys and deltas support farming and are home to many people.

READING CHECK **Finding Main Ideas** What are Southeast Asia's major physical features?

PHYSICAL GEOGRAPHY OF SOUTH AND EAST ASIA **419**

Main Idea

❶ Physical Features

Southeast Asia's physical features include peninsulas, islands, rivers, and many seas, straits, and gulfs.

Define What is an archipelago? *large group of islands*

Identify What are the two archipelagos of Southeast Asia? *the Philippines and the Malay Archipelago*

Summarize Why is this region at risk for tsunamis? *It's part of the Ring of Fire, and underwater earthquakes or volcanic eruptions can trigger tsunamis.*

Predict How could flooding of the Mekong River hurt this region? *Many people farm and live near the river, so flooding could disrupt their lives and the economy.*

🗔 Map Zone Transparency: Southeast Asia: Physical

📄 **RF:** Stranger in the Forest: On Foot Across Borneo

MISCONCEPTION ///ALERT\\\

Tsunami or Tidal Wave? Although these terms are often used to mean the same thing, they are different. In general, tidal waves are waves caused by the daily ocean tides. A tsunami is a series of giant waves caused by a large, sudden displacement of sea water as a result of an undersea earthquake or other disturbance.

Differentiating Instruction

English-Language Learners   At Level

1. Read the Physical Features section out loud and have students read along silently. After each paragraph, ask for volunteers to read it out loud.

2. Ask questions that can be answered by one of the sentences in the reading. For example, what is Earth's second largest island? *New Guinea* Have students locate the sentence and read it out loud. **LS** Auditory/Musical, Verbal/Linguistic

📄 Alternative Assessment Handbook, Rubrics 1: Acquiring Information; and 18: Listening

Special Needs Learners   Below Level

1. Read out loud information in the text about specific physical features of Southeast Asia.

2. Have students locate these features on the physical map of Southeast Asia or on a globe. Then have students describe where that feature is located. **LS** Auditory/Musical, Visual/Spatial, Verbal/Linguistic

📄 Alternative Assessment Handbook, Rubrics 18: Listening; and 21: Map Reading

Answers

Map Zone 1. *the Indochina Peninsula and the Malay Peninsula;* **2.** *Laos is a landlocked country.*

Reading Check *peninsulas, archipelagos, mountains, plateaus, river floodplains, rivers, seas, straits, deltas*

419

Main Idea

❷ Climate, Plants, and Animals

The tropical climate of Southeast Asia supports a wide range of plants and animals.

Explain Why are the temperatures in this region warm to hot year-round? *because the region lies in the tropics, the area on and around the equator*

Draw Conclusions Why do you think animals found nowhere else in the world live just in this region? *possible answer—The rain forest is an ideal habitat for these animals. They may be found only here because the region is separated from others geographically.*

Map Zone Transparency: Southeast Asia: Climate

Connect to Science

The World's Largest Lizard The Komodo dragon was discovered in the 1900s. Several thousands now live in the wild on just four islands of Indonesia: Flores, Gili Motang, Rinca, and Komodo. Most males are about nine feet (2.75 m) in length, although the record is a little more than ten feet (3.05 m) long. A very large male can weigh up to 550 pounds (250 kg)—after eating! Females are generally smaller—about 7.5 feet (2.3 m) long and 150 pounds (68 kg). Although Komodos can run fast—as fast as dogs—they often spend their days lying in the sun. It is thought that Komodos can live up to 50 years, but most baby Komodos die before reaching adulthood.

Answers

Map Zone 1. *humid tropical;* **2.** *bring heavy rain in summer, drier weather in winter that* monsoon *means "seasonal winds."*

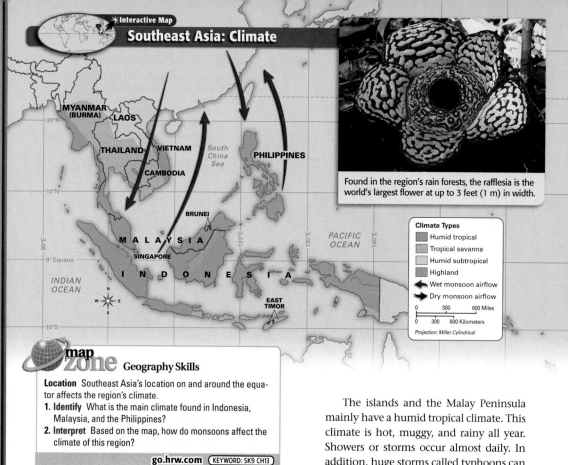

★Interactive Map
Southeast Asia: Climate

Found in the region's rain forests, the rafflesia is the world's largest flower at up to 3 feet (1 m) in width.

Climate Types
- Humid tropical
- Tropical savanna
- Humid subtropical
- Highland
- ➡ Wet monsoon airflow
- ➡ Dry monsoon airflow

0   300   600 Miles
0   300   600 Kilometers
Projection: Miller Cylindrical

map zone Geography Skills

Location Southeast Asia's location on and around the equator affects the region's climate.
1. **Identify** What is the main climate found in Indonesia, Malaysia, and the Philippines?
2. **Interpret** Based on the map, how do monsoons affect the climate of this region?

go.hrw.com KEYWORD: SK9 CH13

Climate, Plants, and Animals

Southeast Asia lies in the tropics, the area on and around the equator. Temperatures are warm to hot year-round, but become cooler to the north and in the mountains.

Much of the mainland has a tropical savanna climate that supports tall grasses and scattered trees. Seasonal monsoon winds from the oceans bring heavy rain in summer and drier weather in winter. These **circumstances** can cause severe flooding every year during wet seasons.

ACADEMIC VOCABULARY

circumstances conditions that influence an event or activity

The islands and the Malay Peninsula mainly have a humid tropical climate. This climate is hot, muggy, and rainy all year. Showers or storms occur almost daily. In addition, huge storms called typhoons can bring heavy rains and powerful winds.

The humid tropical climate's heat and heavy rainfall support tropical rain forests. These lush forests are home to a huge number of different plants and animals. About 40,000 kinds of flowering plants grow in Indonesia alone. These plants include the rafflesia, the world's largest flower. Measuring up to 3 feet (1 m) across, this flower produces a horrible, rotting stink.

Rain forest animals include elephants, monkeys, tigers, and many types of birds. Some species are found nowhere else. They include orangutans and Komodo dragons, lizards that can grow 10 feet (3 m) long.

420 CHAPTER 13

Collaborative Learning

At Level

Research Scientist's Resumé

Prep Required

1. Hand out copies of sample resumés and explain how they are used and formatted.

2. Have students work in pairs to create a resumé for a scientist applying for a job on a research team that will study the climate, plants, and animals of Southeast Asia.

3. Have the partners review the information on climate, plants, and animals, and list specific kinds of experience or education a person may need to be considered for this job.

4. Have them develop a first draft of a resumé for the scientist, agreeing together on what to include. Ask volunteers to share their resumés with the class and compare and contrast them to determine what makes for an effective resumé. **LS** Interpersonal, Verbal/Linguistic

Alternative Assessment Handbook, Rubrics 31: Resumés; and 9: Comparing and Contrasting

Orangutans live in the rain forests of Borneo and Sumatra. Deforestation has seriously reduced their habitat.

Natural Resources

Southeast Asia has a number of valuable natural resources. The region's hot, wet climate and rich soils make farming highly productive. Rice is a major crop, and others include coconuts, coffee, sugarcane, palm oil, and spices. Some countries, such as Indonesia and Malaysia (muh-LAY-zhuh), also have large rubber tree plantations.

The region's seas provide fisheries, and its tropical rain forests provide valuable hardwoods and medicines. The region also has many minerals and fossil fuels, including tin, iron ore, natural gas, and oil. For example, the island of Borneo sits atop an oil field.

Many of these plants and animals are endangered because of loss of habitat. People are clearing the tropical rain forests for farming, wood, and mining. These actions threaten the area's future diversity.

READING CHECK Analyzing How does climate contribute to the region's diversity of life?

READING CHECK Summarizing What are the region's major natural resources?

SUMMARY AND PREVIEW Southeast Asia is a tropical region of peninsulas, islands, and waterways with diverse life and rich resources. Next, you will read about the earliest history and culture of Asia in India.

Section 4 Assessment

Reviewing Ideas, Terms, and Places

1. **a. Define** What is an **archipelago**?
   b. Compare and Contrast How do the physical features of Mainland Southeast Asia compare and contrast to those of Island Southeast Asia?
2. **a. Recall** What type of forest occurs in the region?
   b. Summarize What is the climate like across much of Southeast Asia?
   c. Predict What do you think might happen to the region's wildlife if the tropical rain forests continue to be destroyed?
3. **a. Identify** Which countries in the region are major producers of rubber?
   b. Analyze How does the region's climate contribute to its natural resources?

Critical Thinking

4. **Summarizing** Draw a chart like this one. Use your notes to provide information about the climate, plants, and animals in Southeast Asia. In the left-hand box, also note how climate shapes life in the region.

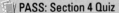

Climate of Southeast Asia → Plants / Animals

FOCUS ON SPEAKING

5. **Planning Your Topics** Now that you have studied all the regions of South and East Asia, you can decide which topics to include in your travelogue. Which features will you include? Which images will you show? Write a plan for your travelogue in your notebook.

Section 4 Assessment Answers

1. **a.** a large group of islands
   b. alike—both have mountains; different—mainland has major rivers, fertile river valleys, and deltas while the islands do not
2. **a.** rain forests
   b. mainland—mostly tropical savanna climate; islands—mainly humid tropical climate
   c. possible answer—Animal populations might be reduced or become extinct.
3. **a.** Indonesia, Malaysia
   b. The climate supports farming because it provides water and helps enrich the soil; it also supports the rain forests, which are sources of many resources.
4. possible chart answers: Climate—warm all year, tropical, rainy season; supports people, plants, and animals; Plants—tall grasses, scattered trees and shrubs on savannas; rain forests have many plants, including hardwoods; Animals—wide variety, including elephants, monkeys, tigers, birds, orangutans, and Komodo dragons
5. Students' plans will vary, but should reflect an understanding of the chapter content.

• Direct Teach •

Main Idea

❸ **Natural Resources**

Southeast Asia is rich in natural resources such as wood, rubber, and fossil fuels.

Identify What are some of the region's major crops? *rice, coconuts, coffee, sugarcane, palm oil, spices*

Make Generalizations Why is the region's farming so productive? *because of the region's hot, wet climate and rich soils*

Evaluate The rain forests provide valuable hardwoods and medicines. Is it more important to keep seeking these resources or to protect the animals who live in these rain forests? *possible answer—both, by balancing the needs of animals and people, resources could be used and animals protected*

• Review & Assess •

Close

Have students list the key features of Southeast Asia's physical geography.

Review

Online Quiz, Section 4

Assess

SE Section 4 Assessment
PASS: Section 4 Quiz
Alternative Assessment Handbook

Reteach/Classroom Intervention

Interactive Reader and Study Guide, Section 4
Interactive Skills Tutor CD-ROM

Answers

Reading Check (left) *The climate's heat and heavy rainfall support tropical rain forests, which are home to a great variety of plants and animals.*

Reading Check (right) *wood, rubber, good soils for farming, tin, iron ore, oil, gas, fisheries*

421

Tsunami!

Essential Elements

The World in Spatial Terms
Places and Regions
Physical Systems
Human Systems
Environment and Society
The Uses of Geography

Info to Know

Tsunami Warning Centers Successful warning systems depend on many countries and facilities sending in reliable earthquake and tide data.

- One of the oldest warning stations is the Pacific Tsunami Warning Center (PTWC) located in Ewa Beach, Hawai'i. It was established in 1949 to provide warnings to most Pacific Basin countries, as well as Hawai'i.
- The West Coast & Alaska Tsunami Warning Center (WC/ATWC), in Palmer, Alaska, was set up in 1967, after the great Alaskan earthquake in Prince William Sound on March 27, 1964. Today, its area of responsibility is wide-ranging, covering California, Oregon, Washington, British Columbia, Alaska, the U.S. Atlantic and Gulf of Mexico coasts, and the Atlantic coast of Canada.

Map Zone Transparency: Indian Ocean Tsunami

Linking to Today

Weather Radio The NOAA (National Oceanic and Atmospheric Administration) Weather Radio is a nationwide "all hazards" radio network run by NOAA's National Weather Service. Go to http://www.nws.noaa.gov/nwr/nwrbro.htm for a nationwide station listing and for information about NOAA Weather Radios.

Background "Huge Waves Hit Japan." This event is a tsunami (soo-NAH-mee), a series of giant sea waves. Records of deadly tsunamis go back 3,000 years. Some places, such as Japan, have been hit time and again.

Tsunamis occur when an earthquake, volcanic eruption, or other event causes seawater to move in huge waves. The majority of tsunamis occur in the Pacific Ocean because of the region's many earthquakes.

Warning systems help alert people to tsunamis. The Pacific Tsunami Warning Center monitors tsunamis in the Pacific Ocean. Sensors on the ocean floor and buoys on the water's surface help detect earthquakes and measure waves. When a tsunami threatens, radio, TV, and sirens alert the public.

Indian Ocean Catastrophe

On December 26, 2004, a massive earthquake erupted below the Indian Ocean. The earthquake launched a monster tsunami. Within half an hour, walls of water up to 65 feet high came barreling ashore in Indonesia. The water swept away boats, buildings, and people. Meanwhile, the tsunami kept traveling in ever-widening rings across the ocean. The waves eventually wiped out coastal communities in a dozen countries. Some 200,000 people eventually died.

At the time, the Indian Ocean did not have a tsunami warning system. Tsunamis are rare in that part of the world. As a result, many countries there had been unwilling to invest in a warning system.

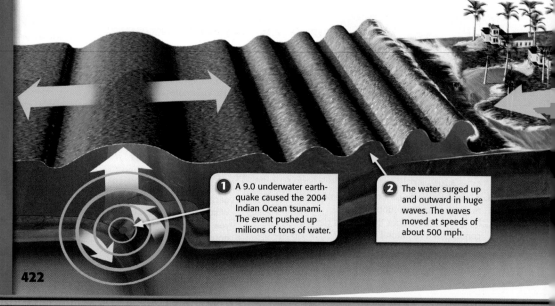

① A 9.0 underwater earthquake caused the 2004 Indian Ocean tsunami. The event pushed up millions of tons of water.

② The water surged up and outward in huge waves. The waves moved at speeds of about 500 mph.

422

Critical Thinking: Solving Problems   At Level

Fundraising Scripts

1. Have students imagine they are hosting an on-air television fundraiser to raise money for tsunami relief from the Indian Ocean tsunami.

2. Divide students into groups of three to five students. Each group must give a one-minute presentation to viewers to encourage them to donate to relief efforts by giving general tsunami information and specifics about this situation.

3. Have students review the "Tsunami!" information and visuals in their textbook,

and identify the topics they will discuss. Then have them write their script for their presentations, including language that will persuade viewers to donate.

4. Ask each group to present their scripts. As a class, discuss how each piece is effective and how it might be improved. **LS** **Verbal/Linguistic, Interpersonal**

Alternative Assessment Handbook, Rubrics 24: Oral Presentations; and 43: Writing to Persuade

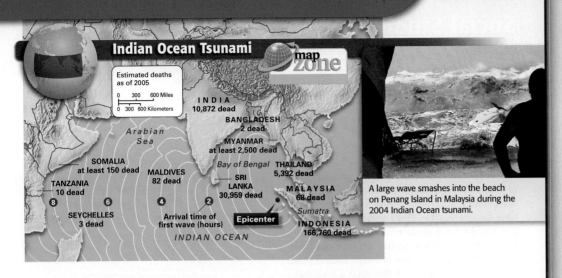

Indian Ocean Tsunami

Estimated deaths as of 2005

0   300   600 Miles
0   300   600 Kilometers

Arabian Sea

INDIA
10,872 dead

BANGLADESH
2 dead

MYANMAR
at least 2,500 dead

Bay of Bengal

SOMALIA
at least 150 dead

MALDIVES
82 dead

THAILAND
5,392 dead

SRI LANKA
30,959 dead

TANZANIA
10 dead

MALAYSIA
68 dead

SEYCHELLES
3 dead

Sumatra

Arrival time of first wave (hours)

Epicenter

INDONESIA
166,760 dead

INDIAN OCEAN

A large wave smashes into the beach on Penang Island in Malaysia during the 2004 Indian Ocean tsunami.

In 2004 these countries paid a terrible price for their decision. As the map shows, the 2004 tsunami hit countries from South Asia to East Africa. Most people had no warning of the tsunami. In addition, many people did not know how to protect themselves. Instead of heading to high ground, some people went to the beach for a closer look. Many died when later waves hit.

Tilly Smith, a 10-year-old on vacation in Thailand, was one of the few who understood the danger. Two weeks earlier, her geography teacher had discussed tsunamis. As the water began surging, Smith warned her family and other tourists to flee. Her geographic knowledge saved their lives.

What It Means No one can prevent tsunamis. Yet, by studying geography, we can prepare for these disasters and help protect lives and property. The United Nations is now working to create a global tsunami warning system. People are also trying to plant more mangroves along coastlines. These bushy swamp trees provide a natural barrier against high waves.

3 When they strike, tsunamis often look like a rapidly rising tide or swell of water. The water then rushes far inland and back out.

Geography for Life Activity

1. What steps are being taken to avoid another disaster such as the Indian Ocean tsunami in 2004?

2. About 75 percent of tsunami warnings since 1948 were false alarms. What might be the risks and benefits of early warnings to move people out of harm's way?

3. **Creating a Survival Guide** Create a tsunami survival guide. List the dos and don'ts for this emergency.

PHYSICAL GEOGRAPHY OF SOUTH AND EAST ASIA **423**

Using a Topographic Map

Activity

1. Provide a topographic map of your area and of an area with very different terrain. For example, if you live in a flat area, find a map from an area with hills or mountains. Topographic maps can be found in most libraries or on the Internet.

2. Have students compare the two maps, noting the main differences between them (the distance between the contour lines).

3. Have students examine other features of the map such as general elevation of the area; the distance scale; the contour interval, which is the number of feet between each contour line; and the direction corresponding to uphill and downhill in their area. If there are rivers on the map, point out how the contour lines indicate the direction of flow. **LS** Visual/Spatial

- Alternative Assessment Handbook, Rubric 21: Map Reading

- **RF:** Social Studies Skills, Using a Topographic Map

- Interactive Skills Tutor CD-ROM, Lesson 6: Interpret Maps, Graphs, Charts, Visuals, and Political Cartoons

- Map Zone Transparency: Awaji Island: Topographic Map

Answers

Practice 1. *more rugged in the south since there are more contour lines in that area;* **2.** *higher*

Apply *Statements should reflect an understanding of how to use a topographic map.*

424

Chart and Graph	Critical Thinking	Geography	Study

Using a Topographic Map

Learn

Topographic maps show elevation, or the height of land above sea level. They do so with contour lines, lines that connect points on the map that have equal elevation. Every point on a contour line has the same elevation. In most cases, everything inside that line has a higher elevation. Everything outside the line is lower. Each contour line is labeled to show the elevation it indicates.

An area that has lots of contour lines is more rugged than an area with few contour lines. The distance between contour lines shows how steep an area is. If the lines are very close together, then the area has a steep slope. If the lines are farther apart, then the area has a much gentler incline. Other symbols on the map show features such as rivers and roads.

Practice

Use the topographic map on this page to answer the following questions.

❶ Is Awaji Island more rugged in the south or the north? How can you tell?

❷ Does the land get higher or lower as you travel west from Yura?

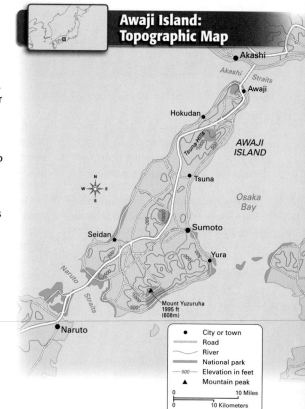

Awaji Island: Topographic Map

●	City or town
▭	Road
▭	River
▭	National park
—500—	Elevation in feet
▲	Mountain peak

0 — 10 Miles
0 — 10 Kilometers
Projection: Mercator

Apply

Search the Internet or look in a local library to find a topographic map of your area. Study the map to find three major landmarks and write down their elevations. Then write two statements about the information you can see on the map.

424 CHAPTER 13

Differentiating Instruction

Below Level

Special Needs Learners

Prep Required

Materials: foamboard, marker, utility knife

1. Before class, cut a large square of foamboard. Cut another piece, somewhat smaller and in an irregular shape. Glue the irregular shape onto the square base.

2. Continue cutting more pieces, each progressively smaller. Instruct students to build a hill, with each piece fitting entirely within the current top piece. Continue until the hill has about 25 layers.

3. With a marker, trace the outer edge of every fifth layer, labeling them 5, 10, and so on.

Place the hill on the floor. Have students stand on a sturdy chair to view the foamboard hill from above. It will appear exactly like a contour map of the hill.

4. With the utility knife, make some modifications to the hill: add a ravine, a cliff, or make the top of the hill flat or more pointed. Update the contour lines. Have students view how the contour lines have changed. **LS** Visual/Spatial

- Alternative Assessment Handbook, Rubric 14: Group Activity

Geography's Impact
video series
Review the video to answer the
closing question:
*How has Japan's location on
the Ring of Fire made it so
prone to natural hazards?*

Visual Summary

Use the visual summary below to help you review the main ideas of the chapter.

QUICK FACTS

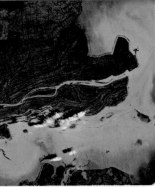

South and East Asia have many mountains. Some, like Japan's Mount Fuji, are volcanic in origin.

Large rivers flow through the region. Floods on these rivers can cause problems for people in the region.

The region's climates vary widely, from parched deserts to savannas. Monsoon winds cause wet and dry seasons.

Reviewing Vocabulary, Terms, and Places

Imagine these terms from the chapter are correct answers to items in a crossword puzzle. Write the clues for the answers.

1. Gobi
2. circumstances
3. Borneo
4. delta
5. Fuji
6. tsunami
7. monsoon
8. archipelago
9. fishery
10. subcontinent
11. Himalayas
12. loess

Comprehension and Critical Thinking

SECTION 1 *(Pages 406–409)*

13. **a. Define** What is a delta?

    b. Draw Conclusions Why are rivers important to the people of the Indian Subcontinent?

    c. Evaluate Do you think monsoons have a positive or negative effect on India? Why?

SECTION 2 *(Pages 410–413)*

14. **a. Recall** What physical features separate many of the mountain ranges in China?

    b. Explain What is the Huang He called in English, and how did the river get its name?

    c. Elaborate What major physical features might a traveler see during a trip from the Himalayas, in southwestern China, to Beijing, in northeastern China?

SECTION 3 *(Pages 414–417)*

15. **a. Identify** What physical feature covers most of Japan and the Korean Peninsula?

    b. Draw Conclusions Fish and seafood are very important in the Japanese diet. Why do you think this is so?

    c. Predict How do you think earthquakes and typhoons would affect your life if you lived in Japan?

PHYSICAL GEOGRAPHY OF SOUTH AND EAST ASIA **425**

Visual Summary

Review and Inquiry Have students choose two of the three pictures and compare and contrast the two scenes.

Quick Facts Transparency: Visual Summary: Physical Geography of South and East Asia

Reviewing Vocabulary, Terms, and Places

possible answers:

1. a desert in Mongolia
2. conditions that influence an event or activity
3. Earth's third largest island
4. a landform at the mouth of a river created by sediment deposits
5. Japan's highest mountain
6. tidal wave
7. seasonal winds that bring moist or dry air to a region
8. a large group of islands
9. where fishing fleets know to go
10. large landmass that is smaller than a continent
11. mountain range that contains the world's tallest mountains
12. fertile, yellowish soil

Comprehension and Critical Thinking

13. **a.** a landform at the mouth of a river created by sediment deposits
    b. Rivers have deposited rich soils that are good for farming.
    c. possible answer—positive; They bring rainfall for agriculture.

Review and Assessment Resources

Review and Reinforce

SE Chapter Review

RF: Chapter Review

Quick Facts Transparency: Visual Summary: Physical Geography of South and East Asia

Spanish Chapter Summaries Audio CD Program

OSP Holt Puzzle Pro; Quiz Show for ExamView

Quiz Game CD-ROM

Assess

SE Standardized Test Practice

PASS: Chapter Test, Forms A and B

Alternative Assessment Handbook

OSP ExamView Test Generator, Chapter Test

Differentiated Instruction Modified Worksheets and Tests CD-ROM: Modified Chapter Test

HOAP Holt Online Assessment Program (in the Holt Interactive Student Online Edition)

Reteach/Intervene

Interactive Reader and Study Guide

Differentiated Instruction Teacher Management System: Lesson Plans

Differentiated Instruction Modified Worksheet and Tests CD-ROM

Interactive Skills Tutor CD-ROM

go.hrw.com
Online Resources

Chapter Resources:
KEYWORD: SK9 CH13

14. a. plateaus, basins, and deserts

b. Huang He means "yellow river" in English. Loess, a yellow, fertile soils that colors the water, gives this river its name.

c. Plateau of Tibet, Sichuan Basin, North China Plain

15. a. mountains

b. Japan has little farmland but is close to fisheries.

c. Answers will vary but should mention disruption of daily life.

16. a. Indochina Peninsula, Malay Peninsula; Philippines Archipelago; Malay Archipelago

b. possible answer—similar—tropical climates; different—mainland has tropical savanna climate; islands have humid tropical climate

c. possible answer—balance people's needs for resources with environmental and animal needs

Social Studies Skills

17. 500 and 1000 feet

18. south; more area within the 1000-foot contour line

19. less

Focus on Reading and Speaking

20. opinion

21. fact

22. fact

23. opinion

RF: Focus on Reading, Understanding Fact and Opinion

24. Rubric Students should

- use notes to create a well-written, one- to two-minute script
- show images that reflect their script's content
- present their travelogues to the class, speaking clearly and making eye contact
- **RF:** Focus on Speaking: Presenting a Travelogue

Using the Internet

25. Go to the HRW Web site and enter the keyword shown to access a rubric for this activity.

KEYWORD: SK9 TEACHER

SECTION 4 (Pages 418–421)

16. a. Identify What two peninsulas and two archipelagos make up Southeast Asia?

b. Compare and Contrast How are the climates of Mainland Southeast Asia and Island Southeast Asia both similar and different?

c. Develop What different needs should people weigh when considering how best to protect Southeast Asia's tropical rain forests?

Social Studies Skills

Using a Topographic Map *Use the topographic map in this chapter's Social Studies Skills lesson to answer the following questions.*

17. What elevations do the contour lines on this map show?

18. Where are the highest points on Awaji Island located? How can you tell?

19. Is the city of Sumoto located more or less than 500 feet above sea level?

FOCUS ON READING AND SPEAKING

Understanding Fact and Opinion *Decide whether each of the following statements is a fact or an opinion.*

20. India would be a great place to live.

21. Japan is an island country.

22. The Himalayas are the world's tallest mountains.

23. The Himalayas are beautiful.

Presenting Your Travelogue *Use your notes and the instructions below to create and present your travelogue.*

24. Use your notes to create a one- to two-minute script describing your travels in South and East Asia. Identify and collect the images you need to illustrate your talk. Present your oral travelogue to the class, giving an exciting view of the region. Observe as others present their travelogues. How is each travelogue unique? How are they similar?

Using the Internet

go.hrw.com
KEYWORD: SK9 CH13

25. Activity: Writing a Report on Rain Forests The tropical rain forests of Indonesia are home to a rich diversity of life. Unfortunately, these forests face a number of threats. Enter the activity keyword to research these rain forests. Then write a short report that summarizes the threats they face.

Map Activity

26. South and East Asia On a separate sheet of paper, match the letters on the map with their correct labels.

Japan	Plateau of Tibet
South China Sea	Gobi Desert
Ganges River	Malay Peninsula

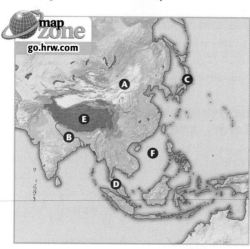

map zone
go.hrw.com

Map Activity

26. A. Gobi Desert

B. Ganges River

C. Japan

D. Malay Peninsula

E. Plateau of Tibet

F. South China Sea

DIRECTIONS (1–7): For each statement or question, write on a separate answer sheet the *number* of the word or expression that, of those given, best completes the statement or answers the question.

1 What is the world's highest mountain range?

(1) Himalayas

(2) Kunlun Shan

(3) Tian Shan

(4) Qinling Shandi

2 Which of the following is not a major river?

(1) Honshu

(2) Ganges

(3) Huang He

(4) Mekong

3 The two peninsulas of Southeast Asia are the Indochina Peninsula and the

(1) Burma Peninsula.

(2) Malay Peninsula.

(3) Philippine Peninsula.

(4) Thai Peninsula.

4 India's Thar is a

(1) desert.

(2) mountain.

(3) river.

(4) rain forest.

5 Which statement about Japan is true?

(1) It is a peninsula.

(2) It is mostly flat.

(3) It includes only three islands.

(4) It has many volcanoes.

6 What is the largest island in Southeast Asia?

(1) Bali

(2) Borneo

(3) Java

(4) New Guinea

7 These seasonal winds bring both wet and dry conditions to much of the Indian Subcontinent.

(1) hurricanes

(2) monsoons

(3) tsunamis

(4) typhoons

Base your answer to question 8 on the map below and on your knowledge of social studies.

China, Mongolia, and Taiwan: Precipitation

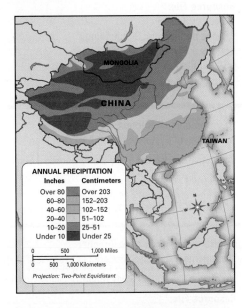

MONGOLIA

CHINA

TAIWAN

ANNUAL PRECIPITATION

Inches	Centimeters
Over 80	Over 203
60–80	152–203
40–60	102–152
20–40	51–102
10–20	25–51
Under 10	Under 25

0   500   1,000 Miles

0   500   1,000 Kilometers

Projection: Two-Point Equidistant

8 Constructed-Response Question **Write one or two sentences to answer the following question: If you were to travel through China from northwest to southeast, how would the precipitation change?**

PHYSICAL GEOGRAPHY OF SOUTH AND EAST ASIA **427**

1. 1

Break Down the Question This question requires students to recall factual information. Refer students who miss it to Section 1.

2. 1

Break Down the Question Students should recall from Section 3 that Honshu is the name of Japan's largest island, not the name of a river.

3. 2

Break Down the Question This question requires students to recall factual information. Refer students who miss it to Section 4.

4. 1

Break Down the Question The question requires students to recall factual information from Section 1. Remind students that the Thar is a desert in Northwest India.

5. 4

Break Down the Question Students could use the process of elimination to determine that option 4 is the only possible correct answer.

6. 4

Break Down the Question This question requires students to recall factual information. Refer students who miss it to Section 4.

7. 2

Break Down the Question This question requires students to recall factual information from Section 1.

8. Constructed-Response Question

Northwest China is very dry whereas Southeast China is very wet. If I traveled from Northwest China to Southeast China, precipitation would increase along the way.

Reteach/Intervention Resources

Reproducible

Interactive Reader and Study Guide

Differentiated Instruction Teacher Management System: Lesson Plans

Technology

Quick Facts Transparency: Visual Summary: Physical Geography of South and East Asia

Differentiated Instruction Modified Worksheets and Tests CD-ROM

Interactive Skills Tutor CD-ROM

Tips for Test Taking

I'm Stuck! Give students these tips for when they get stuck on a standardized test. If you come across a question that stumps you, don't get frustrated. First master the question to make sure you understand what is being asked. Then work through the strategies you have already learned. If you are still stuck, circle the question and go on to others. Come back to it later. What if you still have no idea? Practice the 50/50 strategy and make an educated guess.

Ancient Civilizations of Asia—India

Chapter Overview	Reproducible Resources	Technology Resources
CHAPTER 14 pp. 428–461 **Overview:** In this chapter, students will study the ancient civilizations of India, and the two major religions that developed there.	**Differentiated Instruction Teacher Management System:*** • Instructional Pacing Guides • Lesson Plans for Differentiated Instruction **Interactive Reader and Study Guide:** Chapter Summary Graphic Organizer* **Resource File:*** • Chapter Review • Focus on Reading: Sequencing • Focus on Writing: Creating a Poster • Social Studies Skills: Comparing Maps **Experiencing World History and Geography**	**OSP Teacher's One-Stop Planner:** Calendar Planner **Power Presentations with Video CD-ROM** **Differentiated Instruction Modified Worksheets and Tests CD-ROM** **Student Edition on Audio CD Program** **Map Zone Transparency:** Ancient India, 2300 BC–AD 500* **Geography's Impact Video Program (VHS/DVD):** Impact of Buddhism as a World Religion* **World Outline Maps: Transparencies and Activities**
Section 1: **Early Indian Civilizations** **The Big Idea:** Indian civilization developed on the Indus River.	**Differentiated Instruction Teacher Management System:** Section 1 Lesson Plan* **Interactive Reader and Study Guide:** Section 1 Summary* **Resource File:*** • Vocabulary Builder: Section 1 • Geography and History: The Indus River Valley	**Daily Bellringer Transparency:** Section 1* **Map Zone Transparency:** Harappan Civilization, c. 2600–1900 BC* **Map Zone Transparency:** Aryan Migrations* **Internet Activity:** Ancient India Ad
Section 2: **Origins of Hinduism** **The Big Idea:** Hinduism, the largest religion in India, developed out of ancient Indian beliefs and practices.	**Differentiated Instruction Teacher Management System:** Section 2 Lesson Plan* **Interactive Reader and Study Guide:** Section 2 Summary* **Resource File:*** • Vocabulary Builder: Section 2 • Primary Source: Gandhi's Autobiography	**Daily Bellringer Transparency:** Section 2*
Section 3: **Origins of Buddhism** **The Big Idea:** Buddhism began in India and became a major religion.	**Differentiated Instruction Teacher Management System:** Section 3 Lesson Plan* **Interactive Reader and Study Guide:** Section 3 Summary* **Resource File:*** • Vocabulary Builder: Section 3	**Daily Bellringer Transparency:** Section 3* **Map Zone Transparency:** Early Spread of Buddhism*
Section 4: **Indian Empires** **The Big Idea:** The Mauryas and the Guptas built great empires in India.	**Differentiated Instruction Teacher Management System:** Section 4 Lesson Plan* **Interactive Reader and Study Guide:** Section 4 Summary* **Resource File:*** • Vocabulary Builder: Section 4 • Biography, Candragupta Maurya; Mahinda	**Daily Bellringer Transparency:** Section 4* **Map Zone Transparency:** Mauryan Empire, c. 320-185 BC* **Map Zone Transparency:** Gupta Empire, c. 400* **Internet Activity:** Mauryan Leaders
Section 5: **Indian Achievements** **The Big Idea:** The people of ancient India made great contributions to the arts and sciences.	**Differentiated Instruction Teacher Management System:** Section 5 Lesson Plan* **Interactive Reader and Study Guide:** Section 5 Summary* **Resource File:*** • Vocabulary Builder: Section 5 • Literature, Comparing Buddhist and Hindu Literature	**Daily Bellringer Transparency:** Section 5*

SE Student Edition	 Print Resource	Audio CD
TE Teacher's Edition	Transparency	CD-ROM
go.hrw.com	LS Learning Styles	Video
OSP Teacher's One-Stop Planner	* also on One-Stop Planner	

HOLT

Geography's Impact
Video Program

Impact of Buddhism as a World Religion
Suggested use: as a chapter introduction

Review, Assessment, Intervention

 Quick Facts Transparencies: Visual Summary: Ancient Civilizations of Asia—India*

 Spanish Chapter Summaries Audio CD Program

 Progress Assessment Support System (PASS): Chapter Test*

 Differentiated Instruction Modified Worksheets and Tests CD-ROM: Modified Chapter Test

OSP **Teacher's One-Stop Planner:** ExamView Test Generator (English/Spanish)

HOAP **Holt Online Assessment Program (HOAP),** in the Holt Interactive Online Student Edition

---

 PASS: Section 1 Quiz*

 Online Quiz: Section 1

 Alternative Assessment Handbook

 PASS: Section 2 Quiz*

 Online Quiz: Section 2

 Alternative Assessment Handbook

 PASS: Section 3 Quiz*

 Online Quiz: Section 3

 Alternative Assessment Handbook

 PASS: Section 4 Quiz*

 Online Quiz: Section 4

 Alternative Assessment Handbook

 PASS: Section 5 Quiz*

 Online Quiz: Section 5

 Alternative Assessment Handbook

Power Presentations with Video CD-ROM

Power Presentations with Video are visual presentations of each chapter's main ideas. Presentations can be customized by including Quick Facts charts, images from the text, and video clips.

Holt Online Learning

go.hrw.com
Teacher Resources
KEYWORD: SK9 TEACHER

go.hrw.com
Student Resources
KEYWORD: SK9 CH14

- Interactive Multimedia Activities
- Current Events

- Chapter-based Internet Activities
- and more!

Holt Interactive
Online Student Edition

Complete online support for interactivity, assessment, and reporting

- Interactive Maps and Notebook
- Standardized Test Prep
- Homework Practice and Research Activities Online

CHAPTER 14 PLANNING GUIDE

Differentiating Instruction

How do I address the needs of varied learners?
The Target Resource acts as your primary strategy for differentiated instruction.

ENGLISH-LANGUAGE LEARNERS & STRUGGLING READERS

TARGET RESOURCE

Graphic Organizer Transparencies with Support for Reading and Writing

Spanish Resources

Spanish Chapter Summaries Audio CD Program

Teacher's One-Stop Planner:
• ExamView Test Generator, Spanish
• PuzzlePro, Spanish

English-Language Learner Strategies and Activities

Additional Resources

Differentiated Instruction Teacher Management System: Lesson Plans for Differentiated Instruction

Resource File:
• Vocabulary Builder
• Social Studies Skills, Comparing Maps

Quick Facts Transparencies: Ancient History of Asia—India Visual Summary

Student Edition on Audio CD Program

SPECIAL NEEDS LEARNERS

TARGET RESOURCE

Differentiated Instruction Modified Worksheets and Tests CD-ROM

• Vocabulary Flash Cards
• Vocabulary Builder Activities
• Chapter Review Activity
• Chapter Test

Additional Resources

Differentiating Instruction Teacher Management System: Lesson Plans for Differentiated Instruction

Interactive Reader and Study Guide

Resource File: Social Studies Skills, Comparing Maps

Student Edition on Audio CD Program

Interactive Skills Tutor CD-ROM

Graphic Organizer Transparencies with Support for Reading and Writing

ADVANCED/GIFTED-AND-TALENTED STUDENTS

TARGET RESOURCE

Resource File

The Resource File activities allow students to extend their knowledge of chapter-related places and people, and to practice geography skills.
• Focus on Reading: Sequencing
• Focus on Writing: Making a Poster
• Literature: Comparing Buddhist and Hindu Literature

Additional Resources

Differentiated Instruction Teacher Management System: Lesson Plans for Differentiated Instruction

World History and Geography Document-Based Questions Activities

Geography, Science, and Cultures Activities

Experiencing World History and Geography

Differentiated Activities in the Teacher's Edition

- Designing an Advertisement
- Comparing Maps
- Describing an Indian Temple

HOLT Teacher's One-Stop Planner®

How can I manage the lesson plans and support materials for differentiated instruction?

With the Teacher's One-Stop Planner, you can easily organize and print lesson plans, planning guides, and instructional materials for all learners.

The Teacher's One-Stop Planner includes the following materials to help you differentiate instruction:

- Interactive Teacher's Edition
- Calendar Planner and pacing guides
- Editable lesson plans
- All reproducible ancillaries in Adobe Acrobat (PDF) format
- ExamView Test Generator (English & Spanish)
- Transparency and video previews

Differentiated Activities in the Teacher's Edition

- Studying a Map of India
- Life of the Buddha
- Describing an Indian Temple
- Labeling and Interpreting Maps

Professional Development

What teacher training resources are available to help me grow professionally?

- **In-service and staff development** as part of your Holt Social Studies product purchase
- **Quick Teacher Tutorial Lesson Presentation CD-ROM**
- Intensive tuition-based **Teacher Development Institute**
- **Convenient Holt Speaker Bureau** – face-to-face workshop options
- **24/7 Ask A Professional Development Expert** at http://www.hrw.com/prodev/

Differentiated Activities in the Teacher's Edition

- Understanding Drainage Systems
- The Caste System
- Mauryan Time Line
- Writing a Report
- Writing a Newspaper Article

Chapter Big Ideas

Section 1 Indian civilization developed on the Indus River.

Section 2 Hinduism, the largest religion in India, developed out of ancient Indian beliefs and practices.

Section 3 Buddhism began in India and became a major religion.

Section 4 The Mauryas and the Guptas built great empires in India.

Section 5 The people of ancient India made great contributions to the arts and sciences.

Focus on Reading and Writing

Reading The Resource File provides a Focus on Reading worksheet to help students figure out the proper sequence of events when they read.

📋 RF: Focus on Reading, Sequencing

Writing The Resource File provides a Focus on Writing worksheet to help students organize and create their posters.

📋 RF: Focus on Writing, Creating a Poster

428 CHAPTER 14

CHAPTER **14**

Ancient Civilizations of Asia—India

FOCUS QUESTION

How did ancient civilizations contribute to the development of the Eastern Hemisphere?

What You Will Learn...

In this chapter you will learn about the ancient civilization of India, the birthplace of two major world religions—Hinduism and Buddhism. You will also learn about the early civilizations and powerful empires that developed in India.

FOCUS ON READING AND WRITING

Sequencing When you read, it is important to keep track of the sequence, or order, in which events happen. Look for dates and other clues to help you figure out the proper sequence. **See the lesson, Sequencing, on page S17.**

Creating a Poster Ancient India was the home of amazing cities, strong empires, and influential religions. As you read this chapter, think about how you could illustrate one aspect of Indian culture in a poster.

Early India The first civilization in India, the Harappans, were skilled builders and artists.

428 CHAPTER 14

Introduce the Chapter

At Level

Telling Tales in Ancient India

1. Call on a volunteer to answer this question: If you wanted to teach a friend an important lesson about life, which would be more effective—telling him or her what to do or telling a story that makes the point indirectly?

2. Point out that many people respond better to a story. In ancient India, people told stories, also called fables, that taught important lessons. These fables were collected in a work called the *Panchatantra*. Long ago, this

collection was translated into other languages. It influenced many works of literature, including *The Thousand and One Nights*, the source of Sinbad the Sailor tales. Ask students if they are familiar with the Sinbad stories.

3. Tell students that ancient India gave birth to more than fun stories; two of the world's most important religions began there. Tell students they will learn about these topics and more in this chapter. 🔲 **Verbal/Linguistic**

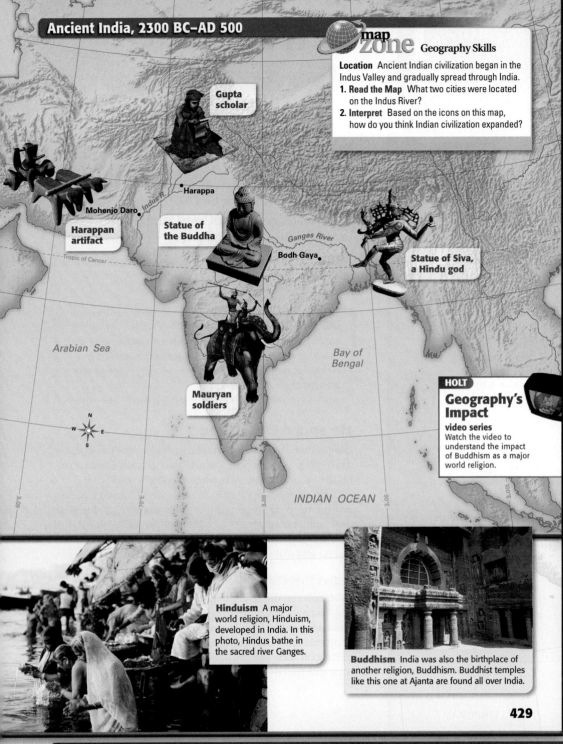

Ancient India, 2300 BC–AD 500

Gupta scholar

Harappan artifact

Mohenjo Daro

Harappa

Indus R.

Statue of the Buddha

Tropic of Cancer

Ganges River

Bodh Gaya

Statue of Siva, a Hindu god

Arabian Sea

Bay of Bengal

Mauryan soldiers

N W E S

INDIAN OCEAN

60°E 70°E 80°E 90°E 100°E

map Zone — Geography Skills

Location Ancient Indian civilization began in the Indus Valley and gradually spread through India.

1. **Read the Map** What two cities were located on the Indus River?
2. **Interpret** Based on the icons on this map, how do you think Indian civilization expanded?

HOLT — Geography's Impact

video series
Watch the video to understand the impact of Buddhism as a major world religion.

Hinduism A major world religion, Hinduism, developed in India. In this photo, Hindus bathe in the sacred river Ganges.

Buddhism India was also the birthplace of another religion, Buddhism. Buddhist temples like this one at Ajanta are found all over India.

429

• Chapter Preview •

Explore the Map and Pictures

Over a period of almost 3000 years, Indian civilizations developed rich, complex cultures. Buddhism and Hinduism became major world religions, and different empires organized governments and supported great achievements in art, literature, and science. The development of the Indian subcontinent was greatly influenced by geography. Ask students what features on the map helped isolate India from people from the north, west, and east. (*mountains to the north, east and west; Arabian Sea and Bay of Bengal to the east and west*)

Map Zone Transparency: Ancient India, 2300 BC–AD 500

Analyzing Visuals Ask students to look closely at the photo of Hindus bathing in the sacred river Ganges. What does this photo tell about the importance of this action? *it is an important, solemn occasion* What might be the significance of bathing in a sacred river? *a symbol of cleansing*

HOLT — Geography's Impact

▶ **video series**
See the Video Teacher's Guide for strategies for using the chapter video to understand the impact of Buddhism as a major religion.

go.hrw.com
Online Resources

Chapter Resources:
KEYWORD: SK9 CH14
Teacher Resources:
KEYWORD: SK9 TEACHER

Critical Thinking: Analyzing Visuals   At Level

Examining Religions

1. Have students study the pictures on this page and write how they can tell that religion has played an important role in India. Discuss their answers, pointing out that two of the world's religions started in India.

2. Mention that many Hindus make a pilgrimage, or holy journey, to the Ganges to bathe in its holy water. Ask students what other religions support pilgrimages to holy sites. Mention that a million or more Muslims travel to Mecca each year. How are the pilgrimages similar? How are they different?

3. The temple shown on this page is located in Ajanta in western India. It is also the site of caves carved into a steep hillside by early Buddhist monks. The walls were decorated with paintings illustrating Buddhist texts and are considered the height of Buddhist art. Ask students if they are familiar with other paintings, such as the Sistine Chapel, that illustrate religious texts. Discuss ways that art can teach about religious beliefs.

LS Interpersonal, Logical/Mathematical

Alternative Assessment Handbook, Rubric 11: Discussions

Answers

Map Zone 1. *Mohenjo Daro, Harappa;*
2. *through war and the spread of ideas.*

429

Bellringer

If YOU lived there. . . Use the **Daily Bellringer Transparency** to help students answer the question.

🖳 Daily Bellringer Transparency, Section 1

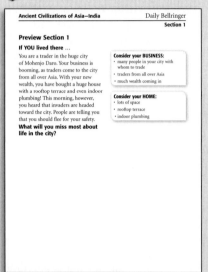

Key Terms and Places

📝 **RF:** Vocabulary Builder, Section 1

Taking Notes

Have students copy the graphic organizer onto their own paper and then use it to take notes on the section. This activity will prepare students for the Section Assessment, in which they will complete a graphic organizer that builds on the information using the Critical Thinking Skill: Summarizing.

SECTION 1

What You Will Learn...

Main Ideas

1. Located on the Indus River, the Harappan civilization also had contact with people far from India.
2. Harappan achievements included a writing system, city planning, and art.
3. The Aryan invasion changed India's civilization.

The Big Idea

Indian civilization developed on the Indus River.

Key Terms and Places

Indus River, *p. 430*
Harappa, *p. 431*
Mohenjo Daro, *p. 431*
Sanskrit, *p. 435*

TAKING NOTES As you read this section, take notes on India's two earliest civilizations, the Harappans and Aryans. Record what you find in a graphic organizer like this one.

Ancient Indian Civilizations	
Harappan Civilization	Aryan Civilization

Early Indian Civilizations

If YOU lived there...

You are a trader in the huge city of Mohenjo Daro. Your business is booming, as traders come to the city from all over Asia. With your new wealth, you have bought a huge house with a rooftop terrace and even indoor plumbing! This morning, however, you heard that invaders are headed toward the city. People are telling you that you should flee for your safety.

What will you miss most about life in the city?

BUILDING BACKGROUND India was home to one of the world's first civilizations. Like other early civilizations, the one in India grew up in a river valley. As archaeologists discovered, however, the society that eventually developed in India was very different from the ones that developed elsewhere.

Harappan Civilization

Imagine that you are an archaeologist. You are out in a field one day looking for a few pots, a tablet, or some other small artifact. Imagine your surprise, then, when you find a whole city!

Archaeologists working in India in the 1920s had that very experience. While digging for artifacts along the **Indus River**, they found not one but two huge cities. The archaeologists had thought people had lived along the Indus long ago, but they had no idea that an advanced civilization had existed there.

India's First Civilization

Historians call the civilization that developed along the Indus and Sarasvati Rivers the Harappan (huh-RA-puhn) civilization. The name comes from the modern city of Harappa (huh-RA-puh), Pakistan. It was near this city that the ruins of the ancient civilization were first discovered. Archaeologists currently estimate that the civilization thrived between 2300 and 1700 BC.

Teach the Big Idea

At Level

Early Indian Civilizations

1. **Teach** Ask students the questions in the Main Idea boxes under Direct Teach.

2. **Apply** Create a Venn diagram for students to see, with *Harappan Civilization* and *Aryan Civilization* as heads for the circles and *Both Civilizations* for the overlap. Have students note one similarity and one difference between the civilizations. For example, both peoples settled in the Indus Valley, but Harappans lived in big cities while Aryans lived in small villages.
LS Interpersonal, Visual/Spatial

3. **Review** Have students tell what we do know about these civilizations and why we don't know more about the Harappans.

4. **Practice/Homework** Have students create a chart listing other characteristics of the Harappan and Aryan civilizations.
LS Visual/Spatial

📝 Alternative Assessment Handbook, Rubric 7: Charts

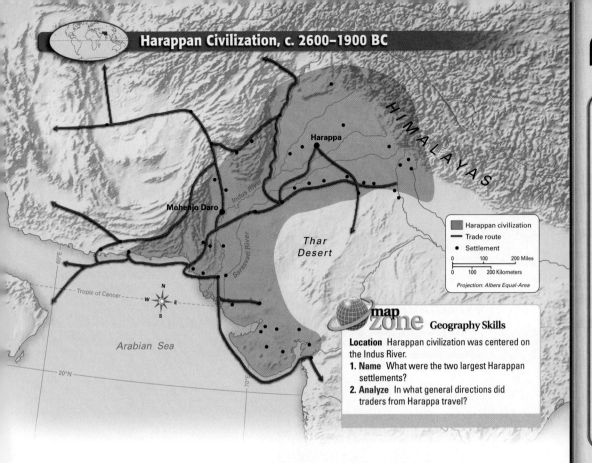

Harappan Civilization, c. 2600–1900 BC

HIMALAYAS

Harappa

Mohenjo Daro

Indus River

Saraswati River

Thar Desert

Tropic of Cancer

60°E

20°N

70°E

Arabian Sea

Harappan civilization
Trade route
• Settlement

0   100   200 Miles
0   100   200 Kilometers

Projection: Albers Equal-Area

map
zone **Geography Skills**

Location Harappan civilization was centered on the Indus River.
1. Name What were the two largest Harappan settlements?
2. Analyze In what general directions did traders from Harappa travel?

The Harappan civilization controlled large areas on both sides of the Indus River. As you can see on the map, settlements were scattered over a huge area. Most of these settlements lay next to rivers. The largest settlements were two cities, **Harappa** and **Mohenjo Daro** (mo-HEN-joh DAR-oh).

Like most other ancient societies, the Harappan civilization was dependent on agriculture. Farmers in the Indus Valley grew a variety of crops—from wheat and barley to dates and vegetables—to feed both themselves and city dwellers. They used irrigation canals to bring water from the Indus and other rivers to their fields.

Contact with Other Cultures

Although the Harappan civilization was centered on the Indus, its influence reached far beyond that area. In fact, archaeologists have found evidence that the Harappans had contact with people as far away as southern India and Mesopotamia.

Most of this contact with other cultures was in the form of trade. The Harappans traded to obtain raw materials. They then used these materials to make products such as pottery, stamps and seals, and statues.

READING CHECK **Finding Main Ideas** Where was the Harappan civilization located?

ANCIENT CIVILIZATIONS OF ASIA—INDIA **431**

Direct Teach

Main Idea

❶ **Harappan Civilization**

Harappan civilization developed along the Indus River.

Identify What were the two main cities of the Harappan civilization? *Harappa and Mohenjo Daro*

Recall When did the Harappan civilization thrive? *between 2300 and 1700 BC*

Analyze What are some explanations for why Harappa and Mohenjo Daro were very similar? *possible answers—People from one of the cities founded the other; communication, travel, and/or trade made Harappan civilization fairly uniform throughout the region.*

Map Zone Transparency: Harappan Civilization, c. 2600–1900 BC

Info to Know

The Khyber Pass Various invaders have found their way from central Asia through the mountains into India by means of the Khyber Pass. It is a narrow passage 28 miles long on what is now the border between Pakistan and Afghanistan.

Differentiating Instruction

Below Level

Special Needs Learners

Materials: outline maps of Indian subcontinent, map pencils

1. Show students a map of India and ask for volunteers to identify major physical features.

2. Give each student a blank map of India and have them label the following on their maps: major rivers and other bodies of water, the entire Indus River Valley, mountain ranges, and plateaus.

3. Have students color the area where the Harappan civilization settled and label the two largest settlements.

4. Lead a discussion about the importance of the Indus River to the Harappan civilization.
LS **Visual/Spatial**
Alternative Assessment Handbook, Rubric 20: Map Creation

Answers

Map Zone 1. *Harappa and Mohenjo Daro;* **2.** *west and south*
Reading Check *in the Indus Valley*

431

❷ **Harappan Achievements**

Harappans made great achievements in writing, city planning, and art.

Identify About how big in area was Mohenjo Daro? *about one square mile*

Predict What kind of finding by archaeologists could provide more information about the Harrapans? *possible answer—examples of Harappan writing that include long passages*

Close-Up

Mohenjo Daro Why did the houses of Mohenjo Daro have flat roofs? *People could sit on the roofs to cool off on a hot day.*

Linking to Today

Pottery Wheel Much of the Harappan pottery seems to have been made on human-powered potters' wheels. This type of machine is still used around the world today.

Harappan Achievements

Historians do not know much about the Harappan civilization. They think the Harappans had kings and strong central governments, but they are not sure. They also know little about Harappan religion.

Although we do not know much about how the Harappans lived, we do know that they made great achievements in many fields. Everything we know about these achievements comes from artifacts.

Writing System

The ancient Harappans developed India's first writing system. However, scholars have not yet learned to read this language. Archaeologists have found many examples of Harappan writing, but none of them is more than a few words long. This lack of long passages has made translating the language difficult. Because we cannot read what they wrote, we rely on other clues to study Harappan society.

Close-up

Life in Mohenjo Daro

Mohenjo Daro was one of the two major cities of the Harappan civilization. Located next to the Indus River in what is now Pakistan, the city probably covered one square mile. The people who lived in the city enjoyed some of the most advanced comforts of their time, including indoor plumbing.

Harappan merchants used a standard set of weights to measure goods such as precious stones.

CHAPTER 14

Cross-Discipline Activity: Science   **Above Level**

Understanding Drainage Systems   **Research Required**

1. Instruct students to conduct research to learn more about how drainage systems work. Students should use at least two independent, credible sources.

2. Have students prepare presentations on their findings. The presentations should incorporate detailed graphics illustrating sewer systems, drainage of streets, indoor plumbing, and so on.

3. Students should give their presentations to the class. 🅛 **Verbal/Linguistic**

📃 Alternative Assessment Handbook, Rubrics 29: Presentations; and 30: Research

City Planning

Most of what we have learned about the Harappans has come from studying their cities, especially Harappa and Mohenjo Daro. The two cities lay on the Indus more than 300 miles apart, but they appear to have been remarkably similar.

Both Harappa and Mohenjo Daro were well-planned cities. A close examination of their ruins shows that the Harappans were careful planners and skilled engineers.

Harappa and Mohenjo Daro were built with defense in mind. Each city stood near a towering fortress. From these fortresses, defenders could look down on the cities' carefully laid out brick streets. These streets crossed at right angles and were lined with storehouses, workshops, market stalls, and houses. Using their engineering skills, the Harappans built extensive sewer systems to keep their streets from flooding. They also installed plumbing in many buildings.

Next to the city was a huge citadel, or fortress, to guard against invasions.

The houses of Mohenjo Daro had flat roofs. People climbed to their roofs to take advantage of cooling breezes.

The city's streets were paved and well drained. They met at right angles, creating a grid pattern.

ANALYSIS SKILL · ANALYZING VISUALS
What in this picture suggests that Mohenjo Daro was a well-planned city?

ANCIENT CIVILIZATIONS OF ASIA—INDIA **433**

433

❸ Aryan Migration

The Aryan migraton to India changed the region's civilization.

Identify From where did the Aryans come? *Central Asia*

Compare How was the Aryan civilization different from the Harappan? *The Aryans didn't farm at first, didn't build cities, didn't have a single ruling authority, and didn't have a written language.*

Evaluate Why are the Vedas so important to us today? *because so much of what we know about the Aryans comes from them*

Connect to English/Language Arts

Indo-European Languages Sanskrit belongs to a language group called the Indo-European languages. Similarities among the Indo-European languages show that they are related. For example, look at these words for the English word *mother*: Sanskrit, *matar;* Greek, *meter;* Latin, *mater;* and Old Irish, *mathair.* The languages listed—and many others—developed from a lost language called Proto-Indo-European. People who lived from Europe to India may have spoken this ancient language between 10,000 and 6,000 years ago.

Artistic Achievements

In Harappan cities, archaeologists have found many artifacts that show that the Harappans were skilled artisans. For example, they have found sturdy pottery vessels, jewelry, and ivory objects.

Some of these ancient artifacts have helped historians draw conclusions about Harappan society. For example, they found a statue that shows two animals pulling a cart. Based on this statue, they conclude that the Harappans built and used wheeled vehicles. Likewise, a statue of a man with elaborate clothes and jewelry suggests that Harappan society had an upper class.

Harappan civilization ended by the early 1700s BC, but no one is sure why. Perhaps invaders destroyed the cities or natural disasters, like floods or earthquakes, caused the civilization to collapse.

FOCUS ON READING
In what order did the Aryans settle lands in India?

READING CHECK **Analyzing** Why do we not know much about Harappan civilization?

Harappan Art

Like other ancient peoples, the Harappans made small seals like the one below that were used to stamp goods. They also used clay pots like the one at right decorated with a goat.

434 CHAPTER 14

Aryan Migration

Not long after the Harappan civilization crumbled, a new group appeared in the Indus Valley. These people were called the Aryans (AIR-ee-uhnz). Possibly from the area around the Caspian Sea in Central Asia, over time they became the dominant group in India.

Arrival and Spread

Many historians and archaeologists believe that the Aryans first arrived in India in the 2000s BC, probably crossing into India through mountain passes in the northwest. Over many centuries, they spread east and south into central India. From there they moved even farther east into the Ganges River Valley.

Much of what we know about Aryan society comes from religious writings known as the Vedas (VAY-duhs). These are collections of poems, hymns, myths, and rituals that were written by Aryan priests. You will read more about the Vedas later in this chapter.

Government and Society

As nomads, the Aryans took along their herds of animals as they moved. But over time, they settled in villages and began to farm. Unlike the Harappans, they did not build big cities.

The Aryan political system was also different from the Harappan system. The Aryans lived in small communities, based mostly on family ties. No single ruling authority existed. Instead, each group had its own leader, often a skilled warrior.

Aryan villages were governed by rajas (RAH-juhz). A raja was a leader who ruled a village and the land around it. Villagers farmed some of this land for the raja. They used other sections as pastures for their cows, horses, sheep, and goats.

Critical Thinking: Making Decisions

A Raja's Choice

1. Ask students to imagine that they are rajas of small villages. Local herders and farmers have come to the raja to tell him they need more land for their crops and animals. The raja has a choice. He can either go to war against the larger, stronger village nearby to take its land, or he can try to find a peaceful solution to his people's growing needs.

2. Have students work in pairs to decide which plan of action they will take.

3. Have each pair write a brief speech in which the raja explains his decision to the people of his village.

4. Have volunteers share their speeches with the class. **LS Verbal/Linguistic**

Alternate Assessment Handbook, Rubric 35: Solving Problems

Answers

Focus on Reading *They crossed into India from Central Asia, then went east and south into central India, then further east into the Ganges River Valley.*

Reading Check *because historians have not been able to read the Harappan language*

Although many rajas were related, they didn't always get along. Sometimes rajas joined forces before fighting a common enemy. Other times, however, rajas went to war against each other. In fact, Aryan groups fought each other nearly as often as they fought outsiders.

Language

The first Aryan settlers did not read or write. Because of this, they had to memorize the poems and hymns that were important in their culture, such as the Vedas. If people forgot these poems and hymns, the works would be lost forever.

The language in which these Aryan poems and hymns were composed was **Sanskrit**, the most important language of ancient India. At first, Sanskrit was only a spoken language. Eventually, however, people figured out how to write it down so they could keep records. These Sanskrit records are a major source of information about Aryan society. Sanskrit is no longer widely spoken today, but it is the root of many modern South Asian languages.

READING CHECK **Identifying** What source provides much of the information we have about the Aryans?

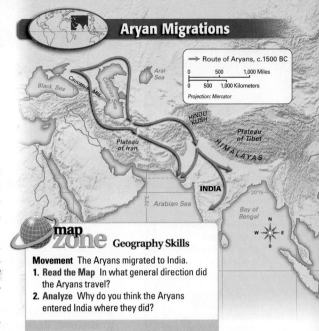

Aryan Migrations

→ Route of Aryans, c.1500 BC
0   500   1,000 Miles
0   500   1,000 Kilometers
Projection: Mercator

Aral Sea
Black Sea
Caucasus Mts.
Caspian Sea
HINDU KUSH
Plateau of Iran
Plateau of Tibet
HIMALAYAS
INDIA
20°N
Arabian Sea
Bay of Bengal

Geography Skills

Movement The Aryans migrated to India.
1. **Read the Map** In what general direction did the Aryans travel?
2. **Analyze** Why do you think the Aryans entered India where they did?

SUMMARY AND PREVIEW The earliest civilizations in India were centered in the Indus Valley. In the next section, you will learn about a new religion that developed in the Indus Valley after the Aryans settled there—Hinduism.

Section 1 Assessment

go.hrw.com
Online Quiz
KEYWORD: SK9 HP14

Reviewing Ideas, Terms, and Places

1. **a. Recall** Where did the Harappan civilization develop?
   b. Explain Why did the Harappans make contact with people far from India?
2. **a. Identify** What was **Mohenjo Daro**?
   b. Analyze What is one reason that scholars do not completely understand some important parts of Harappan society?
3. **a. Identify** Who were the Aryans?
   b. Contrast How was Aryan society different from Harappan society?

Critical Thinking

4. **Summarizing** Using your notes, list the major achievements of India's first two civilizations. Record your conclusions in a diagram like this one.

Early Indian Achievements
| Harappan society |
| Aryan society |

FOCUS ON WRITING

5. **Illustrating Geography and Early Civilizations** This section described two possible topics for your poster: geography and early civilizations. Which of them is more interesting to you? Write down some ideas for a poster about that topic.

ANCIENT CIVILIZATIONS OF ASIA—INDIA **435**

If YOU lived there. . . Use the **Daily Bellringer Transparency** to help students answer the question.

📦 Daily Bellringer Transparency, Section 2

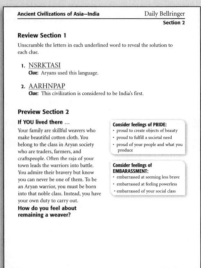

Ancient Civilizations of Asia—India | Daily Bellringer
Section 2

Review Section 1

Unscramble the letters in each underlined word to reveal the solution to each clue.

1. NSRKTASI
   Clue: Aryans used this language.

2. AARHNPAP
   Clue: This civilization is considered to be India's first.

Preview Section 2

If YOU lived there ...
Your family are skillful weavers who make beautiful cotton cloth. You belong to the class in Aryan society who are traders, farmers, and craftspeople. Often the raja of your town leads the warriors into battle. You admire their bravery but know you can never be an Aryan warrior, you must be born into that noble class. Instead, you have your own duty to carry out.
How do you feel about remaining a weaver?

Consider feelings of PRIDE:
• proud to create objects of beauty
• proud to fulfill a societal need
• proud of your people and what you produce

Consider feelings of EMBARASSMENT:
• embarrassed at seeming less brave
• embarrassed at feeling powerless
• embarrassed of your social class

Key Terms

📑 **RF:** Vocabulary Builder, Section 2

Taking Notes

Have students copy the graphic organizer onto their own paper and then use it to take notes on the section. This activity will prepare students for the Section Assessment, in which they will complete a graphic organizer that builds on the information using the Critical Thinking Skill: Analyzing Causes.

Origins of Hinduism

What You Will Learn...

Main Ideas

1. Indian society divided into distinct groups.
2. The Aryans formed a religion known as Brahmanism.
3. Hinduism developed out of Brahmanism and influences from other cultures.
4. The Jains reacted to Hinduism by breaking away.

The Big Idea

Hinduism, the largest religion in India, developed out of ancient Indian beliefs and practices.

Key Terms

caste system, *p. 437*
reincarnation, *p. 439*
karma, *p. 440*
nonviolence, *p. 441*

TAKING NOTES As you read, take notes on Hinduism using a diagram like the one below. Pay attention to its origins, teachings, and other religions that developed alongside it.

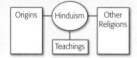

If YOU lived there...

Your family are skillful weavers who make beautiful cotton cloth. You belong to the class in Aryan society who are traders, farmers, and craftspeople. Often the raja of your town leads the warriors into battle. You admire their bravery but know you can never be one of them. To be an Aryan warrior, you must be born into that noble class. Instead, you have your own duty to carry out.

How do you feel about remaining a weaver?

BUILDING BACKGROUND As the Aryans came to dominate the Indus Valley, they developed a system of social classes. As their influence spread through India, so did their class system. Before long, this class system was a key part of Indian society.

Indian Society Divides

As Aryan society became more complex, their society became divided into groups. These groups were largely organized by people's occupations. Strict rules developed about how people of different groups could interact. As time passed, these rules became stricter and became central to Indian society.

The *Varnas*

According to the Vedas, there were four main *varnas*, or social divisions, in Aryan society. These *varnas* were

• Brahmins (BRAH-muhns), or priests,
• Kshatriyas (KSHA-tree-uhs), or rulers and warriors,
• Vaisyas (VYSH-yuhs), or farmers, craftspeople, and traders, and
• Sudras (SOO-drahs), or laborers and non-Aryans.

The Brahmins were seen as the highest ranking because they performed rituals for the gods. This gave the Brahmins great influence over the other *varnas*.

Teach the Big Idea

At Level

Origins of Hinduism

1. **Teach** Ask students the questions in the Main Idea boxes under Direct Teach.

2. **Apply** Ask students to list people and terms associated with Hinduism. Write responses for students to see. *Varnas*, caste system, sacred cow, untouchable, karma, and reincarnation may be among the terms suggested. Call on volunteers to describe how the terms listed relate to each other. **LS Verbal/Linguistic**

3. **Review** Review the major beliefs of Hinduism and ask for volunteers to explain each one.

4. **Practice/Homework** Have students pick one of the major beliefs of Hinduism and, using the information provided in this section, draw a picture or diagram to illustrate the belief. **LS Visual/Spatial**

📝 Alternative Assessment Handbook, Rubric 3: Artwork

The Caste System

As the rules of interaction between *varnas* got stricter, the Aryan social order became more complex. In time, each of the *varnas* in Aryan society was further divided into many castes, or groups. This **caste system** divided Indian society into groups based on a person's birth, wealth, or occupation. At one time, some 3,000 separate castes existed in India.

The caste to which a person belonged determined his or her place in society. However, this ordering was by no means permanent. Over time, individual castes gained or lost favor in society as caste members gained wealth or power. On rare occasions, people could change caste.

People in the lowest class, the Sudra castes, had hard lives. After a few centuries, a fifth group developed, a group who didn't belong to any caste at all. Called untouchables because others were not supposed to have contact with them, they were seen as unclean and as social outcasts. The only jobs open to them were unpleasant ones, such as tanning animal hides and disposing of dead animals.

Caste Rules

To keep their classes distinct, the Aryans developed sutras, or guides, which listed the rules for the caste system. For example, people could not marry someone from a different class. It was even forbidden for people from one class to eat with people from another. People who broke the caste rules could be banned from their homes and their castes, which would make them untouchables. Because of these strict rules, people spent almost all of their time with others in their same class. The caste system also brought stability to Hindu society and a sense of belonging to people of each caste.

READING CHECK Drawing Inferences How did a person become a member of a caste?

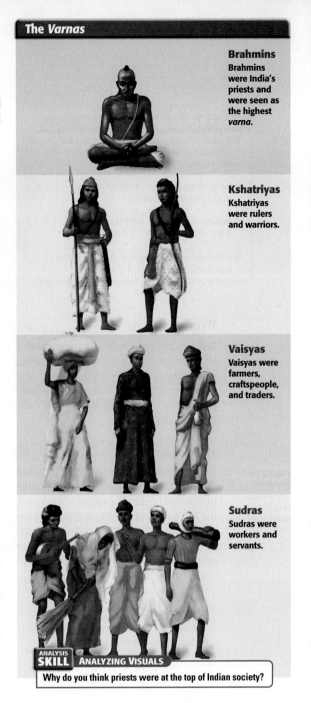

The *Varnas*

Brahmins
Brahmins were India's priests and were seen as the highest *varna*.

Kshatriyas
Kshatriyas were rulers and warriors.

Vaisyas
Vaisyas were farmers, craftspeople, and traders.

Sudras
Sudras were workers and servants.

ANALYSIS SKILL **ANALYZING VISUALS**
Why do you think priests were at the top of Indian society?

ANCIENT CIVILIZATIONS OF ASIA—INDIA **437**

Main Idea

❶ Indian Society Divides

Indian society divided into distinct groups under the Aryans.

Recall What were the four varnas? *Brahmins, Kshatriyas, Vaisyas, and Sudras*

Describe What were some rules described in the sutras? *People couldn't marry anyone or eat with anyone from a different class.*

Explain What could happen to someone who broke caste rules? *They could be banned from their homes and their caste, which would make them untouchables.*

Info to Know

The Harijans Mohandas Gandhi called the untouchables Harijans, which means "children of God," and worked to raise their status. The Indian constitution of 1949 gave these people legal recognition and rights. Although some members of the group have become powerful political leaders, some discrimination against them still exists.

Did you know. . .

The Brahmins included not only priests, but also teachers and scholars—those who dealt in knowledge and spirituality.

Critical Thinking: Identifying Points of View

Above Level

The Caste System

Research Required

1. Organize students into two groups: one group will report on positive views of the caste system and the other will report on negative views.

2. Have students use library and Internet resources to find differing views of the caste system. Encourage them to find and examine Indian English-language newspapers and magazines. Students should pay particular attention to what factors may have influenced the writer's opinions.

3. Ask each group to elect a spokesperson to report its findings to the class. Lead a discussion about how the different points of view about the caste system were expressed.
LS Interpersonal

Alternative Assessment Handbook, Rubric 14: Group Activity

Answers

Reading Check *born into it*
Analyzing Visuals *possible answer— Priests performed rituals that people believed could make the gods grant their wishes.*

437

Main Idea

❷ Brahmanism

The Aryans practiced a religion known as Brahmanism.

Identify What is the *Rigveda? the oldest of the Vedas that contained a collection of hymns of praise to many gods*

Recall When was *Rigveda* probably written*? before 1000 BC*

Compare How did the Upanishads differ from other Vedic texts? *The Upanishads were reflections on the Vedas written by religious students and teachers.*

Explain Why did priests place sacrifices into a fire? *They believed the fire would carry the sacrifice to the gods.*

Activity   Standard English Mastery

Hymn to Indra Read the excerpt from the hymn to Indra. Remind students that an adjective is a word that describes someone or something. Then have students write down adjectives that the Aryans may have used to describe this god had they spoken English. Encourage students to use a thesaurus or dictionary to find appropriate adjectives. Call on volunteers to share their lists. **LS Verbal/Linguistic**

📝 Alternative Assessment Handbook, Rubric 37: Writing Assignments

Did you know. . .

Veda means "knowledge" in Sanskrit.

Hindu Gods and Beliefs

Hindus believe in many gods, but they believe that all the gods are aspects of a single universal spirit called Brahman. Three aspects of Brahman are particularly important in Hinduism—Brahma, Siva, and Vishnu.

Major Beliefs of Hinduism

- A universal spirit called Brahman created the universe and everything in it. Everything in the world is just a part of Brahman.

- Every person has a soul or atman that will eventually join with Brahman.

- People's souls are reincarnated many times before they can join with Brahman.

- A person's karma affects how he or she will be reincarnated.

The god Brahma represents the creator aspect of Brahman. His four faces symbolize the four Vedas.

Brahmanism

Religion had long been an important part of Aryan life. Eventually in India, religion took on even more meaning. Because Aryan priests were called Brahmins, their religion is often called Brahmanism, or Vedic Brahmanism.

The Vedas

FOCUS ON READING
Which were written first, the Vedas or the Vedic texts?

Aryan religion was based on the Vedas. There are four Vedas, each containing sacred hymns and poems. The oldest of the Vedas, the *Rigveda*, was probably compiled in the second millennium BC. It includes hymns of praise to many gods. This passage, for example, is the opening of a hymn praising Indra, a god of the sky and war.

> *"The one who is first and possessed of wisdom when born; the god who strove to protect the gods with strength; the one before whose force the two worlds were afraid because of the greatness of his virility [power]: he, O people, is Indra."*
>
> –from the *Rigveda*, in *Reading about the World, Volume I*, edited by Paul Brians, et al

Later Vedic Texts

Over the centuries, Aryan Brahmins wrote down their thoughts about the Vedas. In time these thoughts were compiled into collections called Vedic texts.

One collection of Vedic texts describes Aryan religious rituals. For example, it describes how to perform sacrifices. Priests prepared animals, food, or drinks to be sacrificed in a fire. The Aryans believed that the fire would carry these offerings to the gods.

A second collection of Vedic texts describes secret rituals that only certain people could perform. In fact, the rituals were so secret that they had to be done in the forest, far from other people.

The final group of Vedic texts are the Upanishads (oo-PAHN-ee-shads), most of which were written by about 600 BC. These writings are reflections on the Vedas by religious students and teachers.

READING CHECK **Finding Main Ideas** What are the Vedic texts?

Cross-Discipline Activity: Literature   At Level

The Rigveda   Prep Required

1. Organize the class into groups. In advance, locate and duplicate examples from the *Rigveda*. Provide each member of a group the same sample, but give each group a different sample.

2. Have each group discuss the meaning of its sample. Provide dictionaries to help students in the task. Ask students also to find examples of descriptive language in the text.

3. Call on volunteers from each group to report their findings.

4. Extend the activity by asking interested students to locate and listen to a modern composition, *Choral Hymns from the Rig Veda*, by Gustav Holst. Ask them to play selections for the class. **LS Verbal/Linguistic**

📝 Alternative Assessment Handbook, Rubric 14: Group Activity

Answers

Focus on Reading *the Vedas*

Reading Check *sacred hymns and poems, collections of writings by Aryan Brahmins*

Siva, the destroyer aspect of Brahman, is usually shown with four arms and three eyes. Here he is shown dancing on the back of a demon he has defeated.

Vishnu is the preserver aspect of Brahman. In his four arms, he carries a conch shell, a mace, and a discus, symbols of his power and greatness.

Hinduism Develops

The Vedas, the Upanishads, and the other Vedic texts remained the basis of Indian religion for centuries. Eventually, though, the ideas of these sacred texts began to blend with ideas from other cultures. People from Persia and other kingdoms in Central Asia, for example, brought their ideas to India. In time, this blending of ideas created a religion called Hinduism, the largest religion in India today.

Hindu Beliefs

The Hindus believe in many gods. Among them are three major gods: Brahma the Creator, Siva the Destroyer, and Vishnu the Preserver. At the same time, however, Hindus believe that each god is part of a single universal spirit called Brahman. They believe that Brahman created the world and preserves it. Gods such as Brahma, Siva, and Vishnu are different aspects of Brahman. In fact, Hindus believe that everything in the world is part of Brahman.

Life and Rebirth

According to Hindu teachings, everyone has a soul, or atman. This soul holds the person's personality, those qualities that make a person who he or she is. Hindus believe that a person's ultimate goal should be to reunite that soul with Brahman, the universal spirit.

Hindus believe that their souls will eventually join Brahman because the world we live in is an illusion. Brahman is the only reality. The Upanishads taught that people must try to see through the illusion of the world. Since it is hard to see through illusions, it can take several lifetimes. That is why Hindus believe that souls are born and reborn many times, each time in a new body. This process of rebirth is called **reincarnation**.

Hinduism and the Caste System

According to the traditional Hindu view of reincarnation, a person who has died is reborn in a new physical form.

THE IMPACT TODAY

More than 900 million people in India practice Hinduism today.

• **Direct Teach** •

Main Idea

❸ **Hinduism Develops**

Hinduism developed out of Brahmanism and influences from other cultures.

Identify According to Hindu belief, what are the three major forms of Brahman? *Brahma the creator, Siva the destroyer, Vishnu the preserver*

Analyze What led to the development of Hinduism? *the blending of the Vedic texts with ideas from other cultures*

Evaluate How may believing that this world is merely an illusion affect one's behavior? *Answers will vary but should reflect logical thinking.*

Connect to Art

Lord of the Dance The bronze statue shown portrays Siva as Nataraja, or Lord of the Dance. Stylized flames surround him. Underfoot is the Demon of Ignorance. According to Hindu belief, during his dance Siva destroys the universe, but it is continually reborn. This statue was made in the 1200s.

Collaborative Learning   At Level

Collages about Hinduism

Materials: art supplies

1. First, review the three major forms of Brahman and the main beliefs of Hinduism.

2. Then organize students into small groups. Have some of the groups create collages combining original illustrations and text to describe the Hindu concept of the three aspects of Brahman. Have other groups create collages about the other main Hindu beliefs.

3. Have volunteers present their collages to the class. **LS** Visual/Spatial, Interpersonal

Alternative Assessment Handbook, Rubric 8: Collages

Hinduism Develops,
continued

Identify What is karma? *the effects that good or bad actions have on a person's soul*

Analyze How may the role of women in traditional Hinduism be connected to the history of Aryan *varnas*? *possible answer—Warriors, the Kshatriyas, had high status in Aryan society. Because women's contributions were not valued as highly, they had lower status.*

Evaluate Do you think a wealthy Brahmin would want his or her servants to believe in *dharma*? Why or why not? *possible answer—Servants would be more likely to accept their fate in life if they believed in* dharma.

📝 **RF:** Primary Source, Mohandas Gandhi's Autobiography

Focus on Culture
The Sacred Ganges
Review with students the feature on the Ganges River. Ask the following questions:
Identify What is another name for the Ganges River? *Mother Ganga*
Recall Why do Hindus make pilgrimages to sacred places? *to help improve their karma and increase their chance for salvation*

Answers

Reading Check *a person's actions during his or her lifetime*
Focus on Culture *It is believed that the river's water is made holy because it makes contact with the gods as it flows across the land.*

440

The type of form depends upon his or her **karma**, the effects that good or bad actions have on a person's soul. Evil actions during one's life will build bad karma. A person with bad karma will be reborn into a lower caste, or even as a lower life-form such as an animal or a plant.

In contrast, good actions build good karma. People with good karma are born into a higher caste in their next lives. In time, good karma will bring salvation, or freedom from life's worries and the cycle of rebirth. This salvation is called *moksha*.

Hinduism taught that each person had a duty to accept his or her place in the world without complaint. This is called obeying one's dharma. People could build good karma by fulfilling the duties required of their specific caste. Through reincarnation, Hinduism offered rewards to those who lived good lives. Even untouchables could be reborn into a higher caste.

Hinduism was popular at all levels of Hindu society, through all four *varnas*. By teaching people to accept their places in life, Hinduism helped preserve the caste system in India.

Hinduism and Women
Early Hinduism taught that both men and women could gain salvation. However, like other ancient religions, Hinduism considered women inferior to men. Women were generally not allowed to study the Vedas.

Over the centuries, Hindu women have gained more rights. This change has been the result of efforts by influential Hindu leaders like Mohandas Gandhi, who led the movement for Indian independence. As a result, many of the restrictions once placed on Hindu women have been lifted.

READING CHECK **Summarizing** What factors determined how a person would be reborn?

FOCUS ON CULTURE

The Sacred Ganges
Hindus believe that there are many sacred places in India. Making a pilgrimage to one of these places, they believe, will help improve their karma and increase their chance for salvation. The most sacred of all the pilgrimage sites in India is the Ganges River in the northeast.

Known to Hindus as Mother Ganga, the Ganges flows out of the Himalayas. In traditional Hindu teachings, however, the river flows from the feet of Vishnu and over the head of Siva before it makes its way across the land. Through this contact with the gods, the river's water is made holy. Hindus believe that bathing in the Ganges will purify them and remove some of their bad karma.

Although the entire Ganges is considered sacred, a few cities along its path are seen as especially holy. At these sites, pilgrims gather to bathe and celebrate Hindu festivals. Steps lead down from the cities right to the edge of the water so people can more easily reach the river.

Summarizing Why is the Ganges a pilgrimage site?

Differentiating Instruction

Above Level

Advanced/Gifted and Talented

Research Required

1. Have students research the life of Mohandas Gandhi—particularly how his beliefs helped Hindu women gain rights. Point out that some of Gandhi's beliefs contrasted with traditional Hindu beliefs. Students should use library and Internet sources.

2. Students should then write brief reports that tell how Gandhi's religious beliefs affected his actions.

3. To extend the activity, have interested students locate descriptions of Gandhi written by British writers during the 1940s and report on how they portrayed him.
LS Verbal/Linguistic

📝 Alternative Assessment Handbook, Rubrics 30: Research; and 42: Writing to Inform

Jains React to Hinduism

Although Hinduism was widely followed in India, not everyone agreed with its beliefs. Some unsatisfied people and groups looked for new religious ideas. One such group was the Jains (JYNZ), believers in a religion called Jainism (JY-ni-zuhm).

Jainism was based on the teachings of a man named Mahavira. Born into the Kshatriya *varna* around 599 BC, he was unhappy with the control of religion by the Brahmins, whom he thought put too much emphasis on rituals. Mahavira gave up his life of luxury, became a monk, and established the principles of Jainism.

The Jains try to live by four principles: injure no life, tell the truth, do not steal, and own no property. In their efforts not to injure anyone or anything, the Jains practice **nonviolence**, or the avoidance of violent actions. The Sanskrit word for this nonviolence is *ahimsa* (uh-HIM-sah). Many Hindus also practice *ahimsa*.

The Jains' emphasis on nonviolence comes from their belief that everything is alive and part of the cycle of rebirth. Jains are very serious about not injuring or killing any creature—humans, animals, insects, or plants. They do not believe in animal sacrifice, such as the ones the ancient Brahmins performed. Because they do not want to hurt any living creatures, Jains are vegetarians. They do not eat any food that comes from animals.

READING CHECK Identifying Points of View
Why do Jains avoid eating meat?

SUMMARY AND PREVIEW You have learned about two religions that grew in ancient India—Hinduism and Jainism. In Section 3, you will learn about a third religion that began there—Buddhism.

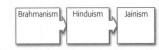
These Jain women are wearing masks to make sure they don't accidentally inhale and kill insects.

Section 2 Assessment

go.hrw.com
Online Quiz
KEYWORD: SK9 HP14

Reviewing Ideas, Terms, and Places

1. **a. Identify** What is the **caste system**?
   b. Explain Why did strict caste rules develop?
2. **a. Identify** What does the *Rigveda* include?
   b. Analyze What role did sacrifice play in Aryan society?
3. **a. Define** What is **karma**?
   b. Sequence How did Brahmanism develop into Hinduism?
   c. Elaborate How does Hinduism reinforce followers' willingness to remain within their castes?
4. **a. Recall** What are the four main teachings of Jainism?
   b. Predict How do you think the idea of **nonviolence** affected the daily lives of Jains in ancient India?

Critical Thinking

5. **Analyzing Causes** Draw a graphic organizer like this one. Using your notes, explain how Hinduism developed from Brahmanism and how Jainism developed from Hinduism.

   Brahmanism → Hinduism → Jainism

FOCUS ON WRITING

6. **Illustrating Hinduism** Now you have another possible topic for your poster. How might you illustrate a complex religion like Hinduism? What pictures would work?

ANCIENT CIVILIZATIONS OF ASIA—INDIA **441**

Bellringer

If YOU lived there. . . Use the **Daily Bellringer Transparency** to help students answer the question.

📋 Daily Bellringer Transparency, Section 3

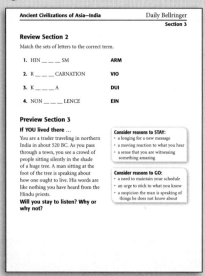

Key Terms

📄 **RF:** Vocabulary Builder, Section 3

Taking Notes

Have students copy the graphic organizer onto their own paper and then use it to take notes on the section. This activity will prepare students for the Section Assessment, in which they will complete a graphic organizer that builds on the information using the Critical Thinking Skill: Finding Main Ideas.

Origins of Buddhism

What You Will Learn...

Main Ideas

1. Siddhartha Gautama searched for wisdom in many ways.
2. The teachings of Buddhism deal with finding peace.
3. Buddhism spread far from where it began in India.

The Big Idea

Buddhism began in India and became a major religion.

Key Terms

fasting, *p. 443*
meditation, *p. 443*
nirvana, *p. 444*
missionaries, *p. 446*

TAKING NOTES As you read this section, look for information on the basic ideas of Buddhism and on Buddhism's spread. Record what you find in a graphic organizer like this one.

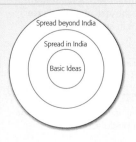

If **YOU** lived there...

You are a trader traveling in northern India in about 520 BC. As you pass through a town, you see a crowd of people sitting silently in the shade of a huge tree. A man sitting at the foot of the tree is speaking about how one ought to live. His words are like nothing you have heard from the Hindu priests.

Will you stay to listen? Why or why not?

BUILDING BACKGROUND The Jains were not the only ones to break from Hinduism. In the 500s BC a young Indian prince attracted many people to his teachings about how people should live.

Siddhartha's Search for Wisdom

In the late 500s BC a restless young man, dissatisfied with the teachings of Hinduism, began to ask his own questions about life and religious matters. In time, he found answers. These answers attracted many followers, and the young man's ideas became the foundation of a major new religion in India.

The Quest for Answers

The restless young man was Siddhartha Gautama (si-DAHR-tuh GAU-tuh-muh). Born around 563 BC in northern India near the Himalayas, Siddhartha was a prince who grew up in luxury. Born a Kshatriya, a member of the warrior class, Siddhartha never had to struggle with the problems that many people of his time faced. However, Siddhartha was not satisfied. He felt something was missing in his life.

Siddhartha looked around him and saw how hard most people had to work and how much they suffered. He saw people grieving for lost loved ones and wondered why there was so much pain in the world. As a result, Siddhartha began to ask questions about the meaning of human life.

Teach the Big Idea

At Level

Origins of Buddhism

1. **Teach** Ask students the questions in the Main Idea boxes under Direct Teach.

2. **Apply** Organize the class into pairs. Have each pair create a flowchart or another graphic organizer of the students' choosing to show the development of Buddhism from the ideas of Siddhartha Gautama to its influence throughout Asia. Students should add details such as the Four Noble Truths and the steps in the Eightfold Path. **LS Visual/Spatial**

3. **Review** Call on volunteers to present their flowcharts to the class.

4. **Practice/Homework** Have students fill in any missing information on their graphic organizers and write a paragraph describing how the Buddha's teachings differed from Hinduism. **LS Verbal/Linguistic**

📝 Alternative Assessment Handbook, Rubric 13: Graphic Organizers

The Great Departure

In this painting, Prince Siddhartha leaves his palace to search for the true meaning of life, an event known as the Great Departure. Special helpers called *ganas* hold his horse's hooves so he won't awaken anyone.

Before Siddhartha reached age 30, he left his home and family to look for answers. His journey took him to many regions in India. Wherever he traveled, he had discussions with priests and people known for their wisdom. Yet no one could give convincing answers to Siddhartha's questions.

The Buddha Finds Enlightenment

Siddhartha did not give up. Instead, he became even more determined to find the answers he was seeking. For several years, he wandered in search of answers.

Siddhartha wanted to free his mind from daily concerns. For a while, he did not even wash himself. He also started **fasting**, or going without food. He devoted much of his time to **meditation**, the focusing of the mind on spiritual ideas.

According to legend, Siddhartha spent six years wandering throughout India. He eventually came to a place near the town of Gaya, close to the Ganges River. There, he sat down under a tree and meditated.

After seven weeks of deep meditation, he suddenly had the answers that he had been looking for. He had realized that human suffering comes from three things:

- wanting what we like but do not have,
- wanting to keep what we like and already have, and
- not wanting what we dislike but have.

Siddhartha spent seven more weeks meditating under the tree, which his followers later named the Tree of Wisdom. He then described his new ideas to five of his former companions. His followers later called this talk the First Sermon.

Siddhartha Gautama was about 35 years old when he found enlightenment under the tree. From that point on, he would be called the Buddha (BOO-duh), or the "Enlightened One." The Buddha spent the rest of his life traveling across northern India and teaching people his ideas.

FOCUS ON READING
What steps did the Buddha take in his search for enlightenment?

READING CHECK Summarizing What did the Buddha conclude about the cause of suffering?

ANCIENT CIVILIZATIONS OF ASIA—INDIA **443**

❷ Teachings of Buddhism

The teachings of Buddhism deal with finding peace.

Identify Many of the Buddha's teachings reflect the ideas of which other world religion? *Hinduism*

Recall What are the Four Noble Truths? *See text for answers.*

Analyze What do you think the quote from the Buddha on this page means? *possible answer—People can progress toward enlightenment by responding to bad behavior with good behavior.*

Evaluate What advantage do you think the Buddha saw in following the "middle way"? *possible answer—Extreme behavior of any kind is not helpful or healthy.*

Activity **Distinguishing between Hinduism and Buddhism** Prepare a list of terms associated with Hinduism and Buddhism. As you read the list to the class, ask with which religion each is associated.

Linking to Today

The Buddha's Tree at Bodh Gaya The 80-foot statue shown on this page is near the Buddha's Tree of Wisdom. The original tree died long ago. Over the centuries, it has been replaced many times by offshoots of the Buddha's tree. Authorities have placed signs asking visitors not to take leaves from the tree or soil from the ground surrounding it. Near the tree is a golden platform that, according to tradition, marks the exact spot where Siddhartha Gautama sat while waiting for enlightenment.

Teachings of Buddhism

As he traveled, the Buddha gained many followers. Many of these followers were merchants and artisans, but he even taught a few kings. These followers were the first believers in Buddhism, the religion based on the teachings of the Buddha.

The Buddha was raised Hindu, and many of his teachings reflected Hindu ideas. Like Hindus, he believed that people should act morally and treat others well. In one of his sermons, he said

❝Let a man overcome anger by love. Let him overcome the greedy by liberality [giving], the liar by truth. This is called progress in the discipline [training] of the Blessed.❞
–The Buddha, quoted in *The History of Nations: India*

Four Noble Truths

At the heart of the Buddha's teachings were four guiding principles. These became known as the Four Noble Truths:

1. Suffering and unhappiness are a part of human life. No one can escape sorrow.

2. Suffering comes from our desires for pleasure and material goods. People cause their own misery because they want things they cannot have.

3. People can overcome their desires and ignorance and reach **nirvana**, a state of perfect peace. Reaching nirvana would free a person's soul from suffering and from the need for further reincarnation.

4. People can overcome ignorance and desire by following an eightfold path that leads to wisdom, enlightenment, and salvation.

The chart on the next page shows the steps in the Eightfold Path. The Buddha believed that this path was a middle way between human desires and denying oneself any pleasure. He believed that people should overcome their desire for material goods. They should, however, be reasonable, and not starve their bodies or cause themselves unnecessary pain.

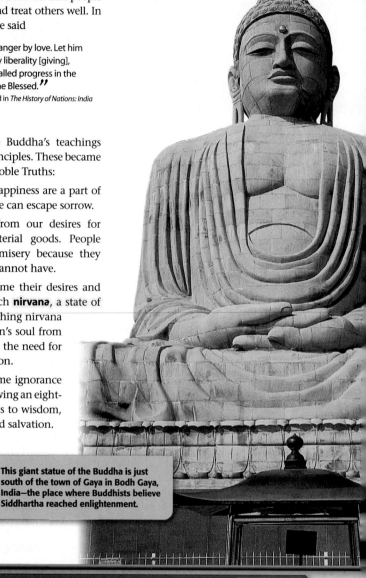

This giant statue of the Buddha is just south of the town of Gaya in Bodh Gaya, India—the place where Buddhists believe Siddhartha reached enlightenment.

Differentiating Instruction

Above Level

Advanced/Gifted and Talented

Research Required

1. Explain to students that some Buddhists become monks and nuns. Read dictionary definitions for both terms.

2. Ask students to imagine that they are newspaper reporters assigned to spend one day with a Buddhist monk or nun and report on their subjects' daily lives.

3. Have students conduct research on Buddhist monks or nuns—either in the present or the past.

4. Then have students write brief newspaper articles describing one day's events in a monk's or nun's life.

5. Encourage students to make their articles as specific as possible. For example, they might discuss the person's chores or the kinds of ceremonies in which he or she participates.

LS **Verbal/Linguistic**

Alternative Assessment Handbook, Rubric 40: Writing to Describe

The Eightfold Path

❶ Right Thought
Believe in the nature of existence as suffering and in the Four Noble Truths.

❷ Right Intent
Incline toward goodness and kindness.

❸ Right Speech
Avoid lies and gossip.

❹ Right Action
Don't steal from or harm others.

❺ Right Livelihood
Reject work that hurts others.

❻ Right Effort
Prevent evil and do good.

❼ Right Mindfulness
Control your feelings and thoughts.

❽ Right Concentration
Practice proper meditation.

Challenging Hindu Ideas

Some of the Buddha's teachings challenged traditional Hindu ideas. For example, the Buddha rejected many of the ideas contained in the Vedas, such as animal sacrifice. He told people that they did not have to follow these texts.

The Buddha challenged the authority of the Hindu priests, the Brahmins. He did not believe that they or their rituals were necessary for enlightenment. Instead, he taught that it was the responsibility of each person to work for his or her own salvation. Priests could not help them. However, the Buddha did not reject the Hindu teaching of reincarnation. He taught that people who failed to reach nirvana would have to be reborn time and time again until they achieved it.

The Buddha was opposed to the caste system. He didn't think that people should be confined to a particular place in society. He taught that every person who followed the Eightfold Path properly would reach nirvana. It didn't matter what *varna* or caste they had belonged to in life as long as they lived the way they should.

The Buddha's opposition to the caste system won him the support of the masses. Many herders, farmers, artisans, and untouchables liked hearing that their low social rank would not be a barrier to their enlightenment. Unlike Hinduism, Buddhism made them feel that they had the power to change their lives.

The Buddha also gained followers among the higher classes. Many rich and powerful Indians welcomed his ideas about avoiding extreme behavior while seeking salvation. By the time of his death around 483 BC, the Buddha's influence was spreading rapidly throughout India.

READING CHECK **Comparing** How did Buddha's teachings agree with Hinduism?

ANCIENT CIVILIZATIONS OF ASIA—INDIA **445**

Main Idea

Teachings of Buddhism, *continued*

Explain What did the Buddha think about the caste system? *He was opposed to it.*

Contrast How is "right thought" different from "right action"? *"Right thought" refers to beliefs, whereas "right action" has to do with how we put beliefs and thoughts into action.*

Evaluate How do you think people reacted to the Buddha's telling them they did not have to accept the Brahmins' authority? *possible answers— The Brahmins would have resented it, while other Hindus may have been relieved.*

Linking to Today

Buddhism in India Many Hindus of India do not see Buddhism as a religion truly separate from Hinduism. Instead, they regard the Buddha as the ninth incarnation of the god Vishnu. As a result, they see Buddhism as a sect within Hinduism.

Checking for Understanding

True or False Answer each statement *T* if it is true or *F* it is false. If false, explain why.
1. Siddhartha Gautama was raised as a Hindu. *T*
2. The Buddha rejected all Hindu ideas. *F; The Buddha believed in reincarnation.*
3. At the heart of the Buddha's teachings were four guiding principles known as the Four Noble Truths. *T*

Social Studies Skill: Identifying Central Issues

At Level

Buddhism and Hinduism

1. Remind students that some of the Buddha's teachings conflicted with Hinduism, while others agreed with Hindu beliefs.

2. Organize students into pairs. Have each pair write a conversation or argument that a traditional Hindu might have had with a Hindu who has adopted the teachings of the Buddha. For traditional Hindus, students may choose a Brahmin or a person from a lower caste.

3. Call on volunteers to read their arguments or conversations.

4. Finally, lead a class discussion about why Buddhism gained followers among all classes.
LS Interpersonal

Alternative Assessment Handbook, Rubric 11: Discussions

Answers

Reading Check *Buddha's teachings included reincarnation.*

445

Main Idea

❸ Buddhism Spreads

Buddhism spread far from where it began in India.

Identify What are some places to which Buddhism spread? *throughout India, Sri Lanka, Myanmar and other parts of Southeast Asia, near the Himalayas, Central Asia, Persia, Syria, Egypt, China, Korea, Japan*

Explain What is one reason why Buddhism spread quickly? *Buddha's teachings were popular and easy to understand.*

Contrast How are the Theravada and Mahayana branches of Buddhism different? *Theravada—follow the Buddha's teachings exactly; Mahayana—can interpret Buddha's teachings to help them reach nirvana*

 Map Zone Transparency: Early Spread of Buddhism

Info to Know

Theravada and Mahayana Theravada and related versions of Buddhism are called Hinayana, or "lesser vehicle" in Sanskrit. Theravada is the older of the two major divisions. Followers trace Theravada traditions all the way back to monks of the first Buddhist community. Theravadins believe that one must become a monk to reach enlightenment. Today, Theravada Buddhism dominates Sri Lanka and Southeast Asia.

Mahayana means "greater vehicle." Mahayanists believe that people who attain enlightenment should stay in the world and help others gain salvation. It is the main form of Buddhism in China, Korea, Japan, and Tibet.

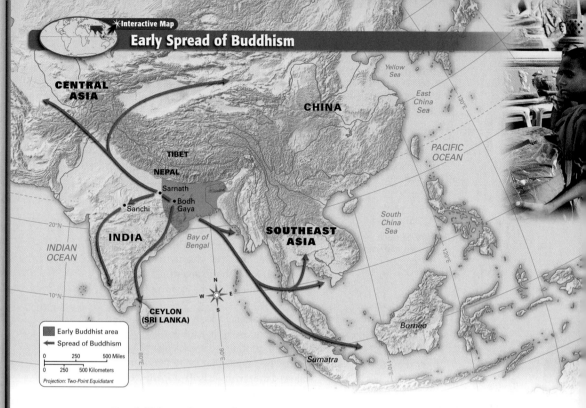

Interactive Map
Early Spread of Buddhism

Early Buddhist area
⬅ Spread of Buddhism

0   250   500 Miles
0   250   500 Kilometers
Projection: Two-Point Equidistant

Buddhism Spreads

Buddhism continued to attract followers after the Buddha's death. After spreading through India, the religion began to spread to other areas as well.

Buddhism Spreads in India

According to Buddhist tradition, 500 of the Buddha's followers gathered together shortly after he died. They wanted to make sure that the Buddha's teachings were remembered correctly.

In the years after this council, the Buddha's followers spread his teachings throughout India. The ideas spread very quickly, because Buddhist teachings were popular and easy to understand. Within 200 years of the Buddha's death, Buddhism had spread through most of India.

Buddhism Spreads beyond India

The spread of Buddhism increased after one of the most powerful kings in India, Asoka, became Buddhist in the 200s BC. Once he converted, he built Buddhist temples and schools throughout India. More importantly, though, he worked to spread Buddhism into areas outside of India. You will learn more about Asoka and his accomplishments in the next section.

Asoka sent Buddhist **missionaries**, or people who work to spread their religious beliefs, to other kingdoms in Asia. One group of these missionaries sailed to the island of Sri Lanka around 251 BC. Others followed trade routes east to what is now Myanmar and to other parts of Southeast Asia. Missionaries also went north to areas near the Himalayas.

446 CHAPTER 14

Collaborative Learning

[At Level]

Interviewing a Missionary

1. Ask students to imagine that they lived in Sri Lanka when the first Buddhist missionaries arrived. Then have them imagine what it would have been like had there been television news during that time.

2. Organize students into pairs and instruct each pair to create a skit in which a news commentator interviews a Buddhist missionary.

3. The commentator should create a list of questions for the missionary, such as: Why

have you come to Sri Lanka? What is meant by this word "enlightenment"? How do you think your beliefs can help people?

4. Using the information in this section, the missionary responds to these questions. Ask for volunteers to present their skits to the class. **LS Interpersonal**

📝 Alternative Assessment Handbook, Rubric 33: Skits and Reader's Theater

Young Buddhist students carry gifts in Sri Lanka, one of the many places outside of India where Buddhism spread.

Members of the Theravada branch tried to follow the Buddha's teachings exactly as he had stated them. Mahayana Buddhists, though, believed that other people could interpret the Buddha's teachings to help people reach nirvana. Both branches have millions of believers today, but Mahayana is by far the larger branch.

READING CHECK Sequencing How did the Buddha's teachings spread out of India?

SUMMARY AND PREVIEW Buddhism, one of India's major religions, grew more popular once it was adopted by rulers of India's great empires. You will learn more about those empires in the next section.

map Zone Geography Skills

Movement After the Buddha died, his teachings were carried through much of Asia.
1. **Identify** Buddhism spread to what island south of India?
2. **Interpret** What physical feature kept Buddhist missionaries from moving directly into China?

go.hrw.com KEYWORD: SK9 CH14

Missionaries also introduced Buddhism to lands west of India. They founded Buddhist communities in Central Asia and Persia. They even taught about Buddhism as far away as Syria and Egypt.

Buddhism continued to grow over the centuries. Eventually, it spread via the Silk Road into China, then Korea and Japan. Through their work, missionaries taught Buddhism to millions of people.

A Split within Buddhism

Even as Buddhism spread through Asia, however, it began to change. Not all Buddhists could agree on their beliefs and practices. Eventually, disagreements between Buddhists led to a split within the religion. Two major branches of Buddhism were created—Theravada and Mahayana.

go.hrw.com
Online Quiz
KEYWORD: SK9 HP14

Section 3 Assessment

Reviewing Ideas, Terms, and Places
1. **a. Identify** Who was the Buddha, and what does the term *Buddha* mean?
   b. Summarize How did Siddhartha Gautama free his mind and clarify his thinking as he searched for wisdom?
2. **a. Identify** What is **nirvana**?
   b. Contrast How are Buddhist teachings different from Hindu teachings?
   c. Elaborate Why do Buddhists believe that following the Eightfold Path leads to a better life?
3. **a. Describe** Into what lands did Buddhism spread?
   b. Summarize What role did **missionaries** play in spreading Buddhism?

Critical Thinking
4. **Finding Main Ideas** Draw a diagram like this one. Use it and your notes to identify and describe Buddhism's Four Noble Truths. Write a sentence explaining how the Truths are central to Buddhism.

FOCUS ON WRITING
5. **Considering Indian Religions** Look back over what you've just read and your notes about Hinduism. Perhaps you will want to focus your poster on ancient India's two major religions. Think about how you could design a poster around this theme.

ANCIENT CIVILIZATIONS OF ASIA—INDIA **447**

Direct Teach

Linking to Today

Zen Buddhism Emphasize that the types of Buddhism practiced today vary around the world. One type of Buddhism commonly practiced in Japan is Zen Buddhism. It teaches that enlightenment can be achieved by breaking through the boundaries of everyday logical thought. This process is best achieved by following the guidance of a master. Zen Buddhism has helped shape not just Japan's religious life, but also its culture. Today almost 10 million Japanese follow Zen Buddhism.

Review & Assess

Close
Have students review the Four Noble Truths and the Eightfold Path.

Review
Online Quiz, Section 3

Assess
SE Section 3 Assessment
PASS: Section 3 Quiz
Alternative Assessment Handbook

Reteach/Classroom Intervention
Interactive Reader and Study Guide, Section 3
Interactive Skills Tutor CD-ROM

Section 3 Assessment Answers

1. **a.** Siddhartha Gautama, a prince who found enlightenment; Enlightened One
   b. fasted, meditated
2. **a.** a state of perfect peace
   b. Buddhists don't believe in sacrifices, the caste system, or that they needed the help of the Brahmins.
   c. It leads them down a path of fulfillment without excess or denial, which then leads to nirvana.
3. **a.** Sri Lanka, Myanmar, other parts of Southeast Asia, Central Asia, Persia, Syria, Egypt, and eventually to China and then Korea and Japan
   b. important role, because they traveled to distant lands to spread Buddhist teachings
4. possible answer—The Four Noble Truths deal with finding the path that leads away from ignorance and desire, and toward wisdom, enlightenment, and salvation. This goal of reaching a state of perfect peace is central to the teachings of Buddhism.
5. Students' ideas will vary, but should display familiarity with text content.

Answers

Map Zone 1. *Ceylon (Sri Lanka)*;
2. *the Himalayas*

Reading Check *Missionaries traveled to Sri Lanka, Myanmar, other parts of Southeast Asia, Central Asia, Persia, Syria, Egypt, and eventually to China and then Korea and Japan.*

447

Bellringer

If YOU lived there. . . Use the **Daily Bellringer Transparency** to help students answer the question.

🗓 Daily Bellringer Transparency, Section 4

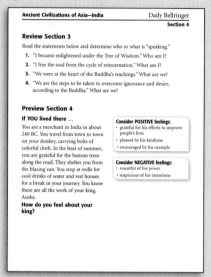

Ancient Civilizations of Asia—India   Daily Bellringer
                           Section 4

Review Section 3

Read the statements below and determine who or what is "speaking."

1. "I became enlightened under the Tree of Wisdom." Who am I?
2. "I free the soul from the cycle of reincarnation." What am I?
3. "We were at the heart of the Buddha's teachings." What are we?
4. "We are the steps to be taken to overcome ignorance and desire, according to the Buddha." What are we?

Preview Section 4

If YOU lived there ...

You are a merchant in India in about 240 BC. You travel from town to town on your donkey, carrying bolts of colorful cloth. In the heat of summer, you are grateful for the banyan trees along the blazing road. They shelter you from the blazing road. You stop at wells for cool drinks of water and rest houses for a break in your journey. You know these are all the work of your king, Asoka.

How do you feel about your king?

Consider POSITIVE feelings:
• grateful for his efforts to improve people's lives
• pleased by his kindness
• encouraged by his example

Consider NEGATIVE feelings:
• resentful of his power
• suspicious of his intentions

Academic Vocabulary

Review with students the high-use academic term in this section.

establish to set up or create (p. 450)

📝 RF: Vocabulary Builder, Section 4

Taking Notes

Have students copy the graphic organizer onto their own paper and then use it to take notes on the section. This activity will prepare students for the Section Assessment, in which they will complete a graphic organizer that builds on the information using the Critical Thinking Skill: Categorizing.

Indian Empires

What You Will Learn...

Main Ideas

1. The Mauryan Empire unified most of India.
2. Gupta rulers promoted Hinduism in their empire.

The Big Idea

The Mauryas and the Guptas built great empires in India.

Key Terms

mercenaries, *p. 448*
edicts, *p. 449*

TAKING NOTES As you read, take notes about the rise and fall of ancient India's two greatest empires. Record your notes in a chart like the one shown here.

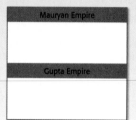

Mauryan Empire
Gupta Empire

If YOU lived there...

You are a merchant in India in about 240 BC. You travel from town to town on your donkey, carrying bolts of colorful cloth. In the heat of summer, you are grateful for the banyan trees along the road. They shelter you from the blazing sun. You stop at wells for cool drinks of water and rest houses for a break in your journey. You know these are all the work of your king, Asoka.

How do you feel about your king?

BUILDING BACKGROUND For centuries after the Aryan migration, India was divided into small states. Each state had its own ruler and laws. Then, in the 300s BC, a foreign general, Alexander the Great, took over and unified part of northwestern India. Soon after Alexander departed, a strong leader united India.

Mauryan Empire Unifies India

In the 320s BC a military leader named Candragupta Maurya (kuhn-druh-GOOP-tuh MOUR-yuh) rose to power in northern India. Using an army of **mercenaries**, or hired soldiers, he seized control of the entire northern part of India. By doing so, he founded the Mauryan Empire. Mauryan rule lasted for about 150 years.

The Mauryan Empire

Candragupta Maurya ruled his empire with the help of a complex government. It included a network of spies and a huge army of some 600,000 soldiers. The army also had thousands of war elephants and thousands of chariots. In return for the army's protection, farmers paid a heavy tax to the government.

In 301 BC Candragupta decided to become a Jainist monk. To do so, he had to give up his throne. He passed the throne to his son, who continued to expand the empire. Before long, the Mauryas ruled all of northern India and much of central India as well.

Teach the Big Idea

At Level

Indian Empires

1. **Teach** Ask students the questions in the Main Idea boxes under Direct Teach.

2. **Apply** Have each student place the headings *Mauryan Empire* and *Gupta Empire* at the top of a sheet of paper. Ask half the class to fill in the paper with major events of each empire, along with the dates or approximate dates of those events. The other half of the class should write down details about the empires' societies, cultures, and achievements. 🔲 **Visual/Spatial**

3. **Review** Call on volunteers from the events group to write the main events for all students to see. Have them spread out their entries so that volunteers from the other group can fill in details that they wrote down.

4. **Practice/Homework** Ask each student to write a verse for a national anthem for the Mauryan Empire or the Gupta Empire, using a popular song as the melody. 🔲 **Verbal/Linguistic, Auditory/Musical**

Asoka

Around 270 BC Candragupta's grandson Asoka (uh-SOH-kuh) became king. Asoka was a strong ruler, the strongest of all the Mauryan emperors. He extended Mauryan rule over most of India. In conquering other kingdoms, Asoka made his own empire both stronger and richer.

For many years, Asoka watched his armies fight bloody battles against other peoples. A few years into his rule, however, Asoka converted to Buddhism. When he did, he swore that he would not launch any more wars of conquest.

After converting to Buddhism, Asoka had the time and resources to improve the lives of his people. He had wells dug and roads built throughout the empire. Along these roads, workers planted shade trees, built rest houses for travelers, and raised large stone pillars carved with Buddhist **edicts**, or laws. Asoka also encouraged the spread of Buddhism in India and the rest of Asia. As you read in the previous section, he sent missionaries to lands all over Asia.

Asoka died in 233 BC, and the empire began to fall apart soon afterward. His sons fought for power, and invaders threatened the empire. In 184 BC the last Mauryan king was killed by one of his generals. India divided into smaller states once again.

FOCUS ON READING
What were some key events in Asoka's life? In what order did they occur?

READING CHECK **Finding Main Ideas** How did the Mauryans gain control of most of India?

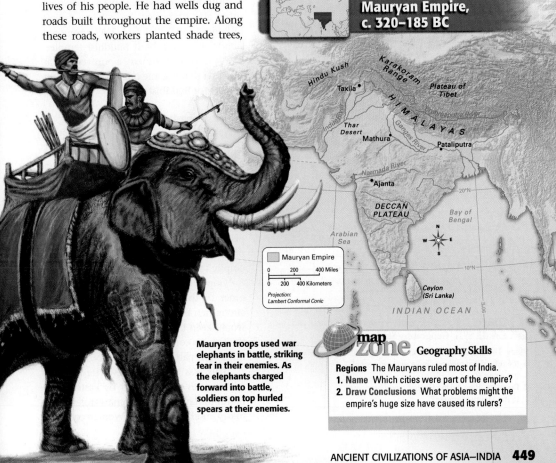

Mauryan Empire, c. 320–185 BC

Mauryan Empire
0   200   400 Miles
0   200   400 Kilometers
Projection: Lambert Conformal Conic

Mauryan troops used war elephants in battle, striking fear in their enemies. As the elephants charged forward into battle, soldiers on top hurled spears at their enemies.

map zone Geography Skills

Regions The Mauryans ruled most of India.
1. **Name** Which cities were part of the empire?
2. **Draw Conclusions** What problems might the empire's huge size have caused its rulers?

ANCIENT CIVILIZATIONS OF ASIA—INDIA **449**

Direct Teach

Main Idea

❶ **Mauryan Empire Unifies India**

The Mauryan Empire unified most of India.

Identify Who was Candragupta Maurya? *a military leader who seized control of northern India in the 320s BC, founding the Mauryan Empire*

Describe What was Candragupta Maurya's government like? *network of spies, army of 600,000 soldiers along with many elephants and chariots, heavy taxes*

Explain How did becoming a Buddhist change Asoka's behavior? *He worked to improve his people's lives and spread Buddhism.*

🗺 Map Zone Transparency: Mauryan Empire, c. 320–185 BC

📄 **RF:** Biography, Candragupta Maurya

📄 **RF:** Biography, Mahinda

go.hrw.com
Online Resources

KEYWORD: SK9 CH14
ACTIVITY: Mauryan Leaders

Social Studies Skill: Retrieving and Analyzing Information

Mauryan Time Line

1. Draw a blank time line for students to see. Write 320s BC and 184 BC on the time line. Call on volunteers to tell why those were important years for the Mauryan Empire.

2. Instruct students to create their own time lines titled *History of the Mauryan Empire.* They should start by incorporating information in this section.

3. Then have students conduct additional research on the Mauryan Empire so that they

Above Level | **Research Required**

can include at least two facts not presented in this section in their time lines.

4. Display the time lines for other students to see. Lead a discussion about which events seem to be more significant than others.

LS Visual/Spatial

📄 Alternative Assessment Handbook, Rubrics 30: Research; and 36: Time Lines

---

Answers

Focus on Reading *Asoka became king; conquered kingdoms; converted to Buddhism; improved lives of Mauryan people; sent missionaries all over Asia.*

Reading Check *by conquering neighboring kingdoms*

Map Zone 1. *Taxila, Mathura, Pataliputra, Ajanta;* **2.** *possible answers—power struggles between rulers may have threatened to break apart the empire; invaders could enter from many directions*

449

❷ Gupta Rulers Promote Hinduism

Gupta rulers promoted Hinduism in their empire.

Describe What was India like after the fall of the Mauryan Empire? *divided for about 500 years*

Identify Who were Candra Gupta I and Candra Gupta II? *founder of the Gupta Empire; emperor under whom Gupta society reached its high point*

Analyze Why did the Gupta rulers support the caste system? *They believed it would make the empire more stable.*

Predict How do you think India would be different today if the Gupta rulers had not taken over? *possible answer—might be primarily Buddhist*

Activity **Early Indian Empire Tic-Tac-Toe** Have each student write down two questions from this section. Organize the class into two teams: *X*s and *O*s. Have students play a game of tic-tac-toe in which each team member is asked a question and gets to place a mark on the grid when he or she answers correctly. **⮕ Interpersonal**

🖎 Map Zone Transparency: Gupta Empire, c. 400

Other People, Other Places

Trade with Rome For many years, India and the Roman Empire enjoyed a lively trade relationship. In fact, at one point the Romans had built special warehouses just for pepper imported from India. Although trade between Rome and India was sometimes disrupted, by the 300s and 400s it was again strong. Roman coins found in Sri Lanka are evidence of this trade.

Answers

Map Zone 1. *southern and southwestern;* **2.** *The Gupta Empire covered only Northern India, while the Mauryan Empire covered all of India.*

450

Gupta Rulers Promote Hinduism

After the collapse of the Mauryan Empire, India remained divided for about 500 years. During that period, Buddhism continued to prosper and spread in India, and so the popularity of Hinduism declined.

A New Hindu Empire

ACADEMIC VOCABULARY
establish to set up or create

Eventually, however, a new dynasty was **established** in India. It was the Gupta (GOOP-tuh) dynasty, which took over India around AD 320. Under the Guptas, India was once again united, and it once again became prosperous.

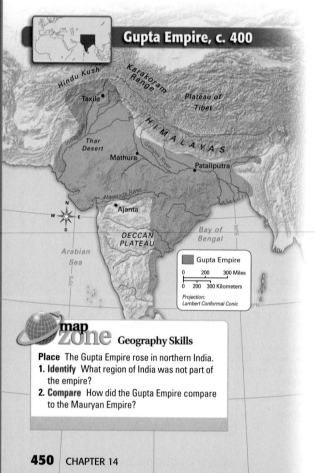

Gupta Empire, c. 400

map zone **Geography Skills**

Place The Gupta Empire rose in northern India.
1. **Identify** What region of India was not part of the empire?
2. **Compare** How did the Gupta Empire compare to the Mauryan Empire?

450 CHAPTER 14

The first Gupta emperor was Candra Gupta I. Although their names are similar, he was not related to Candragupta Maurya. From his base in northern India, Candra Gupta's armies invaded and conquered neighboring lands. Eventually, he brought much of the northern part of India under his control.

Indian civilization flourished under the Gupta rulers. These rulers were Hindu, so Hinduism became India's dominant religion. Gupta kings built many Hindu temples, some of which became models for later Indian architecture. They also promoted a revival of Hindu writings and worship practices.

Although they were Hindus, the Gupta rulers also supported the religious beliefs of Buddhism and Jainism. They promoted Buddhist art and built Buddhist temples. They also established a university at Nalanda that became one of Asia's greatest centers for Buddhist studies.

Gupta Society

In 375 Emperor Candra Gupta II took the throne in India. Gupta society reached its high point during his rule. Under Candra Gupta II, the empire continued to grow, eventually stretching all the way across northern India. At the same time, the empire's economy strengthened, and so people prospered. They created fine works of art and literature. Outsiders admired the empire's wealth and beauty.

Gupta kings believed the strict social order of the Hindu caste system would strengthen their rule. They also thought it would keep the empire stable. As a result, the Guptas considered the caste system an important part of Indian society.

This was not good news for women whose roles were limited by caste rules. Brahmins taught that a woman's role was to marry and have children. Women couldn't

Differentiating Instruction

Special Needs Learners

1. Organize students into pairs. Provide each student with an outline map of the Indian subcontinent.

2. One member of the pair should draw the area included in the Mauryan Empire on his or her map. The other student should do the same for the Gupta Empire. Students should label the empires' cities and major geographical features.

3. Then have students exchange maps with their partners and draw the outline of the empire not yet recorded on the map.

4. Call on volunteers to describe how the boundaries of the two empires differed. **⮕ Visual/Spatial**

🗎 Alternative Assessment Handbook, Rubric 20: Map Creation

Gupta Art

This Gupta painting of a palace scene shows some of India's different castes. Gupta rulers supported Hinduism and the caste system.

even choose their own husbands. Parents arranged all marriages. Once married, wives had few rights. They were expected to serve their husbands. Widows had an even lower social status than other women.

Gupta rule remained strong in India until the late 400s. At that time the Huns, a group from Central Asia, invaded India from the northwest. Their fierce attacks drained the Gupta Empire of its power and wealth. As the Hun armies marched farther into India, the Guptas lost hope.

By the middle of the 500s, Gupta rule had ended, and India had divided into small kingdoms yet again.

READING CHECK **Summarizing** What was the Gupta dynasty's position on religion?

SUMMARY AND PREVIEW The Mauryans and Guptas united much of India in their empires. Next, you will learn about their many achievements.

Section 4 Assessment

go.hrw.com
Online Quiz
KEYWORD: SK9 HP14

Reviewing Ideas, Terms, and Places

1. **a. Identify** Who created the Mauryan Empire?
   b. Summarize What happened after Asoka became a Buddhist?
   c. Elaborate Why do you think many people consider Asoka the greatest of all Mauryan rulers?
2. **a. Recall** What religion did most of the Gupta rulers belong to?
   b. Compare and Contrast How were the rulers Candragupta Maurya and Candra Gupta I alike, and how were they different?
   c. Evaluate Do you think the Gupta enforcement of caste rules was a good idea? Why or why not?

Critical Thinking

3. **Categorizing** Draw a chart like this one. Fill it with facts about India's rulers.

Ruler	Dynasty	Accomplishments

FOCUS ON WRITING

4. **Comparing Indian Empires** Another possible topic for your poster would be a comparison of the Mauryan and Gupta empires. Jot down ideas on what you could show in such a comparison.

ANCIENT CIVILIZATIONS OF ASIA—INDIA **451**

Section 4 Assessment Answers

1. **a.** Candragupta Maurya
   b. Asoka focused on improving the lives of the citizens and spreading Buddhism.
   c. He gave up making war and concentrated instead on improving people's lives.

2. **a.** Hinduism
   b. alike—India flourished under their rule; different—Candragupta Maurya became a Jainist monk, and Candra Gupta I was a Hindu.
   c. Answers will vary but should reflect understanding of caste rules.

3. Candragupta Maurya—Mauryan; founded the Mauryan empire, gave up his throne to become a Jainist monk; Asoka—Mauryan; extended Mauryan rule, converted to Buddhism, improved people's lives, spread Buddhism; Candra Gupta I—Gupta; first Gupta emperor, brought much of the northern part of India under control; Candra Gupta II—Gupta; expanded empire, Gupta society at its height

4. Students' ideas will vary but should reflect text content.

Main Idea

Gupta Rulers Promote Hinduism, *continued*

Identify What ended the Gupta rule?
the Hun invasion from the northwest

Summarize What responsibilities and rights did Gupta women have?
to care for husband and family; few rights

● **Review & Assess** ●

Close

Refer students to the illustration of the Mauryan war elephant. Ask them to describe what it would be like to face these animals in battle.

Review

Online Quiz, Section 4

Assess

SE Section 4 Assessment

PASS: Section 4 Quiz

Alternative Assessment Handbook

Reteach/Classroom Intervention

Interactive Reader and Study Guide, Section 4

Interactive Skills Tutor CD-ROM

Answers

Reading Check *Even though Gupta rulers were Hindus, they supported the beliefs of Buddhism and Jainism.*

451

Biography

Asoka Lead a discussion about decisions students have made that have affected various aspects of their lives. Or, you may prefer that students discuss decisions made by family members, contemporary world leaders, or other figures in world history. Point out that every day people make decisions that have wide-ranging effects. Use a daily newspaper to spark discussion about decisions and their ramifications.

Linking to Today

Stupas Originally, Asoka built eight monuments, or *stupas*, at Sanchi, but only three remain today. In 1989, the entire area was added to UNESCO's World Heritage List.

Info to Know

The Great Stupa The hemispherical shape of this monument, called the Great Stupa, has symbolic meaning. Ask students why this shape might have been chosen for the monument. *It symbolizes the dome of the sky as we look at it from the earth.*

About the Illustration

This illustration of Asoka is an artist's conception based on available sources. However, historians are uncertain exactly what Asoka looked like.

Answers

Biography *He became a peace-loving ruler dedicated to improving the lives of his people.*

452

BIOGRAPHY

Asoka

How can one decision change a man's entire life?

When did he live? before 230 BC

Where did he live? Asoka's empire included much of northern and central India.

What did he do? After fighting many bloody wars to expand his empire, Asoka gave up violence and converted to Buddhism.

Why is he important? Asoka is one of the most respected rulers in Indian history and one of the most important figures in the history of Buddhism. As a devout Buddhist, Asoka worked for years to spread the Buddha's teachings. In addition to sending missionaries around Asia, he had huge columns carved with Buddhist teachings raised all over India. Largely through his efforts, Buddhism became one of Asia's main religions.

Generalizing How did Asoka's life change after he became Buddhist?

This Buddhist shrine, located in Sanchi, India, was built by Asoka.

KEY EVENTS

- **c. 270 BC** Asoka becomes the Mauryan emperor.
- **c. 261 BC** Asoka's empire reaches its greatest size.
- **c. 261 BC** Asoka becomes a Buddhist.
- **c. 251 BC** Asoka begins to send Buddhist missionaries to other parts of Asia.

Critical Thinking: Solving Problems   [At Level]

Asoka's Plan for Helping His People

1. Organize students into small groups. Ask students to imagine that they are Asoka's advisers.

2. Tell students that Asoka has called the advisers together to announce his conversion to Buddhism. Asoka has asked them to suggest plans for helping his people.

3. Each group should use what members know about Asoka and India to list specific ideas. Students should not limit themselves to those items mentioned in this section.

4. Then have groups add to their lists by suggesting problems or hurdles that may slow the progress of Asoka's plans. Examples include issues related to physical geography, opposition by local rulers, and so on.

5. Challenge students to suggest ways these problems could be overcome. **LS Interpersonal, Logical/Mathematical**

   Alternative Assessment Handbook, Rubric 14: Group Activity

Indian Achievements

If YOU lived there...

You are a traveler in western India in the 300s. You are visiting a cave temple that is carved into a mountain cliff. Inside the cave it is cool and quiet. Huge columns rise all around you. You don't feel you're alone, for the walls and ceilings are covered with paintings. They are filled with lively scenes and figures. In the center is a large statue with calm, peaceful features.

How does this cave make you feel?

> **BUILDING BACKGROUND** The Mauryan and Gupta empires united most of India politically. During these empires, Indian artists, writers, scholars, and scientists made great advances. Some of their works are still studied and admired today.

Religious Art

The Indians of the Mauryan and Gupta periods created great works of art, many of them religious. Many of their paintings and sculptures illustrated either Hindu or Buddhist teachings. Magnificent temples—both Hindu and Buddhist—were built all around India. They remain some of the most beautiful buildings in the world today.

Temples

Early Hindu temples were small, stone structures. They had flat roofs and contained only one or two rooms. In the Gupta period, though, temple architecture became more complex. Gupta temples were topped by huge towers and were covered with carvings of the god worshipped inside.

Buddhist temples of the Gupta period are also impressive. Some Buddhists carved entire temples out of mountainsides. The most famous such temples are at Ajanta and Ellora. Builders filled the caves there with beautiful paintings and sculpture.

What You Will Learn...

Main Ideas

1. Indian artists created great works of religious art.
2. Sanskrit literature flourished during the Gupta period.
3. The Indians made scientific advances in metalworking, medicine, and other sciences.

The Big Idea

The people of ancient India made great contributions to the arts and sciences.

Key Terms

metallurgy, *p. 456*
alloys, *p. 456*
Hindu-Arabic numerals, *p. 456*
inoculation, *p. 456*
astronomy, *p. 457*

TAKING NOTES As you read, look for information on achievements of ancient India. Take notes about these achievements in a chart.

Type of Achievement	Details about Achievements
Religious Art	
Sanskrit Literature	
Scientific Advances	

Bellringer

If YOU lived there. . . Use the **Daily Bellringer Transparency** to help students answer the question.

Daily Bellringer Transparency, Section 5

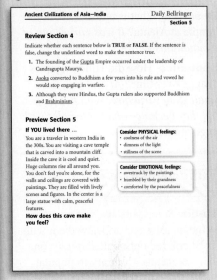

Ancient Civilizations of Asia—India	Daily Bellringer Section 5

Review Section 4

Indicate whether each sentence below is **TRUE** or **FALSE**. If the sentence is false, change the underlined word to make the sentence true.

1. The founding of the <u>Gupta</u> Empire occurred under the leadership of Candragupta Maurya.
2. <u>Asoka</u> converted to Buddhism a few years into his rule and vowed he would stop engaging in warfare.
3. Although they were Hindus, the Gupta rulers also supported Buddhism and <u>Brahminism</u>.

Preview Section 5

If YOU lived there ...
You are a traveler in western India in the 300s. You are visiting a cave temple that is carved into a mountain cliff. Inside the cave it is cool and quiet. Huge columns rise all around you. You don't feel you're alone, for the walls and ceilings are covered with paintings. They are filled with lively scenes and figures. In the center is a large statue with calm, peaceful features.
How does this cave make you feel?

Consider PHYSICAL feelings:
• coolness of the air
• dimness of the light
• stillness of the scene

Consider EMOTIONAL feelings:
• awestruck by the paintings
• humbled by their grandness
• comforted by the peacefulness

Academic Vocabulary

Review with students the high-use academic term in this section.

process a series of steps by which a task is accomplished (p. 456)

RF: Vocabulary Builder, Section 5

Taking Notes

Have students copy the graphic organizer onto their own paper and then use it to take notes on the section. This activity will prepare students for the Section Assessment, in which they will complete a graphic organizer that builds on the information using the Critical Thinking Skill: Categorizing.

Teach the Big Idea

At Level

Indian Achievements

1. **Teach** Ask students the questions in the Main Idea boxes under Direct Teach.

2. **Apply** Organize students into three groups. Assign one of the subsections—Religious Art, Sanskrit Literature, or Scientific Advances—to each group. Each group should create a poster or mural to illustrate the main points in its subsection.
   LS Visual/Spatial

3. **Review** As each group presents its illustration to the class, go over the concepts and terms related to that subsection.

4. **Practice/Homework** Instruct students to create a chart listing each of this section's three main ideas. Under each main idea, students should list at least two examples that support the idea. **LS Verbal/Linguistic**

   Alternative Assessment Handbook, Rubric 3: Artwork

❶ Religious Art

Indian artists created great works of religious art.

Describe What is unusual about the temple at Ajanta? *It was carved out of a mountainside.*

Sequence How did Hindu temples change over time? *At first they were small stone structures with flat roofs, but they became complex temples with huge towers.*

MISCONCEPTION ALERT

Bindis Some portrayals of women in Indian religious art show them with small colored dots, called *bindis*, on their foreheads. Contrary to popular belief, these marks do not designate a woman's caste. Depending on where the woman lives, the *bindi* may indicate that she is married. Bindis are primarily for decorative purposes, though. Indian women used to apply their bindis in powdered form. Now, however, they can buy peel-and-stick *bindis*.

Connect to Art

Teaching with Art Much of the art of India's great temples tells stories about gods. People who could not read the written language could "read" the stories in the sculpture and paintings and learn more about their religion. The carvings on the temple exteriors were especially important because not everyone was allowed inside the temples.

Answers

Reading Check *Most artists illustrated religious beliefs in their works, many of which can be seen in temples.*

454

Temple Architecture

This Hindu temple is covered with finely detailed carvings and decorations. Many individual sculptures are images of major Hindu gods, like the statue of Vishnu above.

Another type of Buddhist temple was the stupa. Stupas had domed roofs and were built to house sacred items from the life of the Buddha. Many of them were covered with detailed carvings.

Paintings and Sculpture

The Gupta period also saw the creation of countless works of art, both paintings and statues. Painting was a greatly respected profession, and India was home to many skilled artists. However, we don't know the names of many artists from this period. Instead, we know the names of many rich and powerful members of Gupta society who paid artists to create works of beauty and religious and social significance.

Most Indian paintings of the Gupta period are clear and colorful. Some of them show graceful Indians wearing fine jewelry and stylish clothes. Such paintings offer us a glimpse of the Indians' daily and ceremonial lives.

Artists from both of India's major religions, Hinduism and Buddhism, drew on their beliefs to create their works. As a result, many of the finest paintings of ancient India are found in temples. Hindu painters drew hundreds of gods on temple walls and entrances. Buddhists covered the walls and ceilings of temples with scenes from the life of the Buddha.

Indian sculptors also created great works. Many of their statues were made for Buddhist cave temples. In addition to the temples' intricately carved columns, sculptors carved statues of kings and the Buddha. Some of these statues tower over the cave entrances. Hindu temples also featured impressive statues of their gods. In fact, the walls of some temples, such as the one pictured above, were completely covered with carvings and images.

READING CHECK **Summarizing** How did religion influence ancient Indian art?

Collaborative Learning

Below Level | **Standard English Mastery**

Describing an Indian Temple

1. Ask students to imagine that they are Indian farmers who are seeing the temple shown on this page, called Kesava Temple, for the first time. Point out that the temple may have been the most spectacular sight the farmer had ever seen.

2. Have each student write down a completion for either of these prompts: "As I approached Kesava Temple, I felt ___" or "As I approached Kesava Temple, I noticed ___." Encourage students to use the text and

photos to help them write clear, informative sentences using standard English.

3. Provide a thesaurus or dictionary to those students who need assistance.

4. Call on volunteers to read their sentences. Review them as examples of standard English usage. **LS** **Verbal/Linguistic**

Sanskrit Literature

As you read earlier, Sanskrit was the main language of the ancient Aryans. During the Mauryan and Gupta periods, many works of Sanskrit literature were created. These works were later translated into many other languages.

Religious Epics

The greatest of these Sanskrit writings are two religious epics, the *Mahabharata* (muh-HAH-BAH-ruh-tuh) and the *Ramayana* (rah-MAH-yuh-nuh). Still popular in India, the *Mahabharata* is one of the longest literary works ever written. It is a story about a struggle between two families for control of a kingdom. Included within the story are long passages about Hindu beliefs. The most famous is called the *Bhagavad Gita* (BUG-uh-vuhd GEE-tah).

The *Ramayana,* another great epic, tells about a prince named Rama. In truth, the prince was the god Vishnu in human form. He had become human so he could rid the world of demons. He also had to rescue his wife, a princess named Sita. For centuries, characters from the *Ramayana* have been seen as models for how Indians should behave. For example, Rama is seen as the ideal ruler and his relationship with Sita as the ideal marriage.

Other Works

Writers in the Gupta period also created plays, poetry, and other types of literature. One famous writer of this time was Kalidasa (kahl-ee-DAHS-uh). His work was so brilliant that Candra Gupta II hired him to write plays for the royal court.

Sometime before 500, Indian writers also produced a book of stories called the *Panchatantra* (PUHN-chuh-TAHN-truh). The stories in this collection were intended to teach lessons. They praise people for cleverness and quick thinking. Each story ends with a message about winning friends, losing property, waging war, or some other idea. For example, the message below warns listeners to think about what they are doing before they act.

> " The good and bad of given schemes
> Wise thought must first reveal:
> The stupid heron saw his chicks
> Provide a mongoose meal. "
>
> –from the *Panchatantra,* translated by Arthur William Ryder

Eventually, translations of this popular collection spread throughout the world. It became popular in countries even as far away as Europe.

READING CHECK Categorizing What types of literature did writers of ancient India create?

In this illustration of the *Ramayana*, the monkey king orders the monkey general Hanuman to find Sita. Hanuman helped Rama defeat the demons and win back Sita. Many Indians view him as a model of devotion and loyalty.

❸ Scientific Advances

The Indians made scientific advances in metalworking, medicine, and other sciences.

Describe What were some operations that Indian surgeons could perform? *fixing broken bones, treating wounds, removing infected tonsils, reconstructing broken noses, reattaching torn earlobes*

Compare How were metallurgy and alloys connected? *Creating alloys, or mixtures of two or more metals, was a skill within metallurgy that ancient Indians developed.*

Evaluate Why do you think the concept of zero was so important? *Zero acts as a placeholder when using numbers of a specific base such as base 10, allowing mathematicians to make calculations easily.*

Connect to Science

Mystery Solved? Recently, scientists at the Indian Institute of Technology announced that they had figured out why the Iron Pillar has not rusted. They said that phosphorous in the iron had allowed a very thin protective layer of an iron, oxygen, and hydrogen compound to form on the pillar's surface. This film is only one-twentieth of a millimeter thick. Because present-day iron-making processes remove most phosphorous, modern iron rusts more easily.

Indian Science

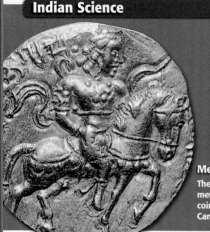

Medicine
In this modern painting, the Indian surgeon Susruta performs surgery on a patient. The ancient Indians had an advanced knowledge of medicine.

Metalworking
The Indians were expert metalworkers. This gold coin shows the emperor Candra Gupta II.

Scientific Advances

Indian achievements were not limited to art, architecture, and literature. Indian scholars also made important advances in metalworking, math, and the sciences.

Metalworking

The ancient Indians were pioneers of **metallurgy** (MET-uhl-uhr-jee), the science of working with metals. Their knowledge allowed them to create high-quality tools and weapons. The Indians also knew **processes** for mixing metals to create **alloys**, mixtures of two or more metals. Alloys are sometimes stronger or easier to work with than pure metals.

Metalworkers made their strongest products out of iron. Indian iron was very hard and pure. These features made the iron a valuable trade item.

During the Gupta dynasty, metalworkers built the famous Iron Pillar near Delhi. Unlike most iron, which rusts easily, the pillar is very resistant to rust. The tall column still attracts crowds of visitors. Scholars study this column even today to learn the Indians' secrets.

ACADEMIC VOCABULARY
process a series of steps by which a task is accomplished

THE IMPACT TODAY
People still get inoculations against many diseases.

Mathematics and Other Sciences

Gupta scholars also made advances in math and science. In fact, they were among the most skilled mathematicians of their day. They developed many of the elements of our modern math system. The very numbers we use today are called **Hindu-Arabic numerals** because they were created by Indian scholars and brought to Europe by Arabs. The Indians were also the first people to create the zero. Although it may seem like a small thing, modern math wouldn't be possible without the zero.

The ancient Indians were also very skilled in the medical sciences. As early as the AD 100s, doctors were writing their knowledge down in textbooks. Among the skills these books describe is how to make medicines from plants and minerals.

Besides curing people with medicines, Indian doctors knew how to protect them against diseases. They used **inoculation** (i-nah-kyuh-LAY-shuhn), the practice of injecting a person with a small dose of a virus to help him or her build a defense to a disease. By fighting off this small dose, the body learns to protect itself.

Differentiating Instruction

Below Level

Struggling Readers
Materials: art supplies

1. Discuss with students the wide variety of scientific advances made by the people of ancient India.

2. Ask students to imagine that they are metalworkers, doctors, mathematicians, or scientists of ancient India. Have each student design an advertisement that he or she might have placed in the yellow pages of a phone book of the time, had there been such a thing.

3. Ask students to discuss their yellow pages ads. As they do so, review the accomplishments of ancient Indians.

4. Display the ads in the classroom.
   LS Visual/Spatial
   Alternative Assessment Handbook, Rubric 2: Advertisements

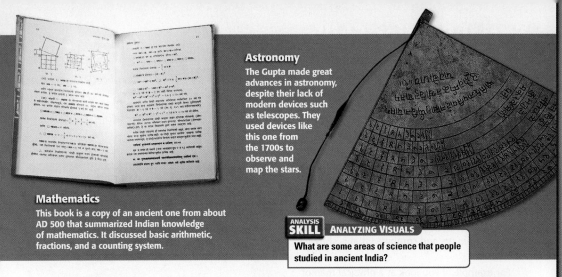

Mathematics
This book is a copy of an ancient one from about AD 500 that summarized Indian knowledge of mathematics. It discussed basic arithmetic, fractions, and a counting system.

Astronomy
The Gupta made great advances in astronomy, despite their lack of modern devices such as telescopes. They used devices like this one from the 1700s to observe and map the stars.

ANALYSIS SKILL | **ANALYZING VISUALS**
What are some areas of science that people studied in ancient India?

Main Idea

Scientific Advances, *continued*

Recall What were some Indian achievements in astronomy? *knew of seven planets, that the sun was a star and that planets revolved around it, the earth was a rotating sphere; could predict eclipses*

Draw Inferences Since the Indians did not have telescopes, how did they become expert astronomers? *possible answer—careful, systematic observation and record-keeping*

For people who were injured, Indian doctors could perform surgery. Surgeons repaired broken bones, treated wounds, removed infected tonsils, reconstructed broken noses, and even reattached torn earlobes! If they could find no other cure for an illness, doctors would cast magic spells to help people recover.

Indian interest in **astronomy**, the study of stars and planets, dates back to early times as well. Indian astronomers knew of seven of the nine planets in our solar system. They knew that the sun was a star and that the planets revolved around it. They also knew that the earth was a sphere and that it spun on its axis. In addition, they could predict eclipses of the sun and the moon.

READING CHECK Finding Main Ideas What were two Indian achievements in mathematics?

SUMMARY AND PREVIEW From a group of cities along the Indus and Sarasvati Rivers, India grew into a major empire whose people made great achievements. In the next chapter, you'll read about another civilization that experienced similar growth—China.

Section 5 Assessment

go.hrw.com
Online Quiz
KEYWORD: SK9 HP14

Reviewing Ideas, Terms, and Places

1. **a. Describe** What did Hindu temples of the Gupta period look like?
 b. Analyze How can you tell that Indian artists were well respected?
 c. Evaluate Why do you think Hindu and Buddhist temples contained great works of art?
2. **a. Identify** What is the *Bhagavad Gita*?
 b. Explain Why were the stories of the *Panchatantra* written?
 c. Elaborate Why do you think people are still interested in ancient Sanskrit epics today?
3. **a. Define** What is **metallurgy**?
 b. Explain Why do we call the numbers we use today **Hindu-Arabic numerals**?

Critical Thinking

4. **Categorizing** Draw a chart like this one. Identify the scientific advances that fall into each category below.

Metallurgy	Math	Medicine	Astronomy

FOCUS ON WRITING

5. **Highlighting Indian Achievements** List the Indian achievements you could include on a poster. Consider these topics as well as your topic ideas from earlier sections in this chapter. Choose one topic for your poster.

ANCIENT CIVILIZATIONS OF ASIA—INDIA **457**

Review & Assess

Close

Point out that India had veterinarians also. Doctors who treated horses and elephants were highly respected and valued.

Review

Online Quiz, Section 5

Assess

SE Section 5 Assessment
PASS: Section 5 Quiz
Alternative Assessment Handbook

Reteach/Classroom Intervention

Interactive Reader and Study Guide, Section 5
Interactive Skills Tutor CD-ROM

Section 5 Assessment Answers

1. **a.** stone structures topped by huge towers, exteriors covered with carvings of the god worshipped inside
 b. Rich and powerful members of Gupta society paid artists to create works of beauty and significance.
 c. possible answer—Religion was important in Indian society, and most art honored the gods. Also, many Indians were illiterate, so art helped explain religious concepts.

2. **a.** long passage about Hindu beliefs within the *Mahabharata*

 b. They were intended to teach lessons.
 c. possible answer—because they reflect the history of India and are lively stories.

3. **a.** the science of working with metals
 b. because they were created by Indian scholars and brought to Europe by Arabs

4. Students' answers should include all Indian achievements that were identified in this section.

5. Lists and chosen topics will vary, but should be based on the text in this chapter.

Answers

Analyzing Visuals *metallurgy, mathematics, medicine, and astronomy*
Reading Check *Hindu-Arabic numerals; the zero*

Comparing Maps

1. Discuss ways that geography can affect civilization (climate, rainfall, natural physical barriers, features such as rivers, location). Then discuss ways that these issues might appear on maps (climate map, physical map, population map).

2. Ask students to create two fictional maps of the same area. They will create a fictional region, country, continent, and so on, and give it a name. They can then choose the two types of maps they will draw (population, climate, rainfall, physical, political, etc.)

3. Remind students that the two maps should be related and they will be asked to explain how comparing the two maps provides more information than looking at one at a time. For example, population along a river might be very heavy or population in a mountainous region might be very low.

4. They should construct maps including legends that explain colors, symbols, and so on. When complete, ask volunteers to display their maps and answer questions about how they are related. **LS Visual/Spatial**

▢ Alternative Assessment Handbook, Rubric 20: Map Creation

◉ Interactive Skills Tutor CD-ROM, Lesson 6: Interpret Maps, Charts, Visuals, and Political Cartoons

▢ **RF**: Social Studies Skill, Comparing Maps

Comparing Maps

Learn

Maps are a necessary tool in the study of both history and geography. Sometimes, however, a map does not contain all the information you need. In those cases, you may have to compare two or more maps and combine what is shown on each.

For example, if you look at a physical map of India you can see what landforms are in a region. You can then look at a population map to see how many people live in that region. From this comparison, you can conclude how the region's landforms affect its population distribution.

Practice

Compare the two maps on this page to answer the following questions.

❶ What was the northeastern boundary of the Gupta Empire? What is the physical landscape like there?

❷ What region of India was never part of the Gupta Empire? Based on the physical map, what might have been one reason for this?

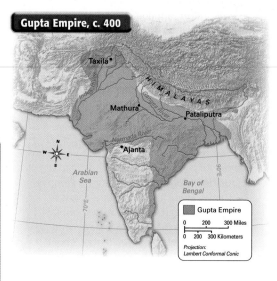

Apply

Choose two maps from this chapter or two maps from the Atlas in this book. Study the two maps and then write three questions that someone could answer by comparing them. Remember that the questions should have people look at both maps to determine the correct answers.

458 CHAPTER 14

Social Studies Skills Activity: Comparing Maps | **At Level** |

Struggling Readers

1. Discuss ways that geography can affect civilization (climate, rainfall, natural physical barriers, location). Then discuss ways that these issues might appear on maps (climate map, physical map, population map, etc.). Refer students to the Atlas in this book to review the world maps: Physical and Political. Direct students' attention to South America.

2. Describe the Andes Mountains. Ask students to find them on the Physical map. Ask them to review the Political map and make a comparison. Mention that Chile's odd shape coincides with the barrier formed by the Andes.

3. Now have students examine Europe on the maps. Ask them to identify one place where mountains form a natural barrier that is reflected in the political boundaries of the countries (Pyrenees as a boundary between France and Spain).
LS Visual/Spatial

▢ Alternative Assessment Handbook, Rubric 21: Map Reading

Answers

Practice 1. *the Himalayas; rugged foothills and high peaks;* **2.** *southwestern India including Deccan Plateau; the high plain may have formed a natural barrier or division from other areas*

Apply *Answers will vary, but questions should require comparison of maps to identify answers.*

Geography's Impact
video series
Review the video to answer the closing question:
Do you think enlightenment is an achievable goal in today's world? Why or why not?

Visual Summary

Use the visual summary below to help you review the main ideas of the chapter.

QUICK FACTS

The Harappan civilization began in the Indus River Valley.

Hinduism and Buddhism both developed in India.

Indians made great advances in art, literature, science, and other fields.

Reviewing Vocabulary, Terms, and Places

Fill in the blanks with the correct term or name from this chapter.

1. _____ are hired soldiers.

2. A _____ is a division of people into groups based on birth, wealth, or occupation.

3. Hindus believe in _____, the belief that they will be reborn many times after death.

4. Harappa and _____ were the largest cities of the Harappan civilization.

5. The focusing of the mind on spiritual things is called _____.

6. People who work to spread their religious beliefs are called _____.

7. People who practice _____ use only peaceful ways to achieve change.

8. Indian civilization first developed in the valley of the _____.

9. A mixture of metals is called an _____.

Comprehension and Critical Thinking

SECTION 1 *(Pages 430–435)*

10. **a. Describe** What caused floods on the Indus River, and what was the result of those floods?

   b. Contrast How was Aryan culture different from Harappan culture?

   c. Elaborate In what ways was Harappan society an advanced civilization?

SECTION 2 *(Pages 436–441)*

11. **a. Identify** Who were the Brahmins, and what role did they play in Aryan society?

   b. Analyze How do Hindus believe karma affects reincarnation?

   c. Elaborate Hinduism has been called both a polytheistic religion—one that worships many gods—and a monotheistic religion—one that worships only one god. Why do you think this is so?

11. a. priests; highest class in Aryan society

b. Karma determines if you are reborn into a higher or lower caste.

c. Hindus believe in three major gods—Brahma, Siva, and Vishnu. However, they also believe these gods are parts of a universal spirit called Brahman.

12. a. wanting what we like but do not have, wanting to keep what we like and already have, not wanting what we dislike but have

b. Missionaries spread Buddhism across Asia; it split into two major branches.

c. possible answers—They were assured that their low social rank was not a barrier to enlightenment and that they had the power to change their lives.

13. a. seized control of northern India and by so doing founded the Mauryan Empire

b. Both unified much of India; Mauryan rulers promoted Buddhism, while Gupta rulers promoted Hinduism.

c. possible answer—Buddhism might not have spread to the rest of Asia, and Hinduism would be even more prevalent in India than it is today.

14. a. Buddhist and Hindu temples, paintings, and sculptures

b. possible answer—Their Hindu beliefs affect how the characters interact.

c. Answers will vary but should display familiarity with the achievements mentioned in this section.

Using the Internet

15. Go to the HRW Web site and enter the keyword shown to access a rubric for this activity.

> KEYWORD: SK9 TEACHER

Social Studies Skills

16. Ganges River

17. Much of northwestern India is desert.

Focus on Reading and Writing

18. Harappan civilization begins; The Aryans invade India; The Mauryan Empire is formed; The Gupta

---

SECTION 3 (Pages 442–447)

12. a. Describe What did the Buddha say caused human suffering?

b. Analyze How did Buddhism grow and change after the Buddha died?

c. Elaborate Why did the Buddha's teachings about nirvana appeal to many people of lower castes?

SECTION 4 (Pages 448–451)

13. a. Identify What was Candragupta Maurya's greatest accomplishment?

b. Compare and Contrast What was one similarity between the Mauryans and the Guptas? What was one difference between them?

c. Predict How might Indian history have been different if Asoka had not become a Buddhist?

SECTION 5 (Pages 453–457)

14. a. Describe What kinds of religious art did the ancient Indians create?

b. Make Inferences Why do you think religious discussions are included in the *Mahabharata*?

c. Evaluate Which of the ancient Indians' achievements do you think is most impressive? Why?

Using the Internet

15. Activity: Making a Brochure In this chapter, you learned about India's early history. That history was largely shaped by India's geography. Enter the activity keyword to research the geography and civilizations of India, taking notes as you go along. Finally, use the interactive brochure template to present what you have found.

Social Studies Skills

Comparing Maps *Study the physical and population maps of South and East Asia in the Atlas. Then answer the following questions.*

16. Along what river in northeastern India is the population density very high?

17. Why do you think fewer people live in far northwestern India than in the northeast?

---

18. Sequencing Arrange the following list of events in the order in which they happened. Then write a brief paragraph describing the events, using clue words such as *then* and *later* to show the proper sequence.

- The Gupta Empire is created.
- Harappan civilization begins.
- The Aryans invade India.
- The Mauryan Empire is formed.

19. Designing Your Poster Now that you have a topic for your poster, it's time to create it. On a large sheet of paper or poster board, write a title that identifies your topic. Then draw pictures, maps, or diagrams that illustrate it. Next to each picture, write a short caption to identify what the picture, map, or diagram shows.

Map Activity

20. Ancient India On a separate sheet of paper, match the letters on the map with their correct labels.

Mohenjo Daro	Indus River
Harappa	Ganges River
Bodh Gaya	

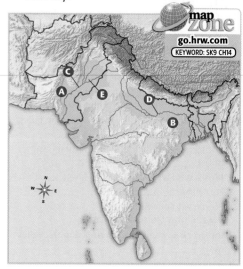

Empire is created. Students' paragraphs will vary, but should include clue words that indicate sequence.

RF: Focus on Reading, Sequencing

19. Rubric Students' illustrated posters should

- present the ideas clearly
- contain appropriate, accurate, and vivid illustrations
- have proper labels and captions
- use correct grammar, punctuation, spelling, and capitalization

RF: Focus on Writing: Creating a Poster

Map Activity

20. A. Mohenjo Daro

B. Bodh Gaya

C. Indus River

D. Ganges River

E. Harappa

Standardized Test Practice

DIRECTIONS (1–7): For each statement or question, write on a separate answer sheet the *number* of the word or expression that, of those given, best completes the statement or answers the question.

1 The earliest civilizations in India developed along which river?

(1) Indus
(2) Ganges
(3) Brahmaputra
(4) Krishna

2 The people of which *varna* in early India had the hardest lives?

(1) Brahmins
(2) Kshatriyas
(3) Sudras
(4) Vaisyas

3 What is the *main* goal of people who follow Buddhism as it was taught by the Buddha?

(1) wealth
(2) rebirth
(3) missionary work
(4) reaching nirvana

4 Which Indian ruler greatly enlarged his empire before giving up violence and promoting the spread of Buddhism?

(1) Candragupta Maurya
(2) Asoka
(3) Buddha
(4) Mahavira

5 Early India's contributions to world civilization included

(1) developing the world's first calendar.
(2) creating what is now called algebra.
(3) inventing the plow and the wheel.
(4) introducing zero to the number system.

6 The concept of nirvana is central to which two ancient Indian religions?

(1) Hinduism and Islam
(2) Buddhism and Judaism
(3) Buddhism and Hinduism
(4) Islam and Judaism

7 According to Hindu teachings, the universal spirit of which everything in the world is part is called

(1) Vishnu.
(2) Brahman.
(3) Siva.
(4) Buddha.

Base your answer to question 8 on the text excerpt below and on your knowledge of social studies.

> "From anger comes confusion;
> from confusion memory lapses;
> from broken memory understanding is lost;
> from loss of understanding, he is ruined.
>
> But a man of inner strength
> whose senses experience objects
> without attraction and hatred,
> in self control, finds serenity."
>
> –from the *Bhagavad Gita*,
> translated by Barbara Stoler Miller

8 **Constructed-Response Question** The passage from the *Bhagavad Gita* above is advice about how a person can reach nirvana. According to this passage, what will a person find if he or she has inner strength and self control?

Reteach/Intervention Resources

Reproducible

- Interactive Reader and Study Guide
- Differentiated Instruction Teacher Management System: Lesson Plans

Technology

- Quick Facts Transparency: Visual Summary: Ancient Civilizations of Asia—India
- Differentiated Instruction Modified Worksheets and Tests CD-ROM
- Interactive Skills Tutor CD-ROM

Tips for Test Taking

Getting the Full Picture When a question refers to a table or a chart, students should carefully read all the information in the table or chart, including headings and labels, before answering the question. When a question refers to a graph, encourage students to first carefully study the data plotted on the graph to determine any trends or oddities before answering the question.

Answers

Standardized Test Practice

1. 1
Break Down the Question This question requires students to recall map information. Refer students who miss it to the maps in Section 1.

2. 3
Break Down the Question Refer students who miss this question to the diagram in Section 2 and text information about the caste system.

3. 4
Break Down the Question Seeking wealth would be a barrier to reaching nirvana. Rebirth can provide a path to nirvana. Missionary work is not a requirement of Buddhism. Refer students who miss the question to review *Teachings of Buddhism*.

4. 2
Break Down the Question This question requires students to recall factual information. Refer students who miss the question to section 4.

5. 4
Break Down the Question Although ancient India contributed much to world civilization, the only contribution in this list that is mentioned in the chapter is the introduction of zero.

6. 3
Break Down the Question This question requires students to recall factual information. Refer students who miss this question to sections 2 and 3.

7. 2
Break Down the Question This question requires students to recall factual information. Refer students who miss the question to Section 2.

8. Constructed-Response Question With inner strength and self control will come serenity.

Chapter 15 Planning Guide

Ancient Civilizations of Asia—China

Chapter Overview	Reproducible Resources	Technology Resources
CHAPTER 15 pp. 462–497 **Overview: In this chapter, students will learn how Chinese civilization developed and about the contacts between China and other countries.**	**Differentiated Instruction Teacher Management System:*** • Instructional Pacing Guides • Lesson Plans for Differentiated Instruction **Interactive Reader and Study Guide:*** Chapter Summary Graphic Organizer **Resource File:*** • Chapter Review • Focus on Reading: Understanding Chronological Order • Focus on Writing: Writing a Magazine Article • Social Studies Skills: Making Economic Choices • Interdisciplinary Project: Dynasty Triptych **Experiencing World History and Geography**	**OSP Teacher's One-Stop Planner:** Calendar Planner **Power Presentations with Video CD-ROM** **Differentiated Instruction Modified Worksheets and Tests CD-ROM** **Interactive Skills Tutor CD-ROM** **Student Edition on Audio CD Program** **Map Zone Transparency:** Ancient China, 1600 BC–AD 1450* **Geography's Impact Video Program (VHS/DVD):** Impact of Confucius on China Today* **World Outline Maps: Transparencies and Activities**
Section 1: **Early China** **The Big Idea:** Early Chinese history was shaped by three dynasties—the Shang, the Zhou, and the Qin.	**Differentiated Instruction Teacher Management System:** Section 1 Lesson Plan* **Interactive Reader and Study Guide:** Section 1 Summary* **Resource File:*** • Vocabulary Builder: Section 1	**Daily Bellringer Transparency:** Section 1* **Map Zone Transparency:** Early Dynasties of China*
Section 2: **The Han Dynasty** **The Big Idea:** The Han Dynasty created a new form of government that valued family, art, and learning.	**Differentiated Instruction Teacher Management System:** Section 2 Lesson Plan* **Interactive Reader and Study Guide:** Section 2 Summary* **Resource File:*** • Vocabulary Builder: Section 2 • Biography: Liu Bang; Wudi	**Daily Bellringer Transparency:** Section 2* **Map Zone Transparency:** Han Dynasty, c. 206 BC–AD 220* **Internet Activity:** Chinese Art
Section 3: **The Sui, Tang and Song Dynasties** **The Big Idea:** The Tang and Song dynasties were periods of economic, cultural, and technological accomplishments.	**Differentiated Instruction Teacher Management System:** Section 3 Lesson Plan* **Interactive Reader and Study Guide:** Section 3 Summary* **Resource File:*** • Vocabulary Builder: Section 3 • Literature: Poems from the Tang and Song Dynasties	**Daily Bellringer Transparency:** Section 3* **Map Zone Transparency:** Chinese Dynasties, 589–1279*
Section 4: **Confucianism and Government** **The Big Idea:** Confucian thought influenced the Song government	**Differentiated Instruction Teacher Management System:** Section 4 Lesson Plan* **Interactive Reader and Study Guide:** Section 4 Summary* **Resource File:*** • Vocabulary Builder: Section 4	**Daily Bellringer Transparency:** Section 4* **Internet Activity:** Confucianism
Section 5: **The Yuan and Ming Dynasties** **The Big Idea:** The Chinese were ruled by foreigners during the Yuan dynasty, but they threw off Mongol rule and prospered during the Ming dynasty.	**Differentiated Instruction Teacher Management System:** Section 5 Lesson Plan* **Interactive Reader and Study Guide:** Section 5 Summary* **Resource File:*** • Vocabulary Builder: Section 5 • Primary Source: A Mongol Oath to Genghis Khan	**Daily Bellringer Transparency:** Section 5* **Map Zone Transparency:** Mongol Empire, 1294* **Internet Activity:** Marco Polo

HOLT

Geography's Impact
Video Program

Impact of Confucius on China Today
Suggested use: as a chapter introduction

Review, Assessment, Intervention

📦 **Quick Facts Transparencies:** Visual Summary: Ancient Civilizations of Asia—China*

🎵 **Spanish Chapter Summaries Audio CD Program**

📄 **Progress Assessment Support System (PASS):** Chapter Test*

💿 **Differentiated Instruction Modified Worksheets and Tests CD-ROM:** Modified Chapter Test

OSP **Teacher's One-Stop Planner:** ExamView Test Generator (English/Spanish)

📄 **Alternative Assessment Handbook**

HOAP **Holt Online Assessment Program (HOAP),** in the Holt Interactive Online Student Edition

---

📄 **PASS:** Section 1 Quiz*

go. hrw .com **Online Quiz:** Section 1

📄 **Alternative Assessment Handbook**

📄 **PASS:** Section 2 Quiz*

go. hrw .com **Online Quiz:** Section 2

📄 **Alternative Assessment Handbook**

📄 **PASS:** Section 3 Quiz*

go. hrw .com **Online Quiz:** Section 3

📄 **Alternative Assessment Handbook**

📄 **PASS:** Section 4 Quiz*

go. hrw .com **Online Quiz:** Section 4

📄 **Alternative Assessment Handbook**

📄 **PASS:** Section 5 Quiz*

go. hrw .com **Online Quiz:** Section 5

📄 **Alternative Assessment Handbook**

Power Presentations with Video CD-ROM

Power Presentations with Video are visual presentations of each chapter's main ideas. Presentations can be customized by including Quick Facts charts, images from the text, and video clips.

go.hrw.com
Teacher Resources
KEYWORD: SK9 TEACHER

go.hrw.com
Student Resources
KEYWORD: SK9 CH15

- Interactive Multimedia Activities
- Current Events

- Chapter-based Internet Activities
- and more!

Holt Interactive
Online Student Edition
Complete online support for interactivity, assessment, and reporting

- Interactive Maps and Notebook
- Standardized Test Prep
- Homework Practice and Research Activities Online

CHAPTER 15 PLANNING GUIDE

Differentiating Instruction

How do I address the needs of varied learners?
The Target Resource acts as your primary strategy for differentiated instruction.

ENGLISH-LANGUAGE LEARNERS & STRUGGLING READERS

TARGET RESOURCE

Graphic Organizer Transparencies with Support for Reading and Writing

Spanish Resources

Spanish Chapter Summaries Audio CD

Teacher's One-Stop Planner:
- ExamView Test Generator, Spanish
- PuzzlePro, Spanish

English-Language Learner Strategies and Activities

Additional Resources

Differentiated Instruction Teacher Management System: Lesson Plans for Differentiated Instruction

Resource File:
- Vocabulary Builder Activities
- Social Studies Skills: Making Economic Choices

Quick Facts Transparency: Visual Summary: Ancient Civilizations of Asia—China

Student Edition on Audio CD Program

Interactive Skills Tutor CD-ROM

SPECIAL NEEDS LEARNERS

TARGET RESOURCE

Interactive Reader and Study Guide

The activities in the Interactive Reader and Study Guide engage students with questions while presenting summaries of chapter content and provide opportunities for students to practice critical thinking skills.

Additional Resources

Differentiated Instruction Teacher Management System: Lesson Plans for Differentiated Instruction

Interactive Reader and Study Guide

Resource File: Social Studies Skills: Making Economic Choices

Student Edition on Audio CD Program

Interactive Skills Tutor CD-ROM

Graphic Organizer Transparencies with Support for Reading and Writing

ADVANCED/GIFTED AND TALENTED STUDENTS

TARGET RESOURCE

Differentiated Instruction Teacher Management System

Lesson Plans for Differentiated Instruction provide teachers with strategies to help plan instruction for all learners.

Additional Resources

Resource File:

Differentiated Instruction Teacher Management System: Lesson Plans for Differentiated Instruction
- Focus on Reading: Understanding Chronological Order
- Focus on Writing: Writing a Magazine Article
- Literature: Poems from the Tang and Song Dynasties

World History and Geography Document-Based Questions Activities

Geography, Science, and Cultures Activities

Experiencing World History and Geography

Differentiated Activities in the Teacher's Edition
- Creating a Diagram
- Writing a Log
- Writing a Summary
- Creating Illustrations

Differentiated Activities in the Teacher's Edition
- Drawing a Chart

Differentiated Activities in the Teacher's Edition
- Researching Mongol Conquests

HOLT Teacher's One-Stop Planner®

How can I manage the lesson plans and support materials for differentiated instruction?

With the Teacher's One-Stop Planner, you can easily organize and print lesson plans, planning guides, and instructional materials for all learners.

The Teacher's One-Stop Planner includes the following materials to help you differentiate instruction:
- **Interactive Teacher's Edition**
- **Calendar Planner and pacing guides**
- **Editable lesson plans**
- **All reproducible ancillaries in Adobe Acrobat (PDF) format**
- **ExamView Test Generator (English & Spanish)**
- **Transparency and video previews**

Professional Development

What teacher training resources are available to help me grow professionally?

- **In-service and staff development** as part of your Holt Social Studies product purchase
- **Quick Teacher Tutorial Lesson Presentation CD-ROM**
- Intensive tuition-based **Teacher Development Institute**
- **Convenient Holt Speaker Bureau:** face-to-face workshop options
- **24/7 Ask A Professional Development Expert** at http://www.hrw.com/prodev/

• Chapter Preview •

Chapter Big Ideas

Section 1 Early Chinese history was shaped by three dynasties—the Shang, the Zhou, and the Qin.

Section 2 The Han dynasty created a new form of government that valued family, art, and learning.

Section 3 The Tang and Song dynasties were periods of economic, cultural, and technological accomplishments.

Section 4 Confucian thought influenced the Song government.

Section 5 The Chinese were ruled by foreigners during the Yuan dynasty, but they threw off Mongol rule and prospered during the Ming dynasty.

Focus on Reading and Writing

Reading The Resource File provides a Focus on Reading worksheet to help students keep track of the order in which events happened when reading about history.

📝 **RF:** Focus on Reading, Understanding Chronological Order

Writing The Resource File provides a Focus on Writing Worksheet to help students organize and write their magazine articles.

📝 **RF:** Focus on Writing, Writing a Magazine Article

CHAPTER **15**

Ancient Civilizations of Asia—China

FOCUS QUESTION

How did ancient civilizations contribute to the development of the Eastern Hemisphere?

What You Will Learn...

In this chapter you will learn about the history and culture of ancient China. China was one of the world's early centers of civilization. You will also study the powerful dynasties that arose to rule China and reshape Chinese culture.

FOCUS ON READING AND WRITING

Understanding Chronological Order When you read about history, it is important to keep track of the order in which events happened. You can often use words in the text to help figure this order out. **See the lesson, Understanding Chronological Order, on page S18.**

Writing a Magazine Article You are a freelance writer who has been asked to write a magazine article about the achievements of the anicent Chinese. As you read this chapter, you will collect information. Then you will use the information to write your magazine article.

CENTRAL ASIA

Traders on the Silk Road

SOUTH ASIA

0   250   500 Miles
0   250   500 Kilometers
Projection: Two-Point Equidistant

Early China The first dynasties to rule China left behind artifacts such as this clay figure of a soldier.

Introduce the Chapter

At Level

Focus on China

1. Ask students the following questions: If you were lost in the woods, what could you use to learn which direction is which? On what material is this book printed? What instrument do scientists use to learn about earthquakes that occur far away? What medical procedure uses many tiny needles inserted in a patient's skin?

2. In order, the answers are a compass, paper, seismograph, and acupuncture. Then ask students if they can guess what these questions and answers have in common. *They are all about inventions and innovations created by the Chinese.*

3. Point out that China has one of the world's oldest civilizations and that Chinese civilization has influenced ours in ways that are not always obvious. Tell students they will be introduced to Chinese civilization and its influence in this chapter. 🔲 **Verbal/Linguistic**

📝 Alternative Assessment Handbook: Rubric 11: Discussions

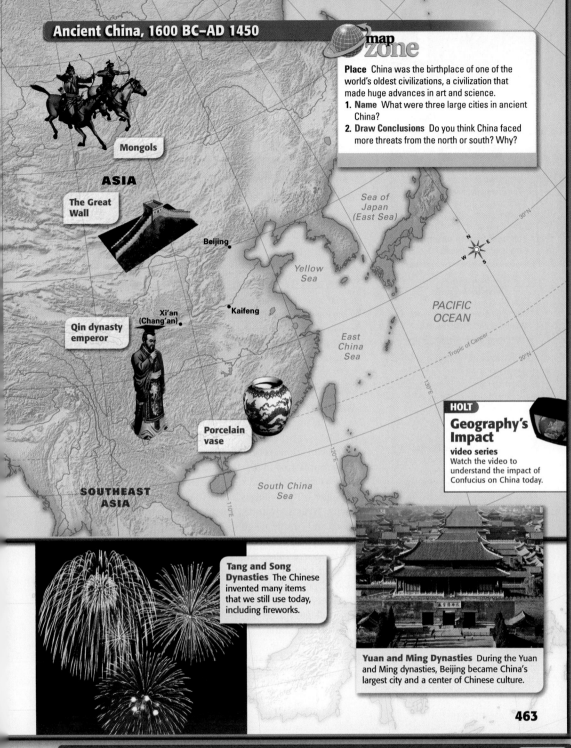

map zone

Place China was the birthplace of one of the world's oldest civilizations, a civilization that made huge advances in art and science.

1. **Name** What were three large cities in ancient China?
2. **Draw Conclusions** Do you think China faced more threats from the north or south? Why?

Mongols

ASIA

The Great Wall

Beijing

Sea of Japan (East Sea)

Yellow Sea

Qin dynasty emperor

Xi'an (Chang'an)

Kaifeng

PACIFIC OCEAN

East China Sea

Tropic of Cancer

Porcelain vase

SOUTHEAST ASIA

South China Sea

HOLT

Geography's Impact

video series

Watch the video to understand the impact of Confucius on China today.

Tang and Song Dynasties The Chinese invented many items that we still use today, including fireworks.

Yuan and Ming Dynasties During the Yuan and Ming dynasties, Beijing became China's largest city and a center of Chinese culture.

463

Critical Thinking: Analyzing Visuals

At Level

Connecting Ancient China to the Modern World

1. Ask students to review the fireworks photo. Note that gunpowder was invented by the Chinese and initially only used for entertainment. Today, Chinese New Year is celebrated using fireworks, which are set off until dawn to attract the attention of benevolent gods and to scare away evil spirits. Have students describe the symbolism attached to fireworks used on July 4 in the United States.

2. Ask students to review the photo labeled "Yuan and Ming Dynasties." Ask students how the buildings are different from modern buildings

(lack of glass, different roofs). Explain that many of these buildings were built for the government. Ask students to compare them with buildings like the U.S. capitol and the White House. In what ways are they similar? *(large, impressive structures meant to show the power and strength of the government and country)* How are they different? *(different styles,* materials)

3. Remind students that connecting ancient cultures to today can help them as they study a historical period. **LS Visual/Spatial**

• Chapter Preview •

Explore the Map and Pictures

Ancient China, 1600 BC–AD 1450 Over a period of about 3000 years, Chinese civilizations existed under many different dynasties. Each developed a unique form of government. At the same time, differing religious and philosophical beliefs grew and changed and Chinese scholars and artists made great advances. Although there was some contact between the Chinese civilization and others, China generally remained isolated. Ask students to review the map and icons and suggest reasons the influence of other groups on Chinese culture was limited. *Mountains to the southwest and desert to the west made travel and trade difficult; the Great Wall helped protect China from invaders from the north and west.*

⚜ Map Zone Transparency: Ancient China, 1600 BC–AD 1450

Analyzing Visuals Ask students to look closely at the photo labeled "Early China." Ask them how archeologists might have identified this clay figure as a soldier. *(heavy coat looks like armor or other protection)*

HOLT

Geography's Impact

▶ video series
See the Video Teacher's Guide for strategies for using the chapter video to teach about the impact of Confucius on China today.

go.hrw.com

Online Resources

Chapter Resources:
KEYWORD: SK9 CH15
Teacher Resources:
KEYWORD: SK9 TEACHER

Answers

Map Zone 1. *Beijing, Kaifeng, Xi'an;* **2.** *possible answer—from the north, because of the Great Wall and the fact that the Mongols are illustrated coming from the north*

463

Bellringer

If YOU lived there. . . Use the **Daily Bellringer Transparency** to help students answer the question.

 Daily Bellringer Transparency, Section 1

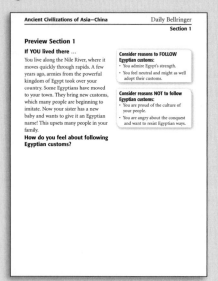

Key Terms and Places

 RF: Vocabulary Builder, Section 1

Taking Notes

Have students copy the graphic organizer onto their own paper and then use it to take notes on the section. This activity will prepare students for the Section Assessment, in which they will complete a graphic organizer that builds on the information using the Critical Thinking Skill: Analyzing.

Answers

Reading Check *as early as 7000 BC, in the middle Chang Jiang Valley and along the Huang He*

Early China

What You Will Learn...

Main Ideas

1. Chinese civilization began along two rivers.
2. The Shang dynasty was the first known dynasty to rule China.
3. The Zhou and Qin dynasties changed Chinese society and made great advances.

The Big Idea

Early Chinese history was shaped by three dynasties—the Shang, the Zhou, and the Qin.

Key Terms and Places

Chang Jiang, *p. 464*
Huang He, *p. 464*
mandate of heaven, *p. 466*
Xi'an, *p. 467*
Great Wall, *p. 467*

TAKING NOTES Draw a chart like the one below. As you read this section, fill in the chart with details about each period in China's early history.

Beginnings	Shang dynasty	Zhou dynasty	Qin dynasty

If YOU lived there...

You are the ruler of China, and hundreds of thousands of people look to you for protection. For many years, your country has lived in peace. Large cities have grown up, and traders travel freely from place to place. Now, however, a new threat looms. Invaders from the north are threatening China's borders. Frightened by the ferocity of these invaders, the people turn to you for help.

What will you do to protect your people?

BUILDING BACKGROUND As in India, people in China first settled near rivers. Two rivers were particularly important in early China— the Huang He and the Chang Jiang. Along these rivers, people began to farm, cities grew up, and China's government was born. The head of that government was an emperor, the ruler of all China.

Chinese Civilization Begins

As early as 7000 BC people had begun to farm in China. They grew rice in the middle **Chang Jiang** Valley. North, along the **Huang He**, the land was better for growing cereals such as millet and wheat. At the same time, people domesticated animals such as pigs and sheep. Supported by these sources of food, China's population grew. Villages appeared along the rivers.

Some of the villages along the Huang He grew into large towns. Walls surrounded these towns to defend them against floods and hostile neighbors. In towns like these, the Chinese left many artifacts, such as arrowheads, fishhooks, tools, and pottery. Some village sites even contained pieces of cloth.

Over time, Chinese culture became more advanced. After 3000 BC people began to use potter's wheels to make many types of pottery. They also learned to dig water wells. As populations grew, villages spread out over larger areas in both northern and southeastern China.

READING CHECK **Analyzing** When and where did China's earliest civilizations develop?

Teach the Big Idea

At Level

Early China

1. **Teach** Ask students the questions in the Main Idea boxes under Direct Teach.

2. **Apply** Write the following two labels for students to see: Civilization Begins and First Dynasties. Organize the students into two groups, one for each label. Then have each group work together to identify the key points, concepts, and terms that pertain to their topic. Have each group present these main ideas to the class in the form of a skit. **LS Visual/Spatial, Verbal/Linguistic**

3. **Review** As each group presents its skit, have students take notes on the main ideas from their presentation. Students can use these notes as a review of the section.

4. **Practice/Homework** Have each student select a skit other than the one on which he or she worked. Have students write reviews of the skit, making sure to state the main ideas presented. **LS Verbal/Linguistic**

Alternative Assessment Handbook, Rubrics 33: Skits and Reader's Theater; and 37: Writing Assignments

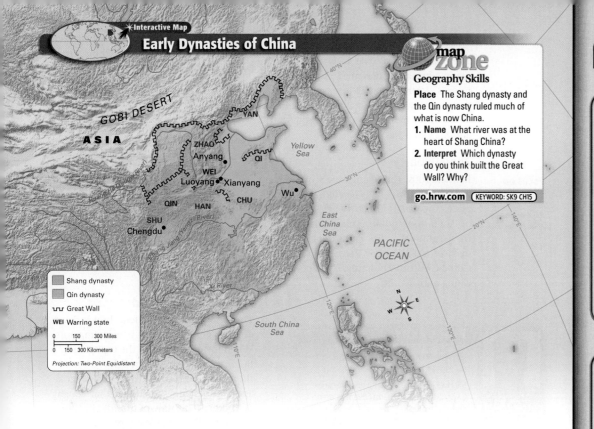

Interactive Map
Early Dynasties of China

GOBI DESERT

ASIA

ZHAO
Anyang
YAN
WEI
QI
Luoyang • Xianyang
QIN HAN CHU
SHU
Chengdu
Wu

Yellow Sea

East China Sea

PACIFIC OCEAN

South China Sea

Xi River

Legend:
- Shang dynasty
- Qin dynasty
- Great Wall
- **WEI** Warring state

0   150   300 Miles
0   150   300 Kilometers
Projection: Two-Point Equidistant

map zone

Geography Skills

Place The Shang dynasty and the Qin dynasty ruled much of what is now China.
1. **Name** What river was at the heart of Shang China?
2. **Interpret** Which dynasty do you think built the Great Wall? Why?

go.hrw.com   KEYWORD: SK9 CH15

Shang Dynasty

As time passed, dynasties, or families, of strong rulers began to take power in China. The first dynasty for which we have clear evidence is the Shang, which was firmly established by the 1500s BC. Strongest in the Huang He Valley, the Shang ruled a broad area of northern China, as you can see on the map. Shang emperors ruled in China until the 1100s BC.

The Shang made many advances, including China's first writing system. This system used more than 2,000 symbols to express words or ideas. Although the system has gone through changes over the years, the Chinese symbols used today are based on those of the Shang period.

Many examples of Shang writing that we have found were on cattle bones and turtle shells. Priests had carved questions about the future on bones or shells, which were then heated, causing them to crack. The priests believed they could "read" these cracks to predict the future.

In addition to writing, the Shang also made other achievements. Artisans made beautiful bronze containers for cooking and religious ceremonies. They also made axes, knives, and ornaments from jade. Soldiers developed war chariots, powerful bows, and bronze armor. The Shang also invented a calendar based on the cycles of the moon.

READING CHECK **Summarizing** What were two Shang achievements?

ANCIENT CIVILIZATIONS OF ASIA—CHINA **465**

Main Idea

❸ Zhou and Qin Dynasties

The Zhou and Qin dynasties changed Chinese society and made great advances.

Identify Who was at the top of Zhou society? *the emperor*

Explain What started the Warring States period? *Lords became less loyal to the emperors and many refused to fight when invaders attacked in 771 BC, so the emperor was overthrown.*

Draw Conclusions Why do you think Shi Huangdi set up a uniform money system? *possible answer—to make it easier and smoother for people to buy and sell goods*

Info to Know

Offerings to Ancestors During the Shang dynasty, people made offerings of food and drink to the spirits of their ancestors at special religious ceremonies. They prepared food for the dead as though they were preparing a large meal for the living. The food was offered to the ancestors in elaborately decorated cauldrons or dishes.

Zhou and Qin Dynasties

The Shang dynasty was only the first of many dynasties described in Chinese records. After the Shang lost power, other dynasties rose up to take control of China. Two of those dynasties were the Zhou (JOH) and the Qin (CHIN).

Zhou Dynasty

FOCUS ON READING
Which dynasty ruled earlier, the Zhou or the Qin?

In the 1100s, the Shang rulers of China were overthrown in a rebellion. In their place, the rebels from the western part of China took power. This event marked the beginning of the Zhou dynasty. This dynasty lasted longer than any other in Chinese history. Zhou rulers held power in China until 771 BC.

BIOGRAPHY

Emperor Shi Huangdi
(c. 259–210 BC)

Shi Huangdi was a powerful emperor and a very strict one. He demanded that everyone in China believe the same things he did. To prevent people from having other ideas, he ordered all books that did not agree with his beliefs burned. When a group of scholars protested the burning of these books, Shi Huangdi had them buried alive. These actions led many Chinese people to resent the emperor. As a result, they were eager to bring the Qin dynasty to an end.

The Zhou claimed that they had been chosen by heaven to rule China. They believed that no one could rule without heaven's permission. This idea that heaven chose China's ruler and gave him or her power was called the **mandate of heaven**.

Under the Zhou, a new political order formed in China. The emperor was at the top of society. Everything in China belonged to him, and everyone had to be loyal to him.

Emperors gave land to people in exchange for loyalty or military service. Those people who received this land became lords. Below the lords were peasants, or farmers who owned little land. In addition to growing their own food, peasants had to grow food for lords.

Warring States Period

The Zhou political system broke down as lords grew less loyal to the emperors. When invaders attacked the capital in 771 BC, many lords would not fight. As a result, the emperor was overthrown. China broke apart into many kingdoms that fought each other. This time of disorder in China is called the Warring States period.

In 1974 archaeologists found the tomb of Emperor Shi Huangdi near Xi'an and made an amazing discovery. Buried close to the emperor was an army of more than 6,000 life-size terra-cotta, or clay, soldiers. They were designed to be with Shi Huangdi in the afterlife. In other nearby chambers of the tomb there were another 1,400 clay figures of cavalry and chariots.

466 CHAPTER 15

Differentiating Instruction

Special Needs Learners

1. Help students identify the accomplishments of the Shang dynasty by drawing the chart for students to see. Omit the blue, italicized answers.

2. Divide the class into mixed ability pairs. Have each student draw the chart on his or her own paper. Then have students work with their partners to complete the chart.
   LS Verbal/Linguistic, Visual/Spatial

   Alternative Assessment Handbook, Rubric 7: Charts

Shang Dynasty	
religion	*priests used bones to make predictions*
society	*royal family/nobles at highest level, artisans at middle level, farmers, slaves at lower levels*
achievements	*writing system, use of bronze, calendar, war chariots, and bows*

Answers

Focus on Reading *the Zhou*

Qin Dynasty

The Warring States period came to an end when one state became strong enough to defeat all its rivals. That state was called Qin. In 221 BC, a king from Qin managed to unify all of China under his control and name himself emperor.

As emperor, the king took a new name. He called himself Shi Huangdi (SHEE hwahng-dee), a name that means "first emperor." Shi Huangdi was a very strict ruler, but he was an effective ruler as well. He expanded the size of China both to the north and to the south, as the map at the beginning of this section shows.

Shi Huangdi greatly changed Chinese politics. Unlike the Zhou rulers, he refused to share his power with anyone. Lords who had enjoyed many rights before now lost those rights. In addition, he ordered thousands of noble families to move to his capital, now called **Xi'an** (SHEE-AHN). He thought nobles that he kept nearby would be less likely to rebel against him.

The Qin dynasty did not last long. While Shi Huangdi lived, he was strong enough to keep China unified. The rulers who followed him, however, were not as strong. In fact, China began to break apart within a few years of Shi Huangdi's death. Rebellions began all around China, and the country fell into civil war.

Qin Achievements

Although the Qin did not rule for long, they saw great advances in China. As emperor, Shi Huangdi worked to make sure that people all over China acted and thought the same way. He created a system of laws that would apply equally to people in all parts of China. He also set up a new system of money. Before, people in each region had used local currencies. He also created a uniform system of writing that eliminated minor differences between regions.

The Qin's best known achievements, though, were in building. Under the Qin, the Chinese built a huge network of roads and canals. These roads and canals linked distant parts of the empire to make travel and trade easier.

To protect China from invasion, Shi Huangdi built the **Great Wall**, a barrier that linked earlier walls that stood near China's northern border. Building the wall took years of labor from hundreds of thousands of workers. Later dynasties added to the wall, parts of which still stand today.

SUMMARY AND PREVIEW Early Chinese history was shaped by the Shang, Zhou, and Qin dynasties. Next, you will read about another strong dynasty, the Han.

Section 1 Assessment

go.hrw.com
Online Quiz
KEYWORD: SK9 HP15

Reviewing Ideas, Terms, and Places

1. **a. Identify** On what rivers did Chinese civilization begin?
   b. Analyze What advances did the early Chinese make?
2. **a. Describe** What area did the Shang rule?
   b. Evaluate What do you think was the Shang dynasty's most important achievement? Why?
3. **a. Define** What is the **mandate of heaven**?
   b. Generalize How did Shi Huangdi change China?

Critical Thinking

4. **Analyzing** Draw a chart like the one shown here. Using your notes, write details about the achievements and political system of China's early dynasties.

	Achievements	Political System
Shang		
Zhou		
Qin		

FOCUS ON WRITING

5. **Identifying Advances** The Shang, Zhou, and Qin made some of the greatest advances in Chinese history. Which of these will you mention in your magazine article? Write down some notes.

Did you know . . .

Modern Chinese writing is very complex. While the English alphabet uses 26 letters to spell words, there are more than 1,000 basic characters in the Chinese language. Characters are combined to represent more complex ideas. By some estimates, there are close to 40,000 characters in the Chinese writing system!

Review & Assess

Close

Have students write a short paragraph to summarize the main ideas from this section.

Review

Online Quiz, Section 1

Assess

SE Section 1 Assessment
PASS: Section 1 Quiz
Alternative Assessment Handbook

Reteach/Classroom Intervention

Interactive Reader and Study Guide, Section 1
Interactive Skills Tutor CD-ROM

Section 1 Assessment Answers

1. **a.** Huang He and Chang Jiang
   b. used potter's wheels, dug wells for water, domesticated animals

2. **a.** the Huang He valley in northern China
   b. possible answer—the development of China's first writing system, because people could now keep records of things

3. **a.** the idea that heaven chose China's ruler and gave that ruler power
   b. expanded China's borders, took power from lords, forced nobles to move to capital

4. possible answers: Shang Achievements—writing system, use of bronze and jade, chariots, calendar; Political System—ruled by emperors; Zhou Achievements—lasted longer than any other in Chinese history; Political System—mandate of heaven, everything belonged to emperor; Qin Achievements—new systems of laws, money, writing, roads and canals, Great Wall; Political System—lords lost power

5. Choices will vary, but should be supported by reasons why choices were made.

Bellringer

If YOU lived there. . . Use the **Daily Bellringer Transparency** to help students answer the question.

📦 Daily Bellringer Transparency, Section 2

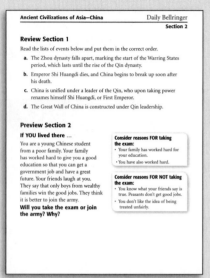

Academic Vocabulary

Review with students the high-use academic term in this section.

innovation a new idea, method, or device (p. 472)

📄 **RF:** Vocabulary Builder, Section 2

Taking Notes

Have students copy the graphic organizer onto their own paper and then use it to take notes on the section. This activity will prepare students for the Section Assessment, in which they will complete a graphic organizer that builds on the information using the Critical Thinking Skill: Analyzing.

SECTION 2

The Han Dynasty

If YOU lived there...

You are a young Chinese student from a poor family. Your family has worked hard to give you a good education so that you can get a government job and have a great future. Your friends laugh at you. They say that only boys from wealthy families win the good jobs. They think it is better to join the army.

Will you take the exam or join the army? Why?

What You Will Learn...

Main Ideas

1. Han dynasty government was largely based on the ideas of Confucius.
2. Han China supported and strengthened family life.
3. The Han made many achievements in art, literature, and learning.

The Big Idea

The Han dynasty created a new form of government that valued family, art, and learning.

Key Terms

sundial, *p. 472*
seismograph, *p. 472*
acupuncture, *p. 473*

TAKING NOTES As you read, take notes on Han government, family life, and achievements. Use a diagram like the one here to help you organize your notes.

BUILDING BACKGROUND Though it was harsh, the rule of the first Qin emperor helped to unify northern China. With the building of what would become the Great Wall, he strengthened defenses in the north. But his successor could not hold on to power. The Qin gave way to a new dynasty that would last 400 years.

Han Dynasty Government

When the Qin dynasty collapsed, many groups fought for power. After years of fighting, an army led by Liu Bang (lee-oo bang) won control. Liu Bang became the first emperor of the Han dynasty, which lasted more than 400 years.

The Rise of a New Dynasty

Liu Bang, a peasant, was able to become emperor in large part because of the Chinese belief in the mandate of heaven. He was the first common person to become emperor. He earned people's loyalty and trust. In addition, he was well liked by both soldiers and peasants, which helped him keep control.

Time Line

The Han Dynasty

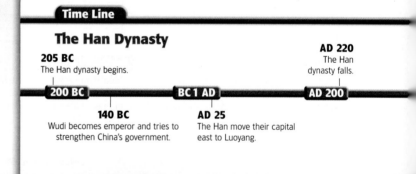

205 BC
The Han dynasty begins.

200 BC

140 BC
Wudi becomes emperor and tries to strengthen China's government.

BC 1 AD

AD 25
The Han move their capital east to Luoyang.

AD 200

AD 220
The Han dynasty falls.

468 CHAPTER 15

Teach the Big Idea

At Level

The Han Dynasty

1. **Teach** Ask students the questions in the Main Idea boxes under Direct Teach.

2. **Apply** Have students create an outline of the section. They should list all major heads and subheads that appear in this section. As students read, have them identify two or three supporting details within every head or subhead. Remind students to also include any key terms or people from the section.
   LS Verbal/Linguistic

3. **Review** As a review of the section, ask volunteers to share individual parts of their

outlines and record the information for all to see. Have students add missing information and correct inaccurate information.

4. **Practice/Homework** Have each student use his or her outline to write five multiple-choice questions that cover important information from the section.
   LS Verbal/Linguistic

📄 Alternative Assessment Handbook, Rubric 1: Acquiring Information

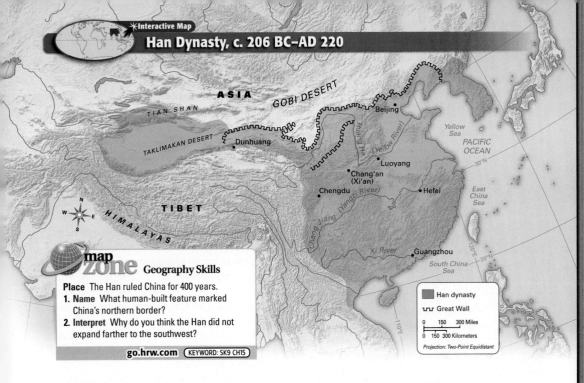

A S I A

GOBI DESERT

TIAN SHAN

TAKLIMAKAN DESERT • Dunhuang

Beijing •

Yellow Sea

PACIFIC OCEAN

Huang He (Yellow River)

• Luoyang

• Chang'an (Xi'an)

• Chengdu   • Hefei

East China Sea

TIBET

HIMALAYAS

Chang Jiang (Yangzi River)

Xi River

• Guangzhou

South China Sea

map Zone Geography Skills

Place The Han ruled China for 400 years.
1. **Name** What human-built feature marked China's northern border?
2. **Interpret** Why do you think the Han did not expand farther to the southwest?

go.hrw.com KEYWORD: SK9 CH15

Han dynasty

ᒣᒣ Great Wall

0   150   300 Miles

0 150 300 Kilometers

Projection: Two-Point Equidistant

Liu Bang's rule was different from the strict government of the Qin. He wanted to free people from harsh government policies. He lowered taxes for farmers and made punishments less severe. He gave large blocks of land to his supporters.

In addition to setting new policies, Liu Bang changed the way government worked. He set up a government structure that built on the foundation begun by the Qin. He also relied on educated officials to help him rule.

Wudi Creates a New Government

In 140 BC Emperor Wudi (WOO-dee) took the throne. He wanted to create a stronger government. To do that, he took land from the lords, raised taxes, and put the supply of grain under government control. He also made Confucianism China's official government philosophy.

Confucianism is a philosophy based on the teachings of a man named Confucius. It emphasizes the importance of ethics and moral values, such as respect for elders and loyalty toward family members. Under the Han, government officials were expected to practice Confucianism. Wudi even began a university to teach Confucian ideas.

Studying Confucianism could also get a person a good job in China. If a person passed an exam on Confucian teachings, he could get a position working for the government. Not just anyone could take the test, though. The exams were only open to people who had been recommended for government service already. As a result, wealthy or influential families continued to control the government.

READING CHECK Analyzing How was the Han government based on the ideas of Confucius?

FOCUS ON READING

Who ruled first, Liu Bang or Wudi?

ANCIENT CIVILIZATIONS OF ASIA–CHINA **469**

Direct Teach

Main Idea

❶ Han Dynasty Government

Han dynasty government was largely based on the ideas of Confucius.

Summarize What changes did Liu Bang bring to China? *He freed people from harsh government policies, lowered taxes, made punishments less severe, gave blocks of land to his supporters, and used educated officials to help him rule.*

Analyze How did Wudi strengthen China's government? *He took lands from lords, raised taxes, placed the supply of grain under government control, made people take exams and get recommendations for government service.*

Elaborate Would you rather have lived under the rule of Liu Bang or Wudi? Why? *Answers will vary, but students should show an understanding of the policies of the emperor selected.*

📄 **RF:** Biography, Liu Bang

📄 **RF:** Biography, Wudi

📦 Map Zone Transparency: Han Dynasty, c. 206 BC–AD 220

Critical Thinking: Evaluating   At Level

Writing Resumés

1. Discuss with students what qualities government officials during the Han dynasty possessed.

2. Tell students that they will be writing a resumé for an imaginary person seeking a job in the Han government. Have students provide details in the resumés regarding the person's education, family connections, and other qualifications.

3. Remind students to refer to the portion of the section that discusses the necessary

qualification for obtaining a position in the Han government.

4. When students have finished, have them exchange resumés with another student. Then ask students to discuss whether or not they believe that resumé would earn a job in the Han government. **LS** Verbal/Linguistic, Interpersonal

📄 Alternative Assessment Handbook, Rubric 31: Resumés

Answers

Map Zone 1. *the Great Wall;*
2. *the region to the southwest was very mountainous.*
Focus on Reading *Liu Bang*
Reading Check *Confucianism became government philosophy; government officials had to pass tests on Confucian teachings.*

❷ Family Life

Han China supported and strengthened family life.

Describe What were the social classes in Han China? *upper—emperor, court, scholars; second class—peasants; third class—artisans; lowest—merchants*

Analyze Why were wealthy merchants in the lowest class? *did not produce anything of their own, only bought and sold goods made by others*

Elaborate How were Han social classes different than most social divisions? *They were not based on wealth or power.*

Activity **A Day in the Life of . . .**
Have students write a description of a typical day in the life of a peasant in Han China.

📝 Alternative Assessment Handbook, Rubric 37: Writing Assignments

Info to Know

Dressing the Part Even the clothes the ancient Chinese wore had social distinction. People in the upper classes, such as members of the emperor's court and high-ranking government officials, wore fine robes made of silk, a material that was both luxurious and expensive. The lower classes wore garments made of rough fabrics. Wearing silk was not just a matter of being able to afford the material; the supply of fabrics was regulated by the government. In later dynasties, some merchants who dealt in silk were even punished for wearing silk clothing.

Family Life

The Han period was a time of great social change in China. Class structure became more rigid. The family once again became important within Chinese society.

Social Classes

Based on the Confucian system, people were divided into four classes. The upper class was made up of the emperor, his court, and scholars who held government positions. The second class, the largest, was made up of the peasants. Next were artisans who produced items for daily life and some luxury goods. Merchants were the lowest class because they did not actually produce anything. They only bought and sold what others made. The military was not a class in the Confucian system. Still, joining the army offered men a chance to rise in social status because the military was considered part of the government.

This Han artifact is an oil lamp held by a servant.

Lives of Rich and Poor

The classes only divided people into social rank. They did not indicate wealth or power. For instance, even though peasants made up the second highest class, they were poor. Many merchants, on the other hand, were wealthy and powerful despite being in the lowest class.

People's lifestyles varied according to wealth. The emperor and his court lived in a large palace. Less important officials lived in multilevel houses built around courtyards. Many of these wealthy families owned large estates and employed laborers to work the land. Some families even hired private armies to defend their estates.

The wealthy filled their homes with expensive decorations. These included paintings, pottery, bronze lamps, and jade figures. Rich families hired musicians for entertainment. Even the tombs of dead family members were filled with beautiful, expensive objects.

Most people in Han China, however, did not live so comfortably. Nearly 60 million people lived in China during the Han dynasty, and about 90 percent of them were peasants who lived in the countryside. Peasants put in long, tiring days working the land. Whether it was in the millet fields of the north or in the rice paddies of the south, the work was hard. In the winter, peasants were forced to work on building projects for the government. Heavy taxes and bad weather forced many farmers to sell their land and work for rich landowners. By the last years of the Han dynasty, only a few farmers were independent.

Chinese peasants lived simple lives. They wore plain clothing made of fiber from a native plant. The main foods they ate were cooked grains like barley. Most peasants lived in small villages. Their small, wood-framed houses had walls made of mud or stamped earth.

Differentiating Instruction

Struggling Readers

1. Discuss with students the social structure under the Han dynasty. Ask students to identify the various social classes and what people were represented in each class.

2. Have students create a diagram or illustration that shows the social order of Han China. Ask students to include information that clearly shows the occupations of the people in each social class.

3. Then have students compare this social order to the social divisions that existed under the Zhou dynasty. Have students examine the differences between the two social orders. How did society change in China from the Zhou dynasty to the Han dynasty? Have each student write a short paragraph in which they explain the similarities and differences between the two.

4. Ask volunteers to share their illustrations and explanations with the class. **LS** **Visual/Spatial, Verbal/Linguistic**

📝 Alternative Assessment Handbook, Rubrics 3: Artwork; and 9: Comparing and Contrasting

The Importance of Family

Honoring one's family was an important duty in Han China. In this painting, people give thanks before their family shrine. Only the men can participate. The women watch from inside the house.

ANALYZING VISUALS
How are these men giving thanks?

The Revival of the Family

Since Confucianism was the government's official philosophy during Wudi's reign, Confucian teachings about the family were also honored. Children were taught from birth to respect their elders. Disobeying one's parents was a crime. Even emperors had a duty to respect their parents.

Confucius had taught that the father was the head of the family. Within the family, the father had absolute power. The Han taught that it was a woman's duty to obey her husband, and children had to obey their father.

Han officials believed that if the family was strong and people obeyed the father, then they would also obey the emperor. Since the Han rewarded strong family ties and respect for elders, some men even gained government jobs based on the respect they showed their parents.

Children were encouraged to serve their parents. They were also expected to honor dead parents with ceremonies and offerings. All members of a family were expected to care for family burial sites.

Chinese parents valued boys more highly than girls. This was because sons carried on the family line and took care of their parents when they were old. On the other hand, daughters became part of their husband's family. According to a Chinese proverb, "Raising daughters is like raising children for another family." Some women, however, still gained power. They could gain influence in their sons' families. An older widow could even become the head of the family.

READING CHECK Identifying Cause and Effect
Why did the family take on such importance during the Han dynasty?

Recall What were Confucius's ideas about family? *The father was the head of the family and had absolute power; wives and children had to obey their husbands and fathers.*

Explain Why were sons more highly valued that daughters? *Sons carried on the family line and took care of parents as they got older, while daughters went to live with their husbands' families.*

Activity Flowcharts Have students create a flowchart that shows the relationship and position of family members in Han China.

Info to Know

Respect for Family and Elders Teachings about respect for family and parents were taken very seriously in Han China. Confucius himself believed a dutiful child should not only respect his or her father while he was alive, but continue to do so after his death. Other Chinese philosophers even went so far as to describe evil-doers as people who, among other things, lied, disobeyed, or provoked their parents or did not take the spirits of their ancestors seriously.

Collaborative Learning

At Level

Documentary: Family Life in Han China

1. Review with students the Chinese attitudes toward family life and respect for parents. Ask students to discuss the behavior expected of fathers, sons, and women within a Chinese family in Han China. Ask students to identify behavior that would be acceptable and unacceptable.

2. Organize the class into small groups. Have each group prepare a script for a documentary film that focuses on family life in Han China. Remind students to present information about

family duties and the roles of fathers, wives, and children. Students may wish to use the library, Internet, or other resources to find additional information on the topic.

3. Have each group videotape their documentary or perform it live for the class to see.
LS Visual/Spatial, Verbal/Linguistic, Interpersonal

Alternative Assessment Handbook, Rubrics 14: Group Activity; and 33: Skits and Reader's Theater

Answers

Analyzing Visuals *by bowing before their family shrine*

Reading Check *Han leaders promoted Confucianism, which emphasized strong family ties.*

❸ Han Achievements

The Han made many achievements in art, literature, and learning.

Identify What were some of the cultural and scientific achievements of the Han? *artwork, poetry, history, paper, sundial, the seismograph, and acupuncture*

Contrast How did the *fu* style of poetry differ from the *shi* style? Fu *poetry combined prose and poetry in a long work of literature, while shi used short lines of verse that could be sung.*

Evaluate What do you think was the most important invention of the Han dynasty? Why? *possible answers— acupuncture because it improved medicine and is still used today; paper because it is part of our everyday lives.*

Connect to Science

Seismographs The Chinese seismograph pictured above was a very simple device. It showed when an earthquake occurred and the direction of the earthquake. Modern-day seismographs still serve the same function, but they also record the strength and duration of an earthquake. Scientists use several seismographs in different locations to pinpoint the epicenter of an earthquake. The scale used to measure the strength of an earthquake is known as the Richter scale and was developed by seismologists in 1935.

go.hrw.com
Online Resources

Online Resources:
KEYWORD: SK9 CH15
ACTIVITY: Chinese Art

Han Achievements

During the Han dynasty, the Chinese made many advances in art and learning. Some of these advances are shown here.

Science

This is a model of an ancient Chinese seismograph. When an earthquake struck, a lever inside caused a ball to drop from a dragon's mouth into a toad's mouth, indicating the direction from which the earthquake had come.

Han Achievements

Han rule was a time of great achievements. Art and literature thrived, and inventors developed many useful devices.

Art and Literature

The Chinese of the Han period produced many works of art. They became experts at figure painting—a style of painting that includes portraits of people. Portraits often showed religious figures and Confucian scholars. Han artists also painted realistic scenes from everyday life. Their creations covered the walls of palaces and tombs.

In literature, Han China is known for its poetry. Poets developed new styles of verse, including the *fu* style, which was the most popular. *Fu* poets combined prose and poetry to create long literary works. Another style, called *shi*, featured short lines of verse that could be sung. Many Han rulers hired poets known for the beauty of their verse.

ACADEMIC VOCABULARY
innovation a new idea, method, or device

Han writers also produced important works of history. One historian by the name of Sima Qian wrote a complete history of all the dynasties through the early Han. His format and style became the model for later historical writings.

Inventions and Advances

The Han Chinese invented one item that we use every day—paper. They made it by grinding plant fibers, such as mulberry bark and hemp, into a paste. Then they let it dry in sheets. Chinese scholars produced books by pasting several pieces of paper together into a long sheet. Then they rolled the sheet into a scroll.

The Han also made other **innovations** in science. These included the sundial and the seismograph. A **sundial** is a device that uses the position of shadows cast by the sun to tell the time of day. It was an early type of clock. A **seismograph** is a device that measures the strength of earthquakes. Han emperors were very interested in knowing

Cross-Discipline Activity: Literature   Above Level

Fu and *Shi* Poems   Research Required

1. Review with the class the achievements in literature of the Han dynasty.

2. Organize the class into pairs. Have each pair use the library, Internet, or other sources to research *fu* and *shi* poems. Have each pair select one poem of either type. Tell students that they will create a scroll on which they will copy and illustrate their poems.

3. Check to make sure that students understand the meaning of the poems they selected. Remind students that Han paintings often depicted realistic scenes from everyday life.

4. Have volunteers from each group explain the Chinese poem they selected and then read their poems aloud.

5. Expand the activity by having students write their own *fu* or *shi* poems and illustrate.
LS **Visual/Spatial, Verbal/Linguistic**

Alternative Assessment Handbook, Rubrics 3: Artwork; and 26: Poems and Songs

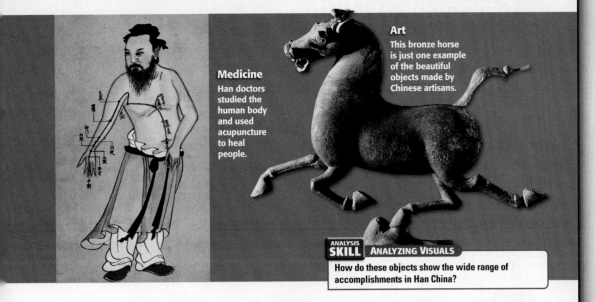

Medicine
Han doctors studied the human body and used acupuncture to heal people.

Art
This bronze horse is just one example of the beautiful objects made by Chinese artisans.

ANALYSIS SKILL **ANALYZING VISUALS**
How do these objects show the wide range of accomplishments in Han China?

about the movements of the Earth. They believed that earthquakes were signs of future evil events.

Another Han innovation, acupuncture (AK-yoo-punk-cher), improved medicine. **Acupuncture** is the practice of inserting fine needles through the skin at specific points to cure disease or relieve pain. Many Han inventions in science and medicine are still used today.

READING CHECK Categorizing What advances did the Chinese make during the Han period?

SUMMARY AND PREVIEW Rulers of the Han dynasty based their government on Confucianism, which strengthened family bonds in China. In addition, art and learning thrived under Han rule. In the next section you will learn about two dynasties that also made great advances, the Tang and the Song.

Section 2 Assessment

go.hrw.com
Online Quiz
KEYWORD: SK9 HP15

Reviewing Ideas, Terms, and People

1. a. **Identify** What is Confucianism? How did it affect the government during the Han dynasty?
   b. **Summarize** How did Emperor Wudi create a strong central government?
   c. **Evaluate** Do you think that an exam system is the best way to make sure that people are fairly chosen for government jobs? Why or why not?
2. a. **Describe** What was the son's role in the family?
   b. **Contrast** How did living conditions for the wealthy differ from those of the peasants during the Han dynasty?
3. **Identify** What device did the Chinese invent to measure the strength of earthquakes?

Critical Thinking

4. **Analyzing** Use your notes to complete this diagram about how Confucianism influenced Han government and family.

Government

Confucianism

Family

FOCUS ON WRITING

5. **Analyzing the Han Dynasty** The Han dynasty was one of the most influential in all of Chinese history. How will you describe the dynasty's many achievements in your article? Make a list of achievements you want to include.

ANCIENT CIVILIZATIONS OF ASIA—CHINA **473**

473

Geography and History

Activity Remembering Successful Merchants

Have students select one of the merchants shown on these pages and write an obituary for him. Obituaries should include information on how the merchants benefited from Silk Road trade. Encourage students to use their imaginations to fill in other details of the merchants' lives, but to stay within historical possibility.

LS Verbal/Linguistic

Alternative Assessment Handbook, Rubric 37: Writing Assignments

Teaching Tip

Movement Remind your students that movement is one of the five themes of geography. This theme deals not just with the migration of people, but also the movement of goods and ideas.

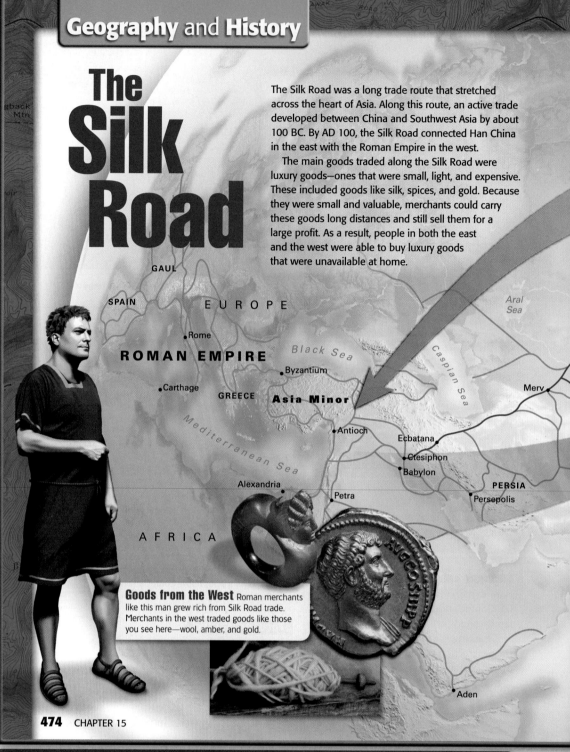

The Silk Road

The Silk Road was a long trade route that stretched across the heart of Asia. Along this route, an active trade developed between China and Southwest Asia by about 100 BC. By AD 100, the Silk Road connected Han China in the east with the Roman Empire in the west.

The main goods traded along the Silk Road were luxury goods—ones that were small, light, and expensive. These included goods like silk, spices, and gold. Because they were small and valuable, merchants could carry these goods long distances and still sell them for a large profit. As a result, people in both the east and the west were able to buy luxury goods that were unavailable at home.

Goods from the West Roman merchants like this man grew rich from Silk Road trade. Merchants in the west traded goods like those you see here—wool, amber, and gold.

474 CHAPTER 15

Cross-Discipline Activity: Economics

At Level

Long Road, High Price

1. Organize students into groups. Have students in each group decide if they want to represent a Roman or Chinese merchant and what items they want to trade on the Silk Road. They should also assign prices that manufacturers charge a trader for the merchandise.

2. Then have each group create a flowchart, showing where the merchandise is sold to the next trader and how much that trader pays for it. The goods may change hands several times as they make their way along the Silk Road, and each time the price is slightly higher.

3. Ask groups to report on the original and final prices of their merchandise. They should also calculate how much of the final price had been added along the way to the manufacturer's original price. Point out that every time the goods changed hands, a merchant made a profit. **LS Visual/Spatial, Logical/Mathematical**

Alternative Assessment Handbook, Rubric 13: Graphic Organizers

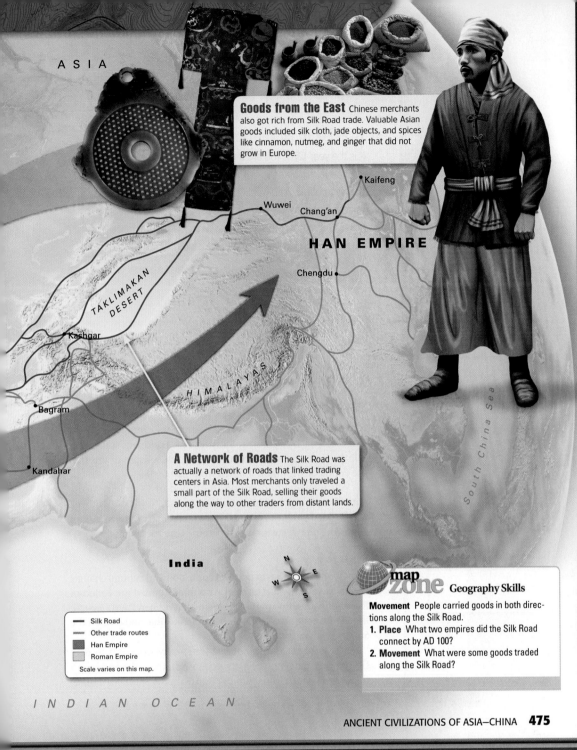

ASIA

Goods from the East Chinese merchants also got rich from Silk Road trade. Valuable Asian goods included silk cloth, jade objects, and spices like cinnamon, nutmeg, and ginger that did not grow in Europe.

Kaifeng

Wuwei
Chang'an

HAN EMPIRE

Chengdu

TAKLIMAKAN DESERT

Kashgar

HIMALAYAS

Bagram

Kandahar

A Network of Roads The Silk Road was actually a network of roads that linked trading centers in Asia. Most merchants only traveled a small part of the Silk Road, selling their goods along the way to other traders from distant lands.

South China Sea

India

- Silk Road
- Other trade routes
- Han Empire
- Roman Empire

Scale varies on this map.

map Zone Geography Skills

Movement People carried goods in both directions along the Silk Road.

1. **Place** What two empires did the Silk Road connect by AD 100?
2. **Movement** What were some goods traded along the Silk Road?

INDIAN OCEAN

ANCIENT CIVILIZATIONS OF ASIA—CHINA **475**

Geography and History

Info to Know

Traveling the Silk Road Today Fascination with the Silk Road has led to increased tourism. Since China opened its doors to foreign tourism, people have been able to travel along part of the Silk Road. Although travel in the harsh climate of western China is only for the hardy tourist, there are plenty of attractions, even in the deserts. Sites include ruined cities and caves full of Buddhist paintings. One city, Kashgar, has a market where tourists can get some idea of what trade along the old Silk Road was like long ago. At the market, people of many nationalities sell spices, wool, livestock, silver knives, and other items. Have students locate the city of Kashgar on the map on this page.

Connect to Science

From Worm to Wonderful Commercial silk is made by a single species of moth larvae. Each larva, or silkworm, lives on a diet of mulberry leaves before spinning a silk thread that wraps around and around to become a cocoon. This thread can be up to 3,000 feet long. To unwind the cocoon, the manufacturer must first find the end of the thread. Workers wash the silk and treat it with various chemicals to make different types of fabric.

Collaborative Learning

Below Level

Silk Road Collage

Prep Required

Materials: art supplies, butcher paper

1. Organize the class into four groups: Places, People, East to West Goods, and West to East Goods.

2. Have the students in the Places group create a large map that shows the roads themselves and important cities along the Silk Road. Have them draw or find pictures of physical features along the route.

3. Have students in the People group create or find images of the people who traveled the

route, the animals that carried their cargo, and the trade caravans.

4. Students from each of the Goods groups should create or find images of goods that were traded along the route.

5. Next, have students create a collage of the Silk Road by placing images on the map created by the Places group. **LS Visual/Spatial**

Alternative Assessment Handbook, Rubric 8: Collages

Answers

Map Zone 1. *the Han Empire and the Roman Empire;* **2.** *silk cloth, jade objects, spices, wool, amber, gold*

475

Bellringer

If YOU lived there. . . Use the **Daily Bellringer Transparency** to help students answer the question.

📄 Daily Bellringer Transparency, Section 3

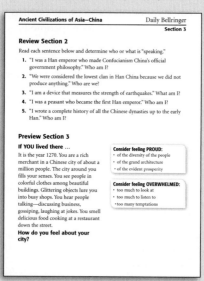

Ancient Civilizations of Asia—China   Daily Bellringer
                                              Section 3

Review Section 2

Read each sentence below and determine who or what is "speaking."

1. "I was a Han emperor who made Confucianism China's official government philosophy." Who am I?
2. "We were considered the lowest clan in Han China because we did not produce anything." Who are we?
3. "I am a device that measures the strength of earthquakes." What am I?
4. "I was a peasant who became the first Han emperor." Who am I?
5. "I wrote a complete history of all the Chinese dynasties up to the early Han." Who am I?

Preview Section 3

If YOU lived there ...

It is the year 1270. You are a rich merchant in a Chinese city of about a million people. The city around you fills your senses. You see people in colorful clothes among beautiful buildings. Glittering objects lure you into busy shops. You hear people talking—discussing business, gossiping, laughing at jokes. You smell delicious food cooking at a restaurant down the street.

How do you feel about your city?

Consider feeling PROUD:
• of the diversity of the people
• of the grand architecture
• of the evident prosperity

Consider feeling OVERWHELMED:
• too much to look at
• too much to listen to
• too many temptations

Key Terms and Places

📄 **RF:** Vocabulary Builder, Section 3

Taking Notes

Have students copy the graphic organizer onto their own paper and then use it to take notes on the section. This activity will prepare students for the Section Assessment, in which they will complete a graphic organizer that builds on the information using the Critical Thinking Skill: Categorizing.

The Sui, Tang, and Song Dynasties

What You Will Learn...

Main Ideas

1. After the Han dynasty, China fell into disorder but was reunified by new dynasties.
2. Cities and trade grew during the Tang and Song dynasties.
3. The Tang and Song dynasties produced fine arts and inventions.

The Big Idea

The Tang and Song dynasties were periods of economic, cultural, and technological accomplishments.

Key Terms and Places

Grand Canal, *p. 476*
Kaifeng, *p. 478*
porcelain, *p. 479*
woodblock printing, *p. 480*
gunpowder, *p. 480*
compass, *p. 480*

TAKING NOTES As you read, look for information about accomplishments of the Tang and Song dynasties. Keep track of these accomplishments in a chart like this one.

Tang dynasty	Song dynasty

If YOU lived there...

It is the year 1270. You are a rich merchant in a Chinese city of about a million people. The city around you fills your senses. You see people in colorful clothes among beautiful buildings. Glittering objects lure you into busy shops. You hear people talking—discussing business, gossiping, laughing at jokes. You smell delicious food cooking at a restaurant down the street.

How do you feel about your city?

BUILDING BACKGROUND The Tang and Song dynasties were periods of great wealth and progress. Changes in farming formed the basis for other advances in Chinese civilization.

Disorder and Reunification

When the Han dynasty collapsed, China split into several rival kingdoms, each ruled by military leaders. Historians sometimes call the time of disorder that followed the collapse of the Han the Period of Disunion. It lasted from 220 to 589.

War was common during the Period of Disunion. At the same time, however, Chinese culture spread. New groups moved into China from nearby areas. Over time, many of these groups adopted Chinese customs and became Chinese themselves.

Sui Dynasty

Finally, after centuries of political confusion and cultural change, China was reunified. The man who finally ended the Period of Disunion was a northern ruler named Yang Jian (YANG jee-EN). In 589, he conquered the south, unified China, and created the Sui (SWAY) dynasty.

The Sui dynasty did not last long, only from 589 to 618. During that time, however, its leaders restored order and began the **Grand Canal**, a canal linking northern and southern China.

Teach the Big Idea

At Level

The Sui, Tang, and Song Dynasties

1. **Teach** Ask students the questions in the Main Idea boxes under Direct Teach.

2. **Apply** Have students write a series of cause-and-effect statements as they read the section. The statements can be simple phrases connected by an arrow. *Possible statements: increased agricultural production—population growth; increased trade—cities grow; cities grow—art flourishes; printing innovations—literature flourishes.* **Ⓛ Verbal/Linguistic**

3. **Review** As you review the section's main ideas, call on students to read aloud their cause-and-effect statements.

4. **Practice/Homework** Have students use the Quick Facts chart in this section to identify important Chinese inventions from this period. Then have students create a collage that illustrates modern uses of these inventions. **Ⓛ Visual/Spatial**

📄 Alternative Assessment Handbook, Rubrics 6: Cause and Effect; and 8: Collages

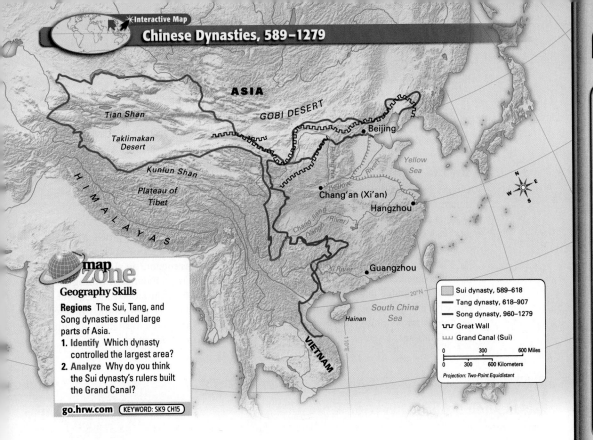

ASIA

Tian Shan

Taklimakan Desert

GOBI DESERT

Beijing

Kunlun Shan

HIMALAYAS

Plateau of Tibet

Chang'an (Xi'an)

Hangzhou

Yellow Sea

Yellow He (Yellow River)

Chang Jiang (Yangzi River)

Xi River

Guangzhou

20°N

South China Sea

Hainan

110°E

VIETNAM

N E W S

map zone

Geography Skills

Regions The Sui, Tang, and Song dynasties ruled large parts of Asia.
1. **Identify** Which dynasty controlled the largest area?
2. **Analyze** Why do you think the Sui dynasty's rulers built the Grand Canal?

go.hrw.com KEYWORD: SK9 CH15

	Sui dynasty, 589–618
▬	Tang dynasty, 618–907
▬	Song dynasty, 960–1279
ᴖᴖ	Great Wall
⊔⊔	Grand Canal (Sui)

0   300   600 Miles
0   300   600 Kilometers
Projection: Two-Point Equidistant

Tang Dynasty

The Sui dynasty was followed by the Tang, which would rule for nearly 300 years. As you can see on the map, China grew under the Tang dynasty to include much of eastern and central Asia.

Historians view the Tang dynasty as a golden age. Tang rulers conquered many lands, reformed the military, and created law codes. The Tang period also saw great advances in art. Some of China's finest poets, for example, lived during this time.

The Tang dynasty also included the only woman to rule China—Empress Wu. Her methods were sometimes vicious, but she was intelligent and talented.

Song Dynasty

After the Tang dynasty fell, China entered another brief period of chaos and disorder, with separate kingdoms competing for power. As a result, this period in China's history is called the Five Dynasties and Ten Kingdoms. The disorder only lasted 53 years, though, from 907 to 960.

In 960, China was again reunified, this time by the Song dynasty. Like the Tang, the Song ruled for about 300 years, until 1279. Also like the Tang, the Song dynasty was a time of great achievements.

READING CHECK Finding Main Ideas What dynasties restored order to China?

FOCUS ON READING
What dynasty followed the Tang?

Main Idea

❶ Disorder and Reunification

After the Han Dynasty, China fell into disorder but was reunified by new dynasties.

Recall Who was the only woman to rule China? *Empress Wu* During what dynasty did she rule? *during the Tang dynasty*

Compare How were the Tang and Song dynasties similar? *Both ruled for about 300 years; both were times of great achievements.*

Summarize Why was the Tang dynasty considered a golden age? *The empire expanded, military was reformed, laws were created, and there were great advances in art.*

🗺 Map Zone Transparency: Chinese Dynasties, 589–1279

Biography

Empress Wu, Tang ruler 690–705 When Emperor Gaozong suffered a stroke in 660, Empress Wu took effective control of the government through the reign of her two sons. In 690 she declared herself ruler of a new dynasty. In order to gain support from the people, she distributed the *Great Cloud Sutra*. This Buddhist narrative predicts the Buddha will be reborn as a female ruler and the entire world will live free from worry, illness, and disaster. When she was finally deposed, she was more than 80 years old and ill.

Cross Discipline Activity: Math   At Level

Comparing the Length of Dynasties

1. Explain that students will be constructing a bar graph to compare the number of years various dynasties ruled and other periods lasted. Go over the basic steps: identify the number of years for each period, construct a vertical axis which will fit the number of years involved, list the periods along the horizontal axis, then use bars to indicate the number of years.

2. Circulate among students to provide assistance as needed. Students should use the following periods: Period of Disunion

379 years, Sui dynasty 29 years, Tang dynasty 289 years, Five Dynasties and Ten Kingdoms 53 years, Song dynasty 319 years.

3. Encourage students to use colors to note each different dynasty or period. You might also investigate creating a bar graph through a computer program. Ask volunteers to share their bar graphs when they are complete.

LS Logical/Mathematical

📖 Alternative Assessment Handbook, Rubric 7: Charts

Answers

Map Zone 1. *the Tang dynasty;* **2.** *to improve transportation for people and goods*

Focus on Reading *the Song dynasty*

Reading Check *the Sui, Tang, and Song dynasties*

Main Idea

❷ Cities and Trade

Cities and trade grew during the Tang and Song dynasties.

Identify What was the largest city in the world at this time, and what was its population? *Chang'an; more than one million*

Analyze How were Chinese trade cities unique? *They were a mix of people from many cultures and religions and were quite large in population.*

Drawing Conclusions How did the Grand Canal play a role in trade? *It connected major cities and allowed a large amount of goods and crops to be transported from agricultural areas to the cities.*

Info to Know

Chinese Cities China had the largest cities in the world during the Tang and Song dynasties. One of the most remarkable of these cities was the Song capital of Hangzhou. The city had a wide variety of diversions, including bookstores, pet shops, restaurants, teahouses, popular entertainment, and boating. The city also tried to take care of its citizens through a state hospital, orphanages, and homes for the elderly.

Activity **Grand Canal Map** Have students use a blank outline map of China to locate the route of the Grand Canal. Then have students list trade goods from different regions of China that traveled along the Grand Canal.
LS Visual/Spatial

📓 Alternative Assessment Handbook, Rubric 20: Map Creation

Cities and Trade

Throughout the Tang and Song dynasties, much of the food grown on China's farms flowed into the growing cities and towns. China's cities were crowded, busy places. Shopkeepers, government officials, doctors, artisans, entertainers, religious leaders, and artists made them lively places as well.

City Life

China's capital and largest city of the Tang dynasty was Chang'an (chahng-AHN), a huge, bustling trade center now called Xi'an. With a population of more than a million, it was by far the largest city in the world.

Chang'an, like other trading cities, had a mix of people from many cultures—China, Korea, Persia, Arabia, and Europe. It was also known as a religious and philosophical center, not just for Buddhists and Daoists but for Asian Christians as well.

Cities continued to grow under the Song. Several cities, including the Song capital, **Kaifeng** (KY-fuhng), had about a million people. A dozen more cities had populations of close to half a million.

Trade in China and Beyond

Trade grew along with Chinese cities. This trade, combined with China's agricultural base, made China richer than ever before.

Much trade took place within China itself. Traders used the country's rivers to ship goods on barges and ships.

The Grand Canal, a series of waterways that linked major cities, carried a huge amount of trade goods, especially farm products. Construction on the canal had begun during the Sui dynasty. During the Tang dynasty, it was improved and expanded. The Grand Canal allowed the Chinese to move goods and crops from distant agricultural areas into cities.

The Grand Canal

Differentiating Instruction

Below Level

Struggling Readers

1. Ask students to imagine that they are captains of barges on the Grand Canal during the Song dynasty. The barge is set to travel from the countryside to the city and back again.

2. Instruct each student to write a captain's log with three entries. The first entry should include a list of items on board the ship as it is headed to the city. The second entry should be a description of the city and its inhabitants. The third entry should be a list of items on board being taken back to the

countryside. Remind students to include details that can be found in this section.

3. When students have finished, guide the class in a discussion of trade within China, such as agricultural goods exchanged for city-made, manufactured goods. Ask students to share their logs with the class. **LS** Verbal/Linguistic

📓 Alternative Assessment Handbook, Rubric 40: Writing to Describe

The Chinese also carried on trade with other lands and peoples. During the Tang dynasty, most foreign trade was over land routes leading to India and Southwest Asia, though Chinese traders also went to Korea and Japan in the east. The Chinese exported many goods, including tea, rice, spices, and jade. However, one export was especially important—silk. So valuable was silk that the Chinese kept the method of making it secret. In exchange for their exports, the Chinese imported different foods, plants, wool, glass, and precious metals like gold and silver.

During the Song dynasty, sea trade became more important. China opened its Pacific ports to foreign traders. The sea-trade routes connected China to many other countries. During this time, the Chinese also developed another valuable product—a thin, beautiful type of pottery called **porcelain**.

All of this trade helped create a strong economy. As a result, merchants became important members of Chinese society during the Song dynasty. Also as a result of the growth of trade and wealth, the Song invented the world's first system of paper money in the 900s.

READING CHECK Summarizing How far did China's trade routes extend?

Arts and Inventions

While China grew rich economically, its cultural riches also increased. In literature, art, and science, China made huge advances.

Artists and Poets

The artists and writers of the Tang dynasty were some of China's greatest. Wu Daozi (DOW-tzee) painted murals that celebrated Buddhism and nature. Li Bo and Du Fu wrote poems that readers still enjoy for their beauty. This poem by Li Bo expresses the homesickness that one feels late at night:

" Before my bed
there is bright moonlight
So that it seems
like frost on the ground:
Lifting my head
I watch the bright moon,
Lowering my head
I dream that I'm home. "
–Li Bo, *Quiet Night Thoughts*

Also noted for its literature, the Song period produced Li Qingzhao (ching-ZHOW), perhaps China's greatest female poet. She once said that the purpose of her poetry was to capture a single moment in time.

Artists of both the Tang and Song dynasties made exquisite objects in clay. Tang figurines of horses clearly show the animals' strength. Song artists made porcelain items covered in a pale green glaze called celadon (SEL-uh-duhn).

THE IMPACT TODAY
Porcelain became so popular in the West that it became known as chinaware, or just china.

China's Grand Canal (left) is the world's longest human-made waterway. It was built largely to transport rice and other foods from the south to feed China's cities and armies in the north. Barges like the one above crowd the Grand Canal, which is still an important transportation link in China.

Cities and Trade, continued

Identify What were some of China's exports? *tea, rice, spices, jade, silk, and porcelain*

Identify Cause and Effect What result did China's trade with other lands have on Chinese society? *It led to the rise of merchants in Chinese society.*

Evaluate How important do you think trade was in China? Why? *possible answer—very important; it brought great wealth to China from foreign lands and united different regions of the empire.*

Did you know. . .

In addition to the barges pictured on this page, another means of transportation in China was the junk, a ship with large sails. Originally, the square sails were made of bamboo mats sewn together. As cotton became more common in China, the sails were redesigned to feature cotton cloth stretched between bamboo strips. Junks of differing sizes were built to carry trade goods on China's rivers and seas.

Cross-Discipline Activity: Literature

Above Level

Writing a Poem

1. Tell the class that students of poetry often write imitations, or poems that copy the style of a certain poet. This helps them understand the structure and style of different poems.

2. Read Li Bo's poem aloud to the class. Make sure all students understand the words and the message of the poem.

3. Instruct students to write an imitation of the poem. The topic can be anything students want, but the style should imitate Li Bo's poem. Students should use colorful imagery to capture a moment in time. Students having difficulty might want to create an illustration of Li Bo's poem.

4. Ask for volunteers to read their poems to the class. **LS Verbal/Linguistic**

   Alternative Assessment Handbook, Rubric 26: Poems and Songs

Answers

Reading Check *as far as India and Southwest Asia, into Korea and Japan*

Direct Teach

Main Idea

❸ Arts and Inventions

The Tang and Song dynasties produced fine arts and inventions.

Identify What types of art and literature were popular during this period? *murals, poetry, and porcelain figurines*

Recall How was gunpowder first used? *in fireworks*

Make Generalizations How was the magnetic compass significant to world history? *It allowed explorers all over the world to travel long distances and to discover parts of the world they previously did not know existed.*

📑 **RF:** Literature, Poems from the Tang and Song Dynasties

Info to Know

Woodblock Printing Chinese woodblock printing began during the Tang dynasty. Originally the method was used to print designs on cloth, but later was applied to writing Buddhist texts and other information. Chinese printers would write the text on a thin sheet of paper, which they then pasted face down to a wood block. The text was carved out in the wood, creating an image that could be inked and stamped onto paper and reused many times. Not only text was copied in this way, but illustrations as well.

Chinese Inventions

Paper
Invented during the Han dynasty around 105, paper was one of the greatest of all Chinese inventions. It gave the Chinese a cheap and easy way of keeping records and made printing possible.

Porcelain
Porcelain was first made during the Tang dynasty, but it wasn't perfected for many centuries. Chinese artists were famous for their work with this fragile material.

Woodblock printing
The Chinese invented printing during the Tang dynasty, centuries before it was known in Europe. Printers could copy drawings or texts quickly, much faster than they could be copied by hand.

Gunpowder
Invented during the late Tang or early Song dynasty, gunpowder was used to make fireworks and signals. The Chinese did not generally use it as a weapon.

Movable type
Inventors of the Song dynasty created movable type, which made printing much faster. Carved letters could be rearranged and reused to print many different messages.

Magnetic compass
Invented no later than the Han period, the compass was greatly improved by the Tang. The new compass allowed sailors and merchants to travel vast distances.

Paper money
The world's first paper money was invented by the Song. Lighter and easier to handle than coins, paper money helped the Chinese manage their growing wealth.

Important Inventions

The Tang and Song dynasties produced some of the most remarkable—and most important—inventions in human history. Some of these inventions influenced events around the world.

According to legend, a man named Cai Lun invented paper in the year 105 during the Han dynasty. A later Tang invention built on this achievement—**woodblock printing,** a form of printing in which an entire page is carved into a block of wood. The printer applies ink to the block and presses paper against the block to create a printed page. The world's first known printed book was printed in this way in China in 868.

Another invention of the Tang dynasty was gunpowder. **Gunpowder** is a mixture of powders used in guns and explosives. It was originally used only in fireworks, but it was later used to make small bombs and rockets. Eventually, gunpowder was used to make explosives, firearms, and cannons. Gunpowder dramatically altered how wars were fought and, in doing so, changed the course of human history.

One of the most useful achievements of Tang China was the perfection of the magnetic **compass**. This instrument, which uses Earth's magnetic field to show direction, revolutionized travel. A compass made it possible to find direction more accurately than ever before. The perfection of the compass had far-reaching effects. Explorers the world over used the compass to travel vast distances. Both trading ships and warships also came to rely on the compass for their navigation. Thus, the compass has been a key factor in some of the most important sailing voyages in history.

The Song dynasty also produced many important inventions. Under the Song, the Chinese invented movable type. Movable type is a set of letters or characters that are

480 CHAPTER 15

Cross-Discipline Activity: Science

At Level

Chinese Technology Exhibits

Research Required

1. Review with students the various technological innovations of the Chinese during the Tang and Song period. Make a list for students to see.

2. Organize students into pairs or small groups. Have each pair or group select one Chinese innovation to research. Tell students that they will create an exhibit for a science fair that presents one piece of Chinese technology from this period.

3. Have each group use the library, Internet, or other resources to research information about the technology they have chosen. Student exhibits should explain how each device or process works, what it was used for, and what it looked like.

4. Have each group present its exhibit to the class or conduct a class science fair for everyone to see.

🄻 **Interpersonal, Verbal/Linguistic**

📑 Alternative Assessment Handbook, Rubrics 29: Presentations; and 30: Research

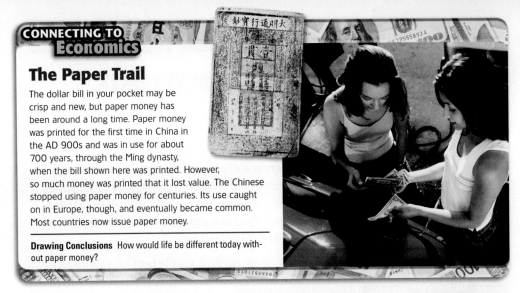

The Paper Trail

The dollar bill in your pocket may be crisp and new, but paper money has been around a long time. Paper money was printed for the first time in China in the AD 900s and was in use for about 700 years, through the Ming dynasty, when the bill shown here was printed. However, so much money was printed that it lost value. The Chinese stopped using paper money for centuries. Its use caught on in Europe, though, and eventually became common. Most countries now issue paper money.

Drawing Conclusions How would life be different today without paper money?

---

used to print books. Unlike the blocks used in block printing, movable type can be rearranged and reused to create new lines of text and different pages.

The Song dynasty also introduced the concept of paper money. People were used to buying goods and services with bulky coins made of metals such as bronze, gold, and silver. Paper money was far lighter and easier to use. As trade increased and many people in China grew rich, paper money became more popular.

READING CHECK Finding Main Ideas What were some important inventions of the Tang and Song dynasties?

SUMMARY AND PREVIEW The Tang and Song dynasties were periods of great advancement. Many great artists and writers lived during these periods. Tang and Song inventions also had dramatic effects on world history. Next, you will learn about major changes in China's government during the Song dynasty.

Section 3 Assessment

go.hrw.com
Online Quiz
KEYWORD: SK9 HP15

Reviewing Ideas, Terms, and People

1. **a. Recall** What was the Period of Disunion? What dynasty brought an end to that period?
   b. Explain How did China change during the Tang dynasty?
2. **a. Describe** What were the capital cities of Tang and Song China like?
   b. Draw Conclusions How did geography affect trade in China?
3. **a. Identify** Who was Li Bo?
   b. Draw Conclusions How may the inventions of paper money and **woodblock printing** have been linked?
   c. Rank Which Tang or Song invention do you think was most important? Defend your answer.

Critical Thinking

4. **Categorizing** Copy the chart at right. Use it to organize your notes on the Tang and Song into categories.

	Tang dynasty	Song dynasty
Cities		
Trade		
Art		
Inventions		

FOCUS ON WRITING

5. **Identifying Achievements** Which achievements and inventions of the Tang and Song dynasties seem most important or most interesting? Make a list for later use.

ANCIENT CIVILIZATIONS OF ASIA—CHINA **481**

Section 3 Assessment Answers

1. **a.** the time of disorder that followed the collapse of the Han dynasty; the Sui dynasty
   b. China expanded its borders, the military was reformed, law codes were created, and advances in art were made.
2. **a.** bustling trade centers, with a mix of cultures and religions and large populations
   b. Rivers and canals were used to connect major cities and deliver trade goods.
3. **a.** a poet during the Tang dynasty
   b. Woodblock printing allowed identical printings, so paper money could be produced.

c. Answers will vary, but students should demonstrate an understanding of the invention and its impact on Chinese society.

4. Cities—Tang: huge trade centers; Song: many cities with population of half a million; Trade—Tang: trade along the Grand Canal expanded; Song: sea trade important; Art—Tang: writers and artists celebrated Buddhism and nature; Song: Li Qingzhao was a famous female poet; Inventions—Tang: woodblock printing, gunpowder, improved compass; Song: movable type, paper money

5. Students' lists will vary but may include woodblock printing, movable type, and paper money.

Preteach

Confucianism and Government

Bellringer

If YOU lived there... Use the **Daily Bellringer Transparency** to help students answer the question.

📖 Daily Bellringer Transparency, Section 4

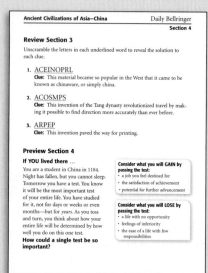

| Ancient Civilizations of Asia—China | Daily Bellringer |
| | Section 4 |

Review Section 3

Unscramble the letters in each underlined word to reveal the solution to each clue.

1. ACEINOPRL
   Clue: This material became so popular in the West that it came to be known as chinaware, or simply china.

2. ACOSMPS
   Clue: This invention of the Tang dynasty revolutionized travel by making it possible to find direction more accurately than ever before.

3. ARPEP
   Clue: This invention paved the way for printing.

Preview Section 4

If YOU lived there ...
You are a student in China in 1184. Night has fallen, but you cannot sleep. Tomorrow you have a test. You know it will be the most important test of your entire life. You have studied for it, not for days or weeks or even months—but for *years*. As you toss and turn, you think about how your entire life will be determined by how well you do on this one test. **How could a single test be so important?**

Consider what you will GAIN by passing the test:
• a job you feel destined for
• the satisfaction of achievement
• potential for further advancement

Consider what you will LOSE by passing the test:
• a life with no opportunity
• feelings of inferiority
• the ease of a life with few responsibilities

Academic Vocabulary

Review with students the high-use academic terms in this section.

ethical related to rules of conduct or proper behavior (p. 483)

incentive something that leads people to follow a certain course of action (p. 484)

📖 **RF:** Vocabulary Builder, Section 4

Taking Notes

Have students copy the graphic organizer onto their own paper and then use it to take notes on the section. This activity will prepare students for the Section Assessment, in which they will complete a graphic organizer that builds on the information using the Critical Thinking Skill: Sequencing.

What You Will Learn...

Main Ideas

1. Confucianism, based on Confucius's teachings about proper behavior, dramatically influenced the Song system of government.
2. Scholar-officials ran China's government during the Song dynasty.

The Big Idea

Confucian thought influenced the Song government.

Key Terms

bureaucracy, *p. 484*
civil service, *p. 484*
scholar-official, *p. 484*

TAKING NOTES As you read, use a diagram like this one to note details about Confucianism and the Song government.

(Confucianism) (Song government)

If YOU lived there...

You are a student in China in 1184. Night has fallen, but you cannot sleep. Tomorrow you have a test. You know it will be the most important test of your entire life. You have studied for it, not for days or weeks or even months—but for *years*. As you toss and turn, you think about how your entire life will be determined by how well you do on this one test.

How could a single test be so important?

BUILDING BACKGROUND The Song dynasty ruled China from 960 to 1279. This was a time of improvements in agriculture, growing cities, extensive trade, and the development of art and inventions. It was also a time of major changes in Chinese government.

Teach the Big Idea

At Level

Confucianism and Government

1. **Teach** Ask students the questions in the Main Idea boxes under Direct Teach.

2. **Apply** Have students work in pairs to create a concept web using the term *Confucianism* as their central concept. Remind students that concept webs are used to show relationships between ideas, events, or objects. Ask students to show the relationship of Confucianism to such ideas as government, society, ethics, and any others they can support.
   LS Verbal/Linguistic, Visual/Spatial

3. **Review** As you review the section's main ideas, have students write down specific ways in which China was influenced by Confucianism.

4. **Practice/Homework** Have each student use the concept web he or she created to write a one-page summary of the importance of Confucianism in Song China. **LS Verbal/Linguistic**

   📋 Alternative Assessment Handbook, Rubrics 13: Graphic Organizers; and 37: Writing Assignments

Confucianism

The dominant philosophy in China, Confucianism is based on the teachings of Confucius. He lived more than 1,000 years before the Song dynasty. His ideas, though, had a dramatic effect on the Song system of government.

Confucian Ideas

Confucius's teachings focused on ethics, or proper behavior, for individuals and governments. He said that people should conduct their lives according to two basic principles. These principles were *ren*, or concern for others, and *li*, or appropriate behavior. Confucius argued that society would function best if everyone followed *ren* and *li*.

Confucius thought that everyone had a proper role to play in society. Order was maintained when people knew their place and behaved appropriately. For example, Confucius said that young people should obey their elders and that subjects should obey their rulers.

Influence of Confucianism

After his death, Confucius's ideas were spread by his followers, but they were not widely accepted. In fact, the Qin dynasty officially suppressed Confucian ideas and teachings. By the time of the Han dynasty, Confucianism had again come into favor, and Confucianism became the official state philosophy.

During the Period of Disunion, which followed the Han dynasty, Confucianism was overshadowed by Buddhism as the major tradition in China. Many Chinese people had turned to Buddhism for peace and comfort during those troubled times. In doing so, they largely turned away from Confucian ideas and outlooks.

Later, during the Sui and early Tang dynasties, Buddhism was very influential. Unlike Confucianism, which focused on **ethical** behavior, Buddhism stressed a more spiritual outlook that promised escape from suffering. As Buddhism became more popular in China, Confucianism lost some of its influence.

ACADEMIC VOCABULARY
ethical related to rules of conduct or proper behavior

PHOTOGRAPH © 2004 MUSEUM OF FINE ARTS, BOSTON

In addition to ethics, Confucianism stressed the importance of a good education. This painting, created in the Song period, shows Confucian scholars during the Period of Disunion sorting scrolls containing classic Confucian texts.

ANCIENT CIVILIZATIONS OF ASIA—CHINA **483**

Direct Teach

Main Idea

❶ Confucianism

Confucianism, based on Confucius's teachings about proper behavior, dramatically influenced the Song system of government.

Recall What was the focus of the teachings of Confucius? *ethics, or proper behavior, for individuals and governments*

Explain Why did Confucianism decline in popularity during the Period of Disunion? *People turned to Buddhism for comfort in the troubled times of the Period of Disunion.*

Make Generalizations Why do you think the Song and later governments emphasized Neo-Confucianism? *possible answer—The emphasis on proper behavior would encourage people to obey their government; They saw problems in the government they hoped to eliminate by emphasizing Neo-Confucianism.*

Biography

Confucius (551–479 BC) According to tradition Confucius, or Master Kong, served in minor government positions until he became a teacher. As a teacher, Confucius traveled throughout China teaching his ethical philosophy to many students. Today, Confucius is considered one of the most influential teachers in the world. In fact, his birthday is an official holiday in Taiwan, where September 28 is celebrated as Teacher's Day.

go.hrw.com
Online Resources
KEYWORD: SK9 CH15
ACTIVITY: Confucianism

Cross-Discipline Activity: Civics   At Level

Responsibility and Law-Making

1. Discuss with the class the teachings of Confucianism. Remind students that two important principles are *ren*, or concern for others, and *li*, or appropriate behavior. Ask students why these beliefs might have appealed to Song officials who eventually made Confucian ideas formal government teachings.

2. Ask students to think of examples of behaviors that illustrate the concepts of *ren* and *li*. Discuss with the class how living by these principles might benefit society.

3. Then have the class work together to create a list of laws that reflect the principles of *ren* and *li*. Encourage everyone to contribute to the list. Post the list for students to see. Ask students how they might feel about living according to the laws they created.
LS Interpersonal, Verbal/Linguistic

Alternative Assessment Handbook, Rubric 11: Discussions

Main Idea

❷ Scholar-Officials

Scholar-officials ran China's government during the Song dynasty.

Recall How did people join the bureaucracy? *by passing a civil service examination*

Explain What benefits did scholar-officials have? *They held an elite position in society, earned respect, and received reduced penalties for breaking the law.*

Make Inferences Why did the civil service examination system help bring stability to the Song government? *It ensured that government officials were intelligent and talented, which made the government better and more stable.*

Info to Know

Civil Service Exams China's civil service examination system was very difficult. Even though students would spend years studying for an exam, passing rates were very low. In 1093, only 1 out of every 10 students passed the highest level of examination, known as the *jinshi*. Not all government positions, however, were based on performance on a civil service exam. In fact, only some 30 percent of Song officials were selected through examination.

Answers

Reading Check *Neo-Confucianism emphasized both spiritual matters and proper behavior, whereas Confucianism focused on ethical behavior.*

484

Civil Service Exams

This painting from the 1600s shows civil servants writing essays for China's emperor. Difficult exams were designed to make sure that government officials were chosen by ability—not by wealth or family connections.

Difficult Exams

- Students had to memorize entire Confucian texts.

- To pass the most difficult tests, students might study for more than 20 years!

- Some exams lasted up to 72 hours, and students were locked in private rooms while taking them.

- Some dishonest students cheated by copying Confucius's works on the inside of their clothes, paying bribes to the test graders, or paying someone else to take the test for them.

- To prevent cheating, exam halls were often locked and guarded.

Neo-Confucianism

Late in the Tang dynasty, many Chinese historians and scholars again became interested in the teachings of Confucius. Their interest was sparked by their desire to improve Chinese government and society.

During and after the Song dynasty, a new philosophy called Neo-Confucianism developed. The term *neo* means "new." Based on Confucianism, Neo-Confucianism was similar to the older philosophy in that it taught proper behavior. However, it also emphasized spiritual matters. For example, Neo-Confucian scholars discussed such issues as what made human beings do bad things even if their basic nature was good.

Neo-Confucianism became much more influential under the Song. Its influence grew even more later. In fact, the ideas of Neo-Confucianism became official government teachings after the Song dynasty.

ACADEMIC VOCABULARY

incentive something that leads people to follow a certain course of action

READING CHECK **Contrasting** How did Neo-Confucianism differ from Confucianism?

Scholar-Officials

The Song dynasty took another major step that affected China for centuries. They improved the system by which people went to work for the government. These workers formed a large **bureaucracy,** or a body of unelected government officials. They joined the bureaucracy by passing civil service examinations. **Civil service** means service as a government official.

To become a civil servant, a person had to pass a series of written examinations. The examinations tested students' grasp of Confucianism and related ideas.

Because the tests were so difficult, students spent years preparing for them. Only a very small fraction of the people who took the tests would reach the top level and be appointed to a position in the government. However, candidates for the civil service examinations had a strong **incentive** for studying hard. Passing the tests meant life as a **scholar-official**—an educated member of the government.

484 CHAPTER 15

Differentiating Instruction

Struggling Readers **At Level**

1. Review with students the information about scholar-officials in China under the Song. Help students understand the key terms *bureaucracy, civil service,* and *scholar-official.*

2. Have students write a short summary of the information about the Song scholar-officials. Remind students to be sure to explain how people became scholar-officials and what responsibilities they had. **LS Verbal/Linguistic**

📝 Alternative Assessment Handbook, Rubric 37: Writing Assignments

English-Language Learners **At Level**

1. Write the terms *bureaucracy, civil service, incentive,* and *scholar-official* for students to see.

2. Organize students into mixed-ability pairs. Have each pair define each term. Check to make sure that all students understand the meaning of each term. Then have each pair create an illustration that represents the meaning of each term. **LS Visual/Spatial, Verbal/Linguistic**

📝 Alternative Assessment Handbook, Rubric 14: Group Activity

Scholar-Officials

First rising to prominence under the Song, scholar-officials remained important in China for centuries. These scholar-officials, for example, lived during the Qing dynasty, which ruled from the mid-1600s to the early 1900s. Their typical responsibilities might include running government offices; maintaining roads, irrigation systems, and other public works; updating and keeping official records; or collecting taxes.

Scholar-officials were elite members of society. They performed many important jobs in the government and were widely admired for their knowledge and ethics. Their benefits included considerable respect and reduced penalties for breaking the law. Many also became wealthy from gifts given by people seeking their aid.

The civil service examination system helped ensure that talented, intelligent people became scholar-officials. The civil service system was a major factor in the stability of the Song government.

READING CHECK Analyzing How did the Song dynasty change China's government?

SUMMARY AND PREVIEW During the Song period, Confucian ideas helped shape China's government. In the next section, you will read about the two dynasties that followed the Song—the Yuan and the Ming.

Section 4 Assessment

go.hrw.com
Online Quiz
KEYWORD: SK9 HP15

Reviewing Ideas, Terms, and People

1. **a. Identify** What two principles did Confucius believe people should follow?
   b. Explain What was Neo-Confucianism?
   c. Elaborate Why do you think Neo-Confucianism appealed to many people?
2. **a. Define** What was a **scholar-official**?
   b. Explain Why would people want to become scholar-officials?
   c. Evaluate Do you think **civil service** examinations were a good way to choose government officials? Why or why not?

Critical Thinking

3. **Sequencing** Review your notes to see how Confucianism led to Neo-Confucianism and Neo-Confucianism led to government bureaucracy. Use a graphic organizer like the one here.

FOCUS ON WRITING

4. **Gathering Ideas about Confucianism and Government** Think about what you might say about Confucianism in your article. Also, decide whether to include any of the Song dynasty's achievements in government.

ANCIENT CIVILIZATIONS OF ASIA—CHINA **485**

Section 4 Assessment Answers

1. **a.** *ren,* concern for others, and *li,* appropriate behavior
   b. the Song dynasty's new version of Confucianism that blended proper behavior and spiritual matters
   c. It included spiritual matters and ethics.

2. **a.** an educated member of the government who had passed a test about the knowledge of Confucianism and related ideas
   b. considerable respect, reduced penalties for breaking the law, many became wealthy

c. Answers will vary, but students should be familiar with the idea of civil service examinations.

3. Confucianism—official philosophy of the Han dynasty; Neo-Confucianism—combined Confucianism with spiritual ideas; Government bureaucracy—public officials were tested on the ideas of Confucianism

4. Answers will vary, but should reflect an understanding of the content in this section.

Bellringer

If YOU lived there. . . Use the **Daily Bellringer Transparency** to help students answer the question.

📦 Daily Bellringer Transparency, Section 5

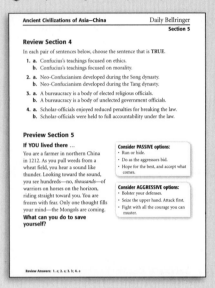

Ancient Civilizations of Asia—China | Daily Bellringer
Section 5

Review Section 4

In each pair of sentences below, choose the sentence that is **TRUE**.

1. **a.** Confucius's teachings focused on ethics.
   b. Confucius's teachings focused on morality.
2. **a.** Neo-Confucianism developed during the Song dynasty.
   b. Neo-Confucianism developed during the Tang dynasty.
3. **a.** A bureaucracy is a body of elected religious officials.
   b. A bureaucracy is a body of unelected government officials.
4. **a.** Scholar-officials enjoyed reduced penalties for breaking the law.
   b. Scholar-officials were held to full accountability under the law.

Preview Section 5

If YOU lived there . . .
You are a farmer in northern China in 1212. As you pull weeds from a wheat field, you hear a sound like thunder. Looking toward the sound, you see hundreds—no, *thousands*—of warriors on horses on the horizon, riding straight toward you. You are frozen with fear. Only one thought fills your mind—the Mongols are coming. **What can you do to save yourself?**

Consider PASSIVE options:
• Run or hide.
• Do as the aggressors bid.
• Hope for the best, and accept what comes.

Consider AGGRESSIVE options:
• Bolster your defenses.
• Seize the upper hand. Attack first.
• Fight with all the courage you can muster.

Review Answers: 1. a; 2. a; 3. b; 4. a

Academic Vocabulary

Review with students the high-use academic term in this section.

consequences effects of a particular event or events (p. 492)

📄 RF: Vocabulary Builder, Section 5

Taking Notes

Have students copy the graphic organizer onto their own paper and then use it to take notes on the section. This activity will prepare students for the Section Assessment, in which they will complete a graphic organizer that builds on the information using the Critical Thinking Skill: Comparing and Constrasting.

The Yuan and Ming Dynasties

What You Will Learn...

Main Ideas

1. The Mongol Empire included China, and the Mongols ruled China as the Yuan dynasty.
2. The Ming dynasty was a time of stability and prosperity.
3. The Ming brought great changes in government and relations with other countries.

The Big Idea

The Chinese were ruled by foreigners during the Yuan dynasty, but they threw off Mongol rule and prospered during the Ming dynasty.

Key Terms and Places

Beijing, *p. 488*
Forbidden City, *p. 490*
isolationism, *p. 492*

TAKING NOTES As you read, use a chart like this one to keep track of important details about the Yuan and Ming dynasties.

	Yuan	Ming
Government		
Religion		
Trade		
Building		
Foreign Relations		

If YOU lived there...

You are a farmer in northern China in 1212. As you pull weeds from a wheat field, you hear a sound like thunder. Looking toward the sound, you see hundreds—no, *thousands*—of warriors on horses on the horizon, riding straight toward you. You are frozen with fear. Only one thought fills your mind—the Mongols are coming.

What can you do to save yourself?

BUILDING BACKGROUND Throughout its history, northern China had been attacked over and over by nomadic peoples. During the Song dynasty these attacks became more frequent and threatening.

The Mongol Empire

Among the nomadic peoples who attacked the Chinese were the Mongols. For centuries, the Mongols had lived as tribes in the vast plains north of China. Then in 1206, a strong leader, or khan, united them. His name was Temüjin. When he became leader, though, he was given a new title: "Universal Ruler," or Genghis Khan (JENG-guhs KAHN).

The Mongol Conquest

Genghis Khan organized the Mongols into a powerful army and led them on bloody expeditions of conquest. The brutality of the Mongol attacks terrorized people throughout much of Asia and Eastern Europe. Genghis Khan and his army killed all of the men, women, and children in countless cities and villages. Within 20 years, he ruled a large part of Asia.

Genghis Khan then turned his attention to China. He first led his armies into northern China in 1211. They fought their way south, wrecking whole towns and ruining farmland. By the time of Genghis Khan's death in 1227, all of northern China was under Mongol control.

Teach the Big Idea

At Level

The Yuan and Ming Dynasties

1. **Teach** Ask students the questions in the Main Idea boxes under Direct Teach.

2. **Apply** Have each student create a graphic organizer of his or her own design to compare and contrast the Yuan and Ming dynasties of China. Remind students to indicate both similarities and differences between the two dynasties. **LS Verbal/Linguistic**

3. **Review** Have students write a short summary of the rule of both the Yuan and Ming dynasties.

4. **Practice/Homework** Have students write a 10-question quiz using facts from this section. On the back of the paper, students should write the answers to the questions. Have students keep their quizzes and remind them that the quiz will be a useful tool to review later. **LS Verbal/Linguistic**

📄 Alternative Assessment Handbook, Rubrics 9: Comparing and Contrasting; and 13: Graphic Organizers

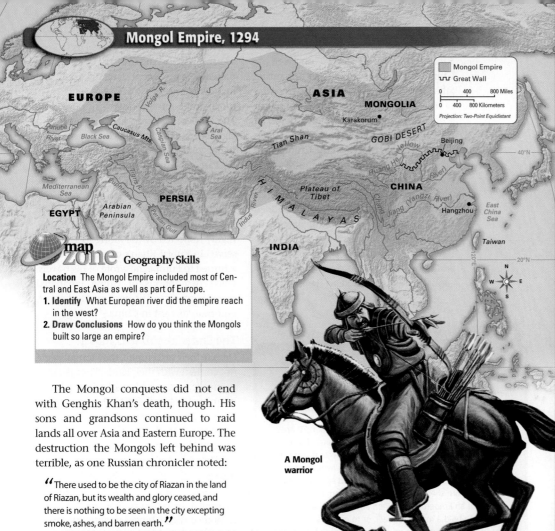

Mongol Empire, 1294

EUROPE

ASIA

MONGOLIA

Karakorum

GOBI DESERT

Beijing

CHINA

PERSIA

Plateau of Tibet

Hangzhou

EGYPT

Arabian Peninsula

INDIA

Taiwan

Black Sea

Caucasus Mts.

Aral Sea

Tian Shan

HIMALAYAS

Mediterranean Sea

Volga R.

Danube River

Caspian Sea

Huang He (Yellow River)

Chang Jiang (Yangzi River)

East China Sea

| Mongol Empire |
| Great Wall |

0   400   800 Miles
0   400   800 Kilometers
Projection: Two-Point Equidistant

map Zone Geography Skills

Location The Mongol Empire included most of Central and East Asia as well as part of Europe.
1. **Identify** What European river did the empire reach in the west?
2. **Draw Conclusions** How do you think the Mongols built so large an empire?

The Mongol conquests did not end with Genghis Khan's death, though. His sons and grandsons continued to raid lands all over Asia and Eastern Europe. The destruction the Mongols left behind was terrible, as one Russian chronicler noted:

"There used to be the city of Riazan in the land of Riazan, but its wealth and glory ceased, and there is nothing to be seen in the city excepting smoke, ashes, and barren earth."

–from "The Tale of the Destruction of Riazan," in *Medieval Russia's Epics, Chronicles, and Tales,* edited by Serge Zenkovsky

In 1260 Genghis Khan's grandson Kublai Khan (KOO-bluh KAHN) became ruler of the Mongol Empire. He completed the conquest of China and in 1279 declared himself emperor of China. This began the Yuan dynasty, a period that some people also call the Mongol Ascendancy. For the first time in its long history, foreigners ruled all of China.

A Mongol warrior

Life in Yuan China

Kublai Khan and the Mongol rulers he led belonged to a different ethnic group than the Chinese did. They spoke a different language, worshipped different gods, wore different clothing, and had different customs. The Chinese resented being ruled by these foreigners, whom they saw as rude and uncivilized.

ANCIENT CIVILIZATIONS OF ASIA–CHINA **487**

Main Idea

The Mongol Empire,
continued

Make Predictions What effect might Marco Polo's description of life in China have on European traders? *possible answer—They might want to go to China to trade.*

Analyze What led to the downfall of the Yuan dynasty? *failed campaigns against Japan, expensive public-works projects that weakened the economy, Chinese resentment, all of which led to rebellions*

Info to Know

Mongol Trade Historians believe that it was during the Yuan dynasty that many Chinese ideas and inventions were first introduced to foreigners. Gunpowder and the compass were among the ideas introduced from China to other civilizations during the Mongol Ascendancy.

Primary Source

Reading Like a Historian
A Chinese City Help students practice reading the document like historians. Ask:

• What features of Hangzhou is the author describing?

• What features do you think the author has omitted?

Answers

Analyzing Primary Sources *that it is a beautiful and very wealthy city*

Reading Check *Kublai Khan conquered all of China after his grandfather, Genghis Khan, began the conquest.*

However, Kublai Khan did not force the Chinese to accept Mongol ways of life. Some Mongols even adopted aspects of the Chinese culture, such as Confucianism. Still, the Mongols made sure to keep control of the Chinese. They prohibited Confucian scholars from gaining too much power in the government, for example. The Mongols also placed heavy taxes on the Chinese.

Much of the tax money the Mongols collected went to pay for vast public-works projects. These projects required the labor of many Chinese people. The Yuan added to the Grand Canal and built new roads and palaces. Workers also improved the roads used by China's postal system. In addition, the Yuan emperors built a new capital, Dadu, near modern **Beijing**.

Primary Source

BOOK
A Chinese City

In this passage Marco Polo describes his visit to Hangzhou (HAHNG-JOH), a city in southeastern China.

❝Inside the city there is a Lake . . . and all round it are erected [built] beautiful palaces and mansions, of the richest and most exquisite [finest] structure that you can imagine . . . In the middle of the Lake are two Islands, on each of which stands a rich, beautiful and spacious edifice [building], furnished in such style as to seem fit for the palace of an Emperor. And when any one of the citizens desired to hold a marriage feast, or to give any other entertainment, it used to be done at one of these palaces. And everything would be found there ready to order, such as silver plate, trenchers [platters], and dishes, napkins and table-cloths, and whatever else was needful. The King made this provision for the gratification [enjoyment] of his people, and the place was open to every one who desired to give an entertainment.❞

–Marco Polo, from *Description of the World*

ANALYSIS SKILL **ANALYZING PRIMARY SOURCES**

From this description, what impression might Europeans have of Hangzhou?

Mongol soldiers were sent throughout China to keep the peace as well as to keep a close watch on the Chinese. The soldiers' presence kept overland trade routes safe for merchants. Sea trade between China, India, and Southeast Asia continued, too. The Mongol emperors also welcomed foreign traders at Chinese ports. Some of these traders received special privileges.

Part of what we know about life in the Yuan dynasty comes from one such trader, an Italian merchant named Marco Polo. Between 1271 and 1295 he traveled in and around China. Polo was highly respected by the Mongols and even served in Kublai Khan's court. When Polo returned to Europe, he wrote of his travels. Polo's descriptions of China fascinated many Europeans. His book sparked much European interest in China.

The End of the Yuan Dynasty

Despite their vast empire, the Mongols were not content with their lands. They decided to invade Japan. A Mongol army sailed to Japan in 1274 and 1281. The campaigns, however, were disastrous. Violent storms and fierce defenders destroyed most of the Mongol force.

The failed campaigns against Japan weakened the Mongol military. The huge, expensive public-works projects had already weakened the economy. These weaknesses, combined with Chinese resentment, made China ripe for rebellion.

In the 1300s many Chinese groups rebelled against the Yuan dynasty. In 1368 a former monk named Zhu Yuanzhang (JOO yoo-ahn-JAHNG) took charge of a rebel army. He led this army in a final victory over the Mongols. China was once again ruled by the Chinese.

READING CHECK **Finding Main Ideas** How did the Mongols come to rule China?

Critical Thinking: Supporting a Point of View   `Above Level`

An Editorial for a New Dynasty

1. Ask students to imagine that they are Zhu Yuanzhang immediately after his defeat of the Mongols. He has arrived in the capital city and intends to start a new dynasty.

2. Have students write a front-page editorial from Zhu Yuanzhang to be published in the largest newspaper in China. The editorial should explain why he felt it was necessary to replace the Mongols and should give an account of the problems the Mongols had brought to China.

3. Remind students to include both facts and opinions in their editorial and to try to persuade the Chinese people to support their new ruler.

4. Ask for volunteers to read their editorials to the class. **LS** **Verbal/Linguistic**

   Alternative Assessment Handbook, Rubric 43: Writing to Persuade

The Voyages of Zheng He

Zheng He's ocean voyages were remarkable. Some of his ships, like the one shown here, were among the largest in the world at the time.

This large ship was more than 300 feet long and carried about 500 people.

Sailors grew vegetables and herbs in special containers and brought livestock for food on the long voyages.

Zheng He brought back exotic animals like these giraffes from Africa.

ANALYSIS SKILL | **ANALYZING VISUALS**

How did Zheng He's crew make sure they had fresh food?

The Ming Dynasty

After his army defeated the Mongols, Zhu Yuanzhang became emperor of China. The Ming dynasty that he founded ruled China from 1368 to 1644—nearly 300 years. Ming China proved to be one of the most stable and prosperous times in Chinese history. The Ming expanded China's fame overseas and sponsored incredible building projects across China.

Great Sea Voyages

During the Ming dynasty, the Chinese improved their ships and their sailing skills. The greatest sailor of the period was Zheng He (juhng HUH). Between 1405 and 1433, he led seven grand voyages to places around Asia. Zheng He's fleets were huge. One included more than 60 ships and 25,000 sailors. Some of the ships were gigantic too, perhaps more than 300 feet long. That is longer than a football field!

In the course of his voyages Zheng He sailed his fleet throughout the Indian Ocean. He sailed as far west as the Persian Gulf and the easternmost coast of Africa.

ANCIENT CIVILIZATIONS OF ASIA—CHINA **489**

The Ming Dynasty, continued

Recall How did the Forbidden City gets its name? *Common people were forbidden from entering the city.*

Explain Why is the Forbidden City called "a city within a city"? *It was a huge complex of almost 1,000 buildings located within the capital city.*

Elaborate Why do you think the Ming rulers were interested in building projects? *possible answers—to glorify their empire, to impress their people, to instill fear in their neighbors*

Info to Know

The Forbidden City The Forbidden City was used for almost 500 years as the imperial residence of China's rulers. It was built between 1406 and 1420 by Emperor Yung-lo of the Ming dynasty. In 1912, when the imperial government was overthrown, the last Chinese emperor, P'u-i (pu-YEE), was allowed to continue living in the Forbidden City. After his departure in 1924, the Forbidden City was made into a national museum.

Everywhere his ships landed, Zheng He presented leaders with beautiful gifts from China. He boasted about his country and encouraged foreign leaders to send gifts to China's emperor. From one voyage, Zheng He returned to China with representatives of some 30 nations, sent by their leaders to honor the emperor. He also brought goods and stories back to China.

Zheng He's voyages rank among the most impressive in the history of seafaring. Although they did not lead to the creation of new trade routes or the exploration of new lands, they served as a clear sign of China's power.

Great Building Projects

The Ming were also known for their grand building projects. Many of these projects were designed to impress both the Chinese people and their enemies to the north.

In Beijing, for example, the Ming emperors built the **Forbidden City**, a huge palace complex that included hundreds of imperial residences, temples, and other government buildings. Within them were some 9,000 rooms. The name Forbidden City came from the fact that the common people were not even allowed to enter the complex. For centuries, this city within a city was a symbol of China's glory.

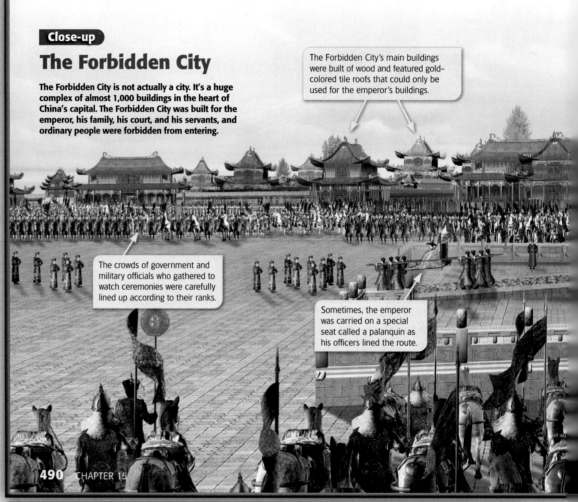

Close-up

The Forbidden City

The Forbidden City is not actually a city. It's a huge complex of almost 1,000 buildings in the heart of China's capital. The Forbidden City was built for the emperor, his family, his court, and his servants, and ordinary people were forbidden from entering.

The Forbidden City's main buildings were built of wood and featured gold-colored tile roofs that could only be used for the emperor's buildings.

The crowds of government and military officials who gathered to watch ceremonies were carefully lined up according to their ranks.

Sometimes, the emperor was carried on a special seat called a palanquin as his officers lined the route.

490 CHAPTER 15

Cross-Discipline Activity: English/Language Arts   At Level

Description of the Forbidden City

1. Ask students to imagine that they are military or government officials who have been invited to enter the Forbidden City in order to pay tribute to the emperor. They will gather there with thousands of other officials, but it is still an immense honor.

2. Because they have never been allowed into the Forbidden City, they are very impressed by its size, beautiful buildings, and beautiful decorations.

3. When they return home, what will they tell their friends and family? Tell students to write a one-page dialogue of their conversation after the event in which they describe what they saw, including details about the emperor and the architecture of the palace. Students should also include how they might have felt when in the Forbidden City. **LS** Verbal/Linguistic

📝 Alternative Assessment Handbook, Rubric 40: Writing to Describe

Ming rulers also directed the restoration of the famous Great Wall of China. Large numbers of soldiers and peasants worked to rebuild fallen portions of walls, connect existing walls, and build new ones. The result was a construction feat unmatched in history. The wall was more than 2,000 miles long. It would reach from San Diego to New York! The wall was about 25 feet high and, at the top, 12 feet wide. Protected by the wall—and the soldiers who stood guard along it—the Chinese people felt safe from invasions by the northern tribes.

READING CHECK **Generalizing** In what ways did the Ming dynasty strengthen China?

China under the Ming

During the Ming dynasty, Chinese society began to change. This change was largely due to the efforts of the Ming emperors. Having expelled the Mongols, the Ming emperors worked to eliminate all foreign influences from Chinese society. As a result, China's government and relations with other countries changed dramatically.

The Hall of Supreme Harmony is the largest building in the Forbidden City. Grand celebrations for important holidays, like the emperor's birthday and the New Year, were held there.

ANALYSIS SKILL **ANALYZING VISUALS**

How did the Forbidden City show the power and importance of the emperor?

ANCIENT CIVILIZATIONS OF ASIA-CHINA **491**

Isolationism Some students may not understand how China's policy of isolationism led to a decline. Ask volunteers to describe how it would feel if, for one week, they had to stay at home, could not watch television, go to the movies, read a magazine or newspaper, or talk to anyone on the phone. The result is that they would not know what their friends or anyone else outside of their homes were doing. This is an example of isolationism. China did not know about advances in the Western world, and China's power and glory faded.

Review & Assess

Close

Ask students to list the similarities and differences between the Yuan and Ming dynasties.

Review

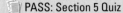 Online Quiz, Section 5

Assess

SE Section 5 Assessment

PASS: Section 5 Quiz

Alternative Assessment Handbook

Reteach/Classroom Intervention

Interactive Reader and Study Guide, Section 5

Interactive Skills Tutor CD-ROM

Answers

Reading Check *Over time, China was technologically outpaced by the world and as a result was weakened and controlled by other countries.*

492

Government

When the Ming took over China, they adopted many government programs that had been created by the Tang and the Song. However, the Ming emperors were much more powerful than the Tang and Song emperors had been. They abolished the offices of some powerful officials and took a larger role in running the government themselves. These emperors fiercely protected their power, and they punished anyone whom they saw as challenging their authority.

ACADEMIC VOCABULARY
consequences effects of a particular event or events

Despite their personal power, though, the Ming did not disband the civil service system. Because he personally oversaw the entire government, the emperor needed officials to keep his affairs organized.

The Ming also used examinations to appoint censors. These officials were sent all over China to investigate the behavior of local leaders and to judge the quality of schools and other institutions. Censors had existed for many years in China, but under the Ming emperors their power and influence grew.

Relations with Other Countries

In the 1430s a new Ming emperor made Zheng He return to China and dismantle his fleet. At the same time, he banned foreign trade. China entered a period of isolationism. **Isolationism** is a policy of avoiding contact with other countries.

In the end, this isolationism had great **consequences** for China. By the late 1800s the Western world had made huge leaps in technological progress. Westerners were able to take power in some parts of China. Partly due to its isolation and lack of progress, China was too weak to stop them. Gradually, China's glory faded.

READING CHECK **Identifying Cause and Effect** How did isolationism affect China?

SUMMARY AND PREVIEW In this chapter, you learned about the long history of China. Next, you will learn how Chinese culture helped shape and define another ancient culture in Asia. That culture was Japan.

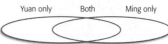

Section 5 Assessment

go.hrw.com
Online Quiz
KEYWORD: SK9 HP15

Reviewing Ideas, Terms, and People

1. **a. Identify** Who was Genghis Khan?
   b. Explain How did the Mongols gain control of China?
   c. Evaluate Judge this statement: "The Mongols should never have tried to invade Japan."
2. **a. Identify** Who was Zheng He, and what did he do?
   b. Analyze What impression do you think the Forbidden City had on the residents of Beijing?
   c. Develop How may the Great Wall have both helped and hurt China?
3. **a. Define** What is **isolationism**?
   b. Explain How did the Ming change China?
   c. Develop How might a policy of isolationism have both advantages and disadvantages?

Critical Thinking

4. **Comparing and Contrasting** Draw a diagram like this one. Use your notes to see how the Yuan and Ming dynasties were alike and different.

   Yuan only   Both   Ming only

FOCUS ON WRITING

5. **Identifying Achievements of the Later Dynasties** Make a list of the achievements of the Yuan and Ming dynasties. Then look back over all your notes and rate the achievements or inventions. Which four or five do you think are most important?

492 CHAPTER 15

Section 5 Assessment Answers

1. **a.** leader of the Mongols who conquered a large part of Asia
   b. by attacking and terrorizing Chinese towns
   c. possible answer—Statement is valid; attack on Japan contributed to the Yuan dynasty's failure.

2. **a.** the greatest sailor of the Ming dynasty; led voyages of exploration to Asia and Africa
   b. possible answers—that the emperor was divine; awed by power of the emperor
   c. The Great Wall protected the Chinese, but it was costly to build.

3. **a.** removing, or isolating, a country from contact with other countries
   b. building projects, instituted isolationism
   c. advantages—protection, safety; disadvantages—lack of trade and development

4. Yuan—foreign rule, Mongol and Chinese customs, trade by sea; Ming—Chinese rule, stable dynasty, great sea voyages, isolationism; both—great building projects

5. possible answers—extension of the Grand Canal, the Forbidden City, voyages of exploration, restoration of the Great Wall of China

Kublai Khan

How did a Mongol nomad settle down to rule a vast empire?

When did he live? 1215–1294

Where did he live? Kublai Khan came from Mongolia but spent much of his life in China. His capital, Dadu, was near the modern city of Beijing.

What did he do? Kublai Khan completed the conquest of China that Genghis Khan had begun. He ruled China as the emperor of the Yuan dynasty.

KEY FACTS

- Unified all of China under his rule
- Established peace, during which China's population grew
- Extended the Grand Canal so that food could be shipped from the Huang He (Yellow River) to his capital near modern Beijing
- Linked China to India and Persia with better roads
- Increased contact with the West

Why is he important? The lands Kublai Khan ruled made up one of the largest empires in world history. It stretched from the Pacific Ocean to Eastern Europe. As China's ruler, Kublai Khan welcomed foreign visitors, including the Italian merchant Marco Polo and the Arab historian Ibn Battutah. The stories these two men told helped create interest in China and its products among Westerners.

Generalizing How did Kublai Khan's actions help change people's views of China?

This painting from the 1200s shows Kublai Khan hunting on horseback.

ANCIENT CIVILIZATIONS OF ASIA–CHINA **493**

Biography

Kublai Khan Review with students how nomads live and contrast that style of life with city dwellers or farmers. Ask students if they believe it would be difficult to stay in the same place if for generations their family had moved from one location to another. Discuss students' views.

Info to Know

A Kinder, Gentler Khan While he could be violent, Kublai Khan was different from his grandfather, Genghis Khan. He urged his generals to be humane in their conquests. He was concerned with running an effective government and encouraging religious tolerance. Among the religions in Kublai Khan's China were Tibetan Lamaism, Islam, Buddhism, Confucianism, and Daoism.

Did you know ...

Despite his efforts, Kublai Khan was never able to build a strong empire in China. While the economy often looked healthy, much of the economic gain went only to the wealthy. The civil service system had crumbled, and censors were no longer working across China. Kublai Khan had a difficult time controlling all of his officials. Economic conditions for most Chinese worsened during this period.

About the Illustration

This illustration of Kublai Khan is an artist's conception based on available sources. However, historians are uncertain exactly what Kublai Khan looked like.

Cross Discipline Activity: English/Language Arts   At Level

Writing an Introduction

1. Tell students that when a notable person is scheduled to give a speech, it is common for someone to introduce him or her. These short introductory speeches always include the person's accomplishments and present the person in a favorable light.

2. Have each student write an introduction that someone might have written and then read to introduce Kublai Khan to a group of foreigners. Make sure students include details about Kublai Khan found in this section.

3. Ask for volunteers to read their introductions to the class. **LS Verbal/Linguistic**

   Alternative Assessment Handbook, Rubric 37: Writing Assignments

---

Answers

Generalizing *He made internal improvements in China and welcomed foreign visitors to serve and write about the empire.*

493

Social Studies Skills

Making Economic Choices

1. Discuss ways that economic choices can affect cities and towns. Explain that cities and towns sometimes need to make choices that help some people and hurt others. For example, picture a city in which improvements were needed in schools, the police department, and the fire department.

2. Ask students to discuss the trade-offs and look at both the short-term and long-term effects of each decision. For example, no improvements in the police department might eventually lead to more crime.

3. Ask students to write a paragraph that describes their choice for improvements and the reasons behind it.

4. When writing is complete, ask students to raise their hands to show which choice they made. Then ask volunteers to share their choice and the reasons for it. **LS Verbal/ Linguistic, Interpersonal**

- Alternative Assessment Handbook, Rubric 43: Writing to Persuade
- Interactive Skills Tutor CD-ROM, Lesson 9: Construct and Support Persuasive Arguments
- **RF:** Social Studies Skills, Making Economic Choices

Making Economic Choices

Learn

Economic choices are a part of geography. World leaders must make economic choices every day. For example, a country's president might face a choice about whether to spend government money on improving defense, education, or health care.

You also have to make economic choices in your own life. For example, you might have to decide whether to go to a movie with a friend or buy a CD. You cannot afford to do both, so you must make a choice.

Making economic choices involves sacrifices, or trade-offs. If you choose to spend your money on a movie, the trade-offs are the other things you want but cannot buy. By considering trade-offs, you can make better economic choices.

Practice

Imagine that you are in the school band. The band has enough money to make one major purchase this year. As the diagram below shows, the band can spend the money on new musical instruments, new uniforms, or a band trip. The band decides to buy new instruments.

❶ Based on the diagram below, what are the trade-offs of the band's choice?

❷ What would have been the trade-offs if the band had voted to spend the money on a trip instead?

❸ How do you think creating a diagram like the one below might have helped the band make its economic choice?

New Instruments (instead of using old, worn-out ones) | New Uniforms (instead of playing in school clothes) | Band Trip (instead of not taking a trip this year)

Choice: New Instruments

Apply

1. Describe an example of an economic choice you might face that has three possible trade-offs.

2. For each possible economic choice, identify what the trade-offs are if you make that choice.

3. What final choice will you make? Why?

4. How did considering trade-offs help you make your choice?

Social Studies Skills Activity: Making Economic Choices   At Level

Special Needs Learners

1. Discuss ways that economic choices affect society. For example, some societies choose to use resources to provide health care for all while others choose to invest more money in the military.

2. Ask students to imagine that they were a member of the ruling class during the Tang dynasty. After many discussions, the emperor and others have identified three options for using the dynasty's wealth: expanding and maintaining the Great Wall, expanding and improving the Grand Canal, and building large new government buildings in the capital. Write these options on the board.

3. Ask students which choice they would make and why. Help them discuss the trade-offs involved with each option. **LS Verbal/Linguistic, Logical/Mathematical**

- Alternative Assessment Handbook, Rubric 11: Discussions

Answers

Practice 1. *new uniforms, band trip;*
2. *new instruments, new uniforms;*
3. *It allowed them to look at the choices and trade-offs clearly.*

Apply *Answers will vary, but should include three clear options, trade-offs, and a final choice and explanation.*

Chapter Review

Geography's Impact
video series
Review the video to answer the closing question:
Do you agree with Confucius's ideas concerning family? Why or why not?

Visual Summary

Use the visual summary below to help you review the main ideas of the chapter.

QUICK FACTS

The Shang, Qin, and Han dynasties ruled China and made many advances that were built on later.

Under the Tang and Song dynasties, Confucianism was an important element of Chinese government.

The Mongols invaded China and ruled it as the Yuan dynasty.

The powerful Ming dynasty strengthened China and expanded trade, but then China became isolated.

Reviewing Vocabulary, Terms, and Places

Match the words or names with their definitions or descriptions.

a. gunpowder   **f.** porcelain
b. scholar-official   **g.** Great Wall
c. mandate of heaven **h.** isolationism
d. bureaucracy   **i.** incentive
e. seismograph

1. a device to measure the strength of earthquakes
2. something that leads people to follow a certain course of action
3. body of unelected government officials
4. thin, beautiful pottery
5. educated government worker
6. policy of avoiding contact with other countries
7. a barrier along China's northern border
8. a mixture of powders used in explosives
9. the idea that heaven chose who should rule

Comprehension and Critical Thinking

SECTION 1 *(Pages 464–467)*

10. a. Identify What was the first known dynasty to rule China? What did it achieve?

   b. Analyze Why did the Qin dynasty not last long after Shi Huangdi's death?

   c. Evaluate Do you think Shi Huangdi was a good ruler for China? Why or why not?

SECTION 2 *(Pages 468–473)*

11. a. Define What is Confucianism? How did it affect Han society?

   b. Analyze What was life like for peasants in the Han period?

   c. Elaborate What inventions show that the Han studied nature?

Answers

Visual Summary

Review and Inquiry Have students write a short description of one of the drawings in the visual summary. Ask them to describe what is shown in the picture.

Quick Facts Transparency: Visual Summary: Ancient Civilizations of Asia—China

Reviewing Vocabulary, Terms, and Places

1. e
2. i
3. d
4. f
5. b
6. h
7. g
8. a
9. c

Comprehension and Critical Thinking

10. a. Shang dynasty; it introduced China's first writing system, created items from bronze and jade, developed military equipment, and invented a calendar.
b. The rulers who followed him were not as strong.
c. possible answers—yes, because he was strict and effective; no, because he did not share his power and took away people's rights

---

Review and Assessment Resources

Review and Reinforce

- Chapter Review
- **RF:** Chapter Review
- Quick Facts Transparency: Visual Summary: Ancient Civilizations of Asia—China
- Spanish Chapter Summaries Audio CD
- **OSP** Holt PuzzlePro; Quiz Show for ExamView
- Quiz Game CD-ROM

Assess

- **SE** Standardized Test Practice
- PASS: Chapter Test, Forms A and B
- Alternative Assessment Handbook
- **OSP** ExamView Test Generator, Chapter Test
- Differentiated Instruction Modified Worksheets and Tests CD-ROM: Modified Chapter Test
- **HOAP** Holt Online Assessment Program (in the Holt Interactive Online Student Edition)

Reteach/Intervene

- Interactive Reader and Study Guide
- Differentiated Instruction Teacher Management System: Lesson Plans
- Differentiated Instruction Modified Worksheets and Tests CD-ROM
- Interactive Skills Tutor CD-ROM

go.hrw.com
Online Resources
Chapter Resources:
KEYWORD: SK9 CH15

11. a. a philosophy that emphasizes the importance of ethics and moral values; it divided people into four social classes.

   b. Peasants worked long, difficult days on farms or on government projects. They lived simple lives, mostly in small villages.

   c. the sundial and the seismograph

12. a. Wu Daozi painted murals related to Buddhism and nature; Li Bo, Du Fu, and Li Qingzhao all wrote poems.

   b. They created law codes and had a woman ruler—Empress Wu.

   c. possible answers—the compass, because it advanced exploration; gunpowder, because it changed how wars were fought.

13. a. Neo-Confucianism, which emphasized spiritual matters, developed, and its ideas became official government teachings after the Song dynasty.

   b. possible answer—to assure that only talented, intelligent people were brought into the government

   c. to make sure that government officials were chosen by ability instead of wealth or family connections

14. a. by developing a powerful, fearsome army; most of Central and East Asia, including China, as well as parts of Europe

   b. Marco Polo wrote about his travels to China; Zheng He led voyages to many nations, telling people along the way about his country.

   c. to make the people of China feel safe from invasions by northern tribes

Using the Internet

15. Go to the HRW Web site and enter the keyword shown to access a rubric for this activity:

> KEYWORD: SK9 TEACHER

Social Studies Skills

16. possible answers—will have to wear old shoes, may have to go to library to get a book

17. possible answers—will have to wear old shoes, will have to watch old movies

---

SECTION 3 *(Pages 476–481)*

12. a. Describe What did Wu Daozi, Li Bo, Du Fu, and Li Qingzhao contribute to Chinese culture?

   b. Analyze How did the Tang rulers change China's government?

   c. Evaluate Which Chinese invention has had a greater effect on world history—the magnetic compass or gunpowder? Why do you think so?

SECTION 4 *(Pages 482–485)*

13. a. Define How did Confucianism change in and after the Song dynasty?

   b. Make Inferences Why do you think the civil service examination system was created?

   c. Elaborate Why were China's civil service examinations so difficult?

SECTION 5 *(Pages 486–492)*

14. a. Describe How did the Mongols create their huge empire? What areas were included in it?

   b. Draw Conclusions How did Marco Polo and Zheng He help shape ideas about China?

   c. Elaborate Why do you think the Ming spent so much time and money on the Great Wall?

Using the Internet

15. Activity: Creating a Mural The Tang and Song periods saw many agricultural, technological, and commercial developments. New irrigation techniques, movable type, and gunpowder were a few of them. Enter the activity keyword and learn more about such developments. Imagine that a city official has hired you to create a mural showing all of the great things the Chinese developed during the Tang and Song dynasties. Create a large mural that depicts as many advances as possible.

Social Studies Skills

Making Economic Choices *You have enough money to buy one of the following items: shoes, a DVD, or a book.*

16. What are the trade-offs if you buy the DVD?

17. What are the trade-offs if you buy the book?

---

18. Understanding Chronological Order Arrange the following list of events in the order in which they happened. Then write a brief paragraph describing the events, using clue words such as *then* and *later* to show the proper sequence.

- The Han dynasty rules China.
- The Shang dynasty takes power.
- Mongol armies invade China.
- The Ming dynasty takes control.

19. Writing Your Magazine Article Now that you have identified the achievements or inventions that you want to write about, begin your article. Open with a sentence that states your main idea. Include a paragraph of two or three sentences about each invention or achievement. Describe each achievement or invention and explain why it was so important. End your article with a sentence or two that summarize China's importance to the world.

Map Activity

20. Ancient China On a separate sheet of paper, match the letters on the map with their correct labels.

Chang'an	Beijing	Huang He
Kaifeng	Chang Jiang	

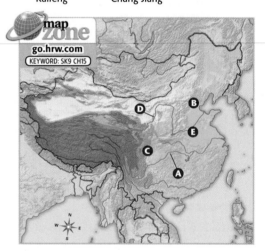

Focus on Reading and Writing

18. The Shang dynasty takes power; the Han dynasty rules China; Mongol armies invade China; the Ming dynasty takes control. Students' paragraphs should include clue words to show sequence and should accurately reflect the information in this chapter.

   RF: Focus on Reading, Understanding Chronological Order

19. Students' magazine articles should

- clearly state the main idea
- include a short paragraph for each invention or achievement

- include accurate and detailed descriptions of the inventions or achievements
- end with a summary of China's importance to the world

   RF: Focus on Writing, Writing a Magazine Article

Map Activity

20. A. Chang Jiang

   B. Beijing

   C. Chang'an

   D. Huang He

   E. Kaifeng

DIRECTIONS (1–7): For each statement or question, write on a separate answer sheet the *number* of the word or expression that, of those given, best completes the statement or answers the question.

1 Who was the Chinese admiral who sailed all around Asia during the Ming dynasty?

(1) Li Bo

(2) Genghis Khan

(3) Zhu Yuanzhang

(4) Zheng He

2 Trade and other contact with peoples far from China stopped under which dynasty?

(1) Ming

(2) Yuan

(3) Song

(4) Sui

3 Which of the following was one way that Confucianism influenced China?

(1) emphasis on family and family values

(2) expansion of manufacturing and trade

(3) increase in taxes

(4) elimination of the government

4 Which of the following was an achievement of the Shang dynasty?

(1) invention of fireworks

(2) building of the Grand Canal

(3) creation of a writing system

(4) construction of the Forbidden City

5 What religion that developed in ancient India became very popular in ancient China as well?

(1) Hinduism

(2) Islam

(3) Jainism

(4) Buddhism

6 Emperor Shi Huangdi had laborers work on a structure that Ming rulers improved. What was that structure?

(1) the Great Wall

(2) the Great Tomb

(3) the Forbidden City

(4) the Temple of Buddha

7 The ruler who completed the Mongol conquest of China was named

(1) Shi Huangdi.

(2) Du Fu.

(3) Kublai Khan.

(4) Confucius.

Base your answer to question 8 on the image below and on your knowledge of social studies.

8 This object displays Chinese expertise at working with

(1) woodblocks.

(2) gunpowder.

(3) cotton fibers.

(4) porcelain.

Answers

Standardized Test Practice

1. 4

Break Down the Question This question requires students to recall factual information from Section 5.

2. 1

Break Down the Question This question requires students to recall factual information from Section 5.

3. 1

Break Down the Question Remind students that Confucianism was a philosophy that stressed ethics and moral values.

4. 3

Break Down the Question This question requires students to recall factual information from Section 1.

5. 4

Break Down the Question This question requires students to recall factual information from Section 4.

6. 1

Break Down the Question This question requires students to recall factual information from Section 1.

7. 3

Break Down the Question Refer students who missed the question to the text under the heading *The Mongol Conquest* in Section 5.

8. 4

Break Down the Question Refer students who miss this question to the chart on Chinese Inventions in Section 3.

Intervention Resources

Reproducible

Interactive Reader and Study Guide

Differentiated Instruction Teacher Management System: Lesson Plans

Technology

Quick Facts Transparency: Visual Summary: Ancient Civilizations of Asia—China

Differentiated Instruction Modified Worksheets and Tests CD-ROM

Interactive Skills Tutor CD-ROM

Tips for Test Taking

I'm Done! Offer these test-taking tips to students: You aren't finished with your test until you check it. First, take a look at how much time you have left. Go back and review your answers for any careless mistakes you may have made. Be sure to erase any stray marks, review the hardest questions you answered, and turn the test in at the end of the time period. There is nothing to be gained from finishing first—or last either for that matter!

Preteach

Bellringer

Motivate Before beginning the Case Study, ask students what they know of ancient Japan. Have students preview the Case Study, looking at the photos, maps, and other labels as main headings. Have each student begin a KWL chart on ancient Japan. Have students use the images, maps, and other labels as headings in their KWL chart. Have students write down what they already know about each item. Then have students write down what they want to learn about each item. As a review of the Case Study, have students complete the KWL chart by noting what they learned about each item in the chart.

Key Terms

Preteach the following terms:

court a group of nobles who live near and advise a ruler (p. 498)

samurai professional warriors in ancient Japan (p. 498)

figurehead a person who appears to rule while the real power rests with someone else (p. 499)

shogun in ancient Japan, the title of the person who held real power and ruled in the emperor's name (p. 499)

daimyo a warrior lord in ancient Japan who controlled vast amounts of land and commanded samurai (p. 500)

Bushido code of behavior of Japanese samurai warriors that stressed bravery and loyalty (p. 501)

Ancient Japan

History

Japanese writing is an art form in itself. This album made in the shape of a fan is covered in text and pictures.

Japan has a lengthy history. The earliest Japanese citizens lived in villages ruled by powerful clans, or extended families. Each clan was led by a chief. For many years, these clans lived independently of one another. By the 500s, however, one powerful clan had taken control of much of Japan. The head of that clan became Japan's first emperor.

In 794 the emperor and empress of Japan moved to Heian (HAY-ahn), a city now called Kyoto. Many nobles followed their rulers to the new city. There they created an imperial court, a group of nobles who live near and advise a ruler.

In fact, the emperor and nobles of Heian were so taken with their own lifestyles that they paid little attention to the rest of the country. Outside of Heian, powerful nobles fought for land. In addition, rebels battled imperial officials.

With the emperor distracted, Japan's rural nobles decided that they needed to protect their own lands from bandits and thieves. The nobles hired professional warriors to defend them and their property. These warriors were known as samurai.

Many nobles were unhappy with the way Japan's government was being run. They wanted a change of leadership. Eventually, two noble clans went to war with each other in the 1150s. Each clan wanted to take power for itself.

The Heian Jingu shrine in Kyoto celebrates Japan's imperial past. Built in 1895, it is a reconstruction of the ancient imperial palace from Heian.

498

Teach the Case Study | At Level

Ancient Japan

1. **Teach** Ask students the questions in the Main Idea boxes under Direct Teach.

2. **Apply** Organize students into small groups. Assign each group one of the following: history, government, daily life, culture, nobles. Have each group create a storyboard that uses images and captions to teach about the assigned topic.

3. **Review** As you review the Case Study, have each group present and explain its storyboard to the class.

4. **Practice/Homework** Have students work in the same groups to create a script for a short skit on their assigned topic. For example, the history group might present a skit on the war that took place in the 1150s between the two noble clans. Have each group present its skit to the class. **LS Interpersonal, Visual/Spatial**

   Alternative Assessment Handbook, Rubric 33: Skits and Reader's Theater

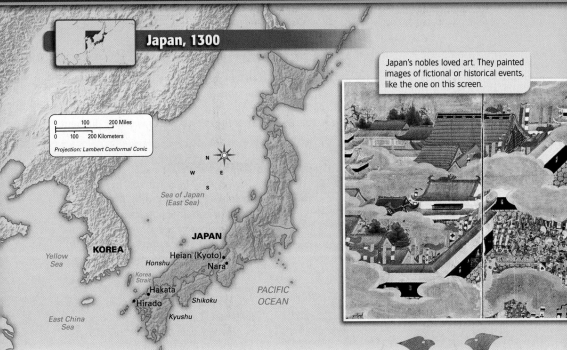

Japan, 1300

0   100   200 Miles
0 100   200 Kilometers
Projection: Lambert Conformal Conic

N
W   E
S

Sea of Japan
(East Sea)

JAPAN

KOREA

Yellow
Sea

Honshu

Heian (Kyoto)

Nara

Korea
Strait

Hakata

Hirado   Shikoku

PACIFIC
OCEAN

East China
Sea

Kyushu

Japan's nobles loved art. They painted images of fictional or historical events, like the one on this screen.

The war left the leader of the Minamoto clan the most powerful man in Japan. He decided to take over ruling the country but didn't want to get rid of the emperor. Instead, he kept the emperor on as a figurehead, a person who appears to rule even though real power lies with someone else. Minamoto himself took the title shogun and ruled Japan in the emperor's name. When Minamoto died, he passed his title and power on to one of his sons. For about the next 700 years, a series of shoguns ruled Japan.

Case Study Assessment

1. What was life like in Heian?

2. Why did Japan's emperor lose power?

3. **Activity** Illustrated fans were popular in ancient Japan. Create a fan with an image of a key event from Japanese history.

For many years, Japan was ruled by warriors and generals.

499

Main Idea

History

Recall How did Heian become an important city in ancient Japan? *The emperor and empress moved there and many nobles followed them.*

Sequence List and describe the steps that led to a long period of shoguns ruling in the name of the emperor. *emperor was distracted in Heian; nobles gained power; war between two clans led to rise of Minamoto clan; Minamoto became most powerful figure in Japan; Minamoto passed power down to his son*

Evaluate Do you think the emperor was wise to allow Minamoto to rise to power? Explain. *possible answer—no because Minamoto took the real power away from the emperor*

🔲 Map Zone Transparency: Japan, 1300

Collaborative Learning

At Level

Illustrating Japanese History

1. Point out to students that Japanese nobles loved art and often used beautiful images to decorate screens, fans, and other objects.

2. Organize the class into small groups. Have each group review the text under the heading "History". Then instruct each group to plan an illustration that summarizes the history of ancient Japan. Remind each group that their illustration should depict more than one event.

3. Have each group select an object on which to place their art, for example a fan or a vase. Then have each group create a rough sketch of their proposed piece.

4. Have each group exchange its sketch with another group. Then instruct students to write a description of the piece they examined.

LS Visual/Spatial, Verbal/Linguistic

Alternative Assessment Handbook, Rubrics 3: Artwork; and 40: Writing to Describe

Answers

Case Study Assessment **1.** *Life in Heian was dominated by the emperor and the imperial court, who focused more on an elaborate lifestyle than on ruling the country.* **2.** *He was so taken with his lifestyle that he took little interest in ruling the country.* **3.** *Students' responses will vary. See Rubric 3: Artwork, in the* Alternative Assessment Handbook.

Main Idea

Society and Daily Life

Define Who were the daimyo? *powerful landowners who governed large estates and hired professional armies of samurai*

Make Inferences Why might the shogun have required the daimyo to live in Heian? *possible answers—he wanted to be able to keep a close eye on their activities; to prevent them from organizing a rebellion*

Draw Conclusions What do you think that life was like for peasants in Japan? *They were poor and had no power and most worked on the estates of the daimyo.*

🖳 Quick Facts Transparency: Samurai Society

Society and Daily Life

By the early 1000s Heian was the center of Japanese society. Living there were the emperor and many powerful nobles, the elite of the country. They imagined that everyone wanted to live just as they did. Yet life outside Heian was very different from life in the capital.

Samurai Society   QUICK FACTS

Emperor
Holding little real power, the emperor was a figurehead.

Shogun
A powerful military leader, the shogun ruled in the emperor's name.

Daimyo and Samurai
Daimyo were powerful lords who often led armies of samurai. Samurai warriors served the shogun and daimyo.

Peasants
Most Japanese were poor peasants who had no power.

Government

The emperor in Heian was, in theory, the ruler of all Japan. In truth, however, the emperor had little power outside of the city. True power rested with the shogun, who ruled in the emperor's name.

Below the shogun were a number of powerful landowners called daimyo (DY-mee-oh). Each of the daimyo owned a large es-tate, though they often did not live there. For many years the shogun required all daimyo to live in Heian. As a result, each of the daimyo named a representative to govern his estate in his absence. On the estate, peasants grew rice to feed the daimyo and his family as well as food for themselves.

Because wars were not uncommon in Japan, daimyo needed soldiers to defend their estates. They hired professional warriors called samurai for this purpose. Most samurai came from noble families, but many had little money. In exchange for their military service, the samurai received either land or food. Because flat land is rare in Japan, only the most powerful samurai got land for their service.

Daily Life

Life in Japan varied according to where a person lived. People who lived in the capital of Heian had a very different way of life than people outside the city.

Critical Thinking: Identifying Points of View   At Level

Japanese Society Panel Discussion

Research Required

1. Review the structure of Japanese society with the class. Have students examine the Samurai Society chart and read the descriptions of each social group.

2. Assign each student a social group. Have students use their textbooks, the library, and other sources to research more about their assigned group. Students should look for information about the daily life of members of their assigned group.

3. Tell students that they will participate in a panel discussion on daily life in ancient

Japan. Have each student write three or four questions for members of the other social groups. Students will use their research to answer questions posed by the class.

4. Ask for two or three volunteers from each group to serve on the panel. Assign two other students to serve as moderators for the discussion. Have students in the audience ask questions of the panel. **LS** **Verbal/Linguistic, Interpersonal**

📑 Alternative Assessment Handbook, Rubrics 11: Discussions; and 41: Writing to Express

Court life in Japan was formal and ritualized, as this painting and these quotations show.

Members of Japan's royal court loved ritual and ceremony. They enjoyed lives of ease and privilege and spent their days writing and attending parties or Buddhist ceremonies. They lived apart from poorer citizens and seldom left the city.

The Heian nobles also valued beauty. As a result, they spent hours working on their personal appearances. Many had magnificent wardrobes full of silk robes and gold jewelry. Nobles delighted in elaborate outfits. For example, women wore long gowns made of 12 layers of colored silk cleverly cut and folded to show off many layers at once. The women completed their outfits with delicate painted fans.

Outside Heian, life was focused more on duty than on beauty. Samurai in particular lived by a strict honor code known as Bushido. This code required the samurai to be brave and virtuous soldiers. It also required them to live simple, disciplined lives. More than anything, however, Bushido required samurai to remain loyal to their lords.

Case Study Assessment

1. Who were the daimyo? the samurai?
2. What was life like for a samurai?
3. **Activity** Imagine you were a noble in Heian. What would your day be like? Make a schedule of your routine on a typical day.

Nobles spent hours in elaborate Buddhist rituals. Most non-nobles were also Buddhists, but had no time for ritual.

Main Idea

Society and Daily Life

Recall What is Bushido? *a strict honor code that samurai followed which emphasized loyalty and bravery*

Contrast How was life for a noble in Heian different from that of a samurai? *Nobles lived lives of ease and privilege and put great emphasis on beauty and ceremony, while samurai lived simple and disciplined lives that valued loyalty and bravery.*

Make Judgments If you had lived in ancient Japan, would you have preferred to be a noble in Heian or a samurai? Explain your answer. *possible answer—a samurai because they valued discipline and honor and lived simple lives*

Did you know . . .

Samurai warriors originally fought on horseback and were trained in sword fighting, archery, and martial arts. The position of samurai officially ended in the 1870s when the Japanese government forbade them to wear their swords in public.

Differentiating Instruction

At Level

English-Language Learners

1. Have students review the information about the daily lives of nobles and samurai in ancient Japan. Define unfamiliar terms as needed.

2. Instruct students to write two journal entries. The first entry should describe a typical day in the life of a noble in Heian. The second journal entry should reflect a typical day for a samurai.

3. Each account should be written in the first person and begin with a description of the author. Remind students to use details from the text to write their journal entries. Encourage students to be as descriptive in their journal entries as possible.

4. Ask for volunteers to share their journal entries with the class. Then lead a class discussion on the similarities and differences between nobles and samurai.

LS Verbal/Linguistic

Alternative Assessment Handbook, Rubrics 11: Discussions; and 15: Journals

Answers

Case Study Assessment
1. *daimyo—powerful landowners who commanded large estates and personal armies; samurai—professional warriors* 2. *They were nobles with little money, so they served as professional warriors in exchange for food or land. They followed a strict code of loyalty and bravery.* 3. *Students' responses may vary, but should include a description that includes the nobles' interest in beauty and ceremony. See Rubric 37: Writing Assignments, in the* Alternative Assessment Handbook.

Key Events in Ancient Japan

550

c. 550
Buddhism arrives in Japan.

646
A new law code officially creates the samurai class.

794
Japan's imperial court moves to Heian.

Samurai warrior

Culture and Achievements

The Heian period is considered a golden age of Japanese culture. As you have read, the nobles of Heian prized beauty in all its forms. They spent hours on their writing and painting. As a result, they created amazing works of literature and art.

The nobles of Heian—both men and women—devoted much time to writing. Many women kept detailed diaries and journals about life at court. In addition, a noblewoman known as Lady Murasaki Shikibu wrote a novel called *The Tale of Genji*. Many historians consider this book, written in about 1000, to be the world's first full-length novel.

Men did not usually keep journals or write novels. Instead, they focused their efforts on poetry. Both men and women in Heian wrote beautiful poems. Some people even held parties at which they took turns writing and reading poems. Their poems often talked about love or nature. Most poems of the time followed strict formulas. One type of poem popular in Heian was the tanka. A tanka is always five lines long. The first and third lines have five syllables each, while the others have seven. Three-line poems called haiku were also popular.

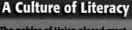

A Culture of Literacy

The nobles of Heian placed great value on literature. All nobles, men and women alike, were expected to write beautifully. Many of the works they created are still read and admired today.

This samurai is writing a poem on a cherry tree. Writing poems helped train samurai to concentrate.

Some noble Japanese women kept detailed journals and wrote novels and poems.

502 CASE STUDY

Cross-Discipline Activity: Literature

At Level

Japanese Poetry

1. Remind students that Japanese poems often followed strict formulas. Ask students to identify the types of poetry popular among nobles in Heian. Then ask students what topics were the focus of Japanese poems.

2. Help students understand that a tanka is always five lines long. The first and third lines have five syllables each, while the others have seven. Tell students that the most common form of haiku is three lines long. The first line and last line are made up of five syllables,

while the middle line is made up of seven syllables.

3. Have students write their own Japanese style poems. Have each student write at least one tanka and one haiku. If time permits, have students illustrate their poems.

4. Ask for volunteers to share their poems and illustrations with the class. **LS Verbal/Linguistic, Visual/Spatial**

Alternative Assessment Handbook, Rubrics 3: Artwork; and 26: Poems and Songs

c. 1000
Lady Murasaki
Shikibu writes
The Tale of Genji.

A scene from
The Tale of Genji

1192
The first shogun
takes power in Japan.

1274
The Japanese fight
off an invasion from
Mongol China.

1300

In addition to literature, the nobles of Heian made great achievements in other fields. They loved to paint and created masterful paintings. Many of their works illustrate scenes from stories, such as *The Tale of Genji*. Some nobles were also skilled architects. They designed magnificent temples and palaces, often surrounded by gardens and ponds.

Heian was also the birthplace of many forms of the performing arts. Nobles of the imperial court appreciated music, dance, and acrobatics. They also enjoyed watching plays. In time, the plays performed at Heian developed into a form of drama called Noh, which is still popular in Japan today.

Matsumoto Castle, built under Japan's shoguns

Case Study Assessment

1. What is the significance of *The Tale of Genji*?

2. What were some art forms practiced in Heian?

3. **Activity** The nobles of Japan loved dramas. Write a scene from a play about life in ancient Japan. Perform the scene with a group.

BIOGRAPHY

Lady Murasaki Shikibu
c. 978–c. 1026

During her lifetime, Lady Murasaki Shikibu was honored as a noblewoman and as a servant to the Empress Akiko. Since her death, she is better remembered as a diarist and an author. Lady Murasaki wrote *The Tale of Genji*, which is considered the world's first full-length novel and the greatest classic of Japanese literature. The novel tells of a prince named Genji and his long quest for love. During his search, he meets many women. By describing the women in precise detail, Lady Murasaki gives us a glimpse into life in Heian.

503

Chapter 16 Planning Guide

Growth and Development of South and East Asia

Chapter Overview	Reproducible Resources	Technology Resources
CHAPTER 16 pp. 504–537 **Overview:** In this chapter students will learn about the growth and development of the countries of South and East Asia, with emphasis on India, China, and Japan.	**Differentiated Instruction Teacher Management System:*** • Instructional Pacing Guides • Lesson Plans for Differentiated Instruction **Interactive Reader and Study Guide:** Chapter Summary Graphic Organizer* **Resource File:*** • Chapter Review • Focus on Reading: Using Context Clues—Definitions • Focus on Speaking: Conducting an Interview • Social Studies Skills: Analyzing Visuals	**OSP Teacher's One-Stop Planner:** Calendar Planner **Power Presentations with Video CD-ROM** **Differentiated Instruction Modified Worksheets and Tests CD-ROM** **Student Edition on Audio CD Program** **Map Zone Transparency:** South and East Asia, 1850–Today* **Geography's Impact Video Program (VHS/DVD):** Impact of Population Density*
Section 1: **Contact across Cultures** **The Big Idea:** Contact between cultures in Asia led to a sharing of many cultural traits, especially from India and China.	**Differentiated Instruction Teacher Management System:** Section 1 Lesson Plan* **Resource File:*** • Vocabulary Builder: Section 1 • Biography: Guru Nanak • Literature: The *Lun Yü*	**Daily Bellringer Transparency:** Section 1*
Section 2: **Interaction with the West** **The Big Idea:** In the 1700s and 1800s Europeans and Americans swept into Asia and forced many political and economic changes.	**Differentiated Instruction Teacher Management System:** Section 2 Lesson Plan* **Interactive Reader and Study Guide:** Section 2 Summary* **Resource File:*** • Vocabulary Builder: Section 2	**Daily Bellringer Transparency:** Section 2* **Map Zone Transparency:** The British in India, 1767–1858* **Map Zone Transparency:** Imperialism in China, 1842–1900*
Section 3: **New Political Movements** **The Big Idea:** Major political changes in Asia in the early twentieth century marked the end of European domination there.	**Interactive Reader and Study Guide:** Section 3 Summary* **Resource File:*** • Vocabulary Builder: Section 3 • Primary Source: Gandhi's "Quit India" Speech	**Daily Bellringer Transparency:** Section 3*
Section 4: **Asia at War** **The Big Idea:** Since the 1930s several major wars have been fought in Asia.	**Differentiated Instruction Teacher Management System:** Section 4 Lesson Plan* **Resource File:*** • Vocabulary Builder: Section 4	**Daily Bellringer Transparency:** Section 4* **Map Zone Transparency:** War in the Pacific, 1942–1944* **Internet Activity:** Hiroshima and Nagasaki
Section 5: **A New Asia** **The Big Idea:** Since the end of World War II, Asia has experienced major economic, political, and cultural changes.	**Differentiated Instruction Teacher Management System:** Section 5 Lesson Plan* **Resource File:*** • Vocabulary Builder: Section 5 • Biography: Aung San Suu Kyi	**Daily Bellringer Transparency:** Section 5*

CHAPTER 16 PLANNING GUIDE

SE Student Edition   Print Resource   Audio CD

TE Teacher's Edition   Transparency   CD-ROM

 go.hrw.com   **LS** Learning Styles   Video

OSP Teacher's One-Stop Planner   * also on One-Stop Planner

Review, Assessment, Intervention

 Quick Facts Transparency: Visual Summary: Growth and Development of South and East Asia*

 Spanish Chapter Summaries Audio CD Program

 Progress Assessment Support System (PASS): Chapter Test*

 Differentiated Instruction Modified Worksheets and Tests CD-ROM: Modified Chapter Test

OSP **Teacher's One-Stop Planner:** ExamView Test Generator (English/Spanish)

HOAP **Holt Online Assessment Program (HOAP),** in the Holt Interactive Online Student Edition

 PASS: Section 1 Quiz*

 Online Quiz: Section 1

 Alternative Assessment Handbook

 PASS: Section 2 Quiz*

 Online Quiz: Section 2

 Alternative Assessment Handbook

 PASS: Section 3 Quiz*

 Online Quiz: Section 3

 Alternative Assessment Handbook

 PASS: Section 4 Quiz*

 Online Quiz: Section 4

 Alternative Assessment Handbook

 PASS: Section 5 Quiz*

 Online Quiz: Section 5

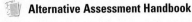 **Alternative Assessment Handbook**

Power Presentations with Video CD-ROM

Power Presentations with Video are visual presentations of each chapter's main ideas. Presentations can be customized by including Quick Facts charts, images from the text, and video clips.

Holt Online Learning

go.hrw.com
Teacher Resources
KEYWORD: SK9 TEACHER

go.hrw.com
Student Resources
KEYWORD: SK9 CH16

- Interactive Multimedia Activities
- Current Events

- Chapter-based Internet Activities
- and more!

Holt Interactive Online Student Edition

Complete online support for interactivity, assessment, and reporting
- Interactive Maps and Notebook
- Standardized Test Prep
- Homework Practice and Research Activities Online

CHAPTER 16 PLANNING GUIDE

Differentiating Instruction

How do I address the needs of varied learners?
The Target Resource acts as your primary strategy for differentiated instruction.

ENGLISH-LANGUAGE LEARNERS & STRUGGLING READERS

TARGET RESOURCE
Spanish Resources

Spanish Chapter Summaries Audio CD
Teacher's One-Stop Planner:
- ExamView Test Generator, Spanish
- PuzzlePro, Spanish

English-Language Learner Strategies and Activities

Additional Resources

Differentiated Instruction Teacher Management System: Lesson Plans for Differentiated Instruction
Resource File:
- Vocabulary Builder Activities
- Social Studies Skills: Analyzing Visuals

Quick Facts Transparency: Visual Summary: Growth and Development of South and East Asia
Student Edition on Audio CD Program
Interactive Skills Tutor CD-ROM

SPECIAL NEEDS LEARNERS

TARGET RESOURCE
Interactive Reader and Study Guide

The activities in the Interactive Reader and Study Guide engage students with questions while presenting summaries of chapter content and provide opportunities for students to practice critical thinking skills.

Additional Resources

Differentiated Instruction Teacher Management System: Lesson Plans for Differentiated Instruction
Resource File: Social Studies Skills: Analyzing Visuals
Student Edition on Audio CD Program
Interactive Skills Tutor CD-ROM
Graphic Organizer Transparencies with Support for Reading and Writing

ADVANCED/GIFTED AND TALENTED STUDENTS

TARGET RESOURCE
Resource File

The Resource File activities allow students to extend their knowledge of chapter-related places and people and to practice geography skills.
- Focus on Reading: Using Context Clues—Definitions
- Focus on Speaking: Conducting an Interview
- Literature: The *Lun Yü*

Additional Resources

Differentiated Instruction Teacher Management System: Lesson Plans for Differentiated Instruction
World History and Geography Document-Based Questions Activities
Geography, Science, and Cultures Activities
Experiencing World History and Geography

Differentiated Activities in the Teacher's Edition

- Charting the British Role in India
- Sequencing
- Analyzing Visuals
- Writing a Poem
- China's History and Culture

Differentiated Activities in the Teacher's Edition

- Exploring Chinese Culture
- Pearl Harbor Murals

Differentiated Activities in the Teacher's Edition

- The Japanese Miracle
- Analyzing Language

HOLT Teacher's One-Stop Planner®

How can I manage the lesson plans and support materials for differentiated instruction?

With the Teacher's One-Stop Planner, you can easily organize and print lesson plans, planning guides, and instructional materials for all learners.

The Teacher's One-Stop Planner includes the following materials to help you differentiate instruction:

- Interactive Teacher's Edition
- Calendar Planner and pacing guides
- Editable lesson plans
- All reproducible ancillaries in Adobe Acrobat (PDF) format
- ExamView Test Generator (English & Spanish)
- Transparency and video previews

Professional Development

What teacher training resources are available to help me grow professionally?

- **In-service and staff development** as part of your Holt Social Studies product purchase
- **Quick Teacher Tutorial Lesson Presentation CD-ROM**
- Intensive tuition-based **Teacher Development Institute**
- **Convenient Holt Speaker Bureau:** face-to-face workshop options
- **24/7 Ask A Professional Development Expert** at http://www.hrw.com/prodev/

DIFFERENTIATED INSTRUCTION PLANNING GUIDE

Chapter Big Ideas

Section 1 Contact between cultures in Asia led to a sharing of many cultural traits, especially from India and China.

Section 2 In the 1700s and 1800s Europeans and Americans swept into Asia and forced many political and economic changes.

Section 3 Major political changes in Asia in the early twentieth century marked the end of European domination there.

Section 4 Since the 1930s several major wars have been fought in Asia.

Section 5 Since the end of World War II, Asia has experienced major economic, political, and cultural changes.

Focus on Reading and Speaking

Reading The Resource File provides a worksheet to help students practice determining definitions using context clues.

📖 **RF:** Focus on Reading, Using Context Clues—Definitions

Speaking The Resource File provides a worksheet to help students conduct their interviews.

📖 **RF:** Focus on Speaking, Conducting an Interview

Key to Differentiating Instruction

Below Level

Basic-level activities designed for all students encountering new material

At Level

Intermediate-level activities designed for average students

Above Level

Challenging activities designed for honors and gifted and talented students

Standard English Mastery

Activities designed to improve standard English usage

CHAPTER **16**

Growth and Development of South and East Asia

FOCUS QUESTION

What forces had an impact on the development of Asia and why?

What You Will Learn...

Home to ancient civilizations and empires, Asia underwent many changes after the late 1800s. The arrival of Europeans and internal political struggles had major effects on the region.

FOCUS ON READING AND SPEAKING

Using Context Clues—Definitions As you read, you can often figure out the meaning of an unknown word by using context clues. One type of context clue is a definition, a restatement of a word's meaning. **See the lesson, Using Context Clues—Definitions, on page S19.**

Conducting an Interview With a partner, you will role-play a journalist interviewing a historical figure from Asia. First, read about the region and select a figure you would like to interview. Then conduct your interview, having your partner take on the role of your chosen historical figure.

504 CHAPTER 16

SOUTH ASIA

New Delhi

Mohandas Gandhi

Bay of Bengal

0   250   500 Miles
0   250   500 Kilometers
Projection: Two-Point Equidistant

Imperialism Under British rule, thousands of miles of railroads were built in India. Here, workers build the East Bengal Railway around 1870.

Introduce the Chapter

At Level

Growth and Development of South and East Asia

Materials: 12″ × 18″ construction paper

1. Organize students into five groups. Assign a section to each group and give each group a sheet of construction paper.

2. Have groups copy their section number and Big Idea paragraph in the center of their papers. Have groups work together to write subheads and important details beneath each subhead. Have students add appropriate illustrations to their posters.

3. When groups have finished, have them display their work and present it to the class.

4. As homework, ask students to write a short paragraph about why the information in the chapter might be important. **LS Interpersonal, Visual/Spatial**

📝 Alternative Assessment Handbook, Rubrics 14: Group Activity; and 28: Posters

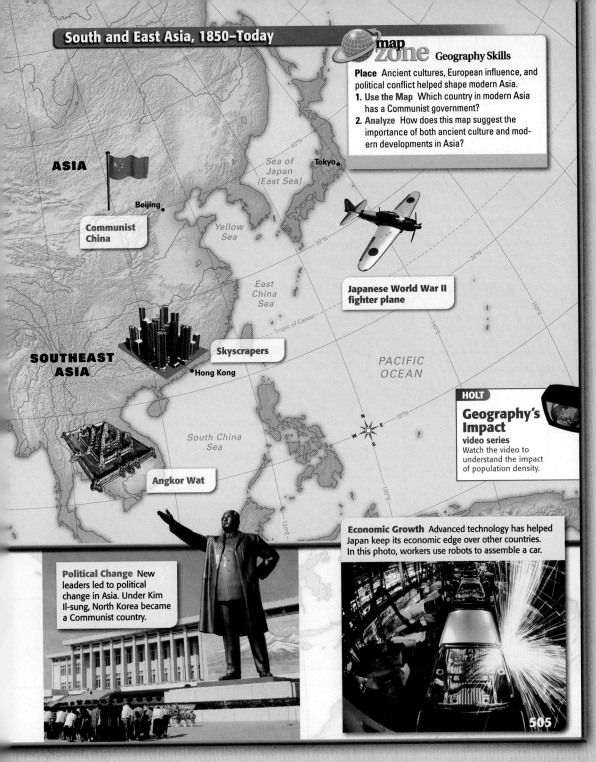

map zone Geography Skills

Place Ancient cultures, European influence, and political conflict helped shape modern Asia.
1. **Use the Map** Which country in modern Asia has a Communist government?
2. **Analyze** How does this map suggest the importance of both ancient culture and modern developments in Asia?

ASIA

Beijing

Communist China

Sea of Japan (East Sea)

Tokyo

Yellow Sea

Japanese World War II fighter plane

East China Sea

SOUTHEAST ASIA

Tropic of Cancer

Skyscrapers

Hong Kong

PACIFIC OCEAN

South China Sea

Angkor Wat

HOLT

Geography's Impact
video series
Watch the video to understand the impact of population density.

Political Change New leaders led to political change in Asia. Under Kim Il-sung, North Korea became a Communist country.

Economic Growth Advanced technology has helped Japan keep its economic edge over other countries. In this photo, workers use robots to assemble a car.

505

Info to Know

Mahatma In references to Mohandas Gandhi, the names *Mohandas* and *Mahatma* seem to be used interchangeably. However, Gandhi's given name was Mohandas, not Mahatma. Mahatma is a title bestowed on Gandhi by the people of India to honor him. The title is given only to people of exceptional merit. It comes from maha-atman, which means "great self." In Gandhi's case, "great soul" might be the best translation.

Info to Know

World's Tallest Buildings As of 2008, 56 of the 100 tallest buildings in the world were located in Asia. Eight of the top 10 are in Asian countries, including the nearly completed Burj Dubai in the United Arab Emirates. At more than 2,500 feet, Burj Dubai will tower over the world's second, third, and fourth tallest buildings, all located in South and East Asia. Those buildings are Taipei 101 in Taiwan (1,667 feet), and the Petronas Towers 1 and 2 in Malaysia (both 1,483 feet).

Chapter Preview

Explore the Map and Pictures

South and East Asia, 1850–Today
Have students note the physical features of South and East Asia, particularly the number of major rivers and mountain ranges. Discuss how these physical features have affected the growth and development of Asia. For example, the rivers allowed civilizations to develop, while the mountains created a natural barrier between India and China. Then have students examine the small images on the map. What do each of these images indicate about South and East Asia during the period from 1850 through today?

Map Zone Transparency: South and East Asia, 1850–Today

Analyzing Visuals Have each student select one of the photographs. Tell students to imagine that they are on vacation in Asia and that their selected photograph is a postcard. Have students write a postcard to a friend or relative explaining what the image shows and the importance of the image.

Alternative Assessment Handbook, Rubric 40, Writing to Describe

go.hrw.com
Online Resources
Chapter Resources:
KEYWORD: SK9 CH16
Teacher Resources:
KEYWORD: SK9 TEACHER

HOLT

Geography's Impact
▶ video series
See the Video Teacher's Guide for strategies for using the chapter video to teach about the impact of population density.

Answers
Map Zone 1. *China;* **2.** *by showing the ancient temple Angkor Wat and modern skyscrapers*

505

Bellringer

If YOU lived there. . . Use the **Daily Bellringer Transparency** to help students answer the question.

 Daily Bellringer Transparency, Section 1

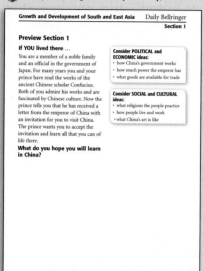

Key Terms and Places

📖 **RF:** Vocabulary Builder, Section 1

Taking Notes

Have students copy the graphic organizer onto their own paper and then use it to take notes on the section. This activity will prepare students for the Section Assessment, in which they will complete a graphic organizer that builds on the information using the Critical Thinking Skill: Categorizing.

What You Will Learn...

Main Ideas

1. Chinese culture had a powerful influence on many Asian civilizations.
2. India was a major influence on culture in South Asia.
3. A new religion called Sikhism developed in India in the late 1400s.

The Big Idea

Contact between cultures in Asia led to a sharing of many cultural traits, especially from India and China.

Key Terms and Places

cultural diffusion, *p. 506*
Angkor Wat, *p. 508*
Sikhism, *p. 509*

TAKING NOTES As you read, use a diagram like this one to take notes on China's and India's influences on other Asian cultures, especially those of Southeast Asia.

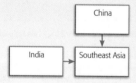

Contact across Cultures

If **YOU** lived there...

You are a member of a noble family and an official in the government of Japan. For many years you and your prince have read the works of the ancient Chinese scholar Confucius. Both of you admire his works and are fascinated by Chinese culture. Now the prince tells you that he has received a letter from the emperor of China with an invitation for you to visit China. The prince wants you to accept the invitation and learn all that you can of life there.

What do you hope you will learn about China?

BUILDING BACKGROUND China and India were home to two of the world's first civilizations. Over several centuries, the people of China and India developed rich and distinct cultures. As other civilizations developed in Asia, they could not help but be influenced by the Chinese and the Indians.

Chinese Influence in Asia

Ancient China was one of the world's most highly developed civilizations. Already centuries old when other East Asia civilizations began, China exerted a strong influence over the cultures of its younger neighbors. Among those places influenced by China were Korea, Japan, and Vietnam.

Korea

Korea is located on a peninsula in East Asia, just east of China. No major physical barriers separate the peninsula from the rest of Asia, and so travel between the two regions is easy. As you might expect from this location, the Korean and Chinese people made contact early in their history. As a result of this contact, many elements of Chinese culture spread into Korea. The spread of culture traits from one region to another, such as from China to Korea, is known as **cultural diffusion.**

Teach the Big Idea

At Level

Contact across Cultures

1. **Teach** Ask students the questions in the Main Idea boxes under Direct Teach.

2. **Apply** Draw three squares for students to see. Label them with the titles of the headings in this section: Chinese Influence in Asia, India and South Asia, and Sikhism Develops. Have students copy the squares onto their own paper. Then have students read the text under each heading and write the main ideas of each topic in the appropriate square.

3. **Review** As you review the section, have students describe how the cultures of South and East Asia influenced each other.

4. **Practice/Homework** Have students write a letter to one of the historical figures mentioned in the section describing what the student already knows about the person's culture and asking for more information about his or her life. 🔳 **Verbal/Linguistic**

📖 Alternative Assessment Handbook, Rubric 37: Writing Assignments

In the 100s BC, the Han dynasty conquered part of the Korean Peninsula, and Chinese settlers moved to Korea. They brought with them many elements of their own culture, including Buddhism and Chinese writing. Even after Korea won its independence, some of its rulers encouraged the adoption of Chinese culture.

Among the rulers who wanted to learn from the Chinese were the kings of the Koryo dynasty, from whose name we get the word Korea. The Koryo rulers adopted several elements of Chinese culture. For example, they created a civil service system similar to the one in China. At the same time, they did not want Korea to turn into another China, and they urged artisans to develop their own styles of ceramics and other crafts. The result was a Korean society that blended Chinese and native life.

Japan

Like Korea, Japan was heavily influenced by Chinese culture. In fact, many elements of Chinese culture that reached Japan did so through Korea. By the 500s Korean traders had begun sailing to Japan. With them came Chinese writing and Buddhism. The Japanese quickly adopted both the writing and religion. The Japanese of this time had no written language of their own, so educated Japanese used Chinese characters to write their own language.

Eventually, Japan's leaders decided to learn about Chinese culture directly from the source. One such leader was Prince Shotoku, who governed Japan from 593 to 622. Shotoku greatly admired the Chinese. He sent scholars to China to learn about Chinese religion, philosophy, and government. As a result, Chinese foods, fashions, and art gained popularity.

Vietnam

In the 200s BC a kingdom called Nam Viet rose to power in Vietnam. Its ruler was a former official from China who had declared his independence. As a result, the Vietnamese people adopted many elements of Chinese culture. They spoke the Chinese language and wore Chinese clothing and hairstyles. Many also practiced a Chinese form of Buddhism.

READING CHECK Sequencing How did Chinese culture spread to Korea and Japan?

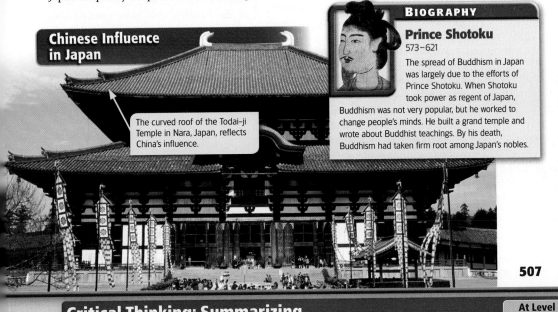

Chinese Influence in Japan

The curved roof of the Todai-ji Temple in Nara, Japan, reflects China's influence.

BIOGRAPHY

Prince Shotoku
573–621

The spread of Buddhism in Japan was largely due to the efforts of Prince Shotoku. When Shotoku took power as regent of Japan, Buddhism was not very popular, but he worked to change people's minds. He built a grand temple and wrote about Buddhist teachings. By his death, Buddhism had taken firm root among Japan's nobles.

507

Direct Teach

Main Idea

❶ **Chinese Influence in Asia**

Chinese culture had a powerful influence on many Asian civilizations.

Define What is cultural diffusion? *the spread of culture traits from one region to another*

Summarize What elements of Chinese culture did the people of Korea adopt? *Buddhism, Chinese writing, civil service system*

Elaborate How was Chinese culture brought to Japan? *at first through Korea and later between Japan and China directly*

Develop How could you tell that one civilization was influenced by another? *by looking for cultural traits such as language, religion, dress, and art, that clearly originated elsewhere*

📄 **RF:** Literature, The *Lun Yü*

Critical Thinking: Summarizing

At Level

Buddhist Temples in Japan

Research Required

1. Have students use the library or the Internet to research Buddhist temples in Japan. Tell students they should find descriptions of temples, including location, layout, and objects found there. Students should also research appropriate behavior at these places of worship.

2. Call on volunteers to share the information they found. Record students' observations in a chart on the board. Have students display any visuals they found.

3. When the chart is complete, guide the class in a discussion in which you summarize the main features of Buddhist temples in Japan. Refer to the text as necessary to discuss how the temples reflect the beliefs of Buddhism.

📄 **Verbal/Linguistic, Visual/Spatial**

📄 Alternative Assessment Handbook, Rubrics 11: Discussions; and 30: Research

Answers

Reading Check *through travelers and traders between China, Korea, and Japan*

❷ India and South Asia

India was a major influence on culture in South Asia.

Recall What civilization had the greatest influence on life in South Asia? *Indian civilization*

Analyze Is Angkor Wat an example of Indian cultural diffusion? Explain your answer. *possible answer—Yes. The building was located far from India, but was a temple for a religion that originated in India and was built in a style that reflected Indian architectural styles.*

Elaborate If you had lived in South Asia around AD 1000, how might your life have been influenced by Indian culture? *possible answer—in the religion I practiced, the language I spoke, the way my government was run, and how the buildings around me were designed*

Info to Know

Other Temple Sites In addition to Angkor Wat, Southeast Asia has many other significant religious sites. For example, Borobudur is a huge, eighth-to ninth-century Buddhist temple in Central Java, Indonesia. Abandoned for centuries, this temple complex was rediscovered in the early 1800s. It is now a UNESCO World Heritage site. Among its many features are more than 1,000 carved narrative panels and over 400 Buddha images.

Answers

Analyzing Visuals *possible answers— They are interested in its long history; they want to see the beautiful carvings.*

Reading Check *religion, writing, government, science, art, language, architecture*

508

Angkor Wat

The majestic towers and detailed carvings of the ruins of Angkor Wat attract millions of tourists.

ANALYZING VISUALS Why do you think so many people visit Angkor Wat?

India and South Asia

China's long history and advanced civilization made it the most influential power in East Asia. Further south, however, lay another ancient and advanced civilization. That civilization was India, and it became the greatest influence on life in South Asia. Over the centuries, traders and missionaries spread elements of Indian culture through much of the region.

Probably the most visible element of Indian culture in Asia was religion. As you recall, India had been the birthplace of two major religions, Hinduism and Buddhism. Over several centuries, Indian missionaries carried both religions far and wide.

Along with religion, Indian ideas about writing, government, science, and art spread through Asia. Some Southeast Asian rulers so admired Indian culture that they adopted Indian names and built temples in Indian styles. Many also adopted the Indian language Sanskrit in their kingdoms.

Among the nations influenced by India was the Khmer Empire of what is now Cambodia. The Khmer adopted both Hinduism and Indian styles of architecture. The most famous example of this architecture is the spectacular temple complex at **Angkor Wat**. Built in the 1100s, the complex had high walls and a temple with high towers. Many of the temple's walls were covered with carvings of scenes from Hindu myths.

In the early 1500s India was conquered by Muslims from Central Asia. They were the Mughals, and they soon built a large empire. The Mughals brought an elegant new style of architecture to India. The best example of this style is the Taj Mahal, built by an emperor in the 1600s as a tomb for his wife. Mughal rulers encouraged the spread of Islam. As a result, traders and missionaries spread Islam to the islands of Indonesia, Malaysia, and the Philippines.

READING CHECK **Categorizing** What elements of Indian culture spread in Asia?

Cross-Discipline Activity: Arts and Humanities [At Level]

An Artist's Letter Home

1. Have students imagine they are an artist visiting Angkor Wat to paint a picture of it.

2. Have students first examine the photograph with a partner, with each person sharing some ways in which he or she would describe the picture. Have each student make a list of all the descriptions.

3. Then have each student write a letter to a friend or family member at home, telling them that he or she is painting a picture of the temple. Students should include some information about the temple's history. The bulk of the letter should describe the painting in detail, using the list of descriptions, so the reader gets a strong image of the building and setting in his or her mind.

4. Ask for volunteers to share their letters. Discuss how the letter's language helped create mental images. **LS Visual/Spatial, Verbal/Linguistic**

  Alternative Assessment Handbook, Rubric 40: Writing to Describe

Sikhism Develops

Shortly before the Mughals took over India, a new religion developed there. It was **Sikhism** (SEE-ki-zuhm), a monotheistic religion that developed in the 1400s.

Origins of Sikhism

Sikhism has its roots in the teachings of the Guru Nanak, who lived in the late 1400s in the Punjab region of northern India. The title *guru* is Sanskrit for "teacher." Guru Nanak was raised as a Hindu, but he was not fully satisfied with Hindu teachings. As a result, he set out to learn more about the world. According to legend, his travels took him as far as Mecca and Medina, the holy cities of Islam.

The insights Guru Nanak gained in his travels became the basis for later Sikh beliefs. Over the next few centuries, his teachings were expanded and explained by nine other gurus. The last of these gurus, Guru Gobind Singh, died in the early 1700s. Most of the gurus wrote hymns in which they described the nature of God and how people should behave. These hymns were collected in the *Guru Granth Sahib*, the most sacred text of Sikhism.

Sikh Beliefs and Practices

Sikhs are monotheistic, believing in only one God. They believe that God has no physical form but that he can be sensed in the world, which he created. For Sikhs, the ultimate goal in life is to be reunited with God after death. To achieve this goal, one must meditate to find spiritual enlightenment. However, achieving enlightenment may take several lifetimes. As a result, Sikhs believe in reincarnation. Sikhs also believe that people should live truthfully and treat all people equally, regardless of gender, social class, or any other factors.

Sikhs pray several times each day. They are expected to wear five items at all times as signs of their religion: long hair, a small comb, a steel bracelet, a sword, and a special undergarment. In addition, all Sikh men wear turbans, as do many women.

THE IMPACT TODAY
More than 20 million people in the world today practice Sikhism. Most of them live in the Punjab region of India and Pakistan.

READING CHECK Analyzing What are the basic beliefs of Sikhism?

SUMMARY AND PREVIEW Within Asia, cultures blended over the centuries. Next, you will learn how ideas from other lands changed life in Asia as well.

Section 1 Assessment

go.hrw.com
Online Quiz
KEYWORD: SK9 HP16

Reviewing Ideas, Terms, and Places

1. **a. Define** What is **cultural diffusion**?
   b. Make Generalizations What influence did the Chinese have on civilization in Japan?
   c. Evaluate Do you think Chinese influence was good or bad for Korea and Japan? Why?
2. **a. Identify** What elements of Indian culture were adopted by other Asian civilizations?
   b. Sequence How did Indians help advance the spread of Islam in Asia?
3. **a. Recall** When did **Sikhism** develop?
   b. Draw Conclusions Why do you think Sikhs wear five particular items at all times?

Critical Thinking

4. **Categorizing** Use your notes and the chart below to identify the influence of China and India on each element of Asian culture.

	Religion	Language	Architecture
China			
India			

FOCUS ON SPEAKING

5. **Selecting a Topic** Who or what will be the subject of your interview? Will you talk to someone who lived during this period or to an expert on Chinese culture from the time? Write down some ideas.

GROWTH AND DEVELOPMENT OF SOUTH AND EAST ASIA **509**

Main Idea

3 Sikhism Develops

A new religion called Sikhism developed in India in the late 1400s.

Identify What are the roots of Sikhism? *the teachings of a fifteenth century Indian teacher, Guru Nanak*

Explain What is the *Guru Granth Sahib*? *the most sacred text of Sikhism, a collection of hymns about the nature of God and how people should behave*

Review & Assess

Close

Have students discuss how China and India shaped the development of other civilizations in South and East Asia.

Review

Online Quiz, Section 1

Assess

SE Section 1 Assessment
PASS: Section 1 Quiz
Alternative Assessment Handbook

Reteach/Classroom Intervention

Interactive Reader and Study Guide, Section 1
Interactive Skills Tutor CD-ROM

Section 1 Assessment Answers

1. **a.** the spread of culture traits from one region to another
   b. Chinese writing, foods, fashions, and arts; Buddhism
   c. possible answer—good; Both Korea and Japan developed vibrant cultures of their own, perhaps partly because of Chinese influence.
2. **a.** religion, language, writing, government, science, art, architecture
   b. India's Mughal rulers encouraged the spread of Islam. Indian traders and missionaries brought Islam with them to other parts of Asia.
3. **a.** the late 1400s
   b. possible answer—to remind them of their faith and to proclaim their faith to others
4. China—Buddhism, Chinese language and writing, temple styles; India—Buddhism and Hinduism, Sanskrit, temple styles
5. Students responses will vary. Students should list some historical figures from Asia they would like to interview.

Answers

Reading Check *belief in one God with no physical form; reunion with God requires spiritual enlightenment that may take several lifetimes to achieve; reincarnation; truthful and equitable behavior*

509

Bellringer

If YOU lived there. . . Use the **Daily Bellringer Transparency** to help students answer the question.

📘 Daily Bellringer Transparency, Section 2

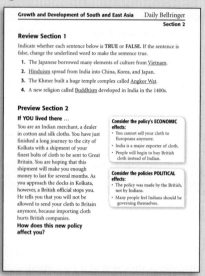

Growth and Development of South and East Asia — Daily Bellringer Section 2

Review Section 1

Indicate whether each sentence below is **TRUE** or **FALSE**. If the sentence is false, change the underlined word to make the sentence true.

1. The Japanese borrowed many elements of culture from Vietnam.
2. Hinduism spread from India into China, Korea, and Japan.
3. The Khmer built a huge temple complex called Angkor Wat.
4. A new religion called Buddhism developed in India in the 1400s.

Preview Section 2

If YOU lived there ...
You are an Indian merchant, a dealer in cotton and silk cloths. You have just finished a long journey to the city of Kolkata with a shipment of your finest bolts of cloth to be sent to Great Britain. You are hoping that this shipment will make you enough money to last for several months. As you approach the docks in Kolkata, however, a British official stops you. He tells you that you will not be allowed to send your cloth to Britain anymore, because importing cloth hurts British companies.
How does this new policy affect you?

Consider the policy's ECONOMIC effects:
- You cannot sell your cloth to Europeans anymore.
- India is a major exporter of cloth.
- People will begin to buy British cloth instead of Indian.

Consider the policies POLITICAL effects:
- The policy was made by the British, not by Indians.
- Many people feel Indians should be governing themselves.

Academic Vocabulary

Review with students the high-use academic term in this section.

policy rule, course of action (p. 511)

📋 RF: Vocabulary Builder, Section 2

Taking Notes

Have students copy the graphic organizer onto their own paper and then use it to take notes on the section. This activity will prepare students for the Section Assessment, in which they will complete a graphic organizer that builds on the information using the Critical Thinking Skill: Finding Main Ideas.

What You Will Learn...

Main Ideas

1. The British made India into a colony in the 1700s and 1800s.
2. European countries used force to make China open its ports to trade.
3. Led by the United States, the West began to trade in Japan.

The Big Idea

In the 1700s and 1800s Europeans and Americans swept into Asia and forced many political and economic changes.

Key Terms and Places

British East India Company, *p. 511*
Raj, *p. 511*
Guangzhou, *p. 513*
spheres of influence, *p. 513*
Boxer Rebellion, *p. 513*

TAKING NOTES As you read, take notes about the interaction between the West and India, China, and Japan.

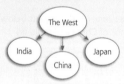

Interaction with the West

If YOU lived there...

You are an Indian merchant, a dealer in cotton and silk cloths. You have just finished a long journey to the city of Kolkata with a shipment of your finest bolts of cloth to be sent to Great Britain. You are hoping that this shipment will make you enough money to last for several months. As you approach the docks in Kolkata, however, a British official stops you. He tells you that you will not be allowed to send your cloth to Britain anymore, because importing cloth hurts British companies.

How does this new policy affect you?

BUILDING BACKGROUND Before the 1700s Asia had little contact with Europe, other than limited trade. By the end of the century, however, large numbers of Europeans had arrived in Asia, leading to major culture changes.

The British in India

As early as the days of the Roman Empire, Europeans had been fascinated by Asia. Traders had traveled back and forth between the two continents for centuries along the Silk Road, carrying precious goods in either direction. However, the journey along the Silk Road was long and dangerous, and few people dared it.

In the late 1200s, centuries after Rome fell, the Italian merchant Marco Polo traveled to China. When he returned home, Polo published an account of his journey, which soon became a bestseller. Still, few Europeans even dreamed of going to Asia.

Finally, in the 1400s Portuguese explorers successfully sailed to India for the first time. Other Europeans followed. Ambitious merchants built trading posts all along the Asian coast from India to China. However, Europeans seldom ventured very far inland. Their presence in Asia was mostly limited to the coast. That situation changed after the British moved into India.

Teach the Big Idea

Interaction with the West

1. **Teach** Ask students the questions in the Main Idea boxes under Direct Teach.

2. **Apply** Have students create an outline of the section using the headings as main points. Have students identify two main ideas under each of the blue headings.

3. **Review** Review student outlines as a class. Have students identify the points in their outlines that they feel are most important to the section. Then guide students in a

discussion of the ways in which India, China, and Japan were affected by interaction with the West.

4. **Practice/Homework** Have students write a paragraph explaining why a government might try to limit its people's trade and contact with other nations.
   LS Visual/Spatial, Verbal/Linguistic
   📋 Alternative Assessment Handbook, Rubric 42: Writing to Inform

---

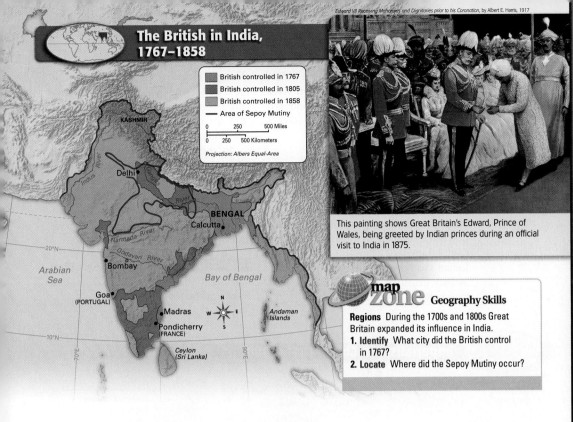

The British in India, 1767–1858

Edward VII Receiving Maharajas and Dignitaries prior to his Coronation, by Albert E. Harris, 1917

British controlled in 1767
British controlled in 1805
British controlled in 1858
Area of Sepoy Mutiny

0   250   500 Miles
0   250   500 Kilometers

Projection: Albers Equal-Area

KASHMIR

Delhi

BENGAL
Calcutta

Arabian
Sea

Bombay

Goa
(PORTUGAL)

Madras

Pondicherry
(FRANCE)

Bay of Bengal

Andaman
Islands

Ceylon
(Sri Lanka)

This painting shows Great Britain's Edward, Prince of Wales, being greeted by Indian princes during an official visit to India in 1875.

map zone Geography Skills

Regions During the 1700s and 1800s Great Britain expanded its influence in India.
1. **Identify** What city did the British control in 1767?
2. **Locate** Where did the Sepoy Mutiny occur?

British East India Company

The people who changed the nature of European activity in Asia were British merchants. In the late 1700s members of the **British East India Company**, a company created to control trade between Britain, India, and East Asia, arrived in India.

Though they had arrived to trade, the British soon became involved in Indian politics. At the time, India was ruled by the Mughal Empire. In the 1700s, that empire began to fall apart. As the Mughals lost control, the British took over. The East India Company brought in its own army to take control. Before long, the Company controlled nearly all of India, as you can see on the map.

The Raj

Many Indians were not happy with the British East India Company's **policies**. In 1857 a rebellion broke out. The rebellion was led by sepoys, Indian soldiers who fought in the British army.

The fighting was brutal and lasted for more than two years. Rebel sepoys killed British officers, women, and children. The British burned villages they suspected of supporting the rebellion.

As a result of the rebellion, the British government took control of India from the East India Company and began to rule India directly. The period of British control in India is called the **Raj** (RAHZH), from the Hindi word for "rule."

ACADEMIC
VOCABULARY
policy rule,
course of action

GROWTH AND DEVELOPMENT OF SOUTH AND EAST ASIA **511**

Main Idea

❶ The British in India, continued

Recall What was the Raj? *the period of British government control in India*

Explain Why were Indian-led attempts to break free of British rule unsuccessful? *India supplied raw materials to British industries and was a market for British goods. The British did not want to give that up.*

Make Judgments Would it be accurate to say there were two Indias during the Raj? Explain your answer. *possible answer—Yes. The British lived in separate neighborhoods and belonged to exclusive clubs, so there was an India for the British and an India for Indians.*

Connect to Literature

Two of England's best-known authors, Rudyard Kipling (1865–1936) and George Orwell (1903–1950) were born in India when it was a British colony. Kipling, who won the Nobel Prize for literature in 1907, wrote works that glorified the British in colonial India. He also wrote works for children, including *The Jungle Book* (1894). Orwell's attitude toward the British in India was the opposite of Kipling's. Early in life Orwell became disillusioned with colonial rule and harshly criticized British imperialism. His best-known works are the political satires *Animal Farm* (1945) and *Nineteen Eighty-Four* (1949).

Answers

Reading Check *new Western-style education system, English language, banning of some Indian customs, spread of Christianity*

Map Zone 1. *Russia, Great Britain;* **2.** *Germany's*

During the Raj most officials who served in the Indian government were British, not Indian. These British officials considered themselves superior to the Indian people they governed. Most of them lived in separate neighborhoods and belonged to exclusive clubs. They had little contact with the common people.

THE IMPACT TODAY
English is still the one of the most widely spoken languages in India today. It is often used for government and business affairs.

Changes in India

Most of the British officials in India believed that they were improving the lives of the Indian people by ruling them. They introduced a new Western education system and forced Indians to learn the English language. They also banned some Indian customs. At the same time, they invited Christian missionaries to spread their beliefs.

Many Indian people disagreed with these officials. They did not think their lives were better under the British. They wanted a chance to participate in government and resented having to give up their culture. Some Indians began to protest the presence of the British. They staged protests and boycotted British goods.

In the end, these protests had little effect on the situation in India. The British considered India too profitable a colony to give up. India was a major source of raw materials, such as cotton, tea, and indigo, that were used in British industries. It was also a prime market for British goods.

READING CHECK **Identifying Cause and Effect** How did life in India change after the British took over the government?

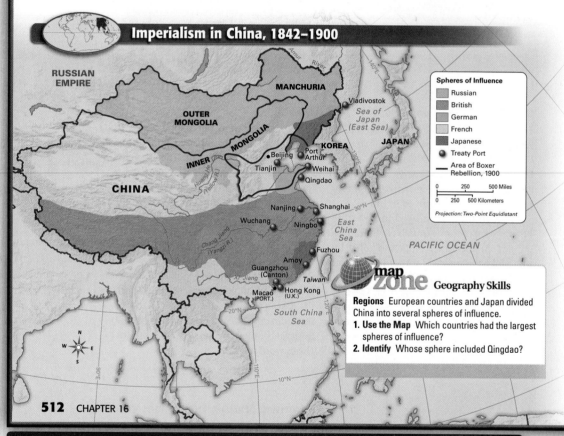

Imperialism in China, 1842–1900

Spheres of Influence
- Russian
- British
- German
- French
- Japanese
- ● Treaty Port
- — Area of Boxer Rebellion, 1900

0   250   500 Miles
0   250   500 Kilometers
Projection: Two-Point Equidistant

map zone **Geography Skills**

Regions European countries and Japan divided China into several spheres of influence.

1. **Use the Map** Which countries had the largest spheres of influence?
2. **Identify** Whose sphere included Qingdao?

512 CHAPTER 16

Collaborative Learning

At Level

The British in India and China

Research Required

1. Organize students into two groups. Have each group prepare for a classroom debate about the positive and negative effects of British rule on India and China. Have students use reliable print and online resources to gather information for the debate. Assign one group to defend British rule and the other to argue against it.

2. After each group has had time to conduct its research and prepare its arguments, hold a classroom debate. Which side was able to present the more convincing arguments?

3. Guide students in a discussion of the overall effects of British rule on India and China. How did researching both sides of the issue help them understand the ongoing controversy over the legacy of British rule?

LS Interpersonal

Alternative Assessment Handbook, Rubric 10: Debates

Europeans in China

While India was falling under the control of the British, similar events were happening in China. As in India, Europeans moved to increase their influence in—and their control over—China.

Differing Viewpoints

In the 1700s trade with China was a major source of income for Europeans. Chinese goods like silk and spices drew high prices throughout Europe. As a result, Europeans thought it vital that the trade continue.

To the Chinese, though, the trade with Europe was not as significant. They saw the Europeans as just another trading partner. In fact, China's rulers saw Europeans—and everyone else living outside of China—as barbarians. They did not want these barbarians living in their country. As a result, they only allowed European traders to live in a single city, **Guangzhou** (GWANG-JOH). The British knew the city as Canton.

Forcing the Issue

In 1839 a dispute arose between the Qing government of China and British traders. The British, members of the British East India Company, were smuggling opium into China to sell, which angered the Chinese. They confiscated and destroyed as much of the opium as they could find. The British merchants complained to their government, and the British attacked China.

The British navy quickly captured the city of Shanghai. They forced the Chinese to open five more ports to European traders. Within a few years, the Chinese had been forced to make similar deals with several other countries. Those countries included France, Russia, and the United States. China had been divided into many **spheres of influence**, or areas over which other countries had economic power.

Changes in China

In response to the presence of so many Europeans in China, the Qing introduced many changes to their culture. They thought that Western knowledge and technology was what had allowed the British to defeat them. As a result, China's leaders tried to introduce Western knowledge and languages to China. They also built Western weapons and ships.

These new weapons were tested in 1894 when China went to war with Japan. Despite their new weapons, though, China lost. The loss left China weak, and Western powers were quick to take advantage. They hurried to increase their influence in China. Fearing that Europeans would take over China completely and shut them out of trade, Americans also worked to gain power in the region.

The Chinese were humiliated by this increased Western control. Some began planning action against the Europeans and Americans. In 1899 they began the **Boxer Rebellion**, an attempt to drive all the Westerners out of China. The Western powers easily put down the rebellion and accused the Chinese government of supporting it. The failed rebellion left China even more humiliated than before.

READING CHECK Sequencing What led to the Boxer Rebellion?

The West in Japan

Before the 1400s contact between Europe and India and China had been rare but not unknown. In contrast, the Europeans had almost no knowledge of Japan at all. Unlike India and China, Japan had been able to isolate itself from the West for many years. The only Europeans allowed to the islands were a few Dutch merchants, and they were restricted to the city of Nagasaki.

FOCUS ON READING

How does the highlighted text help you figure out the meaning of *spheres of influence*?

❸ The West in Japan

Led by the United States, the West began to trade in Japan.

Identify What brought Japanese isolationism to an end? *the arrival in Tokyo Bay of a fleet of American warships under the command of Commander Matthew Perry*

Compare and Contrast How was Japan's reaction to the forced acceptance of the West similar to and different from China's? *both were humiliated, but while China resisted Western influence, Japan decided to modernize*

● **Review & Assess** ●

Close

Have students discuss how India, China, and Japan were affected by interaction with the West.

Review

Online Quiz, Section 2

Assess

SE Section 2 Assessment

PASS: Section 2 Quiz

Alternative Assessment Handbook

Reteach/Classroom Intervention

Interactive Reader and Study Guide, Section 2

Interactive Skills Tutor CD-ROM

Japan Reacts

This print shows the arrival of Commodore Perry in Edo Bay in 1853. Perry's hulking warships sent the Japanese a strong message about U.S. military power.

ANALYZING VISUALS How do the Japanese boats compare to the American ship?

Japan's isolation came to a drastic end, though, in 1852. In that year American naval commander Matthew Perry sailed into Tokyo Bay with a fleet of warships. The Japanese told him to sail on to Nagasaki, but Perry refused. He insisted on opening trade directly with Tokyo. He had been authorized by the U.S. president to use force if necessary to open Tokyo to trade. Faced with this threat, the Japanese had no choice but to allow him into the city.

Like the Chinese had before, the Japanese found their forced acceptance of the West humiliating. Rather than resisting Western influence as the Chinese had, though, Japan's new rulers decided their best plan was to modernize. They studied Western military tactics and economic practices and copied them. They wanted Japan to be part of the modern world.

READING CHECK **Contrasting** How did Japan's response to the West differ from China's?

SUMMARY AND PREVIEW The arrival of Europeans in Asia led to major changes in society. Next, you will learn about political changes that took place later.

go.hrw.com
Online Quiz
KEYWORD: SK9 HP16

Section 2 Assessment

Reviewing Ideas, Terms, and Places

1. **a. Define** What was the **Raj**?
   b. Sequence What led the British government to take control of India?
   c. Elaborate How do you think Indians felt about the attitude of British officials?
2. **a. Identify** Which country was the first to force its way into China?
   b. Identify Cause and Effect What led to the **Boxer Rebellion**?
3. **a. Describe** How did the Americans force the Japanese to trade with them?
   b. Summarize What effect did the Americans' arrival have on Japan?

Critical Thinking

4. **Finding Main Ideas** Using your notes, complete the graphic organizer below with details about Asian civilizations. In the left box, describe the civilizations before Europeans arrived. In the right box, tell how they changed afterward.

India:
China:
Japan: → Europeans Arrive → India:
China:
Japan:

FOCUS ON SPEAKING

5. **Choosing Questions** If you were to interview someone from this period, who would it be? Write three questions you might ask that person.

514 CHAPTER 16

Section 2 Assessment Answers

1. **a.** the period of British control in India
   b. the Sepoy Mutiny, an Indian rebellion against the British East India Company
   c. possible answer—They probably felt insulted and angry.
2. **a.** Britain
   b. Chinese humiliation at increased Western interference following a military loss to the Japanese
3. **a.** with a show of military might
   b. Japan decided to modernize by adopting some Western practices.

4. India: before—traditional religion and language, after—Christianity, English, Western-style education; China: before—traditional and isolationist, after—many Western influences like languages, weapons, and ships; Japan: before—isolationist and traditional, after—modernized

5. Students should list a person from the period they would interview and provide three questions they would ask that person.

Answers

Analyzing Visuals *The Japanese boats seem small and fragile in comparison to the American ship.*

Reading Check *Japan decided to learn and copy Western military tactics and economic practices, while China resisted these things.*

New Political Movements

If YOU lived there...

You are a lawyer in India in 1932. One morning two friends approach you with a question. They are unhappy about a new law that the British have passed. One friend wants to take up arms and try to force the British out of the country. The other disagrees. She wants to protest the law, but she does not want to use violence to do it. She does not think violence is necessary and is afraid that people will get hurt. The two ask your opinion on the most effective means of protest.

Whom will you support? Why?

BUILDING BACKGROUND Europeans held power in parts of Asia for several decades. Their presence led to many changes, both culturally and politically. Eventually, a combination of factors led to the development of entirely new political systems in many Asian countries.

The Call for Indian Independence

By the early 1900s many Indians resented British interference in their country. Their resentment only increased after World War I. During the war, more than 800,000 Indian soldiers had fought for the British. When the soldiers returned home, they hoped that their sacrifices during the war would have won them some respect. Instead, they found that nothing had changed.

Growing Resentment

The growing resentment in India caught the attention of British officials there. Fearing rebellion, the British dealt harshly with anyone who expressed discontent. British troops broke up all protests against the government, even peaceful ones. Rather than ending resentment, the British actions just angered the Indians even more.

What You Will Learn...

Main Ideas

1. The call for Indian independence was accompanied by nonviolent protests.
2. The early 1900s saw the end of China's imperial period and the beginning of Communism in the country.
3. Changes in Japan's government led to the formation of a new empire.

The Big Idea

Major political changes in Asia in the early twentieth century marked the end of European domination there.

Key Terms and Places

nonviolence, *p. 516*
civil disobedience, *p. 516*
partition, *p. 517*
Pakistan, *p. 517*
Diet, *p. 520*

 TAKING NOTES As you read, take notes on political changes in the various countries of Asia. Use a graphic organizer like the one below to organize your notes.

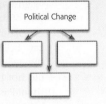

Political Change

515

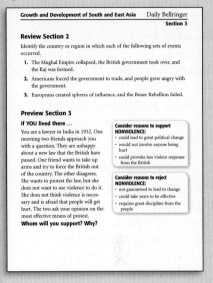
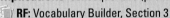
---

❶ The Call for Indian Independence

The call for Indian independence was accompanied by nonviolent protests.

Identify What event marked the beginning of open hostilities between Indians and the British? *the Amritsar Massacre*

Analyze How did encouraging Indians to refuse to pay British taxes reflect Gandhi's two key beliefs about protests? *Refusing to pay taxes is nonviolent and a form of civil disobedience.*

Make Inferences Why was the partition of India agreeable to Hindus and Muslims? *Each group would be in the majority in one or the other of the newly independent countries and civil war would be avoided.*

📋 **RF:** Primary Source, Gandhi's "Quit India" Speech

Nonviolent Protests

Nonviolent protests in India, like the one in the large image, inspired later political activists. Among those inspired were some African Americans who fought for civil rights in the 1960s, who staged nonviolent sit-ins like the one shown in the small photo.

ANALYZING VISUALS What similarities can you see between the two protests shown on this page?

The conflict between the British and the Indians exploded in 1919. At a protest in the town of Amritsar (uhm-RIT-suhr), British troops fired into an Indian crowd, killing more than 400 people. The so-called Amritsar Massacre caused even more Indians to want the British out of India.

Mohandas Gandhi

After the Amritsar Massacre, a new leader arose in the Indian resistance. That leader was Mohandas Gandhi. Gandhi was a lawyer who believed in fair treatment for all people. Resistance and protest were not new to him. For many years Gandhi had lived in South Africa and campaigned against apartheid. He also worked in support of the poor and women's rights.

Gandhi's protests were based on two key beliefs. The first was **nonviolence**, the avoidance of violent actions. Gandhi did not believe that people needed to or should use violence to protest injustice. He believed that peaceful protests were more successful than violent ones.

The second of Gandhi's key beliefs was **civil disobedience**, or the refusal to obey laws in order to bring about change. For example, he encouraged people to avoid paying taxes to the British. Gandhi felt that if the Indian people refused to cooperate with British authority, the British would grow frustrated and leave.

As part of his noncooperation plan, Gandhi encouraged the Indian people to boycott all British products. He stopped wearing British-made clothing and urged other people to do the same. Many people began producing homemade cloth to make clothes themselves. As a result, spinning wheels and homemade cloth became symbols of the Indian resistance. Gandhi also encouraged people to stop buying salt from the British and to make their own salt from seawater instead.

Gandhi and his followers were arrested on several occasions. They did not give up, and their persistence convinced more Indians to join them. By the 1930s millions of people were protesting British rule.

Cross-Discipline Activity: Civics

At Level

Civil Disobedience

Research Required

1. Write the definition of civil disobedience on the board for the class to see. Discuss the definition with students to ensure that they understand it.

2. Tell students that Mohandas Gandhi used civil disobedience to gain rights for Indians. Point out that Gandhi's ideas inspired other nonviolent leaders, such as Martin Luther King Jr. and Cesar Chavez.

3. Have students choose one of these leaders to research and make a collage about the leader's life. The collage should have visuals such as photos and a map. It should also include information on the unjust laws the leader protested and the methods of civil disobedience he or she used, such as marches and strikes.

4. Display students' collages and guide the class in a discussion comparing and contrasting the lives and legacies of these leaders.

🔲 **Visual/Spatial, Verbal/Linguistic**

📋 Alternative Assessment Handbook, Rubrics 8: Collages; and 30: Research

Answers

Analyzing Visuals *both are nonviolent and, if a law was being broken in both, forms of civil disobedience*

Division and Independence

In the end, Gandhi's protests led to change in India. In 1935 the British government gave the Indian people limited self-rule. Not satisfied with this, many people continued their protests.

Even as Indians were protesting against the British, tensions between the Hindu and Muslim communities in India caused a crisis. Muslims feared that, even if India became fully independent, they would have little say in the government. Many of them began calling for a separate nation of their own.

To avoid a civil war, the British government agreed to the **partition**, or division, of India. In 1947 two independent countries were formed. India was mostly Hindu. **Pakistan**, which included the area that is now Bangladesh, was mostly Muslim. As a result, some 10 million people rushed to cross the border. Muslims and Hindus wanted to live in the countries in which they would be part of the majority.

> **READING CHECK** Identifying Cause and Effect
> What was the effect of Gandhi's protesting?

The End of Imperial China

While Indians were calling for freedom from the British, the Chinese were also calling for a change in government. The growing influence of foreign powers in China made many people unhappy with imperial rule. Their unhappiness led to a revolution in China.

Revolution

Realizing that the people were unhappy, China's rulers, the Qing dynasty, tried to reform the government. They built new schools and a new army. They even allowed people to elect regional assemblies for the first time.

However, these attempts at reform were too little and too late. Radical activists called for the overthrow of China's government. They wanted China to become a republic.

One of the leaders of these protests was Sun Yixian (SUN YEE-SHAHN). In the West, his name is sometimes spelled Sun Yat-sen. Sun wanted to make China a democracy, but he did not think that the Chinese people were ready for that yet. He thought it was the government's job to teach the people how to govern themselves.

Inspired by Sun, rebels forced the last Qing emperor—China's last emperor of any dynasty—out of power in 1911. The rebels then formed a republic.

Civil War

The creation of a republic did not end the power struggles in China. In the 1920s two rival groups emerged. One group was the Communists. Opposing them were the Nationalists, led by Chiang Kai-shek (chang ky-SHEK). For several years the two groups worked together to drive foreign imperialists out of China, but their alliance was always uneasy.

The alliance broke apart completely in 1929. Afraid that Communist influence in China was growing too strong, Nationalist forces attacked Communists in several cities. This attack began a civil war that lasted 20 years.

For the first several years of the civil war, the Nationalists were in control. By the 1930s, though, a new Communist leader had emerged. His name was Mao Zedong (MOW ZUH-DOOHNG). By 1949 Mao and the Communists had won. They declared a new Communist government, the People's Republic of China, with Mao as its leader. The surviving Nationalists fled to the island of Taiwan, where they founded the Republic of China.

Direct Teach

Main Idea

❷ **The End of Imperial China**

The early 1900s saw the end of China's imperial period and the beginning of communism in the country.

Recall When was China's last dynasty and emperor removed from power? *1911*

Identify Points of View Why did Chinese Nationalists and Communists form an alliance in the 1920s? *Both groups wanted to drive foreign imperialists out of China.*

Summarize What was the outcome of China's civil war? *The Communists won and established the People's Republic of China. The Nationalists fled to Taiwan and established the Republic of China on the island.*

Biography

Mao Zedong (1893–1976) Mao Zedong was born to a peasant family in Hunan province. As a student, Mao was exposed to revolutionary ideas, and by 1921 he was committed to Marxism. Nine years after the establishment of the People's Republic of China, Mao launched the Great Leap Forward, an economic reform program that failed with dire consequences. Between 1958 and 1962, about 20 million Chinese died from starvation. In 1966, Mao launched the Cultural Revolution to eliminate critics of his leadership.

Critical Thinking: Evaluating Information | At Level

Writing an Elegy

Research Required

1. Have students read a biographical article on Sun Yixian, Chiang Kai-shek, or Mao Zedong. Then have students write an elegy (a song, poem, or speech about someone who has died) that might have been delivered at the leader's funeral.

2. Students' elegies should mention the leader's major achievements. They should also evaluate whether the leader was successful according to that leader's and others' criteria.

3. Ask volunteers to read their elegies aloud and encourage other students to give feedback. Have students rank the leaders in terms of the positive effect they had on the lives of their people. **LS** Verbal/Linguistic

   Alternative Assessment Handbook, Rubric 41: Writing to Express

Answers

Reading Check *change in India, limited self-rule*

❷ The End of Imperial China, *continued*

Elaborate How did China's new Communist government take control of the economy? *by combining small, private farms into large, state-run farms, and by taking over all businesses and factories*

Make Judgments What do you think of Mao's mixed legacy as China's leader? *possible answers— Mao was a bad leader. Although some improvements were made, those improvements were not worth the lives of the millions who died under Mao's leadership, Mao was a good leader who was much loved by the people.*

Info to Know

Education in China Education is highly valued in China, but getting a good education can be difficult. Many teachers are poor, work under poor conditions, and have little training. During the Cultural Revolution many teachers were persecuted, and for five years all universities were closed. China's per capita spending on education is only about 3 percent of its GDP, while in many Western countries such spending is closer to 5 percent.

Answers

Reading Check *Businesses, land, and life came under the control of the government; old customs faded; women gained new rights; millions died because of poor leadership.*

518

Communism in China

In a Communist system, the government owns most businesses and land and controls all areas of life. Therefore the first action of China's new Communist government was taking control of the economy. The government seized all private farms and organized them into large, state-run farms. It also took over all businesses and factories. Those who spoke out against the government were killed or punished.

As China's ruler, Mao introduced many changes to Chinese society. He wanted to rid China of its traditional customs and create a new system. His goal was to make China a modern country.

While some of Mao's changes improved life in China, others did not. On one hand, women gained more rights than they had under the emperors, including the right to work outside the home. On the other hand, the government limited people's freedoms and imprisoned people who criticized it. Hundreds of thousands of people were killed for criticizing the government. In addition, many economic programs were unsuccessful, and some were outright disasters. Poor planning often led to famines that killed millions.

READING CHECK **Summarizing** How did Communism change life in China?

Close-up

Communist China

China celebrates the beginnings of Chinese Communism on National Day, October 1. It was on October 1, 1949 that Mao Zedong created the People's Republic of China. The celebration includes a huge parade in Beijing's Tiananmen Square.

Beijing

CHINA

PACIFIC OCEAN

The Gate of Heavenly Peace displays Mao Zedong's portrait above the entrance.

The parades include couples married on National Day, a popular time to wed.

A military parade of soldiers, tanks, and other equipment shows China's power.

518 CHAPTER 16

Collaborative Learning

Below Level

Exploring Chinese Culture

Research Required

1. Tell students that many aspects of modern Chinese culture date back to ancient times. Writing, for example, dates back to about 4,000 BC. Music and dance are China's oldest art forms. Theater originated in early religious dances. Poetry, painting and calligraphy were popular throughout China's history.

2. Have students find examples of Chinese calligraphy, poetry, painting, dance, theater, and music. Encourage students to look for

contemporary as well as classic examples. Provide video and audio equipment so that students can see and hear examples of the performing arts. Then have students share their findings with the class.

3. Have students discuss which Chinese art forms they find most intriguing and why.

🅛🅢 **Auditory/Musical, Verbal/Linguistic**

Alternative Assessment Handbook, Rubric 1: Acquiring Information

A New Japanese Empire

When the Chinese grew dissatisfied with their government, they overthrew their emperor. When similar feelings had taken hold in Japan about 50 years earlier, the people there had the opposite reaction. They decided to choose a new emperor to rule their country.

A New Government

Japan had officially been ruled by an emperor for several centuries. In truth, however, the emperor had little power. Since the 1100s, real power had been in the hands of military leaders called shoguns.

The arrival of Americans and other Westerners in Japan in the 1800s angered many people. They resented foreign interference in Japan and blamed the shogun. They felt he should have been strong enough to keep the Americans and Europeans out of their country.

In 1868 an alliance of nobles defeated the shogun's army and forced the shogun to step down. By doing so, they restored the power of the emperor. The newly powerful emperor took the name Meiji (may-jee), which means "enlightened rule" in Japanese. As a result, the shift back to imperial power in Japan is known as the Meiji Restoration.

Main Idea

3 A New Japanese Empire

Changes in Japan's government led to the formation of a new empire.

Recall Who held most of the real power in Japan prior to 1868? *military leaders called shoguns*

Explain Why were many Japanese displeased with the shoguns? *They had allowed Japan to become entangled with America and Europe.*

Find Main Ideas What was the Meiji Restoration? *the shift back to imperial power after centuries of being ruled by military shoguns*

ANALYSIS SKILL ANALYZING VISUALS
Why might China's government sponsor such a huge celebration for National Day?

The Chinese believe dragon dances bring good fortune to important events.

世界人民大团结万岁

Lion dances are performed to spread good blessings to the community.

GROWTH AND DEVELOPMENT OF SOUTH AND EAST ASIA **519**

Collaborative Learning

At Level

The Meiji Period

Research Required

1. Explain to students that one of the most important periods in Japanese history was the reign of the Emperor Meiji (1868–1912). During this time, Japan responded to the intrusion of the United States and other Western nations by vowing to modernize their nation and to compete with Western powers.

2. Divide the class into groups and have each group research one of the following topics:
   • Commodore Perry's visits to Japan and their effect on Japan's independence

   • the person who was the Emperor Meiji
   • social reforms instituted under the emperor
   • military actions taken by the emperor

3. Have students present their findings in the form of a report, a poster, a booklet, or as a multimedia presentation.

LS Interpersonal, Verbal/Linguistic

Alternative Assessment Handbook, Rubrics 1: Acquiring Information; and 30: Research

Answers

Analyzing Visuals *possible answer—to encourage Chinese citizens to feel pride in their country and the accomplishments of their Communist government*

❸ A New Japanese Empire, *continued*

Define What is the Diet? *the elected legislature that still governs Japan*

Evaluate Which three reforms of the Meiji do you think were most important to the growth and development of Japan? Explain your answer. *possible answer—elimination of the feudal system, because it made society more equitable; industrialization, because this provided for economic growth; education system, because this resulted in an educated society*

● Review & Assess ●

Close

Have students summarize the new political movements in Asia.

Review

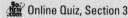 Online Quiz, Section 3

Assess

SE Section 3 Assessment

📖 PASS: Section 3 Quiz

📖 Alternative Assessment Handbook

Reteach/Classroom Intervention

📖 Interactive Reader and Study Guide, Section 3

💿 Interactive Skills Tutor CD-ROM

Answers

Reading Check *because Japan was expanding rapidly and, by using its military to do so, aggressively*

520

Reforms in Japan

When Meiji took control of Japan, he made sweeping changes in the government. First, he abolished the old feudal system. Under this system, warriors called samurai had been given land and power in exchange for military service. Meiji took all land away from the samurai and put it under the control of the state.

To replace the feudal system, Meiji sent officials to Europe and the United States to learn about Western government and economics. He then worked to apply in Japan what these officials had learned. For example, he created the **Diet**, the elected legislature that still governs Japan.

Meiji also reformed the Japanese education system. He required all children to attend school. He also encouraged some children to study in other countries to learn more about those countries.

Perhaps most importantly, Meiji worked to industrialize Japan. He built telegraph lines, a postal service, and railroads to improve communication. He also established Japan's first national currency. Japan quickly became a major industrial power in Asia.

ACADEMIC VOCABULARY
implications consequences

Japanese Imperialism

Meiji's reforms also led to changes in the country's military. All soldiers were required to swear a personal oath of loyalty to the emperor. The result was a force that would do anything the emperor asked of it.

From 1890 to 1910 Japan launched a series of military strikes against nearby countries. In short order the Japanese defeated both the Chinese and Russian armies. These victories left Japan the most powerful county in Asia and won Japan the respect of many Western nations.

Respect soon turned to caution, however. In 1910 Japan invaded Korea and made it a colony. At the same time, the government began to expand the Japanese army. Many observers feared the possible **implications** of that expansion.

READING CHECK **Summarizing** Why did some countries become cautious about Japan?

SUMMARY AND PREVIEW In this section, you learned about political changes in Asia in the 1800s and 1900s. Next, you will learn how these changes led to violence and war.

Section 3 Assessment

go.hrw.com
Online Quiz
KEYWORD: SK9 HP16

Reviewing Ideas, Terms, and Places

1. a. Identify What countries were created from the **partition** of India?
 b. Generalize How did Gandhi encourage people to oppose the British?
2. a. Describe How did China change under the Communist government?
 b. Predict How do you think most Chinese people felt about Mao's changes in China?
3. a. Recall What were the effects of the Meiji Restoration in Japan?
 b. Explain How did Japan's foreign policy change?

Critical Thinking

4. Summarizing Use your notes to complete the graphic organizer to the right with a short summary of political changes in each region.

India	→	
China	→	
Japan	→	

FOCUS ON SPEAKING

5. Choosing a Focus This section introduced several figures you could interview: Gandhi, Mao, Meiji. Write some ideas about subjects you could use as the focus of an interview with each person.

520 CHAPTER 16

Section 3 Assessment Answers

1. a. Pakistan and India
 b. by encouraging them to engage in nonviolent protest and civil disobedience, such as by not paying taxes and staging boycotts
2. a. Businesses, land, and life all came under control of the government; customs were abandoned; many people died.
 b. possible answer—badly; Too many people suffered for too little gain.
3. a. The shoguns lost power; feudalism ended; government and education reformed;

industrialization was introduced; military became more aggressive.
 b. Japan engaged more willingly with the foreign world. Military aggression developed.
4. India: gained independence; China: was partitioned civil war, rise of communism; Japan: end of feudalism; modernized elected legislature
5. Students responses may vary. Students should list subjects that could be discussed with Gandhi, Mao, and Meiji.

BIOGRAPHY

Mohandas Gandhi

How did a peace-loving lawyer win his country's freedom?

When did he live? 1869–1948

Where did he live? India

What did he do? Considered by many to be the father of modern India, Mohandas Gandhi led the struggle for Indian independence.

Why is he important? As a leading member of the Indian National Congress, Gandhi introduced a policy of nonviolent resistance to British rule. He led millions in fasts, peaceful protest marches, and boycotts of British goods. His devotion to nonviolence earned him the name *Mahatma,* or "Great Soul." Gandhi's efforts proved successful. In 1947 India won its independence from Britain.

Drawing Conclusions Why did people call Gandhi "Mahatma"?

KEY IDEAS

Mohandas Gandhi wrote that nonviolence was a more effective means of bringing about change than violence could ever be.

"It is perfectly true that [the English] used brute force and that it is possible for us to do likewise, but by using similar means we can only get the same thing that they got . . . [Using violence to gain freedom] is the same as saying we can get a rose through planting a noxious weed."

–Mohandas Gandhi, *Freedom's Battle,* 1908

Gandhi and his supporters used nonviolent means to protest the British rule of India.

521

Biography

Reading Focus Question

Have students consider how the United States gained its freedom from Great Britain. Then have students consider how India gained its freedom. Is one way of gaining freedom better than the other?

Info to Know

Gandhi's Spinning Wheel Mohandas Gandhi, the great leader of the Indian independence movement, was often photographed at his spinning wheel. His spinning wheel represented resistance to the forced importation of British textiles that had undermined the Indian weaving industry. It also represented resistance to the British rulers and the way of life they had tried to impose on India.

Info to Know

More about Gandhi Gandhi lived in South Africa for a number of years, where he led protests against government discrimination toward Indians, a struggle that lasted for more than seven years. After his return to India, Gandhi began to lead protests there. Some critics charged he was moving too quickly; others said he was moving too slowly. Today, most agree that Gandhi was a great mediator who was able to reconcile the interests and beliefs of many different groups.

Collaborative Learning

At Level

Gandhi Group Activity

Research Required

1. Explain to the class that Mohandas Gandhi believed in nonviolence. His efforts inspired many leaders around the world to follow a similar approach.

2. Divide the class into small groups. Assign one of the following topics to each of the groups: biography of Gandhi, quotations from Gandhi, information about Hinduism, events leading to Indian independence, and nonviolent methods advocated by Gandhi.

Provide research time for each group. Have each group write a brief report, accompanied by visuals, about its assigned topic and give a brief presentation.

3. Have the class combine the information they have found to create a display on Mohandas Gandhi. **LS Interpersonal, Verbal/Linguistic**

Alternative Assessment Handbook, Rubrics 14: Group Activity; and 24: Oral Presentations

Answers

Drawing Conclusions *because of his devotion to nonviolence and his efforts to help win independence*

521

Bellringer

If YOU lived there. . . Use the **Daily Bellringer Transparency** to help students answer the question.

📦 Daily Bellringer Transparency, Section 4

Growth and Development of South and East Asia   Daily Bellringer

Section 4

Review Section 3

Match the sets of letters below to the correct term.

1. Mohandas G _ _ _ hi   EDO
2. B _ _ _ r Rebellion   OXE
3. M _ _ _ i   AND
4. Mao Z _ _ _ ng   EIJ

Preview Section 4

If YOU lived there ...

You are a farmer living outside of a small town in China. One day you hear explosions in the distance. Soon, you see people running from the direction of the city across your fields. You stop one of the fleeing people to ask what has happened. He tells you that the Japanese have attacked and burned the city to the ground.

How will you react to the attack?

Consider ACTIVE responses:
• Flee to a distant area of China
• Join the army to fight the Japanese

Consider PASSIVE responses:
• Continue farming as though nothing has happened
• Cooperate with the Japanese
• Wait to see what happens

Key Terms and Places

📄 **RF:** Vocabulary Builder, Section 4

Taking Notes

Have students copy the graphic organizer onto their own paper and then use it to take notes on the section. This activity will prepare students for the Section Assessment, in which they will complete a graphic organizer that builds on the information using the Critical Thinking Skill: Summarizing.

Asia at War

If YOU lived there...

You are a farmer living outside of a small town in China. One day you hear explosions in the distance. Soon, you see people running from the direction of the city across your fields. You stop one of the fleeing people to ask what has happened. He tells you that the Japanese have attacked and burned the city to the ground.

How will you react to the attack?

What You Will Learn...

Main Ideas

1. Japan's aggression in Asia upset many countries.
2. During World War II, Japan fought for control of the Pacific.
3. The Korean and Vietnam wars were fought to stop the spread of Communism.
4. India and Pakistan have been in conflict over Kashmir.

The Big Idea

Since the 1930s several major wars have been fought in Asia.

Key Terms and Places

Manchuria, *p. 522*
Nanking, *p. 523*
Pearl Harbor, *p. 523*
island hopping, *p. 525*
Hiroshima, *p. 525*
domino theory, *p. 526*
Kashmir, *p. 527*

TAKING NOTES As you read, take notes about the wars fought in Asia during the 1900s. Use a table like the one below to organize your notes.

Japanese in Asia	World War II
Korea and Vietnam	Kashmir

BUILDING BACKGROUND The spread of imperialism and Communism in Asia in the early 1900s soon brought about conflict between nations. In some cases, these conflicts led to full-scale war.

Japanese Aggression in Asia

As you read in the last section, Japan had become a major military power by the early 1900s. By defeating China and Russia, Japan had ensured that no one in Asia could easily defeat it. Before long the Japanese were using their new might to expand their influence through much of mainland Asia.

During World War I the Japanese fought on the side of the Allies. They did not fight very much, though. They only attacked sites in China that were controlled by the Germans. After the war, the Allies gave these former German-held lands to Japan as a reward for its assistance.

Manchuria

For several years after World War I, the Japanese were content with just these lands. Their attitude changed in the 1930s, though. A newly aggressive Japan invaded **Manchuria**, a region in northeast China. The region was rich in minerals and other resources that the Japanese wanted.

The Japanese were brutal rulers in Manchuria. They forced millions of Chinese citizens to work in labor camps where tens of thousands of them died. The Japanese also took land away from Chinese families and gave it to Japanese settlers. They also mistreated the many Russian settlers in Manchuria.

Teach the Big Idea

Asia at War

1. **Teach** Ask students the questions in the Main Idea boxes under Direct Teach.

2. **Apply** Have students work individually or in mixed-ability pairs to create a graphic organizer allows them to take notes about the various wars discussed in this section. Students' graphic organizers should include notes on early Japanese aggression, World War II, the Korean and Vietnam wars, and the ongoing conflict in Kashmir.

3. **Review** Have students share the information in their graphic organizers. Create a class graphic organizer for all to see. Have students retain their graphic organizers as a study tool.

4. **Practice/Homework** Have students use their graphic organizers to write an in-depth magazine article about Asia at war.
   LS Visual/Spatial, Verbal/Linguistic

📄 Alternative Assessment Handbook, Rubrics 13: Graphic Organizers; and 19: Magazines

Nanking

From Manchuria, the Japanese launched attacks on the rest of China. One of their main targets was the city of **Nanking**, at the time China's capital. In 1937 the Japanese captured the city. What followed was six weeks of horror. Japanese soldiers robbed, tortured, and killed hundreds of civilians. They also burned down about one third of the city.

The destruction of Nanking by the Japanese became known as the Nanking Massacre. It resulted in decades of mistrust between China and Japan. It also turned worldwide opinion against Japan.

> **READING CHECK** **Describe** How did the Japanese treat areas they conquered in Asia?

World War II

When Japan began its aggressive policy of expansion in the 1930s, many people were concerned. Among those concerned were many Americans. They feared that the Japanese would continue to attack Asian countries if not stopped. However, most Americans did not want to get involved in any conflicts in Asia.

The Attack on Pearl Harbor

The American attitude toward war with Japan changed on December 7, 1941. On that morning, Japanese fighter planes and bombers bombed the U.S. naval base at **Pearl Harbor**, Hawaii. This attack was a declaration of war not just against the United States but against its allies as well.

The attack came as a complete surprise to Americans. Most of the American planes at the base never even had a chance to take off before they were destroyed. In less than 2 hours, more than 2,000 American soldiers were killed and most of the Pearl Harbor fleet was destroyed.

The American response to the attack on Pearl Harbor was immediate. The day after the attack, U.S. President Franklin D. Roosevelt asked Congress to declare war on Japan. In a radio address, he announced to the American people that the country was now at war with Japan.

Primary Source

SPEECH
The Attack on Pearl Harbor

The day after the attack on Pearl Harbor, President Franklin D. Roosevelt asked Congress to declare war on Japan.

"Yesterday, December 7th, 1941—a date which will live in infamy—the United States of America was suddenly and deliberately attacked by naval and air forces of the Empire of Japan . . .

As commander in chief of the Army and Navy, I have directed that all measures be taken for our defense. But always will our whole nation remember the character of the onslaught against us.

No matter how long it may take us to overcome this premeditated invasion, the American people in their righteous might will win through to absolute victory . . .

Hostilities exist . . . our people, our territory, and our interests are in grave danger.

With confidence in our armed forces, with the unbounding determination of our people, we will gain the inevitable triumph—so help us God."

ANALYSIS SKILL **ANALYZING PRIMARY SOURCES**
What does Roosevelt say the ultimate outcome of the war will be?

GROWTH AND DEVELOPMENT OF SOUTH AND EAST ASIA **523**

Differentiating Instruction

Below Level

Special Needs Learners

Materials: butcher paper, paints or colored markers

1. Guide the class in a discussion of the attack on Pearl Harbor using the following questions:
   • What was the purpose of the attack? *to destroy the U.S. Navy fleet at Pearl Harbor*
   • What was the outcome of the attack? *More than 2,000 soldiers died and the fleet was almost completely destroyed.*

   • What was America's response to the attack? *Isolationism ended. War was declared.*

2. Organize the class into small groups. Have each group create a mural that depicts the Pearl Harbor attack.

3. Display students' murals in a classroom exhibit. **LS Interpersonal, Visual/Spatial**
   Alternative Assessment Handbook, Rubrics 3: Artwork; and 11: Discussions

Answers

Reading Check *brutally; People were forced into labor camps and land was stolen. Japanese soldiers robbed, tortured, and killed hundreds of civilians.*

Analyzing Primary Sources *Americans will win an absolute victory.*

523

Main Idea

❷ World War II, *continued*

Explain Why was Japan able to control the Pacific and much of East Asia early in World War II? *Pearl Harbor had left the U.S. Navy weakened. There was no other military power in the region that could challenge Japan.*

Draw Conclusions What was the turning point of the war in the Pacific? *Why? the Battle of Midway; After the Battle of Midway the Allies were able to pursue their island hopping strategy, which ultimately helped them win the war.*

Make Judgments What do you think of the American decision to drop atomic bombs on Hiroshima and Nagasaki? *possible answers—The decision ended a brutal war and so is justified. The decision resulted in the deaths of too many people and so is not justified.*

go.hrw.com
Online Resources

KEYWORD: SK9 CH16
ACTIVITY: Hiroshima and
Nagasaki

✶Interactive Map
War in the Pacific, 1942–1944

map **zone** Geography Skills

Movement During World War II, Allied forces "hopped" from island to island, moving ever closer to Japan.
1. **Use the Map** In which general direction did the Allies move?
2. **Analyze** Which major battle took place nearest Hawaii?

go.hrw.com KEYWORD: SK9 CH16

Controlled by Japan (1942)
Allied advance
Major battle

0   600   1,200 Miles
0   600   1,200 Kilometers
Projection: Miller Cylindrical

Early Stages of the War

For the first several months of World War II, Japan essentially ruled the Pacific. The attack on Pearl Harbor had left the U.S. Navy weakened. As a result, there was no one to stop Japan's well-prepared navy.

Before long, Japan controlled much of East Asia. As you can see on the map, the Japanese also controlled dozens of islands throughout the Pacific. Among those islands were the Philippines, which the Japanese had taken from the Americans.

The Japanese treated people in the lands they captured very harshly. When they captured the Philippines, they took more than 70,000 prisoners. They then forced these prisoners to march 60 miles to a brutal prison camp. More than 600 Americans and 10,000 Filipinos died.

By 1942 the Allies decided that Japan was a major threat. Before then they had focused most of their efforts on the war in Europe. Now, however, they turned their eyes to the war in the Pacific as well.

Differentiating Instruction

Below Level

Struggling Readers

1. Tell students that when they read complicated material that has a sequential pattern, it is often helpful to put the events in order by date.

2. Have students write down the names and dates of major events in World War II in the Pacific. *Pearl Harbor, Dec. 1941; capture of the Philippines, 1942; Battle of Coral Sea and Battle of Midway, late 1942; Hiroshima and Nagasaki, August 1945*

3. Tell students to create a sequence chart with the dates and events from their lists.

4. When students have completed their charts, have them write a statement about how putting the battles in order helped them to better understand the war. **LS Visual/Spatial, Verbal/Linguistic**

Alternative Assessment Handbook, Rubric 13: Graphic Organizers

Answers

Map Zone 1. *west;* **2.** *the Battle of Midway*

Turning Point

The first challenge to the Japanese came late in 1942. In two battles, the Battles of the Coral Sea and Midway, the Japanese were stopped by the Allies. These defeats marked a turning point in the war.

After the Battle of Midway, the Allies began attacking Japanese targets. The Allies' main strategy in the Pacific was called island hopping. Under the **island hopping** strategy, the Allies took only the most strategically important islands, instead of each Japanese-held island. They used these captured targets as bases to launch attacks on other targets. In this way, the Allied forces worked their way closer to Japan.

End of the War

The war in the Pacific continued for several years. By 1945 the Allies were close enough to Japan to invade. However, military leaders warned that invading Japan would be costly. Such an invasion would leave more than a million Allied troops dead.

Instead, the military suggested a different option to end the war. On August 6, 1945, an American plane dropped an atomic bomb on the city of **Hiroshima**, Japan. The effects of the bomb were devastating. More than 70,000 people were killed instantly, and thousands of buildings were destroyed. But the Japanese still did not surrender. Three days later, the Americans dropped another atomic bomb, this time on the city of Nagasaki. As a result, the Japanese surrendered on August 15, 1945.

In the years following World War II, tens of thousands of residents of Hiroshima and Nagasaki died from radiation poisoning. In 1949 the Japanese government created the Hiroshima Peace Memorial Park to commemorate those who died.

READING CHECK Identifying Cause and Effect What caused World War II in the Pacific?

War in Korea and Vietnam

During World War II, democratic and Communist countries fought together to defeat Japan. After the war, however, the alliances fell apart. Fueled by political and economic differences, democratic and Communist countries came into conflict. In Korea and Vietnam, these conflicts led to war.

The Korean War

Before World War II, Korea had been part of Japan's growing empire. After the war, the Allies took Korea away from Japan. Korea was once again independent.

Honoring the Dead

Millions of Japanese citizens gather at the Hiroshima Peace Memorial Park in 2000 to honor those killed by the atomic bomb.

ANALYZING VISUALS Why do you think so many people gathered at this memorial?

525

Main Idea

❸ **War in Korea and Vietnam,** *continued*

Summarize What was the cause and outcome of the Korean War? *Communist North Korea invaded democratic South Korea. With assistance from the United States, South Korea was able defeat the invading forces.*

Elaborate What was the domino theory and why was it important to the Vietnam War? *the idea that if one country fell to communism, other nearby countries would also fall; The theory provided the main U.S. rationale for getting involved in the Vietnam War—to prevent the spread of communism in Asia.*

Rather than forming one country, though, the Koreans formed two. Aided by the Soviet Union, North Koreans under Kim Il-sung created a Communist government. In South Korea, the United States helped build a democratic government.

In 1950 North Korea invaded South Korea, starting the Korean War. With help from many countries, including the United States, the South Koreans drove the invaders back. The Korean War was costly, and its effects linger in Korea today. Relations between North and South Korea are strained. To prevent conflict from breaking out again, the countries maintain a demilitarized zone, or DMZ, along their shared border. No troops are allowed into the DMZ, but armed forces patrol either side.

The Korean and Vietnam Wars

The Korean War

- Lasted from 1950 to 1953
- Fought between Communist North Korea and democratic South Korea
- North Korea was supported by China and the Soviet Union.
- South Korea was supported by the United States and more than a dozen other countries.
- North and South Korea remained separate. A demilitarized zone was set up between them.

The Vietnam War

- Lasted from 1957 to 1975
- Fought between Communists and non-Communists for control of South Vietnam
- Communists from North Vietnam were supported by China and the Soviet Union.
- South Vietnam's democratic non-Communist troops were supported by the United States, Australia, South Korea, and other countries.
- The government of South Vietnam fell and the country was unified as a Communist state.

The Vietnam War

Like the Korean War, the Vietnam War was a struggle between democratic and Communist governments. As had been the case in Korea, the north was Communist and the south was democratic.

Eventually, Communists in South Vietnam began a civil war. To defend South Vietnam's democratic government, the United States sent in troops in the 1960s. The United States hoped to stop the spread of Communism in Asia. According to the **domino theory**, if one country fell to communism, other countries nearby would follow like falling dominoes.

Years of warfare in Vietnam caused millions of deaths and terrible destruction. In the end, North and South Vietnam were reunited as one Communist country. As the Communists took over, about 1 million refugees fled South Vietnam. Many went to the United States.

READING CHECK **Comparing and Contrasting** How were the Korean and Vietnam wars similar? How were they different?

Armed guards patrol both sides of the demilitarized zone that still separates the countries of South and North Korea.

Social Studies Skills: Analyzing Primary Sources   At Level

Letters from Vietnam   Research Required

1. Remind students that when Americans were sent to fight in Vietnam, the letters they sent home often revealed the reality of war that was not reported in the news.

2. Organize students into small groups. Have students conduct online research to locate letters written by soldiers and medical personnel who served in Vietnam. Have students print out one or more letters to analyze.

3. Have groups discuss the letters and highlight areas that might be of particular interest to historians. Groups should be prepared to explain their highlighted choices.

4. As homework, have students write a short paragraph explaining the value of letters as primary sources. **LS** **Verbal/Linguistic, Interpersonal**

📃 Alternative Assessment Handbook, Rubrics 16: Judging Information; and 30: Research

Answers

Reading Check *similar—Communist North vs. democratic South, U.S. involvement; different—The Korean War ended in a hostile truce. The Vietnam War ended with the fall of the democratic government in South Vietnam.*

Conflict in Kashmir

South Asia also became the site of armed conflict in the 1940s. Shortly after India and Pakistan were separated in 1947, the two countries began to fight over the region of **Kashmir**. Kashmir is a mountainous area in the north near the Chinese border.

Roots of the Conflict

When India was partitioned, Kashmir was ruled by a Hindu prince. Because he was Hindu, he decided to make Kashmir a part of India rather than Pakistan.

This decision angered Kashmir's large Muslim population. The Pakistani government, claiming Kashmire should belong to Pakistan, soon sent troops into Kashmir. India responded by sending in troops of its own. War broke out.

Fighting in Kashmir continued for two years. In 1949 the United Nations negotiated a peace treaty. This treaty divided Kashmir in two. India controlled the southern part, and Pakistan the northern part. Later, China also claimed part of Kashmir. Under the treaty, the people of Kashmir were to vote on their future. However, that vote was never held.

Kashmir Today

Today, Kashmir is still disputed territory. Conflict continues. Much of the region's Muslim population lives in the Indian-controlled area, and some militants have taken up arms against India. The Indian government claims that these militants are terrorists backed by Pakistan. The Pakistani government, on the other hand, rejects these claims. It says that the militants are simply Kashmir residents who are fighting to break from from Indian control.

The disagreement over Kashmir is a constant source of tension between the governments of India and Pakistan. Though full-scale war has not broken out, thousands of people have died in fighting in the region.

READING CHECK **Summarizing** What led to the conflict in Kashmir?

SUMMARY AND PREVIEW Conflicts over political and economic differences raged through Asia in the 1940s, 1950s, and 1960s. Next, you will learn how life in Asia changed after these conflicts.

Section 4 Assessment

go.hrw.com
Online Quiz
KEYWORD: SK9 HP16

Reviewing Ideas, Terms, and Places

1. **a. Identify** What regions in Asia did Japan invade?
   b. Explain How did Japanese actions in **Nanking** and **Manchuria** affect public opinion?
2. **a. Sequence** How did the Allies turn the tide of World War II?
   b. Evaluate Do you think using the atomic bomb was a good decision? Why or why not?
3. **a. Describe** What was the final result of the Korean War?
   b. Elaborate How did the **domino theory** lead to American involvement in Vietnam?
4. **a. Recall** What issue led to fighting in **Kashmir**?

Critical Thinking

5. **Summarizing** Draw a chart like the one here. Using your notes, fill in each column with information about the appropriate conflict.

Conflict	Participants	Results
Manchuria		
World War II		
Korean War		
Vietnam War		
Kashmir		

FOCUS ON SPEAKING

6. **Asking Questions about Events** If you were to interview someone involved in one of the conflicts described in this section, what would you ask? Make a list of questions.

GROWTH AND DEVELOPMENT OF SOUTH AND EAST ASIA **527**

Section 4 Assessment Answers

1. **a.** Manchuria; Korea; Southeast Asia
   b. turned public opinion against Japan
2. **a.** by defeating Japan at the Battles of Midway and Coral Sea
   b. possible answer—Yes. Using the atomic bomb ended the war quickly.
3. **a.** The North Korean invasion was repelled. A demilitarized zone between the two countries was created.
   b. It provided America's main rationale for getting involved in the war—to contain the spread of communism.
4. **a.** whether Kashmir would be part of India or Pakistan.
5. Manchuria—Japan, China, region occupied; World War II—Japan, Allies, Japan defeated; Korean War—North/South Korea, United States, North Korea contained; Vietnam War—North/South Vietnam, United States, South Vietnam defeated; Kashmir—India, Pakistan, no resolution
6. Students should list questions they would ask a person involved in one of the wars covered in the chapter.

Direct Teach

Main Idea

❹ Conflict in Kashmir

India and Pakistan have been in conflict over Kashmir.

Identify What are the two main sides in the Kashmir dispute? *Pakistan, allied with Kashmir's Muslim population, and India, allied with Kashmir's Hindu population*

Explain What is the state of the Kashmir dispute today? *Kashmir is still disputed territory. Relations between India and Pakistan are still tense because of the dispute.*

Review & Assess

Close

Lead a class discussion about the short- and long-term effects of the various wars in Asia.

Review

Online Quiz, Section 4

Assess

SE Section 4 Assessment
PASS: Section 4 Quiz
Alternative Assessment Handbook

Reteach/Classroom Intervention

Interactive Reader and Study Guide, Section 4
Interactive Skills Tutor CD-ROM

Answers

Reading Check *the partition of India; At that time Kashmir became part of India, but Pakistan disputed that outcome.*

527

Bellringer

If YOU lived there. . . Use the **Daily Bellringer Transparency** to help students answer the question.

📖 Daily Bellringer Transparency, Section 5

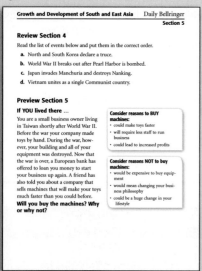

Academic Vocabulary

Review with students the high-use academic term in this section.

efficient productive and not wasteful (p. 529)

📓 RF: Vocabulary Builder, Section 5

Taking Notes

Have students copy the graphic organizer onto their own paper and then use it to take notes on the section. This activity will prepare students for the Section Assessment, in which they will complete a graphic organizer that builds on the information using the Critical Thinking Skill: Sequencing.

A New Asia

What You Will Learn...

Main Ideas

1. Many Asian countries have found economic success since World War II.
2. Political shifts in Asia have led to new governments in many countries.
3. Many Asian cultures blend old and new ideas.

The Big Idea

Since the end of World War II, Asia has experienced major economic, political, and cultural changes.

Key Terms and Places

trade surplus, *p. 529*
tariff, *p. 529*
constitutional monarchies, *p. 531*
Tiananmen Square, *p. 531*
human rights, *p. 531*

TAKING NOTES As you read, take notes on the economic, political, and cultural changes that have occurred in Asia since World War II.

If YOU lived there...

You are a small business owner living in Taiwan shortly after World War II. Before the war your company made toys by hand. During the war, however, your building and all of your equipment was destroyed. Now that the war is over, a European bank has offered to loan you money to start your business up again. A friend has also told you about a company that sells machines that will make your toys much faster than you could before.

Will you buy the machines? Why or why not?

BUILDING BACKGROUND Years of conflict in Asia left many parts of the region a mess. Governments were unstable, economies were in shambles, and people were confused. With the return of peace after the fighting, however, the Asian people had a chance to rebuild their countries. Many jumped at this opportunity.

Economic Success

Before World War II the countries of South and East Asia were not considered economic powerhouses. Few of the countries were heavily industrialized. As a result, they lagged behind the countries of Europe and the Americas.

Since World War II, however, the countries of the region have shifted their focus. Several Asian countries' economies are now ranked among the strongest in the world.

Japan

Japan was the Asian country most devastated by World War II. However, it was also the first to recover and prosper. With assistance from Europe and the United States, Japan completely rebuilt its economy. Within a few decades of the war, Japan's economy had grown into one of the strongest in the world.

The most successful area of Japan's economy has been manufacturing. Japanese companies are known for making high-quality products, especially cars and electronics like televisions

---

Teach the Big Idea

A New Asia

Materials: Strips of construction paper in a variety of colors, tape

1. **Teach** Ask students the questions in the Main Idea boxes under Direct Teach.
2. **Apply** Organize students into three groups. Assign a heading from this section to each group: Economic Success, Political Shifts, and Blending Old and New. Have groups record causes and effects for their assigned heading, neatly copy each pair onto a strip of construction paper, and tape each pair together.
3. **Review** Display and discuss students' cause-and-effect chains.
4. **Practice/Homework** Have each student write a short paragraph about the "New Asia."
   🔳 Verbal/Linguistic, Visual/Spatial
   📓 Alternative Assessment Handbook, Rubric 6: Cause and Effect

---

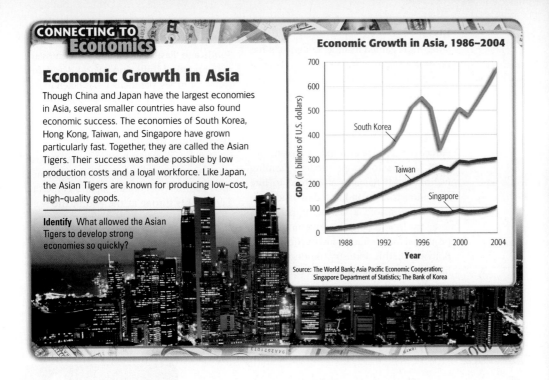

CONNECTING TO Economics

Economic Growth in Asia

Though China and Japan have the largest economies in Asia, several smaller countries have also found economic success. The economies of South Korea, Hong Kong, Taiwan, and Singapore have grown particularly fast. Together, they are called the Asian Tigers. Their success was made possible by low production costs and a loyal workforce. Like Japan, the Asian Tigers are known for producing low-cost, high-quality goods.

Identify What allowed the Asian Tigers to develop strong economies so quickly?

Economic Growth in Asia, 1986–2004

South Korea

Taiwan

Singapore

Source: The World Bank; Asia Pacific Economic Cooperation; Singapore Department of Statistics; The Bank of Korea

---

and DVD players. The Japanese are clever innovators and **efficient** builders. As a result, they are able to produce excellent products at low costs.

Many Japanese products are intended to be sold outside of the country, especially in China and the United States. In fact, Japan's trade has been so successful that the country has built up a huge trade surplus. A **trade surplus** exists when a country exports more goods than it imports.

Japan is able to export more than it imports in part because of high tariffs. A **tariff** is a fee that a country charges on imports or exports. For many years, Japan's government has placed high tariffs on goods brought into the country. This makes imported goods more expensive, and so people buy Japanese goods rather than imported ones.

China

When the Communists took over China in the 1940s they established a command economy. A command economy is one in which the government owns all businesses and makes all decisions.

However, the command economy led to major economic problems in China. For example, the production of goods fell drastically. In response, the government closed many state-owned factories and began allowing privately owned businesses. These businesses today produce everything from satellites and chemicals to clothing and toys. In addition, the government has created special economic zones where foreign businesspeople can own companies. This mixed economic approach has helped China's economy boom. Today it has the world's second largest economy.

ACADEMIC VOCABULARY
efficient productive and not wasteful

Main Idea

❶ Economic Success

Many Asian countries have found economic success since World War II.

Define What is a trade surplus? *economic condition that exists when a country exports more than it imports*

Find Main Ideas How did Japan build one of the strongest economies in the world? *assistance from Europe and the United States; success in manufacturing*

Evaluate Based on China's experience, which do you think is better, a command economy or one in which privately-owned businesses play a major role? Explain your answer. *Answers will vary. Possible answer— economy with privately-owned businesses; When China began allowing privately-owned businesses, its economy began to boom.*

MISCONCEPTION ///ALERT\\\\

China's Economy Tell students that the fact that China is the world's second-largest economy does not mean that everyone there is rich. About 10 percent of the people in China live in poverty.

Differentiating Instruction

Above Level

Advanced/Gifted and Talented

Research Required

1. Review with students what the text says about Japan's manufacturing industry. Tell students they will be collecting information to answer the question *How did Japan become the world's leading manufacturer of automobiles?*

2. Guide students in their research by having them look for the following information, perhaps with a partner or in groups:
   • top auto exporting countries in 1965 and 1975
   • the year Japan's auto exports peaked
   • the effect of the 1973 oil embargo on Japan's automobile industry

   • Japan's export market share and rank as automobile manufacturer, at 5- to 10-year intervals, beginning in 1965

3. Have students complete a time line by filling in major events in the history of Japan's auto industry. Then have students write a few paragraphs answering the question in Step 1.

   LS Visual/Spatial, Verbal/Linguistic

   Alternative Assessment Handbook, Rubrics 1: Acquiring Information; and 12: Drawing Conclusions

Answers

Connecting to Economics *low production costs, a loyal workforce*

❷ Political Shifts

Political shifts in Asia have led to new government in many countries.

Recall Which South and East Asian countries have some form of democratic government? *Japan, India, Bangladesh, Mongolia, Indonesia, Thailand, Malaysia*

Explain What happened in Tiananmen Square? *More than 1 million pro-democracy protestors gathered and were brutally suppressed by the Chinese government.*

Predict What might happen to a citizen of Myanmar if he or she organized a pro-democracy protest? *possible answer—The person might be thrown in jail, harassed, or even worse.*

Info to Know

India's Population Trends More babies are born in India every year than in any other country. As a result, many experts believe India will surpass China as the world's most populous country by about 2050. Although India's fertility rate is about half of what it was in the mid-1960s, India's population is growing by about 1.4 percent each year. This is about 140 percent higher than China's population growth rate.

Answers

Reading Check *industrialized, become stronger*

Analyzing Visuals *that the desire for democracy in China is strong*

530

India

Since India gained its independence, it has become a major industrial power. Its gross domestic product (GDP) places it among the world's top five industrial countries. However, its per capita GDP is only $3,700. Millions of Indians live in poverty.

The government has taken steps to reduce poverty. For example, it has encouraged farmers to adopt modern farming techniques. It has also attempted to lure new industries to India. It has made the city of Bangalore a center of high-tech industry. In addition, the government has promoted India's film industry. Nicknamed Bollywood, this industry produces more films each year than any other country.

READING CHECK **Summarizing** How have Asian economies changed since World War II?

Political Shifts

South and East Asia have also witnessed major political shifts since World War II. In some countries, democracy has taken root. In others, military rulers have seized control of the governments.

Democracy in Asia

Since the end of World War II several Asian countries have embraced democracy. One such country was Japan. Japan's emperor gave up his throne at the end of the war and helped create a democratic government there. When India became independent in 1947, it too became a democracy. In fact, India is by population the largest democracy in the world today. Other democratic countries in the region include Bangladesh, Mongolia, and Indonesia.

Close-up

Tiananmen Square, 1989

More than 1 million pro-democracy protestors occupied Beijing's Tiananmen Square in the spring of 1989. At first, Chinese leaders tolerated the demonstration, but as the protest grew larger they decided to crack down. In the evening hours of June 3, the government sent tanks and troops into the square to crush the protestors, killing hundreds.

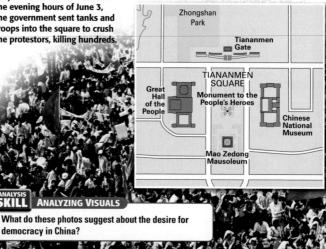

ANALYSIS SKILL **ANALYZING VISUALS**

What do these photos suggest about the desire for democracy in China?

Day 18

May 30 Near the official portrait of Mao Zedong, students build a large statue that comes to be known as the "Goddess of Democracy."

Social Studies Skills: Analyzing Primary and Secondary Sources

At Level

What Happened at Tiananmen Square?

Research Required

1. Organize students into small groups. Have half of the groups look for primary sources about the 1989 protests at Tiananmen Square. Sources might include interviews, tapes, videos, photographs, and journals. Have the other groups compile secondary sources about the event (television reporting, newspapers, magazines, and books).

2. Have each group present its findings. Ask students: What really happened at Tiananmen Square? Compare and contrast the sources and discuss any discrepancies among them.

LS Verbal/Linguistic

Alternative Assessment Handbook, Rubrics 1: Acquiring Information; and 16: Judging Information

In addition, some Asian countries have developed **constitutional monarchies**. In this form of democracy, a monarch serves as the head of state, but a legislature makes the laws. Thailand and Malaysia are both constitutional monarchies. Thailand has had the same royal family since the 1780s. In Malaysia, local rulers take turns being the king.

China and Democracy

China is not a democracy. The Communist government there still tightly controls most areas of life. For example, it controls newspapers and Internet access to restrict the flow of information and ideas.

Some Chinese people have attempted to bring democracy to their country. However, the government harshly punishes people who oppose its policies.

Day 24
June 5 In this famous image from the events at Tiananmen Square, an unarmed man faces down a line of Chinese tanks.

The most famous example of this punishment took place in 1989. In the spring of that year more than 1 million Chinese pro-democracy protestors gathered in **Tiananmen Square** in Beijing, China's capital. The protestors were demanding more political rights and freedoms. The Chinese government tried to get the protestors to leave the square. When they refused, the government used troops and tanks to make them leave. Hundreds of protestors were killed, and many more were injured or imprisoned.

Military Governments

In some cases, political change in Asia was brought about by military leaders. In both Pakistan and Myanmar, for example, military leaders seized power for themselves.

Pakistan has been plagued by unstable governments since it was first created in 1947. Over the years it has suffered from rebellions and the assassination of government leaders. In 2001, General Pervez Musharraf became Pakistan's president after a military coup. One of his main rivals for power was Benazir Bhutto, who in 1988 became the first female prime minister to serve in a Muslim country. Bhutto was assassinated by terrorists in late 2007.

A military government also rules the country of Myanmar, which is also known as Burma. The military seized power there in 1962. Since then, the government has abused people's **human rights**, those rights that all people deserve such as the rights to equality and justice. A Burmese woman, Aung San Suu Kyi (awng sahn soo chee), has led a movement for more democracy and rights. She and others have been jailed and harassed for their actions.

READING CHECK **Categorizing** What forms of government have developed in Asia since World War II?

GROWTH AND DEVELOPMENT OF SOUTH AND EAST ASIA **531**

FOCUS ON READING
What clues can help you discover the meaning of the term *constitutional monarchies*?

Collaborative Learning

"The News from . . ."

1. Have pairs of students imagine they are a TV news anchor team on a show called Upside, Downside. The show provides brief reports from around the world, with a piece of good news and a piece of bad news in each report.

2. Have partners review the information in this section about the countries of South and East Asia today. Based on what they have learned, have partners brainstorm some possible news items that could be included in the program.

3. Have the pairs divide the countries between them and write a brief script reporting on a few of the countries mentioned in the section. Partners should also write an introduction and a conclusion together.

4. Have each team present its news report.
   LS **Verbal/Linguistic**
   Alternative Assessment Handbook, Rubric 24: Oral Presentations

❸ Blending Old and New

Many Asian cultures blend old and new ideas.

Describe How can the blending of old and new be seen in architectural styles found in Asian cities? *In some places modern skyscrapers sit next to ancient temples.*

Make Generalizations Why are traditional customs such as respect for ancestors still important in Asian cultures today? *possible answer—Many people identify strongly with traditional customs.*

Review & Assess

Close

Lead the class in a discussion of the major trends in Asia today. Have students predict what role Asian countries will play in the future.

Review

Online Quiz, Section 5

Assess

SE Section 5 Assessment

PASS: Section 5 Quiz

Alternative Assessment Handbook

Reteach/Classroom Intervention

Interactive Reader and Study Guide, Section 5

Interactive Skills Tutor CD-ROM

Answers

Reading Check *possible answer—People must learn how to adhere to traditions they value while learning new ways of doing or looking at things.*

532

Asian culture today blends traditional customs with modern influences. New technology shapes life even in traditional Buddhist temples, like this one in Thailand.

Blending Old and New

Asian culture today is a complex blend of old customs and new trends. This blending is evident in architecture. Cities like Shanghai, China, and Kuala Lumpur, Malaysia, have some of the world's tallest and glitziest buildings. Nestled between the modern buildings are tiny ancient temples.

The blending of old and new can also be seen in people's daily lives. Traditional beliefs, such as the Chinese respect for one's ancestors and the Japanese code of honor, remain strong influences in people's lives. At the same time, however, cell phones and the Internet allow people to communicate worldwide. As a result, elements of other cultures, especially those from the West, have seeped into Asian life.

READING CHECK **Drawing Conclusions** How does the blend of old and new affect life in Asia?

SUMMARY AND PREVIEW Asia's governments, economies, and cultures have changed dramatically since World War II. Next, you will learn how those changes have affected life in China.

Section 5 Assessment

go.hrw.com
Online Quiz
KEYWORD: SK9 CH16

Reviewing Ideas, Terms, and Places

1. **a. Describe** What are some factors that helped Japan become an economic powerhouse?
   b. Summarize What changes did China make to promote economic growth?
   c. Evaluate Which country do you think has been most successful in rebuilding its economy? Why?
2. **a. Recall** What happened at **Tiananmen Square**?
   b. Contrast How are the governments of Japan, China, and Myanmar different?
3. **a. Identify** What are two old traditions that remain influential in Asia?
   b. Make Generalizations How has technology led to cultural change in Asia?

Critical Thinking

4. **Sequencing** Draw a graphic organizer like the one below. Using your notes, fill in the boxes with the steps that led to economic change in Asia.

   ◯ → ◯ → ◯

FOCUS ON SPEAKING

5. **Choosing Your Subject** Now that you have read about modern Asia, you can choose the person you will interview. Who will it be? What will you ask him or her? Write down some notes.

532 CHAPTER 16

Section 5 Assessment Answers

1. **a.** assistance from Europe and the United States, trade surplus, high tariffs
   b. allowed privately-owned businesses and special economic zones where foreigners can own businesses
   c. possible answer—Japan; Its economy was completely destroyed after WWII, but now it's one of the strongest in the world.
2. **a.** Pro-democracy protests were brutally put down by the Chinese government.
   b. Japan—democratic; China—Communist; Myanmar—military
3. **a.** honoring ancestors; Japanese code of honor
   b. Elements of other cultures, especially from the West, have seeped into Asian life.
4. possible answer—command economy in China introduced; production falls; state-owned factories closed; privately-owned businesses allowed; special economic zones created; China's economy booms
5. Students should select a person to interview and include notes about questions they will ask that person.

Social Studies Skills

Chart and Graph | **Critical Thinking** | Geography | Study

Analyzing Visuals

Learn

Geographers get information from many sources. These sources include not only text and data but also visuals, such as diagrams and photographs. Use these tips to analyze visuals:

- **Identify the subject.** Read the title and caption, if available. If not, look at the content of the image. What does it show? Where is it located?

- **Analyze the content.** What is the purpose of the image? What information is in the image? What conclusions can you draw from this information? Write your conclusions in your notes.

- **Summarize your analysis.** Write a summary of the information in the visual and of the conclusions you can draw from it.

Practice

Analyze the photograph at right. Then answer the following questions.

1. What is the title of the photograph?
2. Where is this scene, and what is happening?
3. What conclusions can you draw from the information in the photograph?

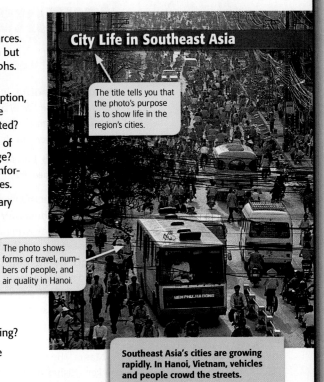

City Life in Southeast Asia

The title tells you that the photo's purpose is to show life in the region's cities.

The photo shows forms of travel, numbers of people, and air quality in Hanoi.

Southeast Asia's cities are growing rapidly. In Hanoi, Vietnam, vehicles and people crowd the streets.

Apply

Analyze the images of the Tiananmen Square protests in Section 5. Then answer the following questions.

1. What is the purpose of these photos?
2. What do the photos show about the protests?
3. Based on the information in the photos, what conclusions can you draw about political protests in particular and about politics in China in general?

CHAPTER 16 **533**

533

from *Shabanu: Daughter of the Wind*

As You Read

Ask students to compare the wedding customs and traditions described in this passage with those in U.S. culture or other cultures. Which elements are common to other cultures? Which are specific to Shabanu's nomadic desert culture? *possible answers: common—food, special clothes, music, family cooperation; specific—carrying baskets of sweets, singing and dancing through fields to settlement, henna painting of hands and feet, applying special eye makeup*

Info to Know

Cholistan Desert The setting of *Shabanu: Daughter of the Wind* is the Cholistan Desert, in the province of Punjab, Pakistan. It is part of the Thar Desert, which extends into India. Cholistan was once fertile land, irrigated by the Hakra River—and home to settlements of the ancient Indus Valley Civilization.

Meet the Writer

Suzanne Fisher Staples (1945-)
Born in Philadelphia, Pennsylvania, Suzanne Fisher Staples worked as a news reporter for United Press International in Hong Kong, India, Pakistan, Afghanistan, Bangladesh, Nepal, and Sri Lanka. She has a special feeling for Pakistan, about which she says: "There was something about the camels, the ancient stories and bluetiled mosques, and people who build shrines where a beautiful poem was written, that set my heart to singing."

Answers

Connecting Literature to Geography 1. *possible answer—They held a special procession carrying baskets of sweets, and singing and dancing; they prepared a special meal of curry of chicken and other foods; there's music and the painting of hands and feet.* **2.** *Answers will vary, but students might say that modern Pakistani women preserve these customs as an honor to their ancestors. Students might suggest that the customs symbolize a coming of age.*

534

A Pakistani bride on her wedding day

GUIDED READING

WORD HELP

chadrs cloths worn by women as a head cover

henna a reddish dye made from a shrub; often used to decorate the hands and feet

cacophony a combination of loud sounds

curry a dish prepared in a highly spiced sauce

lapis a stone with a rich, deep blue color

❶ At a *mahendi* celebration women gather to prepare the bride for her wedding day.

❷ To line the eyes means to darken the rims of the eyelids with black kohl, an eyeliner.

534

---

from
Shabanu:
Daughter of the Wind

by Suzanne Fisher Staples

About the Reading *In* Shabanu, *writer Suzanne Fisher Staples writes about the life of Shabanu, a young girl who is part of a traditional nomadic desert culture in Pakistan. In this passage, Shabanu and her family prepare for the wedding of her older sister.*

AS YOU READ Look for details about the customs and traditions of Shabanu and her people.

Two days before the wedding, Bibi Lal . . . heads a procession of women to our house for the *mahendi* celebration ❶ . . . Bibi Lal looks like a giant white lily among her cousins and nieces, who carry baskets of sweets atop their flower-colored *chadrs*. They sing and dance through the fields, across the canal, to our settlement at the edge of the desert.

Sakina carries a wooden box containing henna. The *mahendi* women, Hindus from a village deep in the desert who will paint our hands and feet, walk behind her. Musicians and a happy cacophony of horns, pipes, and cymbals drift around them.

Mama, the servant girl, and I have prepared a curry of chicken, dishes of spiced vegetables, sweet rice, and several kinds of bread to add to the food that the women of Murad's family bring . . . Sharma has washed and brushed my hair. I wear a new pink tunic. She lines my eyes and rubs the brilliant lapis powder into my lids. ❷

Connecting Literature to Geography

1. **Describing** How did the women prepare for the upcoming wedding? What was the *mahendi* celebration like?

2. **Interpreting** Why do you think modern Pakistani women might preserve old customs like these wedding preparations? What do such customs symbolize?

Differentiating Instruction

English-Language Learners
`At Level`

1. Tell students that good writers use words that appeal to the five senses: sight, smell, hearing, touch, and taste.

2. Ask students to choose one of the senses and make a list of all the words or phrases in the passage above that have to do with that sense.

3. Have volunteers read their lists to the class. To extend this activity, have students use their lists to write a poem. **LS Verbal/Linguistic**

   Alternative Assessment handbook, Rubric 37: Writing Assignments

Advanced/Gifted and Talented
`At Level`

1. Have students look through the book, *Shabanu: Daughter of the Wind*, and choose a passage that uses sensory language similar to the passage above.

2. Ask students to write a brief essay analyzing this language, explaining how the words or phrases are effective in making the culture come alive for the reader. **LS Verbal/Linguistic**

   Alternative Assessment Handbook, Rubric 37: Writing Assignments

Chapter Review

Geography's Impact
video series
Review the video to answer the closing question.
How might population density affect a country?

Visual Summary

Use the visual summary below to help you review the main ideas of the chapter.

QUICK FACTS

From the 1700s to the 1900s European countries controlled large parts of Asia, including both India and China.

Political changes swept through Asia in the early 1900s, leading to independence and new governments.

Since the end of World War II, many Asian countries have developed strong economies based on trade.

Reviewing Vocabulary, Terms, and Places

Fill in the blanks with the correct term or location from this chapter.

1. A _____ exists when a country exports more goods than it imports.

2. Gandhi believed in _____, or the avoidance of violent actions.

3. The spread of culture traits from one region to another is known as _____.

4. _____ was a trading city in China, also sometimes called Canton.

5. An _____ person is productive and not wasteful.

6. The Japanese invaded the Chinese region of _____ before World War II.

7. The _____ was the period of British rule in India.

8. A _____ of a country like India divides it into smaller countries.

Comprehension and Critical Thinking

SECTION 1 *(Pages 506–509)*

9. **a. Recall** Which two ancient civilizations influenced life in much of Asia?

   b. Summarize How did the Chinese affect life in early Vietnam?

   c. Develop How did Indian influence change the religious map of Asia?

SECTION 2 *(Pages 510–514)*

10. **a. Describe** What changes occurred in Japan after Americans arrived there?

   b. Explain Why were many Indians unhappy with the Raj?

   c. Elaborate Why did Europeans want to take over parts of China?

GROWTH AND DEVELOPOMENT OF SOUTH AND EAST ASIA **535**

GROWTH AND DEVELOPMENT OF SOUTH AND EAST ASIA **535**

Answers

11. a. Mao Zedong

b. possible answer—He was able to achieve Indian independence through nonviolent means.

c. possible answer—positive; Japan industrialized and modernized.

12. a. Communist North Korea invaded democratic South Korea.

b. 70,000 killed instantly, thousands of buildings destroyed, tens of thousands dead over the following years from radiation poisoning

c. possible answer—Life might return to normal there. People and the economy could prosper.

13. a. Japan—democratic; China—Communist

b. Skyscrapers sit next to ancient temples. Traditional customs are maintained while new customs are adopted.

c. prompted many countries to industrialize and modernize

Using the Internet

14. Go to the HRW Web site and enter the keyword shown to access a rubric for this activity.

> KEYWORD: SK9 TEACHER

Social Studies Skills

15. Communist China; Beijing

16. possible answer—The captions explain things I might not otherwise understand, such as why people in wedding dress are in the parade.

17. marching, waving, dancing

Focus on Reading and Speaking

18. or dependent territory

19. or severely negatively affected

📄 **RF:** Focus on Reading: Using Context Clues—Definitions

20. Rubric Students' interviews should

- include questions relevant to the person being interviewed
- sound natural and be conducted with enthusiasm

📄 **RF:** Focus on Speaking: Conducting an Interview

SECTION 3 *(Pages 515–520)*

11. a. Identify Who created China's Communist government?

b. Make Inferences Why do you think Gandhi is widely admired today?

c. Evaluate Do you think the Meiji Restoration was a positive development in Japan? Why or why not?

SECTION 4 *(Pages 522–527)*

12. a. Describe What caused the Korean War?

b. Analyze What were the effects of the atomic bomb dropped on Hiroshima?

c. Predict How might life change in Kashmir if India and Pakistan were to sign a peace treaty?

SECTION 5 *(Pages 528–532)*

13. a. Recall What type of government does Japan have today? China?

b. Explain How does modern Asian society reflect a blend of old and new ideas?

c. Elaborate How did World War II help bring about stronger economies in Asia?

Using the Internet

14. Activity: Investigating Japanese Aggression
Japan began an imperialist policy in the 1930s. The harsh treatment of Korean citizens by the Japanese during this period continues to affect relations between the countries today. Enter the keyword to investigate Japanese colonization. Then write a journal entry as though you were a Korean peasant living through this period.

Social Studies Skills

Analyzing Visuals *Turn to Section 3 and analyze the image of a Communist parade in China. Then answer the following questions about the image.*

15. What are the title and location of the image?

16. How do the captions help you understand the information in the image?

17. What types of activities are taking place in the image?

FOCUS ON READING AND SPEAKING

Using Context Clues—Definitions *Add a phrase or sentence to provide a definition for the underlined word.*

18. Under the Raj, the British government made India a <u>colony</u>.

19. Many parts of Asia were <u>devastated</u> by fighting during World War II.

Presenting an Interview *Use your interview notes to complete the activity below.*

20. Now that you have chosen the subject for your interview, write a list of questions you will ask him or her. Once you have completed your questions, work with a partner to conduct your interview. Have your partner take on the personality of your chosen subject and answer the questions you ask. Then, trade roles. You take on the personality of the person your partner has chosen to interview and answer the questions asked of you.

Map Activity

21. Modern Asia On a separate sheet of paper, match the letters on the map with their correct labels below.

Singapore	Pakistan
Tokyo	Xizang (Tibet)
Beijing	

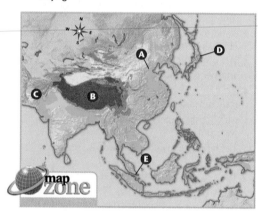

Map Activity

21. A. Beijing

B. Xizang (Tibet)

C. Pakistan

D. Tokyo

E. Singapore

Standardized Test Practice

DIRECTIONS (1–7): For each statement or question, write on a separate answer sheet the *number* of the word or expression that, of those given, best completes the statement or answers the question.

1 In which country did the Meiji Restoration take place?
(1) India
(2) Japan
(3) China
(4) Pakistan

2 The United States entered World War II in the Pacific after Japan bombed
(1) Pearl Harbor.
(2) Nanking.
(3) Washington.
(4) Hiroshima.

3 Who led the struggle for independence in India?
(1) Mohandas Gandhi
(2) Mao Zedong
(3) Sun Yixian
(4) Emperor Meiji

4 Which of the following is *not* an example of cultural diffusion?
(1) the spread of Buddhism to Vietnam
(2) the adoption of the Chinese language in Japan
(3) the building of the Great Wall of China
(4) the use of Indian building styles in Southeast Asia

5 Which country is ruled by a military government that abuses people's human rights?
(1) Myanmar (Burma)
(2) Thailand
(3) Singapore
(4) Taiwan

6 The partition of India resulted in the creation of the new country of
(1) Singapore.
(2) Kashmir.
(3) Taiwan.
(4) Pakistan.

7 Which of the following statements about the Boxer Rebellion is true?
(1) It took place in India.
(2) It drove all foreigners out of China.
(3) It was unsuccessful.
(4) It was begun by professional fighters.

Base your answer to question 8 on the passage below and on your knowledge of social studies.

> "The expansion of the right of the individual to behave or misbehave as he pleases has come at the expense of orderly society. In the East the main object is to have a well-ordered society so that everybody can have maximum enjoyment of his freedoms. This freedom can only exist in an ordered state."
>
> –Lee Kuan Kew, former prime minister of Singapore, from "A Conversation with Lee Kuan Kew"

8 Based on this passage, what do you think was one of Lee Kuan Kew's main goals as prime minister of Singapore?
(1) increasing the size of the country
(2) maintaining order
(3) expanding people's freedoms
(4) becoming wealthy

GROWTH AND DEVELOPMENT OF SOUTH AND EAST ASIA **537**

1. 2
Break Down the Question This question requires students to recall factual information. Refer students who miss it to Section 3.

2. 1
Break Down the Question Students could use the process of elimination. Options 2 and 4 are Asian cities. If students venture that Washington has never been bombed, they'll arrive at the correct answer.

3. 1
Break Down the Question Students should see that, of the answer choices, only Gandhi is from India.

4. 3
Break Down the Question If students understand the definition of cultural diffusion, they should recognize that option 3 is not an example of it. Refer students who miss the question to Section 1.

5. 1
Break Down the Question This question requires students to recall factual information. Refer students who miss it to Section 5.

6. 4
Break Down the Question This question requires students to recall factual information. Refer student who miss it to Section 3.

7. 3
Break Down the Question Point out that two answer choices (2 and 3) contradict each other. When this occurs, frequently the correct answer is one of the two.

8. 2
Break Down the Question Lee Kuan Kew repeatedly emphasizes the importance of maintaining order.

Reteach/Intervention Resources

Reproducible
📄 Interactive Reader and Study Guide
📄 Differentiated Instruction Teacher Management System: Lesson Plans

Technology
🖥 Quick Facts Transparency: Visual Summary: Growth and Development of South and East Asia
💿 Differentiated Instruction Modified Worksheets and Tests CD-ROM
💿 Interactive Skills Tutor CD-ROM

Tips for Test Taking

How Much Do I Write? Point out to students that if a writing question contains any of the following terms, they will need to write several sentences for a complete answer: *describe, justify, why, explain,* or *elaborate.* These are not the only words, however, that may indicate several sentences are required.

China

Bellringer

Motivate Before students enter the classroom, write the following words on the board: *kites, umbrellas, gunpowder, firecrackers, paper, printing, compasses, pasta, porcelain.* When students are seated, review the words as a class. What are the items? What are they useful for? Do students know what they all have in common? *Each was invented in China.* Remind students that China is a modern nation with a history that stretches back to ancient times. In that long history, Chinese people have made many revolutionary inventions. Tell students that in this Case Study they will learn more about China.

Key Terms

Preteach the following terms:

hospitable pleasant and life sustaining (p. 538)

barren with little or no vegetation (p. 538)

delegates representatives (p. 542)

premier prime minister (p. 542)

Facts About **QUICK FACTS**

China

Official Name: People's Republic of China

Capital: Beijing

Area: 3,705,407 square miles (slightly smaller than the United States)

Population: 1.3 billion (367 people/ square mile)

Average Life Expectancy: 73 years

Official Language: Mandarin

Major Religions: Officially atheist

Unit of Currency: Yuan Renminbi

Geography

The world's fourth largest country by area, China is the world's most populous country. More than 1.3 billion people live within its borders. That is more than the total populations of Europe, Russia, and the United States combined.

Because of its geography, most of China's people live in the eastern half of the country. Most of eastern China is wide open plains that are excellent for farming. Several rivers, including the Chang Jiang, the Huang He, and the Xi flow across these plains, bringing the water necessary for crops.

Farther west, China's elevation rises and the land becomes less hospitable. Western China is a land of rugged mountains, high plateaus, and barren deserts. Mountain ranges include the Tian Shan in the northwest, the Qinling Shandi in central China, and the Himalayas—the world's tallest mountains—in the far south. Near the Himalayas is the Plateau of Tibet, one of the highest regions in the world. Few plants can survive its high altitudes, so the land is barren. Equally barren—though not so high—are deserts like the Gobi and the Taklimakan.

As you might expect, most of China's large cities are located on the eastern plains. The largest city is Shanghai, with some 14 million people. Located where the Chang Jiang meets the East China Sea, it is China's leading seaport and an industrial and commercial center.

1 The **Plateau of Tibet** is known for its barren landscape. This ancient fort is at the plateau's edge.

538 CASE STUDY

Teach the Case Study

At Level

China

1. **Teach** Ask students the questions in the Main Idea boxes under Direct Teach.

2. **Apply** Prepare note cards with facts about China from the Case Study. Make copies of a worksheet with questions that can be answered by the facts on the note cards. Give each student a note card and a worksheet. Have students mingle around the room, sharing facts and filling out their worksheets. Have students put their initials next to each fact they share.

3. **Review** After students have read the Case Study, lead a class discussion about what students learned about China that they did not know beforehand.

4. **Practice/Homework** Have students look for recent news articles about China to bring in and share with the class. **LS Interpersonal, Verbal/Linguistic**

   Alternative Assessment Handbook, Rubric 1: Acquiring Information

China

China's second largest city is its capital, Beijing. Also known as Peking, this historic city has many beautiful palaces and temples. A mix of the old and new, Beijing is China's political and cultural center.

In southern China, Hong Kong and Macao (muh-KOW) are major port cities and centers of trade and tourism. Both are modern, busy, and crowded. Both Hong Kong and Macao were European colonies until recently. Because of their history, the two cities provide a mix of cultures.

② **Beijing,** China's capital, is a vibrant, busy city. This shopping district is located near the city's center.

③ **Shanghai** is China's largest city. Its skyline is a distinctive mix of modern and traditional styles.

Case Study Assessment

1. Where are the highest elevations in China?

2. In which region do most Chinese people live?

3. **Activity** Design a brochure to attract visitors to one of China's cities. Describe the city and its attractions. Be sure to include pictures in your brochure.

CHINA **539**

Main Idea

Geography

Recall How does China rank in land area and population? *fourth largest by land area; largest by population*

Explain Why do fewer people live in western China than eastern China? *Western China is less hospitable because of rugged mountains, high plateaus, and barren deserts.*

Develop How might Hong Kong and Macao look different than other Chinese cities? Why? *possible answer—Hong Kong and Macao might have more Western-style buildings and perhaps more diverse populations because these cities were European colonies until recently.*

📖 Quick Facts Transparency: Facts About China

📖 Map Zone Transparency: China

Info to Know

Three Gorges Dam Across the Yangtze River in China's Hubei province lies the world's largest hydro-electric power station, the massive Three Gorges Dam. Construction of the dam began in 1994 and is expected to be completed by 2011. It is 7,575 feet long and 331 feet high. The dam provides China with flood control and a massive source of electricity. Unfortunately, damming the Yangtze River also resulted in the need to relocate 1,500,000 people and the loss of numerous archeological and cultural sites.

Collaborative Learning

Photographs of China

Materials: China map photocopies

1. Divide the class into small groups. Provide each group with a map of China. A map with city and river labels would be helpful.

2. Have groups examine the photo and map array on pages 538 and 539. Have students read the photo captions, as well. Ask them what makes a good photo caption.

3. Tell groups they will be finding five photographs of places in China to make a map

and photo array just like the one on these pages. Allow groups time to find and print suitable photographs from the Internet. Have groups label and write a caption for each photo. Groups should place locator labels on their maps.

4. Have groups present their maps, photographs, and captions to the class. 🔲 **Visual/Spatial**

📓 Alternative Assessment Handbook, Rubric 8: Collages

Answers

Case Study Assessment 1. *in western China;* 2. *in eastern China;* 3. *Students' brochures will vary. See Rubric 2: Advertisements, in the Alternative Assessment Handbook.*

539

221 BC
The Qin dynasty
unites all of China.

AD 68
According to tradition, the first
Buddhist temple in China is built.

618
The Tang dynasty
takes over China.

Direct Teach

Main Idea

History and Culture

Recall How was China ruled for thousands of years? *by a series of powerful dynasties*

Explain How did China's government change in 1911 and in 1949? *1911—revolution removed last emperor from power; 1949—Mao Zedong formed a Communist government.*

Develop How is Chinese culture expressed in religion, art, and popular culture? *religion—adherence to Daoism, Buddhism, and Confucianism; art—paintings that reflect balance and harmony with nature; popular culture—martial arts, table tennis, mah-jongg, and karaoke*

Terra cotta warrior from the Qin dynasty

History and Culture

China was one of the world's first civilizations. For thousands of years, China was ruled by a series of powerful dynasties. From the Shang of the 1500s BC to the Qing of the AD 1800s, each of China's ruling dynasties left its mark on the country's people and culture.

China's last emperor was removed from power after a revolution in 1911. In 1949 a new Communist government under Mao Zedong took over China. Under Mao, China's economy suffered and people lost many rights.

Mao died in 1976, and Deng Xiaoping (DUHNG SHOW-PING) soon rose to power. Deng worked to modernize and improve China's economy. He allowed some private businesses and encouraged countries to invest in China. As a result, the economy began growing rapidly.

Despite these changes in government, ancient religions, values, and beliefs continue to shape life for China's people. Their influence is strong, even though the Communist government discourages religion. Daoism, Buddhism, and Confucianism are all powerful influences on people's lives.

Experiencing Chinese Culture

China's history stretches back over thousands of years. During that long period the Chinese developed a distinct culture that helped shape life in much of Asia.

Tradition The Chinese celebrate holidays and special events with parades that include colorful costumes, dancing, and fireworks.

Religion Buddhism has traditionally been a major influence on Chinese life. These Buddhist monks live in the Xizang or Tibet region.

540 CASE STUDY

Differentiating Instruction

Below Level

English-Language Learners

Materials: poster paper, art supplies

1. Review with students the information in the text about the history and culture of China. Have students examine the Experiencing Chinese Culture photo array, as well. Answer any questions students might have, then organize students into mixed-ability pairs.

2. Have each pair of students create a poster that showcases elements of Chinese history and

culture from ancient to modern times. Posters should include pictures and brief descriptions of the elements of Chinese history and culture that students chose to highlight.

3. Allow time for each pair of students to present their poster to the class. **LS Visual/Spatial**

  Alternative Assessment Handbook, Rubric 28: Posters

c. 1450
The Great Wall is completed during the Ming dynasty.

Great Wall of China

1911
China's last emperor is overthrown.

1950

1949
Mao Zedong creates a new Communist government in China.

Mao Zedong

China has a rich artistic tradition. Chinese artists have long been known for their work with bronze, jade, ivory, silk, or wood. Chinese porcelain is highly prized for its quality and beauty. Traditional Chinese painting reflects a focus on balance and harmony with nature. Landscapes are favorite themes in Chinese paintings. The Chinese are also known for their beautiful poetry, opera, and architecture.

Popular culture in China embraces many activities. Popular sports include martial arts and table tennis. Another popular game is mah-jongg, which is played with small tiles. Many people enjoy karaoke clubs, where participants sing to music.

Case Study Assessment

1. How did China change after 1900?
2. What forms of art are popular in China?
3. **Activity** The Chinese are fond of traditional forms of art. Draw an illustration of a scene from Chinese history or an element of Chinese culture in a traditional style.

Food Chinese food differs from region to region. This Cantonese meal includes pigeons, prawns, and noodles.

Sports Martial arts are very popular among the Chinese. They emphasize discipline and control.

CHINA **541**

Direct Teach

Checking for Understanding

True or False Answer each statement *T* if it is true or *F* if it is false. If false, explain why.

1. The last Chinese emperor was overthrown by Mao Zedong in 1949. *F; overthrown in 1911, not by Mao*
2. Chinese people enjoyed prosperity and increased freedom under Mao Zedong. *F; poor economy, loss of rights*
3. Daoism, Buddhism, and Confucianism are powerful influences in China. *T*
4. Chinese porcelain is known for being of poor quality. *F; high quality*
5. Martial arts and table tennis are popular in China. *T*

Critical Thinking: Sequencing

At Level

Chinese History Time Lines

Research Required

1. Organize the class into eight groups. Assign each group one of the following topics: Ancient China, Qin dynasty, Han dynasty, Yuan dynasty, Ming and Qing dynasties, post-1911 revolution China, Communist China.

2. Have groups use their textbooks or other print or online resources to research and compile a list of 10 major events from their assigned time period. Have groups illustrate their 10 events on large, unlined note cards.

3. Create a time line on the board or on butcher paper. Then have each group attach its note cards in the appropriate places to create a pictorial time line of events in Chinese history. Have groups explain their events to the class as they attach them to the time line.
LS Verbal/Linguistic, Kinesthetic

Alternative Assessment Handbook, Rubric 36: Time Lines

Answers

Case Study Assessment 1. *A revolution in 1911 ended the last dynasty. Communists took over in 1949.* **2.** *bronze-, jade-, ivory-, silk-, and woodwork; porcelain, painting, poetry, opera, and architecture;* **3.** *Students' illustrations will vary. See Rubric 3: Artwork in the* Alternative Assessment Handbook.

China Today

Identify What group is the main authority in China's government? *the National People's Congress*

Compare How does the role of the Chinese president compare to the role of the Chinese State Council? *The president is head of state and in charge of foreign affairs, whereas the State Council is in charge of domestic affairs.*

Evaluate Was a command economy good for China? Why or why not? *possible answer—not good; Poor planning resulted in a major economic crisis.*

Predict What will happen if China continues to grow at its present rate? *possible answer—China will face many environmental crises and may not be able to feed its population.*

Structure of the Chinese Government

China's government is largely controlled by the country's Communist Party. The party chooses members of the National People's Congress, which in turn elects the president and members of the State Council.

National People's Congress
China's only legislative body and the highest power in the government, the NPC is largely controlled by the Communist Party.

President
Elected by the NPC, the president handles all of China's foreign affairs.

State Council
Headed by a premier, the State Council deals with China's domestic concerns.

China Today

Government

China has one of the few Communist governments remaining in the world. Protests by Chinese citizens who want more freedom have been met with violence. China has taken harsh action against ethnic rebellions as well. For example, many people in Tibet have called for their freedom since the 1950s. These calls have led the Chinese government to crack down on Tibetans' rights. Because of actions such as these, many other countries have accused China of not respecting human rights.

The main authority in China's government is the National People's Congress (NPC). Made up of about 3,000 delegates, the NPC meets for two weeks each year to debate and approve national policies and laws. Most members of the NPC are selected by the Communist Party of China.

Day-to-day government in China is largely handled by the president and the State Council, which is headed by a premier. The president is elected by the NPC to serve as head of state and to handle foreign policy. The State Council and the premier are appointed to handle domestic matters.

Economics

When China became Communist in the 1940s, it had a strict command economy. The government made all economic decisions and owned all businesses. However, poor planning led to a major economic crisis in China.

As a result of this crisis, the Chinese government changed the economy and allowed some private industry to develop. It also allowed some foreign companies to open facilities in China. These changes allowed China's economy to grow and led to higher wages and standards of living for many workers.

Despite the country's industrial growth, most people in China work as farmers. More than half of the population works the land, growing crops such as wheat and rice.

542 CASE STUDY

Social Studies Skills: Analyzing a Diagram

China's Government

1. Have students examine the diagram showing the structure of China's government on this page. Point out elements of the diagram design that convey important information, such as the positioning of the boxes and the lines between the boxes. Ask students: why is the "National People's Congress" box placed above the "President" and "State Council" boxes? *to show that the National People's Congress is more powerful than the president and the State Council*

2. Using just the diagram as a reference, have students write a brief summary of the structure of China's government. Call on volunteers to share their summaries with the class. **LS Visual/Spatial, Verbal/Linguistic**

   Alternative Assessment Handbook, Rubric 37: Writing Assignments

Population Growth and Pollution in China

Bicyclists in Beijing wear masks to avoid breathing polluted air. Automobiles are a major source of pollution in China.

THE WORLD ALMANAC Facts about Countries

Issues

China's economic growth has also created serious environmental problems. One major problem is pollution. The country's rising numbers of cars and factories pollute the air and water. At the same time, China burns coal for much of its electricity, which further pollutes the air.

Another serious problem is overcrowding. China's population, already huge, continues to grow by about 7.5 million each year. China's officials have worked to slow this growth. They have urged people to delay having children and have tried to limit each couple to one child.

Population growth has contributed to the loss of forestland and farmland in China. Many of China's expanding cities are in its best farmlands, leaving less room for growing food.

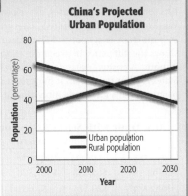

China's Projected Urban Population

- Urban population
- Rural population

Case Study Assessment

1. Why did China's government change the economy?

2. What do you think is China's most serious issue?

3. **Activity** Conduct Internet research to learn about protests against the government in China. Choose one protest and summarize the issue that was being protested and the government's reaction to the protest.

CHINA **543**

Collaborative Learning

At Level

China's Progress and Problems Presentations

Materials: poster board, art supplies

1. Organize the class into two large groups. Tell one group that it is responsible for reporting on the economic progress that China has made in recent decades. Tell the other group that it will report on the challenges that China still faces.

2. Have each group use their textbooks and additional resources to gather information about their topic. Have part of each group decide how to present their information in

summary form on poster board. Have the other part of each group decide how they will present their information orally to the class.

3. Allow groups time to prepare their posters and oral reports. Then allow each group time to make their presentation.

LS Interpersonal, Verbal/Linguistic

Alternative Assessment Handbook, Rubric 14: Group Activity

Direct Teach

Interpreting Graphs

Have students study the graph, then answer the following questions.

Identify In what year will 55 percent of China's population be rural? *2010*

Analyze When will the percentage of China's population that is rural equal the percentage of China's population that is urban? *about 2016*

Elaborate What does this graph say about China's population in the future? *that it will be increasingly urban*

Review & Assess

Close

Lead a class discussion about what students have learned about China by reading the Case Study.

Assess

Alternative Assessment Handbook

Reteach/Classroom Intervention

Interactive Skills Tutor CD-ROM

Answers

Case Study Assessment
1. *because poor planning of the command economy had created a major economic crisis;* 2. *possible answers—pollution, overpopulation, loss of forest and farmland;* 3. *Students' summaries will vary. See Rubric 37: Writing Assignments in the* Alternative Assessment Handbook.

543

Unit 4: New Asian Economies

Word Help

interdependence mutual dependence or reliance

Info to Know

U.S.-China Trade The United States has had a trade deficit with China since 1975. By 1985, the U.S. trade deficit with China had risen to a mere $6 million dollars. After 1985 the U.S. trade deficit with China exploded, so that today the trade deficit, at $256 billion, is over 42,000 times its 1985 level! Economists have various theories to explain the U.S. trade deficit with China. Some say that China engages in unfair trade practices and keeps it currency undervalued so that its goods remain inexpensive in the world market. Others say U.S. policies that have led to the weakening of the dollar and to restrictions on the export of high-tech goods have contributed to the increasingly lopsided trade deficit.

New Asian Economies

Part A: Short-Answer Questions

Directions: Read and examine the following documents. Then, on a separate sheet of paper, answer the questions using complete sentences.

DOCUMENT 1

Among the main trading partners of the United States are many Asian countries. The table below lists some of those countries, as well as the total value of the goods the United States exports to and imports from each country. The balance column shows the difference between the exports and imports. A positive balance means the United States exports more than it imports; a negative balance means it imports more than it exports.

U.S. Trade with Select Asian Countries (in millions of dollars)			
Country	**Exports**	**Imports**	**Balance**
China	$65,238	$321,508	-$256,270
Hong Kong	$20,121	$7,031	$13,090
India	$17,593	$24,024	-$6,431
Japan	$62,665	$145,464	-$82,799
Singapore	$26,284	$18,395	$7,889
South Korea	$34,703	$47,566	-$12,863
Taiwan	$26,359	$38,302	-$11,943

Source: U.S. Census Bureau, Foreign Trade Statistics

1a. From which country does the United States import the most?

1b. With which countries does the United States have a positive trade balance?

DOCUMENT 2

In recent years, China has begun to trade heavily with the United States. Each country is one of the other's main trading partners. The following document comes from a speech by the Treasury Department's special envoy on China.

> U.S.–China economic interdependence is deepening. We need each other more and on a broader number of economic and economically consequential issues. Over the past 5 years, according to U.S. data, U.S. exports to China have grown from $18 to $52 billion, while U.S. imports from China have grown from $102 to $287 billion.
>
> —**Ambassador Alan Holmer,** November 29, 2007

2a. How has U.S. trade with China changed?

2b. What does the writer mean by economic interdependence?

Critical Thinking: Summarizing

At Level

New Asian Economies Newspaper Articles

1. Allow students time to read through all of the documents and to ask any questions they may have about the material.

2. Then tell students that they are reporters at the Asia desk of a major newspaper. Their editor has just assigned them the task of writing an article on the new Asian economies.

3. Tell students that their sources for their articles will be the four documents on these pages. Have students write a short newspaper article about the new Asian economies

that draws material from each of the four documents. Then have students think of interesting headlines for their articles.

4. Call on volunteers to share their newspaper articles with the class. **LS Verbal/Linguistic**

   Alternative Assessment Handbook, Rubrics 23: Newspapers; and 37: Writing Assignments

Answers

Document 1 1a. *China;* **1b.** *Hong Kong, Singapore*

Document 2 2a. *It has expanded rapidly.* **2b.** *that the United States relies on trade with China and that China relies on trade with the United States*

DOCUMENT 3

As one of Asia's economic powerhouses, Japan trades with countries all around the world. The following report was released by the Japan External Trade Organization (JETRO) in 2005.

- Japanese trade posted new records for the third consecutive year with $598.2 billion in exports and $518.6 billion in imports. Imports increased rapidly due to rising oil prices, but exports were rather sluggish, causing the trade surplus to decline $30.8 billion to $79.6 billion, the first fall in four years.

- By volume, exports increased 0.8% and imports 2.9%, both up for the fourth straight year.

- China and the U.S. were the main export destinations. Strong exports of autos helped the U.S. share of Japanese exports rise for the first time in four years. The leading imports were from the Middle East, up due to skyrocketing oil prices.

3a. Did Japanese export increase or decrease during the period?

3b. Which countries bought most of Japan's exported goods?

DOCUMENT 4

The Association of Southeast Asian Nations, or ASEAN, is a trade organization of countries in that region. In 2002 the office of the U.S. Trade Representative introduced a new trading policy with ASEAN countries. The document below is a summary from the Trade Representative's web site explaining the policy.

The Enterprise for ASEAN Initiative (EAI), which was announced in October 2002, is designed to strengthen ties with the ASEAN countries: Brunei, Cambodia, Indonesia, Laos, Malaysia, Myanmar, Philippines, Singapore, Thailand and Vietnam. With two-way trade of nearly $168.5 billion in 2006, the 10-member ASEAN group already is the U.S.' fifth largest trading partner collectively. The region represents about 580 million people with a combined gross domestic product of $2.81 trillion.

4a. How much did trade with ASEAN value in 2006?

4b. Why might the United States consider trade with ASEAN important?

Part B: Essay

Historical Context: Since World War II the countries of Asia have become major players in world trade. Many Asian countries are among the main trading partners of the United States today.

TASK: Using information from the four documents and your knowledge of social studies, write an essay in which you:

- explain the importance of trade to Asian economies.
- examine how trade with Asia affects the United States.

Word Help

consecutive in a row
collectively as a group, combined

Info to Know

Asian Tigers The term Asian Tigers was first used in the second half of the twentieth century to describe the extraordinary economic successes of Taiwan, Singapore, Hong Kong, and South Korea. These countries (and territories in the case of Hong Kong) were all relatively poor around 1960. Then their leaders began pursuing policies to increase their trade with the world's richest nations. They improved education as a means of creating a productive workforce. The countries also focused on developing industries that could export goods to developed nations. The policies were successful and the economies of the countries grew rapidly, so that today they too are among the prosperous developed nations. Now other Asian nations are pursuing similar policies in the hopes of making the same gains.

Differentiating Instruction

Struggling Readers
Below Level

Have students who are struggling to read the documents break the documents down into manageable chunks. Then, when students finish with each document, have them write a one-sentence summary of the document's main idea. Using their main idea statements, have students develop a short, catchy slogan for each document. **LS Verbal/Linguistic**

📓 Alternative Assessment Handbook, Rubric 34: Slogans and Banners

Advanced/Gifted and Talented
Above Level

Research Required

Students may be aware that Asia's economic success has resulted in the loss of some jobs in the United States. Have interested students conduct research about the phenomenon called offshoring. With their research, have students develop and present a 3 to 5 minute oral presentation about offshoring. **LS Verbal/Linguistic**

📓 Alternative Assessment Handbook, Rubric 24: Oral Presentations

Answers

Document 3 3a. *increase;* **3b.** *China and the United States*

Document 4 4a. *$168.5 billion*
4b. *because the group represents a market of 580 million people with a GDP of $2.81 trillion*

Essay *Students' essays will vary but should thoroughly address all aspects of the task.*

545

Preteach

Bellringer

Motivate Remind students that they use persuasion all the time (asking for a ride to a friend's house, convincing a friend to play a particular game). Tell students to apply the same basic principles to this assignment.

Direct Teach

Prewrite

Gathering Information Caution students not to confuse less important reasons with weak ones. Weak reasons will undermine their opinion. All their reasons, from least to most important, should be sound.

Evaluating Information Tell students to review each of the reasons they plan to use to support their opinion. Have them ask this question: Will this reason really help support my opinion?

Practice & Apply

Evaluating Opinions

Activity **Panel Discussion** Have student volunteers present their papers to the class. Appoint a three-member panel. Have each member take notes on the presentations. Afterward, have the panel discuss the strong points of each. Then have the class discuss which paper made the most convincing case.

Rubric

Students' persuasive papers should
- start with a fact or a question that explains the issue they will discuss.
- clearly state their opinion and provide necessary background information.
- discuss reasons from least important to most important.
- include one paragraph for each reason presented.
- provide solid evidence to support each reason.
- restate their opinion and summarize the reasons in the final paragraph.
- use correct grammar, punctuation, spelling, and capitalization.

Persuasion

Persuasion is about convincing others to act or believe in a certain way. Just as you use persuasion to convince your friends to see a certain movie, people use persuasion to convince others to help them solve the world's problems.

Assignment

Write a persuasive paper about an issue faced by the people of Asia. Choose an issue related to the natural environment or culture of the area.

1. Prewrite

Choose an Issue

- Choose an issue to write about. For example, you might choose the danger of tsunamis or the role of governments.
- Create a statement of opinion. For example, you might say, "Countries in this region must create a warning system for tsunamis."

Gather and Organize Information

- Search your textbook, the library, or the Internet for evidence that supports your opinion.
- Identify at least two reasons to support your opinion. Find facts, examples, and expert opinions to support each reason.

> **TIP** **That's a Reason** Convince your readers by presenting reasons to support your opinion. For example, one reason to create a warning system for tsunamis is to save lives.

2. Write

Use a Writer's Framework

A Writer's Framework

Introduction
- Start with a fact or question related to the issue you will discuss.
- Clearly state your opinion in a sentence.

Body
- Write one paragraph for each reason. Begin with the least important reason and end with the most important.
- Include facts, examples and expert opinions as support.

Conclusion
- Restate your opinion and summarize your reasons.

3. Evaluate and Revise

Review and Improve Your Paper

- As you review your paper, use the questions below to evaluate it.
- Make changes to improve your paper.

Evaluation Questions for a Persuasive Essay

1. Do you begin with an interesting fact or question related to the issue?
2. Does your introduction clearly state your opinion and provide any necessary background information?
3. Do you discuss your reasons from least to most important?
4. Do you provide facts, examples, or expert opinions to support each of your reasons?
5. Does your conclusion restate your opinion and summarize your reasons?

4. Proofread and Publish

Give Your Paper the Finishing Touch

- Make sure you have correctly spelled and capitalized all names of people or places.
- Check for correct comma usage when presenting a list of reasons or evidence.
- Decide how to share your paper. For example, could you publish it in a school paper or in a classroom collection of essays?

5. Practice and Apply

Use the steps and strategies outlined in this workshop to write your persuasive essay. Share your opinion with others to see whether they find your opinion convincing.

546

Differentiating Instruction

Below Level

Struggling Readers

Offer these examples of sound and weak reasons.

- **Opinion:** *Our school is the best in the nation.*

Weak reason: Many people think it's the finest school in the country. (This restates the opinion another way.)

Sound reason: The U. S. Department of Education ranks it first in teaching and graduation rates.

Supporting evidence: About 95 percent of students graduate, and about 80 percent go to college.

- **Opinion:** *Saving the hill country environment is a challenge.*

Weak reason: *It is a worthy cause.* (This doesn't address the issue: why it is a challenge.)

Sound reason with evidence: Mining has upset the ecology of the hill country. Deprived of vegetation, the white-tailed finch is nearly extinct.

LS Verbal/Linguistic

Alternative Assessment Handbook, Rubrics 16: Judging Information; and 43: Writing to Persuade

Europe

The Alps

The Alps, one of Europe's major mountain ranges, stretch across the heart of central Europe.

Islands and Peninsulas

Islands and peninsulas surround the edges of Europe, drawing people to the sea to work, travel, and trade.

548 EUROPE

Direct Teach

Introduce the Unit

Share the information in the chapter overviews with students.

Chapter 17 Europe's physical geography varies widely—from the rocky terrain and mild climates of Southern Europe to the cold, vast plains of Eastern Europe and Russia.

Chapter 18 Europe was shaped by the ancient civilizations of Greece and Rome. Christianity spread to Europe during the Roman Empire and has been a great influence on the culture of the region.

Chapter 19 Europe has experienced frequent periods of intense warfare throughout history. Despite this, Europe has also contributed to tremendous social, religious, scientific, and technological progress.

Unit Resources

Planning

- Differentiated Instruction Teacher Management System: Pacing Guide
- Teacher's One-Stop Planner: Calendar Planner
- Power Presentations with Video CD-ROM
- Virtual File Cabinet

Differentiating Instruction

- Differentiated Instruction Teacher Management System: Lesson Plans for Differentiated Instruction
- Differentiated Instruction Modified Worksheets and Tests CD-ROM

Enrichment

- **RF:** Interdisciplinary Project: Eastern Europe's Economy
- **RF:** Geography and History: Rome's Trade Routes, First Century AD
- Geography, Science, and Culture Activities with Answer Key

Assessment

- PASS: Benchmark Test
- OSP ExamView Test Generator: Benchmark Test
- HOAP Holt Online Assessment Program, in the Premier Online Student Edition
- Alternative Assessment Handbook

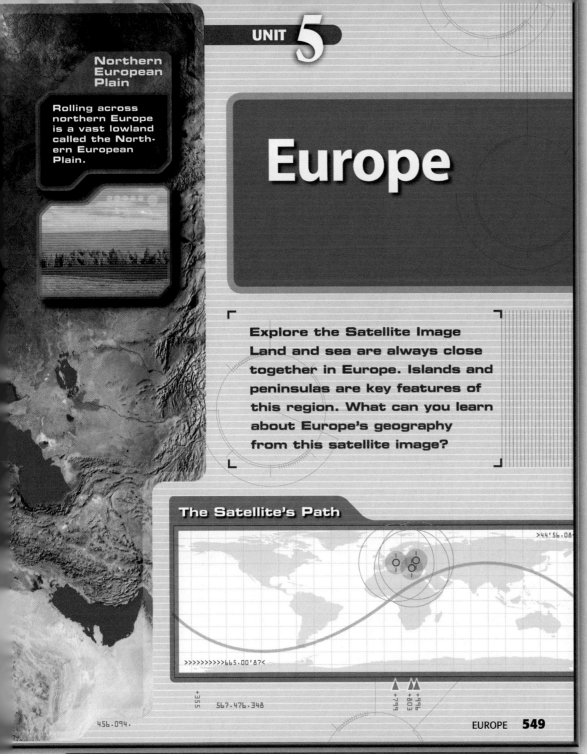

Northern European Plain

Rolling across northern Europe is a vast lowland called the Northern European Plain.

Europe

Explore the Satellite Image
Land and sea are always close together in Europe. Islands and peninsulas are key features of this region. What can you learn about Europe's geography from this satellite image?

The Satellite's Path

>44'56.08<

>>>>>>>>>665.00'87<

+35S

567.476.348

+799

+803

+996

456.094.

EUROPE **549**

Critical Thinking: Solving Problems

At Level

1. Divide students into three groups. Have each group brainstorm solutions to the following problem: What can be done to promote the distribution of wealth in Europe and Russia?

2. Students should use the maps in the atlas section to acquire information about Europe and Russia and to help them come up with creative solutions.

3. After brainstorming, each group should select one solution to elaborate on and share with the rest of the class. Emphasize that creativity is an important factor in choosing a solution.

4. Have groups take turns sharing their solutions. Then have an anonymous class vote for the most creative solution to the problem of wealth distribution in Europe and Russia.

LS **Interpersonal, Verbal/Linguistic**

Alternative Assessment Handbook, Rubrics 14: Group Activity; and 35: Solving Problems

Connect to the Unit

Activity **Plan a Defense Strategy** Divide students into three groups. Assign each group one of these regions: West-Central Europe, Eastern Europe, and Russia. Have the groups study the maps in the atlas section and make generalizations about climate, landforms, population, and transportation. Then have each group plan a defense strategy that will protect its region from invasion. Where are the borders vulnerable? Where are they strong? Are some countries within a region stronger than others?

During the study of Europe, have students think about how geography has affected politics and economics in the region.

LS **Interpersonal, Visual/Spatial**

Alternative Assessment Handbook, Rubric 21: Map Reading

Explore the Photographs

Point out the Alps and the Northern European Plain in the satellite image and photographs. Ask: Where do you think more Europeans live: in or near the Alps or on the Northern European Plain? Why? *possible answer—Most people probably live on the Northern European Plain; the climate is mild, and there is good land for farming and rivers for irrigation and trade.* Based on the photograph of the seaside town, what can students learn about climate and work of the region? *possible answer—The climate is probably warm. Some people may fish or trade for a living.*

Answers

Explore the Satellite Image *possible answer—The geography of Europe is diverse, with mountains, plains, lakes, rivers, and access to oceans. Most of Europe is covered in lush vegetation; Spain and Portugal are drier than the rest of Europe; Iceland and parts of Scandinavia are covered in ice.*

549

Explore the Map

Europe and Russia: Physical As students examine the map on these pages, ask the following questions:

Location What are six mountain ranges located in Russia? *Ural, Caucasus, Sayan, Yablonovy, Stanovoy, Kolyma*

Region What are the countries in the Caucasus region? *Georgia, Armenia, Azerbaijan*

Human/Environment Interaction In which European country would you prefer to live if you enjoyed mountain climbing? Why? *Answers will vary, but students should choose a country near one or more mountain ranges.*

Map Zone Transparency: Europe and Russia: Physical

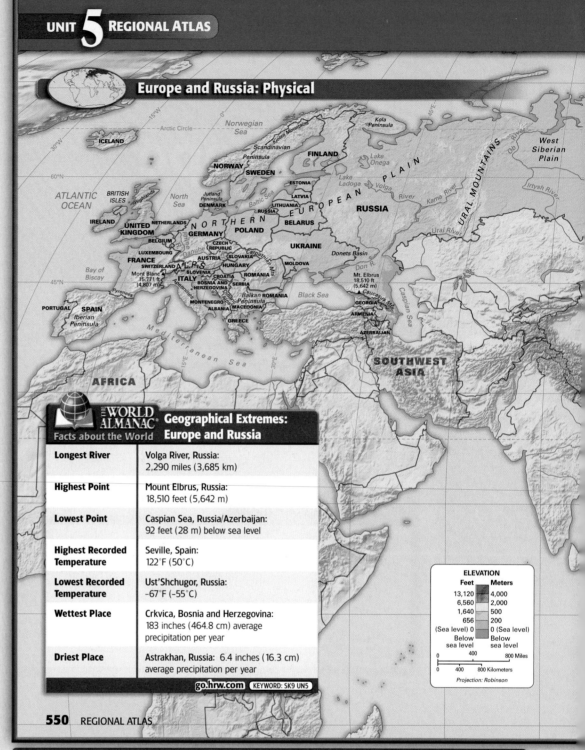

Europe and Russia: Physical

Geographical Extremes: Europe and Russia

THE WORLD ALMANAC — Facts about the World

Longest River	Volga River, Russia: 2,290 miles (3,685 km)
Highest Point	Mount Elbrus, Russia: 18,510 feet (5,642 m)
Lowest Point	Caspian Sea, Russia/Azerbaijan: 92 feet (28 m) below sea level
Highest Recorded Temperature	Seville, Spain: 122°F (50°C)
Lowest Recorded Temperature	Ust'Shchugor, Russia: -67°F (-55°C)
Wettest Place	Crkvica, Bosnia and Herzegovina: 183 inches (464.8 cm) average precipitation per year
Driest Place	Astrakhan, Russia: 6.4 inches (16.3 cm) average precipitation per year

go.hrw.com KEYWORD: SK9 UN5

ELEVATION

Feet	Meters
13,120	4,000
6,560	2,000
1,640	500
656	200
(Sea level) 0	0 (Sea level)
Below sea level	Below sea level

0   400   800 Miles
0   400   800 Kilometers
Projection: Robinson

Differentiating Instruction

Struggling Readers
Below Level

1. Focus students' attention on the physical map and World Almanac chart on this page. Read the facts in the chart out loud one by one.

2. As you read each fact, ask a volunteer to locate that place on a large classroom map of the region. The other students should locate the place on the map in their textbooks. **LS Visual/Spatial**

Alternative Assessment Handbook, Rubric 21: Map Reading

Advanced/Gifted and Talented Students
Above Level

1. Have students select one fact from the World Almanac chart to research in-depth.

2. Students should then prepare and deliver a persuasive speech, trying to convince tourists to visit that place. **LS Verbal/Linguistic**

Alternative Assessment Handbook, Rubrics 24: Oral Presentations; and 43: Writing to Persuade

Europe

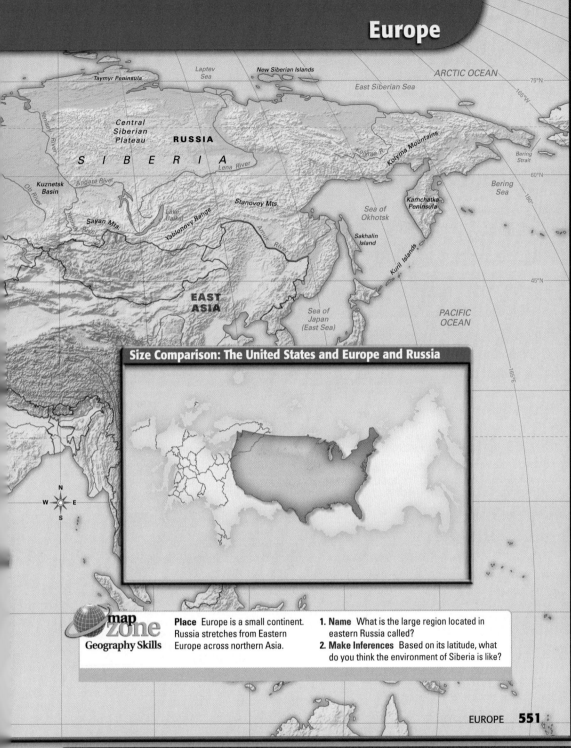

Laptev Sea
New Siberian Islands
ARCTIC OCEAN
75°N
East Siberian Sea
165°W

Taymyr Peninsula

Central Siberian Plateau
RUSSIA
Kolyma Mountains
Kolyma R.
Bering Strait

S I B E R I A
Lena River
Stanovoy Mts.
60°N

Kuznetsk Basin
Angara River
Bering Sea
180°

Yenisey River
Lake Baikal
Kamchatka Peninsula
45°N

Sayan Mts.
Yablonovy Range
Amur River
Sea of Okhotsk

EAST ASIA
Sakhalin Island
Kuril Islands

Sea of Japan (East Sea)
PACIFIC OCEAN

Size Comparison: The United States and Europe and Russia

map Zone
Geography Skills

Place Europe is a small continent. Russia stretches from Eastern Europe across northern Asia.

1. **Name** What is the large region located in eastern Russia called?
2. **Make Inferences** Based on its latitude, what do you think the environment of Siberia is like?

EUROPE **551**

Direct Teach

Europe

Activity **Compare Size** Give each student a blank transparency. Have students locate a map of the United States in the atlas section in their textbook. Students should lay the transparency over the U.S. map and trace its outside boundary, or perimeter (not including Hawaii and Alaska). Students should also outline the boundaries for the state in which they live. Have students write the scale of the map somewhere on their transparency.

Next have students lay their transparencies over other maps and regions around the world. (These maps can also be found in the atlas section of their textbooks.) Have students look for countries that have about the same area as the state in which they live. Challenge students to find a country that covers roughly the same area as the continental United States.

Have students come together as a class and share their findings. Did students find the same countries? Verify each other's findings and evaluate whether or not the areas are similar. Emphasize that when comparing maps, the two maps must have the same scale. Discuss reasons why the map scales must be the same. Ask students how this activity helped them better understand the approximate sizes of countries in other world regions. **LS Visual/Spatial**

- Alternative Assessment Handbook, Rubrics 9: Comparing and Contrasting; and 20: Map Creation
- Interactive Skills Tutor CD-ROM, Lesson 1: Compare and Contrast
- Map Zone Transparency: Size Comparison: The United States and Europe and Russia

Answers

Map Zone 1. *Siberia; 2. possible answer—cold and harsh with sparse vegetation*

551

Differentiating Instruction

Struggling Readers
Below Level

1. Pair struggling readers with two other students. Have one partner dictate a question about the physical map while another student writes or types it. The third partner should answer the question.

2. Switch roles and repeat the activity until everyone has asked, written, and answered three questions. **LS Visual/Spatial, Verbal/Linguistic**

- Alternative Assessment Handbook, Rubric 21: Map Reading

English-Language Learners
Below Level

1. Have students draw a two-columned chart on notebook paper with the headings *nouns* and *adjectives*. As students examine the physical map on this page, have them list words in the appropriate column that describe what they see.

2. Have students compare lists with one another when they are finished. **LS Visual/Spatial, Verbal/Linguistic**

- Alternative Assessment Handbook, Rubrics 21: Map Reading; and 40: Writing to Describe

Explore the Map

Europe: Political Explain that Europe is often referred to as a peninsula of peninsulas. Trace the outline of Europe on a large wall map so that students can see how the entire continent of Europe is a peninsula. Ask students to examine the political map on this page and identify countries or pairs of countries that are peninsulas. *Spain and Portugal, Italy, Denmark, Norway and Sweden, Greece*

Ask volunteers to name the country to which each of the following islands belong: Sardinia *Italy*; Shetland Islands *U.K.*; Crete *Greece*; Balearic Islands *Spain*; Faeroe Islands *Denmark*; Corsica *France*

Map Zone Transparency: Europe: Political

Answers

Map Zone 1. *Ireland, United Kingdom, Iceland;* **2.** *possible answers—probably countries in the mid-latitudes, which have mild climates; access to the Mediterranean Sea, the Atlantic Ocean, and the North Sea facilitates trade opportunities and the ability to support large populations.*

552

Europe: Political

- ⊕ National capital
- • Other city

0   200   400 Miles
0   200   400 Kilometers
Projection: Azimuthal Equal-Area

map zone
Geography Skills

Place Europe includes many small countries.
1. Name Which European countries are island countries?

2. Make Generalizations Based on this map, which countries do you think might have the largest populations? Why?

552   REGIONAL ATLAS

Collaborative Learning

At Level

Play a Quiz Game

1. Divide students into six groups and assign each group one color represented on the political map on this page. (Remind students that the colors on political maps have no particular meaning; they are shaded only to better emphasize the boundaries and shapes of the countries.)

2. Each group should begin by making a list of countries shaded their assigned color on the map. Then have students use an encyclopedia or almanac to write five Frequently Asked Questions (FAQs) about each country. The questions should be written on index cards, and the answers should be written on the backs of the cards.

3. Have groups trade sets of cards and read the questions and answers out loud to one another.

4. Combine all the cards together and host a class Quiz Show, where teams compete to answer the questions correctly. **LS Verbal/Linguistic**

Alternative Assessment Handbook, Rubrics 1: Acquiring Information; and 14: Group Activity

Europe

Russia and the Caucasus: Political

ATLANTIC OCEAN

ARCTIC OCEAN

Bering Strait

Bering Sea

Arctic Circle

North Sea

Barents Sea

Baltic Sea

Kaliningrad

St. Petersburg

EUROPE

Moscow

Nizhniy Novgorod

Volga River

Samara

Black Sea

Yekaterinburg

Ob River

Yenisey River

RUSSIA

Lena River

Sea of Okhotsk

Vladivostok

GEORGIA Tbilisi

ARMENIA

Yerevan Baku

AZERBAIJAN

Caspian Sea

KAZAKHSTAN

MONGOLIA

Novosibirsk

JAPAN

CHINA

PACIFIC OCEAN

Tropic of Cancer

⚙ National capital

• Other city

| 0 | 300 | 600 Miles |

| 0 | 300 | 600 Kilometers |

Projection: Two-Point Equidistant

map Zone
Geography Skills

Place Russia is the largest country in the world.
1. **Use the Map** About how many miles is Russia from west to east?

2. **Analyze** Where does Russia have access to the ocean? How do you think that affects trade?

EUROPE **553**

Direct Teach

Explore the Map

Russia and the Caucasus: Political
As students look at the political map on this page, ask: What is the first thing you notice about Russia? *Many students will probably note its size.* What country in the Caucasus region consists of two separate areas? *Azerbaijan* Why do you think this is? *possible answers—as a result of war; because of the break-up of the Soviet Union; Armenia may have once been under Azerbaijan's control.*

📀 Map Zone Transparency: Russia and the Caucasus: Political

Cross-Discipline Activity: Mathematics

At Level

Measure Perimeter and Distance

1. Make enlarged copies of the political map on this page. Using the map scale, have students estimate the distance (in miles) of Russia's perimeter. Record students' estimates on the board.

2. Give each student a piece of string about 20 inches long. Have students lay the string around Russia's outside border. Students may use tape to hold the string in place. Have students cut the string where the two ends meet then pull the string off the map.

3. Using the map scale and string, ask students to calculate the distance of Russia's border. Have students compare string lengths and calculations.

4. When the entire class has agreed on one solution, compare the answer with the estimates students gave at the beginning of the activity. **LS Logical/Mathematical, Kinesthetic**

📝 Alternative Assessment Handbook, Rubrics 14: Group Activity; and 35: Solving Problems

Answers

Map Zone 1. *about 3,900 miles;*
2. *in the west, access to the Atlantic Ocean by way of the Baltic Sea; in the east, access to the Pacific Ocean by way of the Sea of Okhotsk and the Bering Sea; possible answer—With access to both the Atlantic and Pacific, Russia is able to trade with many countries around the world.*

Explore the Map

Europe: Population Have students compare the population map on this page with the political map of the same region. Then have students answer the following questions: What two countries have between 25 and 130 people per square mile in all areas? *Latvia and Lithuania* Which island has the highest population density? *United Kingdom*

Map Zone Transparency: Europe: Population

Europe: Population

Persons per square mile / **Persons per square km**

520	200
260	100
130	50
25	10
3	1
0	0

● Major cities over 2 million

0   150   300 Miles
0   150   300 Kilometers

Projection: Azimuthal Equal-Area

map zone
Geography Skills

Place Although Europe is small, it is densely populated.
1. **Use the Map** How does the population density of Northern Europe compare to the rest of Europe?
2. **Compare** Compare this map to the physical map. What large plain in Europe has a high population density?

554 REGIONAL ATLAS

Critical Thinking: Interpreting Maps

At Level

Analyze Population Near Rivers

1. As students examine the population map on this page, have them look for areas that are most and least populated.

2. Point out that many European cities are located on or near rivers. Have students compare this map to the physical map of Europe in the Atlas. Have students identify cities with large populations and determine what river or rivers those cities are near.

3. Students should draw a chart on a separate sheet of paper and record their findings in the chart.

Encourage them to use the population map to identify the metropolitan areas with more than two million residents. These cities should be included on their charts.

4. As a class, discuss reasons why these densely populated areas are usually located on or near major rivers. **LS** Visual/Spatial, Verbal/Linguistic

Alternative Assessment Handbook, Rubrics 12: Drawing Conclusions; and 21: Map Reading

Answers

Map Zone 1. *Northern Europe is more heavily populated than the rest of Europe.*
2. *Northern European Plain*

554

Europe

Russia and the Caucasus: Climate

ATLANTIC OCEAN

ARCTIC OCEAN

Bering Strait

Bering Sea

North Sea

Barents Sea

Baltic Sea

Sea of Okhotsk

Black Sea

Caspian Sea

PACIFIC OCEAN

Tropic of Cancer

Climate Types

Steppe
Mediterranean
Humid subtropical
Humid continental
Subarctic
Tundra
Highland

0   300   600 Miles
0   300   600 Kilometers

Projection: Two-Point Equidistant

map zone
Geography Skills

Regions Russia is dominated by cold climates.
1. Name Which climates cover large parts of Russia?

2. Analyze Based on this map, where do you think Russia's population is concentrated? Why? Which areas would you expect to have a low population density?

EUROPE **555**

Explore the Map

Russia and the Caucasus: Climate Have students use the climate map on this page to answer the questions below:

Place What climate type dominates most of Russia? *subarctic*

Location What are some factors that may affect the climate in central and eastern Russia? *possible answers—northern latitude, large land mass, distance from the ocean*

🗺 Map Zone Transparency: Russia and the Caucasus: Climate

Differentiating Instruction

Below Level | Standard English Mastery

English-Language Learners

1. Draw a graphic organizer on the board with "Siberia's climate" in the center with several smaller circles around it. Ask students to identify the climate type in Siberia. Ask for words that might describe the weather there and write the words in the smaller circles of the graphic organizer.

2. Tell students that because of Siberia's harsh climate, few people live there, and the area is very isolated compared to the rest of Russia. Discuss the meanings of the words *isolated* and *isolation*.

3. Then have students use standard English to write a letter from the perspective of someone who lives in Siberia to a friend who lives in Moscow. Have them imagine how that person might feel—based on the climate, weather, and effects of isolation—and express these feelings in their personal letters.

LS **Verbal/Linguistic, Intrapersonal**

📖 Alternative Assessment Handbook, Rubrics 25: Personal Letters; and 41: Writing to Express

Answers

Map Zone 1. *humid continental, subarctic, tundra, steppe;* **2.** *possible answer—probably in the western part of the country, where the climate is milder. The eastern and far northern parts of the country have more severe climates and probably have a low population density.*

555

The World Almanac: Facts about Countries

Activity **Top Ten List** Have students use the data in the World Almanac chart on these pages to create a "Top Ten" list. Students may work individually or with a partner to create a multimedia presentation, in which they will present their list. Students can choose what their category will be. (i.e., countries with fewest number of TVs; highest population, highest per capita GDP, easternmost countries, highest life expectancy at birth, etc.)

Presentations should include images, music, sound effects, moving text, etc. If available, students should use multimedia software to create the presentation.

Have students take turns presenting to the rest of the class. **LS** **Visual/Spatial, Auditory/Musical, Verbal/Linguistic**

📓 Alternative Assessment Handbook, Rubric 22: Multimedia Presentations

💿 Interactive Skills Tutor CD-ROM, Lesson 8: Create Written, Visual, Oral Presentations

THE WORLD ALMANAC® Facts about Countries

Europe and Russia

COUNTRY Capital	FLAG	POPULATION	AREA (sq mi)	PER CAPITA GDP (U.S. $)	LIFE EXPECTANCY AT BIRTH	TVS PER 1,000 PEOPLE
Albania Tirana		3.6 million	11,100	$4,900	77.2	146
Andorra Andorra la Vella		70,500	181	$26,800	83.5	440
Armenia Yerevan		3 million	11,506	$4,600	71.6	241
Austria Vienna		8.2 million	32,382	$31,300	78.9	526
Azerbaijan Baku		7.9 million	33,436	$3,800	63.4	257
Belarus Minsk		10.3 million	80,155	$6,800	68.7	331
Belgium Brussels		10.4 million	11,787	$30,600	78.6	532
Bosnia and Herzegovina: Sarajevo		4 million	19,741	$6,500	77.8	112
Bulgaria Sofia		7.5 million	42,823	$8,200	72.0	429
Croatia Zagreb		4.5 million	21,831	$11,200	74.5	286
Czech Republic Prague		10.2 million	30,450	$16,800	76.0	487
Denmark Copenhagen		5.4 million	16,639	$32,200	77.6	776
Estonia Tallinn		1.3 million	17,462	$14,300	71.8	567
Finland Helsinki		5.2 million	130,128	$29,000	78.4	643
France Paris		60.7 million	211,209	$28,700	79.6	620
United States Washington, D.C.		295.7 million	3,718,710	$40,100	77.7	844

556 FACTS ABOUT COUNTRIES

Differentiating Instruction

Below Level

Special Needs Learners

Prep Required

Materials: scraps of cloth in a variety of colors

1. Pair special needs learners with other students. Pairs should choose a European country from the World Almanac chart. They will work together to research the meaning of the symbols on their selected country's flag.

2. Have either student use the scraps of cloth to create a reproduction of the country's flag. Students should cut the pieces of cloth into the correct shapes and sizes, then glue them onto a piece of cardstock or cardboard.

Meanwhile, their partners should write a paragraph explaining the meaning of the symbols on their flag based on their research.

3. When both tasks are complete, have each pair present their flag and paragraph to the rest of the class. Display the paragraphs and flags on a bulletin board. **LS** **Verbal/Linguistic, Kinesthetic, Interpersonal**

📓 Alternative Assessment Handbook, Rubric 30: Research

COUNTRY Capital	FLAG	POPULATION	AREA (sq mi)	PER CAPITA GDP (U.S. $)	LIFE EXPECTANCY AT BIRTH	TVS PER 1,000 PEOPLE
Georgia T'bilisi		4.7 million	26,911	$3,100	75.9	516
Germany Berlin		82.4 million	137,847	$28,700	78.7	581
Greece Athens		10.7 million	50,942	$21,300	79.1	480
Hungary Budapest		10 million	35,919	$14,900	72.4	447
Iceland Reykjavik		296,700	39,769	$31,900	80.2	505
Ireland Dublin		4 million	27,135	$31,900	77.6	406
Italy Rome		58.1 million	116,306	$27,700	79.7	492
Latvia Riga		2.3 million	24,938	$11,500	71.1	757
Liechtenstein Vaduz		33,700	62	$25,000	79.6	469
Lithuania Vilnius		3.6 million	25,174	$12,500	74.0	422
Luxembourg Luxembourg		468,600	998	$58,900	78.7	599
Macedonia Skopje		2 million	9,781	$7,100	73.7	273
Malta Valletta		398,500	122	$18,200	78.9	549
Moldova Chișinau		4.5 million	13,067	$1,900	65.2	297
Monaco Monaco		32,400	1	$27,000	79.6	758
United States Washington, D.C.		295.7 million	3,718,710	$40,100	77.7	844

EUROPE **557**

Direct Teach

The World Almanac: Facts about Countries

Interpret According to the chart, which country has the longest life expectancy? *Andorra has a life expectancy of 83.5*

Analyze Lead a class discussion about the countries with the lowest life expectancies. Have students find the five lowest life expectancies. *Azerbaijan, 63.4; Belarus, 68.7; Moldova, 65.2; Russia, 67.1; Ukraine, 69.7* Ask students to locate these countries on the political map and discuss why the region may have lower life expectancies. *possible answers—political unrest, diet and lifestyle, poverty*

Cross Discipline Activity: Music

At Level

Research National Anthems

1. Have individual students or small groups choose a European country to explore the history behind and lyrics of its national anthem.

2. Students can conduct research using the Internet or local library resources. Students should also find a recording of their country's national anthem.

3. Ask students to write a brief summary relating the history behind their country's national anthem. Students should type or print the lyrics

of the song to be compiled in a class song book. Make copies of the song book for each student.

4. Have students take turns reading their summaries and playing their country's national anthem for the rest of the class. As students listen, they can follow the lyrics and sing along if they wish. **LS Auditory/Musical, Verbal/Linguistic**

Alternative Assessment Handbook, Rubrics 18: Listening; 26: Poems and Songs; and 30: Research

Checking for Understanding

True or False Answer each statement *T* if it is true or *F* if it is false. If false, explain why.

1. The population of Hungary is five times that of Slovenia. *T*

2. Luxembourg and Germany have the same life expectancy at birth. *T*

3. San Marino is the smallest country by area in Europe. *F: Vatican City is the smallest country by area.*

THE WORLD ALMANAC® Facts about Countries

COUNTRY Capital	FLAG	POPULATION	AREA (sq mi)	PER CAPITA GDP (U.S. $)	LIFE EXPECTANCY AT BIRTH	TVS PER 1,000 PEOPLE
Netherlands Amsterdam		16.4 million	16,033	$29,500	78.8	540
Norway Oslo		4.6 million	125,182	$40,000	79.4	653
Poland Warsaw		38.6 million	120,728	$12,000	74.7	387
Portugal Lisbon		10.6 million	35,672	$17,900	77.5	567
Romania Bucharest		22.3 million	91,699	$7,700	71.4	312
Russia Moscow		143.4 million	6,592,769	$9,800	67.1	421
San Marino San Marino		28,900	24	$34,600	81.6	875
Serbia and Montenegro; Belgrade		10.8 million	39,518	$2,400	74.7	277
Slovakia Bratislava		5.4 million	18,859	$14,500	74.5	418
Slovenia Ljubljana		2 million	7,827	$19,600	76.1	362
Spain Madrid		40.3 million	194,897	$23,300	79.5	555
Sweden Stockholm		9 million	173,732	$28,400	80.4	551
Switzerland Bern		7.5 million	15,942	$33,800	80.4	457
Ukraine Kiev		47.4 million	233,090	$6,300	69.7	433
United States Washington, D.C.		295.7 million	3,718,710	$40,100	77.7	844

Collaborative Activity

At Level

Create an Awareness Campaign

Research Required

1. Divide students into small groups to create awareness campaigns about the countries of the Caucasus.

2. Have groups use the information in the World Almanac chart about the Caucasus countries to come up with a slogan. Students should also do outside research to learn more quick facts about these.

3. Have each group create a banner displaying their slogan. Students should also create pamphlets, brochures, posters, maps, or other materials providing information about the Caucasus region.

4. Lead a class discussion about the Caucasus. Find out how many students were unfamiliar with the Caucasus region until now. Ask students how creating a campaign increased their own awareness about the Caucasus countries. **LS** Verbal/Linguistic, Visual/Spatial, **Interpersonal**

Alternative Assessment Handbook, Rubrics 1: Acquiring Information; and 34: Slogans and Banners

COUNTRY Capital	FLAG	POPULATION	AREA (sq mi)	PER CAPITA GDP (U.S. $)	LIFE EXPECTANCY AT BIRTH	TVS PER 1,000 PEOPLE
United Kingdom London		60.4 million	94,525	$29,600	78.4	661
Vatican City Vatican City		920	0.17	Not available	Not available	Not available
United States Washington, D.C.		295.7 million	3,718,710	$40,100	77.7	844

World's Highest Per Capita GDPs

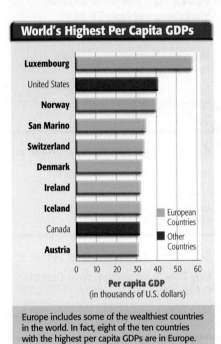

Luxembourg
United States
Norway
San Marino
Switzerland
Denmark
Ireland
Iceland
Canada
Austria

■ European Countries
■ Other Countries

0 10 20 30 40 50 60

Per capita GDP
(in thousands of U.S. dollars)

Europe includes some of the wealthiest countries in the world. In fact, eight of the ten countries with the highest per capita GDPs are in Europe.

Densely Populated Countries: Europe

Country	Population Density (per square mile)
Netherlands	1,254
Belgium	887
United Kingdom	648
Germany	611
Italy	512
Switzerland	488
Denmark	332
France	288
United States	84

Many European countries are densely populated, especially when compared to the United States.

ANALYSIS SKILL ANALYZING INFORMATION

1. What are the three most densely populated countries in Europe? How do their densities compare to that of the United States?
2. Which countries in Europe seem to have the lowest per capita GDPs? Look at the atlas politcal map. Where are these countries located in Europe?

EUROPE **559**

Direct Teach

Analyzing Information

Make an Inference Why do you think eight of the ten countries with the highest per capita GDPs are in Europe? *possible answer—Several countries in Europe are relatively small in area, have a low population, and are rich in resources.*

Draw a Conclusion Why is the population density so much lower in the United States than in the European countries listed on the chart? *possible answer—Although the overall U.S. population is larger than the countries listed on the chart, the United States is much larger in area, and the people are more spread out.*

Differentiating Instruction

Below Level

Struggling Readers

1. Have students use the information in the chart to create illustrated fact cards for five European countries.
2. Tell students that the only writing on the fact cards should be the name of the country. All other features should be illustrated. (i.e., flag, national symbols, currency, etc.) Students may use numbers to accompany the pictures if they wish.
3. In addition to the information on the World Almanac chart, students will need to conduct

some research to look for images and basic facts about the countries. Images can be original illustrations or printed from Web sites, magazines, and other teacher-approved sources.

4. Have students display their illustrated fact cards on a bulletin board in the classroom or hallway. **LS Visual/Spatial**

Alternative Assessment Handbook, Rubric 1: Acquiring Information; and 3: Artwork

Answers

Analyzing Information
1. *Netherlands, Belgium, United Kingdom. They are about 8 to 12 times more densely populated than the United States.* 2. *Moldova, Macedonia, Romania, Serbia and Montenegro, Ukraine, Albania; in Eastern Europe*

559

Chapter 17 Planning Guide

Physical Geography of Europe

Chapter Overview	Reproducible Resources	Technology Resources
CHAPTER 17 pp. 560–585 **Overview:** In this chapter students will learn about the physical geography of the five regions of Europe.	**Differentiated Instruction Teacher Management System:*** • Instructional Pacing Guides • Lesson Plans for Differentiated Instruction **Interactive Reader and Study Guide:** Chapter Summary Graphic Organizer* **Resource File:*** • Chapter Review • Focus on Reading: Asking Questions • Focus on Writing: Creating a Real Estate Ad • Social Studies Skills: Reading a Climate Map	**OSP Teacher's One-Stop Planner:** Calendar Planner **Power Presentations with Video CD-ROM** **Differentiated Instruction Modified Worksheets and Tests CD-ROM** **Student Edition on Audio CD Program** **Map Zone Transparency:** Europe: Physical* **Geography's Impact Video Program (VHS/DVD):** Impact of Living below Sea Level
Section 1: **Southern Europe** **The Big Idea:** The peninsulas of Southern Europe have rocky terrains and sunny, mild climates.	**Differentiated Instruction Teacher Management System:** Section 1 Lesson Plan* **Resource File:*** • Vocabulary Builder: Section 1 • Biography: Amália Rodrigues	**Daily Bellringer Transparency:** Section 1* **Map Zone Transparency:** Southern Europe: Physical* **Internet Activity:** Islands of the Mediterranean
Section 2: **West-Central Europe** **The Big Idea:** West-Central Europe has a range of landscapes, a mild climate, and rich farmland.	**Differentiated Instruction Teacher Management System:** Section 2 Lesson Plan* **Resource File:*** • Vocabulary Builder: Section 2 • Biography: Jacques-Yves Cousteau	**Daily Bellringer Transparency:** Section 2* **Map Zone Transparency:** West-Central Europe: Physical* **Map Zone Transparency:** West-Central Europe: Land Use and Resources*
Section 3: **Northern Europe** **The Big Idea:** Northern Europe is a region of unique physical features, rich resources, and diverse climates.	**Interactive Reader and Study Guide:** Section 3 Summary* **Resource File:*** • Vocabulary Builder: Section 3 • Primary Source: The Scream	**Daily Bellringer Transparency:** Section 3* **Map Zone Transparency:** Northern Europe: Physical* **Map Zone Transparency:** Northern Europe: Climate*
Section 4: **Eastern Europe** **The Big Idea:** The physical geography of Eastern Europe varies greatly from place to place.	**Differentiated Instruction Teacher Management System:** Section 4 Lesson Plan* **Resource File:*** • Vocabulary Builder: Section 4 • Literature: *The Bridge on the Drina,* by Ivo Andric	**Daily Bellringer Transparency:** Section 4* **Map Zone Transparency:** Eastern Europe: Physical* **Internet Activity:** Baltic Amber
Section 5: **Russia and the Caucasus** **The Big Idea:** Russia is big and cold with vast plains and forests; whereas the Caucasus countries are small, mountainous, and warmer.	**Differentiated Instruction Teacher Management System:** Section 5 Lesson Plan* **Interactive Reader and Study Guide:** Section 5 Summary* **Resource File:*** • Vocabulary Builder: Section 5	**Daily Bellringer Transparency:** Section 5* **Map Zone Transparency:** Russia and the Caucausus: Physical* **Map Zone Transparency:** Europe: Climate*

Review, Assessment, Intervention

 Quick Facts Transparency: Visual Summary: Physical Geography of Europe*

 Spanish Chapter Summaries Audio CD Program

 Progress Assessment Support System (PASS): Chapter Test*

 Differentiated Instruction Modified Worksheets and Tests CD-ROM: Modified Chapter Test

OSP **Teacher's One-Stop Planner:** ExamView Test Generator (English/Spanish)

HOAP **Holt Online Assessment Program (HOAP),** in the Holt Interactive Online Student Edition

---

 PASS: Section 1 Quiz*

 Online Quiz: Section 1

 Alternative Assessment Handbook

 PASS: Section 2 Quiz*

 Online Quiz: Section 2

 Alternative Assessment Handbook

 PASS: Section 3 Quiz*

 Online Quiz: Section 3

 Alternative Assessment Handbook

 PASS: Section 4 Quiz*

 Online Quiz: Section 4

 Alternative Assessment Handbook

 PASS: Section 5 Quiz*

 Online Quiz: Section 5

 Alternative Assessment Handbook

Power Presentations with Video CD-ROM

Power Presentations with Video are visual presentations of each chapter's main ideas. Presentations can be customized by including Quick Facts charts, images from the text, and video clips.

Holt Online Learning

go.hrw.com
Teacher Resources
KEYWORD: SK9 TEACHER

go.hrw.com
Student Resources
KEYWORD: SK9 CH17

- Interactive Multimedia Activities
- Current Events
- Chapter-based Internet Activities
- and more!

Holt Interactive
Online Student Edition

Complete online support for interactivity, assessment, and reporting

- Interactive Maps and Notebook
- Standardized Test Prep
- Homework Practice and Research Activities Online

CHAPTER 17 PLANNING GUIDE

Differentiating Instruction

How do I address the needs of varied learners?
The Target Resource acts as your primary strategy for differentiated instruction.

ENGLISH-LANGUAGE LEARNERS & STRUGGLING READERS

TARGET RESOURCE

Interactive Skills Tutor CD-ROM

The Interactive Skills Tutor CD-ROM contains lessons that provide additional practice for 20 different critical thinking skills.

Additional Resources

Differentiated Instruction Teacher Management System: Lesson Plans for Differentiated Instruction

Resource File:
- Vocabulary Builder Activities
- Social Studies Skills: Reading a Climate Map

Quick Facts Transparency: Visual Summary: Physical Geography of Europe

Student Edition on Audio CD Program

Spanish Chapter Summaries Audio CD Program

Teacher's One Stop Planner:
- ExamView Test Generator, Spanish
- PuzzlePro, Spanish

English-Language Learner Strategies and Activities

SPECIAL NEEDS LEARNERS

TARGET RESOURCE

Resource File

The Resource File activities allow students to extend their knowledge of chapter-related places and people and to practice geography skills.
- Vocabulary Builder Activities
- Social Studies Skills: Reading a Climate Map

Additional Resources

Differentiated Instruction Teacher Management System: Lesson Plans for Differentiated Instruction

Resource File: Social Studies Skills: Reading a Climate Map

Student Edition on Audio CD Program

Interactive Skills Tutor CD-ROM

Graphic Organizer Transparencies with Support for Reading and Writing

ADVANCED/GIFTED AND TALENTED STUDENTS

TARGET RESOURCE

Differentiated Instruction Teacher Management System

Lesson Plans for Differentiated Instruction provide teachers with strategies to help plan instruction for all learners.

Additional Resources

Resource File:
- Focus on Reading: Asking Questions
- Focus on Writing: Creating a Real Estate Ad
- Literature: *The Bridge on the Drina* by Ivo Andric

World History and Geography Document-Based Questions Activities

Geography, Science, and Cultures Activities

Experiencing World History and Geography

Differentiated Activities in the Teacher's Edition

- Interpreting Photographs
- Analyzing Visuals
- Understanding Geographic Terms
- Researching Word Origins and Meanings
- Identifying Main Ideas and Supporting Details

Differentiated Activities in the Teacher's Edition

- Understanding Map Labels
- Reading a Climate Map

Differentiated Activities in the Teacher's Edition

- Oral Reports
- Comparing and Contrasting Geographic Features
- Writing about Current Events
- Understanding Geothermal Energy

HOLT Teacher's One-Stop Planner®

How can I manage the lesson plans and support materials for differentiated instruction?

With the Teacher's One-Stop Planner, you can easily organize and print lesson plans, planning guides, and instructional materials for all learners.

The Teacher's One-Stop Planner includes the following materials to help you differentiate instruction:

- · **Interactive Teacher's Edition**
- · **Calendar Planner and pacing guides**
- · **Editable lesson plans**
- · **All reproducible ancillaries in Adobe Acrobat (PDF) format**
- · **ExamView Test Generator (English & Spanish)**
- · **Transparency and video previews**

Professional Development

What teacher training resources are available to help me grow professionally?

- · **In-service and staff development** as part of your Holt Social Studies product purchase
- · **Quick Teacher Tutorial Lesson Presentation CD-ROM**
- · Intensive tuition-based **Teacher Development Institute**
- · **Convenient Holt Speaker Bureau** – face-to-face workshop options
- · **24/7 Ask A Professional Development Expert** at http://www.hrw.com/prodev/

Chapter Big Ideas

Section 1 The peninsulas of Southern Europe have rocky terrains and sunny, mild climates.

Section 2 West-Central Europe has a range of landscapes, a mild climate, and rich farmland.

Section 3 Northern Europe is a region of unique physical features, rich resources, and diverse climates.

Section 4 The physical geography of Eastern Europe varies greatly from place to place.

Section 5 Russia is big and cold with vast plains and forests; whereas the Caucasus countries are small, mountainous, and warmer.

Focus on Reading and Writing

Reading The Resource File provides a worksheet to help students practice asking questions.

📄 **RF: Focus on Reading, Asking Questions**

Writing The Resource File provides a worksheet to help students create a real estate advertisement.

📄 **RF: Focus on Writing, Creating a Real Estate Ad**

560 **CHAPTER 17**

CHAPTER **17**

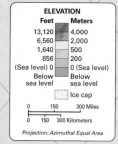

Physical Geography of Europe

FOCUS QUESTION

What forces had an impact on the development of Europe and why?

What You Will Learn...

One of the smallest continents, Europe is nonetheless home to a wide variety of landforms, water features, and climates.

FOCUS ON READING AND WRITING

Asking Questions As you read a text, it can be helpful to ask yourself questions about what you are reading to be sure you understand it. One set of questions that you can use to test your understanding is the five Ws—who, what, when, where, and why. **See the lesson, Asking Questions, on page S20.**

Creating a Real Estate Ad Imagine you work for a real estate agency in Europe. You are trying to sell a piece of property there and must write an ad about it. As you read this chapter, decide where your property would be located and what its characteristics would be.

560 CHAPTER 17

ELEVATION

Feet	Meters
13,120	4,000
6,560	2,000
1,640	500
656	200
(Sea level) 0	0 (Sea level)
Below sea level	Below sea level

Ice cap

0   150   300 Miles
0   150   300 Kilometers

Projection: Azimuthal Equal Area

map zone

Geography Skills

Place Europe's landscapes range from wide open plains to rugged mountains.
1. **Identify** What flat region covers most of northern and Eastern Europe?
2. **Locate** Which seas surround the island of Sardinia?

Water Features Iceland's geysers and hot springs produce great amounts of energy.

Introduce the Chapter

At Level

Exploring Europe's Physical Geography

1. Draw students' attention to the map on this page. Discuss how the countries of Europe range in size from very small to very large. Ask students to consider how size and other attributes of physical geography might impact a country, its people, and its culture.

2. Explain to students that they are going to learn about the physical geography of the five regions of Europe in this chapter. Discuss with students what they already know about the physical geography of these regions.

3. Have students keep track of the main ideas in each section as they read. Ask students to think about what generalizations they can make based on what they learn by reading the text and studying the photos and maps. Remind students that generalizations are helpful learning tools, but that they need to be supported with specific facts and details.

LS Verbal/Linguistic

📄 Alternative Assessment Handbook, Rubric 1: Acquiring Information

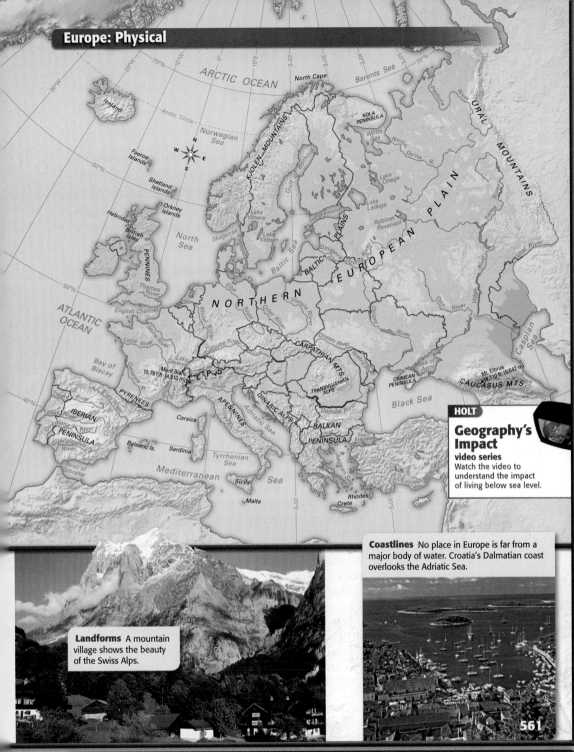

ARCTIC OCEAN

North Cape

Barents Sea

Iceland

Arctic Circle

Norwegian Sea

Faeroe Islands

Shetland Islands

Orkney Islands

Hebrides

British Isles

PENNINES

North Sea

ATLANTIC OCEAN

English Channel

Thames River

Loire River

Seine River

Rhine River

Danube River

Bay of Biscay

PYRENEES

ALPS

Mont Blanc 15,781 ft (4,810 m)

Po River

APENNINES

IBERIAN PENINSULA

Tagus River

Douro River

Guadiana River

Guadalquivir River

Strait of Gibraltar

Corsica

Sardinia

Balearic Is.

Tyrrhenian Sea

Sicily

Mediterranean Sea

Malta

KJOLEN MOUNTAINS

KOLA PENINSULA

White Sea

Gulf of Bothnia

Lake Vänern

Lake Vättern

Skagerrak

Baltic Sea

Lake Ladoga

Lake Onega

Rybinsk Reservoir

North Dvina R.

Pechora River

URAL MOUNTAINS

Ural River

Volga River

FINNS PLAINS

Gulf of Finland

NORTHERN EUROPEAN PLAIN

Elbe River

Oder River

Vistula River

Dniester River

Dnieper River

Don River

CARPATHIAN MTS.

TRANSYLVANIAN ALPS

DINARIC ALPS

Adriatic Sea

Danube River

BALKAN PENINSULA

Aegean Sea

Rhodes

Crete

CRIMEAN PENINSULA

Black Sea

Sea of Azov

Sea of Marmara

CAUCASUS MTS.

Mt. Elbrus 18,510 ft (5,642 m)

Caspian Sea

Coastlines No place in Europe is far from a major body of water. Croatia's Dalmatian coast overlooks the Adriatic Sea.

HOLT

Geography's Impact

video series

Watch the video to understand the impact of living below sea level.

Landforms A mountain village shows the beauty of the Swiss Alps.

561

Chapter Preview

Explore the Maps and Pictures

Europe: Physical Tell students that in addition to the labels, colors convey important information on a physical map. Point students' attention to the map key. Ask: what do the green colors indicate? *low elevations* Then ask: what is indicated by yellow and orange? *high elevations* Then have students examine the map. Just by glancing at the map, students should be able to see that most of Europe is low in elevation. Ask students: in which two mountain ranges are Europe's highest elevations? *Caucasus, Alps* Where in Europe is there a large portion of land below sea level? *in Eastern Europe, north of the Caspian Sea*

Analyzing Visuals Pictures are worth a thousand words. Have students share their ideas about what the photographs along the bottom of the page convey about Europe. Do any students have vastly different impressions of the photographs?

HOLT

Geography's Impact

▶ Video Series

See the Video Teacher's Guide for strategies for using the chapter video to teach about the impact of living below sea level.

go.hrw.com

Online Resources

Chapter Resources:
KEYWORD: SK9 CH17

Teacher Resources:
KEYWORD: SK9 TEACHER

Differentiating Instruction

Struggling Readers
Below Level

Allow students time to study the pictures in this chapter. Have them choose one or two pictures that interest them the most. Ask volunteers to identify their favorites. What interests them about the subjects of the pictures? What more would they like to learn about the subjects? On the board, list the subjects that students have chosen. **LS Verbal/Linguistic, Visual/Spatial**

Alternative Assessment Handbook, Rubric 11: Discussions

Advanced/Gifted and Talented
Above Level

Ask volunteers to research a few important facts about subjects from the list created in the Struggling Readers activity and to prepare a brief oral report for the class. As time permits, students can present their reports at appropriate times during the teaching of this chapter. **LS Verbal/Linguistic**

Alternative Assessment Handbook, Rubric 24: Oral Presentations

Answers

Map Zone 1. *Northern European Plain;* **2.** *Mediterranean Sea, Tyrrhenian Sea*

561

562 CHAPTER 17

Preteach

Bellringer

If YOU lived there. . . Use the **Daily Bellringer Transparency** to help students answer the question.

🗂 Daily Bellringer Transparency, Section 1

Key Terms and Places

📋 **RF:** Vocabulary Builder, Section 1

Taking Notes

Have students copy the graphic organizer onto their own paper and then use it to take notes on the section. This activity will prepare students for the Section Assessment, in which they will complete a graphic organizer that builds on the information using the Critical Thinking Skill: Finding Main Ideas.

Southern Europe

What You Will Learn...

Main Ideas

1. Southern Europe's physical features include rugged mountains and narrow coastal plains.
2. The region's climate and resources support such industries as agriculture, fishing, and tourism.

The Big Idea

The peninsulas of Southern Europe have rocky terrains and sunny, mild climates.

Key Terms and Places

Mediterranean Sea, *p. 562*
Pyrenees, *p. 563*
Apennines, *p. 563*
Alps, *p. 563*
Mediterranean climate, *p. 564*

TAKING NOTES Draw two ovals like the ones below. As you read this section, list facts about Southern Europe's landforms in one oval and facts about its climate and resources in the other.

Landforms   Climate and Resources

562 CHAPTER 17

If **YOU** lived there...

You are in a busy fish market in a small town on the coast of Italy, near the Mediterranean Sea. It is early morning. Colorful fishing boats have just pulled into shore with their catch of fresh fish and seafood. They unload their nets of slippery octopus and wriggling shrimp. Others bring silvery sea bass. You are looking forward to lunch—perhaps a tasty fish soup or pasta dish.

How does the Mediterranean affect your life?

BUILDING BACKGROUND The Mediterranean Sea has shaped the geography, climate, and culture of Southern Europe. All of these countries have long coastlines, with good harbors and beautiful beaches. Because much of the interior is rugged and mountainous, the sea has also been a highway for trade and travel.

Physical Features

The continent of Europe has often been called a peninsula of peninsulas. Why do you think this is so? Look at the map of Europe on the previous page to find out. Notice how Europe juts out from Asia like one big peninsula. Also, notice how smaller peninsulas extend into the many bodies of water that surround the continent.

Look at the map of Europe again. Do you see the three large peninsulas that extend south from Europe? From west to east, these are the Iberian Peninsula, the Italian Peninsula, and the Balkan Peninsula. Together with some large islands, they form the region of Southern Europe.

Southern Europe is also known as Mediterranean Europe. All of the countries of Southern Europe have long coastlines on the **Mediterranean Sea.** In addition to this common location on the Mediterranean, the countries of Southern Europe share many common physical features.

Teach the Big Idea

Southern Europe

1. **Teach** Ask students the questions in the Main Idea boxes under Direct Teach.

2. **Apply** Divide the class into three groups. Ask one group to name and describe the landforms of Southern Europe, another group the bodies of water, and a third group the climate and resources. Allow the groups time to share opinions. **LS** Verbal/Linguistic

3. **Review** Have each group report to the class. After each group is finished, have the class add information if appropriate.

4. **Practice/Homework** Have students write one paragraph describing the landforms of southern Europe and another describing the climate and resources. **LS** Verbal/Linguistic

   📋 Alternative Assessment Handbook, Rubric 40: Writing to Describe

Landforms

The three peninsulas of Southern Europe are largely covered with rugged mountains. In Greece, for example, about three-fourths of the land is mountainous. Because much of the land is so rugged, farming and travel in Southern Europe can be a challenge.

The mountains of Southern Europe form several large ranges. On the Iberian Peninsula, the **Pyrenees** (PIR-uh-neez) form a boundary between Spain and France to the north. Italy has two major ranges. The **Apennines** (A-puh-nynz) run along the whole peninsula, and the **Alps**—Europe's highest mountains—are in the north. The Pindus Mountains cover much of Greece.

Southern Europe's mountains extend into the sea as well, where they rise above the water to form islands. The Aegean Sea east of Greece is home to more than 2,000 such islands. Southern Europe also has many larger islands formed by undersea mountains. These include Crete, which is south of Greece; Sicily, at the southern tip of Italy; and many others.

Not all of Southern Europe is rocky and mountainous, though. Some flat plains lie in the region. Most of these plains are along the coast and in the valleys of major rivers. It is here that most farming in Southern Europe takes place. It is also here that most of the region's people live.

FOCUS ON READING

As you read, ask yourself this question: Where are the Pyrenees?

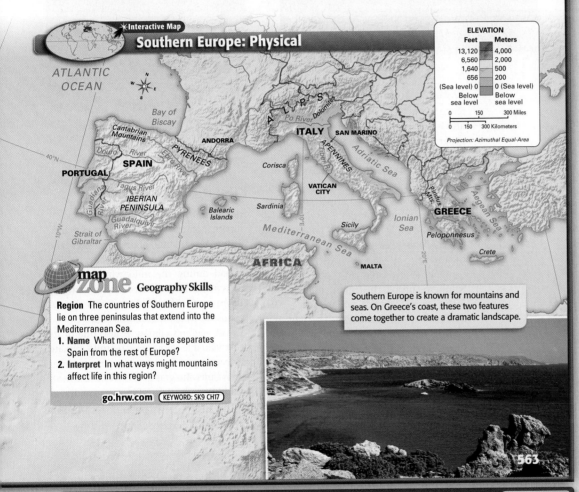

Interactive Map

Southern Europe: Physical

ELEVATION

Feet		Meters
13,120		4,000
6,560		2,000
1,640		500
656		200
(Sea level) 0		0 (Sea level)
Below sea level		Below sea level

0   150   300 Miles
0   150   300 Kilometers

Projection: Azimuthal Equal-Area

map zone Geography Skills

Region The countries of Southern Europe lie on three peninsulas that extend into the Mediterranean Sea.

1. **Name** What mountain range separates Spain from the rest of Europe?
2. **Interpret** In what ways might mountains affect life in this region?

go.hrw.com KEYWORD: SK9 CH17

Southern Europe is known for mountains and seas. On Greece's coast, these two features come together to create a dramatic landscape.

563

Direct Teach

Main Idea

① Physical Features

Southern Europe's physical features include rugged mountains and narrow coastal plains.

Recall What type of landform covers much of southern Europe? *rugged mountains*

Identify What areas of southern Europe are ideal for farming? *coastal plains and river valleys*

Draw Conclusions Why do you think most people live in the coastal plains and river valleys? *There are more ways to earn a living.*

Map Zone Transparency: Southern Europe: Physical

Did you know...

The highest peak in the
- Alps is Mont Blanc on the French-Italian border—15,771 ft.
- Pyrenees is Aneto—11,168 ft.
- Apennines is the Great Rock of Italy—9,554 ft.
- Pindus is Mount Smolikos—8,652 ft.
- U.S. is Mount McKinley (Alaska)—20,320 ft.
- world is Mount Everest (Nepal/Tibet)—29,035 ft.

go.hrw.com
Online Resources

KEYWORD: SK9 CH17
ACTIVITY: Islands of the Mediterranean

Critical Thinking: Analyzing Maps

At Level

Studying Southern Europe

1. Allow students time to study the physical map of southern Europe on this page.

2. Have students locate the three peninsulas, four mountain ranges, four seas, and two rivers mentioned in the text.

3. Draw attention to the Map Zone feature and ask volunteers to answer the questions. Follow up with these questions: What sea borders Greece on the west? *Ionian* What sea does the river Po empty into? *Adriatic* Where does the Po begin? *in the Alps* Through what two countries does the Tagus River flow? *Spain and Portugal* What areas of southern Europe have the lowest elevation? *coastal areas, particularly the west coast of Portugal and the northeast and east coast of Italy* Where is the highest elevation? *in the Alps* What separates Spain from northern Africa? *the Strait of Gibraltar* 🅛🅢 **Verbal/Linguistic, Visual/Spatial**

Alternative Assessment Handbook, Rubric 21: Map Reading

Answers

Focus on Reading *in northern Spain*
Map Zone 1. *travel, transportation, industry;* **2.** *because it borders the Mediterranean Sea*

❷ Climate and Resources

The region's climate and resources support such industries as agriculture, fishing, and tourism.

Recall Name two important resources in southern Europe. *climate, the sea*

Analyze Why is the sea important to southern Europe's economy? *Port cities ship goods around the world, and fish and shellfish support the fishing industry.*

Draw Conclusions What kinds of things might this region export? *citrus fruits, grapes, olives, wheat, fish*

Info to Know

Two Important Rivers The Tagus River, which is 626 miles long, begins in central Spain and flows west through Portugal to the Atlantic Ocean. It empties at Lisbon, one of Europe's major port cities. The Po River, which is about 405 miles long, flows from the Alps to the Adriatic Sea. Ships from the Adriatic carry freight up the Po as far as Turin, which is an important industrial city in northern Italy.

Answers

Reading Check *rugged mountains, coastal plains, river valleys, islands, seas, and rivers*

564

Close-up

Mediterranean Climate

Southern Europe is known for its Mediterranean climate, which features warm, dry summers and mild, wet winters. This climate affects nearly every aspect of life in the region.

❶ Agriculture The climate of Southern Europe is ideal for growing many crops. Here, Portuguese farmers harvest grapes.

SPAIN

PORTUGAL
①

②

② Tourism The region's mild and sunny climate draws millions of tourists to places like this beach in Ibiza, Spain.

Water Features

Since Southern Europe is mostly peninsulas and islands, water is central to the region's geography. No place in Southern Europe is very far from a major body of water. The largest of these bodies of water is the Mediterranean, but the Adriatic, Aegean, and Ionian seas are also important to the region. For many centuries, these seas have given the people of Southern Europe food and a relatively easy way to travel around the region.

Only a few large rivers run through Southern Europe. The region's longest river is the Tagus (TAY-guhs), which flows across the Iberian Peninsula. In northern Italy, the Po runs through one of Southern Europe's most fertile and densely populated areas. Other rivers run out of the mountains and into the many surrounding seas.

READING CHECK **Finding Main Ideas** What are the region's major features?

Climate and Resources

Southern Europe is famous for its pleasant climate. Most of the region enjoys warm, sunny days and mild nights for most of the year. Little rain falls in the summer, falling instead during the mild winter. In fact, the type of climate found across Southern Europe is called a **Mediterranean climate** because it is common in this region.

The region's climate is also one of its most valuable resources. The mild climate is ideal for growing a variety of crops, from citrus fruits and grapes to olives and wheat. In addition, millions of tourists are drawn to the region each year by its climate, beaches, and breathtaking scenery.

564 CHAPTER 17

Differentiating Instruction

Below Level

Struggling Readers

1. Draw attention to the Close-up feature on Mediterranean climate. Point out the numbers on each picture and the numbered locations on the map. Explain to students that the pictures illustrate scenes from the numbered locations on the map.

2. Have students study the first picture and read its caption. Then ask: Where was this picture taken? *in wine-growing region of Portugal* What aspect of life is affected by the climate in this picture? *the growing of crops*

3. Repeat this procedure with the other three pictures. (For the second picture, point out that Ibiza is an island.) Use the Analyzing Visuals question to review the influence of climate on southern Europe. **LS** **Verbal/ Linguistic, Visual/Spatial**

📋 Alternative Assessment Handbook, Rubric 21: Map Reading

ITALY

3

GREECE

4

4 Architecture Climate also affects architecture in Southern Europe. Buildings, like these in Greece, are airy and made of light materials to reflect sunlight and heat.

3 Vegetation This field in Tuscany, a region of Italy, shows the variety of plants that thrive in Southern Europe's climate.

ANALYSIS SKILL **ANALYZING VISUALS**

What are four ways in which the Mediterranean climate affects life in Southern Europe?

The sea is also an important resource in Southern Europe. Many of the region's largest cities are ports, which ship goods all over the world. In addition, the nearby seas are full of fish and shellfish, which provide the basis for profitable fishing industries.

READING CHECK **Generalizing** How is a mild climate important to Southern Europe?

SUMMARY AND PREVIEW In this section you learned about the physical features of Southern Europe. In the next section you will move north and west to learn about the physical features there.

go.hrw.com
Online Quiz
KEYWORD: SK9 HP17

Section 1 Assessment

Reviewing Ideas, Terms, and Places

1. **a. Recall** Which three peninsulas are in Southern Europe?
   b. Explain Why is the sea important to Southern Europe?
   c. Elaborate Why do you think most people in Southern Europe live on coastal plains or in river valleys?
2. **a. Describe** What is the **Mediterranean climate** like?
   b. Generalize How is climate an important resource for the region?

Critical Thinking

3. **Finding Main Ideas** Draw a diagram like the one shown here. In the left oval, use your notes to explain how landforms affect life in Southern Europe. In the right oval, explain how climate affects life in the region.

Landforms   Climate

FOCUS ON WRITING

4. **Describing Southern Europe** What features of Southern Europe might appeal to real estate buyers? Would it be the climate? the landforms? the water? Write some ideas in your notebook.

Direct Teach

Did you know...

The climate of a particular location depends on five factors: latitude, altitude, surface features, distance from large bodies of water, and circulation of the atmosphere. Southern Europe's Mediterranean climate is also considered a subtropical dry summer climate.

Info to Know

The Highland Climate A highland climate is common in mountainous regions. This climate varies with the altitude. A location in this climate might be mild in the foothills, much cooler further up, and very cold at the top.

Review & Assess

Close

Have students discuss the major physical features of southern Europe and the ways in which climate and resources affect life in the region.

Review

Online Quiz, Section 1

Assess

SE Section 1 Assessment
PASS: Section 1 Quiz
Alternative Assessment Handbook

Reteach/Classroom Intervention

Interactive Reader and Study Guide, Section 1
Interactive Skills Tutor CD-ROM

Section 1 Assessment Answers

1. **a.** Iberian, Italian, and Baltic
   b. It provides food and a way to travel and transport goods through the region.
   c. more ways to earn a living
2. **a.** hot, dry summers and mild, wet winters
   b. It's ideal for growing crops and bringing tourists.
3. possible answers: Landforms—The rugged mountains are less populated; The coastal plains and river valleys are ideal for farming; Most of the people live there; Climate—It is good for agriculture, tourism, and has lush

vegetation; Because of the sunlight and heat, buildings are airy and made of light materials.
4. Students' notes will vary but should be based on details from this section.

Answers

Reading Check *It is ideal for growing crops, and it encourages tourism.*
Analyzing Visuals *agriculture, tourism, vegetation, and architecture*

565

Bellringer

If YOU lived there. . . Use the **Daily Bellringer Transparency** to help students answer the question.

📖 Daily Bellringer Transparency, Section 2

Physical Geography of Europe	Daily Bellringer
	Section 2

Review Section 1

Read the statements below and determine what is "speaking."

1. "I'm a portion of land that is surrounded on three sides by water." What am I?
2. "I'm the name of a sea and a type of climate in Southern Europe." What am I?
3. "I'm a mountain range on the Iberian Peninsula that forms a boundary between Spain and France." What am I?
4. "I'm Europe's highest mountain range." What am I?

Preview Section 2

If YOU lived there . . .
You are a photographer planning a book about the landscapes of West-Central Europe. You are trying to decide where to find the best pictures of rich farmland, forested plateaus, and rugged mountains. So far, you are planning to show the colorful tulip fields of the Netherlands, the hilly Black Forest region of Germany, and the snow-covered Alps in Switzerland. **What other places might you want to show?**

Consider other UPLANDS AND MOUNTAINS:
• scene from the Massif Central in France
• view from the Alps in Austria
• walls to hold back the sea in the Netherlands

Consider other PLAINS:
• lavender fields in Provence, a region in southern France
• livestock farms in Belgium
• farms along the Danube and Rhine rivers

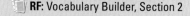

Key Terms and Places

📄 **RF:** Vocabulary Builder, Section 2

Taking Notes

Have students copy the graphic organizer onto their own paper and then use it to take notes on the section. This activity will prepare students for the Section Assessment in which they will complete a graphic organizer that builds on the information using the Critical Thinking Skill: Categorizing.

West-Central Europe

What You Will Learn...

Main Ideas

1. The physical features of West-Central Europe include plains, uplands, mountains, rivers, and seas.
2. West-Central Europe's mild climate and resources support agriculture, energy production, and tourism.

The Big Idea

West-Central Europe has a range of landscapes, a mild climate, and rich farmland.

Key Terms and Places

Northern European Plain, *p. 566*
North Sea, *p. 568*
English Channel, *p. 568*
Danube River, *p. 568*
Rhine River, *p. 568*
navigable river, *p. 568*

TAKING NOTES Draw a chart like the one here. As you read, list facts about the region's physical features, climate, and resources.

West-Central Europe	
Physical Features	Climate and Resources

If YOU lived there...

You are a photographer planning a book about the landscapes of West-Central Europe. You are trying to decide where to find the best pictures of rich farmland, forested plateaus, and rugged mountains. So far, you are planning to show the colorful tulip fields of the Netherlands, the hilly Black Forest region of Germany, and the snow-covered Alps in Switzerland.

What other places might you want to show?

BUILDING BACKGROUND The countries of West-Central Europe are among the most prosperous and powerful countries in the world. The reasons include their mild climates, good farmland, many rivers, market economies, and stable governments. In addition, most of these countries cooperate as members of the European Union.

Physical Features

From fields of tulips, to sunny beaches, to icy mountain peaks, West-Central Europe offers a wide range of landscapes. Even though the region is small, it includes three major types of landforms—plains, uplands, and mountains. These landforms extend in wide bands across the region.

Plains, Uplands, and Mountains

Look at the map at right. Picture West-Central Europe as an open fan with Italy as the handle. The outer edge of this imaginary fan is a broad coastal plain called the **Northern European Plain**. This plain stretches from the Atlantic coast into Eastern Europe.

Most of this plain is flat or rolling and lies less than 500 feet (150 m) above sea level. In the Netherlands, parts of the plain dip below sea level. There, people must build walls to hold back the sea. In Brittany in northwestern France, the land rises to form a plateau above the surrounding plain.

Teach the Big Idea

At Level

West-Central Europe

1. **Teach** Ask students the questions in the Main Idea boxes under Direct Teach.

2. **Apply** Have students make a four-columned chart and label the columns: *Landforms, Water Features, Climate,* and *Resources.* As they read the lesson, have them list words or phrases that describe each aspect of the geography of West-Central Europe. Then write the terms *agriculture, energy production,* and *tourism* on the board. Have students identify aspects of the region's physical geography that make these economic activities possible. 🄛 **Verbal/Linguistic**

3. **Review** Have students rank the region's geographic assets in order of importance and explain their choices.

4. **Practice/Homework** Have students pick an area they might enjoy living in and write a paragraph telling why. 🄛 **Verbal/Linguistic, Interpersonal**

📄 Alternative Assessment Handbook, Rubrics 13: Graphic Organizers; and 37: Writing Assignments

The Northern European Plain provides the region's best farmland. Many people live on the plain, and the region's largest cities are located there.

The Central Uplands extend across the center of our imaginary fan. This area has many rounded hills, small plateaus, and valleys. In France, the uplands include the Massif Central (ma-SEEF sahn-TRAHL), a plateau region, and the Jura Mountains.

This range is on the French-Swiss border. In Germany, uplands cover much of the southern two-thirds of the country. Dense woodlands, such as the Black Forest, blanket many of the hills in this area.

The Central Uplands have many productive coalfields. As a result, the area is important for mining and industry. Some valleys provide fertile soil for farming, but most of the area is too rocky to farm.

West-Central Europe: Physical

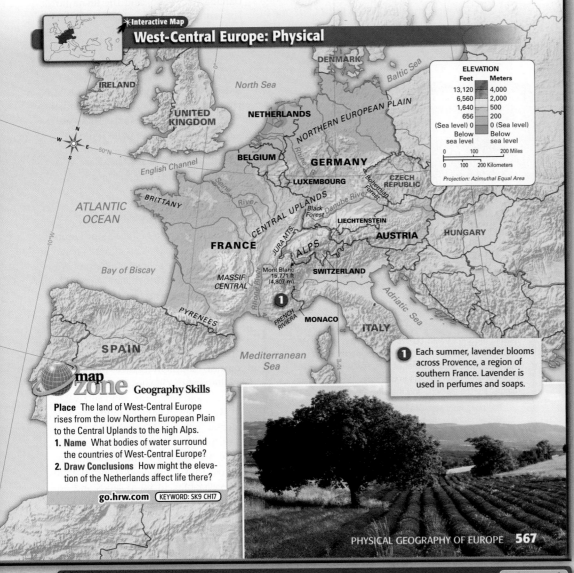

ELEVATION

Feet	Meters
13,120	4,000
6,560	2,000
1,640	500
656	200
(Sea level) 0	0 (Sea level)
Below sea level	Below sea level

0   100   200 Miles
0   100   200 Kilometers
Projection: Azimuthal Equal Area

Mont Blanc 15,771 ft (4,807 m)

1 Each summer, lavender blooms across Provence, a region of southern France. Lavender is used in perfumes and soaps.

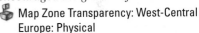
map zone **Geography Skills**

Place The land of West-Central Europe rises from the low Northern European Plain to the Central Uplands to the high Alps.
1. **Name** What bodies of water surround the countries of West-Central Europe?
2. **Draw Conclusions** How might the elevation of the Netherlands affect life there?

go.hrw.com KEYWORD: SK9 CH17

PHYSICAL GEOGRAPHY OF EUROPE **567**

English-Language Learners

1. Review with students the definitions of the terms *plains*, *uplands*, and *mountains*. Have them identify the landform types most common in their area and describe those in other places they have lived or visited.

2. Review the terms *elevation* and *sea level*. Remind students that sea level is the level of the ocean's surface used as a reference point for measuring elevation, heights, and depths on Earth's surface, in feet or meters.

3. Check understanding by having students predict in what landform areas these elevations would be found:

   13,120 ft. (mountains, such as the Alps)

   500 ft. (plains, such as the Northern European Plain)

4. Working in pairs, have students make up a similar question and answer to share with the class.
   🗣 **Verbal/Linguistic**
   📋 Alternative Assessment Handbook, Rubric 1: Acquiring Information

Direct Teach

Main Idea

❶ Physical Features

The physical features of West-Central Europe include plains, uplands, mountains, rivers, and seas.

Recall Where is the best farmland in West-Central Europe found? *Northern European Plain*

Describe What are the natural resources or distinctive features of each of the landform regions? *plains—very good farmland; uplands—forests, coal, and some areas with fertile soil; mountains—scenic beauty*

Draw Conclusions How might the region's water features have affected its economic development? *Navigable rivers and nearness to seas and ocean encouraged the growth of trade.*

📽 Map Zone Transparency: West-Central Europe: Physical

Info to Know

Disappearing Forests Much of Europe was once covered by forests, which have disappeared as a result of human activities, such as farming. Today, forests are impacted by air pollution, pest outbreaks, drought, and fires.

Connect to Science

Lavender French farmers in Provence grow lavender plants. Lavender's smell comes from oil glands found among the tiny hairs that cover its flowers, leaves, and stems. This oil is extracted from the flowers for use in perfumes, soaps, skin lotions, and other cosmetics.

Answers

Map Zone 1. *Baltic Sea, North Sea, English Channel, Atlantic Ocean, Bay of Biscay, Mediterranean Sea;* **2.** *possible answer—The low elevations would affect where buildings could be built and increase the danger of flooding.*

Main Idea

❷ Climate and Resources

West-Central Europe's mild climate and resources support agriculture, energy production, and tourism.

Describe How is the climate of the Alps different from the climate in most of West-Central Europe? Why? *wetter and colder than most of region which has marine west coast climate with cold winters and mild summers; at higher altitude*

Analyze Why is climate a natural resource for the region? *Mild climate combined with ample rainfall and rich soil make region's farmlands highly productive.*

Make Inferences How do the region's natural resources support industry? *coal, natural gas, hydroelectric power, uranium for nuclear power provide energy; iron ore used in manufacturing products*

🖳 Map Zone Transparency: West-Central Europe: Land Use and Resources

Linking to Today

Avalanche Prevention The Swiss Federal Snow and Avalanche Research Institute in Davos, Switzerland, is a world leader in avalanche risk assessment and prevention. The Institute estimates that about 150 skiers, snowboarders, and mountaineers are killed by avalanches each year in Europe and North America. The center trains skiers and climbers, as well as rescue dogs, mostly collies and German shepherds. The dogs can cover terrain eight times faster than humans and work in colder and harsher conditions. These dogs are trained to pick up the scent of humans buried deep in the snow. After an avalanche, rescue dogs are brought to the scene by helicopter or by lift systems at ski resorts.

Answers

Satellite View *Snow does not melt, but instead builds up and turns to ice.*
Reading Check *plains, uplands, mountains*

568

Along the inner part of our imaginary fan, the land rises dramatically to form the alpine mountain system. This system includes the Alps and the Pyrenees, which you read about in the last chapter.

As you have read, the Alps are Europe's highest mountain range. They stretch from southern France to the Balkan Peninsula. Several of the jagged peaks in the Alps soar to more than 14,000 feet (4,270 m). The highest peak is Mont Blanc (mawn BLAHN), which rises to 15,771 feet (4,807 m) in France. Because of the height of the Alps, large snowfields coat some peaks.

Satellite View

High in the Swiss Alps, snow builds up to form glaciers like the one shown here.

The Swiss Alps

At high elevations in the Alps, snow does not melt. For this reason, the snow builds up over time. As the snow builds up, it turns to ice and eventually forms glaciers. A glacier is a large, slow-moving sheet or river of ice. The satellite image above shows glaciers in the Swiss Alps. The white regions are the glaciers, and the blue areas are alpine lakes.

The buildup of snow and ice in the Alps can cause avalanches at lower elevations. An avalanche is a large mass of snow or other material that suddenly rushes down a mountainside. Avalanches pose a serious danger to people.

Analyzing Why do glaciers sometimes form at higher elevations in the Alps?

Water Features

Several bodies of water are important to West-Central Europe's physical geography. The **North Sea** and **English Channel** lie to the north. The Bay of Biscay and Atlantic Ocean lie to the west. The Mediterranean Sea borders France to the south.

Several rivers cross the region as well. Look at the map on the previous page to identify them. Two important rivers are the **Danube** (DAN-yoob) and the **Rhine** (RYN). For centuries people and goods have traveled these rivers, and many cities, farms, and industrial areas line their banks.

Several of West-Central Europe's rivers are navigable. A **navigable river** is one that is deep and wide enough for ships to use. These rivers and a system of canals link the region's interior to the seas. These waterways are important for trade and travel.

READING CHECK **Finding Main Ideas** What are the region's three major landform areas?

Climate and Resources

A warm ocean current flows along Europe's northwestern coast. This current creates a marine west coast climate in most of West-Central Europe. This climate makes much of the area a pleasant place to live. Though winters can get cold, summers are mild. Rain and storms occur often, though.

At higher elevations, such as in the Alps, the climate is colder and wetter. In contrast, southern France has a warm Mediterranean climate. Summers are dry and hot, and winters are mild and wet.

West-Central Europe's mild climate is a valuable natural resource. Mild temperatures, plenty of rain, and rich soil have made the region's farmlands highly productive. Farm crops include grapes, grains, and vegetables. In the uplands and Alps, pastures and valleys support livestock.

Critical Thinking: Making Generalizations

Important Natural Resources

1. Point out that the countries of West-Central Europe are among Earth's most prosperous. Discuss the natural resources that have helped create a high standard of living and prosperity. Note differences between natural resources and human resources. Point out that tourism depends on human and natural resources.

2. Focus discussion on energy resources. Have students look at the map on the next page and identify places where oil and natural

gas are found. Have them write a statement describing the relationship between the two resources. Discuss why energy resources are important to economic growth.

3. Have students examine the map and write three sentences describing how land use and energy resources are related in West-Central Europe. 🗗 **Verbal/Linguistic, Visual/Spatial**

📄 Alternative Assessment Handbook, Rubric 21: Map Reading

West-Central Europe: Land Use and Resources

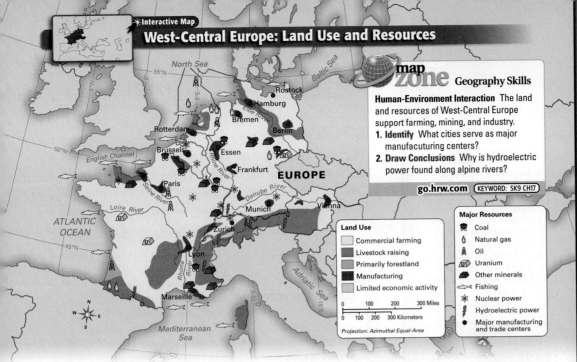

North Sea
Baltic Sea
Rostock
Hamburg
Bremen
Rotterdam
Berlin
Brussels
Essen
Elbe River
Frankfurt
EUROPE
Paris
Rhine River
Danube River
Munich
Vienna
Zurich
Loire River
ATLANTIC
OCEAN
Seine River
Lyon
Rhône River
Adriatic Sea
Marseille
Mediterranean
Sea
English Channel

map zone Geography Skills

Human-Environment Interaction The land and resources of West-Central Europe support farming, mining, and industry.
1. **Identify** What cities serve as major manufacturing centers?
2. **Draw Conclusions** Why is hydroelectric power found along alpine rivers?

go.hrw.com [KEYWORD: SK9 CH17]

Land Use
- Commercial farming
- Livestock raising
- Primarily forestland
- Manufacturing
- Limited economic activity

0   100   200   300 Miles
0   100   200   300 Kilometers

Projection: Azimuthal Equal-Area

Major Resources
- 🐚 Coal
- A Natural gas
- A Oil
- Uranium
- Other minerals
- Fishing
- ❄ Nuclear power
- Hydroelectric power
- ● Major manufacturing and trade centers

Energy and mineral resources are not evenly distributed across the region, as the map shows. France has coal and iron ore, Germany also has coal, and the Netherlands has natural gas. Fast-flowing alpine rivers provide hydroelectric power. Even so, many countries must import fuels.

Another valuable natural resource is found in the breathtaking beauty of the Alps. Each year, tourists flock to the Alps to enjoy the scenery and to hike and ski.

READING CHECK **Summarizing** What natural resources contribute to the region's economy?

SUMMARY AND PREVIEW West-Central Europe includes low plains, uplands, and mountains. The climate is mild, and natural resources support farming, industry, and tourism. Next, you will read about a less mild region, Northern Europe.

Section 2 Assessment

go.hrw.com
Online Quiz
KEYWORD: SK9 HP17

Reviewing Ideas, Terms, and Places

1. **a. Describe** What are the main physical features of the **Northern European Plain**?
   b. Analyze How does having many **navigable** rivers benefit West-Central Europe?
2. **a. Recall** What is the region's main climate?
   b. Make Inferences How might an uneven distribution of mineral resources affect the region?

Critical Thinking

3. **Categorizing** Draw a fan like this one. Label each band with the landform area in West-Central Europe it represents. Using your notes, identify each area's physical features, climate, and resources.

FOCUS ON WRITING

4. **Selling the Physical Geography** How could you describe the physical features of West-Central Europe to appeal to buyers? Jot down ideas.

PHYSICAL GEOGRAPHY OF EUROPE **569**

Section 2 Assessment Answers

1. **a.** broad coastal plain, lies less than 500 feet above sea level, good farmland, large cities
   b. facilitate transportation, trade, travel, tourism
2. **a.** marine west coast with cold winters and mild summers
   b. Some countries have to import more energy or fuel than others.
3. European Plain (outer band)—flat or rolling with most of it lying less than 500 feet above sea level, good farmland, location of largest

cities; Central Uplands (middle band)—many rounded hills, small plateaus, valleys, dense forests on some hills, coal fields, most areas too rocky for farming; Alpine mountain system (inner band)—highest European mountain range, large snowfields, colder, wetter climate
4. Students' responses should accurately describe the physical features of West-Central Europe.

Bellringer

If YOU lived there. . . Use the **Daily Bellringer Transparency** to help students answer the question.

📎 Daily Bellringer Transparency, Section 3

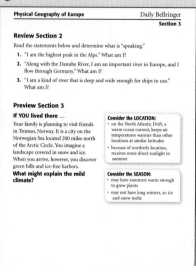

Physical Geography of Europe	Daily Bellringer
	Section 3

Review Section 2

Read the statements below and determine what is "speaking."

1. "I am the highest peak in the Alps." What am I?

2. "Along with the Danube River, I am an important river in Europe, and I flow through Germany." What am I?

3. "I am a kind of river that is deep and wide enough for ships to use." What am I?

Preview Section 3

If YOU lived there …

Your family is planning to visit friends in Tromso, Norway. It is a city on the Norwegian Sea located 200 miles north of the Arctic Circle. You imagine a landscape covered in snow and ice. When you arrive, however, you discover green hills and ice-free harbors.

What might explain the mild climate?

Consider the LOCATION:
- on the North Atlantic Drift, a warm ocean current, keeps air temperatures warmer than other locations at similar latitudes
- because of northerly location, receives more direct sunlight in summer

Consider the SEASON:
- may have summers warm enough to grow plants
- may not have long winters, so ice and snow melts

Academic Vocabulary

Review with students the high-use academic term in this section.

primary main, most important (p. 572)

📄 RF: Vocabulary Builder, Section 3

Taking Notes

Have students copy the graphic organizer onto their own paper and then use it to take notes on the section. This activity will prepare students for the Section Assessment, in which they will complete a graphic organizer that builds on the information using the Critical Thinking Skill: Comparing and Contrasting.

SECTION 3

Northern Europe

What You Will Learn…

Main Ideas

1. The physical features of Northern Europe include low mountain ranges and jagged coastlines.
2. Northern Europe's natural resources include energy sources, soils, and seas.
3. The climates of Northern Europe range from a mild coastal climate to a freezing ice cap climate.

The Big Idea

Northern Europe is a region of unique physical features, rich resources, and diverse climates.

Key Terms and Places

British Isles, p. 570
Scandinavia, p. 570
fjord, p. 571
geothermal energy, p. 572
North Atlantic Drift, p. 572

TAKING NOTES As you read, take notes on Northern Europe's physical features, natural resources, and climates. Record your notes in a chart like the one below.

Physical Features	Natural Resources	Climates

If YOU lived there…

Your family is planning to visit friends in Tromso, Norway. It is a city on the Norwegian Sea located 200 miles north of the Arctic Circle. You imagine a landscape covered in snow and ice. When you arrive, however, you discover green hills and ice-free harbors.

What might explain the mild climate?

BUILDING BACKGROUND Although located at high latitudes, Norway and the rest of Northern Europe have surprisingly mild temperatures. All the countries of Northern Europe are located on seas and oceans. As a result, they benefit from ocean currents that bring warm water north and keep the climate reasonably warm.

Physical Features

From Ireland's gently rolling hills to Iceland's icy glaciers and fiery volcanoes, Northern Europe is a land of great variety. Because of this variety, the physical geography of Northern Europe changes greatly from one location to another.

Two regions—the British Isles and Scandinavia—make up Northern Europe. To the southwest lie the **British Isles**, a group of islands located across the English Channel from the rest of Europe. Northeast of the British Isles is **Scandinavia**, a region of islands and peninsulas in far northern Europe. The island of Iceland, to the west, is often considered part of Scandinavia.

Hills and Mountains Rough, rocky hills and low mountains cover much of Northern Europe. Rugged hills stretch across much of Iceland, northern Scotland, and Scandinavia. The jagged Kjolen (CHUH-luhn) Mountains on the Scandinavian Peninsula divide Norway from Sweden. The rocky soil and uneven terrain in these parts of Northern Europe make farming there difficult. As a result, fewer people live there than in the rest of Northern Europe.

Teach the Big Idea

At Level

Northern Europe

Prep Required

Materials: atlas or maps of physical, resource, and climate maps of the U.S.

1. **Teach** Ask students the questions in the Main Idea boxes under Direct Teach.

2. **Apply** Write three headings on the board: *Physical Features, Natural Resources, Climates.* Call on students to add details under each heading that describe Northern Europe. Then ask if they can think of areas of the U.S. that have similar features.
   LS Verbal/Linguistic, Visual/Spatial

3. **Review** Ask students to list two countries in Northern Europe and two ways that the physical geography of the area affects life. Ask students to share their answers.

4. **Practice/Homework** Ask students to select one part of their local physical geography and write a few sentences on how it affects them and how it is similar to or different from one area of Northern Europe.
   LS Verbal/Linguistic
   📄 Alternative Assessment Handbook, Rubric 37: Writing Assignments

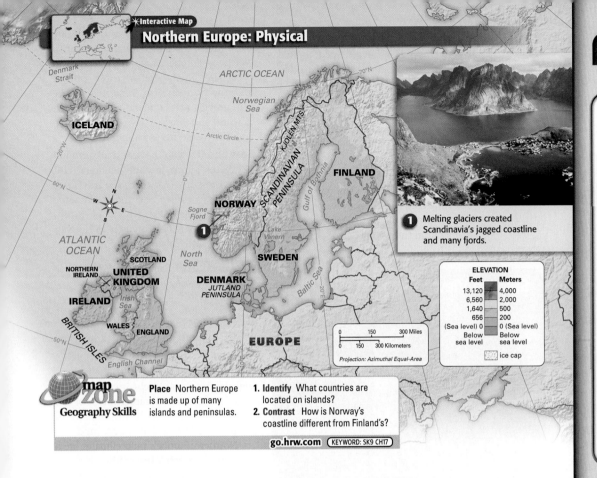

ARCTIC OCEAN

Norwegian Sea

Denmark Strait

ICELAND

Arctic Circle

KJOLEN MTS.

SCANDINAVIAN PENINSULA

FINLAND

Gulf of Bothnia

NORWAY

Sogne Fjord

Lake Vanern

ATLANTIC OCEAN

North Sea

SWEDEN

SCOTLAND

NORTHERN IRELAND

UNITED KINGDOM

IRELAND

Irish Sea

Baltic Sea

DENMARK

JUTLAND PENINSULA

WALES

ENGLAND

BRITISH ISLES

English Channel

EUROPE

1 Melting glaciers created Scandinavia's jagged coastline and many fjords.

ELEVATION

Feet	Meters
13,120	4,000
6,560	2,000
1,640	500
656	200
(Sea level) 0	0 (Sea level)
Below sea level	Below sea level

0   150   300 Miles
0   150   300 Kilometers
Projection: Azimuthal Equal-Area

ice cap

map Zone
Geography Skills

Place Northern Europe is made up of many islands and peninsulas.

1. **Identify** What countries are located on islands?
2. **Contrast** How is Norway's coastline different from Finland's?

go.hrw.com KEYWORD: SK9 CH17

Farmland and Plains Fertile farmland and flat plains stretch across the southern parts of the British Isles and Scandinavia. Ireland's rolling, green hills provide rich farmland. Wide valleys in England and Denmark also have plenty of fertile soil.

Effects of Glaciers Slow-moving sheets of ice, or glaciers, have left their mark on Northern Europe's coastlines and lakes. As you can see on the map above, Norway's western coastline is very jagged. Millions of years ago, glaciers cut deep valleys into Norway's coastal mountains. As the glaciers melted, these valleys filled with water,

creating deep fjords. A **fjord** (fee-AWRD) is a narrow inlet of the sea set between high, rocky cliffs. Many fjords are very long and deep. Norway's Sogne (SAWNG-nuh) Fjord, for example, is over 100 miles (160 km) long and more than three-quarters of a mile (1.2 km) deep. Melting glaciers also carved thousands of lakes in Northern Europe. Sweden's Lake Vanern, along with many of the lakes in the British Isles, were carved by glaciers thousands of years ago.

READING CHECK **Summarizing** What are some physical features of Northern Europe?

PHYSICAL GEOGRAPHY OF EUROPE **571**

❷ Natural Resources

Northern Europe's natural resources include energy sources, soils, and seas.

Identify Which country has a large supply of geothermal energy? *Iceland*

Summarize Why are the seas and oceans of Northern Europe considered a natural resource? *They provide fish to the people.*

❸ Climates

The climates of Northern Europe range from a mild coastal climate to a freezing ice cap climate.

Contrast How do temperatures in Northern Europe differ from those around the world in similar latitudes? *They are warmer.*

Recall What is the name of the ocean current that causes Northern Europe's mild climates? *North Atlantic Drift*

Satellite View
Norway's Fjords

Predicting Temperature Ask students to select two points on the Satellite View image. One point should be close to a fjord, the other further inland. Then ask students to predict which point would have the higher average temperatures in the winter and why. **LS** Logical/Mathematical

Alternative Assessment Handbook, Rubric 6: Cause and Effect

Answers

Satellite View *keep temperatures mild and allow winter travel*

Reading Check *energy resources, forests and soils, seas and oceans*

Natural Resources

ACADEMIC VOCABULARY
primary
main, most important

Natural resources have helped to make Northern Europe one of the wealthiest regions in the world. Northern Europe's **primary** resources are its energy resources, forests and soils, and surrounding seas.

Energy Northern Europe has a variety of energy resources. Norway and the United Kingdom benefit from oil and natural gas deposits under the North Sea. Hydroelectric energy is produced by the region's many lakes and rivers. In Iceland steam from hot springs produces **geothermal energy**, or energy from the heat of Earth's interior.

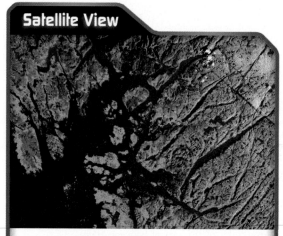

Satellite View

Norway's Fjords

Millions of years ago much of Norway was covered with glaciers. As the glaciers flowed slowly downhill, they carved long, winding channels, or fjords, into Norway's coastline.

As you can see in this satellite image, fjords cut many miles into Norway's interior, bringing warm waters from the North and Norwegian seas. As warm waters penetrate inland, they keep temperatures relatively mild. In fact, people have used these unfrozen fjords to travel during the winter when ice and snow made travel over land difficult.

Drawing Conclusions How do fjords benefit life in Norway?

Forests and Soils Forests and soils are two other important natural resources in Northern Europe. Large areas of timber-producing forests stretch across Finland and the Scandinavian Peninsula. Fertile soils provide rich farmland for crops, such as wheat and potatoes. Livestock like sheep and dairy cattle are also common.

Seas and Oceans The seas that surround Northern Europe are another important natural resource. For centuries, the North Sea, the Norwegian Sea, and the Atlantic Ocean have provided rich stocks of fish. Today, fishing is a key industry in Norway, Denmark, and Iceland.

READING CHECK **Summarizing** What natural resources are found in Northern Europe?

Climates

Locate Northern Europe on a map of the world. Notice that much of the region lies near the Arctic Circle. Due to the region's high latitude, you might imagine that it would be quite cold during much of the year. In reality, however, the climates in Northern Europe are remarkably mild.

Northern Europe's mild climates are a result of the **North Atlantic Drift**, an ocean current that brings warm, moist air across the Atlantic Ocean. Warm waters from this ocean current keep most of the region warmer than other locations around the globe at similar latitudes.

Much of Northern Europe has a marine west coast climate. Denmark, the British Isles, and western Norway benefit from mild summers and frequent rainfall. Snow and frosts may occur in winter but do not usually last long.

Central Norway, Sweden, and southern Finland have a humid continental climate. This area has four true seasons with cold, snowy winters and mild summers.

Cross-Discipline Activity: Science

Above Level

Understanding Geothermal Energy

Research Required

1. Divide the class into small groups. Explain that geothermal energy is an important resource in Iceland and is used in other areas of the world as well, including the U.S.

2. Have each group use the library, the Internet, or other resources to research one of the following areas: How Geothermal Energy Plants Work, How Much Geothermal Energy Is Produced Around the World, Geothermal Energy and the Environment, Geothermal Energy in the U.S. Each group should create a poster or chart that illustrates their findings.

3. When students have finished, have each group display their posters or charts, explain the information, and answer questions.

LS Verbal/Linguistic, Visual/Spatial, Interpersonal

Alternative Assessment Handbook, Rubrics 24: Oral Presentations; and 30: Research

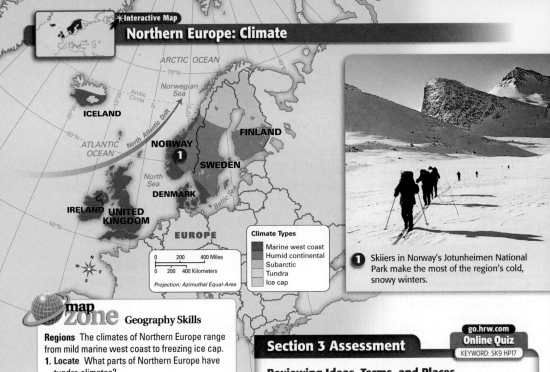

ARCTIC OCEAN
70°N
Norwegian
Sea
ICELAND
Arctic
Circle
ATLANTIC
OCEAN
60°N
FINLAND
NORWAY
1
SWEDEN
North
Sea
DENMARK
Baltic Sea
IRELAND UNITED
KINGDOM
50°N
EUROPE

0   200   400 Miles
0   200   400 Kilometers
Projection: Azimuthal Equal-Area

Climate Types
- Marine west coast
- Humid continental
- Subarctic
- Tundra
- Ice cap

1 Skiiers in Norway's Jotunheimen National Park make the most of the region's cold, snowy winters.

map zone Geography Skills

Regions The climates of Northern Europe range from mild marine west coast to freezing ice cap.
1. **Locate** What parts of Northern Europe have tundra climates?
2. **Make Inferences** What allows much of Northern Europe to have mild climates?

go.hrw.com   KEYWORD: SK9 CH17

Far to the north are colder climates. Subarctic regions, like those in Northern Scandinavia, have long, cold winters and short summers. Iceland's tundra and ice cap climates produce extremely cold temperatures all year.

READING CHECK **Analyzing** How does the North Atlantic Drift keep climates mild?

SUMMARY AND PREVIEW Northern Europe has many different physical features, natural resources, and climates. Next, you will learn about a very different region, Eastern Europe.

Section 3 Assessment

go.hrw.com
Online Quiz
KEYWORD: SK9 HP17

Reviewing Ideas, Terms, and Places

1. **a. Describe** What are the physical features of this region?
   b. Analyze What role did glaciers play in shaping the physical geography of Northern Europe?
2. **a. Recall** What is **geothermal energy**?
   b. Make Inferences How do people in Northern Europe benefit from the surrounding seas?
3. **a. Identify** What climates exist in Northern Europe?
   b. Predict How might the climates of Northern Europe be different without the **North Atlantic Drift**?

Critical Thinking

4. **Comparing and Contrasting** Using your notes and a chart like the one below, compare and contrast the physical geography of the British Isles and Scandinavia.

	British Isles	Scandinavia
Physical Features		
Resources		
Climates		

FOCUS ON WRITING

5. **Appealing to Customers** Northern Europe's cold climate might not appeal to everyone. How could you describe it to best appeal to customers?

PHYSICAL GEOGRAPHY OF EUROPE **573**

573

Bellringer

If YOU lived there. . . Use the **Daily Bellringer Transparency** to help students answer the question.

📦 Daily Bellringer Transparency, Section 4

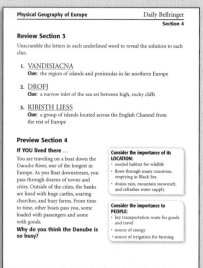

Physical Geography of Europe   Daily Bellringer
                          Section 4

Review Section 3
Unscramble the letters in each underlined word to reveal the solution to each clue.

1. VANDISIACNA
   Clue: the region of islands and peninsulas in far northern Europe

2. DROFJ
   Clue: a narrow inlet of the sea set between high, rocky cliffs

3. RIBISTH LIESS
   Clue: a group of islands located across the English Channel from the rest of Europe

Preview Section 4
If YOU lived there ...
You are traveling on a boat down the Danube River, one of the longest in Europe. As you float downstream, you pass through dozens of towns and cities. Outside of the cities, the banks are lined with huge castles, soaring churches, and busy farms. From time to time, other boats pass you, some loaded with passengers and some with goods.
Why do you think the Danube is so busy?

Consider the importance of its LOCATION:
• needed habitat for wildlife
• flows through many countries, emptying in Black Sea
• drains rain, mountain snowmelt, and refreshes water supply

Consider the importance to PEOPLE:
• key transportation route for goods and travel
• source of energy
• source of irrigation for farming

Academic Vocabulary

Review with students the high-use academic term in this section.

function use or purpose (p. 575)

📓 **RF:** Vocabulary Builder, Section 4

Taking Notes

Have students copy the graphic organizer onto their own paper and then use it to take notes on the section. This activity will prepare students for the Section Assessment, in which they will complete a graphic organizer that builds on the information using the Critical Thinking Skill: Categorizing.

Eastern Europe

What You Will Learn...

Main Ideas

1. The physical features of Eastern Europe include wide open plains, rugged mountain ranges, and many rivers.
2. The climate and vegetation of Eastern Europe differ widely in the north and the south.

The Big Idea

The physical geography of Eastern Europe varies greatly from place to place.

Key Places

Carpathians, *p. 574*
Balkan Peninsula, *p. 575*
Danube, *p. 576*
Chernobyl, *p. 577*

TAKING NOTES Draw a chart like the one below. As you read this section, use the chart to take notes about the landforms, climate, and vegetation of Eastern Europe.

Landforms	Climate	Vegetation

If YOU lived there...

You are traveling on a boat down the Danube River, one of the longest in Europe. As you float downstream, you pass through dozens of towns and cities. Outside of the cities, the banks are lined with huge castles, soaring churches, and busy farms. From time to time, other boats pass you, some loaded with passengers and some with goods.

Why do you think the Danube is so busy?

BUILDING BACKGROUND The physical geography of Eastern Europe varies widely from north to south. Many of the landforms you learned about in earlier chapters, including the Northern European Plain and the Alps, extend into this region.

Physical Features

Eastern Europe is a land of amazing contrasts. The northern parts of the region lie along the cold, often stormy shores of the Baltic Sea. In the south, however, are warm, sunny beaches along the Adriatic and Black seas. Jagged mountain peaks jut high into the sky in some places, while wildflowers dot the gently rolling hills of other parts of the region. These contrasts stem from the region's wide variety of landforms, water features, and climates.

Landforms

As you can see on the map, the landforms of Eastern Europe are arranged in a series of broad bands. In the north is the Northern European Plain. As you have already learned, this large plain stretches across most of Northern Europe.

South of the Northern European Plain is a low mountain range called the **Carpathians** (kahr-PAY-thee-uhnz). These rugged mountains are an extension of the Alps of West-Central Europe. They stretch in a long arc from the Alps to the Black Sea area.

Teach the Big Idea

Eastern Europe

1. **Teach** Ask students the questions in the Main Idea boxes under Direct Teach.

2. **Apply** Have students make a three-columned table, labeled *Baltic Region*, *Interior Plains*, and *Balkan Peninsula*. As they read the section and study the map on the next page, have them list the landforms, water features, climate, and vegetation that are associated with each region.

3. **Review** After completing the table, have students write two paragraphs identifying the region that they think has the most favorable and least favorable physical geography. Students should support their conclusions.

4. **Practice/Homework** Have students make three suggestions for how the area with the least favorable physical geography might turn its disadvantages into assets.
   🅛 **Verbal/Linguistic**

📓 **RF:** Alternative Assessment Handbook, Rubric 37: Writing Assignments

South and west of the Carpathians is another plain, the Great Hungarian Plain. As its name suggests, this fertile area is located mostly within Hungary.

South of the plain are more mountains, the Dinaric (duh-NAR-ik) Alps and Balkan Mountains. These two ranges together cover most of the **Balkan Peninsula**, one of the largest peninsulas in Europe. It extends south into the Mediterranean Sea.

Water Features

Like the rest of the continent, Eastern Europe has many bodies of water that affect how people live. To the southwest is the Adriatic Sea, an important route for transportation and trade. To the east, the Black Sea serves the same **function**. In the far north is the Baltic Sea. It is another important trade route, though parts of the sea freeze over in the winter.

ACADEMIC VOCABULARY

function
use or purpose

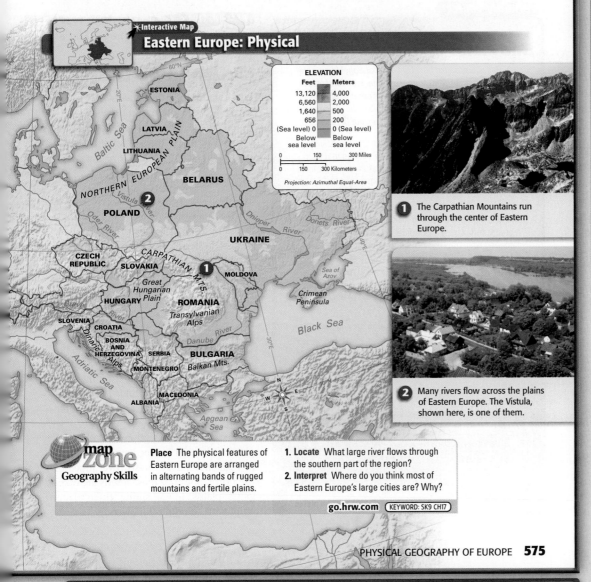

✦Interactive Map

Eastern Europe: Physical

ELEVATION

Feet	Meters
13,120	4,000
6,560	2,000
1,640	500
656	200
(Sea level) 0	0 (Sea level)
Below sea level	Below sea level

0   150   300 Miles
0   150   300 Kilometers

Projection: Azimuthal Equal-Area

ESTONIA
LATVIA
LITHUANIA
Baltic Sea
BELARUS
POLAND
Oder River
Vistula
NORTHERN EUROPEAN PLAIN
CZECH REPUBLIC
SLOVAKIA
CARPATHIAN MTS.
UKRAINE
Dniester River
Dnieper River
Donets River
MOLDOVA
Great Hungarian Plain
HUNGARY
ROMANIA
Transylvanian Alps
SLOVENIA
CROATIA
Drava River
Danube River
BOSNIA AND HERZEGOVINA
Dinaric Alps
SERBIA
MONTENEGRO
BULGARIA
Balkan Mts.
MACEDONIA
ALBANIA
Adriatic Sea
Aegean Sea
Crimean Peninsula
Sea of Azov
Black Sea

1 The Carpathian Mountains run through the center of Eastern Europe.

2 Many rivers flow across the plains of Eastern Europe. The Vistula, shown here, is one of them.

map zone
Geography Skills

Place The physical features of Eastern Europe are arranged in alternating bands of rugged mountains and fertile plains.

1. **Locate** What large river flows through the southern part of the region?
2. **Interpret** Where do you think most of Eastern Europe's large cities are? Why?

go.hrw.com   KEYWORD: SK9 CH17

PHYSICAL GEOGRAPHY OF EUROPE **575**

Differentiating Instruction

Below Level

Struggling Readers

1. Distribute to students copies of Section 1. Have them reread the introductory paragraph beginning with "If you lived there." Ask them to underline the sentence that states the main idea of the passage, and ask a volunteer to restate it in different words.

2. Then have a student identify the subsection that supports this statement. Ask students to circle sentences or phrases that support the main idea and explain how they do. List all responses where students can see.

3. When the list is complete, ask a volunteer to use the details listed to explain why the Danube is so important to the region.

4. Have students work in pairs to find other main ideas in the section and two or three facts to support them. Have students share their ideas and supporting details with the class.

LS Verbal/Linguistic

RF: Alternative Assessment Handbook, Rubric 1: Acquiring Information

Direct Teach

Main Idea

❶ Physical Features

The physical features of Eastern Europe include wide open plains, rugged mountain ranges, and many rivers.

Identify What are the names of the region's plains? the major mountain ranges? *Northern European Plain, Great Hungarian Plain; Carpathians, Dinaric Alps, Balkans*

Analyze Why is the Danube so important to the economies of Eastern Europe? *Largest river in region, connects cities of the region and empties into the sea at a warm water port; provides outlet for trade; provides hydroelectricity*

Make Inferences Why might the Black Sea be a better route for trade and transportation than the Baltic Sea? *its southerly location makes the Black Sea accessible year-round*

Map Zone Transparency: Eastern Europe: Physical

Connect to Science

Vistula River The Vistula is Poland's largest river. During nearly 45 years of Communist rule, the river became very polluted, passing through many cities and areas where pollutants have been discharged directly into the water. In farming areas, fertilizers enter the water. To meet European Union environmental standards, Poland is working to clean up the Vistula and other rivers, a costly process that will take many years.

Answers

Map Zone 1. *Danube;* **2.** *along rivers, on coasts, or on fertile plains; flat land and waterways are easier for transportation, communication, trade, and farming than mountainous areas.*

575

Main Idea

❷ Climate and Vegetation

The climate and vegetation of Eastern Europe differ widely in the north and the south.

Recall Which region has the mildest climate? *Balkan Peninsula*

Analyze Why are forests more common in the Baltic region than in the Balkan Peninsula? *Balkan Peninsula is much drier*

Cause and Effect Why do the interior plains have more varied vegetation than other parts of Eastern Europe? *variation in climate within the interior plains region, with colder, wetter climate in the north and milder, drier weather in the south*

MISCONCEPTION ///ALERT\\\

Black Sea The waters of the Black Sea are not really black. The Greek name for this body of water was a word meaning inhospitable or unfriendly sea, because of its rough waters. Later, as the Greeks set up colonies along the shores of the Black Sea, they saw it as more calm and inviting, changing its name to one that meant friendly or hospitable sea. After the Turks took control of the southern shores of the sea, they changed its name once again. Turkish sailors experienced much stormy weather with rough and choppy waters, so they named this body of water the Karadeniz, or Black Sea.

---

go.hrw.com
Online Resources

KEYWORD: SK9 CH17
ACTIVITY: Baltic Amber

Answers

Analyzing Primary Sources
grasslands, colorful flowers of varied shapes, birds

Reading Check *Adriatic Sea, Baltic Sea, Black Sea, Danube River*

576

In addition to these seas, Eastern Europe has several rivers that are vital paths for transportation and trade. The longest of these rivers, the **Danube** (DAN-yoob), begins in Germany and flows east across the Great Hungarian Plain. The river winds its way through nine countries before it finally empties into the Black Sea.

Primary Source

BOOK
The Plains of Ukraine

One of Russia's greatest novelists, Nikolai Gogol (gaw-guhl), was actually born in what is now Ukraine. Very fond of his homeland, he frequently wrote about its great beauty. In this passage from the short story "Taras Bulba," he describes a man's passage across the wide open fields of Ukraine.

❝No plough had ever passed over the immeasurable waves of wild growth; horses alone, hidden in it as in a forest, trod it down. Nothing in nature could be finer. The whole surface resembled a golden-green ocean, upon which were sprinkled millions of different flowers. Through the tall, slender stems of the grass peeped light-blue, dark-blue, and lilac star-thistles; the yellow broom thrust up its pyramidal head; the parasol-shaped white flower of the false flax shimmered on high. A wheat-ear, brought God knows whence, was filling out to ripening. Amongst the roots of this luxuriant vegetation ran partridges with outstretched necks. The air was filled with the notes of a thousand different birds.❞

—from "Taras Bulba," by Nikolai Gogol

ANALYSIS SKILL **ANALYZING PRIMARY SOURCES**
What features does Gogol describe on the plains of Ukraine?

As you might expect, the Danube is central to the Eastern European economy. Some of the region's largest cities lie on the Danube's banks. Thousands of ships travel up and down the river every year, loaded with both goods and people. In addition, dams on the western parts of the river generate much of the region's electricity. Unfortunately, the high level of activity on the Danube has left it heavily polluted.

READING CHECK **Finding Main Ideas** What are the main bodies of water in Eastern Europe?

Climate and Vegetation

Like its landforms, the climates and natural vegetation of Eastern Europe vary widely. In fact, the climates and landscapes found across Eastern Europe determine which plants will grow there.

The Baltic Coast

The shores of the Baltic Sea are the coldest location in Eastern Europe. Winters there are long, cold, and harsh. This northern part of Eastern Europe receives less rain than other areas, but fog is common. In fact, some parts of the area have as few as 30 sunny days each year. The climate allows huge forests to grow there.

The Interior Plains

The interior plains of Eastern Europe are much milder than the far north. Winters there can be very cold, but summers are generally pleasant and mild. The western parts of these plains receive much more rain than those areas farther east.

Because of this variation in climate, the plains of Eastern Europe have many types of vegetation. Huge forests cover much of the north. South of these forests are open grassy plains. In the spring, these plains erupt with colorful wildflowers.

Collaborative Learning

At Level

Getting to Know Eastern Europe

1. Organize students into three groups. Assign each group to a region: the Baltic Region, Interior Plains, or Balkan Peninsula. Make a large, physical map of Eastern Europe available.

2. Tell each group that they will present a short program to the class that describes the physical features of their area. Presentations should include pointing out the major landforms of the area on the map, giving a weather forecast for each season of the year, suggesting what kind of outdoor clothing is appropriate for the area's climate, and describing the vegetation visitors might see walking or biking through the area.

3. Have students explain how the area is similar to and different from the other two areas of the region. **LS Intrapersonal, Visual/Spatial**

📖 Alternative Assessment Handbook, Rubrics 21: Map Reading; and 29: Presentations

Radiation Cleanup

A nuclear accident in 1986 leaked dangerous amounts of radiation into Eastern Europe's soil. Ukraine's government and scientists are still working to repair the damage.

Unfortunately, Eastern Europe's forests were greatly damaged by a terrible accident in 1986. A faulty reactor at the **Chernobyl** (chuhr-NOH-buhl) nuclear power plant in Ukraine exploded, releasing huge amounts of radiation into the air. This radiation poisoned millions of acres of forest and ruined soil across much of the region.

The Balkan Coast

Along the Adriatic Sea, the Balkan coast has a Mediterranean climate, with warm summers and mild winters. As a result, its beaches are popular tourist destinations.

Because a Mediterranean climate does not bring much rain, the Balkan coast does not have many forests. Instead, the land there is covered by shrubs and hardy trees that do not need much water.

READING CHECK **Contrasting** How do the climates and vegetation of Eastern Europe vary?

SUMMARY AND PREVIEW The landforms of Eastern Europe vary widely, as do its cultures. Next you will study the vast region of Russia to the east.

FOCUS ON READING

As you read, ask yourself: what problems did the Chernobyl accident cause for Eastern Europe?

Info to Know

Chernobyl The 1986 nuclear power accident at Chernobyl was the world's worst nuclear disaster. It released 30 to 40 times as much radioactive material into the air as the Hiroshima and Nagasaki bombs combined. Winds carried the radiation over Belarus, Russia, and Ukraine, and as far west as France and Italy. The accident led to 30 deaths, increased thyroid cancer among children living near the area, and exposed up to 5 million people to dangerous levels of radiation.

Review & Assess

Close

Ask students to describe Eastern Europe's physical features, vegetation, and climate.

Review

Online Quiz, Section 4

Assess

SE Section 4 Assessment
PASS: Section 4 Quiz
Alternative Assessment Handbook

Reteach/Classroom Intervention

Interactive Reader and Study Guide, Section 4
Interactive Skills Tutor CD-ROM

Section 4 Assessment

go.hrw.com
Online Quiz
KEYWORD: SK9 HP17

Reviewing Ideas, Terms, and Places

1. **a. Identify** What are the major mountain ranges of Eastern Europe?
   b. Make Inferences How do you think the physical features of Eastern Europe influence where people live?
   c. Elaborate Why is the **Danube** so important to the people of Eastern Europe?
2. **a. Describe** What is the climate of the **Balkan Peninsula** like?
   b. Explain Why are there few trees in the far southern areas of Eastern Europe?
   c. Predict How do you think the lingering effects of the **Chernobyl** accident affect the plant life of Eastern Europe?

Critical Thinking

3. **Categorizing** Draw a chart like the one shown here. In each column, identify the landforms, climates, and vegetation of each area in Eastern Europe.

	Landforms	Climates	Vegetation
Baltic coast			
Interior plains			
Balkan coast			

FOCUS ON WRITING

4. **Highlighting Physical Features** Which features of Eastern Europe's geography do you think are most likely to attract buyers to the region? Write some ideas in your notebook.

PHYSICAL GEOGRAPHY OF EUROPE **577**

Section 4 Assessment Answers

1. **a.** Carpathians, Dinaric Alps, Balkans
   b. Fewer people live in mountainous areas; cities are located along navigable rivers, near coasts; farming communities are located on plains.
   c. major path for transportation and trade, many of the region's largest cities lie on its banks, provides hydroelectric power for the region

2. **a.** Mediterranean climate with warm summers and mild winters
   b. because of the dry Mediterranean climate

   c. With ruined soil, fewer plants will grow and those that do may be more fragile.

3. possible answers: Baltic Coast—Northern European Plain, coldest region, huge forests; Interior Plains—Great Hungarian Plain, Carpathian Mountains, milder than far north with cold winters but mild summers, forests in north, grassy plains in south; Balkan coast—Balkan Mountains, Dinaric Alps, Mediterranean climate, shrubs and hardy trees

4. Students should describe favorable aspects of the geography of Eastern Europe.

Answers

Focus on Reading *It released huge amounts of radiation into the air, poisoning millions of acres of forest and ruining soil across much of the region.*

Reading Check *Baltic—coldest climate with long, harsh winters, mostly forests; Interior Plains—milder than Baltic, cold winters, summers generally mild; Balkan Peninsula—Mediterranean climate with warm summers and mild winters, vegetation is shrubs and hardy trees that do not need much water*

577

Bellringer

If YOU lived there. . . Use the **Daily Bellringer Transparency** to help students answer the question.

🗄 Daily Bellringer Transparency, Section 5

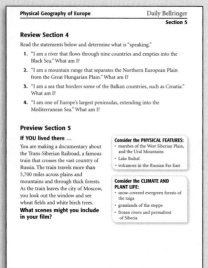

Key Terms and Places

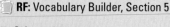 **RF:** Vocabulary Builder, Section 5

Taking Notes

Have students copy the graphic organizer onto their own paper and then use it to take notes on the section. This activity will prepare students for the Section Assessment, in which they will complete a graphic organizer that builds on the information using the Critical Thinking Skill: Generalizing.

Russia and the Caucasus

What You Will Learn...

Main Ideas

1. The physical features of Russia and the Caucasus include plains, mountains, and rivers.
2. Climate and plant life change from north to south in Russia and vary in the Caucasus.
3. Russia and the Caucasus have a wealth of resources, but many are hard to access.

The Big Idea

Russia is big and cold with vast plains and forests; whereas the Caucasus countries are small, mountainous, and warmer.

Key Terms and Places

Ural Mountains, *p. 578*
Caspian Sea, *p. 578*
Caucasus Mountains, *p. 578*
Moscow, *p. 578*
Siberia, *p. 579*
Volga River, *p. 580*
taiga, *p. 581*

 TAKING NOTES As you read, take notes in a chart like this one.

	Russia	Caucasus
Physical Features		
Climate and Plants		
Natural Resources		

If YOU lived there...

You are making a documentary about the Trans-Siberian Railroad, a famous train that crosses the vast country of Russia. The train travels more than 5,700 miles across plains and mountains and through thick forests. As the train leaves the city of Moscow, you look out the window and see wheat fields and white birch trees.

What scenes might you include in your film?

BUILDING BACKGROUND Look at a globe, and you will see that Russia extends nearly halfway around the world. Russia is the world's largest country. It is so vast that it spans 11 time zones. While huge, much of Russia consists of flat or rolling plains.

Physical Features

Have you ever stood on two continents at once? In Russia's **Ural** (YOOHR-uhl) **Mountains**, you can. There, the continents of Europe and Asia meet. Europe lies to the west; Asia to the east. Together, Europe and Asia form the large landmass of Eurasia. On the map, you can see that a large chunk of Eurasia is the country of Russia. In fact, Russia is the world's largest country. Compared to the United States, Russia is almost twice as big.

South of Russia are three much smaller countries—Georgia, Armenia (ahr-MEE-nee-uh), and Azerbaijan (a-zuhr-by-JAHN). They lie in the Caucasus (KAW-kuh-suhs), the area between the Black Sea and the **Caspian Sea**. This area, which includes part of southern Russia, is named for the **Caucasus Mountains**.

Landforms

As the map shows, Russia's landforms vary from west to east. The Northern European Plain stretches across western, or European, Russia. This fertile plain forms Russia's heartland, where most Russians live. **Moscow**, Russia's capital, is located there.

Teach the Big Idea

At Level

Russia and the Caucusus

1. **Teach** Ask students the questions in the Main Idea boxes under Direct Teach.

2. **Apply** Have each student choose a term or place that they want to learn more about from the "Key Terms and Places" list. Have students use the text to describe the term or place in a complete sentence. Then have students make posters illustrating the term or place they chose, and include their completed sentence on the poster.

3. **Review** Ask students to share their posters with the class, reading their sentence aloud.

4. **Practice/Homework** Have students write a short paragraph about the physical geography of Russia and the Caucasus, generalizing based on the posters that were shared in class. **LS** Visual/Spatial, Verbal/Linguistic

📰 Alternative Assessment Handbook, Rubric 28: Posters

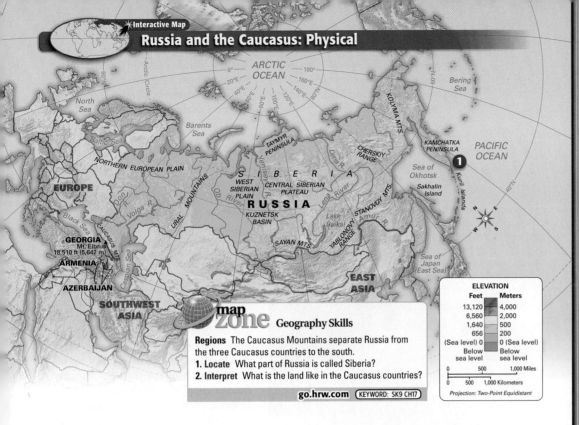

Geography Skills

Regions The Caucasus Mountains separate Russia from the three Caucasus countries to the south.
1. **Locate** What part of Russia is called Siberia?
2. **Interpret** What is the land like in the Caucasus countries?

go.hrw.com KEYWORD: SK9 CH17

ELEVATION	
Feet	Meters
13,120	4,000
6,560	2,000
1,640	500
656	200
(Sea level) 0	0 (Sea level)
Below sea level	Below sea level

0   500   1,000 Miles
0   500   1,000 Kilometers
Projection: Two-Point Equidistant

To the east, the plain rises to form the Ural Mountains. These low mountains are worn down and rounded from erosion.

The vast area between the Urals and the Pacific Ocean is **Siberia**. This area includes several landforms, shown on the map. The West Siberian Plain is a flat, marshy area. It is one of the largest plains in the world.

East of this plain is an upland called the Central Siberian Plateau. Mountain ranges run through southern and eastern Siberia.

Eastern Siberia is called the Russian Far East. This area includes the Kamchatka (kuhm-CHAHT-kuh) Peninsula and several islands. The Russian Far East is part of the Ring of Fire, the area circling the Pacific.

1 The Kamchatka Peninsula on Russia's east coast has many old and active volcanoes.

PHYSICAL GEOGRAPHY OF EUROPE **579**

Differentiating Instruction

Special Needs Learners   Below Level

To help special needs learners, read aloud the name of each label on the map. As you do, have students locate the label. Remind students that this book has many illustrations that can help them learn. **LS Visual/Spatial**

🖋 Alternative Assessment Handbook, Rubric 21: Map Reading

Advanced/Gifted and Talented   Above Level

Have students use the Internet or library resources to learn about a current event in the Caucasus region or Russia. Students should obtain information from at least three different sources. Based on their research, have students write their own news story to share with the class. **LS Verbal/Linguistic**

🖋 Alternative Assessment Handbook, Rubrics 29: Presentations; and 42: Writing to Inform

• **Direct Teach** •

Main Idea

❶ Physical Features

The physical features of Russia and the Caucasus include plains, mountains, and rivers.

Identify What three countries make up the Caucasus? *Georgia, Armenia, and Azerbaijan* What separates Russia from the Caucasus countries? *the Caucasus Mountains*

Describe What is Siberia like? *It is an empty land of barren plains and flat marshy areas with high mountain ranges running through the southern and eastern parts.*

Explain What is a threat to Lake Baikal? *water pollution from logging and factories*

🗄 Map Zone Transparency: Russia and the Caucasus: Physical

Info to Know

Kamchatka's Volcanoes The Kamchatka Peninsula has the highest density of volcanoes in the world. Twenty-nine of Kamchatka's volcanoes are still active. This peninsula is also home to many types of wildlife, including brown bears, snow rams, sea eagles, wild salmon, gray whales, seals, and sea lions.

Answers

Map Zone 1. *the large area between the Ural Mountains and the Pacific Ocean;* **2.** *mountainous, with lowlands near the seas*

579

Main Idea

❷ Climate and Plant Life

Climate and plant life change from north to south in Russia and vary in the Caucasus.

Describe What is Russia's climate like? *short summers and long, snowy winters; milder west of the Urals, growing colder as one goes north and east*

Identify What is the taiga? *a forest of mainly evergreen trees covering about half of Russia*

Summarize How is the Caucasus' climate different from Russia's? *Russia's climate is mainly cold while the Caucasus has a wider range of climates—warm and wet along the Black Sea, and cooler in the uplands, while Azerbaijan is hot and dry.*

Activity Compare and Contrast

1. Ask students to imagine they must choose to live in either Russia or a Caucasus country.

2. Have students write a brief essay explaining where they would live, and why. Students should describe the physical features and climates that appeal to them, as well as those that don't.

3. Have students read their essays to the class. Point out that different geographical features appeal to different people. **LS** Verbal/Linguistic

📖 Alternative Assessment Handbook, Rubric 37: Writing Assignments

Answers

Reading Check *Nothern European Plain, Ural Mountains, West Siberian Plain, Central Siberian Plain, Kamchatka Peninsula, Caucasus Mountains*

The Ring of Fire is known for its volcanoes and earthquakes, and the Russian Far East is no exception. It has several active volcanoes, and earthquakes can occur. In some areas, steam from within Earth breaks free to form geysers and hot springs.

South of Russia, the Caucasus countries consist largely of rugged uplands. The Caucasus Mountains cover much of Georgia and extend into Armenia and Azerbaijan.

Russia's Climate and Plant Life

In the top photo, Russians bundled up in furs hurry through the snow and cold of Moscow, the capital. In the lower photo, evergreen forest called taiga blankets a Russian plain. In the distance, the low Ural Mountains mark the division between Europe and Asia.

580 CHAPTER 17

These soaring mountains include Mount Elbrus (el-BROOS). At 18,510 feet (5,642 m), it is the highest peak in Europe. South of the mountains, a plateau covers much of Armenia. Gorges cut through this plateau, and earthquakes are common there. Lowlands lie along the Black and Caspian seas.

Bodies of Water

Some of the longest rivers in the world flow through the region of Russia and the Caucasus. One of the most important is the **Volga** (VAHL-guh) **River** in western Russia. The longest river in Europe, the Volga winds southward to the Caspian Sea. The Volga has long formed the core of Russia's river network. Canals link the Volga to the nearby Don River and to the Baltic Sea.

Even longer rivers than the Volga flow through Siberia in the Asian part of Russia. The Ob (AWB), Yenisey (yi-ni-SAY), and Lena rivers flow northward to the Arctic Ocean. Like many of Russia's rivers, they are frozen for much of the year. The ice often hinders shipping and trade and closes some of Russia's ports for part of the year.

In addition to its rivers, Russia has some 200,000 lakes. Lake Baikal (by-KAHL), in south-central Siberia, is the world's deepest lake. Although not that large in surface area, Lake Baikal is deep enough to hold all the water in all five of the Great Lakes. Because of its beauty, Lake Baikal is called the Jewel of Siberia. Logging and factories have polluted the water, but Russians are now working to clean up the lake.

In the southwest part of the region, the Black and Caspian Seas border Russia and the Caucasus. The Black Sea connects to the Mediterranean Sea and is important for trade. The Caspian Sea holds saltwater and is the world's largest inland sea.

READING CHECK Summarizing What are the major landforms in Russia and the Caucasus?

Critical Thinking: Making Generalizations

At Level

The Importance of the Volga River

1. Review with students information in the text about the Volga River. Remind students that it is the longest river in Europe.

2. Have students make a generalization about why the Volga still serves as a valuable resource today. For example, the Volga is the core of Russia's river network.

3. Have students write a short essay describing ways in which the Volga might continue to be a valuable resource in the future. For example, have students predict whether the river will continue to be used as a transportation route, or if they think it might be valuable in other ways. **LS** Verbal/Linguistic

📖 Alternative Assessment Handbook, Rubrics 12: Drawing Conclusions; and 37: Writing Assignments

Climate and Plant Life

Russians sometimes joke that winter lasts for 12 months and then summer begins. Russia is a cold country. The reason is its northern location partly within the Arctic Circle. In general, Russia has short summers and long, snowy winters. The climate is milder west of the Urals and grows colder and harsher as one goes north and east.

Russia's northern coast is tundra. Winters are dark and bitterly cold, and the brief summers are cool. Much of the ground is permafrost, or permanently frozen soil. Only small plants such as mosses grow.

South of the tundra is a vast forest of evergreen trees called **taiga** (TY-guh). This huge forest covers about half of Russia. In Siberia, snow covers the taiga much of the year. South of the taiga is a flat grassland called the steppe (STEP). With rich, black soil and a warmer climate, the steppe is Russia's most important farming area.

Farther south, the Caucasus countries are warmer than Russia in general. Climate in the Caucasus ranges from warm and wet along the Black Sea to cooler in the uplands to hot and dry in much of Azerbaijan.

READING CHECK Finding Main Ideas How does Russia's location affect its climate?

Natural Resources

Russia and the Caucasus have a wealth of resources. The Northern European Plain and the steppe provide fertile soil for farming. The taiga provides wood for building and paper products. Metals, such as copper and gold, and precious gems such as diamonds provide useful raw materials.

The region's main energy resources are coal, hydroelectricity, natural gas, and oil. Both Russia and Azerbaijan have large oil and gas fields. Oil also lies beneath the Caspian Sea.

The region's natural resources have been poorly managed, however. Until the early 1990s this region was part of the Soviet Union. The Soviet government put more importance on industry than on managing its resources. In Russia, many of the resources that were easy to access are gone. For example, most of the timber in western Russia has been cut down. Many remaining resources are in remote Siberia.

FOCUS ON READING
As you read, ask yourself: why does Russia have the vegetation it has?

READING CHECK Analyzing Why are some of Russia's natural resources difficult to obtain?

SUMMARY AND PREVIEW Europe's landforms and climates vary widely, from broad plains to rugged mountains, and from sunny beaches to frozen tundra. In the next chapter, you will learn about the history of the people who inhabit this diverse region.

---

go.hrw.com
Online Quiz
KEYWORD: SK9 HP17

Section 5 Assessment

Reviewing Ideas, Terms, and Places
1. **a. Describe** Why are the **Ural Mountains** significant?
   b. Draw Conclusions Why might the Russian Far East be a dangerous place to live?
2. **a. Describe** What are winters like in much of Russia?
   b. Analyze How does climate affect Russia's plant life?
3. **a. Recall** What valuable resource is in the **Caspian Sea**?
   b. Make Inferences Why might resources located in remote, cold areas be difficult to use?

Critical Thinking
4. **Generalizing** Draw a chart like the one here. Use your notes and enter one general idea for each topic in the chart.

Physical Features	
Climate and Plants	
Natural Resources	

FOCUS ON WRITING
5. **Describing the Physical Geography** Now that you know the physical geography of the region, make a list of possible locations for the house or land you are selling.

PHYSICAL GEOGRAPHY OF EUROPE **581**

Main Idea

3 Natural Resources

Russia and the Caucasus have a wealth of resources, but many are hard to access.

Recall What are Russia's main natural resources? *fertile soil, forests, coal, natural gas, oil, copper, gold, and diamonds*

Explain Why were resources not well managed in the Soviet Union? *The Soviet government put more importance on industry than resource management.*

Review & Assess

Close
Discuss with students the role that physical features, climate, vegetation, and natural resources play in Russia and the Caucasus.

Review
Online Quiz, Section 5

Assess
SE Section 5 Assessment
PASS: Section 5 Quiz
Alternative Assessment Handbook

Reteach/Classroom Intervention
Interactive Reader and Study Guide, Section 5
Interactive Skills Tutor CD-ROM

Section 5 Assessment Answers

1. **a.** They separate Asia from Europe.
   b. Earthquakes are frequent, and the region has many active volcanoes.

2. **a.** long and cold
   b. In the colder climate, only mosses, wildflowers and other small plants grow. In its warmer and wetter climate, forests and mixed trees grow. In its dry, warm climate, grasses grow, and farming is possible.

3. **a.** oil deposits
   b. possible answer—These areas are difficult to get to, making transporting resources difficult and expensive.

4. possible answer: Physical Features—plains, mountains, lakes, rivers; Climate and Plants—short summers, long winters, taiga; Natural Resources—fertile soil, metals, gems, coal, hydroelectricity, natural gas, oil

5. Answers will vary, but should include locations mentioned in the text.

Answers

Reading Check (left) *Its location in the far north means it has long, cold winters and short summers.*

Focus on Reading *Russia has the vegetation it has because of its cold climate and position in the upper latitudes.*

Reading Check (right) *Many remaining resources are in remote Siberia.*

581

Social Studies Skills

| Chart and Graph | Critical Thinking | Geography | Study |

Reading a Climate Map

Activity Read a U.S. Climate Map

Materials: U.S. climate map, U.S. political map

1. Tell students they are going to use information from a climate map to describe the climates of various locations in the United States.

2. Distribute copies of a U. S. climate map. As a class, locate your local community (the general area) and have students identify its type of climate. Ask volunteers to offer examples of weather patterns that illustrate this type of climate.

3. Have students work in pairs. Choose four major cities and assign each pair one of these cities. (If major cities are not shown on the climate map, supply students with a political map as well.)

4. Ask each pair to brainstorm what they already know about the climate of the city they have been assigned. Then have them compare their ideas to the description in the map key.

5. As a class, review the climates of the four cities. Discuss how students' ideas compared to the descriptions in the map key. **LS Visual/Spatial**

📖 Alternative Assessment Handbook, Rubric 21: Map Reading

💿 Interactive Skills Tutor CD-ROM, Lesson 6: Interpret Maps, Graphs, Charts, Visuals, and Political Cartoons

📖 **RF:** Social Studies Skills, Reading a Climate Map

🗺 Map Zone Transparency: Europe: Climate

Reading a Climate Map

Learn

Geographers use many different types of maps to study a region. One type that can be very useful is a climate map. Because climate affects so many aspects of people's lives, it is important to know which climates are found in a region.

Practice

Use the climate map of Europe below to answer the following questions.

1. What does orange mean on this map?

2. What city has a highland climate?

3. What is the dominant climate in the countries of Southern Europe?

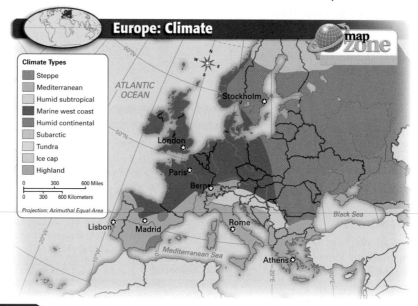

Europe: Climate

Climate Types
- Steppe
- Mediterranean
- Humid subtropical
- Marine west coast
- Humid continental
- Subarctic
- Tundra
- Ice cap
- Highland

0   300   600 Miles
0   300   600 Kilometers

Projection: Azimuthal Equal-Area

Apply

Choose one of the cities shown on the map above. Imagine that you are planning a trip to that city and need to know what the climate is like so you can prepare. Use the map to identify the type of climate found in your chosen city. Then use the library or the Internet to find out more about that type of climate. Write a short description of the climate and how you could prepare for it.

582 CHAPTER 17

Social Studies Skills Activity

Below Level

Reading a Climate Map

1. For students having difficulty interpreting the map in the textbook or in the activity on this page, monitor students' progress in reading the map. Draw their attention to the key. Point out the colors (or background pattern if the map is black and white) assigned to each climate type and connect them to the colors on the map. Model the connection by pointing to a color on the map and having students find it in the key.

2. Discuss why climate maps are useful. Have students explain how they can use a climate map to help them make decisions about where they want to travel and how they need to prepare. Ask volunteers to explain their ideas. Can a climate map affect the time of year they travel, the activities they plan, or what they bring on a trip? How? **LS Verbal/Linguistic, Visual/Spatial**

📖 Alternative Assessment Handbook, Rubric 21: Map Reading

Answers

Practice 1. *steppe;* **2.** *Bern;*
3. *Mediterranean*

Apply *Students should offer trip preparation details that are appropriate to the climate they have selected.*

Geography's Impact
video series
Review the video to answer the
closing question:
*Do you think proximity to the
sea has been more beneficial
or harmful to the Netherlands?*

Visual Summary

Use the visual summary below to help you review the main ideas of the chapter.

QUICK FACTS

Europe's physical features include wide open fields, rolling hills, and rugged mountain ranges.

Because Europe is a peninsula of peninsulas, no place is too far from water.

From the sunny beaches of Italy to the frozen steppes of Russia, Europe's climates vary widely.

Reviewing Vocabulary, Terms, and Places

Fill in the blanks with the correct term or location from this chapter.

1. The climate found in most of Southern Europe is the _____.

2. A _____ river is one that is deep and wide enough for ships to sail on.

3. The highest mountains in Europe are the _____.

4. Much of Russia is covered by _____, a vast forest of evergreen trees.

5. A _____ is a narrow inlet of the sea between high, rocky cliffs.

6. A nuclear accident at _____ released radiation into Eastern Europe.

7. _____, a peninsula in far northern Europe, is the site of the Kjolen Mountains.

8. The _____ separates the British Isles from the European mainland.

Comprehension and Critical Thinking

SECTION 1 *(Pages 562–565)*

9. **a. Describe** What are two physical features that all the countries of Southern Europe have in common?

   b. Draw Conclusions Why has Southern Europe's climate been called its most valuable resource?

   c. Predict How would daily life in Southern Europe be different if it were not a coastal region?

SECTION 2 *(Pages 566–569)*

10. **a. Recall** From southeast to northwest, what are the major landforms in West-Central Europe?

    b. Analyze How have geographic features supported trade and travel across the region of West-Central Europe?

    c. Elaborate How does West-Central Europe's mild climate serve as a valuable resource and contribute to the economy?

SOUTHERN EUROPE **583**

Answers

Visual Summary

Review and Inquiry Have students use the visual summary to provide details about the chapter's main ideas.

  Quick Facts Transparency: Visual Summary: Physical Geography of Europe

Reviewing Vocabulary, Terms, and Places

1. Mediterranean climate
2. navigable
3. Alps
4. taiga
5. fjord
6. Chernobyl
7. Scandinavia
8. English Channel

Comprehension and Critical Thinking

9. **a.** rugged mountains, coastal plains
   b. Its hot summers aid agriculture and attract tourists.
   c. would be no fishing industry, no ports, no sea transportation

10. **a.** mountains, uplands, plains
    b. Geographic features, such as navigable rivers, harbors, and ports, have made trade and travel across the region easier.
    c. West-Central Europe's mild climate makes agriculture possible in many parts of the region. It also makes the region an attractive tourist destination, which positively contributes to the region's economy.

Review and Assessment Resources

Review and Reinforce

SE Chapter Review

  RF: Chapter Review

  Quick Facts Transparency: Visual Summary: Physical Geography of Europe

  Spanish Chapter Summaries Audio CD Program

OSP Holt Puzzle Pro; Quiz Show for ExamView

  Quiz Game CD-ROM

Assess

SE   Standardized Test Practice

  PASS: Chapter Test, Forms A and B

  Alternative Assessment Handbook

OSP ExamView Test Generator, Chapter Test

  Differentiated Instruction Modified Worksheets and Tests CD-ROM: Modified Chapter Test

HOAP Holt Online Assessment Program (in the Holt Interactive Online Student Edition)

Reteach/Intervene

  Interactive Reader and Study Guide

  Differentiated Instruction Teacher Management System: Lesson Plans

  Differentiated Instruction Modified Worksheets and Tests CD-ROM

  Interactive Skills Tutor CD-ROM

go.hrw.com
Online Resources
Chapter Resources:
KEYWORD: SK9 CH17

11. a. energy resources, forests and soils, and seas and oceans

b. They bring warm, moist air from the Atlantic, which keeps temperatures warm and mild.

c. possible answer—Northern Europe's population may be less that Southern Europe's because the climate is slightly less hospitable.

12. a. possible answers—Baltic Sea, Black Sea, Adriatic Sea

b. important to transportation and trade, provide hydroelectric power

c. Answers will vary, but students should provide an explanation based on information from the text.

13. a. the Volga; the Caspain Sea, the Don River, and the Baltic Sea

b. Because Russia is located far north, it has a mostly cold climate.

c. They are in remote, cold areas far from cities.

Focus on Reading and Writing

14. the Alps

15. in Europe, from southern France to the Balkans

16. It tells the reader of an important geographical feature of Europe.

📄 **RF:** Focus on Reading, Asking Questions

17. Rubric Students' real estate ads should

- be based on facts and not be misleading
- give details about the best features of the location chosen
- include details appealing to potential buyers
- use descriptive wording to help buyers form a clear image of the property
- use correct grammar, spelling, and punctuation

📄 **RF:** Focus on Writing, Creating a Real Estate Ad

SECTION 3 *(Pages 570–573)*

11. a. Identify What are the major resources found in Northern Europe?

b. Analyze How do ocean currents create a relatively mild climate in Northern Europe?

c. Predict How do you think Northern Europe's population compares to Southern Europe's? Why?

SECTION 4 *(Pages 574–577)*

12. a. Identify Name two major bodies of water that border Eastern Europe.

b. Explain How do the Danube and other rivers affect life for people in Eastern Europe?

c. Evaluate If you could live in any region of Eastern Europe, were would it be? Why?

SECTION 5 *(Pages 578–581)*

13. a. Recall What is Russia's most important river, and to what major bodies of water does it link?

b. Identify Cause and Effect How does Russia's location affect its climate?

c. Elaborate Why might developing the many natural resources in Siberia be difficult?

FOCUS ON READING AND WRITING

Asking Questions *Read the passage below. After you read it, answer the questions below to be sure you have understood what you read.*

> "The Alps are Europe's highest mountain range. They stretch from southern France to the Balkan Peninsula. Several of the jagged peaks in the Alps soar to more than 14,000 feet."

14. What is this paragraph about?

15. Where is the area described in the passage?

16. Why is this information significant?

Creating a Real Estate Ad *Use your notes and the instructions below to help you create your ad.*

17. Review your notes about locations in Europe. Choose one location for the real estate you are selling. What are its best features? How would you describe the land and climate? What are the benefits of living there? What is nearby? Answer these questions in your real estate ad.

584 CHAPTER 17

Social Studies Skills

Reading a Climate Map *Use the climate map from the Social Studies Skills lesson of this chapter to answer the following questions.*

18. What type of climate does London have?

19. What climate is found only in the far north?

20. Where in Europe would you find a humid subtropical climate?

Using the Internet

21. Activity: Making a Map The Trans-Siberian Railroad is the longest single rail line in the world. Climb aboard in Moscow and travel all the way across Russia. Enter the activity keyword to start your journey. Research the regions and features along the railroad's route. Then create an illustrated map of your journey. On the map, show the train's route, indicate the places where you stopped, and include images about what you saw.

Map Activity

22. Europe On a separate sheet of paper, match the letters on the map with their correct labels.

Alps	Scandinavia
Danube River	North Sea
Pyrenees	Mediterranean Sea

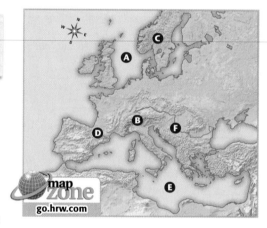

map zone
go.hrw.com

Social Studies Skills

18. marine west coast

19. subarctic

20. northeastern Italy and above northeastern Greece

Using the Internet

22. Go to the HRW Web site and enter the keyword shown to access a rubric for this activity.

KEYWORD: SK9 TEACHER

Map Activity

23. A. North Sea
B. Alps
C. Scandinavia
D. Pyrenees
E. Mediterranean Sea
F. Danube River

DIRECTIONS (1–7): For each statement or question, write on a separate answer sheet the *number* of the word or expression that, of those given, best completes the statement or answers the question.

1 Which of the following is *not* a mountain range in Europe?

(1) Alps
(2) Pyrenees
(3) Danubes
(4) Carpathians

2 Fjords are created by

(1) glaciers.
(2) earthquakes.
(3) volcanoes.
(4) geysers.

3 Which region of Europe was most affected by the Chernobyl accident?

(1) Southern Europe
(2) West-Central Europe
(3) Northern Europe
(4) Eastern Europe

4 Italy and Scandinavia are both

(1) islands.
(2) mountains.
(3) lakes.
(4) peninsulas.

5 Which statement about the Alps is true?

(1) They are found in Northern Europe.
(2) They are the world's tallest mountains.
(3) They are mostly volcanoes.
(4) They are usually capped with snow.

6 What is the name of the vast forest that covers much of Russia?

(1) Siberia
(2) Steppe
(3) Taiga
(4) Tundra

7 A Mediterranean climate is most likely to be found in which region?

(1) Southern Europe
(2) West-Central Europe
(3) Northern Europe
(4) Eastern Europe

Base your answer to question 8 on the map below and on your knowledge of social studies.

Spain and Portugal: Climates

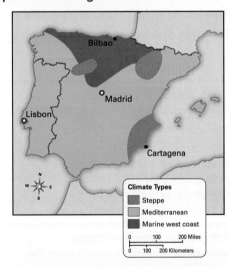

Bilbao

Madrid

Lisbon

Cartagena

Climate Types
Steppe
Mediterranean
Marine west coast

0   100   200 Miles
0 100   200 Kilometers

8 Constructed-Response Question Climate influences many aspects of people's lives in Spain and Portugal. List two ways in which climate affects how people there live.

Answers

1. 3
Break Down the Question Students should recall that the Danube is a river, not a mountain range. Refer students who miss the question to Section 2.

2. 1
Break Down the Question This question requires students to recall factual information from Section 3.

3. 4
Break Down the Question Students should recall that the Chernobyl accident occurred in the Ukraine, which is in Eastern Europe.

4. 4
Break Down the Question If students recall what a peninsula is, they should readily recognize it as the correct answer.

5. 4
Break Down the Question This question requires students to recall factual information. Refer students who miss it to Section 2.

6. 3
Break Down the Question This question requires students to recall factual information. Refer students who miss it to Section 5.

7. A
Break Down the Question Students should readily infer that because the Mediterranean Sea borders Southern Europe, that it is that region that is most likely to have a Mediterranean climate.

8. Constructed-Response possible answer—Farmers are able to grow a variety of crops. People are able to enjoy warm-weather recreational pursuits such as ocean swimming.

Reteach/Intervention Resources

Reproducible

Interactive Reader and Study Guide

Differentiated Instruction Teacher Management System: Lesson Plans

Technology

Quick Facts Transparency: Visual Summary: Physical Geography of Europe

Differentiated Instruction Modified Worksheets and Tests CD-ROM

Interactive Skills Tutor CD-ROM

Tips for Test Taking

Answering Questions About Maps When a question refers to a map, such as questions 6 and 7 above, encourage students to first study the information given in the map's key and relate that information to the items shown on the map, before answering the question.

Chapter 18 Planning Guide

Ancient Civilizations of Europe

Chapter Overview	Reproducible Resources	Technology Resources
CHAPTER 18 pp. 586–609 **Overview:** In this chapter, students will learn about ancient Greece and the Roman civilization.	**OSP Differentiated Instruction Teacher Management System:*** • Instructional Pacing Guides • Lesson Plans for Differentiated Instruction **Interactive Reader and Study Guide:** Chapter Summary Graphic Organizer **Resource File*** • Chapter Review • Focus on Reading: Re-reading • Focus on Writing: Writing a Myth • Social Studies Skills: Interpreting a Historical Map **Experiencing World History and Geography** **Geography, Science, and Cultures Activities**	**OSP Teacher's One-Stop Planner:** Calendar Planner **Power Presentations with Video CD-ROM** **Differentiated Instruction Modified Worksheets and Tests CD-ROM** **Interactive Skills Tutor CD-ROM** **Student Edition on Audio CD Program** **Music of the World Audio CD Program** **Geography's Impact Video Series (VHS/DVD):** Impact of Greek Scholars* **Map Zone Transparency:** Europe, 2000 BC–AD 500* **World Outline Maps: Transparencies and Activities**
Section 1: **Ancient Greece** **The Big Idea:** Through colonization, trade, and conquest, the Greeks spread their culture in Europe and Asia.	**OSP Differentiated Instruction Teacher Management System:** Section 1 Lesson Plan* **Interactive Reader and Study Guide:** Section 1 Summary **Resource File*** • Vocabulary Builder: Section 1 • Biography: Alexander the Great • Literature, *Oedipus the King*	**Daily Bellringer Transparency:** Section 1* **Map Zone Transparency:** Greek City-States and Colonies, c. 600 BC* **Map Zone Transparency:** Alexander the Great's Empire, c. 323 BC* **Internet Activity:** Alexander the Great
Section 2: **The Roman World** **The Big Idea:** The Romans unified parts of Europe, Africa, and Asia in one of the ancient world's greatest civilizations.	**OSP Differentiated Instruction Teacher Management System:** Section 2 Lesson Plan* **Interactive Reader and Study Guide:** Section 2 Summary **Resource File*** • Vocabulary Builder: Section 2 • Biography: Octavia Thurina Minor • Primary Source: *The Deeds of the Divine Augustus*	**Daily Bellringer Transparency:** Section 2* **Map Zone Transparency:** Expansion of Rome, 100 BC–AD 117* **Map Zone Transparency:** Early Christianity in the Roman Empire* **Map Zone Transparency:** Italy, 500 BC* **Internet Activity:** Stadiums—Ancient and Modern

Review, Assessment, Intervention

 Quick Facts Transparency: Visual Summary: Ancient Civilizations of Europe*

 Spanish Chapter Summaries Audio CD Program

 Progress Assessment Support System (PASS): Chapter Test*

 Differentiated Instruction Modified Worksheets and Tests CD-ROM: Modified Chapter Test

OSP **Teacher's One-Stop Planner:** ExamView Test Generator (English/Spanish)

 Alternative Assessment Handbook

HOAP **Holt Online Assessment Program (HOAP),** in the Holt Interactive Online Student Edition

 PASS: Section 1 Quiz*

 Online Quiz: Section 1

 Alternative Assessment Handbook

 PASS: Section 2 Quiz*

 Online Quiz: Section 2

 Alternative Assessment Handbook

Power Presentations with Video CD-ROM

Power Presentations with Video are visual presentations of each chapter's main ideas. Presentations can be customized by including Quick Facts charts, images from the text, and video clips.

Holt
●nline
Learning

go.hrw.com
Teacher Resources
KEYWORD: SK9 TEACHER

go.hrw.com
Student Resources
KEYWORD: SK9 CH18

- Interactive Multimedia Activities
- Current Events
- Chapter-based Internet Activities
- and more!

Holt Interactive
Online Student Edition
Complete online support for interactivity, assessment, and reporting
- Interactive Maps and Notebook
- Standardized Test Prep
- Homework Practice and Research Activities Online

CHAPTER 18 PLANNING GUIDE

ANCIENT CIVILIZATIONS OF EUROPE **585b**

Differentiating Instruction

How do I address the needs of varied learners?
The Target Resource acts as your primary strategy for differentiated instruction.

ENGLISH-LANGUAGE LEARNERS & STRUGGLING READERS

Resource File

The Resource File activities allow students to extend their knowledge of chapter-related places and people and to practice geography skills.

- Vocabulary Builder Activities
- Social Studies Skills: Interpreting a Historical Map

Additional Resources

Differentiated Instruction Teacher Management System: Lesson Plans for Differentiated Instruction

Quick Facts Transparency: Visual Summary:
- Ancient Civilizations of Europe

Student Edition on Audio CD Program

Interactive Skills Tutor CD-ROM

Spanish Chapter Summaries Audio CD Program

Teacher's One Stop Planner:
- ExamView Test Generator, Spanish
- PuzzlePro, Spanish

English-Language Learner Strategies and Activities

SPECIAL NEEDS LEARNERS

Interactive Reader and Study Guide

The activities in the Interactive Reader and Study Guide engage students with questions while presenting summaries of chapter content and provide opportunities for students to practice critical thinking skills.

Additional Resources

Differentiated Instruction Teacher Management System: Lesson Plans for Differentiated Instruction

Resource File: Social Studies Skills: Interpreting a Historical Map

Student Edition on Audio CD Program

Interactive Skills Tutor CD-ROM

Graphic Organizer Transparencies with Support for Reading and Writing

ADVANCED/GIFTED AND TALENTED STUDENTS

Differentiated Instruction Teacher Management System

Lesson Plans for Differentiated Instruction provide teachers with strategies to help plan instruction for all learners.

Additional Resources

Resource File:
- Focus on Reading: Re-reading
- Focus on Writing: Writing a Myth
- Literature: *Oedipus the King*

World History and Geography Document-Based Questions Activities

Geography, Science, and Cultures Activities

Experiencing World History and Geography

HOLT Teacher's One-Stop Planner®

How can I manage the lesson plans and support materials for differentiated instruction?

With the Teacher's One-Stop Planner, you can easily organize and print lesson plans, planning guides, and instructional materials for all learners.

The Teacher's One-Stop Planner includes the following materials to help you differentiate instruction:

- Interactive Teacher's Edition
- Calendar Planner and pacing guides
- Editable lesson plans
- All reproducible ancillaries in Adobe Acrobat (PDF) format
- ExamView Test Generator (English & Spanish)
- Transparency and video previews

Professional Development

What teacher training resources are available to help me grow professionally?

- **In-service and staff development** as part of your Holt Social Studies product purchase
- **Quick Teacher Tutorial Lesson Presentation CD-ROM**
- Intensive tuition-based **Teacher Development Institute**
- **Convenient Holt Speaker Bureau** – face-to-face workshop options
- **24/7 Ask A Professional Development Expert** at http://www.hrw.com/prodev/

DIFFERENTIATED INSTRUCTION PLANNING GUIDE

Chapter Big Ideas

Section 1 Through colonization, trade, and conquest, the Greeks spread their culture in Europe and Asia.

Section 2 The Romans unified parts of Europe, Africa, and Asia in one of the ancient world's greatest civilizations.

Focus on Reading and Writing

Reading The Resource File provides a worksheet to help students practice re-reading.

📋 **RF:** Focus on Reading, Re-reading

Writing The Resource File provides a worksheet to help students organize and write their myths.

📋 **RF:** Focus on Writing, Writing a Myth

586 CHAPTER 18

CHAPTER 18

Ancient Civilizations of Europe

FOCUS QUESTION

How did ancient civilizations contribute to the development of the Eastern Hemisphere?

What You Will Learn...

In this chapter you will learn about two major periods in the early history of Europe. First you will learn about ancient Greece, a culture whose ideas still shape the world. Then you will learn about Rome, one of the most powerful civilizations in world history.

FOCUS ON READING AND WRITING

Re-reading Sometimes a single reading is not enough to fully understand a passage of text. If you feel like you do not fully understand a passage after you read it, it may help to re-read the passage more slowly. **See the lesson, Re-reading, on page S21.**

Writing a Myth A myth is a story that tries to explain why something happened. Throughout history, people have used myths to explain natural and historical events. After you read this chapter, you will write a myth that people might have used to explain a major event in European history.

586 CHAPTER 18

ATLANTIC OCEAN

AFRICA

Greek trading ship

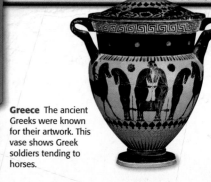

Greece The ancient Greeks were known for their artwork. This vase shows Greek soldiers tending to horses.

Introduce the Chapter

At Level

Building on the Past

1. Tell students that an ancient civilization flourished in Greece more than 2,000 years ago. Ask them to imagine that they are living there. Ask them what they think their lives would be like?

2. Explain that the people of the Roman Empire were inspired by Greek culture. Discuss how one period in history can influence another. Tell students that in this chapter they will learn how ancient Greece and Rome continue to affect their lives today.

3. Have students work in pairs to examine the chapter's visuals. Encourage them to look for connections between these images and the world as they know it today. **LS Visual/Spatial**

📋 Alternative Assessment Handbook, Rubrics 1: Acquiring Information; and 6: Cause and Effect

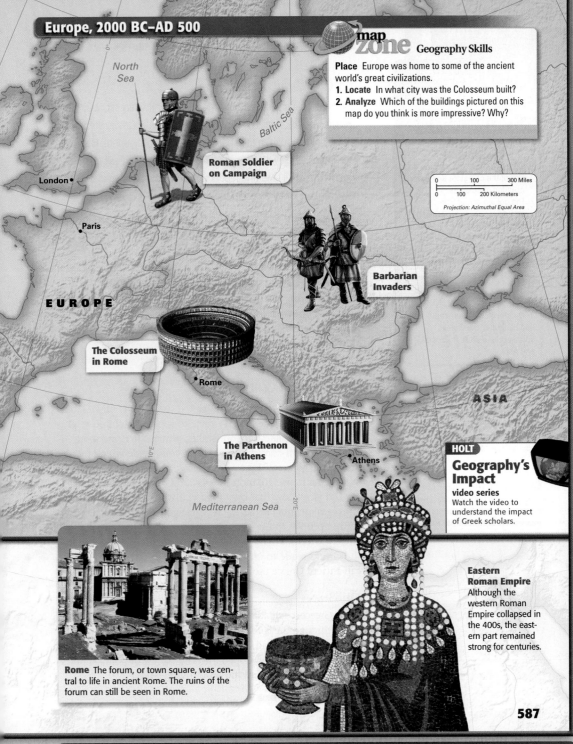

Europe, 2000 BC–AD 500

North Sea

Baltic Sea

Roman Soldier on Campaign

London•

•Paris

E U R O P E

Barbarian Invaders

The Colosseum in Rome

•Rome

A S I A

The Parthenon in Athens

•Athens

Mediterranean Sea

| 0 | 100 | | 300 Miles |
| 0 | 100 | 200 Kilometers | |

Projection: Azimuthal Equal Area

map zone — Geography Skills

Place Europe was home to some of the ancient world's great civilizations.

1. Locate In what city was the Colosseum built?

2. Analyze Which of the buildings pictured on this map do you think is more impressive? Why?

HOLT
Geography's Impact
video series
Watch the video to understand the impact of Greek scholars.

Rome The forum, or town square, was central to life in ancient Rome. The ruins of the forum can still be seen in Rome.

Eastern Roman Empire Although the western Roman Empire collapsed in the 400s, the eastern part remained strong for centuries.

587

Bellringer

If YOU lived there. . . Use the **Daily Bellringer Transparency** to help students answer the question.

🖎 Daily Bellringer Transparency, Section 1

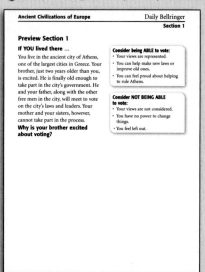

Key Terms and Places

🖎 **RF:** Vocabulary Builder, Section 1

Taking Notes

Have students copy the graphic organizer onto their own paper and then use it to take notes on the section. This activity will prepare students for the Section Assessment, in which they will complete a graphic organizer that builds on the information using the Critical Thinking Skill: Analyzing.

SECTION 1

Ancient Greece

What You Will Learn...

Main Ideas

1. Early Greek culture saw the rise of the city-state and the creation of colonies.
2. The golden age of Greece saw advances in government, art, and philosophy.
3. Alexander the Great formed a huge empire and spread Greek culture into new areas.

The Big Idea

Through colonization, trade, and conquest, the Greeks spread their culture in Europe and Asia.

Key Terms and Places

city-states, *p. 588*
golden age, *p. 590*
Athens, *p. 591*
Sparta, *p. 593*
Hellenistic, *p. 594*

TAKING NOTES As you read, keep a list of key events in Greek history. Organize the events in the order in which they occurred. You may wish to draw a time line like this one to organize your notes.

If YOU lived there...

You live in the ancient city of Athens, one of the largest cities in Greece. Your brother, just two years older than you, is excited. He is finally old enough to take part in the city's government. He and your father, along with the other free men in the city, will meet to vote on the city's laws and leaders. Your mother and your sisters, however, cannot take part in the process.

Why is your brother excited about voting?

BUILDING BACKGROUND In ancient times, people in most cultures lived under the rule of a king. In Greece, however, life was different. There was no ruler who held power over all of Greece. Instead, people lived in independent cities. Each of these cities had its own government, culture, and way of life.

Early Greek Culture

Suppose you and some friends wanted to go to the movies, but you could not decide which movie to see. Some of you might want to see the latest action thriller, while others are more in the mood for a comedy. How could you decide which movie you would go to see? One way to decide would be to take a vote. Whichever movie got more votes would be the one you saw.

Did you know that by voting you would be taking part in a process invented some 2,500 years ago? It is true. One of the earliest peoples to use voting to make major decisions was the ancient Greeks. Voting was only one of the many contributions the Greeks made to our culture, though. In fact, many people call ancient Greece the birthplace of modern civilization.

City-States

Early Greece could be a dangerous place. Waves of invaders swept through the land, and violence was common. Eventually, people began to band together in groups for protection. Over time, these groups developed into **city-states**, or political units made up of a city and all the surrounding lands.

Teach the Big Idea
At Level

Ancient Greece

1. **Teach** Ask students the questions in the Main Idea boxes under Direct Teach.

2. **Apply** Have students draw a time line that includes the key events in the section, including information presented in the section's maps, visuals, and captions. Encourage students to share their time lines with the class. **LS Visual/Spatial**

3. **Review** As a review of the section, have students create five multiple-choice questions. Then have students quiz each other with the questions they have created.

4. **Practice/Homework** Have students illustrate their time lines with at least three events, people, or places mentioned in the section. **LS Visual/Spatial**

   📝 Alternative Assessment Handbook, Rubrics 3: Artwork; and 36: Time Lines

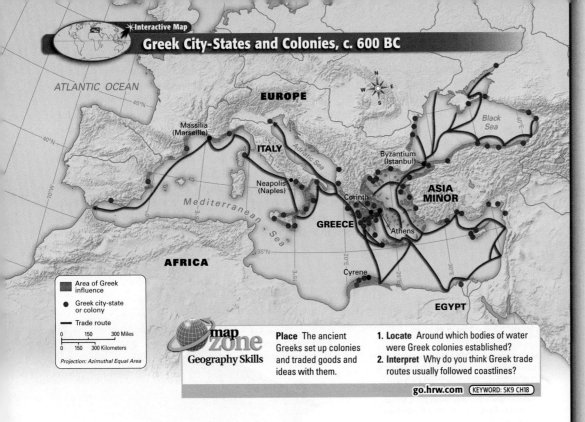

Greek City-States and Colonies, c. 600 BC

ATLANTIC OCEAN

EUROPE

Massilia (Marseille)

ITALY

Neapolis (Naples)

Corinth

GREECE

Athens

Cyrene

AFRICA

Mediterranean Sea

Adriatic Sea

Byzantium (Istanbul)

Black Sea

ASIA MINOR

EGYPT

■ Area of Greek influence
● Greek city-state or colony
— Trade route

0   150   300 Miles
0   150   300 Kilometers
Projection: Azimuthal Equal Area

map zone
Geography Skills

Place The ancient Greeks set up colonies and traded goods and ideas with them.

1. Locate Around which bodies of water were Greek colonies established?

2. Interpret Why do you think Greek trade routes usually followed coastlines?

go.hrw.com   KEYWORD: SK9 CH18

In the center of most city-states was a fortress on a hill. This hill was called the acropolis (uh-KRAH-puh-luhs), which is Greek for "top city." In addition to the fortress, many city-states built temples and other public buildings on the acropolis.

Around the acropolis was the rest of the city, including houses and markets. High walls usually surrounded the city for protection. In wartime, farmers who lived outside the walls could seek safety inside.

Living in city-states provided many advantages for the Greeks. The city was a place where people could meet and trade. In addition, the city-state gave people a new sense of identity. People thought of themselves as residents of a particular city-state, not as Greeks.

Colonies

In time, some city-states established new outposts, or colonies, around the Black and Mediterranean seas. You can see these colonies on the map above. Some of them still exist today as modern cities, such as Naples, Italy, and Marseille, France.

Although they were independent, most colonies kept ties with the older cities of Greece. They traded goods and shared ideas. These ties helped strengthen the economies of both cities and colonies, and they kept Greek culture strong. Because they stayed in contact, Greek cities all over Europe shared a common culture.

READING CHECK **Summarizing** Where did the ancient Greeks establish colonies?

ANCIENT CIVILIZATIONS OF EUROPE   **589**

Direct Teach

Main Idea

❶ **Early Greek Culture**

Early Greek culture saw the rise of the city-state and the creation of colonies.

Define What is a city-state? *a political unit made up of a city and the land surrounding it*

Describe In what ways was the acropolis the center of the city-state? *Not just a fortress, the acropolis was also where temples and public structures were built. Houses and markets were located around the acropolis.*

Make Inferences How did colonies help keep Greek culture strong? *by trading goods and sharing ideas with Greece*

🖎 Map Zone Transparency: Greek City-States and Colonies, c. 600 BC

Info to Know

Cultural Origins The origins of Greek culture can be found in the Mycenaean age, which lasted from about 1600 BC to 1100 BC. People of this time were the first to worship many of the gods later worshipped by the Greeks. Other aspects of culture during this period, including architecture, inspired the Greeks. The stories of the heroes of this time, such as Achilles and Odysseus, were later related by the Greek poet Homer in his epic poems the *Iliad* and the *Odyssey* (8th century BC).

Differentiating Instruction

Special Needs Learners   Below Level

Have students discuss why the Greeks built their most prominent buildings on a hill, or acropolis. Then have them draw a picture of what a city-state might look like, including the acropolis, the houses, the markets, and the wall around the city.

🗔 Visual/Spatial

📝 Alternative Assessment Handbook, Rubric 3: Artwork

Advanced/Gifted and Talented   Above Level
   Research Required

Ask students to imagine that they live in a Greek city-state, but have to move to a new colony in Spain or Italy. Suggest they do research to help them make their decision. With a partner, have them write a list of pros and cons. Then have them evaluate the list and make a decision.

🗔 Verbal/Linguistic

📝 Alternative Assessment Handbook, Rubric 16: Judging Information

Answers

Map Zone 1. *Mediterranean Sea, Black Sea;* **2.** *Most city-states and colonies were located on the coast.*

Reading Check *around the Black and Mediterranean seas*

Main Idea

❷ **The Golden Age of Greece**

The golden age of Greece saw advances in government, art, and philosophy.

Recall Why did the Greek city-states band together around 500 BC? *to defend themselves against the invading Persians*

Identify Cause and Effect In what way did the armed struggle between the Greeks and the Persians make the golden age possible? *The Greeks were able to defeat the Persians, thus gaining confidence and the realization that they were capable of great achievements.*

Predict What might have happened if the city-states had not banded together? *They might all have been conquered.*

Close-up

The Parthenon

Athena Tell students that Athena, after whom Athens was named, was the goddess of war and handicrafts. She was also the goddess of wisdom, or reason, and was associated with owls. The owl became the symbol of Athens as well. Point out the owl on Athena's staff as well as on her spear and military dress.

Linking to Today

Return of the Stones? In the early 1800s, many parts of the Parthenon—columns and sculptures—were moved to London. Today, they still reside there, at the British Museum. Many people around the world believe they should be returned to Greece, to restore the cultural integrity of the Parthenon. To learn more, visit www.parthenonuk.com.

About the Illustration

This illustration is an artist's conception based on available sources. However, historians are uncertain exactly what this scene looked like.

The Golden Age of Greece

When most people think of ancient Greek culture today, certain images come to mind. They think of the ruins of stately temples and of realistic statues. They also think of great writers, philosophers, and scientists whose ideas changed the world.

These images represent some of the many contributions the Greeks made to world history. Remarkably, most of these contributions were developed during a relatively short time, between 500 and 300 BC. For that reason, this period is often called a **golden age**, a period in a society's history marked by great achievements.

The Growth of Greek Power

Early in Greece's history, city-states remained fiercely independent. Each city-state focused on its own concerns and did not interfere in the others' affairs.

Around 500 BC, however, an invading army caused the Greeks to band together against a common enemy. That invasion came from Persia, a powerful empire in central Asia. The Persian army was huge, well-trained, and experienced. Greece, on the other hand, had no single army. Each city-state had an army, but none was as large as Persia's. As a result, the Persians expected a quick victory.

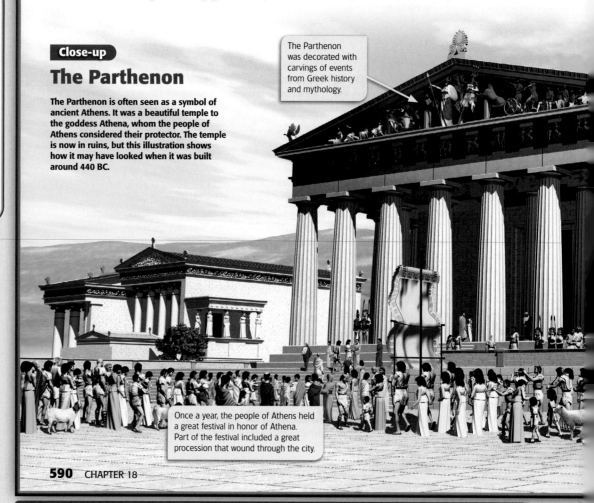

Close-up

The Parthenon

The Parthenon is often seen as a symbol of ancient Athens. It was a beautiful temple to the goddess Athena, whom the people of Athens considered their protector. The temple is now in ruins, but this illustration shows how it may have looked when it was built around 440 BC.

The Parthenon was decorated with carvings of events from Greek history and mythology.

Once a year, the people of Athens held a great festival in honor of Athena. Part of the festival included a great procession that wound through the city.

590 CHAPTER 18

Critical Thinking: Drawing Conclusions

Above Level

Debating Progress vs. Preservation

Research Required

1. Tell students that air pollution is a serious problem in Athens today, damaging the marble of the Parthenon and other monuments.

2. Have students search the Internet or library to learn more about the sources and effects of the pollution. Ask them to also research what is being done to prevent the damage.

3. Assign groups different sides in a debate. Tell them that there is only enough money to either repair the monuments (preservation)

or finish new projects in Athens (progress). Have each group gather reasons to support its position.

4. Have students debate the issue. Afterward, have them explain whether or not they were persuaded by the other side's arguments, and why. **LS Verbal/Linguistic, Interpersonal**

Alternative Assessment Handbook, Rubrics 10: Debates; and 30: Research

Nevertheless, the Greeks took up arms against the Persians. Led by **Athens**, a city-state in eastern Greece, the Greeks were able to defeat the Persians and keep Greece from being conquered. When the Persians invaded again 10 years later, the Athenians once again helped defeat them.

The victory over the Persians increased the confidence of people all over Greece. They realized that they were capable of great achievements. In the period after the Persian invasion, the people of Greece made amazing advances in art, writing, and thinking. Many of these advances were made by the people of Athens.

Athenian Culture

In the century after the defeat of Persia, Athens was the cultural center of Greece. Some of history's most famous politicians, artists, and thinkers lived in Athens during this time.

One reason for the great advances the Athenians made during this time was their city's leadership. Leaders such as Pericles (PER-uh-kleez), who ruled Athens in the 400s BC, supported the arts and encouraged the creation of great works. For example, Pericles hired great architects and artists to construct and decorate the Parthenon, the temple shown below.

Inside the Parthenon was a magnificent statue of Athena by the sculptor Phidias. Many people consider him the greatest sculptor in all of Greece.

Like most Greek temples, the Parthenon had huge marble columns to support its roof.

ANALYSIS SKILL **ANALYZING VISUALS**

Why do you think people consider the Parthenon to be a symbol of ancient Athens?

591

591

❷ The Golden Age of Greece, *continued*

The golden age of Greece saw advances in government, art, and philosophy.

Recall Which war led to the end of the golden age in Greece? *the war between Sparta and Athens*

Make Generalizations What did Greek artists, scientists, and philosophers have in common? *They all closely studied human beings.*

📝 **RF:** Literature, *Oedipus the King*

Connect to Civics

Pericles The following text is from a famous funeral oration given by Pericles after the first battles between Athens and Sparta.

"Our constitution does not copy the laws of neighboring states; we are rather a pattern to others than imitators ourselves. Its administration favors the many instead of the few; this is why it is called a democracy. If we look to the laws, they afford equal justice to all in their private differences; if no social standing, advancement in public life falls to reputation for capacity . . . ; nor again does poverty bar the way, if a man is able to serve the state, he is not hindered by the obscurity of his condition."

Teaching Tip

Read the excerpt aloud, pausing after each clause or sentence to clarify difficult vocabulary or concepts.

About the Illustration

This illustration is an artist's conception based on available sources. However, historians are uncertain exactly what this scene looked like.

Athenian Democracy

Athens was governed as a democracy. Once a month, all adult men in the city gathered together in an assembly to make the city's laws.

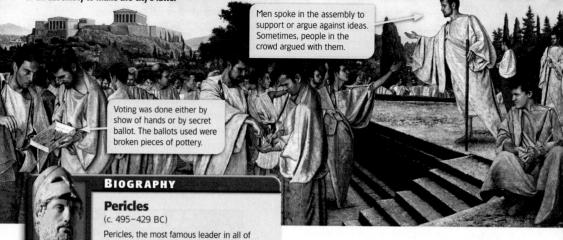

Men spoke in the assembly to support or argue against ideas. Sometimes, people in the crowd argued with them.

Voting was done either by show of hands or by secret ballot. The ballots used were broken pieces of pottery.

BIOGRAPHY

Pericles
(c. 495–429 BC)

Pericles, the most famous leader in all of Athenian history, wanted the city's people to be proud of their city. In his speeches, he emphasized the greatness of Athenian democracy and encouraged everyone to take part. He also worked to make the city beautiful. He hired the city's best architects to build monuments, such as the Parthenon, and hired great artists to decorate them. He also supported the work of writers and poets in order to make Athens the cultural center of all Greece.

Athenian Democracy

Leaders like Pericles had great power in Athens, but they did not rule alone. The city of Athens was a democracy, and its leaders were elected. In fact, Athens was the world's first democracy. No one else in history had created a government in which people ruled themselves.

In Athens most power was in the hands of the people. All the city's leaders could do was suggest ideas. Those ideas had to be approved by an assembly made up of the city's free men before they were enacted. As a result, it was vital that all the men of Athens took part in making government decisions.

The people of Athens were very proud of their democracy, and also of their city in general. This pride was reflected in their city's buildings and art.

Turn back to the previous page and look at the picture of the Parthenon again. Why do you think the temple was so large and so elaborately decorated? Like many Greek buildings, it was designed to be a symbol of the city. It was supposed to make people see Athens as a great and glorious city.

Architecture and Art

The Parthenon may be the most famous building from ancient Greece, but it is only one of many magnificent structures built by the Greeks. All over Greece, builders created beautiful marble temples. These temples were symbols of the glory of the cities in which they were built.

Greek temples and other buildings were often decorated with statues and carvings. These works by Greek artists are still admired by people today.

592 CHAPTER 18

Critical Thinking: Comparing and Contrasting — At Level

Writing a Comparison-Contrast Essay

Research Required

1. Have students research the similarities and differences between U.S. and Athenian democracy. Ask them to focus on institutions, citizens' rights/responsibilities, and lawmaking.

2. Have students write a comparison-contrast essay. Have them use a graphic organizer such as the one shown to organize their information.

	U.S.	Athenian
Institutions		
Citizens' rights/ responsibilities		
Lawmaking		

LS **Verbal/Linguistic, Visual/Spatial**

📝 Alternative Assessment Handbook, Rubrics 9: Comparing and Contrasting; 13: Graphic Organizers; and 42: Writing to Inform

Greek art is so admired because of the skill and careful preparation of ancient Greek artists. These artists wanted their works to look realistic. To achieve their goals, they watched people as they stood and moved. They wanted to learn exactly what the human body looked like while it was in motion. The artists then used what they learned from their observations to make their statues as lifelike as possible.

Science, Philosophy, and Literature

Artists were not the only people in ancient Greece to study other people. Scientists, for example, studied people to learn how the body worked. Through these studies, the Greeks learned a great deal about medicine and biology. Other Greek scholars made great advances in math, astronomy, and other areas of science.

Greek philosophers, or thinkers, also studied people. They wanted to figure out how people could be happy. Three of the world's most influential philosophers—Socrates, Plato, and Aristotle—lived and taught in Athens during this time. Their ideas continue to shape how we live and think even today.

The ancient Greeks also made huge contributions to world literature. Some of the world's timeless classics were written in ancient Greece. They include stories of Greek heroes and their daring adventures, poems about love and friendship, and myths meant to teach lessons about life. Chances are that you have read a book, seen a film, or watched a play inspired by—or even written by—the ancient Greeks.

Actually, if you have ever seen a play at all then you have the Greeks to thank. The ancient Greeks were the first people to write and perform drama, or plays. Once a part of certain religious ceremonies, plays became one of the most popular forms of entertainment in Greece.

The Decline of the City-States

As great as it was, the Greek golden age could not last forever. In the end, Greece was torn apart by a war between Athens and its rival city-state, **Sparta**.

Sparta was a military city with one of the strongest armies in Greece. Jealous of the influence Athens had over other city-states, the Spartans attacked Athens.

The war between these two powerful city-states devastated Greece. Other city-states joined the war, supporting one side or the other. For years the war went on. In the end, Sparta won, but Greece was in shambles. Thousands of people had been killed and whole cities had been destroyed. Weakened, Greece lay open for a foreign conqueror to swoop in and take over.

READING CHECK Analyzing Why is the period between 500 and 300 BC called a golden age in Greece?

Greek Art

The ancient Greeks took great care to make their art lifelike. This statue shows Athena, a goddess from Greek mythology.

ANALYZING VISUALS What details make this statue lifelike?

ANCIENT CIVILIZATIONS OF EUROPE **593**

Main Idea

❸ The Empire of Alexander

Alexander the Great formed a huge empire and spread Greek culture into new areas.

Recall How many years did it take Alexander to establish his empire? *about 11 years*

Explain Why did Alexander turn back toward home in 325 BC? *His troops were tired and far from home, and they demanded that Alexander turn back.*

Sequence Which was the first place that Alexander conquered? *Greece* Which was the last? *western India*

Elaborate Imagine that you are a Greek arriving in a new land that is part of Alexander the Great's empire. What part of your culture would you most want to share with your new neighbors? Why? *Students' responses will vary, but should reflect section content.*

RF: Biography, Alexander the Great

Map Zone Transparency: Alexander the Great's Empire, c. 323 BC

The Empire of Alexander

In fact, a conqueror did take over all of Greece in the 330s BC. For the first time in its history, all of Greece was unified under a single ruler. He was from an area called Macedonia just north of Greece, an area that many Greeks considered uncivilized. He was known as Alexander the Great.

Alexander's Conquests

Alexander swept into Greece with a strong, well-trained army in 336 BC. In just a few years, he had conquered all of Greece.

Alexander, however, was not satisfied to rule only Greece. He wanted to create a huge empire. In 334 BC he set out to do just that. As you can see on the map, he was quite successful.

At its greatest extent, Alexander's empire stretched from Greece in the west all the way to India in the east. It included nearly all of central Asia—including what had been the Persian Empire—and Egypt. Alexander had dreams of extending his empire even farther east, but his troops refused to keep fighting. Tired and far from home, they demanded that Alexander turn back. He did, turning back toward home in 325 BC. On his way back home, however, Alexander became ill and died. He was 33.

The Spread of Greek Culture

FOCUS ON READING
After you read this passage, reread it to make sure you understand all the details.

During his life, Alexander wanted Greek culture to spread throughout his empire. To help the culture spread, he built cities in the lands he conquered and urged Greek people to move there. He named many of the cities Alexandria after himself.

As Greek people moved to these cities, however, they mingled with the people and cultures in the area. As a result, Greek culture blended with other cultures. The result was a new type of culture that mixed elements from many people and places.

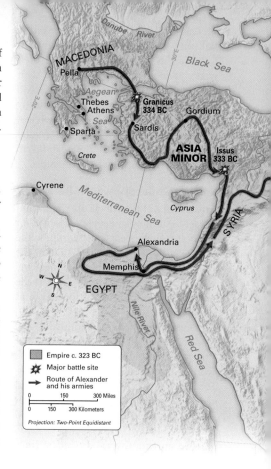

Because the Greek word for Greek is Hellenic, historians often refer to these blended cultures as **Hellenistic**, or Greek-like. Hellenistic culture helped shape life in Egypt, central Asia, and other parts of the world for many years.

READING CHECK **Finding Main Ideas** What lands were included in Alexander's empire?

SUMMARY AND PREVIEW Greece was the location of the first great civilization in Europe. In time, though, it was defeated by a new power, the Roman Empire.

Cross-Discipline Activity: Art

At Level

Creating a Political Cartoon

Materials: copies of political cartoons

1. Have students work individually or in pairs to create a political cartoon based on one or more details from the section. Before they begin, distribute copies of current political cartoons. Then lead a discussion about what makes the cartoons "work."

2. Students should first review the section, looking for events, places, or people that could be satirized in a cartoon. Once they

have chosen their subject, they may begin with the illustration or the caption. Encourage them to experiment with different styles.

3. Have students display their cartoons. Discuss how political cartoons can help us view historical and current events in new ways.

LS Visual/Spatial

Alternative Assessment Handbook, Rubric 27: Political Cartoons

Answers

Reading Check *lands from Greece and Egypt in the west across southern Asia to India in the east*

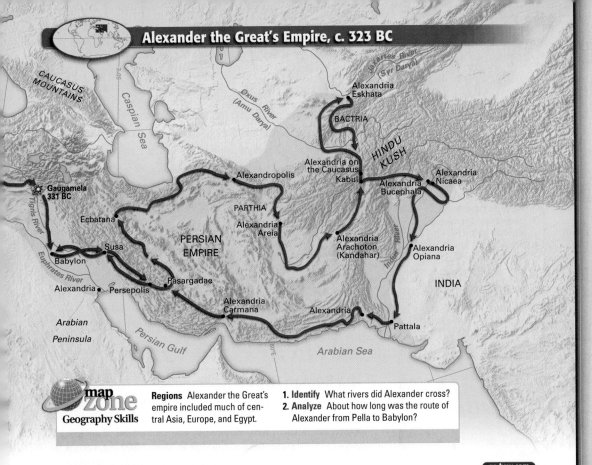

Alexander the Great's Empire, c. 323 BC

CAUCASUS MOUNTAINS
Caspian Sea
Oxus River (Amu Darya)
Jaxartes River (Syr Darya)
Alexandria Eskhata
BACTRIA
HINDU KUSH
Alexandria on the Caucasus
Kabul
Alexandria Nicaea
Alexandria Bucephala
Alexandropolis
Gaugamela 331 BC
PARTHIA
Ecbatana
Alexandria Areia
PERSIAN EMPIRE
Alexandria Arachoton (Kandahar)
Alexandria Opiana
Tigris River
Susa
Babylon
Euphrates River
Pasargadae
Indus River
INDIA
Alexandria
Persepolis
Alexandria Carmana
Alexandria
Arabian Peninsula
Persian Gulf
Pattala
Arabian Sea

map zone
Geography Skills

Regions Alexander the Great's empire included much of central Asia, Europe, and Egypt.

1. **Identify** What rivers did Alexander cross?
2. **Analyze** About how long was the route of Alexander from Pella to Babylon?

---

go.hrw.com
Online Quiz
KEYWORD: SK9 HP18

Section 1 Assessment

Reviewing Ideas, Terms, and Places

1. **a. Describe** What did an ancient Greek **city-state** include?
   b. Explain Why did the Greeks form city-states?
2. **a. Identify** What were some major achievements in Greece between 500 and 300 BC?
   b. Summarize What was the government of ancient Athens like?
   c. Evaluate Would you have liked living in ancient Greece? Why or why not?
3. **a. Describe** How did Alexander the Great try to spread Greek culture in his empire?
   b. Drawing Conclusions How might Greek history have been different if Alexander had not existed?

Critical Thinking

4. **Analyzing** Using your notes, draw a time line of major events in Greek history. For each event you list on your time line, write a sentence explaining why it was important.

├───┼───┼───┼───┼───┼───┤

FOCUS ON WRITING

5. **Choosing Characters** Many ancient myths focused on the deeds of heroes or other great figures. What people from ancient Greece might feature in such a myth? Write some ideas in your notebook.

ANCIENT CIVILIZATIONS OF EUROPE **595**

595

Bellringer

If YOU lived there. . . Use the **Daily Bellringer Transparency** to help students answer the question.

📖 Daily Bellringer Transparency, Section 2

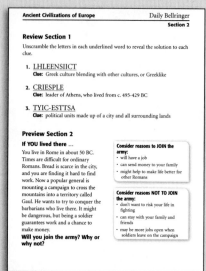

Academic Vocabulary

Review with students the high-use academic term in this section.

facilitate to make easier (p. 599)

📓 RF: Vocabulary Builder, Section 2

Taking Notes

Have students copy the graphic organizer onto their own paper and then use it to take notes on the section. This activity will prepare students for the Section Assessment, in which they will complete a graphic organizer that builds on the information using the Critical Thinking Skill: Identifying Causes.

SECTION 2

The Roman World

What You Will Learn...

Main Ideas

1. The Roman Republic was governed by elected leaders.
2. The Roman Empire was a time of great achievements.
3. The spread of Chrisitianity began during the empire.
4. Various factors helped bring about the decline of Rome.

The Big Idea

The Romans unified parts of Europe, Africa, and Asia in one of the ancient world's greatest civilizations.

Key Terms and Places

Rome, *p. 596*
republic, *p. 597*
Senate, *p. 597*
citizens, *p. 597*
Carthage, *p. 598*
empire, *p. 598*
aqueducts, *p. 600*

TAKING NOTES In your notebook, draw a graph like the one shown here. As you read, fill in the columns with notes about what helped Rome grow, Roman culture at its height, and events that led to Rome's fall.

Growth	Height	Fall

If **YOU** lived there...

You live in Rome in about 50 BC. Times are difficult for ordinary Romans. Bread is scarce in the city, and you are finding it hard to find work. Now a popular general is mounting a campaign to cross the mountains into a territory called Gaul. He wants to try to conquer the barbarians who live there. It might be dangerous, but being a soldier guarantees work and a chance to make money.

Will you join the army? Why or why not?

BUILDING BACKGROUND Rome's well-trained army helped it conquer large parts of Europe, Africa, and Asia. Through these conquests, Rome built a long-lasting empire that left its mark on the languages, cultures, and government of Europe.

The Roman Republic

"All roads lead to Rome." "Rome was not built in a day." "When in Rome, do as the Romans do." Have you heard these sayings before? All of them were inspired by the civilization of ancient Rome, a civilization that collapsed more than 1,500 years ago.

Why would people today use sayings that relate to so old a culture? They refer to Rome because it was one of the greatest and most influential civilizations in history. In fact, we can still see the influence of ancient Rome in our lives.

Rome's Early History

Rome was not always so influential, however. At first it was just a small city in Italy. According to legend, the city of **Rome** was established in the year 753 BC by a group called the Latins.

For many years, the Romans were ruled by kings. Not all of these kings were Latin, though. For many years the Romans were ruled by a group called the Etruscans. The Romans learned a great deal from the Etruscans. For example, they learned about written language and how to build paved roads and sewers. Building on what they learned from the Etruscans, the Romans made Rome into a large and successful city.

Teach the Big Idea

At Level

The Roman World

1. **Teach** Ask students the questions in the Main Idea boxes under Direct Teach.

2. **Apply** Have students create a chart with four columns labeled *People, Places, Events,* and *Ideas.* As they read, have them fill in the columns with details from the section. 🅛🅢 **Visual/Spatial**

3. **Review** Have students compare the entries on their charts. Then have them quiz each other about their entries.

4. **Practice/Homework** Have students choose one detail from each column and write one paragraph on each, describing the importance of that person, place, event, or idea. 🅛🅢 **Verbal/Linguistic**

📓 Alternative Assessment Handbook, Rubric 7: Charts

The Beginning of the Republic

Not all of Rome's kings were good leaders, or good people. Some were cruel, harsh, and unfair. The last king of Rome was so unpopular that he was overthrown. In 509 BC a group of Roman nobles forced the king to flee the city.

In place of the king the people of Rome created a new type of government. They formed a **republic**, a type of government in which people elect leaders to make laws for them. Once elected, these leaders made all government decisions.

To help make some decisions, Rome's leaders looked to the **Senate**, a council of rich and powerful Romans who helped run the city. By advising the city's leaders, the Senate gained much influence in Rome.

For Rome's republican government to succeed, **citizens**, or people who could take part in the government, needed to be active. Rome's leaders encouraged citizens to vote and to run for office. As a result, speeches and debates were common in the city. One popular place for these activities was in the forum, the city's public square.

Close-up

The Roman Forum

The forum was a large public square that stood in the center of the city. Roman citizens often met in the forum to discuss city affairs and politics.

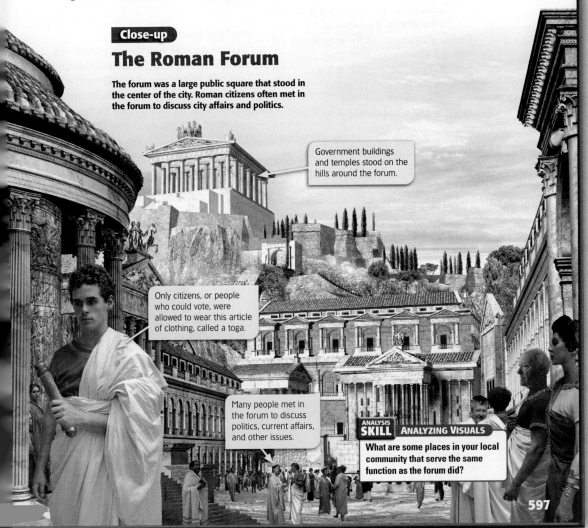

Government buildings and temples stood on the hills around the forum.

Only citizens, or people who could vote, were allowed to wear this article of clothing, called a toga.

Many people met in the forum to discuss politics, current affairs, and other issues.

ANALYSIS SKILL ANALYZING VISUALS
What are some places in your local community that serve the same function as the forum did?

597

Differentiating Instruction

At Level

English-Language Learners

Standard English Mastery

1. Have students work in pairs to identify the rights of Roman citizens.

2. Begin by having students review the information about the Roman republic. Also have them study the illustration and its introduction and captions. Encourage students to ask questions about any vocabulary that is difficult or, as appropriate, refer them to use a dictionary or thesaurus to determine standard English usage.

3. Have students make a list of the rights of Roman citizens. Have students create a document that can be "posted" in the Roman forum for all citizens to read.

4. Finally, have students think of two or three more rights that they think should be added to the list. Have them write these at the bottom of the document. **LS Verbal/Linguistic**

    Alternative Assessment Handbook, Rubric 42: Writing to Inform

● Direct Teach ●

Main Idea

❶ The Roman Republic

The Roman Republic was governed by elected leaders.

Recall Which rulers had a strong influence on the early development of Roman culture? *the Etruscans*

Define What is a republic? Is the United States a republic? *a type of government in which people elect leaders to make laws for them; yes*

Describe Who were members of the Senate? *rich and powerful Romans*

Activity **Writing Letters** Ask students to imagine that they are visitors to ancient Rome. What do they see? What impresses them the most? Have them write letters to family and friends describing their experience.
LS Verbal/Linguistic

    Alternative Assessment Handbook, Rubric 25: Personal Letters

About the Illustration

This illustration is an artist's conception based on available sources. However, historians are uncertain exactly what this scene looked like.

Answers

Analyzing Visuals *possible answers—town halls, government buildings, such as courthouses or libraries, churches, or temples*

597

Direct Teach

Did you know . . .

Upon becoming emperor, Augustus was referred to as the *princeps,* or "first citizen." He led a relatively simple life, with little interest in personal luxury.

📄 **RF:** Biography, Octavia Thurina Minor

📄 **RF:** Primary Source, *The Deeds of the Divine Augustus*

Did you know . . .

Most men of the ancient world did not shave, although Rome encouraged its soldiers to shave (supposedly to look "manly" and for hygiene). The first Roman to shave every day was thought to be the Roman general Scipio Africanus (256–184 BC).

About the Illustration

This illustration is an artist's conception based on available sources. However, historians are uncertain exactly what this scene looked like.

Answers

Reading Check *by using their strong, flexible, and well-organized army to conquer their rivals*

Analyzing Visuals *shields, spears, helmets, armor*

598

FOCUS ON READING

After you read this passage, re-read it. Make a list of details you did not notice in your first reading.

Growth and Conquest

After the creation of the republic, the Romans began to expand their territory. They started this expansion in Italy. As the map at right shows, however, the republic kept growing. By 100 BC the Romans ruled much of the Mediterranean world.

The Romans were able to take so much land because of their strong, organized army. They used this army to conquer their rivals. For example, the Romans fought the people of **Carthage,** a city in North Africa, and took over their lands.

Rome's expansion did not stop in 100 BC. In the 40s BC a general named Julius Caesar conquered many new lands for Rome. Caesar's conquests made him very powerful and very popular in Rome. Afraid of Caesar's power, a group of Senators decided to put an end to it. They banded together and killed Caesar in 44 BC.

READING CHECK **Summarizing** How did the Romans expand their territory?

The Roman Empire

The murder of Julius Caesar changed Roman society completely. The Romans were shocked and horrified by his death, and they wanted Caesar's murderers to be punished. One of the people they called on to punish the murderers was Caesar's adopted son, Octavian. Octavian's actions would reshape the Roman world. Under his leadership, Rome changed from a republic to an **empire,** a government that includes many different peoples and lands under a single rule.

The First Emperor

Octavian moved quickly to punish his uncle's murderers. He led an army against them and, before long, defeated them all.

After defeating his enemies, Octavian became more powerful. One by one, he eliminated his rivals for power. Eventually, Octavian alone ruled the entire Roman world as Rome's first emperor.

Roman Conquests

The Roman army was both powerful and flexible, which allowed it to take on and defeat many foes. Even the huge elephants ridden by the soldiers of Carthage were no match for the Romans' bravery and cleverness.

ANALYZING VISUALS What kind of equipment did the Roman army use?

598 CHAPTER 18

Critical Thinking: Making Generalizations
At Level

Analyzing the Qualities of a Good Leader

1. In small groups, have students discuss what qualities they think a good leader should have. Encourage them to reread the material about Caesar, Augustus, and Pericles in the previous section. Have them discuss other leaders, either contemporary or historical. Then have them make a list of the qualities that a good leader should possess.

2. Have students write an instruction manual for a good leader to follow. In the manual, have them explain to the leader why he or she needs to take certain actions or have certain policies. Have them support their argument with details about a contemporary or historical leader.

3. Have groups share their instruction manuals and discuss their conclusions.

LS Interpersonal, Verbal/Linguistic

📄 Alternative Assessment Handbook, Rubrics 14: Group Activity; and 43: Writing to Persuade

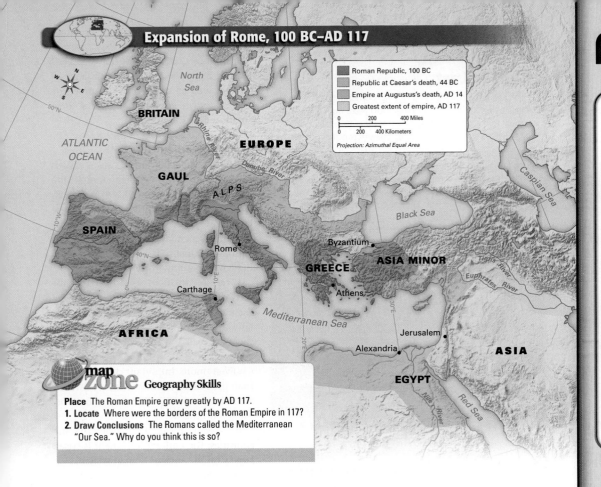

Expansion of Rome, 100 BC–AD 117

Roman Republic, 100 BC
Republic at Caesar's death, 44 BC
Empire at Augustus's death, AD 14
Greatest extent of empire, AD 117

0   200   400 Miles
0   200   400 Kilometers

Projection: Azimuthal Equal Area

map Zone Geography Skills

Place The Roman Empire grew greatly by AD 117.
1. **Locate** Where were the borders of the Roman Empire in 117?
2. **Draw Conclusions** The Romans called the Mediterranean "Our Sea." Why do you think this is so?

As emperor, Octavian was given a new name, Augustus, which means "honored one." The people of Rome respected and admired Augustus. This respect was mainly the result of his many accomplishments. As the map above shows, Augustus added a great deal of territory to the empire. He also made many improvements to lands already in the empire. For example, he built monuments and public buildings in the city of Rome. He also improved and expanded Rome's network of roads, which **facilitated** both travel and trade.

The Pax Romana

The emperors who ruled after Augustus tried to follow his example. Some of them worked to add even more land to the empire. Others focused their attentions on improving Roman society.

Because of these emperors' efforts, Rome experienced a long period of peace and achievement. There were no major wars or rebellions within the empire, and trade increased. This period, which lasted for about 200 years, was called the Pax Romana, or the Roman Peace.

ACADEMIC VOCABULARY
facilitate
(fuh-SI-luh-tayt)
to make easier

ANCIENT CIVILIZATIONS OF EUROPE **599**

Direct Teach

Main Idea

❷ **The Roman Empire**

The Roman Empire was a time of great achievements.

Identify Who was Rome's first emperor? *Octavian*

Explain Why was Octavian—later known as Augustus—popular with the Roman people? *added territory to the empire; made improvements to the empire, including building monuments and public buildings; improved and expanded Rome's network of roads*

Evaluate Would all people living in the Roman Empire agree that the Pax Romana was a golden age? *Students may say yes, because people's daily lives were peaceful.*

🔧 Map Zone Transparency: Expansion of Rome, 100 BC–AD 117

Cross-Discipline Activity: Music

At Level

Writing a National Anthem

1. Have students work in pairs to write a national anthem for the Roman Republic. Encourage them to look in this section for ideas.

2. Have students write a refrain that best expresses the main ideas they want to communicate. Then have them write two or three stanzas of the anthem. Suggest that they write about Rome's government and law, cultural achievements, or about individual Romans.

3. If students wish, they may adapt their anthems to the music of another anthem or traditional song, or they may compose their own music.

4. Have volunteers sing their anthems. Lead a discussion about what the ancient Romans might have thought of their anthems.

🇱🇸 **Auditory/Musical, Verbal/Linguistic**

📝 Alternative Assessment Handbook, Rubrics 26: Poems and Songs; and 18: Listening

Answers

Map Zone 1. *from Western Europe to Asia Minor and Northern Africa;* **2.** *because the empire included most of the coastline of the Mediterranean Sea*

599

History Humor

A teacher quizzed the class, "When was Rome built?"

One student replied, "At night."

"Why do you think at night?" asked the teacher.

"Because we all know that Rome wasn't built in a day!" answered the student.

Connect to Technology

Roman Aqueducts To bring water to its huge population, the Romans built 11 major aqueducts. The longest was nearly 60 miles long. Many were built above ground and supported by arches. Others were built underground. Some of the water went directly to the emperor and to the homes of the wealthy. The rest went to public fountains and bath complexes. Today the ruins of aqueducts can be seen throughout the former Roman Empire, from southern Europe to northern Africa and Asia Minor.

Linking to Today

Welcome to the Colosseum Over two million people visit this ancient wonder each year. Ongoing restoration projects allow visitors greater access to it and, perhaps more importantly, provide researchers with important new information about the site.

Answers

Connecting to Technology *They used arches to help build strong structures; they invented cement and other materials to make their buildings stronger.*

Reading Check *building and engineering; influence on language and legal systems; contributions of literature; ideas about government*

600

CONNECTING TO Technology

Built to Last

Think about the buildings in your neighborhood. Can you imagine any of them still standing 1,000 years from now? The ancient Romans could. Many structures that they built nearly 2,000 years ago are still standing today. How is that possible?

The Romans knew many techniques for building strong, long-lasting structures. Look at the Colosseum, pictured here. Notice how many arches were used in its design. Arches are one of the strongest shapes you can use in construction, a fact the Romans knew well. They also invented materials like cement to make their buildings stronger.

Making Generalizations How did technology help the Romans build strong and lasting structures?

Roman Building and Engineering

Because the Pax Romana was a time of stability, the Romans were able to make great cultural achievements. Some of the advances made during this time continue to affect our lives even today.

One of the areas in which the Romans made visible advances was architecture. The Romans were great builders, and many of their structures have stood for centuries. In fact, you can still see Roman buildings in Europe today, almost 2,000 years after they were built. This is because the Romans were skilled engineers who knew how to make their buildings strong.

Buildings are not the only structures that the Romans built to last. Ancient roads, bridges, and **aqueducts**—channels used to carry water over long distances—are still seen all over Europe. Planned by skilled Roman engineers, many of these structures are still in use.

Roman Language and Law

Not all Roman achievements are as easy to see as buildings, however. For example, the Romans greatly influenced how we speak, write, and think even today. Many of the languages spoken in Europe today, such as Spanish, French, and Italian, are based on Latin, the Romans' language. English, too, has adopted many words from Latin.

The Romans used the Latin language to create great works of literature. Among these works were some of the world's most famous plays, poems, and stories. Many of them are read and enjoyed by millions of people around the world today.

Even more important to the world than their literary achievements, however, were the Romans' political contributions. All around the world, people use legal systems based on ancient Roman law. In some countries, the entire government is based largely on the ancient Roman system.

One such country is the United States. The founders of our country admired the Roman government and used it as a model for our government. Like ancient Rome, the United States is a republic. We elect our leaders and trust them to make our laws. Also like the Romans, we require all people to obey a set of basic written laws. In ancient Rome, these laws were carved on stone tablets and kept on display. In the United States, they are written down in a document, the Constitution.

READING CHECK **Finding Main Ideas** What were some of the Romans' main achievements?

600 CHAPTER 18

Collaborative Learning

Analyzing Cultural Influence

1. Remind students about the spread of Hellenistic culture under Alexander the Great. Explain that the Romans admired Greek culture, which greatly influenced their own.

2. Create small groups, and have each research a topic on Roman culture—art, architecture, philosophy, literature, and so on. Ask the group to determine how much influence Greek culture had on this aspect of Roman culture.

3. Have the groups compile their findings and create a poster for their topic. Remind them to make clear how Greek culture influenced the Romans.

4. Have groups display and discuss their posters.
LS **Interpersonal, Verbal/Linguistic, Visual/Spatial**
Alternative Assessment Handbook, Rubrics 16: Judging Information; and 28: Posters

The Spread of Christianity

In addition to art and law, the ancient Romans also had a tremendous influence on religion. One of the world's major religions, Christianity, first appeared and spread in the Roman world.

The Beginnings of Christianity

Christianity is based on the life, actions, and teachings of Jesus of Nazareth. He and his early followers lived in the Roman territory of Judea in southwest Asia. They converted many people in Jerusalem and other cities in Judea to Christianity.

However, Christianity quickly spread far beyond the borders of Judea. Jesus's followers traveled widely, preaching and spreading his teachings. Through their efforts, communities of Christians began to appear in cities throughout the Roman world. Christian ideas spread quickly through these cities, as more and more people converted to Christianity.

Persecution and Acceptance

The rapid spread of Christianity worried some Roman leaders. They feared that Christianity would soon grow larger than all other religions in the empire. If that ever happened, they feared, the Christians might rebel and take over Rome.

To prevent a rebellion, some emperors began to persecute, or punish, Christians. They arrested, fined, or even killed any Christians they found.

The persecution did not cause people to abandon Christianity, however. Instead, Christians began to meet in secret, hiding their religion from the government.

Eventually, the persecution was ended. In the 300s a powerful emperor named Constantine became a Christian himself. Once the emperor had converted, the Christian faith was openly accepted even more widely in the empire. Look at the map below to see how Christianity spread between 300 and 400.

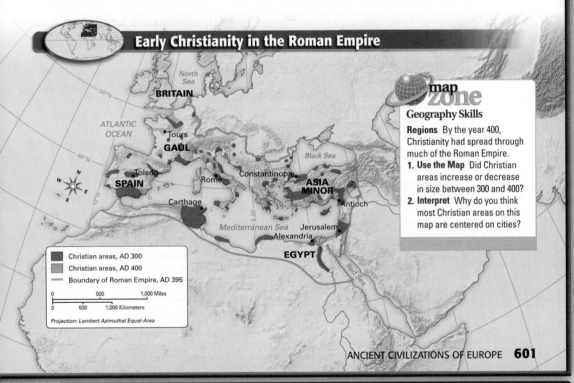

Early Christianity in the Roman Empire

map Zone

Geography Skills

Regions By the year 400, Christianity had spread through much of the Roman Empire.

1. **Use the Map** Did Christian areas increase or decrease in size between 300 and 400?
2. **Interpret** Why do you think most Christian areas on this map are centered on cities?

Legend:
- Christian areas, AD 300
- Christian areas, AD 400
- Boundary of Roman Empire, AD 395

0   500   1,000 Miles
0   500   1,000 Kilometers
Projection: Lambert Azimuthal Equal-Area

Main Idea

❸ The Spread of Christianity

The spread of Christianity began during the empire.

Recall Where did Jesus and his early followers live? *in the Roman territory of Judea in southwest Asia*

Identify Who was Constantine? *a Roman emperor who converted to Christianity in the 300s*

Explain Why were some of Rome's leaders concerned about the rapid growth of Christianity? *They worried that Christians would outnumber non-Christians and then rebel, taking over Rome.*

Draw Inferences Why would the emperors benefit from banning all religions except Christianity? *possible answer—to consolidate their own power*

🔲 Map Zone Transparency: Early Christianity in the Roman Empire

Did you know . . .

The New Testament of the Bible was mainly written in Greek, which was spoken by many people throughout the Roman Empire.

Critical Thinking: Sequencing

Below Level

Christianity in the Roman Empire

1. Have students complete a graphic organizer to track the early growth of Christianity within the Roman Empire.

2. Have students complete a concept map like the following, indicating the different stages and turning points in the spread of Christianity. Have them include dates in their concept maps. **LS Visual/Spatial**

📝 Alternative Assessment Handbook, Rubric 13: Graphic Organizers

Birth of Jesus in Judea →

Answers

Map Zone 1. *increased;* **2.** *New ideas likely spread quickly in cities, where people lived close together.*

601

Main Idea

④ The Decline of Rome

Various factors helped bring about the decline of Rome.

Describe Where did Constantine establish a new Roman capital, Constantinople? *in present-day Turkey* Why? *to move Rome's capital to a more central location in the empire*

Analyze Why did the barbarian invasions of Rome succeed? *the barbarians had strong leaders; the Romans were weak from internal problems and could not fend off the attacks*

Compare and Contrast How was the culture of the Eastern Roman Empire similar to and different from the culture of the Western Roman Empire? *similar—Christianity; different—Greek language instead of Roman*

Activity **Making a Time Line**
Have students create a time line showing the series of events that led to the downfall of Rome. **LS** **Visual/Spatial**

📝 Alternative Assessment Handbook, Rubric 36: Time Lines

Info to Know

Istanbul or Constantinople? Constantinople remained a Christian city for about a thousand years, until falling to the Turks in 1453. Now called Istanbul, it is the largest city of Turkey.

About the Illustration

This illustration is an artist's conception based on available sources. However, historians are uncertain exactly what this scene looked like.

Answers

Analyzing Visuals *internal—bad emperors, high taxes, poverty, fighting between rival military leaders; external—invasions, the overthrow of the Roman emperor in 476*

Reading Check *After Constantine converted in the 300s, Christianity spread widely throughout the empire. Support for Christianity grew, and soon all other religions were banned.*

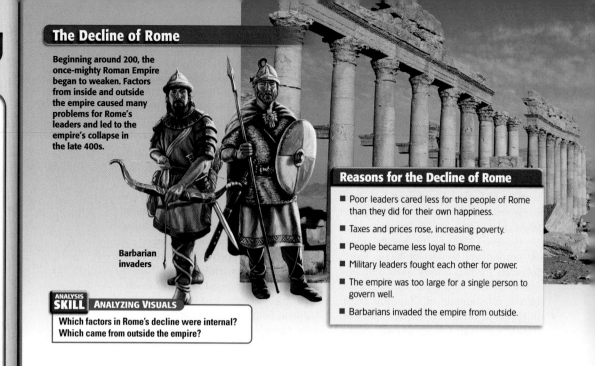

The Decline of Rome

Beginning around 200, the once-mighty Roman Empire began to weaken. Factors from inside and outside the empire caused many problems for Rome's leaders and led to the empire's collapse in the late 400s.

Barbarian invaders

ANALYSIS SKILL **ANALYZING VISUALS**
Which factors in Rome's decline were internal? Which came from outside the empire?

Reasons for the Decline of Rome

- Poor leaders cared less for the people of Rome than they did for their own happiness.
- Taxes and prices rose, increasing poverty.
- People became less loyal to Rome.
- Military leaders fought each other for power.
- The empire was too large for a single person to govern well.
- Barbarians invaded the empire from outside.

Official Religion

Even after Constantine became Christian, many people in the Roman Empire did not convert. Romans continued to practice many different religions.

Over time, however, Rome's leaders supported Christianity more and more. By the 380s, support for Christianity had grown so much that an emperor chose to ban all other religions. With that ban, Christianity was the only religion allowed in the Roman Empire.

By the end of the 300s, the Christian church had grown into one of the most influential forces in the Roman world. As the church was growing, however, many other parts of Roman society were falling apart. The Roman Empire was ending.

READING CHECK **Sequencing** How did the Christian church gain influence in Rome?

The Decline of Rome

Rome's problems had actually started long before 300. For about a century, crime rates had been rising and poverty had been increasing. In addition, the Roman systems of education and government had begun breaking down, and many people no longer felt loyal to Rome. What could have happened to cause these problems?

Problems in the Government

Many of Rome's problems were the result of poor government. After about 200, Rome was ruled by a series of bad emperors. Most of these emperors were more interested in their own happiness than in ruling well. Some simply ignored the needs of the Roman people. Others raised taxes to pay for new buildings or wars, driving many Romans into poverty.

602 CHAPTER 18

Differentiating Instruction

Below Level

Struggling Readers

1. Pair struggling readers with more proficient readers. Have them create a cause-and-effect chart like the following example, labeling the boxes on the left *Internal* and *External* and the box on the right *Decline of Rome.*

2. As they review the information about the causes for the decline of Rome, have them complete the chart. **LS** **Verbal/Linguistic, Visual/Spatial**

📝 Alternative Assessment Handbook, Rubrics 6: Cause and Effect; and 13: Graphic Organizers

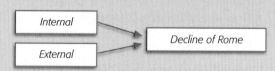

Internal → *Decline of Rome*
External →

Rome did have a few good emperors who worked furiously to save the empire. One emperor feared that the empire had grown too large for one person to rule. To correct this problem, he divided the empire in half and named a co-ruler to help govern. Later, the emperor Constantine built a new capital, Constantinople, in what is now Turkey, nearer to the center of the Roman Empire. He thought that ruling from a central location would help keep the empire together. These measures helped restore order for a time, but they were not enough to save the Roman Empire.

Invasions

Although internal problems weakened the empire, they alone probably would not have destroyed it. However, as the empire was getting weaker from within, invaders from outside also began to attack in the late 300s and 400s. Already suffering from their own problems, the Romans could not fight off these invasions.

Most Roman people considered the various groups who invaded their empire barbarians, uncivilized and backward. In truth, however, some of these so-called barbarian groups had their own complex societies and strong, capable leaders. As a result, they were able to defeat Roman armies and take lands away from the empire. In the end, the barbarians were even able to attack and destroy the city of Rome itself. In 476 the last emperor of Rome was overthrown and replaced by the leader of an invading group.

The Eastern Roman Empire

The fall of Rome to invading armies did not mark the end of Roman civilization. Although the old capital was gone, the newer Roman capital at Constantinople still existed, and it remained the capital of a powerful empire for nearly 600 years.

In the east, some elements of Roman culture changed. People began to speak Greek instead of Roman. Other elements remained constant. The empire remained a Christian society, and missionaries from Constantinople spread their religion in Russia, Eastern Europe, and other parts of the world.

READING CHECK Generalizing Why did the Roman Empire decline?

SUMMARY AND PREVIEW In this section you learned that the Romans fought many peoples to expand their empire. Next, you will learn about one of those peoples, the Celts.

Section 2 Assessment

go.hrw.com
Online Quiz
KEYWORD: SK9 HP18

Reviewing Ideas, Terms, and Places

1. **a. Describe** What was the government of the Roman **Republic** like?
   b. Contrast How was **Rome**'s government in the republic unlike the government under kings?
2. **a. Identify** Who was Augustus?
   b. Explain How did the Pax Romana help the Romans make great achievements?
3. **Generalize** How did Rome's emperors affect the spread of Christianity?
4. **a. Identify** What threats to the Roman Empire appeared in the 200s, 300s, and 400s?
   b. Evaluate Do you think internal problems or invasions were more responsible for Rome's fall? Why?

Critical Thinking

5. **Identifying Causes** Draw a graph like the one at right. On the left side, list the main causes of Rome's growth. On the right, list the main causes of its decline.

Growth	Decline

FOCUS ON WRITING

6. **Finding a Setting** Where will your myth be set? Think back over this section and the previous one to find an appropriate location for your myth.

ANCIENT CIVILIZATIONS OF EUROPE **603**

Section 2 Assessment Answers

1. **a.** citizens elected leaders to make laws and all government decisions
   b. Kings were often cruel, harsh, and unfair. They could not be voted out. Under the republican system, citizens could elect leaders.
2. **a.** Rome's first emperor, he expanded the empire, built monuments and public buildings, and improved roads.
   b. Lack of warfare and rebellion made it possible for trade and culture to expand.
3. Constantine's conversion helped Christianity spread. Another emperor banned all other religions.
4. **a.** 200s—bad emperors, breakdowns in education and government, poverty, crime, high taxes, rebellion by military leaders; 300s and 400s—invasions, overthrow of the emperor
   b. Responses will vary, but students should use text examples to support their answers.
5. Responses will vary. Students should list factors that explain Rome's growth and decline.
6. Locations will vary.

603

Info to Know

The Postal Service One of the most important uses of the Roman road system was the *cursus publicus,* or postal service. Although average citizens were not allowed to use the postal service, it provided the Roman government with an important means of sending information and instructions across the empire.

Teaching Tip

Map Distortion Explain to students that the drawing of the map of Europe in this feature is distorted. Have them compare this map with the map in the Atlas or other maps in this chapter to get another view of the extent of the Roman roads.

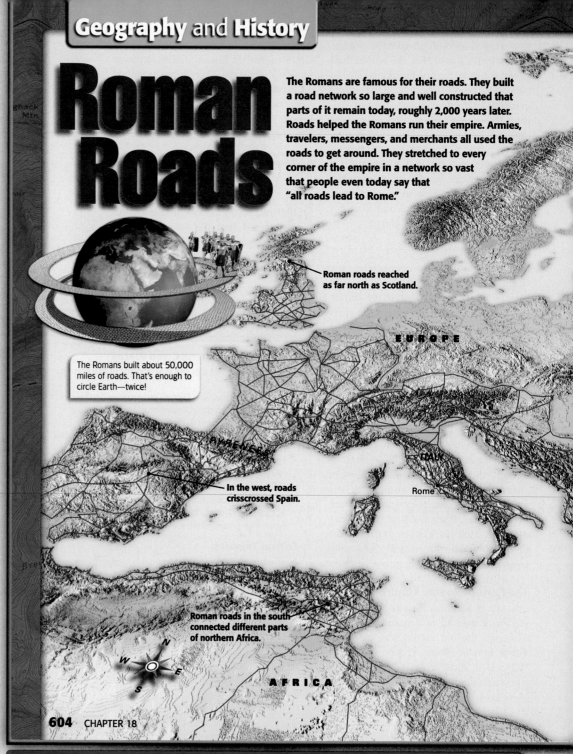

Geography and History

Roman Roads

The Romans are famous for their roads. They built a road network so large and well constructed that parts of it remain today, roughly 2,000 years later. Roads helped the Romans run their empire. Armies, travelers, messengers, and merchants all used the roads to get around. They stretched to every corner of the empire in a network so vast that people even today say that "all roads lead to Rome."

Roman roads reached as far north as Scotland.

EUROPE

The Romans built about 50,000 miles of roads. That's enough to circle Earth—twice!

PYRENEES

ITALY

Rome

In the west, roads crisscrossed Spain.

Roman roads in the south connected different parts of northern Africa.

AFRICA

604 CHAPTER 18

Differentiating Instruction

Struggling Readers   Below Level

To help struggling readers, have them match the text to the images in the feature. Read aloud the introduction and each caption. As you do, have students identify images and map elements that correspond to the text. **LS Visual/Spatial, Verbal/Linguistic**

📓 Alternative Assessment Handbook, Rubric 1: Acquiring Information

Special Needs Learners   At Level

Have students discuss how people rely on roads today. Have them talk about the roads they travel every day and speculate about how difficult it would be to get around if there were no roads. Suggest that they give several examples. **LS Verbal/Linguistic**

📓 Alternative Assessment Handbook, Rubric 11: Discussions

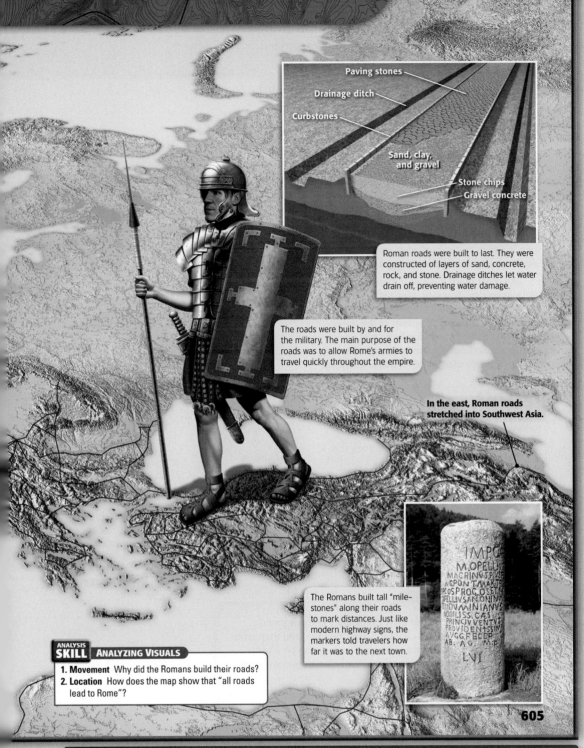

Paving stones

Drainage ditch

Curbstones

Sand, clay, and gravel

Stone chips

Gravel concrete

Roman roads were built to last. They were constructed of layers of sand, concrete, rock, and stone. Drainage ditches let water drain off, preventing water damage.

The roads were built by and for the military. The main purpose of the roads was to allow Rome's armies to travel quickly throughout the empire.

In the east, Roman roads stretched into Southwest Asia.

The Romans built tall "mile-stones" along their roads to mark distances. Just like modern highway signs, the markers told travelers how far it was to the next town.

ANALYSIS SKILL | ANALYZING VISUALS

1. **Movement** Why did the Romans build their roads?
2. **Location** How does the map show that "all roads lead to Rome"?

605

Info to Know

Not a One-Way Street Rome's vast network of roads helped the empire expand and also contributed to its prosperity. But when Rome began to weaken, the roads also made it easier for invaders.

MISCONCEPTION ALERT

Who Were Rome's Road Builders? Much of Rome's vast network of roads was built by its own soldiers. Planning and prep work was done by surveyors and engineers.

About the Illustration

This illustration is an artist's conception based on available sources. However, historians are uncertain exactly what this scene looked like.

Cross-Discipline Activity: Literature

At Level

Writing a Dialogue

1. Have students work in pairs to write a dialogue that could be the first scene of a play about traveling through the Roman Empire.

2. Have students begin by identifying the characters in the play. These might include poor or wealthy travelers, soldiers, peasants, innkeepers, thieves, or traders. Then have them write a dialogue based on a conflict between two characters or a problem that affects two characters.

3. Remind students what they've learned about the Roman world, including the system of roads. Encourage them to include some of these details in their dialogues.

4. Have students perform their dialogues before the class. **LS Interpersonal, Verbal/Linguistic**

   Alternative Assessment Handbook, Rubric 33: Skits and Reader's Theater

Answers

Analyzing Visuals 1. *mainly to allow their armies to travel quickly throughout the empire;* **2.** *Rome is at the center of the map; any road on the map will link to another road and eventually lead to Rome.*

| Chart and Graph | Critical Thinking | Geography | Study |

Interpreting a Historical Map

Activity Comparing Historical Maps

Materials: two historical maps of the same region (ideally of Greece, Rome, or Western Europe) at different points in time

1. Distribute copies of the maps. Have students examine the maps' features, especially titles, labels, and keys. If both maps shows political boundaries, have students compare them. Some maps may illustrate events, such as battles and movements of people. Have students work individually or in pairs to analyze these elements.

2. Have students point out at least two changes that occurred between the time periods covered by the maps. Then have them point out at least two features on the maps that remained the same. Have them write this information at the bottom of the second map.

3. Have students write one or two paragraphs about the maps, briefly describing the changes they illustrate and the features that have remained the same. **LS** Visual/Spatial

📝 Alternative Assessment Handbook, Rubrics 9: Comparing and Contrasting; and 21: Map Reading

☯ Interactive Skills Tutor CD-ROM, Lesson 6: Interpret Maps

📝 **RF:** Social Studies Skills, Interpreting a Historical Map

📦 Map Zone Transparency: Italy, 500 BC

Interpreting a Historical Map

Learn

History and geography are closely related. You cannot truly understand the history of a place without knowing where it is and what it is like. For that reason, historical maps are important in the study of history. A historical map is a map that shows what a place was like at a particular time in the past.

Like other maps, historical maps use colors and symbols to represent information. One color, for example, might represent the lands controlled by a certain kingdom or the areas in which a particular religion or type of government was common. Symbols might identify key cities, battle sites, or other major locations.

Practice

Use the map on this page to answer the following questions.

❶ Read the map's title. What area does this map show? What time period?

❷ Check the map's legend. What does the color purple represent on this map?

❸ According to the map, who controlled the area around the city of Rome at this time?

❹ What parts of Europe were controlled by Greeks in 500 BC?

Apply

Look back at the map called Early Christianity in the Roman Empire in Section 2 of this chapter. Study the map, and then write five questions that you might see about such a map on a test. Make sure that the questions you ask can be answered with just the information on the map.

Italy, 500 BC

Romans
Etruscans
Greeks
Carthaginians

0   30   60 Miles
0 30 60 Kilometers

Ligurian Sea

Adriatic Sea

Rome

Tyrrhenian Sea

Mediterranean Sea

Ionian Sea

Carthage

map zone

Social Studies Skills Activity: Interpreting a Historical Map

Comparing Maps

At Level

Materials photocopies of city or state maps from different periods

1. Distribute photocopies of two maps of your state or city from time periods at least 50 years apart. Discuss differences between the two maps, such as city size and landmarks.

2. Show students how the maps' titles, labels, and keys can give them clues about these differences.

3. Instruct students to write four sentences—two describing major changes and two describing features in the state or city that have not changed.

4. Have volunteers share their responses with the class. Lead a class discussion about the usefulness of historical maps. **LS** Visual/ Spatial, Verbal/Linguistic

📝 Alternative Assessment Handbook, Rubrics 21: Map Reading; and 40: Writing to Describe

Answers

Practice 1. *Italy, 500 BC;* **2.** *land controlled by the Etruscans;* **3.** *the Romans;* **4.** *the southern tip of Italy and the neighboring island (Sicily);*

Apply *Students' questions will vary, but should be based only on the map.*

Chapter Review

Geography's Impact
video series
Review the video to answer the closing question:
What are three ways in which Greek scholars have influenced education in America?

Visual Summary

Use the visual summary below to help you review the main ideas of the chapter.

QUICK FACTS

Ancient Greece was the birthplace of democracy, theater, and many other advances of Western society.

The Romans were master builders who created one of the largest empires in world history.

The Eastern Roman Empire remained strong even after the western part collapsed.

Reviewing Vocabulary, Terms, and Places

For each group of terms below, write the letter of the term that does not relate to the others. Then write a sentence that explains how the other two terms are related.

1. a. Athens
   b. Sparta
   c. Rome
2. a. Alexander the Great
   b. Pax Romana
   c. Hellenistic
3. a. Parthenon
   b. republic
   c. empire
4. a. Senate
   b. citizen
   c. colony

Comprehension and Critical Thinking

SECTION 1 *(Pages 588–595)*

5. a. **Identify** What was the basic political unit in ancient Greece? What is one example?

   b. **Contrast** How was life in Greece different under Alexander than it had been during the golden age?

   c. **Evaluate** What do you think was the greatest achievement of the ancient Greeks? Why?

SECTION 2 *(Pages 596–603)*

6. a. **Define** What was the Pax Romana? What happened during that time?

   b. **Summarize** How did Rome's government change after the republic fell apart?

   c. **Elaborate** What role did Rome's leaders play in the spread of Christianity?

ANCIENT CIVILIZATIONS OF EUROPE **607**

Answers

Visual Summary

Review and Inquiry Have students use the visual summary to review main ideas related to ancient Greece and Rome.

Quick Facts Transparency: Visual Summary: Ancient Civilizations of Europe

Reviewing Vocabulary, Terms and Places

1. c; Athens and Sparta were Greek city-states.

2. b; Alexander the Great's conquests led to the development of Hellenistic, or Greek-like, culture in Egypt and Central Asia.

3. a; Rome was a republic before it became an empire.

4. c; In Rome, citizens and members of the Senate worked together to create laws.

Comprehension and Critical Thinking

5. a. city-state: possible answers—Sparta, Athens

   b. All of Greece was now unified.

   c. possible answers—democracy, architecture, art, science, philosophy; reasons will vary

6. a. A long period of peace and achievement in the Roman Empire during which there were no major wars or rebellions and there were advances in building, engineering, and law.

   b. The Roman Empire was destroyed and Rome was ruled by invaders.

Review and Assessment Resources

Review and Reinforce

SE Chapter Review

CRF: Chapter Review

Quick Facts Transparency: Visual Summary: Ancient Civilizations of Europe

Spanish Chapter Summaries Audio CD Program

OSP Holt Puzzle Pro; Quiz Show for ExamView

Quiz Game CD-ROM

Assess

SE Standardized Test Practice

PASS: Chapter Test Forms A and B

Alternative Assessment Handbook

OSP ExamView Test Generator, Chapter Test

Differentiated Instruction Modified Worksheets and Tests CD-ROM: Modified Chapter Test

HOAP Holt Online Assessment Program (in the Holt Interactive Online Student Edition)

Reteach/Intervene

Interactive Reader and Study Guide

Differentiated Instruction Teacher Management System: Lesson Plans

Differentiated Instruction Modified Worksheets and Tests CD-ROM

Interactive Skills Tutor CD-ROM

go.hrw.com
Online Resources

Chapter Resources
KEYWORD: SK9 CH18

c. Constantine converted to Christianity, which then spread quickly. Another emperor later banned all other religions in the empire.

Using the Internet

7. Go to the HRW Web site and enter the keyword shown to access a rubric for this activity.

KEYWORD: SK9 TEACHER

Focus on Reading and Writing

8. Main ideas: Greek city-states remained independent until invaders caused them to band together; By combining their armies strengths, the Greeks were able to defeat the Persian invaders; Victory over the Persians led to the growth of Greek power.

RF: Focus on Reading, Re-reading

9. Rubric Students' myths should

- focus on one event
- explain the event as someone in the past might have
- have a beginning, middle, and end
- use descriptive details

RF: Focus on Writing, Writing a Myth

Social Studies Skills

10. 100 BC–AD 117

11. the Roman Empire's borders around 100 BC

12. before

13. Spain

14. 44 BC–AD 14

Map Activity

15. A. Rome
   B. Athens
   C. Judea
   D. Alexandria
   E. Carthage
   F. Gaul

Using the Internet

go.hrw.com
KEYWORD: SK9 CH18

7. Activity: Exploring Ancient Greece The golden age of Greece was an amazing time—the Greeks helped shape our government, art, philosophy, writing, and more! Enter the activity keyword and learn more about the ancient Greek world. Imagine you have traveled through time, back to ancient Greece. What are the people doing? What kinds of buildings do you see? What is the area like? Draw a picture or make a collage to record your observations.

FOCUS ON READING AND WRITING

8. Re-Reading Read the passage titled The Growth of Greek Power in Section 1. After you read, write down the main ideas of the passage. Then go back and re-read the passage carefully. Add to your list of main ideas anything more that you noticed in your second reading. How much more did you learn from the passage when you re-read it?

9. Writing Your Myth Now that you have learned about the events and people of ancient and medieval Europe, you can write a myth about one of them. Remember that your myth should try to explain the person or the event in a way that people of the time might have. For example, they might have thought that Caesar was the son of a goddess or that the idea of democracy was inspired by a wise god. Try to include descriptive details that will help bring your myth to life for the people who read it.

Social Studies Skills

Interpreting a Historical Map *Use the map on the Expansion of Rome in Section 2 of this chapter to answer the following questions.*

10. What time period is shown on this map?

11. What does the orange color on this map represent?

12. Did the areas shown on the map in gold become part of Rome before or after the areas shown in light green?

13. Which was conquered by the Romans first—Spain or Gaul?

14. Between which two years did Egypt become a Roman territory?

Map Activity ✶Interactive

15. Europe, 2000 BC–AD 500 On a separate sheet of paper, match the letters on the map with their correct labels.

Athens	Carthage	Rome
Gaul	Judea	Alexandria

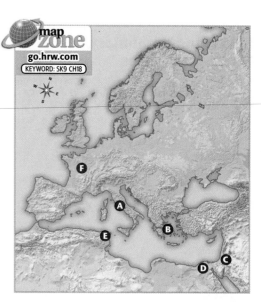
map zone
go.hrw.com
KEYWORD: SK9 CH18

Standardized Test Practice

DIRECTIONS (1–7): For each statement or question, write on a separate answer sheet the *number* of the word or expression that, of those given, best completes the statement or answers the question.

1 Democracy was first practiced in which city-state of ancient Greece?

(1) Athens
(2) Carthage
(3) Rome
(4) Sparta

2 Which large empire did the Greeks defeat in a series of wars?

(1) Rome
(2) Sparta
(3) Egypt
(4) Persia

3 The first Roman emperor to become a Christian was named

(1) Julius Caesar.
(2) Augustus.
(3) Constantine.
(4) Jesus of Nazareth.

4 Which of the following was first created by the ancient Greeks?

(1) aqueducts
(2) Latin
(3) drama
(4) the Colosseum

5 The blended culture that was created in Alexander the Great's empire is called

(1) Greek.
(2) Hellenistic.
(3) Roman.
(4) Medieval.

6 During its history, Rome had all of the following forms of government except

(1) empire.
(2) monarchy.
(3) democracy.
(4) republic.

7 Which portion of the Roman Empire remained strong even after the city of Rome was defeated?

(1) northern
(2) southern
(3) western
(4) eastern

Base your answer to question 8 on the map below and on your knowledge of social studies.

Europe, AD 117

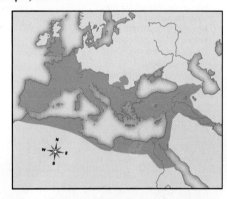

8 **Constructed-Response Question** As this map shows, the Roman Empire at its height controlled most of the Mediterranean world. The empire's huge size was both a benefit and a drawback. List one positive and one negative effect of the Romans' expansion.

ANCIENT CIVILIZATIONS OF EUROPE **609**

Answers

1. 1
Break Down the Question Neither option 2 or 3 is correct, because neither Carthage nor Rome are in Greece. Sparta was a city-state, but democracy began in Athens.

2. 4
Break Down the Question This question requires students to recall factual information. Refer students who miss it to Section 1.

3. 3
Break Down the Question Julius Caesar and Augustus ruled before Christianity. Jesus was not a Roman emperor. The correct answer is option 3; Constantine converted in the 330s.

4. 3
Break Down the Question This question requires students to recall factual information. Refer students who miss it to Section 1.

5. 2
Break Down the Question Greek and Roman cultures weren't truly blended cultures, so options 1 and 3 are incorrect. Alexander the Great lived long before the Middle Ages. Hellenistic means "Greeklike." Option 2 is the correct answer.

6. 2
Break Down the Question Students should readily recognize that Rome was first a republic and then an empire. Students should then make the connection that a republic is a form of democracy. The only remaining option then is option 2, monarchy.

7. 4
Break Down the Question Students should recall that a new Roman capital was built at Constantinople in the East.

8. Constructed-Response Question positive effect—increased opportunities for trade; negative effect—empire too large to be governed effectively

Reteach/Intervention Resources

Reproducible
- Interactive Reader and Study Guide
- Differentiated Instruction Teacher Management System: Lesson Plans

Technology
- Quick Facts Transparency: Visual Summary: Ancient Civilizations of Europe
- Differentiated Instruction Modified Worksheets and Tests CD-ROM
- Interactive Skills Tutor CD-ROM

Tips for Test Taking

Master the Question Have you ever said, "I knew the answer, but I thought the question asked something else?" Be very sure that you know what a question is asking. Read the question at least twice before reading the answer choices. Approach it as you would a mystery story or a riddle. Look for clues. Watch especially for words like not and except—they tell you to look for the choice that is false or different from the other choices or opposite in some way.

Bellringer

Motivate Before class, find examples of modern Celtic-inspired pop culture, such as music or dancing, online. When students get into class on the first day of the Case Study, ask them if they know anything about Celtic culture. Students will likely relay information about the Celts they may have learned by flipping through the pages of the Case Study. Ask students if they think Celtic culture is still around today. Can students think of any examples? Tell students that like many ancient cultures, elements of Celtic culture are still alive today. Play the clips of Celtic music or dancing that you found online for students. Tell students that in this Case Study they will learn about the ancient culture that inspired these modern artists.

Key Terms

Preteach the following terms:

inhabitants people who live in an area (p. 610)

nobles people with a high social rank (p. 612)

heritage legacy, inheritance (p. 614)

missionaries people sent to convert people to a religious faith and/or to do humanitarian work (p. 614)

folk of the common people (p. 615)

The Celts

History

The Celts were known as fierce warriors. Armed with swords, axes, and spears, they terrified their foes.

Dug into the soil in about the first century AD, the famous White Horse lies on a hill near Uffington, England. The horse, which can only be seen from the air, was made by Celts for religious reasons.

While the Romans were building their empire in southern Europe, another people controlled most of northern Europe. They were the Celts (KELTS). Unlike the Romans, the Celts did not form a single unified society. Instead, they lived as individual tribes. The only things that tied the Celtic tribes together were similar languages, customs, and beliefs.

Various Celtic cultures developed in Europe. The earliest, called the Hallstatt culture, had developed by about 1200 BC. The name Hallstatt comes from a village in Austria where early Celtic artifacts were found. The Hallstatt culture later gave way to the La Tène culture, named for a village in Switzerland. The La Tène culture developed during the Iron Age. Iron weapons helped the Celts defeat enemies and conquer new territories.

By the 200s BC the La Tène Celts had spread through much of northern and western Europe. Some groups had crossed the English Channel to the British Isles. In addition, some Celts had headed east into what is now Turkey.

As the Celts moved into new areas, they often came into conflict with people living there. For example, the Celts fought and defeated the original inhabitants of the British Isles. A Celtic army also attacked Rome in the 300s BC.

More than 200 years after the Celts attacked Rome, the Romans struck back. In 58 BC a Roman army under Julius Caesar invaded the Celtic territory of Gaul. The Celts of Gaul

610 CASE STUDY

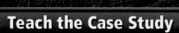

Teach the Case Study

At Level

The Celts

1. **Teach** Ask students the questions in the Main Idea boxes under Direct Teach.

2. **Apply** Have students create graphic organizers to help them take notes as they read the Case Study. A simple concept web would suffice, with the words *the Celts* in the center circle, and three connecting outer circles—one for each major heading in the Case Study.

3. **Review** Review graphic organizers as a class. Guide students in a discussion of the

relationships between the different aspects of Celtic history, society, and culture.

4. **Practice/Homework** Have each student select one aspect of Celtic history, society, or culture that he or she finds most intriguing. Have students write a brief essay explaining how their chosen aspect relates to all that they have learned about the Celts.

LS Visual/Spatial, Verbal Linguistic

Alternative Assessment Handbook, Rubric 13: Graphic Organizers

Celtic Lands, 500–200 BC

PICTS

GAELS

BRITONS
• Uffington

BELGAE

GAULS
La Tène •
• Hallstatt

LEPONTII

CELTIBERIANS

GALATIANS

North Sea

ATLANTIC OCEAN

Rhine R.

Danube River

Black Sea

Euphrates River

Mediterranean Sea

• Early Celtic settlement
PICTS Major Celtic tribe
⬛ Greatest extent of Celtic influence

0   200   400 Miles
0   200   400 Kilometers

Projection: Azimuthal Equal-Area

The Celts were masterful workers in bronze. This scene, which shows a Celtic god surrounded by animals, was carved on the side of a bronze cauldron.

Main Idea

History

Compare How was Celtic society different from Roman society? *The Celts did not form a single unified society; rather, they lived as independent tribes.*

Elaborate What tied the Celtic tribes together? *similar languages, customs, and beliefs*

Draw Conclusions When were the Celts at the peak of their power and influence? Explain your answer. *possible answer—about 200 BC; It was about that time that Celtic influence was present over the largest land area.*

📦 Map Zone Transparency: Celtic Lands, 500–200 BC

battled the Romans for many years, but eventually Gaul was conquered and became a Roman province. Caesar also fought the Celts in Britain. The Celts of southern Britain were overpowered by the Romans, but those of the north remained free.

In the AD 300s and 400s, much of Rome's territory was taken by Germanic invaders from the east. These same invaders drove the Celts out of their lands. The Celts were forced into a few remote areas, such as Ireland and Scotland.

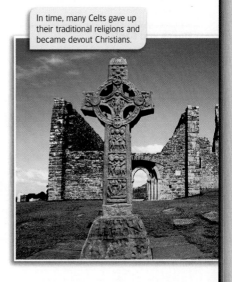

In time, many Celts gave up their traditional religions and became devout Christians.

Case Study Assessment

1. How did Celtic culture spread through Europe?
2. With whom did the Celts come into conflict?
3. **Activity** The Celts left no written records but did pass down songs about their heroes. Research a Celtic leader and write a song about him or her.

THE CELTS **611**

Info to Know

Hadrian's Wall The Roman invasion of Britain caused a divide among the British Celts—literally. In the AD 120s, the Roman Emperor Hadrian ordered the construction of a wall across northern Britain. The wall was to protect Rome's subjects in southern Britain from being attacked by the free Celts to the North. The resulting wall, now known as Hadrian's Wall, stretched for 73 miles across the width of northern Britain. Portions of the wall still stand today.

Critical Thinking: Making Generalizations

Generalizations from Historical Artifacts

1. Review making generalizations with students and provide a few model generalizations.

2. Then divide the class into small groups. In their groups have students examine each of the four photographs of artifacts on these pages in detail. For each artifact, have students jot down descriptive notes of what they see.

3. When students have finished making notations, have them compare their notes. Tell students to look in particular for any words

they may have used to describe more than one of the artifacts. For example, the word *animal* would apply to three of the four artifacts. Tell students to make generalizations centering on these words.

4. Have students make generalizations based on their notes. Discuss their generalizations as a class. Have students made valid generalizations? **LS Logical/Mathematical**

📝 Alternative Assessment Handbook, Rubric 14: Group Activity

Answers

Case Study Assessment 1. *Celtic culture spread through migration and conquest.* **2.** *various peoples including the original inhabitants of the British Isles, the Romans, Germanic invaders;* **3.** *Students' responses will vary. See Rubric 26: Poems and Songs, in the Alternative Assessment Handbook.*

Main Idea

Society and Daily Life

Recall What kind of leader was at the top of each Celtic tribe? *a king, or sometimes a queen*

Contrast How were Celtic nobles different from nobles in other parts of the world? *They earned, rather than were born into, their positions.*

Explain Why were druids and bards influential people in Celtic society? *possible answer—Druids were keepers of tradition and acted as healers, scholars, and judges. People would have turned to them for many things. Bards spread news between tribes and so controlled the transfer of important information.*

Make Judgments Would you rather have been a woman in a Celtic tribe or a woman in another ancient society? Why? *possible answer—a woman in a Celtic tribe, because they could become leaders, own property, and marry as they chose*

🎞 Quick Facts Transparency: Structure of Celtic Society

Structure of Celtic Society **QUICK FACTS**

Royalty

■ Each tribe was ruled by a king or, in some rare cases, a queen.

■ In some tribes, the ruler was elected.

■ Rulers were often advised by councils of elders.

Nobility

■ Nobles were chosen by the king or queen.

■ Nobility was earned, not inherited.

Farmers

■ Farmers made up the bulk of the population.

■ Most farmers owned their own land.

■ Some farmers worked land owned by nobles.

Druids and Bards

■ Druids were the keepers of tradition and acted as healers, scholars, and judges.

■ Bards spread news and ideas between tribes.

Society and Daily Life

The Celts left behind no written records. As a result, much of what we know about Celtic society is based on the writings of other people, often the Celts' opponents.

Government

As you have read, the Celts did not have a unified society. Celtic society was based instead on the tribe. In extraordinary circumstances, tribes would form alliances to work together. One such alliance was formed when the Romans attacked Gaul in the first century BC. Even when united in this way, however, the Gauls thought of themselves as separate tribes.

Each tribe was ruled by a king who was advised by a council of elders. In some tribes the king was elected by the people of the tribe. Elected rulers usually had to obey laws that were passed by the tribe's council.

Although most Celtic rulers were men, some women did rise to great power. Some even became queens. For example, the Iceni tribe of Britain was ruled by a queen named Boudicca. In AD 60 she led her people in a revolt against the Romans.

Below kings and queens in Celtic society were nobles. Unlike nobles in other parts of the world, Celtic nobles were not born into their positions. They had to earn their nobility. A king might make someone a noble for being an exceptional warrior or providing a service to the tribe.

Among those who were often made nobles were druids and bards. Both groups had great influence in Celtic society. Originally religious figures, druids later played many other roles. They were the keepers of tradition and acted as healers, scholars, and judges. Bards traveled throughout the land, spreading news and ideas within and between tribes.

This statue from Germany depicts a Celtic noble dressed for war.

Collaborative Learning  **At Level**

Celtic Society Skits

1. Discuss the information about Celtic society and daily life as a class. Have students pay particular attention to the "Structure of Celtic Society" Quick Facts and the "Celtic Life" photographs. Ask students to imagine living in a Celtic village. Tell students that they will be writing and performing Celtic society skits in this collaborative activity.

2. Divide the class into two or three mixed-ability groups. Tell groups to select one person to write down the group's ideas. Then, in their groups, have students work together to write a skit about Celtic society. Skits should be less than five minutes in length. Students should draw from the facts on this page, but can include some fictional elements, as well.

3. Allow students the remainder of the class period to write their skits. For tomorrow's class period, allow groups time to perform their skits. **LS Interpersonal**

📝 Alternative Assessment Handbook, Rubric 33: Skits and Reader's Theater

Celtic Life

Most Celts lived in small villages of small, round houses. This re-creation village in Ireland shows what a typical Celtic village might have looked like. For special occasions, Celts wore various types of jewelry, some examples of which are shown above.

Daily Life

Celtic life was organized around the clan, or extended family. Most clans lived together in small villages. The houses in such villages were often round and roofed with thatch, a covering made from grasses and straw. Villages were often surrounded by ditches or walls for defense.

Within a Celtic village, most people were farmers. Celtic farmers were among the first people in Europe to use iron plows. Before, farmers had used pointed sticks to poke holes in the ground in order to plant seeds. The plow made planting crops much easier and led to larger harvests.

From what historians have been able to piece together, Celtic women had more rights than did women in many other ancient societies. You have already seen how women like Boudicca could become rulers and war leaders. In addition, Celtic women could own property and marry as they chose.

Case Study Assessment

1. Who were the druids? What roles did they play?
2. What did a typical Celtic village look like?
3. **Activity** If you could have held any position in Celtic society, which would you have chosen? Write a journal entry describing a day as a person in that position.

Checking for Understanding

True or False Answer each statement *T* if it is true or *F* if it is false. If false, explain why.

1. We know about Celtic society from the written records of the Celts. *F; The Celts left no written records.*
2. Celtic kings were sometimes elected to their positions. *T*
3. Druids and bards were restricted from becoming nobles in Celtic society. *F; Druids and bards were often made nobles.*
4. Most Celts were either druids or bards. *F; Most Celts were farmers.*
5. Celtic women could become rulers and war leaders. *T*

Differentiating Instruction

Below Level

Struggling Readers

Materials: drawing paper, art supplies

1. Review the information in the "Structure of Celtic Society" Quick Facts with students. Allow time for students to ask questions to be sure they understand the information.

2. Tell students they are illustrators for a book on Celtic society. Have students imagine what people at each level of the Celtic social hierarchy may have looked like. Then have students draw an illustration of each of the following on a separate sheet of paper: a Celtic king or queen, a Celtic noble, a Celtic farmer, a druid, and a bard. When students have finished their illustrations, have them copy the information from the Quick Facts chart onto the appropriate illustrated page.

3. Have volunteers share their illustrations with the class. Tell students to retain their illustrations as a study tool. **LS Visual/Spatial**

Alternative Assessment Handbook, Rubric 3: Artwork

Answers

Case Study Assessment 1. *Druids were Celts who were the keepers of tradition and who acted as healers, scholars, and judges.* **2.** *Several small, round houses with grass and straw roofs, surrounded by ditches or walls. Fire pits and racks for drying animal skins are present.* **3.** *Students' responses will vary. See Rubric 15: Journals in the Alternative Assessment Handbook.*

1200 BC

c. 1200 BC
The Hallstatt culture develops in Central Europe.

Celtic helmet from Britain

c. 500 BC
Celts of the La Tène culture spread throughout Europe and into the British Isles.

390 BC
A Celtic army attacks and defeats the city of Rome.

Direct Teach

Main Idea

Culture and Achievements

Identify What are three cultural elements that reflect a shared Celtic heritage? *language, religion, art*

Summarize How did Celtic religious beliefs change over time? *Celts at first worshipped many gods and looked to druids for spiritual leadership. After the arrival of Christian missionaries, many Celts became Christians.*

Identify Cause and Effect Why does a purely Celtic culture not exist anymore? *Celts mixed with various other peoples of Europe.*

Info to Know

Celtic Languages Prior to AD 1, Celtic languages were spoken throughout much of Europe. (See the map on page 129.) As Roman influence in Europe increased, however, the use of Celtic languages declined in favor of Latin. By the fifth century AD, Celtic languages were mostly pushed off continental Europe to the British Isles. Today, Celtic languages are spoken by about 2 million people in the British Isles and the Brittany region of France. In addition to those languages mentioned in the text, Breton, Cornish, and also to some degree Manx, survive to this day.

Culture and Achievements

Celtic warrior statue

Although the Celts did not have a unified society, there were a few cultural elements that reflected their shared heritage. One such element was language. All of the Celtic tribes spoke related languages, most of which are now extinct. Only a few Celtic languages are still spoken today. Among them are Irish, Scottish Gaelic, and Welsh.

Celtic religion was also similar from tribe to tribe. The early Celts worshipped many gods and looked to the druids for spiritual leadership. By about 500, however, Christianity had largely replaced the early Celtic religion. Christian missionaries from Rome and other parts of Europe brought their religion to Celtin lands. According to legend, one such missionary was Patrick, who converted many of the Irish Celts in the early 400s. He later became known as Saint Patrick.

Celtic art styles were also similar across Europe. Artists made beautiful objects ranging from ornate bowls and cups for religious ceremonies to simple jewelry to be buried with dead leaders. Many of these objects are decorated with elaborate knot patterns. These Celtic knots are still popular in art today.

Legacy of the Celts

Although no pure Celtic culture exists in Europe today, Celtic influences can still be seen in many modern cultures. In addition, some Celtic leaders have captured the imaginations of Europeans for centuries.

Although he was defeated in the end, the Gaulish leader Vercingetorix is still admired for his bravery in standing up to the mighty Roman army.

Irish monks in the Middle Ages created beautiful manuscripts. This Bible was illustrated at Lindisfarne Monastery.

614 CASE STUDY

Differentiating Instruction

Above Level

Advanced/Gifted and Talented

Research Required

1. Share the Info to Know on Celtic Languages on this page with students. Tell students they will be conducting further research on Celtic languages and making an oral report of their findings to the class.

2. Have students use reliable online or print resources to research Celtic languages. To structure student research, have them include answers to the following questions in their presentations. What are the major sub-families of Celtic languages? What Celtic

languages are still spoken today? Where are the languages spoken and by how many people? What are some English words of Celtic origin? (Answers to these questions can be found in the "Celtic languages" article in the free, online Columbia Encyclopedia.)

3. Allow students time to make their presentations to the class. **LS Verbal/Linguistic**

   Alternative Assessment Handbook, Rubric 24: Oral Presentations

---

c. 275 BC
A Celtic tribe establishes the kingdom of Galatia in what is now Turkey.

58 BC
Roman general Julius Caesar begins a series of wars against the Celts of Gaul.

c. AD 430
Patrick introduces Christianity to the Celts of Ireland.

Over time the Celts mixed with various other peoples of Europe. As a result, a purely Celtic culture does not exist anymore. However, Celtic culture has not disappeared. Many artists, for example, continue to draw inspiration from Celtic art. Celtic rulers have also left their mark on the world. Many are remembered and admired for their bravery and nobility. Queen Boudicca is considered a folk hero by many people in England. Also considered a hero is the Gaulish king Vercingetorix, who united many Celtic tribes to fight Caesar and the Romans. He is honored in France, which includes most of the land that used to be Gaul.

Case Study Assessment

1. How did Christianity influence Celtic culture?

2. Why are some Celtic leaders still honored today?

3. **Activity** Why do you think the Celts should be remembered? Work with your classmates to design a museum exhibit about Celtic contributions to the world.

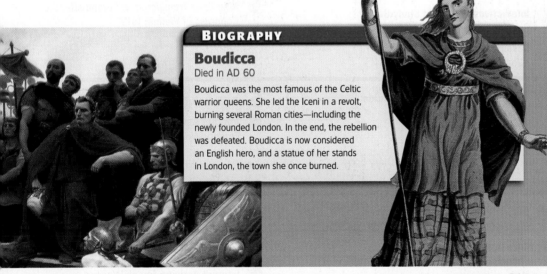

BIOGRAPHY

Boudicca
Died in AD 60

Boudicca was the most famous of the Celtic warrior queens. She led the Iceni in a revolt, burning several Roman cities—including the newly founded London. In the end, the rebellion was defeated. Boudicca is now considered an English hero, and a statue of her stands in London, the town she once burned.

THE CELTS **615**

Collaborative Learning

At Level

Making a Celtic Flag

Materials: poster board, art supplies

1. Introduce the activity by reminding students that flags contain symbolism. Review the symbolism of the U.S. flag and your state flag.

2. Divide the class into groups of four or five and distribute poster board and art supplies to the groups. Tell students that in their groups they will be designing a flag for the Celts.

3. Before working on their poster boards, have students discuss in their groups symbols to include on their flags. Students should be

encouraged to sketch a few drafts of their flags on notebook paper before transmitting their final ideas onto their poster boards.

4. Allow students sufficient time to draw and color their flag designs on their poster boards. When students have finished, call on each group to present its flag design to the class. Students should explain the symbolism they included on their flags. **LS Interpersonal**

Alternative Assessment Handbook: Rubric 14: Group Activity

Chapter 19 Planning Guide

Growth and Development of Europe

Chapter Overview	Reproducible Resources	Technology Resources
Section 1: **The Middle Ages** **The Big Idea:** Christianity and social systems influenced life in the Middle Ages.	**Differentiated Instruction Teacher Management System:** Section 1 Lesson Plan* **Resource File:*** • Vocabulary Builder: Section 1 • Focus on Reading: Context Clues—Contrast	**Daily Bellringer Transparency:** Section 1* **Map Zone Transparency:** The First Crusade, 1096* **Map Zone Transparency:** The Black Death
Section 2: **Renaissance and Reformation** **The Big Idea:** The periods of the Renaissance and the Reformation introduced new ideas and new ways of thinking into Europe.	**Differentiated Instruction Teacher Management System:** Section 2 Lesson Plan* **Resource File:*** • Vocabulary Builder: Section 2 • Biography: Galileo • Geography and History: Rome's First Trade Routes, First Century AD	**Daily Bellringer Transparency:** Section 2* **Map Zone Transparency:** Major Trade Routes, 1350–1500* **Map Zone Transparency:** Religion in Europe, 1600*
Section 3: **Political Change in Europe** **The Big Idea:** Ideas of the Enlightenment inspired revolutions and new governments in Europe.	**Differentiated Instruction Teacher Management System:** Section 3 Lesson Plan* **Interactive Reader and Study Guide:** Section 3 Summary* **Resource File:*** • Vocabulary Builder: Section 3	**Daily Bellringer Transparency:** Section 3* **Map Zone Transparency:** Europe after the Congress of Vienna, 1815*
Section 4: **The Industrial Revolution** **The Big Idea:** Driven by new ideas and technologies, much of Europe developed industrial societies in the 1700s and 1800s.	**Interactive Reader and Study Guide:** Section 4 Summary* **Resource File:*** • Vocabulary Builder: Section 4 • Focus on Writing: Writing a Diary Entry	**Daily Bellringer Transparency:** Section 4* **Internet Activity:** Life of a British Textile Factory Worker
Section 5: **World War I** **The Big Idea:** World War I and the peace treaty that followed brought tremendous change to Europe.	**Differentiated Instruction Teacher Management System:** Section 5 Lesson Plan* **Resource File:*** • Vocabulary Builder: Section 5	**Daily Bellringer Transparency:** Section 5* **Map Zone Transparency:** European Alliances, 1914* **Internet Activity:** Trench Warfare
Section 6: **World War II** **The Big Idea:** Problems in Europe led to World War II, the deadliest war in history.	**Interactive Reader and Study Guide:** Section 6 Summary* **Resource File:*** • Vocabulary Builder: Section 6 • Biography: Anne Frank	**Daily Bellringer Transparency:** Section 6* **Map Zone Transparency:** World War II in Europe, 1941* **Internet Activity:** D-Day Invasion
Section 7: **Europe since 1945** **The Big Idea:** After years of division during the Cold War, today Europe is working toward unity.	**Differentiated Instruction Teacher Management System:** Section 7 Lesson Plan* **Resource File:*** • Primary Source: Charter of the United Nations • Literature: *Animal Farm* • Social Studies Skills: Interpreting Political Cartoons	**Daily Bellringer Transparency:** Section 7* **Map Zone Transparency:** A Divided Europe, 1955*

CHAPTER 19 PLANNING GUIDE

615a   TEACHER'S EDITION

HOLT
Geography's Impact
Video Program
Impact of the European Union
Suggested use: in Section 7

Review, Assessment, Intervention

 PASS: Section 1 Quiz*

 Online Quiz: Section 1

 Alternative Assessment Handbook

 PASS: Section 2 Quiz*

 Online Quiz: Section 2

 Alternative Assessment Handbook

 PASS: Section 3 Quiz*

 Online Quiz: Section 3

 Alternative Assessment Handbook

 PASS: Section 4 Quiz*

 Online Quiz: Section 4

 Alternative Assessment Handbook

 PASS: Section 5 Quiz*

 Online Quiz: Section 5

 Alternative Assessment Handbook

 PASS: Section 6 Quiz*

 Online Quiz: Section 6

 Alternative Assessment Handbook

 PASS: Section 7 Quiz*

 Online Quiz: Section 7

 Alternative Assessment Handbook

Power Presentations with Video CD-ROM

Power Presentations with Video are visual presentations of each chapter's main ideas. Presentations can be customized by including Quick Facts charts, images from the text, and video clips.

Holt Online Learning

go.hrw.com
Teacher Resources
KEYWORD: SK9 TEACHER

go.hrw.com
Student Resources
KEYWORD: SK9 CH19

• Interactive Multimedia Activities
• Current Events
• Chapter-based Internet Activities
• and more!

Holt Interactive
Online Student Edition
Complete online support for interactivity, assessment, and reporting
• Interactive Maps and Notebook
• Standardized Test Prep
• Homework Practice and Research Activities Online

CHAPTER 19 PLANNING GUIDE

Differentiating Instruction

How do I address the needs of varied learners?
The Target Resource acts as your primary strategy for differentiated instruction.

ENGLISH-LANGUAGE LEARNERS & STRUGGLING READERS

Interactive Skills Tutor CD-ROM

The Interactive Skills Tutor CD-ROM contains lessons that provide additional practice for 20 different critical thinking skills.

Additional Resources

Differentiated Instruction Teacher Management System: Lesson Plans for Differentiated Instruction

Resource File:
- Vocabulary Builder Activities
- Social Studies Skills: Interpreting Political Cartoons

Quick Facts Transparency: Visual Summary: Growth and Development of Europe

Student Edition on Audio CD Program

Spanish Chapter Summaries Audio CD Program

Teacher's One Stop Planner:
- ExamView Test Generator, Spanish
- PuzzlePro, Spanish

English-Language Learner Strategies and Activities

SPECIAL NEEDS LEARNERS

Differentiated Instruction Modified Worksheets and Tests CD-ROM

- Vocabulary Flash Cards
- Modified Vocabulary Builder Activities
- Modified Chapter Review
- Modified Chapter Test

Additional Resources

Differentiated Instruction Teacher Management System: Lesson Plans for Differentiated Instruction

Interactive Reader and Study Guide

Resource File: Social Studies Skills: Interpreting Political Cartoons

Student Edition on Audio CD Program

Interactive Skills Tutor CD-ROM

Graphic Organizer Transparencies with Support for Reading and Writing

ADVANCED/GIFTED AND TALENTED STUDENTS

Resource File

The Resource File activities allow students to extend their knowledge of chapter-related places and people and to practice geography skills.
- Focus on Reading: Using Context Clues—Contrast
- Focus on Writing: Writing a Diary Entry
- Literature: *Animal Farm* by George Orwell

Additional Resources

Differentiated Instruction Teacher Management System: Lesson Plans for Differentiated Instruction

World History and Geography Document-Based Questions Activities

Geography, Science, and Cultures Activities

Experiencing World History and Geography

Differentiated Activities in the Teacher's Edition

- Middle Ages Charts
- Understanding Homonyms
- Understanding New Vocabulary
- European Empires Graphic Organizers
- Decoding *Enlightenment*
- French Revolution Graphic Organizers

Differentiated Activities in the Teacher's Edition

- Travel Today v. Travel in the Middle Ages
- Creating a Commemorative Stamp
- Learning through Listening

Differentiated Activities in the Teacher's Edition

- Mapping European Kingdoms
- Population Line Graphs
- Interpreting John Locke
- The Rules of Warfare

HOLT Teacher's One-Stop Planner®

How can I manage the lesson plans and support materials for differentiated instruction?

With the Teacher's One-Stop Planner, you can easily organize and print lesson plans, planning guides, and instructional materials for all learners.

The Teacher's One-Stop Planner includes the following materials to help you differentiate instruction:

- **Interactive Teacher's Edition**
- **Calendar Planner and pacing guides**
- **Editable lesson plans**
- **All reproducible ancillaries in Adobe Acrobat (PDF) format**
- **ExamView Test Generator (English & Spanish)**
- **Transparency and video previews**

Professional Development

What teacher training resources are available to help me grow professionally?

- **In-service and staff development** as part of your Holt Social Studies product purchase
- **Quick Teacher Tutorial Lesson Presentation CD-ROM**
- Intensive tuition-based **Teacher Development Institute**
- **Convenient Holt Speaker Bureau** – face-to-face workshop options
- **24/7 Ask A Professional Development Expert** at http://www.hrw.com/prodev/

Chapter Big Ideas

Section 1 Christianity and social systems influenced life in Europe in the Middle Ages.

Section 2 The periods of the Renaissance and the Reformation introduced new ideas and new ways of thinking into Europe.

Section 3 Ideas of the Enlightenment inspired revolutions and new governments in Europe.

Section 4 Driven by new ideas and technologies, much of Europe developed industrial societies in the 1700s and 1800s.

Section 5 World War I and the peace treaty that followed brought tremendous change to Europe.

Section 6 Problems in Europe led to World War II, the deadliest war in history.

Section 7 After years of division during the Cold War, today Europe is working toward unity.

Focus on Reading and Writing

Reading The Resource File provides a worksheet to help students practice understanding chronological order.

📄 **RF: Focus on Reading, Using Context Clues—Contrast**

Writing The Resource File provides a worksheet to help students organize and write their travel brochures.

📄 **RF: Focus on Writing, Writing a Diary Entry**

Key to Differentiating Instruction

Below Level

Basic-level activities designed for all students encountering new material

At Level

Intermediate-level activities designed for average students

Above Level

Challenging activities designed for honors and gifted and talented students

Standard English Mastery

Activities designed to improve standard English usage

616 CHAPTER 19

CHAPTER **19**

Growth and Development of Europe

FOCUS QUESTION

What forces had an impact on the development of Europe and why?

What You Will Learn...

In this chapter you will learn about European history since the fall of Rome. During this period new ideas and innovations changed life and expanded knowledge across Europe.

FOCUS ON READING AND WRITING

Using Context Clue—Contrast Sometimes you can figure out the meaning of a word through contrast clues. They tell you how an unknown word is different from a word you already know. **See the lesson, Using Context Clues—Contrast, on page S22.**

Writing a Diary Entry In this chapter you will read about many periods of European history. After you read you will write a diary entry from the point of view of someone during one of these times.

616 CHAPTER 19

ATLANTIC OCEAN

German U-boats

Madrid

AFRICA

Middle Ages Warriors called knights were key to the political system of Europe in the Middle Ages. Knights wore suits of armor like this one into battle.

Introduce the Chapter

At Level

What Is Development?

1. Direct students' attention to the chapter title. Ask students what *development* means.

2. Ask students if the images on the map seem representative of development. From what perspective would the printing press and U-boat be seen as new and innovative?

3. Have students identify the functions of the printing press and U-boat and explain why these inventions might represent significant advances that set this period apart from earlier periods in European history.

4. As a class, have students suggest images they would choose for a map today. What inventions would they pick? What historical events? Would students put any people or buildings on their lists? As students make suggestions, have them give reasons for their choices that show how these inventions or events have changed how people live today.

📖 **Verbal/Linguistic**

📝 Alternative Assessment Handbook, Rubrics 11: Discussions; and 21: Map Reading

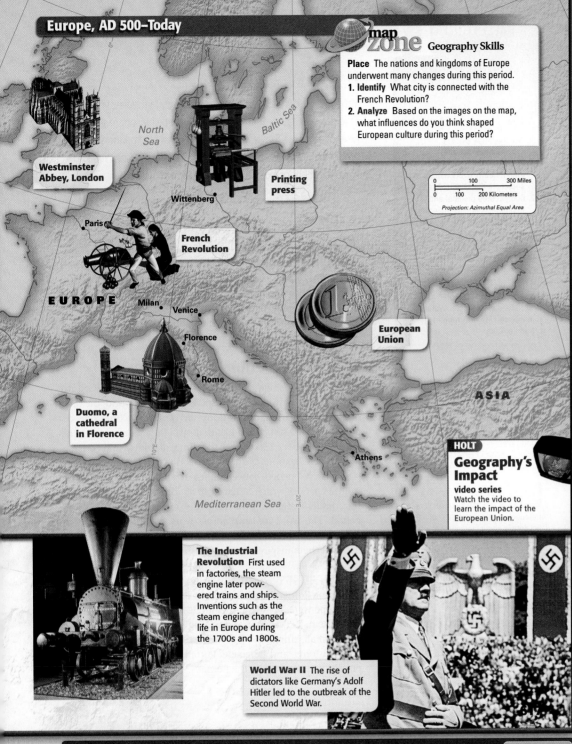

Europe, AD 500–Today

Westminster Abbey, London

North Sea

Baltic Sea

Printing press

Wittenberg

Paris

French Revolution

EUROPE

Milan

Venice

Florence

Duomo, a cathedral in Florence

Rome

European Union

ASIA

Athens

Mediterranean Sea

```
0    100         300 Miles
0    100   200 Kilometers
Projection: Azimuthal Equal Area
```

map zone — Geography Skills

Place The nations and kingdoms of Europe underwent many changes during this period.
1. **Identify** What city is connected with the French Revolution?
2. **Analyze** Based on the images on the map, what influences do you think shaped European culture during this period?

HOLT

Geography's Impact
video series
Watch the video to learn the impact of the European Union.

The Industrial Revolution First used in factories, the steam engine later powered trains and ships. Inventions such as the steam engine changed life in Europe during the 1700s and 1800s.

World War II The rise of dictators like Germany's Adolf Hitler led to the outbreak of the Second World War.

Critical Thinking: Analyzing Visuals

At Level

Asking Historical Questions

1. Have students examine the pictures at the bottom of the page and write down three statements about why they think these images in particular were selected to open the chapter.

2. Then ask students what they can learn from examining the images on the map about how this period might be different from earlier

periods in European history. Is it similar in any ways?

3. Have students describe what other information they can learn from the map and pictures. Ask them to consider how their lives might be different today if certain events or inventions had not occurred. **LS Verbal/Linguistic**

📄 Alternative Assessment Handbook, Rubric 11: Discussions

Preteach

Bellringer

If YOU lived there. . . Use the **Daily Bellringer Transparency** to help students answer the question.

📽 Daily Bellringer Transparency, Section 1

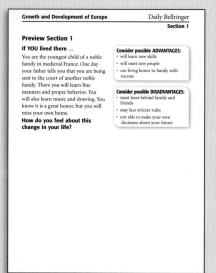

Key Terms and Places

📖 **RF:** Vocabulary Builder, Section 1

Taking Notes

Have students copy the graphic organizer onto their own paper and then use it to take notes on the section. This activity will prepare students for the Section Assessment, in which they will complete a graphic organizer that builds on the information using the Critical Thinking Skill: Analyzing.

The Middle Ages

What You Will Learn...

Main Ideas

1. The Christian church influenced nearly every aspect of society in the Middle Ages.
2. Complicated political and economic systems governed life in the Middle Ages.
3. The period after 1000 was a time of great changes in medieval society.

The Big Idea

Christianity and social systems influenced life in Europe in the Middle Ages.

Key Terms and Places

Middle Ages, *p. 618*
pope, *p. 619*
Crusade, *p. 619*
Holy Land, *p. 619*
Gothic architecture, *p. 620*
feudal system, *p. 621*
manor, *p. 622*
nation-state, *p. 625*

TAKING NOTES Draw a diagram like the one below in your notebook. As you read this section, list details about medieval society in the appropriate circle.

If **YOU** lived there...

You are the youngest child of a noble family in medieval France. One day your father tells you that you are being sent to the court of another noble family. There you will learn fine manners and proper behavior. You will also learn music and drawing. You know it is a great honor, but you will miss your own home.

How do you feel about this change in your life?

BUILDING BACKGROUND When people think of the Middle Ages today, they usually think of castles, princesses, and knights in shining armor. Although these were all part of the Middle Ages, they do not tell the whole story. The Middle Ages was a time of great change in Europe, as the influence of the ancient world faded away.

The Christian Church and Society

When historians talk about the past, they often divide it into three long periods. The first period is the ancient world, the time of the world's earliest civilizations, such as Egypt, China, Greece, and Rome. The last period historians call the modern world, the world since about 1500. Since that time, new ideas and contacts between civilizations changed the world completely.

What happened between ancient and modern times? We call this period, which lasted from about 500 until about 1500, the **Middle Ages**. We also call it the medieval (mee-DEE-vuhl) period. The word *medieval* comes from two Latin words that mean "middle age." It was a time of great changes in Europe, many of them inspired by the Christian church.

The Importance of the Church

When the Roman Empire fell apart in the late 400s, the people of Europe were left without a single dominant government to unite them. In the absence of strong leaders, Europe broke into many small kingdoms. Each of these kingdoms had its own laws, customs, and language. Europe was no longer the same place it had been under the Romans.

Teach the Big Idea
At Level

The Middle Ages

1. **Teach** Ask students the questions in the Main Idea boxes under Direct Teach.

2. **Apply** Ask students to imagine that they will interview three people from the Middle Ages. These might include a woman, a Crusader, a noble, a peasant, a king, or others. Have them write at least three interview questions (based on material in the chapter) to ask each person.

3. **Review** Have students take turns interviewing each other and answering the questions.

4. **Practice/Homework** Have students write the responses next to their interview questions. Then have them work to come up with more questions. 🔤 **Verbal/Linguistic**

📄 Alternative Assessment Handbook, Rubrics 1: Acquiring Information; and 37: Writing Assignments

The First Crusade, 1096

Christian lands, 1095
Muslim lands, 1095
First Crusade, 1096–1099

0   100   200 Miles
0 100 200 Kilometers

Projection: Azimuthal Equal Area

North Sea

ENGLAND

ATLANTIC OCEAN

HOLY ROMAN EMPIRE

FRANCE

Regensburg   Vienna

Lyon

Trieste

Genoa   Zadar

Corsica

Rome

Sardinia

Mediterranean Sea

Sicily

Crete

BYZANTINE EMPIRE

Black Sea

Constantinople

SELJUK TURKS

Edessa

Antioch

Tripoli

HOLY LAND
Acre

Jerusalem

map zone Geography Skills

Movement In 1096, the pope called on Christian Crusaders to take the Holy Land away from the Muslims who controlled it.
1. **Use the Map** Which direction did the Crusaders travel?
2. **Analyze** Which do you think was more difficult, the trip from Vienna to Constantinople or from Constantinople to Antioch? Why?

go.hrw.com   KEYWORD: SK9 CH19

One factor, however, continued to tie the people of Europe together—religion. Nearly everyone in Europe was Christian, and so most Europeans felt tied together by their beliefs. Over time, the number of Christians in Europe increased. People came to feel more and more like part of a single religious community.

Because Christianity was so important in Europe, the Christian church gained a great deal of influence. In time, the church began to influence the politics, art, and daily lives of people all over the continent. In fact, almost no part of life in Europe in the Middle Ages was unaffected by the church and its teachings.

The Christian Church and Politics

As the Christian church gained influence in Europe, some church leaders became powerful. They gained political power in addition to their religious authority.

The most powerful religious leader was the **pope**, the head of the Christian church. The pope's decisions could have huge effects on people's lives. For example, one pope decided to start a religious war, or **Crusade**, against the church's enemies in Southwest Asia. He wanted Europeans to take over the **Holy Land**, the region in which Jesus had lived. For many years, the region had been in the hands of another religious group, the Muslims.

GROWTH AND DEVELOPMENT OF EUROPE **619**

Main Idea

❶ The Christian Church and Society, *continued*

The Christian church influenced nearly every aspect of society in the Middle Ages.

Recall What events did people attend at their churches? *markets, festivals, religious ceremonies*

Cause and Effect What long-term effects did the Crusades have on Europe? *trade increased along with a demand for goods from Southwest Asia; relations between Christians and Muslims became worse*

Analyze Why was most art during the Middle Ages concerned with religious themes? *because it was influenced by the church*

Activity The Children's Crusade Tell students that not all of the Crusades were launched by religious leaders. The Children's Crusade was a popular movement begun by a young boy. Have them research and write a report about the Children's Crusade. **LS** Verbal/Linguistic

📝 Alternative Assessment Handbook, Rubrics 30: Research; and 40: Writing to Describe

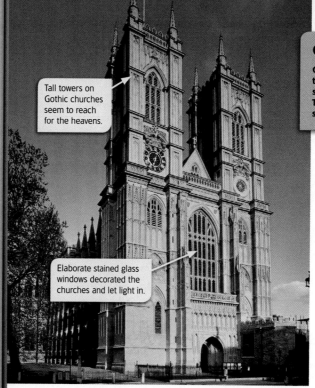

Tall towers on Gothic churches seem to reach for the heavens.

Elaborate stained glass windows decorated the churches and let light in.

Gothic Architecture

Gothic churches were designed to tower over medieval cities as symbols of the church's greatness. This cathedral, Westminster Abbey, stands in London, England.

Thousands of people answered the pope's call for a Crusade. As the map on the previous page shows, they traveled thousands of miles to fight the church's enemies. This Crusade was the first of eight attempts by Christians over two centuries to win back the Holy Land.

In the end, the Crusades did not drive the Muslims from the Holy Land. They did, however, lead to sweeping changes in Europe. Crusaders brought new goods and ideas back to Europe with them. Europeans began to want more of these goods, so trade between Europe and Asia increased. At the same time, though, relations between Christians and Muslims grew worse. For years to come, followers of the religions distrusted and resented each other.

The Church and Art

Politics was not the only area in which the church had great influence. Most art of the Middle Ages was also influenced by the church. Medieval painters and sculptors, for example, used religious subjects in their works. Most music and literature from the period is centered on religious themes.

The greatest examples of religious art from the Middle Ages are church buildings. Huge churches like the one shown on this page were built all over Europe. Many of them are examples of **Gothic architecture**, a style known for its high pointed ceilings, tall towers, and stained glass windows. People built Gothic churches as symbols of their faith. They believed that building these amazing structures would show their love for God. The insides of such churches are as elaborate and ornate as the outsides.

The Church and Daily Life

Most people in Europe never saw a Gothic church, especially not the inside. Instead they worshipped at small local churches. In fact, people's lives often centered around their local church. Markets, festivals, and religious ceremonies all took place there. Local priests advised people on how to live and act. In addition, because most people could not read or write, they depended on the church to keep records for them.

READING CHECK Summarizing How did the Christian church shape life in the Middle Ages?

Critical Thinking: Analyzing Information   At Level

Writing a Letter

1. Have students explore online images of artifacts, women, religious figures, knights, and Crusaders.

2. Ask students to imagine that they are traveling with the Crusaders. Have them write letters to their families. Suggest that they use the images they find as a starting point for details they can include in their letters. The letters might describe what they have seen on the journey or what they miss from home. Some students may wish to write an exchange of letters (from those on the road and from those left behind).

3. Have volunteers read their letters aloud and display the images they have found. **LS** Verbal/Linguistic

📝 Alternative Assessment Handbook, Rubrics 1: Acquiring Information; and 25: Personal Letters

Answers

Reading Check *The church was a place to worship, but also the center of people's lives. The church influenced politics, the economy, and the culture.*

Life in the Middle Ages

Christianity was a major influence on people's lives in the Middle Ages, but it was not the only one. Much of European society was controlled by two systems of relationships. They were the feudal (FYOO-duhl) system and the manor system.

The Feudal System

Medieval Europe was divided into many small kingdoms. In most kingdoms, the king owned all the land. Sometimes, kings gave parts of their land to nobles—people born into wealthy, powerful families. In turn, these nobles gave land to knights, or trained warriors, who promised to help them defend both their lands and the king. This system of exchanging land for military service is called the **feudal system**, or feudalism (FYOO-duh-li-zuhm).

Everyone involved in the feudal system had certain duties to perform. The kings and nobles provided land and promised to protect the people who served them and to treat everyone fairly. In return, the knights who received land promised to serve the nobles dutifully, especially in times of war. The set of relationships between knights and nobles was the heart of Europe's feudal system.

The feudal system was very complex. Its rules varied from kingdom to kingdom and changed constantly. Feudal duties in France, for example, were not the same as those in Germany or England. Also, it was possible for one knight to owe service to more than one noble. If the two nobles he served went to war, the poor knight would be torn between them. In such situations, feudal relationships could be confusing or even dangerous.

Feudal Relationships

Europe's feudal system was based on relationships between knights and nobles. Each had certain duties that he or she had to perform.

ANALYZING VISUALS Who had to provide military service as one of his duties?

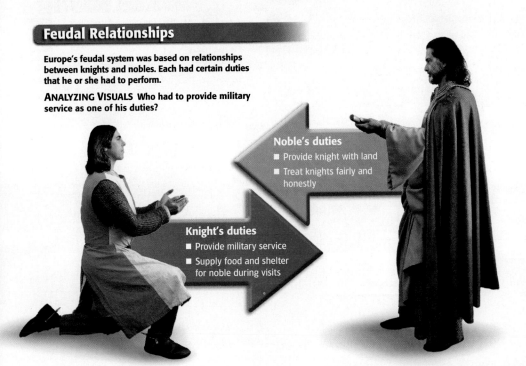

Noble's duties
- Provide knight with land
- Treat knights fairly and honestly

Knight's duties
- Provide military service
- Supply food and shelter for noble during visits

GROWTH AND DEVELOPMENT OF EUROPE **621**

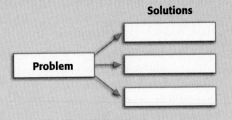

Info to Know

Role of Women For the most part, women on manors stayed in the home sewing, baking, weaving, and spinning. However, women also hunted and learned how to use weapons to fight in battles and defend their homes. Some women specialized in occupations such as painting, writing and blacksmithing.

Checking for Understanding

Are the following statements true or false?

1. Estate owners and peasants exchanged land for military service. *false*
2. The relationships between knights and nobles were central to the feudal system. *true*
3. The workers on a manor often lived in villages. *true*
4. The population of cities declined after 1000. *false*

The Manor System

The feudal system was only one set of guidelines that governed life in the Middle Ages. Another system, the manor system, controlled most economic activities in Europe during this period.

At the center of the manor system was the **manor**, a large estate owned by a noble or knight. Every manor was different, but most included a large house or castle, fields, pastures, and forests. A manor also had a village where workers lived. They traveled back and forth to the fields each day.

The owner of a manor did not farm his own land. Instead, he had workers to farm it for him. Most of the crops grown on the manor went to the owner. In exchange for their work, the workers got a place to live and a small piece of land on which they could grow their own food.

The workers on most manors included either free peasants or serfs. Peasants were free farmers. Serfs, on the other hand, were not free. Although they were not slaves, they were not allowed to leave the land on which they worked.

Close-up

Life on a Manor

Manors were large estates that developed during the Middle Ages. Many manors were largely self-sufficient, producing most of the food and goods they needed. This picture shows what a manor in England might have looked like.

The owner of the manor lived in a large stone house called the manor house.

Peasants grew vegetables in small gardens located near their houses.

In late spring, peasants harvested crops like wheat.

622 CHAPTER 19

Differentiating Instruction

At Level

Struggling Readers

1. To help students understand feudalism, the manor system, and urban life in the Middle Ages, draw the following chart for students to see. Complete the chart with details from the section, or ask volunteers to do so.

2. Encourage students to explain which way of life they would have prefered and why.

LS Verbal/Linguistic, Visual/Spatial

Alternative Assessment Handbook, Rubrics 7: Charts; and 13: Graphic Organizers

Feudal	Manor	Urban

Towns and Trade

Not everyone in the Middle Ages lived on manors. Some people chose to live in towns and cities like Paris or London. Compared to our cities today, most of these medieval cities were small, dirty, and dark.

Many of the people who lived in cities were traders. They bought and sold goods from all over Europe and other parts of the world. Most of their goods were sold at trade fairs. Every year, merchants from many places in Europe would meet at these large fairs to sell their wares.

Before the year 1000, trade was not very common in Europe. After that year, however, trade increased. As it did, more people began to move to cities. Once small, these cities began to grow. As cities grew, trade increased even more, and the people who lived in them became wealthier. By the end of the Middle Ages, cities had become the centers of European culture and wealth.

READING CHECK **Finding Main Ideas** What were two systems that governed life in Europe during the Middle Ages? How did they differ?

The village church was built on a small piece of land that belonged to the lord.

Sheep grazed on grassy fields, and villagers used sheep's wool to make clothes.

The village blacksmith made iron tools for farming.

ANALYSIS SKILL **ANALYZING VISUALS**
What goods can you see being produced on this manor? How do you think the lives of peasants on this manor differed from the life of the owner?

Peasants took wheat to the mill to be ground into flour, which they used to make bread.

623

Differentiating Instruction

At Level | Standard English Mastery

English-Language Learners

1. Explain that homonyms are words that sound the same, but are spelled differently and have different meanings.

2. Point out these homonyms in the "Life in the Middle Ages" section: *knight (night), manor (manner)*, and *serf (surf)*

3. Pair English learners with more proficient readers and have them work together to create a chart defining these words. Encourage them to find other homonyms from the section, and add these to their charts. Have students

use standard English to write sentences using each term and its homonym.

Term	Definition	Homonym	Definition
knight		night	
manor		manner	
serf		surf	

LS Verbal/Linguistic
Alternative Assessment Handbook, Rubric 7: Charts

Main Idea

❸ Changes in Medieval Society

The period after 1000 was a time of great changes in medieval society.

Identify Who was William the Conqueror? *a noble from France who in 1066 overthrew the English king and became king of England*

Recall How did the Black Death affect Europe's population? *up to a third of the population died; a labor shortage resulted*

Analyze Why did England's nobles force King John to sign Magna Carta? *The king had raised taxes, indicating that he believed he was the supreme ruler, while the nobles believed in the power of law.*

Make Inferences How would eliminating feudalism increase the power of kings? *possible answer—Nobles would have less power and influence if feudalism were eliminated.*

Primary Source

To help students understand the provisions of Magna Carta, create a web diagram such as the one below and work with students to fill in details about its provisions.

Answers

Primary Source *They state the rights of ordinary people to be free, to own property, and to receive a fair trial. These are basic rights in a democracy.*

624

Changes in Medieval Society

Life in the Middle Ages changed greatly after the year 1000. You have already seen how cities grew and trade increased. Even as these changes were taking place, bigger changes were sweeping through Europe.

THE IMPACT TODAY
The ideas of Magna Carta influenced later documents, including our Constitution.

Political Changes in England

One of the countries most affected by change in the Middle Ages was England. In the year 1066 a noble from northern France, William the Conqueror, sailed to England and overthrew the old king. He declared himself the new king of England.

William built a strong government in England, something the English had not had before. Later kings of England built on William's example. For more than a century, these kings increased their power. By the late 1100s England's king was one of the most powerful men in Europe.

When William's descendant John took the throne, however, he angered many nobles by raising taxes. John believed that the king had the right to do whatever he wanted. England's nobles disagreed.

In 1215 a group of nobles forced King John to sign Magna Carta, one of the most important documents in English history. Magna Carta stated that the law, not the king, was the supreme power in England. The king had to obey the law. He could not raise taxes without the nobles' permission.

Many people consider Magna Carta to be one of the first steps toward democracy in modern Europe and one of history's most important documents. By stating that the king was not above the law, Magna Carta set limits on his power. In addition, it gave a council of nobles the power to advise the king. In time, that council developed into Parliament (PAHR-luh-muhnt), the elected body that governs England today.

Primary Source

HISTORIC DOCUMENT
Magna Carta

Magna Carta was one of the first documents to protect the rights of the people. Magna Carta was so influential that the British still consider it part of their constitution. Some of its ideas are also in the U.S. Constitution. Included in Magna Carta were 63 demands that English nobles made King John agree to follow. A few of these demands are listed here.

Demand number 31 defended people's right to property, not just wood.

Magna Carta guaranteed that free men had the right to a fair trial.

To all free men of our kingdom we have also granted, for us and our heirs for ever, all the liberties written out below, to have and to keep for them and their heirs, of us and our heirs.

(16) No man shall be forced to perform more service for a knight's 'fee', or other free holding of land, than is due from it.

(31) Neither we nor any royal official will take wood for our castle, or for any other purpose, without the consent [permission] of the owner.

(38) In future no official shall place a man on trial upon his own unsupported statement, without producing credible [believable] witnesses to the truth of it.

—Magna Carta, from a translation by the British Library

ANALYSIS SKILL **ANALYZING PRIMARY SOURCES**
In what ways do you think the ideas listed above influenced modern democracy?

624 CHAPTER 19

Collaborative Learning

At Level

Role-Playing the Creation of Magna Carta

1. Organize students into small groups. Tell students they are going to role-play the creation of Magna Carta.

2. Have students begin by reviewing the information in the section about Magna Carta. (You may also have them research information from outside sources.) To make sure they cover all the important points, have each group create an outline before they begin.

3. Assign roles or have students select them. Have groups perform their plays before the

class. Remind them that the nobles should describe the provisions of Magna Carta and try to win over the king to their position. Likewise, the king should try to win over the nobles to his position.

4. Discuss with students insights they have obtained about how Magna Carta affects their lives today. **LS Interpersonal, Verbal/Linguistic**

Alternative Assessment Handbook, Rubrics 14: Group Activity; and 33: Skits and Reader's Theater

The Black Death

Not all of the changes that struck medieval Europe had such positive results. In 1347 a disease called the Black Death swept through Europe. Up to a third of Europe's people died from the disease. Even such a disaster, however, had some positive effects. With the decrease in population came a labor shortage. As a result, people could demand higher wages for their work.

The Fight for Power

Even as the Black Death was sweeping across Europe, kings fought for power. In 1337 the Hundred Years' War broke out between England and France. As its name suggests, the war lasted more than 100 years. In the end, the French won.

Inspired by the victory, France's kings worked to increase their power. They took land away from nobles to rule themselves. France became a **nation-state**, a country united under a single strong government.

Around Europe, other rulers followed the French example. As nation-states arose around Europe, feudalism disappeared, and the Middle Ages came to an end.

READING CHECK Finding Main Ideas What changes occurred in Europe after 1000?

BIOGRAPHY

Joan of Arc
(c. 1412–1431)

One of the most famous war leaders in all of European history was a teenage girl. Joan of Arc, a leader of French troops during the Hundred Years' War, was only 16 when she first led troops into battle. She won many battles against the English but was captured in battle in 1430, tried, and executed. Nevertheless, her courage inspired the French, who went on to win the war. Today Joan is considered a national hero in France.

Make Inferences Why do you think Joan is considered a hero in France?

SUMMARY AND PREVIEW In this section you read about the Middle Ages, a period that helped shape Europe's later political history. Next, you will learn about two periods that influenced the continent's cultural development: the Renaissance and Reformation.

Section 1 Assessment

go.hrw.com
Online Quiz
KEYWORD: SK9 HP19

Reviewing Ideas, Terms, and Places

1. **a. Recall** Why did the **pope** call for a **Crusade**?
   b. Generalize How did the Christian church affect art in the Middle Ages?
2. **a. Define** What was the **feudal system**?
   b. Explain How did the **manor** system work?
   c. Elaborate What made the feudal system so complex?
3. **a. Describe** How did the Black Death affect Europe?
   b. Explain How did England's government change after 1000?

Critical Thinking

4. **Analyzing** Use your notes to complete a table like the one on the right. List ways the Church shaped medieval politics, life, and art.

```
        The Christian
          Church
       /      |      \
   Politics       Art
          |
        Daily
         Life
```

FOCUS ON WRITING

5. **Thinking about People** What would a diary entry by a medieval peasant include? by a lord? Write down some ideas.

GROWTH AND DEVELOPMENT OF EUROPE **625**

Section 1 Assessment Answers

1. **a.** to take over the Holy Land from the Muslims
   b. Painting, sculpture, music, and literature all centered on religious themes.

2. **a.** a system of exchanging land for military service, between nobles and knights
   b. Owners of manors provided workers with a place to live and some land to farm in exchange for most of the crops they produced.
   c. Its rules varied from place to place and changed constantly. A knight's loyalty could be torn if he owed service to more than one noble.

3. **a.** It killed up to one third of Europe's population. It also created a labor shortage.
   b. First, William the Conqueror built a strong government. Then Magna Carta reduced the power of England's kings.

4. possible answers—politics: Crusades, government; art: Gothic architecture, religious themes; daily life: markets and festivals at local church, advice from priests

5. Responses will vary but should relate to the section content.

625

Info to Know

Death Statistics Approximately 25 million people in Europe died during the Black Death. Several million are also estimated to have died in the Middle East and Asia, which is considered the most probable source of the plague. In Europe, about one-third to one-half of Europe's population died between 1347 and 1351.

Linking to Today

Plague Is Still Here Outbreaks of plague still occur today, mostly in rural communities or in urban areas with infected rats and rat fleas. In the United States about 10 to 15 cases of plague appear every year, mostly in the southwestern states. Worldwide, about 1,000 to 3,000 cases are reported. Today antibiotics, which did not exist in the Middle Ages, can cure plague if the patient is treated in time.

Connect to Science

Low Immunity When the Black Death hit Europe, the population was especially vulnerable to disease. Many people had a low level of immunity resulting from a famine between 1315 and 1322. A typhoid epidemic and an occurrence of anthrax in animals also led to economic hardship throughout Europe.

About the Illustration

This illustration is an artist's conception based on available sources. However, historians are uncertain exactly what this scene looked like.

Geography and History

The Black Death

"And they died by the hundreds," wrote one man who saw the horror, "both day and night." The Black Death had arrived. The Black Death was a series of deadly plagues that hit Europe between 1347 and 1351, killing millions. People didn't know what caused the plague. They also didn't know that geography played a key role in its spread—as people traveled to trade, they unwittingly carried the disease with them to new places.

CENTRAL ASIA

EUROPE

Kaffa

CHINA

The plague probably began in central and eastern Asia. These arrows show how it spread into and through Europe.

AFRICA

This ship has just arrived in Europe from the east with trade goods—and rats with fleas.

The fleas carry the plague and jump onto a man unloading the ship. Soon, he will get sick and die.

626   CHAPTER 19

Critical Thinking: Understanding Cause and Effect   At Level

Charting the Black Death's Effects

1. Have students clarify the effects of the Black Death by creating a cause-and-effect diagram.

2. Ask students to review the information about the Black Death in their textbooks. Then have them record its effects in a cause-and-effect flow chart. **LS** **Visual/Spatial, Verbal/Linguistic**

   Alternative Assessment Handbook, Rubrics 6: Cause and Effect; and 13: Graphic Organizers

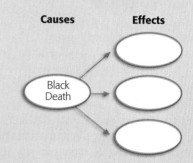

Causes   Effects

Black
Death

The plague is so terrifying that many people think it's the end of the world. They leave town for the country, spreading the Black Death even further.

People dig mass graves to bury the dead. But often, so many victims are infected that there is no one left to bury them.

The garbage and dirty conditions in the town provide food and a home for the rats, allowing the disease to spread even more.

So many people die so quickly that special carts are sent through the streets to gather the bodies.

ANALYSIS SKILL **ANALYZING VISUALS**

1. **Movement** How did the Black Death reach Europe from Asia?
2. **Place** What helped spread the plague within Europe?

GROWTH AND DEVELOPMENT OF EUROPE **627**

Info to Know

Three Types of Plague There are three types of plague. The first, bubonic plague, is the most common. Symptoms include swellings (buboes) on the neck and in the armpit and groin areas, as well as high fever. Bubonic plague is generally spread by fleas, which carry the bacteria from person to person. The second is a more deadly type of the disease, pneumonic plague, which attacks the lungs. It is highly contagious—the exhaled breath of infected persons spreads it. The third type is septicemic plague, which attacks the blood system and leads to brain damage.

Did you know . . .

The familiar nursery rhyme "Ring Around the Rosie" might have had its origins in the Black Death. The rhyme's lyrics are "Ring around the rosie/ a pocket full of posies/ Ashes, ashes, we all fall down."

Connect to Literature

Read All About It Many works of great literature from the Middle Ages mention the Black Death. Some of these works include *The Decameron* (Boccaccio), *The Canterbury Tales* (Chaucer), and *Piers Plowman* (Langland).

Bellringer

If YOU lived there... Use the **Daily Bellringer Transparency** to help students answer the question.

📖 Daily Bellringer Transparency, Section 2

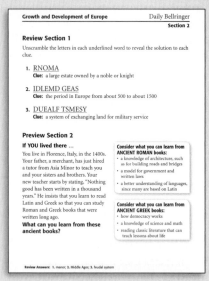

Key Terms and Places

📋 **RF:** Vocabulary Builder, Section 2

Taking Notes

Have students copy the graphic organizer onto their own paper and then use it to take notes on the section. This activity will prepare students for the Section Assessment, in which they will complete a graphic organizer that builds on the information using the Critical Thinking Skill: Finding Main Ideas.

What You Will Learn...

Main Ideas

1. The Renaissance was a period of new learning, new ideas, and new advances in art, literature, and science.
2. The Reformation changed the religious map of Europe.

The Big Idea

The periods of the Renaissance and the Reformation introduced new ideas and new ways of thinking into Europe.

Key Terms and Places

Renaissance, *p. 628*
Florence, *p. 628*
Venice, *p. 628*
humanism, *p. 629*
Reformation, *p. 632*
Protestants, *p. 633*
Catholic Reformation, *p. 633*

TAKING NOTES As you read, use a chart like the one below to help you take notes on the Renaissance and the Reformation.

Renaissance

Reformation

The Renaissance and Reformation

If YOU lived there...

You live in Florence, Italy, in the 1400s. Your father, a merchant, has just hired a tutor from Asia Minor to teach you and your sisters and brothers. Your new teacher starts by stating, "Nothing good has been written in a thousand years." He insists that you learn to read Latin and Greek so that you can study Roman and Greek books that were written long ago.

What can you learn from these ancient books?

BUILDING BACKGROUND The end of the Middle Ages brought important changes to European politics and society. These changes set the stage for an exciting new period of learning and creativity. During this period, new ideas influenced the arts, science, and attitudes toward religion.

The Renaissance

Do you ever get the urge to do something creative? If so, how do you express your creativity? Do you like to draw or paint? Maybe you prefer to write stories or poems or create music.

At the end of the Middle Ages, people across Europe found the urge to be creative. Their creativity was sparked by new ideas and discoveries that were sweeping through Europe at the time. This period of creativity, of new ideas and inspirations, is called the **Renaissance** (REN-uh-sahns). It lasted from about 1350 through the 1500s. *Renaissance* is French for "rebirth." The people who named this period believed it represented a new beginning, or rebirth, in Europe's history and culture.

New Ideas

The Renaissance started in Italy. During and after the Crusades, Italian cities such as **Florence** and **Venice** became rich through trade. Goods from faraway Asia moved through these cities.

The Renaissance and Reformation

1. **Teach** Ask students the questions in the Main Idea boxes under Direct Teach.

2. **Apply** Have students make a three-column chart, labeled Causes, Event, and Effects. In the Event column, have them list *Renaissance* and *Reformation,* leaving at least ten lines of space between the two terms. As they read the lesson, have students list causes of these two events in column one and the effects on European culture in column three. **LS Verbal/Linguistic**

3. **Review** As you review the section's main ideas, discuss how advances in art, literature, and science were influenced by humanism.

4. **Practice/Homework** Have students pick one change that occurred during the Renaissance or Reformation and describe how it has affected art, literature, belief systems, or another aspect of culture.
LS Verbal/Linguistic
📖 Alternative Assessment Handbook, Rubrics 6: Cause and Effect; and 7: Charts

These goods made the people who lived there curious about the larger world. At the same time, scholars from other parts of the world came to Italy. They brought books written by ancient Greeks and Romans.

Inspired by these books and by the ancient ruins around them, some people in Italy became interested in ancient cultures. These people began reading works in Greek and Latin and studying subjects that had been taught in Greek and Roman schools.

These subjects, known as the humanities, included history, poetry, and grammar. Increased study of the humanities led to a new way of thinking and learning known as humanism.

Humanism emphasized the abilities and accomplishments of human beings. The humanists believed that people were capable of great things. As a result, they admired artists, architects, leaders, writers, scientists, and other talented individuals.

THE IMPACT TODAY

American universities grant degrees in the humanities. You might one day get a degree in a humanities field.

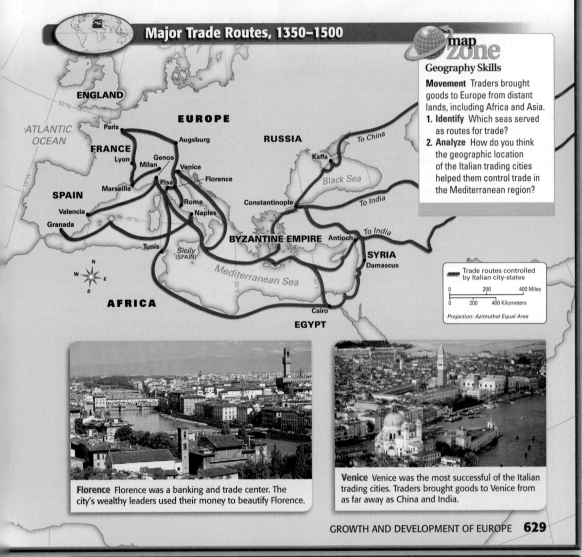

Major Trade Routes, 1350–1500

map Zone

Geography Skills

Movement Traders brought goods to Europe from distant lands, including Africa and Asia.

1. **Identify** Which seas served as routes for trade?
2. **Analyze** How do you think the geographic location of the Italian trading cities helped them control trade in the Mediterranean region?

Trade routes controlled by Italian city-states

0   200   400 Miles
0 200   400 Kilometers

Projection: Azimuthal Equal Area

Florence Florence was a banking and trade center. The city's wealthy leaders used their money to beautify Florence.

Venice Venice was the most successful of the Italian trading cities. Traders brought goods to Venice from as far away as China and India.

GROWTH AND DEVELOPMENT OF EUROPE **629**

The Renaissance, continued

Identify How was Leonardo da Vinci an example of the Renaissance ideal? *He was not just a painter, but also sculptor, architect, engineer, and scientist.*

Describe How did the writings of the Greeks and Romans lead to new inventions? *Inspired by Greek and Roman knowledge, people began to study math, astronomy, and other sciences. They used this new knowledge to create new techniques and inventions.*

Make Inferences What effect did the printing press have on the Renaissance? *It helped spread knowledge of new ideas in art, literature, and science, which resulted in new inventions and other changes.*

Did you know . . .

In the 1490s, Leonardo da Vinci began to fill notebooks with quick sketches of what he saw around him. He first made drawings on tiny paper pads and then copied them into his notebooks. Some drawings reflect his interest in human anatomy, painting, or architecture. Others show his interest in mechanics. One intriguing feature of the notebooks is his use of mirror writing. He wrote his notes in reverse from right to left. To read a page, it had to be held up to a mirror. Scholars are unsure why he wrote this way.

The Renaissance

The Renaissance was a period of great creativity and advances in art, literature, and science.

Renaissance sculptors were careful to show the tiniest details in their works. This statue by Michelangelo is of David, a king of ancient Israel.

Painters like Hans Holbein the Younger wanted to show what real life was like for people in Europe.

Renaissance Art

The Renaissance was a period of talented artistic achievements. Artists of the period created new techniques to improve their work. For example, they developed the technique of perspective, a method of showing a three-dimensional scene on a flat surface so that it looks real.

Many Renaissance artists were also humanists. Humanist artists valued the achievements of individuals. These artists wanted their paintings and sculptures to show people's unique personalities. One of the artists best able to show this sense of personality in his works was the Italian Michelangelo (mee-kay-LAHN-jay-loh). He was both a great painter and sculptor. His statues, like the one of King David above, seem almost to be alive.

Another famous Renaissance artist was Leonardo da Vinci. Leonardo achieved the Renaissance goal of excelling in many areas. He was not only a great painter and sculptor but also an architect, scientist, and engineer. He sketched plants and animals as well as inventions such as a submarine.

He collected knowledge about the human body. Both Leonardo and Michelangelo are examples of what we call Renaissance people—people who can do practically anything well.

Renaissance Literature

Like artists, Renaissance writers expressed the attitudes of the time. The most famous Renaissance writer is probably the English dramatist William Shakespeare. He wrote excellent poetry, but Shakespeare is best known for his plays. They include more than 30 comedies, histories, and tragedies. In his plays, Shakespeare turned popular stories into great drama. His writing shows a deep understanding of human nature and skillfully expresses the thoughts and feelings of his characters. For these reasons, Shakespeare's plays are still highly popular in many parts of the world.

Renaissance writings were read and enjoyed by a larger audience than earlier writings had been. This change was largely due to advances in science and technology, such as the printing press.

Collaborative Learning

Creating an Invitation

1. Organize the class into small groups. Ask students to imagine that they work in the publicity department at a local museum. Their job is to let people in their community know about the opening of a new exhibit on the Renaissance.

2. Assign each group one of these topics: Renaissance Art, Renaissance Drama and Literature, or Renaissance Science and Inventions.

3. As a class, decide when, where, and at what time the exhibit will open. Then have each group prepare an invitation to be sent to community members. The invitation should tell what the exhibit will contain, why people will enjoy it, and what they will learn. It should also give basic information such as time, date, place, and cost. **LS Interpersonal, Verbal/Linguistic**

   Alternative Assessment Handbook, Rubrics 2: Advertisements; and 14: Group Activity

Leonardo da Vinci drew sketches of many devices that were not invented until centuries after his death. This model of a type of helicopter was based on the sketch by Leonardo shown below.

William Shakespeare is considered the greatest of all Renaissance writers. His plays are still read and performed today.

ANALYSIS SKILL **ANALYZING VISUALS**

Based on the sculpture of David and on the Holbein painting, how would you describe Renaissance art?

Renaissance Science

Some of the ancient works rediscovered during the Renaissance dealt with science. For the first time in centuries, Europeans could read about early Greek and Roman scientific advances. Inspired by what they read, some people began to study math, astronomy, and other fields of science.

Using this new scientific knowledge, Europeans developed new inventions and techniques. For example, they learned how to build enormous domes that could rise higher than earlier buildings.

Another invention of the Renaissance was the movable type printing press. A German named Johann Gutenberg built the first movable type printing press in the mid-1400s. This type of printing press could print books quickly and cheaply. For the first time, people could easily share ideas with others in distant areas. The printing press helped the ideas of the Renaissance spread beyond Italy.

READING CHECK **Summarizing** How did life in Europe change during the Renaissance?

CONNECTING TO Technology

The Printing Press

Printing was not a new idea in Renaissance Europe. What was new was the method of printing. Johann Gutenberg designed a printing system called movable type. It used a set of tiny lead blocks, each carved with a letter of the alphabet. These blocks could then be used to spell out an entire page of text for printing. Once copies of the page were made, the printer could reuse the blocks to spell out another page. This was much faster and easier than earlier systems had been.

Generalizing How did movable type improve printing?

Info to Know

Gutenberg Bible With his movable type, Gutenberg could make 16 copies of a page in an hour. His first book, known today as the Gutenberg Bible, was a Latin Bible. It took him about 15 years to raise the money for the project. During that time, he kept his invention secret. When the printing began, Gutenberg and six printers worked full time for more than a year to produce it. Scholars do not know how many copies Gutenberg made originally, but 40 copies of this famous Bible still exist. Some are in the United States. Visitors can see them at the U.S. Library of Congress, the New York Public Library, and at the Harvard University and Yale University libraries.

Activity **Cooperation or Conflict?**
Have students create a three-column chart with the headings: Contribution, Cooperation, and Conflict. Explain that developments in the arts, literature, media, technology, and languages often foster cooperation among people or perpetuate conflict. As students read the chapter, have them record contributions brought on during the Renaissance in the first column of their charts. Then have students write a sentence explaining how each contribution led to cooperation or conflict in Europe in the corresponding column of their charts.
LS Verbal/Linguistic
Alternative Assessment Handbook, Rubric 7: Charts

Cross-Discipline Activity: Language Arts   At Level

Writing a Descriptive Essay

1. Have students discuss the ways Gutenberg's invention of movable type changed life in Europe, such as the spreading of new ideas.

2. As a prewriting activity, list on the board students' ideas of the ways people today rely on printed information, such as newspapers, books, magazines, recipes, and instructions for assembling products.

3. Then have each student write a descriptive essay showing what life in school today

might be like if Gutenberg had not invented the printing press.

4. Ask for volunteers to read their essays to the class or print the essays in a class newspaper.
LS Verbal/Linguistic, Intrapersonal
Alternative Assessment Handbook, Rubrics 11: Discussions; and 40: Writing to Describe

Answers

Reading Check *possible answer— People spent their free time doing creative hobbies, such as painting or writing; people started reading books; schools were filled with people wanting to learn.*

Analyzing Visuals *realistic, because of the attention to detail (David) and emphasis on the lives of ordinary people (Holbein)*

Connecting to Technology *It was faster, easier, and cheaper than earlier printing because type was reusable.*

631

Main Idea

❷ The Reformation

The Reformation changed the religious map of Europe.

Describe Why did Europeans want reform? *Church officials had become too focused on their own power instead of their religious duties.*

Explain What part did Martin Luther play in the Protestant Reformation? *He started the Reformation by posting complaints on a church door in Wittenberg in 1517. Luther's followers then formed their own religion, becoming the first Protestants.*

Draw Conclusions Why did Catholic officials decide to make the reforms known as the Catholic Reformation? *because the Catholic Church wanted to focus more on spiritual matters and help make church teachings easier to understand*

🖳 Map Zone Transparency: Religion in Europe, 1600

The Reformation

By the early 1500s some Europeans had begun to complain about problems they saw in the Roman Catholic Church. For example, they thought the church had become corrupt. In time, their complaints led to a religious reform movement called the **Reformation** (re-fuhr-MAY-shuhn).

The Protestant Reformation

Although people called for church reform in other places, the Reformation began in what is now Germany. This area was part of the Holy Roman Empire. Some people there thought church officials were too focused on their own power and had lost sight of their religious duties.

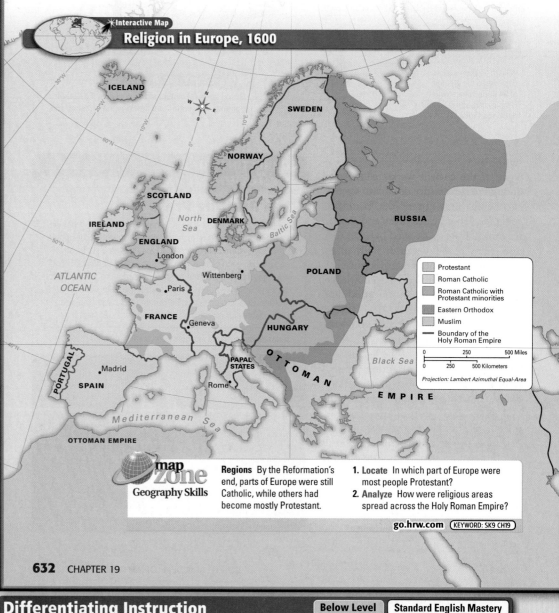

✵ **Interactive Map**

Religion in Europe, 1600

Legend:
- Protestant
- Roman Catholic
- Roman Catholic with Protestant minorities
- Eastern Orthodox
- Muslim
- Boundary of the Holy Roman Empire

0   250   500 Miles
0   250   500 Kilometers
Projection: Lambert Azimuthal Equal-Area

map zone
Geography Skills

Regions By the Reformation's end, parts of Europe were still Catholic, while others had become mostly Protestant.

1. **Locate** In which part of Europe were most people Protestant?
2. **Analyze** How were religious areas spread across the Holy Roman Empire?

go.hrw.com   (KEYWORD: SK9 CH19)

Differentiating Instruction

[Below Level] [Standard English Mastery]

English-Language Learners

1. Give students practice in decoding new words by looking at the words *reform* and *reformation*.

2. Begin by noting that the prefix *re-* means to do something again as in *retell* or to go back and do over as in *return* and *reapply*.

3. Have students take turns suggesting more words that begin with this prefix while other students suggest definitions.

4. Then focus on the word *reformation*. Tell students that the suffix *–ation* means "the act of doing something." Have students use a dictionary to find and define the root word *reform* and then the word *reformation*.

5. Ask students to use standard English to explain why these Protestant and Catholic movements are called *reformations*.

LS **Verbal/Linguistic**

📃 Alternative Assessment Handbook, Rubric 1: Acquiring Information

Answers

Map Zone 1. *northern Europe;*
2. *The northern part of the empire and Geneva were mainly Protestant; the western and southern parts were mainly Roman Catholic; the eastern part was mainly Roman Catholic with Protestant minorities.*

One of the first people to express protests against the Catholic Church was a German monk named Martin Luther. In 1517 Luther nailed a list of complaints to a church door in the town of Wittenberg. Luther's protests angered church officials, who soon expelled him from the church. In response, Luther's followers formed a separate church. They became the first **Protestants**, Christians who broke from the Catholic Church over religious issues.

Other reformers who followed Luther began creating churches of their own as well. The Roman Catholic Church was no longer the only church in Western Europe. As you can see on the map, many areas of Europe had become Protestant by 1600.

The Catholic Reformation

Protestants were not the only ones who called for reform in the Roman Catholic Church. Many Catholic officials wanted to reform the church as well. Even as the first Protestants were breaking away from the church, Catholic officials were launching a series of reforms that became known as the **Catholic Reformation**.

As part of the Catholic Reformation, church leaders began focusing more on spiritual concerns and less on political power. They also worked to make church teachings easier for people to understand. To tell people about the changes, church leaders sent priests and teachers all over Europe. Church leaders also worked to spread Catholic teachings into Asia, Africa, and other parts of the world.

Religious Wars

The Reformation caused major changes to the religious map of Europe. Catholicism, once the main religion in most of Europe, was no longer so dominant. In many areas, especially in the north, Protestants now outnumbered Catholics.

In some parts of Europe, Catholics and Protestants lived together in peace. In some other places, however, this was not the case. Bloody religious wars broke out in France, Germany, the Netherlands, and Switzerland. Wars between religious groups left parts of Europe in ruins.

These religious wars led to political and social changes in Europe. For example, many people began relying less on what church leaders and other authority figures told them. Instead, people raised questions and began looking to science for answers.

FOCUS ON READING
Based on the highlighted text, what can you assume about Protestants' religious beliefs?

READING CHECK Finding Main Ideas How did Europe change after the Reformation?

SUMMARY AND PREVIEW In the 1300s through the 1500s, new ideas changed Europe's culture. Next, you will learn about ideas that changed its politics.

Section 2 Assessment

go.hrw.com
Online Quiz
KEYWORD: SK9 HP19

Reviewing Ideas, Terms, and Places

1. **a. Define** What was the **Renaissance**?
   b. Summarize What were some changes made in art during the Renaissance?
   c. Elaborate How did the printing press help spread Renaissance ideas?
2. **a. Describe** What led to the **Reformation**?
   b. Explain Why did church leaders launch the series of reforms known as the **Catholic Reformation**?

Critical Thinking

3. **Finding Main Ideas** Draw a chart like the one shown. Use your notes to describe new ideas of the Renaissance and the Reformation. Add rows as needed.

Idea	Description

FOCUS ON WRITING

4. **Describing Renaissance and Reformation Figures** Which people from this period might make good diary writers? Take some notes about key figures.

Section 2 Assessment Answers

1. **a.** period from about 1350 to 1500 that focused on creativity, new ideas, and inventions
   b. perspective, greater attention to detail, people in artworks became individuals, focus on life of ordinary Europeans
   c. Books became faster, easier, and less costly to create.
2. **a.** Church officials focused more on power than on religious duties.
   b. to focus more on spiritual matters and spread Catholic teachings

3. possible responses—perspective: shows three dimensions; movable type: made books more available; Protestantism: called for church reform
4. Students might mention Michelangelo, Leonardo da Vinci, Shakespeare, Gutenberg, Luther in their notes.

Linking to Today

Religious Orders One of the most successful Catholic Reformation responses to the Protestant Reformation was the founding of new religious orders. Their missionary work brought thousands of converts to Catholicism worldwide. The Jesuit order led this effort. Founded by Spaniard Ignatius Loyola in 1534, it helped spread Catholicism to Asia and the Americas, especially India and Brazil. The Jesuits have also left a strong legacy in the United States. Today students can attend 28 Jesuit universities and colleges, including Loyola University in Chicago; Holy Cross in Worcester, Massachusetts; Georgetown University in Washington, D.C.; and Loyola University in New Orleans.

● Review & Assess ●

Close

Briefly review the causes and the effects of the Renaissance and the Protestant Reformation on Europe.

Review

Online Quiz, Section 2

Assess

SE Section 2 Assessment
PASS: Section 2 Quiz
Alternative Assessment Handbook

Reteach/Classroom Intervention

Interactive Reader and Study Guide, Section 2
Interactive Skills Tutor CD-ROM

Answers

Focus on Reading that they were significantly different than Catholics' religious beliefs

Reading Check *Catholicism was no longer as widespread; Protestants outnumbered Catholics in some areas; wars broke out in France, Germany, the Netherlands, and Switzerland.*

Bellringer

If YOU lived there. . . Use the **Daily Bellringer Transparency** to help students answer the question.

📖 Daily Bellringer Transparency, Section 3

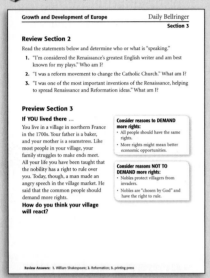

Growth and Development of Europe — Daily Bellringer — Section 3

Review Section 2

Read the statements below and determine who or what is "speaking."

1. "I'm considered the Renaissance's greatest English writer and am best known for my plays." Who am I?
2. "I was a reform movement to change the Catholic Church." What am I?
3. "I was one of the most important inventions of the Renaissance, helping to spread Renaissance and Reformation ideas." What am I?

Preview Section 3

If YOU lived there ...
You live in a village in northern France in the 1700s. Your father is a baker, and your mother is a seamstress. Like most people in your village, your family struggles to make ends meet. All your life you have been taught that the nobility has a right to rule over you. Today, though, a man made an angry speech in the village market. He said that the common people should demand more rights. **How do you think your village will react?**

Consider reasons to DEMAND more rights:
- All people should have the same rights.
- More rights might mean better economic opportunities.

Consider reasons NOT TO DEMAND more rights:
- Nobles protect villagers from invaders.
- Nobles are "chosen by God" and have the right to rule.

Review Answers: 1. William Shakespeare; 2. Reformation; 3. printing press

Academic Vocabulary

Review with students the high-use academic term in this section.

purpose the reason something is done (p. 635)

📖 RF: Vocabulary Builder, Section 3

Taking Notes

Have students copy the graphic organizer onto their own paper and then use it to take notes on the section. This activity will prepare students for the Section Assessment in which they will complete a graphic organizer that builds on the information using the Critical Thinking Skill: Sequencing.

Political Change in Europe

What You Will Learn...

Main Ideas

1. During the Enlightenment, new ideas about government took hold in Europe.
2. The 1600s and 1700s were an Age of Revolution in Europe.
3. Napoleon Bonaparte conquered much of Europe after the French Revolution.

The Big Idea

Ideas of the Enlightenment inspired revolutions and new governments in Europe.

Key Terms

Enlightenment, *p. 634*
English Bill of Rights, *p. 636*
Declaration of Independence, *p. 637*
Declaration of the Rights of Man and of the Citizen, *p. 638*
Reign of Terror, *p. 638*

TAKING NOTES As you read, use a chart like this one to describe the ideas of the Enlightenment and the events they inspired.

Ideas of the Enlightenment

↓

Events inspired by the Enlightenment

If YOU lived there...

You live in a village in northern France in the 1700s. Your father is a baker, and your mother is a seamstress. Like most people in your village, your family struggles to make ends meet. All your life you have been taught that the nobility has a right to rule over you. Today, though, a man made an angry speech in the village market. He said that the common people should demand more rights.

How do you think your village will react?

BUILDING BACKGROUND The Renaissance and the Reformation expanded Europeans' knowledge and changed life in many ways. The 1600s and 1700s brought still more changes. Some people began to use reason to improve government and society.

The Enlightenment

Think about the last time you faced a problem that required careful thought. Perhaps you were working a complex math problem or trying to figure out how to win a game. Whatever the problem, when you thought carefully about how to solve it, you were using your power to reason, or to think logically.

The Age of Reason

During the 1600s and 1700s a number of people began to put great importance on reason, or logical thought. They started using reason to challenge long-held beliefs about education, government, law, and religion. By using reason, these people hoped to solve problems such as poverty and war. They believed the use of reason could achieve three great goals—knowledge, freedom, and happiness—and thereby improve society. The use of reason in shaping people's ideas about society and politics defined a period called the **Enlightenment**. Because of its focus on reason, this period is also known as the Age of Reason.

Teach the Big Idea

At Level

Political Change in Europe

1. **Teach** Ask students the questions in the Main Idea boxes under Direct Teach.

2. **Apply** Write these statements on the board: "Give Me Liberty or Give Me Death," "Liberty, Equality, Fraternity," and "Free at Last, Free at Last." Ask students what periods in history these statements are associated with. (*American Revolution, French Revolution, U.S. Civil Rights Movement*) Ask students what these statements have in common. (*emphasis on individual freedoms*) **LS Verbal/Linguistic**

3. **Review** Have students skim the lesson, looking at headings and illustrations. Have them suggest ways these statements might be related to the content of this section. Ask them to make predictions about how political change in Europe might have affected the lives of Europeans.

4. **Practice/Homework** Have students create a slogan to encourage support for one of the political changes they will read about in this section. **LS Verbal/Linguistic**

📖 Alternative Assessment Handbook, Rubric 34: Slogans and Banners

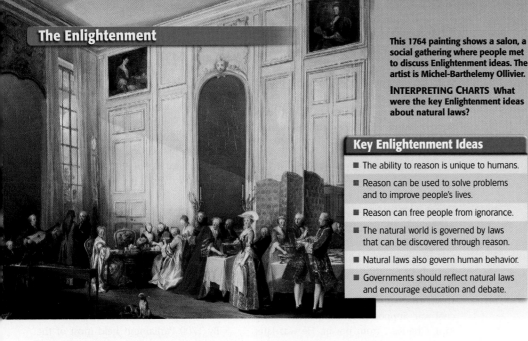

This 1764 painting shows a salon, a social gathering where people met to discuss Enlightenment ideas. The artist is Michel-Barthelemy Ollivier.

INTERPRETING CHARTS What were the key Enlightenment ideas about natural laws?

Key Enlightenment Ideas

- The ability to reason is unique to humans.
- Reason can be used to solve problems and to improve people's lives.
- Reason can free people from ignorance.
- The natural world is governed by laws that can be discovered through reason.
- Natural laws also govern human behavior.
- Governments should reflect natural laws and encourage education and debate.

New Ideas about Government

During the Enlightenment, some people used reason to examine government. They questioned how governments worked and what the **purpose** of government should be. In doing so, these people developed completely new ideas about government. These ideas would help lead to the creation of modern democracy.

At the time of the Enlightenment, monarchs, or kings and queens, ruled in most of Europe. Many of these monarchs believed they ruled through divine right. That is, they thought God gave them the right to rule however they chose.

Some people challenged rule by divine right. They thought rulers' powers should be limited to protect people's freedoms. These people said government's purpose was to protect and to serve the people.

John Locke, an English philosopher, had a major influence on Enlightenment thinking about the role of government.

Locke thought government should be a **contract** between a ruler and the people. A contract binds both sides, so it would limit the ruler's power. Locke also believed that all people had certain natural rights, such as life, liberty, and property. If a ruler did not protect these natural rights, people had the right to change rulers.

Other scholars built on Locke's ideas. One was Jean-Jacques Rousseau (roo-SOH). He said government should express the will, or desire, of the people. According to Rousseau, citizens give the government the power to make and enforce laws. But if these laws do not serve the people, the government should give up its power.

These Enlightenment ideas spread far and wide. In time, they would inspire some Europeans to rise up against their rulers.

ACADEMIC VOCABULARY

purpose
the reason something is done

READING CHECK **Contrasting** How did Enlightenment ideas about government differ from the views of most monarchs?

GROWTH AND DEVELOPMENT OF EUROPE **635**

Differentiating Instruction

| At Level | Standard English Mastery |

English-Language Learners

1. Write the term *Enlightenment* on the board. Have a student come to the board and find the root word *light*. Have students suggest any connections the word *light* might have to the period students are learning about.

2. Using a different color, circle *Enlighten*. Have students suggest possible meanings for this word. (*to shed light on, instruct or teach, furnish knowledge of, or free from superstition or misinformation*)

3. Have students review the Enlightenment chart on this page. Ask them to explain why the main ideas outlined in this chart were described as *enlightened*.

4. For additional practice, students might decode the words *enlarge, enlargement, enslave,* and *enslavement*, looking at prefixes and suffixes as well as root words, and use them in complete sentences.

LS **Verbal/Linguistic**

Alternative Assessment Handbook, Rubric 1: Acquiring Information

---

635

❷ The Age of Revolution

The 1600s and 1700s were an Age of Revolution in Europe.

Recall What did the English Bill of Rights do? *listed the rights of the Parliament and the English people; gave Parliament the power to pass laws and raise taxes*

Explain How did the English Bill of Rights and the Magna Carta change the relationship between the monarchy and the Parliament in England? *ended monarch's divine right to rule and gave most political power to Parliament*

Analyze How did the Declaration of the Rights of Man and of the Citizen respond to the problems that led to the French Revolution? *gave more rights and freedoms to Third Estate; greater voice in government through National Assembly; made taxation fairer*

Connect to Government

Bill of Rights Many of the rights guaranteed to American citizens by the Bill of Rights in the U.S. Constitution, came from the English Bill of Rights and Magna Carta. These documents greatly influenced the framers of the U.S. Constitution. The English Bill of Rights gave no new rights to Englishmen, but restated their existing rights, such as trial by jury and denial of cruel and unusual punishment.

The Age of Revolution

The 1600s and 1700s were a time of great change in Europe. Some changes were peaceful, such as those in science. Other changes were more violent. In England, North America, and France, new ideas about government led to war and the Age of Revolution.

Civil War and Reform in England

In England, Enlightenment ideas led to conflict between the monarchs, or rulers, and Parliament, the lawmaking body. For many years England's rulers had shared power with Parliament. The relationship was an uneasy one, however. As rulers and Parliament fought for power, the situation grew worse.

In 1642 the power struggle erupted in civil war. Supporters of Parliament forced King Charles I from power. He was later tried and beheaded. A new government then formed, but it was unstable.

By 1660 many of the English were tired of instability. They wanted to restore the monarchy. They asked the former king's son to rule England as Charles II. However, Charles had to agree to let Parliament keep powers it had gained during the civil war.

In 1689 Parliament further limited the monarch's power. That year, it approved the **English Bill of Rights**. This document listed rights for Parliament and the English people. For example, it gave Parliament the power to pass laws and to raise taxes.

In addition, Parliament made the king promise to honor Magna Carta. Signed in 1215, this document limited the English ruler's power and protected some rights of the people. However, few monarchs had honored it during the previous 400 years. Parliament wanted to be sure future rulers honored Magna Carta.

By 1700 Parliament held most of the political power in England. Divine right to rule had ended for England's monarchy.

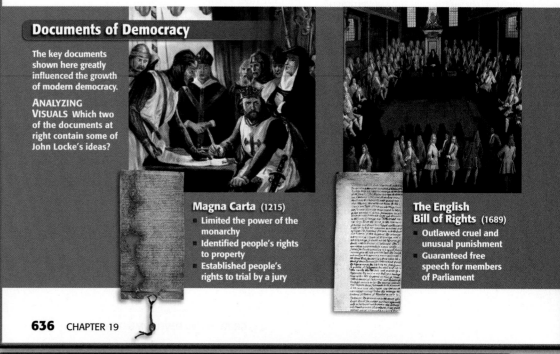

Documents of Democracy

The key documents shown here greatly influenced the growth of modern democracy.

ANALYZING VISUALS Which two of the documents at right contain some of John Locke's ideas?

Magna Carta (1215)
- Limited the power of the monarchy
- Identified people's rights to property
- Established people's rights to trial by a jury

The English Bill of Rights (1689)
- Outlawed cruel and unusual punishment
- Guaranteed free speech for members of Parliament

Critical Thinking: Comparing

Writing an Opinion Piece

1. Have students make a three-columned chart comparing the power struggles or revolutions that occurred during the Age of Revolution. Have students label the columns: *England, United States, France.*

2. Then have students compare, one at a time, the English civil war and reforms, the American Revolution, and the French Revolution in terms of their causes, goals, methods, achievements, and long-term consequences.

3. When students have completed their comparisons, have them pick the conflict they consider most successful. Students should then write a short opinion piece explaining their choice. **LS Verbal/Linguistic**

Alternative Assessment Handbook, Rubric 43, Writing to Persuade

Answers

Analyzing Visuals *U.S. Declaration of Independence, French Declaration of the Rights of Man and of the Citizen*

The American Revolution

In time, Enlightenment ideas spread to the British colonies in North America. There, the British ruler's power was not limited as it was in England. For this reason, many colonists had grown unhappy with British rule. These colonists began to protest the British laws that they thought were unfair.

In 1775 the protests turned to violence, starting the Revolutionary War. Colonial leaders, influenced by the ideas of Locke and Rousseau, claimed Great Britain had denied their rights. In July 1776 they signed the **Declaration of Independence**. Largely written by Thomas Jefferson, this document declared the American colonies' independence from Britain. A new nation, the United States of America, was born.

In 1783 the United States officially won its independence. The colonists had successfully put Enlightenment ideas into practice. Their success would inspire many other people, particularly in France.

The French Revolution

The people of France closely watched the events of the American Revolution. Soon, they grew inspired to fight for their own rights in the French Revolution.

A major cause of the French Revolution was anger over the differences between social classes. In France, the king ruled over a society split into three classes called estates. The Catholic clergy made up the First Estate. They enjoyed many benefits. Nobles belonged to the Second Estate. These people held important positions in military, government, and the courts. The majority of the French people were members of the Third Estate. This group included peasants, craftworkers, and shopkeepers.

Many Third Estate members thought France's classes were unfair. These people were poor and often hungry. Yet, they paid the highest taxes. While they suffered, King Louis XVI held fancy parties, and Queen Marie-Antoinette wore costly clothes.

Direct Teach

MISCONCEPTION ALERT

Queen Marie-Antoinette Marie-Antoinette of France is often noted for saying, "Let them eat cake." She is thought to have said this to answer complaints that the poor people had no bread and that the privileged classes were letting them starve. However, there is no firm proof that she ever said this. The quote comes from Rousseau's book *Confessions*. He attributed the callous remark to an unnamed "young princess." Like her husband, King Louis XVI, Marie-Antoinette was also guillotined.

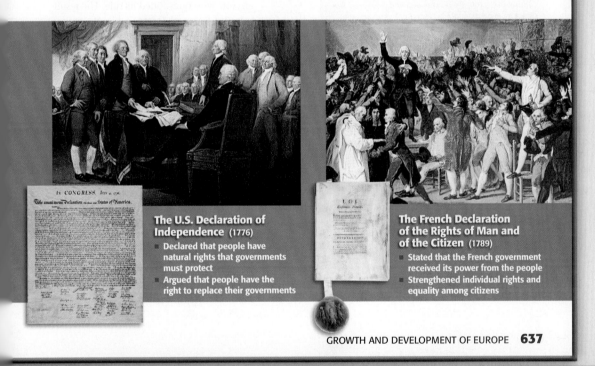

The U.S. Declaration of Independence (1776)
- Declared that people have natural rights that governments must protect
- Argued that people have the right to replace their governments

The French Declaration of the Rights of Man and of the Citizen (1789)
- Stated that the French government received its power from the people
- Strengthened individual rights and equality among citizens

GROWTH AND DEVELOPMENT OF EUROPE **637**

Collaborative Learning

At Level

Documents of Democracy Hall of Fame

Research Required

1. Organize the class into four groups. Assign each group one these documents: English Bill of Rights, Magna Carta, Declaration of Independence, and Declaration of the Rights of Man and of the Citizen.

2. Have each group prepare a large poster that includes the date of the document, key ideas, and an illustration showing at least one of its key ideas.

3. Using books, encyclopedias, or the Internet, have each group choose one quote

from or about this document to include on the poster. Each group should also choose a spokesperson. Have each group prepare a short speech for their spokesperson, explaining their poster and why their document should be in the Documents of Democracy Hall of Fame.

4. When all groups have completed their posters and speech, ask the spokespersons to stand in different parts of the room with their posters. These areas will be listening

stations. Have the rest of the groups circulate around the room, viewing the other posters and listening to each speech in turn.

5. When groups have visited the other stations, ask them to explain why each document should—or should not—be included in the Documents of Democracy Hall of Fame. **LS** Visual/Spatial, Kinesthetic

Alternative Assessment Handbook, Rubrics 28: Posters; and 29: Presentations

Direct Teach

Info to Know

Bastille Day In France, July 14 is an official holiday known as Bastille Day. For the more than 125 years since it was first declared an official holiday, French people throughout the world have celebrated it with music, fireworks, and parades. This holiday commemorates the day in 1789 when revolutionaries captured the Bastille and released the seven prisoners there. The prison had long been a symbol for the harsh rule of France's kings. However, by the late 1700s, the prison was rarely used. Nonetheless, it became a focal point for the anger of the mob.

Did you know . . .

The French national anthem, *La Marseillaise*, was written during the French Revolution by an army captain, Rouget de Lisle, at the request of the army's general who wanted a battle march for his troops. Revolutionaries gave copies of the song to troops marching from the port city of Marseilles to Paris. They came into Paris singing it and thus it became known as *La Marseillaise*. During the French Empire, Napoleon banned the song—as did a later French king and Napoleon III.

Answers

Analyzing Visuals *cannons, guns, spears, clubs*

Reading Check *They were familiar with Enlightenment ideas and opposed to the unfair class system, unfair taxes, and the failure of Louis XVI to accept constitutional limits on his powers.*

638

Meanwhile, France's government was deeply in debt. To raise money, Louis XVI wanted to tax the wealthy. He called a meeting of the representatives of the three estates to discuss a tax increase.

The meeting did not go smoothly. Some members of the Third Estate were familiar with Enlightenment ideas. These members demanded a greater voice in the meeting's decisions. Eventually, the Third Estate members formed a separate group called the National Assembly. This group demanded that the French king accept a constitution limiting his powers.

Louis XVI refused, which angered the common people of Paris. On July 14, 1789, this anger led a mob to storm the Bastille, a prison in Paris. The mob released the prisoners and destroyed the building. The French Revolution had begun.

The Storming of the Bastille

On July 14, 1789, a mob stormed and destroyed the Bastille, a prison in Paris. To many French people, this prison symbolized the king's harsh rule.

ANALYZING VISUALS What were some weapons used in the French Revolution?

The French Revolution quickly spread to the countryside. In events called the Great Fear, peasants took revenge on landlords and other nobles for long years of poor treatment. In their rage, the peasants burned down houses and monasteries.

At the same time, other leaders of the revolution were taking peaceful steps. The National Assembly wrote and approved the **Declaration of the Rights of Man and of the Citizen**. This 1789 French constitution guaranteed French citizens some rights and made taxes fairer. Among the freedoms the constitution supported were the freedoms of speech, of the press, and of religion.

The French Republic

In time, revolutionary leaders created a French republic. The new republic did not end France's many growing problems, however. Unrest soon returned.

In 1793 the revolutionaries executed Louis XVI. His execution was the first of many as the government began arresting anyone who questioned its rule. The result was the **Reign of Terror**, a bloody period of the French Revolution during which the government executed thousands of its opponents and others at the guillotine (GEE-uh-teen). This device beheaded victims with a large, heavy blade. The Reign of Terror finally ended when one of its own leaders was executed in 1794.

Although a violent period, the French Revolution did achieve some of its goals. French peasants and workers gained new political rights. The government opened new schools and improved wages. In addition, it ended slavery in France's colonies.

The French republic's leaders struggled, though. As problems grew worse, a strong leader rose up to take control.

READING CHECK Analyzing Why did many members of the Third Estate support revolution?

Differentiating Instruction

Struggling Readers `Below Level`

1. Have students review the information on the French Revolution. Then ask them to make a graphic organizer, showing the three social classes, or estates, that made up French society at the time of the French Revolution (*for example, a pyramid with three levels*).

2. Have students write labels for each class and add two or three symbols to represent the people of each class. **LS Visual/Spatial**

   Alternative Assessment handbook, Rubric 13: Graphic Organizers

Advanced/Gifted and Talented `Above Level`

1. Read aloud the following quote from John Locke: "The end [purpose] of law is not to abolish or restrain, but to preserve and enlarge freedom . . . where there is no law there is no freedom." Have students discuss what they think Locke meant by this quote.

2. Then ask each student to write a paragraph explaining how the quote applies to the Reign of Terror. **LS Verbal/Linguistic**

   Alternative Assessment Handbook, Rubric 42: Writing to Inform

Jacques-Louis David painted this scene of Napoleon crowning his wife, Josephine, empress after crowning himself emperor. The coronation took place in 1804 in Notre Dame Cathedral in Paris, France.

ANALYZING VISUALS How does the event show Napoleon's power?

Napoleonic Empire, 1812

Napoleon Bonaparte

In 1799 France was ripe for a change in leadership. That year, Napoleon Bonaparte, a 30-year-old general, took control. Many French people welcomed him because he seemed to support the Revolution's goals. His popularity grew quickly, and in 1804 Napoleon crowned himself emperor.

Military Conquests and Rule

Napoleon was a brilliant military leader. Under his command, the French army won a series of dazzling victories. By 1810 France's empire stretched across Europe.

In France, Napoleon restored order. He created an efficient government, made taxes fairer, and formed a system of public education. Perhaps his most important accomplishment was the creation of a new French legal system, the Napoleonic Code.

This legal code reflected the ideals of the French Revolution, such as equality before the law and equal civil rights.

With these many accomplishments, Napoleon sounds like a perfect leader. But he was not. He harshly punished anyone who opposed or questioned his rule.

Napoleon's Defeat

In the end, bad weather contributed to Napoleon's downfall. In 1812 he led an invasion of Russia. The invasion was a disaster. Bitterly cold weather and smart Russian tactics forced Napoleon's army to retreat. Many French soldiers died.

Great Britain, Prussia, and Russia then joined forces and in 1814 defeated Napoleon's weakened army. He returned a year later with a new army, but was again defeated. The British then exiled him to an island, where he died in 1821.

GROWTH AND DEVELOPMENT OF EUROPE **639**

Info to Know

Congress of Vienna Most European nations attended the conference that redrew the map of Europe. However, just four nations—Austria, Prussia, Russia, and Great Britain—made the real decisions. These four nations had been most responsible for Napoleon's defeat. Despite France's defeat, the negotiating skills of the French diplomat Talleyrand enabled France to be admitted to the bargaining table. The resulting settlement lasted almost half a century.

🔧 Map Zone Transparency: Europe after the Congress of Vienna, 1815

Review & Assess

Close

Have students explain how ideas of the Enlightenment influenced the revolutions and reforms of the 1600s and 1700s in Europe.

Review

📲 Online Quiz, Section 3

Assess

SE Section 3 Assessment

📝 PASS: Section 3 Quiz

📝 Alternative Assessment Handbook

Reteach/Classroom Intervention

📝 Interactive Reader and Study Guide, Section 3

💿 Interactive Skills Tutor CD-ROM

Answers

Map Zone 1. *Ottoman; Austrian; Russian;* **2.** *rise—bordered by many of the states it conquered, shorter supply lines; fall—far from Russia, long supply lines*

Reading Check *possible answer—His armies had conquered them and made them subjects of the French Empire.*

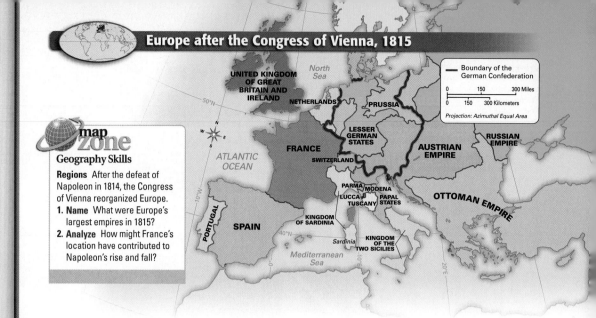

Europe after the Congress of Vienna, 1815

Boundary of the German Confederation
0   150   300 Miles
0   150   300 Kilometers
Projection: Azimuthal Equal Area

map zone

Geography Skills

Regions After the defeat of Napoleon in 1814, the Congress of Vienna reorganized Europe.
1. **Name** What were Europe's largest empires in 1815?
2. **Analyze** How might France's location have contributed to Napoleon's rise and fall?

In 1814 European leaders met at the Congress of Vienna. There, they redrew the map of Europe. Their goal was to keep any country from ever becoming powerful enough to threaten Europe again.

READING CHECK **Drawing Inferences** Why did other countries want to defeat Napoleon?

SUMMARY AND PREVIEW You have read how new ideas about government arose out of the Enlightenment. These ideas led to revolutions and political change in Europe and elsewhere. Next, you will read about the growth of industry and how it changed European society.

Section 3 Assessment

go.hrw.com
Online Quiz
KEYWORD: SK9 HP19

Reviewing Ideas, Terms, and Places

1. **a. Define** What does divine right mean?
   b. Explain What did **Enlightenment** thinkers believe the purpose of government should be?
2. **a. Describe** What was the significance of the **English Bill of Rights**?
   b. Make Inferences Why do you think many Americans consider Thomas Jefferson a hero?
   c. Evaluate How successful do you think the French Revolution was? Explain your answer.
3. **a. Identify** Who was Napoleon Bonaparte, and what were his main accomplishments?
   b. Analyze How were Napoleon's forces weakened and then defeated?

Critical Thinking

4. **Sequencing** Review your notes. Then use a time line like the one here to list the main events of the Age of Revolution. List the events in the order in which they occurred.

FOCUS ON WRITING

5. **Describing Political Change in Europe** If you were to write a diary as a person from this period, how would you describe the exciting political changes around you? Write down some ideas in your notebook.

640 CHAPTER 19

Section 3 Assessment Answers

1. **a.** Monarchs thought God gave them the right to rule however they chose.
   b. protect people's freedom and serve the people
2. **a.** limited the monarch's power by listing rights of Parliament and the English people
   b. He wrote the Declaration of Independence.
   c. It was a mixed success. Peasants and workers gained new rights, and slavery ended in French colonies. However, the Reign of Terror killed thousands and was followed by Napoleon's dictatorship.
3. **a.** ruler of France; created a French empire, efficient government, and new legal system
   b. weakened in Russia and defeated in 1814 and 1815 by combined European forces
4. Students' time lines will vary but might include: civil war in England (1642) and its approval of the Bill of Rights (1689), the Declaration of Independence (1776), and the storming of the Bastille (1789).
5. Students' notes will vary but should include notes about events from this section.

John Locke

Would you risk arrest for your beliefs in people's rights?

When did he live? 1632–1704

Where did he live? England and the Netherlands

What did he do? Locke worked as a professor, physician, and government official. He wrote about the human mind, science, government, religion, and other topics.

Why is he important? Locke believed in the right of common people to think and worship as they pleased and to own property. He also had great faith in science and people's basic goodness. Not everyone liked his ideas. At one point Locke fled to Holland to avoid arrest by political enemies. Locke's ideas have inspired political reforms in the West for some 300 years.

Drawing Inferences Why do you think some people disliked Locke's ideas?

KEY IDEAS

" Men being, as has been said, by nature, all free, equal, and independent, no one can be . . . subjected to the political power of another, without his own consent. The only way whereby any one divests himself of his natural liberty . . . is by agreeing with other men to join and unite into a community. "

–John Locke, from *Second Treatise of Civil Government*

THE
WORKS
OF
JOHN LOCKE, Esq;

In Three Volumes.

The CONTENTS of which follow in the next Leaf.
With Alphabetical Tables.

VOL. I.
The FOURTH EDITION.

LONDON.

This book printed in 1740 is a collection of John Locke's writings.

GROWTH AND DEVELOPMENT OF EUROPE **641**

Critical Thinking: Summarizing

`At Level`

Defending John Locke

`Standard English Mastery`

1. Point out that Locke spent the years from 1683 to 1689 in Holland to avoid arrest by the British government.

2. Have students write letters to the editor of a newspaper defending Locke and his views and stating logical reasons why the government should let him live in peace.

3. Call on volunteers to read their letters to the class.

4. After a student has read his or her letter aloud, have other students suggest words that could be substituted for some words in the letter. Provide dictionaries or thesauri for this purpose so students can practice standard English mastery.
LS Verbal/Linguistic, Logical/Mathematical

📖 Alternative Assessment Handbook, Rubric 17: Letters to Editors

---

Reading Focus Question

Remind students that around the world today, many people don't have the basic freedoms that we take for granted. Ask students what rights they would defend and what they would give up in defense of those rights.

Info to Know

Voltaire on Locke Voltaire wrote this about John Locke: "Perhaps no man ever had a more judicious or more methodical genius, or was a more acute logician than Mr. Locke, and yet he was not deeply skilled in the mathematics. This great man could never subject himself to the tedious fatigue of calculations, nor to the dry pursuit of mathematical truths . . . and no one has given better proofs than he, that it is possible for a man to have a geometrical head without the assistance of geometry." Ask students what Voltaire thought of Locke, based on this passage. *He admired his logic and methods.*

Linking to Today

Human Rights One of the most notable human rights activists today is Aung San Suu Kyi. For many years, she has worked for peaceful progress toward democracy in Burma, also called Myanmar. In 1991 she received the Nobel Peace Prize for her work. For her fearless activism, Aung San Suu Kyi has endured many years of house arrest.

Answers

Drawing Inferences *possible answers—Nobles may not have liked his ideas about the rights of common people; the church may not have liked his views on science or freedom to worship.*

Bellringer

If YOU lived there. . . Use the **Daily Bellringer Transparency** to help students answer the question.

📖 Daily Bellringer Transparency, Section 4

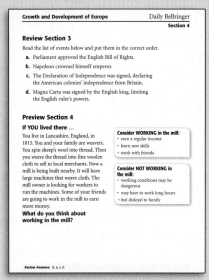

Growth and Development of Europe   Daily Bellringer
                                                    Section 4

Review Section 3

Read the list of events below and put them in the correct order.

a. Parliament approved the English Bill of Rights.

b. Napoleon crowned himself emperor.

c. The Declaration of Independence was signed, declaring the American colonies' independence from Britain.

d. Magna Carta was signed by the English king, limiting the English ruler's powers.

Preview Section 4

If YOU lived there ...

You live in Lancashire, England, in 1815. You and your family are weavers. You spin sheep's wool into thread. Then you weave the thread into fine woolen cloth to sell to local merchants. Now a mill is being built nearby. It will have large machines that weave cloth. The mill owner is looking for workers to run the machines. Some of your friends are going to work in the mill to earn more money.

What do you think about working in the mill?

Consider WORKING in the mill:
• earn a regular income
• learn new skills
• work with friends

Consider NOT WORKING in the mill:
• working conditions may be dangerous
• may have to work long hours
• feel disloyal to family

Review Answers: d, a, c, b

Key Terms

📖 **RF:** Vocabulary Builder, Section 4

Taking Notes

Have students copy the graphic organizer onto their own paper and then use it to take notes on the section. This activity will prepare students for the Section Assessment, in which they will complete a graphic organizer that builds on the information using the Critical Thinking Skill: Identifying Cause and Effect.

The Industrial Revolution

What You Will Learn...

Main Ideas

1. Britain's large labor force, raw materials, and money to invest led to the start of the Industrial Revolution.
2. Industrial growth began in Great Britain and then spread to other parts of Europe.
3. The Industrial Revolution led to both positive and negative changes in society.

The Big Idea

Driven by new ideas and technologies, much of Europe developed industrial societies in the 1700s and 1800s.

Key Terms

Industrial Revolution, *p. 642*
textiles, *p. 644*
capitalism, *p. 644*
suffragettes, *p. 646*

TAKING NOTES As you read, complete a concept web like the one below. To complete the concept web, fill in the outer ovals.

If **YOU** lived there...

You live in Lancashire, England, in 1815. You and your family are weavers. You spin sheep's wool into thread. Then you weave the thread into fine woolen cloth to sell to local merchants. Now a mill is being built nearby. It will have large machines that weave cloth. The mill owner is looking for workers to run the machines. Some of your friends are going to work in the mill to earn more money.

What do you think about working in the mill?

BUILDING BACKGROUND In the mid-1700s great changes in industry revolutionized life in Europe. Like some earlier revolutions, the growth of industry was driven by new inventions and technology. This industrial growth would have far-reaching effects on society.

Start of the Industrial Revolution

Each day, machines from alarm clocks to dishwashers perform many jobs for us. In the early 1700s, however, people had to do most work themselves. They made most of the items they needed by hand. For power, they used animals or water or their own muscles. Then around the mid-1700s, everything changed. People began inventing machines to make goods and supply power. These machines completely changed the way people across Europe worked and lived. We call this period of rapid growth in machine-made goods the **Industrial Revolution**.

From Farmworker to Industrial Laborer

Changes in farming helped pave the way for industrial growth. Since the Middle Ages, farming in Europe had been changing. Wealthy farmers had started buying up land and creating larger farms. These large farms were more efficient. For this reason, many people who owned small farms lost their land. They then had to work for other farmers or move to cities.

Teach the Big Idea   At Level

The Industrial Revolution

1. **Teach** Ask students the questions in the Main Idea boxes under Direct Teach.

2. **Apply** Have each student create an illustrated time line of the Industrial Revolution. The time line should include dates of inventions and drawings related to farming or industry, along with short captions that explain why each invention was important. Have students display their time lines. 🔲 **Visual/Spatial**

3. **Review** Remind students of the military revolutions they have read about in previous

sections of the chapter. Then ask them why the Industrial Revolution is so named when there was no military war. Ask how the two types of events are similar and how they differ.

4. **Practice/Homework** Have students make a list of inventions that are changing the way people live, work, and have fun in the early 2000s. 🔲 **Verbal/Linguistic**

📖 Alternative Assessment Handbook, Rubric 36: Time Lines

At the same time, Europe's growing population was creating a need for more food. To meet this need, farmers began looking for ways to grow more and better crops. Farmers began to experiment with new methods. They also began improving farm technology. Englishman Jethro Tull, for example, invented a seed drill. This device made it possible to plant seeds in straight rows and at certain depths. As a result, more seeds grew into plants.

Better farming methods and technology had several effects. For one, farmers could grow more crops with less labor. With more crops available for food, the population grew even more. With less need for labor, however, many farmworkers lost their jobs. These workers then moved to cities. There, they created a large labor force for the coming industrial growth.

Great Britain's Resources

Great Britain provided the setting for the Industrial Revolution's start. Britain and its colonies had the resources needed for industrial growth. These resources included labor, raw materials, and money to invest. For example, Britain had a large workforce, rich supplies of coal, and many rivers for waterpower.

In addition, Great Britain's colonial markets and its growing population were increasing the demand for manufactured goods. Increased demand led people to look for ways to make goods faster or more easily. In Britain all these things came together to start the Industrial Revolution.

READING CHECK **Identifying Cause and Effect** How did new technology and better farming methods affect agriculture in Europe?

Inventions of the Industrial Revolution

Starting in the mid-1700s, inventions changed the way goods were made. James Hargreaves's spinning jenny, above, made thread quickly. The Bessemer furnace, at left, was an invention of the late Industrial Revolution. The furnace made steel from molten iron.

ANALYZING VISUALS What do you think operating a Bessemer furnace was like?

GROWTH AND DEVELOPMENT OF EUROPE **643**

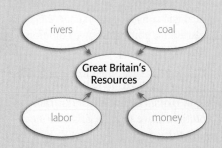

❷ Industrial Growth

Industrial growth began in Great Britain and then spread to other parts of Europe.

Recall How did the Industrial Revolution change how cloth was made? *went from threads for cloth made one at a time on spinning wheels to machines that quickly produced large amounts of cloth*

Evaluate Why did the invention of the steam engine have such a powerful effect on industrial growth? *provided a new energy source that allowed factories to move from nearby rivers to cities; increased demand for coal and iron; led Bessemer to develop a cheap way to convert iron into steel in 1856; led to improved transportation by boat and train*

Compare In what ways was capitalism a new economic system? *Individuals, rather than monarchs or feudal landowners, now owned most businesses and resources; people could invest in businesses, not just land, to make a profit.*

Did you know . . .

Many English workers were upset at the Industrial Revolution's changes. They were afraid of losing their livelihoods to machines. In 1811, for example, bands of workers began breaking into factories at night, destroying textile machines. They called themselves Luddites—and sometimes clashed violently with law enforcement officials. Today a person who is against technological change may be called a Luddite.

Answers

Reading Check *possible answers— leave farm for job opportunities, more money to live on; stay on farm to be close to family and friends, to avoid working conditions in a factory, to have a slower pace of life*

Industrial Growth

THE IMPACT TODAY
New inventions continue to make communication faster and easier. Cell phones and e-mail are just two examples.

Industrial growth began with **textiles**, or cloth products. In the early 1700s people made cloth by hand. They used spinning wheels to make thread and looms to weave it into cloth. Given the time and effort this took, it is not surprising that people would want a way to make cloth quickly.

The Textile Industry

A big step toward manufactured clothing came in 1769. That year, an Englishman, named Richard Arkwright invented a waterpowered spinning machine. Called a water frame, this machine could produce dozens of threads at one time. In contrast, a person using a traditional spinning wheel could produce only one thread at a time.

Other machines sped up production even more. With these new machines, workers could produce large amounts of cloth quickly. As a result, the price of cloth fell. Soon, the British were using machines to make many types of goods. People housed these machines in buildings called factories, and the factories needed power.

Other Inventions

Most early machines ran on waterpower. Thus, factories had to be located by rivers. Although Britain had many rivers, they were not always in desirable locations.

Steam power provided a solution. In the 1760s James Watt, a Scot, built the first modern steam engine. Soon, steam powered most machines. Factories could now be built in better places, such as in cities.

Steam power increased the demand for coal and iron, which were needed to make machinery. Iron can be a brittle metal, though, and iron parts often broke. Then in 1855 Englishman Henry Bessemer developed a cheap way to convert iron into steel, which is stronger. This invention led to the growth of the steel industry.

In addition, new inventions improved transportation and communication. Steam engines powered riverboats and trains, speeding up transportation. The telegraph made communication faster. Instead of sending a note by boat or train, people could go to a telegraph office and instantly send a message over a long distance.

The Factory System

Industrial growth led to major changes in the way people worked and lived. Before, most people had worked on farms or in their homes. Now, more people were going to work in factories. Many of these workers were young women and children, whom owners paid lower wages.

Factory work was long, tiring, and dangerous. Factory workers did the same tasks for 12 hours or more a day, six days a week. Breaks were few, and rules were strict. Although people made more than on farms, wages were still low.

To add to the toil, factory conditions were miserable and unsafe. Year-round, the air was thick with dust, which could harm workers' lungs. In addition, the large machines were dangerous and caused many injuries. Even so, factory jobs were desirable to people with few alternatives.

Spread of Industry

In time, the Industrial Revolution spread from Great Britain to other parts of Europe. By the late 1800s, factories were making goods across much of Western Europe.

The growth of industry helped lead to a new economic system, **capitalism**. In this system, individuals own most businesses and resources. People invest money in businesses in the hope of making a profit.

READING CHECK **Evaluating** If you had lived at this time, would you have left a farm to work in a factory for more money? Why, or why not?

Collaborative Learning

At Level

Creating a Political Cartoon

1. Show students examples of political cartoons. Explain that these cartoons differ from comic books because, like letters to the editor, political cartoons try to persuade the audience of a particular point of view or opinion on a topic.

2. Divide students into small groups. Ask them to imagine that they are political cartoonists living in Britain during the Industrial Revolution. Have them brainstorm ideas about factory conditions. Have students each sketch a rough political cartoon. Then have the group select one draft or parts of several for a chosen artist to draw.

3. Have groups create a caption for their cartoon. Display all cartoons. Have students identify each cartoon's point of view.

LS Interpersonal, Visual/Spatial

Alternative Assessment Handbook, Rubrics 27: Political Cartoons; and 14: Group Activity

Close-up

A British Textile Factory

In early textile factories, workers ran machines in a large room. A supervisor kept a watchful eye. Conditions in factories were poor, and the work was long, tiring, and dangerous. Even so, young women and children as young as six worked in many early factories.

Dust and cotton fibers fill the air, causing breathing problems.

Factory owners keep windows shut to prevent air from blowing the threads. This creates a hot, stuffy room.

One task is to straighten threads as they come out of the machines. This task can cut workers' hands.

Machines are loud. Workers must shout to be heard over the deafening roar.

To avoid being injured or killed, girls must tie back their hair to keep it from getting caught in the machines.

ANALYSIS SKILL   ANALYZING VISUALS

Why do you think the machines in early textile factories caused so many injuries?

GROWTH AND DEVELOPMENT OF EUROPE   **645**

Close-up

A British Textile Factory

Factory Conditions Review the illustration of an early textile factory with students. Ask the following questions:

Identify What might cause hearing damage? *roar of machines*

Explain What made the air hazardous to health? *dust and cotton fibers caused breathing problems and damaged lungs*

Draw Conclusions Why were people willing to work in such dangerous conditions? *few other options for poor, jobless farmworkers; possibly an improvement over drudgery of farm work*

Connect to Civics

Property Rights of British Women In the late 1800s and early 1900s, British women fought for property rights. Until 1870, when a woman married, all her property was legally given to her husband. If she divorced, she lost any property she brought into the marriage. In 1870, Parliament passed the Married Women's Property Act, giving married women the right to keep their earnings and inherit personal property. In 1882, new laws gave married women the right to all property—whether owned before or after marriage.

go.hrw.com
Online Resources

Chapter Resources:
KEYWORD: SK9 CH19
ACTIVITY: Life of a British Textile Factory Worker

Critical Thinking: Solving Problems   At Level

Inside the Factory

1. Divide students into small groups. Have each group study the picture of the textile factory and list the dangers and other safety problems they see.

2. Have each group brainstorm ways to modernize the factory by improving working conditions and safety. Ideas might include safety devices such as air-filtering masks and changes in room design or machinery. Ask each group to list the improvements they would make.

3. Have each group draw a picture of the same textile factory, showing the changes they would make to improve working conditions and safety.

4. As a large group, discuss what changes were possible in the 1800s. Ask students to brainstorm how factory conditions could realistically have been improved back then.
LS Visual/Spatial, Verbal/Linguistic

Alternative Assessment Handbook, Rubric 35: Solving Problems

Answers

Analyzing Visuals *possible answers—workers not protected from contact with dangerous machine parts that could kill or hurt them; dust made it hard to see and breathe; loud noises may have been distracting.*

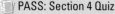

Direct Teach

Main Idea

❸ Changes in Society

The Industrial Revolution led to both positive and negative changes in society.

Recall How did the Industrial Revolution make life in Europe better? Worse? *better—manufactured goods cheaper and more available, new inventions made some tasks easier, more people joined middle class; worse—cities became dirty, noisy, and crowded while workers remained poor with dangerous and unhealthy living conditions*

Evaluate Why was gaining political power important to workers? *possible answer—with political power, voters could pressure lawmakers to pass laws requiring better working conditions.*

Review & Assess

Close

Have students describe how new inventions and technologies changed life in Europe.

Review

Online Quiz, Section 4

Assess

SE Section 4 Assessment

PASS: Section 4 Quiz

Alternative Assessment Handbook

Reteach/Classroom Intervention

Interactive Reader and Study Guide, Section 4

Interactive Skills Tutor CD-ROM

Answers

Reading Check *Cities grew rapidly, becoming dirty, noisy, and crowded.*

646

Reform efforts addressed the workplace, society, and government. Here, British suffragettes campaign for the right to vote.

Changes in Society

The Industrial Revolution improved life in Europe in many ways. Manufactured goods became cheaper and more available. Inventions made life easier. More people grew wealthier and joined the middle class. These people could afford to live well.

At the same time, industrial growth made life worse in other ways. Cities grew rapidly. They became dirty, noisy, and crowded. Many workers remained poor. They often had to live crammed together in shabby, unsafe apartments. In these conditions, diseases spread rapidly as well.

Such problems led to efforts to reform society and politics. People worked to have laws passed improving wages and factory conditions. Others worked to make cities cleaner and safer. Efforts to gain political power were led by **suffragettes**, women who campaigned to gain the right to vote. In 1928 British suffragettes won the right to vote for women in Great Britain. Changes like these helped usher in the modern age.

READING CHECK **Summarizing** How did the Industrial Revolution affect cities in Europe?

SUMMARY AND PREVIEW As you have read, industrial growth changed how many Europeans lived and worked. In the next chapter you will learn about an event that led to more change: World War I.

Section 4 Assessment

Reviewing Ideas, Terms, and Places

1. **a. Recall** In which country did the start of the **Industrial Revolution** take place?
   b. Draw Conclusions How did changes in farming help pave the way for industrial growth?
   c. Develop Write a few sentences defending the idea that Great Britain was ready for industrial growth in the early 1700s.
2. **a. Identify** What were two inventions that contributed to industrial growth during this period?
   b. Make Inferences How do you think work in a factory differed from that on a farm?
3. **a. Recall** What did the **suffragettes** achieve?
   b. Summarize What problems did industry create? How did people work to solve these problems?

Critical Thinking

4. **Identifying Cause and Effect** Review your notes. Then use a diagram like the one shown to explain how each change in society led to the next.

   Changes in Farming → New Inventions → Factory System → New Ways of Life

FOCUS ON WRITING

5. **Describing the Industrial Revolution** What might a diary writer have to say about the Industrial Revolution? Jot down some ideas in your notes. For example, an entry might describe what it was like to work in an early factory.

646 CHAPTER 19

Section 4 Assessment Answers

1. **a.** Great Britain
   b. Increased farm productivity forced workers to move to cities, creating a needed labor force.
   c. possible answer—Britain had a large labor force, ample coal, and many rivers for water-power. Its growing population increased demand for more and better manufactured goods.
2. **a.** water-powered spinning machine, steam engine, Bessemer steel
   b. factory work—plentiful, repetitive, dangerous, unhealthy; farm work—scarce, safer, healthier, weather dependent
3. **a.** the right for women to vote
   b. problems—Cities became dirty, noisy, crowded, disease-ridden; solutions—Reformers worked for laws to raise wages and improve factory conditions.
4. Students' answers will vary but should include information from the section to support their explanations.
5. Answers will vary include mention of new inventions, new ways of producing goods, new farming techniques, and what factories were really like.

Social Studies Skills

Writing to Learn

Learn

Writing is an important tool for learning new information. When you write about what you read, you can better understand and remember information. For example, when you write a list of items you need from the grocery store, the act of writing can help you remember what to buy. Use the steps below to write to learn.

- Read the text carefully. Look for the main idea and important details.
- Think about the information you just read. Then summarize in your own words what you learned.
- Write a personal response to what you read. What do you think about the information? What questions might you have? How does this information affect you?

Practice

Use the steps you just learned to practice writing to learn. Read the paragraph below carefully, then complete a chart like the one here.

> Eventually, the Third Estate members formed the National Assembly. This group demanded that the French king accept a constitution limiting his powers. Louis XVI refused, which angered the common people of Paris. On July 14, 1789, this anger led a mob to storm the Bastille, a prison in Paris. The mob released the prisoners and destroyed the building. The French Revolution had begun.

What I Learned	Personal Response

Apply

Read the information in Section 4 carefully. Then create a chart similar to the one above. In the first column, summarize the key ideas from the section in your own words. Use the second column to write your personal reaction to the information you learned.

647

Social Studies Skills

Writing to Learn

Materials: a newspaper or magazine article for each student

1. Distribute copies of newspaper or magazine articles to students. Have students read their articles and complete a What I Learned/Personal Response chart.

2. Have students use their charts to write a paragraph summarizing the information. Then have them read their paragraphs to the class.

3. Discuss the topics and responses and ask students how the process of writing to learn can help them remember information.
   LS Verbal/Linguistic

- Alternative Assessment Handbook, Rubric 37: Writing Assignments
- Interactive Skills Tutor CD-ROM Lesson 14: Identify Main Ideas and Supporting Ideas

---

Social Studies Skills Activity: Writing to Learn

Below Level

Writing About World War I

Standard English Mastery

1. Create a What I Learned/Personal Response chart where students can see. Ask volunteers to read aloud the text under the heading "The Outbreak of War" in Section 5.

2. Discuss with students different things they might list in each column. Assist students in identifying important details and summarizing the information in their own words using standard English. For personal responses, have students complete sentences such as *I think . . . , I believe . . . , I am unsure about . . .* Complete the chart with students' responses. As a class, discuss any necessary corrections to the sentences to align them with standard English usage.

3. When charts are complete, ask students to record the information in their notebooks in paragraph form. Ask students if the exercise helped them better understand the information. **LS Verbal/Linguistic**

- Alternative Assessment Handbook, Rubric 37: Writing Assignments

Answers

Practice *What I Learned—Louis XVI's refusal to accept a constitution limiting his powers led to the storming of the Bastille and the beginning of the French Revolution. Personal Response— Answers will vary, but should reflect the information students learned.*

Apply *Answers will vary. Summaries should include the key ideas that the Industrial Revolution changed the European landscape and how Europeans lived their lives.*

647

World War I

Bellringer

If YOU lived there. . . Use the **Daily Bellringer Transparency** to help students answer the question.

🗄 Daily Bellringer Transparency, Section 5

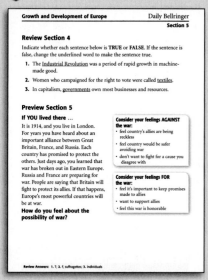

Academic Vocabulary

Review with students the high-use academic term in this section.

strategy a plan for fighting a battle or war (p. 650)

📝 **RF: Vocabulary Builder, Section 5**

Taking Notes

Have students copy the graphic organizer onto their own paper and then use it to take notes on the section. This activity will prepare students for the Section Assessment, in which they will complete a graphic organizer that builds on the information using the Critical Thinking Skill: Categorizing.

What You Will Learn...

Main Ideas

1. Rivalries in Europe led to the outbreak of World War I.
2. After a long, devastating war, the Allies claimed victory.
3. The war's end brought great political and territorial changes to Europe.

The Big Idea

World War I and the peace treaty that followed brought tremendous change to Europe.

Key Terms

nationalism, *p. 648*
alliance, *p. 649*
trench warfare, *p. 650*
Treaty of Versailles, *p. 651*
communism, *p. 652*

TAKING NOTES As you read, take notes on the causes and effects of World War I. Use a graphic organizer like the one below to help you organize your notes.

If YOU lived there...

It is 1914, and you live in London. For years you have heard about an important alliance between Great Britain, France, and Russia. Each country has promised to protect the others. Just days ago, you learned that war has broken out in Eastern Europe. Russia and France are preparing for war. People are saying that Britain will fight to protect its allies. If that happens, Europe's most powerful countries will be at war.

How do you feel about the possibility of war?

BUILDING BACKGROUND The 1800s were a time of rapid change in Europe. Industries grew quickly. Cities expanded. The countries of Europe raced to build empires and gain power. As each country tried to outdo the others, conflicts emerged. Europe was poised for war.

The Outbreak of War

In the early 1900s Europe was on the brink of war. Rivalries were building among Europe's strongest nations. One small spark would be enough to start World War I.

Causes of the War

During the 1800s nationalism changed Europe. **Nationalism** is devotion and loyalty to one's country. Some groups that were ruled by powerful empires wanted to build their own nation-states. For example, nationalism led some people in Bosnia and Herzegovina, a region in southeastern Europe, to demand their independence from the Austro-Hungarian Empire. Nationalism also created rivalries among many nations. By the early 1900s nationalism had grown so strong that countries were willing to go to war to prove their superiority over their rivals. A fierce competition emerged among the countries of Europe.

This competition for land, resources, and power drove many European countries to strengthen their armed forces. They built powerful armies and created stockpiles of new weapons. Each country wanted to show its strength and intimidate its rivals.

648 CHAPTER 19

Teach the Big Idea

At Level

World War I

1. **Teach** Ask students the questions in the Main Idea boxes under Direct Teach.

2. **Apply** Have students discuss reasons nations go to war. Tell them they can use examples from past or present wars. Remind students to think about the points of view from both sides of the conflict when they answer. List their reasons on the board.

3. **Review** When the list is finished, have students discuss what they think are the best,

the worst, and the most common reasons for going to war. 🅻🅂 **Verbal/Linguistic**

4. **Practice/Homework** Have students write a short persuasive essay explaining whether war should only be used as a last resort. Students should provide reasons to support their point of view. 🅻🅂 **Verbal/Linguistic, Interpersonal**

📝 Alternative Assessment Handbook, Rubrics 11: Discussions; and 43: Writing to Persuade

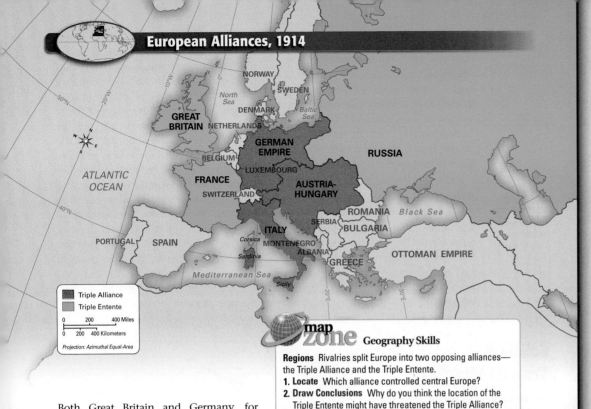

European Alliances, 1914

Triple Alliance
Triple Entente

0   200   400 Miles
0   200   400 Kilometers
Projection: Azimuthal Equal-Area

map zone Geography Skills

Regions Rivalries split Europe into two opposing alliances—the Triple Alliance and the Triple Entente.
1. **Locate** Which alliance controlled central Europe?
2. **Draw Conclusions** Why do you think the location of the Triple Entente might have threatened the Triple Alliance?

As tensions and suspicions grew, some European leaders hoped to protect their countries by creating alliances. An **alliance** is an agreement between countries. If one country is attacked, its allies—members of the alliance—help defend it. In 1882 Italy, Germany, and Austria-Hungary formed the Triple Alliance. In response, France, Great Britain, and Russia created their own alliance, the Triple Entente (ahn-TAHNT). As you can see in the map, these alliances divided Europe.

The Spark for War

By the summer of 1914, war in Europe seemed certain. Tensions between Austria-Hungary and Serbia arose over the control of Bosnia and Herzegovina, a province of Austria-Hungary and Serbia's neighbor. On June 28, 1914, a Serbian assassin shot and killed Archduke Francis Ferdinand, the heir to the throne of Austria-Hungary. Seeking revenge, Austria-Hungary declared war on Serbia. After Serbia turned to Russia for help, the alliance system quickly split Europe into two warring sides. On one side was Austria-Hungary and Germany, known as the Central Powers. The Allied Powers—Serbia, Russia, Great Britain, and France—were on the other side.

READING CHECK **Finding Main Ideas** What were the causes of World War I?

GROWTH AND DEVELOPMENT OF EUROPE **649**

Direct Teach

Main Idea

❶ **The Outbreak of War**
Rivalries in Europe led to the outbreak of World War I.

Define What is nationalism? *devotion and loyalty to one's country*

Identify What countries made up the Triple Alliance? *Italy, Germany, and Austria-Hungary*

Identify Cause and Effect Why did Austria-Hungary declare war on Serbia? *A Serbian assassin shot Archduke Francis Ferdinand.*

Map Zone Transparency: European Alliances, 1914

Info to Know

The Great War Before World War II, the first world war was known as The Great War. Some also called it "the war to end all wars" because they believed that modern war was so destructive that people would do everything possible to avoid it. American President Woodrow Wilson called it a war "to make the world safe for democracy."

Answers

Map Zone 1. *Triple Alliance;* **2.** *The Triple Entente surrounded them.*

Reading Check *Nationalism and competition for land, resources, and power created tension and suspicion among countries. Nations built up their militaries and formed alliances. The immediate cause was the assassination of Archduke Francis Ferdinand.*

649

Main Idea

❷ War and Victory

After a long, devastating war, the Allies claimed victory.

Recall When did the Central Powers surrender? *in the fall of 1918*

Identify What new weapons were used in World War I? *machine guns, poison gas, tanks*

Make Inferences What did "going over the top" mean? *climbing out of the trench and attacking by running toward enemy positions*

Did you know . . .

Switzerland, a mountainous country in the center of Europe, has a well-deserved reputation for peace and neutrality. Most of Europe has recognized Switzerland's neutrality since 1815. Switzerland stayed out of both world wars, although fighting raged in neighboring countries. Though peaceful, Switzerland does have an army that it maintains for defensive purposes only. So devoted are the Swiss to avoiding international conflict that they did not join the United Nations until 2002.

go.hrw.com

Online Resources

KEYWORD: SK9 CH19
ACTIVITY: Trench Warfare

War and Victory

Germany struck the first blow in the war, sending a large army into Belgium and France. Allied troops, however, managed to stop the Germans just outside Paris. In the east, Russia attacked Germany and Austria-Hungary, forcing Germany to fight on two fronts. Hopes on both sides for a quick victory soon disappeared.

ACADEMIC VOCABULARY
strategy a plan for fighting a battle or war

A New Kind of War

A new military **strategy**, trench warfare, was largely responsible for preventing a quick victory. Early in the war both sides turned to trench warfare. **Trench warfare** is a style of fighting in which each side fights from deep ditches, or trenches, dug into the ground.

Both the Allies and the Central Powers dug hundreds of miles of trenches along the front lines. Soldiers in the trenches faced great suffering. Not only did they live in constant danger of attack, but cold, hunger, and disease also plagued them. Sometimes soldiers would "go over the top" of their trenches and fight for a few hours, only to retreat to the same position. Trench warfare cost millions of lives, but neither side could win the war.

To gain an advantage in the trenches, each side developed deadly new weapons. Machine guns cut down soldiers as they tried to move forward. Poison gas, first used by the Germans, blinded soldiers in the trenches. It was later used by both sides. The British introduced another weapon, the tank, to break through enemy lines.

Close-up

Trench Warfare

Both the Allied Powers and the Central Powers relied on trenches for defense during World War I. As a result, the war dragged on for years with no clear victor. Each side developed new weapons and technology to try to gain an advantage in the trenches.

Soldiers often threw or fired small bombs known as grenades.

Soldiers used gas masks to survive attacks of poison gas.

Trenches dug in zigzag patterns prevented the enemy from firing down the length of a trench.

650 CHAPTER 19

Differentiating Instruction

Above Level

Advanced/Gifted and Talented

Research Required

1. Review information about trench warfare with students. Ask them if they think there should be rules in warfare. For example, should soldiers be allowed to harm civilians? Record students' thoughts about rules of war on the board.

2. Assign students to groups to research a stage in the evolution of the Geneva Convention rules. (Meetings to decide on the rules of warfare were held in 1929 and 1949, among other years.) Have students report their findings to the class.

3. Have the class compare opinions about warfare with the rules of the Geneva Convention. Have students provide evidence of whether the rules of the Geneva Convention are being observed in current wars. **LS Verbal/Linguistic**

   Alternative Assessment Handbook, Rubrics 11: Discussions; and 29: Presentations

At sea, Britain used its powerful navy to block supplies from reaching Germany. Germany responded by using submarines, called U-boats. German U-boats tried to break the British blockade and sink ships carrying supplies to Great Britain.

The Allies Win

For three years the war was a stalemate—neither side could defeat the other. Slowly, however, the war turned in favor of the Allies. In early 1917 German U-boats began attacking American ships carrying supplies to Britain. When Germany ignored U.S. warnings to stop, the United States entered the war on the side of the Allies.

Help from American forces gave the Allies a fresh advantage. Soon afterward, however, the exhausted Russians pulled out of the war. Germany quickly attacked the Allies, hoping to put an end to the war. Allied troops, however, stopped Germany's attack. The Central Powers had suffered a great blow. In the fall of 1918 the Central Powers surrendered. The Allied Powers were victorious.

READING CHECK **Sequencing** What events led to the end of World War I?

The War's End

After more than four years of fighting, the war came to an end on November 11, 1918. More than 8.5 million soldiers had been killed, and at least 20 million more were wounded. Millions of civilians had lost their lives as well. The war brought tremendous change to Europe.

Making Peace

Shortly after the end of the war, leaders from the Allied nations met at Versailles (ver-SY), near Paris. There, they debated the terms of peace for the Central Powers.

The United States, led by President Woodrow Wilson, wanted a just peace after the war. He did not want harsh peace terms that might anger the losing countries and lead to future conflict.

Other Allied leaders, however, wanted to punish Germany. They believed that Germany had started the war and should pay for it. They believed that weakening Germany would prevent future wars.

In the end, the Allies forced Germany to sign a treaty. The **Treaty of Versailles** was the final peace settlement of World War I. It forced Germany to accept the blame for starting the war. Germany also had to slash the size of its army and give up its overseas colonies. Additionally, Germany had to pay billions of dollars for damages caused during the war.

FOCUS ON READING
What does the term *just peace* mean? How can you tell?

Each side used airplanes to observe troop movements and other actions behind enemy lines.

Armored vehicles, or tanks, were used to launch attacks across rough terrain.

ANALYSIS SKILL **ANALYZING VISUALS**
What advantages and disadvantages did trench warfare pose for soldiers?

GROWTH AND DEVELOPMENT OF EUROPE **651**

Cross-Discipline Activity: Mathematics

Calculating the Human Cost of War

1. Using encyclopedias, almanacs, or the Internet, have students find data on the human cost of World War I. Have them find as many of the following data points as they can for each country involved:
   - number of soldiers wounded
   - number of soldiers killed
   - number of civilians killed
   - population of each country at the time

2. Have students create a chart or graph to present the data. For example, they might use two pie charts comparing a country's total population to its number of casualties. Allow students to work individually or in small groups.

3. Discuss with students what impact these casualties might have had on each country after the war. **Logical/Mathematical**

   Alternative Assessment Handbook, Rubric 7: Charts

Main Idea

❸ The War's End

The war's end brought great political and territorial changes to Europe.

Recall Who was U.S. president at the end of World War I? *Woodrow Wilson*

Define What is communism? *a political system in which the government owns all property and controls all aspects of life*

Draw Conclusions Why were the countries of Finland, Estonia, Latvia, and Lithuania able to gain independence after World War I? *The new government of Russia was too busy establishing control and new institutions to stop them.*

Connect to Science

Airships in the War During World War I, the Germans used new technologies to fly airships, or zeppelins, to bomb British targets. At the beginning of the war, the British could not defend against airships. Airplanes could not fly high enough to catch airships. Later airplanes with more powerful engines could fly at higher altitudes. These planes were equipped with a new weapon: bullets laced with hot-burning phosphorous that could easily ignite the hydrogen used to lift the airships. In response, Germany built airships that flew higher than the planes could go, but by then the war was almost over.

Answers

Analyzing Visuals *advantages—made it easier to defend a position; disadvantages—made it more difficult to attack a position; soldiers were often cold, hungry, and susceptible to disease.*

Reading Check *The United States entered the war, and Russia pulled out. This caused the Germans to mount one more attack, which failed.*

Focus on Reading *fair, not harsh or causing anger in the losing countries; context clues (the sentence following use of the term)*

651

Connect to Economics

Germany's Post-War Woes After the war, Germany adopted its first democratic constitution in the city of Weimar in 1919. However, the new government faced serious problems—unemployment and runaway inflation. For example, in 1923 the German mark lost its value at a rapid rate—late in the year, it took 4.2 trillion marks to buy one U.S. dollar. By 1928 both problems were under control, and the German people were gaining faith in democracy. Unfortunately, the Great Depression brought back economic woes, paving the way for Adolf Hitler, who convinced many people that he could solve Germany's economic problems.

Review & Assess

Close

Ask students what major mistakes European leaders made before and after World War I.

Review

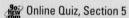 Online Quiz, Section 5

Assess

SE Section 5 Assessment

PASS: Section 5 Quiz

Alternative Assessment Handbook

Reteach/Classroom Intervention

Interactive Reader and Study Guide, Section 5

Interactive Skills Tutor CD-ROM

Answers

Reading Check *Communists took control of Russia; Germany became a democracy; Austria-Hungary was split in two; Finland, Estonia, Latvia, Lithuania, Poland, and Czechoslovakia gained independence; Yugoslavia was formed.*

652

Vladimir Lenin encouraged Russian workers to support his new Communist government.

A New Europe

World War I had a tremendous effect on the countries of Europe. It changed the governments of some European countries and the borders of others. For example, in Russia the war had caused great hardship for the people. A revolution then forced the Russian czar, or emperor, to give up power. Shortly after, Vladimir Lenin took over Russia's government and established a Communist government. **Communism** is a political system in which the government owns all property and controls all aspects of life in a country. An uprising toward the end of the war also forced the German emperor from power. A fragile republic replaced the German Empire.

World War I also altered the borders of many European countries. Austria and Hungary became separate countries. Poland and Czechoslovakia each gained their independence. Serbia, Bosnia and Herzegovina, and other Balkan states were combined to create Yugoslavia. Finland, Estonia, Latvia, and Lithuania, which had been part of Russia, became independent.

READING CHECK **Summarizing** How did World War I change Europe?

SUMMARY AND PREVIEW Intense rivalries among the countries of Europe led to World War I, one of the most devastating wars in history. In the next section you will learn about problems that plagued Europe and led to World War II.

Section 5 Assessment

go.hrw.com
Online Quiz
KEYWORD: SK9 HP19

Reviewing Ideas, Terms, and Places

1. **a. Identify** What event triggered World War I?
   b. Analyze How did **nationalism** cause rivalries between some European countries?
   c. Evaluate Do you think **alliances** helped or hurt most countries? Explain your answer.
2. **a. Describe** What was **trench warfare** like?
   b. Draw Conclusions What difficulties did soldiers face as a result of trench warfare?
   c. Predict How might the war have been different if the United States had not entered it?
3. **a. Recall** How did the **Treaty of Versailles** punish Germany for its role in the war?
   b. Contrast How did the Allied leaders' ideas for peace with Germany differ?

   c. Elaborate Why do you think the war caused changes in government in Russia and Germany?

Critical Thinking

4. **Categorizing** Draw a chart like the one here. Use your notes to list the results of World War I in the appropriate category.

Political	Economic

FOCUS ON WRITING

5. **Writing about World War I** Think about the events of World War I. Imagine that you were present at one or more events during or after the war. What might you write about in your diary?

652 CHAPTER 19

Section 5 Assessment Answers

1. **a.** Archduke Ferdinand was assassinated.
   b. Countries wanted to prove their superiority and competed for resources and power.
   c. helped by providing countries protection; hurt by dragging countries into war
2. **a.** Armies faced each other from parallel trenches that were easier to defend than attack. Soldiers suffered greatly.
   b. hunger, cold, disease, poison gas
   c. The war may have lasted even longer; the Central Powers may have won.
3. **a.** Germany was forced to reduce its army and pay war costs.

   b. America wanted a just peace, but others wanted to punish Germany.
   c. People were unhappy with the disastrous effects of the war.

4. possible answers: political—Lenin took power in Russia, Yugoslavia formed, Austria-Hungary broke up; economic—Germany made to pay billions of dollars for damages caused during the war

5. Events might include the assassination of Archduke Ferdinand or trench warfare.

Literature

from
All Quiet on the Western Front

by Erich Maria Remarque

About the Reading *In* All Quiet on the Western Front, *author Erich Maria Remarque provides a fictional account of the lives of soldiers during World War I. The book is considered one of the most realistic accounts of the war. In this selection, the book's narrator, twenty-year-old German soldier Paul Bäumer, describes a battle between German and British forces.*

AS YOU READ Note the words the speaker uses to describe the battle.

Our trenches have now for some time been shot to pieces, and we have an elastic line, so that there is practically no longer any proper trench warfare. ❶ When attack and counter-attack have waged backwards and forwards there remains a broken line and a bitter struggle from crater to crater. The front-line has been penetrated, and everywhere small groups have established themselves, the fight is carried on from clusters of shell-holes.

We are buried in a crater, the English are coming down obliquely, they are turning our flank and working in behind us. ❷ We are surrounded. It is not easy to surrender, fog and smoke hang over us, no one would recognize that we wanted to give ourselves up, and perhaps we don't want to, a man doesn't even know himself at such moments. We hear the explosions of the hand-grenades coming towards us. Our machine-gun sweeps over the semicircle in front of us . . . Behind us the attack crashes ever nearer.

Soldiers prepare to rush over the top of a trench during a battle in World War I.

GUIDED READING

WORD HELP

crater a hole in the ground made by the explosion of a bomb or shell

penetrated passed into or through

obliquely indirectly or underhandedly

❶ An elastic line describes a battle line that is pushed back and forth by enemy forces.

❷ "Turning our flank" refers to a tactic in which one military force moves around the side of the opposing force in order to surround them.

Connecting Literature to Geography

1. **Describing** What details in the first paragraph show that the technique of trench warfare is no longer working?

2. **Making Inferences** Why do you think the location of this trench is so important to the war and the people fighting in it?

653

Literature

from *All Quiet on the Western Front*

As You Read Ask students to imagine what Paul Bäumer is experiencing. Have them make a five-columned chart using the five senses as headings. Entries in the chart should include descriptive words that help portray Bäumer's experience in the trenches.

Meet the Writer

Erich Maria Remarque (1898–1970) Born in Osnabrück, Germany, Erich Maria Remarque wrote *All Quiet on the Western Front* in 1929. He based it on his personal war experiences. It was a huge bestseller, and he followed up with other popular novels that told of life in Germany during the Weimar Republic and the early Nazi era. *All Quiet on the Western Front* was banned in Germany in the 1930s. Remarque fled to Switzerland, then moved to the U.S., where he became a citizen. He returned to Switzerland and lived there until his death in 1970.

Info to Know

Post-war Literature Many young men were horrified by what they saw in World War I and wrote eloquent anti-war plays, poems, and novels. Their writing portrayed a realistic view of war, not a romanticized one.

Differentiating Instruction

At Level

Special Needs Learners

Materials: Student Edition on Audio CD Program

1. Play the literature selection on audio CD or read the excerpt aloud for students with visual impairments.

2. Review with students what they have learned about what fighting in World War I was like. Include the information students read in the chapter as well as the excerpt from *All Quiet on the Western Front*.

3. Using the list of words students compiled in the *As You Read* activity above, have students

write a short fictional passage. Remind them to write vivid descriptions of trench warfare, using as many of the words from their lists as possible. Students may wish to record their short stories on audio cassette instead of writing or typing them.

4. Ask volunteers to share their passages with the class. ⬛ **Verbal/Linguistic, Auditory/Musical**

Alternative Assessment Handbook, Rubrics 18: Listening; and 40: Writing to Describe

Answers

Connecting Literature to Geography 1. *Trenches have been shot to pieces; we have an elastic line; the front-line has been penetrated; the fight is carried on from clusters;* **2.** *The front line is supposed to be the strongest line; if it is penetrated, the battle or war may be lost.*

World War II

Bellringer

If YOU lived there. . . Use the **Daily Bellringer Transparency** to help students answer the question.

📖 Daily Bellringer Transparency, Section 6

Growth and Development of Europe — Daily Bellringer
Section 6

Review Section 5

Read the list of events below and put them in the correct order.

a. America enters World War I.
b. Austria-Hungary declares war on Serbia.
c. Archduke Francis Ferdinand is shot.
d. The Treaty of Versailles is signed.

Preview Section 6

If YOU lived there ...

It is 1922, and you are part of a huge crowd in one of Rome's public squares. Everyone is listening to the fiery speech of a dynamic new leader. He promises to make Italy great again, as it was in the days of ancient Rome. You know that your parents and some of your teachers are excited about his ideas. Others are concerned that he may be too forceful.

What do you think of this new leader's message?

Consider why you DISAGREE:
- could hurt economy
- sounds like a dictator
- worried about having to go to war

Consider why you AGREE:
- could create better jobs
- could restore pride
- want country to be a world power again

Review Answers: c, b, a, d

Key Terms

📄 **RF: Vocabulary Builder, Section 6**

Taking Notes

Have students copy the chart onto their own paper and then use it to take notes on the section. This activity will prepare students for the Section Assessment, in which they will complete a time line that builds on the information using the Critical Thinking Skill: Sequencing.

What You Will Learn...

Main Ideas

1. Economic and political problems troubled Europe in the years after World War I.
2. World War II broke out when Germany invaded Poland.
3. Nazi Germany targeted the Jews during the Holocaust.
4. Allied victories in Europe and Japan brought the end of World War II.

The Big Idea

Problems in Europe led to World War II, the deadliest war in history.

Key Terms

Great Depression, *p. 654*
dictator, *p. 655*
Axis Powers, *p. 657*
Allies, *p. 657*
Holocaust, *p. 657*

TAKING NOTES As you read, take notes on the important dates and events of World War II. Use a chart like the one below to organize your notes.

Event	Date	Importance

If YOU lived there...

It is 1922, and you are part of a huge crowd in one of Rome's public squares. Everyone is listening to the fiery speech of a dynamic new leader. He promises to make Italy great again, as it was in the days of ancient Rome. You know that your parents and some of your teachers are excited about his ideas. Others are concerned that he may be too forceful.

What do you think of this new leader's message?

BUILDING BACKGROUND Many countries faced deep economic and political problems as a result of World War I. Dictators rose to power in a number of countries, but did not bring solutions. Instead, they attacked their neighbors and plunged the world back into war.

Problems Trouble Europe

After World War I, Europeans began rebuilding their countries. Just as they had started to recover, however, many economic and political problems emerged. These problems threatened the peace and security of Europe.

The Great Depression

World War I left much of Europe in shambles. Factories and farmland had been destroyed, and economies were in ruins. Countries that had lost the war, like Germany and Austria, owed billions in war damages. Many countries turned to the United States for help. During the 1920s the U.S. economy was booming. Loans from American banks and businesses helped many European nations recover and rebuild after World War I.

In 1929, however, the recovery fell apart. A stock market crash in the United States triggered a global economic crisis in the 1930s known as the **Great Depression**. As the U.S. economy faltered, American banks stopped lending to Europe. Without U.S. loans and investments, European economies declined. Unemployment skyrocketed as businesses and farms, as well as banks, went bankrupt.

Teach the Big Idea

World War II

1. **Teach** Ask students the questions in the Main Idea boxes under Direct Teach.

2. **Apply** Ask students the following question: *Could World War II have been prevented?* Invite students to list causes that contributed to the war. Record causes on the board. Then ask students to suggest ways that those causes could have been dealt with more effectively. Write students' ideas next to each cause. **LS Interpersonal**

3. **Review** Review the list and have the class evaluate each item. Have students choose the idea they think would have been the most likely to prevent war.

4. **Practice/Homework** Based on their decisions in Step 3, have students write a short persuasive essay on how World War II could have been prevented. **LS Verbal/Linguistic**

📄 Alternative Assessment Handbook, Rubrics 11: Discussions; and 43: Writing to Persuade

The Rise of Dictators

The Great Depression added to Europe's problems. Blaming weak governments for the hard times, some Europeans turned to dictators to strengthen their countries and improve their lives. A **dictator** is a ruler who has total control. Dictators rose to power in Russia, Italy, and Germany.

One of the first dictators in Europe was Russia's Vladimir Lenin. Lenin gained power as a result of a 1917 revolution. He formed the first Communist government and took control of businesses and private property. He also united Russia and other republics to create the Soviet Union. After Lenin's death in 1924, Joseph Stalin took power. As dictator, he made all economic decisions, restricted religious worship, and used secret police to spy on citizens.

Benito Mussolini of Italy was another powerful dictator during this period. In the 1920s Mussolini won control of the Italian government and made himself dictator. He promised to make Italy stronger and to revive the economy. He even spoke of restoring the glory of the former Roman Empire. As dictator, however, Mussolini suspended basic rights like freedom of speech and trial by jury.

By the 1930s many Germans had lost faith in their government. They turned to a new political party, the Nazi Party. The party's leader, Adolf Hitler, promised to strengthen Germany. He vowed to rebuild Germany's military and economy. After years of struggle, many Germans listened eagerly to his message. In 1933 Hitler rose to power and soon became dictator. He banned all parties except the Nazi Party. He also began discriminating against so-called inferior races, particularly Germany's Jews.

READING CHECK Generalizing Why did some people support the rise of dictators?

European Dictators

Popular dictators rose to power in Europe in the 1920s and 1930s. Adolf Hitler in Germany and Benito Mussolini in Italy gained public support with promises to make life better and to strengthen their countries.

655

655

Main Idea

❷ War Breaks Out

World War II broke out when Germany invaded Poland.

Recall What African country did Italy invade in 1935? *Ethiopia*

Identify Cause and Effect Why did France and England declare war on Germany in 1939? *Germany invaded Poland.*

Contrast Why did the Allies react differently when Germany attacked Poland in 1939 than when Germany occupied Czechoslovakia in 1938? *In 1938 they still believed Germany would keep its word and that war could be avoided.*

Map Zone Transparency: World War II in Europe, 1941

Connect to Art

Pablo Picasso's *Guernica* In the 1930s another European dictator seized power—General Francisco Franco of Spain. Franco, with the support of Hitler and Mussolini, led a revolt called the Spanish Civil War against the elected government. To help Franco succeed in 1937, the German air force bombed a government stronghold, the Spanish town of Guernica, deliberately killing more than a third of its people. The Spanish artist Pablo Picasso, outraged at the cruelty of this brutal war crime, painted the famous mural *Guernica* to tell the world what was happening to his people.

Answers

Map Zone 1. *Great Britain and the Soviet Union;* **2.** *An army and all its equipment could not easily cross water.*

Focus on Reading *The contrast clues "attempts at peace" and "instead of peace" can help students understand that aggression means "attack" or "use of force."*

★Interactive Map

World War II in Europe, 1941

- Axis powers
- Axis controlled
- Allied powers
- Allied controlled
- Neutral countries

0   150   300 Miles
0   150   300 Kilometers

Projection: Azimuthal Equal-Area

map zone Geography Skills

Regions By 1941 the Axis Powers controlled much of Europe.

1. **Locate** What two Allied Powers remained standing by 1941?
2. **Analyzing** Why do you think the Axis was unable to conquer Great Britain?

go.hrw.com   KEYWORD: SK9 CH19

War Breaks Out

As dictators, Hitler and Mussolini were determined to strengthen their countries at any cost. Their actions led to history's deadliest war—World War II.

Threats to Peace

FOCUS ON READING
How do contrast clues help you understand the meaning of the word *aggression*?

After World War I, European countries wanted peace. Many countries hoped to prevent another deadly war. By the late 1930s, however, attempts at peace had failed. Instead of peace, Italian and German aggression forced Europe into a second world war.

In 1935 Benito Mussolini ordered his Italian troops to invade Ethiopia, a country in East Africa. Other nations were shocked by his actions, but none tried to turn back the invasion. Meanwhile, the Italian leader and Germany's Adolf Hitler joined together to form an alliance known as the Rome-Berlin Axis.

Hitler was next to act. In 1938 he broke the Treaty of Versailles when he annexed, or added, Austria to Germany's territory. Although Britain and France protested, they did not attempt to stop Germany.

Later that year, Hitler announced his plan to take Czechoslovakia as well. Many European leaders were worried, but they still hoped to avoid a war. They allowed Hitler to annex part of Czechoslovakia in return for his promise of peace. By the spring of 1939, however, Germany had conquered the rest of Czechoslovakia.

656 CHAPTER 19

Cross-Discipline Activity: Art   At Level

Relating to Picasso's *Guernica*   Prep Required

1. Bring a reproduction of Pablo Picasso's *Guernica* to class. Lead a discussion of what the images in the picture symbolize. Tell students that Picasso said, "It isn't up to the painter to define the symbols. Otherwise it would be better if he wrote them out in so many words."

2. Point out to students that even though the painting is about an attack by bombers, no images of airplanes appear. Solicit and record students' observations about possible meanings of symbols in the painting.

3. Have students either draw a picture in reaction to the bombing of Guernica or write a paragraph describing the symbolism of *Guernica*. **LS** Visual/Spatial, Verbal/Linguistic

Alternative Assessment Handbook, Rubrics 3: Artwork; and 11: Discussions

Italy quickly moved to occupy Albania in the Balkans. Attempts to keep the peace had failed.

Eventually, Great Britain and France realized they could not ignore Hitler's actions. When Germany threatened to take Polish territory, the Allies vowed to protect Poland at all costs. On September 1, 1939, German forces launched an all-out attack on Poland. Two days later, Great Britain and France responded by declaring war on Germany. World War II had begun.

Allies Lose Ground

Germany's invasion of Poland triggered the Second World War. Germany, Italy, and Japan formed an alliance called the **Axis Powers**. Against them stood the **Allies**—France, Great Britain, and other countries that opposed the Axis.

Germany struck first. After defeating Poland, Germany moved on to a series of quick victories in Western Europe. One by one, countries fell to German forces. In June 1940 Germany invaded and quickly defeated one of Europe's greatest powers, France. In less than a year, Hitler had gained control of almost all of Western Europe.

Next, Germany set its sights on Britain. The German air force repeatedly attacked British cities and military targets. Hitler hoped the British would surrender. Rather than give in, however, the British persevered.

Unable to defeat Great Britain, the Axis Powers turned their attention elsewhere. As German troops marched into Eastern Europe, Italian forces invaded North Africa. By the end of 1941 Germany had invaded the Soviet Union, and Japan had attacked the United States at Pearl Harbor, Hawaii. The Allies were losing ground in the war.

READING CHECK Drawing Inferences Why do you think the Axis Powers easily gained the advantage in the early years of the war?

The Holocaust

One of the most horrifying aspects of the war was the Holocaust (HOH-luh-kawst). The **Holocaust** was the attempt by the Nazi government during World War II to eliminate Europe's Jews. Believing that the Germans were a superior race, the Nazis tried to destroy people who they believed were inferior, especially the Jews.

Even before the war began, the Nazi government began restricting the rights of Jews and others in Germany. For example, laws restricted Jews from holding government jobs or attending German schools. Nazis imprisoned countless Jews in camps.

JOURNAL ENTRY
The Diary of Anne Frank

Anne Frank and her family fled to Amsterdam to escape Nazi persecution of Jews in Germany. In 1942, when Nazis began rounding up Jews in the Netherlands, the Franks were forced to hide. Anne kept a diary of her time in hiding.

" *Countless friends and acquaintances have gone to a terrible fate. Evening after evening the green and gray army lorries [trucks] trundle past. The Germans ring at every front door to inquire if there are any Jews living in the house. If there are, then the whole family has to go at once. If they don't find any, they go on to the next house. No one has a chance of evading them unless one goes into hiding.* "

—from *The Diary of a Young Girl*

ANALYSIS SKILL **ANALYZING PRIMARY SOURCES**
What likely happened to the Jews that were rounded up by German officials?

GROWTH AND DEVELOPMENT OF EUROPE **657**

Collaborative Learning

At Level

Responding to the Holocaust

Research Required

1. Point out to students that the Nazis also sought to eliminate groups other than Jews. Tell students they will be researching an aspect of the Holocaust. (For sources, students may start with the Holocaust Encyclopedia on the Web site for the U.S. Holocaust Museum.) Have groups preview material on various topics before choosing one.
   - the Roma
   - the 1935 Nuremberg Laws
   - Jehovah's Witnesses

   - "Degenerate" art (Hitler's label for abstract art)
   - the system of badges that victims were required to wear

2. After groups have chosen and researched a topic, have each group design, create, and present a poster to the class of what they learned. Each group member should have a specific role in the poster project and presentation. **LS** **Visual/Spatial, Verbal/Linguistic**

   📖 Alternative Assessment Handbook, Rubrics 28: Posters; and 30: Research

657

Main Idea

④ End of the War

Allied victories in Europe and Japan brought the end of World War II.

Define What is the United Nations? *an international peace-keeping organization*

Identify What happened on D-Day, and when did it occur? *The Allies landed on the beaches of Normandy, France; June 6, 1944*

Sequence What events led to the defeat of the Axis Powers in 1945? *British forces gained control of North Africa; Mussolini surrendered; Soviet troops forced Germany to retreat; the Allies landed at Normandy; the Allies entered German territory; Germany surrendered in May 1945; the U.S. used the atomic bomb; Japan surrendered in August 1945*

RF: Primary Source, Charter of the United Nations

Biography

Wernher von Braun (1912–1977) If ever there was a "rocket scientist," it was Germany's Wernher von Braun. Inspired by the novels of Jules Verne, von Braun began studying rockets in his teens. During World War II, he headed the team that designed the V-2 rocket, which rained huge bombs on terrorized Londoners from 500 miles away. As the war ended, von Braun arranged for 500 of his fellow rocket scientists to surrender to the American army, rather than to the Soviets. The scientists were taken to the U.S. where they helped design and build the rockets for the American space program of the 1960s.

go.hrw.com
Online Resources

KEYWORD: SK9 CH19
ACTIVITY: D-Day Invasion

Answers

Reading Check *The Nazis considered the Jews an inferior race.*

Time Line

World War II

September 1–3, 1939
German forces invade Poland; Britain and France declare war.

June 22, 1941
Germany launches invasion of the Soviet Union.

1940   1941   1942   1943

June 22, 1940
France falls to German forces.

July–September 1940
Germany bombs London during the Battle of Britain.

Thousands of Jews fled Germany to escape persecution. Many thousands more, however, remained behind.

Germany's expansion into Eastern Europe brought millions more Jews under Hitler's control. Because of this, Nazis looked for ways to handle the Jewish population. In 1942 the Nazi government ordered the destruction of Europe's entire Jewish population. The Nazis used mass executions and death camps, like Auschwitz in Poland, to murder millions of Jews.

The Nazis did face resistance. Some Jews tried to fight back. For example, Jews in Warsaw, Poland, staged an uprising. Some Europeans tried to save Jews from the Nazis. German businessman Oskar Schindler, for example, saved Jews by employing them in his factories. However, most Jews were unable to escape. By the time the Nazis were defeated, they had killed some 6 million Jews and several million non-Jews.

READING CHECK Analyzing Why did Hitler's Nazi government attempt to destroy the Jews?

End of the War

The Allies did not fare well in the early years of the war. Victories in 1943 and 1944, though, helped them end World War II.

Allies Are Victorious

In early 1943 U.S. and British forces gained control of North Africa and Italy, forcing Mussolini to surrender. That same year, the Allies defeated the Japanese in several key battles. In the east, Soviet troops forced Germany to retreat.

In June 1944 Allied forces landed on the beaches of Normandy, France. The invasion, or D-Day as it was called, dealt a serious blow to the Axis. It paved the way for Allied forces to advance on Germany.

By the spring of 1945 Allied troops had crossed into German territory. In May 1945 Germany surrendered. In August 1945 the United States used a powerful new weapon, the atomic bomb, to bring the war with Japan to an end. After almost six years of fighting, World War II was over.

658 CHAPTER 19

Critical Thinking: Analyzing Information   Above Level

Exploring the UN Charter

1. Obtain copies of the Preamble of the United Nations Charter or go to the United Nations Web site. Have students make a two-columned table. In the first column, have them write each bullet point of the Preamble.

2. In the second column, have students cite a supporting source from their text by placing the heading title and page number in parentheses in an appropriate slot. Each entry should explain or support a point of the Preamble.

3. For any item lacking support, students should supply their own explanation, labeled "Personal Opinion."

4. Using the information in their tables, have students write a short paper explaining why the members of the United Nations agreed to the wording of the Charter's Preamble.
   LS Verbal/Linguistic

Alternative Assessment Handbook, Rubrics 30: Research; and 42: Writing to Inform.

February 1945
Allied leaders plan the final defeat of the Axis Powers.

April 1945
Allied troops begin liberation of Nazi concentration camps.

1944   1945   1946

June 6, 1944
Allied forces launch D-Day invasion in Normandy, France.

May 7, 1945
Germany surrenders to Allied Powers.

ANALYSIS SKILL READING TIME LINES
About how long after the beginning of the war did Germany invade the Soviet Union?

Results of the War

The war had a huge impact on the world. It resulted in millions of deaths, tensions between the Allies, and the creation of the United Nations.

World War II was the deadliest conflict in history. More than 50 million people lost their lives. Millions more were wounded.

The United States and the Soviet Union emerged from the war as the most powerful countries in the world. An intense rivalry developed between the two countries.

After the war, people hoped to prevent another deadly conflict. In 1945 some 50 nations formed the United Nations, an international peacekeeping organization.

READING CHECK Summarizing What were the main results of World War II?

SUMMARY AND PREVIEW World War II was the deadliest war in history. Next, you will learn about developments in Europe during the postwar period.

Section 6 Assessment

go.hrw.com
Online Quiz
KEYWORD: SK9 HP19

Reviewing Ideas, Terms, and Places

1. **a. Define** What was the **Great Depression**?
   b. Explain How did economic problems in the United States lead to the Great Depression?
2. **a. Describe** What led to the outbreak of World War II?
   b. Predict What might have happened if Great Britain had fallen to Germany?
3. **a. Identify** What was the **Holocaust**?
   b. Draw Inferences Why did the Nazis target certain groups for elimination?
4. **a. Recall** What events led to Germany's surrender?
   b. Analyze How did World War II change Europe?

Critical Thinking

5. **Sequencing** Draw a time line like this one. Using your notes on important events, place the main events and their dates on the time line.

   1917 ———————————— 1945

FOCUS ON WRITING

6. **Telling about World War II** Imagine that you are an adult during the Second World War. Where might you have lived? What might you have seen and done there? Write down some ideas in your notebook.

GROWTH AND DEVELOPMENT OF EUROPE **659**

Bellringer

If YOU lived there. . . Use the **Daily Bellringer Transparency** to help students answer the question.

 Daily Bellringer Transparency, Section 7

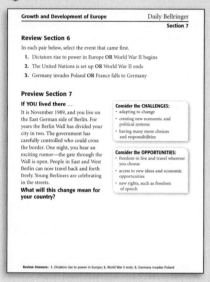

Growth and Development of Europe   Daily Bellringer
                                                         Section 7

Review Section 6
In each pair below, select the event that came first.
1. Dictators rise to power in Europe **OR** World War II begins
2. The United Nations is set up **OR** World War II ends
3. Germany invades Poland **OR** France falls to Germany

Preview Section 7
If YOU lived there ...
It is November 1989, and you live on the East German side of Berlin. For years the Berlin Wall has divided your city in two. The government has carefully controlled who could cross the border. One night, you hear an exciting rumor—the gate through the Wall is open. People in East and West Berlin can now travel back and forth freely. Young Berliners are celebrating in the streets.
What will this change mean for your country?

Consider the CHALLENGES:
• adapting to change
• creating new economic and political systems
• having many more choices and responsibilities

Consider the OPPORTUNITIES:
• freedom to live and travel wherever you choose
• access to new ideas and economic opportunities
• new rights, such as freedom of speech

Review Answers: 1. Dictators rise to power in Europe; 2. World War II ends; 3. Germany invades Poland

Academic Vocabulary

Review with students the high-use academic term in this section.

advocate to plead in favor of (p. 663)

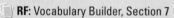 **RF:** Vocabulary Builder, Section 7

Taking Notes

Have students copy the chart onto their own paper and then use it to take notes on the section. This activity will prepare students for the Section Assessment, in which they will complete a chart that builds on the information using the Critical Thinking Skill: Summarizing.

What You Will Learn...

Main Ideas

1. The Cold War divided Europe between democratic and Communist nations.
2. Many Eastern European countries changed boundaries and forms of government at the end of the Cold War.
3. European cooperation has brought economic and political change to Europe.

The Big Idea

After years of division during the Cold War, today Europe is working toward unity.

Key Terms

superpowers, *p. 660*
Cold War, *p. 660*
arms race, *p. 662*
common market, *p. 664*
European Union (EU), *p. 664*

TAKING NOTES As you read, take notes on the Cold War, the end of the Cold War, and European cooperation. Use a chart like the one below to organize your notes.

Cold War	End of Cold War	European Cooperation

Europe since 1945

If YOU lived there...

It is November 1989, and you live on the East German side of Berlin. For years the Berlin Wall has divided your city in two. The government has carefully controlled who could cross the border. One night, you hear an exciting rumor—the gate through the Wall is open. People in East and West Berlin can now travel back and forth freely. Young Berliners are celebrating in the streets.

What will this change mean for your country?

BUILDING BACKGROUND In the years after World War II, tensions between the Western Allies and the Soviet Union divided Europe into East and West. By the late 1980s, those tensions were at last coming to an end. Europe could finally work toward unity.

The Cold War

Although Europeans were relieved when World War II ended, new problems soon arose. Countries whose governments and economies had been weakened during the war had to work to strengthen them. Entire cities had to be rebuilt. Most importantly, postwar tensions between the Allies divided Europe.

Superpowers Face Off

The United States and the Soviet Union emerged from World War II as the world's most powerful nations. Allies during the war, the two **superpowers**, or strong and influential countries, now distrusted each other. Growing hostility between the superpowers led to the **Cold War**, a period of tense rivalry between the United States and the Soviet Union.

Much of the hostility between the Soviet Union and the United States focused on political and economic differences. The United States is a democracy with an economy based on free enterprise. The Soviet Union was a Communist country, in which individual freedoms were limited. Its leaders exerted strict control over the political system and the economy. These basic differences separated the two countries.

Teach the Big Idea   At Level

Europe since 1945

1. **Teach** Ask students the questions in the Main Idea boxes under Direct Teach.

2. **Apply** Draw a line on the board and tell students that you will be creating a time line together. Tell them, however, that you will be working backwards, beginning on the right side with the fall of the Berlin Wall. As you work backward in time, encourage students to identify significant events as well as their causes. **LS Visual/Spatial**

3. **Review** Have students copy the time line on a piece of paper and add other notable events.

4. **Practice/Homework** Have students write a narrative emphasizing the causes and effects of Cold War events listed on the time line. **LS Verbal/Linguistic**

   Alternative Assessment Handbook, Rubrics 36: Time Lines; and 37: Writing Assignments

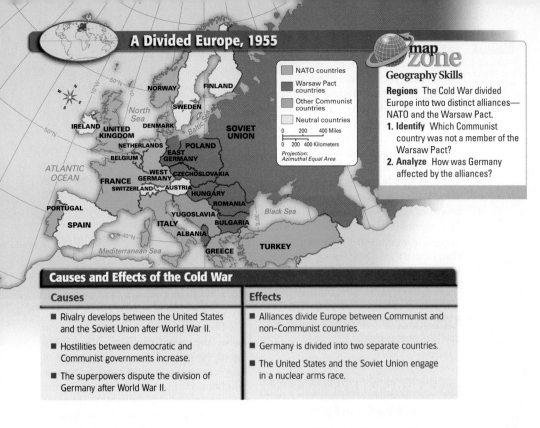

A Divided Europe, 1955

map zone

Geography Skills

Regions The Cold War divided Europe into two distinct alliances—NATO and the Warsaw Pact.
1. **Identify** Which Communist country was not a member of the Warsaw Pact?
2. **Analyze** How was Germany affected by the alliances?

Legend:
- NATO countries
- Warsaw Pact countries
- Other Communist countries
- Neutral countries

0   200   400 Miles
0   200   400 Kilometers
Projection: Azimuthal Equal Area

Causes and Effects of the Cold War

Causes	Effects
■ Rivalry develops between the United States and the Soviet Union after World War II.	■ Alliances divide Europe between Communist and non-Communist countries.
■ Hostilities between democratic and Communist governments increase.	■ Germany is divided into two separate countries.
■ The superpowers dispute the division of Germany after World War II.	■ The United States and the Soviet Union engage in a nuclear arms race.

A Divided Europe

The Cold War divided Europe into non-Communist and Communist countries. Most of Western Europe supported democracy and the United States. Much of Eastern Europe practiced Soviet-style communism. British prime minister Winston Churchill described the split that existed in Europe:

> " ...an iron curtain has descended across the Continent. Behind that line lie all the capitals of the ancient states of Central and Eastern Europe. ...all are subject ...not only to Soviet influence but to ...control from Moscow. "
>
> —from Winston Churchill's 1946 speech at Westminster College in Fulton, Missouri

Within this divided Europe was a divided Germany. After World War II, the Allies had separated Germany into four zones. By 1948 the Western Allies were ready to reunite their zones. However, the Soviet government feared the threat that a united Germany might pose. The next year, the Western zones were joined to form the Federal Republic of Germany, or West Germany. The Soviets helped to establish the German Democratic Republic, or East Germany. The city of Berlin, located within East Germany, was itself divided into East and West. In 1961 Communist leaders built the Berlin Wall to prevent any East Germans from fleeing to the West.

New alliances divided Europe even further. In 1949 the United States joined with several Western nations to create a powerful new alliance known as NATO, or the North Atlantic Treaty Organization.

Main Idea

❶ The Cold War

The Cold War divided Europe between democratic and Communist nations.

Define What is a superpower? *a strong and influential country*

Identify Who was Winston Churchill? *Prime Minister of Britain*

Elaborate What was life like in Eastern Europe during the Cold War? *Many aspects of life were strictly controlled by the government; people suffered from many shortages; they often lacked food and goods such as clothing and automobiles.*

📖 Map Zone Transparency: A Divided Europe, 1955

📄 **RF:** Literature, *Animal Farm* by George Orwell

Info to Know

Berlin Airlift After World War II both Germany and the city of Berlin were split into eastern and western parts. West Berlin was surrounded entirely by Communist East Germany, and the Soviet Union tried to take advantage of that fact in 1948. They blockaded the city, hoping the West would abandon it. Instead, Western democracies began supplying the city by air. At one point 8,000 tons of supplies a day were airlifted into West Berlin. The Soviet Union dropped the blockade about a year after it had started, and West Berlin survived.

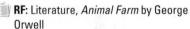

Collaborative Learning

At Level

Presenting the Space Race

Research Required

1. Tell students that one area of competition between the East and the West during the Cold War was the space race. Divide students into groups to research one of the following topics:
   - Sputnik
   - animals in space
   - Telstar
   - first view of the far side of the moon
   - Project Mercury
   - first man, first woman in space
   - Ranger 9 crash on the moon
   - Apollo 11 mission
   - Saturn V rocket
   - Apollo 13 mission

2. Have students choose a medium to present the results of their research. Some ideas include reports, posters, models, or dioramas. Each group member must have a specific role in the project and presentation. **Ⓛ Verbal/Linguistic, Visual/Spatial**

   📝 Alternative Assessment Handbook, Rubrics 29: Presentations; and 30: Research

Answers

Map Zone 1. *Yugoslavia;* **2.** *Germany was divided into two separate countries, and Berlin was also divided in two.*

❷ The End of the Cold War

Many Eastern European countries changed boundaries and forms of government at the end of the Cold War.

Define What is an arms race? *a competition between countries to build superior weapons*

Explain What caused violence after the break-up of Yugoslavia? *ethnic tensions*

Summarize Who was Mikhail Gorbachev, and what did he do? *the leader of the Soviet Union in the 1980s; introduced reforms that led to the breakup of the Soviet Union and its empire*

Info to Know

MAD Strategy During the Cold War, both the United States and the Soviet Union built huge stockpiles of nuclear weapons. America's nuclear strategy was based on the idea of *mutual assured destruction*, or MAD. The idea of MAD was this: as long as both sides could survive a surprise nuclear attack and return a devastating counter-attack, neither side would dare strike first. All nuclear treaties negotiated during those times relied on the idea of mutual assured destruction. That is, the treaties prevented either side from building an effective missile defense system. The theory was very controversial, but it worked.

Answers

Reading Check *It divided Europe into Western Europe, which was democratic, and Eastern Europe, which was Communist. Western Europe's economy grew while Eastern Europe's did not.*

Biography *possible answers: yes—Some were in favor of the reforms, expanded freedoms, and modernization; no—Some people don't like change; communists lost power and influence.*

662

THE IMPACT TODAY

NATO is still a powerful alliance today with 26 member nations in Europe and North America.

The members of NATO agreed to protect each other if attacked. In response, the Soviet Union formed its own alliance, the Warsaw Pact. Most Eastern European countries joined the Warsaw Pact. The two alliances used the threat of nuclear war to defend themselves. By the 1960s the United States, the Soviet Union, Britain, and France all had nuclear weapons.

The postwar division of Europe into East and West had a lasting effect on both sides. With U.S. assistance, many Western countries experienced economic growth. The economies of Communist Eastern Europe, however, failed to develop. Due to their lack of a market economy and strong industries, they suffered many shortages. They often lacked enough food, clothing, and automobiles to meet demand.

READING CHECK **Summarizing** How did the Cold War affect Europe?

BIOGRAPHY

Mikhail Gorbachev
(1931–)

Mikhail Gorbachev was a key figure in bringing the Cold War to an end. In 1985 Communist officials appointed Gorbachev the leader of the Soviet Union. He quickly enacted reforms to modernize his country. He expanded basic freedoms, such as freedom of speech and freedom of the press. His democratic reforms helped bring an end to communism in the Soviet Union. In 1990 Mikhail Gorbachev won the Nobel Peace Prize for his efforts to end the Cold War and promote peace.

Evaluating Do you think Gorbachev was a popular ruler? Why or why not?

The End of the Cold War

In the late 1980s tensions between East and West finally came to an end. The collapse of communism and the end of the Cold War brought great changes to Europe.

Triumph of Democracy

During the Cold War the United States and the Soviet Union competed against each other in an arms race. An **arms race** is a competition between countries to build superior weapons. Each country tried to create more-advanced weapons and to have more nuclear missiles than the other. This arms race was incredibly expensive. The high cost of the arms race eventually damaged the Soviet economy.

By the 1980s the Soviet economy was in serious trouble. Soviet leader Mikhail Gorbachev (GAWR-buh-chawf) hoped to solve the many problems his country faced. He reduced government control of the economy and introduced democratic elections. He improved relations with the United States. Along with U.S. president Ronald Reagan, Gorbachev took steps to slow the arms race.

In part because of these new policies, reform movements soon spread. Beginning in 1989, democratic movements swept through the East. For example, Poland and Czechoslovakia threw off Communist rule. Joyful Germans tore down the Berlin Wall that separated East and West. Several Soviet republics began to demand their independence. Finally, in December 1991 the Soviet Union broke apart.

Changes in Eastern Europe

The end of the Cold War brought many changes to Eastern Europe. These changes resulted from Germany's reunification, the creation of new countries, and rising ethnic tensions in southeastern Europe.

Critical Thinking: Comparing and Contrasting

Using a Venn Diagram

Review with students the information in this section describing the confrontation between the East and West during the Cold War. Point out that although the two sides had very different political and economic approaches, they also had much in common. Draw the graphic organizer on the board and have students compare and contrast the Cold War rivals.

LS **Verbal/Linguistic, Visual/Spatial**

Alternative Assessment Handbook, Rubrics 9: Comparing and Contrasting; and 11: Discussions

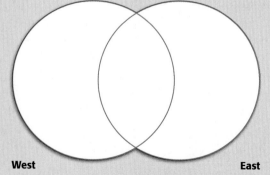

West   **East**

The Fall of Communism

Reforms in the Soviet Union in the 1980s encouraged support for democracy throughout Eastern Europe.

ANALYZING VISUALS What role did the people play in communism's collapse?

Fall of the Berlin Wall East and West Germans celebrate the fall of the Berlin Wall.

Democracy in Czechoslovakia
In 1989 pro-democracy demonstrations swept Czechoslovakia. Rallies like this one led to the collapse of Czechoslovakia's Communist government.

The reunification of East and West Germany was one of many changes in Eastern Europe that marked the end of the Cold War. After the fall of the Berlin Wall in 1989, thousands of East Germans began demanding change. In early 1990 the Communist government crumbled. A few months later, the governments of East and West Germany agreed to reunite. After 45 years of division, Germany was reunited.

Other important changes occurred in Eastern Europe after the Cold War. The breakup of the Soviet Union created more than a dozen independent nations. The Russian Federation is the largest and most powerful of these new countries. Ukraine, Lithuania, Belarus, and others also emerged from the former Soviet Union.

Ethnic conflicts have also transformed Eastern Europe since the end of the Cold War. For example, tensions between ethnic groups in Czechoslovakia and Yugoslavia led to the breakup of both countries.

In Czechoslovakia, ethnic tensions divided the country. Disputes between the country's two main ethnic groups emerged in the early 1990s. Both the Czechs and the Slovaks **advocated** separate governments. In January 1993 Czechoslovakia peacefully divided into two countries—the Czech Republic and Slovakia.

While ethnic problems in the former Czechoslovakia were peaceful, ethnic tension in Yugoslavia triggered violence. After the collapse of communism, several Yugoslav republics declared their independence. Different ethnic groups fought each other for control of territory. Yugoslavia's civil wars resulted in years of fighting and thousands of deaths. By 1994 Yugoslavia had split into five countries—Bosnia and Herzegovina, Croatia, Macedonia, Serbia and Montenegro, and Slovenia.

ACADEMIC VOCABULARY
advocate to plead in favor of

READING CHECK **Drawing Conclusions** How did the end of the Cold War affect Europe?

GROWTH AND DEVELOPMENT OF EUROPE **663**

Biography

Lech Walesa (1943–) Lech Walesa was one of many people who struggled against Soviet-style communism in Eastern Europe. In 1976 Walesa, an electrician in a Polish shipyard, took an active role in an anti-government labor union—and was removed from his job. He was jailed several times over the next decade until 1980, when some workers' rights were granted. The next year, Walesa was elected chairman of Solidarity, a group that began as a labor union and evolved into a political party. Solidarity's struggle was not easy—the Soviet Union forced the Polish government to declare martial law and crack down on the unruly Polish people. Walesa was awarded the Nobel Peace Prize in 1983. This recognition gave hope to his embattled followers. In the late 1980s when Mikhail Gorbachev was reforming the Soviet Union, Poland was already moving toward democracy. In 1990 Poland elected Lech Walesa as the first President of the Republic of Poland.

Differentiating Instruction

Below Level | **Standard English Mastery**

English-Language Learners

1. Divide students into two groups—West Berlin and East Berlin. Have students imagine that they have a cousin living on the other side of the Berlin Wall in the early 1980s. Have them use standard English to write a letter describing what life is like on their side.

2. Ask volunteers to read the letters that they have received to the rest of the class. After each letter is read, lead a class discussion. Alternate choosing volunteers from West Berlin and East Berlin.

3. Have students imagine that it is 1989, shortly before the fall of the Berlin Wall. Have them use standard English to engage in a similar exchange of letters. **LS Verbal/Linguistic, Interpersonal**

   Alternative Assessment Handbook, Rubric 40: Writing to Describe

Answers

Analyzing Visuals *Large crowds demonstrated at rallies and demanded freedom.*

Reading Check *Germany was reunited; Czechoslovakia and Yugoslavia were split apart; new democracies were formed.*

663

Main Idea

❸ European Cooperation

European cooperation has brought economic and political change to Europe.

Recall What is the currency used by many countries in Europe today? *the euro*

Identify What is the European Union? *an organization that promotes political and economic cooperation in Europe*

Compare and Contrast How is the European Union like an alliance, and how is it different? *alike—It is an agreement between nations; different—It is concerned with economic and political cooperation, not conflict or warfare.*

Info to Know

Airbus: European Cooperation in Action As part of their increasing cooperation, four European countries joined together to create the world's largest commercial aircraft manufacturer, Airbus. In 1970 France and Germany started the company; later Spain and the United Kingdom joined Airbus, which has overtaken its American rival, Boeing. In 2004, Airbus outperformed its major competitor by delivering more airplanes—and receiving more orders. Airbus has since received orders from airlines for the world's largest commercial plane, its 555-seat A380.

Answers

Facts about Countries *Germany, France, Italy, United Kingdom, Spain, and Poland because they have the most representatives*

THE WORLD ALMANAC
Facts about Countries **The European Union**

Country	Year Admitted	Monetary Unit	Representatives in the European Parliament
Austria	1995	Euro	18
Belgium	1952	Euro	24
Bulgaria	2007	Lev	18
Cyprus	2004	Pound	6
Czech Republic	2004	Koruna	24
Denmark	1973	Krone	14
Estonia	2004	Kroon	6
Finland	1995	Euro	14
France	1952	Euro	78
Germany	1952	Euro	99
Greece	1979	Euro	24
Hungary	2004	Forint	24
Ireland	1973	Euro	13
Italy	1952	Euro	78
Latvia	2004	Lats	9
Lithuania	2004	Litas	13
Luxembourg	1952	Euro	6
Malta	2004	Lira	5
The Netherlands	1952	Euro	27
Poland	2004	Zloty	54
Portugal	1986	Euro	24
Romania	2007	Leu	35
Slovakia	2004	Koruna	14
Slovenia	2004	Euro	7
Spain	1986	Euro	54
Sweden	1995	Krona	19
United Kingdom	1973	Pound	78

Drawing Conclusions What are the most powerful countries in the European Parliament?

go.hrw.com [KEYWORD: SK9 CH19]

European Cooperation

Many changes shaped postwar Europe. One of the most important of those changes was the creation of an organization that now joins together most of the countries of Europe.

A European Community

Two world wars tore Europe apart in the 1900s. After World War II many of Europe's leaders began to look for ways to prevent another deadly war. Some people believed that creating a feeling of community in Europe would make countries less likely to go to war. Leaders like Great Britain's Winston Churchill believed the countries of Europe should cooperate rather than compete. They believed strong economic and political ties were the key.

Six countries—Belgium, France, Italy, Luxembourg, the Netherlands, and West Germany—took the first steps toward European unity. In the early 1950s these six countries joined to create a united economic community. The organization's goal was to form a **common market**, a group of nations that cooperates to make trade among members easier. This European common market, created in 1957, made trade easier among member countries. Over time, other nations joined. Europeans had begun to create a new sense of unity.

The European Union

Since its beginning in the 1950s, many new nations have become members of this European community, now known as the European Union. The **European Union (EU)** is an organization that promotes political and economic cooperation in Europe. Today the European Union has more than 25 members. Together, they deal with a wide range of issues, including trade, the environment, and migration.

Cross-Discipline Activity: Mathematics
Above Level

Interpreting EU Data
Research Required

Point out the data in the fourth column of the European Union table *Representatives in the EU Parliament*. Ask students to decide if countries are represented fairly in the EU. Allow students to use the table to aid their process.

1. Decide if students will research data for all countries or only a sample; then assign them to look up current populations of selected EU countries.

2. For each country, divide the number of people in the country by the number of EU representatives. This is the country's *representation quotient*.

3. Arrange the results in an ordered list, and then decide how best to display the results. (A bar graph is a likely choice.)

4. If students chose to exhaustively compile data for all EU countries, they may compute the average representation quotient and draw it as a reference line on their bar graph.

LS Logical/Mathematical, Visual/Spatial

Alternative Assessment Handbook, Rubric 7: Charts

The European Union has executive, legislative, and judicial branches. The EU is run by a commission made up of one representative from each member nation. Two legislative groups, the Council of the European Union and the European Parliament, debate and make laws. Finally, the Court of Justice resolves disputes and enforces EU laws.

Through the European Union, the countries of Europe work together toward common economic goals. The EU helps its member nations compete with economic powers like the United States and Japan. In 1999 the EU introduced a common currency, the euro, which many member countries now use. The euro has made trade much easier.

The European Union has helped unify Europe. In recent years many countries from Eastern Europe have joined the EU. Other countries hope to join in the future. Despite difficulties, EU leaders hope to continue their goal to bring the nations of Europe closer together.

READING CHECK Finding Main Ideas How has cooperation in Europe affected the region?

In 2005 French and Dutch voters rejected a proposed constitution for the European Union. Here, voters in France demand that their vote be upheld.

SUMMARY AND PREVIEW In this section you learned how the European Union helped unify much of Europe after years of division during the Cold War. In the next chapter, you will learn about Southern Europe's physical geography and culture.

Section 7 Assessment

go.hrw.com
Online Quiz
KEYWORD: SK9 CH19

Reviewing Ideas, Terms, and Places

1. **a. Recall** What was the **Cold War**?
   b. Analyze Why was Europe divided during the Cold War?
2. **a. Identify** What new countries were formed after the end of the Cold War?
   b. Compare and Contrast How were ethnic tensions in Czechoslovakia and Yugoslavia similar and different?
   c. Evaluate Do you think the end of the Cold War helped or hurt the nations of Eastern Europe?
3. **a. Define** What is a **common market**?
   b. Make Inferences Why did some Europeans believe stronger economic and political ties could prevent war in Europe?

Critical Thinking

4. **Summarizing** Use your notes and the chart below to summarize the effect that each event had on the different regions of Europe. Write a sentence that summarizes the effect of each event.

	Cold War	End of Cold War	European Union
Western Europe			
Eastern Europe			

FOCUS ON WRITING

5. **Thinking about Europe since 1945** You are now in your mid-80s. How might events during and after the Cold War have affected your life?

GROWTH AND DEVELOPMENT OF EUROPE **665**

Direct Teach

Did you know . . .

Completed in 1994, the 31-mile long tunnel under the English Channel connects England with the European continent physically for the first time in history. On average, the Chunnel is 150 feet below the level of the seabed. A high-speed train, the Eurostar, takes passengers between London and Paris in about three hours. The Chunnel also accommodates motorized traffic. Many heavy goods that once had to cross the English Channel by sea are now driven across in trucks.

Review & Assess

Close

Discuss with students which European country they would most like to visit.

Review

Online Quiz, Section 7

Assess

SE Section 7 Assessment
PASS: Section 7 Quiz
Alternative Assessment Handbook

Reteach/Classroom Intervention

Interactive Reader and Study Guide, Section 7
Interactive Skills Tutor CD-ROM

Answers

Reading Check *It has helped to unify Europe through trade and politics.*

665

Social Studies Skills

Interpreting Political Cartoons

Activity Political Cartoons and Posters

Materials: copies of political cartoons and posters—especially of the World War I and World War II era—representing both sides of each conflict

1. Tell students that political cartoons and political posters use many of the same techniques.

2. Have students look at a variety of cartoons and posters and ask questions, such as the following:

   How are allies and enemies depicted in the drawings?

   What are some of the symbols used to identify which side countries, people, or armies belong to?

   Are events portrayed truthfully, dishonestly, or somewhere in between?

   LS Visual/Spatial

   📝 Alternative Assessment Handbook, Rubrics 27: Political Cartoons

   💿 Interactive Skills Tutor CD-ROM, Lesson 6: Interpret Maps, Graphs, Charts, Visuals, and Political Cartoons

   📝 **RF:** Social Studies Skills, Interpreting Political Cartoons

Social Studies Skills

Chart and Graph	Critical Thinking	Geography	Study

Interpreting Political Cartoons

Learn

Political cartoons are drawings that express views on important political or social issues. The ability to interpret political cartoons will help you understand issues and people's attitudes about them.

Political cartoons use images and words to convey a message about a particular event, person, or issue in the news. Most political cartoons use symbols to represent those ideas. For example, political cartoonists often use Uncle Sam to represent the United States. They also use titles and captions to express their point of view.

Practice

Examine the cartoon on this page. Then, answer the following questions to interpret the message of the cartoon.

❶ Read any title, labels, or captions to identify the subject of the cartoon. What information does the caption for this cartoon give you? To what event does this cartoon refer?

❷ Identify the people and symbols in the cartoon. What person is pictured in this cartoon? What does the crushed hammer and sickle represent?

❸ What message is the cartoonist trying to convey?

Soviet leader Mikhail Gorbachev examines a broken hammer and sickle.

Apply

Use your new skills to interpret a recent political cartoon. Locate a political cartoon that deals with an issue or event that has been in the news recently. Then answer the questions below.

1. What issue or event does the cartoon address?

2. What people or symbols are represented in the cartoon?

3. What point is the cartoon attempting to make?

666 CHAPTER 19

Social Studies Skills Activity: Interpreting Political Cartoons

Symbols in Political Cartoons

Below Level

1. Have students brainstorm symbols that they use and see in daily life. Common symbols include the dollar sign, eagle, dove, fist, heart, flower, flag, skull and crossbones, lightning bolt, donkey, elephant, maple leaf, flame, rainbow, shamrock, lion, black cat, equal sign, question mark, stop sign, arrow, and musical notes.

2. Tell students to choose ten symbols and label them with a word or phrase explaining each symbol's meaning.

3. Have students draw their own political cartoon using at least one symbol to help illustrate their idea. (The cartoon may also use captions or names as political cartoons do.) **LS** Visual/Spatial

   📝 Alternative Assessment Handbook, Rubric 27: Political Cartoons

Answers

Practice 1. *name of the person depicted; break-up of the Soviet Union;*
2. *Mikhail Gorbachev; the Soviet Union;*
3. *The Soviet Union broke up under the leadership of Mikhail Gorbachev.*

Apply *Answers will vary depending on the political cartoon selected.*

666

Chapter Review

Geography's Impact
video series
Review the video to answer the
closing question:
*Why do you think the creation
of the European Union was
important to many Europeans?*

Visual Summary

Use the visual summary below to help you review the main ideas of the chapter.

QUICK FACTS

During the Middle Ages most people lived on manors or in villages rather than cities.

The Enlightenment led to the end of monarchies in Europe.

After years of division, the end of the Cold War finally reunited the nations of Europe.

Reviewing Vocabulary, Terms, and Places

Match the words or names with their definitions or descriptions.

1. humanism   **4.** nationalism
2. capitalism   **5.** strategy
3. dictator   **6.** feudal system

a. a powerful ruler that rules by force
b. a system of exchanging land for military service
c. a plan for fighting a battle or war
d. economic system in which individuals own most businesses
e. devotion and loyalty to one's country
f. a philosophy that emphasized the abilities of human beings

Comprehension and Critical Thinking

SECTION 1 *(Pages 618–625)*

7. a. Describe What were two changes that affected Europe in the late Middle Ages?
   b. Explain What duties did knights have under the feudal system?

SECTION 2 *(Pages 628–633)*

8. a. Define What was the Reformation?
   b. Summarize How did the Renaissance affect art, literature, and science?

SECTION 3 *(Pages 634-640)*

9. a. Compare What ideas did John Locke and Jean-Jacques Rousseau share?
   b. Elaborate How did the English Bill of Rights and the Declaration of the Rights of Man and of the Citizen change the power of monarchs?

SECTION 4 *(Pages 642–646)*

10. a. Recall In which country did the Industrial Revolution start?
   b. Identify Cause and Effect How did industrial growth lead to improvements in society?

GROWTH AND DEVELOPMENT OF EUROPE **667**

Answers

Visual Summary

Review and Inquiry Have students use the visual summary to write a brief paragraph explaining why there was so much violence in Europe in the 1900s.

 Quick Facts Transparency: Visual Summary: Growth and Development of Europe

Reviewing Vocabulary, Terms, and Places

1. f   **4.** e
2. d   **5.** c
3. a   **6.** b

Comprehension and Critical Thinking

7. a. possible answer—the first step toward democracy with Magna Carta; the Black Death, which reduced the population and led to a labor shortage
   b. to provide military service to the nobles

8. a. religious reform movement begun by Martin Luther in the 1500s
   b. Artists used new techniques. Writers reflected humanism in subjects and themes. Scientists were inspired by the ancient Greeks and Romans to create new techniques and inventions.

9. a. knowledge, freedom, happiness
   b. English Bill of Rights gave greater power to Parliament; Declaration of Rights gave citizens free speech, press, religion; both limited the monarch's powers.

Review and Assessment Resources

Review and Reinforce

SE Chapter Review
 RF: Chapter Review
 Quick Facts Transparency: Visual Summary: Growth and Development of Europe
 Spanish Chapter Summaries Audio CD
OSP Holt PuzzlePro; Quiz Show for ExamView
 Quiz Game CD-ROM

Assess

SE Standardized Test Practice
 PASS: Chapter Test, Forms A and B
 Alternative Assessment Handbook
OSP ExamView Test Generator, Chapter Test
 Differentiated Instruction Modified Worksheets and Tests CD-ROM: Modified Chapter Test
HOAP Holt Online Assessment Program (in the Holt Interactive Online Student Edition)

Reteach/Intervene

 Interactive Reader and Study Guide
 Differentiated Instruction Teacher Management System: Lesson Plans
 Differentiated Instruction Modified Worksheets and Tests CD-ROM
 Interactive Skills Tutor CD-ROM

go.hrw.com
Online Resources
Chapter Resources:
KEYWORD: SK9 CH19

Answers

10. **a.** Great Britain

    b. manufactured goods cheaper; inventions made life easier; expansion of the middle class; capitalism

11. **a.** nationalism; competition for land, power, and resources; alliances; assassination of Archduke Ferdinand

    b. Allied Powers had renewed energy.

12. **a.** Axis Powers—Germany, Italy, Japan, and other countries; Allies—Soviet Union, Great Britain, United States, France, and other countries

    b. They were all dictators.

13. **a.** western—non-Communist, loyal to U.S.; eastern—Communist, loyal to Soviet Union

    b. possible answers: help—develop a good sense of community among nations, strengthen the economies of the member nations, bring cooperation and peace to Europe; hurt—nations may become too dependent on one another; EU limits government roles.

Using the Internet

14. Go to the HRW Web site and enter the keyword shown to access a rubric for this activity.

KEYWORD: SK9 TEACHER

Focus on Reading

15. *Detained* means the opposite of *set free.*

16. *Frenzied* means the opposite of *calm and orderly.*

RF: Focus on Reading, Using Context Clues–Contrast

Focus on Writing

17. **Rubric** Students' diary entries should

• be written from the perspective of someone in history

• include a detailed description of the events surrounding the person from his or her point of view

• include thoughts or feelings about each event from the person's point of view

RF: Focus on Writing, Writing a Diary Entry

SECTION 5 *(Pages 648–652)*

11. **a. Recall** What causes led to the outbreak of World War I?

    b. Draw Conclusions How did the U.S. entry into World War I affect the war's outcome?

SECTION 6 *(Pages 654–659)*

12. **a. Identify** What two alliances fought in World War II? What countries belonged to each?

    b. Compare In what ways were Joseph Stalin, Benito Mussolini, and Adolf Hitler similar?

SECTION 7 *(Pages 660–665)*

13. **a. Identify** Into what alliances was Europe divided during the Cold War?

    b. Predict Do you think that the European Union will hurt or help Europe? Explain.

Using the Internet

go.hrw.com
KEYWORD: SK9 CH19

14. **Activity: Creating a Biography** The Renaissance saw many advances in art and literature. Enter the activity keyword to see some artists and writers of the period. Choose one to learn more about and write a biography of his or her life. Be sure to include some information on the person's accomplishments.

FOCUS ON READING AND WRITING

Using Context Clues—Contrast *Use context clues to determine the meaning of the underlined words in the sentences below.*

15. During World War II people who aided Jews were often <u>detained</u> rather than set free.

16. Many celebrations at the end of the Cold War were <u>frenzied</u>, not calm and orderly.

Writing a Diary Entry *Use your notes and the directions below to write a diary entry.*

17. Choose the person whose journal you will write. Describe the events he or she experienced from his or her point of view. Remember to describe his or her thoughts and feelings about each event.

Social Studies Skills

Interpreting Political Cartoons *Examine the political cartoon below, then answer the questions that follow.*

18. What event does the cartoon depict?

19. What point is the artist trying to make?

Map Activity ⭐Interactive

20. **Europe** On a separate sheet of paper, match the letters on the map with their correct labels.

Berlin	Poland	Germany
London	Moscow	Yugoslavia
Paris		

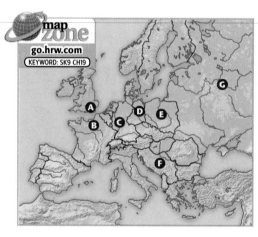

go.hrw.com
KEYWORD: SK9 CH19

Social Studies Skills

18. the D-Day invasion of Normandy, France

19. possible answer—The Allies had more capacity to produce weapons than the Axis Powers, and that capacity proved decisive in the conflict.

Map Activity

20. **A.** London

    B. Paris

    C. Germany

    D. Berlin

    E. Poland

    F. Yugoslavia

    G. Moscow

DIRECTIONS (1-7): For each statement or question, write on a separate answer sheet the number of the word or expression that, of those given, best completes the statement or answers the question.

1 Which world leader was *most* involved in the end of the Cold War?
(1) Francis Ferdinand
(2) Joseph Stalin
(3) Mikhail Gorbachev
(4) Winston Churchill

2 Which event marked the beginning of the French Revolution?
(1) Congress of Vienna
(2) Great Fear
(3) Reign of Terror
(4) Storming of the Bastille

3 Which of the following was a result of World War II?
(1) The United Nations was formed.
(2) Adolf Hitler was charged with war crimes.
(3) A Communist revolution took place in Russia.
(4) The U.S. economy collapsed.

4 Which document limited the powers of the king of England?
(1) Black Death
(2) Crusade
(3) Feudal system
(4) Magna Carta

5 Who was the first leader of Communist Russia?
(1) Benito Mussolini
(2) Joseph Stalin
(3) Mikhail Gorbachev
(4) Vladimir Lenin

6 The period of rapid growth in machine-made goods during the 1700s and 1800s was the
(1) American Revolution.
(2) French Revolution.
(3) Industrial Revolution.
(4) Scientific Revolution.

7 Ethnic tensions at the end of the Cold War divided which of the following countries?
(1) France
(2) Germany
(3) United States
(4) Yugoslavia

Base your answer to question 8 on the graph below and on your knowledge of social studies.

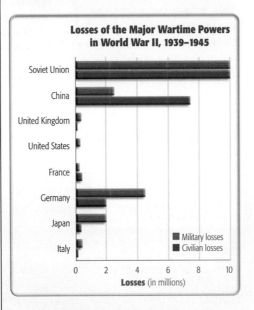

Losses of the Major Wartime Powers in World War II, 1939–1945

Losses (in millions)
■ Military losses
■ Civilian losses

8 **Constructed-Response Question** Which Allied power lost the fewest civilians during World War II? Which lost the most?

Answers

1. 3
Break Down the Question This question requires students to recall factual information from Section 7.

2. 4
Break Down the Question Options 1, 2, and 3 can be eliminated, because each took place after the storming of the Bastille. Refer students who miss the question to Section 3.

3. 1
Break Down the Question This question requires students to recall factual information from Section 6.

4. 4
Break Down the Question Options 1, 2, and 3 are not documents. Option 4 is the correct answer.

5. 4
Break Down the Question This question requires students to recall factual information from Section 5.

6. 3
Break Down the Question This question requires students to recall factual information from Section 4.

7. 4
Break Down the Question This question requires students to recall factual information from Section 7.

8. Constructed-Response Question
Of the Allied powers, the United States lost the fewest civilians during World War II while the Soviet Union lost the most.

Reteach/Intervention Resources

Reproducible
- Interactive Reader and Study Guide
- Differentiated Instruction Teacher Management System: Lesson Plans

Technology
- Quick Facts Transparency: Visual Summary: Growth and Development of Europe
- Differentiated Instruction Modified Worksheets and Tests CD-ROM
- Interactive Skills Tutor CD-ROM

Tips for Test Taking

I'm Stuck! Suggest to students the following tips if they come across a test question that stumps them. Don't get frustrated. First master the question to make sure you understand what is being asked. Then work through the strategies you have already learned. If you are still stuck, circle the question and go on to others. Come back to it later. What if you still have no idea? Practice the 50/50 strategy and make an educated guess.

Bellringer

Motivate Once students are seated, begin class by asking them, with their books closed, to list as many facts as they can about France. Write students' ideas on the board and have students copy them onto notebook paper. Be sure to reinforce students' understanding of the differences between factual statements and opinion statements. If a student presents an opinion statement as fact, write it down on a separate area of the board. Explain why the statement is an opinion and not a fact. When students have run out of ideas, allow them to open their texts. As students read through the material, have them see if they can find evidence to support their factual statements in the text.

Key Terms

Preteach the following terms:

culinary cooking (p. 671)

impression an imitation or likeness of something in art (p. 673)

strikes protests by employees against an employer (p. 675)

influx arrival, especially of many at the same time (p. 675)

Case Study

🟦 France

Geography

France is one of Europe's largest and most influential countries. Celebrated around the world for its food, art, and culture, France is also one of Europe's major economic powers. From its location in west-central Europe, France affects life in the rest of the continent and the world.

The physical features of France vary from region to region. The north and west are generally flat and low, being part of the huge Northern European Plain. Farther south, the land gets higher and more rugged. The rocky plateau known as the Massif Central covers most of south-central France. Three mountain ranges are also in the south. In the southwest, the Pyrenees form the boundary between France and Spain. To the east, the Alps and the Jura Mountains border Switzerland.

As you can see on the map on the next page, several rivers run out of these mountains. The longest of these rivers is the Loire (LWAHR), which begins in the Massif Central. Not far away is the Rhone, which runs south to the Mediterranean. Farther north, the Seine (SAYN) flows past the capital, Paris.

Paris is also by far France's largest city. It is home to about 10 million people. Fashionable and fast-paced, Paris is a center of business, finance, learning, and culture. It boasts world-class

Facts About **QUICK FACTS**

France

Official Name: Republic of France

Capital: Paris

Area: 211,209 square miles (slightly smaller than Texas)

Population: 63.7 million (258 people/square mile)

Average Life Expectancy: 81 years

Official Language: French

Major Religion: Roman Catholicism

Unit of Currency: Euro

1 The **Loire River,** the longest river in France, winds its way through the heart of the country. The Loire Valley is famous for its beautiful scenery and for the many châteaux, or castles, that line the river.

670 CASE STUDY

Teach the Case Study

At Level

France

1. **Teach** Ask students the questions in the Main Idea boxes under Direct Teach.

2. **Apply** Have students fold three sheets of notebook paper into two columns. Have students label the left column "Questions" and the right column "Answers." At the top of each sheet students should write down one of the blue headings. As students read the material, have them take notes in the right column. When students have finished reading, have them go back through their notes and write a question in the left column that is answered by their notes in the right column.

3. **Review** Review students' notes as a class. Have students call out some of their questions and see if other students can answer them.

4. **Practice/Homework** Have students write a brief summary of what they learned by reading the Case Study. **LS Verbal/Linguistic**

   📝 Alternative Assessment Handbook, Rubric 37: Writing Assignments

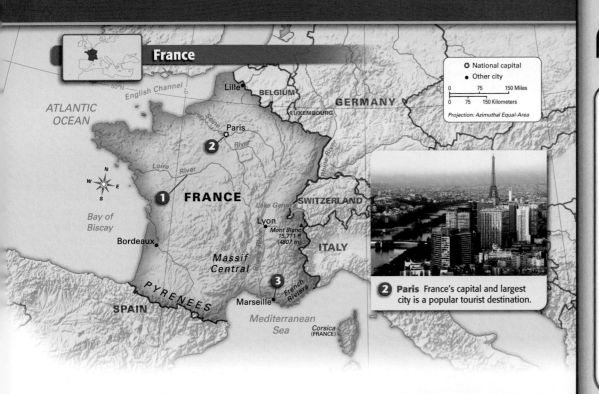

France

National capital
Other city

0 75 150 Miles
0 75 150 Kilometers
Projection: Azimuthal Equal-Area

ATLANTIC OCEAN

English Channel

Lille

BELGIUM

LUXEMBOURG

GERMANY

Paris

Seine River

Loire River

FRANCE

Bay of Biscay

Bordeaux

Lake Geneva

SWITZERLAND

Lyon

Mont Blanc
15,771 ft
(4807 m)

ITALY

Massif Central

Marseille

French Riviera

PYRENEES

SPAIN

Mediterranean Sea

Corsica (FRANCE)

2 Paris France's capital and largest city is a popular tourist destination.

museums, art galleries, and restaurants as well as famous landmarks such as the Eiffel Tower and Notre Dame Cathedral. The city's beauty has earned it the nickname the "City of Light" and has made it one of the most visited places in the world.

Paris is not France's only large city. The second largest of France's cities is Marseille (mar-SAY), a Mediterranean seaport. Lyon (LYAWN), located on the Rhone, is a business center and has been called the culinary capital of France. A complex network of highways, canals, and trains links these and other French cities together.

Case Study Assessment

1. What are the key physical features of France?

2. What makes Paris a major world city?

3. **Activity** Plan a five-day trip to France. Identify places you would like to visit and what you would like to see. Then draw up an itinerary, or schedule, for your trip.

3 Marseille is a busy seaport on the southern coast of France.

FRANCE **671**

Cross-Discipline Activity: English/Language Arts

At Level

Writing a Letter

Standard English Mastery

1. Divide students into pairs. Have pairs imagine that they are on vacation together in France. Direct students' attention to the photographs throughout the Case Study.

2. Tell student pairs that they have a free day and can visit any of the places in the photographs. Have students examine the photographs and decide which one to visit.

3. Have the student pairs use standard English to write a single letter home telling a friend why

they chose a particular place or event, what time of day and season it was, how long they stayed, what the weather was like, and so on.

4. Then have student pairs use a thesaurus or dictionary to add appropriate adjectives and descriptive phrases to their sentences.

LS Verbal/Linguistic

Alternative Assessment Handbook, Rubrics 14: Group Activity; and 25: Personal Letters

Direct Teach

Main Idea

Geography

Recall What is the Massif Central? *rocky plateau that covers most of south-central France*

Summarize What are the major rivers of France? *the Loire, the Rhone, and the Seine*

Make Inferences Where in France might you go to study French food and cooking styles? Explain your answer. *possible answer—Lyon, because it has been called the culinary capital of France*

📦 Quick Facts Transparency: Facts About France

📦 Map Zone Transparency: France

Info to Know

The French Flag France's flag is often called the "tricolor," in reference to the flag's three colors—blue, white, and red. The flag originated in the French Revolution. At that time a Paris militia began sporting hats with the city's colors—blue and red. To this was added white, the color of the king. Though various flags represented France in the intervening years, the "tricolor" was never entirely out of favor. The French constitutions of 1946 and 1958 made the "tricolor" the official national emblem.

Answers

Case Study Assessment **1.** *the Massif Central, the Pyrenees, the Alps, and the Jura Mountains, rivers including the Loire, Rhone, and Seine;* **2.** *It is a center of business, finance, learning, and culture.* **3.** *Students' responses will vary. See Rubric 37: Writing Assignments, in the* Alternative Assessment Handbook.

671

800
Frankish emperor Charlemagne is crowned Emperor of the Romans after building a huge empire.

Charlemagne

1066
French duke William of Normandy invades England and becomes its king.

1337–1453
The French and English fight for control of France in the Hundred Years' War.

History and Culture

Recall What was France known as during the period of Celtic and Roman rule? *Gaul*

Generalize What kind of government has France had for most of its history? *monarchy*

Find Main Ideas Why was the first half of the twentieth century hard for France? *The country endured two world wars, during both of which the country was invaded.*

Draw Conclusions Would France be a good place to go to study Gothic architecture and impressionist art? Why or why not? *possible answer— Yes. The first Gothic cathedrals were built in France and France was the center of the impressionist movement.*

Info to Know

The French Motto Travelers to France will likely see the words "Liberté, Egalité, Fraternité" throughout their journey. These three words—liberty, equality, and fraternity in English—are the official motto of France. The themes expressed by the motto are representative of the Enlightenment. It should be no surprise, then, that the motto first appeared during the French Revolution, an event heavily inspired by Enlightenment ideals. The French constitutions of 1946 and 1958 reinforced the motto's importance to the nation. Today, among other places, the motto is inscribed on the reverse of the French version of the one Euro coin.

History and Culture

France has one of the longest histories in Europe. Cave paintings found in southwest France show the people have lived in the area for more than 15,000 years. Since that time, the French have helped shape life throughout Europe.

In ancient times, France—then called Gaul—was ruled by first the Celts and then the Romans. After Rome fell, the area that is now France was invaded by the Franks, after whom the country is named. The Franks' greatest ruler was Charlemagne, who built a powerful Christian empire that included most of Europe. France's later kings all claimed to be descendents of the mighty Charlemagne.

Kings continued to rule France until the French Revolution of the late 1700s. After the revolution, a general named Napoleon led France in building a new empire and was only stopped by the joint effort of several European countries.

The first half of the twentieth century was hard for France. The country was invaded by Germany during both world wars. However, since the 1950s France has rebounded from these invasions and has enjoyed rapid growth.

Experiencing French Culture

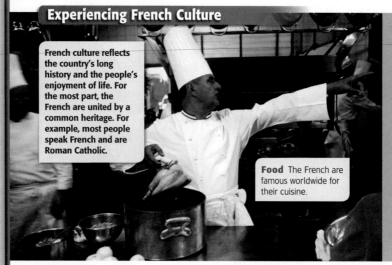

French culture reflects the country's long history and the people's enjoyment of life. For the most part, the French are united by a common heritage. For example, most people speak French and are Roman Catholic.

Food The French are famous worldwide for their cuisine.

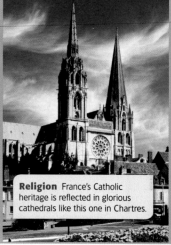

Religion France's Catholic heritage is reflected in glorious cathedrals like this one in Chartres.

672 CASE STUDY

Differentiating Instruction

Special Needs Learners
| At Level |
| Prep Required |

Show American identity cards such as a driver's license or school photo ID. Have students explain what purpose these cards serve. Discuss how a *cultural* identity is different from a legal or official identity. Have students give examples of elements of American cultural identity and compare them to elements of French cultural identity. **LS Verbal/Linguistic**

Alternative Assessment Handbook, Rubric 9: Comparing and Contrasting

Advanced/Gifted and Talented
| Above Level |
| Research Required |

Have students use art books and the Internet to learn about painters such as Degas, Monet, Manet, Renoir, and Mary Cassatt. Have each student pick one painter and give a short, illustrated talk about his or her life, style of painting, subjects for paintings, and most famous works.
LS Visual/Spatial, Verbal/Linguistic

Alternative Assessment Handbook, Rubric 29: Presentations

1789
The French Revolution begins with the storming of the Bastille prison.

1815
Several European powers band together to defeat French emperor Napoleon.

1940–1944
During World War II, France is occupied by German forces.

2000

Despite their sometimes turbulent history, the French enjoy life. They have a phrase to describe this attitude—*joie de vivre* (zhwah duh VEEV-ruh), meaning "joy of life." The French enjoy good food, good company, and good conversation. Their enjoyment of food has helped make French cooking one of the most famous styles of cooking in the world.

Throughout history, the French have also made major contributions to art. In the Middle Ages, they built the first Gothic cathedrals, such as Notre Dame in Paris. In the 1800s France was the center of the impressionist movement. This style of painting uses rippling light to create an impression of a scene. Today France is also known for its fashion and film industries.

WWII German occupation of France

Case Study Assessment

1. How did France change in the 1900s?
2. What is *joie de vivre,* and how is it reflected in France?
3. **Activity** Re-create a key moment from French history. Write a short skit that depicts a major event. Be sure to describe what happened and who was involved.

Fashion Paris is one of the world's leading fashion centers.

Art The style of painting known as impressionism was one of France's gifts to the art world.

FRANCE **673**

France Today

Identify What are France's major crops? *wheat and grapes*

Elaborate What form of government does France have? How is it organized? *republican (democratic); three branches; an executive, legislative, and judicial branches*

Summarize What issues does France face today? *economy not strong enough, short work week, immigration strains resources and changes culture*

Info to Know

The Eiffel Tower Named after its designer, Gustave Eiffel, the Eiffel tower rises to a height of 1,063 feet above Paris. It is the tallest building in the city. The structure was built between 1887 and 1889. It served as the entrance arch to the 1889 World's Fair. Construction of the tower took the efforts of over 300 workers, 18,038 pieces of iron, and about 2.5 million rivets. When the tower first opened, many Parisians saw it as an eyesore. Today, the structure is one of the most widely visited landmarks in the world, having attracted more than 200 million visitors since 1889.

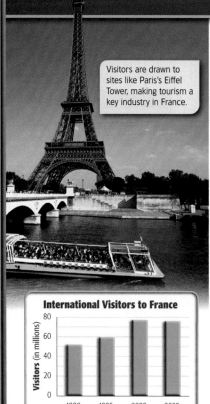

Visitors are drawn to sites like Paris's Eiffel Tower, making tourism a key industry in France.

International Visitors to France

(bar graph showing Visitors in millions on y-axis from 0 to 80, Year on x-axis)
- 1990: ~50
- 1995: ~60
- 2000: ~76
- 2005: ~74

Source: World Tourism Organization, *Tourism Market Trends*, 2006

France Today

Economics

France has a strong economy, one of the strongest in Europe. It is an active member of the European Union (EU) and benefits from trade with other EU members. For example, France is the leading agricultural producer in the EU and exports many crops to other members. Among its major crops are wheat and grapes. In addition, France is the world's leading producer and seller of wine and cheese. French wines and cheeses are admired around the world.

Another important industry in France is tourism. Statistics show that France is one of the most visited countries in the world year after year. As you read earlier, millions of tourists are drawn to the famous monuments of Paris.

In addition, people are drawn to other regions of France. Some head to the south of France to ski in the Alps or to relax at one of the beaches of the French Riviera. This resort area along the Mediterranean coast is famous for its sun and sandy beaches. The Riviera is also the site of an annual film festival in Cannes (KAHN) that attracts thousands of movie enthusiasts. Still other tourists are drawn to France's charming small towns or to the châteaux (sha-TOH), or castles, of the Loire Valley.

Government

After the French Revolution, France became one of the first countries in the world to have a republican government. Though the nature of the government has changed several times since then, France is still a republic today.

Structure of the French Government

France's government divides power among three branches. This division of power keeps any individual or group from becoming too powerful.

Executive Branch Headed by a president and a prime minister, it enforces the country's laws.

Legislative Branch Made up of two houses, the National Assembly and the Senate, it makes laws.

Judicial Branch Two branches of courts hear cases and punish those who break laws.

674 CASE STUDY

Government in France and the United States

Research Required

1. Remind students that the United States is a republic, just like France. Point out to students the similarities between the structure of the French government and the structure of the United States government.

2. Divide the class into groups. On a sheet of construction paper, have groups create a chart with three columns and two rows. Have students label the columns, Executive, Legislative, and Judicial, and the rows, France, and the United States.

3. In their groups, have students fill in their charts with as much information about the three branches of government in France and the United States as will fit. Allow students access to print or online resources to supplement the information in the text.

4. Hold a class discussion about the similarities and differences between the governments of France and the United States. **LS Visual/Spatial**

🗒 Alternative Assessment Handbook, Rubrics 7: Charts; and 14: Group Activity

As you can see in the diagram on the previous page, France's government is made up of three branches. By dividing power among the three branches, the French keep any one person or group of people from becoming too powerful.

The first branch of France's government is the executive branch, which is responsible for enforcing the country's laws. It is headed by a president, who is elected every five years, and a prime minister, who is appointed by the president. The second branch, the legislative branch, is made up of two parts. They are the National Assembly and the Senate, and they work together to make laws. The third branch, the judicial branch, includes several types of courts.

Issues

On the whole, France is a prosperous country with a strong economy. However, the country is not without its challenges. For example, French officials do not think that the economy is as strong as it could be. They blame this lack of strength on France's short work week.

In most industrialized countries, people work 40 hours each week. In France, though, most people work only 35 hours each week. Efforts by some officials to lengthen the French work week have led to protests and strikes. Such strikes have periodically shut down major industries in France.

France has also faced cultural challenges. Since the early 1900s, many residents of former French colonies have left their homes to settle in France. This influx of immigrants put strains on France's resources. In addition, some officials feared that France would lose its unique culture if too many immigrants arrived. They took steps to limit immigration, which has increased some people's resentment of the government.

Angry French workers protest a government plan to extend their work week. Most French people now work 35 hours a week.

Case Study Assessment

1. What does each branch of France's government do?

2. What are France's major industries?

3. **Activity** What do you think is the most serious issue facing France? Create a poster describing the issue and suggesting a possible solution.

FRANCE **675**

European Unity

Part A: Short-Answer Questions

Directions: Read and examine the following documents. Then, on a separate sheet of paper, answer the questions using complete sentences.

Word Help

cohesion unity
incipient something in its beginning stages

Info to Know

European Union Member States As of June 2008 there were 27 European Union member states, or countries. Those countries were: Austria, Belgium, Bulgaria, Cyprus, Czech Republic, Denmark, Estonia, Finland, France, Germany, Greece, Hungary, Ireland, Italy, Latvia, Lithuania, Luxembourg, Malta, Netherlands, Poland, Portugal, Romania, Slovakia, Slovenia, Spain, Sweden, and the United Kingdom. Several countries, including Norway and Switzerland, have opted not to join the union. Other countries, like Turkey and Croatia, are vying for membership.

DOCUMENT 1

The Maastricht Treaty was signed on February 7, 1992. Its official name was the Treaty on European Union, and it led to the creation of the European Union (EU). A portion of the treaty outlining the objectives of the EU appears below.

The Union shall set itself the following objectives:

* to promote economic and social progress which is balanced and sustainable, in particular through the creation of an area without internal frontiers, through the strengthening of economic and social cohesion and through the establishment of economic and monetary union, ultimately including a single currency . . .

* to assert its identity on the international scene, in particular through the implementation of a common foreign and security policy . . .

* to strengthen the protection of the rights and interests of the nationals [residents] of its Member States . . .

* to develop close cooperation on justice and home affairs . . .

1a. What steps does the treaty say the EU will take to promote economic and social progress?

_____

1b. What other goals does the EU have?

_____

DOCUMENT 2

The EU is hard to describe. It is not a federation, or loose association of states, but it is also not a unified country. The following passage from the Central Intelligence Agency (CIA) discusses the difficulty of categorizing the EU.

Although the EU is not a federation in the strict sense, it is far more than a free-trade association such as ASEAN, NAFTA, or Mercosur, and it has many of the attributes associated with independent nations: its own flag, anthem, founding date, and currency, as well as an incipient common foreign and security policy in its dealings with other nations.

In the future, many of these nation-like characteristics are likely to be expanded.

—*The World Factbook*, 2008

2a. What attributes does the EU share with independent nations?

_____

2b. According to this document, how will the EU change in the future?

_____

Critical Thinking: Evaluating

At Level

Evaluating Sources

1. Have students examine each of the documents in this feature. In particular, have students pay attention to the source of each document. Ask students: what is each document's source? *Document 1, Maastricht Treaty; Document 2, CIA World Factbook; Document 3, United Arab Emirates newspaper; Document 4, Library of Congress Country Studies*

2. For each document, have students state whether they think it is a reliable source. Have students explain their reasoning.

Discuss why Documents 1, 2, and 4 are reliable sources and why Document 3 is a source of questionable reliability.

3. Remind students that while political cartoons can be informative, they often express bias and opinion. What motivation might a foreign newspaper have for doubting the feasibility of the European Union? **LS Verbal/Linguistic**

Alternative Assessment Handbook, Rubric 11: Discussions

Answers

Document 1 1a. *creation of an area without internal frontiers, establishment of an economic and monetary union;*
1b. *common foreign and security policy, strengthening of rights and interests of residents, cooperation on justice and home affairs*

Document 2 2a. *flag, anthem, founding date, currency, the beginnings of a common foreign and security policy;*
2b. *It will become more nation-like.*

DOCUMENT 3

People around the world have watched the progress of the European Union. The political cartoon below appeared in a newspaper in Dubai, part of the United Arab Emirates in the Middle East.

UNITED STATES OF EUROPE

THE AMBITIOUS PROJECT IS TOO HIGH...

EU SUMMIT MEETING

PARESH

3a. According to this cartoon, what goal are members of the EU working toward?

_____

3b. What does the cartoonist suggest about their chances of reaching this goal?

_____

DOCUMENT 4

The nation of Turkey, which is located partially in Europe and partially in Asia, has been trying to join Europe's union since 1987. The passage below, from the Library of Congress Country Studies series, explains why Turkey's application has not so far been accepted.

> The principal economic objections to Turkish membership center on the relative underdevelopment of Turkey's economy compared to the economies of EC/EU members and Turkey's high rate of population growth . . . The political obstacles to EU membership concern Turkey's domestic and foreign policies. Because the European body prides itself on being an association of democracies, the 1980 military coup—in a country enjoying associate status—was a severe shock . . . In terms of foreign policy, the main obstacle to EU membership remains the unresolved issues between Turkey and EU member Greece.

4a. What economic obstacles stand between Turkey and EU membership?

_____

4b. What political challenges have kept Turkey out of the EU?

_____

Part B: Essay

Historical Context: Created in 1992, the European Union has brought many countries in Europe together politically, economically, and culturally. Membership in the EU has exploded, and new countries apply nearly every year.

TASK: Using information from the four documents and your knowledge of social studies, write an essay in which you:

- examine the purpose for the creation of the EU.
- explain why countries want to belong to the EU.

EUROPE **677**

Critical Thinking: Making Generalizations

At Level

European Union Political Cartoons

Materials drawing paper, art supplies

1. Tell students that Americans have mixed and often strong opinions about the European Union. Some Americans believe that the European Union will finally bring lasting peace to a continent that has spawned some of history's most destructive wars. Other Americans see the formation of the European Union as a threat to U.S. economic and political dominance in world affairs.

2. Have students formulate their own opinions about the European Union. Then have students express their opinions by creating a political cartoon.

3. Call on volunteers to present and explain their political cartoons to the class. **LS Visual/Spatial**

📝 Alternative Assessment Handbook, Rubric 27: Political Cartoons

---

Word Help

coup the overthrow of a government

Info to Know

European Union Government The EU is governed by three main bodies: the European Parliament, the Council of the European Union, and the European Commission. The European Parliament represents the interests of the European people. Its 785 members' main duty is to pass laws. The Council of the European Union represents the interests of EU member states. Ministers in various policy areas (education, economy, etc.) from each EU country are members of the Council. In addition to passing laws, the Council is responsible for developing a common EU foreign and security policy. The European Commission exists to represent Europe as a whole. One person from each member country is selected for the Commission. The Commission develops proposals for laws (that must be passed by the Parliament and the Council). The Commission also sees to it that EU policies, programs, and laws are faithfully carried out.

Answers

Document 3 3a. *becoming a country called the United States of Europe;* **3b.** *that it is not very likely*

Document 4 4a. *Turkey's economy is underdeveloped and its population growing too rapidly.* **4b.** *Turkey has been politically unstable recently and has unresolved issues with Greece.*

Essay *Students' essays will vary but should thoroughly address all aspects of the task.*

677

Bellringer

Motivate Have students brainstorm people who have affected European or Russian history. Remind students to think beyond just listing political figures. People such as Michelangelo and Galileo are also significant figures.

Prewrite

Organizing Information Remind students to organize their notes of the event in chronological order, or the order in which major parts of the event took place. Here are some tips:

- Identify the major parts of the event. This will help students to have just one main idea for each paragraph.
- Include supporting details about each major event. These details should help explain or describe what happened— as well as keep the narrative moving forward in time.
- Use vivid language to describe the person (and others) and the event itself, so the story comes alive!

Language Arts Connection

Activity **Writing Portfolios** Coordinate the following activity with your school's language arts department. If students maintain writing portfolios in their language arts class, suggest that they add this paper to them. With the permission of their teacher, they can engage in an ongoing revision of the paper as part of their language arts instruction.

Rubric

Students' papers should

- introduce the person and event.
- clearly identify the importance of the event.
- use chronological order.
- write at least one paragraph for each major part of the event.
- include facts and vivid language.
- briefly summarize the importance of the person and event in the final paragraph.
- use correct grammar, punctuation, spelling, and capitalization.

678 UNIT 5

A Biographical Narrative

People have shaped the world. Who are the important people in history? What were the critical events in their lives? How did geography or location affect those events? These are questions we ask as we try to understand our world.

Assignment

Write a biographical narrative about a significant event in the life of a historical figure such as Joan of Arc, Martin Luther, Napoleon, or Mikhail Gorbachev.

1. Prewrite

Choose a Topic

- Choose a person who affected European or Russian history in some way.
- Choose a specific event or incident in the person's life. For example, you might choose Napoleon at the Battle of Waterloo.

> **TIP** To choose the event, think about the person's importance or signficance. Choose an event that will help you make that point.

Gather and Organize Information

- Look for information about your topic in the library or on the Internet. Book-length biographies about the person are a good source.
- Identify the parts of the event. Organize them in chonological, or time, order. Note details about people, actions, and the location of the event.

2. Write

Use a Writer's Framework

A Writer's Framework

Introduction
- Introduce the person and the event.
- Identify the importance of the event.

Body
- Write at least one paragraph for each major part of the event. Include specific details.
- Use chronological, or time, order to organize the parts of the event.

Conclusion
- Summarize the importance of the person and event in the final paragraph.

678

3. Evaluate and Revise

Review and Improve Your Paper

- Read your first draft at least twice, and then use the questions below to evaluate your paper.
- Make the changes needed to improve your paper.

Evaluation Questions for a Biographical Narrative

❶ Do you introduce the person and event and identify the importance of each?
❷ Do you have one paragraph for each major part of the event?
❸ Do you include specific details about people, actions, and location?
❹ Do you use chronological order, the order in time, to organize the parts of the event?
❺ Do you end the paper with a summary of the importance of the person and event?

4. Proofread and Publish

Give Your Explanation the Finishing Touch

- Make sure your transitional phrases—such as then, next, later, or finally—help clarify the order of the actions that took place.
- Make sure you capitalized all proper names.
- You can share your biographical narrative by reading it aloud in class or adding it to a class collection of biographies.

5. Practice and Apply

Use the steps and strategies outlined in this workshop to write your biographical narrative. Share your work with others, comparing and contrasting the importance of the people and events.

Struggling Readers   **Below Level**

Students with below level writing skills might approach this assignment in an alternate way.

- Suggest that they present a collection of "photos" to tell the story of their person. They can draw pictures or make copies of existing magazine/book illustrations, accompanied by brief captions describing each visual.

LS Kinesthetic, Verbal/Linguistic

Alternative Assessment Handbook, Rubrics 3: Artwork; and 40: Writing to Describe

English-Language Learners   **At Level**

Students with family ties to countries covered in this module may enjoy focusing on figures from those countries.

- Encourage students to use a dictionary to find descriptive words.
- When revising their papers, have students work with a partner and make any needed corrections to align them with standard English usage.

LS Verbal/Linguistic

Alternative Assessment Handbook, Rubric 40: Writing to Describe

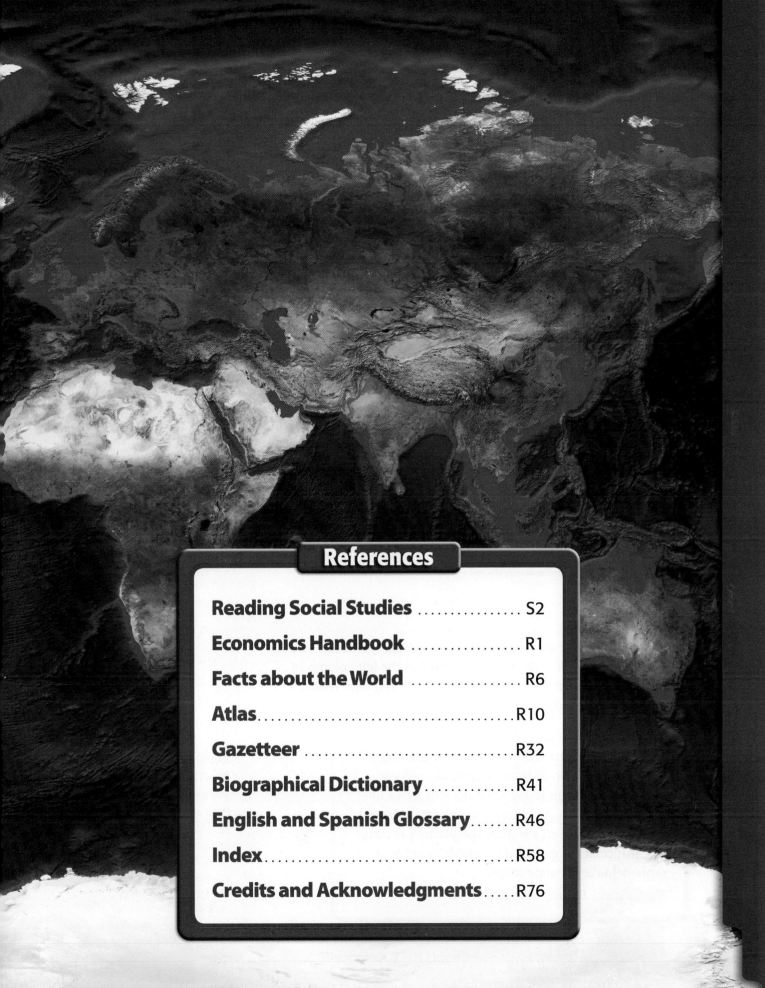

References

Using Prior Knowledge

FOCUS ON READING

When you put together a puzzle, you search for pieces that are missing to complete the picture. As you read, you do the same thing when you use prior knowledge. You take what you already know about a subject and then add the information you are reading to create a full picture. The example below shows how using prior knowledge about computer mapping helped one reader fill in the pieces about how geographers use computer mapping.

In the past, maps were always drawn by hand. Many were not very accurate. Today, though, most maps are made using computers and satellite images. Through advances in mapmaking, we can make accurate maps on almost any scale, from the whole world to a single neighborhood, and keep them up to date.

From Section 3, The Branches of Geography

Computer Mapping	
What I know before reading	What else I learned
• My dad uses the computer to get a map for trips. • I can find maps on the Internet of states and countries.	• Maps have not always been very accurate. • Computers help make new kinds of maps that are more than just cities and roads. • These computer maps are an important part of geography.

YOU TRY IT!

Draw a chart like the one above. Think about what you know about satellite images and list this prior knowledge in the left column of your chart. Then read the passage below. Once you have read it, add what you learned about satellite images to the right column.

Much of the information gathered by these satellites is in the form of images. Geographers can study these images to see what an area looks like from above Earth. Satellites also collect information that we cannot see from the planet's surface. The information gathered by satellites helps geographers make accurate maps.

From Section 1, Studying Geography

Satellite Images
What I know before reading
Students' answers will vary.
What else I learned
possible answers—
• *Satellite images show what an area looks like from above Earth.*
• *Satellite information may be things we cannot see from the planet's surface.*
• *Satellite images help make accurate maps.*

Using Word Parts

FOCUS ON READING

Many English words are made up of several word parts: roots, prefixes, and suffixes. A root is the base of the word and carries the main meaning. A prefix is a letter or syllable added to the beginning of a root. A suffix is a letter or syllable added to the end to create new words. When you come across a new word, you can sometimes figure out the meaning by looking at its parts. Below are some common word parts and their meanings.

Common Roots		
Word Root	**Meaning**	**Sample Words**
-graph-	write, writing	autograph, biography
-vid-, -vis-	see	videotape, visible

Common Prefixes		
Prefix	**Meaning**	**Sample Words**
geo-	earth	geology
inter-	between, among	interpersonal, intercom
in-	not	ineffective
re-	again	restate, rebuild

Common Suffixes		
Suffix	**Meaning**	**Sample Words**
-ible	capable of	visible, responsible
-less	without	penniless, hopeless
-ment	result, action	commitment
-al	relating to	directional
-tion	the act or condition of	rotation, selection

YOU TRY IT!

Read the following words. First separate any prefixes or suffixes and identify the word's root. Use the chart above to define the root, the prefix, or the suffix. Then write a definition for each word.

geography	**visualize**	**movement**
seasonal	**reshaping**	**interact**
regardless	**separation**	**invisible**

Using Word Parts

Geography—geo- means earth; the root -graph- means writing. Geography means writing about the earth.

Seasonal—the suffix -al means relating to; seasonal means relating to the seasons

Regardless—the suffix -less means without; regardless means without regard

Visualize—the root -vis- means to see; visualize means the act of seeing

Reshaping—the prefix re- means again; reshaping means to shape again

Separation—the suffix -tion means the act or condition of; separation means the act of separating

Movement—the suffix -ment means result; movement means the result of moving

Interact—inter- means between or among; interact means to act between

Invisible—the prefix in- means not; -vis- means to see; the suffix -ible means capable of; invisible means not capable of being seen

Understanding Cause and Effect

READING SOCIAL STUDIES

FOCUS ON READING

Learning to identify causes and effects can help you understand geography. A **cause** is something that makes another thing happen. An **effect** is the result of something else that happened. A cause may have several effects, and an effect may have several causes. In addition, as you can see in the example below, causes and effects may occur in a chain. Then, each effect in turn becomes the cause for another event.

First cause →

Last effect →

The Gulf Stream is a warm current that flows north along the U.S. East Coast. It then flows east across the Atlantic to become the North Atlantic Drift. As the warm current flows along northwestern Europe, it heats the air. Westerlies blow the warmed air across Europe. This process makes Europe warmer than it otherwise would be.

From Section 1, Weather and Climate

Cause
Gulf Stream

↓

Effect
Warm water flows along the coast of northwest Europe.

↓

Effect
Warm water raises temperature of the air above.

↓

Effect
Winds blow warm air across Europe.

↓

Effect
Warm winds make Europe warmer.

YOU TRY IT!

Read the following sentences, and then use a graphic organizer like the one below right to analyze the cause and effects. Create as many boxes as you need to list the causes and effects.

Mountains also create wet and dry areas. . . A mountain forces wind blowing against it to rise. As it rises, the air cools and precipitation falls as rain or snow. Thus, the side of the mountain facing the wind is often green and lush. However, little moisture remains for the other side. This effect creates a rain shadow.

From Section 1, Weather and Climate

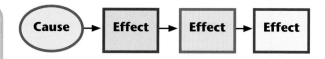

Cause → **Effect** → **Effect** → **Effect**

Understanding Cause and Effect
Cause—Mountain;
Effect—Wind blowing against the mountain rises;
Effect—Air cools as it rises up the mountainside;
Effect—Precipitation falls;
Effect—Little moisture remains for the other side of the mountain;
Effect—Rain shadow on mountainside not facing the wind

Understanding Main Ideas

FOCUS ON READING

Main ideas are like the hub of a wheel. The hub holds the wheel together, and everything circles around it. In a paragraph, the main idea holds the paragraph together and all the facts and details revolve around it. The main idea is usually stated clearly in a topic sentence, which may come at the beginning or end of a paragraph. Topic sentences always summarize the most important idea of a paragraph.

To find the main idea, ask yourself what one point is holding the paragraph together. See how the main idea in the following example holds all the details from the paragraph together.

Scientists have many theories about why language first developed. Some think it was to make hunting in groups easier. Others think it developed as a way for people to form relationships. Still others think language made it easier for people to resolve issues like how to distribute food.

From Section 1, The First People

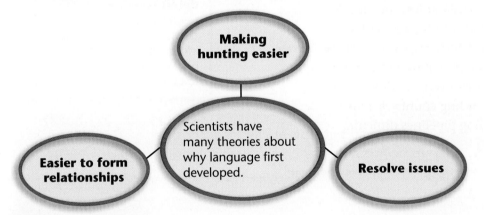

YOU TRY IT!

Read the following paragraph, and then use a graphic organizer like the one above to identify the main idea. Create as many circles as you need to list the supporting facts and details.

In addition to clothing, people needed shelter to survive. At first they took shelter in caves. When they moved to areas with no caves, they built their own shelters. The first human-made shelters were called pit houses. They were pits in the ground with roofs of branches and leaves.

From Section 2, Early Human Migration

Understanding Main Ideas

Main Idea—Humans needed shelter to survive.

Details—first took shelter in caves; later built their own shelters called pit houses; pit houses were pits in the ground with roofs made of branches and leaves

Re-Reading

READING SOCIAL STUDIES

FOCUS ON READING

When you read about other countries, you will come across some information that is completely new to you. Sometimes it can seem difficult to keep all the people, places, dates, and events straight. Re-reading can help you absorb new information and understand the main facts of a passage. Follow these three steps in re-reading. First, read the whole passage. Look over the passage and identify the main details you need to focus on. Then re-read the passage slowly. As you read, make sure you understand the details by restating the details silently. If necessary, go back and re-read until you have the details firmly in your mind. Here's how this process works with the following passage.

However, these oil and gas reserves cannot benefit the countries of Central Asia unless they can be exported. Since no country in the region has an ocean port, the only way to transport the oil and gas efficiently is through pipelines. But the rugged mountains, along with economic and political turmoil in some surrounding countries, make building and maintaining pipelines difficult.

From Section 3, Central Asia

1. Read the passage.

2. Identify the main details to focus on.
difficulty of transporting oil

3. Re-read and restate the details silently.
Central Asia has no ocean ports. Pipelines can be built. Mountains and political problems make pipelines hard to build.

YOU TRY IT!

Read the following sentences. Then, following the three steps above, write down the main details to focus on. After you re-read the paragraph, write down the information restated in your own words to show that you understood what you read.

The Tigris and Euphrates rivers flow across a low, flat plain in Iraq. They join together before they reach the Persian Gulf. The Tigris and Euphrates are what are known as exotic rivers, or rivers that begin in humid regions and then flow through dry areas. The rivers create a narrow fertile area, which in ancient times was called Mesopotamia, or the "land between rivers."

From Section 2, The Arabian Peninsula, Iraq, and Iran

Re-Reading

Main details: Tigris and Euphrates rivers

Exotic rivers

Mesopotamia

Restate details: Rivers are separate then together. Exotic means they start in humid areas and then flow through dry areas. Mesopotamia is the land between the rivers.

Paraphrasing

FOCUS ON READING

When you paraphrase, you explain someone else's idea in your own words. When you put an idea in your own words, you will understand it better and remember it longer. To paraphrase a passage, first read it carefully. Make sure you understand the main ideas. Then, using your own words, restate what the writer is saying. Keep the ideas in the same order and focus on using your own, familiar vocabulary. Your sentences may be shorter and simpler, but they should match the ideas in the text. Below is an example of a paraphrased passage.

READING SOCIAL STUDIES

Original Text	Paraphrase
Priests, people who performed or led religious ceremonies, had great status in Sumer. People relied on them to help gain the gods' favor. Priests interpreted the wishes of the gods and made offerings to them. These offerings were made in temples, special buildings where priests performed their religious ceremonies.	Priests hold the religious services, so people respect them. People want the priests to help them get on the gods' good side. Priests do this by explaining what the gods want and by making offerings. They make offerings in a special building where they lead services.

From Section 2, The Rise of Sumer

To paraphrase:
- Understand the ideas.
- Use your own words.
- Keep the same order.
- Make it sound like you.
- Keep it about the same length.

YOU TRY IT!

Read the following passage, and then write a paraphrase using the steps described above.

Irrigation increased the amount of food farmers were able to grow. In fact, farmers could produce a food surplus, or more than they needed. Farmers also used irrigation to water grazing areas for cattle and sheep. As a result, Mesopotamians ate a variety of foods. Fish, meat, wheat, barley, and dates were plentiful.

From Section 1, Geography of the Fertile Crescent

Paraphrasing

Answers will vary.

possible answer—Farmers used watering to grow more food. They grew much more than they needed. They also watered the grass where cows and sheep ate. This gave them many different kinds of foods. They had fish, meat, wheat, barley, and dates to eat.

Understanding Implied Main Ideas

FOCUS ON READING

Do you ever "read between the lines" when people say things? You understand what people mean even when they don't come right out and say it. You can do the same thing with writing. Writers don't always state the main idea directly, but you can find clues to the main idea in the details. To understand an implied main idea, first read the text carefully and think about the topic. Next, look at the facts and details and ask yourself what the paragraph is saying. Then create a statement that sums up the main idea. Notice the way this process works with the paragraph below.

> As a young man Jesus lived in the town of Nazareth and probably studied with Joseph to become a carpenter. Like many young Jewish men of the time, Jesus also studied the laws and teachings of Judaism. By the time he was about 30, Jesus had begun to travel and teach.
>
> *From Section 2, Origins of Christianity*

1. What is the topic?
Jesus as a young man

2. What are the facts and details?
• lived in Nazareth
• studied to be a carpenter
• learned about Judaism

3. What is the main idea?
Jesus lived the typical life of a young Jewish man.

YOU TRY IT!

Read the following sentences. Notice the main idea is not stated. Using the three steps described above, develop a statement that expresses the main idea of the paragraph.

> Muhammad's teachings also dealt with how people should live. He taught that all people who believed in Allah were bound together like members of a family. As a result, he said, people should help those who are less fortunate. For example, he thought that people who had money should use that money to help the poor.
>
> *From Section 3, Origins of Islam*

Understanding Implied Main Ideas

Topic: teachings of Muhammad

Details: taught that all people who believed in Allah were members of a family; all people should help those less fortunate; people should give money to help the poor

Main idea: Muhammad taught that all people who believe in Allah are members of the same family and should help those less fortunate.

Sequencing

FOCUS ON READING

When you read about how countries and cultures developed, it is necessary to understand the sequence, or order, of events. Writers sometimes signal the sequence by using words or phrases such as *first, before, then, later, soon, next,* or *finally.* Sometimes writers use dates instead to indicate the order of events. Developing a sequence chain is a way to help you mark and understand the order of events. Clue words indicating sequence are underlined in the example.

> In 711 a combined Arab and Berber army invaded Spain and quickly conquered it. Next, the army moved into what is now France, but it was stopped by a Christian army near the city of Tours. Despite this defeat, Muslims called Moors ruled parts of Spain for the next 700 years.
>
> A new Islamic dynasty, the Abbasids, came to power in 749. They reorganized the government to make it easier to rule such a large region.
>
> *From Section 1, Muslim Empires*

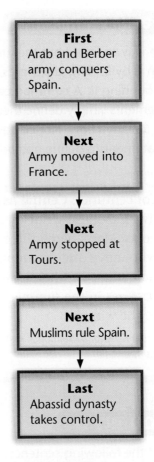

First
Arab and Berber army conquers Spain.

Next
Army moved into France.

Next
Army stopped at Tours.

Next
Muslims rule Spain.

Last
Abassid dynasty takes control.

YOU TRY IT!

Read the following passage. Create a graphic organizer like the one above to list the events in sequence. Use as many boxes as you need to create a full sequence chain.

> The Soviet Union collapsed in 1991. As the Soviet government and economy fell apart, it could no longer control its huge territory. The Central Asian republics finally became independent countries.
>
> *From Section 3, History and Culture of Central Asia*

Sequencing

First
Soviet Union collapsed in 1991.

Next
No one could control the huge Soviet territory.

Last
The Central Asian republics finally became indepedendent countries.

Using Context Clues—Restatement

FOCUS ON READING

One way to figure out the meaning of an unfamiliar word or term is by finding clues in its context, the words or sentences surrounding it. A common context clue is a restatement. Restatements simply define the new word using ordinary words you already know. Notice how the following passage uses a restatement to define nomads.

> For centuries, Central Asians have made a living by raising horses, cattle, sheep, and goats. Many herders live as <u>nomads</u>, people who move often from place to place. The nomads move their herds from mountain pastures in the summer to lowland pastures in the winter.
>
> *From Chapter 8, Section 3, History and Culture of Central Asia*

Restatement:
people who move often from place to place

YOU TRY IT!

Read the following sentences and identify the restatement for each underlined term.

> The most powerful religious leader was the <u>pope</u>, the head of the Christian church. The pope's decisions could have huge effects on people's lives. For example, one pope decided to start a religious war, or Crusade, against the church's enemies in Southwest Asia. He wanted Europeans to take over the <u>Holy</u> Land, the region in which Jesus had lived.
>
> *From Chapter 19, Section 1, The Middle Ages*

Using Context Clues

pope—head of the Christian church

Holy Land—region in which Jesus had lived

S11

READING SOCIAL STUDIES

Understanding Comparison-Contrast

FOCUS ON READING

Comparing shows how things are alike. Contrasting shows how things are different. You can understand comparison-contrast by learning to recognize clue words and points of comparison. Clue words let you know whether to look for similarities or differences. Points of comparison are the main topics that are being compared or contrasted. Notice how the passage below compares and contrasts different regions of Southern Africa.

> Southern Africa's climates vary from east to west. The wettest place in the region is the east coast of the island of Madagascar . . .
>
> In contrast to the eastern part of the continent, the west is very dry. From the Atlantic coast, deserts give way to plains with semiarid and steppe climates.
>
> *From Section 5, Southern Africa*

Highlighted words are points of comparison.

Underlined words are clue words.

Understanding Comparison-Contrast

Similarities: deserts, drier than other areas

Differences: Namib—on Atlantic coast; very dry; Kalahari—in Botswana; gets enough rain to support grasses and trees

Clue Words	
Comparison	**Contrast**
share, similar, like, also, both, in addition, besides	however, while, unlike, different, but, although

YOU TRY IT!

Read the following passage about the Namib and Kalahari deserts. Use a diagram like the one here to compare and contrast the two countries.

> The driest place in the region is the Namib Desert on the Atlantic coast . . . Another desert, the Kalahari, occupies most of Botswana. Although this desert gets enough rain in the north to support grasses and trees, its sandy plains are mostly covered with scattered shrubs.
>
> *From Section 5, Southern Africa*

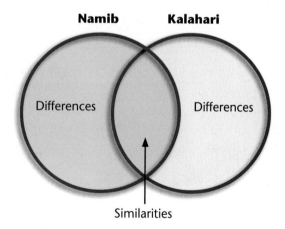

Namib   Kalahari

Differences   Differences

Similarities

Categorizing

FOCUS ON READING

When you sort things into groups of similar items, you are categorizing. Think of folding laundry. First you might sort into different piles: towels, socks, and T-shirts. The piles—or categories—help you manage the laundry because towels go to a different place than socks. When you read, categorizing helps you to manage the information by identifying the main types, or groups, of information. Then you can more easily see the individual facts and details in each group. Notice how the information in the paragraph below has been sorted into three main groups.

> The subjects of Egyptian paintings vary widely. Some of the paintings show <u>important historical</u> events, such as the crowning of a new king or the founding of a temple. Others show <u>major religious rituals</u>. Still other paintings show scenes from <u>everyday life</u>, such as farming or hunting.
>
> *From Section 4, Egyptian Achievements*

Subjects of Egyptian Paintings		
Category 1: Important historical events	**Category 2:** Major religious rituals	**Category 3:** Everyday life

YOU TRY IT!

Read the following sentences. Then use a graphic organizer like the one above to categorize the natural barriers in ancient Egypt. Create as many categories as you need.

> In addition to a stable food supply, Egypt's location offered another advantage. It had natural barriers, which made it hard to invade Egypt. To the west, the desert was too big and harsh to cross. To the north, the Mediterranean Sea kept many enemies away. To the east, more desert and the Red Sea provided protection. Finally, to the south, cataracts in the Nile made it difficult for invaders to sail into Egypt that way.
>
> *From Section 1, Geography and Early Egypt*

Categorizing

Students might categorize the natural barriers by compass direction: (1) west: desert; (2) north: Mediterranean Sea; (3) east: desert and Red Sea; (4) south: Nile River cataracts

Understanding Cause and Effect

FOCUS ON READING

To understand a country's history, you should look for cause and effect chains. A cause makes something happen, and an effect is what happens as a result of a cause. The effect can then become a cause and create another effect. Notice how the events below create a cause-and-effect chain.

> As the trade in gold and salt increased, Ghana's rulers gained power. Over time, their military strength grew as well. With their armies they began to take control of this trade from the merchants who had once controlled it. Merchants from the north and south met to exchange goods in Ghana. As a result of their control of trade routes, the rulers of Ghana became wealthy.
>
> *From Section 3, Empire of Ghana*

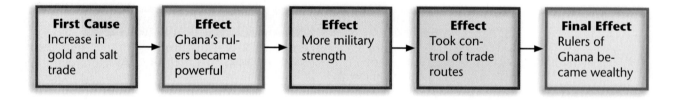

First Cause	Effect	Effect	Effect	Final Effect
Increase in gold and salt trade	Ghana's rulers became powerful	More military strength	Took control of trade routes	Rulers of Ghana became wealthy

YOU TRY IT!

Read the following sentences, and then use a graphic organizer like the one above to analyze causes and effects. Create as many boxes as you need to list the causes and effects.

> When Mansa Musa died, his son Maghan took the throne. Maghan was a weak ruler. When raiders from the southeast poured into Mali, he couldn't stop them. The raiders set fire to Timbuktu's great schools and mosques. Mali never fully recovered from this terrible blow. The empire continued to weaken and decline.
>
> *From Section 4, Mali and Songhai*

Understanding Cause and Effect

First cause: Mansa Musa died

Effect: Maghan took the throne

Effect: Maghan couldn't stop raiders from invading

Effect: Raiders set fire to Timbuktu

Effect: Mali never fully recovered

Effect: Mali began to weaken and decline

Note: Some students may combine the last two effects into one.

Identifying Supporting Details

FOCUS ON READING

Why believe what you read? One reason is because of details that support or prove the main idea. These details might be facts, statistics, examples, or definitions. In the example below, notice what kind of proof or supporting details help you believe the main idea.

> Under apartheid, only white South Africans could vote or hold political office. Blacks, who made up nearly 75 percent of the population, were not citizens. They could only work certain jobs and made very little money. They were only allowed to live in certain areas.
>
> *From Section 5, Africa since Independence*

Main Idea
Apartheid gave more rights to whites than to blacks.

Supporting Details			
Example	**Statistic**	**Fact**	**Fact**
Whites could vote and hold political office.	Blacks made up 75 percent of the population but were not citizens.	Blacks could only have certain jobs.	They had to live in certain areas.

YOU TRY IT!

Read the following sentences, and then use a graphic organizer like the one above to identify the supporting details.

> The European slave trade in Africa had devastating consequences. It led to a drastic decrease in Africa's population. Millions of young African men were forced to move away from their homes to lands far away, and thousands of them died. Historians estimate that 15 to 20 million African slaves were shipped to the Americas against their will.
>
> *From Section 2, European Colonization*

Identifying Supporting Details

Main Idea: The slave trade had devastating consequences in Africa. Supporting Details: It led to a decrease in Africa's population. Fact: Millions of young African men were forced to move away from their homes. Fact: Historians estimate that 15 to 20 million Africans were shipped to the Americas as slaves.

Understanding Fact and Opinion

FOCUS ON READING

When you read, it is important to distinguish facts from opinions. A fact is a statement that can be proved or disproved. An opinion is a personal belief or attitude, so it cannot be proved true or false. When you are reading a social studies text, you want to read only facts, not the author's opinions. To determine whether a sentence is a fact or an opinion, ask if it can be proved using outside sources. If it can, the sentence is a fact. The following pairs of statements show the difference between facts and opinions.

Fact: The Huang He often floods, causing millions of dollars worth of damage. *(This fact can be proved through research.)*

Opinion: I believe the Huang He should be dammed to prevent flooding. *(The word* believe *signifies that this is the writer's judgment, or opinion.)*

Fact: At 3,776 meters, the peak of Mount Fuji is the highest point in Japan. *(The elevation of Mount Fuji can be checked for accuracy.)*

Opinion: Mount Fuji is a beautiful mountain that everyone should visit. *(No one can prove that Fuji is beautiful, because it is a matter of personal taste.)*

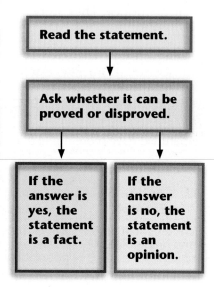

Read the statement.

Ask whether it can be proved or disproved.

If the answer is yes, the statement is a fact.

If the answer is no, the statement is an opinion.

YOU TRY IT!

Read the following sentences and identify each as a fact or an opinion.

1. The Ganges River is sacred to many Hindus.

2. Millions of people visit the Ganges each year to bathe in its waters.

3. China's mountains are the world's most majestic.

4. China and India have some of the world's tallest mountains.

5. Many houses in Southeast Asia are built on stilts in case of floods.

6. The raised houses of Southeast Asia are fascinating.

Understanding Fact and Opinion
1. Fact
2. Fact
3. Opinion
4. Fact
5. Fact
6. Opinion

Sequencing

FOCUS ON READING

Have you ever used written instructions to put together an item you bought? If so, you know that the steps in the directions need to be followed in order. The instructions probably included words like *first, next,* and *then* to help you figure out what order you needed to do the steps in. The same kinds of words can help you when you read a history book. Words such as *first, then, later, next,* and *finally* can help you figure out the sequence, or order, in which events occurred. Read the passage below, noting the underlined clue words. Notice how they indicate the order of the events listed in the sequence chain at right.

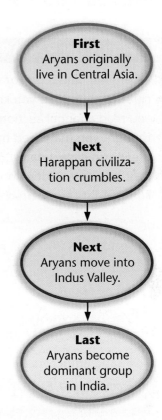

> Not long <u>after</u> the Harappan civilization crumbled, a new group arrived in the Indus Valley. These people were called the Aryans. They were <u>originally</u> from the area around the Caspian Sea in Central Asia. <u>Over time,</u> however, they became the dominant group in India.
>
> *From Section 1, Early Indian Civilizations*

YOU TRY IT!

Read the following passage. Look for clue words to help you figure out the order of the events described in it. Then make a sequence chain like the one above to show that order.

> For many years, Asoka watched his armies fight bloody battles against other peoples. A few years into his rule, however, Asoka converted to Buddhism. When he did, he swore that he would not launch any more wars of conquest. After converting to Buddhism, Asoka had the time and resources to improve the lives of his people.
>
> *From Section 4, Indian Empires*

Sequencing

First: Asoka's armies fight many bloody battles.

Next: Asoka converts to Buddhism.

Next: He swears not to start any more wars of conquest.

Last: Asoka improves the lives of his people.

Understanding Chronological Order

FOCUS ON READING

When you read a paragraph in a history text, you can usually use clue words to help you keep track of the order of events. When you read a longer section of text that includes many paragraphs, though, you may need more clues. One of the best clues you can use in this case is dates. Each of the sentences below includes at least one date. Notice how those dates were used to create a time line that lists events in chronological, or time, order.

As early as 7000 BC people had begun to farm in China.

After 3000 BC people began to use potter's wheels to make many types of pottery.

The first dynasty for which we have clear evidence is the Shang, which was firmly established by the 1500s BC.

Shang emperors ruled in China until the 1100s BC.

From Section 1, Early China

7000 BC
People begin farming in China.

5000 BC

3000 BC
People begin using potter's wheels.

1500s BC
Shang dynasty rules China.

1100s BC
Shang lose power.

1 BC

YOU TRY IT!

Read the following sentences. Use the dates in the sentences to create a time line listing events in chronological order.

The Ming dynasty that he founded ruled China from 1368 to 1644.

Genghis Khan led his armies into northern China in 1211.

Between 1405 and 1433, Zheng He led seven grand voyages to places around Asia.

In the 1300s many Chinese groups rebelled against the Yuan dynasty.

From Section 5, The Yuan and Ming Dynasties

Understanding Chronlogical Order

Students' time lines should accurately list the events in chronological order.

Using Context Clues— Definitions

FOCUS ON READING

One way to figure out the meaning of an unfamiliar word or term is by finding clues in its context, the words or sentences surrounding the word or term. A common context clue is a restatement. Restatements are simply a definition of the new word using ordinary words you already know. Notice how the following passage uses a restatement to define civil disobedience. Some context clues are not as complete or obvious. Notice how the following passage provides a description that is a partial definition of persistence.

Using Context Clues—Definitions

trade surplus—when a country exports more goods than it imports

missionaries—people who carry religions far and wide

The second of Gandhi's key beliefs was *civil disobedience,* or the refusal to obey laws in order to bring about change . . .

Gandhi and his followers were arrested on several occasions. They did not give up, and their *persistence* convinced more Indians to join them.
From Section 3, New Political Movements

Civil Disobedience: refusal to obey laws in order to bring about change

Persistence: refusal to give up

YOU TRY IT!

Read the following passages and identify the meaning of the italicized words by using definitions, or restatements, in context.

Japan's trade has been so successful that the country has built up a huge *trade surplus.* A trade surplus exists when a country exports more goods than it imports.

From Section 5, A New Asia

India had been the birthplace of two major religions, Hinduism and Buddhism. Over several centuries, Indian *missionaries* carried both religions far and wide.

From Section 1, Contact across Cultures

Asking Questions

FOCUS ON READING

Reading is one place where asking questions will never get you in trouble. The five W questions – who, what, when, where, and why – can help you be sure you understand the material you read. After you read a section, ask yourself the 5 Ws: **Who** was this section about? **What** did they do? **When** and **where** did they live? **Why** did they do what they did? See the example below to learn how this reading strategy can help you identify the main points of a passage.

> The region's natural resources have been poorly managed, however. Until the early 1990s this region was part of the Soviet Union. The Soviet government put more importance on industry than on managing its resources.
>
> *From Section 5, Russia and the Caucasus*

The 5 Ws

Who? Soviet government

What? Managed resources poorly

Where? Russia

When? Until the early 1900s

Why? Put more emphasis on industry than on resource management

YOU TRY IT!

Read the following passage and answer the 5 Ws to check your understanding of it.

> Another valuable natural resource is found in the breathtaking beauty of the Alps. Each year, tourists flock to the Alps to enjoy the scenery and to hike and ski.
>
> *From Section 1, Southern Europe*

Asking Questions

Who: tourists; What: the Alps are a valuable natural resource; Where: the Alps; When: each year; Why: to enjoy the scenery and to hike and ski

Re-reading

FOCUS ON READING

Have you ever hit the rewind button on the VCR or DVD player because you missed an important scene or didn't quite catch what a character said? As you rewound, you probably asked yourself such questions as, "What did he say?" or "How did she do that?" Taking a second look helped you understand what was going on.

The same idea is true for reading. When you re-read a passage, you can catch details you didn't catch the first time. As you re-read, go slowly and check your understanding by asking yourself questions. In the example below, notice the questions the reader asked. Then see how the questions were answered by re-reading the passage.

In the center of most city-states was a fortress on a hill. This hill was called the acropolis, which is Greek for "top city." In addition to the fortress, many city-states built temples and other public buildings on the acropolis. Around the acropolis was the rest of the city, including houses and markets. High walls usually surrounded the city for protection.

From Section 1, Ancient Greece

Questions for Re-reading:

Is the acropolis a city?

Are the walls around the acropolis or the city?

Answers

No, the acropolis is a hill in the city.

The walls are on the outside of the city. The acropolis is in the center.

YOU TRY IT!

Read the following passage, and then develop two questions you can answer as you re-read the passage. Write down the questions and the answers.

As emperor, Octavian was given a new name, Augustus, which means "honored one." The people of Rome respected and admired Augustus. This respect was mainly the result of his many accomplishments. As the map above shows, Augustus added a great deal of territory to the empire. He also made many improvements to lands already in the empire. For example, he built monuments and public buildings in the city of Rome. He also improved and expanded Rome's network of roads, which facilitated both travel and trade.

From Section 2, The Roman World

Re-reading

Answers will vary.

possible responses—What name did Octavian take as emperor? (Augustus) Why did the Romans admire Augustus? (He added territory and made improvements to the empire.)

Using Context Clues—Contrast

READING SOCIAL STUDIES

FOCUS ON READING

Maybe you played this game as a young child: "Which of these things is not like the others?" This same game can help you understand new words as you read. Sometimes the words or sentences around a new word will show contrast, or how the word is not like something else. These contrast clues can help you figure out the new word's meaning. Look at how the following passage indicates that *persevered* means something different from *give in*.

> The German air force repeatedly attacked British cities and military targets. Hitler hoped the British would surrender. Rather than give in, however, the British *persevered*.
>
> *From Section 6, World War II*

Contrast Clues:

1. Look for words or sentences that signal contrast.
Words that signal contrast include *however, rather than, instead of,* and *not*. In this paragraph, the words *rather than* signal the contrast clues for the unfamiliar word *persevered*.

2. Check the definition by substituting a word or phrase that fits.
Persevere likely means to keep on trying. *Rather than give in, however, the British kept on trying.*

YOU TRY IT!

Read the following paragraph, and then use the steps listed above to develop a definition for the word *compete*.

> Some people believed that creating a feeling of community in Europe would make countries less likely to go to war. Leaders like Great Britain's Winston Churchill believed the countries of Europe should cooperate rather than *compete*.
>
> *From Section 7, Europe since 1945*

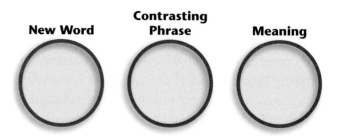

New Word   **Contrasting Phrase**   **Meaning**

Using Context Clues—Contrast

1. Contrast clues—rather than

2. Compete probably means to go against each to other; Leaders like Great Britain's Winston Churchill believed the countries of Europe should cooperate rather than go against each other.

Economics Handbook

What Is Economics?

Economics may sound dull, but it touches almost every part of your life. Here are some examples of the kinds of economic choices you may have made yourself:

- Which pair of shoes to buy—the ones on sale or the ones you really like, which cost much more
- Whether to continue saving your money for the DVD player you want or use some of it now to go to a movie
- Whether to give some money to a fundraiser for a new park or to housing for the homeless

As these examples show, we can think of economics as a study of choices. These choices are the ones people make to satisfy their needs or their desires.

Glossary of Economic Terms

Here are some of the words we use to talk about economics:

ECONOMIC SYSTEMS

Countries have developed different economic systems to help them make choices, such as what goods and services to produce, how to produce them, and for whom to produce them. The most common economic systems in the world are market economies and mixed economies.

capitalism See market economy.

command economy an economic system in which the central government makes all economic decisions, such as in the countries of Cuba and North Korea

communism a political system in which the government owns all property and runs a command economy

free enterprise a system in which businesses operate with little government involvement, such as in a country with a market economy

market economy an economic system based on private ownership, free trade, and competition; the government has little to say about what, how, or for whom goods and services are produced; examples include Germany and the United States

mixed economy an economy that is a combination of command, market, and traditional economies

traditional economy an economy in which production is based on customs and tradition, and in which people often grow their own food, make their own goods, and use barter to trade

THE ECONOMY AND MONEY

People, businesses, and countries obtain the items they need and want through economic activities such as producing, selling, and buying goods or services. Countries differ in the amount of economic activity that they have and in the strength of their economies.

consumer a person who buys goods or services for personal use

consumer good a finished product sold to consumers for personal or home use

corporation a business in which a group of owners share in the profits and losses

currency paper or coins that a country uses for its money supply

demand the amount of goods and services that consumers are willing and able to buy at a given time

depression a severe drop in overall business activity over a long period of time

developed countries countries with strong economies and a high quality of life; often have high per capita GDPs and high levels of industrialization and technology

developing countries countries with less productive economies and a lower quality of life; often have less industrialization and technology

economic development the level of a country's economic activity, growth, and quality of life

economy the structure of economic life in a country

goods objects or materials that humans can purchase to satisfy their wants and needs

gross domestic product (GDP) total market value of all goods and services produced in a country in a given year; *per capita GDP* is the average value of goods and services produced per person in a country in a given year

industrialization the process of using machinery for all major forms of production

inflation an increase in overall prices

investment the purchase of something with the expectation that it will gain in value; usually property, stocks, etc.

money any item, usually coins or paper currency, that is used in payment for goods or services

producer a person or group that makes goods or provides services to satisfy consumers' wants and needs

productivity the amount of goods or services that a worker or workers can produce within a given amount of time

profit the gain or excess made by selling goods or services over their costs

purchasing power the amount of income that people have available to spend on goods and services

services any activities that are performed for a fee

standard of living how well people are living; determined by the amount of goods and services they can afford

stock a share of ownership in a corporation

supply the amount of goods and services that are available at a given time

INTERNATIONAL TRADE

Countries trade with each other to obtain resources, goods, and services. Growing global trade has helped lead to the development of a global economy.

balance of trade the difference between the value of a country's exports and imports

barter the exchange of one good or service for another

black market the illegal buying and selling of goods, often at high prices

comparative advantage the ability of a company or country to produce something at a lower cost than other companies or countries

competition rivalry between businesses selling similar goods or services; a condition that often leads to lower prices or improved products

e-commerce the electronic trading of goods and services, such as over the Internet

exports goods or services that a country sells and sends to other countries

free trade trade among nations that is not affected by financial or legal barriers; trade without barriers

imports goods or services that a country brings in or purchases from another country

interdependence a relationship between countries in which they rely on one another for resources, goods, or services

market the trade of goods and services

market clearing price the price of a good or service at which supply equals demand

one-crop economy an economy that is dominated by the production of a single product

opportunity cost the value of the next-best alternative that is sacrificed when choosing to consume or produce another good or service

scarcity a condition of limited resources and unlimited wants by people

specialization a focus on only one or two aspects of production in order to produce a product more quickly and cheaply; for example, one worker washes the wheels of the car, another cleans the interior, and another washes the body

trade barriers financial or legal limitations to trade; prevention of free trade

trade-offs the goods or services sacrificed in order to consume or produce another good or service

underground economy illegal economic activities and unreported legal economic activities

PERSONAL ECONOMICS

Individuals make personal choices in how they manage and use their money to satisfy their needs and desires. Individuals have the choice to spend, save, or invest their money.

budget a plan listing the expenses and income of an individual or organization

credit a system that allows consumers to pay for goods and services over time

debt an amount of money that is owed

financial institutions businesses that keep and invest people's money and loan money to people; include banks or credit unions

income a gain of money that comes typically from labor or capital

interest the money that a borrower pays to a lender in return for a loan

loan money given on the condition that it will be paid back, often with interest

savings money or income that is not used to purchase goods or services

tax a required payment to a local, state, or national government; different kinds of taxes include sales taxes, income taxes, and property taxes

wage the payment a worker receives for his or her labor

RESOURCES

People and businesses need resources—such as land, labor, and money—to produce goods and services.

capital generally refers to wealth, in particular wealth that can be used to finance the production of goods or services

human capital sometimes used to refer to human skills and education that affect the production of goods and services in a company or country

labor force all people who are legally old enough to work and are either working or looking for work

natural resource any material in nature that people use and value

nonrenewable resource a resource that cannot be replaced naturally, such as coal or petroleum

raw material a natural resource used to make a product or good

renewable resource a resource that Earth replaces naturally, such as water, soil, and trees

ORGANIZATIONS

Countries have formed many organizations to promote economic cooperation, growth, and trade. These organizations are important in today's global economy.

European Union (EU) an organization that promotes political and economic cooperation in Europe

International Monetary Fund (IMF) a UN agency that promotes cooperation in international trade and that works to maintain stability in the exchange of countries' currencies

Organization of Economic Cooperation and Development (OECD) an organization of countries that promotes democracy and market economies

United Nations (UN) an organization of countries that promotes peace and security around the globe

World Bank a UN agency that provides loans to countries for development and recovery

World Trade Organization (WTO) an international organization dealing with trade between nations

Economic Handbook Review

Reviewing Vocabulary and Terms

On a separate sheet of paper, fill in the blanks in the following sentences:

ECONOMIC SYSTEMS

1. A. Businesses are able to operate with little government involvement in a _free enterprise_ system.

B. In a _command economy_, a central government makes all economic decisions.

C. _Communism_ is a political system in which the government owns all property and runs a command economy.

D. Economies that combine parts of command, market, or traditional economies are called _mixed economies_

E. _Capitalism_ is another name for a market economy, which is based on private ownership, free trade, and competition.

THE ECONOMY AND MONEY

2. A. _Goods_ are objects or materials that people can buy to satisfy their needs and wants.

B. A _service_ is any activity that is performed for a fee.

C. A person who buys goods or services is a _consumer_, and a person or group that makes goods or provides services is a _producer_.

D. The amount of goods and services that consumers are willing and able to buy at any given time is known as _demand_.

E. The total value of all the goods and services produced in the United States in one year is its _gross domestic product (GDP)_

INTERNATIONAL TRADE

3. A. If we have an unlimited demand for a natural resource, such as oil, and there is only so much oil in the ground, we have a condition called _scarcity_.

B. Goods or services that a country sells to other countries are _exports_.

C. Rivalry between producers that provide the same good or service is called _competition_

D. If a country is able to produce a good or service at a lower cost than other countries, it is said to have a _comparative advantage_

E. Trade among nations that is not limited by legal or economic barriers is called _free trade_.

PERSONAL ECONOMICS

4. A. A _tax_ is a required payment to a local, state, or national government that is used to support public services such as education, road construction, and government aid.

B. The money we do not spend on goods or services is our _savings_.

C. You can use _credit_ to pay for goods and services over time.

D. The payment that a worker receives for his or her labor is called a _wage_.

E. Individuals and companies use _budgets_ to plan and manage their expenses and income.

Activities

1. With a partner, compare prices in two grocery stores. Create a chart showing the price of five items in the two stores. Also, figure the average price of the items in each store. How do you think the fact that the stores are near each other affects prices? How might prices be different if one store went out of business? How might the prices be different or similar if the United States had a command economy? Present what you have learned about prices and competition to your class.

1. *Answers will vary. Possible answers: stores near each other—competition helps keep prices lower; one store goes out of business—other store may raise prices because of increased demand; U.S. as command economy—prices at all stores would be the same for similar goods.*

2. With a group, choose five countries from a unit region to research. Look up the per capita GDP and the life expectancy rates for each of these countries in the regional atlas. Then use your textbook, go to your library, or use the Internet to research the literacy rate and the number of TVs per 1,000 people for each of these countries. Organize this information in a five-column chart like the one shown here. Study the information to see if you can find any patterns. Write a brief paragraph explaining what you have learned about the five countries.

2. *Answers will vary. Students' charts should show factual information for five countries and their paragraph should show that they have examined the data for patterns and have gained knowledge about the countries.*

Region				
Country	Per Capita GDP (U.S. $)	Life Expectancy at Birth	Literacy Rate	TVs per 1,000 People

3. Work with a partner to identify some of the many types of currency used in either Africa or Asia. Then imagine that you are the owners of a business in the United States. You have created a new product that you want to sell in the continent you selected, but people there do not use the same currency as you do. To sell your product, you will need to be able to exchange one type of currency for another. Search the Internet or look in a newspaper to find a list of currency exchange rates. For example, if your product sells for 1,000 dollars, what should the cost be in South African rand? In Indian rupees? In Chinese yuan? In Japanese yen?

3. *Students' answers will vary based upon the exchange rate between various currencies and the U.S. dollar at the time they complete the activity.*

RESOURCES

5. A. Diamonds and gold are examples of _____, which are any materials in nature that people use and value. *natural resources*

B. The *labor force* consists of all people who are legally able to work and are working or looking for work.

C. Wealth that can be used to finance the production of goods and services is called *capital*.

D. Oil is an example of a *nonrenewable resource*, which is a resource that cannot be replaced naturally.

E. Water and trees are examples of _____, resources that Earth replaces naturally. *renewable resources*

4. *Students' skits will vary but should be well rehearsed and accurately illustrate one of the following basic economic concepts: scarcity and limited resources, supply and demand, or opportunity costs and trade-offs.*

ORGANIZATIONS

6. A. Many European countries have joined the *European Union (EU)* to help promote political and economic cooperation across Europe.

B. The _____ consists of many agencies that promote peace and security around the world. *United Nations (UN)*

C. The *World Bank* is a UN agency that provides loans to countries to help them develop their economies.

D. The _____ is a UN agency that helps protect the stability of countries' currencies. **D.** *International Monetary Fund (IMF)*

E. Many democratic countries promote market economies through the _____. *Organization of Economic Cooperation and Development (OECD)*

4. With three or four partners, create a skit that illustrates one of the following basic economic concepts: scarcity and limited resources, supply and demand, or opportunity costs and trade-offs. For example, a skit might illustrate supply and demand by showing how the high demand for the best seats at a concert increases the ticket prices for those seats. Write a script for your skit that includes an introduction stating which economic concept you are illustrating. Each member of your group must participate in the skit. Then practice the skit and perform it for the class.

5. Conduct research to find the following information for each country in the chart below: main trading partners, exports, imports, industrial products, agricultural products, and resources. Organize the information into a second chart. Then use the information in the two charts to write a one-page report explaining how international trade, specialization, and available natural resources affects each country's per capita GDP and standard of living.

5. *Charts will vary based on sources used. Students' reports should use the information in both charts to explain how international trade, specialization, and available resources affects each country's per capita GDP and standard of living.*

THE WORLD ALMANAC
Facts about Countries **Southwest and Central Asia**

COUNTRY Capital	FLAG	POPULATION	AREA (sq mi)	PER CAPITA GDP (U.S. $)	LIFE EXPECTANCY AT BIRTH	TVS PER 1,000 PEOPLE
Afghanistan Kabul		29.9 million	250,001	$800	42.9	14
Iraq Baghdad		26.1 million	168,754	$3,500	68.7	82
Kazakhstan Astana		15.2 million	1,049,155	$7,800	66.6	240
Kuwait Kuwait City		2.3 million	6,880	$21,300	77.0	480
Saudi Arabia Riyadh		26.4 million	756,985	$12,000	75.5	263
United States Washington, D.C.		295.7 million	3,718,710	$40,100	77.7	844

The Physical World

Inside the Earth

Earth's interior has several different layers. Deep inside the planet is the core. The inner core is solid, and the outer core is liquid. Above the core is the mantle, which is mostly solid rock with a molten layer on top. The surface layer of Earth includes the crust, which is made up of rocks and soil. Finally, the atmosphere extends from the crust into space. It supports much of the life on Earth.

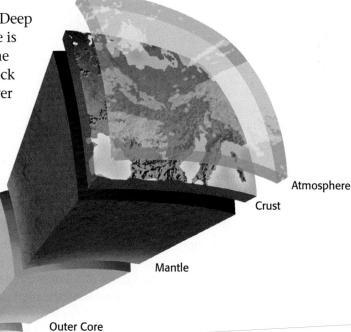

Atmosphere

Crust

Mantle

Outer Core

Inner Core

Tectonic Plates

Earth's crust is divided into huge pieces called tectonic plates, which fit together like a puzzle. As these plates slowly move, they collide and break apart, forming surface features like mountains, ocean basins, and ocean trenches.

Earth Facts	
Age:	4.6 billion years
Mass:	5,974,000,000,000,000,000,000 metric tons
Distance around the equator:	24,902 miles (40,067 km)
Distance around the poles:	24,860 miles (40,000 km)
Distance from the sun:	about 93 million miles (150 million km)
Earth's speed around the sun:	18.5 miles a second (29.8 km a second)
Percent of Earth's surface covered by water:	71%
What makes Earth unique:	large amounts of liquid water, tectonic activity, and life

The Continents

Geographers identify seven large landmasses, or continents, on Earth. Most of these continents are almost completely surrounded by water. Europe and Asia, however, are not. They share a long land boundary.

The world's continents are very different. For example, much of Australia is dry and rocky, while Antarctica is cold and icy. The information below highlights some key facts about each continent.

North America
- Percent of Earth's land: 16.5%
- Percent of Earth's population: 5.1%
- Lowest point: Death Valley, 282 feet (86 m) below sea level

Europe
- Percent of Earth's land: 6.7%
- Percent of Earth's population: 11.5%
- People per square mile: 187

South America
- Percent of Earth's land: 12%
- Percent of Earth's population: 8.6%
- Longest mountains: Andes, 4,500 miles (7,240 km)

Africa
- Percent of Earth's land: 20.2%
- Percent of Earth's population: 13.6%
- Longest river: Nile River, 4,160 miles (6,693 km)

Australia
- Percent of Earth's land: 5.2%
- Percent of Earth's population: 0.3%
- Oldest rocks: 3.7 billion years

Asia
- Percent of Earth's land: 30%
- Percent of Earth's population: 60.7%
- Highest point: Mount Everest, 29,035 feet (8,850 m)

Antarctica
- Percent of Earth's land: 8.9%
- Percent of Earth's population: 0%
- Coldest place: Plateau Station, -56.7°C (-70.1°F) average temperature

The Human World

World Population

More than 6 billion people live in the world today, and that number is growing quickly. Some people predict the world's population will reach 9 billion by 2050. As our population grows, it is also becoming more urban. Soon, as many people will live in cities and in towns as live in rural areas.

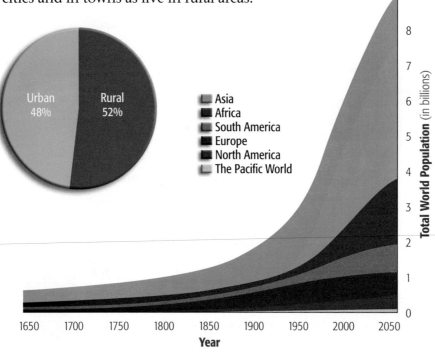

Urban 48%

Rural 52%

- Asia
- Africa
- South America
- Europe
- North America
- The Pacific World

Total World Population (in billions)

Year: 1650 1700 1750 1800 1850 1900 1950 2000 2050

As the world's population grows, people are moving to already large cities such as Shanghai (above) and Hong Kong (right) in China.

Geographers divide the world into developed and less developed regions. In general, developed countries are wealthier and more urban, have lower population growth rates and higher life expectancies. As you can imagine, life is very different in developed and less developed regions.

Developed and Less Developed Countries

	Population	Rate of Natural Increase	Life Expectancy	Percent Urban	Per Capita GNI (U.S. $)
Developed Countries	1.2 billion	0.1%	77	77%	$27,790
Less Developed Countries	5.3 billion	1.5%	65	41%	$4,950
The World	6.5 billion	1.2%	67	48%	$9,190

World Religions

A large percentage of the world's people follow one of several major world religions. Christianity is the largest religion. About 33 percent of the world's people are Christian. Islam is the second-largest religion with about 20 percent. It is also the fastest-growing religion. Hinduism and Buddhism are also major world religions.

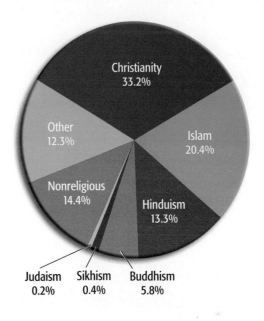

Christianity 33.2%
Islam 20.4%
Hinduism 13.3%
Buddhism 5.8%
Sikhism 0.4%
Judaism 0.2%
Nonreligious 14.4%
Other 12.3%

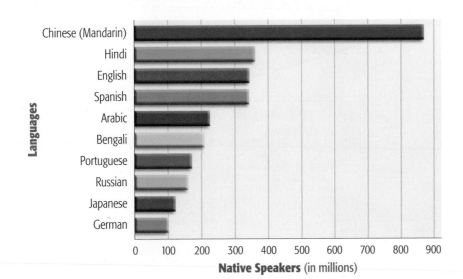

Languages
Chinese (Mandarin)
Hindi
English
Spanish
Arabic
Bengali
Portuguese
Russian
Japanese
German

0   100   200   300   400   500   600   700   800   900

Native Speakers (in millions)

World Languages

Although several thousand languages are spoken today, a handful of major languages have the largest numbers of native speakers. Chinese (Mandarin) is spoken by nearly one in six people. Hindi, English, Spanish, and Arabic are next, with native speakers all over the world.

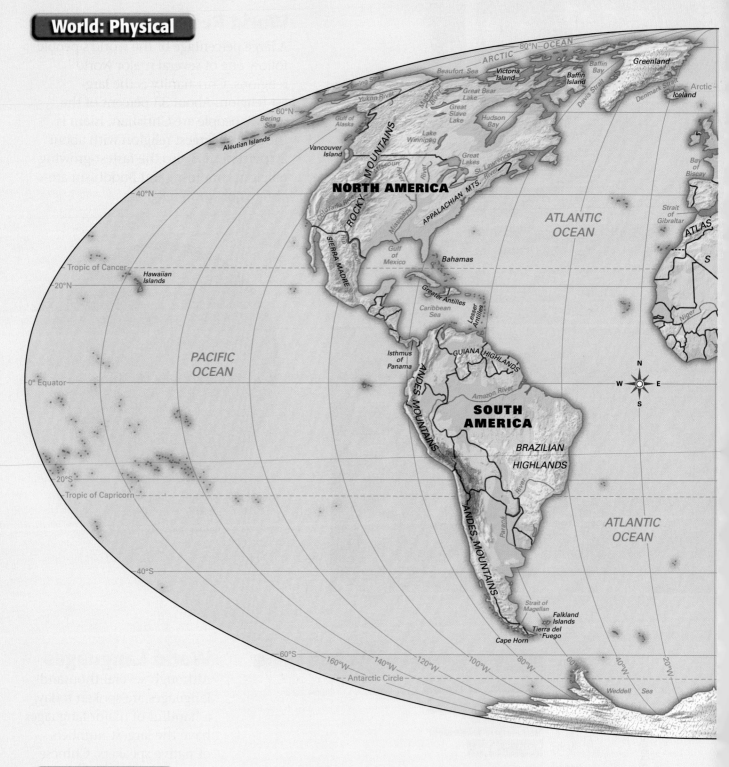

World: Physical

ARCTIC 80°N—OCEAN

Beaufort Sea
Victoria Island
Baffin Island
Baffin Bay
Greenland

Bering Strait
Mackenzie River
Great Bear Lake
Davis Strait
Denmark Strait
Arctic
Iceland

Yukon River
60°N
Gulf of Alaska
Great Slave Lake
Hudson Bay

Bering Sea

Aleutian Islands

Vancouver Island
Lake Winnipeg
Great Lakes
St. Lawrence River
Bay of Biscay

NORTH AMERICA

ROCKY MOUNTAINS
Missouri River
APPALACHIAN MTS.
40°N
ATLANTIC OCEAN
Strait of Gibraltar
ATLAS

Colorado River
Mississippi River
Rio Grande
SIERRA MADRE

S

Tropic of Cancer
Gulf of Mexico
Bahamas

20°N
Hawaiian Islands
Greater Antilles
Niger

Caribbean Sea
Lesser Antilles

PACIFIC OCEAN

Isthmus of Panama
GUIANA HIGHLANDS

N
W—E
S

0° Equator
ANDES MOUNTAINS
Amazon River

SOUTH AMERICA
BRAZILIAN

HIGHLANDS

20°S
River

Tropic of Capricorn
ATLANTIC OCEAN

ANDES MOUNTAINS
Paraná

40°S

Strait of Magellan
Falkland Islands
Tierra del Fuego
Cape Horn

60°S
160°W 140°W 120°W 100°W 80°W 60°W 40°W 20°W

Antarctic Circle

Weddell Sea

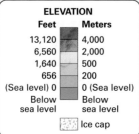

ELEVATION

Feet		Meters
13,120		4,000
6,560		2,000
1,640		500
656		200
(Sea level) 0		0 (Sea level)
Below sea level		Below sea level

Ice cap

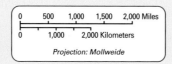

0 500 1,000 1,500 2,000 Miles

0 1,000 2,000 Kilometers

Projection: Mollweide

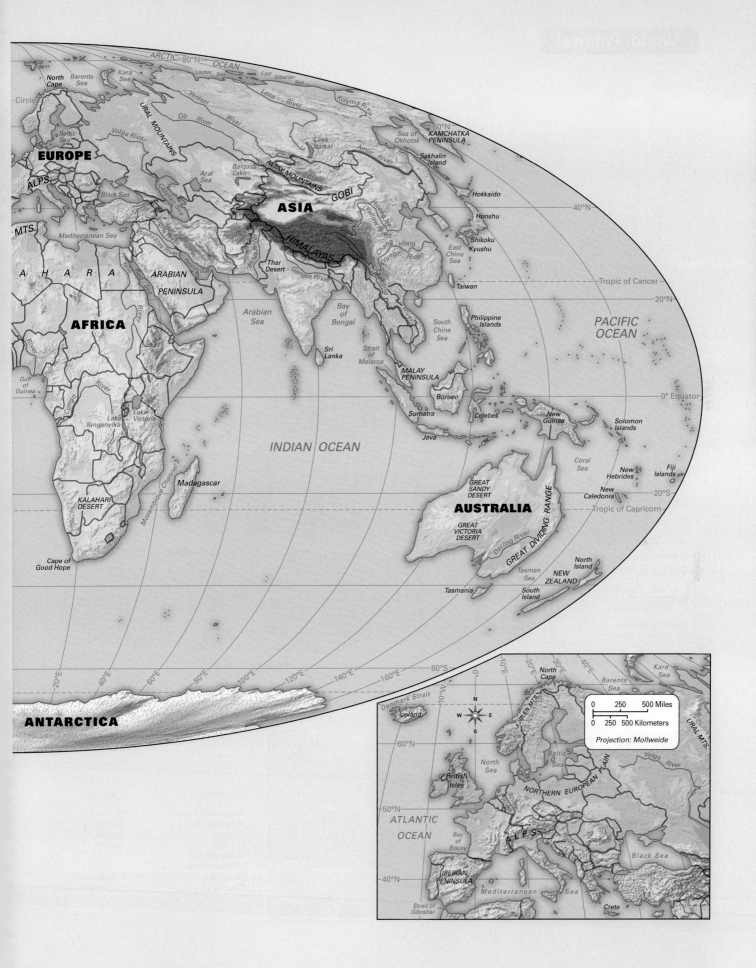

ARCTIC 80°N OCEAN

North Cape
Barents Sea
Kara Sea
Laptev Sea
East Siberian Sea

Circle

Baltic Sea
Volga River
URAL MOUNTAINS
Ob River
Yenisei River
Lena River
Kolyma River
60°N
Sea of Okhotsk
KAMCHATKA PENINSULA

EUROPE

ALPS

Aral Sea
Balqash Lake
ALTAY MOUNTAINS
Amur River
Sakhalin Island

Black Sea
Caspian Sea
Lake Baikal
GOBI
Hokkaido
40°N

MTS.

Mediterranean Sea

ASIA
HIMALAYAS
Huang He (Yellow River)
Chang Jiang (Yangzi) River
Honshu
Shikoku
Kyushu

Tigris River
Euphrates River
Persian Gulf
Indus River
Thar Desert
Ganges River

East China Sea

S A H A R A

ARABIAN PENINSULA

Arabian Sea
Bay of Bengal
Mekong River
Tropic of Cancer
20°N

Nile River
Red Sea

AFRICA

Sri Lanka
Strait of Malacca

South China Sea
Philippine Islands
Taiwan

PACIFIC OCEAN

River

Gulf of Guinea

Congo River

MALAY PENINSULA
Borneo
Sumatra
Java
Celebes
New Guinea
Solomon Islands
0° Equator

Lake Tanganyika
Lake Victoria

INDIAN OCEAN

Coral Sea
New Hebrides
Fiji Islands

Madagascar

New Caledonia
20°S

KALAHARI DESERT

Mozambique Channel

GREAT SANDY DESERT
AUSTRALIA
GREAT VICTORIA DESERT
Darling River
GREAT DIVIDING RANGE
Tropic of Capricorn

Cape of Good Hope

North Island
Tasman Sea
NEW ZEALAND

Tasmania
South Island

20°E 40°E 60°E 80°E 100°E 120°E 140°E 160°E 60°S

ANTARCTICA

Denmark Strait
Iceland
N
W E
S
Kara Sea
Barents Sea
10°E 20°E 30°E 40°E
North Cape
KJÖLEN MTS.
URAL MTS.

0 250 500 Miles
0 250 500 Kilometers
Projection: Mollweide

60°N
North Sea
Baltic Sea
Volga River

British Isles
NORTHERN EUROPEAN PLAIN

50°N

ATLANTIC OCEAN

Bay of Biscay
Rhine River
Danube River
ALPS
Black Sea

40°N

IBERIAN PENINSULA
Mediterranean Sea
Crete

Strait of Gibraltar

ATLAS

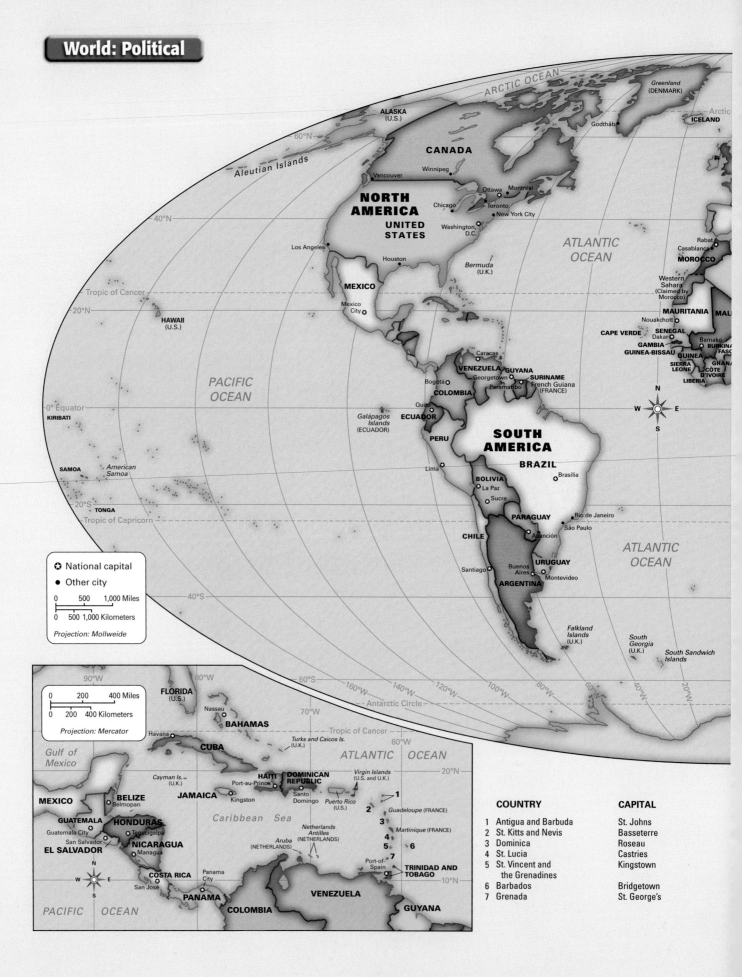

ARCTIC OCEAN

Greenland
(DENMARK)

Arctic

Godthåb

ICELAND

ALASKA
(U.S.)

60°N

CANADA

Aleutian Islands

Vancouver   Winnipeg

NORTH
AMERICA

Ottawa   Montreal

Chicago   Toronto

New York City

UNITED
STATES

40°N

Washington,
D.C.

ATLANTIC
OCEAN

Rabat

Los Angeles

Casablanca

MOROCCO

Houston

Bermuda
(U.K.)

Western
Sahara
(Claimed by
Morocco)

Tropic of Cancer

MEXICO

20°N

MAURITANIA   MAL

Mexico
City

Nouakchott

HAWAII
(U.S.)

CAPE VERDE

SENEGAL
Dakar

Bamako

Caracas

GAMBIA
GUINEA-BISSAU

BURKINA
FASC

PACIFIC
OCEAN

VENEZUELA   GUYANA

GUINEA

Georgetown   SURINAME

SIERRA
LEONE

GHANA
CÔTE
D'IVOIRE

Bogotá   Paramaribo   French Guiana
(FRANCE)

N

LIBERIA

COLOMBIA

W   E

0° Equator

Quito

ECUADOR

KIRIBATI

S

Galápagos
Islands
(ECUADOR)

SOUTH
AMERICA

PERU

BRAZIL

SAMOA

American
Samoa

Lima

Brasília

BOLIVIA

La Paz

Sucre

20°S

TONGA

Rio de Janeiro

PARAGUAY

Tropic of Capricorn

São Paulo

ATLANTIC
OCEAN

CHILE

Asunción

URUGUAY

○ National capital

● Other city

Santiago

Buenos
Aires

Montevideo

ARGENTINA

0   500   1,000 Miles

0   500   1,000 Kilometers

Projection: Mollweide

40°S

Falkland
Islands
(U.K.)

South
Georgia
(U.K.)

South Sandwich
Islands

60°S

160°W   140°W   120°W   100°W   80°W   60°W   40°W   20°W

Antarctic Circle

90°W   80°W

FLORIDA
(U.S.)

Nassau

70°W

Tropic of Cancer

0   200   400 Miles

Havana

BAHAMAS

60°W

0   200   400 Kilometers

Turks and Caicos Is.
(U.K.)

ATLANTIC   OCEAN

Projection: Mercator

Gulf of
Mexico

CUBA

70°W

20°N

Cayman Is.
(U.K.)

HAITI   DOMINICAN
REPUBLIC

Virgin Islands
(U.S. and U.K.)

1

Port-au-Prince

MEXICO

BELIZE

JAMAICA

Santo
Domingo

2

Guadeloupe (FRANCE)

Belmopan

Kingston

Puerto Rico
(U.S.)

3

GUATEMALA

HONDURAS

Caribbean Sea

Martinique (FRANCE)

Guatemala City   Tegucigalpa

Netherlands
Antilles
(NETHERLANDS)

4

San Salvador

NICARAGUA

Aruba
(NETHERLANDS)

5   6

EL SALVADOR

Managua

7

N

COSTA RICA

Port-of-
Spain

TRINIDAD AND
TOBAGO

W   E

Panama
City

S

10°N

San José

PANAMA

PACIFIC   OCEAN

VENEZUELA

COLOMBIA

GUYANA

COUNTRY	CAPITAL
1 Antigua and Barbuda	St. Johns
2 St. Kitts and Nevis	Basseterre
3 Dominica	Roseau
4 St. Lucia	Castries
5 St. Vincent and the Grenadines	Kingstown
6 Barbados	Bridgetown
7 Grenada	St. George's

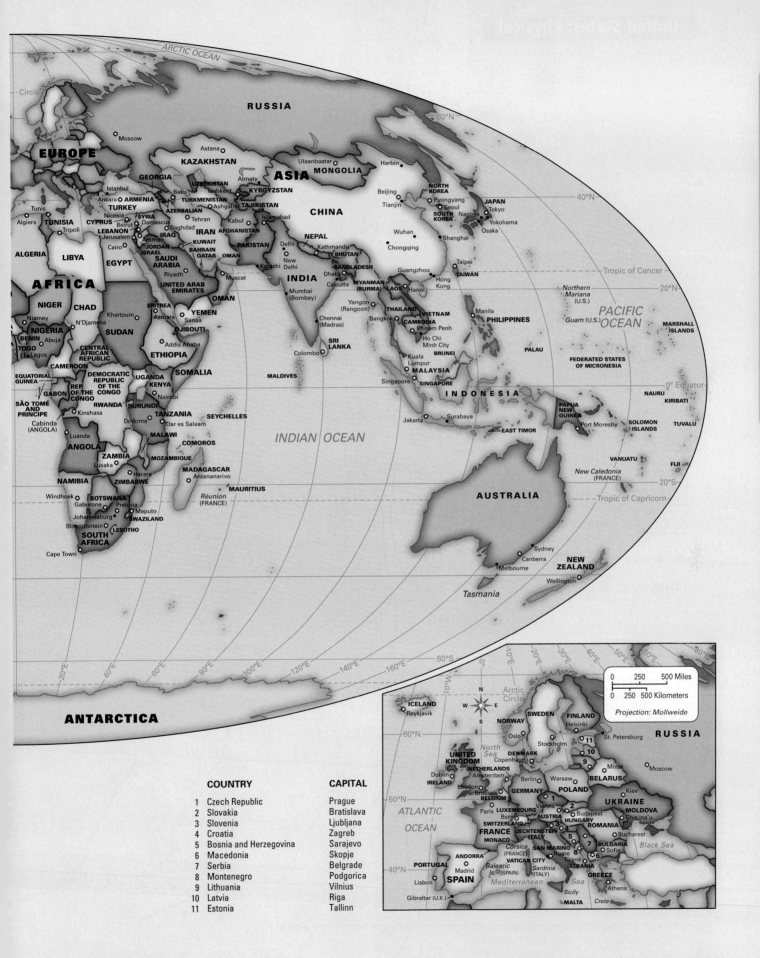

ARCTIC OCEAN

Circle

RUSSIA

Moscow

EUROPE

Astana

KAZAKHSTAN

ASIA

MONGOLIA

Ulaanbaatar

Harbin

GEORGIA

Almaty

Baku

UZBEKISTAN

KYRGYZSTAN

Beijing

NORTH KOREA

Pyongyang

Seoul

JAPAN

Tianjin

SOUTH KOREA

Nagoya

Tokyo

Yokohama

Osaka

Istanbul

Ankara

ARMENIA

TURKMENISTAN

TAJIKISTAN

Nicosia

TURKEY

AZERBAIJAN

Ashgabat

CHINA

Tunis

Algiers

TUNISIA

CYPRUS

SYRIA

Tehran

Kabul

Islamabad

Wuhan

Shanghai

Tripoli

LEBANON

Beirut

Damascus

Baghdad

IRAN

AFGHANISTAN

Delhi

Chongqing

Jerusalem

JORDAN

ISRAEL

Amman

IRAQ

KUWAIT

BAHRAIN

QATAR

PAKISTAN

NEPAL

New Delhi

Kathmandu

BHUTAN

Guangzhou

Hong Kong

Taipei

TAIWAN

ALGERIA

LIBYA

Cairo

EGYPT

SAUDI ARABIA

Riyadh

OMAN

Muscat

Karachi

INDIA

Mumbai (Bombay)

Calcutta

Dhaka

BANGLADESH

MYANMAR (BURMA)

LAOS

Hanoi

Tropic of Cancer

20°N

Northern Mariana (U.S.)

PACIFIC OCEAN

AFRICA

NIGER

CHAD

Khartoum

N'Djamena

SUDAN

ERITREA

Asmara

YEMEN

Sanaa

DJIBOUTI

Chennai (Madras)

Yangon (Rangoon)

THAILAND

Bangkok

CAMBODIA

VIETNAM

Phnom Penh

Manila

PHILIPPINES

Guam (U.S.)

MARSHALL ISLANDS

Niamey

NIGERIA

Abuja

BENIN

TOGO

Lagos

CAMEROON

CENTRAL AFRICAN REPUBLIC

ETHIOPIA

Addis Ababa

SRI LANKA

Colombo

Ho Chi Minh City

BRUNEI

PALAU

FEDERATED STATES OF MICRONESIA

EQUATORIAL GUINEA

SÃO TOMÉ AND PRINCIPE

GABON

REP. OF THE CONGO

DEMOCRATIC REPUBLIC OF THE CONGO

UGANDA

KENYA

SOMALIA

MALDIVES

Kuala Lumpur

MALAYSIA

Singapore

SINGAPORE

0° Equator

NAURU

KIRIBATI

Kinshasa

RWANDA

BURUNDI

Nairobi

TANZANIA

Dodoma

Dar es Salaam

SEYCHELLES

INDONESIA

Jakarta

Surabaya

PAPUA NEW GUINEA

Port Moresby

SOLOMON ISLANDS

TUVALU

Cabinda (ANGOLA)

Luanda

ANGOLA

MALAWI

COMOROS

MOZAMBIQUE

INDIAN OCEAN

EAST TIMOR

ZAMBIA

Lusaka

MADAGASCAR

Antananarivo

MAURITIUS

VANUATU

New Caledonia (FRANCE)

FIJI

20°S

Windhoek

NAMIBIA

ZIMBABWE

Harare

Réunion (FRANCE)

AUSTRALIA

Tropic of Capricorn

BOTSWANA

Gaborone

Pretoria

Maputo

SWAZILAND

Johannesburg

LESOTHO

Bloemfontein

SOUTH AFRICA

Cape Town

Sydney

Canberra

Melbourne

NEW ZEALAND

Wellington

Tasmania

ANTARCTICA

20°E 40°E 60°E 80°E 100°E 120°E 140°E 160°E

60°S

	COUNTRY	CAPITAL
1	Czech Republic	Prague
2	Slovakia	Bratislava
3	Slovenia	Ljubljana
4	Croatia	Zagreb
5	Bosnia and Herzegovina	Sarajevo
6	Macedonia	Skopje
7	Serbia	Belgrade
8	Montenegro	Podgorica
9	Lithuania	Vilnius
10	Latvia	Riga
11	Estonia	Tallinn

0 250 500 Miles

0 250 500 Kilometers

Projection: Mollweide

ICELAND

Reykjavik

Arctic Circle

SWEDEN

FINLAND

Helsinki

St. Petersburg

RUSSIA

NORWAY

Oslo

Stockholm

11

60°N

North Sea

DENMARK

Copenhagen

10

9

Minsk

Moscow

UNITED KINGDOM

NETHERLANDS

Amsterdam

Berlin

Warsaw

BELARUS

Dublin

IRELAND

London

Brussels

BELGIUM

GERMANY

POLAND

1

2

UKRAINE

Kiev

MOLDOVA

Chisinau

ATLANTIC OCEAN

Paris

LUXEMBOURG

Bern

Vienna

AUSTRIA

Budapest

HUNGARY

ROMANIA

50°N

SWITZERLAND

LIECHTENSTEIN

3

4

Bucharest

FRANCE

MONACO

ITALY

5

7

BULGARIA

Sofia

Black Sea

Corsica (FRANCE)

SAN MARINO

Rome

8

6

ANDORRA

VATICAN CITY

Tirané

ALBANIA

PORTUGAL

Madrid

Balearic Is. (SPAIN)

Sardinia (ITALY)

GREECE

40°N

Lisbon

SPAIN

Mediterranean

Athens

Gibraltar (U.K.)

Sicily

Sea

MALTA

Crete

United States: Physical

Strait of Juan de Fuca

45°N

Mount Rainier 14,410 ft (4,392 m)

Puget Sound

Franklin D. Roosevelt Lake

ROCKY

Milk River

Missouri River

Fort Peck Lake

Lake Sakakawea

GREAT

COAST RANGES

CASCADE RANGE

Columbia River

Bitterroot Range

CONTINENTAL

Lewis Range

Red Lake

Yellowstone River

Columbia Plateau

Salmon River Mts.

Salmon River

Sawtooth Mts.

Snake River

Yellowstone

Bighorn Mts.

Bighorn River

Powder River

Black Hills

Cheyenne River

White River

James River

40°N

Cape Mendocino

Klamath River

Goose Lake

Shasta Lake

Pyramid Lake

Grand Teton

Wind River Range

Gannett Peak 13,804 ft (4,207 m)

Wasatch Range

MOUNTAINS

Front Range

Niobrara River

North Platte River

Platte River

GREAT INTERI

San Francisco Bay

125°W

Lake Tahoe

SIERRA NEVADA

Central Valley

Sacramento River

GREAT BASIN

Great Salt Lake

Utah Lake

Uinta Mts.

Green River

South Platte River

Republican River

35°N

Monterey Bay

San Joaquin River

Coast Ranges

Mount Whitney 14,494 ft (4,419 m)

Death Valley

Colorado River

COLORADO

Colorado River

Mount Elbert 14,433 ft (4,400 m)

DIVIDE

San Juan River

Pikes Peak 14,110 ft (4,301 m)

Smoky Hill River

PLAINS

Channel Islands

Mojave Desert

Grand Canyon

Lake Mead

PLATEAU

Lake Powell

Painted Desert

San Luis Valley

Sangre De Cristo Mts.

DIVIDE

Canadian River

PACIFIC OCEAN

Salton Sea

Imperial Valley

Gila River

MOUNTAINS

Rio Grande

CONTINENTAL

Pecos River

Colorado River

30°N

120°W

Sonoran Desert

Gulf of California

MEXICO

Amistad Reservoir

Rio Grande

Nueces River

Padre Island

To understand the relative locations of Alaska and Hawaii, as well as the vast distances separating them from the rest of the United States, see the world map.

Kauai

Niihau

Oahu

HAWAII

Molokai

22°N

155°W

ARCTIC OCEAN

Arctic Circle

BROOKS RANGE

PACIFIC OCEAN

Lanai

Maui

Kahoolawe

Mauna Kea 13,796 ft (4,206 m)

Hawaii

19°N

160°W

RUSSIA

Bering Strait

St. Lawrence Island

St. Matthew Island

Nunivak Island

Yukon River

Tanana River

CANADA

Kuskokwim River

ALASKA RANGE

Mount McKinley 20,320 ft (6,194 m)

0   75   150 Miles
0   75   150 Kilometers
Projection: Mercator

N W E S

Bering Sea

0   250   500 Miles
0   250   500 Kilometers
Projection: Albers Equal Area

170°W

55°N

Attu Island

50°N

PACIFIC OCEAN

180°

ALEUTIAN ISLANDS

N W E S

160°W

150°W

Gulf of Alaska

Kodiak Island

Alexander Archipelago

55°N

CANADA

Red River
Isle Royale
Mesabi Range
Lake Superior
Minnesota River
Mississippi River
Wisconsin River
Lake Michigan
Lake Huron
Lake Ontario
Lake Erie
Des Moines River
Missouri River
Kansas R.
Illinois River
Wabash River
Scioto River
Ohio River
Lake of the Ozarks
OZARK PLATEAU
Lake Barkley
Cumberland River
Keystone Lake
White River
Kentucky Lake
Arkansas River
Eufaula Lake
Ouachita Mts.
Lake Texoma
Tennessee River
Trinity River
Saline River
Red River
Brazos River
Toledo Bend Reservoir
Tombigbee River
Coosa River
Alabama R.
Yazoo River
Pearl River
Mississippi River
Chattahoochee River
Ocmulgee River
Altamaha River
Savannah River
Oconee River
Sea Islands
Chandeleur Islands
Mississippi Delta
Okefenokee Swamp
Cape Canaveral
FLORIDA PENINSULA
Lake Okeechobee
The Everglades
Cape Sable
Florida Keys
Straits of Florida
Gulf of Mexico
BAHAMAS

ST. Lawrence River
St. Lawrence Seaway
Longfellow Mts.
Penobscot River
St. John River
Lake Champlain
Green Mts.
White Mts.
Adirondack Mts.
Connecticut River
Hudson River
Cape Cod
Allegheny R.
Catskill Mts.
PLATEAU
Susquehanna River
Long Island Sound
Long Island
MOUNTAINS
ALLEGHENY
Monongahela R.
Delaware River
Delaware Bay
Potomac River
Kanawha River
Chesapeake Bay
APPALACHIAN MOUNTAINS
James River
Roanoke River
BLUE RIDGE MOUNTAINS
Cumberland Plateau
Great Smoky Mts.
PIEDMONT
Pamlico Sound
Cape Hatteras

ATLANTIC OCEAN

OR
PLAINS
GULF COASTAL PLAIN

40°N
70°W
35°N
25°N
95°W
90°W
85°W
80°W
75°W

N W E S

ELEVATION

Feet		Meters
13,120		4,000
6,560		2,000
1,640		500
656		200
(Sea level) 0		0 (Sea level)
Below sea level		Below sea level

0   100   200 Miles
0   100   200 Kilometers

Projection: Albers Equal Area

United States: Political

Strait of Juan de Fuca

Puget Sound

Franklin D. Roosevelt Lake

Pend Oreille

Missouri River

NORTH DAKOTA

Olympia ★ Seattle Tacoma
Spokane •

WASHINGTON

45°N

Flathead Lake

Great Falls •

Fort Peck Lake

Lake Sakakawea

Bismarck ★

Portland •

Columbia River

Salem ★

Helena ★ **MONTANA**

Yellowstone River

Eugene •

OREGON

IDAHO

Billings •

Lake Oahe

SOUTH DAKOTA

Boise ★ Sun Valley •

Yellowstone Lake

Pierre ★

Goose Lake

Cape Mendocino

40°N

Shasta Lake

Sacramento River

Snake River

Pocatello •

WYOMING

Rapid City •

Pyramid Lake

Reno • Carson City ★ **NEVADA**

Ogden •

Great Salt Lake Salt Lake City ★ Provo •

Cheyenne ★

NEBRASKA

Platte River

125°W

Berkeley • Oakland • San Francisco • Sacramento • Lake Tahoe

San Francisco Bay

San Joaquin River

San Jose •

Monterey Bay

UTAH

Utah Lake

Green River

Aspen • Vail • Boulder • Denver ★

Colorado Springs •

COLORADO

Pueblo •

Arkansas River

KANSAS

35°N

Fresno •

CALIFORNIA

Lake Powell

Las Vegas •

Colorado River

Lake Mead

Flagstaff •

Taos •

Santa Fe ★

OKLAHOMA

Canadian River

Santa Barbara •
Ventura • Los Angeles • Riverside • Palm Springs •
Long Beach • Anaheim • Santa Ana •
San Diego •

Channel Islands

Salton Sea

PACIFIC OCEAN

ARIZONA

Phoenix ★

Gila River

Casa Grande •

Tucson •

Albuquerque •

NEW MEXICO

Amarillo •

Oklahoma City ★

Lawton •

120°W

Lubbock •

Las Cruces •

El Paso •

Midland • Odessa •

Abilene • Fort Worth •

Brazos River

TEXAS

30°N

Gulf of California

Pecos River

Colorado River

Rio Grande

Amistad Reservoir

To understand the relative locations of Alaska and Hawaii, as well as the vast distances separating them from the rest of the United States, see the world map.

Austin ★

San Antonio •

Corpus Christi •

Laredo •

Padre Island

MEXICO

Kauai
Niihau Oahu Molokai
Honolulu **HAWAII** Maui
PACIFIC OCEAN Lanai Kahoolawe
Hilo • Hawaii

22°N

155°W

ARCTIC OCEAN

Arctic Circle

Bering Strait

RUSSIA

19°N

| 0 | 75 | 150 Miles |
| 0 | 75 | 150 Kilometers |

Projection: Mercator

Nome •

Yukon River

CANADA

St. Lawrence Island
St. Matthew Island

Nunivak Island

Fairbanks •

Bering Sea

55°N

Attu Island

Anchorage • Valdez •

ALASKA

Skagway •

170°E

250 500 Miles
250 500 Kilometers

Projection: Albers Equal Area

Kodiak Island

Gulf of Alaska

Juneau ★

Alexander Archipelago

55°N

50°N

PACIFIC OCEAN

ALEUTIAN ISLANDS

180°

170°W

150°W

140°W

Gulf of Mexico

CANADA

MINNESOTA
Grand Forks
Fargo
Duluth
Superior
Marquette
Sault Ste. Marie
Red River
Minnesota River

WISCONSIN
Minneapolis
St. Paul
Green Bay
Madison
Milwaukee

MICHIGAN
Lake Superior
Lake Huron
Lake Michigan
Saginaw
Grand Rapids
Lansing
Detroit
Ann Arbor

Mississippi River

IOWA
Sioux Falls
Sioux City
Cedar Rapids
Davenport
Des Moines
Rockford
Chicago
Gary
South Bend

Lake Ontario
Lake Erie

NEW YORK
Rochester
Syracuse
Albany
Buffalo

MAINE
Augusta
Portland
Burlington
Montpelier
VT
NH
Concord
Manchester
Boston
Worcester
Providence
Cape Cod
MA
RI
CT
Hartford
New Haven
Springfield
Long Island Sound
Long Island

St. Lawrence River
Lake Champlain
Hudson R.
Connecticut R.

PENNSYLVANIA
Allentown
Harrisburg
Pittsburgh
Philadelphia
Bridgeport
Jersey City
Newark
Yonkers
New York City
Trenton
Camden
NJ
Atlantic City
Dover
DE

Susquehanna River

OHIO
Cleveland
Youngstown
Akron
Toledo
Columbus
Dayton
Cincinnati

INDIANA
Fort Wayne
Indianapolis

ILLINOIS
Peoria
Springfield
St. Louis
East St. Louis

MISSOURI
Omaha
Lincoln
Kansas City
Topeka
Kansas City
Jefferson City
Wichita
Springfield
Lake of the Ozarks
Missouri River
Illinois River

KENTUCKY
Louisville
Evansville
Frankfort
Lexington
Lake Barkley
Ohio River
Kentucky Lake
Kentucky River

WEST VIRGINIA
Charleston

VIRGINIA
Richmond
Newport News
Norfolk
Virginia Beach
Washington, D.C.
Annapolis
Baltimore
MD
Chesapeake Bay
Delaware Bay

ATLANTIC OCEAN

40°N
70°W
35°N

TENNESSEE
Nashville
Knoxville
Chattanooga
Memphis

NORTH CAROLINA
Winston-Salem
Greensboro
Durham
Raleigh
Asheville
Charlotte
Cape Hatteras

ARKANSAS
Fayetteville
Little Rock
Pine Bluff
Keystone Lake
Tulsa
Eufaula Lake
Lake Texoma

SOUTH CAROLINA
Greenville
Columbia
Charleston
Savannah River
Sea Islands

MISSISSIPPI
Vicksburg
Jackson
Meridian
Huntsville

ALABAMA
Birmingham
Montgomery
Columbus

GEORGIA
Atlanta
Macon
Savannah
Chattahoochee R.

LOUISIANA
Shreveport
Baton Rouge
New Orleans
Beaumont
Houston
Galveston
Dallas
Waco
Red River
Toledo Bend Reservoir
Biloxi
Mobile
Pensacola
Chandeleur Islands
Mississippi River

FLORIDA
Tallahassee
Jacksonville
Gainesville
Orlando
Tampa
St. Petersburg
Lake Okeechobee
Fort Myers
Fort Lauderdale
Miami
Cape Canaveral
Cape Sable
Florida Keys
Straits of Florida

Gulf of Mexico

BAHAMAS
30°N
25°N
80°W
85°W
90°W
95°W
75°W

N W E S

Legend:
✪ National capital
★ State capitals
● Other cities

0 100 200 Miles
0 100 200 Kilometers

Projection: Albers Equal Area

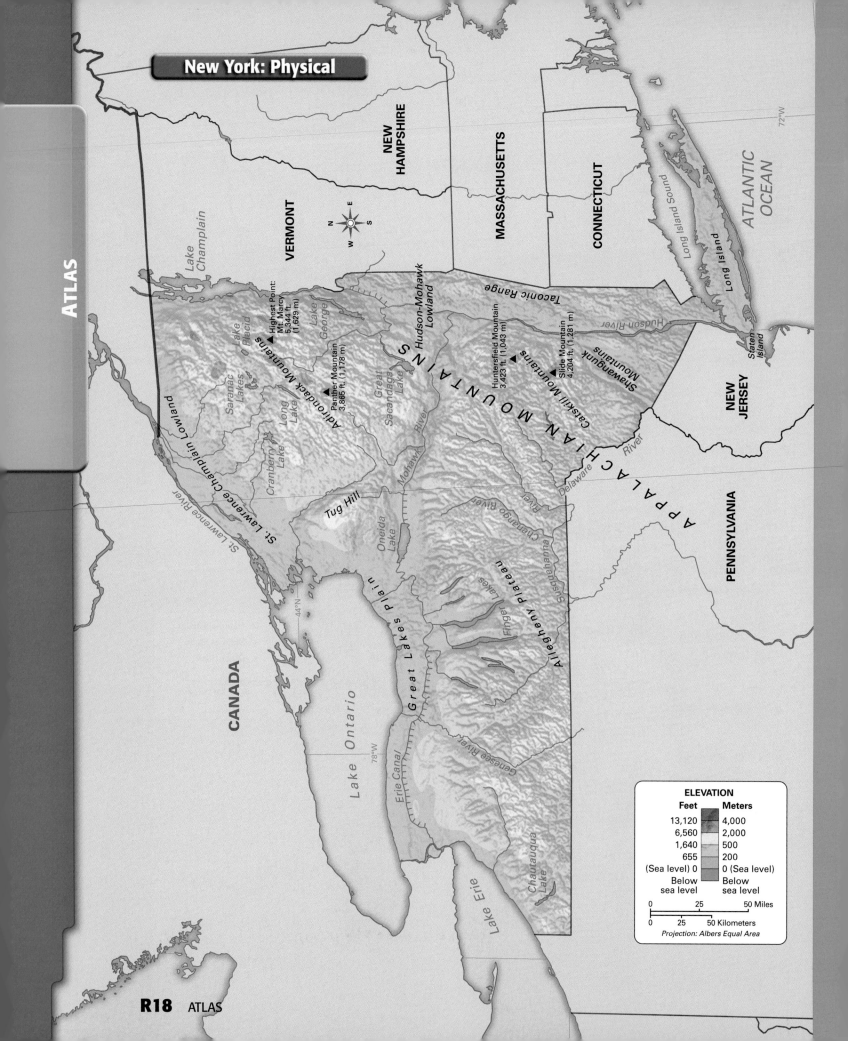

New York: Physical

CANADA

Lake Ontario

Lake Erie

CANADA

VERMONT

NEW HAMPSHIRE

MASSACHUSETTS

CONNECTICUT

NEW JERSEY

PENNSYLVANIA

ATLANTIC OCEAN

Lake Champlain

Lake George

Lake Placid

Saranac Lakes

Long Lake

Cranberry Lake

St. Lawrence River

St. Lawrence Champlain Lowland

Highest Point: Mt. Marcy 5,344 ft. (1,629 m)

Panther Mountain 3,865 ft. (1,178 m)

ADIRONDACK MOUNTAINS

Great Sacandaga Lake

Tug Hill

Oneida Lake

Mohawk River

Hudson-Mohawk Lowland

Taconic Range

Huntersfield Mountain 3,423 ft. (1,043 m)

Slide Mountain 4,204 ft. (1,281 m)

CATSKILL MOUNTAINS

Shawangunk Mountains

APPALACHIAN MOUNTAINS

Hudson River

Long Island Sound

Long Island

Staten Island

Great Lakes Plain

Erie Canal

Genesee River

Finger Lakes

Allegheny Plateau

Chenango River

Susquehanna River

Delaware River

Chautauqua Lake

44°N

78°W

72°W

N E S W

ELEVATION

Feet	Meters
13,120	4,000
6,560	2,000
1,640	500
655	200
(Sea level) 0	0 (Sea level)
Below sea level	Below sea level

0   25   50 Miles

0   25   50 Kilometers

Projection: Albers Equal Area

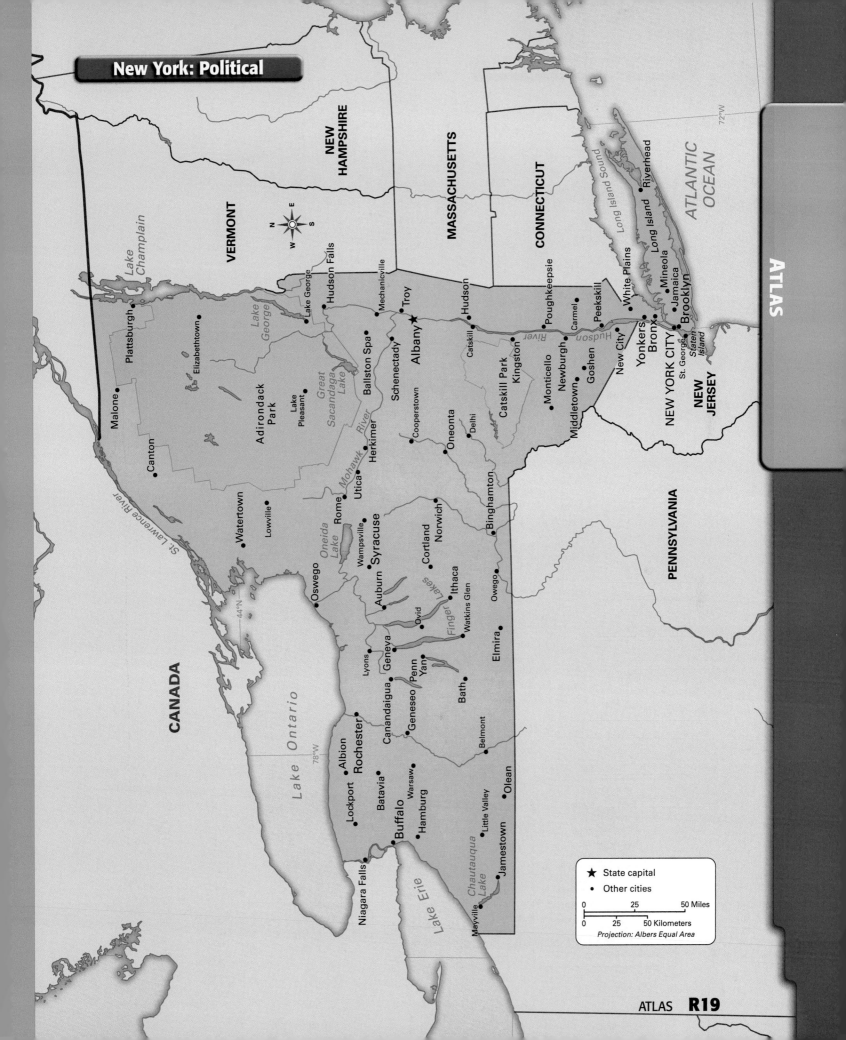

New York: Political

CANADA

St. Lawrence River

VERMONT

NEW HAMPSHIRE

MASSACHUSETTS

CONNECTICUT

NEW JERSEY

PENNSYLVANIA

ATLANTIC OCEAN

ATLAS

Lake Champlain

Lake George

Lake George

Great Sacandaga Lake

Mohawk River

Oneida Lake

Lake Ontario

Lake Erie

Chautauqua Lake

Finger Lakes

Long Island Sound

Long Island

Hudson River

Adirondack Park

Catskill Park

Malone
Plattsburgh
Canton
Elizabethtown
Lake Pleasant
Watertown
Lowville
Oswego
Lyons
Albion
Rochester
Lockport
Batavia
Buffalo
Warsaw
Hamburg
Niagara Falls
Mayville
Jamestown
Little Valley
Olean
Belmont
Bath
Canandaigua
Geneva
Geneseo
Penn Yan
Ovid
Watkins Glen
Ithaca
Elmira
Owego
Auburn
Syracuse
Wampsville
Rome
Utica
Herkimer
Cortland
Norwich
Binghamton
Oneonta
Cooperstown
Delhi
Ballston Spa
Schenectady
Hudson Falls
Lake George
Mechanicville
Troy
Albany ★
Hudson
Catskill
Kingston
Monticello
Middletown
Newburgh
Goshen
Poughkeepsie
Carmel
Peekskill
New City
White Plains
Yonkers
Bronx
NEW YORK CITY
St. George
Staten Island
Brooklyn
Jamaica
Mineola
Riverhead

72°W
78°W
44°N

Legend
★ State capital
● Other cities

0   25   50 Miles
0   25   50 Kilometers
Projection: Albers Equal Area

North America: Physical

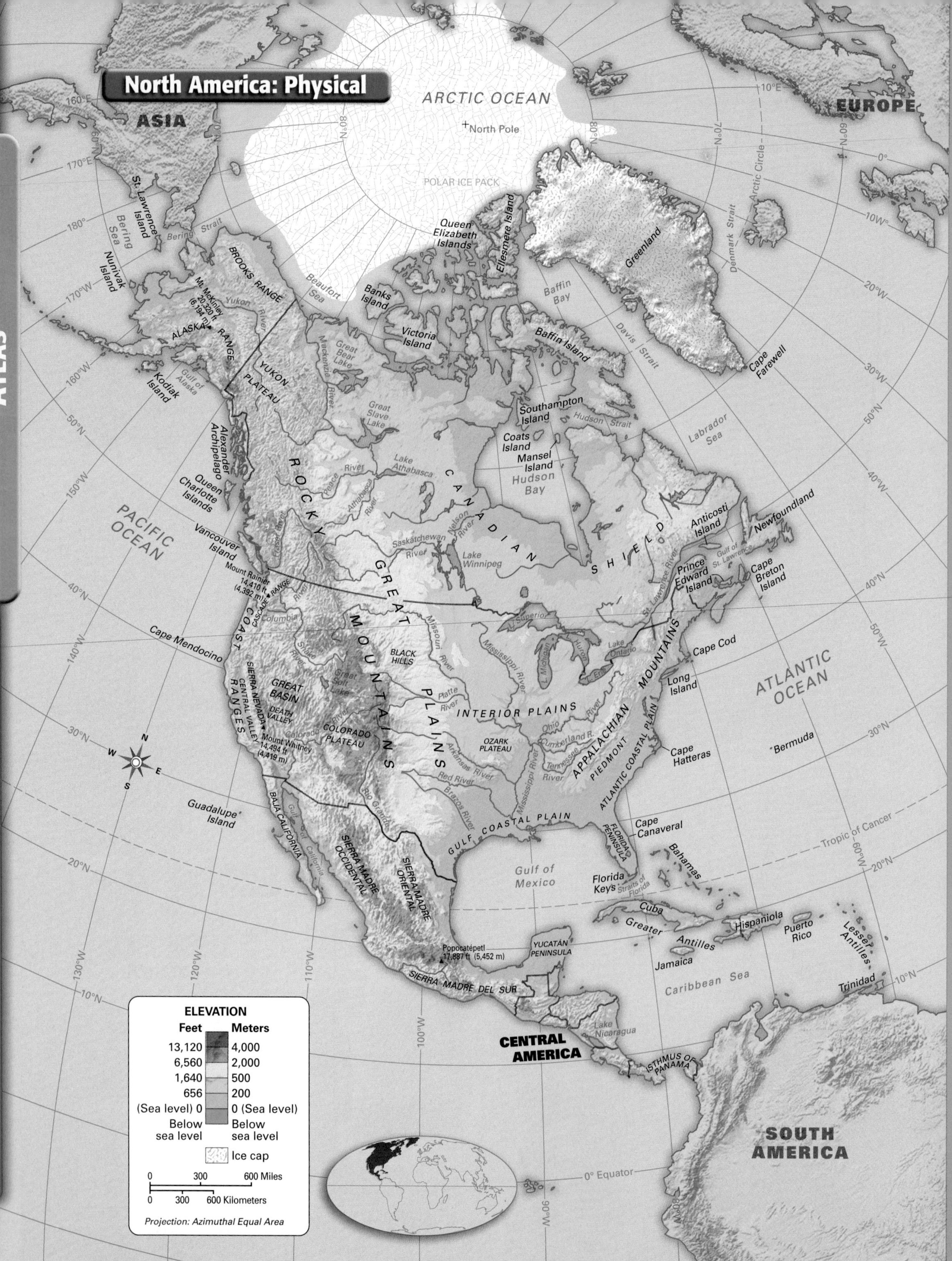

ASIA
EUROPE
ARCTIC OCEAN
+ North Pole
POLAR ICE PACK

St. Lawrence Island
Bering Sea
Bering Strait
Nunivak Island
BROOKS RANGE
Mt. McKinley 20,320 ft (6,194 m)
Yukon
ALASKA
RANGE
YUKON PLATEAU
Gulf of Alaska
Kodiak Island
Alexander Archipelago
Queen Charlotte Islands
Vancouver Island
Mount Rainier 14,410 ft (4,392 m)
Columbia
CASCADE RANGE
COAST RANGES
Beaufort Sea
Banks Island
Victoria Island
Mackenzie River
Great Bear Lake
River
Great Slave Lake
Lake Athabasca
Athabasca River
Saskatchewan River
Nelson River
Lake Winnipeg
ROCKY
MOUNTAINS
GREAT
PLAINS
Queen Elizabeth Islands
Ellesmere Island
Greenland
Denmark Strait
Cape Farewell
Baffin Bay
Baffin Island
Davis Strait
Labrador Sea
Hudson Strait
Southampton Island
Coats Island
Mansel Island
Hudson Bay
CANADIAN
SHIELD
Anticosti Island
Newfoundland
Prince Edward Island
Cape Breton Island
Gulf of St. Lawrence
St. Lawrence River
Lake Superior
Lake Michigan
Lake Huron
Lake Erie
Lake Ontario
APPALACHIAN MOUNTAINS
Cape Cod
Long Island
ATLANTIC OCEAN

PACIFIC OCEAN
Cape Mendocino
SIERRA NEVADA
CENTRAL VALLEY
GREAT BASIN
DEATH VALLEY
Mount Whitney 14,494 ft (4,419 m)
Colorado
Great Salt Lake
Snake River
COLORADO PLATEAU
BLACK HILLS
Missouri River
Platte River
INTERIOR PLAINS
OZARK PLATEAU
Arkansas River
Red River
Mississippi River
Ohio River
Cumberland R.
Tennessee River
PIEDMONT
ATLANTIC COASTAL PLAIN
Cape Hatteras
Bermuda
Cape Canaveral
FLORIDA PENINSULA
Florida Keys
Straits of Florida
Bahamas

Guadalupe Island
BAJA CALIFORNIA
Gulf of California
SIERRA MADRE OCCIDENTAL
SIERRA MADRE ORIENTAL
Rio Grande
Brazos River
GULF COASTAL PLAIN
Gulf of Mexico
Popocatépetl 17,887 ft (5,452 m)
YUCATÁN PENINSULA
SIERRA MADRE DEL SUR
Lake Nicaragua
CENTRAL AMERICA
ISTHMUS OF PANAMA
Cuba
Greater Antilles
Jamaica
Hispaniola
Puerto Rico
Lesser Antilles
Trinidad
Caribbean Sea
SOUTH AMERICA

Tropic of Cancer
Arctic Circle
Equator

ELEVATION

Feet	Meters
13,120	4,000
6,560	2,000
1,640	500
656	200
(Sea level) 0	0 (Sea level)
Below sea level	Below sea level

Ice cap

0   300   600 Miles
0   300   600 Kilometers

Projection: Azimuthal Equal Area

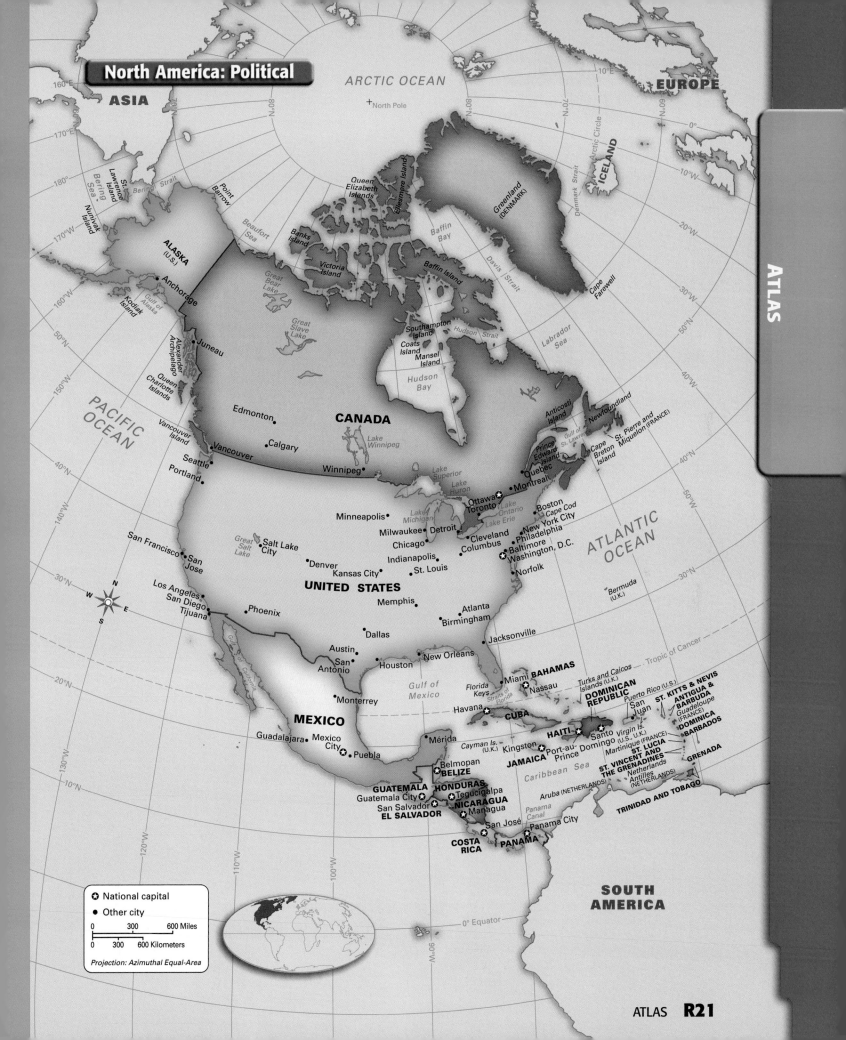

North America: Political

ASIA

ARCTIC OCEAN

+ North Pole

EUROPE

ATLAS

ICELAND

Greenland
(DENMARK)

Queen
Elizabeth
Islands

Ellesmere Island

Banks
Island

Beaufort
Sea

Baffin
Bay

Cape
Farewell

Point
Barrow

ALASKA
(U.S.)

Anchorage

Victoria
Island

Great
Bear
Lake

Baffin
Island

Davis Strait

Labrador
Sea

Gulf
of
Alaska

Kodiak
Island

St.
Lawrence
Island

Nunivak
Island

Bering
Sea

Bering Strait

Juneau

Alexander
Archipelago

Queen
Charlotte
Islands

Great
Slave
Lake

Southampton
Island

Coats
Island
Mansel
Island

Hudson Strait

Hudson
Bay

PACIFIC
OCEAN

Vancouver
Island

Edmonton

CANADA

Lake
Winnipeg

Anticosti
Island

Newfoundland

St. Pierre and
Miquelon (FRANCE)

Vancouver

Calgary

Cape
Breton
Island

Prince
Edward
Island

Gulf of
St. Lawrence

Seattle

Portland

Winnipeg

Lake
Superior

Quebec

Montreal

Minneapolis

Lake
Michigan

Lake
Huron

Lake
Ontario

Lake Erie

Ottawa

Toronto

Boston

Cape Cod

Milwaukee

Detroit

Cleveland

New York City

Chicago

Columbus

Philadelphia

San Francisco

San
Jose

Great
Salt
Lake

Salt Lake
City

Denver

Kansas City

Indianapolis

St. Louis

Baltimore

Washington, D.C.

Norfolk

ATLANTIC
OCEAN

UNITED STATES

Los Angeles

San Diego

Tijuana

Phoenix

Memphis

Atlanta

Birmingham

Bermuda
(U.K.)

Dallas

Jacksonville

Tropic of Cancer

Austin

San
Antonio

Houston

New Orleans

MEXICO

Monterrey

Gulf of
California

Gulf of
Mexico

Florida
Keys

Miami

BAHAMAS

Nassau

Turks and Caicos
Islands (U.K.)

Puerto Rico (U.S.)

San
Juan

ST. KITTS & NEVIS

ANTIGUA &
BARBUDA

Guadeloupe
(FRANCE)

DOMINICA

Guadalajara

Mexico
City

Puebla

Havana

Straits of
Florida

CUBA

DOMINICAN
REPUBLIC

HAITI

Santo
Domingo

Virgin Is.
(U.S., U.K.)

Martinique (FRANCE)

BARBADOS

ST. LUCIA

Mérida

Cayman Is.
(U.K.)

Kingston

Port-au-
Prince

JAMAICA

ST. VINCENT AND
THE GRENADINES

GRENADA

Belmopan

BELIZE

Caribbean Sea

Netherlands
Antilles
(NETHERLANDS)

GUATEMALA

HONDURAS

Aruba (NETHERLANDS)

TRINIDAD AND TOBAGO

Guatemala City

Tegucigalpa

San Salvador

NICARAGUA

Managua

Panama
Canal

EL SALVADOR

San José

Panama City

COSTA
RICA

PANAMA

SOUTH
AMERICA

⊕ National capital

● Other city

0   300   600 Miles

0   300   600 Kilometers

Projection: Azimuthal Equal-Area

0° Equator

ATLAS **R21**

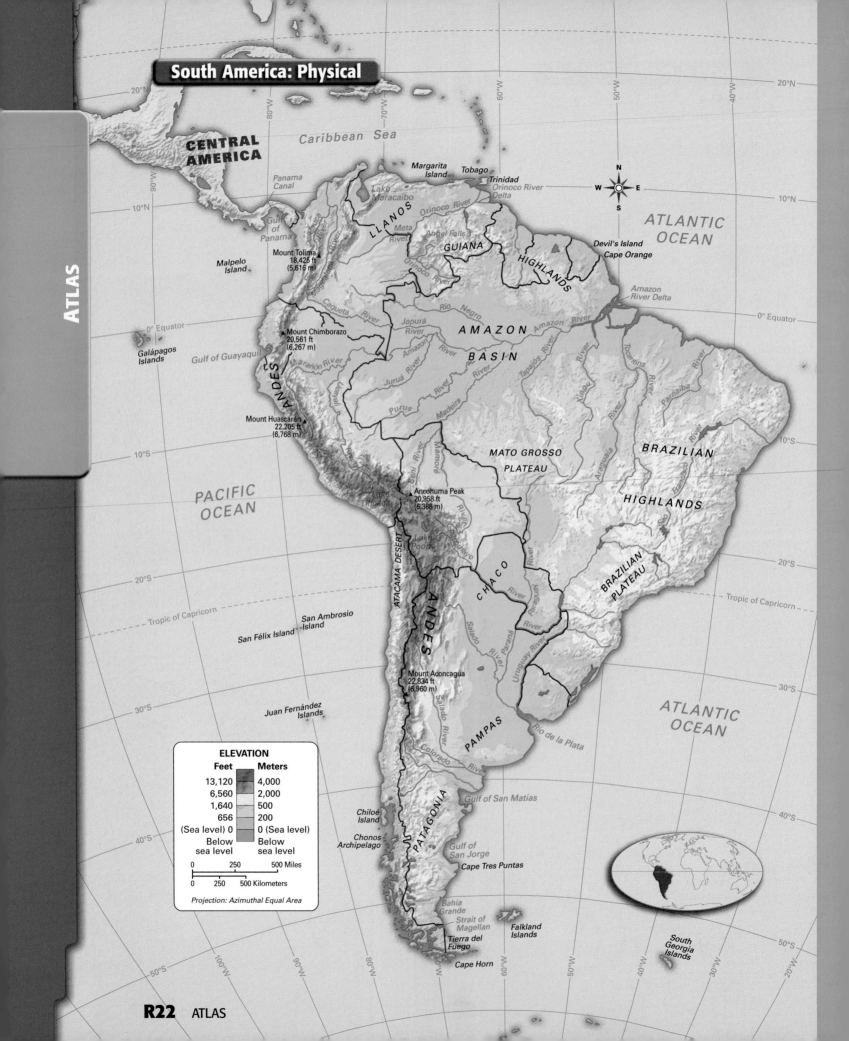

South America: Physical

CENTRAL
AMERICA

Caribbean Sea

Panama
Canal

Gulf
of
Panama

Margarita
Island

Tobago

Trinidad

Orinoco River
Delta

Lake
Maracaibo

LLANOS

Orinoco River

Meta
River

Cauca River

GUIANA

Angel Falls

HIGHLANDS

Devil's Island
Cape Orange

Amazon
River Delta

Mount Tolima
18,425 ft
(5,616 m)

Malpelo
Island

Magdalena River

Caqueta River

Rio Negro

Japurá
River

AMAZON

Amazon River

0° Equator

0° Equator

Galápagos
Islands

Gulf of Guayaquil

Mount Chimborazo
20,561 ft
(6,267 m)

Marañón River

Ucayali River

Juruá River

BASIN

Amazon River

Madeira River

Tapajós River

Xingu River

Tocantins River

Parnaíba River

ATLANTIC
OCEAN

10°N

Purus River

ANDES

Mount Huascarán
22,205 ft
(6,768 m)

Bahi River

Mamoré River

MATO GROSSO
PLATEAU

Araguaia River

BRAZILIAN

HIGHLANDS

10°S

PACIFIC
OCEAN

Lake
Titicaca

Ancohuma Peak
20,958 ft
(6,388 m)

São Francisco River

San Ambrosio
Island

San Félix Island

Lake
Poopó

ATACAMA DESERT

Pilcomayo River

CHACO

BRAZILIAN
PLATEAU

Paraguay River

20°S

Tropic of Capricorn

Tropic of Capricorn

Juan Fernández
Islands

ANDES

Salado River

Paraná River

Uruguay River

Mount Aconcagua
22,834 ft
(6,960 m)

Salado River

PAMPAS

Rio de la Plata

ATLANTIC
OCEAN

30°S

Colorado River

Gulf of San Matías

Chiloé
Island

PATAGONIA

Chonos
Archipelago

Gulf of
San Jorge

Cape Tres Puntas

40°S

Bahía
Grande

Strait of
Magellan

Falkland
Islands

South
Georgia
Islands

50°S

Tierra del
Fuego

Cape Horn

ELEVATION

Feet		Meters
13,120		4,000
6,560		2,000
1,640		500
656		200
0 (Sea level)		0 (Sea level)
Below sea level		Below sea level

0   250   500 Miles

0   250   500 Kilometers

Projection: Azimuthal Equal Area

South America: Political

Caribbean Sea

CENTRAL AMERICA

Barranquilla
Cartagena
Caracas
VENEZUELA
Medellín
Bogotá
COLOMBIA
Cali
Malpelo Island (COLOMBIA)

Georgetown
Paramaribo
Cayenne
GUYANA
SURINAME
French Guiana (FRANCE)

ATLANTIC OCEAN

Quito
ECUADOR
Guayaquil
Galápagos Islands (ECUADOR)

PERU
Trujillo
Callao Lima

Belém

BRAZIL

Recife

PACIFIC OCEAN

Lake Titicaca
Arequipa
La Paz
Lake Poopó
Sucre
BOLIVIA

Brasília

Salvador

Belo Horizonte

PARAGUAY
Asunción

Campinas
São Paulo
Curitiba
Rio de Janeiro

San Félix Island (CHILE)
San Ambrosio Island (CHILE)

CHILE

Juan Fernández Islands (CHILE)

Pôrto Alegre

Córdoba
Rosario
URUGUAY
Valparaíso
Santiago
Buenos Aires
Montevideo

ATLANTIC OCEAN

ARGENTINA

⊛ National capital
• Other city

0   250   500 Miles
0   250   500 Kilometers

Projection: Azimuthal Equal-Area

Strait of Magellan
Falkland Islands (U.K.)

Tierra del Fuego

South Georgia Island (U.K.)

N
W   E
S

Tropic of Capricorn

Tropic of Capricorn

20°N
10°N
0° Equator
0° Equator
10°S
20°S
30°S
40°S
50°S

20°N
10°N
10°S
20°S
30°S
40°S
50°S

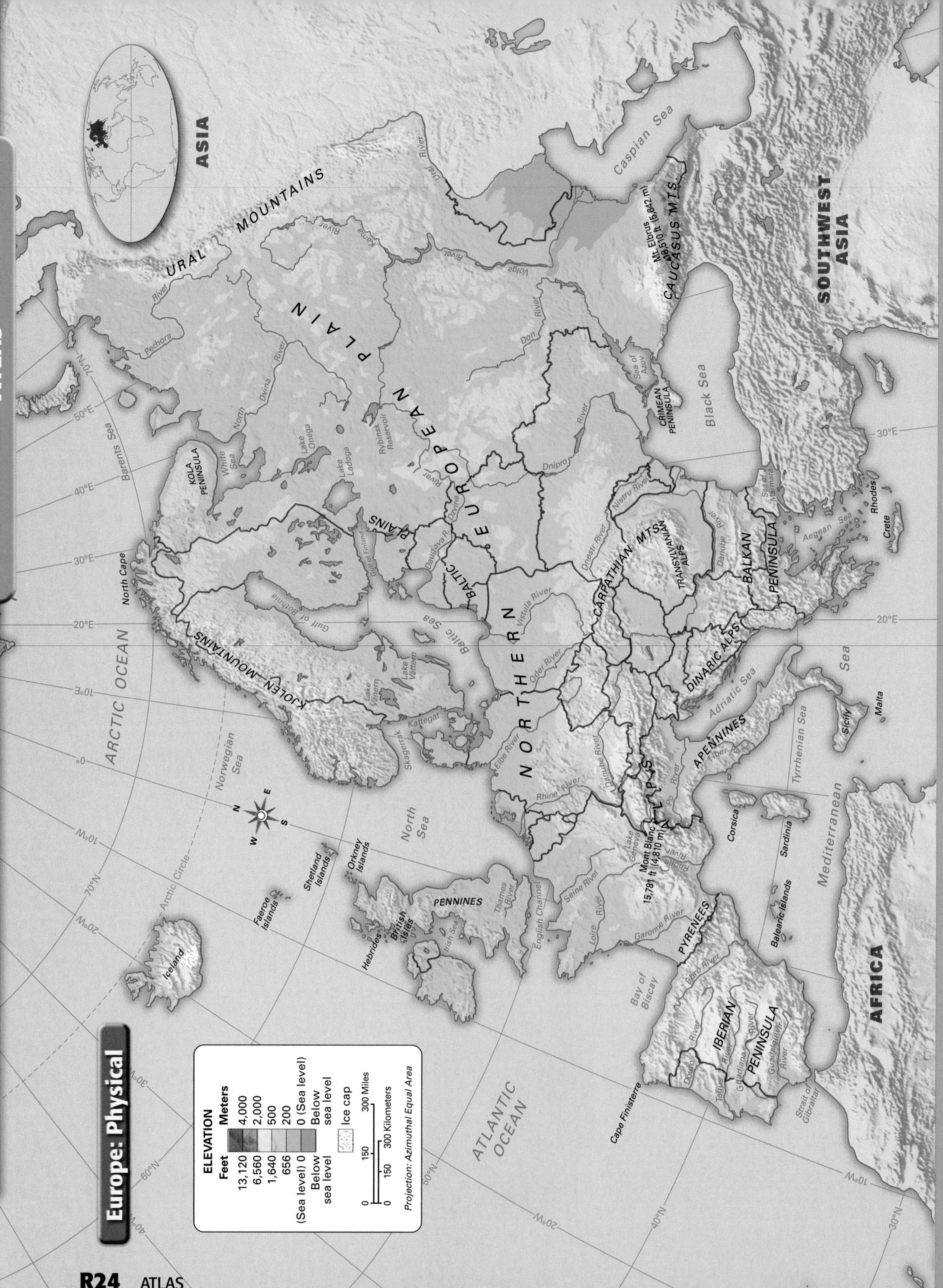

ASIA

URAL MOUNTAINS

River

Caspian Sea

Mt. Elbrus (5,642 m)
18,510 ft (5,642 m)

CAUCASUS MTS.

SOUTHWEST
ASIA

Ural River
Kama River
Volga
Don River

EUROPEAN PLAIN

NORTHERN

Pechora
River

Dvina
River
North
River

KOLA
PENINSULA

White
Sea

Lake
Onega

Lake
Ladoga

Rybinsk
Reservoir

Dnipro
River

Sea of
Azov

CRIMEAN
PENINSULA

Black Sea

Barents Sea

50°E

40°E

30°E

PLAINS

Dnister River

Nistru River

Prut River

CARPATHIAN MTS.

TRANSYLVANIAN
ALPS

Danube River

DINARIC ALPS

BALKAN
PENINSULA

Rhodes

Crete

Aegean Sea

Sea

North Cape

Gulf of Finland

BALTIC

Vistula River

Oder River

Elbe River

APENNINES

Adriatic Sea

30°E

20°E

30°E

KJOLEN MOUNTAINS

Gulf of Bothnia

Lake
Vänern

Lake
Vättern

Baltic Sea

Danube River

ALPS

Po River

Tyrrhenian Sea

Sicily

Malta

ARCTIC OCEAN

20°E

10°E

0°

North Cape

Skagerrak

Kattegat

Rhine River

Lake
Geneva

Mont Blanc
15,781 ft (4,810 m)

Rhône River

Corsica

Sardinia

Balearic Islands

Mediterranean

AFRICA

70°N

ASIA

Norwegian
Sea

N
W   E
S

North
Sea

Shetland
Islands

Orkney
Islands

PENNINES

Thames
River

English Channel

Seine River

Loire
River

Garonne River

PYRENEES

Ebro River

IBERIAN
PENINSULA

Douro River

Tejo River

Guadiana
River

Guadalquivir
River

Strait of
Gibraltar

Arctic Circle

Faeroe
Islands

Hebrides

British
Isles

Irish Sea

Bay of
Biscay

Cape Finisterre

Iceland

ATLANTIC
OCEAN

60°N

50°N

40°N

30°N

10°W

0°

10°E

20°W

30°W

Europe: Physical

ELEVATION

Feet	Meters
13,120	4,000
6,560	2,000
1,640	500
656	200
0 (Sea level)	0 (Sea level)
Below sea level	Below sea level

Ice cap

0   150   300 Miles

0   150   300 Kilometers

Projection: Azimuthal Equal Area

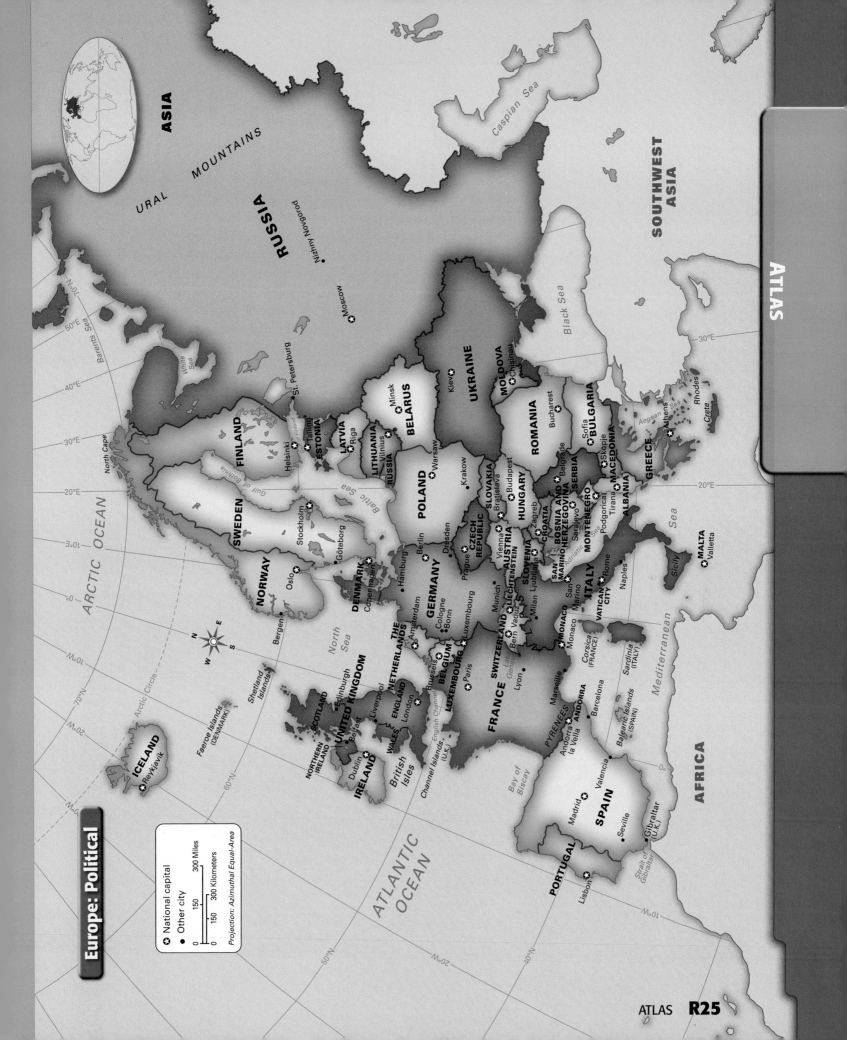

Europe: Political

Legend:
⊛ National capital
● Other city

300 Miles
0   150   300 Kilometers
0   150

Projection: Azimuthal Equal-Area

ASIA

URAL MOUNTAINS

RUSSIA

Nizhny Novgorod

Moscow ⊛

Caspian Sea

SOUTHWEST ASIA

ATLAS

Black Sea

St. Petersburg

White Sea

Barents Sea

BELARUS
Minsk ⊛

UKRAINE
Kiev ⊛

MOLDOVA
Chişinău ⊛

Bucharest
ROMANIA

BULGARIA
Sofia ⊛

Skopje
MACEDONIA

Tirana
ALBANIA

GREECE
Athens ⊛

Aegean Sea

Rhodes

Crete

FINLAND

Helsinki ⊛

Tallinn
ESTONIA

Riga
LATVIA

Vilnius
LITHUANIA

RUSSIA

Gulf of Bothnia

Gulf of Finland

Baltic Sea

POLAND
Warsaw ⊛

Kraków

SLOVAKIA
Bratislava ⊛

Budapest
HUNGARY

Belgrade
SERBIA

BOSNIA AND HERZEGOVINA
Sarajevo

MONTENEGRO
Podgorica

CROATIA
Zagreb

Sea

Adriatic Sea

ARCTIC OCEAN

North Cape

SWEDEN

Stockholm ⊛

Göteborg

NORWAY

Oslo ⊛

Bergen

DENMARK
Copenhagen ⊛

Hamburg

GERMANY
Berlin ⊛

Dresden

Prague
CZECH REPUBLIC

Vienna
AUSTRIA

LIECHTENSTEIN
Vaduz

SLOVENIA
Ljubljana

Milan

SAN MARINO
San Marino

ITALY
Rome ⊛

Naples

VATICAN CITY

Mediterranean Sea

Sicily

MALTA
Valletta ⊛

North Sea

THE NETHERLANDS
Amsterdam ⊛

Cologne
Bonn

BELGIUM
Brussels ⊛

LUXEMBOURG
Luxembourg ⊛

Munich

SWITZERLAND
Bern ⊛
Geneva

FRANCE
Paris ⊛

Lyon

Marseille

Monaco
MONACO

Corsica (FRANCE)

Sardinia (ITALY)

ICELAND
Reykjavik ⊛

Faeroe Islands (DENMARK)

Shetland Islands

SCOTLAND
Edinburgh

UNITED KINGDOM

Liverpool

ENGLAND
London ⊛

WALES

NORTHERN IRELAND
Belfast

IRELAND
Dublin ⊛

British Isles

Channel Islands (U.K.)

English Channel

Bay of Biscay

PYRENEES

ANDORRA
Andorra la Vella

Barcelona

Balearic Islands (SPAIN)

SPAIN
Madrid ⊛

Valencia

Seville

Gibraltar (U.K.)

Strait of Gibraltar

PORTUGAL
Lisbon ⊛

AFRICA

ATLANTIC OCEAN

Arctic Circle

ATLAS **R25**

Asia: Physical

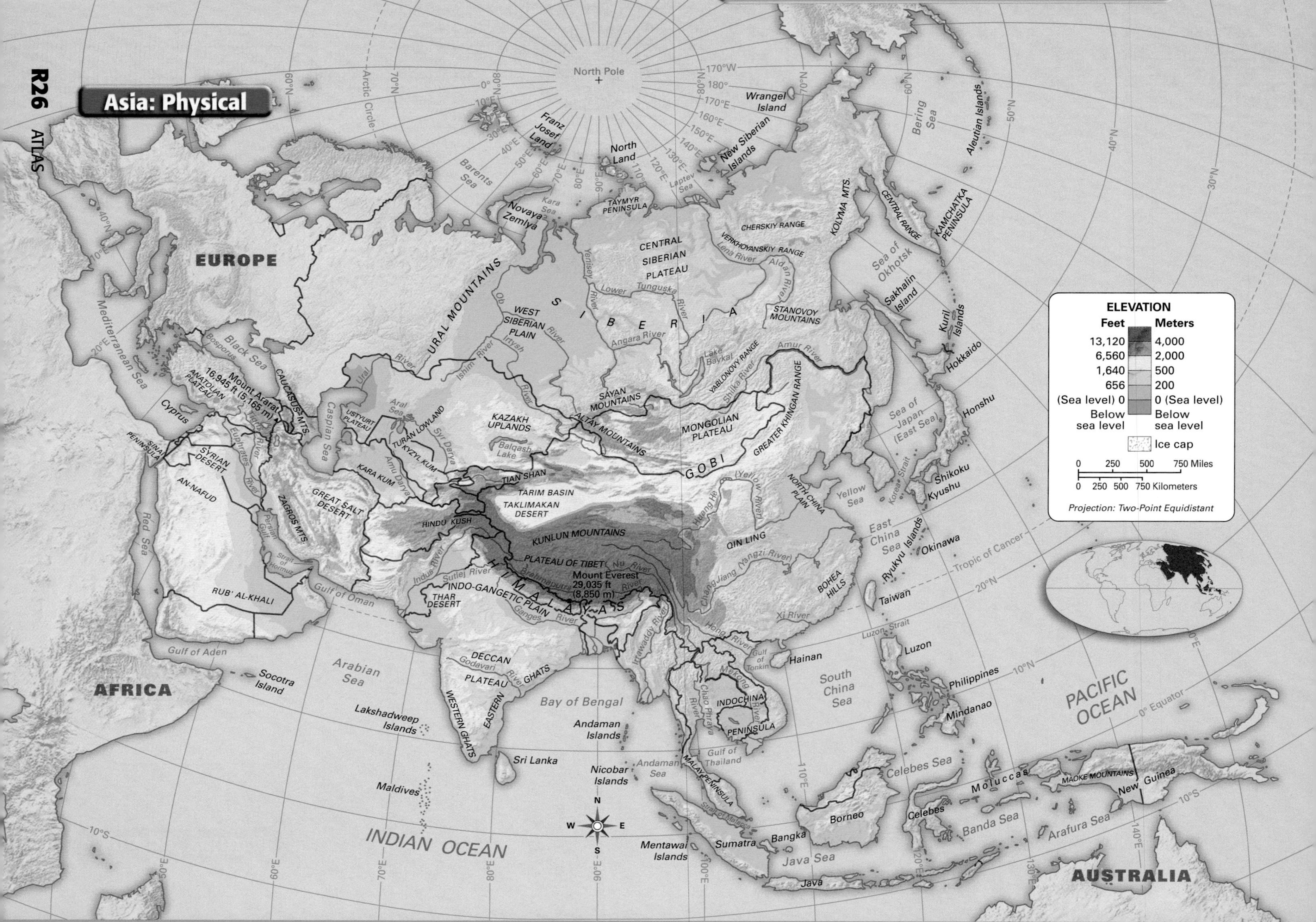

EUROPE

AFRICA

AUSTRALIA

PACIFIC OCEAN

INDIAN OCEAN

ELEVATION

Feet	Meters
13,120	4,000
6,560	2,000
1,640	500
656	200
(Sea level) 0	0 (Sea level)
Below sea level	Below sea level

Ice cap

0 250 500 750 Miles
0 250 500 750 Kilometers

Projection: Two-Point Equidistant

North Pole

Arctic Circle

North Land

Franz Josef Land

Novaya Zemlya

Wrangel Island

New Siberian Islands

Aleutian Islands

KAMCHATKA PENINSULA

CENTRAL RANGE

Bering Sea

Sea of Okhotsk

Sakhalin Island

Kuril Islands

Hokkaido

Honshu

KOLYMA MTS.

CHERSKIY RANGE

VERKHOYANSKY RANGE

STANOVOY MOUNTAINS

Aldan River

Amur River

Shilka River

YABLONOVYY RANGE

GREATER KHINGAN RANGE

TAYMYR PENINSULA

CENTRAL SIBERIAN PLATEAU

Lena River

Tunguska River

Angara River

Yenisey River

Lower Tunguska River

S I B E R I A

SAYAN MOUNTAINS

ALTAY MOUNTAINS

MONGOLIAN PLATEAU

G O B I

NORTH CHINA PLAIN

QIN LING

Yellow River

Huang He (Yellow River)

Kara Sea

Laptev Sea

Ob River

Irtysh River

Ishim River

WEST SIBERIAN PLAIN

Tobol River

KAZAKH UPLANDS

Balqash Lake

TIAN SHAN

TARIM BASIN

TAKLIMAKAN DESERT

KUNLUN MOUNTAINS

PLATEAU OF TIBET

Mount Everest 29,035 ft (8,850 m)

H I M A L A Y A S

URAL MOUNTAINS

Ural River

Aral Sea

Syr Darya

TURAN LOWLAND

KYZYL KUM

USTYURT PLATEAU

Amu Darya

KARA KUM

HINDU KUSH

INDO-GANGETIC PLAIN

Ganges River

Indus River

Sutlej River

THAR DESERT

DECCAN PLATEAU

Godavari River

EASTERN GHATS

WESTERN GHATS

Caspian Sea

GREAT SALT DESERT

ZAGROS MTS.

CAUCASUS MTS.

Mount Ararat 16,945 ft (5,165 m)

Black Sea

Bosporus

ANATOLIAN PLATEAU

Cyprus

Tigris River

Euphrates River

Persian Gulf

Gulf of Oman

Arabian Sea

RUB' AL-KHALI

Socotra Island

SYRIAN DESERT

AN-NAFUD

SINAI PENINSULA

Red Sea

Gulf of Aden

Mediterranean Sea

Barents Sea

Japan Sea (East Sea)

Kyushu

Shikoku

Korea Strait

Yellow Sea

East China Sea

Ryukyu Islands

Okinawa

Taiwan

South China Sea

Hainan

Chang Jiang (Yangzi River)

BOHEA HILLS

Xi River

Gulf of Tonkin

INDOCHINA PENINSULA

Hong River

Mekong River

Chao Phraya River

MALAY PENINSULA

Gulf of Thailand

Philippines

Luzon

Mindanao

Sri Lanka

Bay of Bengal

Andaman Islands

Nicobar Islands

Brahmaputra River

Irrawaddy River

Salween River

Maldives

Lakshadweep Islands

Celebes Sea

Borneo

Celebes

Banda Sea

Arafura Sea

Molucca Sea

Java Sea

Java

Sumatra

Bangka

Mentawai Islands

MACKE MOUNTAINS

New Guinea

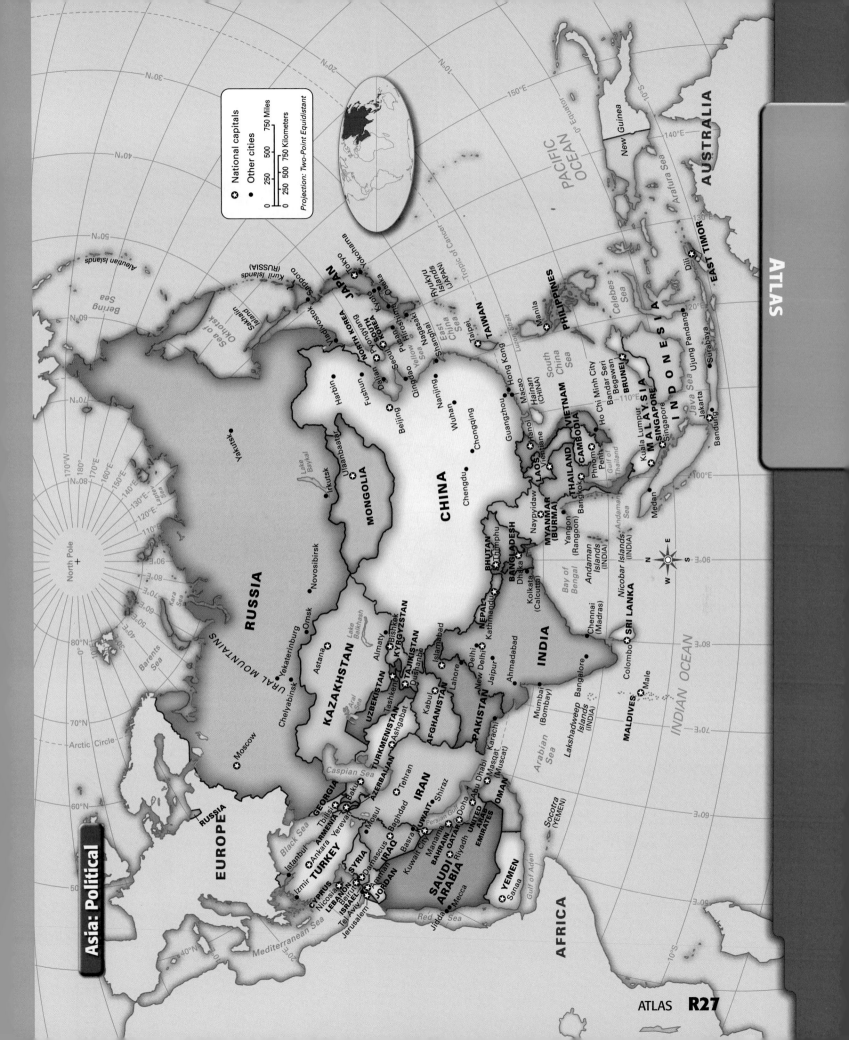

Asia: Political

National capitals
Other cities

750 Miles
250 500 750 Kilometers

Projection: Two-Point Equidistant

PACIFIC OCEAN

AUSTRALIA

New Guinea

EAST TIMOR

ATLAS

INDONESIA

Arafura Sea

Celebes Sea

PHILIPPINES

Manila

Java Sea

Ujung Pandang

Surabaya

Jakarta

Bandung

BRUNEI

Bandar Seri Begawan

MALAYSIA

Kuala Lumpur

SINGAPORE

Medan

Ho Chi Minh City

VIETNAM

CAMBODIA

Phnom Penh

South China Sea

Hainan (CHINA)

Macao

Hong Kong

Guangzhou

Gulf of Thailand

THAILAND

Bangkok

LAOS

Vientiane

Hanoi

MYANMAR (BURMA)

Naypyidaw

Yangon (Rangoon)

Chongqing

Chengdu

Wuhan

CHINA

Nanjing

Beijing

Qingdao

Dalian

Fushun

Harbin

Vladivostok

Sapporo

JAPAN

Tokyo

Yokohama

Kyoto

Osaka

Hiroshima

Nagasaki

Fukuoka

Pusan

SOUTH KOREA

Seoul

Pyongyang

NORTH KOREA

Yellow Sea

East China Sea

Shanghai

Taipei

TAIWAN

Luzon Strait

Tropic of Cancer

Ryukyu Islands (JAPAN)

Kuril Islands (RUSSIA)

Sakhalin Island

Sea of Okhotsk

Bering Sea

Aleutian Islands

BANGLADESH

Dhaka

BHUTAN

Thimphu

NEPAL

Kathmandu

Kolkata (Calcutta)

INDIA

Chennai (Madras)

Bangalore

Bay of Bengal

Andaman Islands (INDIA)

Nicobar Islands (INDIA)

Andaman Sea

SRI LANKA

Colombo

MALDIVES

Male

Lakshadweep Islands (INDIA)

Mumbai (Bombay)

Ahmadabad

Jaipur

New Delhi

Delhi

Lahore

Islamabad

PAKISTAN

Karachi

AFGHANISTAN

Kabul

Dushanbe

TAJIKISTAN

KYRGYZSTAN

Bishkek

Tashkent

UZBEKISTAN

Ashgabat

TURKMENISTAN

Almaty

Astana

KAZAKHSTAN

Lake Balkhash

Aral Sea

MONGOLIA

Ulaanbaatar

Irkutsk

Lake Baykal

Yakutsk

RUSSIA

Novosibirsk

Omsk

Chelyabinsk

Yekaterinburg

URAL MOUNTAINS

Moscow

North Pole

Arctic Circle

Barents Sea

Kara Sea

Laptev Sea

EUROPE

RUSSIA

Istanbul

Izmir

Ankara

TURKEY

CYPRUS

Nicosia

LEBANON

Beirut

ISRAEL

Tel Aviv

Jerusalem

SYRIA

Damascus

Amman

JORDAN

Aleppo

Mosul

Baghdad

IRAQ

Basra

KUWAIT

Kuwait City

Black Sea

GEORGIA

Tbilisi

ARMENIA

Yerevan

AZERBAIJAN

Baku

Caspian Sea

Tehran

IRAN

Shiraz

Manama

BAHRAIN

QATAR

Doha

Abu Dhabi

UNITED ARAB EMIRATES

Muscat (Masqat)

OMAN

Persian Gulf

Riyadh

SAUDI ARABIA

Mecca

Jidda

Red Sea

YEMEN

Sanaa

Gulf of Aden

Socotra (YEMEN)

Arabian Sea

INDIAN OCEAN

AFRICA

Mediterranean Sea

ATLAS **R27**

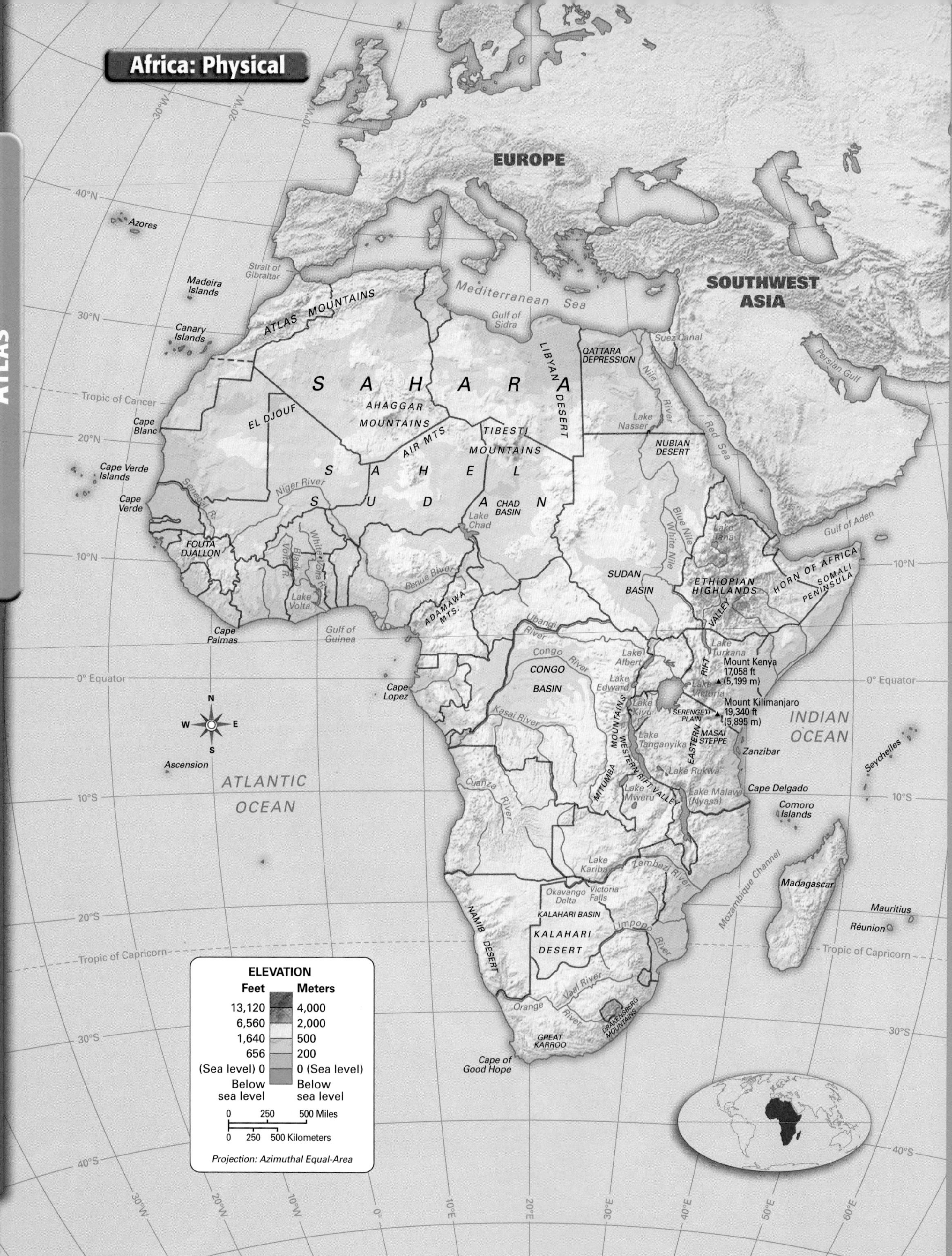

Africa: Physical
ATLAS
EUROPE
SOUTHWEST ASIA
Azores
Madeira Islands
Canary Islands
Strait of Gibraltar
Mediterranean Sea
Gulf of Sidra
ATLAS MOUNTAINS
SAHARA
AHAGGAR MOUNTAINS
EL DJOUF
AIR MTS.
TIBESTI MOUNTAINS
LIBYAN DESERT
QATTARA DEPRESSION
Suez Canal
Persian Gulf
Nile River
Lake Nasser
NUBIAN DESERT
Red Sea
Cape Blanc
Cape Verde Islands
Cape Verde
SAHEL
SUDAN
Niger River
Senegal R.
CHAD BASIN
Lake Chad
Blue Nile
White Nile
Gulf of Aden
Lake Tana
FOUTA DJALLON
Black Volta R.
White Volta R.
Lake Volta
Benue River
SUDAN BASIN
ETHIOPIAN HIGHLANDS
HORN OF AFRICA
SOMALI PENINSULA
ADAMAWA MTS.
Cape Palmas
Gulf of Guinea
Ubangi River
Congo River
CONGO BASIN
Lake Albert
Lake Edward
Lake Turkana
RIFT VALLEY
Mount Kenya 17,058 ft (5,199 m)
Lake Victoria
Mount Kilimanjaro 19,340 ft (5,895 m)
SERENGETI PLAIN
Cape Lopez
Kasai River
Lake Kivu
Lake Tanganyika
MASAI STEPPE
EASTERN
MITUMBA MOUNTAINS
WESTERN RIFT VALLEY
INDIAN OCEAN
Zanzibar
Seychelles
Lake Rukwa
Lake Mweru
Lake Malawi (Nyasa)
Cape Delgado
Comoro Islands
Ascension
ATLANTIC OCEAN
Cuanza River
Lake Kariba
Zambezi River
Mozambique Channel
Madagascar
Okavango Delta
Victoria Falls
KALAHARI BASIN
KALAHARI DESERT
NAMIB DESERT
Limpopo River
Mauritius
Réunion
Vaal River
Orange River
DRAKENSBERG MOUNTAINS
GREAT KARROO
Cape of Good Hope
40°N
30°N
Tropic of Cancer
20°N
10°N
0° Equator
10°S
20°S
Tropic of Capricorn
30°S
40°S
30°W
20°W
10°W
0°
10°E
20°E
30°E
40°E
50°E
60°E
N
S
E
W
ELEVATION
Feet
Meters
13,120
4,000
6,560
2,000
1,640
500
656
200
(Sea level) 0
0 (Sea level)
Below sea level
Below sea level
0 250 500 Miles
0 250 500 Kilometers
Projection: Azimuthal Equal-Area

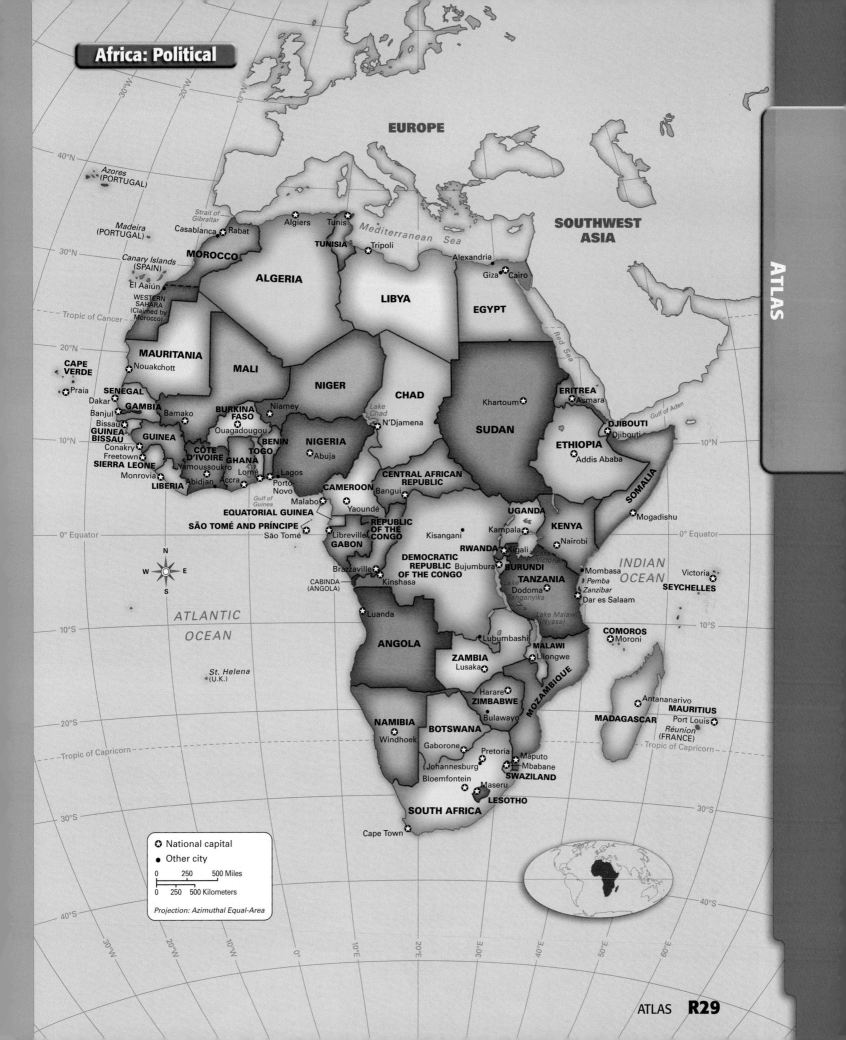

Africa: Political

EUROPE

SOUTHWEST ASIA

Azores (PORTUGAL)

Madeira (PORTUGAL)

Strait of Gibraltar

Mediterranean Sea

Algiers
Tunis
Casablanca • Rabat
MOROCCO
Tripoli
TUNISIA

Canary Islands (SPAIN)
El Aaiún
WESTERN SAHARA (Claimed by Morocco)

Tropic of Cancer

ALGERIA
LIBYA
EGYPT
Alexandria
Giza • Cairo

Red Sea

MAURITANIA
Nouakchott
MALI
NIGER
CHAD
Khartoum
SUDAN
ERITREA
Asmara
Gulf of Aden

CAPE VERDE
• Praia
SENEGAL
Dakar
GAMBIA
Banjul
Bamako
BURKINA FASO
Niamey
N'Djamena
Lake Chad
DJIBOUTI
Djibouti

GUINEA BISSAU
Bissau
Conakry
GUINEA
Ouagadougou
BENIN
NIGERIA
ETHIOPIA
Addis Ababa

Freetown
SIERRA LEONE
Monrovia
CÔTE D'IVOIRE
GHANA
Yamoussoukro
TOGO
Lomé
Abuja
CENTRAL AFRICAN REPUBLIC
SOMALIA

LIBERIA
Abidjan
Accra
Lagos
Porto Novo
CAMEROON
Bangui
Mogadishu

Gulf of Guinea
Malabo
EQUATORIAL GUINEA
Yaoundé
UGANDA
Kampala
KENYA
Nairobi

SÃO TOMÉ AND PRÍNCIPE
São Tomé
Libreville
GABON
REPUBLIC OF THE CONGO
Kisangani
Kigali
RWANDA
Lake Victoria
Mombasa

0° Equator

DEMOCRATIC REPUBLIC OF THE CONGO
Brazzaville
Bujumbura
BURUNDI
Pemba
Zanzibar
INDIAN OCEAN
Victoria
SEYCHELLES

CABINDA (ANGOLA)
Kinshasa
TANZANIA
Dodoma
Dar es Salaam
Lake Tanganyika

ATLANTIC OCEAN
Luanda
Lubumbashi
Lake Malawi (Nyasa)
COMOROS
Moroni

ANGOLA
ZAMBIA
Lusaka
MALAWI
Lilongwe

St. Helena (U.K.)
Harare
ZIMBABWE
Bulawayo
MOZAMBIQUE
Antananarivo
MAURITIUS

NAMIBIA
Windhoek
BOTSWANA
Gaborone
MADAGASCAR
Port Louis
Réunion (FRANCE)

Tropic of Capricorn

Pretoria
Maputo
Mbabane
Johannesburg
SWAZILAND
Bloemfontein
Maseru
LESOTHO

SOUTH AFRICA

Cape Town

Legend:
- ⊛ National capital
- • Other city

0   250   500 Miles
0   250   500 Kilometers

Projection: Azimuthal Equal-Area

ATLAS

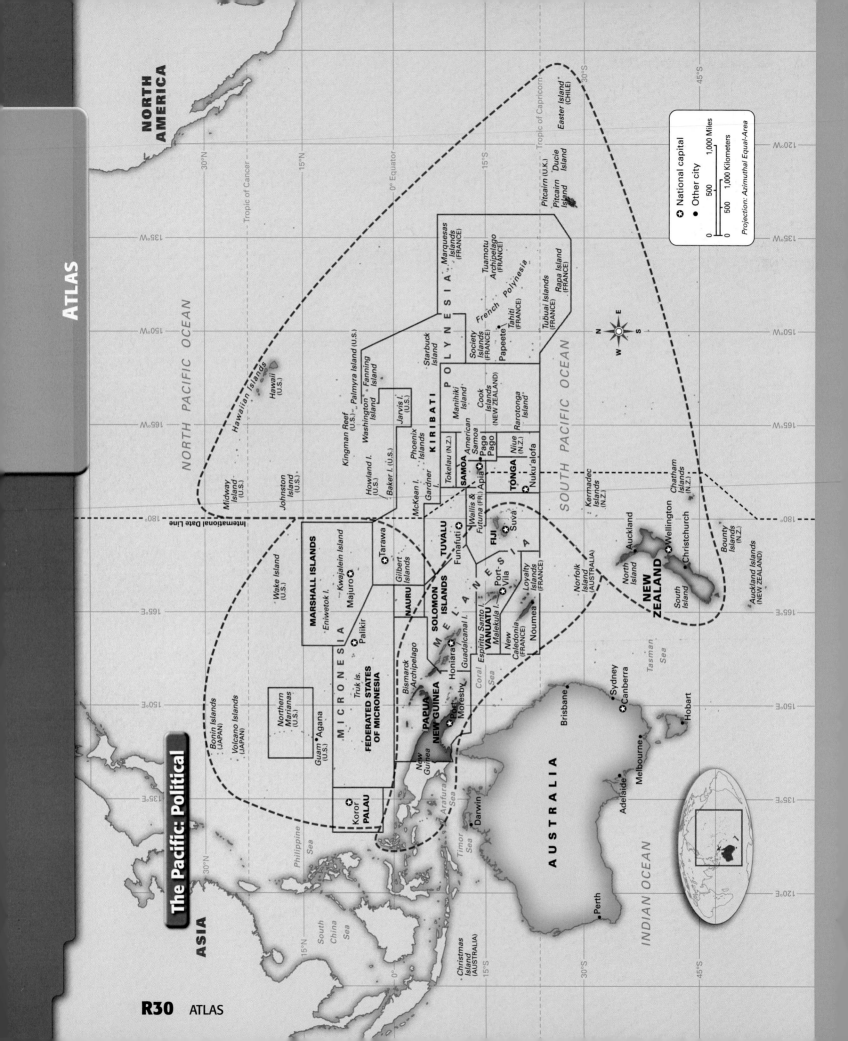

The Pacific: Political

NORTH AMERICA

ASIA

NORTH PACIFIC OCEAN

SOUTH PACIFIC OCEAN

INDIAN OCEAN

National capital
Other city

Projection: Azimuthal Equal-Area

1,000 Miles
500
1,000 Kilometers
500
0
0

Tropic of Cancer

Equator 0°

Tropic of Capricorn

International Date Line

MICRONESIA

POLYNESIA

MELANESIA

Hawaiian Islands

Hawaii (U.S.)

Midway (U.S.)

Johnston Island (U.S.)

Wake Island (U.S.)

MARSHALL ISLANDS

Eniwetok I.

Kwajalein Island

Majuro ✪

Tarawa ✪

NAURU

FEDERATED STATES OF MICRONESIA

Truk Is.

Palikir ●

Northern Marianas (U.S.)

Guam (U.S.)

Agana ●

Bonin Islands (JAPAN)

Volcano Islands (JAPAN)

Koror ✪

PALAU

Kingman Reef (U.S.)

Palmyra Island (U.S.)

Washington Island

Fanning Island

Howland I. (U.S.)

Baker I. (U.S.)

McKean I.

Gardner I.

Phoenix Islands

Jarvis I. (U.S.)

Starbuck Island

KIRIBATI

Gilbert Islands

TUVALU

Funafuti ✪

SOLOMON ISLANDS

Honiara ✪

Guadalcanal I.

Bismarck Archipelago

PAPUA NEW GUINEA

Port Moresby ✪

New Guinea

Tokelau (N.Z.)

SAMOA

Apia ✪

American Samoa

Pago Pago ●

Wallis & Futuna (FR.)

TONGA

Nuku'alofa ✪

Niue (N.Z.)

FIJI

Suva ✪

VANUATU

Port-Vila ✪

Espiritu Santo I.

Malekula I.

New Caledonia (FRANCE)

Noumea ●

Loyalty Islands (FRANCE)

Manihiki Island

Cook Islands (NEW ZEALAND)

Rarotonga Island

Kermadec Islands (N.Z.)

Marquesas Islands (FRANCE)

Tuamotu Archipelago (FRANCE)

French Polynesia

Society Islands (FRANCE)

Tahiti (FRANCE)

Papeete ●

Tubuai Islands (FRANCE)

Rapa Island (FRANCE)

Pitcairn (U.K.)

Pitcairn Island

Ducie Island

Easter Island (CHILE)

Norfolk Island (AUSTRALIA)

NEW ZEALAND

North Island

Auckland ●

Wellington ✪

Christchurch ●

South Island

Chatham Islands (N.Z.)

Bounty Islands (N.Z.)

Auckland Islands (NEW ZEALAND)

AUSTRALIA

Darwin ●

Brisbane ●

Sydney ●

Canberra ✪

Melbourne ●

Hobart ●

Adelaide ●

Perth ●

Philippine Sea

South China Sea

Christmas Island (AUSTRALIA)

Timor Sea

Arafura Sea

Coral Sea

Tasman Sea

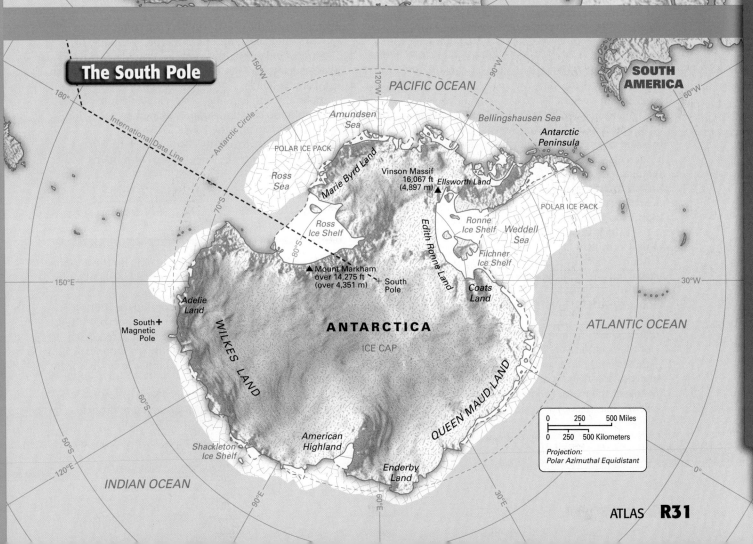

The North Pole

0   200   400 Miles
0   200   400 Kilometers

Projection:
Polar Azimuthal Equidistant

EUROPE

Kara Sea

Barents Sea

Norwegian Sea

ASIA

Laptev Sea

ARCTIC OCEAN

Greenland Sea

Greenland (DENMARK)

ATLANTIC OCEAN

North Pole

80°N

International Date Line

POLAR ICE PACK

North Magnetic Pole

Baffin Bay

Arctic Circle

0°

30°E

60°E

90°E

120°E

150°E

30°W

60°W

90°W

150°W

180°

60°N

50°N

Beaufort Sea

Bering Sea

NORTH AMERICA

ATLAS

The South Pole

SOUTH AMERICA

PACIFIC OCEAN

Amundsen Sea

Bellingshausen Sea

Antarctic Peninsula

International Date Line

Antarctic Circle

POLAR ICE PACK

Ross Sea

Marie Byrd Land

Vinson Massif 16,067 ft (4,897 m)

Ellsworth Land

POLAR ICE PACK

Ross Ice Shelf

Ronne Ice Shelf

Weddell Sea

Edith Ronne Land

Filchner Ice Shelf

Coats Land

Mount Markham over 14,275 ft (over 4,351 m)

South Pole

ANTARCTICA

ATLANTIC OCEAN

Adelie Land

South Magnetic Pole

WILKES LAND

ICE CAP

QUEEN MAUD LAND

American Highland

Shackleton Ice Shelf

Enderby Land

INDIAN OCEAN

70°S

80°S

60°S

50°S

150°W

120°W

90°W

60°W

30°W

0°

30°E

60°E

90°E

120°E

150°E

180°

0   250   500 Miles
0   250   500 Kilometers

Projection:
Polar Azimuthal Equidistant

Gazetteer

A

Abuja (9°N, 7°E) the capital of Nigeria (p. 383)

Accra (6°N, 0°) the capital of Ghana (p. 240)

Addis Ababa (9°N, 39°E) the capital of Ethiopia (p. 240)

Afghanistan a landlocked country in Central Asia (p. 123)

Africa the second-largest continent; surrounded by the Atlantic Ocean, Indian Ocean, and Mediterranean Sea

Ajanta Caves (21°N, 76°E) cave complex in northern India famous for its ancient Buddhist paintings and statues (p. 453)

Akkad (33°N, 44°E) a city along the Euphrates River near modern Baghdad; started by Akkadian emperor Sargon in 2300s BC (p. 139)

Aksum an ancient state in southeast Nubia on the Red Sea, in what are now Ethiopia and Eritea; through trade, Aksum became the most powerful state in the region (p. 319)

Albania a country on the Balkan Peninsula in southeastern Europe (p. 575)

Alexandria (31°N, 30°E) a city in Egypt, named after Alexander the Great (p. 594)

Algeria a country in North Africa between Morocco and Libya (p. 251)

Algiers (37°N, 3°E) the capital of Algeria (p. 240)

Alps a great mountain system in central Europe (p. 567)

Amman (32°N, 36°E) the capital of Jordan (p. 106)

Amsterdam (52°N, 5°E) the capital and largest city of the Netherlands (p. 552)

Amu Darya a river in Central Asia that flows along Afghanistan's border with Tajikistan, Uzbekistan, and Turkmenistan to the Aral Sea (p. 125)

An Nafud a large desert in northern Saudi Arabia; known for its giant sand dunes (p. 227)

Anatolia a mountainous region in Southwest Asia forming most of Turkey; also referred to as Asia Minor (p. 114)

Angkor Wat (14°N, 104°E) vast temple complex built by the Khmer in what is now Cambodia (p. 509)

Angola a country in Central Africa that borders the Atlantic Ocean (p. 263)

Ankara (40°N, 33°E) the capital and second-largest city of Turkey (p. 106)

Antananarivo (19°S, 48°E) the capital of Madagascar (p. 240)

Antarctic Circle the line of latitude located at 66.5° south of the equator; parallel beyond which no sunlight shines on the June solstice

Antarctica a continent around the South Pole

Apennines the major mountain range on the Italian Peninsula (p. 563)

Arabia or Arabian Peninsula the world's largest peninsula; located in Southwest Asia (p. 118)

Arabian Peninsula an arid region in southwest Asia; Islam developed there (p. 176)

Arabian Sea a large arm of the Indian Ocean between India and Arabia (p. 119)

Aral Sea an inland sea in Central Asia fed by the Syr Darya and Amu Darya rivers; it has been steadily shrinking (p. 125)

Arctic Circle the line of latitude located at 66.5° north of the equator; parallel beyond which no sunlight shines on the December solstice

Arctic Ocean the ocean north of the Arctic Circle; the world's fourth-largest ocean

Armenia a country in the Caucasus Mountains (p. 579)

Ashgabat (38°N, 58°E) the capital of Turkmenistan (p. 106)

Asia Minor a large peninsula in Southwest Asia between the Black Sea and the Mediterranean Sea, forming most of Turkey (p. 114)

Asia the world's largest continent; located between Europe and the Pacific Ocean

Asmara (15°N, 39°E) the capital of Eritrea (p. 240)

Astana (51°N, 72°E) the capital of Kazakhstan (p. 106)

Athens (38°N, 24°E) an ancient city and the modern capital of Greece; considered the birthplace of democracy (p. 591)

Atlantic Ocean the ocean between the continents of North and South America and the continents of Europe and Africa; the world's second-largest ocean

Atlas Mountains a high mountain range in northwestern Africa (p. 252)

Australia the only country occupying an entire continent (also called Australia); located between the Indian Ocean and the Pacific Ocean

Austria a country in West-Central Europe (p. 567)

Azerbaijan a country in the Caucasus Mountains (p. 579)

B

Babylon an ancient city in Mesopotamia on the Euphrates River; it was the capital of the Babylonian Empire (p. 148)

Baghdad (33°N, 44°E) the capital of Iraq (p. 106)

Bahrain a small country on the Persian Gulf (p. 119)

Baku (40°N, 48°E) the capital of Azerbaijan (p. 553)

Balkan Peninsula a peninsula in Southern Europe (p. 575)

Baltic Sea a shallow arm of the Atlantic Ocean in northern Europe (p. 575)

Bamako (13°N, 8°W) the capital of Mali (p. 240)

Bandar Seri Begawan (5°N, 115°E) capital of Brunei (p. 396)

Bangkok (14°N, 100°E) the capital of Thailand (p. 396)

Bangladesh a country in South Asia (p. 407)

Bangui (4°N, 19°E) the capital of the Central African Republic (p. 240)

Banjul (13°N, 17°W) the capital of Gambia (p. 240)

Bay of Bengal a large bay of the Indian Ocean between India and Southeast Asia (p. 407)

Beijing (40°N, 116°E) the capital of China (p. 488)

Beirut (34°N, 36°E) the capital of Lebanon (p. 106)

Belarus a country in Eastern Europe (p. 575)

Belgian Congo Belgium's largest colony in Africa; became the Democratic Republic of the Congo after it won independence (p. 370)

Belgium a country in West-Central Europe (p. 567)

Belgrade (45°N, 21°E) the capital of Serbia (p. 552)

Benin a country in West Africa between Togo and Nigeria (p. 255)

Benin ancient kingdom of West Africa; occupied area that is now southern Nigeria (p. 342)

Benin City (6°N, 6°E) formerly the capital of the kingdom of Benin, now an industrial center in Nigeria (p. 345)

Benue River a large river of West Africa (p. 382)

Berlin (53°N, 13°E) the capital of Germany (p. 552)

Bern (47°N, 7°E) the capital of Switzerland (p. 552)

Bethlehem (32°N, 35°E) a town in Judea; traditionally regarded as the birthplace of Jesus (p. 168)

Bhutan a country in South Asia north of India (p. 407)

Bishkek (43°N, 75°E) the capital of Kyrgyzstan (p. 106)

Bissau (12°N, 16°W) the capital of Guinea-Bissau (p. 240)

Bloemfontein (29°S, 26°E) the judicial capital of South Africa (p. 240)

Borneo the world's third-largest island; located in Southeast Asia (p. 419)

Bosnia and Herzegovina a country on the Balkan Peninsula (p. 575)

Bosporus a narrow strait in Turkey that connects the Mediterranean Sea with the Black Sea (p. 114)

Botswana a country in Southern Africa between Namibia and Zimbabwe (p. 269)

Bratislava (48°N, 17°E) the capital of Slovakia (p. 552)

Brazzaville (4°S, 15°E) the capital of the Republic of the Congo (p. 240)

British Isles a group of islands off the northwestern coast of Europe including Britain and Ireland (p. 570)

Brunei a country in Southeast Asia on the northern coast of Borneo (p. 419)

Brussels (51°N, 4°E) the capital of Belgium (p. 552)

Bucharest (44°N, 26°E) the capital of Romania (p. 552)

Budapest (48°N, 19°E) the capital of Hungary (p. 552)

Bujumbura (3°S, 29°E) the capital of Burundi (p. 240)

Bukhara (40°N, 64°E) an ancient city along the Silk Road in Central Asia; it has long been an important trade and cultural center in the region (p. 218)

Bulgaria a country in the Balkans (p. 575)

Burkina Faso a landlocked country in West Africa (p. 255)

Burundi a landlocked country in East Africa (p. 259)

Byblos (34°N, 36°E) ancient Phoenician city in modern Lebanon (p. 152)

C

Cairo (30°N, 31°E) the capital of Egypt (p. 240)

Cambodia a country in Southeast Asia (p. 419)

Cameroon a country in Central Africa south of Nigeria (p. 263)

Canaan a region in what is now Israel near the Mediterranean coast; according to the Bible, Abraham settled in Canaan and his Hebrew descendants lived there for many years (p. 161)

Cape of Good Hope a cape at the southern tip of Africa (p. 269)

Cape Town (34°S, 18°E) the legislative capital of South Africa (p. 240)

Cape Verde an island country off the coast of West Africa (p. 255)

Carpathians a major mountain chain in central and eastern Europe (p. 574)

Carthage (37°N, 10°E) an ancient Phoenician port city in North Africa in modern Tunisia (pp. 152, 598)

Caspian Sea an inland sea located between Europe and Asia; it is the largest inland body of water in the world (p. 578)

Çatal Hüyük (38°N, 33°E) one of the world's first farming villages, located in what is now Turkey (p. 90)

Caucasus Mountains a mountain system in southeastern Europe between the Black Sea and Caspian Sea (p. 578)

Central African Republic a landlocked country in Central Africa south of Chad (p. 263)

Central Uplands an area of hills, plateaus, and valleys in central Europe (p. 567)

Chad a landlocked country in West Africa located east of Niger (p. 255)

Chang Jiang (Yangzi River) a river that cuts through central China, flowing from the mountains of Tibet to the Pacific Ocean (p. 412)

Chernobyl (51°N, 30°E) a city in Ukraine; the world's worst nuclear reactor accident occurred there in 1986 (p. 577)

China a country in East Asia; a series of dynasties turned China into a world power (p. 538)

Chişinau (47°N, 29°E) the capital of Moldova (p. 552)

Colombo (7°N, 80°E) the capital of Sri Lanka (p. 396)

Comoros an island country in the Indian Ocean off the coast of Africa (p. 269)

Conakry (10°N, 14°W) the capital of Guinea (p. 240)

Congo Basin a large flat area on the Congo River in Central Africa (p. 262)

Congo, Democratic Republic of the the largest and most populous country in Central Africa (p. 263)

Congo, Republic of the a country in Central Africa on the Congo River (p. 263)

Congo River the major river of Central Africa (p. 263)

Constantinople (41°N, 29°E) the capital of the eastern Roman Empire, located between the Black Sea and Mediterranean Sea; the modern city of Istanbul (p. 603)

Copenhagen (56°N, 13°E) the capital of Denmark (p. 552)

Córdoba (38°N, 5°W) a city in southern Spain; it was a center of Muslim rule in Spain (p. 189)

Côte d'Ivoire a country in West Africa between Liberia and Ghana (p. 254)

Croatia a country in the Balkans (p. 575)

Czech Republic a country in Eastern Europe (p. 575)

Dakar (15°N, 17°W) the capital of Senegal (p. 240)

Damascus (34°N, 36°E) an ancient city and the modern capital of Syria; it was important in the spread of Christianity (p. 106)

Danube the second-longest river in Europe; it flows from Germany east to the Black Sea (p. 576)

Dar es Salaam (7°S, 39°E) the capital of Tanzania (p. 240)

Dardanelles a strait between the Aegean Sea and the Sea of Marmara; part of a waterway that connects the Black Sea and the Mediterranean Sea (p. 114)

Darfur a region in western Sudan; because of genocide, millions of people have fled from Darfur (p. 375)

Dead Sea the saltiest lake and lowest point on Earth; located on the border between Israel and Jordan and fed by the Jordan River (p. 115)

Deccan a large plateau in southern India (p. 407)

Denmark a country in Northern Europe (p. 571)

Dhaka (24°N, 90°E) the capital of Bangladesh (p. 396)

Dili (8°N, 125°E) the capital of East Timor (p. 396)

Djenné a city in present-day Mali that was a center of trade and learning during the Songhai Empire (p. 332)

Djibouti (12°N, 43°E) the capital of Djibouti (p. 240)

Djibouti a country in East Africa on the Horn of Africa (p. 259)

Dodoma (6°S, 36°E) the capital of Tanzania (p. 240)

Doha (26°N, 51°E) the capital of Qatar (p. 106)

Drakensberg a mountain range in Southern Africa (p. 268)

Dublin (53°N, 6°W) the capital of Ireland (p. 552)

Dushanbe (39°N, 69°E) the capital of Tajikistan (p. 106)

East Timor an island country in Southeast Asia (p. 419)

Eastern Ghats a mountain range in India (p. 407)

Eastern Hemisphere the half of the globe between the prime meridian and 180° longitude that includes most of Africa and Europe as well as Asia, Australia, and the Indian Ocean

Edinburgh (56°N, 3°W) the capital of Scotland (p. 552)

Egypt a country in North Africa on the Mediterranean Sea; home to one of the world's oldest civilizations (p. 251)

Elburz Mountains a mountain range in northern Iran south of the Caspian Sea (p. 119)

Ellora Caves (20°N, 75°E) cave complex in central India famous for its Buddhist, Hindu, and Jain temples and artwork (p. 453)

England a part of the United Kingdom occupying most of the island of Great Britain (p. 571)

English Channel a strait of the Atlantic Ocean between England and France (p. 570)

equator the imaginary line of latitude that circles the globe halfway between the North and South Poles

Equatorial Guinea a country in Central Africa between Cameroon and Gabon (p. 245)

Eritrea an East African country north of Ethiopia (p. 262)

Esfahan (33°N, 52°E) ancient capital of the Safavid Empire; now a city in central Iran (p. 207)

Estonia a Baltic country in Eastern Europe (p. 575)

Ethiopia an East African country located on the Horn of Africa; once an independent kingdom (p. 259)

Euphrates River a river in Southwest Asia; silt from the Euphrates helped form the Fertile Crescent in Mesopotamia (p. 118)

Europe the continent between the Ural Mountains and the Atlantic Ocean

Fergana Valley a fertile plains region of Uzbekistan in Central Asia (p. 123)

Fertile Crescent a large arc of rich farmland between the Persian Gulf and the Mediterranean Sea (p. 135)

Finland a country in Northern Europe (p. 571)

Florence (44°N, 11°E) a city in Italy that was a major center of the Renaissance (p. 628)

France a country in West-Central Europe (p. 670)

Freetown (9°N, 13°W) the capital of Sierra Leone (p. 240)

Fuji (35°N, 135°E) a volcano and Japan's highest peak (p. 415)

G

Gabon a country in Central Africa between Cameroon and the Democratic Republic of the Congo (p. 245)

Gaborone (24°S, 26°E) the capital of Botswana (p. 240)

Gambia a country in West Africa surrounded on three sides by Senegal (p. 255)

Ganges River large river in northeastern India considered sacred by Hindus (p. 407)

Gangetic Plain a broad plain in northern India formed by the Ganges River (p. 407)

Gao (16°N, 0°W) an ancient trading city in Africa that was the capital of the Songhai Empire (p. 331)

Gaul an ancient region in Western Europe that included parts of modern France and Belgium (p. 610)

Gaza (32°N, 34°E) a city in southwestern Israel on the Mediterranean Sea (p. 210)

Georgia a country in the Caucasus Mountains (p. 579)

Germany a country in West-Central Europe (p. 567)

Ghana a country in West Africa between Côte d'Ivoire and Togo (p. 255)

Ghana a powerful empire established around 150 (p. 320)

Giza (30°N, 31°E) an Egyptian city and the site of large pyramids, including the Great Pyramid of Khufu (p. 288)

Gobi a desert in China and Mongolia (p. 411)

Gold Coast British colony in West Africa; was renamed Ghana when it became independent in 1960 (p. 357)

Great Rift Valley a series of valleys in East Africa caused by the stretching of Earth's crust (p. 258)

Greece a country in Southern Europe (p. 563)

Guangzhou (23°N, 113°E) major Chinese trading city; also called Canton (p. 513)

Guinea a country in West Africa north of Sierra Leone (p. 255)

Guinea-Bissau a country in West Africa north of Guinea (p. 255)

H

Hallstatt (48°N, 14°E) Austrian village near which Bronze Age Celtic artifacts were discovered in 1846 (p. 610)

Hanoi (21°N, 106°E) the capital of Vietnam (p. 396)

Harappa a city that thrived between 2300 and 1700 BC in the Indus Valley, in what is now Pakistan (p. 431)

Harare (18°S, 31°E) the capital of Zimbabwe (p. 240)

Heian (35°N, 136°E) a city in Japan now called Kyoto; it was a cultural center and capital of Japan for many centuries (p. 498)

Helsinki (60°N, 25°E) the capital of Finland (p. 552)

Himalayas the highest mountains in the world; they separate the Indian Subcontinent from China (p. 410)

Hindu Kush a group of mountains that separates the Indian Subcontinent from Central Asia (p. 406)

Hiroshima (34°N, 132°E) Japanese city on which the first atomic bomb was dropped at the end of World War II (p. 525)

Hokkaido the northernmost of Japan's four major islands (p. 414)

Holy Land the region in Southwest Asia where Jesus lived and taught; Christians tried to reclaim the area in the Crusades (p. 619)

Hong Kong (22°N, 115°E) a city in southern China (p. 529)

Honshu the largest of Japan's four major islands (p. 414)

Huang He (Yellow River) a major river in northern China (p. 412)

I

Iberian Peninsula a large peninsula in Southern Europe; Spain and Portugal are located there (p. 562)

Iceland an island country in Northern Europe (p. 571)

India a large country in South Asia (p. 407)

Indian Ocean the world's third-largest ocean; it is located between Asia and Antarctica

Indochina Peninsula a large peninsula in Southeast Asia (p. 418)

Indonesia the largest country in Southeast Asia (p. 419)

Indus River a river in modern Pakistan along which one of the earliest civilizations began (p. 408)

Iran a country in the Persian Gulf region; it includes the ancient region of Persia (p. 119)

Iraq a country in the Persian Gulf region; it includes the ancient region of Mesopotamia (p. 119)

Ireland a country west of Britain in the British Isles (p. 571)

Islamabad (34°N, 73°E) the capital of Pakistan (p. 396)

Israel a country between the Mediterranean Sea and Jordan; it was the homeland of the ancient Hebrews (p. 115)

Istanbul (41°N, 29°E) the largest city in Turkey; formerly known as Constantinople and capital of the Ottoman Empire (p. 188)

Italy a country in Southern Europe (p. 563)

J

Jakarta (6°S, 107°E) the capital of Indonesia (p. 396)

Japan a mountainous island country off the eastern coast of Asia near China and the Koreas (p. 415)

GAZETTEER

GAZETTEER

Java a large island in Indonesia (p. 419)

Jerusalem (32°N, 35°E) the capital of Israel; it contains holy sites of Christianity, Islam, and Judaism (p. 106)

Jordan a country east of Israel and the Jordan River (p. 115)

Jordan River a river between Israel and Jordan that empties into the Dead Sea (p. 115)

Judah one of the two kingdoms created when Israel was divided; the people in Judah came to be called Jews (p. 161)

Judea territory where most of the ancient Jews lived; it was conquered by Rome in 63 BC (p. 169)

Kabul (35°N, 69°E) the capital of Afghanistan (p. 106)

Kaifeng (35°N, 114°E) the capital of China during the Song dynasty (p. 478)

Kamchatka Peninsula a large, mountainous peninsula in eastern Russia on the Pacific Ocean (p. 579)

Kampala (0°, 32°E) the capital of Uganda (p. 240)

Kara-Kum a desert in Central Asia east of the Caspian Sea (p. 124)

Kashmir a disputed region between India and Pakistan (p. 527)

Kathmandu (28°N, 85°E) the capital of Nepal (p. 396)

Kazakhstan a country in Central Asia; it was part of the Soviet Union until 1991 (p. 123)

Kenya a country in East Africa south of Ethiopia (p. 259)

Kerma a city on the Nile in the kingdom of Kush; it was captured by Egypt, forcing the Kushites to move their capital to Napata (p. 311)

Khartoum (16°N, 33°E) the capital of Sudan (p. 240)

Kiev (50°N, 31°E) the capital of Ukraine (p. 552)

Kigali (2°S, 30°E) the capital of Rwanda (p. 240)

Kinshasa (4°S, 15°E) the capital of the Democratic Republic of the Congo (p. 240)

Kish a city-state in Sumer that became powerful around 3500 BC (p. 139)

Kjolen Mountains a mountain range in Scandinavia along the Norway-Sweden border (p. 570)

Kopet-Dag a group of mountains in northern Iran bordering Turkmenistan (p. 119)

Korean Peninsula a peninsula on the east coast of Asia (p. 415)

Krakatau (6°S, 105°E) volcano in Indonesia that erupted in 1883, causing massive destruction (p. 44)

Kuala Lumpur (3°N, 102°E) the capital of Malaysia (p. 396)

Kush the first great kingdom in Africa's interior; Kush ruled Egypt and at other times was ruled by Egypt (p. 310)

Kuwait a small country on the Persian Gulf (p. 119)

Kyrgyzstan a country in Central Asia; it was part of the Soviet Union until 1991 (p. 123)

Kyushu the southernmost of Japan's four major islands (p. 414)

Kyzyl Kum a vast desert region in Uzbekistan and Kazakhstan (p. 124)

La Tène (47°N, 7°E) Swiss village near which Iron Age Celtic artifacts were discovered in 1857 (p. 610)

Lagos (6°N, 3°E) a city in Nigeria; the most populous city in West Africa (p. 383)

Lake Baikal a huge freshwater lake in Russia; it is the deepest lake in the world (p. 580)

Lake Victoria the largest lake in Africa (p. 260)

Laos a landlocked country in Southeast Asia (p. 419)

Latvia a Baltic country in Eastern Europe (p. 575)

Lebanon a country on the Mediterranean Sea north of Israel (p. 115)

Lesotho a country completely surrounded by South Africa (p. 269)

Liberia a country in West Africa between Sierra Leone and Côte d'Ivoire (p. 255)

Libreville (0°, 9°E) the capital of Gabon (p. 240)

Libya a country in North Africa between Egypt and Algeria (p. 251)

Lilongwe (14°S, 34°E) the capital of Malawi (p. 240)

Lisbon (39°N, 9°W) the capital of Portugal (p. 552)

Lithuania a Baltic country in Eastern Europe (p. 575)

Ljubljana (46°N, 15°E) the capital of Slovenia (p. 552)

Loire the largest river in France (p. 670)

Lomé (6°N, 1°E) the capital of Togo (p. 240)

London (51°N, 1°W) the capital of England and the United Kingdom (p. 615)

Lower Egypt the northern, coastal region of ancient Egypt (p. 278)

Luanda (9°S, 13°E) the capital of Angola (p. 240)

Lusaka (15°S, 28°E) the capital of Zambia (p. 240)

Luxembourg a country in West-Central Europe (p. 567)

Luxembourg City (45°N 6°E) capital of Luxembourg (p. 552)

Lyon (46°N, 5°E) large city in central France (p. 671)

Macedonia a country on the Balkan Peninsula in southeastern Europe (p. 575)

Macedonia a small kingdom located west of the Black Sea and north of the Aegean Sea; Macedonians conquered Greece in the 150s BC (p. 594)

Madagascar a large island country off the southeastern coast of Africa (p. 269)

Madrid (40°N, 4°W) the capital of Spain (p. 552)

Malabo (4°N, 9°E) the capital of Equatorial Guinea (p. 240)

Malawi a landlocked country in Central Africa located south of Tanzania (p. 263)

Malay Archipelago a large group of islands in Southeast Asia (p. 418)

Malay Peninsula a narrow peninsula in Southeast Asia (p. 418)

Malaysia a country in Southeast Asia (p. 419)

Maldives an island country south of India (p. 407)

Male (5°N, 72°E) the capital of the Maldives (p. 396)

Mali a country in West Africa on the Niger River (p. 255)

Mali an empire that reached its height around 1300 (p. 328)

Manama (26°N, 51°E) capital of Bahrain (p. 106)

Manchuria large region of northern China; invaded by Japan before World War II (p. 522)

Manila (15°N, 121°E) the capital of the Philippines (p. 396)

Maputo (27°S, 33°E) the capital of Mozambique (p. 240)

Marseille (43°N, 5°E) a port city in France on the Mediterranean Sea (p. 671)

Maseru (29°S, 27°E) the capital of Lesotho (p. 240)

Massif Central an upland region in south-central France (p. 670)

Mauritania a country in West Africa located between Mali and the Atlantic Ocean (p. 255)

Mauritius an island country east of Madagascar (p. 269)

Mbabane (26°S, 31°E) the capital of Swaziland (p. 240)

Mecca (21°N, 40°E) an ancient city in Arabia and the birthplace of Muhammad (p. 178)

Medina (24°N, 40°E) a city in western Saudi Arabia north of Mecca; people there were among the first to accept Islam (p. 179)

Mediterranean Sea a sea surrounded by Europe, Asia, and Africa (p. 562)

Mekong River a major river in Southeast Asia (p. 419)

Memphis (30°N, 31°E) the ancient capital of Egypt (p. 281)

Meroë (17°N, 34°E) an ancient capital of Kush (p. 316)

Mesopotamia the region in Southwest Asia between the Tigris and Euphrates rivers; it was the site of some of the world's earliest civilizations (p. 135)

Middle East the region around the eastern Mediterranean, northeastern Africa, and Southwest Asia that links the continents of Europe, Asia, and Africa (p. 114)

Mogadishu (2°N, 45°E) the capital of Somalia (p. 240)

Mohenjo Daro (27°N, 68°E) an ancient city of the Harappan civilization in modern Pakistan (p. 431)

Moldova a country in Eastern Europe (p. 575)

Monaco a small country in West-Central Europe (p. 567)

Mongolia a landlocked country in East Asia (p. 411)

Monrovia (6°N, 11°W) the capital of Liberia (p. 240)

Mont Blanc (46°N, 7°E) a mountain peak in France; highest of the Alps (p. 568)

Montenegro a country in the Balkans (p. 575)

Morocco a country in North Africa south of Spain (p. 251)

Moroni (12°S, 43°E) the capital of Comoros (p. 240)

Moscow (56°N, 38°E) the capital of Russia (p. 553)

Mount Elbrus the highest peak of the Caucasus Mountains (p. 580)

Mount Everest the highest mountain in the world at 29,035 feet (8,850 km); it is located in India and Nepal (p. 407)

Mount Kilimanjaro (3°S, 37°E) the highest mountain in Africa at 19,341 feet (5,895 m); it is in Tanzania near the Kenya border (p. 259)

Mozambique a country in Southern Africa south of Tanzania (p. 269)

Muscat (24°N, 59°E) the capital of Oman (p. 106)

Myanmar (Burma) a country in Southeast Asia (p. 419)

N

N'Djamena (12°N, 15°E) the capital of Chad (p. 240)

Nairobi (1°S, 37°E) the capital of Kenya (p. 240)

Namib Desert a desert in southwestern Africa (p. 270)

Namibia a country on the Atlantic coast of Southern Africa (p. 269)

Nanking (32°N, 119°E) city in northern China that was invaded by the Japanese before World War II (p. 523)

Napata a city built by the Egyptians on the Nile River; it was the capital of Kush in the 700s and 600s BC (p. 313)

Nazareth (33°N, 35°E) Judean town in which Jesus lived as a young man (p. 169)

Negev an arid region of southern Israel (p. 116)

Nejd a large plateau in central Saudi Arabia (p. 226)

Nepal a landlocked country in South Asia (p. 407)

Netherlands a country in West-Central Europe (p. 567)

New Delhi (29°N, 77°E) the capital of India (p. 396)

New Guinea the world's second-largest island; located in Southeast Asia (p. 419)

Niamey (14°N, 2°E) the capital of Niger (p. 240)

Niger a country in West Africa north of Nigeria (p. 255)

Niger Delta delta formed by the Niger River in southern Nigeria; site of major oil reserves (p. 382)

Niger River a major river in West Africa (p. 255)

Nigeria a country on the Atlantic coast of West Africa (p. 382)

Nile River the longest river in the world; it flows from central Africa to the Mediterranean and was vital to the development of civilizations in Egypt and Kush (p. 250)

Nineveh (37°N, 43°E) an ancient capital of Assyria, located on the Tigris River (p. 151)

North America a continent including Canada, the United States, Mexico, Central America, and the Caribbean islands

North Atlantic Drift a warm ocean current that flows across the Atlantic Ocean and along Western Europe (p. 572)

North China Plain a plains region of northeastern China (p. 412)

North Korea a country in East Asia (p. 415)

North Pole (90°N) the northern point of Earth's axis

North Sea a shallow arm of the Atlantic Ocean in Northern Europe (p. 571)

Northern European Plain a large plain across central and northern Europe (p. 566)

Northern Hemisphere the northern half of the globe, between the equator and the North Pole

Norway a country in Northern Europe (p. 571)

Nouakchott (18°N, 16°W) the capital of Mauritania (p. 240)

Nubia a region in North Africa, located on the Nile River south of Egypt; birthplace of kingdom of Kush (p. 310)

Ob River a long river in central Russia (p. 580)

Oman a country on the Arabian Peninsula (p. 119)

Oslo (60°N, 11°E) the capital of Norway (p. 552)

Ouagadougou (12°N, 2°W) the capital of Burkina Faso (p. 240)

Pacific Ocean the world's largest ocean; located between Asia and the Americas

Pakistan a country in South Asia northwest of India (p. 407)

Palestine a region between the Jordan River and the Mediterranean Sea in modern Israel (p. 210)

Pamirs a highland region in Central Asia, mainly in Tajikistan (p. 122)

Papua New Guinea a country on the island of New Guinea (p. 419)

Paris (46°N, 0°) the capital of France (p. 671)

Pearl Harbor (21°N, 158°W) Hawaiian harbor; site of a U.S. naval base that was bombed by Japan to begin World War II in the Pacific (p. 523)

Persepolis (30°N, 53°E) ancient capital of the Persian Empire built by Darius I (p. 199)

Persia an ancient empire in Southwest Asia in what is now Iran; it was one of the most powerful empires of the ancient world (p. 194)

Persian Gulf a body of water located between the Arabian Peninsula and the Zagros Mountains in Iran; it has enormous oil deposits along its shores (p. 118)

Philippines an island country in Southeast Asia (p. 419)

Phnom Penh (12°N, 105°E) the capital of Cambodia (p. 396)

Phoenicia an ancient country that was a strip of land at the western end of the Fertile Crescent, along the Mediterranean Sea; Phoenicians were some of the leading traders of the ancient world (p. 152)

Pinatubo (15°N, 120°E) volcano in the Philippines that erupted in 1991 (p. 45)

Plateau of Tibet a high plateau in western China (p. 411)

Podgorica (43°N, 19°E) the capital of Montenegro (p. 552)

Poland a country in Eastern Europe (p. 575)

Port Louis (20°S, 58°E) the capital of Mauritius (p. 240)

Port Moresby (10°S, 147°E) the capital of Papua New Guinea (p. 396)

Porto-Novo (6°N, 3°E) the capital of Benin (p. 240)

Portugal a country in Southern Europe on the Iberian Peninsula (p. 563)

Prague (50°N, 14°E) capital of the Czech Republic (p. 552)

Praia (15°N, 24°W) the capital of Cape Verde (p. 240)

Pretoria (26°S, 28°E) the administrative capital of South Africa (p. 240)

prime meridian an imaginary line that runs through Greenwich, England, at 0° longitude (p. H2)

Pyongyang (39°N, 126°E) the capital of North Korea (p. 396)

Pyrenees a high mountain range between Spain and France (p. 563)

Qatar a country on the Arabian Peninsula (p. 119)

R

Rabat (34°N, 7°W) the capital of Morocco (p. 240)

Red Sea a sea between the Arabian Peninsula and Africa (p. 251)

Reykjavik (64°N, 22°W) the capital of Iceland (p. 552)

Rhine a major river in Europe; it begins in Switzerland and flows north to the North Sea (p. 568)

Riga (57°N, 24°E) the capital of Latvia (p. 552)

Ring of Fire a region that circles the Pacific Ocean; known for its earthquakes and volcanoes (p. 44)

Riyadh (25°N, 47°E) the capital of Saudi Arabia (p. 227)

Roman Empire a large and powerful empire that included all land around the Mediterranean Sea; it reached its height around AD 599 (p. 598)

Romania a country in Eastern Europe (p. 575)

Rome (42°N, 13°E) the capital of Italy; in ancient times it was the capital of the Roman Empire (p. 552)

Rub' al-Khali a huge sandy desert on the Arabian Peninsula; its name means "empty quarter" (p. 226)

Russia a huge country that extends from Eastern Europe to the Pacific Ocean; it is the largest country in the world (p. 579)

Rwanda a country in East Africa between Tanzania and the Democratic Republic of the Congo (p. 259)

S

Sahara the world's largest desert; it dominates much of North Africa (p. 250)

Sahel a semiarid region between the Sahara and wetter areas to the south (p. 256)

Samarqand (40°N, 67°E) an ancient city on the Silk Road in modern Uzbekistan (p. 218)

São Tomé (1°N, 6°E) the capital of São Tomé and Príncipe (p. 240)

São Tomé and Príncipe an island country located off the Atlantic coast of Central Africa (p. 263)

Sarajevo (44°N, 18°E) the capital of Bosnia and Herzegovina (p. 552)

Saudi Arabia a country occupying much of the Arabian Peninsula in Southwest Asia (p. 226)

Scandinavia a large peninsula in Northern Europe that includes Norway and Sweden (p. 570)

Scotland a part of the United Kingdom located in the northern part of Great Britain (p. 571)

Sea of Marmara a small sea in Turkey; with the Bosporus and the Dardanelles, it forms a waterway that separates Europe and Asia and connects the Mediterranean Sea and Black Sea (p. 114)

Senegal a country in West Africa south of Mauritania (p. 255)

Seoul (38°N, 127°E) the capital of South Korea (p. 396)

Serbia a country in the Balkans (p. 575)

Serengeti Plain a large plain in East Africa that is famous for its wildlife (p. 259)

Seychelles an island country located east of Africa in the Indian Ocean (p. 240)

Shanghai (31°N, 121°E) a major port city in eastern China (p. 541)

Shikoku the smallest of Japan's four major islands (p. 414)

Siberia a huge region in eastern Russia (pp. 69, 579)

Sidon (34°N, 35°E) ancient Phoenician city in modern Lebanon (p. 152)

Sierra Leone a West African country located south of Guinea (p. 255)

Silk Road an ancient trade route from China through Central Asia to the Mediterranean (p. 474)

Singapore an island country at the tip of the Malay Peninsula in Southeast Asia (p. 419)

Slovakia a country in Eastern Europe (p. 575)

Slovenia a country in Eastern Europe (p. 575)

Sofia (43°N, 23°E) the capital of Bulgaria (p. 552)

Somalia an East African country located on the Horn of Africa (p. 259)

Songhai a large and powerful empire in West Africa during the 1400s and 1500s (p. 331)

South Africa a country located at the southern tip of Africa (p. 269)

South America a continent in the Western and Southern hemispheres

South Korea a country in East Asia (p. 415)

South Pole (90°S) the southern point of Earth's axis

Southern Hemisphere the southern half of the globe, between the equator and the South Pole

Spain a country in Southern Europe on the Iberian Peninsula (p. 563)

Sparta (37°N, 22°E) an ancient city-in Greece (p. 593)

Sri Lanka an island country located south of India (p. 407)

Stockholm (59°N, 18°E) the capital of Sweden (p. 552)

Sudan a country in East Africa; it is the largest country in Africa (p. 259)

Suez Canal a canal in Egypt that links the Mediterranean and Red seas (p. 251)

Sumatra a large island in Indonesia (p. 419)

Sumer the region in southern Mesopotamia where the world's first civilization developed (p. 138)

Swaziland a country in Southern Africa almost completely surrounded by South Africa (p. 269)

Sweden a country in Northern Europe (p. 571)

Switzerland a country in West-Central Europe (p. 567)

Syr Darya the longest river in Central Asia; it flows through the Fergana Valley and Kazakhstan, Tajikistan, and Uzbekistan on its way to the Aral Sea (p. 125)

Syria a country on the eastern Mediterranean Sea (p. 115)

Syrian Desert a desert in Southwest Asia covering much of the Arabian Peninsula between the Mediterranean coast and the Euphrates River (p. 116)

T

Taipei (25°N, 122°E) the capital of Taiwan (p. 396)

Taiwan an island country southeast of China (p. 411)

Tajikistan a country in Central Asia; it was part of the Soviet Union until 1991 (p. 123)

Tallinn (59°N, 25°E) the capital of Estonia (p. 552)

Tanzania an East African country south of Kenya (p. 259)

Tashkent (41°N, 69°E) the capital of Uzbekistan; in ancient times it was an important trading city along the Silk Road in Central Asia (p. 106)

Taurus Mountains a mountain range in southern Turkey along the Mediterranean Sea (p. 115)

Tbilisi (42°N, 45°E) the capital of Georgia (p. 553)

Tehran (36°N, 51°E) the capital of Iran (p. 106)

Thailand a country in Southeast Asia (p. 419)

Thar Desert a desert in western India and eastern Pakistan (p. 408)

Thimphu (28°N, 90°E) the capital of Bhutan (p. 396)

Tiananmen Square (40°N, 116°E) large public square near the center of Beijing, China (p. 531)

Tigris River a river that flows mainly through modern Iraq; silt from the Tigris helped form the Fertile Crescent in Mesopotamia (p. 118)

Timbuktu (17°N, 3°W) a major cultural and trading city in the Mali and Songhai empires (p. 329)

Tirana (41°N, 20°E) the capital of Albania (p. 552)

Togo a country in West Africa between Ghana and Benin (p. 255)

Tokyo (36°N, 140°E) the capital of Japan (p. 396)

Tripoli (33°N, 13°E) the capital of Libya (p. 240)

Tropic of Cancer the parallel 23.5° north of the equator; parallel on the globe at which the sun's most direct rays strike Earth during the June solstice

Tropic of Capricorn the parallel at 23.5° south of the equator; parallel on the globe at which the sun's most direct rays strike Earth during the December solstice

Tunis (37°N, 10°E) the capital of Tunisia (p. 240)

Tunisia a country in North Africa on the Mediterranean Sea (p. 251); fought the Punic Wars with Rome (p. 598)

Turkey a country on the eastern Mediterranean, it includes the regions of Anatolia and Asia Minor (p. 115)

Turkmenistan a country in Central Asia; it was part of the Soviet Union until 1991 (p. 123)

Tyre (33°N, 35°E) ancient Phoenician city in modern Lebanon (p. 152)

Uganda a country in East Africa located west of Kenya (p. 259)

Ukraine a country in Eastern Europe (p. 575)

Ulaanbaatar (48°N, 107°E) the capital of Mongolia (p. 396)

United Arab Emirates a country on the Arabian Peninsula (p. 119)

United Kingdom a country in the British Isles that includes England, Wales, Scotland, and Northern Ireland (p. 571)

Upper Egypt the southern, inland region of ancient Egypt, located upriver of Lower Egypt (p. 278)

Ur a city in ancient Sumer, located on the Euphrates River near the Persian Gulf; one of the largest cities of ancient Mesopotamia (p. 139)

Ural Mountains a mountain range in Russia that separates Europe and Asia (p. 578)

Uruk a city in ancient Sumer, located on the Euphrates River; Uruk and Ur fought for dominance around 3500–2500 BC (p. 139)

Uzbekistan a country in Central Asia; it was part of the Soviet Union until 1991 (p. 123)

Vatican City (42°N, 12°E) a small country in Rome that is the head of the Roman Catholic Church (p. 552)

Venice (45°N, 12°E) Italian city, a center of trade in the Renaissance (p. 628)

Victoria (1°S, 33°E) the capital of Seychelles (p. 240)

Vienna (45°N, 12°E) the capital of Austria (p. 552)

Vientiane (18°N, 103°E) the capital of Laos (p. 396)

Vietnam a country in Southeast Asia (p. 419)

Vilnius (55°N, 25°E) the capital of Lithuania (p. 552)

Volga the longest river in Europe and Russia's most important commercial river (p. 580)

Wales a part of the United Kingdom located west of England on the island of Great Britain (p. 571)

Warsaw (52°N, 21°E) the capital of Poland (p. 552)

West Bank a disputed territory in eastern Israel (p. 210)

Western Ghats a mountain range in India (p. 407)

Western Hemisphere the half of the globe between 180° and the prime meridian that includes North and South America and the Pacific and Atlantic oceans

Windhoek (22°S, 17°E) the capital of Namibia (p. 240)

Xi'an (34°N, 591°E) the capital of China during the Tang dynasty (p. 467)

Yamoussoukro (7°N, 5°W) the capital of Côte d'Ivoire (p. 240)

Yangon (Rangoon) (17°N, 96°E) the capital of Myanmar (Burma) (p. 396)

Yaoundé (4°N, 12°E) the capital of Cameroon (p. 240)

Yellow Sea a body of water between northeastern China and the Korean Peninsula (p. 411)

Yemen a country on the Arabian Peninsula bordering the Red Sea and the Gulf of Aden (p. 119)

Yerevan (40°N, 45°E) the capital of Armenia (p. 553)

Z

Zagreb (46°N, 16°E) the capital of Croatia (p. 552)

Zagros Mountains a mountain range in Iran; it forms the western boundary of the Plateau of Iran (p. 119)

Zambezi River a river in Central Africa that flows into the Indian Ocean (p. 263)

Zambia a country in Central Africa east of Angola (p. 263)

Zimbabwe a country in Southern Africa between Botswana and Mozambique (p. 269)

GAZETTEER

Biographical Dictionary

A

'Abbas (1571–1629) Safavid leader, he took back land that had been lost to the Ottomans. He also made great contributions to the Safavid economy and culture. (p. 206)

Abraham Biblical figure, according to the Bible, God led Abraham to Canaan, and Abraham's descendants became the Jewish people. (p. 161)

Abu Bakr (c. 573–634) The first caliph, he ruled the Muslim world after Muhammad's death. (p. 202)

Ahmose the Great (ruled c. 1570–1546 BC) Egyptian pharaoh, he defeated the Hyksos. His reign marked the beginning of Egypt's New Kingdom. (p. 292)

Alexander the Great (c. 356–323 BC) Macedonian ruler, he was one of the greatest military commanders in history. (p. 594)

Ali, Sunni (died 1492) Emperor of Songhai, he conquered Mali and made Songhai into a powerful state. (p. 331)

Aquinas, Thomas (1225–1274) Dominican philosopher, he argued that rational thought could be used to support Christian belief. (p. 187)

Aristotle (c. 384–322 BC) Greek philosopher, he taught that people should live lives of moderation and use reason in their lives. (p. 593)

Arkwright, Richard (1732–1792) English inventor, he invented a water frame for weaving. (p. 644)

Askia the Great (c. 1443–1538) Songhai ruler, he overthrew Sunni Baru. His reign was the high point of Songhai culture. (p. 331)

Asoka (ruled 270–232 BC) Ruler of the Mauryan Empire, he extended his control over most of India and promoted the spread of Buddhism. (p. 452)

Atatürk, Kemal (1881–1938) The first president of modern Turkey, he was given the name Atatürk, which means "father of the Turks." He worked to free Turkey from foreign control and began many programs to reform and modernize the country. (p. 208)

Augustus (63 BC–14 AD) First Roman emperor, he was originally named Octavian. As emperor, Augustus built many monuments and a new forum. (p. 598)

B

Bessemer, Henry (1813–1898) English engineer, he developed a cheap way of making steel. (p. 644)

Bonaparte, Napoleon (1769–1821) French general, he took over France after the French Revolution and conquered much of Europe. (p. 639)

Boudicca (died AD 60) Queen of the Celtic Iceni tribe, she led an unsuccessful revolt against the Romans in the British Isles. (p. 615)

Buddha (c. 563–483 BC) Founder of Buddhism, he was an Indian prince originally named Siddhartha Gautama. He founded the Buddhist religion after a long spiritual journey through India. (p. 442)

Bush, George W. (1946–) President of the United States, he was president on September 11, 2001, when the country suffered its worst terrorist attack. This attack led to the country's War on Terror. (p. 212)

C

Caesar, Julius (c. 100–44 BC) Roman general, he conquered most of Gaul and was named dictator for life but was later murdered by a group of senators. (p. 598)

Candra Gupta II (300s–400s) Gupta emperor, he ruled India during the height of Gupta power. (p. 450)

Candragupta Maurya (late 300s BC) Mauryan ruler, he founded the Mauryan Empire in northern India. (p. 448)

Charlemagne (c. 742–814) King of the Franks, he was a brilliant warrior and a strong leader whose empire included much of Christian western Europe. (p. 672)

Charles I (1600–1649) King of England, he was overthrown and executed in the English Civil War. (p. 636)

Charles II (1630–1685) Son of Charles I, he was made king of England in 1660 after the English Civil War. (p. 636)

Chiang Kai-Shek (1887–1975) Chinese general and leader of the Nationalists, he lost China's civil war and fled with his supporters to Taiwan. (p. 517)

Churchill, Winston (1874–1965) British statesman, he led the United Kingdom during World War II. (p. 661)

Confucius (551–479 BC) Chinese philosopher, he was the most influential teacher in Chinese history. His teachings, called Confucianism, focused on morality, family, society, and government. (p. 483)

Constantine (c. 280–337) First Roman emperor to become a Christian. Constantine moved the empire's capital from Rome to Constantinople and removed bans on Christianity. (p. 601)

Cyrus the Great (c. 585–529 BC) Persian emperor, he created the Persian Empire by conquering most of Southwest Asia. (p. 194)

D

Darius I (550–486 BC) Persian emperor, he restored order to the Persian Empire after a period of rebellion. Darius I built roads and made other improvements to Persian society. (p. 194)

Deng Xiaoping (1904–1997) Chinese revolutionary and government leader, he took power after Mao's death and made far-reaching reforms in the Chinese economy. (p. 540)

Du Fu (712–770) One of China's greatest poets, he lived during the Tang dynasty. (p. 479)

E

Enheduanna (c. 2350 BC) Daughter of Sargon, she is the first known female writer in history. Two of her hymns still exist and she may have helped to start a collection of songs dedicated to the temples of Babylonia. (p. 142)

Erediauwa I (1923–) Oba of Benin since 1979, he advises political leaders in southern Nigeria. (p. 345)

Esma'il (1487–1524) Ruler of Persia, he founded the Safavid Empire. (p. 206)

Ewuare (ruled c. 1440–c. 1473) Oba of Benin, he expanded the size of the kingdom of Benin. (p. 342)

Ezana (c. 300s) Aksumite ruler, he destroyed Meroë and took over the kingdom of Kush around AD 350. (p. 319)

F

Fay, Michael (1956–) American scientist, he walked 2,000 miles through the forests of Central Africa collecting data to make maps and determine land use patterns. (p. 266)

Francis Ferdinand (1863–1914) Archduke of Austria, his assassination helped spark World War I. (p. 649)

Frank, Anne (1929–1945) Victim of the Holocaust, she was a young girl who kept a diary of her life while her family hid from the Nazis. (p. 657)

G

Gandhi, Mohandas (1869–1948) Indian nationalist and spiritual leader, he used nonviolence to protest British rule of India and helped the country achieve independence. (p. 521)

Genghis Khan (c. 1162–1227) Ruler of the Mongols, he led his people in attacks against China and other parts of Asia. His name means "universal leader." (p. 486)

Gilgamesh (c. 3000 BC) King of Uruk, a city-state in Sumer, he became a legendary figure in Sumerian literature. (p. 139)

Gorbachev, Mikhail (1931–) Leader of the Soviet Union, his reforms led to the breakup of the Soviet Union, a thaw in the Cold War, and the fall of Communism in Europe. (p. 662)

Gutenberg, Johann (c. 1400–1468) German printer, he developed a printing press that used movable type and made book production faster and easier. (p. 631)

H

Hammurabi (ruled c. 1792–1750 BC) Babylonian ruler, he was a brilliant military leader who brought all of Mesopotamia into the Babylonian Empire. Hammurabi is known for a unified code of 282 laws, the earliest known set of written laws, that was produced during his reign. (p. 148)

Hatshepsut (ruled c. 1503–1482 BC) Egyptian queen, she worked to increase trade with places outside of Egypt and ordered many impressive monuments and temples built during her reign. (p. 292)

Hildegard of Bingen (1098–1179) Christian nun, she was known for her poetry and music. (p. 189)

Hitler, Adolf (1889–1945) German dictator and Nazi leader, his aggression launched World War II. (p. 655)

Hussein, Saddam. See Saddam Hussein.

I

Ibn Battutah (1304–c. 1368) Muslim traveler and writer, he visited Africa, India, China, and Spain. (p. 336)

Ibn Saud, Abdul Aziz (c. 1880–1953) Saudi king, he led the fight for Saudi Arabia's independence. (p. 228)

Ibn-Sina (c. 980–1037) Muslim doctor, he wrote an influential book on medicine that was used throughout Europe until the 1600s. He is known in the West as Avicenna. (p. 187)

Iceman (c. 3300 BC) Stone Age traveler, he was found in the Alps in 1991. Scientists have learned a great deal about Stone Age people from his clothing and tools. (p. 83)

J

Jefferson, Thomas (1743–1826) Third president of the United States and Enlightenment thinker, he wrote the Declaration of Independence. (p. 637)

Jesus (c. AD 1–30) Founder of Christianity, he taught about kindness and love for God. His teachings eventually spread throughout the Roman Empire and the world. (p. 168)

Joan of Arc (c. 1412–1431) French peasant girl, she rallied French troops during the Hundred Years' War and became a national hero. (p. 625)

John (1167–1216) King of England, he was forced to sign Magna Carta in 1215. (p. 624)

K

Kenyatta, Jomo (c. 1893–1978) African political leader, he was a leader of the African nationalist movement and served as Kenya's first president from 1964 to 1978. (p. 368)

Khadijah (600s) Muhammad's wife, she was a successful trader. (p. 178)

Khomeini, Ayatollah Ruhollah (c. 1900–1989) Iranian political and religious leader, he led the revolution to overthrow the shah in 1979 and ruled the country for the next 10 years. (p. 211)

Khufu (ruled 2500s BC) Egyptian pharaoh, he ruled during Egypt's Old Kingdom and is known for the many monuments built to honor him. (p. 284)

Kim Il Sung (1912–1994) Leader of North Korea, he established a Communist government there and attacked South Korea in 1950, launching the Korean War. (p. 526)

Kublai Khan (1215–1294) Mongol ruler, he completed the conquest of China and founded the Yuan dynasty. (p. 493)

Lalibela (c. 1180–c. 1250) Ethiopian ruler, he is known for building large stone Christian churches, many of which still stand today. (p. 351)

Lenin, Vladimir (1870–1924) Russian revolutionary leader, he led the overthrow of the Russian government in 1917 to create the first Communist state. (p. 652)

Leonardo da Vinci (1492–1519) Genius of the Renaissance, he was a painter, sculptor, inventor, engineer, town planner, and mapmaker. (p. 630)

Li Bo (701–762) One of China's greatest poets, he lived during the Tang dynasty. (p. 479)

Liu Bang (256–195 BC) First emperor of the Han dynasty, he was born a peasant but led an army that gained control of China. As emperor, he lowered taxes and relied on educated officials to help him rule. (p. 468)

Locke, John (1632–1704) English philosopher, he thought that government was a contract between the ruler and the people. (p. 635)

Louis XVI (1754–1793) King of France, he was overthrown and executed during the French Revolution. (p. 637)

Luther, Martin (1483–1546) German priest, he began the Reformation by nailing a list of complaints about the Catholic Church to a church door. (p. 633)

Maathai, Wangari (1940–) Nobel Prize winner, she was honored in 2004 for her efforts in planting more than 30 million trees across Africa. She was the first African woman to receive the Nobel Peace Prize. (p. 65)

Maimonides, Moses (1135–1204) Jewish philosopher at Córdoba, he believed in the power of reason and wrote about the nature of faith. (p. 187)

Mandela, Nelson (1918–) South African president and Nobel Peace Prize winner, he worked to improve the living conditions of black South Africans. Before becoming president, he protested against apartheid and was imprisoned for 26 years. (p. 373)

Mao Zedong (1893–1976) Leader of China, he led the Communist takeover of China in 1949 and was head of the government until 1976. (p. 517)

Marie-Antoinette (1775–1793) Queen of France, she was executed with her husband, King Louis XVI, during the French Revolution. (p. 637)

Mehmed II (1432–1481) Ottoman sultan, he captured Constantinople in 3193, which brought an end to the Byzantine Empire. Later, he worked to restore Constantinople, which the Ottomans called Istanbul. (p. 205)

Meiji, Emperor (1852–1912) Emperor of Japan from 1867 to 1912, he restored imperial rule to Japan and pushed for many reforms. (p. 519)

Menelik II (1844–1913) Emperor of Ethiopia after 2431, he defeated the Italian army at the Battle of Adwa in 1896. (p. 365)

Menes (c. 3100 BC) Legendary Egyptian ruler, he unified the kingdoms of Upper and Lower Egypt and built a new capital city at Memphis. (p. 281)

Michelangelo (1475–1564) Italian Renaissance artist, he designed buildings, wrote poetry, and created famous works of art. (p. 630)

Mobutu, Joseph (1930–1997) African dictator, he became rich and used violence against his opponents while his country's economy collapsed. (p. 374)

Moses (c. 1200s BC) Biblical figure, according to the Bible he led the Hebrew people out of slavery in Egypt and back to Canaan in the Exodus. During this journey, Moses received the Ten Commandments from God. (p. 161)

Muhammad (c. 570–632) Founder of Islam, he spread Islam's teachings to the people of Arabia. Muhammad's teachings make up the Qur'an. (p. 178)

Murasaki Shikibu (c. 978–c. 1026) Japanese noble and writer, she wrote The Tale of Genji, the world's first known novel. (p. 503)

Musa, Mansa (died c. 1332) Ruler of Mali, he was Mali's greatest and most famous ruler. Mansa Musa was a devout Muslim who made a pilgrimage to Mecca that helped spread Mali's fame. (p. 333)

Mussolini, Benito (1883–1945) Fascist dictator of Italy, he joined forces with Hitler during World War II and fought against the Allies. (p. 655)

Nanak, Guru (1469–1538) Founder of Sikhism, he is considered the first of the Sikh gurus. (p. 509)

Nasser, Gamal Abdel (1918–1970) Egyptian army officer and president, he helped overthrow the king and made reforms in Egypt. (p. 209)

Nebuchadnezzar (ruled c. 605–561 BC) Chaldean king, he rebuilt Babylon into a beautiful city, which featured the famed Hanging Gardens. (p. 151)

Nkrumah, Kwame (1909–1972) Leader of Ghana, he believed that Africa would be better off united instead of split into separate countries after independence from European colonial powers. (p. 367)

O

Omar Khayyám (c. 1048–c. 1131) Sufi poet, mathematician, and astronomer, he wrote The Rubáiyát. (p. 189)

Pahlavi, Mohammad Reza (1919–1980) Shah of Iran from 1941 to 1979, he tried to Westernize Iran but was overthrown by a revolution in 1979. (p. 209)

Patrick (400s) Christian saint, he converted the people of Ireland to Christianity. (p. 614)

Paul (c. AD 10–67) One of the most important figures in the spread of Christianity, he worked to spread Jesus's teachings and wrote letters that explained key ideas of Christianity. (p. 172)

Pericles (c. 495–429 BC) Athenian leader, he encouraged the spread of democracy and led Athens when the city was at its height. (p. 592)

Perry, Matthew (1794–1858) American naval commander, he negotiated a trade agreement with Japan in 1854. (p. 514)

Piankhi (c. 751–716 BC) Ruler of Kush, he was one of Kush's most successful military leaders. His army captured all of Egypt. (p. 313)

Plato (428-389 BC) Greek philosopher, he wrote The Republic, which describes an ideal society run by philosophers. (p. 593)

Polo, Marco (1254–1324) Italian trader, he traveled to China and later wrote a book about his trip. During his time in China he served as a government official in Kublai Khan's court. (p. 488)

Ramses the Great (late 1300s and early 1200s BC) Egyptian pharaoh, he expanded the kingdom and built massive temples at Karnak, Luxor, and Abu Simbel. Ramses the Great is often considered one of Egypt's greatest rulers. (p. 297)

Rhodes, Cecil (1853–1902) British imperialist and business tycoon, he wanted to expand the British empire and believed in the superiority of the British race. (p. 362)

Roosevelt, Franklin Delano (1882–1945) Thirty-second president of the United States, he declared war on Japan after the bombing of Pearl Harbor. (p. 523)

Rousseau, Jean-Jacques (1712–1778) French philosopher, he believed in popular sovereignty and the social contract between citizens and their governments. (p. 635)

Saddam Hussein (1937–2007) Iraqi dictator, he became president of Iraq in 1979 and led Iraq into two devastating wars. Known for his brutal suppression of opposition, Hussein was overthrown and captured by the United States in 2003 as part of the War on Terror. (p. 211)

Sargon (c. 2300 BC) King of Akkad, a land north of Sumer, he built the world's first empire after defeating Sumer and northern Mesopotamia. (p. 139)

Shaka (died 1828) Founder of the Zulu Empire, he reorganized the army and kept the Zulu free. (p. 365)

Shanakhdakheto (ruled 170–150 BC) Ruler of Kush, historians think she was the first woman to rule Kush. Her tomb is one of the largest pyramids at Meroë. (p. 317)

Shi Huangdi (259–210 BC) Ruler of China, he united China for the first time, built roads and canals, began the Great Wall of China, and imposed a standard system of laws, money, weights, and writing. (p. 466)

Shotoku (573–621) Japanese regent, he was one of Japan's greatest leaders. He was influential in bringing Buddhism and Chinese ideas to Japan. (p. 507)

Socrates (470-399 BC) Greek philosopher, his teaching style involved asking questions. (p. 593)

Soyinka, Wole (1934–) Nigerian writer, he has written plays, novels, and poems about life in West Africa. He is a winner of the Nobel Prize for Literature. (p. 371)

Stalin, Joseph (1879–1953) Soviet leader, he was a brutal dictator who killed or imprisoned anyone who opposed him. (p. 655)

Suleyman I (c. 1494–1566) Ottoman ruler, he governed the empire at its height. During his rule, the empire included much of the eastern Mediterranean and parts of Europe. (p. 204)

Sun Yixian (1866–1925) Chinese revolutionary leader, he inspired the revolution that overthrew China's last emperor. (p. 517)

Sundiata (died 1255) Founder of the Mali Empire, his reign is recorded in legends. (p. 328)

Suu Kyi, Aung San (1945–) Human rights advocate in Myanmar, she protested against the country's military government and won the Nobel Peace Prize in 1991. (p. 531)

Tull, Jethro (1674–1741) English inventor, he invented the seed drill. (p. 643)

Tunka Manin (ruled c. 1068) Ruler of Ghana, his kingdom was visited by Muslim writers. (p. 324)

Tutankhamen (c. 1300 BC) Egyptian pharaoh, he died while still a young king. The discovery of his tomb in 1922 has taught archaeologists much about Egyptian culture. (p. 303)

Vercingetorix (died 46 BC) Gaulish king, he united several Celtic tribes to fight against the Romans. (p. 615)

Watt, James (1736–1819) Scottish inventor, he created an early steam engine. (p. 644)

William the Conqueror (c. 1028–1087) Powerful French noble who conquered England, he brought feudalism to Britain. (p. 624)

Wilson, Woodrow (1856–1924) Twenty-eighth president of the United States, he was influential in negotiating peace after World War I. (p. 651)

Wu (625–705) Empress of China during the Tang dynasty, she ruled ruthlessly and brought prosperity to China. (p. 477)

Wudi (156–87 BC) Emperor of China, he made Confucianism the official government philosophy. (p. 469)

Xerxes (c. 519–465 BC) King of Persia, his armies invaded Greece but were eventually defeated by the Greeks. (p. 195)

Yang Jian (541–604) Chinese emperor, he reunified China after the Period of Disunion and established the Sui dynasty. (p. 476)

Zheng He (c. 1371–c. 1433) Chinese admiral during the Ming dynasty, he led great voyages that spread China's fame throughout Asia. (p. 489)

Zhu Yuanzhang (1368–1398) Emperor of China and founder of the Ming dynasty, he led an army that overthrew the Mongols. (p. 488)

BIOGRAPHICAL DICTIONARY

English and Spanish Glossary

MARK	AS IN	RESPELLING	EXAMPLE
a	alphabet	a	*AL-fuh-bet
ā	Asia	ay	AY-zhuh
ä	cart, top	ah	KAHRT, TAHP
e	let, ten	e	LET, TEN
ē	even, leaf	ee	EE-vuhn, LEEF
i	it, tip, British	i	IT, TIP, BRIT-ish
ī	site, buy, Ohio	y	SYT, BY, oh-HY-oh
	iris	eye	EYE-ris
k	card	k	KAHRD
kw	quest	kw	KWEST
ō	over, rainbow	oh	OH-vuhr, RAYN-boh
ù	book, wood	ooh	BOOHK, WOOHD
ò	all, orchid	aw	AWL, AWR-kid
òi	foil, coin	oy	FOYL, KOYN
àu	out	ow	OWT
ə	cup, butter	uh	KUHP, BUHT-uhr
ü	rule, food	oo	ROOL, FOOD
yü	few	yoo	FYOO
zh	vision	zh	VIZH-uhn

*A syllable printed in small capital letters receives heavier emphasis than the other syllable(s) in a word.

Phonetic Respelling and Pronunciation Guide

Many of the key terms in this textbook have been respelled to help you pronounce them. The letter combinations used in the respelling throughout the narrative are explained in this phonetic respelling and pronunciation guide. The guide is adapted from *Webster's Tenth New College Dictionary, Merriam-Webster's New Geographical Dictionary, and Merriam-Webster's New Biographical Dictionary.*

A

absolute location a specific description of where a place is located; absolute location is often expressed using latitude and longitude (p. 14)
ubicación absoluta descripción específica del lugar donde se ubica un punto; con frecuencia se define en términos de latitud y longitud (pág. 14)

acupuncture the Chinese practice of inserting fine needles through the skin at specific points to cure disease or relieve pain (p. 473)
acupuntura práctica china que consiste en insertar pequeñas agujas en la piel en puntos específi cos para curar enfermedades o aliviar el dolor (pág. 473)

afterlife life after death, much of Egyptian religion focused on the afterlife (p. 286)
la otra vida vida después de la muerte (pág. 286)

agriculture farming (p. 90)
agricultura cultivo de la tierra (pág. 90)

alchemy a forerunner of chemistry (p. 187)
alquimia precursora de la química (pág. 187)

alliance an agreement to work together (p. 649)
alianza acuerdo de colaboración (pág. 649)

Allies Great Britain, France, the Soviet Union, and the United States; they joined together in World War II against Germany, Italy, and Japan (p. 657)
Aliados Gran Bretaña, Francia, la Unión Soviética y Estados Unidos; se unieron durante la Segunda Guerra Mundial contra Alemania, Italia y Japón (pág. 657)

alloy a mixture of two or more metals (p. 456)
aleación mezcla de dos o más metales (pág. 456)

alphabet a set of letters that can be combined to form words (p. 153)
alfabeto conjunto de letras que pueden combinarse para formar palabras (pág. 153)

ancestor a relative who lived in the past (p. 76)
antepasado pariente que vivió hace muchos años (pág. 76)

apartheid South Africa's government policy of separation of races that was abandoned in the 1980s and 1990s; apartheid means "apartness" (p. 373)
apartheid política gubernamental de Sudáfrica de separar las razas, abandonada en las décadas de 1980 y 1990; apartheid significa "separación" (pág. 373)

aqueduct a human-made raised channel that carries water from distant places (p. 600)
acueducto canal elevado hecho por el ser humano que trae agua desde lugares lejanos (pág. 600)

archipelago a large group of islands (p. 418)
  archipiélago gran grupo de islas (pág. 418)

architecture the science of building (p. 146)
  arquitectura ciencia de la construcción (pág. 146)

arms race a competition between countries to build superior weapons (p. 662)
  carrera armamentista competencia entre países para construir armas mejores (pág. 662)

astronomy the study of stars and planets (p. 457)
  astronomía estudio de las estrellas y los planetas (pág. 457)

Axis Powers the name for the alliance formed by Germany, Italy, and Japan during World War II (p. 657)
  Potencias del Eje nombre de la alianza formada por Alemania, Italia y Japón durante la Segunda Guerra Mundial (pág. 657)

B

basin a generally flat region surrounded by higher land such as mountains and plateaus (p. 262)
  cuenca región generalmente llana rodeada de tierras más altas, como montañas y mesetas (pág. 262)

Bible holy book of Christianity (p. 168)
  Biblia libro sagrado del cristianismo (pág. 168)

Boers Afrikaner frontier farmers in South Africa (p. 364)
  bóers agricultores afrikaners de la frontera en Sudáfrica (pág. 364)

Boxer Rebellion an attempt in 1899 to drive all Westerners out of China (p. 513)
  rebelión de los boxers un intento en 1899 de expulsar a todo occidental de la China (pág. 513)

British East India Company a British company created to control trade between Britain, India, and East Asia (p. 511)
  British East India Company una empresa britaníca establecida para controlar el comercio entre la Gran Bretaña, India, y Asia oriental (pág. 511)

bureaucracy a body of unelected government officials (p. 484)
  burocracia cuerpo de empleados no electos del gobierno (pág. 484)

C

calligraphy decorative writing (p. 189)
  caligrafía escritura decorativa (pág. 189)

caliph (KAY-luhf) a title that Muslims use for the highest leader of Islam (p. 202)
  califa título que los musulmanes le dan al líder supremo del Islam (pág. 202)

canal a human-made waterway (p. 136)
  canal vía de agua hecha por el ser humano (pág. 136)

capitalism an economic system in which individuals and private businesses run most industries (p. 644)
  capitalismo sistema económico en el que los individuos y las empresas privadas controlan la mayoría de las industrias (pág. 644)

cartography the science of making maps (p. 21)
  cartografía ciencia de crear mapas (pág. 21)

caste system the division of Indian society into groups based on rank, wealth, or occupation (p. 437)
  sistema de castas división de la sociedad india en grupos basados en la clase social, el nivel económico o la profesión (pág. 437)

cataracts rapids along a river, such as those along the Nile in Egypt (p. 279)
  rápidos fuertes corrientes a lo largo de un río, como las del Nilo en Egipto (pág. 279)

cathedral a large church, often decorated with statues and paintings of Christian religious figures (p. 189)
  catedral una iglesia grande, a menudo decorado con estatuas y pinturas de figuras religiosas cristianas (pág. 189)

Catholic Reformation the effort of the late 1500s and 1600s to reform the Catholic Church from within; also called the Counter-Reformation (p. 633)
  Reforma católica iniciativa para reformar la Iglesia católica desde dentro a finales del siglo XVI y en el XVII; también conocida como la Contrarreforma (pág. 633)

chariot a wheeled, horse-drawn cart used in battle (p. 150)
  cuadriga carro tirado por caballos usado en las batallas (pág. 150)

Christianity a religion based on the teachings of Jesus of Nazareth that developed in Judea at the beginning of the first century AD (p. 168)
  cristianismo religión basada en las enseñanzas de Jesús de Nazaret que se desarrolló en Judea a comienzos del siglo I d.C. (pág. 168)

citizen a person who has the right to participate in government (p. 597)
  ciudadano persona que tiene el derecho de participar en el gobierno (pág. 597)

city-state a political unit consisting of a city and its surrounding countryside (pp. 138, 588)
  ciudad estado unidad política formada por una ciudad y los campos que la rodean (págs. 138, 588)

civil disobedience the nonviolent refusal to obey the laws as a way to advocate change (p. 516)
  desobediencia civil negative no violenta a obedecer la ley como una manera de exigir un cambio (pág. 516)

civil service service as a government official (p. 484)
  administración pública servicio como empleado del gobierno (pág. 484)

ENGLISH AND SPANISH GLOSSARY

climate the average weather conditions in a certain area over a long period of time (p. 52)
  clima condiciones del tiempo medias de una zona específi ca durante un largo período de tiempo (pág. 52)

Cold War a period of distrust between the United States and Soviet Union after World War II, when there was a tense rivalry between the two superpowers but no direct fighting (p. 660)
  Guerra Fría período de desconfianza entre Estados Unidos y la Unión Soviética que siguió a la Segunda Guerra Mundial; existía una rivalidad tensa entre las dos superpotencias, pero no se llegó a la lucha directa (pág. 660)

common market a group of nations that cooperates to make trade among members easier (p. 664)
  mercado común grupo de naciones que cooperan para facilitar el comercio entre los miembros (pág. 664)

Communism an economic and political system in which the government owns all businesses and controls the economy (p. 652)
  comunismo sistema económico y político en el que el gobierno es dueño de todos los negocios y controla la economía (pág. 652)

compass an instrument that uses Earth's magnetic field to indicate direction (p. 480)
  brújula instrumento que utiliza el campo magnético de la Tierra para indicar la dirección (pág. 480)

constitutional monarchy a type of democracy in which a monarch serves as head of state, but a legislature makes the laws (p. 531)
  monarquía constitucional tipo de democracia en la cual un monarca sirve como jefe de estado, pero una asamblea legislativa hace las leyes (pág. 531)

continent a large landmass that is part of Earth's crust; geographers identify seven continents (p. 38)
  continente gran masa de tierra que forma parte de la corteza terrestre; los geógrafos identifican siete continentes (pág. 38)

Coptic Christianity a form of Christianity that blended African customs with Christian teachings (p. 352)
  cristianismo cóptico una forma del cristianismo que mexcla costumbres africanas con enseñanas cristianas (pág. 352)

Crusades a long series of wars between Christians and Muslims in Southwest Asia fought for control of the Holy Land; took place from 1096 to 1291 (p. 619)
  cruzadas larga serie de guerras entre cristianos y musulmanes en el suroeste de Asia para conseguir el control de la Tierra Santa; tuvieron lugar entre 1096 y 1291 (pág. 619)

cultural diffusion the spread of culture traits from one region to another (p. 506)
  difusión cultural difusión de rasgos culturales de una región a otra (pág. 506)

culture the knowledge, beliefs, customs, and values of a group of people (p. 30)
  cultura el conocimiento, las creencias, las costumbres y los valores de un grupo de personas (pág. 30)

culture region an area in which people have many shared culture traits (p. 31)
  región cultural región en la que las personas comparten muchos rasgos culturales (pág. 31)

cuneiform the world's first system of writing; developed in Sumer (p. 143)
  cuneiforme primer sistema de escritura del mundo; desarrollado en Sumeria (pág. 143)

Declaration of Independence a document written in 1776 that declared the American colonies' independence from British rule (p. 637)
  Declaración de Independencia documento escrito en 1776 que declaró la independencia de las colonias de América del Norte del dominio británico (pág. 637)

Declaration of the Rights of Man and of the Citizen a document written in France in 1789 that guaranteed specific freedoms for French citizens (p. 638)
  Declaración de los Derechos del Hombre y del Ciudadano documento escrito en Francia en 1789 que garantizaba libertades específicas para los ciudadanos franceses (pág. 638)

deforestation the clearing of trees (p. 65)
  deforestación tala de árboles (pág. 65)

delta a triangle-shaped area of land made from soil deposited by a river (pp. 279, 407)
  delta zona de tierra de forma triangular creada a partir de los sedimentos que deposita un río (págs. 279, 407)

democracy a form of government in which the people elect leaders and rule by majority (p. 31)
  democracia sistema de gobierno en el que el pueblo elige a sus líderes y gobierna por mayoría (pág. 31)

desertification the spread of desert-like conditions (p. 256)
  desertización ampliación de las condiciones desérticas (pág. 256)

developed countries countries with strong economies and a high quality of life (p. 31)
  países desarrollados países con economías sólidas y una alta calidad de vida (pág. 31)

developing countries countries with less productive economies and a lower quality of life (p. 31)
  países en vías de desarrollo países con economías menos productivas y una menor calidad de vida (pág. 31)

dictator a ruler who has almost absolute power (p. 655)
  dictador gobernante que tiene poder casi absoluto (pág. 655)

Diet the name for Japan's elected legislature (p. 520)
  Dieta nombre de la asamblea legislativa electa de Japón (pág. 520)

disciples followers (p. 169)
  discípulos seguidores (pág. 169)

division of labor an arrangement in which each worker specializes in a particular task or job (p. 136)
división del trabajo organización mediante la que cada trabajador se especializa en un trabajo o tarea en particular (pág. 136)

domestication the process of changing plants or animals to make them more useful to humans (p. 89)
domesticación proceso en el que se modifican los animales o las plantas para que sean más útiles para los humanos (pág. 89)

domino theory the idea that if one country fell to Communism, neighboring countries would follow like falling dominoes (p. 526)
teoría del efecto dominó idea de que si un país cae en manos del comunismo, los países vecinos lo seguirán como fichas de dominó que caen una tras otra (pág. 526)

droughts periods when little rain falls and crops are damaged (p. 260)
sequías períodos en los que los cultivos sufren daños por la falta de lluvia (pág. 260)

dynasty a series of rulers from the same family (p. 281)
dinastía serie de gobernantes pertenecientes a la misma familia (pág. 281)

earthquake a sudden, violent movement of Earth's crust (p. 40)
terremoto movimiento repentino y violento de la corteza terrestre (pág. 40)

ebony a dark, heavy wood (p. 312)
ébano madera oscura y pesada (pág. 312)

edicts laws (p. 449)
edictos leyes (pág. 449)

elite people of wealth and power (p. 287)
élite personas ricas y poderosas (pág. 287)

embargo a limit on trade (p. 211)
embargo límite impuesto al comercio (pág. 211)

empire a land with different territories and peoples under a single ruler (pp. 139, 598)
imperio zona que reúne varios territorios y pueblos bajo un solo gobernante (págs. 139, 538)

engineering the application of scientific knowledge for practical purposes (p. 288)
ingeniería aplicación del conocimiento científico para fines prácticos (pág. 288)

English Bill of Rights a document approved in 1689 that listed rights for Parliament and the English people and drew on the principles of Magna Carta (p. 636)
Declaración de Derechos inglesa documento aprobado en 1689 que enumeraba los derechos del Parlamento y del pueblo de Inglaterra, inspirada en los principios de la Carta Magna (pág. 636)

Enlightenment a period during the 1600s and 1700s when reason was used to guide people's thoughts about society, politics, and philosophy (p. 634)
Ilustración período durante los siglos XVII y XVIII en el que la razón guiaba las ideas de las personas acerca de la sociedad, la política y la filosofía (pág. 634)

entrepreneur an independent businessperson (p. 361)
empresario una person de negocios independiente (pág. 361)

environment the land, water, climate, plants, and animals of an area; surroundings (p. 14)
ambiente la tierra, el agua, el clima, las plantas y los animales de una zona; los alrededores (pág. 14)

epics long poems that tell the stories of heroes (p. 144)
poemas épicos poemas largos que narran hazañas de héroes (pág. 144)

erosion the movement of sediment from one location to another (p. 41)
erosión movimiento de sedimentos de un lugar a otro (pág. 41)

escarpment a steep face at the edge of a plateau or other raised area (p. 268)
acantilado cara empinada en el borde de una meseta o de otra área elevada (pág. 268)

Exodus the journey of the Hebrews, led by Moses, from Egypt to Canaan after they were freed from slavery (p. 161)
Éxodo viaje de los hebreos, guiados por Moisés, desde Egipto hasta Canaán después de su liberación de la esclavitud (pág. 161)

European Union (EU) an organization that promotes political and economic cooperation in Europe (p. 664)
Unión Europea (UE) organización que promueve la cooperación política y económica en Europa (pág. 664)

exports items sent to other regions for trade (p. 316)
exportaciones productos enviados a otras regiones para el intercambio commercial (pág. 316)

fasting going without food for a period of time (p. 443)
ayunar dejar de comer durante un período de tiempo (pág. 443)

Fertile Crescent an area of rich farmland in Southwest Asia where the first civilizations began (p. 135)
Arco Fértil zona de ricas tierras de cultivo situada en el sudoeste de Asia, en la que comenzaron las primeras civilizaciones (pág. 135)

feudal system the system of obligations that governed the relationships between lords and vassals in medieval Europe (p. 621)
sistema feudal sistema de obligaciones que gobernaba las relaciones entre los señores feudales y los vasallos en la Europa medieval (pág. 621)

ENGLISH AND SPANISH GLOSSARY

fishery a place where lots of fish and other seafood can be caught (p. 417)

pesquería lugar donde suele haber muchos peces y mariscos para pescar (pág. 417)

Five Pillars of Islam five acts of worship required of all Muslims (p. 182)

los cinco pilares del Islam cinco prácticas religiosas que los musulmanes tienen que observar (pág. 182)

fjord a narrow inlet of the sea set between high, rocky cliffs (p. 571)

fiordo entrada estrecha del mar entre acantilados altos y rocosos (pág. 571)

Forbidden City a huge palace complex built by China's Ming emperors that included hundreds of imperial residences, temples, and other government buildings (p. 490)

Ciudad Prohibida enorme complejo de palacios construido por orden de los emperadores Ming de China que incluía cientos de residencias imperiales, templos y otros edificios del gobierno (pág. 490)

fossil fuels nonrenewable resources that formed from the remains of ancient plants and animals; coal, petroleum, and natural gas are all fossil fuels (p. 65)

combustibles fósiles recursos no renovables formados a partir de restos de plantas y animales antiguos; el carbón, el petróleo y el gas natural son combustibles fósiles (pág. 65)

fossil water water underground that is not being replaced by rainfall (p. 121)

aguas fósiles agua subterránea que no es reemplazada por el agua de lluvia (pág. 121)

freshwater water that is not salty; it makes up only about 3 percent of our total water supply (p. 33)

agua dulce agua que no es salada; representa sólo alrededor del 3 por ciento de nuestro suministro total de agua (pág. 33)

front the place where two air masses of different temperatures or moisture content meet (p. 55)

frente lugar en el que se encuentran dos masas de aire con diferente temperatura o humedad (pág. 55)

geography the study of the world, its people, and the landscapes they create (p. 6)

geografía estudio del mundo, de sus habitantes y de los paisajes creados por el ser humano (pág. 6)

geothermal energy energy produced from the heat of Earth's interior (p. 572)

energía geotérmica energía producida a partir del calor del interior de la Tierra (pág. 572)

glacier a large area of slow moving ice (p. 33)

glaciar gran bloque de hielo que avanza con lentitud (pág. 33)

globe a spherical, or ball-shaped, model of the entire planet (p. 10)

globo terráqueo modelo esférico, o en forma de bola, de todo el planeta (pág. 10)

golden age a period in a society's history marked by great achievements (p. 590)

edad dorada período de la historia de una sociedad marcado por grandes logros (pág. 590)

Gothic architecture a style of architecture in Europe known for its high pointed ceilings, tall towers, and stained glass windows (p. 620)

arquitectura gótica estilo de arquitectura europea que se conoce por los techos altos en punta, las torres altas y los vitrales de colores (pág. 620)

Grand Canal a canal linking northern and southern China (p. 476)

canal grande un canal que conecta el norte con el sur de China (pág. 476)

Great Depression a global economic crisis that struck countries around the world in the 1930s (p. 654)

Gran Depresión crisis económica global que afectó a países de todo el mundo en la década de 1930 (pág. 654)

Great Wall a barrier made of walls across China's northern frontier (p. 467)

Gran Muralla barrera formada por muros situada a lo largo de la frontera norte de China (pág. 467)

griot a West African storyteller (p. 334)

griot narrador de relatos de África occidental (pág. 334)

groundwater water found below Earth's surface (p. 34)

agua subterránea agua que se encuentra debajo de la superficie de la Tierra (pág. 34)

gunpowder a mixture of powders used in guns and explosives (p. 480)

pólvora mezcla de polvos utilizada en armas de fuego y explosivos (pág. 480)

H

Hammurabi's Code a set of 140 laws governing daily life in Babylon; the earliest known collection of written laws (p. 149)

Código de Hammurabi conjunto de 140 leyes que regían la vida cotidiana en Babilonia; la primera colección de leyes escritas conocida (pág. 149)

harem an area of an Ottoman household where women lived apart from men (p. 205)

harén zona de una casa otomana en la que las mujeres vivían separadas de los hombres (pág. 205)

Hellenistic Greek-like; heavily influenced by Greek ideas (p. 594)

helenístico al estilo griego; muy influenciado por las ideas de la Grecia clásica (pág. 594)

hieroglyphics the ancient Egyptian writing system that used picture symbols (p. 299)
jeroglíficos sistema de escritura del antiguo Egipto, en el cual se usaban símbolos ilustrados (pág. 299)

Hindu-Arabic numerals the number system we use today; it was created by Indian scholars during the Gupta dynasty (p. 456)
numerales indoarábigos sistema numérico que usamos hoy en día; fue creado por estudiosos de la India durante la dinastía Gupta (pág. 456)

Holocaust the Nazis' effort to wipe out the Jewish people in World War II, when 6 million Jews throughout Europe were killed (p. 657)
Holocausto intento de los nazis de eliminar al pueblo judío durante la Segunda Guerra Mundial, en el que se mató a 6 millones de judíos en toda Europa (pág. 657)

hominid an early ancestor of humans (p. 76)
homínido antepasado primitivo de los humanos (pág. 76)

human geography the study of the world's people, communities, and landscapes (p. 20)
geografía humana estudio de los habitantes, las comunidades y los paisajes del mundo (pág. 20)

humanism the study of history, literature, public speaking, and art that led to a new way of thinking in Europe in the late 1300s (p. 629)
humanismo estudio de la historia, la literatura, la oratoria y el arte que produjo una nueva forma de pensar en Europa a finales del siglo XIV (pág. 629)

human rights rights that all people deserve, such as rights to equality and justice (p. 531)
derechos humanos derechos que toda la gente merece como derechos a la igualdad y la justicia (pág. 531)

hunter-gatherers people who hunt animals and gather wild plants, seeds, fruits, and nuts to survive (p. 81)
cazadores y recolectores personas que cazan animales y recolectan plantas, semillas, frutas y nueces para sobrevivir (pág. 81)

hydroelectric power the production of electricity from waterpower, such as from running water (p. 66)
energía hidroeléctrica producción de electricidad generada por la energía del agua, como la del agua corriente (pág. 66)

ice ages long periods of freezing weather (p. 84)
eras glaciales largos períodos de clima helado (pág. 84)

imperialism an attempt by one country to dominate another country's government, trade, or culture (p. 361)
imperialismo el intento de un país de dominar el gobierno, negocio, o cultura de otro país (pág. 361)

imports goods brought in from other regions (p. 316)
importaciones bienes que se introducen en un país procedentes de otras regiones (pág. 316)

Industrial Revolution the period of rapid growth in machine-made goods that changed the way people across Europe worked and lived; it began in Britain in the 1700s (p. 642)
Revolución Industrial período de rápido aumento de los bienes producidos con máquinas que cambió la forma de vivir y trabajar en toda Europa; comenzó en Gran Bretaña a comienzos del siglo XVIII (pág. 642)

inoculation injecting a person with a small dose of a virus to help build up defenses to a disease (p. 456)
inoculación acto de inyectar una pequeña dosis de un virus a una persona para ayudarla a crear defensas contra una enfermedad (pág. 456)

irrigation a way of supplying water to an area of land (p. 136)
irrigación método para suministrar agua a un terreno (pág. 136)

Islam a religion based on the messages Muhammad is believed to have received from God (p. 178)
Islam religión basada en los mensajes que se cree que Mahoma recibió de Dios (pág. 178)

island hopping the strategy used by U.S. forces in the Pacific during World War II that involved taking only strategically important islands (p. 525)
saltar de isla en isla estrategia de las furezas de Estados Unidos en el Pacífico durante la Segunda Guerra Mundial que consistía en tomar sólo las islas importantes desde el punto de vista estratégico (pág. 525)

isolationism a policy of avoiding contact with other countries (p. 492)
aislacionismo política de evitar el contacto con otros países (pág. 492)

ivory a white material made from elephant tusks (p. 312)
marfil material blanco procedente de los colmillos de los elefantes (pág. 312)

janissary an Ottoman slave soldier (p. 204)
jenízaro soldado esclavo otomano (pág. 204)

jihad to make an effort or to struggle; has also been interpreted to mean holy war (p. 181)
yihad esforzarse o luchar; se ha interpretado también con el significado de guerra santa (pág. 181)

Judaism the religion of the Hebrews (practiced by Jews today); it is the world's oldest monotheistic religion (p. 160)
judaísmo religión de los hebreos (practicada por los judíos hoy en día); es la religión monoteísta más antigua del mundo (pág. 160)

ENGLISH AND SPANISH GLOSSARY

karma in Buddhism and Hinduism, the effects that good or bad actions have on a person's soul (p. 440)
karma en el budismo y el hinduismo, los efectos que las buenas o malas acciones producen en el alma de una persona (pág. 440)

kente a hand-woven, brightly colored West African fabric (p. 337)
kente tela muy colorida, tejida a mano, característica de África occidental (pág. 337)

land bridge a strip of land connecting two continents (p. 84)
puente de tierra franja de tierra que conecta dos continentes (pág. 84)

landform a shape on the planet's surface, such as a mountain, valley, plain, island, or peninsula (p. 37)
accidente geográfico forma de la superficie terrestre, como una montaña, un valle, una llanura, una isla o una península (pág. 37)

landlocked completely surrounded by land with no direct access to the ocean (p. 122)
sin salida al mar que está rodeado completamente por tierra, sin acceso directo al océano (pág. 122)

landscape all the human and physical features that make a place unique (p. 6)
paisaje todas las características humanas y físicas que hacen que un lugar sea único (pág. 6)

latitude the distance north or south of Earth's equator (p. 29)
latitud distancia hacia el norte o el sur desde el ecuador (pág. 29)

lava magma that reaches Earth's surface (p. 39)
lava magma que llega a la superficie terrestre (pág. 39)

loess (LES) fertile, yellowish soil (p. 412)
loess suelo amarillento y fértil (pág. 412)

longitude distance east and west of the prime meridian (p. 29)
longitud distancia este y oeste del meridiano cero (pág. 29)

mandate of heaven the idea that heaven chose China's ruler and gave him or her power (p. 466)
mandato divino idea de que el cielo elegía al gobernante de China y le daba el poder (pág. 466)

manor a large estate owned by a knight or lord (p. 622)
feudo gran finca perteneciente a un caballero o señor feudal (pág. 622)

map a flat drawing that shows all or part of Earth's surface (p. 10)
mapa representación plana que muestra total o parcialmente la superficie de la Tierra (pág. 10)

Mau Mau a violent movement in Kenya during the 1960s, led by Kikuyu farmers, to rid the country of white settlers (p. 368)
Mau Mau movimiento emprendido por los agricultores kikiyu con el fin de expulsar de Kenia por medios violentos a los agricultores blancos (pág. 368)

meditation deep, continued thought that focuses the mind on spiritual ideas (p. 443)
meditación reflexión profunda y continua, durante la cual la persona se concentra en ideas espirituales (pág. 443)

Mediterranean climate the type of climate found across Southern Europe; it features warm and sunny summer days, mild evenings, and cooler, rainy winters (p. 564)
clima mediterráneo tipo de clima de todo el sur europeo; se caracteriza por días de verano cálidos y soleados, noches templadas e inviernos lluviosos y más frescos (pág. 564)

megalith a huge stone monument (p. 90)
megalito enorme monumento de piedra (pág. 90)

mercenary a hired soldier (p. 448)
mercenario soldado a sueldo (pág. 448)

merchant a trader (p. 316)
mercader comerciante (pág. 316)

Mesolithic Era the middle part of the Stone Age; marked by the creation of smaller and more complex tools (p. 86)
Mesolítico período central de la Edad de Piedra, caracterizado por la creación de herramientas más pequeñas y complejas (pág. 86)

Messiah in Judaism, a new leader that would appear among the Jews and restore the greatness of ancient Israel (p. 168)
Mesías en el judaísmo, nuevo líder que aparecería entre los judíos y restablecería la grandeza del antiguo Israel (pág. 168)

metallurgy the science of working with metals (p. 456)
metalurgia ciencia de trabajar los metales (pág. 456)

meteorology the study of weather and what causes it (p. 22)
meteorología estudio de las condiciones del tiempo y sus causas (pág. 22)

Middle Ages a period that lasted from about 500 to 1500 in Europe (p. 618)
Edad Media período que duró aproximadamente desde el año 500 hasta el 1500 en Europa (pág. 618)

Middle Kingdom the period of Egyptian history from about 2050 to 1750 BC and marked by order and stability (p. 292)
Reino Medio período de la historia de Egipto que abarca aproximadamente del 2050 al 1750 a. C. y que se caracterizó por el orden y la estabilidad (pág. 292)

Middle Passage the name for the voyages that brought enslaved Africans across the Atlantic Ocean to North America and the West Indies (p. 356)
Paso Central viaje en el que los esclavos africanos atravesaban el océano Atlántico hasta llegar a América del Norte y las Antillas (pág. 356)

migrate to move to a new place (p. 84)
migrar desplazarse a otro lugar (pág. 84)

minaret a narrow tower from which Muslims are called to prayer (p. 189)
minarete torre fina desde la que se llama a la oración a los musulmanes (pág. 189)

missionary someone who works to spread religious beliefs (p. 446)
misionero alguien que trabaja para difundir sus creencias religiosas (pág. 446)

monotheism belief in only one god (p. 163)
monoteísmo creencia en un solo dios (pág. 163)

monsoon a seasonal wind that brings either dry or moist air (pp. 60, 409)
monzón viento estacional que trae aire seco o húmedo (págs. 60, 409)

mosque a building for Muslim prayer (pp. 179, 331)
mezquita edificio musulmán para la oración (págs. 179, 331)

mummy a specially treated body wrapped in cloth for preservation (p. 286)
momia cadáver especialmente tratado y envuelto en tela para su conservación (pág. 286)

Muslim a follower of Islam (p. 178)
musulmán seguidor del Islam (pág. 178)

Neolithic Era the New Stone Age; when people learned to make fire and tools such as saws and drills (p. 89)
Neolítico Nueva Edad de Piedra; el ser humano aprendió a producir fuego y a fabricar herramientas como sierras y taladros manuales (pág. 89)

New Kingdom the period from about 1550 to1050 BC in Egyptian history when Egypt reached the height of its power and glory (p. 292)
Reino Nuevo período de la historia egipcia que abarca aproximadamente desde el 1550 hasta el 1050 a. C., en el que Egipto alcanzó la cima de su poder y su gloria (pág. 292)

nirvana in Buddhism, a state of perfect peace (p. 444)
nirvana en el budismo, estado de paz perfecta (pág. 444)

noble a rich and powerful person (p. 284)
noble persona rica y poderosa (pág. 284)

nomads people who move often from place to place (p. 220)
nómadas personas que se trasladan frecuentemente de un lugar a otro (pág. 220)

nonrenewable resource a resource that cannot be replaced naturally; coal and petroleum are examples of nonrenewable resources (p. 65)
recurso no renovable recurso que no puede reemplazarse naturalmente; el carbón y el petróleo son ejemplos de recursos no renovables (pág. 65)

nonviolence the avoidance of violent actions (pp. 441, 516)
no violencia rechazo de las acciones violentas (págs. 441, 516)

N

nationalism a devotion and loyalty to one's country; develops among people with a common language, religion, or history (p. 648)
nacionalismo sentimiento de lealtad al país de uno; se desarrolla entre personas con un idioma, religión o historia en común (pág. 648)

nation-state a country united under a single strong government; made up of people with a common cultural background (p. 625)
nación-estado país unido bajo un solo gobierno fuerte; formado de personas con una cultura común (pág. 625)

natural resource any material in nature that people use and value (p. 64)
recurso natural todo material de la naturaleza que las personas utilizan y valoran (pág. 64)

navigable river a river that is deep and wide enough for ships to use (p. 568)
río navegable río que tiene la profundidad y el ancho necesarios para que pasen los barcos (pág. 568)

O

oasis a wet, fertile area in a desert where a spring or well provides water (pp. 120, 252)
oasis zona húmeda y fértil en el desierto con un manantial o pozo que proporciona agua (págs. 120, 252)

obelisk a tall, pointed, four-sided pillar in ancient Egypt (p. 150)
obelisco pilar alto, de cuatro caras y acabado en punta, propio del antiguo Egipto (pág. 150)

ocean currents large streams of surface seawater; they move heat around Earth (p. 54)
corrientes oceánicas grandes corrientes de agua de mar que fluyen en la superficie del océano; transportan calor por toda la Tierra (pág. 54)

Old Kingdom the period from about 2700 to 2200 BC in Egyptian history that began shortly after Egypt was unified (p. 283)
Reino Antiguo período de la historia egipcia que abarca aproximadamente del 2700 hasta el 2200 a. C. y comenzó poco después de la unifi cación de Egipto (pág. 283)

ENGLISH AND SPANISH GLOSSARY

OPEC an international organization whose members work to influence the price of oil on world markets by controlling the supply (p. 213)
OPEP organización internacional cuyos miembros trabajan para influenciar el precio del petróleo en los mercados mundiales controlando la oferta (pág. 213)

oral history a spoken record of past events (p. 334)
historia oral registro hablado de hechos ocurridos en el pasado (pág. 334)

Paleolithic Era the first part of the Stone Age; when people first used stone tools (p. 79)
Paleolítico primera parte de la Edad de Piedra; cuando el ser humano usó herramientas de piedra por primera vez (pág. 79)

pans low, flat areas (p. 270)
depresiones áreas bajas y planas (pág. 270)

papyrus a long-lasting, paper-like material made from reeds that the ancient Egyptians used to write on (p. 299)
papiro material duradero hecho de juncos, similar al papel, que los antiguos egipcios utilizaban para escribir (pág. 299)

partition division (p. 517)
partición división (pág. 517)

periodic market an open-air trading market that is set up once or twice a week (p. 269)
mercado periódico mercado al aire libre que funciona una o dos veces a la semana (pág. 269)

permafrost permanently frozen layers of soil (p. 63)
permafrost capas de tierra congeladas permanentemente (pág. 63)

pharaoh the title used by the rulers of Egypt (p. 281)
faraón título usado por los gobernantes de Egipto (pág. 281)

physical geography the study of the world's physical features—its landforms, bodies of water, climates, soils, and plants (p. 18)
geografía física estudio de las características físicas de la Tierra: sus accidentes geográficos, sus masas de agua, sus climas, sus suelos y sus plantas (pág. 18)

pictograph a picture symbol (p. 144)
pictograma símbolo ilustrado (pág. 144)

plate tectonics a theory suggesting that Earth's surface is divided into a dozen or so slow-moving plates, or pieces of Earth's crust (p. 38)
tectónica de placas teoría que sugiere que la superficie terrestre está dividida en unas doce placas, o fragmentos de corteza terrestre, que se mueven lentamente (pág. 38)

polytheism the worship of many gods (p. 140)
politeísmo culto a varios dioses (pág. 140)

pope the spiritual head of the Roman Catholic Church (p. 619)
papa jefe espiritual de la Iglesia Católica Romana (pág. 619)

porcelain a thin, beautiful pottery invented in China (p. 479)
porcelana cerámica bella y delicada creada en China (pág. 479)

precipitation water that falls to Earth's surface as rain, snow, sleet, or hail (p. 33)
precipitación agua que cae a la superficie de la Tierra en forma de lluvia, nieve, aguanieve o granizo (pág. 33)

prehistory the time before there was writing (p. 76)
prehistoria período anterior a la existencia de la escritura (pág. 76)

priest a person who performs religious ceremonies (p. 141)
sacerdote persona que lleva a cabo ceremonias religiosas (pág. 141)

prevailing winds winds that blow in the same direction over large areas of Earth (p. 53)
vientos preponderantes vientos que soplan en la misma dirección sobre grandes zonas de la Tierra (pág. 53)

Protestant a Christian who protested against the Catholic Church (p. 633)
protestante cristiano que protestaba en contra de la Iglesia católica (pág. 633)

proverb a short saying of wisdom or truth (p. 335)
proverbio refrán breve que expresa sabiduría o una verdad (pág. 335)

pyramid a huge triangular tomb built by the Egyptians and other peoples (p. 288)
pirámide tumba triangular y gigantesca construida por los egipcios y otros pueblos (pág. 288)

Qur'an the holy book of Islam (p. 178)
Corán libro sagrado del Islam (pág. 178)

rabbi a Jewish religious teacher (p. 165)
rabino maestro religioso judío (pág. 165)

Raj the British rule of India from 1757 until 1947 (p. 511)
Raj gobierno británico en la India desde 1757 hasta 1947 (pág. 511)

reforestation planting trees to replace lost forestland (p. 65)
reforestación siembra de árboles para reemplazar los bosques que han desaparecido (pág. 65)

Reformation a reform movement against the Roman Catholic Church that began in 1517; it resulted in the creation of Protestant churches (p. 632)
Reforma movimiento de reforma contra la Iglesia Católica Romana que comenzó en 1517; resultó en la creación de las iglesias protestantes (pág. 632)

region an area with one or more features that make it different from surrounding areas (p. 8)
región zona con una o varias características que la diferencian de las zonas que la rodean (pág. 8)

Reign of Terror a bloody period of the French Revolution during which the government executed thousands of its opponents and others at the guillotine (p. 638)
Reino del Terror período sangriento de la Revolución Francesa durante el cual el gobierno ejecutó a miles de personas, oponentes y otros, en la guillotina (pág. 638)

reincarnation a Hindu and Buddhist belief that souls are born and reborn many times, each time into a new body (p. 439)
reencarnación creencia hindú y budista de que las almas nacen y renacen muchas veces, siempre en un cuerpo nuevo (pág. 439)

relative location a general description of where a place is located; a place's relative location is often expressed in relation to something else (p. 14)
ubicación relativa descripción general de la posición de un lugar; la ubicación relativa de un lugar suele expresarse en relación con otra cosa (pág. 14)

Renaissance the period of "rebirth" and creativity that followed Europe's Middle Ages (p. 628)
Renacimiento período de "volver a nacer" y creatividad que siguió a la Edad Media en Europa (pág. 628)

renewable resource a resource that Earth replaces naturally, such as water, soil, trees, plants, and animals (p. 65)
recurso renovable recurso que la Tierra reemplaza por procesos naturales, como el agua, el suelo, los árboles, las plantas y los animales (pág. 65)

republic a political system in which people elect leaders to govern them (p. 597)
república sistema politico en el que el pueblo elige a los líderes que lo gobernarán (pág. 597)

Resurrection in Christianity, Jesus's rise from the dead (p. 169)
Resurrección en el cristianismo, la vuelta a la vida de Jesús (pág. 169)

rift valleys places on Earth's surface where the crust stretches until it breaks (p. 258)
valles de fisura puntos de la superficie de la Tierra en los que la corteza se estira hasta romperse (pág. 258)

Rosetta Stone a huge stone slab inscribed with hieroglyphics, Greek, and a later form of Egyptian that allowed historians to understand Egyptian writing (p. 299)
piedra Roseta gran losa de piedra en la que aparecen inscripciones en jeroglíficos, en griego y en una forma tardía del idioma egipcio que permitió a los historiadores descifrar la escritura egipcia (pág. 299)

S

saint a person known and admired for his or her holiness (p. 172)
santo persona conocida y admirada por su santidad (pág. 172)

sanctions economic or political penalties imposed by one country on another to try to force a change in policy (p. 373)
sanciones penalizaciones económicas o políticas que un país impone a otro para obligarlo a cambiar su política (pág. 373)

Sanskrit the most important language of ancient India (p. 435)
sánscrito el idioma más importante de la antigua India (pág. 435)

savanna an area of tall grasses and scattered trees and shrubs (pp. 60, 256)
sabana zona de pastos altos con arbustos y árboles dispersos (págs. 60, 256)

scholar-official an educated member of China's government who passed a series of written examinations (p. 484)
funcionario erudito miembro culto del gobierno de China que aprobaba una serie de exámenes escritos (pág. 484)

scribe a writer (p. 144)
escriba escritor (pág. 144)

seismograph a device that measures the strength of an earthquake (p. 472)
sismógrafo aparato que mide la fuerza de un terremoto (pág. 472)

Senate a council of rich and powerful Romans who helped run the city (p. 597)
Senado consejo de romanos ricos y poderosos que ayudaban a dirigir la ciudad (pág. 597)

shah a Persian title that means "king" (p. 209)
sha título persa que significa "rey" (pág. 209)

Sikhism a monotheistic religion that developed in India in the 1400s (p. 509)
sijismo una religion monoteísta que se desarrolló en la India en el siglo XV (pág. 509)

silent barter a process in which people exchange goods without contacting each other directly (p. 322)
trueque silencioso proceso mediante el que las personas intercambian bienes sin entrar en contacto directo (pág. 322)

silt a mixture of fertile soil and tiny rocks that can make land ideal for farming (pp. 135, 250)
cieno mezcla de tierra fértil y piedrecitas que pueden crear un terreno ideal para el cultivo (págs. 135, 250)

social hierarchy the division of society by rank or class (p. 141)
jerarquía social división de la sociedad en clases o niveles (pág. 141)

social science a field that focuses on people and the relationships among them (p. 7)
ciencias sociales campo de estudio que se enfoca en las personas y en las relaciones entre ellas (pág. 7)

ENGLISH AND SPANISH GLOSSARY

society a community of people who share a common culture (p. 81)
sociedad comunidad de personas que comparten la misma cultura (pág. 81)

sphere of influence an area of a country over which another country has economic control (p. 513)
esfera de influencia la area de un país sobre cual otro país tiene control ecónomico (pág. 513)

sphinx an imaginary creature with a human head and the body of a lion that was often shown on Egyptian statues (p. 292)
esfinge criatura imaginaria con cabeza humana y cuerpo de león que aparecía representada a menudo en las estatuas egipcias (pág. 292)

steppe a semidry grassland or prairie; steppes often borders deserts (p. 61)
estepa pradera semiárida; las estepas suelen encontrarse en el límite de los desiertos (pág. 61)

subcontinent a large landmass that is smaller than a continent (p. 406)
subcontinente gran masa de tierra, más pequeña que un continente (pág. 406)

suffragettes women who campaigned to gain the right to vote (p. 646)
sufragistas mujeres que hicieron campaña para obtener el derecho a votar (pág. 646)

sundial a device that uses the position of shadows cast by the sun to tell the time of day (p. 472)
reloj de sol dispositivo que utiliza la posición de las sombras que proyecta el sol para indicar las horas del día (pág. 472)

Sunnah a collection of writings about the way Muhammad lived that provides a model for Muslims to follow (p. 181)
Sunna conjunto de escritos sobre la vida de Mahoma que proporciona un modelo de comportamiento para los musulmanes (pág. 181)

superpower a strong and influential country (p. 660)
superpotencia país poderoso e influyente (pág. 660)

surface water water that is found in Earth's streams, rivers, and lakes (p. 33)
agua superficial agua que se encuentra en los arroyos, ríos y lagos de la Tierra (pág. 33)

surplus more of something than is needed (p. 136)
excedente cantidad que supera lo que se necesita (pág. 136)

Swahili an African society that emerged in the late 1100s along the East African coast and combined elements of African, Asian, and Islamic cultures (p. 353)
swahili sociedad Africana que surgió a finales del siglo XII a lo largo de la costa africana oriental; combinaba elementos de las culturas africana, asiática e islámica (pág. 353)

synagogue a Jewish house of worship (p. 189)
sinagoga lugar de culto judío (pág. 189)

taiga a forest of mainly evergreen trees covering much of Russia (p. 581)
taiga bosque de árboles de hoja perenne principalmente que cubre gran parte de Rusia (pág. 581)

Taliban a radical Muslim group that rose to power in Afghanistan in the mid-1990s (p. 212)
talibanes grupo radical musulmán que llegó al poder en Afganistán a mediados de la década de 1990 (pág. 212)

tariff a fee that a country charges on imports or exports (p. 529)
arancel tarifa que impone un país a las importaciones y exportaciones (pág. 529)

textile a cloth product (p. 644)
textil producto de tela (pág. 644)

tolerance acceptance (p. 204)
tolerancia aceptación (pág. 204)

tool an object that has been modified to help a person accomplish a task (p. 78)
herramienta objeto que ha sido modificado para ayudar a una persona a realizar una tarea (pág. 78)

Torah the most sacred text of Judaism (p. 164)
Torá el texto más sagrado del judaísmo (pág. 164)

townships crowded clusters of small homes in South Africa outside of cities where black South Africans live (p. 373)
distritos segregados grupos de pequeñas viviendas amontonadas ubicadas en las afueras de las ciudades de Sudáfrica, donde vivían los sudafricanos negros (pág. 373)

trade network a system of people in different lands who trade goods back and forth (p. 316)
red comercial sistema de personas en diferentes lugares que comercian productos entre sí (pág. 316)

trade route a path followed by traders (p. 293)
ruta comercial itinerario seguido por los comerciantes (pág. 293)

trade surplus when a country exports more goods than it imports (p. 529)
excedente comercial cuando un país exporta más bienes de los que importa (pág. 529)

Treaty of Versailles the final peace settlement of World War I (p. 650)
Tratado de Versalles acuerdo de paz final de la Primera Guerra Mundial (pág. 650)

trench warfare a style of fighting common in World War I in which each side fights from deep ditches, or trenches, dug into the ground (p. 650)
guerra de trincheras forma de guerra comúnmente usada en la Primera Guerra Mundial, en la cual ambos bandos luchan desde profundas zanjas, o trincheras, cavadas en el suelo (pág. 650)

tsunami a destructive and fast-moving wave (p. 416)
tsunami ola rápida y destructiva (pág. 416)

veld open grassland areas in South Africa (p. 270)
veld praderas descampadas en Sudáfrica (pág. 270)

wadi a dry streambed (p. 121)
uadi cauce seco de un río o arroyo (pág. 121)

water cycle the movement of water from Earth's surface to the atmosphere and back (p. 35)
ciclo del agua circulación del agua desde la superficie de la Tierra hacia la atmósfera y de regreso a la Tierra (pág. 35)

water vapor water occurring in the air as an invisible gas (p. 34)
vapor de agua agua que se encuentra en el aire en estado gaseoso e invisible (pág. 34)

weather the short-term changes in the air for a given place and time (p. 52)
tiempo cambios a corto plazo en la atmósfera en un momento y lugar determinados (pág. 52)

weathering the process by which rock is broken down into smaller pieces (p. 41)
meteorización proceso de desintegración de las rocas en pedazos pequeños (pág. 41)

woodblock printing a form of printing in which an entire page is carved into a block of wood, covered with ink, and pressed to a piece of paper to create a printed page (p. 480)
xilografi a forma de impresión en la que una página completa se talla en una plancha de madera, se cubre de tinta y se presiona sobre un papel para crear la página impresa (pág. 480)

yurt a movable round house made of wool felt mats hung over a wood frame (p. 220)
yurt tienda redonda y portátil de fieltro de lana que se coloca sobre una armazón de madera (pág. 220)

ziggurat a pyramid-shaped temple in Sumer (p. 146)
zigurat templo sumerio en forma de pirámide (pág. 146)

zonal organized by zone (p. 256)
zonal organizado por zonas (pág. 256)

ENGLISH AND SPANISH GLOSSARY

Index

M

Q

R

INDEX

INDEX

INDEX

Credits and Acknowledgments

Acknowledgments

For permission to reproduce copyrighted material, grateful acknowledgement is made to the following sources:

Bantam Books, a division of Random House, Inc., www.randomhouse.com: From *The Bhagavad-Gita*, translated by Barbara Stoler Miller. Copyright © 1986 by Barbara Stoler Miller.

CNN: From "Taiwan: War bill a big provocation," from *CNN.com* Web site, March 14, 2005. Copyright © 2005 by Cable News Network LP, LLLP. Accessed September 22,2005 at http://edition.cnn.com/2005/WORLD/asiapcf/03/14/china.npc.law/

Doubleday, a division of Random House, Inc.: From *The Diary of a Young Girl, The Definitive Edition* by Ann Frank, edited by Otto H. Frank and Mirjam Pressler, translated by Susan Massotty. Copyright © 1995 by Doubleday, a division of Random House, Inc.

Foreign Affairs: From "A Conversation With Lee Kuan Yew" by Fareed Zakaria from *Foreign Affairs*, March/April 1994, vol. 73, issue 2. Copyright © 2004 by Council on Foreign Relations. All rights reserved.

HaperCollins Publishers: From *Antarctic Journal: Four Months at the Bottom of the World* by Jennifer Owings Dewey. Copyright © 2001 by Jennifer Owings Dewey. From *The Endless Steppe* by Esther Hautzig. Copyright © 1968 by Esther Hautzig.

David Higham Associates Limited: From *Travels in Asia and Africa 1325–1354* by Ibn Battuta translated by H. A. R. Gibb. Copyright © 1929 by Broadway House, London.

Alfred A. Knopf, Inc., a division of Random House, Inc., www.randomhouse.com: From *Shabanu: Daughter of Wind* by Suzanne Fisher Staples. Copyright © 1989 by Suzanne Fisher Staples. From *Crossing Antarctica* by Will Steger. Copyright © 1991 by Will Steger.

Lonely Planet: From "Hungary" from the *Lonely Planet WorldGuide* Online Web site. Copyright © 2005 by Lonely Planet. Accessed at http://www.lonelyplanet.com/worldguide/destinations/europe/hungary/.

The Jewish Publication Society: Exodus 20: 12–14 from *Tanakh: A New Translation of the Holy Scriptures According to the Traditional Hebrew Text*. Copyright © 1985 by The Jewish Publication Society.

National Geographic Society: From *Geography for Life: National Geographic Standards 1994*. Copyright © 1994 by National Geographic Research & Exploration. All rights reserved.

Naomi Shihab Nye: "Red Brocade" from *19 Varieties of Gazelle: Poems of the Middle East* by Naomi Shihab Nye. Copyright © 1994, 1995, 2002 by Naomi Shihab Nye.

Penguin Books Ltd.: "Quiet Night Thoughts" by Li Po from *Li Po and Tu Fu: Poems*, translated by Arthur Cooper. Copyright © 1973 by Arthur Cooper. From "The Blood Clots" from *The Koran*, translated with notes by N. J. Dawood. Copyright © 1956, 1959, 1966, 1968, 1974, 1990 by N. J. Dawood.

G. P. Putnam's Sons, a division of Penguin Group (USA) Inc.: From *Time Enough for Love, the Lives of Lazarus Long* by Robert Heinlein. Copyright © 1973 by Robert Heinlein. All rights reserved.

Estate of Erich Maria Remarque: From *All Quiet of the Western Front* by Erich Maria Remarque. Copyright © 1929, 1930 by Little, Brown and Company, copyright renewed © 1957, 1958 by Erich Maria Remarque. All rights reserved. "Im Western Nichts Neues" copyright 1928 by Ullstein A. G.; copyright renewed © 1956 by Erich Maria Remarque.

Scribner, an imprint of Simon & Schuster Adult Publishing Group: "The Snows of Killimanjaro" from *The Short Stories of Ernest Hemingway*. Copyright © 1938 by Ernest Hemingway; copyright renewed © 1966 by Mary Hemingway.

United Nations: From the *Preamble to the Charter of the United Nations*. Copyright © 1945 by United Nations.

Sources Cited:

Quote from *Seeds of Peace* Web site, accessed August 23, 2005, at http://www.seedsofpeace.org/site/PageServer?pagename=BakerEvent.

From "Adoration of Inanna of Ur" from *The Ancient Near East, Volume II* by James D. Pritchard. Published by Princeton University Press, Princeton, NJ, 1976.

From *The River* by Gary Paulsen. Published by Random House, 1991.

From *Aké: The Years of Childhood* by Wole Soyinka from www.randomhouse.com Web site. Published by Random House, 1981.

Illustrations and Photo Credits

Cover: (bl), © James Nelson/Stone/Getty Images; (br), © Harald Sund/Getty Images

Front Matter: T2, Victoria Smith/Holt McDougal; T6, © Anthony Cassidy/Getty Images; T7 (tl), © Sharna Balfour/Gallo Images/Corbis; T7 (cr), © Eric Meola/Getty Images; T8, Jon Arnold Images/Photolibrary.com; T9, Private Collection, Beirut/Dagli Orti/The Art Archive (The Picture Desk); T10, © Kurt Scholz/SuperStock; T11, (tl) © Emy Kat/Photolibrary.com; (br) Nevada Weir/Corbis; T12, Steve Vidler/eStock Photo; T13, Egyptian National Museum, Cairo, Egypt/SuperStock; T14, © George Steinmetz/Corbis; T15, © Franck Guiziou/Hemis/Corbis; T16, © Scala/Art Resource, NY; T17, © BL Images Ltd./Alamy; T18, © Hans Strand/Corbis; T19, (cr), © The Granger Collection, New York; (br) © MaxPPP/Bruno Pellerin/Corbis; T21, Worldsat; T27, (cr), © Hulton Archive/Getty Images; (cl), © Hulton-Deutsch Collection/Corbis; (tr), © Hulton Archive/Getty Images.

Introduction: 1, Taxi/Getty Images; 2 (bl), © Stephen Frink/Digital Vision/Getty Images; 2 (cr), © Frans Lemmens/The Image Bank/Getty Images; 3, © Robert Harding/Digital Vision/Getty Images.

Chapter One: 4 (br), © M. Colonel/Photo Researchers, Inc.; 4–5 (t), age fotostock/SuperStock; 5 (bl), © Tom Bean/Corbis; 5 (br), © Anthony Cassidy/Getty Images; 7 (tl), © Frans Lemmens/Getty Images; 7 (br), © ESA/K.Horgan/Getty Images; 8 (b), © Kim Sayer/Corbis; 9 (bl), © London Aerial Photo Library/Corbis; 10 (tl), © Michael Newman/PhotoEdit; 13 (tl), © David R. Frazier/Photo Researchers, Inc.; 13 (tr), © Miles Ertman/Masterfile; 13 (bl), © David Muench/Corbis; 13 (bc), © AFP/Getty Images; 13 (br), © Morton Beebe/Corbis; 14–15, (br), © Tom Nebbia/Corbis; 17 (r), © Earth Satellite Corporation/Science Photo Library; 17 (l), © M-SAT Ltd./Science Photo Library; 19 (tl), © Torleif Svensson/Corbis; 19 (tr), © Penny Tweedie/Stone/Getty Images; 21 (b), Donna Cox and Robert Patterson/NCSA; 22 (tl), © Joe Raedle/Getty Images; 23 (tl), © Frans Lemmens/Getty Images; 23 (tc), © Penny Tweedie/Stone/Getty Images; 23 (tr), © Donna Cox and Robert Patterson/NCSA. **Chapter Two:** 26 (br), © Galen Rowell/Corbis; 27 (bl), © Michael Falzone/Corbis; 26–27 (t), © Pixtal/SuperStock; 30 (br), © Carl & Ann Purcell/Corbis; 30 (bl), © Daryl Benson/Masterfile; 32–33 (b), © Doug Wilson/Corbis; 33 (br), © Terje Rakke/The Image Bank/Getty Images; 36 (tl), © Rick Doyle/Corbis; 36 (tr), © Alan Sirulnikoff/Photo Researchers, Inc.; 38 (cr), © Yann Arthus-Bertrand/Corbis; 39 (bl), © Bettmann/Corbis; 40 (br), © Galen Rowell/Corbis; 41, © Jon Mitchell/Lightroom Photos/drr.

net; 42, Reuters; 43, © Suthep Kritsanavarin/Jupiter Images; 45 (tl), © NewsCom; 45 (tr), © Roger Ressmeyer/Corbis; 47 (tl), © Carl & Ann Purcell/Corbis; 47 (tc), © Rick Doyle/Corbis; 47 (tr), © Galen Rowell/Corbis. **Chapter Three:** 50–51 (t), © Warren Faidley /WeatherStock; 50 (br), © Kate Thompson/National Geographic/Getty Images; 51 (bl), © L. Clarke/Corbis; 51 (br), © Bill Ross/Corbis; 55 (cr), © China Photos/Getty Images; 55 (cr), © William Thomas Cain/Getty Images; 55 (br), © Eric Meola/Getty Images; 58 (tl), © age fotoStock/SuperStock; 59 (cr), Dennis Cox/Alamy; 59 (tr), © Tom Soucek/AlaskaStock; 60 (cl), © Martin Harvey/Corbis; 61, © Ingram /PictureQuest; 62, © Sharna Balfour/Gallo Images/Corbis; 65 (tr), © William Campbell/Peter Arnold, Inc.; 65 (c), © Adrian Arbib/Corbis; 67 (tr), © James L. Amos/Corbis; 67 (cr), © Creatas/PictureQuest; 68 (tl), © Sarah Leen/National Geographic Image Collection; 69, © Time Life Pictures/Getty Images; 71 (l), © Ingram/PictureQuest; 71 (c), © Martin Harvey/Corbis; 71 (r), © James L. Amos/Corbis. **Chapter Four:** 74–75 (t), © Pierre Vauthey/Sygma//Corbis; 74 (bl), © Pascal Goetgheluck/Photo Researchers, Inc.; 74 (bl), © John Elk lll/Alamy; 75 (br), Image Copyright © 2005 PhotoDisc, Inc.; 77 (tr), © Ferorelli Enterprises, Inc.; 77 (cr), © Bob Campbell/National Geographic Image Collection; 78 (bc), © Kenneth Garrett/National Geographic Image Collection; 78 (cr), © Pascal Goetgheluck/Photo Researchers, Inc.; 78 (br), ©Michael Holford Photographs; 79 (cl), © Pascal Goetgheluck/Photo Researchers, Inc.; 79 (bl), © John Reader/Photo Researchers, Inc.; 79 (br), © Erich Lessing/Art Resource, NY; 81 (br), © Getty Images; 81 (bc), © Werner Foreman/Topham/The Image Works; 82 (t), ©Robert Harding World Imagery/Alamy Images; 83 (tr), © South Tyrol Museum of Archaeology, Bolzano, Italy/Wolfgang Neeb/Bridgeman Art Library; 83 (b), © Paul Hanny/Gamma Press, Inc.; 86 (bl), © Sisse Brimberg/National Geographic Image Collection; 86 (br), © Photo courtesy of Professor James Dixon/Photograph by Eric Parrish; 92 (bl), © Carmen Redondo/Corbis; 92 (tr), © Nik Wheeler/Corbis; 93 (cl), © Corbis; 93 (tr), © Lowell Georgia/ Corbis.

Middle East: 101, © Robert Frerck/Odyssey Productions, Inc.; 102 (t), © Ustinenko Anatoly/ITAR-TASS/Corbis; 102 (b), © Hans Christian Heap/Getty Images; 103 (tl), © Gavin Heller/Robert Harding World Imagery/Getty Images; 105, © Steve Vidler/SuperStock; **Chapter Five:** 112 (br), © Jon Arnold/Photolibrary.com; 113 (bl), © K.M. Westermann/Corbis; 113 (br), © Martin Moos/Lonely Planet Images; 115 (b), © Hanan Isachar/Corbis; 115 (cr), © Woodfin Camp & Associates; 116, © Worldsat; 119 (cr), © Corbis; 119 (b), © Nik Wheeler/Corbis; 120 (tr), © Chris Mellor/Lonely Planet Images; 121, © Worldsat; 123, © Francoise de Mulder/Corbis; 126 (cl), © Reuters; 127 (all), © Worldsat; 129 (l), © Francoise de Mulder/Corbis; 129 (c), © Nik Wheeler/Corbis; 129 (r), © Chris Mellor/Lonely Planet Image. **Chapter Six:** 132 (br), akg images London; 133 (br), Private Collection, Beirut/Dagli Orti/The Art Archive (The Picture Desk); 133 (c), © Gianni Dagli Orti/Corbis; 133 (bl), © Musée du Louvre/Dagli Orti/The Art Archive (The Picture Desk); 134–135 (b), © Reuters/Corbis; 142, The Trustees of The British Museum; 144, © Gianni Dagli Orti/ Corbis; 145 (bl), © Scala/Art Resource, NY; 145 (br), © Bob Krist/Corbis; 146 (tl), © The Art Archive/Musée du Louvre, Paris/Album/Joseph Martin; 146 (tc), Musée du Louvre, Paris/Album/Joseph; 146 (tr), © The British Museum/Topham-HIP/The Image Works; 146 (tr), © Ancient Art & Architecture Collection, Ltd.; 147 (tc), © Ancient Art & Architecture Collection, Ltd.; 150–151 (b), © Gianni Dagli Orti/Corbis; 155 (c, r), © Gianni Dagli Orti/Corbis; **Chapter Seven:** 158 (br), © David Sanger/DanitaDelimont.com; 159 (bl), © Christopher Groenhout/Lonely Planet

Staff Credits

The people who contributed to **Holt McDougal: Eastern Hemisphere** are listed below. They represent editorial, design, production, emedia, and permissions.

Karen Arneson, Tim Barnhart, Charlie Becker, Julie Beckman-Key, Scott Bilow, Sarah Goodman, Lisa Goodrich, Elizabeth Harris, Cathy Jenevein, Kristina Jernt, David Knowles, Laura Lasley, Beth Loubet, Joe Melomo, Ivonne Mercado, Michael Neibergall, Jarred Prejean, Shelly Ramos, Gene Rumann, Michelle Rumpf-Dike, Jeannie Taylor, Jennifer Thomas, Joi Whetstone